American Journal of International Law

anuary 1982
Vol. 76 No. 1

Published by

American Society of International Law

PATRONS OF THE SOCIETY

Honorable ARTHUR H. DEAN
Honorable HERMAN PHLEGER
GENEVIEVE E. TILLAR (deceased)
W. ROBERT MORGAN
BRUNSON MACCHESNEY (deceased)
ALONA E. EVANS (deceased)
JOHN N. HAZARD

In Memoriam

DR. JAMES BROWN SCOTT
HENRY C. MORRIS
ARTHUR K. KUHN
ALEXANDER FREEMAN
STANLEY P. SMITH

PATRONAGE, GIFTS AND BEQUESTS

Upon donation to the Society of $5,000 or more by gift or bequest, any member of the Society or individual eligible for membership may be elected a Patron of the Society. Upon donation of at least $5,000 in the name of a deceased person, such person may be elected a Patron posthumously.

Gifts and bequests may be made in the name of the American Society of International Law, Washington, D.C. Such contributions are deductible from federal returns for income, estate and gift tax purposes. The Society is incorporated by Act of Congress approved September 20, 1950 (64 Stat. 869).

MANLEY O. HUDSON MEDAL

The American Society of International Law bestows from time to time without regard to nationality a gold medal to commemorate the life work of Manley O. Hudson. Such awards are made for preeminent scholarship and achievement in international law and in the promotion of the establishment and maintenance of international relations on the basis of law and justice. Medals have been awarded to Manley O. Hudson (1956), Lord McNair (1959), Philip C. Jessup (1964), Charles De Visscher (1966), Paul Guggenheim (1970), Myres S. McDougal (1976), Eduardo Jiménez de Aréchega (1978), Richard Reeve Baxter (1981), and Oscar Schachter (1981).

AMERICAN JOURNAL OF INTERNATIONAL LAW

VOL. 76 | January 1982 | NO. 1

CONTENTS

PAGE

The Third United Nations Conference on the Law of the Sea: The Tenth Session (1981) *Bernard H. Oxman* 1

U.S. Fishery Management and the New Law of the Sea *W. T. Burke* 24

Satellite Communication and Spectrum Allocation *Martin A. Rothblatt* 56

Technology and International Negotiations *Jonathan I. Charney* 78

Notes and Comments

The Warsaw Treaty of 1970 and the Western Boundary of Poland *Ludwik Gelberg* 119
The Good Offices of the United Nations Secretary-General in the Field of Human Rights *B. G. Ramcharan* 130
Reporting Under the Covenant on Civil and Political Rights: The First Five Years of the Human Rights Committee *Dana D. Fischer* 142

Contemporary Practice of the United States Relating to International Law *Marian Nash Leich* 154

Judicial Decisions *Monroe Leigh* 160

Current Developments

The 1981 Session of the Institut de Droit International *Oscar Schachter* 176
The Sinai Multinational Force and Observers *Marian Nash Leich* 181
The Hague Convention Abolishing the Requirement of Legalization for Foreign Public Documents *Marian Nash Leich* 182

Book Reviews and Notes *Edited by Leo Gross*

McDougal, Myres S., Harold D. Lasswell, and Lung-chu Chen. *Human Rights and World Public Order. The Basic Policies of an International Law of Human Dignity* 184
Falk, Richard A., and Samuel S. Kim (eds.). *The War System: An Interdisciplinary Approach* 186
Kalshoven, Frits, Pieter Jan Kuyper, and Johan G. Lammers (eds.). *Essays on the Development of the International Legal Order* 188
Pettman, Ralph. *State and Class: A Sociology of International Affairs* 190
Horn, Norbert (ed.). *Legal Problems of Codes of Conduct for Multinational Enterprises.* Vol. I 191
Gardner, James A. *Legal Imperialism: American Lawyers and Foreign Aid in Latin America* 196
Decaux, Emmanuel. *La réciprocité en droit international* 198

Recueil des Cours de l'Académie de droit international de La Haye, 1978. 3 vols. 199
van Dijk, P. *Judicial Review of Governmental Action and the Requirement of an Interest to Sue* 204
Valticos, Nicolas. *International Labour Law* 205
Joyce, James Avery. *World Labour Rights and Their Protection* 205
Best, Geoffrey. *Humanity in Warfare* 208
Schindler, Dietrich, and Jiří Toman (eds.). *The Laws of Armed Conflicts. A Collection of Conventions, Resolutions and other Documents* (2d rev. and completed ed.) 209
Ferencz, Benjamin B. *An International Criminal Court. A Step Toward World Peace: A Documentary History and Analysis.* 2 vols. 211
Nordquist, Myron, S. Houston Lay, and Kenneth R. Simmonds (comps. and eds.). *New Directions in the Law of the Sea.* Vols. VII and VIII 212
Nordquist, Myron, and Kenneth R. Simmonds (comps. and eds.). *New Directions in the Law of the Sea.* Vols. IX and X 212
Matte, Nicolas Mateesco. *Traité de Droit Aérien-aéronautique* (3d ed.) 214
Baccelli, Guido Rinaldi. *La Collaboration Internationale en Matière Aéroportuaire* 215
Larson, Joyce E. (ed.). *New Foundations for Asian and Pacific Security* 216
Soviet Yearbook of International Law, 1979 217
Allen, J. de V., A. J. Stockwell, and L. R. Wright (eds.). *A Collection of Treaties and other Documents affecting the States of Malaysia 1761–1963.* 2 vols. 218

Briefer Notices: Fikentscher, 219; Nguyen, 220; Riklin (ed.), 221; Brownlie (ed.), 221; *The Italian Yearbook of International Law.* Vol. III, 1977, 222; *The Caribbean Yearbook of International Relations: 1977,* 222; Dowrick (ed.), 223; Huynh (comp.), 223.

Books Received 224

International Legal Materials. Contents, Vol. XX, No. 5 (September 1981) 230

The views expressed in the articles, editorial comments, book reviews and notes, and other contributions which appear in AJIL are those of the individual authors and are not to be taken as representing the views of the Board of Editors or of the American Society of International Law.

Manuscripts in triplicate may be sent to the Editors-in-Chief of AJIL, Professors Oscar Schachter and Louis Henkin, Columbia University School of Law, New York, N.Y. 10027. Subscriptions, orders for back numbers, correspondence with reference to AJIL and books for review should be sent to the AMERICAN JOURNAL OF INTERNATIONAL LAW (ISSN 0002-9300), 2223 Massachusetts Avenue, N.W., Washington, D.C. 20008.

AJIL is published in January, April, July, and October and is supplied to all members of the American Society of International Law. The annual subscription to nonmembers of ASIL is $52.00, plus $2.50 for all foreign subscriptions (including ASIL Proceedings). Available back numbers of AJIL will be supplied at $11.00 each. ($21 of membership fee is allotted to AJIL subscription.)

EDITORIAL OFFICE:
BOX 44
COLUMBIA UNIVERSITY SCHOOL OF LAW
NEW YORK, N.Y. 10027

BUSINESS OFFICE:
2223 MASSACHUSETTS AVENUE, N.W.
WASHINGTON, D.C. 20008

Second-class postage paid at Washington, D.C. and additional mailing office

Postmaster: If undeliverable, send notice on Form 3579 to: American Journal of International Law 2223 Massachusetts Ave., N.W. Washington, D.C. 20008

Printed by Lancaster Press, Lancaster, Pa. 17604

The American Society of International Law

The American Society of International Law was organized in 1906 "to foster the study of international law and to promote the establishment and maintenance of international relations on the basis of law and justice."

The Society serves as a meeting place and forum for scholars, teachers, officials, lawyers, and others, from some one hundred countries. In April, it holds a three-day Annual Meeting at which current problems of international law are discussed. The Society also sponsors regional meetings outside of Washington in cooperation with other institutions. Salient questions of international law and relations are considered in depth by panels and study groups organized by the Society's Board of Review and Development. Works of scholarship are often published under the Society's auspices in connection with studies sponsored by the Board, many in the Society's series of *Studies in Transnational Legal Policy*.

The Society periodically issues four publications:

The American Journal of International Law, the leading journal in the field of international law, has been published since 1907. The *Proceedings of the American Society of International Law* carries the papers and discussion of the annual meeting of the Society.

International Legal Materials, a bimonthly, is a unique international collection of texts of current official documents, including legislation, treaties, court decisions, and reports. Subscription rates are $24 a year for members of the Society, $65 for others.

The quarterly *Newsletter* provides members with news of the Society and other organizations in the field.

Society membership is open to all persons of whatever nationality and profession who are interested in its objectives. Dues are: regular, $55; special category, $30 for persons *not* resident in a member country of the Organisation for Economic Co-operation and Development; intermediate, $25; student, $15. Membership application form is printed at the back of each issue of AJIL.

THE THIRD UNITED NATIONS CONFERENCE ON THE LAW OF THE SEA: THE TENTH SESSION (1981)

*By Bernard H. Oxman**

I. Introduction

The tenth session of the Third United Nations Conference on the Law of the Sea met in New York from March 9 to April 24, 1981 and resumed in Geneva from August 3 to August 28, 1981. The Drafting Committee and its organs also met from January 12 to February 27 in New York and from June 29 to July 31 in Geneva.[1]

The ninth session had ended a year earlier with the issuance of a revised text by the collegium[2] of the conference entitled Draft Convention on the Law of the Sea (Informal Text).[3] The concluding procedural note[4] by the President contained the following observations:

> The programme of work for the tenth session must provide for the adoption of the Convention during 1981 and the signature of the Final Act at a date to be determined in consultation with the Government of Venezuela.
>
> When the Conference resumes its work at the tenth session, some remaining questions will have to be considered, among them:
> (a) participation;
> (b) the mandate of the Preparatory Commission, including recommendations that would enable the system of exploration and exploitation to be initiated and also ensure that the Enterprise operate efficiently as early as possible after the Convention enters into force; and
> (c) the treatment to be accorded to preparatory investments made before

* Professor of Law, University of Miami School of Law; United States Representative and Vice Chairman of the U.S. delegation, and Chairman of the English Language Group of the Drafting Committee, at the tenth session of the Law of the Sea Conference. The views expressed herein are those of the author and do not necessarily represent the views of the Department of State, the U.S. Government, or the English Language Group or Drafting Committee of the Conference.

[1] This article is a sequel to Stevenson & Oxman, *The Preparations for the Law of the Sea Conference*, 68 AJIL 1 (1974); *The Third United Nations Conference on the Law of the Sea: The 1974 Caracas Session*, 69 AJIL 1 (1975);—*The 1975 Geneva Session*, 69 AJIL 763 (1975); and Oxman, *The Third United Nations Conference on the Law of the Sea: The 1976 New York Session*, 71 AJIL 247 (1977);—*The 1977 New York Sessions*, 72 AJIL 57 (1978);—*The Seventh Session (1978)*, 73 AJIL 1 (1979);—*The Eighth Session (1979)*, 74 AJIL 1 (1980);—*The Ninth Session (1980)*, 75 AJIL 211 (1981).

[2] The collegium consists of the President of the conference, the Chairmen of the three main committees, the Rapporteur-General, and the Chairman of the Drafting Committee.

[3] UN Doc. A/CONF.62/WP.10/Rev.3 (1980) [hereinafter cited as DC(IT)]. The procedure is set forth in UN Doc. A/CONF.62/62 (1978), 10 Third United Nations Conference on the Law of the Sea, Official Records 6 (1978) [hereinafter cited as Off. Rec.], *discussed in* 73 AJIL at 3–5 and 74 *id.* at 2. The ninth session is discussed by the author at 75 AJIL 211, note 1 *supra*.

[4] UN Doc. A/CONF.62/BUR.13/Rev.1 (1980).

the Convention enters into force, provided that such investments are compatible with the Convention and would not defeat its object and purpose.

During the same period, the three Main Committees and the Plenary will have to examine the recommendations of the Drafting Committee.

At the same time, consultations will have to take place between delegations in an effort to bring the Conference as close as possible to consensus on issues that have not found adequate solution in the text as revised.

It was contemplated in this regard that consultations would continue on the question of delimitation between states with opposite or adjacent coasts.[5]

The story of the tenth session of the conference is almost entirely the story of the consequences of events that occurred after the end of the ninth session:

- In December 1980, Ambassador Hamilton Shirley Amerasinghe of Sri Lanka, President of the conference since its inception, and President of the UN Sea-bed Committee that prepared for it, died.

- In January 1981, the Reagan administration took office and Republicans assumed majority control of the U.S. Senate.

- On March 2, 1981, the following statement was issued by the U.S. Department of State:

> After consultations with the other interested Departments and Agencies of the United States Government, the Secretary of State has instructed our representative to the UN Law of the Sea Conference to seek to ensure that the negotiations do not end at the present session of the Conference, pending a policy review by the United States Government. The interested Departments and Agencies have begun studies of the serious problems raised by the Draft Convention, and these will be the subject of a thorough review which will determine our position toward the negotiations.

- On March 7, 1981, Ambassador James L. Malone was named Special Representative of the President for the Law of the Sea Conference, leading a new U.S. delegation on which several officials were replaced by the new administration.

When the tenth session began, principal responsibility fell on the Asian Group to present an acceptable nominee to replace Ambassador Amerasinghe. By the end of the first week, after some straw polls within the group, Ambassadors Nandan of Fiji and Pinto of Sri Lanka withdrew, and the Asian Group nominated Ambassador T. T. B. Koh of Singapore.[6] He was elected by acclamation on March 13.

II. The Review

The U.S. policy review posed questions of both process and substance. A commonly repeated reaction, "We cannot turn back the clock to 1974," reveals the extent to which these questions are interrelated.[7]

[5] *See* DC(IT) Arts. 15, 74, 83, 121, 298(1)(a), and 309.

[6] Soviet allies in the Asian Group expressed reservations but did not prevent the nomination by consensus.

[7] This reaction is mistakenly perceived by some as merely a reference to personalities.

The Chairman of the Group of 77 summarized the reaction to the new United States position as follows:[8]

> The Conference concluded its 9th resumed session with the hope that the long and costly process of negotiating the Law of the Sea Convention both in terms of manpower and finances was nearing an end and that a new chapter of international understanding and cooperation was about to be written. It was with disbelief and consternation therefore that the group received the news just before the beginning of the 10th, and what was to have been the last negotiating session of the Conference, that the new U.S. administration had decided to undertake a "comprehensive policy review" relating to the Law of the Sea Convention and had instructed its delegation to ensure that the negotiations would not be concluded at that session.

In testimony before Congress, Ambassador Malone summarized the reasons for the U.S. actions:[9]

> When this Administration took office, it was confronted with an Informal Draft Convention on the Law of the Sea containing a number of provisions raising concerns on which I shall elaborate shortly. We were informed that the Conference was on the verge of finalizing this text and that there was an expectation that the negotiations would conclude in 1981.
>
> Many of the provisions of the draft convention prompted substantial criticism from industry, Congress, and the American public. There was also some question whether this draft Convention was consistent with the stated goals of the Reagan Administration. Therefore, the Administration decided that it would be better to face criticism in the U.N. than to proceed prematurely to finalize a treaty that might fail to further our national interests. Many comments were made by foreign delegates and in the U.S. press about the manner in which we announced our decision to conduct a policy review and to appoint a new chief negotiator. Let me report . . . that the decision to conduct the review was made as rapidly as possible, consistent with the many burdens and competing priorities faced by any new Administration. A change in the leadership of the American delegation was essential, in order to ensure that other countries clearly understood our seriousness of purpose with respect to the review. That action was also necessary in order to send the signal to other delegations that the U.S. could not be induced to return immediately, and thus prematurely, to the bargaining table by offers of minor technical changes to the draft convention. I am sure you can also appreciate that it would be less difficult for a new head of delegation to adhere to a negotiating posture that diverged from our past approach.

Process

The review was announced:

- almost 15 years after three separate events that eventually led to the

[8] Statement by Mr. Inam Ul-Haque (Pakistan) on behalf of the Group of 77, Informal Plenary, Aug. 10, 1981 (copy supplied by the speaker).

[9] Testimony by Ambassador James L. Malone before the Subcommittee on Oceanography of the House Merchant Marine and Fisheries Committee, April 28, 1981 (copy circulated by the Department of State).

conference: the circulation of a Soviet note to 60 countries inquiring about the possibility of a new conference on the law of the sea to fix the breadth of the territorial sea at 12 nautical miles; the subsequent circulation of draft articles on the territorial sea and straits by the United States and the USSR, and on fisheries by the United States; and the statements in the United Nations by James Roosevelt of the United States and Arvid Pardo of Malta regarding the establishment of an international regime for the seabeds beyond the limits of coastal state jurisdiction, which captured the attention of many nonexperts;

- over 10 years after the UN General Assembly decided to convene a comprehensive conference on the law of the sea and requested its Sea-bed Committee to prepare for it; and

- over 7 years after the conference was convened, during which time its annual and semi-annual sessions have themselves totaled more than 1 year of meetings (excluding numerous intersessional meetings).

Throughout this period the conference endeavored to elaborate by consensus a single comprehensive "package deal" of disparate and complex elements. "As the conference progressed it was heralded by world opinion as a new ingenious approach to the decision-making process in the UN machinery which in politically loaded UN conferences would give new vitality and possibilities to the United Nations and thus to the world as a whole."[10] The author of this statement, Ambassador Evensen of Norway, outlined his view of the problem as follows:[11]

> We all accepted as self-evident that a conference of this magnitude and complexity would be time-consuming. We wanted to have all states in on the final result. It is a conference where we had to find acceptable compromises between the super-powers, between East and West, between the developing countries and the industrialized countries, between neighbours with fundamentally opposite views in actual disputes. . . . It was equally clear that we could not deal with all of the hundreds and hundreds of issues at once.
>
> We had to proceed from issue to issue, from chapter to chapter. We had to work in main committees, in all types of formal and informal groups in order to build with infinite care, a compromise package comprising the totality. In this stepwise approach we also had to build up confidence based on the self-evident assumption that delegations and states, although not formally bound would stand by their express or tacit commitments. If one main state or group of states rescind one main element of the package, the whole package would fall apart and the compromise package elaborated with such finesse, perhaps even ingenuity, over the years would collapse like a house of cards. A lack of understanding of this main element of the gentleman's agreement accepted by *all* in 1973, would spell disaster for the consensus principle.
>
> If this was not the case the whole consensus principle would be so

[10] Statement by Ambassador Jens Evensen (Norway), Informal Plenary, Aug. 10, 1981 (copy supplied by the speaker).

[11] *Ibid.*

discredited that it would be hopelessly doomed as a viable procedure in protracted multilateral negotiation, especially in the UN framework.

Some sympathetic delegates felt, however, that the argument was pressed a bit far when Ambassador Evensen drew analogies from the rules in Articles 7 and 18 of the Vienna Convention on the Law of Treaties.[12]

Nevertheless, the Soviet Union itself pressed the theme of obligations arising out of the structural imperatives alluded to by Ambassador Evensen. Referring to the right to conduct a review, the Soviet Deputy Foreign Minister observed with characteristic acerbity:

> True, newly-established governments in all countries have such a right. Throughout the work of the Conference new governments in a number of countries succeeded the former ones. However, they conducted such "reviews" observing the elementary norms of international courtesy and the fundamental principles of succession and fulfilling in good faith the obligations assumed. It is easy to imagine where international conferences would be if every new government considered itself entitled to conduct similar endless "reviews" of the previously reached agreements and to make all other participants in international forums wait till such "reviews" are completed.[13]

The Chairman of the Group of 77 sharpened and narrowed the issues to those of "realism" and "good faith negotiations":[14]

> Even if the United States had not participated in the Conference for all these years, and was a newcomer to the negotiations, it would be unrealistic for it to seek to undo what had been achieved already, as a condition for its participation in the treaty. The United States government cannot reject the work of over 150 nations including its own predecessor governments for almost a decade, for in doing so it would be destroying the principle of good faith negotiations. There have been scores of changes in regimes

[12]

> I believe that analogies from the aforementioned Vienna Convention on the Law of Treaties are helpful in this connection. During our negotiations for a package-deal our states were represented by their respective ambassadors to the United Nations or with specially appointed heads of delegation who had full powers to negotiate, of course with the limitation this entails as to adoption, signature and ratification. But at least there were widespread assumptions and expectations that states would stand by their commitments given in compromise negotiations. If not the whole package-deal principle would be a hoax. Thus, in a sense the Vienna Convention art. 7 on full powers is applicable to the package deal negotiations. We who represented our respective Governments had full powers in relation to the package-deal commitments.
>
> I feel that analogies from art. 18 of the Vienna Convention likewise are appropriate. Article 18 states that when a state has signed a treaty it is obligated to refrain from acts that "defeat the object and purpose" of that treaty. Would not similar consideration of equitable behavior entail that wholesale renunciation of perhaps the most essential part of the package-deal, namely part XI, should be considered to defeat "the object and purpose" of the gentleman's agreement we arrived at in 1973?

Ibid. Vienna Convention on the Law of Treaties, UN Doc. A/CONF.39/27 (1969), *entered into force* Jan. 27, 1980, *reprinted in* 63 AJIL 875 (1969), 8 ILM 679 (1969).

[13] Statement by Deputy Foreign Minister Semyon P. Kozyrev (USSR), General Committee, Aug. 3, 1981 (informal English translation supplied by Soviet delegation).

[14] Statement by Mr. Ul-Haque, note 8 *supra*.

in different countries since the work on the treaty was started, but no new regime had so far disowned what its predecessors had striven to achieve in the field of international cooperation for the exploitation of the resources of the seabed which have been universally recognized as being the Common Heritage of Mankind.

I would like to reiterate on behalf of the group its firm and unequivocal position that the Convention on the Law of the Sea must be adopted. We cannot allow the work of so many nations over so many years to be scuttled. Neither our desire for universality, nor our perference for consensus should be construed to mean that any one country or a group of countries, large or small, weak or powerful will be allowed to detract from the basic objective that the sea and its resources must be governed by international law and regulations which are fair and equitable.

The Soviet Union and its East European allies finally carried their lines of argument to an unexpected conclusion, arguably abandoning the consistent adherence to the principle of consensus that has characterized Soviet multilateral diplomacy for decades, albeit in language carefully limited to adopting the Convention "as a whole" and "on the basis of the existing draft":[15]

The Group continues to come out for the adoption of the convention by consensus. However, if some delegations continue to oppose adopting the convention on the basis of the existing draft and thus to impede achieving a consensus, the Group of Socialist Countries of Eastern Europe will be prepared to cooperate with the majority in the Conference and to adopt the convention as a whole by a vote.

The motivations for these arguments are generally the same as those that underlie the "delicate balance" argument whenever it is made in defense of hard-won compromise: genuine belief that the compromise is the best attainable, fatigue and impatience resulting from the time and effort devoted to working out the compromise, and tactical resistance to demands for new concessions. Since the "delicate balance" argument is invariably made in the face of reluctance by a party to accept the compromise, it is frequently accompanied by appeals to protect the integrity of the negotiating process, intimations that the negotiator has somehow bound his principal to accept the result, and threats to exclude the reluctant party from the club.[16]

In response, the United States strongly reaffirmed its support for the process of consensus. That support was echoed by virtually all of its allies.

Some delegations have said to us that one of the principal values of the

[15] Letter from Dr. Andrzej Olszowka (Poland) on behalf of the Group of Socialist Countries of Eastern Europe, Aug. 20, 1981, forwarding the decision by the group adopted at its meeting on Aug. 18, 1981. UN Doc. A/CONF.62/L.77 (1981).

[16] The logic of these arguments tends to restrain the temptation to threaten to change the substance of the compromise in a manner detrimental to the reluctant party. In this case, the temptation is further reduced by the knowledge that, in terms of altering substantive articles, it is virtually impossible to shoot at the United States without hitting the Soviet Union, major U.S. allies, and powerful developing countries. Nevertheless, as the East European statement on voting demonstrates, it is not inconceivable that the Soviet Union would—in "zero-sum" terms—accept some injury for the sake of inflicting greater harm on its adversaries. It did exactly that on the issue of marine scientific research in a fit of pique at the United States; the same could happen again.

> Law of the Sea Conference is that it has established the rule of consensus as a precedent for global conferences. We share that view. To the extent it has been possible to make great progress in these negotiations and in other forums where the rule of consensus was used, it is because States with vital interests knew that their views would not be over-ridden by a large majority of States seeking to protect contrary interests.[17]

The United States made clear that it was not bound by the text, while at the same time demonstrating sensitivity to the underlying structural concerns of other delegations:

> No nation is committed to the text in the sense that it is bound by it. In this regard, I would like to quote from the Conference President's preparatory note to the draft convention: "This text like its predecessor will be informal in character. It is a negotiating text and not a negotiated text, and does not prejudice the position of any delegation."[18]
>
> We have nevertheless tried to be mindful of the fact that a great deal of work has been done by this Conference over the last decade. As we conduct the review, we are therefore making every effort to avoid burdening the Conference with issues that are not vitally important to the acceptability of a treaty to the United States Administration or the United States Senate.[19]
>
> Mr. President, several speakers have placed great emphasis on the importance of continuity in the conduct of long-term international negotiations. We recognize this. But there are other values that are also relevant. One of them is the right of the people in a democratic society to elect a new government. We do not expect the world to come to a halt because we have a new President and a new majority in the Senate. But it would be fundamentally unfair and unproductive were we to shirk our responsibility to ascertain the relationship between this Draft Convention and the policies and goals of the United States Government in the coming years.[20]

On the issue of participation in the Convention, the United States was equally forthright:

> Mr. Chairman, on the basis of the foregoing difficulties and others that I have not taken the time to mention, it is the best judgment of this Administration that this draft convention would not obtain the advice and consent of the Senate. Of course, since the treaty would require implementing legislation, the House would also have a major role that must be considered. We have reason to doubt that the House of Representatives would pass the necessary legislation to give effect to a treaty containing provisions such as these. The provisions I have mentioned raise questions for this Administration. We must seriously consider whether those provi-

[17] Statement by Ambassador James L. Malone (U.S.), Informal Plenary, Aug. 5, 1981 (copy circulated by U.S. delegation).

[18] Testimony by Ambassador Malone, note 9 *supra*.

[19] Statement by Ambassador Malone, note 17 *supra*.

[20] Statement by Ambassador Malone, Plenary, March 17, 1981 (copy circulated by U.S. delegation).

> sions should be included in a treaty to which the U.S. would become a party, unless there were a countervailing national policy interest.[21]
>
> Our review of the Draft Convention has revealed that Part XI of the text would, in its present form, be a stumbling block to treaty ratification.[22]

The United States delegation did not favor holding a resumed session in the summer, and made clear that its policy review would not be completed by then.[23]

Thus, at the start of the resumed session, Ambassador Malone stated:[24]

> The review of the Draft Convention has not been completed. Indeed, it is now entering its most crucial stage.
>
> Substantial time has been devoted to identifying those areas which give us concern. Most of that work has been completed. We do not believe, however, that it would be prudent for us to recommend that the President make decisions about our final position without fully understanding how other nations feel about the issues raised by these areas of concern.

He stressed his conviction "that this Conference can benefit most from structured and sober discussion of these matters in a series of informal meetings."

The idea of special meetings to consider U.S. concerns aroused considerable debate, in large measure because many delegations wished to avoid an open-ended commitment to renegotiate when the United States had not affirmed its support for a treaty in principle and was not in a position to make concrete proposals or to give an exhaustive list of its problems. This brought into sharp focus the underlying issue of process raised by the U.S. review. Professor Riphagen of the Netherlands attempted to synthesize these considerations as follows:

> Doubts have been expressed in various quarters about the utility of the dialogue on which we have recently embarked. Mr. President, let me state at the outset that I do *not* share those doubts. Most of us have gone through all those years of negotiations and consultations, and it is understandable that many of us feel that the results achieved up to now are, if not perfect from any point of view, indeed the best results we could ever achieve.

[21] Testimony by Ambassador Malone, note 9 *supra*.

[22] Statement by Ambassador Malone, note 17 *supra*.

[23]

> *Mr. Oxman* (United States of America) said that his Government was certain that its policy review would not be completed before the autumn of 1981 and felt that it would be advantageous if all delegations were to engage in bilateral and multilateral consultations before taking a final position. Accordingly, the United States believed it would be preferable to delay the next session until early in 1982; at that time his Government would be able to state its definitive views. However, it had become clear to his delegation that others wished to have a session of the Conference in August. While his delegation had taken those views into account, it was not prepared to regard the August session as the final one. . . . An August session for the purpose of informal consultation could contribute to an understanding of the views of others before final decisions were made. The review would be completed after that. . . .

General Committee, Apr. 14, 1981, UN Doc. A/CONF.62/BUR/SR.62 (1981) (prov.).

[24] Statement by Ambassador Malone, note 17 *supra*.

But, Mr. President, we remain under the duty to strive for a *generally* acceptable regime of the seas, in other words towards consensus.

This is not merely so because our rules of procedure so prescribe, but far more important, because the subject matter itself—the legal regime of the seas—so requires. Ever since the idea—if not the word—that the seas are the common heritage of mankind has come to be accepted—and we commemorate in the year after next that one of the greatest proponents of that idea, Hugo Grotius, was born 400 years ago—the necessity of a *general* regime to be complied with by *all* states was implied. Now that we are in the process of a new progressive development of such a general regime, we should not lose sight of this goal. We are not drafting a *manifesto*, to which some may attach their signature and others not, but we are trying to lay down a legal regime, which by that very token must *work* in the present-day world, which means that it must be accepted by all concerned.

On the other hand, Mr. President, this selfsame object and purpose of our conference, the elaboration of a new and detailed regime for the oceans, also imposes *restraints* upon all of us. We do not start from scratch but have to fill in, as it were, a pre-existing framework.[25]

Substance

The first concrete indication of various concerns identified in the review came in a nonexhaustive enumeration presented in congressional testimony in the spring:

—The Draft Convention places under burdensome international regulation the development of all of the resources of the seabed and subsoil beyond the limits of national jurisdiction, representing approximately two-thirds of the earth's submerged lands. These resources include polymetallic nodules. They also include mineral deposits beneath the surface of the seabed about which nothing is known today, but which may be of very substantial economic importance in the future.

—The Draft Convention would establish a supranational mining company, called the Enterprise, which would benefit from significant discriminatory advantages relative to the companies of industrialized countries. Arguably, it could eventually monopolize production of seabed minerals. Moreover, the Draft Convention requires the U.S. and other nations to fund the initial capitalization of the Enterprise, in proportion to their contributions to the U.N.

—Through its transfer of technology provisions, the Draft Convention compels the sale of proprietary information and technology now largely in U.S. hands. Under the Draft Convention, with certain restrictions, the Enterprise, through mandatory transfer, is guaranteed access on request to the seabed mining technology owned by private companies and also technology used by them but owned by others. The text further guarantees similar access to privately-owned technology by any developing country

[25] Statement by Professor Riphagen (Netherlands), Informal Meeting, Aug. 17, 1981 (copy supplied by speaker).

planning to go into seabed mining. We must also carefully consider how such provisions relate to security-related technology.

—The Draft Convention limits the annual production of manganese nodules from the deep seabed, as well as the amount which any one company can mine for the first twenty years of production. The stated purpose of these controls is to avoid damaging the economy of any country which produces the same commodities on land. In short, it attempts to insulate land-based producers from competition with seabed mining. In doing so, the draft treaty could discourage potential investors, thereby creating artificial scarcities. In allocating seabed production, the International Seabed Authority is granted substantial discretion to select among competing applicants. Such discretion could be used to deny contracts to qualified American companies.

—The Draft Convention creates a one-nation, one-vote international organization which is governed by an Assembly and a 36-member Executive Council. In the Council, the Soviet Union and its allies have three guaranteed seats, but the U.S. must compete with its allies for any representation. The Assembly is characterized as the "supreme" organ and the specific policy decisions of the Council must conform to the general policies of the Assembly.

—The Draft Convention provides that, after fifteen years of production, the provisions of the treaty will be reviewed to determine whether it has fulfilled overriding policy considerations, such as protection of land-based producers, promotion of Enterprise operations and equitable distribution of mining rights. If two-thirds of the States Parties to the treaty wish to amend provisions concerning the system of exploitation, they may do so after five years of negotiation and after ratification by two-thirds of the States Parties. If the U.S. were to disagree with duly ratified changes, it would be bound by them nevertheless, unless it exercised its option to denounce the entire treaty.

—The Draft Convention imposes revenue-sharing obligations on seabed mining corporations which would significantly increase the costs of seabed mining.

—The Draft Convention imposes an international revenue-sharing obligation on the production of hydrocarbons from the continental shelf beyond the 200-mile limit. Developing countries that are net-importers of hydrocarbons are exempt from the obligation.

—The Draft Convention contains provisions concerning liberation movements, like the PLO, and their eligibility to obtain a share of the revenues of the Seabed Authority.

—The Draft Convention lacks any provisions for protecting investments made prior to entry into force of the Convention.[26]

Ambassador Elliot L. Richardson, the Public Chairman of the Department of State's Advisory Committee on the Law of the Sea and former head of the

[26] Testimony by Ambassador Malone, note 9 *supra*.

U.S. delegation, while decrying "the remarkable persistence of distortions of the Draft Convention,"[27] himself outlined the following areas for improvement:

> In the case, for example, of U.S. membership on the Council of the Authority, the provision for the selection by each interest-group of its own representatives was put forward by the U.S. delegation last year in the belief that this would solve the problem. It was accepted by the Group of 77 with the same understanding. Having thus in substance already acquiesced in a "guaranteed seat for the United States," it is likely that the 77 would now agree to make the guarantee more explicit.
>
> Again, take the allegation that liberation movements like the PLO would be eligible for a share of the net revenues of the Seabed Authority. Although, as noted above, we have in fact secured effective means of preventing such an outcome, this too is a result that could be reinforced, if not in the text, at least in the official record at the final stage of the Conference.

Not all criticisms of the Draft Convention are distortions, of course. The Interdepartmental Group on the Law of the Sea had already targeted a number of needed improvements even before the review was announced. The IG proposals would have addressed most of the concerns identified by Assistant Secretary Malone when he testified on April 28 before the Subcommittee on Oceanography of the House Merchant Marine and Fish-

[27] Testimony by Ambassador Elliot L. Richardson, House Foreign Affairs Committee, May 14, 1981 (copy supplied by witness). He identified the following as the "most frequently repeated misstatements":

> 1. That the treaty would not give the U.S. assured access to seabed minerals. In fact, the text expressly gives companies sponsored by a member state the right to apply for a "plan of work," spells out the qualifications of applicants in clear, objective terms, and directs the International Seabed Authority to approve a plan of work proposed by an applicant meeting the specified financial and technical standards.
>
> 2. That the U.S. would not be assured of a seat on the Council of the Authority although the Eastern bloc would be guaranteed three seats. Actually, the provisions for membership on the Council would assure the Western industrial countries six to nine seats; each interest group whose representation is required would designate its own representatives. The United States, either as the probably largest investor in deep-seabed mining (one of the represented interest groups) or as the largest importer or consumer of deep seabed minerals (a second interest group), would have as much practical assurance of being named to one of these groups as would the Soviet Union of being named as one of the Eastern bloc representatives.
>
> 3. That U.S. companies would be required to sell sensitive national-security-related technology. On the contrary, the U.S. Government would presumably deny an export license for any such sale. The text provides that "nothing in this Convention shall be deemed to require a State Party, in the fulfilment of its obligations under the relevant provisions of this Convention, to supply information the disclosure of which is contrary to the essential interests of its security."
>
> 4. That a company seeking an ocean-mining contract would be required to transfer its technology without adequate compensation. In fact, the technology-transfer obligation applies "only if the Enterprise finds that it is unable to obtain the same or equally efficient and useful technology on the open market" and then only on "fair and reasonable commercial terms and conditions," subject to binding commercial arbitration of any dispute as to those terms and conditions. In passing, I would note that a number of companies have already come forward to offer seabed mining systems to the future Enterprise.

> eries Committee. The most important of these proposals—and concerns—was the protection of investments made prior to the Draft Conventions's entry into force. Other such matters were the transfer of technology owned by subcontractors, the "Brazil clause," the number of ratifications required for the entry into force of amendments emanating from the Review Conference, and the exemption of net importers from sharing the revenue from the exploitation of hydrocarbons in the continental shelf beyond the 200-mile limit. Although not on either Mr. Malone's or the IG's list, other desirable changes which the Conference would undoubtedly agree to put on its agenda would be a clause more positively encouraging the exploitation of seabed resources and a fixed date for the start-up of the production-ceiling formula.
>
> Although Mr. Malone also referred to the burden imposed on seabed-mining corporations by the Convention's revenue-sharing provisions, this is a concern which should, in all fairness, be dealt with under domestic law. All that is necessary is to give revenue-sharing payments to the Authority the same treatment as taxes paid to a foreign government. Indeed, this has all along been advocated by the State Department. If this were done, the present text [on financial arrangements] is likely to be acceptable to U.S. mining companies.

During the resumed tenth session, the United States delegation spelled out its concerns with the deep seabed mining regime in greater detail in various ad hoc meetings scheduled to avoid the appearance of interference with the regular schedule of the conference. The Chairman of the Group of 77 defended the texts as representing maximal concessions of his group. From these and other exchanges, all concerned will now have to decide on the negotiability of a package of changes that is sufficient for the United States and its allies.

In this regard, the author would offer certain personal observations:

- Adoption of the Convention as is, without significant negotiation and substantial improvement, increases the likelihood that it will never enter into force for the United States and a considerable number of other important countries.

- The credibility of any package of improvements may depend on whether it is perceived that negotiation of the package can be completed in 1982, albeit with intense effort, goodwill, and some luck.

- Pressure for significant changes in texts other than those concerning deep seabed mining may stimulate or heighten pressure for the definitive termination of all negotiation by influential developing countries and the USSR with the acquiescence or support of a significant number of U.S. allies, and may increase the risk of retaliatory changes in substantive texts that can affect customary law.

- The U.S. concerns about certain aspects of representation, voting, and independence of the Council; production policy and controls; the review clause; lacunae in the contract approval system; technology transfer; resources other than nodules; settlement of deep seabed disputes; and preparatory investment protection enjoy significant, if inchoate, sympathy among developing countries. But this sympathy relates almost exclusively to practical, not philosophical, problems.

- Since all concerned are in a political position where they cannot afford too much loss of face, technical changes drafted in a manner intelligible mainly to competent lawyers and diplomats may be the only way to achieve improvements on some issues.

• There is no reason whatsoever why consumers and miners should have to worry about the scores of provisions whose main problem is not the intended content of the package but the opaque, grudging, or legally defective manner in which they are drafted. If the conference is unwilling to entrust a Drafting Committee with improving the ratifiability of the Convention in this regard, some simple mechanism should be devised for the specific purpose of making changes (of substance, if need be) to conform the text rapidly to what is manifestly intended and sensible.

• Political issues relating to dependencies and liberation movements, including the so-called transitional provision, will be resolved in a manner fully acceptable to the Western powers so long as ratification by them is perceived to be an attainable goal.

III. Efforts to Show Progress

The resumed tenth session was marked by considerable effort to show tangible progress. Aside from the perceived need of some delegates to explain the time and expense devoted to the session, the main purpose was to demonstrate a determination to press ahead to completion of the Convention. The results of these efforts include the following:

• the conference, by indicative vote, selected Jamaica as the site of the Sea-Bed Authority and the Federal Republic of Germany as the site of the Tribunal on the Law of the Sea;

• a new, altered provision on delimitation of the economic zone and the continental shelf between states with opposite or adjacent coasts was inserted in the text by the collegium despite significant criticism and hesitation;

• the President issued a report containing a new proposed text on participation by international organizations;

• the Drafting Committee pressed ahead at great speed and "deferred" almost all efforts to correct the more serious errors in the text, leaving those who have not participated in its work with the superficial impression that most of the Convention is "finished";

• the Working Group of 21 continued its work on the resolution to establish a Preparatory Commission; and

• the Draft Convention was revised and reissued with a "higher status."

Site Selection

For some time now, Fiji, Jamaica, and Malta have been candidates for the site of the proposed Sea-Bed Authority, and the Federal Republic of Germany, Portugal, and Yugoslavia have been candidates for the site of the proposed Tribunal on the Law of the Sea. During the first part of the tenth session, the six candidates decided that the matter would be resolved during the third week of the resumed session.

On August 22, in accordance with the decision of the candidates, the Plenary held an indicative vote by secret ballot on both sites pursuant to which the losing candidates would withdraw. A preliminary effort to postpone the voting failed narrowly in a roll-call vote marked by unusual confusion among the East Europeans. Prior to the voting, it was made clear that the site selection will apply only if the state selected is a party to the Convention when it enters into force.[28]

In both elections, no candidate received an absolute majority on the first ballot. On each second ballot, the candidate that won a plurality on the first ballot was elected: Jamaica for the Authority and the Federal Republic of Germany for the Tribunal.[29]

Delimitation of the Economic Zone and the Continental Shelf Between States with Opposite or Adjacent Coasts

The normative provisions on delimitation of the economic zone and the continental shelf have been replaced by the following: "The delimitation of the exclusive economic zone between States with opposite or adjacent coasts shall be effected by agreement on the basis of international law, as referred to in article 38 of the Statute of the International Court of Justice, in order to achieve an equitable solution."[30]

The specific reference to delimitation in the footnote to Article 309 on the possible need for reservations has been deleted. Oddly enough, this deletion merely makes the footnote more open-ended.

The proposed text, worked out in secret by Ireland and Spain representing their respective groups, and Fiji representing the President, was available even in private only for a few days. Its hasty insertion in the Draft Convention was questioned publicly by Arab countries, Iran, Israel, the United States, and Venezuela, and privately by others.

The main pressure for some change in the text came from the advocates of emphasis on equitable principles rather than equidistance.[31] Among other things, with this text they have achieved the elimination of any express reference to equidistance, and the limitation of the entire provision to a rule of delimitation by agreement that does not, as such, purport to lay down a normative rule to be applied in the absence of agreement. In return, they changed the reference to "equitable principles" to a vaguer notion that agreements should achieve an

[28] Ambassador Evensen added the point that the selection should cease to apply if the state denounces the Convention.

[29] For the Sea-Bed Authority, the votes on the first ballot were: Fiji, 14; Jamaica, 69; Malta, 56; abstentions, 5; blank, 1; on the second ballot: Jamaica, 76; Malta, 66; abstentions, 5. For the Tribunal, the votes on the first ballot were: FRG, 67; Portugal, 15; Yugoslavia, 59; abstentions, 3; blank, 1; on the second ballot: FRG, 78; Yugoslavia, 61; absentions, 4; blank, 2.

[30] Draft Convention, note 43 *infra*, Art. 74(1). Art. 83(1) contains an identical provision on the continental shelf.

[31] In part because of the U.S. policy review, and in part because of concerns regarding Canadian reaction on the collegium, these advocates encouraged the appearance of distance between themselves and a U.S. delegation sympathetic to their substantive attitudes.

equitable solution. One can hardly imagine that the parties would characterize their agreements otherwise.

Since both Ireland and Spain are involved in delimitation disputes, their respective neighbors naturally watched the negotiations closely; they presumably concluded that their opponents were forced to concede as much as, if not more than, they gained. It was inevitable, of course, that any resultant text would have to be accepted by both sides. Still, one might have expected more than a text that says nothing of significance while, worse still, trying to give a contrary impression by introducing unnecessary language and avoiding recognized terminology associated with the jurisprudence and scholarship on the subject.

If "the main purpose of a Convention on the Law of the Sea is to reduce the possibility of disputes and conflict between States, and to help resolve differences that do arise by narrowing and reformulating them in generally acceptable legal terms," the U.S. representative observed, then this is not the time for the conference "to give up and move forward with an anodyne text that cannot achieve these purposes and that may indeed have the opposite effect of adding confusion to the law, . . . a text that delegations on both sides privately look upon with embarrassment."[32]

There is perhaps no better evidence of the failure of the conference to think about this text than the inclusion of an express cross-reference to Article 38 of the Statute of the International Court of Justice. That article contains the 60-year-old reference to "civilized" nations that is regarded by some developing-country lawyers as a product of colonialist attitudes. Such an express cross-reference would surely have encountered difficulty if it had been closely scrutinized at a conference that even refused to use the word "customary" to preface a reference to international law in the Preamble.

If inclusion of this text is illustrative of the lengths the conference is willing to go to appear to "make progress," there is little ground for optimism about either the process or the result. One must hope it is an isolated aberration that will be corrected, and that will not be repeated.

Participation of International Organizations

As a result of several meetings held on the subject, the President issued a new text on participation of international organizations[33] "constituted by States to which such member States have transferred competence over matters governed by this Convention, including the competence to enter into treaties in respect of such matters." His report makes clear that this excludes "agencies of the United Nations System."[34]

The European Economic Community was the principal organization in mind. It is doubtful, however, whether equally complex problems of divided competence and responsibility, coupled with third-party dispute settlement, were previously encountered in the negotiation of other treaties to which the Eu-

[32] Statement by Ambassador Malone, Plenary, Aug. 28, 1981 (copy supplied by speaker).
[33] Conf. Doc. FC/27 (1981) (new text in Ann. 2).
[34] *Id.* at 1.

ropean Economic Community is authorized to become party. Certainly, no such treaty has the scope of the Draft Convention on the Law of the Sea.

For an organization to become a party to the Convention, a majority of states members must be parties.[35] In its instrument of acceptance, the organization must file a declaration "specifying the matters governed by this Convention in respect of which competence has been transferred to the organization by its members which are State Parties." States parties that are members of the organization must do the same. The declarations must be kept up to date.

An organization is a party "to the extent that it has competence in accordance with the declarations" and certain supplementary information; states members may not exercise that competence. Thus, the organization takes the place of states parties with respect to matters on which they have transferred competence to it. It may not "implement the Convention in such a manner as to benefit a State member which is not a party to the Convention," and its participation may not "entail an increase of the representation that . . . member States which are States Parties would otherwise be entitled to, including rights in decision-making."

Responsibility for failure to comply with obligations under the Convention is divided between the organization and its members on the basis of the allocation of competence or by agreement between them. However, failure to provide information on request as to who has responsibility in respect of any specific matter, or the provision of contradictory information by the organization and the state concerned, results in joint and several responsibility. The obligations of the organization under the Convention to "third States"—that is, states that are not members of the organization—prevail over its obligations under the agreement establishing the organization.

Provision is made for situations where the organization and a member state "are joint parties to a dispute, or [presumably separate] parties in the same interest." Were they allowed to be separate parties *not* in the same interest, the odd arithmetic of Annex VII, Article 3(g) would give the organization and its members more arbitrators than a single adversary. This is one example of the overall difficulty with that article, which can accidentally produce arbitration panels tilted against one of the parties in disputes involving more than two parties who assert they are not in the same interest. (This in a treaty where arbitration would be the residual compulsory dispute settlement mechanism.) The English Language Group of the Drafting Committee has recommended a technical solution,[36] but some delegation may regard the effort to find an obviously needed correction as a substantive endeavor beyond the competence of the committee. Nevertheless, it is a hopeful sign that the Drafting Committee was able—albeit obliquely—to deal in part with a similar problem in Annex V, Article 3(g) on compulsory conciliation by eliminating the reference to the

[35] It becomes a party by signature followed by an "act of formal confirmation," or by accession. The term "act of formal confirmation" is used in the International Law Commission's Draft Articles on Treaties Concluded Between States and International Organizations or Between International Organizations.

[36] Conf. Doc. ELGDC/26 (1981).

possibility of expanding the conciliation panel to accommodate parties not in the same interest.[37] This is significant because of the provision for compulsory conciliation of certain delimitation, fisheries, and marine scientific research disputes that might involve more than two parties.[38]

The Drafting Committee

The new text issued by the collegium contains over fifteen hundred changes in the six language texts recommended by the Drafting Committee and approved by the Informal Plenary. They cover all Second and Third Committee texts, and some First Committee and dispute settlement texts.

The unusually long hours and intense efforts of participants in the work of the Drafting Committee have resulted in a text that is significantly better drafted and more internally consistent within each language and among the six language versions. It is impossible to summarize such an exercise. It may be useful, however, both to observers of the Law of the Sea Conference and to others to reflect on the strengths and weaknesses of the procedures employed. The principal source of concern in this regard is not the work that the Drafting Committee has done, which has been almost universally welcomed, but the kind of work that the Drafting Committee has not been able to do.

The most novel procedure is the use of six open-ended language groups that meet separately, but simultaneously, on the same articles to make proposals in their respective languages and to consider the proposals of other language groups. This reduces the need for simultaneous interpretation, allows states not members of the committee and Secretariat experts to participate actively, and expedites consideration of proposals in a given language. Moreover, it channels most joint discussion (with simultaneous interpretation) to open meetings of the coordinators where virtually all debate is limited in fact to the six coordinators and the Chairman, arguably to advantage. However, it also reduces regular contact among those who attend different language group meetings. Given the difficulties of eliminating misunderstandings about drafting proposals across the barrier of simultaneous interpretation, this has necessitated informal consultations without interpreters, which the Chairman rightly encourages.

Most proposals of most language groups affect only the text in their language, although this is least true of the English Language Group. In practice, the system frequently approximates the more traditional approach in which one text—usually the English text—is drafted for meaning, and the remaining texts are then brought into conformity with it.

The basic problem is the limitation of the mandate accorded the Drafting Committee, which has discouraged some delegations from sending their most experienced personnel. Proposals to correct serious defects in the text are met with objections that they affect substance or will take too long to consider.

[37] The addenda to UN Docs. A/CONF.62/L.67 and L.75 contain the recommendations of the Drafting Committee presented during the tenth session. The proposal in question is in UN Doc. L.75/Add.10, and was incorporated into the new text, note 43 *infra*.

[38] DC(IT) Arts. 297 and 298.

When this occurs in conjunction with a strict and very rapid "no objection" procedure for dealing with proposals, the chances of making an important correction are seriously reduced. All too frequently, highly skilled and respected participants—especially present and former members of the International Law Commission—easily agree on a drafting improvement among themselves, only to see their suggestions blocked by a young delegate who will rarely, if ever, be blamed by his government for refusing to accept a drafting change in a text that his principals negotiated.

A typical example of the problems facing the Drafting Committee can be found in the very first article, which defines the "Area" as the seabed and subsoil and the ocean floor "beyond the limits of national jurisdiction." This definition was drawn from the Declaration of Principles on the Sea-bed[39] and, indeed, from the name of the committee that prepared the Declaration. The language was vague because, prior to the conference, there was no agreement on the names, nature, or limits of coastal zones.

The Draft Convention describes precise coastal zones with precise limits, in particular the territorial sea, the exclusive economic zone, and the continental shelf. Not one of the provisions regarding these areas uses the term "national jurisdiction." *Expressis verbis,* there are no "limits of national jurisdiction" in the Convention. Indeed, flag states exercise "national" jurisdiction wherever their ships go.

One would have thought it an easy matter to revise the definition of the Area to cross-reference the coastal limits established by the Convention itself. The work of the English Language Group on the matter—a group that functions by consensus and includes a large number of delegates from Asia, Africa, and the Caribbean—however, aroused such a storm of protest from Spanish-speaking delegations—particularly those whose countries face the rich nodule deposits of the Pacific—that all discussion had to cease. Thus, for all the attention being paid to the content of the common heritage principle, the Draft Convention does not contain a correct definition of the limits of the "Area" that is the common heritage, and accordingly does not contain a properly drafted prohibition on claims beyond 200 miles or the continental margin.

Another example concerns texts copied from earlier documents that are now utterly without rational meaning. What is the function of saying the continental shelf texts are without prejudice to tunneling from land in a convention that does not contain a depth-of-exploitability criterion and that establishes a definitive limit of the continental shelf?[40] What is the function of a paragraph that permits submission of a dispute to settlement procedures "specified" in a declaration, when there is no provision for choosing—only for excluding—dispute settlement procedures in the declaration concerned?[41] Proposals to correct these errors in the Drafting Committee failed.

[39] Declaration of Principles Governing the Sea-bed and the Ocean Floor, and the Sub-soil thereof, beyond the Limits of National Jurisdiction, UNGA Res. 2749 (XXV) (1970).

[40] DC(IT) Art. 85, derived from Art. 7 of the Convention on the Continental Shelf, 1958, 15 UST 471, TIAS No. 5578, 499 UNTS 311, *reprinted in* 52 AJIL 858 (1958). *Compare* Art. 76 of the Draft Convention *with* Art. 1 of the Convention on the Continental Shelf.

[41] DC(IT) Art. 298, para. 4. Art. 298(1)(a) of the ICNT had contained a requirement that a state indicate an alternative procedure that it would accept for settling delimitation disputes. This was eliminated in the ICNT/Rev.2 and subsequent texts.

A further example concerns internal consistency of texts. Article 297(1) excludes from compulsory jurisdiction the exercise by a coastal state of its sovereign rights, and thus embraces the continental shelf as well as the economic zone. Paragraph 3(a) of the same article refers to compulsory jurisdiction over all fisheries disputes, and then excludes sovereign rights only with respect to the living resources in the economic zone. Is it conceivable that paragraph 3 subjects continental shelf fishing rights to compulsory jurisdiction, when the substantive articles themselves exclude sedentary species from the obligation to give access to foreign states?[42] Again the effort to correct an obvious error failed.

One could understand a narrow reading of the mandate of the Drafting Committee if the substantive committees had, or desired to establish, a procedure for technical correction of the text. In reality, most delegations fear that meetings of substantive organs could reopen more than just technical problems. The result thus far is that failure to correct a technical problem in the Drafting Committee means it will not be corrected. If the conference is serious about creating a legally binding treaty, this situation needs to be changed, with all texts—including those already dealt with by the Drafting Committee—subject to an efficient system for technical correction. The strict "no objection" procedure—in each language group, in the committee, and in Informal Plenary—should be adequate guarantee that no delegation thereby risks a detrimental change in any aspect of the package (the true meaning of a "substantive" change).

The New Text

At the conclusion of the tenth session, the conference took a measured step in the direction both of negotiation with the United States and of final adoption of a text. It revised the text essentially to incorporate over fifteen hundred Drafting Committee changes. Without making it a formal text closed to negotiation and open to formal amendment, the conference gave the text a "higher status" by deleting the words "informal text" in its title and giving it an official limited document number.[43] The existing procedure for changing the text is retained, namely, a finding of a substantially improved prospect of consensus.

> It will be the official draft convention of the Law of the Sea of the Conference subject, however, to the following three conditions:
>
> *First,* the door would be kept open for the continuation of consultations and negotiations on certain outstanding issues. The results of these consultations and negotiations, if they satisfy the criterion in A/CONF.62/62,[44] will be incorporated in the Draft Convention by the collegium without the need for formal amendments.
>
> *Secondly,* the Drafting Committee will complete its work, and its further recommendations, approved by the Informal Plenary, will be incorporated in the text.

[42] DC(IT) Arts. 68 and 77.

[43] UN Doc. A/CONF.62/L.78 (1981).

[44] UN Doc. A/CONF.62/62, 10 Off. Rec. 6 (1978); relevant texts and author's comments are in 73 AJIL at 4–5.

Thirdly, in view of the fact that the process of consultations and negotiations on certain outstanding issues will continue, the time has, therefore, not arrived for the application of rule 33 of the Rules of Procedure of the Conference. At this stage, delegations will not be permitted to submit amendments. Formal amendments may only be submitted after the termination of all negotiations.[45]

IV. Conclusion

The conference decided to hold its "final decision-making session for the adoption of the Convention" in New York for 8 or 9 weeks in March–April 1982, a schedule intended to allow time for negotiation with the United States[46] and completion of work on outstanding issues. A "final intersessional meeting" of the Drafting Committee is planned for 6 weeks in January–February 1982 "to complete its work." The conference called for arrangements to be made with Venezuela "for the signature of the Final Act and the opening of the Convention for signature in Caracas in early September 1982."[47]

The author doubts that the problems facing the Law of the Sea Conference can be resolved properly without intensified assistance from the bar, a profession whose leading members are uniquely sensitive to the difficulties of building and sustaining a public order whose existence many others merely take for granted.

The invisible hand that makes productive private activity possible is law. Some commentators seem hardly to comprehend that there is more to international law than mere advocacy. A government may be able to stop or slow the emergence of a new rule, but it is difficult for any government on its own to impose a new rule that serves the functions of law, or to stop an existing rule from collapsing.

It may be useful in this regard to remind the public in all countries that the law of the sea and the proposed Convention deal with much more than the philosophy of regulating manganese nodule mining. They deal with military and commercial navigation, overflight, and communications (as the successful exercise by the U.S. Navy of the freedoms of the sea in the Gulf of Sidra during the resumed tenth session made clear); fisheries; continental shelf gas and oil; prevention of pollution; marine scientific research; and settlement of disputes; as well as important practical questions of real concern to prospective seabed miners.

Before resuming negotiations, all countries need to weigh the relative costs of abandoning the possibility of a convention that can be widely accepted as

[45] UN Doc. A/CONF.62/BUR.14 (1981). The President commented that the outstanding issues were those referred to in UN Docs. A/CONF.62/BUR.13 and A/CONF.62/WP.10/Rev.3* (arguably the introductory note), both of which contain open-ended references to issues of concern to delegations. Rule 33 of the Rules of Procedure deals with amendments to proposals.

[46] Needless to say, the effort would lack credibility if the conference in fact proceeded, as currently projected, to apply rule 33—that is, to take up formal amendments—after the first 3 weeks. As for the dangers of voting on formal amendments, they are if anything greater than those previously described by the author. *See* 74 AJIL at 46–47; 75 *id.* at 212.

[47] UN Doc. A/CONF.62/BUR.14, note 45 *supra.*

against making the changes necessary to accommodate the United States and other Western countries. Too much emphasis on the problem of process is self-defeating. One must consider dispassionately the value in their present form of provisions found offensive by the U.S. Government because, if necessary changes are not made, those provisions may never apply to the states from whom the relevant concessions were sought. Could there be an effective Enterprise or production limitation? Whose technology would be transferred? Whose activities would be organized and controlled? Who would be affected by the review conference?

Ambassador Koh has stated that the Convention would be adopted, preferably with, but if necessary, without the United States. Implicit in this remark may be an assumption, at times articulated by developing country representatives, that major Western countries, including Japan and the states of the European Community, will ratify a law of the sea convention over the opposition of the United States. What is remarkable about some discussions of this hypothesis is the lack of appreciation of the extent of public opposition to certain aspects of the Draft Convention in Western countries outside the United States.

One need identify but a few factors:

- The inclusion of any so-called transitional provision regarding dependencies or disputed areas, or a provision on participation of so-called national liberation movements, would eliminate virtually any possibility of significant acceptance.

- Financing the Enterprise is disliked by almost all Western treasuries and economists; both land-based producers and potential seabed producers believe they are in effect being asked to finance a competitor.

- Agencies concerned with assistance to developing countries share that dislike; they see few benefits to the least developed countries flowing from the Enterprise, and are fearful of competition for funds and loan guarantees in a period of shrinking budgets.

- Other aspects of the deep seabed mining regime that trouble the United States also trouble other potential deep seabed mining states. Even France's new Socialist Government has approved deep seabed mining legislation.[48]

- The provision for revenue sharing from the continental shelf beyond 200 miles is much less popular in the Western broad margin states than their Governments—ever fearful of provoking a reaction at the conference on the outer limits of the continental shelf—are saying.

- There is pressure on some governments not to forgo the option of claiming broader environmental and fisheries rights, including control over stocks of coastal species that extend beyond 200 miles.

- Not all Western Governments share the general enthusiasm for the articles on straits or the economic zone, while many states that approve of those articles regard the rights elaborated as already established and vested under customary law.

[48] [1981–82] J.O. 1902 (Oct. 9, 1981, Senate text).

- For at least some countries, one incentive for the treaty would be the substantive and dispute settlement rights they would acquire vis-à-vis the United States only if it were a party.

In general, a state is likely to be reluctant to assume obligations that another similarly situated state is not assuming. This is so sometimes because the absolute burdens—be they monetary or be they duties to others such as landlocked and geographically disadvantaged countries—may thus be increased, and sometimes because those obligations may put the state or its nationals at a relative disadvantage with respect to another state.

The failure of the United States to accept the obligations of the Law of the Sea Convention would inevitably affect the ability of others to persuade their constituencies to accept them. It would give rise to political restraints on ratification by major allies, as well as misgivings of principle regarding the entry into force of a treaty that, without the world's major power, cannot purport to establish a global regime.

Moreover, the member states of the European Community have made clear that concurrent acceptance of the Convention by the Community itself is a legal necessity for them. If a decision by the Council of Ministers of the Community to accept the Convention in practice requires a consensus of the ten member states,[49] and if such acceptance is a prerequisite to ratification by any member state, widespread Western adherence over the objections of the United States becomes ever more problematical.

Public threats to adopt the Convention and isolate the United States from its principal allies are neither credible (in part because of their premature publicity) nor conducive to the completion of a "convention on the law of the sea" in any meaningful sense of the word, namely, one accepted by the major Western industrial and maritime powers. Such threats have the decided disadvantage of making treaty supporters appear to be timorous and weak. Worse still, they risk coloring the treaty so strongly as a (Soviet-promoted) act of defiance of the United States as to doom any real political possibility of substantial Western ratification under any circumstances. This is particularly true if, as the Secretary of State advised the Senate Foreign Relations Committee less than a month after the end of the tenth session, "the United States does intend to continue to participate fully in this Conference with the clear objective of bringing it to a successful conclusion."[50]

It is possible, of course, to imagine a process of negotiation with the United States and its principal allies that is sufficiently sensitive, intense, and flexible to persuade significant Western opinion-leaders that the results should be acceptable. At that time, Western Governments would have to make a decision. If the negotiating process had itself encouraged concerted action by the United States and its allies all along, the probability of a concerted positive decision

[49] There might in fact be more than ten EEC members by the time the issue arises, including Spain, a straits state with major fishing interests, which is not generally noted for its enthusiasm for the Convention.

[50] Secretary of State Alexander M. Haig, Senate Foreign Relations Committee Hearing, Sept. 17, 1981 (preliminary transcript).

would be increased. In any event, the credibility—in a real sense, the legitimacy—of action taken in that situation would be far different.

It is not productive to argue about who gains or loses most from the treaty as a whole. That question turns on a subjective evaluation of priorities about which no two individuals, not to mention states, would agree. The main point is that no one can gain and retain the benefits of a convention on the law of the sea unless it is widely ratified.

U.S. FISHERY MANAGEMENT AND THE NEW LAW OF THE SEA

*By W. T. Burke**

The coming into force for the United States and other nations of a law of the sea treaty may affect fishery management in the United States under the Fishery Conservation and Management Act (FCMA) in a number of different ways.[1] This discussion examines some possible ways and focuses particularly upon possible incompatible provisions in terms of the objectives of fishery management, subsidiary standards for management, conservation and allocation measures, the species within United States authority, the allocation of fishery management authority between state and federal governments, transboundary stocks and high seas/fishery zone stocks, enforcement authority and activity, and lastly, the amendment of regulations adopted under the FCMA to conform to the LOS treaty.

I. Objectives of Fishery Management

Clarification of U.S. fishery management objectives is a basic initial task. A recent and valuable report on fisheries management by the Working Party of the FAO Advisory Committee on Marine Resources Research provides helpful observations on the importance of this task for fisheries management and summarizes traditional objectives.

> As in other activities, the establishment of a clearly defined objective, or set of objectives, is an essential starting point for fishery management. The declared objectives will govern the detailed nature, scope and content of the management schemes that are adopted, including the requirements

* Professor of Law, University of Washington School of Law.

This paper was originally drafted as part of a project of the Fisheries Task Group of the Oceans Policy Committee of the National Research Council. Members of this group read and commented on an earlier draft. Others also kind enough to read earlier drafts include Dayton L. Alverson, Francis T. Christy, Jr., Edward D. Evans, Jr., August Felando, Christopher L. Koch, Elizabeth R. Mitchell, Brian Rothschild, William L. Sullivan, Jr., and unnamed commentators in the National Marine Fisheries Service. I am grateful for comments received, but none of the readers bear any responsibility for statements in the article nor do the latter necessarily reflect the views of any agency of the U.S. Government or of any other entity.

[1] The FCMA was adopted in 1976 as Pub. L No. 94–265 and amended in 1978 by Pub. L. No. 95–354 and again in 1980 by Pub. L. No. 96–561. It is classified in 16 U.S.C. §§1801–1857 and in certain other sections of Title 16 and in 22 U.S.C. §§1972–1973.

The LOS treaty could of course be "adopted" by the LOS Conference but never come into force for the United States. Mere adoption by the LOS Conference would have no effect on U.S. management under the FCMA. It is generally accepted (and is the administration's position) that if the United States signs such a treaty, this would oblige the United States, prior to its ratification of the treaty, to act in such a way as not to defeat the object and purposes of the treaty. Letter of Dec. 21, 1979, from Elliot L. Richardson to Senator Warren G. Magnuson. It is not clear that this obligation would signify any need for a particular change in management and this discussion does not seek to identify such changes. As noted in the text, U.S. law seeks to provide for changes in implementing regulations after U.S. ratification of the treaty, but before it comes into force.

for data and research, and they provide the yardstick against which the success or failure of management can be assessed.

There has been considerable debate regarding the appropriate definition of a fishery management objective. Discussions on an appropriate objective have intensified with the changing legal regime. Before these changes in effective ownership, marine fisheries were international, based, with few exceptions, on common property resources. The fisheries of the different countries taking part in the overall fishery activity were governed by different social, economic and political climates. As a consequence, and not surprisingly, the objectives of fishery management which became most acceptable to the international fishery community, and which were embodied in international fishery management conventions, were ones defined on the basis of criteria relating to the biological properties of the exploited resources and the catches attainable from them.

The most widely used objective was maximum sustainable yield or some variant of it. The merit and attractiveness of maximum sustainable yield was its apparently unambiguous definition, its focus on the maximizing of fish production for food and industrial purposes, and the fact that it could be estimated—at least to a reasonable approximation—with the scientific tools available. It was frequently the upper bound for a range of advocated strategies and thus a basis for compromise. When the simplified context of MSY calculations is altered to allow for species interactions, climatic trends, and alternative definitions of benefits, it is no longer a simple matter to define and calculate MSY.

. . . .

Biologically based objectives such as maximum sustainable yield may result in a management system which "works" and achieves benefits to the community in the form of higher sustained fish supplies than would probably be attained in the absence of management, but the biological objectives in themselves do not satisfy specific important socio-economic concerns in fishery management. As has been pointed out by fishery economists for many years, management based on a biological objective such as MSY will inevitably result in over-capacity in the fishery and the dissipation of the potential economic benefits which might be achieved if "optimization" involved socio-economic objectives with biological constraints. Economists argue that an objective, aimed at maximizing economic yield . . . , would be more appropriate than the biologically based one. The result of doing so might be some sacrifice of average physical yield from the particular stock in question, and in the level of direct employment in that fishery, in return for more long-term stability in the fishery and an increase in the contributions made by the fishery to the economies of the participating countries. Many other objectives have been advocated on some fisheries management situations. These include maximization of employment or achieving a target income distribution and maintaining high catch rates for recreational fisheries.[2]

For the purpose of the present discussion the major objectives of U.S. fishery management are considered to be conservation and allocation, *i.e.*, how much

[2] FOOD AND AGRICULTURE ORGANIZATION (FAO), REPORT OF THE ACMRR WORKING PARTY ON THE SCIENTIFIC BASIS OF DETERMINING MANAGEMENT MEASURES 24 (FAO Fisheries Report No. 236, 1980).

fish (or other living marine resource) can be taken and who gets it, with the former understood to relate both to target species and to species otherwise affected either as incidental catch, as part of the predator-prey relationship, or in the affected food chain.[3] Because management objectives are so important, as noted in the ACMRR Report, it is worthwhile to examine them in relation to the draft LOS treaty, even though it will be concluded that there is no incompatibility between them.

With respect to the conservation objective, some discussion will be devoted to whether or not the FCMA and necessarily related enactments combine to establish a management scheme sufficiently comprehensive to meet the requirements of draft LOS treaty Article 61(3) and (4) regarding associated and dependent species. On allocation there also appears to be no incompatibility between the two; whatever the draft treaty enjoins will be found to be consistent with FCMA objectives.

It is not easy to distill a succinct, coherent, and clear statement of the objectives established for fishery management by the FCMA.[4] The Act specifies that "conservation and management measures shall prevent overfishing,"[5] and the findings, purposes, and stated policy in combination lend support to the view that this may be considered the principal conservation objective of the legislation. Despite this emphasis the Act does not define "overfishing." It nonetheless seems safe to conclude that the Act's conservation objective is to avoid overfishing in the sense of preventing fishing pressure that is excessive because it might lead to irreversible effects.[6] An accompanying objective is to rebuild stocks that are overfished.

In a major departure from most prior management practice, the Act does not require that management seek to maintain target fishery stocks at a level of abundance that permits the taking of the maximum sustainable yield (MSY).[7]

[3] As the ACMRR Report notes, there are many possible objectives for management. The conservation and allocation objectives are selected here because they seem particularly significant in an examination of an international agreement. There is a widespread common interest in assuring that living resources are maintained in reasonable abundance and that these resources are shared among those interested. Most of the other objectives noted are important for their impact on these two and for exclusively national policy.

[4] Questions about the original objectives of the FCMA are examined in Christy, *The Fishery Conservation and Management Act of 1976: Management Objectives and the Distribution of Benefits and Costs*, 52 WASH. L. REV. 657 (1977); and Young, The Political Economy of Fish: The Fishery Conservation and Management Act of 1976, at 13–18 (unpub., Dec. 1980).

[5] Section 301(a)(1). This is the initial part of national Standard 1; the remaining words are "while achieving, on a continuing basis, the optimum yield from each fishery."

[6] FCMA §301(a)(2), (3), (4), (5), and (6) are all findings that deal with overfishing. Of the seven separate standards in §301, only two ((1) and (7)) do not feature reference to overfishing. Section 3(2)(B)(ii) defines conservation and management measures to include those designed to assure that "irreversible or long-term adverse effects on fishery resources and the marine environment are avoided."

[7] FAO, ACMRR REPORT, *supra* note 2, at 24. Nearly all international fishery agreements prior to the advent of 200-mile fishing zones set out to maintain abundance of a fishery at a level that would provide the MSY. The Oct. 1, 1969 Protocol to ICNAF amended that Convention to authorize regulatory measures to achieve "optimum utilization." Protocol to the International Convention for the Northwest Atlantic Fisheries Relating to Panel Membership and to Regulatory Measures, 23 UST 1504, TIAS No. 7432.

The latter concept enters into the Act not as an objective of management but as a benchmark for expressing the optimum yield (OY) of a fishery. It was apparently recognized that OY is a very general notion and that it might help to clarify the objectives OY summarizes by requiring that it be expressed in terms of expected benefits that justify departure from MSY. Professor (now Dean) Don Bevan explained and urged this approach in a letter to Senator Magnuson of September 19, 1975:

> I should like to suggest another definition of optimum yield, which I think is extremely important in applying management in practice. I would completely reject Option B (Option B suggested utilizing maximum economic yield) but point out that Option A can be defined by different interests in different ways and it may make it difficult to apply a practical application of a quantitative figure in an actual fishery. Optimum yield can be taken to mean what anyone wants it to mean. I would suggest that an analogy from navigation is useful in providing a definition of optimum yield. If we know a starting point and know our distance and direction from it, we can locate a position with exactness. I suggest that optimum yield be defined in the same way, that the base line be the maximum sustained yield, and that optimum yield be defined as a measured deviation from maximum sustained yield, together with the reasons for moving from the maximum sustained yield. This definition provides several advantages. First, in order to define maximum sustained yield, sufficient biological observations need to be taken and a sufficient knowledge of stock has to be on hand to understand how the stock will respond to various levels of fishing. And second, those interests who choose to move away from maximum sustained yield, and I can think of many valid reasons to do so, will be required to quantitatively state the movement necessary and what gain is to be expected from over or underfishing. If this is done, we can have some numbers which different interests can evaluate and perhaps a consensus can be obtained more easily.[8]

Accordingly, the second (and partly procedural) component of the definition of OY declares that it "is prescribed as such on the basis of the maximum sustainable yield from such fishery, as modified by any relevant economic, social, or ecological factor."[9]

The FCMA conservation objective for nontarget species—incidental catch or other affected species—is recorded in general provisions that require "to the extent practicable" management of interrelated stocks as a unit or in close coordination[10] and call for account to be taken of, and allowance made for, variations and contingencies concerning fish and fish resources.[11] The term "fishery resource" refers to "any fishery, any stock of fish, any species of fish, and any habitat of fish,"[12] and such terms are not limited to target species. In

[8] Quoted in Bevan, The Function of Optimum Yield Under the Fishery Conservation and Management Act of 1976 (unpub., dated April 18, 1980).

[9] FCMA §3(18).

[10] National Standard 3 provides: "To the extent practicable, an individual stock of fish shall be managed as a unit throughout its range, and interrelated stocks of fish shall be managed as a unit or in close coordination." FCMA §301(a)(3).

[11] National Standard 6 provides: "Conservation and management measures shall take into account and allow for variations among, and contingencies in fisheries, fishery resources, and catches." FCMA §301(a)(6).

[12] FCMA §3(9).

specifying an "optimum yield," the fishery management Council or the Secretary of Commerce has ample authority to reflect the effects of fishing upon nontarget species; the optimum yield is to be prescribed on the basis of MSY from a fishery "as modified by any relevant economic, social or ecological factor." It is not difficult to spell out of these provisions a statutory objective and obligation to see that associated and dependent stocks or species are not seriously threatened or endangered by exploitation of a target species or stock.[13]

The FCMA itself does not include marine mammals but it does require that fishery regulations defer to the protection requirements of the Marine Mammal Protection Act (MMPA)[14] for such animals. The technical reason for this is in section 303, which declares:

> Any fishery management plan which is prepared by any Council, or by the Secretary, with respect to any fishery, shall—
>
> (1) contain the conservation and management measures, applicable to foreign fishing and fishing by vessels of the United States, which are . . .
>
> (C) consistent with the national standards, the other provisions of this chapter, and any other applicable law. . . .[15]

This means that the objectives and provisions of the MMPA must be regarded as constraints or conditions with which FCMA must comply. Most specifically, a management plan and regulations must recognize the obligation to maintain the optimum sustainable population of marine mammals.[16]

The allocation objectives of the Act are to assert U.S. exclusive authority to forbid foreign fishing except of stocks that are surplus to U.S. fish-harvesting capacity[17] and to realize the "optimum yield" from a fishery. The latter concept bears on allocation because it is defined as "the amount of fish—(A) which will provide the greatest overall benefit to the Nation, with particular reference to food production and recreational opportunities."[18]

This concept of "greatest overall benefit to the Nation" is sufficiently loose that officials have a very wide range of discretion in determining what amounts of fish may be considered "optimum." It has been said that optimum yield is whatever it is said to be so long as it is said carefully.[19] The significance of this for allocation is that, because the OY concept is very general, it is easier for

[13] Decisions under the FCMA must comply also with the Endangered Species Act, 87 Stat. 884 (1973). *See* note 15 *infra.*

[14] 16 U.S.C. §§1361–1407 (1972).

[15] Section 303(a)(1).

[16] While the concept of the optimum sustainable population is the key element of the MMPA, there are a number of other potential requirements in the Act which may constrain management decisions under the FCMA. For discussion of these, see Child & Haley, *The Marine Mammal Protection Act and the Fishery Conservation and Management Act: The Need for Balance*, 56 WASH. L. REV. 365 (1981); see also Hammond, Fisheries Management under the Fishery Conservation and Management Act, the Marine Mammal Protection Act, and the Endangered Species Act (Final Report to the U.S. Marine Mammal Commission, May 1980) (NTIS No. PB80–180 599).

[17] The Act forbids foreign fishing in the exclusive fishing zone (and outside it for anadromous and continental shelf resources) except by agreement and in accord with the Act. Section 201(a). For discussion of the formula for determining allowable foreign fishing, see *infra* pp. 37–40.

[18] Section 3(18). Section 301 requires that management plans and regulations achieve the OY.

[19] Bevan, *supra* note 8, at 1.

fish catches to be established either at levels that do not permit or require allocation of a surplus to foreign fleets or at levels that minimize the surplus. The FCMA objective (and standard) of optimum yield thus gives such wide latitude to managers that total or partial exclusion of foreign fishing, despite a (undeclared) biological surplus over U.S. fishing capacity, appears to be consistent with the Act.

The draft LOS treaty[20] addresses both of the major problems of fishery management, conservation (Article 61) and allocation to users (Articles 61 and 62), and confers exclusive authority on coastal states to make decisions on such issues (Articles 56, 61, and 62). Provisions on dispute settlement (part XV) establish that these decisions are subject to the discretion of the coastal state, which cannot be obliged to submit disputes concerning them to dispute settlement as provided in the treaty. The ultimate thrust of the draft treaty on living resources is to permit the coastal state either itself to take the entire allowable catch and exclude foreigners from the 200-mile zone or, if it decides a surplus exists, to grant access on terms and conditions that are satisfactory to it and do not arbitrarily restrict foreign fishing for the surplus.[21]

Within this context the major stated objectives of management are:

> (1) to ensure that living resources in the zone are not endangered by overexploitation (Article 61(2));
>
> (2) to maintain associated or dependent species above levels at which their reproduction may become seriously threatened (Article 61(4));
>
> (3) to provide for harvesting the entire allowable catch of living resources within the zone. The portion in excess of the domestic harvesting capacity shall be made available by agreement to foreign fishing subject to coastal regulations.

A major unstated objective, but a clear effect of the several provisions, is to allow the coastal state to manage fisheries, within the above "limits," so as to derive the optimum benefit therefrom, as it may define optimum benefit. In doing so it is not encumbered by any obligation to make resources available to other states, except as it sees fit to do so. The only coastal state obligation in this regard is to establish an allowable catch, whose dimensions are solely within its discretion to determine, and, if it cannot harvest this catch, to grant access to other states on such terms and conditions as it is willing to accept and are not unreasonable.[22]

The first of the two conservation goals of the LOS treaty is ambiguously

[20] United Nations, Third Conference on the Law of the Sea, Draft Convention on the Law of the Sea (Informal Text), UN Doc. A/CONF.62/WP.10/Rev.3, and Add. 1 and Corrs. 1–6 (1980), *reproduced in* 19 ILM 1131 (1980).

[21] The doctrine of abuse of rights in Article 300 of the treaty makes provision for an attack on unreasonable, arbitrary exercises of lawful authority, although this does not appear to effect any change in the dispute settlement provisions. Article 297(3)(b) provides a compulsory conciliation procedure for specific alleged arbitrary actions and perhaps this procedure could be invoked to give effect to Article 300.

[22] The Draft Convention does not expressly incorporate the reasonableness standard, but it is presumed to be as applicable to these choices as any other. As noted in note 21 *supra*, the Article 300 provision on abuse of rights lays to rest contentions about application of a standard of reasonableness.

stated and the extent of the obligation is therefore not clear. Article 61(2) provides that the coastal state must "ensure" that "the maintenance of the living resources in the economic zone is not endangered by over-exploitation." The expression "maintenance of living resources" is vague in at least two respects and the meaning of the concept "endangered" is also not obvious.

With respect to the former phrase, the term "maintenance" does not indicate what level of the resources is to be maintained and held safe from overexploitation. A second ambiguity arises from the term "living resources," and specifically whether the reference is to a stock, population, or species. This latter may be largely a theoretical difference and not a practical one in view of the difficulty in identifying component stocks and populations in a fishery and determining what is harvested from them.

The concept "endangered" might be interpreted as implying a threat to survival, *i.e.*, in danger of extinction, but it seems doubtful if this is very meaningful or helpful. In the first place, the possibility of extinction of a genuine marine finfish as a result of overfishing is so remote that it is not a reasonable objective of conservation. So far as is known, no marine finfish have been reduced to extinction by overexploitation in the past several thousand years, although some have been exploited intensely for hundreds of years.[23] Moreover, if one is concerned about promoting continued exploitation of marine fish, the occasion for apprehension about endangering a resource comes much earlier than any realistic worry over extinction.

Alternative interpretations might be that endangering in this context refers to reductions in abundance that amount to commercial extinction or, more strictly, to reductions of such magnitude that a species is likely to become endangered unless protective action is taken. Seriously reduced stock might support a marginal fishery, although the added mortality might tip the balance toward irreversibility and this should be prevented.

It is not known what an appropriate interpretation might be, but we are able to exclude one alternative. Article 61(3) states that the measures to avoid endangering are also to "maintain or restore populations of harvested species at levels which can produce the maximum sustainable yield, as qualified by relevant environmental and economic factors." Accordingly, the coastal state may establish such management objectives as environmental and economic factors, among others,[24] and may suggest and pursue such amounts of harvested

[23] Species listed as endangered under the ESPA include one marine finfish, the *totoaba* in the Gulf of California. 50 C.F.R. §17.11 (1980). The reasons for this listing are not known, but it seems unlikely to be related to exploitation.

Although referring to a stock in a specific locale, the following report nonetheless requires mention:

> A scientist from the U.K. Directorate of Fisheries Laboratory has reported that the once-abundant skate, a member of the ray family, has practically disappeared from the Irish Sea. It is believed that the mortality due to commercial fishing exceeded the maximum level which the species could withstand without collapsing. Research vessels have failed to find a single specimen of skate for the last 15 years.

NOAA, Office of International Fisheries Affairs, The Latest Developments in World Fisheries, May 1981, pt. I, at 5.

[24] *See* p. 36 *infra* for comment on the omission of social factors in this formulation.

fish as are appropriate to those objectives, including yield figures in excess of MSY if this is in its interest. Exceeding MSY temporarily does not constitute overfishing in the sense of threatening irreversible effects; hence such action does not endanger maintenance of living resources in the exclusive economic zone.[25]

In sum, this particular objective appears to have no significant implications for management under FCMA because it demands no more than the FCMA already requires by way of avoiding overfishing. Conservation measures that avoid overfishing, as mandated by the FCMA, would also see that a resource is not endangered by overexploitation. The general language of the treaty referring to "living resources" seems immaterial in connection with the FCMA because the latter defines "stock of fish" as a "species, subspecies, geographical grouping, or other category of fish capable of management as a unit."

The second conservation objective of the draft treaty, concerning "the effects on species associated with or dependent upon harvested species," is anything but modest. According to Article 61(4), the coastal state, in establishing conservation and management measures, "shall take into consideration the effects on species associated with or dependent upon harvested species with a view to maintaining or restoring populations of such associated or dependent species above levels at which their reproduction may become seriously threatened." A recent study observed that the terms "associated or dependent species" have as yet no common usage and are vague in nature.[26]

For this discussion this objective embraces two different situations: (1) effects on associated species, which is here interpreted to include incidental catches or by-catches, and (2) effects on dependent species such as predator-prey or more distant food or other biological relationships. These situations are mentioned also in Article 61(3), which requires that in determining conservation and management measures the coastal state should take into account the interdependence of stocks.

Each of these effects may relate to other finfish or to mammals. Insofar as incidental catch or otherwise affected dependent species are marine fish, the limitation imposed by this objective on coastal state measures seems minimal. As noted above, it is extremely difficult to harvest a marine finfish species to the degree that its reproduction is threatened. If it is difficult (and perhaps impossible in any practical sense) to do this by targeting on a species, it is even less likely, in most instances,[27] that such an impact would be brought about by incidental catch or by reducing food levels or the like. Indeed, there may be reason to doubt that fishery management science is developed to the point

[25] Gulland points out that harvesting beyond the MSY level may be a wise choice for a sole owner of a resource, but he distinguishes this sharply from what happens in practice where "the unreasonable logic of open access drives the effort past the MSY level unless all participants can agree on regulations to control effort." J. GULLAND, GOALS AND OBJECTIVES OF FISHERY MANAGEMENT 5 n.1 (FAO Fisheries Technical Paper No. 166, 1977, Doc. No. FIRS/T166). The result is the same in either instance.

[26] Dawson, *Glossary of Terms and Concepts Used in Fishery Management*, in ACMRR REPORT, *supra* note 2, at 117.

[27] Where a stock is naturally small or has been severely reduced by natural or fishing mortality, the effects of by-catch might be to take a larger portion of the stock than that taken by the directed fishery.

that such a precise determination could even be made.[28] On the other hand, the very fact of uncertainty about impacts on associated or dependent species of marine fish may suggest to some that the coastal state must exercise caution in adopting particular measures and that this consideration mandates a more restrictive regime than would otherwise be the case.

The situation with respect to incidental catch of (or other impact on) marine mammals is different, for it is quite conceivable that these populations can be seriously reduced by fishing activities either directly as incidental catch or, perhaps, indirectly by deprivation of food. Because their rate of reproduction is far lower than that of marine fish, a marine mammal species can be reduced to extinction. Nonetheless, this standard does not represent a very onerous obligation for the United States, although it might be a useful one when compared with the U.S. Marine Mammal Protection Act, which requires maintenance of the "optimum sustainable population" as a condition of receiving permission to take marine mammals incidentally. No one is too clear about the meaning of OSP, but its definition by an agency concerned places the lowest point in the range of value assigned to OSP at a much higher level than the one at which reproduction of a species is threatened.[29]

It seems probable that the FCMA and the treaty are compatible on provisions concerning dependent and associated species, both fish and marine mammals. As noted earlier, specific FCMA provisions and other applicable law stipulate a level of protection that meets treaty standards.[30]

While no detailed assessment of the matter has been made for this paper, some observers doubt that U.S. fishery management officials take adequate account of the effects of fishing on marine mammals.[31] That this might be so does not determine the relationship between FCMA (and MMPA) and the draft LOS treaty.

The same general point can be made concerning management efforts to take account of effects of fishing on associated or dependent finfish (or molluscs or crustacea) species. This is an extremely difficult and complex task, which may

[28] The question concerns the capacity for ecosystem management. In an earlier report the ACMRR Working Party, whose final report is quoted in the text at footnote 2 *supra*, stated:

> The management implication of the term "ecosystem management" presumes a reasonable understanding of the physical and chemical environment and the biological species which describe an ecosystem plus an understanding of the interactions among and between the species complex and their environment. Effective ecosystem management would also require an understanding of the flow of material energy and nutrients within the ecosystem. At present the totality of interactions is not sufficiently understood in any marine ecosystem to allow for a comprehensive ecosystem management.

FAO, REPORT OF THE ACMRR WORKING PARTY ON THE SCIENTIFIC BASIS OF DETERMINING MANAGEMENT MEASURES 20 (FAO Fisheries Circular No. 718, 1979). *See* ACMRR REPORT, *supra* note 2; Dawson, *supra* note 26, at 121, where it is stated that "[e]cosystems are not sufficiently understood at this time to allow the relationships to be readily separated or the necessary analyses to be made"; note 32 *infra*.

[29] 50 C.F.R. §216.3 (1979).

[30] P. 28 *supra*.

[31] Child & Haley, *supra* note 16; Hammond, *supra* note 16; letter of Jan. 18, 1979 from John Twiss, Executive Director of Marine Mammal Commission to J. H. Branson, Executive Director, North Pacific Fishery Management Council.

indeed be beyond management capacity at the present time.[32] Nonetheless, the FCMA provisions are consistent with the draft treaty.

The draft treaty's allocational, or distributional, objective for the coastal state is virtually, but not quite, exhausted by provisions aimed essentially at authorizing it to establish the allowable catch at whatever amount or level will satisfy its own interests. If this happens to be the same as the harvesting capacity of the coastal state's fishing fleet, then there is no obligation to permit access by foreign vessels. If the allowable catch does exceed domestic harvesting capacity, then the coastal state is obliged to give access to other states. However, this obligation is imperfect because access is by agreement only, and then in accordance with terms and conditions, some of which might make access an uneconomic proposition. Nonetheless, the nonexhaustive listing in Article 62(4) of a variety of regulatory actions by the coastal state does not mean that the coastal state may deny access to a surplus by unreasonable or arbitrary regulations. Regulations must be consistent with the coastal state's obligation to give access, as established in Article 62(2). It would be inconsistent with the treaty to promulgate invidious regulations that made it wholly impractical to fish at all.

The FCMA and the treaty appear to be compatible in most circumstances with respect to this objective of allocation. The obligation under the treaty is to establish an allowable catch, not to establish it at any particular level above a minimum. There is thus no obligation to create a surplus by setting the allowable catch above harvesting capacity. Under the FCMA the same sequence occurs: the optimum yield may be virtually whatever the Council wants it to be, and only if the OY is set larger than U.S. harvesting capacity is there any need to provide the allocation of the allowable level of foreign fishing. It is permissible under the FCMA to determine that OY is no greater than U.S. harvesting capacity and the treaty demands no more. On the other hand, if it is decided that a surplus exists, the FCMA calls for foreign fishing to be allowed as does the treaty. This point is further examined below in connection with the issue of distributing a surplus.

II. Subsidiary Standards for Management

FCMA section 301 (16 U.S.C. §1851) lists seven standards with which fishery management plans must be consistent, two of which bear consideration in relation to international standards or obligations found in the treaty. Standard 2 declares: "Conservation and management measures shall be based upon the best available scientific information." Standard 5 states: "Conservation and

[32] The Fishery Management Plan for the Bering Sea and Aleutian Islands groundfishery, in discussing fishery-marine mammal interactions, states:

> The Plan development Team for this FMP is acutely aware and is striving for an "ecosystem approach" for managing the marine resources. It will, however, be some time (3–5 years) before an appropriate ecosystem model has become far enough developed, and empirically tested, to begin to be relied upon for resource management.

44 Fed. Reg. 66,367, 66,421 (1979).

management measures shall, where practicable, promote efficiency in the utilization of fishery resources; except that no such measure shall have economic allocation as its sole purpose."

The draft treaty has a version of Standard 2 that differs in several respects. It is found in Article 61(2) but probably is applicable to all purposes served by conservation and management measures: "The coastal State, taking into account the best scientific evidence available to it, shall ensure through proper conservation and management measures that the maintenance of the living resources in the exclusive economic zone is not endangered by over-exploitation." A first point is that instead of requiring that measures be *based* upon the "best," the draft treaty declares that the coastal state shall take the "best" into account. This appears to be a more lenient requirement than in the FCMA because "taking into account" demands a lesser showing than "based upon." On the other hand, it hardly seems likely that "taking into account," as sloppy and indeterminate as this phrase may be, was intended to leave the coastal state free to resort to evidence of lesser quality. It seems more likely that this phrase is a diplomatic euphemism for "using."

A second point is that "best" in the treaty text qualifies "scientific evidence available" rather than "information." Although Dawson uses the terms interchangeably, she comments that the draft treaty formulation "implies that scientific data will be used to determine specific levels of allowable catch and/or harvesting capacity."[33] In such an interpretation the term "evidence" connotes direct influence or determinative effect upon a particular decision. In such a view it may be fair to say that information is not evidence unless it is sufficiently pertinent and weighty to be influential. The significance of such a distinction, presumably, would be that even the "best scientific information" cannot be used to justify, or as a basis for, a particular decision, unless it is interpreted to be "evidence" by criteria of pertinence and persuasiveness.

If such an interpretation of the draft treaty standard and the difference from that in the FCMA were valid, it might have a very large impact on management under the latter. A major criticism sometimes made of the FCMA standard is that it authorizes measures based on poor or inadequate scientific information which is nonetheless the best available. The critics would prefer that in this situation no action be taken and that there be a requirement for a certain minimum body of data for a management plan. One assessment stated:

> The absence of certain types of biological data can have a critical impact on certain of the most fundamental determinations that must be reflected in a management plan. For example, the calculation of optimum yield must begin with a determination of the maximum sustainable yield ("MSY"), a biological concept. Each of the various ways of determining MSY, however, rests in part on tenuous assumptions and data which is often incomplete or speculative. The "soft" data generally available for these biological calculations contrast sharply with the much harder data nearly always available concerning the economic requirements of the fishery. As a result, the pressure to "fudge" the MSY calculation is great where a conservative calculation could intervene with the perceived eco-

[33] Dawson, *supra* note 26, at 117.

nomic requirements of the fishery. The calculation of MSY for the surf clam fishery as the historic average harvest over a period that includes egregious overharvesting, and that thus builds into the calculation the historical factors that led to the near collapse of the fishery, is a case in point.[34]

It is difficult to conclude that the term "evidence" rather than "information" can be given so much significance that this alone warrants refusal to take (or not to take) a particular action because a quantum of scientific information is alleged to be inadequate. The result might well be to hamstring and perhaps cripple a timely and needed management measure because of uncertainty about the quantum of scientific information to support it. The situation would be ripe for legal delays and disruptions arising from differences about the interpretation of scientific data. At the same time, action based on poor data, or good data badly interpreted, can also have harmful consequences. All that is suggested here is that the slight word difference between the draft treaty and FCMA is not a sufficient basis for changing the policy now followed in implementing the FCMA.

National Standard 5 may be inconsistent with the LOS draft because the latter gives greater scope to coastal fishery management for economic purposes, but this does not necessarily mean the provisions are incompatible. Standard 5 declares that while conservation and management measures should promote efficiency "where practicable, . . . no such measure shall have economic allocation as its sole purpose." No such restraint can be derived from the treaty. Nonetheless, the grant of broader authority by the latter does not require that it be exercised; hence there appears to be no incompatibility in the requirements of the treaty in relation to the FCMA.[35]

III. Conservation and Allocation Measures

1. Allowable Catch

The FCMA and the draft treaty appear to be wholly consistent. The latter simply states that the coastal state shall determine the allowable catch. In doing so it is obliged to ensure, taking account of the best available scientific evidence, that "the maintenance of the living resources of the exclusive economic zone is not endangered by over-exploitation."[36] As noted earlier, the FCMA does

[34] Petition of the Environmental Defense Fund for the Amendment of the Guidelines for Development of Fishery Management Plans (50 C.F.R. Part 602) 7 (Oct. 10, 1979).

[35] Nonetheless, it needs to be noted that the treaty authorizes what the FCMA specifically prohibits. Presumably, implementing legislation for the LOS treaty should take account of this difference.

[36] Article 61(2) also states: "As appropriate, the coastal State and competent international organizations, whether subregional, regional or global, shall co-operate to this end." The requirements of such an obligation appear to be no more than prudent policy would dictate with regard to any policy matter. Whether a particular undertaking or initiative is "appropriate" is for the entities involved to decide, *i.e.*, the coastal state and the organization concerned. It seems highly doubtful if this places any significant legal constraint on the coastal state. Judgment would be based on an assessment of factors pertinent to all the interests at stake, including certainly the exclusive interests of the coastal state.

not authorize U.S. regulations that would result in physical extinction of a species or stock or in such reduction that a species or stock or population could be considered threatened.

2. Yield Determination

The FCMA objective of managing to secure the "optimum yield" also appears to be consistent with the draft treaty. The FCMA definition of optimum yield has two components, one expressing the objective (content) and the other providing for the concrete means of formulating and expressing it (procedural).[37] Thus, the goal or objective of OY is to "provide the greatest overall benefit to the Nation, with particular reference to food production and recreational opportunities." The procedural means for formulating and expressing this goal are to prescribe "on the basis of the maximum sustainable yield from such fishery, as modified by any relevant economic, social, or ecological factor."

The draft treaty does not explicitly provide for a specific management objective, but implicitly the various provisions, as noted earlier, permit coastal states to determine their own objectives within certain broad constraints. The procedural component of the treaty comparable to that in the FCMA declares that "[s]uch [conservation and management] measures shall also be designed to maintain or restore populations of harvested species at levels which can produce the maximum sustainable yield, as qualified by relevant environmental and economic factors." It does not seem likely that this treaty provision on yield can reasonably be interpreted to differ in any material way from the counterpart provision in the FCMA. The slight difference in the reference to qualifying factors does not seem significant.

In particular, it does not appear significant that the term "social factors" is not among those mentioned as justifying a departure from MSY. The other treaty provisions in toto convey ample authority on the coastal state to take such factors into account. There can be no serious doubt that the coastal state has full discretion under the treaty to set the allowable catch as it determines may satisfy its own interests, subject only to rather general conservation restrictions. To conclude that the omission of this term in a provision intended to free the coastal state from required adherence to an outdated single objective for conservation[38] is a limitation on the authority of that state to take significant social

[37] I am obliged to Brian Rothschild for suggesting this way of looking at the OY concept although he did not use the terms "content" and "procedure."

[38] Virtually all previous multilateral fishing agreements, including the 1958 Geneva Convention on Conservation of the Living Resources of the High Seas, enshrined maximum sustainable yield as the management goal in their original charters. ("Optimum sustainable yield" is the exact term used in this treaty, but this is widely understood to refer to MSY.) The draft LOS treaty provision is a deliberate departure from this approach and was intended to reflect the multiple objectives now generally understood as appropriate goals.

Expert observers do not read the draft treaty formula as excluding social factors. The Glossary compiled by Dawson states:

> The use of MSY as a measure of "maximum potential productivity" expanded until MSY became the objective of fishery management instead of its foundation. The notion prevailed that what was biologically right for the resource was right for the fishery as a whole.

conditions into account in its domestic or foreign management scheme would be a travesty of treaty interpretation.

While the ultimate objective of U.S. management is to secure the optimum yield and while the OY may be set at larger than the MSY, it is still an important objective of the FCMA to avoid overfishing. Because MSY is a long-term average, it would be quite normal that in any given year the allowable biological catch and the OY might exceed the MSY. If this were not the case, the MSY figure itself would be different. Thus, it is generally accepted that setting OY at greater than MSY does not mean disregard for the concept of overfishing. On this point the FCMA and the treaty do not differ.

3. Conditions of Access to a Surplus

Once a surplus is determined to exist under the FCMA (the procedures for this determination are mentioned below), the Act requires that it be made available to foreign fishing either immediately or in the next harvesting season (these points are also discussed below). The FCMA prescribes for allocation among foreign nations according to certain criteria[39] which emphasize trade in and

---

> This notion has been eroded considerably. . . . Although the ICNT continues to adhere to MSY as the biological basis for the management of living marine resources, it also provides that MSY be qualified (*i.e.*, in some instances modified) by relevant social, economic and environmental factors.

Dawson, *supra* note 26, at 125.

[39] The FCMA was amended in late 1980 to provide a different listing of factors. The original list was short, mentioning (1) extent of traditional fishing, (2) extent of cooperation in, and substantial contribution to, fishery research and identification of fishery resources, and (3) cooperation in enforcement and conservation and management measures. Section 201(e) now lists the following, which are applicable to the 1981 harvesting season and thereafter:

> (A) whether, and to what extent, such nations impose tariff barriers or nontariff barriers on the importation, or otherwise restrict the market access, of United States fish or fishery products;
> (B) whether, and to what extent, such nations are cooperating with the United States in the advancement of existing and new opportunities for fisheries trade, particularly through the purchase of fish or fishery products from United States processors or from United States fishermen;
> (C) whether, and to what extent, such nations and the fishing fleets of such nations have cooperated with the United States in the enforcement of United States fishing regulations;
> (D) whether, and to what extent, such nations require the fish harvested from the fishery conservation zone for their domestic consumption;
> (E) whether, and to what extent, such nations otherwise contribute to, or foster the growth of, a sound and economic United States fishing industry, including minimizing gear conflicts with fishing operations of United States fishermen, and transferring harvesting or processing technology which will benefit the United States fishing industry;
> (F) whether, and to what extent, the fishing vessels of such nations have traditionally engaged in fishing in such fishery;
> (G) whether, and to what extent, such nations are cooperating with the United States in, and making substantial contributions to fishery research and the identification of fishery resources; and
> (H) such other matters as the Secretary of State, in cooperation with the Secretary, deems appropriate.

The last factor, a catchall phrase, gives the Secretary of State wide discretion to make allocation decisions serve whatever policy goals are deemed appropriate from time to time. This catchall appeared in the original FCMA; hence the Secretary was not originally precluded from using the newly mentioned criteria as a basis for allocation.

development of U.S. fisheries and assistance to U.S. management efforts. The treaty differs from the FCMA because it mandates a priority in such considerations but does not exclude those in the FCMA; "all relevant factors" shall be taken into account.[40] But the order of listing the factors differs substantially from that originally proposed by the United States,[41] placing last "the need to minimize economic dislocation in States whose nationals have habitually fished in the zone or which made substantial efforts in research and identification of stocks." *First* consideration is due the coastal state's own economy and other national interests, and then attention is due the rights of landlocked states and states with special geographical characteristics and the requirements of developing states in the subregion or region in harvesting part of the surplus. In contrast, the original FCMA first mentioned traditional fishing states and then referred to other factors. The 1980 amendment to the FCMA allocation formula mentions traditional fishing, but the main emphasis is upon U.S. development and trade interests. On this point there is certainly no incompatibility between the draft treaty and the FCMA.[42]

It does not appear that the priority established by the draft LOS treaty for relevant factors is greatly significant for the United States. Perhaps the reference to developing states might indicate the necessity of giving more weight in allocation decisions than would otherwise be given to the needs of Mexico and

[40] The draft LOS treaty does not specifically declare that the order of listing is an order of priority, but this was the contemporary understanding.

I have no documented evidence for such understanding, but I do have clear recollection of discussion of this point with the principal U.S. fisheries negotiator prior to the LOS Conference who was also well informed about the negotiations during the conference. Two points supported by documentation can be made about the listing of factors in Article 62. As noted in the text, they reverse the order of listing in the United States proposal which was expressly labeled to be in order of priorities. *See* note 41 *infra*. The second point is that the reference to Articles 69 and 70 appears to assure that the developing states dealt with in those articles receive some priority in access to the zones of their region, and this appears to have been the intent of the drafters. *See* Report of Ambassador Nandan, 10 THIRD UNITED NATIONS CONFERENCE ON THE LAW OF THE SEA, OFFICIAL RECORDS 88 (1978).

[41] The U.S. proposal concerning coastal and anadromous living resources called for "maximum utilization" (not optimum) and declared that the coastal state should provide access to resources not fully utilized by its vessels "on the basis of the following priorities," mentioning first states that have traditionally fished a resource, other states in the region, and, finally, all states. The change in this order resulting from the negotiations was not inadvertent. *See* Report of the Committee on the Peaceful Uses of the Sea-bed and the Ocean Floor Beyond the Limits of National Jurisdiction, 27 UN GAOR, Supp. (No. 21) 176, UN Doc. A/8721 (1972).

[42] FCMA section 201(e)(1)(E) raises a question in relation to Article 62(4)(a), which lists the following among the regulations the coastal state may establish: "Licensing of fishermen, fishing vessels and equipment, including payment of fees and other forms of remuneration, which, in the case of developing coastal States, may consist of adequate compensation in the field of financing, equipment and technology relating to the fishing industry. . . ." The question is whether the United States as a developed country could consistently with the treaty require these forms of compensation, as the FCMA contemplates. An affirmative answer is indicated. Article 64 is not intended to be an exhaustive statement of authorized terms and conditions, as indicated by the phrase "*inter alia*" in relation to the listing. The only limitation on such conditions is compliance with the Convention, and determining the form of compensation from foreign fishing is certainly not in violation of any provision of the Convention except as the determination may be arbitrary and unreasonable, a limitation applicable to any exercise of lawful authority pursuant to the treaty.

some Caribbean nations. The latter nations, if any of them fish in the U.S. zone, might benefit under the provisions of Article 70, which deals with "States with special geographical characteristics," but this article does not seriously qualify the exclusive authority of the United States to make allocation decisions in its own interest.[43]

It should be emphasized that the differences in factors mentioned above do not affect the basic obligation to give access to a surplus if one is determined to exist. The FCMA and the draft treaty are consistent on this point. The grant of access to a surplus required by the latter is by agreement and is subject to terms, conditions, and regulations, some of which are set out in Article 62(4).

A general problem concerning access to a surplus, to whomever it may be allocated, potentially arises from the regulations establishing conditions of access. U.S. foreign fishing regulations set numerous conditions, including the payment of fees, partial release of a surplus through withholding of part thereof as a reserve, setting of detailed times and places for fishing, and so forth. It is conceivable that the effect of a particular condition is to make it impractical to fish. For example, the foreign fishing fee may make it uneconomical to fish or regulations impose logistic problems that so inhibit or impede fishing that it cannot be undertaken. As noted earlier, this raises the problem of the reasonableness of the terms and conditions. Presumably, these would be assessed in terms of their relationship to legitimate management objectives and to alternative measures.

An illustrative possible problem is the practice of withholding part of the total allowable level of foreign fishing (TALFF) as a reserve against possible increased catch by the U.S. harvesting industry. While the reserve concept is compatible in principle with the draft treaty, whether it is consistent in practice would appear to depend on the mechanism for establishing and releasing the surplus. The draft LOS treaty requirement of giving access to a surplus, to be meaningful, means that the surplus is available in a practical sense as well as formally. Coastal state insistence on unreasonable conditions that make it impractical to harvest would offend the injunction to give access. In concrete terms, coastal state regulations that are unreasonable in requirements of vessel size, seasons, areas, or timing of announced availability would not be consistent with the draft treaty. For example, if withheld reserves are not released with adequate notice to foreign fishermen of their availability, it may be impossible or impractical for the foreigners to get access. The treaty specifically requires due notice of conservation and management regulations.

The possible problem of precluding access by imposing large fees on foreign fishing probably cannot be answered apart from specific contexts. Can a coastal state ever be justified in setting such a price on access to fish in its zone that a waste of the resource is an acceptable result? As a general proposition the answer should be negative, although perhaps there are conceivable circumstances in which total exclusion by such means is acceptable. What they might

[43] The priority for landlocked and geographically disadvantaged states, which is expressed in Articles 62, 69, and 70, is subject to Article 61, which permits the coastal state to exercise complete discretion in establishing the allowable catch. In addition, Articles 69 and 70 make cross-reference to Article 62, which authorizes a wide range of specific regulations.

be is unknown. Certainly, as a matter of policy a coastal state should avoid the imposition of such fees that foreigners cannot economically engage in fishing.

Recent amendments to the FCMA (now officially the MFCMA) provide for new and complicated optional methods for calculating the total allowable level for foreign fishing in the U.S. fishery.[44] Under some circumstances, apparently, the new methods, if used, could result in a TALFF which would exceed that determined according to the traditional method of TALFF = OY − DAH (domestic annual harvest). No problem of compatibility with the draft treaty would arise in this instance where the TALFF is actually allocated to foreign fishermen when the fish are normally available (see below on this latter point). In some other circumstances, it appears that the TALFF would be less than the amount of fish surplus to domestic harvesting capacity. Although the amendments appear to tie the reductions in TALFF to increases in domestic harvesting capacity, as evidenced by actual increases in domestic harvesting over previous seasons, the reductions appear to be greater than the increases and to leave an unfished surplus. This does not appear to be compatible with the draft LOS treaty.

The amendments might also be incompatible where access to the surplus is not wholly withheld but rather delayed to the next season, as permitted by section 201(d)(4). While this theoretically preserves access to the surplus, it does so only at a probable greater cost to the foreign fishermen. On the other hand, the delay is justified only if immediate allocation is determined to be detrimental to the development of the U.S. fishing industry. Such a trade-off seems to be within the treaty as a regulation under paragraphs (3) and (4) of Article 62, which are designed to give access to the surplus while serving also the economic interests of the coastal state. The additional cost imposed by delay should not be determinative since many valid regulations might increase the cost of fishing.

The new method for calculating TALFF is an optional one. While a management council makes the initial choice of using the old method or the new, it is not clear that this choice actually determines the TALFF. The lack of clarity in this respect arises because of the provision of section 204(d)(4) that when a Council uses the new method of determining TALFF, if the Secretary of Commerce (in consultation with the Secretary of State) approves of the determination by the Council of the amount of OY that will not be harvested by U.S. fishing vessels, then the Secretary of State shall allocate that portion to foreign fishing, subject to the exception already noted.[45] Because it is the decision on the amount that will not be harvested that actually determines the level of foreign fishing, it appears that this decision is not made by a Council but by federal officials. It is not clear that this was the result intended by the drafters.

[44] The "American Fisheries Promotion Act," Title II of Public Law 96–561 (96th Cong., 2d Sess.), in section 230 amends section 201(d) of the FCMA. It also changes the official title of the latter to the Magnuson Fishery Conservation and Management Act.

[45] The decision whether to postpone the allocation is clearly that of the Secretary, in consultation with the Secretary of Commerce, on the basis of the Council recommendation.

IV. Species Coverage

Ratification and implementation of the LOS treaty could have effects on the regulation of three species of fish for which the FCMA makes different provisions: tuna, anadromous fish, and sedentary species.

1. Tuna

The FCMA singles out tuna from all other highly migratory species and makes them exempt from U.S. exclusive fishery management authority in the fisheries conservation zone. Although the draft LOS treaty has a separate article (Article 64) on some highly migratory species (some tuna and several other species which are listed in an Annex),[46] the predominant view is that these species are treated exactly the same as other living resources in the sense that they fall within exclusive coastal authority in the economic zone. The following discussion first examines some bases for the view that tuna are not subject to exclusive coastal authority in the zone and also considers possible interpretations of the obligations in Article 64. The discussion then turns to the conflict between the FCMA and a draft treaty that does make tuna subject to coastal state authority in the zone.

The contention that coastal state authority does not include the highly migratory species (HMS) mentioned in Annex I rests on arguments of varying plausibility. One is that the separate provision on high seas/economic zone stocks in Article 63 establishes that these species are not within coastal state authority in the zone. In this view the reference to living resources in Articles 56 (the basic article on coastal authority in the zone) and 61 and 62 (the basic general articles on living resources) cannot be interpreted to include HMS. This contention is difficult to understand in the face of the apparently unambiguous language of Article 64(2) that Article 64(1) is "*in addition to* other provisions of this Part" (emphasis added). It is argued that this form of cross-reference is unique and should be understood as meaning "instead of" or "exclusive of." While this cross-reference does not appear elsewhere in the treaty, this does not suffice to reverse the otherwise apparent meaning of "in addition to," which obviously *assumes* the applicability of the other provisions of part V.

It is also relevant that Annex I species include cetaceans but that these are clearly subject to coastal state authority subject to the limitation of Article 65. This certainly makes it more difficult to read Article 64 as excluding tuna from any coastal state authority.

A more plausible basis for the contention about Article 64 is that it makes different provision for Annex I species than for other species that migrate great

[46] Annex I of the Draft Convention actually lists ten species of tuna, two species each being incorporated under items 7 and 8. Three tuna species are omitted from Annex I: southern bluefin tuna (*Thunnus maccoyii*), longtail tuna (*Thunnus tonggol*), and black skipjack (*Euthynnus lineatus*). The term "tuna" has meanings that vary among concerned government agencies (in the United States, the Food and Drug Administration and the Bureau of Customs have different interpretations) and by nation. Klawe, *What is a Tuna?*, 39 Marine Fisheries Rev. 1 (No. 11, 1977), offers guidance through this scientific and linguistic quagmire.

distances in the ocean and for other species that inhabit both the zone and the high seas. Article 63 applies to the "same stock or stocks of associated species" that "occur both within the exclusive economic zone and in an area beyond and adjacent to the zone." For such stocks the coastal state and "states fishing for such stocks in the adjacent area" are obliged to seek "to agree upon the measures necessary for the conservation of these stocks in the adjacent area." In contrast, the coastal state's duty under Article 64 is to "co-operate" with other states whose nationals fish in the region for Annex I species both for conservation and for optimum utilization "throughout the region, both within and beyond the exclusive economic zone."

Although there are thus some differences in the coastal state's duties under the two articles, the substance of the coastal state's rights appears to be the same under both. Nothing in the language quoted goes to alter the all-inclusiveness of Articles 56, 61, and 62, especially in light of the provision in Article 64(2) that Article 64(1) applies "in addition to" other provisions of part V. Articles 63 and 64 require the coastal state either to seek to agree or to cooperate with certain other states, but either duty is fully consistent with, and can indeed be argued to rest upon, the full authority of the coastal state over living resources in its zone. It is true that the Article 63 duty to seek to agree applies to "measures necessary for conservation" outside the zone, whereas Article 64 calls for cooperation within and beyond the zone. But the duty to cooperate is not inconsistent with "sovereign rights" nor with recognition that final decisions on the cooperative action that results, or the unilateral action required if cooperation breaks down, are in coastal state hands.

If the coastal state has such authority over Annex I species, as appears to be the case, what is the substance of its obligation under Article 64 to cooperate with other states?

One plausible interpretation is that the coastal state must cooperate by negotiating with other states regarding conservation and utilization, but it retains the exclusive authority to make final decisions in its zone on the substantive conservation measures and on the sharing of catches within its zone. Outside the zone the initiation of conservation and sharing the catch also requires the agreement of all concerned. A requirement of negotiation for conservation and optimum utilization within and without the zone makes sense because it fits the nature of the resources in question; *i.e.*, because they are highly mobile and can be caught within and without the zone, the coastal state cannot conserve them acting alone nor can other fishing states do this on their own. To the extent amounts caught within the zone are dependent on harvesting outside, it is also true that allocation cannot be considered an isolated task within the zone and the coastal state cannot determine this independently.

In the end, Article 64 of the draft LOS treaty appears to preserve the full authority of the coastal state to make the final choices in the zone, but the injunction that it cooperate with other states (and vice versa) is recognition that these decisions cannot simply reflect the exclusive interests of the coastal state. To the extent that highly migratory species are available outside coastal authority, as by definition they are in one or another degree, the questions of how much of the stock can be taken, where, and by whom cannot really be resolved without international cooperation. The ultimate authority of the coastal state in its zone works in such a context to pressure all concerned to reach an agreement that balances the interests involved so that all are "satisfied." While the noncoastal fishing states do not have the weapon of exclusion to force agreement on more favorable terms, their actions can have serious impact on future conditions to the disadvantage of the coastal state; hence such states are not without strength. The balance in pressure between the coastal state and other states depends upon the accessibility of HMS to those concerned. The more fishing must be conducted within the zone, the more influence the coastal officials may exert. Contrariwise, the greater the success normally enjoyed by those fishing outside the zone, the greater the pressure on the coastal state to conclude an arrangement satisfactory to the other states.

Although not a view shared by the United States, the majority view of the draft treaty would authorize the United States to create fishery management plans for the several species of tuna caught within the fishery conservation zone. Nonetheless, the United States need not exercise this authority and it could continue to arrange for tuna management by international agreement. On the other hand, the United States could conclude a management plan and then enter into an international agreement compatible with the plan.

The purpose of the FCMA in exempting tuna from U.S. jurisdiction and control is twofold: to protect U.S. distant-water tuna vessels from the exercise of coastal state jurisdiction and control and to manage tuna by international agreement. Protection is sought by a sanctioning procedure established in section 202(e) (nonrecognition of foreign claims to a fishery conservation zone) and section 205 (import prohibition). Section 403 further seeks to assist tuna vessels by providing for reimbursement of fines and other charges.

Section 202(e) records the "sense of the Congress" that the United States not recognize a foreign fishery conservation zone beyond the territorial sea (to the extent the United States recognizes the latter) if the foreign nation "fails to recognize and accept that highly migratory species are to be managed by applicable international fishery agreements, whether or not such nation is a party to any such agreement." A refusal to recognize the foreign claim to a fishery zone under these circumstances can result (and has resulted) in sanctions against a foreign state that seeks to enforce its claim against U.S. tuna vessels.

If the United States ratifies the LOS treaty, it would recognize, as noted earlier, exclusive coastal authority over tuna, subject only to the obligation to cooperate as recorded in Article 64. Although, as also noted earlier, the practical effect of Article 64 leads to international agreement on the significant questions of conservation and allocation of tuna stocks, the article preserves the ultimate authority of the coastal state to make its own final decision in the zone if "co-operation" breaks down. Accordingly, by accepting the LOS treaty the United States would effectively "fail to recognize" that tuna "are to be managed by applicable international fishery agreements." This would appear to deprive section 202(e)(2) of any continued employment.

Section 205, "Import Prohibitions," provides for use of an automatic import prohibition as a sanction by the United States against a number of fishery-related actions by other nations to which the United States objects. Such actions that would be relevant to an ultimately effective LOS treaty are (1) refusal to allow U.S. fishing vessels to fish for highly migratory species in accordance with an applicable international fishery agreement, (2) noncompliance by a foreign nation with its obligations under "any existing fishery agreement concerning fishing by fishing vessels of the United States in any fishery over which that nation asserts exclusive fishery management authority," and (3) seizure of a U.S. fishing vessel as a consequence of a claim of jurisdiction not recognized by the United States. The question is what effect would be left in these provisions of section 205 if the United States accepted an international agreement that includes tuna among living resources subject to exclusive coastal authority.

With respect to (1), section 205(a)(2) could no longer be invoked by the United States to justify an import prohibition when a coastal state refused to allow U.S. tuna vessels to harvest tuna in its fishery or economic zone. The United States would have accepted such an exercise of coastal state authority and this would supersede the provision in section 205. Similarly, with respect to (3) above, a seizure of a U.S. tuna vessel to enforce a coastal state law within 200 miles would seem no longer to provide a basis for a U.S. sanction under section 205 because the United States would have accepted such coastal state jurisdiction.

On the other hand, it is conceivable that the import prohibition might continue to serve as a sanction where the foreign nation excluded tuna fishing in alleged violation of the LOS agreement itself or some other fishery agreement that might continue to be applicable. The question here would be whether the foreign action was compatible with the agreement in question, not whether the coastal state could claim exclusive authority.

Once having accepted the LOS treaty, the United States could refuse to adopt unilateral regulations for tuna and continue to insist upon international management. Or it could exercise its authority under the newly accepted treaty, and an amended FCMA, solely to promulgate regulations that are identical to, or substantially the same as, measures established by international agreement. Could the United States still lawfully employ a section 205 import prohibition as a sanction when a foreign nation adopted exclusive regulations forbidding U.S. fishing for tuna within 200 miles? This seems extremely doubtful in light of the U.S. acceptance of the agreement providing for coastal state jurisdiction. To invoke a sanction in these circumstances would be wholly inconsistent with its prior agreement. The fact that the United States did not choose to exercise its authority would be irrelevant to its obligation to accept such exercise by others, at least so long as the foreign action did not otherwise violate law.

FCMA section 403 (amending the Fishermen's Protective Act to update its provisions on foreign seizure of U.S. vessels) would appear to be partially negated if the United States is authorized to exercise exclusive jurisdiction over tuna pursuant to its acceptance and ratification of the LOS treaty. Such recognition of exclusive jurisdiction over tuna would eliminate protective action for a seizure of a U.S. tuna vessel on the basis of a 200-mile fishery jurisdiction claim. In addition, section 403(2) contemplates instances in which the foreign claim to jurisdiction is recognized by the United States, but the foreign seizure of a U.S. fishing vessel is unacceptable and objectionable for other reasons. On such occasions protective measures under the Fishermen's Protective Act[47] would still be in order.

2. Salmon

The LOS draft and the FCMA extend coastal state control over similarly defined anadromous species. The draft states in Article 66(1) that "States in whose rivers anadromous stocks originate shall have the primary interest in and responsibility for such stocks." The FCMA claims exclusive authority over "species of fish which spawn in fresh or estuarine waters of the United States and which migrate to ocean waters." If "originate" means "spawn," then the United States has claimed only what is allowed by the treaty. In this interpretation the state with authority is the spawning state, not necessarily the state from whose waters the fish exit to the ocean; the spawning state need not be a "coastal" state. There are several instances of this situation involving Canada and the United States.[48]

If "originate" means that jurisdiction over salmon is conferred upon the state from whose waters the fish enter the ocean rather than upon the state in whose waters they spawn, then the United States is exercising less authority in some instances than the draft treaty provides. In such a situation the FCMA and the draft treaty would conflict because the latter obligates the coastal state with jurisdiction to take action to conserve and to interact with other states for this purpose. Similarly, by this interpretation there would be instances in which the United States, pursuant to the FCMA, would be asserting an authority greater than that permitted and displacing another state (Canada) that should have authority to regulate. These differences between the authority claimed and that conferred by the treaty may be insignificant if the states involved agree on resolving the issue, as do Canada and the United States.

In other respects the FCMA asserts authority not recognized by the draft treaty. Section 102 extends U.S. authority throughout the migratory range of anadromous species except when they are within another state's recognized jurisdiction.[49] Under Article 66(2) of the draft treaty, the state of origin may prescribe regulations for salmon fishing throughout its 200-mile zone and also beyond. Salmon fishing is to be conducted only within the 200-mile limit except when "this would result in economic dislocation for a State other than the State of origin." In addition, while the state of origin may establish total allowable

[47] 22 U.S.C. §§1971–1977.

[48] Seven are identified in section V of Agreed Summary Record of Canada/United States Discussions on a Comprehensive Agreement on the Management and Development of Pacific Salmon Stocks of Mutual Concern, Lynnwood, Washington, October 20–25, 1980. This document records specific arrangements for certain transboundary rivers and agreement on general principles applicable to others.

[49] Under FCMA section 202(a)(4), the Secretary of State is expressly given authority to negotiate regarding conservation and management of anadromous species and highly migratory species.

catches for its stocks, it can do so only "after consultation with other States" fishing these stocks beyond any zone and in another state's zone. For fishing beyond the economic zone, the "States concerned shall maintain consultations with a view to achieving agreement on terms and conditions of such fishing giving due regard to conservation requirements and needs of the State of origin in respect of these stocks." The state of origin has the further obligation to "co-operate in minimizing economic dislocation in such other States fishing these stocks."

While the draft treaty provides for continued high seas fishing where its cessation would result in economic dislocation, the treaty does appear to require prior agreement between the fishing state and the state of origin on the terms and conditions of such activity. The text contemplates that regulations, terms, and conditions are to be promulgated by the state of origin after consultations with a view to agreement "giving due regard to the conservation requirements and needs of the State of origin in respect of these stocks." The preeminent position of the latter state is further indicated because it is obligated to minimize economic dislocation (Article 66(3)(b)), which strongly suggests that the state of origin has final authority over the levels of effort and catch. Subparagraph (c) seems particularly significant in this context. It specifies that high seas fishing states participate "by agreement with the State of origin in measures to renew anadromous stocks, particularly by expenditures for that purpose," and, as a consequence, "shall be given special consideration by the State of origin in the harvesting of stocks originating in its rivers." This provision appears clearly to anticipate prior agreement on conservation and management measures and on the sharing of costs for conservation, and to establish these as preconditions to special consideration by the state of origin. Such special consideration is the allowance of fishing beyond the economic zone, which greatly complicates the problem of management and is contrary to the normal pattern of fishing envisaged by Article 66.

The most pronounced difference between the FCMA and the draft treaty is that the latter requires that enforcement of regulations beyond 200 miles "shall be by agreement between the State of origin and the other States concerned." Presumably, this accord would simply be a part of the overall agreement required prior to any high seas fishing for salmon.

These various provisions could require departures from the provisions of the FCMA. Insofar as the United States were to act under the FCMA to regulate or to curb salmon fishing beyond 200 miles (the United States does not currently do so), it would have to comply with the above requirements of the treaty when the latter becomes the law of the land. This could mean that the United States could not prohibit fishing for salmon under some circumstances despite the absence of a surplus under FCMA procedures, that the terms and conditions of fishing might be different from those the United States would establish on its own, and that the total allowable catch might be calculated differently. If a foreign vessel were to violate U.S. regulations applicable beyond 200 miles, the United States could not enforce them unless this were consistent with a prior agreement with the flag state.

3. Sedentary Species

In an interesting contrast, the draft treaty allows coastal states much greater authority over sedentary species than that embodied in the FCMA, where these are treated the same as fish except that they are managed beyond the 200-mile zone as well as within. Under the treaty the provisions of part V on the economic zone do not apply at all to sedentary species as defined in the treaty[50] (and in the FCMA which employs the same definition). Accordingly, no obligations regarding yields or surplus are applicable to coastal state regulation of these species.[51] Under the FCMA, sedentary species are subject to the same management obligations as any other species and, accordingly, the management councils and the Secretary must determine the MSY, the OY, the TALFF, and so forth. Thus, U.S. fishery management recognizes greater foreign rights to these resources than it is required to by the draft treaty.

V. Transboundary Stocks and High Seas/Fishery Zone Stocks

The FCMA and the draft treaty both envision the need for international agreement to deal with nonmigratory, and some highly migratory, species whose habitat extends beyond a single or any economic zone. In addition to treaties and boundary agreements, both of which could include provisions on transboundary stocks, the FCMA states that the Secretary of State "may enter into such other negotiations . . . as may be necessary and appropriate to further the purposes, policy, and provisions of this Act."[52]

Treaty Article 63 is not inconsistent with the FCMA. With respect to transboundary stocks (the same stock or associated species), the coastal states "shall seek either directly or through appropriate subregional or regional organizations to agree upon the measures necessary to co-ordinate and ensure the conservation and development of such stocks without prejudice to the other provisions of this Part." Very similar provision is made for zone stocks fished on the adjacent high seas, the only difference being that there is no reference to development and the states concerned are to seek to agree only upon the necessary conservation measures.

Professor Knight asserts that Article 52 of the Revised Single Negotiating Text (RSNT) of the treaty (now Article 63) obliges states with transboundary stocks to agree upon the necessary measures for conservation and development.[53]

[50] Article 68 states that part V does not apply to sedentary species, as defined in Article 77, paragraph 4.

[51] Article 77 in part VI provides that the coastal state exercises sovereign rights over the continental shelf for the purpose of exploring and exploiting its natural resources, and the latter are defined in paragraph 4 to include sedentary species. There are no other provisions on such species in this part. Article 76 defines the shelf so that it may extend beyond 200 nautical miles. The FCMA also contemplates the exercise of exclusive fishery management authority over shelf resources beyond 200 nautical miles. FCMA §102.

[52] FCMA §202(a)(5).

[53] Knight, Effect of a Law of the Sea Treaty on the Fishery Conservation and Management Act of 1976, at 13 (Report to Gulf Regional Fishery Management Council, 1977). Professor Knight

This seems to be incorrect. Article 63 does not require an agreement—it requires only that the states seek to agree. If they do not conclude an agreement after good faith negotiations, there is no default on either side.

It should be noted, however, that while there is no formal requirement of an agreement, the practical necessities of the situation might well impose it, just as in the case of tuna noted previously. Depending on the distribution of stocks and their abundance within and outside the zone, the coastal state may or may not be able to manage stocks successfully. In any event, the draft treaty has no provision for the contingency of no agreement.

Article 117 is directly relevant in this connection because it concerns the obligations of all states, *i.e.*, distant water and coastal, to take or to cooperate in taking "such measures for their respective nationals as may be necessary for the conservation of the living resources of the high seas." Again agreement is not required, but conservation may well be impossible unless it is forthcoming. Because the coastal state has exclusive authority over stocks during their time in the zone, its position would appear to be the preeminent one, but the extent to which this is true will vary by species and by other facets of the situation.[54]

Professor Knight notes that these transboundary stock agreements might be used by the federal Government to bypass Council management authority. Apart from the fact that Councils are not authorized to make final management decisions (except that no limited access scheme can be adopted without approval of a majority of the appropriate Council), an agreement having the effect of bypassing a Council would have to take the form of a treaty or of a congressional-executive agreement, and both require some form of participation by the Senate or the whole Congress.[55] An executive agreement concluded through the President's powers alone probably cannot override a prior inconsistent federal statute where Congress has exercised its constitutional powers.[56] This point has

---

adds that "Article 52 [of the Revised Single Negotiating Text] would place the United States under a legal obligation to enter into agreements or arrangements with States through whose exclusive economic zones stocks of fish from the U.S. fishery conservation zone might migrate." *Ibid.*

[54] There could be instances in which the coastal state may be required to take cooperative action by means solely available to it. Such a situation might arise, for example, because food species for a high seas stock are found wholly within the economic zone during a part of their life history. A variety of interrelationships of stocks might so burden the coastal state. On the other hand, there may be occasions where states fishing beyond 200 nautical miles must accommodate to coastal regulations. The exact relationship of Articles 63(2) and 117 is not wholly clear.

[55] The "bypassing" referred to in the text presumably would involve a management plan and regulations contrary to those recommended by a Council for adoption by the Secretary. The Secretary (of Commerce) need not adopt either a recommended plan or the recommended implementing regulations. If, however, the Secretary were to adopt the plan and regulations and an inconsistent international agreement were negotiated by the Secretary of State and put into effect, it might be argued that the agreement superseded the earlier action by the Secretary of Commerce. This sequence of events could raise substantial legal questions including at least two constitutional issues: (1) whether the provision in section 202(a)(5) authorizing negotiations not prohibited by section 202(c) is constitutional, and (2) whether, if the Secretary's later agreement is an executive agreement, it could override prior federal law. *See* Note, *Congressional Authorization and Oversight of International Fishery Agreements under the FCMA of 1976*, 52 WASH. L. REV. 495 (1977).

[56] United States v. Capps, 204 F.2d 655 (4th Cir. 1953).

never been definitely established by the Supreme Court; hence the qualification "probably" is employed.

VI. Scientific Research

When the FCMA was adopted in early 1976, the United States still maintained its position in the LOS negotiations that scientific research in the economic zone ought not be subject to the exclusive jurisdiction of coastal states and it was not impossible that elements of this view might ultimately prevail. Congress sought to support this position (and other U.S. positions) by expressly limiting the extension of U.S. jurisdiction to fishery conservation and management. In addition, FCMA section 2(10) declared that "fishing" "does not include any scientific research activity which is conducted by a scientific research vessel." Implementation of this exclusion in practice has the effect of asserting control over some fishery research because foreign research operators routinely request approval of their operations beforehand. The object of these requests is apparently to avoid possible difficulties.

The U.S. negotiating position found little support in the LOS negotiations with the result that the draft treaty provides for coastal state consent to all research within the economic zone and attaches a variety of obligations and conditions, and some safeguards, to the research and consent processes. Accordingly, the draft treaty would permit the United States to establish research controls that are not envisaged by the FCMA (except in minor part, *i.e.*, fisheries research by a fisheries vessel). This difference is not an incompatibility between the draft treaty and existing law; therefore, the latter can be maintained while fully accepting the former. Such acceptance, even if not implemented by U.S. legislation, thus constitutes recognition of other nations' jurisdiction over research in their respective zones.

This latter point has importance for U.S. policy, which has been to refuse to seek clearances for U.S. vessels planning to do research in areas of claimed but unrecognized national jurisdiction. After the draft LOS becomes effective, the United States would have recognized such claims and could proceed to secure clearances for U.S. vessels. It would not be necessary, and no more desirable than it has been in the past, for the United States to claim control over foreign research in U.S. waters.

VII. Allocation of State and Federal Authority Over Fisheries

The fishery conservation zone established by the FCMA has an inner boundary which begins at the seaward boundary of each of the coastal U.S. states. The latter is defined in the Submerged Lands Act as follows:

> The seaward boundary of each original coastal State is approved and confirmed as a line three geographical miles distant from its coast line. . . . Any State admitted subsequent to the formation of the Union which has not already done so may extend its seaward boundaries to a line three geographical miles distant from its coast line. . . . Nothing in this section

> is to be construed as questioning or in any manner prejudicing the existence of any State's seaward boundary beyond three geographical miles if it was so provided by its constitution or laws prior to or at the time such State became a member of the Union or if it has heretofore been approved by Congress.[57]

Two states, Texas and Florida, have seaward boundaries extending 9 miles into the Gulf of Mexico.

Section 306 of the FCMA preserves existing state fishery management jurisdiction within state boundaries although it also provides for a procedure through which federal regulatory authority may be extended within a state's boundaries. Section 306(a) states: "Except as provided in subsection (b), nothing in this Act shall be construed as extending or diminishing the jurisdiction or authority of any State within its boundaries." Subsection (b) establishes a procedure for federal preemption where it is found that fishing in a fishery covered by a fishery management plan implemented under the Act is engaged in predominately within the fishery conservation zone and beyond such zone and where coastal state action (or lack of action) has results "which will substantially and adversely affect the carrying out of such fishery management plan."

This distribution of state-federal authority is unaffected by the provisions of the LOS treaty. It is true that the treaty provides that nation-states are permitted to establish a 12-mile territorial sea, but this authorization is permissive only and not mandatory.[58] To the extent congressional, as opposed to executive, action is needed, Congress would need to take some affirmative action, in addition to Senate consent to ratification of the treaty, before boundaries of the component states would be extended to 12 miles.

If Congress did act to extend the U.S. territorial sea to 12 miles, it might be argued that this would not necessarily by itself extend state boundaries to that distance unless Congress expressly so provided. It has long been clear that the limits of United States authority in the oceans are more extensive as a national authority than as that of the component coastal states.

If Congress did extend state boundaries to 12 miles, this would seriously affect the exercise of federal fishery management authority and could exacerbate management problems considerably. Section 306 could take on even greater importance in some instances because of greater, but still less than predominant, fishing in the state zone. Where such fishing reaches a significant level, effective management would require that the section 306 preemption procedure be followed so that all of the fishery falls within a single management entity's control. In other instances, however, the extended state boundary might embrace the predominant part of a fishery and effectively oust federal authority. In either event, however, management difficulties would seem to be greater than under the present system. In the former instance, there might be a need for a hearing

[57] 43 U.S.C. §1312.

[58] Article 3 of the draft LOS treaty provides that states have the right to establish a breadth for the territorial sea up to 12 miles. This formulation contemplates that states may set limits less than 12. Extending the limit to 12 miles is not a cost-free exercise, hence it ought not be assumed that the limit should be extended automatically.

if a state contested the federal view,[59] and even if the Secretary prevailed, it could bode ill for continued amicable and effective cooperation between state and federal officials. Where the Secretary cannot preempt state management, the difficulties would be magnified because it might then become very difficult and perhaps impossible to manage a stock as a unit throughout its range or to manage interrelated stocks properly.[60]

VIII. Enforcement

The draft treaty specifically excludes imprisonment for a violation of coastal state fisheries regulations in the exclusive economic zone, unless the states concerned agree otherwise. The United States has negotiated agreements which, by very general provisions incorporating U.S. law, have the effect of allowing for imprisonment; hence the section 309(b) provision for a fine or imprisonment or both for foreign fishing violators is consistent with the draft treaty. Interestingly, only foreign fishermen may be imprisoned for violation of fishing regulations, but domestic fishermen can be imprisoned for resisting boarding or otherwise interfering with enforcement and are subject to a civil penalty for violation of a fishing regulation.

The draft treaty declares that "arrested vessels" are to be "promptly released upon the posting of reasonable bond or other security," which virtually rules out involuntary forfeiture of a vessel. The FCMA in section 310 provides that vessels may be forfeited for commission of any act prohibited in section 307. However, section 310 also makes provision for posting of a bond to stay the execution of process in rem against a vessel.

Professor Knight notes that Article 73(3) of the draft treaty only forbids imprisonment for violations of fisheries regulations. He declares that FCMA section 307 provides for imprisonment only for obstruction and resistance and for fishing without a permit. He concludes: "Violations of regulations, made unlawful by §307(1)(A), are not made subject to imprisonment penalties. Thus, Article 61(3) of the RSNT [now 73(3) of the draft LOS treaty] would not appear to significantly alter the imprisonment rights presently contained in the FCMA."[61] This interpretation of the FCMA may not be correct. Criminal penalties attach to violation of section 307(2), which makes it unlawful for foreign vessels to engage in fishing "within the fishery conservation zone, or for any anadromous species or Continental Shelf fishery resource beyond such zone, unless such fishing is authorized by, and conducted in accordance with, a valid and applicable permit." Thus, even if the foreigner has a permit to fish

[59] There might be disagreement whether state action would "substantially and adversely affect" implementation of a management plan or whether the fishery was predominately within the fishery conservation zone and beyond.

[60] Ecosystem management would appear to be an impossibility unless the various management entities closely coordinate their plans and actions. Even if the federal management scheme does not apply to a stock because it is mostly fished within state boundaries, the impact of such fishing might be felt upon other species that are fully subject to an FMP. Yet in the circumstances envisaged, a Regional Council and the Secretary could not regulate the state fishery.

[61] Knight, *supra* note 53, at 11–12.

in the zone, he may be in violation of section 307(2) if he does not fish in accordance with the permit. The fishing permit incorporates all applicable fishery regulations. Hence, failure to comply with applicable regulations subjects the foreign fisherman to possible imprisonment. Such an outcome would be inconsistent with Article 73(3) of the draft treaty unless there is agreement otherwise as in this instance.

IX. Timing of Amendments to Regulations Adopted Under FCMA

Through section 401, "Effect on Law of the Sea Treaty," the FCMA seeks to deal with the impact of U.S. ratification of a comprehensive LOS treaty that includes provisions on fisheries. Section 401 declares:

> If the United States ratifies a comprehensive treaty, which includes provisions with respect to fishery conservation and management jurisdiction, resulting from any United Nations Conference on the Law of the Sea, the Secretary, after consultation with the Secretary of State, may promulgate any amendment to the regulations promulgated under this Act if such amendment is necessary and appropriate to conform such regulations to the provisions of such treaty, in anticipation of the date when such treaty shall come into force and effect for, or otherwise be applicable to, the United States.

It is plain from section 401 that Congress in 1976 contemplated retention of the FCMA after U.S. ratification of the LOS treaty, at the least until it came into force and perhaps later. Under normal circumstances the treaty would, when effective, supersede inconsistent provisions of the FCMA and subsequent lawful regulations would have to be consistent with these new provisions of the law.[62] But section 401 appears to deal with a somewhat different situation, namely, the promulgation of amended regulations to conform with the treaty after U.S. ratification but *prior* to the time the treaty comes into force for the United States. If the conformed regulations still complied with the FCMA, no legal issue would arise, but it might be that the amended regulations would not be in conformity with the FCMA. In the absence of an effective treaty, such amended regulations would have no statutory base other than section 401 itself, nor would the treaty provide authority because, by definition, it would not be in force.

In this latter, perhaps unlikely event, section 401 appears to raise a constitutional question. Can Congress lawfully delegate to the executive branch the task of making regulations that implement provisions of a treaty not yet in force and whose provisions could be only vaguely anticipated? That would seem to delegate authority to the Executive to repeal FCMA *pro tanto*, without present guidelines. Delegation in matters relating to foreign affairs is subject to far less stringent limitations than in domestic affairs.[63] But there seems to be no prec-

[62] The principal commentary on this set of problems is Jacobson & Cameron, *Potential Conflicts Between a Future Law of the Sea Treaty and the Fishery Conservation and Management Act of 1976*, 52 Wash. L. Rev. 451 (1977). *See also* Knight, *supra* note 53, which discusses the Revised Single Negotiating Text and the FCMA but is still useful and relevant.

[63] United States v. Curtiss-Wright Export Corp., 299 U.S. 304 (1936); *but cf.* Kent v. Dulles, 357 U.S. 116 (1958).

edent for delegating authority, without guidelines, to repeal statutory provisions, even in foreign affairs. Of course, there is a general guideline: the authority granted is to conform the regulations to particular treaty obligations which the United States will have assumed. And the authority to issue the regulations would take effect only after the United States has ratified the treaty, so that the Senate, at least, would have participated in preparing the guidelines for amending the regulations.

In any event, the main point here for fishery management is that the Secretary of Commerce is authorized by FCMA section 401 to promulgate amended regulations conforming to the LOS treaty after the United States ratifies it and before it comes into force.

The general subject area that may call for amended regulations includes foreign fishing for salmon, specific optimum yield determinations, factors relevant to foreign fishery allocations, and foreign fishery fees. On all these points the draft treaty has provisions that may or do differ from those in the FCMA. Interestingly, tuna are now excluded from U.S. jurisdiction under the FCMA and there can be no regulations directly regulating tuna fishing; hence it would appear one could not introduce amended regulations to manage tuna. Regulations for this purpose might thus have to await the time the treaty comes into force for the United States.

This latter point might involve a more general problem. Section 401 authorizes only amendment of outstanding regulations and not the initial adoption of new regulations. Because such regulations assume the existence of a subject matter upon which regulations may be based, it would appear that section 401 authorizes action only in instances where the United States has already asserted its jurisdictional authority through the FCMA. Accordingly, the Secretary would be unable lawfully to promulgate regulations for a subject matter brought under U.S. jurisdiction only by the new treaty. This affects tuna, as noted above.

Another reading of section 401 also avoids constitutional issues. It may be that section 401 means only that the executive branch may anticipate approval of the LOS treaty and its coming into force by prospective adoption of regulations. These regulations would become effective only when the treaty itself did so. This interpretation is not convincing because the executive branch could do this in any event.

Conclusions

That the draft LOS treaty and the FCMA are, with few exceptions, in fundamental accord is not surprising. Both reflect a strong effort to protect coastal interests. The LOS negotiations were dominated from the beginning by concern for exclusive coastal interests and for provision of the necessary authority to safeguard those interests. The result is a draft treaty that greatly enlarges the extent of coastal state fishery jurisdiction, establishes that in virtually all respects coastal state authority is exclusive and final, places few limitations on the exercise of that authority, and incorporates only very general obligations that demand little of the coastal state. This LOS mood was matched closely by the dominant political sentiment in the United States in 1975–1976 (and in 1980), which resulted in an FCMA that is strongly directed toward exclusion of foreign fishing and protection of U.S. fishery interests, primarily industrial.

The incompatibilities between these two exercises stem in major part from the fact that the United States also has a major distant-water fishery interest and, in lesser intensity, from the desire to provide even less favorable treatment of foreign fishing than the treaty requires.

Thus, the most noticeable single difference in the draft treaty and U.S. law consists of the treatment given species of great interest in the domestic fishing industry—tuna and salmon. Acceptance of a treaty that recognizes exclusive coastal jurisdiction over tuna means that provisions of U.S. law seeking protection of U.S. flag vessels fishing for tuna in distant waters would be nullified or seriously eroded. Continuing the nonrecognition and importation sanctions would appear to be impossible or very difficult to bring about, at best. On anadromous species too, the FCMA might require modification to take account of foreign high seas fishing, the calculation of the total allowable catch, the terms and conditions of foreign fishing, and, perhaps, provisions requiring agreement on enforcement measures. It is possible, however, that some of these difficulties might be resolved through further agreements with states fishing for salmon on the high seas.

Neither the treaty nor the FCMA requires a coastal state to declare a surplus over harvesting capacity even if one exists. The treaty obligates the coastal state to give access to such surplus as it does establish, but the FCMA may no longer, after the 1980 amendments, meet this requirement. It is not entirely clear whether the new method of calculating the total allowable level of foreign fishing results in withholding a part of a surplus; if this is the result, the FCMA, as amended, is incompatible with the treaty.

The conditions on access to a surplus that are imposed under the FCMA appear to fall within those specifically mentioned in the treaty which, in any event, does not seek to provide an exhaustive listing. It is not so clear, however, that all U.S. regulations implementing management plans are always consistent with the treaty in the sense that they do not arbitrarily restrict or limit access by foreign fishermen. Such determinations would need to be made in particular instances and this discussion has not attempted the examination required.

The treaty directions for allocation of a surplus place very little limitation on coastal authority. Factors relevant to this decision are mentioned in both the treaty and the FCMA, but neither is exhaustive and the weighting indicated in the draft treaty places no meaningful restriction on U.S. authority except for the possibility of greater deference to certain Caribbean nations who might meet the treaty criteria of special geographical characteristics. The FCMA gives the Secretary of State sufficient discretion that such deference could be accommodated without difficulty, but this discretion itself probably should be limited to require allocation in such instances as might arise.

The draft treaty differs considerably from the FCMA on marine scientific research, an activity of importance for fishery management. Whereas the FCMA excludes research from U.S. jurisdiction, the draft treaty would permit the United States to exercise exclusive authority to approve and to regulate research in the 200-mile zone.

The enforcement provisions of the draft treaty conflict with those in the FCMA because the latter permits imprisonment as a penalty for violations of U.S. law irrespective of the views of foreign fishing nations. The treaty excludes such a penalty unless the nations agree. In practice, the United States has secured such agreement, but the FCMA still should probably be amended to provide for this approach.

A final potential difficulty concerns the treaty provision stating the right of each state to establish a 12-mile territorial sea. Under U.S. law, this limit is 3 miles, except for Texas and Florida on the Gulf of Mexico, and this is the boundary between state and federal authority over fisheries as provided in the FCMA. Such a limit would remain even if the United States accepted the treaty and it came into effect. If the territorial sea and the state boundaries are extended to 12 miles, there could be a profound impact on fishery management because of the greater importance of state authority over fisheries. This is a problem of national law that deserves detailed examination.

SATELLITE COMMUNICATION AND SPECTRUM ALLOCATION

*By Martin A. Rothblatt**

I. Introduction

The orbit/spectrum resource is one of the world's most important reservoirs of value. This resource has a dual "orbit/spectrum" nature because its value can only be realized through the simultaneous exploitation of both the geostationary orbit and the electromagnetic spectrum.[1] The geostationary orbit, a ring of space six earth radii above the equator, is where a communications satellite must be placed in order to assume a fixed position in the sky.[2] These fixed or "geostationary" positions are extremely desirable because they allow the satellite to serve as a dependable relay platform for messages sent between large numbers of geographically isolated communicators.[3]

Messages quickly reach and return from the orbiting communications satellite as signal patterns impressed upon certain frequency bands of the electromag-

* Of the District of Columbia Bar.

[1] Indications of orbit/spectrum value include global communications satellite industry revenues of between $1,500 million and $2,000 million a year: Astrain, Telecommunications and the Economic Impact of Communications Satellites 1 (paper delivered at 31st Congress of the International Astronautical Federation, Tokyo, 1980); and an estimated total American investment in geostationary orbit space between 1975 and 1984 of about $2,000 million: Morgan, *The Next Decade: An Economic Outlook for the Eighties*, SATELLITE COM., Jan. 1981, at 37.

This article examines the international regulatory regime governing the orbit/spectrum resource's satellite communications values. For an excellent survey of international legal issues involved in the simultaneous exploitation of earth orbits and the electromagnetic spectrum for remote sensing/earth observation values, see Mossinghoff & Fuqua, *United Nations Principles on Remote Sensing: Report on Developments, 1970–1980*, 8 J. SPACE L. 103 (1980).

[2] The international legal definition of "geostationary satellite orbit" is the "orbit in which a satellite must be placed to be a geostationary satellite." International Telecommunication Union, World Administrative Radio Conference Radio Regulations (1979) [hereinafter cited as ITU Radio Regulations], Art. N1, §8, No. 3133A. A "geostationary satellite" is legally defined as a "geosynchronous satellite whose circular and direct orbit lies in the plane of the Earth's equator and which thus remains fixed relative to the Earth; by extension, a satellite which remains approximately fixed relative to the Earth." *Id.*, Art. N1, §8, No. 3133. "Geosynchronous satellite" is legally defined as an "earth satellite whose period of revolution is equal to the period of rotation of the Earth about its axis." *Id.*, Art. N1, §8, No. 3132. *See* Gehrig, *Geostationary Orbit—Technology and Law*, in PROCEEDINGS OF THE 19TH COLLOQUIUM ON THE LAW OF OUTER SPACE 267 (1977), for a critical analysis of these definitions.

[3] For a discussion of nongeostationary orbits and their disadvantages, see J. MARTIN, COMMUNICATIONS SATELLITE SYSTEMS 41–61 (1978). Satellites are able to serve as relay platforms because they are high enough to be in the line of sight of up to 40% of the earth's surface. *Ibid.* Satellites in geostationary positions will soon be replaced with larger, permanent "space information stations," which have "an advantage over single-purpose satellites in terms of conservation of orbital and spectrum resources, economies of scale, and greater capabilities." D. SMITH, SPACE STATIONS: INTERNATIONAL LAW AND POLICY 60 (1979).

netic spectrum.[4] Because these spectrum frequencies vary greatly in their ability to pierce the earth/space frontier, it is necessary to specify a frequency band when discussing the orbit/spectrum resource.[5] While current technology allows communications satellite systems to exploit the resource across a wide array of frequencies, there are three particular bands that have especially desirable signal propagation characteristics: the C band, the Ku band, and the Ka band.[6] These three portions of orbit/spectrum have been, and will continue to be, the subject of new international law and serious international concern.[7] The purpose of this article is to describe the basic legal principle that underlies international regulation of the orbit/spectrum resource,[8] and to introduce a jurimetric means of addressing international concern about the precise nature of this principle's application.[9]

II. Maximum Channel Dispersion: The Basic Legal Regulatory Principle

International regulation of orbit/spectrum is based upon application of the principle of maximum channel dispersion to the resource development technology of geostationary satellite communications. This principle requires the

[4] For very clear descriptions of those portions of the electromagnetic spectrum used for telecommunications, see M. FRANKLIN, MASS MEDIA LAW 536–39 (1977); and J. MARTIN, *supra* note 3, at 132–47.

[5] J. MARTIN, *supra* note 3, at 136; S. H. LAY & H. TAUBENFELD, THE LAW RELATING TO THE ACTIVITIES OF MAN IN SPACE 103–12 (1970). The spectrum's extensive and intensive margins are explained in H. LEVIN, THE INVISIBLE RESOURCE (1971).

[6] The frequencies used for Western Hemisphere public communications satellite service in these bands are 5.925–6.425 GHz uplink and 3.7–4.2 GHz downlink for the C band; 11.7–12.7 GHz downlink and 14.0–14.5 GHz uplink for the Ku band; and 17.7–21.2 GHz downlink and 27.5–31.0 GHz uplink for the Ka band. ITU Radio Regulations, *supra* note 2, Art. N7, §4. *See also* Jackson, *The Allocation of the Radio Spectrum*, SCIENTIFIC AM., Feb. 1980, at 34–39.

From a signal propagation standpoint, the C band is "ideal" and accounts for the great majority of satellite communications traffic. J. MARTIN, *supra* note 3, at 138. However, Ku-band conditions are also quite favorable and most new communications satellite systems will utilize this band. Rothblatt, *International Regulation of Digital Communications Satellite Systems*, 32 FED. COM. L.J. 403–11 (1980). Although Ka-band signals propagate better than those transmitted at some neighboring frequencies, further technology development is needed to handle the band's characteristic rain attenuation problems. J. MARTIN, *supra* note 3, at 139. NASA is developing this technology, and the satellite industry is depending upon the Ka band to satisfy mammoth satellite communications needs in the next decade. Dement, *Satellite Orbit Saturation Requires New Technology to Meet Demands*, COM. NEWS, March 1981, at 54–55.

[7] *See* notes 66–98 and accompanying text, *infra*.

[8] *See* notes 10–65 and accompanying text, *infra*.

[9] *See* notes 99–115 and accompanying text, *infra*.

The attorney who is somewhat unfamiliar with satellite communications may wish to consider the advice of Eilene Galloway, one of the world's most respected space law scholars: "The revolution in science and technology imposes an obligation on the scientific community to keep the legal profession informed of the latest developments. National and international lawyers have the matching responsibility of absorbing new facts into the framework of social order." Galloway, *The Community of Law and Science*, in PROCEEDINGS OF THE 1ST COLLOQUIUM ON THE LAW OF OUTER SPACE 59 (1959). *See also* Clarke, 6 J. BRIT. INTERPLAN. SOC'Y 75 (1946) ("Morals and ethics must not lag behind science, otherwise the social system will breed poisons which will cause its own destruction").

objective of international orbit/spectrum resource development law to be to maximize the availability of satellite communications pathways ("channels").

To maximize the availability of satellite channels means to increase, to the greatest extent possible, each of the three functional dimensions whose product makes up a channel. The first dimension, channel depth, describes how many messages can be conveyed at any one time.[10] The second dimension, channel distribution, describes how many different places the messages can reach.[11] The third dimension, channel directionality, describes from how many different places messages can be sent.[12] Hence, when a communication satellite system produces channels from the orbit/spectrum resource, the system is, in essence, dispersing the ability to convey an amount of information (depth) to a number of places (distribution) from a number of sources (directionality). Since every channel is the product of its depth, distribution, and directionality, it will be useful to review international legal support for the maximum channel dispersion principle separately for each of these three dimensions.

[10] "Bits per second" (bps) are the standard units employed to measure how many messages can be conveyed at any one time. Since it requires 56,000 bps to convey the human voice telephonically, a channel with depth of 56,000 bps could convey one voice message at a time, a channel with depth of 112,000 bps could convey about two simultaneous voice messages, and so on.

As an example of growth in the depth of international channels, consider that telegraph cables (1880) conveyed less than 10^3 bps, radio broadcasting (1930) conveyed about 10^5 bps, early telephone submarine cables and television (1955) conveyed about 10^7 bps, modern satellites and fiber optics (1980) can convey about 10^9 bps, and future space information stations (1995) will convey about 10^{12} bps. Pelton, *Global TV 2000*, SATELLITE COM., April 1981, at 18.

[11] Unless the depth described in note 10 is distributed somewhere, one does not have a channel; pathways must lead somewhere. On an international level of analysis, well-distributed channels are those which deliver depth to many or all countries, while poorly distributed channels do not deliver messages much beyond the country of origin. International satellite communications channels distribute depth much more widely than do submarine cables because the former blanket the earth with global and semi-global beams, while the latter terminate at a handful of "landings." For an excellent discussion of the ability of domestic communication satellites greatly to improve the distribution of local broadcast stations and cable systems, see Station Representatives Association, Satellites and Broadcast Stations: A Guide to Present and Potential Satellite Technology, Uses, Regulation and Economic Impact (1980).

[12] Unidirectional channels, such as broadcast stations, convey information from only one composite source. Multidirectional channels, such as telephone networks, convey information from millions of discrete sources. In technical telecommunications terminology, directionality is a function of "switching" capability, the ratio of potential sources to potential receivers in a media system or subsystem. It is possible to attain high switching ratios, that is, high directionality, with either wire or wireless channels. Traditionally, however, wire channels have dominated long-distance switched telecommunications because it was not technologically possible adequately to control isotropic information dispersal in wireless radio (or even natural aural) channels. Isotropically dispersed phenomena, like broadcast information, lose strength as the square of the distance traveled, which necessitates very complex, powerful source capabilities and results in very small source/receiver directionality ratios. With advances in microwave technology it has become possible to control isotropic information dispersal in radio channels and thereby deliver enough information to receivers without a wire to make source capabilities increasingly common, hence directionality ratios increasingly high.

These technological trends are demonstrated in the recently launched Satellite Business System and recently approved Xerox Telecommunications Network, each of which provides deep wireless channels with source-to-receiver directionality ratios of about one—the maximum attainable ratio. Kaplan, *Three Systems Defined*, IEEE SPECTRUM, Oct. 1979, at 44.

Channel Depth

Channel depth or "message volume per unit of time" may be enhanced in two important ways. One way is to develop the orbit/spectrum resource at ever higher frequencies.[13] The other is to encourage as much use of the resource as practicable at a given frequency.[14] International law appears to require maximum efforts at increasing channel depth along each of these lines.

Higher frequency cultivation is encouraged by international agreements that both set aside desirable frequency bands for public communications satellite service and grant to early users of these bands a limited form of protection from subsequent harmful radio interference.[15] Desirable frequency bands for public communications satellite service have been reserved through international agreements reached at the International Telecommunication Union (ITU).[16] These agreements, which appear in the form of a voluminous "Table of Frequency Allocations,"[17] are made pursuant to the ITU's constitutional mandate "to promote the development of technical facilities," to "effect allocation of the radio frequency spectrum," and, "in particular," to encourage the development of "*space techniques*" so that "*full advantage* [may be] taken of their possibilities."[18]

The ITU's commitment to develop the orbit/spectrum resource by taking "full advantage" of "space techniques"[19] finds strong support in the world's major source of international space law, the Outer Space Treaty of 1967.[20] Articles I and II of this Treaty proscribe hindering the development of the geostationary orbit by declaring it to be "the province of all mankind," "free for exploration and use by all States," and "not subject to national appropriation by claim of sovereignty, by means of use or occupation, or by any other means."[21]

[13] *See, e.g.*, J. MARTIN, TELECOMMUNICATIONS AND THE COMPUTER 156–86 (2d ed. 1976).

[14] *Ibid.*

[15] *See generally* D. LEIVE, INTERNATIONAL TELECOMMUNICATIONS AND INTERNATIONAL LAW: THE REGULATION OF THE RADIO SPECTRUM 19–29 (1970).

[16] The first international communications satellite service agreements may be found at International Telecommunication Union Radio Regulations (Geneva, 1959), *entered into force* Oct. 23, 1961, 12 UST 2377, TIAS No. 4893. For a critical analysis of early ITU satellite communications regulation, see D. SMITH, INTERNATIONAL TELECOMMUNICATIONS CONTROL (1969).

[17] ITU Radio Regulations, *supra* note 2, Art. N7, §5, Nos. 3450–3816M.

[18] International Telecommunication Convention (Málaga-Torremolinos, 1973), Art. 4(1)(b), (2)(a), (2)(c), 28 UST 2497, TIAS No. 8572 (entered into force for the United States, April 7, 1976) [hereinafter cited as International Telecommunication Convention] (emphasis supplied). Earlier versions of the Convention may be found at International Telecommunication Convention (Atlantic City, 1947), 63 Stat. 1399, TIAS No. 1901; International Telecommunication Convention (Buenos Aires, 1952), 6 UST 1213, TIAS No. 3266; International Telecommunication Convention (Geneva, 1959), 12 UST 1761, TIAS No. 4892; International Telecommunication Convention (Montreux, 1965), 18 UST 575, TIAS No. 6267.

[19] International Telecommunication Convention, *supra* note 18, Art. 4(2)(c).

[20] Treaty on Principles Governing the Activities of States in the Exploration and Use of Outer Space, Including the Moon and Other Celestial Bodies, *opened for signature* Jan. 27, 1967, 18 UST 2410, TIAS No. 6347, 610 UNTS 205 (entered into force for the United States on Oct. 10, 1967) [hereinafter cited as Outer Space Treaty of 1967].

[21] *Id.*, Arts. I, II. For an analysis of these rules, see S. H. LAY & H. TAUBENFELD, *supra* note 5, at 63–102.

This is consistent with Professor McDougal's well-considered finding that spatial-extension resources, such as the geostationary orbit. and flow resources, such as the electromagnetic spectrum, will generally yield "the greatest production and widest distribution of values" when the governing legal rules keep the resource "open to inclusive enjoyment by many or all participants."[22]

A further means of encouraging development of the resource at higher frequencies is to place earlier utilizers of these frequencies in a better legal position than later entrants. At the heart of granting a preferred position to the early entrant is the practical fact that when one country's planned communications satellite system has the potential of interfering with another country's operating system, it is much easier to eliminate the potential interference by modifying the planned system rather than the operating system.[23] Legally, the earlier satellite communications system is able to secure a right to "international recognition" by being the first to use a share of orbit/spectrum and to notify that use to the ITU's International Frequency Registration Bureau (IFRB).[24]

The value of the "international recognition" right acquired through first use and notification is a preferred position in the ITU's mandatory technical coordination procedures.[25] This preferred position means that if a satellite system operating in accordance with the ITU "Convention, Table of Frequency Allocations and other provisions of the Radio Regulations"[26] receives harmful interference from an uncoordinated, subsequently deployed satellite system, "the latter [satellite system] must, upon receipt of advice thereof, immediately eliminate this harmful interference."[27] Hence, although early users of a space service frequency band are obligated to engage in a technical coordination process, they can never be forced to modify their system substantively so as to allow more room for a new system.[28] Since latecomers to a band can always be forced to absorb most of the compromises required to eliminate interference and thus to achieve coordination, there is often a clear incentive to move into new frequency bands as quickly as is technologically possible.[29]

Additional legal support for the preferred position of early users of orbit/spectrum may be found in Article IX of the Outer Space Treaty.[30] This article requires a state to "undertake appropriate international consultations before proceeding" with any space activity it has reason to believe "would cause potentially harmful interference" to the outer space activities of other states.[31]

In addition to developing the orbit/spectrum resource at new frequency bands, channel depth is also greatly enhanced by making as much use of the

[22] M. McDougal, H. Lasswell, & I. Vlasic, Law and Public Order in Space 774–76, 781 (1963).

[23] Robinson, *Regulating International Airwaves: The 1979 WARC*, 21 Va. J. Int'l L. 1, 45 n.139 (1980).

[24] Christol, *The International Telecommunication Union and the International Law of Outer Space*, in Proceedings of the 22d Colloquium on the Law of Outer Space 43 (1980).

[25] ITU Radio Regulations, *supra* note 2, Art. 9A.

[26] *Id.*, Art. 9A, §4, No. 639BM.

[27] *Id.*, Art. 9A, §6, No. 639DD–DE.

[28] *See, e.g., id.*, Art. 9A, §2, No.639AZ.

[29] In practice, the exigencies of the negotiating process generally require both sides to come to an accommodation. *See* Colino, *International Cooperation Between Communications Satellite Systems: An Overview of Current Practices and Future Prospects*, 5 J. Space L. 65 (1977).

[30] Outer Space Treaty of 1967, note 20 *supra*.

[31] *Id.*, Art. IX.

resource as possible at existing frequency bands.[32] International law seeks to maximize this aspect of channel depth by minimizing occasions for harmful interference between different communications satellite systems.[33] This potential for harmful interference is the principal limit upon the number of geostationary channels that may be simultaneously dispersed at a given frequency band.[34]

In view of the deleterious effect of harmful interference upon channel depth, Article 4 of the International Telecommunication Convention requires the ITU:

> (1) to "effect allocation of the radio frequency spectrum and registration of radio frequency assignments *in order to avoid harmful interference between* radio stations of different countries,"[35] and
>
> (2) to "*coordinate efforts to eliminate harmful interference* between radio stations of different countries and to improve the use made of the radio frequency spectrum."[36]

Further support for an international legal norm of maximum channel depth is found in Articles 10 and 33 of the International Telecommunication Convention.[37] These articles commit the ITU to "the operation of the *maximum* practicable number of radio channels in those portions of the spectrum where harmful interference may occur," to the "effective and economical use of the geostationary satellite orbit," and to the minimization of wasteful use of the orbit/spectrum resource.[38]

Thus, by minimizing technical inefficiency and harmful interference, international satellite communications law seeks to maximize the number of messages that may be conveyed via geostationary channels on any one frequency and at any one time. This objective of maximum channel depth is also the aim of legal rules designed to encourage the initial development of the resource at a new frequency band. These rules flow from the International Telecommunication Convention and the Outer Space Treaty, the two most significant sources of international orbit/spectrum development law. It therefore seems clear that at least in terms of channel depth, the maximum channel dispersion principle does indeed underlie international regulation of orbit/spectrum.

Channel Distribution

Distribution, it will be recalled, describes the number of different places to which a channel can convey a message.[39] International space law supports

[32] In satellite communications jargon this is referred to as "frequency reuse," and is actually a form of multiplexing or "channel sharing."

[33] "Harmful interference" is legally defined as unwanted energy due to emissions that "seriously degrades, obstructs, or repeatedly interrupts a radiocommunication service operating in accordance with [the Radio] Regulations." ITU Radio Regulations, *supra* note 2, Art. N1, §7, No. 3140A, 3142. "Confusion as to assigned frequencies—or worse yet, no assignment at all—would defeat the maximum beneficial use of space communications facilities." C. CHRISTOL, THE INTERNATIONAL LAW OF OUTER SPACE 396 (1966).

[34] Gehrig, *supra* note 2, at 269.

[35] International Telecommunication Convention, *supra* note 18, Art. 4(2)(a).

[36] *Id.*, Art. 4(2)(b). *See* early discussion of the application of these commands to space communications in A. HALEY, SPACE LAW AND GOVERNMENT 168–76 (1963).

[37] *Id.*, Arts. 10, 33.

[38] *Ibid.*

[39] *See* note 11 and accompanying text, *supra.*

maximum channel distribution by promoting the establishment of geostationary satellite communications channels to as many different countries as possible.

Distribution of telecommunications pathways is clearly maximized in the ITU duty to "foster the creation, development and improvement of telecommunication equipment and networks in developing countries *by every means at its disposal*."[40] The particular goal of distributing satellite channels finds strong support in Article 33 of the International Telecommunication Convention, in certain resolutions adopted at the recent 1979 World Administrative Radio Conference (WARC–79), in the Outer Space Treaty, and in the INTELSAT Agreement.

Article 33 of the International Telecommunication Convention provides: "In using frequency bands for space radio services Members shall bear in mind that *radio frequencies and the geostationary satellite orbit* are limited natural resources, that they *must be used efficiently and economically so that countries or groups of countries may have equitable access to both*. . . ."[41]

By insisting upon "equitable access" to orbit/spectrum for all countries, Article 33 tries to ensure that geostationary bandwidth does not only flow to the first few countries operating satellite communications systems.[42] However, ITU concern over the distribution of satellite channels has grown steadily since Article 33 was adopted in 1973.[43] It now appears quite possible that Article 33 will be amended and strengthened at the 1982 ITU Plenipotentiary Conference in Nairobi, Kenya,[44] because the 1971 ITU Resolution from which it flowed, known as Resolution Spa 2–1, was replaced at WARC–79 with the more strongly worded Resolution AY.[45] This new resolution, whose provisions will be "taken into account" by the ITU organs that suggest changes in its Convention, considers "all countries [to] have *equal* rights" in the use of orbit/spectrum, and resolves that those operating communications satellite systems "*take all practicable measures* to realize the possibility of the use of new space systems by other countries or groups of countries."[46]

In addition to ITU sources, the goal of maximum distribution of geostationary channels finds strong support in Article I of the Outer Space Treaty. This article deems outer space to be "the province of all mankind" and requires it

[40] International Telecommunication Convention, *supra* note 18, Art. 4(2)(e) (emphasis supplied).

[41] *Id.*, Art. 33 (emphasis supplied).

[42] *See* C. CHRISTOL, SATELLITE POWER SYSTEM INTERNATIONAL AGREEMENTS 44 (U.S. Dep't of Energy Research, 1978). These countries include Canada, Indonesia, the Soviet Union, and the United States.

[43] The adoption of Article 33 is discussed by the ITU's Secretary-General in Mili, *World Administrative Radio Conference for the Planning of the Broadcasting-Satellite Service in Frequency Bands 11.7–12.2 GHz (in Regions 2 and 3) and 11.7–12.5 GHz (in Region 1)*, in PROCEEDINGS OF THE 20TH COLLOQUIUM ON THE LAW OF OUTER SPACE 346 (1978).

[44] The Plenipotentiary Conference is the ITU's "supreme organ"; it meets about once a decade, it is composed of all ITU member countries, and "it is responsible for revising the International Telecommunication Convention and for establishing general policies and programs." D. LEIVE, *supra* note 15, at 32.

[45] International Telecommunication Union, Final Acts of the World Administrative Radio Conference (1979) [hereinafter cited as WARC–79 Final Acts], Res. AY.

[46] *Ibid.* (emphasis supplied).

to be used "for the benefit and in the interests of all countries, irrespective of their degree of economic or scientific development."[47]

One final major source of international law on orbit/spectrum resource development is the Agreement Relating to the International Telecommunications Satellite Organization, a multilateral treaty among 106 signatories and the organic act of the INTELSAT international satellite communications consortium.[48] The Agreement reveals the need for greater geostationary channel distribution to be the very reason for INTELSAT's formation. Article II, for example, states that INTELSAT is being established with "full regard" for international principles requiring "expanded telecommunications services to all areas of the world," the utilization of "the most advanced technology available" for these services, and the resultant establishment, "for the benefit of all mankind," of "the most efficient and economic facilities possible consistent with the best and most equitable use of the radio frequency spectrum and of orbital space."[49]

With so very many countries committed through INTELSAT and/or the ITU not only to the global distribution of geostationary channels, but also to the maximization of this goal with the "*most* advanced technology," the "*most* efficient and economic facilities," and the *best* use of the orbit/spectrum resource,[50] it seems quite clear that at least in terms of channel depth and channel distribution, the maximum channel dispersion principle underlies international regulation of this resource.

Channel Directionality

Directionality is the dimension of a channel that describes the number of different places from which a message may be sent. To maximize channel directionality means to give as many communicators as possible the technical option of initiating messages.[51] This dimension may be contrasted with channel distribution, which provides as many communicators as possible with the technical option of receiving messages, and with channel depth, which simply addresses the volume of messages moving between communicators.

[47] Outer Space Treaty of 1967, *supra* note 20, Art. I. *See also* General Assembly Resolutions 1802 and 1721 specifying that "communication by satellite offers great benefits to mankind" and "should be available to the nations of the world as soon as practicable on a global and non-discriminatory basis," *analyzed in* C. CHRISTOL, *supra* note 33, at 404–06.

[48] Agreement Relating to the International Telecommunications Satellite Organization, 23 UST 3813, TIAS No. 7532 (1973) [hereinafter cited as INTELSAT Agreement]. *See generally* R. COLINO, THE INTELSAT DEFINITIVE ARRANGEMENTS: USHERING IN A NEW ERA IN SATELLITE TELECOMMUNICATIONS (1973); Doyle, *Permanent Arrangements for the Global Commercial Communications Satellite System of Intelsat*, in PROCEEDINGS OF THE 17TH COLLOQUIUM ON THE LAW OF OUTER SPACE 123 (1975); Pelton, *The Intelsat Global Satellite System and the Pacific: Past, Present and Future*, in PACIFIC TELECOMMUNICATIONS CONFERENCE 2E–23 (1979).

[49] INTELSAT Agreement, *supra* note 48, Preamble, Art. II.

[50] *Id.*, Art. II (emphasis supplied); The International Telecommunication Union is one of "the public international organizations through which major efforts have been undertaken to maximize space communications." C. CHRISTOL, *supra* note 33, at 394.

[51] *See* note 12 and accompanying text, *supra*.

The ITU supports constant growth in channel directionality by calling upon states to increase the usefulness and public availability of electronic bandwidth,[52] to "recognize the right of the public to correspond" by means of international telecommunications service,[53] and to keep channel access costs "at levels as low as possible."[54] Growth in the directionality of satellite communications channels is also supported by the same authority that supports the broader distribution of these channels.[55] The ITU Radio Regulations do have separate provisions for "broadcasting-satellite service," a unidirection channel, and for "fixed-satellite service," a multidirectional channel.[56] However, the sanctity of these service classifications is increasingly problematic and none of the international legal authority cited for maximum channel distribution is limited to unidirectional channels.[57]

The INTELSAT Agreement, for example, decrees the subject organization's "prime objective" to be that "the space segment required for international public telecommunications services of high quality and reliability . . . be available *on a non-discriminatory basis to all areas of the world*."[58] "Public telecommunications services" is defined to include multidirectional channels such as telex, telephony, and data transmission.[59] Thus, through the INTELSAT Agreement, 106 nations have specifically committed themselves to the global distribution of multidirectional channels.[60] This momentous undertaking has been addressed with great success, and has assumed the proportions of a relentless effort to provide ever more multidirectional channels to ever more areas of the world.[61]

Much of this effort is occurring outside the INTELSAT organization. Regional communications satellite consortia are forming to distribute multidirec-

[52] International Telecommunication Convention, *supra* note 18, Art. 4(1)(b).

[53] *Id.*, Art. 18. *See also id.*, Art. 34(1) (binding stations "to exchange radiocommunications reciprocally without distinction as to radio system" employed).

[54] *Id.*, Art. 4(2)(d).

[55] *See* notes 40–50 and accompanying text, *supra.*

[56] The broadcasting-satellite service is legally defined as "a radiocommunication service in which signals transmitted or retransmitted by space stations are intended for direct reception by the general public." ITU Radio Regulations, *supra* note 2, Art. N1, §3, No. 84AP. The legal definition of fixed-satellite service is "a radiocommunication service *between* earth stations." *Id.*, Art. N1, §3, No. 84AG (emphasis supplied).

[57] "The continuing implementation of digital communications and other new technology tends to merge all services into a common system." Rutkowski, *The 1979 World Administrative Radio Conference: The ITU in a Changing World*, 13 INT'L LAW. 289, 301 n.35 (1979). Future Canadian Anik satellites and Indian Insat satellites will be hybrid broadcasting and fixed-satellite service systems. *See also* note 12 *supra.*

[58] INTELSAT Agreement, *supra* note 48, Art. III (emphasis supplied).

[59] *Id.*, Art. I(k).

[60] Each party signs the INTELSAT Agreement "[w]ith full regard for the principles" that "communication by means of satellites should be available to the nations of the world as soon as practicable on a global and non-discriminatory basis," and that "satellite telecommunications should be organized in such a way as to permit all peoples to have access to the global satellite system." *Id.*, Art. II, Preamble.

[61] Pelton, *supra* note 10, at 18–29; Pollack, *Technologies for Future Intelsat Satellites*, 17 J. SPACECRAFT 4 (1980).

tional channels among their member countries,[62] and a new international organization, INMARSAT, was recently established to "serve *all* areas where there is need for maritime communications" with multidirectional channels "open for use by ships of *all* nations."[63] Hence it appears that the global commitment to maximize the depth and distribution aspects of satellite communications channels is accompanied by an undertaking also to increase, to the greatest extent possible, the directional aspects of these channels.

From this exposition of the international legal support for maximum growth in each of the three functional dimensions of a geostationary satellite communications channel, it follows logically that international law supports the maximum dispersion of total geostationary bandwidth.[64] Since orbit/spectrum is simply a "reservoir" or "storehouse" of geostationary bandwidth,[65] one may fairly and confidently conclude that international regulation of this resource is indeed premised upon application of the maximum channel dispersion principle to the resource development technology of geostationary satellite communications.

III. A Jurimetric Means of Accommodating Different Legal Perspectives on Applying the Maximum Channel Dispersion Principle

That the maximum channel dispersion principle actually exists, of course, is universally agreed.[66] However, the precise application of any legal principle to a dynamic environment is uncertain and often controversial.[67]

[62] The Agreement of the Arab Corporation for Space Communications, *reprinted in* SENATE COMM. ON AERONAUTICAL AND SPACE SCIENCES, 94TH CONG., 2D SESS., SPACE LAW: SELECTED BASIC DOCUMENTS 400–16 (Comm. Print 1976); request of African Post and Telegraph Union for a definitional study of a regional African communications satellite system, *reported in* SATELLITE COM., Dec. 1980, at 6. *See also* inventory of probable regional communications satellite systems in A. CHAYES, SATELLITE BROADCASTING 8–9 (1973).

[63] Convention on the International Maritime Satellite Organization, TIAS No. 9605 (1979), Arts. 3, 5(3), 7(1). *See generally* Sondaal, *The Current Situation in the Field of Maritime Communication Satellites: Inmarsat*, 8 J. SPACE L. 21 (1980); Jasentuliyana, *The Establishment of an International Maritime Satellite System*, 2 ANNALS AIR & SPACE L. 323 (1977).

[64] "Bandwidth" simply means information or message-carrying ability in common usage. Technically speaking, bandwidth defines the range of cycles per second in a frequency band.

[65] *See* notes 1–6 and accompanying text, *supra*.

[66] *See* notes 13–63 and accompanying text, *supra*.

[67] America's foremost international space law expert, Dr. Carl Q. Christol, wisely cautions in this regard:

> [I]t should be kept in mind that while definitions may be suitable for a specific object, having, for example, tangible qualities, or for private relationships, as in a contract situation, the utility of endeavoring to define a principle may be questioned. It is generally acknowledged that principles do not lend themselves readily to definitional labels. The latter serve as arbitrary limitations on growth and destroy the usefulness of principles.

With particular reference to the common heritage of mankind principle, Christol observes that while "it may be imagined that through a definition it [is] possible to achieve a degree of present specificity . . . , unfortunately, for this perspective, the history of the law has demonstrated that words have a habit of changing their meanings. As a result a definitional fetish may produce deep-

The current global rush to exploit the orbit/spectrum resource is certainly a "dynamic environment."[68] It should come as no surprise, therefore, that the international community is unsure about the precise application of the maximum channel dispersion principle to the resource. For example, geostationary satellite communications systems are operating under "experimental" ITU Resolutions on even such basic matters as the duration of a system's right to international recognition.[69] It is to the different legal perspectives, and to a jurimetric means of accommodating them, that this final section is addressed.

The Legal Perspectives

There are essentially two different legal perspectives on the correct application of the maximum channel dispersion principle to orbit/spectrum. According to one view, the dispersion of geostationary bandwidth is best maximized by adopting orbit/spectrum development rules that particularly emphasize and promote channel depth. According to the other perspective, this goal is best attained by adopting orbit/spectrum development rules that particularly emphasize and promote channel distribution.

The most recent institutional clash of these two perspectives occurred at

---

seated frustrations." Finally, as to the fundamental nature of international legal principles, Christol astutely notes their "essential quality of *starting points for legal reasoning.*" Consequently, a priori definitional approaches "contribute more to the obscuring of goals than to [the] providing [of] guidance in the use of the yet unperfected [principle]," and "serve more to prevent the gathering of practical meaning than to enhance it." Christol, *The Common Heritage of Mankind Provision in the 1979 Agreement Governing the Activities of States on the Moon and Other Celestial Bodies*, 14 INT'L LAW. 429, 479 (1980), *reprinted* at invitation of Sen. Adlai E. Stevenson *in The Moon Treaty: Hearings Before the Subcomm. on Science, Technology, and Space of the Senate Comm. on Commerce, Science, and Transportation*, 96th Cong., 2d Sess. 186–218 (1980).

[68] In addition to the hundreds of satellites the United States and the Soviet Union have each launched, and the communications satellite systems operated by INTELSAT, INMARSAT, Canada, and Indonesia, there are developmental satellites in orbit of European, Japanese, Chinese, and Indian origin. The Nordic states, the Arab states, Nigeria, Colombia, Brazil, Australia, and Thailand have also expressed serious interest in orbiting their own communications satellites. *See, e.g.*, Robinson, *supra* note 23, at 2 n.1. Certain portions of orbit/spectrum are under particularly intense development. Hill, *Corporate Star Wars: Domsats Battle for the Geostationary Orbit*, SATELLITE COM., Aug. 1980, at 12; Grenier, Popot, Lombard, & Payet, *Telecom I, a National Satellite for Domestic and Business Services*, in 3 INTERNATIONAL CONFERENCE ON COMMUNICATIONS 49.5.1 (1979) (discusses difficulty in finding suitable orbital location for new French business satellite). Indeed, computer models have already predicted significant collision probabilities, over 10-year periods, in the geostationary orbit. Rothblatt, *International Liability of the United States for Space Shuttle Operations*, 13 INT'L LAW. 471, 474 (1979). And an American administrative agency, NOAA, has already undertaken "the first mass shifting of satellites in space" to "eliminate the possibility of a collision in the busy geostationary corridor." SATELLITE COM., April 1981, at 5.

[69] Considering "that it would be advantageous to introduce an experimental procedure to gain experience from application of the new concept of notifying the period of validity of an assignment in space radiocommunications," the World Administrative Radio Conference resolves that (until 1984) "if a notifying administration which wishes to extend the period of operation originally shown on the assignment notice of a frequency assignment of an existing space station informs the [IFRB] accordingly . . . , the Board shall amend as requested the period of operation originally recorded in the Master Register." WARC–79 Final Acts, *supra* note 45, Res. BY.

WARC–79. The controversial issue was whether orbit/spectrum at desirable frequency bands should be rationed among the nations of the world.[70]

To ration orbit/spectrum at a frequency band means first to divide the band into a set of much narrower sub-bands. This set of sub-bands is then associated with each available position in the geostationary orbit. Each sub-band at each orbital position constitutes a unique, interference-free "channel." The channels are then parceled out to all countries in accordance with "the special characteristics of the countries (size, time zones, language differences, etc.)."[71] In formal ITU parlance, this entire rationing process is called "planning."[72] A 1977 ITU Plan covers the broadcasting-satellite service downlink, for Ku-band frequencies, in ITU Regions 1 (Europe, the USSR, and Africa) and 3 (Asia, Oceana).

The traditional alternative to the planning or "rationing approach" is the orbit/spectrum "engineering approach." Under this approach, rights to transmit in a frequency band from a position in the geostationary orbit are acquired by being the first to notify such an operation to the IFRB of the ITU. Subsequent satellite systems employing the same frequency band from nearby orbital positions are accommodated through a programmed process of mutual technical coordination.[73]

Perspective Favoring Orbit/Spectrum Rationing. The nations that favor rationing take the view that maximum geostationary channel dispersion requires decidedly prodistribution rules for orbit/spectrum development.[74] These nations have expressed concern that the distributional tenets of the extant legal regime, such as Article 33 of the ITU Convention, are too weak.[75] In particular, these nations fear that in the near future the present regulatory framework might inhibit the distribution of geostationary channels for domestic telecommunications services by imposing increasingly high coordination costs upon late developers.[76] Indeed, there are already reports of "administrative difficulties in completing advanced coordination procedures for two domestic systems, Indonesia's Palapa and India's Insat."[77] This is especially interesting since Indonesia and India are actually among the earliest orbit/spectrum developers.[78]

[70] Robinson, *supra* note 23, at 27–28.

[71] WARC–79 Final Acts, *supra* note 45, App. 29A, Art. 12.9.1.

[72] For a very clear description of planning, see AV. WK. & SPACE TECH., Sept. 10, 1979, at 75–77.

[73] *See* notes 23–29 and accompanying text, *supra.*

[74] *See, e.g.*, statements made by the Indian, Chinese, Iraqi, and Colombian delegates to WARC–79, *reproduced verbatim in* Rutkowski, Six Ad-Hoc Two: The Third World Speaks Its Mind 7–12 (1979) (unpub. paper available from the author at FCC Office of Science & Technology, Washington, D.C.). *See also* ITU-WARC, India, Proposals for the Work of the Conference, Doc. No. 78 (Sept. 18, 1979); ITU-WARC, Iraq, Draft Resolution Relating to Planning the Radiocommunication Satellite Services Using the Geostationary Orbit, Doc. No. 359 (Oct. 13, 1979).

[75] This concern led to the adoption of Res. AY, notes 43–46 and accompanying text, *supra.*

[76] The Chairman of the U.S. delegation to WARC–79 recently observed that these nations are supporting planning "largely out of fear that developed countries were preempting the orbital positions and frequencies and consequently emerging needs would not be met." Robinson, *supra* note 23, at 27.

[77] *Id.* at 45 n.139.

[78] *See* note 68 *supra.*

Those who believe that rationing is necessary to ensure maximum dispersion of geostationary bandwidth also steadfastly insist that their approach in no way detracts from channel depth. For example, annexes to a scheduled plan for Ku-band broadcasting-satellite service mandate ten specific depth-enhancing techniques to "be applied to the *maximum* extent technically and economically practicable consistent with the capability of systems to fulfill the requirements for which they were designed."[79]

The ITU does not consider a plan's country-by-country channel assignments to constitute national "appropriations" of orbital space.[80] Appropriations of orbital arc would be in clear contravention of Article I of the Outer Space Treaty,[81] which has been shown to support maximum channel depth, and could even lead, in WARC-79 Ambassador Glen Robinson's view, to a "geostationary OPEC."[82]

More than one observer believes that about as much geostationary bandwidth will flow to early orbit/spectrum developers with rationing as without.[83] This is because the planning criteria by which channels are distributed are rough measures of a country's "need" for satellite communications service.[84] Even if the inflexibility of rationing causes some decrease in the growth rate of channel depth, it is argued that total channel dispersion will still be maximized because the plan-induced increments in channel distribution will more than offset the coincident dip in channel depth.[85]

Perspective Opposing Orbit/Spectrum Rationing. Those in opposition to orbit/spectrum rationing believe that maximum geostationary channel dispersion requires unimpeded technological efforts at ever greater channel efficiency. These nations are concerned because they see the ITU Plans as imposing severe handicaps on technological innovation. In particular, these nations fear that rationing will either freeze technology at the level existing when a plan is

[79] WARC-79 Final Acts, *supra* note 45, App. 29A, Ann. 7 (emphasis supplied).

[80] Butler, *World Administrative Radio Conference for Planning Broadcasting Satellite Service*, 5 J. SPACE L. 93, 98 (1977).

[81] Note 20 *supra. See also* C. JENKS, SPACE LAW 200 (1965), for pre-1967 observation: "The general principle that outer space and celestial bodies are not subject to national appropriation can therefore, and indeed must, now be regarded as firmly established."

To be distinguished, however, are clear national or private exclusive property rights in *values exploited from* a space resource through national or private resource development activities.

By analogy, while it is universally agreed that no "State may validly purport to subject any part of the high seas to its sovereignty," Draft Convention on the Law of the Sea (Informal Text), UN Doc. A/CONF.62/WP.10/Rev.3 and Add.1 and Corrs. 1-6, Art. 89, no one questions the exclusive property rights of fishing concerns in the fish they exploit or of ocean transport concerns in their income from moving goods over conducive waters. Similarly, while no state may subject regions of the geostationary orbit to its sovereignty, property rights in exploited information channels and in the signals they conduct are clearly recognized. *See, e.g.*, Ferrer, *The Brussels Convention Concerning the Protection of Signals Transmitted from Satellites*, in PROCEEDINGS OF THE 17TH COLLOQUIUM, *supra* note 48, at 26.

[82] Robinson, *supra* note 23, at 49.

[83] *Id.* at 46-47; Rutkowski, *supra* note 57, at 308.

[84] Rutkowski, *supra* note 57, at 308. *See also* text accompanying note 71 *supra.*

[85] *See, e.g.*, delegate statements quoted in Rutkowski, *supra* note 74, at 8.

approved, or will lead to massive future waste of the resource as plans "become obsolete with changes in both satellite and earth terminal requirements."[86] Indeed, orbit/spectrum waste will already certainly occur in the only planned space service band: the Region 1 and 3 Ku-band broadcasting-satellite service (downlink).[87] This plan was based on a specified minimum separation distance between satellites that recent technological advances have made unnecessarily extravagant.[88] This is particularly disturbing since the plan was just drafted in 1977 and is not even scheduled to be reviewed for 20 years.[89] Satellite technology, on the other hand, advances so quickly that 20 years ago geostationary satellites did not even exist!

Those who oppose orbit/spectrum rationing because of its detrimental impact upon channel depth also maintain that rationing undermines maximum channel distribution. A United States WARC–79 spokesman pointed out, for example, that "an unplanned assignment system would insure better that all future [satellite communications] needs would be met because it would conserve over time more of the resource for distribution as needed."[90]

A sharper criticism of planning rests upon the practical observations that dedicated communications satellite systems are costly ventures, and that nothing will facilitate channel distribution faster than major cuts in these costs.[91] However, it was just observed that ITU Plans discourage major technological advances that could greatly increase channel depth and greatly decrease costs. Even if it is conceded that the coordination procedures of the present regime impose greater administrative costs as channel distribution in a particular frequency band expands,[92] opponents of orbit/spectrum rationing will maintain that these coordination costs are trivial compared to the tremendous obstacles created by a rigid ITU Plan.

Result of the WARC–79 Clash Over Rationing: Resolution BP. As a result of the clash of legal perspectives at WARC–79 over the role of orbit/spectrum rationing in maximizing the dispersion of geostationary bandwidth, the conference formally resolved to convene a special World Administrative Radio Conference on the Uses of the Geostationary Orbit (GEO-WARC). The chief task of this GEO-WARC is to "decide which space services and frequency bands should be planned."[93] Reaching these decisions will be very difficult

[86] Robinson, *supra* note 23, at 44.

[87] WARC–79 Final Acts, *supra* note 45, App. 29A.

[88] Robinson, *supra* note 23, at 44 n.132.

[89] WARC–79 Final Acts, *supra* note 45, App. 29A, Art. 16.

[90] U.S. DEP'T OF STATE, REPORT OF THE CHAIRMAN OF THE UNITED STATES DELEGATION TO THE WORLD ADMINISTRATIVE RADIO CONFERENCE OF THE INTERNATIONAL TELECOMMUNICATION UNION, SEPT. 24–DEC. 6, 1979, at 78–79 (1980) (statement of U.S. spokesman regarding Resolution BP).

[91] The current rapid proliferation of satellite communications systems is certainly a function of the 18 to 1 reduction in satellite rates (in real dollars) since 1965; "satellite communications are becoming less and less expensive when compared to the price of competing items such as paper, gasoline and air transportation. Eventually the impact of this ever-lower true cost of satellite communications must be even greater." Morgan, *supra* note 1, at 26.

[92] *See* notes 77–78 and accompanying text, *supra*.

[93] WARC–79 Final Acts, *supra* note 45, Res. BP.

because, as discussed above, it is usually not apparent to all whether channel dispersion is maximized with planning or without planning.

The resolution itself, denominated "BP," is quite noncommittal on the issue.[94] Its stated objective, "to guarantee in practice" for all countries equitable access to the geostationary-satellite orbit and the frequency bands allocated to space services, is so vague as to do little more than apply the maximum dispersion principle to the resource.[95]

The key phrase, "guarantee in practice," may mean almost anything. One can argue quite convincingly that equitable access is "guaranteed in practice" today since no one has ever been prevented from orbiting a communications satellite system[96] and since the INTELSAT system will provide access to domestic satellite communications channels for as little as $200,000 a year.[97] While Resolution BP does charge the GEO-WARC with actually preparing a plan for those frequency bands it decides to plan, it also charges the GEO-WARC with establishing "guidelines for regulatory procedures" for any frequency bands it decides not to plan.[98]

In sum, there is great uncertainty and controversy over which legal rules best apply the maximum channel dispersion principle to orbit/spectrum. A special worldwide conference called GEO-WARC will be convened to address this issue. This article next articulates a jurimetric approach to orbit/spectrum development law that can reduce international uncertainty about the substantive application of the maximum channel dispersion principle and facilitate the decision-making process at GEO-WARC.

The Jurimetric Approach

Jurimetrics, the application of formal analysis and/or quantitative methods to legal decision making, is especially useful when the decision to be made is a function of one or more quantifiable considerations. The decision orbit/spectrum regulators must make is "which space services and frequency bands should be planned." This decision is a function of whether or not planning maximizes the dispersion of geostationary channels for each frequency band and space service.[99] A channel is but the product of its depth, distribution, and direction-

[94] *Cf.* Robinson, *supra* note 23, at 28, for the view that neither the U.S. position, which sought a completely open-ended agenda for GEO-WARC, nor the proplanning position, which sought a completely predetermined agenda, eventually prevailed.

[95] WARC–79 Final Acts, *supra* note 45, Res. BP.

[96] Robinson, *supra* note 23, at 45 ("The Third World fears of being preempted by earlier developed-country exploitation were belied by experience because no one could show that there had been any such preemption, despite considerable satellite activity by both developing and developed countries").

[97] Quarter transponders are available at the rate of $800,000 per full preemptible transponder.

[98] WARC–79 Final Acts, *supra* note 45, Res. BP. The resolution also invites the ITU's technical advisory committee, the CCIR, to provide "technical information concerning principles, criteria and technical parameters including those required for planning space services." This clearly contemplates the provision as well of technical information required for schemes less detailed than planning.

[99] *See* notes 6 and 56 *supra*.

ality.[100] If each of these three dimensions can be quantified, their product will quantify channel dispersion. By comparing the values obtained for channel dispersion under planned and unplanned regimes it may be possible to determine which regime maximizes channel dispersion. This jurimetric conclusion should then be of some value to international lawmakers in making the very difficult decisions of GEO-WARC.

Channel Depth. Channel depth is generally quantified in terms of cycles per second (Hz) of bandwidth. The basic depth of the broadcasting-satellite service Ku-band downlink, for example, is 500 MHz (million cycles per second) per interference-free orbital position.[101] The jurimetric question to address is whether more of this channel depth is realized under an engineered orbit/spectrum or a rationed orbit/spectrum.

Without rationing, each country is entitled to receive an entire 500 MHz of channel depth per satellite position, less any fraction of this depth already being developed by another satellite system with which harmful interference would occur.[102] In practice, no satellite system has yet been forced to share any of the legally allotted channel depth with another foreign satellite system. Technical coordination has always been able to eliminate harmful interference. Hence, the total amount of basic channel depth available to a country under orbit/spectrum engineering is 500 MHz times A, where A equals the total number of orbital positions from which an acceptable signal can reach a country.[103]

It is possible, however, that in the future technical coordination may require two or more countries to share the bandwidth available from an orbital position. In this case the total amount of basic channel depth available to a country under orbit/spectrum engineering is 500 MHz times K times A, where K is the average fraction of 500 MHz to which a country is entitled.[104] Since no country has yet been forced to share this bandwidth, today K equals 1.

With rationing, each country is entitled to receive about 20 MHz of channel depth per satellite position to which it is entitled.[105] Hence, the total amount of basic channel depth available to a country under orbit/spectrum rationing is 20 MHz times A times j, where j equals the fraction of acceptable orbital

[100] *See* notes 10–12 and accompanying text, *supra.*

[101] *See* note 6 *supra.* It is assumed that the 1000 MHz allocation will be split in half between fixed and broadcasting services. In ITU Region 1 (Europe, the USSR, Africa), however, 800 MHz of bandwidth has been allocated to the broadcasting-satellite service.

[102] ITU Radio Regulations, *supra* note 2, Art. N7, §5 and, for example, Art. 9A.

[103] The term "basic channel depth" is employed to streamline the analysis by disregarding the many technical factors that may affect channel depth, but are either equally applicable under planned and unplanned regimes, or only operate to further increase the channel depth available under an unplanned regime.

[104] This "basic channel depth" could, of course, increase multiplicatively (but for the simplifying assumption of n.103) through the application of techniques such as contiguous spot beams, scanning spot beams, and satellite platforms. *See* Goldman & Edelson, *On Several Communications Satellite Designs Using Large Space Antennas*, in PACIFIC CONFERENCE, *supra* note 48, at 3B-5; Reudink & Yeh, *Rapid-Scan Area-Coverage Communication Satellite*, 17 J. SPACECRAFT 9 (1980); Katz & Donavan, *The Design of Communications Systems on Large Space Platforms*, in 1 INTERNATIONAL CONFERENCE ON COMMUNICATIONS 9.4.1 (1980).

[105] WARC–79 Final Acts, *supra* note 45, App. 29A, Art. 11.3.

positions A to which the country is entitled.[106] Under the 1977 plan, j ranges from 11/6 to 2/35, and has a modal value of 4/35.[107]

It is therefore very clear that channel depth is maximized at a much higher level under orbit/spectrum engineering than under orbit/spectrum planning. While there is 500 MHz times A channel depth available to each country without planning, there is only about 2.3 MHz times A channel depth available to the typical country with a plan.[108] This is an extremely significant drop of two orders of magnitude.

Channel distribution. Channel distribution, it will be recalled, describes the number of *different* places to which messages may be conveyed. Although the greatest amount of channel distribution available from a position in the geostationary orbit is 40 percent of the earth's surface, technical channel depth requirements and international legal restrictions mandate that "all technical means available shall be used to reduce, to the maximum extent practicable, the radiation over the territory of other countries unless an agreement has been previously reached with such countries."[109]

Basically then, each position in the geostationary orbit can distribute channels to all countries capable of receiving an acceptable signal from that orbital position.[110] Let B stand for this number of countries.

Without rationing, each orbital position is capable of distributing B channels. With rationing, each orbital position is only allowed to distribute B times h channels, where h equals the fraction of possible countries B to which that orbital position is entitled to convey signals.[111] Under the 1977 plan, h ranged from about 24/42 in Region 3 to 40/105 in Region 1.[112] Therefore, about twice as much channel distribution is possible without rationing.

Channel Directionality. Channel directionality describes the number of different countries from which channels can be conveyed. On this article's level of analysis, channel directionality values will not differ from channel distribution values because each analytical unit, the country, is only conveying mes-

[106] As a simplifying assumption, "acceptable orbital positions A" is here defined as the number of available orbital positions in the ITU region in which a country falls.

[107] The Soviet Union, for example, with a j value of 11/6, is entitled to two 20-MHz channels at almost every one of Region 1's 35 available orbital positions. The typical country, however, with a j value of 4/35, is entitled to only one 20-MHz channel at each of only four of Region 1's 35 available orbital positions A. *See* notes 70–73 and accompanying text, *supra.*

[108] Under orbit/spectrum rationing, 20 MHz times 4/35 times A equals 2.3 MHz times A.

[109] ITU Radio Regulations, *supra* note 2, Art. 7, §1A, No. 428A.

[110] As a simplifying assumption, it will be deemed that a country can receive an acceptable signal from any orbital position in its ITU region. This assumption would generally only be valid through the use of two or more satellites connected by embryonic intersatellite link technology. The ITU has defined these links and allocated much bandwidth to them. ITU Radio Regulations, *supra* note 2, Art. N1, §3, No. 84ATF, Art. N7, §5. To the extent that this assumption is not currently justifiable, the jurimetric difference between channel distribution with and without planning loses significance.

[111] It seems likely, however, that B times h equals that fraction of an ITU region's orbital positions which do in fact provide a country with an acceptable signal. *See ibid.*

[112] Hence countries were entitled to receive signals from about half of each region's available orbital positions. *See* WARC–79 Final Acts, note 45 *supra*, App. 29A, Art. 12.

sages back to itself.[113] Channel directionality with a plan, therefore, will always be less than or equal to channel directionality without a plan.[114]

Jurimetric Conclusion. Jurimetric analysis clearly indicates that proper application of the maximum channel dispersion principle to the orbit/spectrum resource requires a regulatory framework based upon the engineering and not the rationing approach. The engineering approach maximizes geostationary channel dispersion better than rationing because it offers at least as much distribution and directionality and much greater depth.

Practical Recommendations

International law prescribes maximum development of orbit/spectrum as a matter of basic principle.[115] The international community, however, is uncertain and disagrees as to which particularized legal rules best implement this overarching principle.[116] A jurimetric analysis of the issue indicates that legal rules based upon traditional orbit/spectrum engineering implement the maximum channel dispersion principle to a far greater extent than do rules based upon an ITU Plan.[117] This jurimetric analysis should be further articulated and used as a regulatory guide at the upcoming 1983 Region 2 Administrative Radio Conference for Ku-band broadcasting-satellite service and at the 1984 World Administrative Radio Conference on the Uses of the Geostationary Orbit.

The 1983 Region 2 Administrative Radio Conference. As developed above, it appears that an ITU Plan for Region 2 in the Ku-band downlink, scheduled to be implemented at a Regional Conference in 1983, is not in the best interests of any country, is contrary to fundamental principles of international law, and sets a very poor precedent for the rational development of other space resources.[118] Region 2 countries may wish to reconsider the appropriateness of orbit/spectrum planning, and if a minority of states is unsuccessful in preventing the adoption of an orbit/spectrum plan, they may wish to enter appropriate reservations with respect to the plan and to challenge its legality before the International Court of Justice, a municipal court, and/or a specially designated arbitral tribunal.

For example, should a country desire to use more than or other than its rationed share of orbit/spectrum, such a country and other affected countries[119] could refer the matter to the International Court of Justice pursuant to Articles 34, 35, and 36 of the Court's organic Statute.[120] The legal grounds for such

[113] *See* note 109 and accompanying text, *supra.*

[114] *See* note 110 *supra.*

[115] *See* notes 13–65 and accompanying text, *supra.*

[116] *See* notes 70–98 and accompanying text, *supra.*

[117] *See* notes 101–114 and accompanying text, *supra.*

[118] *See* NASA, SPACE RESOURCES AND SPACE SETTLEMENTS (J. Billingham & W. Gilbreath, eds. 1979); G. O'NEILL, THE HIGH FRONTIER (1977).

[119] This includes all other countries entitled under a plan to the orbital position in controversy. WARC–79 Final Acts, *supra* note 45, App. 29A, Art. 4.3.

[120] ICJ, ACTS AND DOCUMENTS CONCERNING THE ORGANIZATION OF THE COURT, No. 4, Statute of the Court, Arts. 34, 35, 36 (1978).

a challenge could include inconsistency with the maximum channel dispersion principle, contravention of the ITU Convention's mandate to take "full advantage" of the possibilities of space techniques,[121] and derogation of the Outer Space Treaty's commands that space is to be *used* for the benefit of all countries, that space is free for *use* by all states in accordance with international law, and that space is not subject to national appropriation by *any* means.[122]Although no ITU Radio Regulation has yet been interpreted by an international arbitral or judicial tribunal, leading ITU scholars agree that "the time for judicial settlement has arrived, if it is not past due."[123]

The 1984 GEO-WARC. GEO-WARC's initial task is to decide which space services and associated frequency bands to plan. If the jurimetric conclusions arrived at above prove to be generally true for all space services and associated frequency bands, then the conference should conclude that no planning is necessary. In this event, the conference would be obligated to "establish guidelines for regulatory procedures in respect of services and frequency bands not [planned]."[124]

These guidelines should, of course, promote the maximum dispersion of geostationary bandwidth. If an inadequate supply of orbit-to-country pathways is inhibiting channel distribution, the guidelines must include affirmative means of ensuring it without diminishing total channel dispersion.

Professor Robinson has suggested that "guaranteed options to certain orbit positions" may be an acceptable means of accomplishing broader channel distribution.[125] Under the guaranteed option approach, "developed countries occupying orbit positions might agree to time limits on their occupancy or might agree to be 'bumped' from their positions if no slots were available within a specified period to accommodate developing country requirements."[126]

The guaranteed option approach is subject to criticism on the grounds that it fails to address whether the incumbent or the newcomer is maximizing channel dispersion. The incumbent, for example, may be similar to Indonesia's Palapa system, which distributes bandwidth throughout an entire region.[127] Hence, solutions based upon stereotypes may prove counterproductive; appropriate distribution-enhancing regulations must be comparative in nature if the total dispersion of geostationary bandwidth is to be maximized.

[121] International Telecommunication Convention, *supra* note 18, Art. 4(2)(c).

[122] Outer Space Treaty of 1967, *supra* note 20, Arts. I, II (emphasis supplied).

[123] D. LEIVE, *supra* note 15, at 22 (quoting J. TOMLINSON, THE INTERNATIONAL CONTROL OF RADIOCOMMUNICATION 290–91 (1945)).

[124] WARC–79 Final Acts, *supra* note 45, Res. BP.

[125] Robinson, *supra* note 23, at 46.

[126] *Ibid.* n.141.

[127] A regional communications satellite system maximizes channel dispersion to a greater extent than a purely domestic system capable of conveying the same amount of channel depth because the former distributes this depth to several countries and total channel dispersion is the product of depth, distribution, and directionality. Notes 10–12 and accompanying text, *supra. See, e.g.*, D. SMITH, INSTITUTIONAL CONFIGURATION FOR LARGE SPACE COMMUNICATIONS STRUCTURES: A BASIS FOR THE DEVELOPMENT OF INTERNATIONAL SPACE COMMUNICATIONS NORMS 10 (International Commission for the Study of Communications Problems, Doc. No. 88, 1979) (suggests ITU grant orbit/spectrum priorities to regional geostationary platforms because these systems "promise service capability for a vastly greater number of users than conventional [domestic] satellites").

One very attractive approach to meeting GEO-WARC's agenda involves much greater ITU participation in the establishment of satellite communications systems. Such an approach would generate three sets of "guidelines for regulatory procedures":

(1) Constant jurimetric analysis of orbit/spectrum development rates in order to generate objective forecasts as to when portions of the resource will be approaching full development.

(2) Convening subregional conferences among administrations who feel their future needs will be adversely affected by the forecasted status of a portion of the resource. The sole agenda item of these conferences would be to determine interest in ITU facilitation of a subregional communications satellite system.

(3) ITU facilitation of subregional communications satellite systems among countries desiring them, with system architecture and financing depending on the particular case.

While detailed substantive proposals for these regulatory guidelines fall well beyond the confines of this article, certain brief explanatory comments are appropriate.

The first task, constant jurimetric analysis of orbit/spectrum development rates, could be added to the "essential duties" of the IFRB, a true clearinghouse of information on orbit/spectrum development.[128] The forecast as to when a "full development" zone is being approached should be based on, and updated in light of, annual CCIR "technological capability" forecasts,[129] and the level of full development should be determined outside the IFRB.[130] For example, GEO-WARC might determine that a zone of full development is reached when 50 percent of the satellite channels available at a particular band from any ten contiguous orbital positions will be employed within the next 5 years.

Step 2, the holding of subregional conferences to determine interest in ITU facilitation of subregional satellite systems, is necessary to discover whether the IFRB jurimetric forecast provides any real basis for concern about maximum channel dispersion. It may very well be that everyone's needs are currently being met or will foreseeably be met. On the other hand, countries may perceive real problems in meeting their geostationary bandwidth needs in light of an orbit/spectrum development forecast.

[128] *See, e.g.*, International Telecommunication Convention, *supra* note 18, Art. 10, and ITU Radio Regulations, *supra* note 2, Art. 9A.

[129] The ITU's technical advisory committee, the CCIR, advises the ITU on technical radiocommunications matters; "satellites and space communication for all applications have been a major preoccupation of CCIR now for twenty years." Kirby, *CCIR Past, Present, and Future*, in 1 INTERNATIONAL CONFERENCE ON COMMUNICATIONS 9.1.2 (1979).

[130] The determination of what constitutes a "full development zone" is well beyond the IFRB's acknowledged competence, but the application of standards set elsewhere to the changing orbit/spectrum development environment is a traditional IFRB function. Resolution BP invites the IFRB to report "information about difficulties . . . in gaining access to suitable orbital locations and frequencies, and to circulate this report to administrations at least one year before [GEO-WARC]." WARC-79 Final Acts, *supra* note 45, Res. BP. This type of report is a solid step towards the periodic orbit/spectrum development forecasts suggested in the text.

Drawing up this set of guidelines would serve a useful function because it would focus the attention of states concerned about channel distribution upon their common aim and provide them with impartial leadership toward their goal. On the basis of the guidelines, the end result of the subregional conferences should be a decision either to request or not to request specialized ITU organizational assistance in addressing subregional satellite communications needs. A specific ITU entity should be responsible for providing this type of specialized assistance.

In the final step, ITU facilitation of subregional communications satellite systems, the ITU's specialized assistance group would work with the concerned administrations at determining, procuring, and perhaps establishing the satellite system that best addresses their needs. The system might involve no more than the lease of one or more INTELSAT transponders, or it might involve the formation of a new satellite consortium.[131] The satellite systems could be financed by the states themselves, by commercial investors, or by international development agencies.[132] Clearly, each case will be unique.

IV. Conclusion

It has been demonstrated that the orbit/spectrum resource is a great reservoir of telecommunications pathways and that the maximum dispersion of these pathways is mandated by international law. In implementing this mandate, at least two different perspectives have surfaced as to which legal rules yield the desired result. It is the function of an upcoming GEO-WARC to resolve this dispute for each currently regulated fraction of orbit/spectrum.

A jurimetric analysis has been introduced and tentatively applied to the Ku-band broadcasting-satellite service. As a result of this preliminary jurimetric analysis, one must conclude that the engineering regime, and not the rationing regime, best maximizes the dispersion of geostationary bandwidth.

Finally, a suggested augmentation of the traditional regime has been presented which directly addresses international concern that growth in the distributional dimension of channel dispersion becomes problematic as portions of orbit/spectrum approach full development. This addition provides a "fail-safe" means of preventing any sudden unavailability of new geostationary channels at any given frequency band. This would be accomplished by maintaining a vigilant watch on orbit/spectrum development rates, alerting ITU members whose interests might be jeopardized by these rates, and helping concerned ITU members to organize satellite systems that "guarantee in practice" their right of equitable access to the resource.

[131] INTELSAT's satellite systems expert Dr. Joseph Pelton estimates that the international consortium will be able to lease enough transponders to support 36 separate domestic satellite communications systems by 1985. Pelton, Intelsat and the Age of the Technological Already 3 (paper delivered at Fifth Conference on Satellite Communications for Public Service Users, Washington, D.C., 1980).

[132] There is perhaps no wiser investment a developing state or development aid source can make than in telecommunications infrastructure and software. The basis for this advice has been summarized with brilliant simplicity as follows: "Information is the necessary, if not sufficient, condition for advancement." Robinson, *supra* note 23, at 40 n.120.

Incessant growth in communications pathways, a hallmark of human civilization, now takes on unparalleled significance due to the crushing onslaught of global population and energy problems. With the whole world scrambling for the same scarce energy pools, it is in everyone's interest to proliferate as many multidirectional wideband channels as possible. Not much reflection is required to convince oneself that communication directly conserves energy by minimizing physical transportation costs and directly improves productivity by pooling geographically dispersed expertise. These considerations can only be magnified by the presence of a global population that has more than quadrupled since it reached a historical peak at the turn of the century.

The fate of this crucial channel proliferation effort lies largely in the hands of orbit/spectrum regulators. Unwise regulatory decisions that retard channel dispersion will be very costly in terms of energy and productivity. It is the resource-poor and people-rich developing countries that feel these costs most severely. Regulatory decisions that promote maximum channel dispersion will conserve energy and enhance productivity. Hence, while international orbit/spectrum lawmakers shoulder an awesome responsibility, they also enjoy a powerful opportunity.

Structuring a legal regime that maximizes channel dispersion in the dynamic orbit/spectrum environment will not be easy, given the diverse perspectives of our global community. It is nevertheless an eminently worthwhile challenge. It is also quite possible that a jurimetric approach to orbit/spectrum regulation will be of help to international lawmakers in their vital quest for universal agreement on the legal routes that increase, to the greatest extent possible, the depth, distribution, and directionality of geostationary satellite communications channels.

TECHNOLOGY AND INTERNATIONAL NEGOTIATIONS

*By Jonathan I. Charney**

I. INTRODUCTION

International law needs to respond to the dual pressures for change brought on by rapid technological development and the promulgation of the "New International Economic Order." While a number of major international negotiations have been mounted in recent years to respond to these pressures, all of them have failed to meet expectations. The value of international law in shaping and stabilizing international behavior will certainly diminish unless the performance of these international negotiations is improved or other methods for effectuating change are found. It is the purpose of this article to explore some of the procedures that the international community has used to respond to these pressures and to suggest areas for improvement or further exploration.[1]

Two of the major developments in international law since the end of the Second World War have been the attention that has been given to questions of international economic and industrial development and the increased use of multilateral treaty negotiations.[2] The rapid pace of significant scientific and technological advances has increased pressure on the international system to accommodate these developments. Technological advances have historically been an important factor in the development of international law and relations.[3] World War II saw the dawn of the nuclear age, which brought forth significant legal activity relating to the military and peaceful uses of nuclear energy. The international legal system received an additional jolt in the late 1950's when the space age began with artificial earth satellites, which were followed shortly thereafter by space travel. The military and economic implications of this technology have only begun to be explored. Less dramatic but equally significant developments have taken place in the oceans where petroleum exploitation has moved rapidly seaward and the mining of the deep seabed has become possible,

* Professor of Law, Vanderbilt University School of Law. The research for this article was supported by grants from the Vanderbilt University Research Council and the Vanderbilt University School of Law.

[1] For a symposium on the substantive aspects of this problem, see *The Third World Challenge*, 59 FOREIGN AFF. 366 (1980–1981).

[2] W. FRIEDMANN, THE CHANGING STRUCTURE OF INTERNATIONAL LAW 11–12, 123–26 (1964). Many of these activities take place within international organizations or continuing conferences such as the General Agreement on Tariffs and Trade (GATT), the International Civil Aviation Organization (ICAO), the International Bank for Reconstruction and Development (IBRD, World Bank), the International Monetary Fund (IMF), the International Telecommunication Union (ITU), the World Administrative Radio Conference (WARC), and the United Nations Conference on Trade and Development (UNCTAD). The value of international agreements is discussed in R. BILDER, MANAGING THE RISKS OF INTERNATIONAL AGREEMENT 6–7 (1981).

[3] M. MCDOUGAL, H. LASSWELL, & I. VLASIC, LAW AND PUBLIC ORDER IN SPACE 179 (1963).

albeit not yet commercially viable. Telecommunications, weather modification, and biological engineering are other areas where new technologies have or are about to have significant impacts on international law and relations.

In recent years, these advances often have given rise to multilateral negotiations aimed at producing international agreements to govern the new activities. While traditionally the international law relevant to new technological developments has slowly evolved out of the customs and practices of nations before being codified in international agreements, this gestation period has been considerably shortened in the last half of the 20th century. In the past the world and its resources have been large enough to assure that only a few national activities had an impact on the interests of other nations. This was particularly true in the world's commons, such as the oceans, where the concept of *res communis* has held sway for many years. Increased competition for resources and the global implications of some of the new technological developments have forced nations to realize that today individual nations cannot act in those areas without producing impacts on other nations. Consequently, the need for the early development of legal norms of behavior has increased.

Contributing to this situation is a parallel political development. International relations could be characterized by an analogy to free market competition where nations jockey for positions of power, wealth, and influence by acting independently or in concert with other nations with similar interests. While this continues to be true, the promulgation of the New International Economic Order (NIEO) by the United Nations General Assembly and the continued activities of the Group of 77 (representing more than 120 developing countries) in the United Nations and other multilateral forums appear to have had a significant impact on the conduct of international relations.[4] The NIEO is premised on the assumption that there should be a shift of political and economic power from the developed to the developing countries. While few developed countries have embraced the substance of this doctrine, they have all accepted its procedural point that the developing countries, usually acting as a group, have a right to negotiate with the developed countries on the substantive objectives of the NIEO, *i.e.*, the shift of wealth and power. In no sector of international relations is this more apparent than in that pertaining to new technological developments. In that area, where some important rights and benefits are not yet fully vested, the NIEO provides the basis for the developing countries' claim to the right to participate in the earliest stages of legal and commercial development. Their objective is to assure themselves a "fair share" of the benefits from those activities and to prevent the developed countries from extending their "hegemony" to the new areas.

For either or both of these reasons, interdependence and the NIEO, there

[4] Declaration on the Establishment of a New Economic Order, GA Res. 3201 (S-VI) (1974). *See also* Charter of Economic Rights and Duties of States, GA Res. 3281 (XXIX) (1974). For an informative discussion of the underlying pressures for systemic changes, see, ul Haq, *Negotiating the Future*, 59 FOREIGN AFF. 398 (1980–1981). The recent Cancún meeting of the leaders of 22 industrialized and developing nations was convened for the purpose of finding means to break the deadlock on these issues. *See* Riding, *Cancún Parley Concludes Without Agreement*, N.Y. Times, Oct. 24, 1981, at A4, cols. 3–5.

is increased pressure on nations to respond by negotiating international agreements at an early date before custom and practice have had an opportunity to define the legal options. Unfortunately, the record of the international community in these efforts is rather poor. The quality of activities at the UN General Assembly (UNGA) and its related bodies has deteriorated perceptibly in recent years. They often provide an arena for political grandstanding rather than responsible forums for negotiation and compromise. While one of the premier exercises of this kind, the Third United Nations Conference on the Law of the Sea (UNCLOS III), may be headed for eventual agreement, the negotiation has been very difficult and costly; no one knows whether the convention it may produce will ever come into force. The commodity negotiations under the auspices of the United Nations Conference on Trade and Development (UNCTAD), the International Telecommunication Union's World Administrative Radio Conferences (ITU WARC), the negotiations at the Commission for International Economic Cooperation (CIEC), and the conference of the United Nations Educational, Scientific and Cultural Organization (UNESCO) on the new world information and communications order, to name a few, have been arduous and relatively unproductive.

The question naturally arises, What, if anything, should individual nations or the international community as a whole do about this problem? At the macro level, the current international situation has been characterized as "functional eclecticism" or "incrementalism," which means that a relatively disorganized international community reacts in an ad hoc manner to direct needs and demands.[5] Modifications in the system are undertaken by trial and error in order to respond to direct and specific pressures. There exists no grand institutional design. Consequently, special identified short-term interests are more influential, and those concerned with second and third levels of interest are in weaker positions.[6] Some suggest that alternative organizational approaches might present better opportunities for success. The functionalist school of thought would seek to expand a web of nonpolitical international institutional arrangements so that ultimately all international questions would be encompassed within a world community managed by an international bureaucracy.[7] Others argue that the international system, and particularly the United Nations, should be reorganized to bring into focus the interdependence of international issues. Broad objectives could then be stated, and related interests would be addressed and reconciled within a single forum.[8] Another alternative might be to terminate the ties of all international organizations to these subjects.

[5] Brown & Fabian, *Toward Mutual Accountability in the Nonterrestrial Realms*, 29 INT'L ORGANIZATION 877, 882 (1975); and Ruggie, *International Responses to Technology: Concepts and Trends, id.* at 557, 578.

[6] Ruggie, *supra* note 5, at 578. Ruggie & Haas, *Environmental and Resource Interdependencies: Reorganizing for the Evolution of International Regimes*, in 1 REPORT OF THE COMMISSION ON THE ORGANIZATION OF THE GOVERNMENT FOR THE CONDUCT OF FOREIGN POLICY, App. B, at 218, 220 (1975) [hereinafter cited as MURPHY COMMISSION REPORT].

[7] E. HAAS, BEYOND THE NATION-STATE: FUNCTIONALISM AND THE INTERNATIONAL ORGANIZATION 6 (1964).

[8] Ruggie, *supra* note 5, at 582. Ruggie & Haas, *supra* note 6, at 224. The conceptual bases for the reorganization would be the quality of life, the global environment, food and population, and energy and minerals. *Id.* at 225–28.

While there may be theoretical merit to these proposals, no serious thought at the political level has been given to substantially changing the international system in this regard, nor can it be expected that any such changes will take place in the foreseeable future without a third world war, a global economic collapse, or an unforeseen development of tremendous significance.[9] If the macro system is presumed to remain in place, the only possible changes are likely to be incremental and probably only interstitial. This article will address certain procedural adjustments that might be made to facilitate the orderly and sound development of legal rules demanded by the new technological and political developments discussed above. It will focus on the response that nations should make to the dual pressure to develop an international law adequate to the needs brought about by new technological developments and the NIEO. The stages of legal development in these areas can be divided into two time segments: the period prior to the introduction of direct negotiations aimed at creating an international agreement and the period after the beginning of those negotiations. The discussion below will focus on those time periods and will use the recent negotiations on the law of the sea, particularly the issues relating to deep seabed mining, as a basis for illustrating the problems that need to be considered.[10]

II. The Period Prior to Focused Negotiations

The period prior to the holding of negotiations on an international agreement begins when serious thought is given to the need for new international law. In the course of such a period the subject receives increased attention, which will produce one of three results: the law will remain static, the law will change through the development of general international law, or the negotiation of a

[9] Even the highly visible Brandt Commission Report (NORTH-SOUTH: A PROGRAM FOR SURVIVAL (W. Brandt & A. Sampson eds., 1980)) cannot be characterized as suggesting a systemic change. *See* Lescaze, *Brandt Commission Seeks Revived North-South Dialogue*, Washington Post, Feb. 13, 1980, at A25, cols 1–6. There is little indication that many of its substantive proposals will be implemented.

[10] The law of the sea is a particularly appropriate vehicle for illustrating these issues. Throughout its long and well-documented history there has been a constant interplay of politics and technology. Furthermore, the series of negotiations that has now culminated at the Third United Nations Conference on the Law of the Sea has brought this subject to an advanced stage. Thus, the LOS negotiations provide a complete record of the international issues that are the focus of this paper. At the same time, the law of the sea is not so atypical that the observations that might be made on the basis of this record are not generalizable.

For a comprehensive series of articles on the UNCLOS III negotiations, see Stevenson & Oxman, *The Preparations for the Law of the Sea Conference*, 68 AJIL 1 (1974); *The Third United Nations Conference on the Law of the Sea: The 1974 Caracas Session*, 69 *id.* at 1 (1975);—*The 1975 Geneva Session*, *id.* at 763; and Oxman, *The Third United Nations Conference on the Law of the Sea: The 1976 New York Session*, 71 *id.* at 247 (1977);—*The 1977 New York Sessions*, 72 *id.* at 57 (1978);—*The Seventh Session (1978)*, 73 *id.* at 1 (1979);—*The Eighth Session (1979)*, 74 *id.* at 1 (1980); —*The Ninth Session (1980)*, 75 *id.* at 211 (1981); and —*The Tenth Session (1981)*, *supra* at p. 1. Some procedural aspects of the negotiations are discussed in B. BUZAN, SEABED POLITICS (1976); Miles, *The Structure and Effects of the Decision Process in the Seabed Committee and the Third United Nations Conference on the Law of the Sea*, 31 INT'L ORGANIZATION 158 (1977); B. BUZAN, A SEA OF TROUBLES? SOURCES OF DISPUTE IN THE NEW OCEAN REGIME (Adelphi Paper No. 143, 1978); Buzan, *United We Stand . . .: Informal Negotiating Groups at UNCLOS III*, 4 MARINE POL'Y 183 (1980); Buzan, *Negotiating by Consensus: Developments in Technique at the United Nations Conference on the Law of the Sea*, 75 AJIL 324 (1981).

new international agreement will be undertaken. There appear to be four critical aspects of this period that warrant particular attention. First, there is the pressure to commence international negotiations on a new international agreement. For many, the conduct of such negotiations and the production of a draft convention are the preferred objective once it is determined that new law is required. Others would exercise more discretion. A second important concern is the flow of information about the subject that appears to demand new international law. In the case of new technological developments or issues requiring fairly sophisticated technical analyses, the management of information at the early stages of this process can have a critical impact on subsequent progress. Third, it is important to give serious consideration to the use of international forums whose function is not the production of binding international agreements. While they may not serve as a source of law, such forums can play a critical role in the development of the legal issues. Finally, if a formal negotiation is to be undertaken, the participating nations must be committed to negotiating an agreement. One cannot assume that participation in formal negotiations is equivalent to a commitment to negotiate in good faith towards an agreement.

SETTING THE STAGE FOR THE LAW OF THE SEA CONFERENCE

To determine when the negotiation period for the Third United Nations Conference on the Law of the Sea began, one might have to go as far back as the period prior to the 1930 Hague Codification Conference, which considered the law of the sea.[11] While that conference produced no law of the sea convention, the 1958 United Nations Law of the Sea Conference did, and its preparatory work started years before.[12] The Second United Nations Conference on the Law of the Sea in 1960 did not produce an international agreement, although it was clearly called for that purpose.[13] In part, the Third United Nations Conference on the Law of the Sea was born out of the failures of the prior conferences, but it also resulted from new technological and political demands that took on added significance in the mid-1960's and the 1970's. Thus, focus on the most recent effort began shortly after the failure of the second conference.

[11] LEAGUE OF NATIONS, ACTS OF THE CONFERENCE FOR THE CODIFICATION OF INTERNATIONAL LAW, HELD AT THE HAGUE FROM MARCH 13TH TO APRIL 12TH, 1930, Doc. C.351.M.145.1930.V, Vol. I, at 50–54, 123–37; Doc. C.74.M.39.1929.V, Vol. II; and Doc. C.351(b).M.145(b).1930.V, Vol. III. These documents are *reproduced in* LEAGUE OF NATIONS CONFERENCE FOR THE CODIFICATION OF INTERNATIONAL LAW (S. Rosenne ed. 1975).

[12] Preparations for this conference began in 1949. Report of the International Law Commission Covering the work of its eighth session, 11 UN GAOR, Supp. (No. 9) 2, UN Doc. A/3159 (1956), *reprinted in* 2 Y.B. INT'L L. COMM'N 253 (1956), 51 AJIL 154 (1957). The first conference produced four conventions: Convention on the High Seas, 13 UST 2312, TIAS No. 5200, 450 UNTS 82, *reprinted in* 52 AJIL 842 (1958); Convention on the Continental Shelf, 15 UST 471, TIAS No. 5578, 499 UNTS 311, *reprinted in* 52 AJIL 858 (1958); Convention on the Territorial Sea and the Contiguous Zone, 15 UST 1606, TIAS No. 5639, 516 UNTS 205, *reprinted in* 52 AJIL 834 (1958); Convention on Fishing and Conservation of the Living Resources of the High Seas, 17 UST 138, TIAS No. 5969, 559 UNTS 285, *reprinted in* 52 AJIL 851 (1958).

[13] *See* Dean, *The Second Geneva Conference on the Law of the Sea: The Fight for Freedom of the Seas*, 54 AJIL 751 (1960); Jessup, *The Law of the Sea Around Us*, 55 *id.* at 104 (1961).

It is commonly believed that the prospects for commercial exploitation of deep seabed manganese nodules by the developed Western countries prompted the rapid decision by the international community to seek a new convention on the law of the sea. Clearly, Arvid Pardo's 1967 speech in the United Nations General Assembly spurred movement towards the negotiations even though the manganese nodule issue may not have been the original motivation for the calling of a new conference.[14] Many believed that the untold riches of the deep seabed were about to be appropriated by certain Western countries, and that other nations would be excluded from these benefits. Similar fears arose about the ever improving technology to exploit hydrocarbon deposits on the continental shelf and in deeper waters. Consequently, the General Assembly passed a series of resolutions seeking to freeze the status quo, and the international community moved rapidly towards preparatory meetings and then the commencement of formal negotiations in 1973. Because many nations believed that the early entry into force of a multilateral treaty would be the only way to prevent a few nations from dominating deep seabed mining, little thought was given to alternatives or to the conduct of alternative prenegotiation activities that would maximize the opportunity for success at the negotiations.[15]

Seabed mining was certainly not the only reason for holding a new conference. Prior to the Pardo speech, some of the global powers had considered ways to curb the encroachments on their military mobility (especially in straits) caused by the expansion of zones of national jurisdiction.[16] This concern arose from the failure of previous law of the sea negotiations to fix the seaward limits of the territorial sea and other resource zones. By linking the demand of the global powers for navigational freedoms with the pressure to avoid a grab of the deep seabed by developed countries, it was believed that a satisfactory compromise of both interests could be reached.

During the period after Pardo's speech, the international community focused primarily on setting the stage for an early universal negotiation. As the agenda was considered, each interest group suggested additional subjects that it wanted to see improved. Since it was generally accepted that a universal negotiation was the only feasible route, it was difficult to reject agenda items that might deter participation by some nations. Consequently, the final agenda consisted of a compendium of all law of the sea subjects; the conference was committed to reconsidering the entire law of the sea.[17]

[14] Note verbale to Secretary-General U Thant, UN Doc. A/6695 (1967). *See generally* Swing, *Who Will Own the Oceans?*, 54 FOREIGN AFF. 527 (1976).

[15] The informal conferences held by the Law of the Sea Institute and Pacem in Maribus played a role in this regard, but were more informational than anything else.

[16] For a discussion of this issue, see Burke, *Submerged Passage Through Straits: Interpretations of the Proposed Law of the Sea Treaty Text*, 52 WASH. L. REV. 193, 195–200 (1977). *See also* Knauss, *The Military Role in the Ocean and its Relation to the Law of the Sea*, in THE LAW OF THE SEA: A NEW GENEVA CONFERENCE 77 (Proceedings of the Sixth Annual Conference of the Law of the Sea Institute, L. Alexander ed. 1972).

[17] *See* Organization of the second session of the Conference and Allocation of Items: Report of the General Committee, UN Doc. A/CONF.62/28 (1974), 3 THIRD UNITED NATIONS CONFERENCE ON THE LAW OF THE SEA, OFFICIAL RECORDS [hereinafter cited as UNCLOS III, OFF. REC.] 57 (1975).

For a similar reason, the preparation of national negotiating positions was the focus of domestic attention, and inadequate consideration was given to managing the preconference period so as to maximize the opportunity for success at the negotiations. Because attention was centered on the opening of the conference and the General Assembly had dedicated itself to freezing all developments outside the negotiations, there was little use of other forums and events to refine the issues that would be considered.[18] Consequently, the participating nations were far apart when the negotiation period began. This contributed to the slow and frustrating pace of the preparatory meetings and of the conference itself.

THE PRENEGOTIATION PERIOD IN PERSPECTIVE

While the Law of the Sea Conference is unique in many ways, the procedural problems that arose during the prenegotiation period have been faced in other settings. These experiences suggest possible ways to improve the prospects for success in other areas in the future.

Pressure for Early International Negotiations

It may be true that "[n]o nation goes out of its way to propose the creation of international arrangements for jointly managing a resource: unilateral or bilateral methods are always preferred."[19] Current international pressures, however, make the conduct of international negotiations and the contemplation of international institutional arrangements difficult to avoid for the subjects under consideration in this article. Interdependence and the NIEO doctrine are two of the major reasons for this situation.[20]

Debates over the appropriateness and timing of international negotiations have a long history. At the close of World War II the United States pressed for early negotiations to avoid the spread of nuclear weapons. The timing and conduct of the ill-fated Baruch Plan remain a subject of continuing debate.[21] Considerable controversy also arose in connection with efforts to conduct early negotiations on outer space law.[22] In an incisive critique, McDougal and Lipson

[18] Question of the Reservation Exclusively for Peaceful Purposes of the Sea-bed and Ocean Floor, and the Sub-soil thereof, Underlying the High Seas beyond the Limits of Present National Jurisdiction, and the Use of their Resources in the Interests of Mankind [Moratorium Resolution], GA Res. 2574D (XXIV) (1970); Declaration of Principles Governing the Sea-bed and the Ocean Floor, and the Sub-soil thereof, beyond the Limits of National Jurisdiction, GA Res. 2749 (XXV) (1970). For a review of the UN activities from 1967 to 1970, see B. BUZAN, SEABED POLITICS, *supra* note 10, at 65–116. *See also* note 15 *supra*.

[19] Ruggie & Haas, *supra* note 6, at 218.

[20] "Interdependence" is used here to mean "mutual sensitivity." *See* Baldwin, *Interdependence and Power: A Conceptual Analysis*, 34 INT'L ORGANIZATION 471 (1980).

[21] HOUSE COMM. ON INTERNATIONAL RELATIONS, SCIENCE, TECHNOLOGY AND AMERICAN DIPLOMACY: AN EXTENDED STUDY OF THE INTERACTIONS OF SCIENCE AND TECHNOLOGY WITH UNITED STATES FOREIGN POLICY [hereinafter cited as EXTENDED STUDY OF AMERICAN DIPLOMACY] 77–122 (Comm. Print 1977).

[22] The arguments are collected in L. LIPSON & N. KATZENBACH, REPORT TO THE NATIONAL AERONAUTICS AND SPACE ADMINISTRATION ON THE LAW OF OUTER SPACE 51–59 (1961).

listed six arguments that they believed were stimulating calls for early negotiations on the subject:

(1) paper agreements solve problems whether or not effective sanctions exist to assure compliance;

(2) the necessary objective of negotiations is agreement;

(3) almost any agreement is better than no agreement;

(4) overall solutions that fail are superior to particular adjustments that succeed;

(5) international control of appropriation or ownership is somehow demanded by the supposed supranationality of extraterrestrial activity; and

(6) the tidiness of a treaty is so preferable to an uncertain legal situation that it may be worth a substantial price.[23]

In their opinion, these assumptions are debatable, if not altogether wrong. Little adjustment would be required to apply this list to other subjects, and the negative assessment of rushing into early agreements would be equally persuasive.

In part, the difficulties faced over the law of the sea stem from the problem highlighted by McDougal and Lipson. The elementary nature of international law makes it unrealistic to expect to resolve major political issues simply through the generation of a new international agreement. The participants at the conference were wise enough to realize that a paper agreement without real political agreement would be futile. Consequently, the negotiations have proceeded at a snail's pace in order to permit the political issues to be resolved, primarily outside the conference (*e.g.*, the 200-mile zone). The early calling of the conference might have accelerated this process, but it is problematical whether it was necessary to the outcome.

Other pragmatic considerations should also be taken into account in the course of deciding when and whether to start a negotiation. Perhaps the greatest difficulty faced at early negotiations called to respond to new technological developments relates to foreseeability. Unfortunately, the impacts that new technological developments will have on international society are almost impossible to foresee at an early date. A classic example of this difficulty was the attempts to define the boundary between airspace and outer space.[24] Reputable students of the subject saw their early proposals quickly discarded as new developments changed the situation.[25] Thus, premature international agreements can produce "solutions" that may not only be technically incorrect but unworkable. Later efforts to correct them may be difficult, if not fruitless.[26]

[23] McDougal & Lipson, *Perspectives for a Law of Outer Space,* 52 AJIL 407, 420 (1958).

[24] *Id.* at 424–25.

[25] *Id.* at 425; Jaffee, *Reliance upon International Custom and General Principles in the Growth of Space Law,* 7 ST. LOUIS U.L.J. 125, 130 (1962); M. MCDOUGAL, H. LASSWELL, & I. VLASIC, *supra* note 3, at 323–49.

[26] Schachter, *The Prospects for a Regime in Outer Space and International Organization,* in LAW AND POLITICS IN SPACE 95, 99 (M. Cohen ed. 1964). Apparently, this issue has been revived in light of the development of the United States space shuttle. *See* Kopel, *The Question of Defining Outer Space,* 8 J. SPACE L. 154 (1980).

A similar problem applies to the deep seabed. Deep seabed mining of large volumes of manganese nodules has not yet taken place; in the late 1960's and early 1970's, the technology was barely off the drawing board. Many of the facts on which the early stages of the negotiations were predicated are now outdated. Even now, the nature of the activity and its requirements and consequences are barely known. Thus, a sense of uncertainty has pervaded the entire process and there is a substantial risk that any detailed regime established now might rapidly become obsolete.

On the other hand, deferred resolution of legal questions may also present difficulties. In the absence of a relatively mature legal regime the commercial development of new technologies may be deterred. The history of the deep seabed mining industry presents a graphic illustration of such a case: the absence of a clear legal regime has deterred investors and corporate decision makers from moving forward.

Arguments for the early negotiation of new legal regimes are also supported by those nations that view multilateral negotiations as an opportunity to exercise leverage over international decision making. They believe that there would be no such leverage if the decisions were made through the development of customary international law. The developing nations holding this view may be joined by developed nations that do not have the new technology at hand: they, too, may lack the power to directly influence the development of the pertinent customary international law and would expect their leverage to increase at an international negotiation. This confluence of interests was often demonstrated at the deep seabed mining negotiations. While some will argue that the power relationships at multilateral conferences parallel those found in the outside world, it would be more accurate to recognize that the dynamics of such a forum moderate differences in power.[27]

Finally, the timing of the negotiation may have an impact on the difficulties faced by the participants. It could be argued that a very early negotiation might be easier to conduct because it might precede the identification of particular national interests. Thus, the negotiation could proceed at a more theoretical level and enable the participants to develop an "ideal" system that would guide and moderate future pressures.[28] The contrary arguments may be more persuasive. It would appear that the mere call for negotiations stimulates national demands that fail to take full account of real national interests in the subject.[29] In the absence of substantial knowledge about the subject, those demands might very well be extremely unrealistic; resolving those demands can require additional negotiating time and effort.

The deep seabed negotiations are a case in point. Serious discussion of a legal regime for deep seabed mining began in 1967 when few knew very much about the potential industry. At that time it was generally believed that com-

[27] G. SCHWARZENBERGER, POWER POLITICS: A STUDY OF WORLD SOCIETY 109 (3d ed. 1964).

[28] *See, e.g., Sovereignty in Space*, NEWSWEEK, Dec. 19, 1955, at 82; Haley, *Law of Outer Space—A Problem for International Agreement*, 7 AM. U. L. REV. 70, 76 (1958); Clarke, *The Challenge of the Spaceship*, 6 J. BRIT. INTERPLAN. SOC'Y 66–81 (1946).

[29] Schachter, *supra* note 26, at 98. *See also* McDougal & Lipson, *supra* note 23, at 414.

mercial exploitation would begin at an early date. There were equally unrealistic expectations that manganese nodule exploitation would produce a tremendous volume of metals, which, in turn, would generate substantial income for the mining companies and the international community.[30] The competing producers of these metals from land-based sources therefore decided that it was important to deter, if not stop, deep seabed mining. Moreover, a number of developing countries placed a premium on obtaining the financial benefits of deep seabed mining and technology transfer, while the major consumer nations strongly favored the early and unimpeded commencement of industrial activity. Thus, by the time the negotiations at the conference began in 1973, deep seabed mining was not treated as a minor activity that might take place in the distant future but as an imminent and major industrial activity that might have direct impact on national interests. Considerable time and effort had to be devoted to the elimination of national positions generated by the call for the conference at a time when there was inadequate information about deep seabed mining.

[30] The economic viability of deep seabed mining was extensively considered in the course of the multi-session consideration of deep seabed mining legislation before the U.S. Congress. That history is reviewed in Caron, *Municipal Legislation for Exploitation of the Deep Seabed*, 8 OCEAN DEV. & INT'L L. 259 (1980). On June 28, 1980, President Carter signed the legislation into law: the Deep Seabed Hard Mineral Resources Act, P.L. 96–283. The economic issues were explored in a recent book entitled DEEPSEA MINING (J. T. Kildow ed. 1980). *See also* D. LEIPZIGER & J. MUDGE, SEABED MINERAL RESOURCES AND THE ECONOMIC INTERESTS OF DEVELOPING COUNTRIES (1976).

That there has been misinformation about the importance of deep seabed mining has been clear for some time. Many were led to believe that commercial operations would begin by the mid-1970's; it now appears that the earliest possible date will be the late 1980's. While the uncertain political-legal situation may have contributed to this delay, basic technological and economic obstacles also have to be overcome. Early projections presumed that there would be a rapid rise in the number of commercial mine sites once commercial production became possible; these projections are now considered to have been unduly optimistic aside from the potential legal constraints on production. While some counseled against accepting these optimistic forecasts, the industry, which projected an early development of major nodule exploitation, dominated the information flow. Without accusing industry spokesmen of intentionally misleading their governments and the international community, it should be pointed out that an optimistic forecast could serve their interest in many ways: *i.e.*, in obtaining favorable internal company decisions, in obtaining financing from external sources, and in persuading their home governments to seek a favorable legal regime at an early date. *See* the voluminous congressional testimony on the economic issues given during consideration of the Deep Seabed Hard Mineral Resources Act and its predecessor bills, *supra*. A genealogical table of the bills that led up to this legislation is found in Caron, *supra*, at 287. Some of the older and more optimistic reports on the economic viability of deep seabed mining include: Drechsler, *The Value of Subsea Mineral Resources*, in A NEW GENEVA CONFERENCE, *supra* note 16, at 112–13; Rothstein & Kaufman, *The Approaching Maturity of Deep Ocean Mining—The Pace Quickens*, MINING ENGINEERING, April 1971, at 31, 33; Additional Notes on the Possible Economic Implications of Mineral Production from the International Sea-bed Area: Report of the Secretary-General, UN Doc. A/AC.138/73, at 9–10 (1972). *Contra*, Sorensen & Mead, *A Cost-Benefit Analysis of Ocean Mineral Resource Development: The Case of Manganese Nodules*, AM. J. AGRICULTURAL ECON., December 1968, at 1611. *See generally* R. WRIGHT, OCEAN MINING, AN ECONOMIC EVALUATION (Staff Study, Ocean Mining Administration, U.S. Dept. of the Interior, 1976); and Charney, *The Equitable Sharing of Revenues from Seabed Mining*, in H. G. KNIGHT, J. CHARNEY, & J. JACOBSON, POLICY ISSUES IN OCEAN LAW 53 (1975).

Deep seabed mining is still not commercially viable and is unlikely to be so for at least another decade. Furthermore, the scale and economic significance of the industry will be much more modest than projected in the early 1970's. While some of the industry's problems were caused by the international political issues it inspired, its health has been greatly influenced by continuing economic and technological difficulties.

A further obstacle that appears to be symptomatic of early international negotiations relating to new technological developments stems from the information gap likely to exist at those negotiations. New technologies are usually produced and held by a limited number of countries or their nationals. Consequently, many delegations at multilateral negotiations on these subjects will be dependent upon their adversaries for vital information. This creates suspicions, which further complicate the negotiations. It has been pointed out that the Soviet suspicions of the United States at the Baruch Plan negotiations may have been enhanced by this circumstance.[31]

This problem was particularly severe in the deep seabed negotiations. The technology developed for the exploitation of the deep seabed in the late 1960's and the 1970's was the product of a very few companies located in selected Western developed countries.[32] Those companies maintained strict control over the flow of information about their activities and the potential of the industry. The limited information generally available to the conference came directly or indirectly from the industry. In addition, many delegations believed that the delegations from the countries whose companies were engaged in deep seabed development had been fully informed so that they could accurately identify their national interests and appropriate negotiating positions.[33] It took a long time to moderate those suspicions and to fill the information vacuum.

Finally, in an early negotiation the participants' positions may be too far apart to be effectively reconciled at formal negotiations. The process of international law development consists of a continuous narrowing of differences among nations. Early in that process national opinions on the appropriate law might be very diverse. It is clear that the more diverse the national objectives are when a formal negotiation begins, the more difficult the negotiation will be.[34] Thus, during a period of gestation prior to negotiations the gap is narrowed

[31] EXTENDED STUDY OF AMERICAN DIPLOMACY, *supra* note 21, at 77.

[32] In the mid-1970's, the nations directly involved in explorations related to nodule mining included Belgium, West Germany, France, Canada, Great Britain, Japan, and the United States. The firms were Deepsea Ventures (a consortium of Tenneco, U.S. Steel, Union Minière of Belgium, and some Japanese companies); the Kennecott Consortium (Kennecott Copper, Rio Tinto Zinc, Consolidated Gold Fields, Noranda Mines, and Mitsubishi); the International Nickel Company of Canada Consortium (the German AMR group, SEDCO, and a Sumitomo-led Japanese group (DOMCO)). Also, it was mistakenly believed that the Summa Corporation was involved; however, it was actually developing a system to try to recover a Soviet submarine for the CIA. D. LEIPZIGER & J. MUDGE, *supra* note 30, at 128 n.15. *See also* B. BUZAN, SEABED POLITICS, *supra* note 10, at 80.

[33] In truth, the industry had so effectively controlled information on deep seabed mining that the developed country delegations had little knowledge that was not derived from the industry and already generally known.

[34] J. RUBIN & B. BROWN, THE SOCIAL PSYCHOLOGY OF BARGAINING AND NEGOTIATION 145 (1975); P. GULLIVER, DISPUTES AND NEGOTIATIONS 145 (1979).

through interstate communications and experimentation. Arguably, the efficiency of the lawmaking process and the quality of results may be improved if prior to formal negotiations these differences are narrowed through the use of other methods of communication, including the development of customary law.

There is little doubt that the wide disparity of positions that nations brought to UNCLOS III contributed to the negotiating difficulties. Precious little effort was made to narrow these differences prior to the negotiations. Where customary international law developed in concert with the negotiations, substantive issues were resolved readily. Such was the case with the 200-mile zone. Although it was billed as the big issue to be negotiated, developments outside the conference made it apparent that there would be a 200-mile zone of national jurisdiction and the issue rapidly receded at the negotiations.[35] No independent progress was made on the deep seabed issues and that question continued to fester throughout.

This discussion of the factors relevant to a decision to conduct an early negotiation makes it clear that conflicting judgments are involved. There are a number of factors unique to the immaturity of the international legal system that argue against the early development of binding international agreements. McDougal presented them well in his discussion of the outer space debate. The conduct of negotiations in response to new technologies presents additional arguments against early negotiations. Rapid changes in information about a new technology and its societal implications are not easily accommodated by international institutions. Since the rate of change will slow over the period subsequent to an initial technological breakthrough, deferral to a time of slower change and greater knowledge may be advisable. On the other hand, the potential for orderly relations expected from early agreement has appeal, particularly for those interested in harnessing the new technology for commercial use and others interested in the political leverage to be derived from early negotiation. It is questionable whether an early agreement can actually produce the desired order and whether early negotiation is the only way to obtain political leverage by those not holding the technology. Absent these two objectives, the arguments in favor of deferred negotiations are rather persuasive. Thus, it may be better to focus on ways of accommodating the contrary interests. For example, commercialization might be handled better at the earlier stages by domestic activities or limited international arrangements. Global power struggles, such as that over the NIEO, might be resolved better at the general political level first or at those negotiations that are truly ripe for substantive agreement.[36] While the task of deflecting these pressures will not be easy, resistance to premature negotiations may be advisable. It is important that all of these interests be considered before the international community becomes committed to a negotiation to produce a new international agreement. Decisions to negotiate legal regimes at an early date should therefore not be made hastily.

[35] *Compare* Stevenson & Oxman, *Preparations for the Law of the Sea Conference*, *supra* note 10, at 13–23, *with* Stevenson & Oxman, *The 1974 Caracas Session*, *supra* note 10, at 15–17.

[36] *See* the proposed agenda discussed in ul Haq, *supra* note 4.

Information Flow

During the period prior to negotiations an important factor to consider is how much knowledge of the subject under consideration is held by the participating nations and diplomats. Clearly, in 1967 few knew anything about deep seabed mining, and only a limited group of diplomats knew much about other evolving commercial, scientific, and military uses of the oceans. Thus, at the early stages, it was necessary to educate foreign offices and diplomats so that they would be prepared to conduct the necessary consultations and negotiations.[37]

There has been considerable discussion in the literature of the need to assure that the international community, especially the diplomatic corps, is well informed about new technological, scientific, and business developments.[38] It is argued that armed with the necessary knowledge, these officials would better understand when there is an actual need for new arrangements. The increased lead time that would often result would give them a greater opportunity for planning and preparation. Various international organizations sponsor research and issue reports on these developments, as do national governments. By studying such information before entering into negotiations, it is maintained, foreign offices, diplomatic corps, and international organizations would improve the consideration of the new demands.

Attention has been given to this objective within the United States. Suggestions include assuring that State Department personnel are technologically literate by exposing them to the fields of science and technology. Others suggest that experts be included within the State Department staff, that better linkages be forged with specialized government departments that can feed the information into the State Department, that more productive contacts be created between the State Department and the private sector of business and academia, and that more future-oriented studies be commissioned.[39]

It may very well be valuable to provide more and better information to the diplomatic corps, but whether the facilitation of the flow of information and its assimilation would actually change the way nations behave in these areas can be questioned. While futurology is in vogue,[40] it is not sufficiently reliable over long time spans for national action. It has been pointed out that

> [d]uring each twenty-five year period in the course of the last hundred years, there has been at least one major change in international alignments, one major change in the institutions and politics of one major power, and one major change in technology; and none of those changes would have been easy to predict from the facts known twenty-five years before.[41]

[37] *See* B. BUZAN, SEABED POLITICS, *supra* note 10, at 71; *see also* note 15 *supra.*

[38] *See* EXTENDED STUDY OF AMERICAN DIPLOMACY, *supra* note 21, in general and at 1491–1502, 1682–86, and 1702; Keohane & Nye, *Organizing for Global Environmental and Resource Independence*, 1 MURPHY COMMISSION REPORT, *supra* note 6, App. B, at 46, 61–62.

[39] *See* note 38 *supra.*

[40] UNESCO, THINKING AHEAD 151 (1977).

[41] Deutsch, *Outer Space and International Politics: A Look to 1988*, in OUTER SPACE IN WORLD POLITICS 139 (J. Goldsen ed. 1963).

Even improved accuracy may not be sufficient to change national and international behavior. Foreign offices are usually so pressed by immediate needs that they are rarely able or willing to make the necessary resource and political commitments to developments likely to take place far in the future. Furthermore, even if successful, the enormous effort required to maintain expertise in all areas of development would entail the acquisition of information and personnel that would so overload the system that the benefits sought would be lost.[42] Finally, direct political, military, and economic pressures are more likely to dominate critical decisions to initiate negotiations and to identify national objectives than is technical information which tends to play only a supporting role.

In sum, while a well-informed international community and diplomatic corps may be better able to address new and pressing needs and might even be able to perceive a new need at a marginally earlier time, it seems unlikely that the time frame for useful and productive responses will be substantially changed by better information flow and its assimilation. A more feasible, albeit modest, goal might be to assure the rapid acquisition of information as needed. This approach would make the best use of the limited resources and assimilative capacities available.

Nonbinding Forums

Another aspect of international law development is the role played by multilateral forums that do not negotiate international agreements. Many have suggested that resolutions by the United Nations General Assembly present a valuable vehicle for law development.[43] While nations discuss the subject on the agenda and often negotiate the text of the resolutions, their nonbinding nature arguably provides necessary flexibility and may eliminate some of the problems of timing and national claims posed by the negotiation of binding agreements. General Assembly resolutions have played a beneficial role in the formative stages of some international law development, particularly in human rights law and the law of outer space.

The mere placement of a new item on the agenda of the General Assembly necessarily provokes national attention and international discussion. Debate on the subject will also ensue. Because they are not automatically binding as law, the resulting resolutions are tentative and flexible, and thus permit practice and later resolutions to make the necessary adjustments. On the other hand, the very forum and the nonbinding nature of the resolutions may create counterproductive forces: the high visibility of the General Assembly, the absence of real political and economic stakes, and the recent use of the forum as a premier staging ground for the high politics of the NIEO argue against using UNGA resolutions as devices for establishing needed and useful legal norms. For ex-

[42] Bergman, *Organizing the U.S. Government Response to Global Population Growth*, 1 MURPHY COMMISSION REPORT, *supra* note 6, App. B, at 65, 80.

[43] Schachter, *Scientific Advances and International Law Making*, 55 CAL. L. REV. 423, 424–27 (1967); M. BEDJAOUI, TOWARDS A NEW INTERNATIONAL ECONOMIC ORDER 138–42 (1979).

ample, UNGA discussion of the law of the sea tended to freeze positions rather than to encourage a process of accommodation and exploration.

A more promising vehicle for law development may be proceedings at ad hoc international conferences such as the Stockholm Conference on the World Environment and the Rome World Food Conference. Their resolutions have even less juridical significance than UNGA resolutions, but they can serve a valuable function.[44] As separate ad hoc conferences they force nations to address a specific subject both over the course of the conference and during the preparatory work. Since they are diplomatic conferences attended by governmental representatives, the realities of international politics are not totally absent. The delegations that attend these conferences, however, tend to have more expertise in the subject area than those at the UN General Assembly. Consequently, communication tends to be focused more on the particular agenda item. Since the early development of law in these areas is more likely to require low-level activities than the high politics found at the General Assembly, these ad hoc forums present better opportunities for narrowing national differences and developing an international consensus. The negotiation of the final resolution and its issuance can play the valuable role of focusing attention on methods of resolving the outstanding legal and political issues.

Pace of Prenegotiation Activity

The use of international diplomatic forums for purposes other than negotiating international agreements is a significant vehicle for law development that can facilitate movement towards negotiated agreements. The pace of that movement, however, must be carefully adjusted. Arguably, in the case of the law of the sea negotiations the matter moved too quickly at first. Within 3 years of Arvid Pardo's 1967 speech to the General Assembly calling attention to the need for deep seabed law, a series of UNGA resolutions were passed that committed the international community to negotiating an international agreement.[45] With hindsight, it would appear that little would have been lost had more time been devoted to gathering the necessary information and narrowing national differences. If the subject had been mature for negotiation, the conference agenda might have been more manageable, the negotiating obstacles less formidable, and the atmosphere more conducive to the settlement of the issues. Instead, the difficulties and hostilities generated in the early stages of the negotiations probably increased the obstacles to success. During the more than a decade of negotiations, high seas freedoms have continued to erode, deep seabed mining has not begun, and the entry into force of a law of the sea convention remains a long way off.[46]

[44] *See* Sohn, *The Stockholm Declaration on the Human Environment*, 14 HARV. INT'L L.J. 423 (1973).

[45] This history is recounted in Swing, *supra* note 14. *See also* note 18 *supra*.

[46] There have been international law developments that were molded by activity at the conference in the same way that nonbinding conference proceedings discussed above have influence on law development. The fact that this was a treaty negotiation, however, stimulated national claims and positions that may prove counterproductive in the long run.

Obtaining a Commitment to Negotiate

Even if an issue is considered to be ripe for negotiation, it is not certain that nations will be prepared to make the political commitment to hammer out an agreement. Arguably, this was the real problem faced at the Law of the Sea Conference; while some nations seriously sought an agreement, others may not have had that objective. As a consequence of the failure to produce an agreement over many years of negotiation, the optimal time for agreement may have been passed. The discussion of this problem can be divided into two parts. First, how does the first nation or group of nations become committed to the development of an international agreement? Second, how do the interested nations obtain the commitment of other nations whose participation in the negotiation is desired?

A nation will find it more difficult to undertake affirmative foreign policy initiatives than to react to initiatives taken by others. In fact, it has been argued recently that United States foreign policy has been primarily reactive in nature and that there is a need for more initiatives.[47] The same can be said for most nations' foreign policy, but accomplishing such a shift will not be easy. Two of the most important factors in determining whether this shift can be accomplished are the flow of information into the foreign policy sector and the domestic political environment. It was pointed out above that many suggestions have been made to augment the flow of information to the diplomatic corps and to assure its integration into the decision-making system. To the extent that this information is successfully absorbed, it will equip the diplomatic corps with foresight on potential problems and needs that might require new international agreements. If such sensitivity became worldwide, nations might be better prepared to take initiatives on law development as needs arise.

The second factor is less mechanical and more political. Even assuming perfect knowledge and an established need for law development, no move is likely to be made unless the initiator has a clearly defined policy objective that can be translated into specific initiatives. In part, the recent inability of the United States to take international initiatives is due to its ambivalence on a number of broad international political issues. It has tended to wait until domestic demands have become strong enough to motivate action or until it has become necessary to react to initiatives taken by other nations. If the broad issues were resolved, the specific objectives might be clearly identified soon enough to stimulate foreign policy initiatives before decisions are forced by other pressures.

Unfortunately, it is doubtful whether any major nation, particularly the United States, could so reconcile its multiple and often conflicting interests that a forward-thinking foreign policy could be developed for many issues. Thus, more pragmatic proposals would focus on the ability to identify at the earliest possible stage the actual pressures for law development and the relevant specific foreign policy objectives. The effective flow of information into the foreign policy system thus becomes the most promising method for improving national

[47] EXTENDED STUDY OF AMERICAN DIPLOMACY, *supra* note 21, at page 1491.

reactions, while the clarification of general policy objectives would merit continuous, albeit somewhat fruitless, efforts.

Once a government decides to seek new international law through the negotiation of an international agreement, the task before it is to stimulate the interest of other states that it wants to join in the agreement. The nature of the subject under discussion here makes it probable that the ultimate objective will be to establish new law susceptible of global acceptance.

The most direct approach is to generate worldwide interest in the conduct of a global negotiation, as was done for UNCLOS III. Thus, the interested nations would seek to spread the necessary publicity about the subject and the need for agreement. UNGA discussions and resolutions and those of ad hoc diplomatic conferences can contribute significantly to this process. The calling of a negotiating conference itself would more often than not stimulate a commitment by many nations. Informed foreign offices and international civil servants would also be part of the strategy. If steps were taken to assure the availability of relevant information to foreign offices, they could more easily determine their national interests and plan a course of action. A closely related role would be played by experts in the pertinent technical fields. International professional conferences and publications as well as discussions in the popular press serve to bring the technological and legal requirements to the attention of concerned parties.[48]

This approach assumes that open encouragement to negotiate will lead to a commitment to do so, once the potential participants see the need for an agreement and the interest of other nations. Further support can often be obtained by linking various nations' related objectives or even through the normal course of international diplomatic efforts to encourage participation.

These efforts would normally work well when the need for a negotiation is directly felt by all participants because of the nature of the subject matter, *e.g.*, the environment. The need for agreement on new technology may not be felt equally. Those holding the technology may be under more pressure to obtain an agreement in order to facilitate the use of the technology; those lacking the technology may only be interested in obtaining access to it or in gaining leverage over the activity.

One response to this situation has been the more aggressive approach taken in the Antarctic Treaty Consultative Meetings and other specialized international groups. Rather than generally stimulating global interest in the development of a new agreement, the most interested states have directly taken the initiative by negotiating international agreements within the small group.[49] By

[48] The obverse is also true. The experience of the Law of the Sea Conference has shown that nations will be wary of committing themselves to the completion of a negotiation if they believe that their lack of information puts them at a severely disadvantageous position relative to other participants (unless, of course, they have identified an independent need for agreement). This places a premium on the timely and credible distribution of relevant information through government and private channels.

[49] The most recent example of this procedure is the Convention on the Conservation of Antarctic Marine Living Resources, *opened for signature* Aug. 1, 1980 to December 31, 1980, *reprinted in* 19 ILM 841 (1980). *See also* Agreed Measures for the Conservation of Antarctic Fauna and Flora, *reprinted in* CONGRESSIONAL RESEARCH SERVICE, 95TH CONG., 1ST SESS., TREATIES AND OTHER

initiating the agreements and making it clear that they intend to go forward regardless of the participation of others, they create pressure on other nations either to become involved if they want to participate in the new system or to acquiesce in the initiative. This approach certainly permits the more developed nations to exercise considerable leverage over the course of events and to stimulate the conduct of negotiations, but it also poses the risk of provoking adverse reactions if the agreement is not acceptable to a significant number of nonparticipants. Nevertheless, it may facilitate the rapid creation of new international law.[50]

There are many other ways to encourage the development of new legal norms. While methods differ and the degree of control exercised by the most interested nations will vary, the main objective should be to identify and, if necessary, create a situation that will lead to the development of new law either by direct negotiation or by obtaining general acquiescence in the actions of some states. What is critical is that once there is a need for new norms, the international community should be able to develop those norms in a timely fashion. Significant attention should be given to the method used to develop interest; a negotiation in which a considerable number of participants are not committed to producing an agreement may be worse than no negotiation at all.

III. The Negotiation Period

It would be unduly formalistic to assume that negotiations commence only with the opening of a formal negotiating conference. In fact, negotiations take place throughout both periods under discussion. More significantly, the tenor of law development changes when it becomes clear that it will be formalized by means of a new international agreement. At that stage focus shifts from the more general methods of law development to the orchestration of diplomatic negotiations. Thus, for UNCLOS III the shift took place in 1970 when the General Assembly's Declaration of Principles Governing the Sea-bed was passed and the preparatory meetings began.[51]

OPTIONS

Even after negotiations have been initiated, there is a considerable range of negotiating objectives possible. The potential objectives of the legal systems under negotiation have been divided by Ruggie into three categories: the purpose of the international regime, its instrumentalities, and its functions.[52] Its purpose

---

International Agreements on Fisheries, Oceanographic Resources, and Wildlife Involving the United States 28–34 (Comm. Print 1977); Convention for the Conservation of Antarctic Seals, *opened for signature* June 1, 1972, TIAS No. 8826 (*entered into force* March 11, 1978), *reprinted in* 11 ILM 251 (1972).

[50] The question of international participation in the development of the Antarctic mineral resource regime is discussed in Charney, *Future Strategies for an Antarctic Mineral Resource Regime—Can the Environment be Protected?*, in The New Nationalism and the Use of Common Spaces: Issues in Marine Pollution and the Exploitation of Antarctica 206 (J. Charney ed. 1981).

[51] *See* note 18 *supra*.

[52] Ruggie, *supra* note 5, at 571.

might be: (1) to acquire a capability, (2) to make effective use of a capability, or (3) to cope with the consequence of a capability. The instrumentalities that might carry out the objective include: (1) a common framework for national behavior, (2) a joint facility for national behavior, (3) a common policy for integrating national behavior, and (4) a common policy that substitutes for independent national behavior. Finally, an international regime might function in any of three ways: (1) informational, (2) managerial, or (3) executive.[53] The selection of any option will necessarily affect the nature of the negotiation, its timing, and the difficulties faced by the participants. Each option has its appropriate place in a response to new technological developments.

Unfortunately, there is no international consensus on the appropriateness of any objective as applied to specific international issues. In fact, the objectives sought by nations are often closely related to their interest in the subject matter. Thus, a nation with technology that is seeking a hospitable environment for its use will be likely to desire a loosely structured regime allowing national freedom of action. In contrast, a nation seeking to use the negotiation to obtain the benefits of others' technological developments or additional political leverage will be likely to prefer a more comprehensive regime that circumscribes the behavior of the nations holding the technology.

In part, much of the negotiation on the deep seabed regime at UNCLOS III turned on that issue. The solution attempted was to direct the negotiations towards the more pragmatic questions of deep seabed mining and to construct a regime by avoiding the structural issue. As a consequence, the deep seabed negotiations combined objectives, which only compounded the negotiating difficulties.[54] Perhaps it was the collective fault of the participants that the search for compromise forced the integration of these various approaches. No nation appeared to have sought the collage of purposes, instrumentalities, and functions. Rather, it resulted from a series of pragmatic attempts to compromise often inconsistent positions. The combination of forces brought to bear on these negotiations thus encouraged this complex result.[55] Unfortunately, it is the very

[53] *Ibid.*

[54] Since it was assumed that deep seabed mining would not be operating commercially at the commencement of the new regime, the negotiations had as one aim facilitating the acquisition of that capability. In addition, the Enterprise was to have as its initial objective the acquisition of deep seabed mining capabilities. Another purpose of the regime, once the capability was acquired, was to use that capability by conducting deep seabed mining. Finally, the negotiations addressed the consequences of deep seabed mining by drafting provisions on its environmental impact, the sale of metals, and the amelioration of any adverse economic impact on competing producers.

The instrumentalities proposed for this regime were equally comprehensive. Depending on the nature of a specific activity, at least three of the four alternatives would be utilized. The rules applicable to seabed prospecting could best be considered as establishing a common framework for national behavior. Commercial exploration and exploitation by contractors would probably be considered a common policy for integrating national behavior; and the operations of the Enterprise would be a common policy substituting for independent national behavior. Similarly, depending on the particular activity, the seabed regime would act in an informational, managerial, or executive role.

[55] In part, it is that fear which may have motivated the so-called L–5 to vehemently protest the new Moon Treaty. Agreement Governing the Activities of States on the Moon and Other Celestial Bodies, *opened for signature* Dec. 18, 1979, UN Doc. A/34/664, *reprinted in* 18 ILM 1434 (1979).

complexity of the result that may doom the agreement. The expenditure of greater efforts to resolve the issue of objectives might have produced more viable results.

MANAGEMENT OF ISSUES INVOLVING ADVANCED TECHNOLOGY

Beyond the selection of negotiating objectives is the even more complex series of issues raised by the substantive questions. In addition to the normal difficulties faced at international negotiations, the technological foundations of the subject matter raise certain problems. The management of such questions often involves consideration of the advanced technology that gave rise to the negotiations and technical analyses of its impacts. Technical matters have regularly been considered at the UNCTAD commodity negotiations, the WARC, the International Atomic Energy Agency, the Antarctic Consultative Meetings, the Outer Space Committee, and UNCLOS III, among others. The integration of this material into political negotiations requires considerable thought, which it unfortunately has not often received. There are a number of ways that technical issues can be managed. Several approaches were used at the law of the sea negotiations with varying degrees of success.

The Deep Seabed Mining Negotiations

The deep seabed negotiations at UNCLOS III concerned the establishment of a legal regime to govern the commercial exploitation of deep seabed minerals, particularly manganese nodules. The task facing the negotiators was to fashion an entirely new legal system for a technology that had never been put to commercial use. While debate has raged over the question of what law would be applicable to those activities in the absence of an international agreement, efforts at the conference focused on establishing an international organization to oversee the exploitation of seabed resources.

Economic Implications of Deep Seabed Mining. At the outset it was decided that the negotiation of a regime on deep seabed mining would require the delegates to focus on the likely economic and industrial consequences of deep seabed mining. Even before the formal negotiations began, the secretariats of the United Nations and of UNCTAD had been asked to undertake relevant technical studies. They produced a number of well-distributed reports on manganese nodule mining.[56] Nevertheless, these reports did not induce a shift in

---

See Dangerous Defects in the Draft UN Moon Treaty (Letter to the Editor by K. Eric Drexler, Director L-5 Society), N.Y. Times, Oct. 9, 1979, at A22, cols. 3–5. *See generally* Christol, *The Common Heritage of Mankind Provision in the 1977 Agreement Governing the Activities of States on the Moon and Other Celestial Bodies*, 14 INT'L LAW. 429 (1980).

[56] *See* Report of the Secretary-General, Economic Significance, in terms of Sea-bed Mineral Resources, of the Various Limits Proposed for National Jurisdiction, UN Doc. A/AC.138/87, at 27–28 (1973) [hereinafter cited as Economic Significance]; UN DEP'T OF ECONOMIC AND SOCIAL AFFAIRS, MINERAL RESOURCES OF THE SEA (UN Doc. ST/ECA/125, 1970); Report of the Secretary-General, Economic Implications of Sea-bed Mineral Development in the International Area, UN Doc. A/CONF.62/25 (1974), 3 UNCLOS III, OFF. REC. 4 (1975); Report of the Secretary-

the focus of the debate from the broad political issues of the North-South confrontation to the mining regime ostensibly under negotiation. In great part this was due to the fact that the adversaries still believed that their opponents might capitulate on the general political issues at the conference and that a more pragmatic compromise solution would therefore not be required to bring the negotiations to a successful conclusion. The resolution of this basic issue took a considerable amount of time and effort; some would say that it has never been fully resolved. But the reports did provide information on the subject of deep seabed mining and its potential importance, and thus may have contributed in a general way to the shift in the discussions towards the specifics of the mining regime, which took place at a later date.

While these studies did contain valuable information that had not previously been available to the negotiators in a useful form, their utility was limited because questions were raised about their reliability. Financial and technical limitations precluded the independent verification of a large part of the data used in those reports. In fact, almost all of the basic data used came directly or indirectly from the deep seabed mining companies, which exercised considerable control over the flow of information. Similarly, the objectivity and credibility of the analyses made in the reports were controversial. Some of the reports were produced by UNCTAD, which was known to have a political bias in favor of the developing countries. Studies by the countries most interested in deep seabed mining conflicted with these reports. Since the reports by the UN Secretariat and UNCTAD were unsigned and no vehicle for otherwise supporting their credibility was initially provided, their usefulness appeared to be limited to the provision of general background information. Consequently, the question of the economic implications of deep seabed mining remained an open matter when the Caracas session of the conference opened in 1974.

General, Possible Impact of Sea-bed Mineral Production in the Area Beyond National Jurisdiction on World Markets, with Special Reference to the Problems of Developing Countries: A Preliminary Assessment, UN Doc. A/AC.138/36 (1971); Report of the Secretary-General, Possible Methods and Criteria for the Sharing by the International Community of Proceeds and Other Benefits Derived from the Exploitation of the Resources of the Area Beyond the Limits of National Jurisdiction, UN Doc. A/AC.138/38 (1971); Progress Report by the Secretary-General, Sea-bed Mineral Resources: Recent Developments, UN Doc. A/AC.138/90 (1973); Report by the UNCTAD Secretariat, The Effects of Production of Manganese from the Sea-bed, with Particular Reference to the Effects on Developing Country Producers of Manganese Ore, UN Doc. TD/B/483 (1974); An Econometric Model of the Manganese Ore Industry, UN Doc. TD/B/483/Add.1 (1974); Report by the UNCTAD Secretariat, The Effects of Possible Exploitation of the Sea-bed on the Earnings of Developing Countries from Copper Exports, UN Doc. TD/B/484 (1974); Report by the UNCTAD Secretariat, Commodity Problems and Policies, Mineral Production from the Area of the Sea-bed Beyond National Jurisdiction: Issues of International Commodity Policy, UN Doc. TD/B/113, Supp. No. 4 (1972); Report by the FAO Secretariat, Possible Adverse Effects of the Exploitation of the Sea-bed Beyond National Jurisdiction on Fishery Resources, UN Doc. TD/B/447 (1973); Note by the UNCTAD Secretariat, Exploitation of the Mineral Resources of the Sea-bed Beyond National Jurisdiction: Issues of International Commodity Policy, UN Doc. TD/B/449 (1973); Exploitation of the Mineral Resources of the Sea-bed Beyond National Jurisdiction: Issues of International Commodity Policy, Case Study of Cobalt, UN Doc. TD/B/449/Add.1 (1973).

The significance of the economic questions made it necessary to bring more information to the attention of the delegates. By the middle of the Caracas session the Chairman of the First Committee, where the deep seabed regime was to be negotiated, invited the experts from the UN Secretariat and UNCTAD to attend a committee meeting to discuss their reports and to answer questions.[57] That exercise did permit the delegates to focus on the economic issues. Little observable progress was made, however, owing in part to the combative approaches taken by the participants. The experts sought to defend their written products in the face of attempts by some developed countries to discredit them for both substantive and procedural reasons.

A further effort to address the economic implications was undertaken at off-the-record "seminars" of the committee devoted to elucidating the economic issues. In preparation for the seminars, the chairman asked each interested state to bring its own expert to the committee. These experts were to enter into a discussion of the economic issues after presenting any economic data and analyses they believed would be helpful. In the short lead time that the delegations had, "experts" were brought in for this purpose. Initially, they were to speak in their individual capacity. Fearing inappropriate statements, however, the committee decided that the "experts" should speak from the seats of their sponsoring delegations. Some delegations did not even bother to replace their political representatives with new "experts." The seminars were held in the committee's regular meeting room and a very large number of delegations attended, many expecting to become better informed on the issues. It soon became apparent that the "experts" were under a tight rein and little was to be learned from the seminars.

Some delegations also distributed reports that provided written arguments in support of their previously established positions.[58] No substantial progress on the issues could be observed after the seminars; even the Chairman's tentative conclusions on the results of the exercise were strongly challenged by a number of especially interested delegations.[59] As a consequence, there was little perceptible movement from the general debate, which had taken its cue from the more global North-South debate.

Subsequent to the economic seminars, there were no further significant efforts

[57] *See* 2 UNCLOS III, OFF. REC., Meetings 9 and 10 of Comm. I, at 45–52 (1975). In preparation for this discussion the committee Chairman issued a summary of the relevant documents that had been previously presented to the conference, Note by the Chairman of the First Committee, UN Doc. A/CONF.62/C.1/L.2 (1974), 3 UNCLOS III, OFF. REC. 151 (1975).

[58] United States of America: Working Paper on the Economic Effects of Deep Sea-bed Exploitation, UN Doc. A/CONF.62/C.1/L.5, 2 UNCLOS III, OFF. REC. 164; Seminar on Economic Implications of Sea-bed Mineral Development, Statement by Mr. Gavin Moncrieff (United Kingdom, July 31, 1974) (unpub.). *See also* Statement by Leigh S. Ratiner, Alternate United States Representative, Comm. I (Aug. 8, 1974). This statement was made at an informal meeting of Committee I and is unpublished. Much of the substance was repeated, however, at a formal meeting of Committee I, 2 UNCLOS III, OFF. REC. 64–66.

[59] *See* Statement by U.S. Representative Ratiner at the 14th meeting of Committee I on Aug. 19, 1974, 2 UNCLOS III, OFF. REC. 75. Chairman Engo's summary of the seminar is found in *id.* at 68–70.

within the formal framework of the conference to inform the participating delegates on the details of the economic issues. The negotiations focused more attention on the noneconomic legal issues of structuring the deep seabed regime, particularly on the international organization that would conduct or manage deep seabed mining, the International Sea-Bed Authority. Nevertheless, information on the subject did continue to flow to the delegates from published studies, informal discussions, and conferences initiated by governments, industry, and nongovernmental organizations.[60] Over the years, the general level of knowledge on these economic issues increased substantially.

The issue of the economic implications of deep seabed mining remained unresolved over many sessions. As matters evolved, discussions turned toward limitations on the volume of seabed production in an attempt to assure the land-based producers that the competition would not get too intense. The computation of the future world nickel demand and the potential consequences of any limitation on the deep seabed mining industry were hotly debated items. Analysis of these issues entailed the use of highly sophisticated computational skills and prognostications about the future nickel market as well as an understanding of the growth needs of a viable deep seabed mining industry.

Canada was particularly involved in this negotiation and had a significant interest in its outcome because it is a major nickel producer and would have to compete with seabed production. It sought a formula that would severely limit the amount of seabed mining. At one point in the discussions at a well-attended meeting of a First Committee working group, Canada made a notable attempt to strengthen its argument by presenting a series of computer projections analyzing the impact of various production control formulas under discussion.[61]

[60] A particularly significant role was played by an interested and active nongovernmental organization (NGO), the Ocean Education Project (OEP), which periodically sponsored informal seminars for interested delegates. It held approximately 60 luncheons and seminars on UNCLOS III matters. This NGO was established by the World Federation Association and Friends World Committee for Consultation for the purpose of assisting the negotiations. Its active leaders were strongly committed to the success of the negotiations, including the establishment of a strong and viable deep seabed mining regime. Most of the active participants were U.S. citizens, but they had little or no political power, domestic or international. Their activities were periodically reported in the occasional conference newspaper *Neptune*, sponsored by OEP and the Law of the Sea Project of the United Methodist Church.

In addition to the continued flow of information, there were efforts by small and fairly secret groups of interested states directly to negotiate a political settlement of the economic issues. Once agreement was reached within those groups, the members sought to legitimatize their agreement by orchestrating the consideration of the subject at a rather large Committee I working group or similar body. While they did have periods of apparent success, opposition ultimately developed to their agreements (usually from excluded participants) and the initiatives collapsed. These abortive efforts took place during negotiations that preceded the issuance of the Informal Single Negotiating Text, UN Doc. A/CONF.62/WP.8 (1975), 4 UNCLOS III, OFF. REC. 137 (1975) [hereinafter ISNT] and in the interval before the issuance of the Revised Single Negotiating Text, UN Doc. A/CONF.62/WP.8/Rev.1 (1976), 5 *id.* at 125 (1976) [hereinafter RSNT].

[61] This took place during a meeting of the Committee I Chairman's Working Group, chaired by Ambassador Jens Evensen of Norway, on the afternoon of May 26, 1977. No records of this meeting have been issued. The document contained printouts from a computer program which projected the number of manganese nodule mine sites during the period 1985 to 2000, based on various assumptions. The tables were headed "Program: Group of 77 Hi Formulation Offshore Minerals Section: RMCB, EMR" (unpub.). At an annual growth rate of 6%, it projected a total of 23.8899 mine sites in the year 2000.

While it did get the attention of delegates, it does not appear that the analysis helped to move the negotiations forward. Immediately after the presentation, delegates began to question the many assumptions upon which the Canadian projections were based and the general validity of the analysis. There was neither sufficient time nor an appropriate procedure available for the analysis to be fully explained or tested. Nevertheless, this initiative may have stimulated serious efforts to resolve the land-based producers' concerns.

Some time after Canada's presentation it did become clear that a production control provision would be politically acceptable to the conference negotiators at that time.[62] That provision had to take account of both the uncertainties of the metals market and the aspirations of the deep seabed mining industry. Thus, it was generally agreed to develop a floating production limit applicable to a fixed-time period that would be tied to the world consumption of nickel.[63] Before the actual limits could be negotiated, it was decided that two technical questions had to be resolved. First, it was necessary to reach a general understanding on the future of the world nickel market and, second, a technically viable production control formula had to be devised that would permit the political negotiation to focus on the identification of a specific number that, when plugged into the production control formula, would actually determine the size of the limit on production. Recognizing the impossibility of negotiating the entire text of a production control article in the First Committee, the participants agreed to charge a small group of "technical experts" with responding to these needs. The Sub-Group of Technical Experts, often called the Archer group in recognition of its chairman, Alan Archer of the United Kingdom delegation, was established.[64] While no delegations were named to the working group and participation was open to all interested delegations, about 30 representatives from all states with substantial interests in the subject regularly participated in the off-the-record work of the group. It met regularly during the course of the Geneva session in 1978 and less so at a subsequent session. Although the issues under consideration had significant political and

[62] With the U.S. review of UNCLOS III announced by the Reagan administration in March 1981, this issue, in addition to many others, may be reopened. *See* UN THIRD CONFERENCE ON THE LAW OF THE SEA (RESUMED 10TH SESSION), REPORT SUBMITTED TO THE HOUSE COMM. ON FOREIGN AFFAIRS, 97TH CONG., 1ST SESS. (Comm. Print 1981). As an analysis of the dynamics of the international negotiations, the observations made here remain unchanged. It is still an open question whether the solution of this and other issues will ultimately be found to be politically acceptable, as expressed through a binding international agreement.

[63] The formula provided that the maximum quantity of nickel that can be produced from seabed mining will not exceed a certain percent of the growth segment of world nickel consumption. RSNT, pt. I, Text Presented by the Chairman of the First Committee, Art. 9.4(ii) and Ann. 1, para. 21; *see* Introductory Note by the Chairman of the First Committee, pt. IV, 5 UNCLOS III, OFF. REC. 125; Informal Composite Negotiating Text, UN Doc. A/CONF.62/WP.10 (1977), 8 UNCLOS III, OFF. REC. (1978) [hereinafter ICNT], Art. 150.1(g); ICNT/Rev. 1, UN Doc. A/CONF.62/WP.10/Rev.1. (1979), Art. 150.1(g); and ICNT/Rev.2, UN Doc. A/CONF.62/WP.10/Rev.2 (1980), Art. 151.

[64] The Archer Group of Technical Experts, begun at the intersessional meetings, was made a subgroup of Negotiating Group 1 (NG 1), which had been assigned the responsibility of negotiating the system of exploration and exploitation and resource policy (Chairman: Frank Njenga, Kenya). *See* Oxman, *The Seventh Session, supra* note 10, at 10, and U.S. Delegation Report, 7th sess., UNCLOS III, at 13 (1978) (unpub.).

economic implications, important aspects of production control were addressed and resolved to the satisfaction of the participants and, ultimately, of the committee.[65]

The use of this group of instructed experts was one of the few clearly successful procedures for the consideration of technical questions attempted at the negotiations. There are at least two reasons why this approach succeeded. In the first place, the issue was finally ripe for substantial progress. The charge to the group centered on fulfilling technical requirements that grew out of political agreement on the framework for resolving the issue. Equally important was the approach used to fashion the group and its activities. While its size was not predetermined, the number of active participants was small enough to permit effective communication but large enough to permit all interested parties to be represented. The Archer group was not secret, nor were its results predetermined or predesigned. It was clearly a functioning arm of the negotiations established and designed to meet specific needs. Interested delegations assigned individuals who had the necessary expertise or were able to become informed. The able Chairman facilitated the discussions and saw to it that they concentrated on the technical questions needing answers for the political negotiations. As its work progressed, the professionalism that characterized the group became known to the conference. In the end, the group was able to resolve many difficult technical issues and it produced a production control formula that simplified and focused the outstanding political issues.[66]

Financial Arrangements between Exploiters and the Authority. Another subject on which technical information became important to the progress of the deep seabed negotiations was the determination of the charges to be imposed on the exploiters of the deep seabed nodules. Obviously, the potential exploiters and their supporting countries wanted the charges to be small and certainly not so large that they would deter deep seabed mining. Other participants sought to maximize the charges. They wanted to distribute the income to injured land-based producers, to developing countries, and to the International Sea-Bed Authority and its industrial arm, the Enterprise. Some land-based producers even sought a tax structure that would deter deep seabed mining altogether. Thus, the financial arrangements developed into a critical substantive issue on which there was a wide range of positions.

[65] *See* Negotiating Group 1 Sub-Group of Technical Experts, Progress Report, Conf. Doc. NG1/7, 10 UNCLOS III, OFF. REC. 28 (1978); Negotiating Group 1 Sub-Group of Technical Experts, Second Progress Report, UNCLOS III, Conf. Doc. NG1/9 (May 9, 1978); and NG-1 Sub-Group of Technical Experts, Final Report, UNCLOS III, Conf. Doc. NG1/11 (May 11, 1978). *See also* U.S. Delegation Report, *supra* note 64; and Oxman, *supra* note 64.

[66] The political negotiation of the production control article within UNCLOS III at that time was held in another subgroup of NG 1, the Production Control Group chaired by Ambassador Satya Nandan (Fiji) (Nandan group). *See* Oxman, *The Eighth Session, supra* note 10, at 11; U.S. Delegation Report, 8th Sess., UNCLOS III, at 14–17 (1979) (unpub.); and U.S. Delegation Report, 9th Sess., UNCLOS III, at 17 (1980) (unpub.). This work was incorporated into the ICNT/Rev.2, *supra* note 63, Art. 151. *See generally* ICNT, *supra* note 63, Art. 150; ICNT/Rev.1, *supra* note 63, Arts. 150 and 151; Draft Convention on the Law of the Sea (Informal Text), UN Doc. A/CONF.62/WP.10/Rev.3, Art. 151 (1980) [hereinafter DC(IT)]; Draft Convention on the Law of the Sea, UN Doc. A/CONF.62/L.78, Art. 151 (1981) [hereinafter DC].

The first effort to address the problem of taxation directly took place at the sixth session in New York in 1977. First Committee Chairman Engo (Cameroon) personally established the Chairman's Expert Advisory Group on Financial Arrangements to consider these questions. It was chaired by a member of the Australian delegation. Certain interested delegations were invited to present their views and to bring along their experts on the financial aspects of deep seabed mining or related subjects. Some representatives of industry also attended these meetings and presented their views. Discussions took place in private, but all of the taxation schemes that were received by the Chairman were incorporated into a paper that was distributed to one of the larger informal working groups of the First Committee.[67] Nevertheless, this work does not appear to have resulted in any marked progress on the issue. There were a number of procedural deficiencies that contributed to the group's failure,[68] but the effort may have been doomed from the start since there had been no political agreement on either the substance of the taxation issue or a framework for resolving it.

In the year that followed, the range of disagreement narrowed substantially. Although the matter was far from settled, most delegates decided that the financial arrangements were not the appropriate vehicle for limiting deep seabed mining. Schemes that would make deep seabed mining financially prohibitive would not be negotiable. At this point it became clear that the financial impact on the industry of various approaches would have to be considered. Unfortunately, there was no agreement on the financial picture of the industry then or in the future. Since there had never been any commercial exploitation of the deep seabed and the activity had few parallels to current industrial activity, the conference participants were dependent upon expert opinions. The studies issued early in the negotiations not only were controversial but also were woefully out of date and lacked the detail necessary to devise a taxation scheme. Opinions expressed by various delegates enjoyed equally low credibility.

The United States decided to try to fill this information gap. The vehicle

[67] *See* Chairman's Expert Advisory Group on Financial Arrangements, Financial Terms of Contracts, First Committee (June 27, 1977) (unpub.). Related documents issued to the committee to assist in educating the participants on this issue included: Costs of the Authority and Contractual Means of Financing its Activities, UN Doc. A/CONF.62/C.1/L.19 (1977); and Note by the Secretariat, Hypothetical Computation of Production of Nickel from the Area (May 27, 1977) (unpub.). The work of the Chairman's Advisory Group on Financial Arrangements found its way into the ICNT, *supra* note 63, Ann. II, para. 7, but it was highly qualified; *see* footnote * at para. 7, and the Explanatory Memorandum by the President of the Conference on Document A/CONF.62/WP.10, UN Doc. A/CONF.62/WP.10/Add.1 (1977), 8 UNCLOS III, OFF. REC. 65, 66–67 (1978).

[68] Unlike the Archer group, this group held its meetings in relative secrecy and there was a notable absence of the sense of expert consultation. In fact, there were a number of important participants who were under the impression that the Chairman alone would determine the results of the group, and that they were obliged to convince him to adopt their views. Thus, the atmosphere appeared to be one of advocacy rather than expert inquiry and analysis. In the end, the Chairman did not attempt to resolve the issues. Rather, the resulting document incorporated every type of tax presented to the group into one taxing scheme, an approach not acceptable to any but the most ardent opponents of deep seabed mining. A rumored power conflict between two of the major conference actors may have contributed to the failure of this effort.

used was a study prepared by the Massachusetts Institute of Technology (MIT) on the financial aspects of deep seabed mining.[69] While its origins lay in student seminar work under the direction of Professor J. D. Nyhart of MIT, the document distributed to the conference was produced under contract to the United States Government. The United States made a substantial effort to establish the credibility of the study and this effort paid off when the Chairman of the negotiating group responsible for resolving the financial arrangements issue selected the study as a primary basis for his analyses.

In April 1978, Ambassador Tommy Koh of Singapore had been appointed Chairman of Negotiating Group 2, which had jurisdiction over the financial arrangements issue.[70] Shortly after assuming that position, he established a smaller Working Group of Technical Experts. It was understood that representatives of specific delegations would participate in the group but that attendance was open to any interested delegation. While the delegates who did attend were not generally as technically qualified as the participants in the Archer group, Koh quickly turned the discussion into a highly technical seminar, and the group as a whole slowly educated itself on the financial issues and potential solutions. Although the discussions periodically lapsed into political rhetoric and some delegations sought to stand on previously taken political positions, most of the time and effort was devoted to a slow and careful analysis of the financial issues. This took place in a relatively collegial atmosphere, which permitted the group to make tangible progress.[71]

It soon became apparent to the participants in the working group that they needed to reach a working understanding of the financial aspects of the deep seabed mining industry. Koh sought information from all sources, but it was the MIT study proffered by the United States that attracted serious attention and developed into the yardstick against which all proposals were measured.

One might question why the MIT study was accepted when the reports to the economic seminars in Caracas and the computer analysis submitted by Canada were not. Certainly, the observation that the MIT study presented the "truth" would beg the question. It appears that the success of the MIT study can be more appropriately attributed to its perceived credibility. The U.S. efforts in this regard were most effective.[72]

[69] J. NYHART, L. ANTRIM, A. CAPSTAFF, A. KOHLER, & D. LESHAW, A COST MODEL OF DEEP OCEAN MINING AND ASSOCIATED REGULATORY ISSUES (Report No. MITSG 78-4, 1978).

[70] UN Doc. A/CONF.62/62, 10 UNCLOS III, OFF. REC. 6 (1978); Note by Ambassador T. T. B. Koh, Chairman of Negotiating Group 2, Conf. Doc. NG2/1 (April 19, 1978) (unpub.); and Oxman, *The Seventh Session, supra* note 10, at 11-13.

[71] Various experts were brought to the group to aid the Chairman and the participating delegations when necessary. Throughout much of its work, the Chairman invited an expert from the United Nations Development Programme (UNDP) to aid in some technical analysis. Assistance was also given by various expert members of participating delegations and the Secretariat. Ambassador Koh made a particular effort to assemble a group of qualified assistants to help him and the Group of Technical Experts to address the relevant issues, and a number of delegations brought with them or were represented by persons expert in the areas under discussion.

[72] At least five factors appear to have contributed to this success. First, the report was presented not as the product of an interested delegation but rather as the product of a highly reputable academic institution with known expertise in the general area. Second, the report did not appear fully to confirm the political positions taken by the sponsoring delegation. In fact, the United States

In the end, the group proved again that the participants in this highly political multilateral negotiation could successfully tackle and resolve the most difficult issues involving a mixture of political and technical issues.[73] The proposals produced by the Koh group contained detailed provisions for the transfer of an appropriate portion of revenue from the exploiters to the Authority. The amount would vary depending upon a number of factors and specific choices to be made by the exploiters. Some of these variables were stage of development, amount of return on investment realized, duration of the activities, and value of resources produced. The terms and concepts used in the proposals were as sophisticated as any provision found in resource development agreements made in the course of international business transactions. No significant difficulty was encountered when the working group's recommendations were incorporated into the new working text.[74]

Other Law of the Sea Conference Issues

Technical questions were not unique to the deep seabed negotiations at the Law of the Sea Conference. They were clearly relevant to the negotiations over the limits of the continental shelf, the delimitation of archipelagic boundaries, the regime for marine living resources, and the regime for the marine environment. Of those four issues only the first, the limits of the continental shelf, proved difficult to resolve. This was due in part to the way relevant technical information was handled.

---

was required to modify some of its positions in light of the findings of the report. Thus, the credibility of the study was further established. Third, the principal author of the study and his technical assistants were made available to the interested delegates and the conference staff for informal discussions and other meetings so that questions could be raised about the report and interested participants could become well informed. The participants were even able to request additional computer analyses from MIT to determine the impact of various proposals and changed assumptions. Fourth, in addition to a readable statement of the ultimate conclusions and the basic reasons for those conclusions, the report contained a full presentation of the details underlying the entire report. Fifth, no other delegation or authority presented an analysis of the potential industry that even approached the level of sophistication of the MIT study. These factors certainly facilitated the acceptance of the study by the working group.

[73] The work of the Koh group is documented in some of the materials issued by NG 2. *See, e.g.*, Note by Ambassador T. T. B. Koh, *supra* note 70; Financial Terms of Contracts, Some Issues and Questions, Conf. Doc. NG2/2 (April 26, 1978); Financial Arrangements of the Authority, Conf. Doc. NG2/4 (May 4, 1978), 10 UNCLOS III, OFF. REC. 54; Financial Terms of Contracts, Explanatory Notes on the Technical Terminology, Conf. Doc. NG2/6 (May 8, 1978), *id.* at 70; Financial Terms of Contracts, The Chairman's Suggested Compromise Proposals, Conf. Doc. NG2/7 (May 12, 1978), *id.* at 58; Financial Terms of Contracts, The Chairman's Explanatory Memorandum on Document NG2/7, Conf. Doc. NG2/8 (May 11, 1978), *id.* at 63; Report of the Chairman of Negotiating Group 2 to the First Committee, Conf. Doc. NG2/9 (May 16, 1978), *id.* at 52; and Second Report by the Chairman of Negotiating Group 2, UN Doc. A/CONF.62/C.1/L.22, 11 UNCLOS III, OFF. REC. 103 (1980). *See also* U.S. Delegation Report, *supra* note 64, at 16–19; U.S. Delegation Report, 8th Sess., *supra* note 66, at 17–22; and U.S. Delegation Report, 9th Sess., *supra* note 66, at 20–21. For a discussion of the negotiation of the financial arrangements issue by the U.S. representative to the Koh group, see Katz, *Financial Arrangements for Seabed Mining Companies: An NIEO Case Study*, 13 J. WORLD TRADE L. 209 (1979).

[74] *See* ICNT/Rev.2, *supra* note 63, Ann. III, Art. 13, and DC, *supra* note 66, Ann. III, Art. 13. *See also* Oxman, *The Eighth Session, supra* note 10, at 13–15.

Limits of the Continental Shelf. One of the major unresolved issues left over from the first United Nations Conference on the Law of the Sea of 1958 was the definition of the exact seaward limit of coastal states' jurisdiction over the adjacent continental shelf.[75] With the rapid development of technology for exploiting hydrocarbons in the oceans, pressure mounted for the resolution of this issue. Thus, it was high on the agenda of UNCLOS III. While the negotiations were largely confined to the search for language to define the geographical limits of the continental shelf regime, at stake were conflicting national interests in the redistribution of wealth, access to hydrocarbons, and territorial control, as well as unspoken questions of military mobility and flexibility.[76] This conflict assured that the issue would be difficult to resolve.

Early in the negotiations it appeared that a fixed-distance limit for the regime of the continental shelf would be strongly resisted by a large number of delegations. Attention then turned to delimitation formulas that took into account the hydrographic contours of the seabed and its geologic characteristics.[77] As

[75] Article 1 of the Convention on the Continental Shelf, *supra* note 12, defines the continental shelf as

> the seabed and subsoil of the submarine areas adjacent to the coast but outside the area of the territorial sea, to a depth of 200 metres or, beyond that limit, to where the depth of the superjacent waters admits of the exploitation of the natural resources of the said areas. . . .

A thorough analysis of the relevant negotiating history is found in Oxman, *The Preparation of Article 1 of the Convention on the Continental Shelf*, 3 J. MAR. L. 245, 445, and 683 (1972).

[76] Some countries wanted to maximize the seaward limits of the continental shelf either to assure their access to valuable hydrocarbons believed to be there or merely to assure national control over a maximum area of seabed. Others, not likely to gain from an expansive definition of the continental shelf, sought a narrow definition, often combined with a demand for the international sharing of revenues to be derived from the continental shelves of all nations. While this latter group included those nations which were seeking a more equitable distribution of the benefits likely to be realized by the few nations with valuable continental shelf resources, there were others with more direct interests. Some of those countries sought a narrow limit in order to contain potential interferences with high seas freedoms; others sought to limit competing production of hydrocarbons.

[77] The early negotiating texts left the limits of the continental shelf vague. ISNT, *supra* note 60, pt. II, Art. 62; RSNT, *supra* note 60, pt. II, Art. 64; ICNT, *supra* note 63, Art. 76. Beginning with the ICNT/Rev.1, the formulation became more technical and specific. ICNT/Rev.1, *supra* note 63, Art. 76; ICNT/Rev.2, *supra* note 63, Art. 76. Although the text remained static for some time, efforts to develop a precise technical definition began at an early date. *See* RSNT, pt. II, Introductory Note by the Chairman of the Second Committee, 5 UNCLOS III, OFF. REC. 152, 153 (1967). *See also* ICNT, Memorandum by the President, *supra* note 67, at 68. Negotiating Group 6 was established at the seventh session of the conference in 1978 to address this issue. The Chairman of the Second Committee, Andrés Aguilar (Venezuela), chaired this negotiating group. Three alternatives, in addition to the formula found in the ICNT, were before the NG 6 at that time. The Irish formula would determine the limit of the continental shelf by first locating the base of the continental slope. The limit of the continental shelf would be located seaward of that point by use of one of two formulas chosen by the coastal state. Under one alternative, the state could claim an additional 60 nautical miles. Under the other, the state could go beyond the base of the continental slope to where the depth of sediments was no less than 1% of the distance between that point and the foot of the slope. Informal Suggestion by Ireland, Article 76, Definition of the Continental Shelf, Conf. Doc. NG6/1 (May 1, 1978). The Arab Group proposed to limit the extent of the continental shelf absolutely to 200 miles from the coastline. Informal Suggestion by the Arab Group, Article 76, Definition of the Continental Shelf, Conf. Doc. NG6/2 (May 11, 1978). The Soviet Union's position was that the limit of the continental shelf should stop at 300 nautical miles. Conf. Doc. C.2/Informal Meeting/14 (April 27, 1978). Those proposals are published in UN Doc. A/CONF.62/C.2/L.99 (1979) at Anns. I–III, 11 UNCLOS III, OFF. REC. 121 (1980). *See generally* Oxman, *The Seventh Session, supra* note 10, at 19–22.

a consequence, it became difficult for many delegations to appreciate the impact that specific boundary formulations would have on the actual limits of the continental shelf. While all could measure a fixed distance from the coastline, few had confidence in their ability to apply formulas that relied on seabed topography and geology. In fact, there was precious little public information on which the necessary calculations could be based. The lack of adequate data was particularly serious for areas adjacent to developing countries where ocean floor surveys had not been conducted. This uncertainty led many delegations to seek information about the actual geographic and resource implications for their countries of the various formulations under consideration.

In the course of the negotiations there were four public attempts to develop maps of the ocean floor that would assist the participants in their understanding of the various boundary formulas under consideration. The United States issued a small-scale map early in the discussions.[78] An attempt to illustrate various proposed boundary formulations was prepared by the UN Secretariat at the request of the conference in 1977.[79] In May of 1978, Bulgaria and the USSR requested that the conference authorize the International Oceanographic Commission to prepare updated and more detailed maps; this request was reluctantly made by the Plenary, but no maps were produced.[80] Finally, the Soviet Union

[78] This map purported to illustrate the seabed gradient of every continental margin, which provided a general picture of the situation but was not very useful for analyzing specific boundary formulas. In the first place, it was of such a small scale that little detailed information could be derived. Second, the map did not provide all the data needed to apply the various formulas under negotiation and to compare their relative impacts. OFFICE OF THE GEOGRAPHER, DEP'T OF STATE, MAJOR TOPOGRAPHIC DIVISIONS OF THE CONTINENTAL MARGINS (Map. No. 78784 8-70).

[79] *See* Preliminary Study Illustrating Various Formulae for the Definition of the Continental Shelf, UN Doc. A/CONF.62/C.2/L.98 and Adds. 1-3 (1978). These maps did illustrate various boundary delimitation formulas. Unfortunately, after they were issued, questions were raised about the accuracy of the assumptions made in their preparation. *See* Study of the Implications of Preparing Large-scale Maps for the Third United Nations Conference on the Law of the Sea, UN Doc. A/CONF.62/C.2/L.99, *supra* note 77. Furthermore, the small scale used made it difficult to appreciate the full impact of various formulas. Since representatives of the expert group that prepared the maps, the Lamont-Doherty Geological Observatory, were not made available to the conference, there was no opportunity for an interchange that might have allayed the doubts of some delegations. Finally, as the negotiations proceeded, changes were made in the boundary formulas under consideration; this caused the utility of these maps to decrease over time. Despite their limitations, these maps were often referred to in the course of the negotiations.

[80] This last request for a series of UN-prepared maps comparing the various formulas was made in May 1978 at the end of the seventh session of the conference. UN Doc. A/CONF.62/SR.103, 9 UNCLOS III, OFF. REC. 65-66 (1980). Mr. Yankov (Bulgaria) suggested that a competent organization be invited to prepare a map of the ocean regions indicating the practical consequences of the various boundary delimitation formulas. The USSR and Bulgaria wanted the International Oceanographic Commission (IOC), a subsidiary organ of UNESCO, to prepare a set of large-scale maps illustrating the current boundary formulas. Unlike the prior requests, this one was actively resisted by some countries, particularly those seeking expansive coastal state jurisdiction. *Id.* at 66-69. Delegations from Australia and Peru questioned the feasibility of the Bulgarian proposal. After some conflict, it was agreed that a phased request would be made to the IOC. *Ibid.* Ultimately, the IOC agreed to prepare the maps, but apparently because of ambiguities in the request and an inadequate data base, it was determined that the maps could not be prepared. *See* UN Doc. A/CONF.62/C.2/L.99, *supra* note 77. The effort was then abandoned. This left the delegates in the position of negotiating boundary formulas whose impacts admittedly could not be determined, at least on the basis of the generally available information.

made a presentation on the boundary issue to all interested delegates at informal meetings that it held for that purpose during the 1979 Geneva session of the conference.[81]

The treatment of this issue varied substantially from that given to technical questions at the deep seabed negotiations. In the instant case no conference committee, formal or informal, directly considered the technical information. Rather, it was treated as information for participating delegations to use in the development of their own positions and in private negotiations. No significant effort was made to explain the bases upon which the maps were prepared or their accuracy. The uncertainty thus permitted to fester, added to the slow and thorny course of these negotiations.

Recently, a political accommodation on the boundary issue was apparently reached.[82] It is not clear, however, what impact was produced by the shift from an approach that could readily be understood by all participants to one that few, if any, fully understood. The presentation of technical formulations created an information gap that produced suspicion. The efforts to fill that gap became a political issue and thus presented further obstacles to negotiation. On the other hand, the increased sophistication of the new formulations may have given the negotiators the tools for creating a compromise solution that would not have been possible under the more simplified approach.

Archipelagoes. One aspect of the archipelagic deliberations at UNCLOS III was the negotiation of rules permitting the archipelagic states to establish extended jurisdictional lines adjacent to their various islands. While the archipelagic states wanted the right to establish zones as they desired, various other states interested in high seas freedoms sought to limit those zones and to limit their impact on those freedoms. Early in the conference the negotiators fastened on an approach that would protect the high seas freedoms sought by the maritime states and would limit the scope of the archipelagic zones by the use of a mathematical formula that took into account the length of the boundary lines and the ratio of water to land within the lines.[83] Various alternative formulations were considered in negotiations among the interested parties and the matter was settled at an early date.[84] The success of this mathematical formulation was in part due to the willingness of the interested delegations to

[81] The Soviet experts brought with them various maps and illustrations with the clear purpose of discrediting the so-called Irish formula for setting the limits of the continental shelf and of defending their own proposal to place an absolute limit on the breadth of the continental shelf at 300 miles. While the Soviet position was forcefully presented, it also appears to have had little impact, perhaps due to the unabashed advocacy nature of the presentation. *See generally* note 77 *supra*.

[82] It is an extremely complex multifactor formula. *See* DC, *supra* note 66, Art. 76.

[83] ISNT, *supra* note 60, pt. II, Arts. 117–131. *See* Hodgson & Smith, *The Informal Single Negotiating Text (Committee II): A Geographic Perspective,* 3 OCEAN DEV. & INT'L L. 225, 241–44 (1976).

[84] Substantively, this text has remained virtually static during the course of UNCLOS III. *See* RSNT, *supra* note 60, pt. II, Arts. 118–127; ICNT, *supra* note 63, Arts. 46–54; ICNT/Rev.1, *supra* note 63, Arts. 46–54; ICNT/Rev.2, *supra* note 63, Arts 46–54; DC(IT), *supra* note 66, Arts. 46–54; and DC, *supra* note 66, Arts. 46–54.

bring their technical experts to the political negotiations. These experts helped to develop the formulas and then applied them to specific geographic areas, which demonstrated to the negotiators the true impact of the proposals under consideration. By facilitating the communication between the technical analysis and the political negotiation, an agreement was reached and the issue was settled, despite the fact that territorial and resource interests were directly at stake. The early resolution of this issue at the conference presents an informative contrast to the continental shelf issue just discussed.[85]

Marine Living Resources and the Marine Environment. The negotiations on marine living resources and the marine environment also involved questions requiring some technical information. While both of these issues met with their share of difficulty at the conference, their technically related aspects do not appear to have significantly contributed to that difficulty. This conclusion can be reached even though little effort was made to deliver such information to the conference. There appear to be at least three reasons for this situation. First, while a full grasp of the subjects in question requires considerable technical knowledge, the general parameters of the relevant data were known by most, if not all, delegations. The necessary information was not closely held. Since there were many knowledgeable persons, there was little possibility that counterproductive suspicions between opposing delegations would be aroused. Second, many international organizations commanded interest and expertise in these subjects, and it was known that they would provide information to any interested delegation. Third, the negotiation of these subjects was kept at a fairly general level, and the task of fashioning more detailed provisions was left to more specialized agencies. In comparison to the issues discussed above, there was less need for the conference to address the technical questions. These three factors combined made it possible to find acceptable formulations without the problems created when technical questions became an issue.

Conclusion

Although technical questions did become central to the deep seabed negotiations, they did not obstruct agreement once the scope of the political settlement was established. In fact, the use of technical information and analysis facilitated agreement. No sources of information used were accepted as unbiased by all participants, and little information was uncontroversial. Nonetheless, the credibility of the sources, techniques of distribution, and availability of experts as explicators of the technical information had a strong influence on its utility. The consideration of technical questions by political representatives and instructed experts appeared to be most successful when moderate-sized informal groups were asked to produce technical information needed either to fill a gap in an already agreed political structure or to help build support for a political solution that was on the verge of being accepted by the participants.

[85] Of course, the limited number of archipelagic states limited the number of geographic conditions to be considered and the number of highly interested parties; also, the formula relied on known geographic information, unlike the later continental shelf formulas.

A similar close integration of technical analyses and political negotiations was successful in the archipelagic line negotiations. In contrast, it can be argued that the failure to integrate the technical analyses into the continental shelf negotiations contributed to the difficulties encountered there. The alternative to addressing the technical issues is to avoid the negotiation of details that require their consideration, which was successfully done in the negotiations on marine living resources and the marine environment—but only by deferring those issues to other forums. Consequently, the agreement is general and avoids most of the tough issues; nevertheless, it provides a basic framework for the development of the necessary details.

Role of Technical Information at Multilateral Negotiations

While the Law of the Sea Conference is unique in many respects, the history discussed above provides an insight into the conduct of modern international negotiations involving technical issues. There appears to be a close relationship between the management of technical issues and substantive results. If the subject is highly technical and a significant number of delegates believe they are underinformed, while others with conflicting interests appear to be better informed, the suspicions thus generated may inhibit progress. Although suspicions may be avoided if the absolute unavailability of the information is established, such a situation may encourage the settlement of issues by forming political coalitions that are artificial and fail to reflect real national and international interests. If the information becomes known at a subsequent date, agreements reached earlier may be destabilized.[86] Similarly, the misuse of technical information may create suspicions that cannot easily be overcome. In short, the management of technical questions requires planning and coordination with the political decisions.

While any number of factors may be relevant to the use of technical information, some may be expected to arise in most negotiations.

Timing of the Negotiations

As discussed above, the timing of the negotiations in relation to the availability and distribution of the essential knowledge is an important factor. Insufficient

[86] It is important to ensure that the information delivered to a conference is accurate. A classic case of a conference that proceeded on the basis of inadequate data is the first United Nations Conference on the Law of the Sea of 1958. The Convention on the Continental Shelf produced by that conference did not establish a definite limit to the continental shelf and no substantial effort was undertaken to fix that limit. *Supra* note 75. The failure to define the limit contributed to the massive expansion of coastal state jurisdiction in the 1960's and 1970's and the calling of UNCLOS III. This omission by the delegates to UNCLOS I occurred because they were led to believe that uses of the seabed at distances and depths beyond the area indisputably within the regime of the continental shelf would not take place for a great many years, if ever. *See* L. Henkin, Law for the Sea's Mineral Resources 4 and 37 (ISHA Monograph No. 1, 1968). Not only was this area reached very quickly, but the then current activities were rapidly approaching those limits. This unfortunate result took place despite the fact that the International Law Commission, which conducted the preparatory work, made efforts to incorporate the relevant data into its work.

consideration was given to this factor at the deep seabed negotiations of the Law of the Sea Conference. They took place, perhaps, at the worst possible time for their successful resolution. In the late 1960's and early 1970's, the industry sought to convince the international community that deep seabed mining would be feasible in the near future. No nation made a serious, independent effort to verify these assertions. In fact, the industry was not yet well developed, and the data were so closely held (or not even available) that it became difficult to separate real national interests from unfounded hopes and fears. National economic interests were identified on the meager basis of these assertions and this led to the early establishment of negotiating positions that bore little relationship to reality or to well-chosen strategic objectives.

The costs imposed by this poor beginning were more than the time and effort needed to set the record straight. The lost initiative damaged the international and domestic credibility of UNCLOS III; that initiative has never been recaptured. Irreversible and, perhaps, unwise decisions taken at the early stages of the negotiations may have contributed to these difficulties.[87] Consequently, the likelihood that nations will accept the final compromises and bring the convention into force has suffered. In addition, this record has raised questions about the utility of similar multilateral negotiations. It will not be known for some time whether the long negotiations permitted a thorough consideration of all issues or merely forced acquiescence in an unworkable system produced by too many hands over too many years.

Alternatives do present themselves: either conduct the negotiations at a very early date when all interests are remote and unfocused,[88] or delay the negotiations until a full consideration of the relevant technical information and national interests is possible. Unfortunately, it is unrealistic to expect nations to be able to control the time period in which a major multilateral legal issue is negotiated. A negotiation might start at an early date, but it would be far more difficult to conclude it during an early time period. Contributing to the delay would be a lack of interest and the press of other business. Yet deferred negotiation might be an equally costly option. It could impose unacceptable costs on the interested parties due to the resulting uncertainties and the absence of an effective legal regime during a critical period. Often it will take decades for interests to ripen fully and for information to become widely available. Cer-

[87] One critical choice was to abandon the joint venture system for exploiting the deep seabed in favor of the so-called parallel system in which state and private business entities would be able to exploit the seabed directly, as would the internationally established Enterprise. While the system does put the two sides in competition, the supporters of both sides will not be willing to accept the demise of their favored side of the system even though the risks of deep seabed mining will be high. The fragility of this arrangement is recognized, and the fact that a single joint venture system was cast aside early in the negotiations has been regretted by some.

[88] While the negotiation of a comprehensive legal regime may be possible at such an early date, a better choice might be to establish a basic legal structure that would facilitate the development of additional parts of the legal regime as required. To some extent, that was the route taken for the Antarctic Treaty of 1959, 402 UNTS 71, 12 UST 794, TIAS No. 4780. *See* Bilder, *The Present Legal and Political Situation in Antarctica,* in THE NEW NATIONALISM, *supra* note 50, at 167. *See generally A Symposium, Antarctic Resources: A New International Challenge,* 33 U. MIAMI L.R. 285 (1978).

tainly, few international issues can be stalled for that length of time. These considerations further support the holding of prenegotiation activities designed to refine the political and legal options. Such refinements might allay pressures for early negotiation. Nevertheless, it is necessary to focus attention on improving the negotiations regardless of their timing.

Scope of the Negotiating Objectives and Solutions

While it may not be feasible to delay the negotiations, it may still be possible to exclude difficult technical issues or to defer them until a more appropriate time. The scope of the negotiating objectives is critical in this regard. Clearly, the objectives that required the most comprehensive and detailed international agreement were pursued at the deep seabed negotiations.[89] More limited objectives could have been chosen, at least as a first step towards a more comprehensive approach.[90]

A more limited approach was successfully taken in the negotiations on marine living resources and the marine environment by deferring resolution of certain technical issues. There are also advantages to deferring issues that require the consideration of unavailable or highly contentious data. Issues that loom large at an early date might be resolved easily once more information is acquired and assimilated.

Solutions to the issues presented at the negotiations should also be tailored to avoid complex technical problems. In the case of the negotiations on the limits of the continental shelf, the decision to turn from the distance criteria and other readily understood factors to more technical esoteric hydrographic and geological factors contributed to the difficulties faced on that question and, perhaps, to the resultant delays.

Management of the Technical Questions

If the resolution of the issues under negotiation requires that technical subjects be considered, attention must be directed to structuring the deliberations so that they can efficiently satisfy the negotiators' needs and facilitate the political discussions. There appear to be three stages in the management of technical questions: the generation of relevant information, its delivery to the negotiators, and its integration into the product of the negotiations. The factors to be considered in evaluating procedures used at all three stages are their credibility and political responsiveness.

[89] *See* text at note 52 *supra.*

[90] The United States seriously considered a simplification of the text in 1978, but the deep seabed mining industry successfully thwarted this effort. At that stage it may have been too late to move away from a detailed text anyway. *See* Oxman, *The Seventh Session, supra* note 10, at 15–16. It is expected that a number of technical issues relevant to deep seabed mining will be delegated to a preparatory commission. DC, *supra* note 66, Art. 308(4). The question of tailoring the scope and content of international agreements to limit risks and to take account of uncertainties is discussed in R. BILDER, *supra* note 2.

Information Generation. While the accuracy of any piece of information or analysis could be debated endlessly, it should be clear that the kind of information dealt with in this article will rarely be accepted as correct strictly on the merits.[91] Such information must obtain political acceptance. Apparently, the more responsive the source of the information is to the needs of the negotiations, the greater the chances are that the information will receive the necessary political acceptance. At the deep seabed negotiations, both the technical formulations developed by a small group to fill specific needs of the negotiators and the calculations of the experts used to negotiate the archipelagic lines found ready acceptance. It was far more difficult to utilize the Secretariat's early studies on the deep seabed regime, perhaps in part because they were not narrowly drawn to respond to specific negotiating requirements.

Thus, a critical question about the generation of such information is the nature of the source. Several choices are generally available: the staff of the international organization sponsoring the negotiations, the staff of other international organizations, experts hired by the sponsoring organization at the request of the negotiators, the participating delegations themselves, experts hired by the participating delegations, and nongovernmental organizations associated with the negotiations. While each of these sources may be appropriate in certain situations, some generalizable observations can be made.[92]

As mentioned above, the acceptance of information often depends on the apparently conflicting balance of credibility and political responsiveness. The ideal source would then appear to be a distinguished organization that is generally known for its accuracy and objectivity and is also closely involved in the negotiations. In a few circumstances this vehicle has been successfully used. Thus, the Scientific Committee on Antarctic Research (SCAR) has served as an important source of information and analysis for the Antarctic Consultative Parties during their more than 20 years of activity.[93] A similar role in the outer

[91] "Neutral disinterested" experts may be available if the negotiation involves a small number of participants and does not concern universal issues. In large negotiations involving the "big" issues, however, sometimes even the appearance of neutrality or independence will be impossible. The absence of neutral players is a significant obstacle to such universal negotiations in many respects. The increased importance of committee chairmen at UNCLOS III is one response to the problem; it is a solution that has had mixed results. Arguably, no scientific and social science information is neutral. M. McDougal, H. Lasswell, & I. Vlasic, *supra* note 3, at 1096; UNESCO, *supra* note 40, at 151; Keohane & Nye, *supra* note 38, at 63; Haas, *Is There a Hole in the Whole? Knowledge, Technology, Interdependence, and the Construction of International Regimes*, 29 Int'l Organization 827, 875 (1975).

[92] The type of information sought is an important variable, *i.e.*, computations, judgment, or compromise. E. Haas, note 7 *supra*, at 105, 110, and 127. No single theory or model will fit all situations. E. Haas, M. Williams, & D. Babai, Scientists and World Order: Uses of Technical Knowledge in International Organizations 335 (1977).

[93] *See, e.g.*, Possible Environmental Effects of Mineral Exploration and Exploitation in Antarctica (J. H. Zumberge ed., 1979); Zumberge, *Potential Mineral Resources Availability and Possible Environmental Problems in Antarctica*, in The New Nationalism, *supra* note 50, at 115; Final Report of the Tenth Antarctic Treaty Consultative Meeting, Ann. 6, Report of the Group of Ecological, Technological and Other Related Experts on Mineral Exploitation and Exploration in Antarctica (1979). The meetings of the Antarctic Consultative Parties are a creature of the Antarctic Treaty, *supra* note 88.

space negotiations has been played by the Committee on Space Research (COSPAR).[94] Since such associations are rare, the utility of this approach is somewhat limited. Absent a comparable continuing affiliation, the use of independent experts would not necessarily commend itself because they would be unlikely to be sensitized to the political forces at work.

While the secretariat of the sponsoring organization might appear to be an ideal vehicle in some circumstances, it may also have limited utility and merit. It might be well atuned to the political dynamics of the negotiations and staffed with qualified personnel. The identification of such a mission for the staff might even make for better utilization of the international organization.[95] The fact that little information is neutral, however, does raise some difficult problems. An obstacle to a successful negotiation could be created if the sponsoring organization were to be perceived as favoring particular participants. The suspicions that can develop and the resulting reluctance to take advantage of the available services of the secretariat can prejudice the course of the negotiations. Clearly, the difficulties faced at the UNCTAD commodity negotiations have been compounded by the overt support for the Group of 77 by the UNCTAD staff.[96] The quickest way for a sponsoring organization to be suspected of active bias is to issue a report that conflicts with the negotiating objectives of a participant in the negotiations. Thus, it may be advisable to limit the sponsoring organization's input to facilitating the negotiations in other ways.

The use of the participating delegations or their governmental staff would assure political responsiveness and, often, a quality product. That product, however, may suffer from credibility problems because it will automaticallv be assumed to be contrived to support the position of the originating government. If the delegation that produces the information is perceived as neutral on the issue, this problem may not arise. Other more involved delegations, however, will have a heavy burden to establish their credibility. The personal reputation and credibility of the individual or agency directly producing the information may help in this regard.

A far better approach in critical situations may be to take advantage of the credibility of an independent research institution. It must be willing to invest

[94] *See* Jessup & Taubenfeld, *The United Nations Ad Hoc Committee on Peaceful Uses of Outer Space,* 53 AJIL 877, 878 (1959); Taubenfeld, *Weather Modification and Control: Some International Legal Implications,* 55 CAL. L. REV. 493, 505 (1967). A similar approach has been recommended in the field of weather and climate modification. S. BROWN, N. CORNELL, L. FABIAN, & E. WEISS, REGIMES FOR THE OCEAN, OUTER SPACE AND WEATHER 237–38 (1977).

[95] E. HAAS, *supra* note 7, at 445; Schachter, *Some Reflections on International Officialdom,* in INTERNATIONAL ORGANIZATION; LAW IN MOVEMENT 53, 61–62 (J. Fawcett & R. Higgins eds. 1974).

[96] Draft Agreement Establishing the Common Fund for Commodities, UN Doc. TD/IPC/CONF/L.15 and Corr. 1 (1980), *reprinted in* 19 ILM 896 (1980). *See* R. ROTHSTEIN, GLOBAL BARGAINING: UNCTAD AND THE QUEST FOR A NEW INTERNATIONAL ECONOMIC ORDER (1979); P. REYNOLDS, INTERNATIONAL COMMODITY AGREEMENTS AND THE COMMON FUND (1978); Wasserman, *UNCTAD: The Common Fund,* 13 J. WORLD TRADE L. 355 (1979). There is a great deal of debate about the economic ramifications of the various commodity agreements. *See generally* A. LAW, INTERNATIONAL COMMODITY AGREEMENTS (1975); D. MCNICOL, COMMODITY AGREEMENTS AND PRICE STABILIZATION: A POLICY ANALYSIS (1978); F. ADAMS & S. KLEIN, STABILIZING WORLD COMMODITY MARKETS (1978).

the time necessary to become familiar with the political situation while still standing behind its product. This approach was notably successful in the case of the MIT report.

Similarly, it may be advisable to encourage more independent expert groups to develop a working knowledge of international negotiations related to their area of expertise, as illustrated by SCAR and COSPAR. Focus could be on long-term negotiations and international organizations. Serious recommendations made to the International Council of Scientific Unions (ICSU) by delegations or the sponsoring international organizations might be the appropriate route to follow in this regard.[97]

Introducing Information into the Negotiation. Equally critical to the use of technical information is its delivery to the negotiators. If the information results from the work of negotiators at the conference, the question, of course, will not arise. Otherwise, the method of delivery must be considered, especially if the information bears on a controversial matter. In this regard, comparison of the Canadian and MIT studies is informative. In the first place, the release of the MIT study appeared to coincide with the time when the political disagreements had narrowed to the point that the technical information could be helpful in resolving the remaining differences.[98] The Canadian study may have been premature, and thus it became embroiled in the more controversial political debate. Second, the MIT study was packaged and introduced to maximize its credibility. Although both were conceived to serve advocacy positions, the aura of credibility surrounding the MIT study certainly facilitated its introduction and ultimate acceptance.[99] Finally, the forums that considered the studies differed substantially. The Canadian study was first discussed at a large Committee I working group, the MIT study at a small informal group of so-called technical experts. Since there was less political conflict in the latter forum, the MIT study probably had a better chance of being sold to the more specialized group as a prelude to tacit acceptance by the remaining participants. Thus, the timing, credibility, and forum would appear to be important considerations.

A more diffuse approach may be more appropriate in certain circumstances. In cases where the information needs are not highly specialized but involve a basic understanding of a new technology or industrial activity, the use of many sources might be commended. Rather than concentrating on the delivery of a single report, multiple sources might be used so that the general level of knowledge is raised and the appearance of a monopoly of information is dispelled. Thus, governments interested in this approach would encourage research and publication by many sources at the international and domestic level and urge conference participants and observers to hold meetings and discussions to consider the relevant information. In part, the early stages of the deep seabed negotiations served that function. In addition, the general press and scholarly publications devoted considerable space to deep seabed mining. The Secretariat's studies contributed to this information flow, and nongovernmental organizations held seminars and other semi-social functions at which deep seabed mining was

[97] *See* Keohane & Nye, *supra* note 38, at 61. [98] *See* Haas, *supra* note 91, at 850.
[99] *See* text at notes 69–74 *supra*.

a topic. Industry representatives participated in informal luncheon clubs and other activities devoted to open discussion of the industry and its technology (within certain limits, of course). Over time this flow of information increased the level of knowledge and may have tempered some of the original hostility.

Evaluating and Integrating Technical Data into the Negotiation. The use of the Technical Experts Group to integrate the MIT study into the negotiations represented one effective method of managing externally generated information. Once the report received the imprimatur of the Chairman and was used by the group itself, it became extremely difficult to challenge both the study and the group's conclusions.[100] Whether such a group will be successful may be largely dependent upon four characteristics: its size, the quality of its leadership, and the procedures adopted.[101]

Thus, the experience of the deep seabed financial arrangements—the route from expert opinion to a technical expert committee of delegates to informal political negotiations and beyond—appears to commend itself. More direct introduction of information may be less time-consuming, but it also presents additional risks. The handling of the financial arrangements issue contrasts dramatically with the continental shelf boundary negotiations. In the latter case, there was never sufficient opportunity to analyze alternative formulas based on the available maps and other data, which contributed to the unnecessarily slow progress made on the issue.

The use of technical working groups at international negotiations is not unique to UNCLOS III. The technique has been used for years—and with notable success—at the meetings of the consultative parties to the Antarctic Treaty, where technical working groups serve as a regular conduit for reports from SCAR and other sources.

An additional lesson can be learned from the Antarctic Consultative Meetings and other successful negotiations involving technical issues: the value of staffing

[100] A similar legitimization experience was observed in the ILO Committee of Experts; E. Haas, *supra* note 7, at 252–59.

[101] The Archer and Koh groups at UNCLOS III were particularly successful. While the reasons for the success of particular negotiating groups may be hard to establish, it is possible to identify some general characteristics that appear to optimize the opportunity for success. In a recent article Barry Buzan identified three characteristics of a successful negotiating group established to address important political issues: size, quality of membership, and quality of leadership. Buzan, *United We Stand, supra* note 10, at 199. With some modification and the addition of a fourth characteristic, this list can be used to identify the salient qualities of a successful negotiating group established to address technical issues:

> (1) *Size*: Preferably between 12 and 30 participants should be included to assure the inclusion of the key interests and necessary experts while permitting operational efficiency.
>
> (2) *Quality of membership*: The group should include persons of high intellectual caliber who represent important interests and others with technical expertise.
>
> (3) *Quality of leadership*: The chairman should be a person of exceptional qualities including personal prestige, mastery of the subject and the political setting, a reputation for impartiality and fair dealing, support from his or her delegation, and a large capacity for work.
>
> (4) *Procedures*: The meetings of the group should be announced to the conference participants but closed to the public and conducted in a relatively informal collegial atmosphere, preferably in one language without a record. The agenda of the group should be well defined and manageable.

delegations with persons qualified in the relevant technical areas. Such experts facilitate the communication of technical information, and therefore its evaluation and possible integration into the negotiations.[102] When the information emanates from a variety of sources, as discussed above, its integration into the negotiations would tend to be more general and less direct than when it is obtained from a single source for limited purposes.

IV. Conclusion

The viability of the pertinent international law is open to question in areas that are subject to the dual pressures of rapid technological advances and efforts to have the entire community of nations actively participate in the development of that law. As a result, the international community is faced with a difficult management problem. The lack of expeditious progress at recent international negotiations and the high risks of failure have created a need to improve these processes. While there appear to be a number of improvements that can be recommended, the realities of the international system limit the possibility for substantial change and improvement. Beneficial results might be obtained from efforts directed at three fronts. First, there is a need to facilitate the early and effective integration into the foreign policy apparatus of information on new technological developments that may require new international law. Second, before the international community is committed to the development of formal international agreements, especially when poorly understood technical matters are involved, considerable time and effort should be devoted to narrowing national differences and the range of legal solutions. International negotiations that drag on for years and regularly court failure are no substitute for deferred negotiations that stand a greater chance of success. Large-scale international negotiations are suffering from a bad press, which directly affects their productivity. If the new technologies and new political realities are to be adequately served by the international community, the international legal system must reestablish its credibility in these areas.

Arguably, the deferral of international negotiations and an improved rate of success may prejudice the NIEO by enabling the developed countries with the technology to shape the law unilaterally. This argument may not be correct. The early commencement of international negotiations does not guarantee, and in fact may not significantly advance, their early or successful conclusion. Rather, the problems created by an early start of negotiations might prove to be counterproductive for all interests. Even the proponents of the NIEO might

[102] While this should be the responsibility of the home governments, there are ways that the conference organizers may encourage the accreditation of technically competent persons. Not only can it be understood that each delegation will have technical support, but the conference structure can make it clear that technically qualified persons will be required for certain conference activities, such as participation in a standing technical committee.

For financial and other legitimate reasons, all nations may not be able to have their own experts in all relevant fields. In such situations nations with similar interests should be encouraged to obtain the necessary expertise jointly. Encouragement and even financial support for these cooperative activities might be given by the appropriate international organizations and forums, *e.g.*, the UNGA, UNCTAD, the Group of 77, regional organizations, and development programs.

be better served by the successful management of prenegotiation activities that develop an international consensus concerning their objectives.

These prenegotiation activities should at least include the following: (1) a serious consideration of the real value of an international agreement as opposed to the development of law through more diffuse methods; (2) a review of the state of the technology that is relevant to the negotiations (relevant factors include its rate of change and the availability of information about it); (3) an examination of the pressures for early agreement, such as commercialization, to determine whether agreement is really needed and whether alternative methods of satisfying the demand can be found; (4) an exploration of procedures that would narrow national differences before the commencement of negotiations; and (5) a determination that participants in the negotiation will be committed to a negotiated settlement rather than a counterproductive exercise in international diplomatic maneuvers.

Finally, the process of generating technical information and integrating it into international negotiations requires the concerted attention of the international community. International law and international negotiations are still at very rudimentary stages of development. Nevertheless, they must respond to the needs of a world that is increasingly shaped by technological developments and sophisticated technical analyses of events. International law and international negotiations must be made capable of responding to these needs and using these tools. This can only be done if international negotiations are organized so that they can make effective use of relevant technical information. A serious part of conference planning should be devoted to defining the scope of negotiating objectives, the composition of delegations, the availability of credible experts, the selection of various negotiating groups of experts, and the manner of distributing relevant information. Unless the international legal system is capable of responding to these requirements, it will become increasingly anachronistic.

NOTES AND COMMENTS

The Warsaw Treaty of 1970 and the Western Boundary of Poland

From time to time voices appear in West German political and legal literature that question and relativize the legal character of the treaties concluded by the Federal Government and the socialist countries as part of the so-called *Ostpolitik*, and especially of the provisions concerning the final regulation of territorial issues. Sometimes these voices are opposed by those who truly accept the policy of normalizing relations with the socialist countries and détente in Europe. Thus, the issue of boundaries provoked vivid discussion in the Federal Republic in 1979 in connection with the publication of new school atlases.[1] The debate also caused tensions during the election campaign for the Bundestag in 1980 and has been continued in foreign periodicals.[2]

It seems reasonable to recall certain facts omitted or distorted by some West German authors and to comment on their interpretation of the legal issues referred to above. Those who argue against the permanent character of the so-called Eastern treaties and their final settlement of territorial questions as foundations of the process of normalization refer mostly to their own Constitution (which they interpret to suit their arguments), to resolutions passed by the Bundestag when the treaties with the USSR and Poland were ratified, and to decisions of the Federal Constitutional Court[3]—that is, to unilateral acts having no binding force for parties to international agreements. A party to a treaty cannot invoke provisions of its internal legislation as justification for its failure to perform the treaty.[4] Nor can it invoke the independence of its judiciary—even on the highest level—when decisions violating provisions of binding international agreements are made.

The main argument, which is intended to serve as a battering ram against

[1] *See* 8 Informationen über Bildungsmedien in der Bundesrepublik Deutschland, Grenzdarstellungen in Schulatlanten (1979), with papers by I. von Münch, J. A. Frowein, and D. Blumenwitz; and the statements of C. E. Langen in Frankfurter Allgemeine Zeitung, Feb. 8, 1979, *Das östliche Deutschland in den Karten der Schulatlanten,* and of many other politicians in Die Welt, Feb. 17–21, 1979 (*Die Grenzen sind provisorisch*). Several authors expressed the view that the Oder-Neisse boundary should be presented in atlases as a "*sui generis*" boundary, different from state boundaries recognized from the point of view of international law.

[2] *See* in particular Arndt, *Legal Problems of the German Eastern Treaties*, 74 AJIL 122 (1980).

[3] Several West German authors have expressed critical opinions about the decisions of the Federal Constitutional Court in international cases. *E.g.,* Professor Frowein states: "The Federal Constitutional Tribunal is the highest German Court which obviously can never interpret the treaties as an international court whose decisions could be binding for both parties" (this and other translations by the author). Europa-Archiv, No. 19, 1979, at 592.

[4] Article 27 of the Vienna Convention on the Law of Treaties of 1969. I. Seidl-Hohenveldern stresses that "[n]o state may refrain from complying with international obligations on the grounds that they contradict its constitution," and cites an American case, Shufeldt v. Republic of Guatemala, 5 ILR 179, 181 (1930). *See* his *Beseitigung der Verfolgungshindernisse für NS-Verbrechen,* Zeitschrift für Rechtspolitik, October 1974, at 226.

the very essence of the normalization treaties, is based on the thesis that the German Reich still exists within the boundaries of 1937. Contrary to the evident fact that the Reich was completely defeated in 1945 and that two independent German Republics, *i.e.*, the Federal Republic of Germany and the German Democratic Republic, were created on its ruins in 1949, the Federal Constitutional Court in its decisions maintains the fiction that the German Reich still exists[5] and enjoys the rights of a subject of public international law (although it has no capacity to undertake legal acts because it lacks state organs).

The Vice-President of the Social Democratic fraction in the Bundestag, Professor H. Ehmke, reproached the supporters of this thesis, stating that they are defending "a legal state of shadows" (*ein juristisches Schattenreich*).[6] It should be added here that none of the 160 states in the world today—including close allies of the Federal Republic—recognizes the continued existence of the German Reich.[7] It ceased to exist as a result of *dismembratio* when two sovereign states were created on its territory, states that have been members of the United Nations for 8 years. Agreements concluded between these states are valid agreements from the point of view of international law, and the boundary between them constitutes a boundary between two independent subjects of international law.

We would also like to recall certain events and legal acts that led to the establishment of a new postwar Polish boundary on the Oder and Neisse Rivers. The armed aggression of the Reich against Poland in 1939, which violated numerous international agreements and the basic principles and norms of the law of war, and the realization on occupied Polish territory of a plan to exterminate its population, which resulted in the death of over six million people, mostly civilians, constituted a severe and flagrant breach of international law for which the German state was responsible to the Polish state. Mainly to compensate Poland, at least in part, for these acts (and for severe material damage, devastation, and plunder of cultural goods), the Three Powers of the anti-Hitler coalition, after lengthy negotiations in Potsdam, decided to transmit the territories east of the Oder and Neisse Rivers to Poland, the first victim of Hitler's aggression and later a significant contributor to the victory over the Third Reich. The separation of the eastern territories was also viewed as a means of depriving Germany of the potential to repeat acts of aggression in

[5] Referring to its former decision, the Federal Constitutional Court stated the following: "The German Reich still exists . . . [and] continues to have legal competence, but because of deficiency in organization, and particularly a lack of institutions, it is not capable of acting." 36 BVerfGE 1, 16 (1974).

[6] Bundestag Minutes (131st mtg.) 10,353 (Jan. 24, 1979).

[7] Frowein states in this case: "The continued existence of the German Reich outside the boundaries of the Federal Republic of Germany is quite artificial from the point of view of international law. The Federal Republic of Germany has no international practice at all to prove such existence." *See* EUROPA-ARCHIV, No. 19, 1979, at 596. And Professor R. Bernhardt stresses: "The national consciousness . . . the implied wish to become reunified cannot eliminate the real fact that the existence of any state requires effective state authority and that for all of Germany such authority has neither existed for the last 35 years nor is it in sight." *See* his *Deutschland nach 30 Jahren Grundgesetz*, in VERÖFFENTLICHUNGEN DER VEREINIGUNG DER DEUTSCHEN STAATSRECHTSLEHRER 16 (1979).

the future and of securing the peace and safety of its eastern neighbors, which constitute a permanent object of German expansionism (*Drang nach Osten*). Moreover, the Allies generally felt at Potsdam that there was an organic connection between the security of Poland and the security and peace of Europe and the world.

The total defeat of the Third Reich and its unconditional surrender enabled the Allies to enforce Germany's responsibility for acts of aggression against Poland and other states, as well as for damages inflicted on them by Germany's flagrant violation of the laws of war. The author of the formula "unconditional surrender," U.S. President Roosevelt, proposed it to Prime Minister Churchill at Casablanca on October 24, 1943. It was later accepted as a common goal by the Allies and proclaimed a way to end the war with the Axis states. From Allied documents of the period, it appears that unconditional surrender meant "no negotiated peace," and as such excluded the possibility of any talks with the Fascist Governments of the Axis.[8] In other words, unilaterally established terms of peace were to be dictated by the Allies after the unconditional surrender of the Axis. Germany's unconditional surrender on May 8, 1945 was not a military surrender exclusively, as some West German authors claim, even though its armed forces were completely defeated; it was also an unconditional surrender by the German Government and state.[9]

In the Act of Military Surrender of May 8, 1945, which deals first of all with matters concerning the surrender of the German armed forces, paragraph 4 states the following: "This act of military surrender is without prejudice to, and will be superseded by any general instrument of surrender imposed by, or on behalf of the United Nations and applicable to Germany and the German armed forces as a whole." Such an instrument was the Declaration signed a month later at Berlin, on June 5, in which the Governments of the Four Powers "assumed supreme authority with respect to Germany, including all the powers possessed by the German Government, the High Command and any state, municipal or local government or authority." These rights, significantly greater in extent than those of an occupying power envisaged in the fourth Hague Convention of 1907, are closely connected to the unconditional surrender of Germany. In the above-mentioned Berlin Declaration, the Four Powers also declared that they "will hereafter determine the boundaries of Germany or any part thereof and the status of Germany or of any area at present being part of German territory." It was thus a distinct announcement that the victorious

[8] In a note to the British Government of Jan. 14, 1944, Churchill explained that

> [b]y "unconditional surrender" I mean that the Germans have no right to any particular form of treatment. . . . For instance, the Atlantic Charter would not apply to them as a matter of right. On the other hand, the victorious nations owe it to themselves to observe the obligations of humanity and civilisation.

See his 4 THE SECOND WORLD WAR: THE HINGE OF FATE 689 (1950).

[9] In a declaration of the Federal Government of Oct. 21, 1949, Adenauer stated in the Bundestag: "The tragedy of the German nation did not commence only in 1945 after its surrender, which unconditionally transferred all military and state power to the conquerors, but in 1933 when Hitler came to power." *See* introduction and presentation of Ingo von Münch, in DOKUMENTE DES GETEILTEN DEUTSCHLAND 202 (1968).

powers meant to diminish the territory of Germany after its unconditional surrender, an intention that was realized by the Potsdam Agreement of August 2, 1945.

It seems worth recalling that the intention to reduce German territory after its defeat could not have been a surprise to Germany. During the conference of the Three Powers at Yalta, which ended on February 11, 1945, almost 3 months before the surrender of the Reich, these powers declared *expressis verbis*: "We have agreed on common policies and plans for enforcing the unconditional surrender terms which we shall impose together on Nazi Germany after German armed resistance has been finally crushed"; and "We recognize that Poland must receive substantial accession of territory in the North and West." The Allies' intention substantially to reduce German territory in favor of Poland was thus known to the Government of the Reich when it was forced to sign the act of unconditional surrender.

The formal decision to separate the German territories east of the Oder and Neisse Rivers and to transmit them to Poland and the USSR was made in the Potsdam Agreement.[10] The territories transmitted to Poland were characterized as "former German territories," which proves that the signatories of the Agreement had decided to separate them permanently from Germany. Moreover, unlike the remaining German territory, these areas were not subjected to occupation by the Four Powers, occupation by nature being temporary only, but to the administration of Poland,[11] which introduced legislation, established organs of authority, and incorporated the areas into the rest of its territory in order to exercise its sovereignty. At the time, not a single state protested or even expressed reservations about these acts by Poland. Clear approval by some states and the lack of protest by others could only have amounted to the tacit consent of the international community to the permanent incorporation of these areas into the Polish state.

The best proof of the final, rather than provisional, character of this separation of certain territories from Germany is the parallel decision, also made by the Three Powers at Potsdam, to transfer the German population still remaining in Poland to Germany (chapter XIII of the Potsdam Agreement). This transfer applied to Germans both in prewar Polish territories and in areas accorded to Poland by the Potsdam Agreement. It was carried out with the

[10] Referring to decisions made in Yalta, the three heads of government agreed that

> the former German territories east of a line running from the Baltic Sea . . . and thence along the Oder River to the confluence of the eastern Neisse River and along the Western Neisse to the Czechoslovak frontier, including that portion of East Prussia not placed under the administration of the USSR . . . and including the area of the former free city of Danzig, shall be under the administration of the Polish State [with a reservation that] the three Heads of Government reaffirm their opinion that the final delimitation of the western frontier of Poland should await the peace settlement.

[11] Professor M. Lachs (member of the International Court of Justice) writes: " 'Administration' therefore, as opposed to 'occupation' implied the permanent character of the authority concerned, thus becoming an equivalent to the word 'sovereignty'. And it cannot be denied that it has been frequently used in the past to convey this meaning." THE POLISH-GERMAN FRONTIER: LAW, LIFE AND LOGIC OF HISTORY 21 (Warsaw 1964).

complete understanding of the Allied Control Council in Germany and was obviously meant to be irreversible. It would be absurd to suggest that the Allies would have decided on so meaningful an action as the transfer of millions of people only to allow it to be repeated later in the other direction.

The question arises: What was the meaning of the formula contained in the Potsdam Agreement that the "final delimitation of the western frontier of Poland should await the peace settlement"? This type of statement is used in preliminary treaties to ensure that insignificant corrections of boundary lines can be effected later on the basis of local conditions. Similar statements were also contained in the armistice agreements with former allies of the Reich when they dealt with territorial changes. The peace treaties that were concluded afterward only confirmed the provisions on boundaries contained in the armistice agreements (with Italy, Finland, and Hungary).

In the absence of a peace treaty with Germany, on July 5, 1950, Poland concluded with the GDR, *i.e.*, the German state established in the eastern part of the former Reich, the Agreement Concerning the Demarcation of the Established and the Existing Polish-German State Frontier. The Agreement stated that both parties, "wishing to stabilize and strengthen mutual relations on the basis of the Potsdam Agreement which established the frontier on the Oder and the Western Neisse," recognize the frontier as "an inviolable frontier of peace and friendship which does not divide but unites the two peoples." Recognition by the GDR of the boundary on the Oder and Neisse Rivers established by the Potsdam Agreement constituted "the peace settlement" mentioned in that Agreement. It is of fundamental importance because it was an act of the German state that succeeded the Reich, whose eastern border is constituted by the line along the Oder and Neisse Rivers. For 20 years until 1970, the second German state, the FRG, although it has no common frontier with Poland, raised reservations about the western border of Poland and the Zgorzelec Agreement between Poland and the GDR. According to the West German Government of the time, which claimed to represent the whole German nation (*Alleinvertretungsanspruch*),[12] the GDR was not entitled to conclude treaties concerning German territory. It should be added that without waiting for a peace treaty, the Federal Government itself concluded several treaties concerning the boundaries (*i.e.*, small areas) with some of its neighbors.[13] At any rate, the FRG's questioning of the state character of the GDR and its right to conclude international agreements became pointless after the Basic Treaty between the two German states was concluded.

[12] Incidentally speaking, those claims were not shared by many states. Thus, *e.g.*, the British Foreign Secretary explained in 1964 that a tripartite statement by the United States, the United Kingdom, and France of 1950 did "not constitute recognition of the Government of the Federal Republic as the de jure Government of all Germany," as cited by K. Skubiszewski in *Poland's Western Frontier and the 1970 Treaties,* 67 AJIL 23, 26 (1973).

[13] With France, the Netherlands, Luxembourg, and Belgium. The final Protocol of Sept. 24, 1956 to the Treaty with the latter concerning correction of the frontier (*Grenzberichtigungsvertrag*) reads as follows: "In signing this Treaty the Government of the Federal Republic of Germany and the Royal Government of Belgium have agreed to consider the boundary established under this Treaty as final for both Parties." Cited by Frowein in his *Stellungnahme zu dem Beitrag von Prof. Dr. D. Blumenwitz, supra* note 1, at 50.

On December 7, 1970, the Treaty between Poland and the FRG concerning the Basis for Normalization of their Mutual Relations was signed in Warsaw.[14] The parties agreed

> that the existing frontier, which, in accordance with chapter IX of the decisions of the Potsdam Conference of 2 August 1945, runs from the Baltic Sea immediately west of Świnoujście along the Odra [Oder] River to the point of junction with the Nysa Łużycka [Lausitzer Neisse] River and along . . . [this river] to the frontier with Czechoslovakia, constitutes the western State frontier of the Polish People's Republic.

It should be stressed that the description of the western Polish frontier contained in the Warsaw Treaty of 1970 is identical to the one contained in the Potsdam Agreement of 1945 and the Zgorzelec Agreement of 1950. This confirmation is important. The territorial question is crucial for the Treaty of Warsaw and that is why the parties deal with it in Article I of the Treaty.[15] Recognition by the FRG of the Oder-Neisse line as a state frontier of Poland was considered a *conditio sine qua non* for initiation of the process of normalization between the states.

Some West German authors express the opinion—and do it quite earnestly!—that in due time the great powers of the anti-Hitler coalition decided to maintain and even guarantee the prewar German frontiers of 1937.[16] However, the authors of this thesis have forgotten to justify or at least to make it seem plausible that those powers would respect and even guarantee the inviolability of the state territory of an aggressor after its defeat and surrender, when during the war (*durante bello*) Germany had unilaterally annexed a number of areas of European countries. For example, by the decree of October 9, 1939, Hitler annexed the so-called *eingegliederte Ostgebiete*, almost a hundred thousand square kilometers, which comprised truly Polish areas that had never belonged to Germany, parts of France and Belgium, and all of Luxembourg. Germany had also announced that if it won the war, it would annex more areas belonging to European countries, especially vast territories in the east (the Ukraine, Crimea, the Caucasus, and the Baltic area). In addition, a number of official pronouncements by states in the anti-Hitler coalition as well as treaties contradict this thesis. They indicate clearly that the intention was to reduce the territory of Germany after its defeat in favor of the victims of its aggression (*e.g.*, the Report of the Crimea Conference of February 11, 1945).

[14] 830 UNTS 327.

[15] A statement of Arndt, *supra* note 2, at 128 ("[d]uring the negotiations . . . , Poland regarded the question of its western boundary as the most important . . . and therefore insisted that it be dealt with in the first article. A compromise was worked out . . . after the Polish Government yielded . . . to accept the renunciation of force as the paramount commitment by placing it in the preamble, even before Article I") seems to be a misunderstanding. In reality, the question of renunciation of force is dealt with in Article II of the Warsaw Treaty, and there is nothing about it in the short preamble, which ends with the following formula: "Conscious of the fact that the inviolability of the frontiers of all European States and respect for their territorial integrity and sovereignty within their present frontiers are a basic condition for peace."

[16] *See, e.g.*, Blumenwitz, *Die Darstellung der Grenzen Deutschlands in Schulatlanten*, in 8 INFORMATIONEN ÜBER BILDUNGSMEDIEN, *supra* note 1, at 28 *ff*.

It is also worth mentioning that the same treatment, *i.e.*, considerable reduction of territory in favor of the victims of aggression, was applied to other Axis states. Moreover, these reductions did not result from negotiations with the defeated states, since territorial clauses had already been fixed by the Allied powers and given effect in the pretreaty proceedings at the moment of those states' surrender. Thus, Japan emerged from World War II with significant territorial losses: almost half of its prewar territory (about three hundred thousand kilometers) was separated from it. Italy, Finland, and Hungary also sustained territorial losses. In all these cases the decision of the Three Powers was made before the surrender. Later acts, prepared with the participation of the defeated as armistices or eventually peace treaties, only served as formal confirmation of decisions taken by the Three Powers.[17]

It should be added that the peace treaties concluded in 1947 with the former European allies of the Reich provided that the treaties would enter into force after their ratification by the victorious powers, and that ratification (*i.e.*, consent) by the defeated state was not necessary.[18] There is no reason to suppose that less severe measures were contemplated for the German Reich, the main power of the Axis, since Germany indeed bore greater fault in beginning World War II, not to mention its engagement in lawless and extreme conduct. Acts of the coalition during the period 1944–1945 prove quite the opposite.

A number of West German authors often claim that like other decisions made by the Three Powers at the end of World War II or directly thereafter, the Potsdam Agreement is not binding on the FRG because it was not a participant. The Agreement would thus constitute for the FRG *res inter alios actae*.[19] The fact is that the FRG did not take part in the Potsdam Conference for the simple reason that this Republic did not yet exist; it was created 4 years later. No one should forget that German representatives were totally excluded from Potsdam although a number of decisions of vital importance to Germany's future were made there. This situation resulted from the unconditional surrender of the Reich and the assumption of supreme authority over Germany by the Governments of the Four Powers. On the basis of the Berlin Declaration of June 5, 1945, the Potsdam Agreement was considered binding by the German Democratic Republic. The FRG, on the other hand, from the very moment of its creation claimed to be a successor of the German Reich and for a long

[17] As a French author remarks, by the peace treaties of 1947 the defeated countries

> ont été obligées de consentir, soit sous la forme de la *cession*, soit sous celle de la *reconnaissance*, aux abandons de territoire imposés par les vainqueurs. La différence entre le règlement de paix prévu pour l'Allemagne et les *traités de paix* avec . . . les anciens pays satellites de l'Axe ne résidait donc pas, pour ce qui est des clauses territoriales, dans la négociation: dans les deux cas, les décisions arrêtées par les Alliés n'étaient pas négociables.

Meyrowitz, *Le Traité de Varsovie du 7 décembre 1970,* 75 REV. GÉNÉRALE DROIT INT'L PUBLIC 944, 974 n.53 (1971).

[18] Article 90 of the Peace Treaty with Italy of 1947 reads: "The present Treaty . . . shall be ratified by the Allied and Associated Powers. It shall also be ratified by Italy. It shall come into force immediately upon the deposit of ratification by the USSR, the UK, the USA, and by France. . . ." Identical statements are contained in other peace treaties of 1947, *e.g.*, with Hungary (Art. 42) and Finland (Art. 36).

[19] Arndt, *supra* note 2, at 129–30.

time identified itself as the sole successor. Thus, one could conclude that it took over not only the rights but also the responsibilities resulting from Germany's unconditional surrender and the Potsdam decisions taken in consequence of that surrender. It is beyond comprehension how the FRG can question the binding character of the Potsdam decisions and other Allied resolutions because they were taken in the absence of German representatives, and at the same time invoke other actions in which it obviously took no part either (*e.g.,* concerning Berlin). The thesis that the decisions on Germany made by the victorious powers are nonbinding as far as the FRG is concerned, and simultaneous selective acceptance of some of these decisions, could mean that the respective Allied treaties have constituted *pacta in favorem tertii, i.e.,* that they were concluded in favor of Germany or its legal successors.[20] However, such reasoning leads to absurdity. It is sufficient to recall some provisions on Germany in the Potsdam Agreement (chapter III):

> The Allied Armies are in occupation of the whole of Germany and the German people have begun to atone for the terrible crimes committed under the leadership of those whom in the hour of their success, they openly approved and blindly obeyed.
>
> . . . .
>
> . . . [T]he Allies will take in agreement together, now and in the future, the other measures necessary to assure that Germany never again will threaten her neighbors or the peace of the world.
>
> . . . .
>
> 3. The purposes of occupation of Germany . . . are:
>
> . . . .
>
> (ii) To convince the German people that they have suffered a total military defeat and that they cannot escape responsibility for what they have brought upon themselves, since their own ruthless warfare and the fanatical Nazi resistance have destroyed German economy and made chaos and suffering inevitable.

The entire Potsdam Agreement of 1945, and especially its chapter III entitled "Germany," gives no reason to conclude that the parties intended to accord rights to defeated Germany, which had signed an unconditional surrender.

The fact that former German areas east of the Oder-Neisse line now belong to Poland and the USSR is sometimes contested in the FRG in connection with certain terms of the Potsdam Agreement (however, in other cases its binding force is recognized by the FRG!), such as "the final delimitation of the frontier should await a peace settlement." Professor J. A. Frowein believes that the fact that rights were made subject to an eventual peace treaty (*Friedensvertragsvorbehalt*) dissolves the obligation the FRG assumed in Article I of the Warsaw

[20] Professor Menzel points out this contradiction: "It is somewhat strange that we refer to the Potsdam Agreement which we used to ignore and considered as *res inter alios gesta*. When referring to a peace settlement this Potsdam Agreement suddenly becomes attractive and we treat it as a treaty *in favorem tertii.*" OSTVERTRÄGE-BERLIN-STATUS-MÜNCHNER ABKOMMEN-BEZIEHUNGEN ZWISCHEN DER BRD UND DER DDR. VORTRÄGE UND DISKUSSIONEN EINES SYMPOSIUMS VON MÄRZ 1971, at 134 (Veröffentlichungen des Instituts für Internationales Recht an der Universität Kiel, 1971).

Treaty of 1970.[21] It is well known that although more than 35 years have passed since the end of the war, no peace treaty has ever been concluded with Germany. In the meantime, all those matters ordinarily regulated by peace treaties were settled with both German states, the legal successors of the Reich (territorial and military questions, reparations, war criminals, etc.). No genuine politician in the FRG or anywhere else in the world truly believes nowadays that such a treaty will ever be concluded with Germany or its successors. Postwar international practice, involving over a hundred more or less significant armed conflicts, proves that they are not ended by peace treaties.[22] We must also remember that territorial questions were settled by the common decision of the victorious powers, which was dictated to the defeated Axis states after World War II and that the peace treaties concluded later only formally approved those previous decisions.[23]

The rights and responsibilities of the Four Powers are often invoked in the FRG, as well as their "duty" to ensure the unification of Germany within the frontiers of 1937, as they had allegedly guaranteed. But Allied documents for the period 1944–1945 show that the powers reserved for themselves only those rights towards defeated Germany which would guarantee that it would never again be able to violate the peace or endanger the security of its neighbors. In the report of the Crimea Conference of February 11, 1945, the heads of government of the Three Powers declared: "It is our inflexible purpose to destroy German militarism and nazism and to insure that Germany will never again be able to disturb the peace of the world."[24] All the actions of the Allies after Germany's surrender pursued these ends. Neither the state nor the German nation was ever a party to these actions.

In the Potsdam Agreement the Allies declared that after the de-Nazification, demilitarization, and democratization of Germany, they intended to set up certain essential central administrative departments under the direction of the Allied Control Council, which would lead to step-by-step reconstruction of the

[21] Although Frowein was of the opinion that

> in accordance with Article I of the Warsaw Treaty the Oder-Neisse boundary is for the Federal Republic of Germany explicitly the state frontier between Poland and the GDR. The territory to the east of this frontier is Polish state territory . . . and the so-called peace treaty reservation [*Friedensvertragsvorbehalt*] is in this respect for the FRG a condition that dissolves the obligation assumed under Article I of the Warsaw Treaty.

See EUROPA-ARCHIV, No. 19, 1979, at 591–92.

[22] As von Münch remarks: "Contemporary wars are rarely ended by peace treaties." *See* his *Abnormalitäten der Normalisierung—Gedanken zum deutsch-polnischen Verhältnis,* LIBERAL, No. 7–8 (1979).

[23] According to a French author:

> Le système de la déclaration de Berlin du 5 juin 1945 et celui de l'accord de Potsdam excluaient . . . le consentement de l'Allemagne. Sous l'angle de l'accord de Potsdam, les deux Etats allemands actuels . . . ne sauraient avoir plus de droits que n'aurait possédé un gouvernement central allemand, s'il avait pu être constitué à l'époque.

Meyrowitz, *supra* note 17, at 981.

[24] A similar formula is contained in the Potsdam Agreement: "The Allies will take . . . measures necessary to assure that Germany never again will threaten her neighbors or the peace of the world."

German state (chapters III and IV of the Agreement). This declaration created no duty or responsibility for the Allies towards Germany, which was not a party to the Potsdam Agreement. This plan was later abandoned because of the French Government's disapproval. Plans to restore the unity of the German state were scuttled by the Anglo-Saxon powers when they established the "bi-zonia," and later the "tri-zonia," and finally by the establishment in 1949 of the Federal Republic of Germany in the western part of the former Reich. Influential political circles of the FRG played an active role in this division of Germany (under the slogan "freedom before unity," *Freiheit vor Einheit*). At present, considering the development of the international situation and the admission of two sovereign German Republics, *i.e.,* the GDR and the FRG, into the United Nations as peace-loving countries (Article 4 of the Charter), as well as the fact that their mutual relations and relations with other states in this Organization are based on the principle of "sovereign equality," the rights of the Allied powers are naturally considerably limited. Rights other than those concerning West Berlin consist in their guarantee that security will not be endangered or the peace violated in Central Europe.[25] In practice, the rights of the Allied powers in this domain may be realized within the Security Council, the UN organ with primary competence in matters concerning peace and security, of which the former partners in the anti-Hitler coalition are permanent members.

One of the main arguments put forth in the FRG against the final settlement of the Oder-Neisse border is that a guarantee concerning this border was given by the FRG only in its own behalf and that it will be valid only as long as this state exists. But every state, not only the FRG, has the right to incur international obligations only on its own behalf. Attempts by the Federal Government in the past to act on behalf of all of Germany have always been rejected by Poland and many other states. From the point of view of international law, the notion that the territorial obligations of the FRG would not be binding on a united German state is erroneous, since when two states are unified, their frontiers with neighboring states do not change. Thus, the formation of the German Empire in 1871 did not involve any change in the frontiers of the acceding states with their foreign neighbors.

In the present case, both German Republics, the legal successors to the former German Reich, recognized in freely negotiated agreements with Poland that the border on the Oder and Neisse Rivers constitutes the western frontier of Poland (the Zgorzelec Agreement of 1950 with the GDR and the Warsaw Treaty of 1970 with the FRG). The thesis, developed in the FRG during the Cold War period, that it is the responsibility and duty of the Allies to reconstruct the unity of Germany finds no support in the documents of the war period and is one of many equilibristic concepts that have emanated from the FRG and constitute a source of illusions only.[26] Could the Allied powers—notwithstand-

[25] In a mutual exchange of Declarations before signing the Moscow Treaty, both parties expressed agreement that "the remaining rights of the Four Powers in Germany . . . would not be affected by the Moscow Treaty." Thus, they were talking only about rights, not of duties or responsibilities.

[26] As Frowein states: "There is no doubt from the point of view of international law that the four victorious powers in World War II still have the legal ability to participate in the decisions concerning a possible general settlement for Germany." *See* his *Die deutsche Grenzen im völkerrechtlichen Sicht,* in INFORMATIONEN ÜBER BILDUNGSMEDIEN, *supra* note 1, at 22.

ing the fact that they belong to two antagonistic military and political camps—enforce unification upon two sovereign German states, members of the United Nations, if both of them or even only one of them resists? Can one speak now with all seriousness about limiting the rights of the FRG in accordance with the "responsibilities" of these powers, as do some authors in the FRG, and even about enlarging those limitations?[27] As was pointed out, the FRG, which sometimes attempts to act on behalf of all of Germany, now fails to execute responsibilities it has undertaken. One may ask with Skubiszewski, "if the Federal Republic is identical with the all-German state, which in some mysterious way still leads an abstract existence, how can it deny that its treaties will apply to that state when one day it becomes endowed with an actual government?"[28] The allusion of those West German circles to the possibility that revision of the boundaries with their neighbors will become the order of the day if the two German states are unified must naturally keep a policy of territorial revisionism alive in the FRG. Such attitudes can make difficult—if not totally destroy—the already very slight, unrealistic prospects for the unification of Germany.[29]

LUDWIK GELBERG*

[27] As Rauschning states:

> Despite the authority reserved by the Allied powers, the Federal Republic of Germany is not so incapable of acting that it cannot for its own part declare recognition or waiver. . . . On the other hand, it should not be expected that the Western powers could now or at any time in the future defend German territorial claims given up by the German Government itself. Accordingly, reference to the competence or reserved authority of the Allied powers is not an appropriate basis for questioning the finality of the territorial settlements of the Warsaw Treaty.

See OSTVERTRÄGE, *supra* note 20, at 166.

[28] Skubiszewski, *supra* note 12, at 26. Frowein also points out these contradictions:

> On the one hand, the Federal Republic of Germany cannot while concluding the Warsaw Treaty make a declaration effective in light of international law that it is not able to act for all-Germany but for itself and on the other hand, when carrying out the Treaty provisions claim that it defends, to a certain degree, the interests of the German Reich since the boundaries of the German Reich exceed the territory of the FRG. This would be a contradiction that could not be solved.

Frowein, *supra* note 7, at 595.

[29] As was correctly pointed out by the Vice-President of the SPD parliamentary fraction, Professor H. Ehmke, on Jan. 24, 1979 in the Bundestag: "I am convinced that neither our Western nor our Eastern neighbors would be ready for anything as far as the German division is concerned if it was not clear that the present western frontier of Poland would remain as it is." Bundestag Minutes, *supra* note 6, at 10,356.

* Professor of International Law, Polish Academy of Sciences.

THE GOOD OFFICES OF THE UNITED NATIONS SECRETARY-GENERAL IN THE FIELD OF HUMAN RIGHTS

INTRODUCTION

At the end of his term of office, the late Secretary-General U Thant lamented "the great humanitarian emergencies which the United Nations is still not equipped to meet" and underlined the principle that "the Secretary-General's obligations under the Charter must include any humanitarian action that he can take to save the lives of large numbers of human beings."[1] Similarly, in his first annual report to the General Assembly, in 1972, Secretary-General Waldheim asserted that "the unwritten moral responsibility which every Secretary-General bears does not allow him to turn a blind eye when innocent civilian lives are placed in jeopardy on a large scale."[2] He amplified this principle in his annual report of 1980, where he stated that "I have always regarded it as my duty to exercise my good offices in human rights matters and I shall continue to assist in any way I can."[3]

One of the major weaknesses in the arrangements of the United Nations for promoting and protecting human rights is the lack of adequate methods for dealing with urgent situations of violations of human rights. Consequently, the international community invariably looks to the Secretary-General of the United Nations to fill the breach by interceding discreetly on a humanitarian basis. Often, such intercession by the Secretary-General is the only form of response available and acceptable.

In customary international law, "humanitarian intercession" indicated a friendly interposition by a government or other international actor aimed at inducing another government or authority to treat persons under its jurisdiction with respect for the principles of humanity. As opposed to "diplomatic intercession of a humanitarian nature on behalf of certain foreign nationals," Sohn and Buergenthal distinguish "forcible intervention by States to protect their own nationals" and "forcible intervention to protect the nationals of the State against which the intervention has been launched." State practice shows that humanitarian intercession and good offices were intertwined. Thus, Sohn and Buergenthal cite as evidence of the practice of humanitarian intercession U.S. diplomatic correspondence involving requests to the President of the United States "to exercise his good offices in behalf of the oppressed people of Armenia."[4]

In contemporary practice the term "good offices" is usually employed to refer

[1] U Thant, *The Role of the Secretary-General, infra* note 11, at 185. *See also* U THANT, VIEW FROM THE UNITED NATIONS 27 (1978).

[2] UN Doc. A/8701/Add.1, section IX (1972).

[3] UN Doc. A/35/1, section IX (1980).

[4] L. SOHN & T. BUERGENTHAL, INTERNATIONAL PROTECTION OF HUMAN RIGHTS 179, 182 (1973). *See also* R. LILLICH & F. NEWMAN, INTERNATIONAL HUMAN RIGHTS: PROBLEMS OF LAW AND POLICY 485–544 (1979); O. Strauss, *Humanitarian Diplomacy of the United States*, 6 ASIL, PROC. 45–54 (1912).

to humanitarian intercessions by the Secretary-General. But good offices traditionally developed in the area of the settlement of international disputes, and the extension of the term to the humanitarian field has not been without challenge. Thus, at the 35th session of the United Nations General Assembly, in 1980, when a wide-ranging debate took place on good offices in the field of human rights, it was contended that good offices were properly used by the Secretary-General "only when his action had a bearing on international peace and security" and that "good offices constituted a means for the settlement of disputes and presupposed at least two parties agreeing to their use."

On the other hand, it was pointed out that in the field of human rights the good offices role of the Secretary-General had generally been recognized for a long time, and reference was made to a UN press release issued on April 29, 1967 announcing that the Permanent Representatives of Poland and Czechoslovakia, on behalf of a group of socialist countries, had requested that the Secretary-General use his "good offices" with a view to ending persecutions in Greece and to preventing the possible execution of political leaders who had been detained.[5] This debate took place over a draft resolution submitted by the delegation of Canada, which was aimed at developing the full potential of the good offices role of the Secretary-General to enable the United Nations system to cope more adequately with situations of mass and flagrant violations of human rights.[6] Eventually, the Third Committee of the General Assembly decided, on a procedural motion, not to vote on the draft resolution. The general view in the committee was that the Secretary-General should be left free to decide on the manner and modalities of the exercise of good offices in the field of human rights and that the function should not be restricted or regulated in any way.[7]

In view of this reluctance of some states to "legislate" on the subject, it follows necessarily that the nature and characteristics of the concept of good offices in the field of human rights must be determined by reference to the relevant international practice and to such rules or principles of international customary law as may have emerged from that practice. An examination of the relevant rules and practice will be attempted in the following pages. It will be submitted that the exercise by the Secretary-General of good offices in the field of human rights has become part of international customary law.

I. The Nature of Good Offices Regarding Human Rights

In their traditional meaning, good offices "consist in a third party—Government, international organization, individual—attempting to bring conflicting parties to a negotiating table without interfering in the negotiation themselves."[8]

[5] *See* UN Press Release SG/SM/699, April 29, 1967.

[6] UN Doc. A/C.3/35/L.78 (1980).

[7] For the records of the discussion, see UN Doc. A/C.3/35/SR.56–62 (1980).

[8] V. Pechota, The Quiet Approach: A Study of the Good Offices Exercised by the Secretary-General in the Cause of Peace 13 (UNITAR 1972). *See* similarly Darwin, *Mediation and Good Offices*, in International Disputes: The Legal Aspects 83 (Report of a Study Group of the David Davies Memorial Institute of International Studies, 1972). *Cf.* ch. III (Good offices), Art. 10(1), of the Second Report on the Peaceful Settlement of International Disputes, in International Law Association, Report of the 56th Conference 43, 48 (1974).

Good offices as a means of settling international disputes have a long history among the instruments of diplomacy. In more recent times the concept may be traced to Articles 2 and 3 of the Hague Conventions of 1899 and 1907 on the Pacific Settlement of Disputes.

As a method for furthering peaceful solutions of international disputes, the good offices of the Secretary-General have been defined by Pechota as "the informal contacts and friendly suggestions made as far as circumstances allow by the Secretary-General, which are designed to facilitate the settlement of a dispute between two or several of the Organization's Member States."[9] The same writer classifies the good offices of the Secretary-General into: (1) forms of diplomatic assistance such as informal contacts and consultations with parties to a dispute; (2) diplomatic action designed to express international concern, to induce the parties into talks before a favorable atmosphere fades away or before they reach a point of no return, and to assist them in finding a suitable framework for settlement; (3) mediation, conciliation, and coordination; and (4) inquiries, fact-finding, the supervision of plebiscites, elections, or referenda, and the determination of legal rights and duties in a specific situation. Within the third category, namely mediation, conciliation, and coordination, the author includes "various activities aimed at assisting the parties in alleviating human sufferings or easing other burdens such as refugee problems entailed in certain conflicts" but adds that "such activities can hardly be described as good offices in the usual meaning of the term."[10] Perhaps he meant the "traditional" rather than the "usual" meaning of the term, for he himself acknowledges among the categories of involvement by the Secretary-General in the exercise of good offices, "humanitarian problems," including the situation of minorities within some states.[11]

In the League of Nations system for the international protection of minorities, resolutions of the League Council provided for the handling of "exceptional and extremely urgent cases,"[12] and stipulated that in such cases the Secretary-General of the League should simultaneously inform the state concerned and the members of the Council of the matter. Minorities Committees, for their part, made it their practice to try to settle questions raised in communications by means of informal negotiations with the state concerned.[13]

The exercise of good offices with respect to human rights or humanitarian matters is quite extensive in present-day international organizations, such as

[9] V. PECHOTA, *supra* note 8, at 2. [10] *Id.* at 17.

[11] *Ibid.* On the good offices of the Secretary-General generally, see Simmonds, *Good Offices and the Secretary-General*, 29 NORDISK TIDSSKRIFT FOR INTERNATIONAL RET OG JUS GENTIUM 330 (1959); U Thant, *A Quiet United Nations Road to Accord*, UN MONTHLY CHRONICLE, No. 7, July 1970, at 122; U Thant, *The United Nations and some problems of public understanding, id.,* No. 1, Jan. 1971, at 98; U Thant, *The Role of the Secretary-General, id.,* No. 9, Oct. 1971, at 178.

[12] *See* especially Council resolution of June 27, 1921, referred to in The International Protection of Minorities, note 13 *infra*, at 27.

[13] *See* The International Protection of Minorities under the League of Nations 27–32, UN Doc. E/CN.4/Sub.2/6 (1947). *See also* P. DE AZCARATE, LEAGUE OF NATIONS AND NATIONAL MINORITIES: AN EXPERIMENT (1945); J. BARROS, OFFICE WITHOUT POWER: SECRETARY-GENERAL SIR ERIC DRUMMOND, 1919–1933, at 97–98 (1979).

the United Nations, the United Nations High Commissioner for Refugees (UNHCR), the International Labour Organisation (ILO), the United Nations Educational, Scientific and Cultural Organization (UNESCO), and the International Committee of the Red Cross (ICRC). In many of these organizations, good offices with respect to human rights or humanitarian matters are exercised at various levels: by the head or by other members of the secretariat; by organs, as well as by their presidents, chairmen, or members. In some instances there are express mandates to exercise such good offices, while in others they are based on the concept of inherent or implied competence.

In the ILO, good offices are exercised by the Director-General and, under his direction, by members of the International Labour Office. There are elements of good offices in the procedure of direct contacts introduced in 1968 for the purpose of permitting a representative of the ILO Director-General to examine directly with the competent government services, practical or legal difficulties encountered in the application of a ratified convention.[14]

In UNESCO, Decision 104/EX3.3, adopted by the Executive Board in 1978, consolidated the role of the Director-General in respect of intercessions on humanitarian grounds and representations of a conciliatory nature. In the Office of the United Nations High Commissioner for Refugees, a recent High Commissioner expressed the view that good offices "remain as useful as ever for contingencies and situations on the fringe of the normal activities of the High Commissioner's Office."[15]

The International Committee of the Red Cross exercises various kinds of good offices or related functions. Article 4 of the Statutes of the ICRC states that "the ICRC may also take any humanitarian initiative which comes within its role as a specifically neutral and independent institution and consider any question requiring examination by such an institution."[16]

With respect to international or regional instruments on human rights, reference may be made to Article 28 of the European Convention on Human Rights (friendly settlement of complaints); Article 48(1) of the American Convention on Human Rights (friendly settlement of complaints); and Article 41(e) of the International Covenant on Civil and Political Rights (good offices).

The foregoing review shows the broad scope and variety of types of good offices exercised in the human rights and humanitarian field. In essence they can all be grounded in a basic rationale: Is there a humanitarian need and how can it be addressed? The practice of good offices in the field of human rights within organizations such as the League of Nations, the United Nations, the UNHCR, the ILO, UNESCO, the ICRC, the Council of Europe, and the

[14] *See* ILO Doc. GB/205/21/7: past practice concerning special inquiries with particular reference to human rights questions, paras. 27–29.

[15] S. Aga Khan, *Legal Problems Relating to Refugees and Displaced Persons*, 149 RECUEIL DES COURS 287, 349 (1976 I).

[16] D. TANSLEY, FINAL REPORT: AN AGENDA FOR THE RED CROSS: RE-APPRAISAL OF THE ROLE OF THE RED CROSS 72 (1975). *See also* D. P. FORSYTHE, PRESENT ROLE OF THE RED CROSS IN PROTECTION 30–48 (Background Paper No. 1 of the Joint Committee for the Re-appraisal of the Role of the Red Cross, 1975).

OAS shows that among the purposes for which such good offices have been exercised are:

(1) To promote human rights generally, including the ratification of human rights treaties.

(2) To facilitate the establishment or restoration of an attitude of respect for human rights.

(3) To alleviate situations of gross violations of human rights.

(4) To ease tensions and facilitate the movement of refugees.

(5) To initiate consultations to help reach solutions to human rights problems.

(6) To assist individuals or groups.

(7) To assist in the drafting of legislation or the establishment of national or local institutions for the promotion and protection of human rights.

(8) To resolve practical or legal difficulties encountered in the application of a human rights convention.

(9) To provide for contingencies, cases, or situations outside regular mandates or to provide ad hoc protection where there is a lack of specific authorization.

(10) To support the activities of human rights organs through discreet facilitative action behind the scenes.

(11) To fill gaps left by human rights organs, particularly in responding to urgent situations.

(12) To bring about friendly settlements to complaints.

(13) To provide equitable relief in cases where the strict application of rules might result in lack of justice.

(14) To engage in fact-finding, diplomatic, mediatory, or conciliatory activities.

(15) To respond to human needs generally, particularly in situations of emergencies or entailing human suffering.

Good offices, in most organizations, have been tackled in a flexible manner and little attempts have been made to regulate the function.

II. Legal Bases

For the United Nations Secretary-General to exercise good offices in the field of human rights, there may be several bases. He may be exercising a power conferred upon him by the Charter, the General Assembly, the Security Council, or some other authoritative organ such as the Economic and Social Council or, under its authority, the Commission on Human Rights. Good offices may be exercised at the request of the government concerned; in other instances they may be exercised without an invitation by, or even against the wishes of, the government concerned. In practice, whatever the legal basis, the methods and modalities do not vary greatly.

In the following section, there will be set out some of the legal bases which may be invoked either separately or cumulatively, depending on the case or situation in question, to support the exercise of good offices in the field of human rights. In the first place, the Secretariat, as a principal organ of the United Nations, is enjoined in the Charter to foster international cooperation for the promotion and encouragement of respect for human rights. Secondly, the good offices functions of the Secretary-General in the field of human rights could also be based on Article 97 of the Charter, which makes the Secretary-General the chief administrative officer of the Organization. Administration may be perceived in both procedural and substantive terms. Procedurally, it is to service the Organization and to implement the resolutions and decisions of United Nations organs. Substantively, however, the Secretary-General, as chief administrative officer, is also under a duty to promote the implementation of the purposes and principles of the Organization. If, therefore, it happens—as is constantly the case—that none of the relevant human rights organs is in session and that they have no arrangements for intersessional activity, would it not be appropriate for the Secretary-General to intercede provisionally, in order to seek to provide interim relief until one of the organs concerned becomes seized of the matter? Such an "emergency response" has developed in practice as an acknowledged and essential function of the administrative heads of the European and Inter-American Commissions on Human Rights (their respective Secretaries). The concept of interim measures or provisional measures is also one that is well known in international jurisprudence.

Thirdly, good offices may be exercised in the context of the novel powers of the Secretary-General under Article 99 of the Charter, which states that the Secretary-General of the United Nations may bring to the attention of the Security Council any matter which, in his opinion, may threaten the maintenance of international peace and security. Professor Hersch Lauterpacht was of the view "that Article 99 presents considerable potentialities for bringing to the Security Council's attention violations of human rights so grave that they threaten the maintenance of international peace and security." Moreover, he felt, "[t]he clause of domestic jurisdiction of Article 2, paragraph 7, presents no impediment in the way of the exercise of this particular function of the Secretary-General. The matters referred to in Article 99 are not, by definition, essentially within the domestic jurisdiction of any State."[17]

In a recent instance, the question was raised whether the Secretary-General should invoke Article 99 of the Charter in situations involving serious violations of human rights. On April 8, 1979, Martin Ennals, Secretary-General of Amnesty International, addressed a telegram to the United Nations Secretary-General requesting that he use his authority under Article 99 to convene a meeting of the Security Council to consider urgent measures to stop current

[17] H. LAUTERPACHT, INTERNATIONAL LAW AND HUMAN RIGHTS 187 (1950). *See also* L. GOODRICH, E. HAMBRO, & P. SIMONS, THE CHARTER OF THE UNITED NATIONS (1969); Schwebel, *The Origins and Development of Article 99 of the Charter*, 28 BRIT. Y.B. INT'L L. 371 (1952).

waves of political executions and murders across the world. On April 10, 1979, the Secretary-General replied that despite the seriousness of the problem and his distress at the increased number of executions, "invocation of Article 99 is not the most appropriate way to deal with the problem since that article deals explicitly and exclusively with matters involving international peace and security."

It has long been recognized in international law that serious violations of human rights could involve threats to the maintenance of international peace and security. They could therefore be proper grounds for the invocation of Article 99 by the Secretary-General; whether the violations do actually give rise to a threat to international peace and security is a matter of fact to be determined in each case. For present purposes, however, it is submitted that in the context of exercising his competence under Article 99, the Secretary-General could engage in exercises akin to good offices with respect to situations of massive and flagrant violations of human rights.

Fourthly, the doctrine of inherent or implied powers has frequently been invoked as a basis for the exercise of good offices. Indeed, the practice is so extensive that it may be said that the competence of the Secretary-General to exercise good offices has concretized into a rule of customary law within the United Nations. It could be argued that the Secretary-General has powers inherent in his office to undertake all kinds of conceivable good offices. Secretary-General Hammarskjöld felt that action on his part, without any mandate from an organ of the United Nations, was justified "should this appear to him necessary in order to help in filling any vacuum that may appear in the systems which the Charter and traditional diplomacy provide for the safeguard of peace and security."[18]

An inherent or implied competence of the Secretary-General is supported by the practice of many policy-making organs, including the General Assembly, the Economic and Social Council, and the Commission on Human Rights. Thus, United Nations human rights organs have expressly recognized and appreciated the good offices of the Secretary-General in the field of human rights (see Resolution 1979/36 of the Economic and Social Council, Resolution 34/175 of the General Assembly, and Resolution 27 (XXXVI) of the Commission on Human Rights). The latter resolution, for example, "requested the Secretary-General to continue and intensify the good offices envisaged in the Charter of the United Nations in the field of human rights." The above-mentioned resolutions, together with the related practice, lend strong support to the doctrine of implied powers as well as to the view that the competence of the Secretary-General to exercise good offices in the field of human rights is now a part of international customary law. The relevant practice will now be reviewed.

III. The Practice

Pechota reported that "the requests pouring into the Secretary-General's office include many in the field of human rights," and he added that "the

[18] 12 UN GAOR (690th plen. mtg.), paras. 72–73 (1957).

Secretary-General cannot shun such issues, especially if some expectation of assistance had been encouraged by the United Nations' resolute stands on the principles involved. There is reason to expect that discreet facilitative action in the area may soon become one of the major fields in which good offices are exercised."[19]

All four Secretaries-General of the United Nations, so far, have engaged in good offices in human rights or humanitarian matters.[20] Trygve Lie disclosed in his memoirs some of the efforts that he had undertaken on behalf of the Greek children taken to Communist countries during the guerrilla war in Greece. He reported that he had discussed the matter during visits to Marshal Tito of Yugoslavia,[21] Foreign Minister Siroky of Czechoslovakia,[22] and Marshal Stalin of the USSR.[23] He also reported on the conversations he had had with Marshal Tito concerning Bishop Aloysius Stepinac.[24]

Dag Hammarskjöld's general approach was that the Secretary-General should not be expected to exercise his good offices unless guidance could be found either in the Charter or in a decision of a major organ. He normally undertook good offices missions only at the request of governments, and he refused to take initiatives if he believed that either his right to do so or his chances of success were seriously in doubt. Pursuant to a decision of the Security Council, he addressed the human rights problems in South Africa during meetings with South African leaders in 1961, and sought to find arrangements for safeguarding human rights in accordance with United Nations principles.[25]

In his memoirs, *View From the United Nations*, U Thant gave a glimpse into some of the human rights good offices in which he had engaged:

> Regarding the problem of Soviet Jews, Mr. Tekoah[26] had been in touch with me, on a personal and confidential basis, since the middle of 1969. . . . I . . . decided that I would utilize the good offices of my two Russian aides . . . as channels of communication between myself and Moscow. Whenever I received petitions from Mr. Tekoah, I passed them on to one of them for transmission to Moscow. Even my closest colleagues did not know the procedure I was employing, since I felt that complete discretion alone would bear results.[27]

These efforts, he said, had met with much success.

[19] V. PECHOTA, *supra* note 8.

[20] Secretaries-General of the League of Nations also made intercessions on humanitarian matters. *See, e.g.*, on the humanitarian efforts of Secretary-General Drummond, J. BARROS, *supra* note 13, at 105–06.

[21] T. LIE, IN THE CAUSE OF PEACE 243 (1954).

[22] *Id.* at 289.

[23] *Id.* at 304.

[24] *Id.* at 242–43.

[25] B. URQUHART, HAMMARSKJÖLD 496–97 (1972). *See also*, on Hammarskjöld's exercise of good offices in general, pp. 308–14.

[26] The Israeli Ambassador.

[27] U THANT, *supra* note 1, at 351–52. In the UN relief operations to Bangladesh (1971), Secretary-General U Thant, relying upon the purposes of the Charter, invoked his responsibility to ensure that human well-being was protected and humanitarian principles upheld. *See* Morse, *Practice Norms and Reform of International Rescue Operations*, 157 RECUEIL DES COURS 121, 150 (1977 IV).

U Thant reported that he applied

> [s]ome general rules . . . to any exercise of good offices. Obviously efforts of this kind must be fully in accordance with the general principles of the United Nations Charter. Then the Secretary-General must reach a considered judgement as to whether his intervention is likely to be helpful, or whether, on the contrary, it will be ineffective, or even positively harmful. On this basis he must himself decide whether or not to accede to a request to take an initiative to exercise his good offices in a particular situation.

He added that "[o]nce the Secretary-General has decided to act, some other general rules apply. . . . [C]onfidence, mutual respect and absolute discretion are vital to success, and the less publicity there is, the better."[28]

In his annual reports on the work of the Organization between 1972 and 1981, Secretary-General Waldheim has consistently referred to his good offices in the field of human rights.[29] He summarized his approach in a book published in 1978:

> [J]e dispose d'une certaine marge de manoeuvre me permettant d'exercer mon influence dans la défense des droits de l'homme. Pour cela, je me conforme à un critère fondamental: le bien-être de la personne ou des personnes concernées. Le plus souvent, j'offre mes bons offices, à titre officieux, en me plaçant sur un terrain purement humanitaire. J'intercède pour assurer la vie sauve à un condamné à mort, pour favoriser la réunion de familles, pour obtenir des "clarifications" sur les conditions de détention de prisonniers ou sur le traitement réservé à une minorité nationale. J'assure toujours le gouvernement concerné de mon souci de ne pas m'ingérer dans ses affaires intérieures, tout en lui faisant valoir qu'un geste positif de sa part ne manquerait pas de relever son prestige dans l'opinion mondiale. Toute publicité à ma démarche risquerait de faire avorter l'entreprise. Aucun Etat, en effet, ne tient à donner l'impression qu'il a cédé à une quelconque sollicitation étrangère.
>
> Cependant, j'ai aussi recours aux interventions publiques quand j'estime que celles-ci sont nécessaires. Ainsi ai-je lancé, par exemple, un appel public au gouvernement ougandais pour lui demander d'autoriser une enquête impartiale sur les circonstances de la mort de l'archevêque Janani Luwum et de deux ministres. Cela ne m'a pas empêché de poursuivre des contacts confidentiels dans cette affaire.[30]

A review of the policy of Secretary-General Waldheim discloses that in dealing with individual cases in the context of the exercise of good offices, he uses his personal judgment as to whether an intercession on his part would be appropriate or useful. In this regard, he is guided mainly by the welfare of the persons concerned and acts mainly on humanitarian grounds, mindful, as a general rule, of the injunction against intervention in internal affairs. He takes into account the circumstances and responsibilities of the government(s) concerned and normally acts confidentially and discreetly, although, on occasions, he may speak out publicly when necessary. He may occasionally send a rep-

[28] U Thant, *A Quiet Road, supra* note 11, at 124–25.

[29] *See*, in particular, UN Docs. A/8701/Add.1, section IX (1972); A/9601/Add.1, at 8 (1974); A/31/1/Add.1, at 9 (1976); A/32/1, at 6–7 (1977); A/33/1 (1978); A/34/1 (1979); A/35/1, section IX (1980); OPI/622, at 16–17 (1978); UN Press Release SG/SM/321, at 6 (1977).

[30] K. Waldheim, Un Métier unique au monde 102 (1978).

resentative to consult with the government concerned. *Ratione materiae*, he may intercede in cases involving: danger of loss of life; torture or other serious abuses against the physical or mental integrity of persons; prisoners of conscience, where there are special reasons for acting; cases arousing widespread concern at the international level; and cases where there are other, strong humanitarian grounds for acting.

To qualify for action by the Secretary-General, certain elements should usually be present, such as a denial of justice (for example, a deliberate bypassing of the regular judicial processes or political subversion of these processes). In other words, the Secretary-General should not normally be expected to act where, for example, someone has been sentenced to death after having been found guilty through fair process of law, although he has done so on occasions, such as when former President Bhutto of Pakistan faced sentence of death. Usually, also, the Secretary-General should have enough evidence to demonstrate cause for legitimate concern on his part.

Among the types of action taken by the Secretary-General are the following. Where there is evidence giving cause for concern but the facts are not sufficiently clear, the Secretary-General may indicate his concern by asking for information as to the well-being of the person(s) concerned. In appropriate cases he may ask the government to take measures to guarantee the safety or well-being of the person concerned. In other types of cases he may ask for a stay of execution pending further review of the case. In some cases, where he has enough facts and there are reasons for doing so, he may ask the government to exercise clemency or to grant a pardon. In appropriate cases he may ask the government to consider allowing a person to leave instead of executing him.

The role of the Secretary-General in dealing with situations of gross violations of human rights has not been developed as much as his good offices role in dealing with individual cases. The objectives of the Secretary-General in discharging a role in this field seem to be:

(1) to ascertain the facts in a situation of gross violations of human rights;

(2) to maintain communications and contacts with the government concerned;

(3) to try to influence the government concerned to adopt measures that could lead to a cessation of violations and the restoration of human rights, and, in this regard, to utilize whatever possibilities of assistance available in the United Nations, such as technical assistance and advisory services;

(4) to express, if necessary, the conscience of the international community regarding the situation in question, particularly in the face of an uncooperative or recalcitrant government.

In seeking to realize the above-mentioned objectives, the Secretary-General has so far adopted the following approaches, *inter alia*: he may establish contacts with the governments concerned; he may send a representative for discussion with the government concerned; he may personally make a visit on the spot; he may designate a special representative to deal with the situation; he may seek to provide international humanitarian assistance, particularly through the office of the United Nations High Commissioner for Refugees; he may offer

United Nations technical assistance; he may convene an international conference to consider the situation; he may establish an inquiry into the situation; and he may, if he considers it necessary, comment on the situation publicly or express his concern about it.

An example of the approach of the Secretary-General to the handling of situations of gross violations of human rights was that of Chile in 1975. In its Resolution 3219 (XXIX), adopted in 1974, the General Assembly requested that the President of its 29th session and the Secretary-General assist in any way they might deem appropriate in the reestablishment of basic human rights and fundamental freedoms in Chile. The actions taken by the Secretary-General under this resolution were described in a report that he submitted to the 30th session of the General Assembly.[31] The Secretary-General and the Under-Secretary-General for Political and General Assembly Affairs held frequent meetings with the Permanent Representative of Chile to the United Nations. The Secretary-General also met with the Minister for External Relations of Chile, and the Under-Secretary-General visited Chile between February 23 and 28, 1975. On a subsequent occasion, the United Nations Legal Counsel also visted Chile.

An examination of the methods recently employed by the Secretary-General in the case of the American hostages in Iran shows that they included: definition of the issues; consultations, contacts, and representations; a visit on the spot; the making of proposals; the conduct of negotiations; and the establishment of a commission of inquiry.[32]

Conclusions

The following concluding observations may be offered.

(1) The good offices of the United Nations Secretary-General in the field of human rights have become a fully established part of, to use the words of Hammarskjöld, the "common law of organized international co-operation," and therefore of international customary law.

(2) Good offices in the field of human rights have certain characteristics that distinguish them from traditional good offices or that may not even exist in contemporary good offices in the settlement of international disputes generally. Among these the following may be mentioned:

(a) There may be only one government involved.

(b) The matter may be internal to a state (though not within its exclusive domain).

(c) The consent of the state concerned is not necessarily a prerequisite to the good offices initiative, though its cooperation will be essential to success.

(d) Good offices may be exercised with respect to situations involving gross violations as well as with respect to individual cases.

[31] UN Doc. A/10295 (1975).

[32] *See* para. 43 of the ICJ Judgment in the Case Concerning United States Diplomatic and Consular Staff in Tehran (USA v. Iran), [1980] ICJ Rep. 3, *reproduced in* UN Doc. S/13989 (1980), 74 AJIL 746 (1980).

(3) Good offices initiatives must be in accordance with the general principles of the United Nations Charter. However, the requirements of the International Bill of Human Rights must also be taken into account. Good offices should be carried out in a spirit of mutual respect and with discretion.

(4) The exercise of good offices by the United Nations Secretary-General is always discretionary. No element of compulsion or automaticity can or should be injected into this function.

(5) In the practice of Secretary-General Waldheim on individual cases in which he exercises good offices, he acts on the following principles, *inter alia*:

(a) He uses his personal judgment as to whether an intercession on his part would be appropriate or helpful.

(b) He is guided mainly by the welfare of the persons concerned.

(c) He acts mainly on humanitarian grounds, mindful as a general rule of the injunction against intervention in internal affairs.

(d) He takes into account the circumstances and responsibilities of the government(s) concerned.

(e) He normally acts confidentially and discreetly, but on occasions he may speak out publicly when necessary.

(f) He may on occasion send a representative to consult with the government concerned.

(6) In dealing with situations of gross violations of human rights Secretary-General Waldheim has adopted the following approaches, *inter alia*:

(a) He may establish contacts with the governments concerned.

(b) He may send a representative for discussion with the government concerned.

(c) He may personally make a visit on the spot.

(d) He may designate a special representative to deal with the situation.

(e) He may seek to provide international humanitarian assistance, particularly through the Office of the United Nations High Commissioner for Refugees.

(f) He may offer United Nations technical assistance.

(g) He may convene an international conference to consider the situation.

(h) He may establish an inquiry into the situation.

(i) He may, if he considers it necessary, comment on the situation publicly or express his concern about it.

B. G. RAMCHARAN*

* Special Assistant to the Director, UN Division of Human Rights, Geneva. All views expressed are those of the author in his purely personal capacity.

REPORTING UNDER THE COVENANT ON CIVIL AND POLITICAL RIGHTS: THE FIRST FIVE YEARS OF THE HUMAN RIGHTS COMMITTEE

I. INTRODUCTION

The Human Rights Committee (HRC), the body mandated to supervise the implementation of the International Covenant on Civil and Political Rights,[1] has now been in existence for 5 years. Because both state-to-state complaints and individual communications are optional, the examination of the reports of the states parties is the major component of the Committee's work.[2]

This Note will assess the effectiveness of the reporting system as it has evolved in the Committee's first 5 years. The Committee and its members will be examined against five criteria: the quality and independence of the individuals charged with examining the reports; the degree of cooperation shown by the governments in providing full information; the possibility of obtaining and using information from sources other than the reporting state; the power of the examining organ to make specific recommendations on the law and practice of the reporting state as a result of the examination process; and changes in the law and practice of the reporting state as a result of the examination process.[3]

II. THE QUALITY AND INDEPENDENCE OF HRC MEMBERS

The Covenant and the Provisional Rules of Procedure make formal provision for the independence of the members of the Committee.[4] Eighteen nationals

[1] There have been few studies of the practice of the Human Rights Committee. *See* Nowak, *Die Durchsetzung des Internalen Paktes über bürgerliche und politische Rechte,* 7 EUROPÄISCHE GRUNDRECHTE ZEITSCHRIFT 532 (1980); Novak, *The Effectiveness of the International Covenant on Civil and Political Rights—Stocktaking After the First Eleven Sessions of the UN-Human Rights Committee,* 1 HUMAN RIGHTS L.J. 136 (1980); Opsahl, *The Protection of Human Rights in the Council of Europe and the United Nations,* 26 EUROPEAN Y.B. 92 (1980); Graefrath, *Trends Emerging in the Practice of the Human Rights Committee,* GDR COMM. FOR HUMAN RIGHTS BULL. No. I/80, 1980, at 3; Ramcharan, *Implementing the International Covenants on Human Rights,* in HUMAN RIGHTS: THIRTY YEARS AFTER THE UNIVERSAL DECLARATION 159 (B. Ramcharan ed. 1979); Bossuyt, *Le Règlement Intérieur du Comité des droits de l'homme,* 14 REV. BELGE DROIT INT'L 104 (1978–1979); Schwelb, *The International Measures of Implementation of the International Covenant on Civil and Political Rights and of the Optional Protocol,* 12 TEX. INT'L L. REV. 141 (1977).

[2] As of July 31, 1981, of the 66 states parties to the Covenant, only 25 had accepted the Optional Protocol and only 14 had made the declaration envisaged under Article 41, paragraph 1. Report of the Human Rights Committee, 36 UN GAOR, Supp. (No. 40), UN Doc. A/35/40, at 1 (1981). A list of the states parties to the Covenant and to the Optional Protocol, with an indication of those which have made the declaration under Article 41, paragraph 1, is contained in Annex I of that report (hereinafter the annual reports will be cited by date only, *e.g.,* 1981 Report).

[3] The first four criteria are adaptations of those set forth by A. H. Robertson, as elements necessary to make a reporting system effective, in *The Implementation System: International Measures,* in INTERNATIONAL COVENANTS ON HUMAN RIGHTS: THE CIVIL AND POLITICAL COVENANT 332 (L. Henkin ed. 1981).

[4] Covenant. Art. 28; Provisional Rules of Procedure, rule 16.

of the states parties are to be elected by secret ballot from a list of persons nominated by those states. They are to be persons of "high moral character and recognized competence in the field of human rights" who serve in their personal capacities. As in most international bodies, consideration is to be given to the geographical distribution of membership and to the representation of "the different forms of civilization and of the principal legal systems."

With a few notable exceptions, the individuals elected to serve on the Committee have been very able persons with impressive credentials. The majority have had legal training. Many are professors of law. "Assertive" is a word frequently applied to the Committee as a whole.

Ultimately, the states parties control the composition of the Committee through the electoral process. It is not clear at this point how they will use this tool once the work of the Committee becomes more widely known. After the members hit their stride in questioning, no state party has been spared tough scrutiny. From the viewpoint of the Western countries, the questioning of the United Kingdom[5] and the Federal Republic of Germany[6] was particularly noteworthy. The Committee's thorough questioning of the Soviet Union marked the first time that country had accepted scrutiny of its human rights policies by an international body.[7]

The independence of the members of the Committee appears to be real, but their views and approach to its function are naturally colored by their different backgrounds. The members have made a conscious effort to avoid Cold War overtones and to be evenhanded in their questioning; nevertheless, they genuinely disagree on many important matters.

To date, the Committee has made no formal interpretative rulings on the substantive articles of the Covenant, but in their questioning of the state representatives, its members have been interpreting the Covenant from the very beginning. Indeed, the interchange involved in the examination of the reports is essentially a struggle for leverage in the interpretative process. The early practice of the Committee reveals a body divided on many issues, including most of the important ones; the most contentious involve the permissibility of the particular restrictions and limitations justified under sections of the Covenant. At a very general level, the division of the Committee on these issues has tended to be defined by the members from Eastern Europe on one side, and the members from Western Europe and Canada on the other, with the other members finding their places at various points in between. However, a closer look obscures this initial impression. First, the members from Eastern European countries are hardly monolithic in their views. Second, several members from the developing countries play a pivotal role in the decision-making process. Frequently, they supply a driving force in asserting the prerogatives of the Committee. Finally, the differences among the "Western" members are sometimes serious enough to delay and even thwart agreement. Although the deliberations of the Committee on individual communications under the Op-

[5] UN Docs. CCPR/C/SR.67, 69, and 70 (1978).

[6] UN Docs. CCPR/C/SR.92, 94, and 96 (1978).

[7] UN Docs. CCPR/C/SR.108, 109, and 112 (1978).

tional Protocol are closed, the author has been told that ideologically cast positions are even less frequent in this setting.

The most important characteristic of the Committee, which distinguishes it from most international bodies, is the mutual respect and esprit de corps so evident among the members; they have shown a willingness to seek a middle ground between often widely divergent positions. The continuance of this salutary state of affairs largely depends on the reelection of key members. The reelection of several of the particularly effective members in 1978 and 1980 is an auspicious sign for the future of the Committee.

III. The Cooperation of Governments

Under Article 40 of the Covenant, the states parties are required to submit reports on the measures they have adopted that give effect to the rights recognized in the Covenant and the progress made in the enjoyment of those rights. The reports are to indicate the factors and difficulties affecting the implementation of the Covenant. The states parties are to submit their first report 1 year after the Covenant enters into force for them and thereafter when the Committee so requests.[8] The Committee is to "study" the reports and "transmit its reports and such general comments as it may consider appropriate, to the states parties."[9]

To assist the states parties, the HRC formulated general guidelines on the content and form of the reports.[10] Although it was not expressly stated, these guidelines were really directed toward the preparation of states' initial reports. During the 13th session (July 1981), the Committee adopted new guidelines for subsequent reports.[11] The primary purpose of both sets of guidelines is to elicit as much information as possible on the laws and practices relating to the rights protected in the Covenant. Members have repeatedly expressed interest in information on practice as opposed to law on the books. Although some governments have been more forthcoming than others, the Committee has only declared one report unsatisfactory. Referring to discrepancies between the report of Chile on one hand, and the report of the Ad Hoc Working Group of the Commission on Human Rights to Inquire into the Situation of Human Rights in Chile and UN documents generally on the other, the Committee requested a new report.[12] This precedent-setting decision has not been repeated, though members commented on the inadequacy of the reports of Tanzania, Mali, and Kenya, none of which exceeded six pages.[13]

The great majority of states parties have at least formally fulfilled their reporting obligations under the Covenant. However, some have either failed

[8] Covenant, Art. 40, para. 1.

[9] Covenant, Art. 40, para. 4.

[10] 1977 Report at 35.

[11] 1981 Report, Ann. I.

[12] For the full examination of the Chilean report, see UN Docs. CCPR/C/SR.127–130 (1979). A summary of the discussion can be found in the 1979 Report at 17–27.

[13] Kenya: UN Docs. CCPR/C/1/Add.47 (1979) and CCPR/C/SR.271–292 (1981); Tanzania: UN Docs. CCPR/C/1/Add.48 (1979) and CCPR/C/SR.281, 282, and 288 (1981); Mali: UN Docs. CCPR/C/1/Add.49 (1979) and CCPR/C/SR.283, 284, and 289 (1981).

to submit an initial report[14] or have not yet submitted the additional information they promised during the consideration of their initial reports.

At its inception, the HRC adopted the procedure followed by the Committee on the Elimination of Racial Discrimination (CERD): a representative of the reporting state is invited to introduce the report and answer questions.[15] Thus far no state has failed to send a representative for this purpose. He is expected to reply immediately to the Committee's questions and comments; so far as he is unable to do so, he may refer questions to his government for written replies at a later date. The representative of every state that has come before the Committee except two (Libya and Kenya) has answered at least some of the questions immediately, and many have made very substantial responses. A number of states have responded to requests for detailed and precise information by promising a supplementary report. As of the 13th session (July 1981), 44 states have undergone the initial examination and the Committee has considered nine supplementary reports.[16]

For its initial examination of the additional written replies submitted after the first appearance of a state party, the Committee has experimented with a method of work different from that used for the first examination of a report.[17] In the "second round" the members ask questions on a topic-by-topic basis, and the state representative answers all or some of them before a new topic is introduced. The second appearance of a state before the Committee has given the members an opportunity to refer to information provided during the initial examination and to repeat questions whose original answers were considered unsatisfactory. Some members hoped that this "second round" would develop into more of a discussion or exchange of views with the states representatives on important issues arising from the information in the initial report and in response to questions asked during the first round. Although the "second round" procedure has been applied at least in part in every examination of supplementary information, the Eastern European members declined to participate in it between the eighth and the tenth sessions.[18] This posture can be traced to differences within the Committee on its responsibilities with regard to the reporting procedure. A compromise reached by the Committee in October 1981 (to be discussed below) has eased at least some of these difficulties.

Even the most skeptical observers have been impressed by the apparent seriousness that many states from different parts of the world, with diverse political systems, have taken toward their reporting obligation, as reflected by the quality of the reports and the caliber of the representatives, as well as their willingness to answer the Committee's questions.

[14] *See* 1981 Report, Ann. III.

[15] In the practice of CERD, this was a procedural innovation. *See* Buergenthal, *Implementing the UN Racial Convention,* 12 TEX. INT'L L.J. 187, 199–201 (1977).

[16] These figures are based on the author's examination of the Committee's annual reports to the General Assembly.

[17] This procedure was used for the first time during the fifth session (Oct.–Nov. 1978) in the examination of the supplementary report of Ecuador. *See* UN Doc. CCPR/C/SR.118 (1978).

[18] *See, e.g.,* the summary records of the "second round" appearances before the Committee of representatives of Denmark, UN Doc. CCPR/C/SR.251 (1980); Hungary, UN Docs. CCPR/C/SR.225 and 228 (1980); Finland, UN Docs. CCPR/C/SR.170–172 (1979).

IV. Information from Sources Other Than the Reporting State

A particularly weak link in most reporting systems is the examining body's lack of an independent fact-finding capability. The question whether the Committee members may avail themselves of information other than that provided by the states parties has prompted much discussion among the members.[19]

One possible source of other, perhaps critical, information on certain aspects of state practice relevant to the Covenant is the specialized agencies. Article 40(3) authorizes the UN Secretary-General, after consultations with the Committee, to "transmit to the specialized agencies concerned, copies of such parts of the reports as fall within their fields of competence." Although provisions for cooperation with the specialized agencies were included in the Provisional Rules of Procedure, the Committee has been very slow in pursuing this avenue.[20] At the beginning of the eighth session (October 1979), the Committee decided that "[i]nformation, mainly on the specialized agencies' interpretation of, and practice in relation to, the corresponding provisions of their instruments, should be made available to the members of the Committee on a regular basis, and that information can be made available to them on request during meetings of the Committee. . . ."[21] This has since been done, particularly by the International Labour Organisation. The specialized agencies do not have the right to comment on state reports. They may do so only if requested by the Committee, and such a request has never been made.[22]

Another source of information not contained in the reports is the nongovernmental organizations (NGO's) that have consultative status with ECOSOC. While NGO's have no authority to present information to the Committee as a whole, unofficial contact with its members is another matter. It is clear from the questioning of the state representatives that information supplied by NGO's has been used by most members in formulating questions. In addition, members of the Committee often meet in their individual capacities with various "interested persons" in connection with a particular report. Some members find

[19] *See* UN Docs. CCPR/C/SR.56, 73, 82, 99, and 105 (1978), and 180 and 181 (1979) for the most important discussions.

[20] *See* rule 62, paragraph 2, of the Provisional Rules of Procedure.

[21] 1980 Report at 94–95.

[22] With regard to the desirability of the specialized agencies submitting comments on the reports submitted to the Committee by states parties to the Covenant, it was agreed that the decision of the Committee as recorded in paragraph 605 of the Committee's Report to the General Assembly at its thirty-third session (A/33/40) still remained valid, it being understood that the Committee could revert to the matter at a later stage and, in light of the experience it had gained, seek ways of further strengthening its cooperation with the specialized agencies.

Id. at 95. In its earlier decision of July 27, 1978, referred to above:

> The Committee agreed to the transmittal by the Secretary-General to the specialized agencies concerned of the relevant parts of the reports of states parties, contained in its published documents, which might fall within their field of competence. The Committee also agreed that the specialized agencies should not be invited to submit any comments on those parts of the reports since the Covenant contained no provision to that effect.

1978 Report at 105.

the NGO representatives particularly useful in providing information about non-European states. One member estimated to this writer that the Committee would have been 50 percent less effective without NGO expertise. For instance, despite the incompleteness of the Summary Records, they show that during the examination of the Colombian report, several members referred to a document by Amnesty International on the current situation in the country.[23] The Colombian representative then attempted to show that the charges were not founded.[24]

Early in the Committee's practice, there appeared to be an understanding among the majority of its members that information could be used from any outside source but that the source could not be referred to directly. The question was less one of substance than of procedure, *i.e.*, phrasing. More recent practice seems to have been even more flexible.

V. The Power to Make Recommendations

Under Article 40(4), the Committee is mandated to "*study*" state reports and to "transmit" "its reports" on them. In addition, the Committee "shall transmit" such "*general comments*" as it may consider appropriate (emphasis added). In the first 5 years of practice, the Committee has been refining the "study" stage of its reporting procedure. Some members point out that, despite improvements, the study phase remains individual and uncoordinated. No other way of study has taken place, such as by the appointment of a working group or rapporteur to analyze the reports and additional information, and to propose requests for supplementary materials or questions to be put by the Committee. Some members have felt that the study so far carried out has been incomplete and even left to hazard, but until recently all efforts to move beyond the study stage have been thwarted by seemingly irreconcilable differences within the Committee.

Their disparate conceptions of the Committee's role have divided the members on the meaning of "its reports" and "general comments" from the beginning. The positions were staked out during the Committee's third session and have remained basically unchanged.[25] At one extreme, it was argued that Article 40(4) requires the Committee to prepare a report on each report submitted by a state party. In this view, the reporting function is simply a means to an end, since the parties' reports are intended to enable the Committee to determine whether states are in fact giving effect to the rights recognized in the Covenant. At the other extreme, it was argued that the reports referred to do not differ from the annual report required under Article 45. Most importantly, according to this argument, the Committee is not called upon to make an appraisal or to determine whether a given state has fulfilled its obligations.

Similarly, adherents of the first position contended that the power of making general comments is not limited to recommendations directed at all the states parties. The Committee may make comments on a particular state provided that they are general in character, *i.e.*, that they do not relate to named indi-

[23] UN Doc. CCPR/C/SR.222 (1980). [24] UN Doc. CCPR/C/SR.226 (1980).
[25] *See* UN Docs. CCPR/C/SR.48, 49, 50, 55, 73 (1978).

viduals. The other position held that the "general comments" provision precludes recommendations addressed to particular states.

When this question first arose, the positions outlined above were taken by the Western and Eastern European members, respectively. During the tenth session (July 1980), however, in a lengthy discussion of the issue, the members from the developing countries made their positions known: for the first time, the Eastern European members were clearly isolated in their restrictive interpretation.[26]

By the 11th session (October 1980), there seemed to be agreement on the *need* to decide how to proceed beyond the "study" stage of state reports; the serious differences, however, remained. The consensus that broke the impasse eluded the members until the very last moments of the session.[27] Although many compromises were necessary to achieve consensus, the major compromise consisted of agreement to proceed with the adoption of non-country-specific comments in exchange for the possibility of further consideration of issuing separate Committee reports on each state report.[28] The members who interpret Article 40(4) restrictively also agreed to agree on a procedure for periodically examining state reports, as provided for under Article 40(1)(b), which helped defuse the conflict over the "second round" procedure.

The Committee began implementing the consensus agreement in July 1981 with a decision on periodicity, the formulation of new guidelines for the subsequent reports, and the first "general comments" under Article 40(4).

In accordance with Article 40(1)(b), the Committee agreed to ask: (1) states parties whose initial reports were submitted before the end of the 13th session to submit subsequent reports every 5 years from the consideration of either their initial report or the additional information on that report; and (2) other states parties to submit reports every 5 years from the date when their initial report was due. This procedure does not prejudice the power of the Committee to request a subsequent report whenever it deems appropriate.[29]

Retaining the format of the guidelines for the initial reports, the subsequent reports are to concentrate especially on, *inter alia*: (1) completing the information already before the Committee by taking into account the questions raised and including information on questions not previously answered or not fully answered; (2) changes or proposed changes in the laws and practices relevant to the Covenant; and (3) factors affecting and difficulties experienced in the implementation of the Covenant.[30]

Based on its examination of 44 initial reports and nine supplementary reports, the Committee drafted several sets of general comments which it felt would assist the states parties in implementing the Covenant. The first three sets of comments offer specific suggestions on the procedural aspects of reporting, for

[26] *See* UN Docs. CCPR/C/SR.231 and 232 (1980).

[27] For the full text of the Paper Concerning Further Work on State Reports, see 1981 Report, Ann. VI.

[28] *Ibid.* The agreed statement is preceded by the phrase, "Without prejudice to the further consideration of the Committee's duties under Article 40, paragraph 4."

[29] 1981 Report, Ann. IV.

[30] *Id.*, Ann. V.

example by emphasizing: punctuality in fulfilling the reporting obligation within the time limit prescribed by Article 40(1) (General Comment 1/13); completeness of reports following the Committee's guidelines and sufficient attention to factors and difficulties affecting the implementation of the Covenant (General Comment 2/13); ways to ensure that individuals are acquainted with their rights under the Covenant and that all administrative and judicial authorities are aware of the state's obligations under the Covenant (General Comment 3/13). The last two sets of comments suggest improvements in reporting compliance with Articles 3, 2(1), and 26 (General Comment 4/13) and with Article 4 (General Comment 5/13).[31]

On balance, the compromise reached on Article 40(4) during the 11th session amounts to one step backward and two steps forward. The Committee is no closer than it was when the issue first arose to making specific recommendations on the law and practice of the states parties. Any effort by what was then clearly a majority of the Committee to force the issue by a vote would have imperiled its give-and-take working atmosphere. By agreeing to the phrase "without prejudice to the further consideration of the Committee's duties under Article 40(4)," the Eastern European members merely refrained from insisting on a formal interpretation of the only action they are willing to take anyway, *i.e.*, cooperation in the formulation of non-country-specific general comments.

The efforts to implement the compromise underline both the strengths and the weaknesses of consensus as a method of decision making.[32] On the one hand, the Committee would have lost its impressive momentum if no compromise had been reached. Often, "the best is the enemy of the good," as one member quipped during the discussion. In this case, it was a question of inaction or proceeding on the basis of the lowest common denominator. On the other hand, a consensus with which the vast majority of the Committee is dissatisfied is bound to wobble when attempts are made to implement it. The theoretical debate on the meaning of Article 40(4) continues to brew and has intruded itself constantly into the implementation efforts.

It was argued that the decision to ask for periodic reports and the formulation of guidelines on their preparation before the Committee had reached agreement on the results of its initial examination of the state reports, was a retrograde step. In the absence of such an assessment, states parties could claim that their reports had been favorably received by the Committee, and as long as the Committee refrained from expressing an opinion, such claims could not be challenged. If the Committee's questions went unanswered, the state party should be so informed; but the Committee could only do so by means of an

[31] *Id.*, Ann. VII.

[32] Under Article 39(2)(b) of the Covenant, decisions of the Committee are to be made by a majority vote of the members present. However, when the Committee adopted its Provisional Rules of Procedure, there was considerable discussion as to whether decisions would be taken by majority vote or consensus. *See* UN Docs. CCPR/C/SR.3, 4, 6, 7, and 14 (1977). The compromise is reflected in rule 51, which provides that the decisions of the Committee shall be made by a majority of the members present—but with a footnoted qualification: "The members of the Committee generally expressed the view that its method of work normally should allow for attempts to reach decisions by consensus before voting. . . ." 1977 Report, Ann. II. The Committee has conducted its business by consensus through the 13th session.

assessment.[33] One member wondered why the Committee "continued to give instructions to the states parties" in the form of new guidelines for the subsequent reports when it had not yet implemented Article 40(4). "The Committee was tackling its business in the wrong order and should instead be formulating its comments on each of the reports already submitted to it."[34] Finally, the need for country-specific comments was repeatedly voiced when the Committee sought agreement on its first general comments.[35]

Another weakness of decision making by consensus is that often the only thing that can be agreed upon is to postpone resolution of a point of serious disagreement. For instance, the decision on periodicity was delayed by failure to agree on how to deal with supplementary information. After the initial examination of state reports, frequently state representatives have promised both to complete answers to the members' questions and to supply additional information in writing. In nine cases the Committee has examined this supplementary information (the "second round") well within any of the time frames discussed for the examination of the second periodic report. It was argued that any decision on periodicity must build on the "second round" procedure, which encouraged states parties to respond to the initial consideration of their reports without delay.[36] If the states parties were not encouraged to submit this kind of information promptly and if the Committee did not study it promptly, it might well be that the supplementary information requested by the Committee would not be submitted until the following report, *i.e.,* 4 or 5 years after the questions had been asked.[37] After a great deal of discussion in both closed and open session, the Committee was forced to delay deciding how to handle supplementary information submitted by a state before its next scheduled periodic report.[38]

Although some will doubt the efficacy of non-country-specific general comments, the first efforts of the Committee are not without merit. It is to be hoped that future general comments will be addressed increasingly to the application and content of specific articles of the Covenant. The substantive provisions of the Covenant are designed to set a minimum standard. Although the Committee is divided on the interpretation of considerable portions of that standard, on issues not implicating distinctly "political" freedoms, the division slackens somewhat. Here, there appears to be, if not agreement, then the faint promise of agreement on the interpretation of some parts of the standard. Those sections of the Covenant dealing with equality and nondiscrimination (Articles 2(1), 3, 23(4), and 26) and with deprivation of liberty and guarantees for persons accused of crime (Articles 9, 10, 14, and 15) hold the most promise of becoming a real minimum standard within the theoretical one. The general comments may be a vehicle for articulating these areas of near agreement. But the dis-

[33] UN Doc. CCPR/C/SR.306 (1981). [34] *Ibid.*

[35] UN Docs. CCPR/C/SR.304 and 309 (1981).

[36] UN Doc. CCPR/C/SR.296 (1981). [37] UN Doc. CCPR/C/SR.299 (1981).

[38] The vehicle for future agreement is the concluding sentence of the decision: "This is without prejudice to the power of the Committee, under article 40, paragraph 1(b), of the Covenant, to request a subsequent report whenever it deems appropriate." 1981 Report, Ann. IV.

cussion of the first general comments, which deal with Articles 2(1), 3, 26, and 4, shows how difficult this task will be. Several members doubted the wisdom of imposing a particular interpretation of the Covenant by consensus.[39] It would not be surprising if the Committee were forced to resort to voting on such matters in the future.

For practical purposes, the search for agreement on the meaning of the Committee's "reports" has been shelved for the time being, and with it the possibility that the Committee will make specific recommendations on the law and practice of individual state parties. As a result, those members favoring reports on particular states are likely to insert much more comment on a state's compliance with the provisions of the Covenant into the questioning process. Persons familiar with the practice of the Committee will recall the high quality of the comments thus far, and can be encouraged by the prospect of an increase of comments over straight questioning.

The Committee's failure to agree on a method of assessing the compliance of states parties should be viewed in the context of the procedural innovation borrowed from the practice of CERD, which provides for the presence of a state's representative while the Committee is considering that state's report. Consequently, the Committee can attend to direct criticisms of the state's compliance without adopting a formal ruling and the state in question can remedy the default without suffering a formal adverse determination. In the long run, this procedure may prove to be more effective in promoting implementation of the Covenant than formal determinations of noncompliance.[40]

Although great efforts have been made to maintain an atmosphere of "constructive dialogue" during the examination of the reports, most members of the Committee have not been reticent in expressing their opinion on the adequacy of a state's compliance with specific provisions of the Covenant. Of course, the absence of a technical authority to compel compliance, coupled with the confidence that adverse remarks will be lost in the mountains of documents generated daily by the United Nations system, will be viewed as an effective shield by some states parties. However, the experience of the Committee thus far gives reason to believe that the questioning will reveal previously unnoticed problems in compliance.

VI. Changes in the Law and Practice of the Reporting State

The key test of the Committee's reporting system is whether it has effected change in the law and practice of the states parties.[41] It is still too early to adduce many examples of completed changes in the law. That said, one can note with some optimism some of the developments to date.

In several instances the Committee's questioning has resulted in a reexamination of national law. When the Canadian delegation responded to the Com-

[39] UN Doc. CCPR/C/SR.309 (1981). [40] *See* Buergenthal, *supra* note 15, at 201.

[41] Such change is not to be confused with changes in national law made by states parties *prior* to ratification.

mittee's questions, it listed a number of statutory provisions that some members had found not entirely in conformity with the Covenant. It was promised that all of them would be brought to the attention of the appropriate Canadian authorities.[42]

Both times Sweden came before the Committee, members expressed concern about the Swedish act on antisocial behavior and the possible harmful consequences in other countries if that act were taken as a model.[43] It was suggested that since the act had never been applied in practice, its repeal should be considered. The representative of Sweden said that he would take up the matter with the appropriate authorities.[44] At the beginning of the 12th session, the representative of the Secretary-General announced that the Swedish Parliament had recently promulgated an act repealing the law as from January 1, 1982.[45]

When the representative of Senegal appeared before the Committee, some members expressed reservations about the consistency with the Covenant of legislation that limited the number of political parties to four and obliged Senegalese citizens to obtain an exit visa in order to leave the country.[46] Noting this discussion, the Government of Senegal informed the Committee through the Secretary-General that the legislation in question in one case had been repealed by a constitutional instrument establishing a multiparty system, and in the other case had been replaced by new legislation abolishing the obligation to obtain an exit visa.[47]

Some states parties, finding parts of their existing legislation to be at variance with provisions of the Covenant, made reservations at the time of ratification. The Committee has urged those states to make the changes necessary to enable them to withdraw their reservations. In some cases it has indicated that the reservations were unnecessary; Finland is expected eventually to withdraw many of its reservations on this basis.[48] Likewise, having subsequently modified its legislation, Norway withdrew its reservation to Article 6(4) on application of the death penalty.[49]

During the examination of the report of Suriname, one could foresee the possibility of a more explicitly advisory role for the Committee under certain circumstances. Several months earlier, the Government that had submitted the report was overthrown by a coup d'état. Since it was not possible to predict the form of the new Constitution, the Committee thought it might be most useful to highlight certain matters regarding implementation of the Covenant for consideration by the committee that was to draft constitutional amendments.[50]

[42] 1980 Report at 39; UN Docs. CCPR/C/SR.205, 206, 207, 208, and 211 (1980).

[43] 1978 Report at 13; UN Docs. CCPR/C/SR.52 and 53 (1978); 1980 Report at 19; UN Docs. CCPR/C/SR.188 and 189 (1979).

[44] UN Doc. CCPR/C/SR.189 (1979).

[45] UN Doc. CCPR/C/SR.263 (1981).

[46] UN Docs. CCPR/C/SR.213 and 214 (1980).

[47] UN Doc. CCPR/C/SR.295 (1981).

[48] *See* UN Docs. CCPR/C/SR.30 (1978); and 170–172 (1979).

[49] The Committee was informed of this development in Norway's supplementary report, which has been submitted but not yet examined. *See* UN Doc. CCPR/C/1/Add.52 (1979).

[50] *See* UN Docs. CCPR/C/SR.223, 224, and 227 (1980); 1980 Report at 63.

The Committee should take care to give maximum publicity to undertakings by governments to alter their domestic law or practice in response to their obligations under the Covenant. By publicizing the positive aspects of compliance with international human rights norms, the Committee can play an important role in removing the stigma that many states continue to feel is attached to any international oversight of domestic human rights practices.

VII. Conclusion

In its first 5 years of practice, the Committee has achieved an impressive momentum, but it can be derailed in the future at any one of several points: the states parties could cease cooperating; tighter strictures could be placed on the use of sources of information other than the reports; the states parties could ensure an ineffective Committee through the electoral process; and finally, the willingness to seek a middle ground between opposing positions might stop short of finding a way to move from "general" general comments to specific recommendations on the law and practice of individual state parties. The realization of any one of these possibilities would weaken the effectiveness of the Committee. If more than one occurs, the Committee will degenerate into an empty political forum, a familiar fate indeed of United Nations bodies. The possibility for such forums to exert enough influence to effect change in the law and practice of states is notoriously minute.

Dana D. Fischer*

Corrections

In a reference to the 1928 Inter-American Convention on Private International Law (the Bustamante Code) in James Crawford's *Execution of Judgments and Foreign Sovereign Immunity* in the October 1981 issue of the *Journal* (footnote 8, at page 822), it was erroneously stated that the Convention never came into force. Fifteen Latin American countries ratified the Convention, which, in addition to its listing in the *League of Nations Treaty Series*, is included as No. A–31 in the *Organization of American States Treaty Series*.

Also in the October issue, in the first paragraph of Armin Rosencranz's Note on the ECE Convention on Long Range Transboundary Air Pollution (at page 975), it was stated that the Convention was signed by 34 member countries of the UN Economic Commission for Europe. Although 34 countries did in fact sign, only 31 were official members of the 34-nation ECE. Albania, Malta, and Cyprus did not sign, and three nonmember states, Liechtenstein, San Marino, and the Vatican, did sign. The European Economic Community was also a signatory.

* Scholar-in-Residence, Institut Universitaire de Hautes Études Internationales, Geneva. A study of the reporting system of the Human Rights Committee will be published under the auspices of the American Society of International Law in 1982.

I am grateful to the many members of the Human Rights Committee who made helpful comments on an earlier draft of this manuscript.

CONTEMPORARY PRACTICE OF THE UNITED STATES RELATING TO INTERNATIONAL LAW

MARIAN NASH LEICH*

The material in this section is arranged according to the system employed in the annual *Digest of United States Practice in International Law*, published by the Department of State.

EXTRADITION

(U.S. *Digest*, Ch. 3, §5)

Guidelines for U.S. Foreign Service

On July 16, 1981, the Department of State released to all Foreign Service posts a revised directive on international extradition. In view of the great increase in the number of extradition and international law enforcement cases handled by the posts, particularly by consulates (and consulates general) and consular sections of Embassies, the revised directive contained more detail than the former instruction on "what to do and how to do it."

Excerpts follow from Transmittal Letter OCS-4 of July 16, 1981, codified to Volume 7, *Overseas Citizens Services* (formerly *Consular Affairs*), chapter 600, of the *Foreign Affairs Manual*, the internal operating instructions of the Department of State and the Foreign Service of the United States:

600. *International Extradition*

601. *Extradition in General*

Extradition is the process by which a person located in one country is surrendered to another country for trial or punishment. There are a substantial number of international extraditions to and from the United States each year. Speedy trial requirements in the United States and formal or informal cooperation between law enforcement agencies create significant responsibilities for active involvement of posts abroad in international law enforcement. This involvement may include formal presentation of provisional arrest and extradition requests, informal contacts with foreign officials, and follow-up reporting.

Extradition is a formal process conducted pursuant to a treaty. The United States has extradition treaties in force with most countries in Europe and Latin America. There are not as many extradition treaties in force with countries in Asia and Africa. The most recent edition of *Treaties in Force* will indicate whether an extradition treaty is in force between the United States and the particular country.

Extradition treaties specify the crimes for which extradition may be granted, and defenses to extradition which may be raised. The United

* Office of the Legal Adviser, Department of State.

States cannot extradite a person unless there is an extradition treaty in force with the requesting country and the case falls within the terms of the treaty. As a rule, the U.S. Government does not request the surrender of fugitives when there is no extradition treaty in force with the country in which the fugitive is located. In such cases, the United States normally refrains from requesting more than informal cooperation. . . .

The Office of the Legal Adviser . . . is the action office on all extradition cases, and posts should address any inquiries to that office. . . .

602. *Extradition from Foreign Countries of United States Fugitives*

602.1 *Foreign Service Responsibility in Extradition*

Despite the existence of INTERPOL, legal attachés, DEA agents, and other law enforcement international contacts, the extradition process must be conducted through diplomatic channels. Except in the case of dependent areas, small posts, or posts where the regularity of extraditions so requires, diplomatic representatives shall be responsible for extradition. . . .

No extradition (as opposed to provisional arrest) of a fugitive from the United States who is found in a foreign country should be initiated except through the U.S. embassy abroad on instructions from the Department of State. A post should seek instructions from the Department before initiating or participating in an extradition request, even when another agency represented at post seems to be well informed about the case and requests embassy assistance. It is sometimes difficult to tell when an offense is covered by a treaty; once a person is provisionally arrested (see Sec. 602.2), there is a limited time during which supporting evidence must be prepared, authenticated, perhaps translated, and transmitted; and treaties preclude prosecution of offenses other than that for which extradition was granted. . . .

602.2 *Provisional Arrest*

In case of urgency it may be necessary to arrange for the immediate arrest of the fugitive to prevent his further flight while the documents and evidence in support of a formal extradition request are being prepared. This is known as "provisional arrest." Instructions requiring the diplomatic representatives of the United States to request the provisional arrest of the fugitive are conveyed to the post by the Department. Usually such instructions will be initially conveyed by telegram. . . . In urgent cases, the instructions may be conveyed telephonically followed by confirmation telegram. Neither diplomatic nor consular officers are to take any part in the arrest or detention of a criminal absent specific instructions from the Department.

Upon receipt of provisional arrest instructions, the post should make the request by the most expeditious means. In all cases, the request should be made or confirmed by diplomatic note (some foreign governments will not make a provisional arrest without a written request). A note requesting provisional arrest of a fugitive will provide essentially the same information as a request for extradition. . . .

. . . .

A few treaties permit provisional arrest via direct contact between the

U.S. Justice Department and its foreign counterpart. The post should seek instructions from the Department before participating in such a case.

602.3 *Preparation of Extradition Documents*

The documentation in support of an extradition request is ordinarily prepared by the law enforcement authorities (either federal or state) responsible for the criminal charges against the fugitive. These authorities deliver the documents to the Department of Justice. That agency thoroughly reviews the documents for sufficiency and compliance with the applicable treaty, then delivers the documents to the Department of State for final screening and action. When the documents are in order, the seal of the Department of State is affixed, and the documents are sent to the appropriate post with instructions for formally requesting extradition. If necessary, the Department arranges to have the documents translated into the language of the requested country and/or certified by that country's diplomatic representatives in Washington. (Note: In some cases translation by the Department into the applicable language may be impossible within prescribed time limits. In such cases the post may be instructed to arrange for local translation of the certified and authenticated U.S. documents. . . .)

602.4 *Certification of U.S. Extradition Documents*

When extradition documents are received from the Department, a diplomatic or consular officer at the post may, if the applicable treaty so requires or if otherwise requested by the host government, certify the seal of the Department. . . .

Some of the more recent treaties require that the documents be certified by the requested country's diplomatic representatives in the United States. If such certification has been made, there is no need for the U.S. diplomatic or consular officer to certify the seal of the Department.

602.5 *Presentation of Request and Documents*

The request for extradition and supporting documents should be presented to the competent authorities of the foreign government in accordance with the provisions of the applicable treaty. In virtually all cases, the request is made by diplomatic note. . . .

In most countries, the extradition request and supporting documents are presented to the Foreign Ministry, and the case then is handled by the officers of the government to which the request is made. In some countries, however, the case is handled by a private attorney retained by the United States Government or the State within the United States seeking extradition. In such cases, one copy of the documents should be turned over to the private attorney, and another copy presented to the appropriate foreign government authorities, pursuant to the specific instructions of the Department. In every case, the documents should be presented in accordance with local regulations or practice.

There may be subtleties of local extradition law or practice which are unknown or unappreciated in Washington, particularly with respect to countries where an extradition is a rare occurrence. Therefore, it is especially useful for the officer handling the case at the post to establish personal contact with the foreign official (usually in the Justice Ministry) or private counsel handling the case in the judicial process, and find out if there are any apparent deficiencies and how to correct them.

602.6 *Hiring Local Attorneys*

In most cases, the officials of the requested country will make all of the necessary arrangements for bringing about the arrest, detention and extradition of the fugitive. In those few instances where this is not so, the post may request authority to secure the services of a local attorney for assistance in the matter. . . .

. . . .

602.8 *Foreign Country's Decision on Extradition*

When extradition is granted, the post should promptly notify the Department and include, where appropriate, the local deadline for the transfer of the prisoner. . . .

. . . .

If extradition is denied, a detailed explanation for the denial should be obtained from the foreign government and transmitted to the Office of the Legal Adviser as soon as possible. In the event of an adverse judicial decision, the post should inform the Department immediately by telegram, advising of relevant procedures and deadlines for appeal. Copies of any relevant court decisions are also helpful to the Department in its review of the denial and should be forwarded when possible.

603. *Extradition from the United States of Foreign Fugitives*

603.1 *How a Request is Made*

A request by a foreign government for the extradition of a fugitive located in the United States must be addressed to the Department of State. Such a request is usually made by the government's embassy in Washington, D.C. However, such a request might be made directly to the post by the officials of the host country. In that event, the Department should be notified at once. The post should never contact U.S. law enforcement authorities (Federal or State) directly to arrange a fugitive's arrest in the United States, unless instructed to do so by the Department.

603.2 *General U.S. Extradition Procedure*

The officials of the host country's government may contact the post for information on U.S. extradition. The following information may be helpful in responding to such inquiries.

A foreign government's extradition request must meet the requirements of the applicable treaty. These usually include requirements that the request be supported by copies of the documents formally charging the fugitive with an offense, the outstanding order for the fugitive's arrest, and the relevant criminal statutes (including those defining the offense, setting forth the punishment for the offense, and indicating the applicable statute of limitations). In addition, the package should contain evidence from which the fugitive can be identified (e.g., photographs or fingerprint cards, if available, or a detailed physical description).

Moreover, almost every extradition treaty to which the United States is a party demands that the request be supported either by such evidence as would justify the fugitive's committal for trial had the crime been committed in the United States, or by proof that the fugitive is the person convicted in the requesting country. Therefore, a request for the extradition must be accompanied by sufficient evidence (such as statements or depositions from the victims, the witnesses, or the investigating officials) to show probable cause to believe that an extraditable offense was committed and that the fugitive committed it. When a fugitive has been convicted of the offense for which extradition is sought, evidence of this fact should be included in the package.

A person may be extradited from the United States only if there is an extradition treaty in force with the foreign country requesting extradition. In addition, Federal law in the United States requires that a judicial hearing be held to determine if extradition is in order. The fugitive may be released on bond pending this hearing only if special circumstances are shown. At the hearing, the fugitive may be represented by counsel, and can raise any of the defenses to extradition specified in the treaty or available under international law. The Department of Justice will argue on behalf of the requesting country at the hearing when it is obliged to do so by treaty or when that country agrees to provide reciprocal representation; otherwise, the requesting country must retain private counsel to argue the case in favor of extradition.

If the judge or magistrate conducting the hearing is convinced that the evidence is sufficient to sustain the charge under the provisions of the applicable treaty, he or she must order the fugitive incarcerated, and transmit the evidence submitted by the foreign government and a copy of the testimony taken at the hearing to the Secretary of State (18 U.S.C. 3184). Thereafter, the Secretary of State may, in his or her discretion, order that the person be surrendered (18 U.S.C. 3186). The fugitive must then be removed from the United States within two calendar months of the judicial officer's committal order, or he or she may be released from custody (18 U.S.C. 3188). The requesting country must pay all of the expenses incurred in connection with an extradition request (18 U.S.C. 3195) unless the treaty otherwise specifies or unless other arrangements have been made.

The officials of the host country's government may ask the post for advice on the likely success of a particular proposed extradition request. The post should be aware that determining whether extradition may be granted in a specific case is sometimes a difficult task requiring familiarity with the decisions of U.S. courts in similar cases (many of which are not published). For this reason, the post should seek guidance from the Department before venturing an opinion.

. . . .

603.4 *Certification of Foreign Extradition Documents*

603.4-1 *Basis of Requirement*

18 U.S.C. 3190 provides that the documentation submitted by a foreign government in support of a request for extradition is admissible at the extradition hearing if it is authenticated so as to be admissible for similar purposes in the tribunals of the requesting country, and that the certificate to this effect by the principal diplomatic or consular officer of the United

States resident in that foreign country shall be conclusive proof of authentication in the manner required. Therefore, all documentation submitted by the foreign government should be certified in accordance with these provisions. The authentication of the signature or official character of a foreign official named in the documents . . . does not satisfy the requirements for certification under this section.

. . . .

603.4–3 *Who May Certify*

The certificate may be signed only by the chief of mission over his title as Ambassador, or Chargé d'affaires *ad interim*, or by a principal consular officer (including the chief consular officer in the embassy) accredited to the country requesting extradition. If at all possible, the chief of mission should sign the certification.

JUDICIAL DECISIONS

MONROE LEIGH

Act of state doctrine—Foreign Sovereign Immunities Act—judicial restraint in foreign policy arena

INTERNATIONAL ASSOCIATION OF MACHINISTS AND AEROSPACE WORKERS v. ORGANIZATION OF PETROLEUM EXPORTING COUNTRIES. 649 F.2d 1354. U.S. Court of Appeals, 9th Cir., July 6, 1981.

The International Association of Machinists and Aerospace Workers (IAM), an American labor union, brought an antitrust action in the U.S. District Court for the Central District of California against the Organization of Petroleum Exporting Countries (OPEC) and its 13 member nations.[1] The suit was precipitated by dramatic increases in oil prices during the 1970's, which IAM attributed to price fixing by OPEC in violation of section 1 of the Sherman Act (15 U.S.C. §1). IAM sought treble damages and injunctive relief under the Clayton Act (15 U.S.C. §§15, 16). The district court dismissed defendant OPEC on the ground that it had been improperly served, and determined that monetary damages were foreclosed as to all defendants by application of the indirect purchaser rule of *Illinois Brick Co. v. Illinois* (431 U.S. 720 (1977)). As for the remaining claim for injunctive relief, the court held that it lacked jurisdiction under the Foreign Sovereign Immunities Act of 1976 (28 U.S.C. §§1330 and 1602–1611) (FSIA).[2] IAM appealed the dismissal of the claim for injunctive relief.

The U.S. Court of Appeals for the Ninth Circuit affirmed the dismissal, but on alternative grounds. The appeals court reasoned that the doctrine of sovereign immunity was technically inapposite to the summary dismissal of the plaintiff's claims. However, it held that many of the political considerations on which the district court had focused in fashioning its sovereign immunity decision justified judicial avoidance of the controversy through application of the act of state doctrine.

Central to the district court's decision had been its finding that OPEC's alleged price fixing was a sovereign rather than a commercial act. In reaching this conclusion the district court had reasoned that OPEC's *purpose* in setting uniform oil prices was to guarantee control of the member nations' natural resources, which control, the court concluded, was an essentially sovereign function.

On appeal, IAM argued that the district court's application of a "purpose" test rather than an "activity" standard ignored clear congressional mandate.

[1] The defendants did not appear in the district court proceedings. Their position was argued to the court by amici and additional information was supplied by court-appointed experts.

[2] 477 F.Supp. 553 (C.D. Cal. 1979). The district court also held that had there been jurisdiction, two alternative grounds for dismissal were present: first, that the OPEC nations were not "persons" within the meaning of the Sherman Act; second, that there was no proximate cause linking the oil price increases and OPEC activities.

The court of appeals agreed with IAM's argument, noting that IAM's position was supported both by the FSIA's legislative history and by the language of the statute itself. Thus, the court observed, Congress, in enacting the FSIA, had declared that the courts should determine whether an activity was sovereign or commercial by applying an objective nature-of-the-act test, that is, by focusing on "the course of conduct or particular transaction or act, rather than by refer[ring] to its purpose" (28 U.S.C. §1603(d)).

However, the appeals court agreed with the thrust of the district court's opinion: that an American trial court was an inappropriate forum to attempt to decide an international political dispute with such serious ramifications. Accordingly, although the appeals court concluded that the district court technically had the power to adjudicate OPEC's potential liability under American antitrust law, it determined that the district court could properly and prudentially refrain from hearing the case by invoking the act of state doctrine.

As the court explained, the act of state doctrine "declares that a United States court will not adjudicate a politically sensitive dispute which would require the court to judge the legality of the sovereign act of a foreign state." Judicial deference, under this doctrine, is grounded both in the

> institutional limitations of the courts and the peculiar requirements of successful foreign relations. . . . When the courts engage in piecemeal adjudication of the legality of the sovereign acts of states, they risk disruption of our country's international diplomacy. The executive may utilize protocol, economic sanction, compromise, delay, and persuasion to achieve international objectives. Ill-timed judicial decisions challenging the acts of foreign states could nullify these tools and embarrass the United States in the eyes of the world.[3]

The appeals court analogized the act of state doctrine to the political question doctrine in domestic law. Both, the court noted, require deference to the legislative and executive branches in those cases where the politically sensitive nature of the dispute makes the court ill-equipped to resolve the controversy. Another similarity between the two doctrines is that their specific "applicability is not subject to clear definition. The courts balance various factors to determine whether the doctrine should apply."[4]

However, the court noted crucial differences between the act of state doctrine and sovereign immunity under the FSIA:

> The law of sovereign immunity goes to the jurisdiction of the court. The act of state doctrine is not jurisdictional. . . . Rather, it is a prudential doctrine designed to avoid judicial action in sensitive areas. Sovereign immunity is a principle of international law, recognized in the United States by statute. It is the states themselves, as defendants, who may claim sovereign immunity. The act of state doctrine is a domestic legal principle, arising from the peculiar role of American courts. It recognizes not only the sovereignty of foreign states, but also the spheres of power of the coequal branches of our government. Thus a private litigant may raise the act of state doctrine, even when no sovereign state is a party to the action.[5]

[3] 649 F.2d 1354, 1358.

[4] *Id.* at 1359.

[5] *Ibid.*

The court explained that the act of state doctrine was a more flexible rule of application than the sovereign immunity doctrine. Most importantly for the instant case, the Ninth Circuit Court of Appeals held that the act of state doctrine contained no "commercial activity" exception. Thus, a court need not decide whether sovereign activity or commercial activity was implicated. Rather, it could adopt a balancing approach, weighing the commercial nature of the controversy against the foreign policy implications of attempting to adjudicate the matter, in deciding whether it is prudential to hear the suit.

The court noted that application of the act of state doctrine allowed it to exercise discretion in ascertaining the potential impact of international disputes. Citing the Supreme Court's holding in *Banco Nacional de Cuba v. Sabbatino*, the court explained that "some aspects of international law touch more sharply on national nerves than do others; the less important the implications of an issue are for our foreign relations, the weaker the justification for exclusivity in the political branches."[6]

Finally, the court stated that while the decision to deny judicial relief should not be made lightly, the decision was appropriate where, as here, there was great potential for interference with foreign relations. The court noted that both the Second and Fifth Circuits[7] had similarly applied either the act of state doctrine or the political question doctrine to avoid judicial entanglement in world oil politics. The court also observed that avoidance was prudent in this case in light of several other practical considerations: the likelihood that the court's order would prove ineffective; the absence of internationally accepted legal standards upon which to base judgment; and the lack of international consensus in the area of antitrust law.

While the *IAM* decision reflects a realistic assessment of the limitations of American judicial power in the current international oil arena, one is left wondering why either the court of appeals or the district court did not dispose of the case on the basis of the antitrust laws by holding that state actions in controlling the price of oil in the interest of conservation were not within the prohibitions of the U.S. antitrust laws.[8] By holding instead that the act of state doctrine applied and was not subject to a "commercial" exception, the court rejected a promising escape which four Justices of the Supreme Court had sought to open in the *Dunhill* case.[9]

Act of state doctrine—nationalization of assets—assignment of counterclaim

EMPRESA CUBANA EXPORTADORA, INC. v. LAMBORN & CO. 652 F.2d 231. U.S. Court of Appeals, 2d Cir., June 11, 1981.

Lamborn & Co. (Lamborn), a Delaware corporation engaged in the sugar brokerage business, contracted to purchase a quantity of sugar from an entity

[6] *Id.* at 1360 (quoting Banco Nacional de Cuba v. Sabbatino, 376 U.S. 398, 428 (1964)).

[7] Hunt v. Mobil Oil Corp., 550 F.2d 68, 78 (2d Cir.), 71 AJIL 780 (1977), *cert. denied*, 434 U.S. 984 (1977); Occidental of Umm al Qaywayn, Inc. v. A Certain Cargo of Petroleum Laden Aboard the Tanker *Dauntless Coloctronis*, 577 F.2d 1196 (5th Cir. 1978), *cert. denied*, 442 U.S. 928 (1979), 73 AJIL 141 (1979).

[8] *Cf.* Parker v. Brown, 317 U.S. 341 (1943).

[9] Alfred Dunhill of London, Inc. v. Republic of Cuba, 425 U.S. 682 (1976), 70 AJIL 828 (1976).

wholly owned by the Republic of Cuba. The purchase by Lamborn was made as agent for Craig & Co. (Craig), a New York partnership with offices in New York and Havana. Payment representing 95 percent of the estimated purchase price of the sugar was made by Lamborn, but a balance of $32,088 remained due and owing to the seller. Meanwhile, the Havana offices of Craig were nationalized pursuant to Cuban law, and although Cuban law provided for reimbursement, none was ever made for Craig's assets. Subsequently, Craig assigned to Lamborn all of its claims against the Cuban Government arising from the nationalization.

The Republic of Cuba, seeking the balance of payment for the sugar, filed suit against Lamborn in the U.S. District Court for the Southern District of New York. In the course of the litigation, the district court allowed the Republic of Cuba to amend its complaint in order to substitute Empresa Cubana Exportadora, Inc. (Cubazucar), a Cuban governmental entity, as plaintiff.[1] Lamborn asserted both a counterclaim against Cubazucar and a third-party claim against the Republic of Cuba for the value of Craig's seized assets.

The district court awarded Cubazucar damages of $32,088 plus interest for the unpaid sugar, while dismissing both Lamborn's counterclaim and third-party claim.[2] Citing its own decision in *Banco Nacional de Cuba v. Chase Manhattan Bank*,[3] the district court reasoned that the defendant should not be permitted to assert an assigned counterclaim against Cubazucar because to hold otherwise could encourage prospective defendants to buy up unrelated claims against foreign government plaintiffs. The district court also based the dismissal of the counterclaim on New York Judiciary Law sections 489 and 495, which prohibit corporations from taking the assignment of claims with intent to bring suit on them. The court dismissed the third-party claim against the Republic of Cuba on the ground that it was barred by the act of state doctrine. The U.S. Court of Appeals for the Second Circuit affirmed the decision, but on somewhat different grounds.

The court of appeals held first that Lamborn was not precluded from asserting against Cubazucar the claims against the Cuban Government assigned to it by Craig. The court reasoned that since both Lamborn and Craig were closely affiliated in the same sugar business, and since Craig was not a stranger to the commercial transaction that gave rise to Cubazucar's claim against Lamborn, the *Chase* decision cited by the district court was distinguishable. The district court's fear of encouraging a stampede of unrelated claims against foreign states was considered unfounded. Moreover, New York Judiciary Law section 489 was held not to bar Lamborn from raising the assigned claim. The court pointed out that this law was designed to prevent champertous agreements and hence did not apply to situations involving an assignment "between two closely affiliated business enterprises, both of which had been parties to the transaction."[4]

For other reasons, however, the court did not permit Lamborn to raise Craig's claim as a defense to Cubazucar's action for nonpayment on the debt. Thus,

[1] Republic of Cuba v. Lamborn & Co., No. 61 Civ. 1847-CLB (S.D.N.Y. Nov. 1, 1979).

[2] Empresa Cubana Exportadora de Azucar y sus Derivados v. Lamborn & Co., No. 61 Civ. 1847-CLB (S.D.N.Y. July 31, 1980).

[3] 505 F.Supp. 412 (S.D.N.Y. 1980).

[4] 652 F.2d 231, 236.

although Lamborn argued that Cuba's seizure of the Craig assets amounted to payment of Lamborn's obligation under the sugar contract, the court was not persuaded in light of the apparent lack of proof of intent by Cuba to extinguish the contractual debt through receipt (*i.e.*, seizure) of the assets.

Lamborn further maintained that as assignee it was entitled to assert a counterclaim or setoff against its contractual debt in the amount of the value of the seized assets. Cubazucar responded first by contending that it was a juridically separate entity and not to be considered the alter ego of the Republic of Cuba. Second, and more important, Cubazucar argued that any such counterclaim was barred by the act of state doctrine.

Relying on *Banco Nacional de Cuba v. Sabbatino*,[5] which also involved a counterclaim, the court held that the act of state doctrine precluded direct claims by Lamborn or Craig, as well as any counterclaims or setoffs based on the seizure of assets by Cuba:

> [T]he Judicial Branch will not examine the validity of a taking of property within its own territory by a foreign sovereign government, extant and recognized by this country at the time of suit, in the absence of a treaty or other unambiguous agreement regarding controlling legal principles, even if the complaint alleges that the taking violates customary international law.[6]

The court could find no relevant factors militating against the application of the act of state doctrine to the case before it. According to the court, the Hickenlooper Amendment (22 U.S.C. §2370(e)2 (1964)), passed by Congress in response to *Sabbatino* in order to bar the invocation of the act of state doctrine when a confiscation violates international law, did not apply to the present facts. This was because the amendment, as interpreted by the Second Circuit,[7] applies only in cases involving expropriated property that has found its way back into the United States. Since the seized assets of Craig were still in Cuba, the court reasoned, the Hickenlooper Amendment did not apply.

The court also found it unnecessary to consider an exception to the act of state doctrine based on executive branch assertions of adverse effects on American foreign policy interests.[8] The court reasoned that in the absence of any express opinion by the executive branch, there was no reason to believe that the application of the doctrine would prove inconsistent with U.S. State Department policy towards Cuba. Nor was there any basis for considering an exception to the act of state doctrine on the ground that the act was commercial in character,[9] since the act here, the expropriation, was clearly governmental.

The court next attempted to clarify the difference between sovereign immunity and the act of state doctrine with regard to the assertion of counterclaims against a foreign state. According to the court, sovereign immunity is based on the prerogative right not to have sovereign property subject to suit. However,

[5] 376 U.S. 398 (1964).

[6] 652 F.2d at 237 (quoting Banco Nacional de Cuba v. Sabbatino, 376 U.S. at 428).

[7] Banco Nacional de Cuba v. First Nat'l City Bank, 431 F.2d 394 (2d Cir. 1970), *rev'd on other grounds*, 406 U.S. 759 (1972).

[8] *See* First Nat'l City Bank v. Banco Nacional de Cuba, 406 U.S. 759.

[9] *See* the opinions in Alfred Dunhill of London, Inc. v. Republic of Cuba, 425 U.S. 682 (1976).

once a sovereign submits to the judicial process by initiating an action in American courts, notions of fair play and constructive waiver mandate subjection of the foreign state to counterclaims. The act of state doctrine, on the other hand, concerns itself with "the limits for determining the validity of an otherwise applicable rule of law"; it reflects a presumption that the relevant transaction by the foreign state should be held valid.[10] Hence, sovereign immunity implicates a court's jurisdictional power over foreign governments, while the act of state doctrine implicates a rule to be applied as a matter of conflict of laws.

In reaching its decision, the court admitted that the application of the act of state doctrine may very well lead to inequitable results, as in the case at hand where the foreign state is permitted to collect its direct claim while avoiding counterclaim liability for its uncompensated seizure. "Nevertheless," the court concluded, "otherwise applicable policy considerations" require that the doctrine not be abandoned merely because the sovereign appears as plaintiff. "Any other result would inevitably force us to examine the validity of each property seizure made abroad by a foreign sovereign, which is something the Supreme Court has forbidden us to do."[11]

Aliens—Immigration and Nationality Act—"good moral character" clause

NEMETZ v. IMMIGRATION & NATURALIZATION SERVICE. 647 F.2d 432. U.S. Court of Appeals, 4th Cir., April 24, 1981.

In 1976, petitioner Nemetz, an alien who had resided in Virginia for 9 years, petitioned for naturalization. His petition was denied by the Immigration and Naturalization Service (Service) on the ground that, in view of his admitted homosexual relations with his roommate, he had failed to prove "good moral character," one of the standards for naturalization under the applicable statute. The U.S. District Court for the Eastern District of Virginia affirmed the denial, finding that Nemetz had failed to rebut the inference that he had committed sodomy in violation of Virginia law (*see* Va. Code §18.2–361) and therefore had failed to meet his burden of proving good moral character.[1] The U.S. Court of Appeals for the Fourth Circuit reversed, holding that whether a person is of good moral character for purposes of naturalization is a question of federal law, requiring the development of a federal standard to assure the "uniform rule of naturalization" contemplated by the Constitution (Article I, section 8, clause 4). Since the petitioner's alleged homosexual acts were private and consensual, they could not serve as a basis for denial of a finding of good moral character. Thus, the court of appeals ordered the petition for naturalization granted.

The Immigration and Nationality Act requires that one seeking naturalization be of good moral character (*see* 8 U.S.C. 1427(a)), but precludes such a finding if the alien has "been convicted of a crime involving moral turpitude" or "admit[s] having committed such a crime [or] committing acts which constitute the essential elements of such a crime" (8 U.S.C. §§1101(f)(3),

[10] 652 F.2d at 238 (quoting Banco Nacional de Cuba v. Sabbatino, 376 U.S. at 438).

[11] 652 F.2d at 239.

[1] 485 F.Supp. 470 (E.D. Va. 1980).

1182(a)(9)). The court of appeals stated that in light of this standard, the central issue before it was whether the district court properly referred to the Virginia sodomy statute to determine whether the appellant had committed a crime of moral turpitude, *i.e.*, whether it was appropriate for the court to look to state law in determining the issue of good moral character in a naturalization case.

Nemetz argued that since the Constitution requires by its terms a "uniform rule of naturalization," it was improper to refer to a Virginia statute for purposes of defining moral turpitude. The court agreed, noting that reference to state laws, which vary from state to state, can only lead to differing and often inconsistent results. Thus, it was conceded at oral argument that if Nemetz had lived in Illinois, for example, where consensual sodomy between adults has been decriminalized, the Service would not have been able to oppose his petition on the grounds of bad moral character. Accordingly, the court held that the development of a federal standard for making such a determination provides the only certain means of creating the uniform rule required by the Constitution.

The Service maintained, however, that reference to state law was correct because Congress had traditionally deferred to the states to set standards with respect to matters of public morality and that the immigration laws contemplate such deference. The court conceded that Congress has in the past allowed the states great latitude with respect to morality; however, it concluded that such latitude cannot be granted when the resulting inconsistencies undermine a uniform rule of naturalization.

The court of appeals conceded that in attempting to determine which crimes will preclude a finding of good moral character for naturalization purposes, federal courts can appropriately look to state laws in the initial stages of the determination. Moreover, resolution of most cases on this basis will not be problematic, since crimes against the public are generally treated uniformly throughout the country, differences for the most part being in degree rather than in kind. The difficulty arises, however, with respect to private acts which are the subject of radically different legislative treatment by the states. In such cases the "appropriate test . . . is [to determine] whether the act is harmful to the public or is offensive merely to a personal morality. . . . Only those acts harmful to the public will be appropriate bars to a finding of good moral character under the scheme of §§1101(f)(3) and 1182(a)(9)."[2] In this manner, the court concluded, naturalization cases will be subject to uniform resolution and the constitutional requirement will be fulfilled.[3]

Arbitration—confirmation of foreign arbitral award by United States court pending review of award by foreign court

FERTILIZER CORP. OF INDIA v. IDI MANAGEMENT, INC. 517 F.Supp. 948. U.S. District Court, S.D. Ohio, June 9, 1981.

Fertilizer Corporation of India (FCI) obtained an arbitral award in India against IDI Management, Inc. (IDI), an Ohio corporation engaged in the

[2] 647 F.2d 432, 436.

[3] *See* Wadman v. Immigration & Naturalization Service, 329 F.2d 812 (9th Cir. 1964).

design and construction of fertilizer plants, in a dispute that arose over the daily production of a nitrophosphate plant that IDI had constructed for FCI near Bombay, India. IDI petitioned an Indian court to have the award set aside, while FCI petitioned another Indian court for confirmation. While both of these actions were pending, FCI filed a petition for enforcement of the award in the United States District Court for the Southern District of Ohio under the Convention on the Recognition and Enforcement of Foreign Arbitral Awards (Convention),[1] ratified by India in 1961 and by the United States in 1970. The U.S. district court considered and rejected five separate defenses to enforcement of the award, but exercised its discretionary power under Article VI of the Convention to adjourn the enforcement action pending decision by the Indian court on IDI's petition to set aside the award.

As its first defense, IDI asserted that application of the Convention would be retroactive, and therefore improper, because the parties had entered into the contract in 1962, 8 years before the United States ratified the Convention. In dismissing this defense, the court observed that the award itself was not rendered until 1976, at which time both nations were parties to the Convention.[2] Moreover, the Convention merely provides a forum for arbitration and does not affect any substantive rights created by contract. As a remedial device, the court concluded, the Convention could properly be accorded retroactive effect.

Second, IDI asserted that an Indian court would not enforce the award if it had been rendered in the United States, and that the reciprocity in enforcement required by the Convention therefore did not exist. Article I, paragraph 3 of the Convention permits a contracting state to apply the Convention only to awards arising out of relationships considered "commercial" in that state and to apply the Convention only to awards made in another state. Article XIV states that a contracting state may invoke the Convention "only to the extent that it is itself bound to apply the Convention." IDI argued that India has narrowly construed the term "commercial" so as to exclude most such relationships and that Article XIV required the district court to determine the extent of India's application of the Convention and enforce the award only if an Indian court would do so. The court ruled, however, that the Convention merely required it to determine that India was a party to the Convention and, since the United States had adopted the clause restricting its application to commercial disputes, to determine that the contract in issue was considered commercial under the laws of the United States.

IDI's third defense rested upon the public policy of the United States requiring arbitrators to be free from even the appearance of bias. The arbitrator appointed by FCI had served as counsel to FCI in two other cases, and IDI vigorously asserted that this fact was never disclosed before issuance of the award. Nondisclosure of this relationship, IDI protested, was fatal to enforce-

[1] 9 U.S.C. §201 *et seq.* (1976), 21 UST 2517, TIAS No. 6997, 330 UNTS 3.

[2] The Courts of Appeals for the Sixth, Fifth, and Second Circuits have upheld jurisdiction based upon the Convention in similar cases. *See, e.g., In re* Arbitration Between Audi NSO Auto Union Aktiengesellschaft v. Overseas Motors, Inc., 595 F.2d 1222 (6th Cir. 1979); Imperial Ethiopian Gov't v. Baruch-Foster Corp., 535 F.2d 334 (5th Cir. 1976); Fotochrome, Inc. v. Copal Co., 517 F.2d 512 (2d Cir. 1975).

ment of the award even though no actual bias could be shown. The court did not "take lightly IDI's charge" but concluded that, in view of the fact that all three arbitrators were unanimous, nondisclosure of this prior relationship had not "so tainted the proceedings as to nullify the award."[3]

IDI's fourth defense was that the award was unenforceable because it was not binding within the meaning of the Convention. Article V disallows enforcement of any award that has not yet become binding. IDI argued that the award would not become binding until the Indian court completed its review of the merits of the case. In disposing of this argument, the district court pointed out that the parties' contract and the arbitration rules adopted therein by reference explicitly provided that such awards would be final and binding. Moreover, the Indian Arbitration Act, which applies to all arbitral awards issued in India, also provides that such awards are binding. Thus, the court found the award to be enforceable despite the pendency of the appeal before the Indian court.[4]

In the court's view, IDI's fifth affirmative defense was less easily dismissed. IDI argued that the award was unenforceable because the arbitrators had exceeded their authority in awarding consequential damages. The parties' contract expressly excluded damages for lost profits, and Article V(1)(c) of the Convention provides that a court may refuse to enforce an award that deals with a dispute "not falling within the terms of the submission to arbitration." The parties had formally submitted the consequential damages issue to arbitration, although IDI continued to dispute the propriety of such an award throughout the proceedings. The arbitrators nevertheless concluded that there had been a "fundamental breach" and that in such a situation the limitation-of-damages clause no longer applied. While the district court could not "say with certainty" that a breach of contract found to be "fundamental" would abrogate an express clause prohibiting consequential damages, the court declared that the arbitrators, in making such an award, had not exceeded their powers under the Convention.[5]

Despite all five of these conclusions, the district court refused for the time being to enforce the award against IDI. The court reasoned that since the contract was executed and performed in India, and the arbitration was held there, Indian law governed the rights of the parties under the contract. Indian courts possess broad powers to review awards for which reasons are given, and

[3] 517 F.Supp. 948, 954. The court's rejection of this defense comports with a recent line of decisions by the Second Circuit that have construed the Convention's public policy defense narrowly so as to deny enforcement "only where enforcement would violate the forum state's most basic notions of morality and justice." Parsons & Whittemore Overseas Co., Inc. v. Société Génerale de l'Industrie du Papier (RAKTA), 508 F.2d 969, 974 (2d Cir. 1974). *See also* International Produce, Inc. v. A/S Rosshavet, 638 F.2d 548 (2d Cir. 1981); Andros Compania Maritima v. Marc Rich & Co., 579 F.2d 691 (2d Cir. 1978).

[4] While concluding that the award was procedurally final for the purposes of enforcement, the court recognized the potential difficulties raised by enforcement of an award that was currently being reviewed. Thus, the court exercised its broad discretionary power to suspend enforcement pending the outcome of the case on appeal.

[5] 517 F.Supp. at 959.

an award may be set aside if an Indian court discerns an error of law on the face of the arbitration record. Thus, if the Indian court reviewing the award against IDI found the "fundamental breach" theory to be erroneous, it could set the award aside. In order to avoid becoming embroiled in an issue of Indian law, the district court relied on Article VI of the Convention, which authorizes a court to adjourn a decision on the enforcement of an award if an application to set it aside has been filed with a competent authority. Wishing to avoid inconsistent results in the enforcement and final determination of the award in question, the district court held that its decision would be adjourned pending a final decision by the Indian court on the issues of Indian law.

Jurisdiction—federal question—private right of action under the law of nations—subject matter jurisdiction under Alien Tort Claims Act

HANOCH TEL-OREN v. LIBYAN ARAB REPUBLIC. 517 F.Supp. 542. U.S. District Court, District of Columbia, June 30, 1981.

Following an attack on a bus traveling between Haifa and Tel Aviv, Israel, individuals injured in the attack and personal representatives of those who died brought suit in the United States District Court for the District of Columbia against the Libyan Arab Republic, the Palestine Liberation Organization, and others;[1] they alleged multiple tortious acts and sought compensatory and punitive damages. Without reaching the merits of plaintiffs' claims, the district court held that (1) the court lacked federal question jurisdiction; (2) the Alien Tort Claims Act did not create subject matter jurisdiction; and (3) suit was barred in the District of Columbia by the 1-year limitation period for international torts.[2] Accordingly, plaintiffs' claims were dismissed.

To establish federal question jurisdiction under 28 U.S.C. section 1331, plaintiffs asserted that an implied cause of action arose from various federal criminal statutes[3] and the federal common law including the law of nations. Finding the federal criminal statutes to be inapplicable on their face,[4] the court focused its analysis on the question of when an implied private cause of action arises from international treaties and the law of nations. Plaintiffs cited numerous treaties and international conventions which, they argued, offered them

[1] Other defendants included the Palestine Information Office (PIO), the National Association of Arab Americans (NAAA), and the Palestine Congress of North America (PCNA).

[2] Plaintiffs also asserted jurisdiction on the basis of the diversity statute, 28 U.S.C. §1332, and the Foreign Sovereign Immunities Act of 1976, 28 U.S.C. §§1330, 1602–1611 (FSIA). The court held, however, that the presence of aliens on both sides of the case removed the power of the federal court to hear the action under the diversity statute. With regard to the FSIA, the court held, first, that sovereign immunity is still in effect for tort claims unless injury or death occurs within American borders, and second, that the Act could only serve as a basis for jurisdiction of suits against foreign states, which exempted the NAAA, the PCNA, and the PIO.

[3] Plaintiffs relied on: 18 U.S.C. §§956 and 960, which protect foreign governments by making unlawful any conspiratorial activity in the United States in preparation to injure a foreign government; 18 U.S.C. §957, which protects the United States by punishing any activity with the aid of any foreign government aimed at violations of American law; and 18 U.S.C. §§1651–1661, which focus on activity on the high seas.

[4] *See* note 3 *supra*.

a basis for federal jurisdiction.[5] Relying on Chief Justice Marshall's analysis in *Foster v. Neilson* (27 U.S. (2 Pet.) 253 (1829)), the court held that a treaty must provide expressly for, or clearly imply, a private right of action before a federal court may obtain subject matter jurisdiction over an individual's claim under that treaty. After reviewing in some detail the treaties and conventions relied on by the plaintiffs, the court found that none expressly provided for, or clearly implied, a private right of action. The court noted that two guidelines help to determine when a treaty might confer a private right of action: (1) the provisions of the treaty must be more than executory, *i.e.*, a treaty that merely calls for signatory nations to enact legislation implementing the agreement confers no private right of action; and (2) a treaty may be enforceable in individual actions if it manifests an intent that private actions be implied. Similarly, the court found no private right of action under international law apart from treaties. To imply a right of action in U.S. courts on the basis of international law when international law itself does not imply a private right of action, "sanctions judicial interference with foreign affairs and international relations, traditionally an area where courts have chosen to stay their hands absent some fundamental constitutional violation."[6]

Plaintiffs asserted a separate basis of jurisdiction under the Alien Tort Claims Act (28 U.S.C. §1350) (ATCA), which provides that "[t]he district courts shall have original jurisdiction of any civil action by an alien for a tort only, committed in violation of the law of nations or a treaty of the United States." For jurisdiction to vest under section 1350, the court said, three elements must be present: (1) the claim must be made by an alien; (2) a tort must be alleged; and (3) the tort must be in violation of the law of nations or of a treaty of the United States. The court found that the first two elements could be satisfied in this case. As to the third element, however, it concluded that three of the defendants had not been sufficiently linked to the alleged torts. As regards all the defendants, the court concluded that section 1350 "serves merely as an entrance into the federal courts and in no way provides a cause of action to any plaintiff."[7] In short, unless a treaty or the law of nations provides an individual right of action, no jurisdictional grant, be it federal question or the ATCA, can itself confer subject matter jurisdiction.

Finally, the court held that even if it had found the requisite subject matter jurisdiction, plaintiffs' claims were barred by the 1-year statute of limitations for intentional torts under District of Columbia law (D.C. Code 12–301(4)).

With this decision, the court refused to apply the broad jurisdictional analysis of *Filartiga v. Peña-Irala*[8] in the District of Columbia. In *Filartiga,* the U.S.

[5] These treaties and international conventions included the Charter of the United Nations; the Declaration on Principles of International Law concerning Friendly Relations and Co-operation among States, GA Res. 2625 (XXV) (Oct. 24, 1970); the Universal Declaration of Human Rights, GA Res. 217(A) (III) (Dec. 10, 1948); the International Covenant on Civil and Political Rights, GA Res. 2200(A) (XXI) (Dec. 16, 1966); the Hague Conventions of 1899 (II) and 1907 (IV) on the Laws and Customs of War on Land; the Convention on the Prevention and Punishment of the Crime of Genocide, GA Res. 260A (III) (Dec. 9, 1948); the American Convention of Human Rights, OAS TS No. 36 (Nov. 22, 1969).

[6] 517 F.Supp. 542, 548.

[7] *Id.* at 549.

[8] 630 F.2d 876 (2d Cir. 1980), 75 AJIL 149 (1981).

Court of Appeals for the Second Circuit interpreted the ATCA as conferring federal subject matter jurisdiction over a private tort action between two Paraguayan nationals involving acts of torture perpetrated in that country. It did not require that international law must itself provide an individual remedy in order for U.S. courts to have jurisdiction. By finding human rights norms to have been incorporated into the law of nations, courts choosing to follow *Filartiga's* lead could provide relief for at least some human rights violations through the ATCA. If affirmed by the court of appeals, however, *Hanoch Tel-Oren* would severely limit access to federal courts in the District of Columbia for private human rights claims.

Sovereign immunity—Foreign Sovereign Immunities Act—commercial activity, property rights, and tortious conduct exceptions

De Sanchez v. Banco Central de Nicaragua. 515 F.Supp. 900. U.S. District Court, E.D. La., April 20, 1981.

In 1979, during a period of civil unrest in Nicaragua, plaintiff, a Nicaraguan citizen, sought to redeem a certificate of deposit with Banco Nacional de Nicaragua, a Nicaraguan commercial bank, in the amount of $150,000. Because Banco Nacional lacked sufficient American dollars to honor the certificate, it asked Banco Central de Nicaragua (Banco Central), with which it held an account, for the dollars. Banco Central complied, debiting Banco Nacional's account and issuing to plaintiff a $150,000 check on its account with Citizens and Southern International Bank (C & S), an American commercial bank located in New Orleans. After leaving Nicaragua, plaintiff arrived in the United States and presented her check at C & S for payment. C & S refused on the ground that it had been instructed by the president of Banco Central to stop all payments from the account. Plaintiff brought suit against both Banco Central and C & S to recover the amount of the check. Banco Central moved to dismiss plaintiff's suit, contending that the Foreign Sovereign Immunities Act (28 U.S.C. §§1330, 1602–1611) (FSIA) barred the court from assuming jurisdiction over it. The district court denied the motion to dismiss.

The court focused its inquiry on three of the exceptions to sovereign immunity contained in the FSIA.[1] First, the court assessed whether Banco Central's conduct giving rise to the plaintiff's claims could be characterized as "commercial activity" within the meaning of section 1605(a)(2). That exception exempts a foreign state from immunity in any case in which the action is based upon a commercial activity carried on in the United States by the foreign state or upon an act performed in the United States in connection with a commercial activity of the foreign state elsewhere.

Basing its conclusion on sworn statements of various officials of Banco Central, the court held that the bank issued the check to the plaintiff as part of its governmental function to maintain foreign exchange rates through regulation of foreign currency transactions. In this regard, the court noted that Banco

[1] Whether Banco Central was an "agency or instrumentality of a foreign state" within the meaning of the FSIA (28 U.S.C. §1603(b)) was not in issue, as both sides agreed that it was such an entity.

Central earned no fee from the transaction and that an official of the junta Government had authorized the order to stop payment on any check drawn on Banco Central's account with C & S because of the critically low level of Banco Central's international currency reserves. The court thus found that both Banco Central's issuance of the check to plaintiff and its repudiation of its payment obligation were governmental acts that failed to give rise to the section 1605(a)(2) commercial activity exception.

The court next turned to the applicability of section 1605(a)(3), which provides an exception to the immunity of a foreign state in suits involving "rights in property taken in violation of international law." Under this exception, the property must be (1) present in the United States and used in connection with a commercial activity carried on in this country by the foreign state; or (2) owned by an agency or instrumentality of the foreign state that is engaged in a commercial activity in the United States. With regard to the first branch of the exception, the court admitted that to the extent that Banco Central holds funds with C & S to facilitate foreign currency exchanges, it does not hold property that is used in connection with a commercial activity. However, "[u]nder the second category, the property need not be present in connection with a commercial activity of the agency or instrumentality,"[2] as long as such entity conducts commercial activities in the United States.

The court determined that Banco Central did, in fact, conduct commercial activities in this country on the basis of evidence that checks from the C & S account were used to pay for letters of credit issued through C & S for Nicaraguan imports and to pay for principal and interest on credit extended to Banco Central by C & S. Accordingly, the court held that the application of section 1605(a)(3) defeated the defendant's claim of sovereign immunity.

Finally, the court held that jurisdiction existed under section 1605(a)(5), which denies immunity to foreign states sued for tortious conduct that causes, *inter alia*, damage to or loss of property in the United States. The court held that for purposes of the FSIA, the tort of conversion encompasses the wrongful prevention of the exercise of intangible rights represented by a document, such as a check, even if the document itself is not converted. In addition, the court rejected Banco Central's contention that liability under section 1605(a)(5) is limited to tortious conduct resulting in "casualty-type" damage.

The *de Sanchez* decision is notable in three respects. First, one wonders if the court was correct in classifying Banco Central's conduct as governmental under the standard of section 1605(a)(2). While it would seem to be true that the bank's maintenance of foreign exchange rates through the regulation of foreign currency transactions had a governmental purpose, it would also seem that the activity in question in this case—the issuance of appellant's check—was distinctly commercial in nature. In this respect, the court appears to misapply the operative language of the Foreign Sovereign Immunities Act.[3]

[2] 515 F.Supp. 900, 910 (quoting H.R. REP. No. 94-1487, 94th Cong., 2d Sess., *reprinted in* [1976] U.S. CODE CONG. & ADMIN. NEWS 6604, 6618) [hereinafter cited as HOUSE REP.].

[3] The Act states at 28 U.S.C. §1603(d) that "[t]he commercial character of an activity shall be determined by reference to the nature of the course of conduct or particular transaction or act, rather than by reference to its purpose." *See also* HOUSE REP. at 6615.

Second, it might be questioned whether the court's reading of the scope of section 1605(a)(5) is too expansive. The court itself cites persuasive authority that this exception is concerned wholly with "noncommercial" torts;[4] and while the exception may encompass torts beyond those involving physical casualties, the court has some difficulty justifying the application of the exception to the conversion of intangible property rights.

Finally, the court's reliance on section 1605(a)(3), depending as it does on a violation of international law, would appear to be misplaced. In this regard it should be observed that *de Sanchez* is one of several recent cases in which a plaintiff sought to remove the immunity of a foreign sovereign on the basis of a transaction involving a U.S. banking institution. In *Verlinden B.V. v. Central Bank of Nigeria*,[5] the U.S. Court of Appeals for the Second Circuit held that the federal courts lack judicial power to decide cases brought by aliens against foreign sovereigns where no federal claim is alleged. In *Texas Trading & Milling Corp. v. Federal Republic of Nigeria*,[6] a companion case to *Verlinden*, the Second Circuit held that an American company could sue a foreign central bank under section 1605(a)(2) where the transaction involved a letter of credit arrangement with an American bank. Like *Verlinden*, the *de Sanchez* case was brought by an alien plaintiff and therefore raises serious questions of subject matter jurisdiction.[7] Unlike both of the recent holdings of the Second Circuit, however, the court in *de Sanchez* relied on section 1605(a)(3), which applies only to cases involving a violation of international law. According to the court, the plaintiff alleged four bases for recovery: breach of a duty to honor the check, breach of contract, misrepresentation, and conversion—none of which on their face involve a violation of an international standard. Moreover, the court makes no attempt to relate these claims to an international law violation.[8] Thus, it appears that the court made the questionable assumption that an inferable allegation of a violation of international law was sufficient to meet the section 1605(a)(3) standard, an assumption, which, if followed by other courts, could substantially diminish the protection available to foreign sovereigns under this section.

Sovereign immunity—"in the United States" clause of Foreign Sovereign Immunities Act—territorial waters

PEREZ v. THE BAHAMAS. 652 F.2d 186.
U.S. Court of Appeals, D.C. Cir., April 28, 1981.

Appellant brought a private tort action in federal court against the Government of the Bahamas for gunshot wounds incurred when Bahamian govern-

[4] 515 F.Supp. at 913 (citing HOUSE REP. at 6619–20).

[5] 647 F.2d 320 (2d Cir. 1981), 75 AJIL 965 (1981).

[6] 647 F.2d 300 (2d Cir. 1981), 75 AJIL 968 (1981).

[7] *Cf.* Filartiga v. Peña-Irala, 630 F.2d 876 (2d Cir. 1980), 75 AJIL 149 (1981), in which the Second Circuit held that an allegation of torture in violation of international legal norms was sufficient to permit an alien to bring suit under the FSIA.

[8] The only reference by the court to the international law standard is a footnote citation to the House Report, which states that "[t]he term 'taken in violation of international law' would include the nationalization or expropriation of property without payment of the prompt and adequate and effective compensation required by international law." 515 F.Supp. at 910 n.10.

mental gunboats opened fire on a United States fishing vessel while appellant was on board. The shooting occurred less than a half mile from the Great Isaac Cay, an island of the Bahamas. The U.S. Court of Appeals for the District of Columbia Circuit affirmed the district court's holding that it lacked subject matter and personal jurisdiction under the Foreign Sovereign Immunities Act of 1976 (28 U.S.C. §§1330, 1602–1611) (FSIA).

The FSIA renders a foreign sovereign immune from suit unless certain statutory exceptions are met. On appeal, appellant relied principally on section 1605(a)(5), which provides in part:

> (a) A foreign state shall not be immune from the jurisdiction of courts of the United States or of the States in any case—
>
> . . .
>
> (5) . . . in which money damages are sought against a foreign state for personal injury or death, or damage to or loss of property, occurring in the United States and caused by the tortious act or omission of that foreign state or of any official or employee of that foreign state while acting within the scope of his office or employment. . . .

Section 1603(c) specifies that "[t]he 'United States' includes all territory and waters, continental or insular, subject to the jurisdiction of the United States."

Maintaining that the shooting occurred "in the United States," appellant relied (1) on the 200-mile fishery conservation zone of the Fishery Conservation and Management Act of 1976 (16 U.S.C. §§1801–1822) (FCMA), and (2) on the special maritime jurisdiction of the United States for criminal law enforcement (18 U.S.C. §7(1)). The court, however, found the issue concluded by the fact that the shooting occurred in Bahamian territorial waters.

The court held, first, that for purposes of the FCMA, the territorial waters of the United States and the Bahamas are defined by a median line halfway between the two countries (42 Fed. Reg. 12937–38 (1977)). Second, the only waters subject to special maritime jurisdiction for law enforcement purposes are the high seas, and the territorial waters of a nation do not come within the definition of the high seas. Thus, under either rationale, the court said, appellant failed to establish that the tort occurred "in the United States" for purposes of the FSIA.

In this case, the court was confronted with the geographical proximity of the United States and the Bahamas. In this very particular situation, the court could resolve the territorial question by relying specifically on the Secretary of State's regulations under the Fishery Conservation and Management Act. Thus, with regard to the Bahamas, the court established that any tort committed by that Government within the halfway line between the two countries is not subject to review by the U.S. federal courts. The effect of this holding would appear to be that any tortious act by a foreign sovereign that occurs within its territorial waters is immune from scrutiny in federal courts under section 1605(a)(5). The court did not resolve, however, whether a federal court has jurisdiction over a tort committed within the 200-mile fishery conservation boundary but outside the territorial waters of another country.

Current Developments Regarding Judicial Decisions Reported in the Journal, 1980–1981

Alberta Gas Chemicals, Inc. v. United States, 496 F.Supp. 1332, 75 AJIL 666; *decision on the merits,* 515 F.Supp. 780.

Avigliano v. Sumitomo Shoji American, Inc., 638 F.2d 552, 75 AJIL 671; *cert. granted,* 50 U.S.L.W. 3334 (1981).

Filartiga v. Peña-Irala, No. 79–6090 (2d Cir. 1980), 75 AJIL 149; *reported at* 630 F.2d 876.

Letelier v. Republic of Chile, 488 F.Supp. 665, 74 AJIL 940; *decision on the merits,* 502 F.Supp. 259.

Markham v. Pitchess, 605 F.2d 436, 74 AJIL 935; *cert. denied*, 100 S.Ct. 2985, 447 U.S. 904.

New England Merchants Nat'l Bank v. Iran Power Generation & Transmission Co., 495 F.Supp. 73, 75 AJIL 374; *procedural motion denied,* 508 F.Supp. 47; *common issues of law addressed*, 508 F.Supp. 49.

New England Merchants Nat'l Bank v. Iran Power Generation & Transmission Co., 502 F.Supp. 120, 75 AJIL 375; *procedural motion denied*, 508 F.Supp. 47; *common issues of law addressed*, 508 F.Supp. 49; *remanded for consideration of Executive Orders and Treasury regulations*, 646 F.2d 779.

Pfeifer v. United States Bureau of Prisons, 615 F.2d 873, 74 AJIL 943; *cert. denied*, 100 S.Ct. 2993, 447 U.S. 908.

Rosado v. Civiletti, Nos. 80–2001/2 (2d Cir. 1980), 74 AJIL 679; *reported at* 621 F.2d 1179; *cert. denied*, 101 S.Ct. 153, 449 U.S. 856.

United States v. Mann, 615 F.2d 668, 74 AJIL 944; *cert. denied,* 101 S.Ct. 1694.

United States v. Monroy, 614 F.2d 61, 74 AJIL 942; *cert. denied,* 101 S.Ct. 250, 449 U.S. 892.

United States v. Perez-Herrera, 610 F.2d 289, 74 AJIL 937; *rehearing en banc denied*, 613 F.2d 315.

United States v. Rubies, 162 F.2d 397, 74 AJIL 945; *cert. denied*, 100 S.Ct. 2162, 446 U.S. 940; *rehearing denied*, 101 S.Ct. 28, 448 U.S. 912.

Zenith Radio Corp. v. Matsushita Electric Industrial Co., Ltd., 494 F.Supp. 1263, 75 AJIL 379; *discovery rulings,* 505 F.Supp. 1125, 505 F.Supp. 1190, 505 F.Supp. 1313.

CURRENT DEVELOPMENTS

The 1981 Session of the Institut de Droit International

The Institut de Droit International adopted two substantive resolutions in the field of private international law at its 60th session held in Dijon, France in August–September 1981. These resolutions are reproduced below.

The first resolution, entitled "The Problem of Choice of Time in Private International Law," was adopted after consideration of two reports by Professor Ronald Graveson, rapporteur of the 24th Commission. Professor Graveson's main report was presented to the Athens session of the Institute in 1979 and reported in the *Annuaire* of the Institut for that session (volume 58, part II, at pages 179–90). A supplementary report was presented to the Dijon session together with a revised draft resolution (59 *id.*, part I, at pages 285–88). The observations of members of the commission on the subject and the discussions of the plenary session are found in volumes 58 and 59 of the *Annuaire*.

The second resolution is entitled "The Scope of Application of Rules of Conflict of Laws or of Uniform Substantive Law Contained in Treaties." The rapporteur was Professor Alfred E. von Overbeck for the 23d Commission. Professor von Overbeck's report and the observations of commission members are in the *Annuaire,* volume 59, part II.

In the field of public international law, the plenary session of the Institut discussed at some length the topic, "The Effects of Armed Conflicts on Treaties." It had before it two reports and a draft resolution by Professor Bengt Broms, rapporteur for the Fifth Commission. These documents, together with observations of commission members, are in the *Annuaire,* volume 59, part I, at pages 201–83. The plenary session records are in volume 59, part II. The Institut did not adopt a substantive resolution but instead suggested that the commission submit a further study in which

> it would take positions on the questions raised in the plenary meetings, in particular:
>
> —the relationship between the notions of "state of war" and armed conflict;
> —the applicability of the customary rules of international law concerning treaties and of the provisions of the Vienna Convention on the Law of Treaties concerning the termination and suspension of treaties;
> —the influence on the subject under study of the rules of the Charter of the United Nations on the prohibition of the use of force;
> —in consequence of what has been suggested above, the cases where a party has legal grounds not to execute a treaty.

The Institut also discussed a report on "Legal Aspects of the Creation of Deepwaterports and Artificial Islands." It congratulated Professor Fritz Münch, the rapporteur of the Third Commission, for his work and requested that he submit a complementary report at the next session. The report of Professor Münch and the observations of commission members are in volume 59, part I of the *Annuaire,* at pages 1–78.

Volume 59 of the *Annuaire* also includes reports and observations of the 12th Commission on "New Problems of the International Legal System of Extradition with Special Reference to Multilateral Treaties." Professor Karl Doehring is the rapporteur of that commission.

During the session, commission meetings were held on the following topics:

- the distinction between international texts of legal effect and those without legal effect (7th Commission);
- the law applicable to interstate enterprises (9th Commission); and
- the elaboration of multilateral conventions and quasi-legislative resolutions (13th Commission).

New commissions were established for two topics:

- nonappearance before the International Court of Justice; and
- the distribution among states of spheres of action other than territorial demarcation.

Professor Robert Jennings was elected as President and Great Britain selected as the place of the next biennial session in 1983. Other administrative action included the election of Nicolas Valticos to succeed Paul De Visscher as Secretary-General and the election of 11 associate members. Stephen Schwebel, member of the International Court of Justice, is one of the newly elected associate members.

The texts of the two resolutions on private international law are as follows:

I. The Problem of Choice of Time in Private International Law[1]

(24th Commission)

The Institute of International Law,

Recalling the Resolution on the Intertemporal Problem in Public International Law adopted at its Wiesbaden Session in 1975;

Noting that certain problems of time in private international law differ from those in public international law;

Considering it desirable accordingly to propose appropriate solutions to the problem of time in systems of private international law generally;

Considering that the application of the following principles will facilitate the achievement of just and equitable solutions;

I

Adopts this Resolution:

1. The temporal effect of change in a rule of private international law shall be determined by the legal system to which that rule belongs.

2. The temporal effect of changes in the facts that constitute the basis for assuming jurisdiction or for selecting the applicable law, whether such changes result from the action of a natural or legal person or from that

[1] Dated Aug. 29, 1981. The English text is authentic.

of a legislative, judicial or executive authority, shall be determined as follows:

(a) changes during the course of the proceedings in the facts that constitute the basis for assuming jurisdiction shall not deprive a court of its existing jurisdiction or normally affect the recognition or enforcement of its judgements in other States;

(b) in the case of changes in the facts that constitute the basis for selecting the applicable law, by applying that law, from amongst those under consideration, the application of which corresponds most closely to the objectives of the forum's system of choice of law.

3. The temporal effect of change in the applicable law shall be determined by that law.

4. The legal relevance of facts occurring before or after the legally decisive event, except in so far as relevant for the purposes of assuming jurisdiction or of choice of law, shall be determined by the applicable law.

5. The effect of retrospective legal provisions, whether legislative, executive or judicial, should normally be determined by reference to the legal system in which they originate.

6. Particularly in continuous legal situations of personal status, property or obligation, personal status established and rights acquired before the happening of a relevant change of law should be protected so far as possible.

7. In any case in which, on the occasion of regulating the conflict in time, the effects of a legal situation may be subjected to a law different from that applicable to the conditions of its formation, the solution adopted should take into consideration the need to ensure continuity and cohesion of the total regime of the situation under review.

II

Recommends that:

In order to avoid any cause of uncertainty or dispute, every international instrument or statute relating to matters of private international law should include provisions indicating the solution that ought to be given to such problems of applicable time as might arise in the course of its application.

II. The Scope of Application of Rules of Conflict of Laws or of Uniform Substantive Law Contained in Treaties[2]

(23rd Commission)

The Institute of International Law,

Observing the increasing number of rules of conflict of laws or of uniform substantive law that are contained in treaties and the difficulties encountered in determining their scope of application,

Makes the following Recommendations in aid of the drafting of future treaties:

[2] Dated Sept. 1, 1981. This is a translation of the authentic French text.

I. *Treaties covered by the Recommendations*

Article 1

1. These recommendations apply to multilateral and bilateral treaties containing rules:

(a) on the applicable law;
(b) on the jurisdiction of courts and other authorities;
(c) on the recognition and enforcement of foreign decisions and on judicial assistance;
(d) of uniform substantive law.

2. The Recommendations are concerned only with the scope of application of such rules and do not deal with the entry into force of a treaty either between contracting States or in the legal system of any such State.

II. *Issues to be regulated in the treaties*

Article 2

1. It is desirable that all the treaties referred to contain in particular precise provisions relating to the following issues:

(a) the subject-matter covered by the rules which they contain;
(b) the territorial application of such rules (provisions on territorial application);
(c) the application of such rules to facts that occurred before the entry into force of the treaty (provisions on the application in time);
(d) conflicts with other treaties covering the same subject-matter;
(e) the operation of the treaty in relation to States having a non-unified legal system and, where appropriate, its application to situations which concern several units of one of such States;
(f) the meaning of such terms as "law", "national law", "internal law", if used in the treaty;
(g) the scope of clauses on reciprocity, if any;
(h) issues on which reservations are permitted and, if appropriate, the effect of such reservations.

2. Since the content of provisions on these issues will depend on the subject-matter of the treaty, the only recommendations which it seems possible to make at the present time relate to provisions on territorial application, to reservations and to the application in time. On the last point, the Institute refers to the Resolution on the Problem of Time in Private International Law which it also adopted at its Dijon Session.

III. *Conditions of territorial application*

Article 3

The provisions on territorial application shall define the scope of the treaty rules with respect to:

(a) purely internal situations subject to national law;
(b) situations which have no significant link with a contracting State.

Article 4

1. Treaties on the applicable law or on the jurisdiction of courts and other authorities which permit the parties to choose the applicable law or

the competent authority shall specify whether the parties may use this option in purely internal situations.

2. Treaties on the jurisdiction of courts and other authorities shall contain provisions on territorial application specifying the links which the situations covered must have with a contracting State.

3. Treaties on the recognition and enforcement of foreign decisions shall precisely indicate the decisions to which they refer.

4. Treaties on the applicable law which only govern situations having certain links with a contracting State shall contain provisions on territorial application that describe the situations covered. Treaties which do not contain such limitations should make this clear by means of an express provision which could be worded as follows: "The rules of this Treaty shall apply even to a situation that has no link with a contracting State".

Article 5

1. Where the application of uniform substantive law is limited to situations involving a foreign element, the treaty shall contain a provision specifying that element.

2. Treaties which contain rules of uniform substantive law shall restrict the application of such law to situations that have a significant link with at least one contracting State. To this end, the treaties may:

(a) contain applicability provisions that directly specify the situations to which the uniform substantive law applies; or

(b) contain their own provisions on the applicable law, or refer to provisions on the applicable law that are contained in another treaty which is binding upon all parties to the treaty on uniform substantive law; or

(c) combine the methods of subparagraphs (a) and (b) above.

3. Under the system described in subparagraph (b) of the preceding paragraph, the uniform substantive law shall apply if the provision on the applicable law designates the law of a contracting State and if the uniform substantive law is applicable pursuant to the provision referred to in paragraph 1 of this Article.

4. Treaties which contain rules of uniform substantive law shall specify whether the persons concerned may agree to deviate from provisions that determine the territorial application of such rules.

Article 6

1. Article 4 also applies to rules of uniform substantive law that are contained as ancillary provisions in a treaty covered by that Article.

2. Article 5, except where otherwise expressly provided in the treaty, applies to rules of conflict of laws in a treaty which contains mainly rules of uniform substantive law.

Article 7

The criteria that determine territorial application shall be clearly defined. In particular, one should indicate:

(a) the time at which a criterion is to be assessed;

(b) the subsidiary solution to be used whenever a criterion would result in the designation either of several legal systems or of none at all.

IV. *Reservations*

Article 8

Reservations to a treaty which applies even if a situation has no link with a contracting State have no reciprocal effects.

Article 9

Whenever reservations to a treaty which is restricted in its application to situations that have some link with a contracting State are to be given reciprocal effects, one should specify in the treaty the factor which, in connecting the situation with the State that has made the reservation, produces these effects.

Article 10

Whenever reservations are permitted by a treaty which contains rules on the recognition and enforcement of foreign decisions, the recognition and enforcement of the decisions of a State that has made such a reservation shall be subject, unless otherwise provided, to similar limitations in the other contracting States.

OSCAR SCHACHTER

THE SINAI MULTINATIONAL FORCE AND OBSERVERS

Under the Treaty of Peace between Egypt and Israel, signed March 26, 1979, and related documents, the parties envisaged the establishment of a UN peacekeeping force and observers to supervise the implementation, and employ best efforts to prevent any violation, of the terms of Annex I to the Treaty, the Protocol Concerning Israeli Withdrawal and Security Arrangements.[1] The Protocol sets forth arrangements designed to enhance the parties' mutual confidence in the security of the Sinai border area upon final Israeli withdrawal from the Sinai behind the international boundary between Egypt and the former mandated territory of Palestine. Article 1 of the Protocol provided (para. 1) that Israel would complete withdrawal of all its armed forces and civilians from the Sinai not later than 3 years from the date of exchange of instruments of ratification of the Treaty (*i.e.*, by April 25, 1982).

In response to a formal request from the Permanent Representative of Egypt, the President of the Security Council confirmed on May 18, 1981, that Council members had been unable to reach the necessary agreement on establishing the UN peacekeeping force and observers. Israel and Egypt, with the full participation of the United States, entered into discussions on an agreement to create a multinational force and observers as an alternative when it became apparent that there would be no UN force.

On July 17, 1981, representatives of Egypt and Israel, together with Ambassador Michael Sterner, Deputy Assistant Secretary of State for Near Eastern and South Asian Affairs, representing the United States, initialed a protocol and related documents, that constitute the international agreement establishing the Multinational Force and Observers (MFO) and determining its functions.[2]

[1] For the Peace Treaty and Annex I, see 18 ILM 362 (1979).

[2] For the Protocol, see 81 DEP'T STATE BULL., No. 2054, Sept. 1981, at 44, 20 ILM 1190 (1981).

Formal signature of the Protocol by Egyptian Ambassador to the United States Ashraf A. Gorbal and Israeli Ambassador to the United States Ephraim Evron took place at a ceremony at the Department of State on August 3, 1981, witnessed by Secretary of State Alexander M. Haig, Jr., for the United States Government.

Paragraph 2 of the Protocol states that the Treaty provisions relating to the establishment, functions, and responsibilities of the UN Forces and Observers shall apply *mutatis mutandis* to the establishment, functions, and responsibilities of the MFO "or as provided in this Protocol." Paragraph 3 of the Protocol confirms that the provisions of Article IV of the Treaty and the Agreed Minute shall apply to the MFO, but eliminates Security Council authority over removal of the Force and Observers. Paragraph 4 requires the parties to agree on the nations from which the MFO will be drawn. Paragraph 5 states that the mission of the MFO shall be to undertake the functions and responsibilities stipulated in the Treaty for the UN Forces and Observers, and that the details about its international nature, size, structure, and operation will be set out in an attached annex, which is an integral part of the Protocol.

Paragraph 6 of the Protocol states that the parties shall appoint a Director-General who shall be responsible for the MFO's direction and who shall, subject to the parties' approval, appoint a Commander to be responsible for the daily command of the MFO, with details again to be set out in the attached annex. Under paragraph 7, MFO expenses not covered by other sources are to be borne equally by the parties. Paragraph 8 provides for resolution of disputes arising from the interpretation and application of the Protocol in accordance with Article VII of the Treaty.

On December 29, 1981, President Reagan signed into law, as Public Law No. 97–137, legislation authorizing U.S. participation in the Multinational Force and Observers.

MARIAN NASH LEICH
Office of the Legal Adviser, Department of State

THE HAGUE CONVENTION ABOLISHING THE REQUIREMENT OF LEGALIZATION FOR FOREIGN PUBLIC DOCUMENTS

On October 15, 1981, the Convention Abolishing the Requirement of Legalization for Foreign Public Documents[1] entered into force for the United States. The purpose of the Convention is to abolish the requirement that public documents intended for use in a country other than their country of origin be legalized (*i.e.*, authenticated, or certified) by a diplomatic or consular officer of the country of use, who is stationed in the country of the document's origin (the legalization being often the last step in the "chain-certificate" method of document certification).

As a result of the Convention, contracting states are to exempt from such legalization documents to which the Convention applies that originate in any

[1] *Done* Oct. 5, 1961, TIAS No. 10072, 28 U.S.C.A. App., Rules of Civil Procedure No. 44 (Supp. 1981). Vol. VIII of the 1982 edition of the *Martindale-Hubbell Law Directory* will contain the text of the Convention and other information.

other contracting state. The only formality that may be required to certify (1) the authenticity of the signature, (2) the capacity in which the person signing the document has acted, and, (3) where appropriate, the identity of the seal or stamp that it bears, is the addition of a standard certificate ("*apostille*," so entitled and making reference in the title in French to the 1961 Hague Convention). The standard certificate bears one signature, issued by a designated competent authority of the state from which the document emanates. Contracting states are also required to take the necessary steps to prevent their diplomatic or consular agents from performing legalizations in cases where the Convention provides for exemption from legalization.

The Convention applies under its Article 1 to four categories of documents: (1) documents emanating from a judicial or other tribunal, including documents from a public prosecutor, clerk of court, or process server; (2) administrative documents; (3) notarial acts; and (4) private documents bearing official certifications, such as a certificate of registration or an official authentication of a signature. Article 1 specifically excludes two categories of documents from the Convention's scope: documents executed by diplomatic or consular officers, and administrative documents dealing directly with commercial or customs operations (that normally do not require diplomatic or consular certification).

Authorities in the United States who are competent to issue the standard certificate (*apostille*) include the Authentication Officer/Acting Authentication Officer of the Department of State; clerks and deputy clerks of the Supreme Court, the U.S. Courts of Appeals, all U.S. District Courts, the Court of Claims, the Court of Customs and Patent Appeals, and the Court of International Trade; and certain officers of the individual states and other subdivisions.

This Convention is the third in the field of international judicial assistance produced by the Hague Conference on Private International Law to which the United States has become a party. It complements the Convention on the Service Abroad of Judicial and Extrajudicial Documents in Civil or Commercial Matters[2] and the Convention on the Taking of Evidence Abroad in Civil or Commercial Matters.[3]

MARIAN NASH LEICH
Office of the Legal Adviser, Department of State

[2] *Done* Nov. 15, 1965, TIAS No. 6638, 20 UST 361 (entered into force for the United States Feb. 10, 1969).

[3] *Done* March 18, 1970, TIAS No. 7444, 23 UST 2555 (entered into force for the United States Oct. 7, 1972).

BOOK REVIEWS AND NOTES

EDITED BY LEO GROSS

Human Rights and World Public Order. The Basic Policies of an International Law of Human Dignity. By Myres S. McDougal, Harold D. Lasswell, and Lung-chu Chen. New Haven and London: Yale University Press, 1980. Pp. xxiv, 1016. Indexes. $45.

According to the authors' preface, this work "is designed to outline a comprehensive framework for inquiry about human rights and to suggest certain preliminary clarifications of such rights by criteria appropriate to a world public order of human dignity" (p. xvii). The framework is a restatement of the policy-science approach developed by Lasswell, McDougal, and their various Yale associates in numerous other international law contexts such as the use of coercion, the law of outer space, the law of the sea, and interpretation of agreements. The book "recommends a conception of human rights in terms of the shaping and sharing of values in community process and seeks to locate such rights in their most comprehensive community context and in relation to all relevant processes of authoritative decision" (*ibid.*). Over four hundred pages are devoted to "outlining" the "framework." Then follow about 350 pages devoted to "Trends in Decision and Conditioning Factors: Claims Relating to Respect." In this section the authors consider "respect," defined as "freedom of choice, equality, and recognition" (p. 85), as the "core value of human rights" in the particular contexts of slavery, elimination of caste, elimination of apartheid, equality of opportunity and freedom from discrimination, racial discrimination, sex-based discrimination, religious discrimination, discrimination because of nonconforming political opinion, discrimination in choice of language, protection of aliens from discrimination, and protection of the aged from discrimination. About 70 pages are then devoted to a section on "Future Prospects," entitled "The Aggregate Interest in Shared Respect and Human Rights: The Harmonization of Public Order and Civic Order Claims Relating to Comprehensive Public Order." Here the basic message is that, in addition to the need to honor claims by individuals to respect and other values, some accommodation must be made in respect of the claims of other individuals and those of society. The book concludes with a hundred-page "Appendix" entitled "Nationality and Human Rights: The Protection of the Individual in External Arenas."

The range of material consulted and faithfully summarized by the authors is overwhelming; the scholarship is prodigious. There are only occasional lapses in the accuracy of the factual information. (For example, the discussion at pages 506–07 bemoaning the absence of a permanent body of experts on slavery completely overlooks the Group of Experts on Slavery, which has operated since 1974 under the auspices of the Sub-Commission on Prevention of Discrimination and Protection of Minorities.) There is much here that is stimulating. I found the discussion of the role of nongovernmental organizations (NGO's) in the international legal process particularly interesting. This part of the outline should provide the impetus for further detailed work on the role of individual NGO's, such as the International Commission of Jurists, the International Association for Democratic Lawyers, and the International League for Human Rights, by a careful review of their day-to-day activities over time. The examination of claims relating to respect in particular contexts is also well done. The chapter on apartheid is one of the best discussions in print of that complex problem.

Nevertheless, this is both an anticlimactic and a disappointing book. It is anticlimactic since the gist of it, and indeed many of its specific chapters, has already appeared in the journal literature. The previous appearance of much of the material in the journals also explains why the book is so disappointing. Its origins show. There is much repetition and the parts simply do not fit together into a coherent whole. Only the hardiest of readers will make it from cover to cover. It is not just that the writing abounds with jargon and overworked buzzwords, like "comprehensive," "constitutive process," and "authoritative decision." Savage editorial discipline should have been exercised to cut the book by half. For example, the material in chapter 1 on "Human Rights in Comprehensive Context," that in chapter 3 on "Claims Made to Authority for the Protection of Human Rights," and that in chapter 5 on the "Basic Policies of a Comprehensive Public Order of Human Dignity" could be readily combined and reduced—with vastly greater "clarification" achieved. In fact, the best parts of the book are pages 161–363 ("The Global Constitutive Process of Authoritative Decision") and pages 451–796 ("Claims Relating to Respect"). With a little care in explication, the sum total of the book's contribution to our understanding of human rights could have been entrusted to these chapters, and the others omitted.

The authors' inability to part with the tiniest morsel of their material is unwittingly symbolized by the lengthy appendix on nationality and the explanation of it in the preface. In their preface (p. xxii) the authors note that when they first began their study they had hoped to explore in detail the human rights dimensions of all the eight major values—respect, power, enlightenment, well-being, wealth, skill, affection, rectitude—with which they customarily work. They were unable to obtain the resources to do so. The appendix on nationality

> was designed to be part of a comprehensive study of human rights in relation to the value of power. We include it in this volume partly because of the importance of the problems of nationality and partly to suggest a model for the study of other claims in relation to power [*ibid.*].

The temptation to include it should have been resisted. Insofar as the appendix material complements that in the chapter on the respect value and the rights of aliens, it should have been integrated into that chapter. For the rest, a footnote to the material in its original form in the *Yale Law Journal* would have sufficed. The same principle could have been applied to many of the earlier chapters.

There is some very important material in this book, the product of some of the best jurisprudential minds of our century. Surely they could find a better way to make their thoughts accessible to the lesser mortals who constitute their potential readership.

ROGER S. CLARK
Rutgers School of Law at Camden

The War System: An Interdisciplinary Approach. Edited by Richard A. Falk and Samuel S. Kim. Boulder: Westview Press, 1980. Pp. xvi, 659. $35, cloth; $15, paper.

The aim of this interdisciplinary anthology concerning human conflict is explicitly normative: to find the underlying sources of the "war system" (*i.e.*, "an all-embracing structure of mutually interlocking organizational and behavioral variables, in which violence or force is accepted and legitimized as the ultimate arbiter of social conflicts at all levels of human society") in order to overcome it. In pursuit of this goal, the editors have judiciously selected 27 previously published works, organized largely by discipline—moral and philosophical, ethological and psychological, cultural and anthropological, sociopsychological, sociological, socioeconomic, decision-making, international systemic and normative—and presented with original, often synthetic, and always insightful introductions.

Not surprisingly, but somewhat regrettably, the explicit normative aims of the editors have influenced their selection criteria. For example, as they explicitly reject the notion that "nothing much can be done to abolish the war system," they chose to include a devastating critique (by Kim) of the Lorenzian theory of aggression, rather than let Lorenz and his many fellow travelers speak for themselves. Similarly, as the editors reject the "utopian blueprint school," which envisages a warless future achieved by adoption of legal or constitutional blueprints for general disarmament or world government, such as those most frequently identified with Clark and Sohn, the readings by Stanley Hoffmann and Hedley Bull provide an effective counterpoint to an argument not faithfully presented. Furthermore, as can be inferred from the "disciplinary" enumeration above, several extraordinarily important contributions to the study of the "war system" have been omitted. For example, the editors dismiss as too dependent on rationality the contributions of game theory, without letting the mathematicians have their day in court. Equally as curious is the omission of any of the work on arms races by Lewis Richardson or his followers. If length were a problem, then an early work by Daniel Ellsberg, *The Crude Analysis of Strategic Choices*, might have been included. Surely the exclusionary principle could not have been availability of the selections, for some of those reprinted herein are easily accessible to any student of peace studies; others are from much more obscure sources.

The selection criteria mentioned by the editors include both methodology and substance. Thus, a few of the more primitive empirical works in the field are included, whereas more recent work is not even discussed. Similarly, the editors seem concerned about presenting readings that provide policy-relevant hypotheses, such as those fruitfully abundant in the decision-making section. Presumably, this is part of their rationale for the de-emphasis of international legal accounts. But such a concern certainly should have raised questions about the inclusion of Fabbro's account of *Peaceful Societies*, to say nothing of the methodologically suspect study by Otterbein. In addition, the editors note that some of the works included focus on structural variables and others on process; some focus on antecedent and others on dependent variables. The consequence of this latter catholicity is some confusion, especially as the aim of the book is expected to be a contribution to the elimination of the "war system." Much more laudable is the consistent commitment to interdisciplinary research, even where—as in anthropology—the editors perceive a dearth of significant work.

International law scholars, however, will be sadly disappointed to see their discipline represented by two political scientists (Hoffmann and Bull) and only one international lawyer (Falk), who is found writing about the future of world order, rather than the effectiveness of contemporary legal norms. Without wishing to suggest a criticism of any of these three works—among the most insightful in the book—I still think it disappointing that none of the recent work on civil wars, atomic diplomacy, or aggression is included. Perhaps an excerpt from Julius Stone might have been appropriate. Finally, it should be noted that the selections are not really about why war? (*contra* p. 7), but rather why human conflict?

Although it would be foolhardy to attempt to recount here the contents of each of the essays contained in this long volume, it may be possible to capture the essence of its teachings. For example, the book opens—somewhat surprisingly—with Thomas Nagel's inquiry into the moral bases of the rules of war "beyond legal restrictions," an essay more notable as a specimen of contemporary philosophical methodology than for any substantive contribution. This is followed by an interesting, if somewhat irrelevant, essay by Falk on the anarchist orientation to global reform. The section concludes with an essay by Margaret Fisher on conflict strategies, especially Gandhian *satyagraha* and Agonology. Why there isn't an extended discussion of just and unjust wars by Grotius or Michael Walzer in a section entitled moral and philosophical inquiries is not quite clear. The sociocultural rubric contains an abbreviated, but well-selected version of Ted Gurr's classic work on civil violence. The problem with that selection, as well as several others, is the ambiguity of the editors' definition of war. They are explicit in their rejection of Small and Singer's understanding of interstate war as being too narrow, but they go little further.

The volume also contains Galtung's classic essay, *A Structural Theory of Imperialism*—the relevance to the subject at hand being a bit subtle—as well as Robert Jervis's *Hypotheses on Misperception*, Glenn Paige's on Korea and Cuba, and Ole Holsti's on crisis decision making. In each of these cases the republished works are among their best known, but not their most recent and refined.

Less obvious is the reason for representing Quincy Wright in the sociological selection by one of his less distinguished works.

In any event, the republication of such a rich diversity of works is to be appreciated. This work presents, in a single place, a wide assortment of approaches to the study of conflict, including many that smaller libraries may indeed lack. Moreover, there is no question that the editors have succeeded in advancing their case for the wisdom of interdisciplinary research; whether their work—flawed by an ambiguity of definition and some seemingly inexplicable lacunae as well as inclusions—achieves their higher aim of ridding the world of the "war system" is less clear. Most readers will emerge from this book persuaded of the multi-causality of conflict, but without any clear understanding of the causal paths to conflict. Perhaps a concluding essay—of the quality of the introductory sections in each part—would have aided in this regard.

MICHAEL G. SCHECHTER
James Madison College
Michigan State University

Essays on the Development of the International Legal Order. Edited by Frits Kalshoven, Pieter Jan Kuyper, and Johan G. Lammers. Alphen aan den Rijn and Rockville: Sijthoff & Noordhoff, 1980. Pp. xi, 226. Dfl.100; $50.

A *Festschrift* such as this book of essays dedicated to the memory of Professor Jonkheer Haro Frederik van Panhuys (1917–1976) often fails to have a unifying substantive theme, and on that score the present book is worse than average; it appears to be nothing more than what the writers happened to be writing at the time they were asked for contributions. Making matters more difficult for the scholar is the fact that good essays in books such as these tend to get "lost" since, unlike articles in journals, they are ignored by many indexes and compilations. On the other hand, one would not want to discourage the idea of honoring scholars by such appropriate academic testimonials. On balance, then, a *Festschrift* may enrich the literature, which makes it an agreeable task for a reviewer to mention the noteworthy essays contained therein.

An important essay in this collection is *General Principles of Law Recognized by Civilized Nations* by Lammers, one of the three editors of the volume. The notion of "general principles" in Article 38 of the ICJ Statute is the subject of voluminous literature, amply cited by Professor Lammers; however, the literature on the whole is extremely disappointing. Many extravagant assertions have been made, but very little in the way of theory has been offered to back them up. The present essay at least indicates some of the problems, although it too lacks a theoretical basis. For example, Lammers believes that principles of law which are only recognized on a regional scale could nevertheless be used by the Court in cases involving countries within that region. He likens this to the Court's use of regional custom as in the *Asylum* and *Right of Passage* cases, as contrasted to Article 38 which refers to custom as "general practice." But there are two fundamental problems with Lammers's analogy. First, regional or special custom is entirely different from general custom in that the latter need not entail a showing of specific implied or expressed consent on the part of the state against which the custom is asserted.[1] Second, because of this consent

[1] I have developed this argument in D'Amato, *The Concept of Special Custom in International Law*, 63 AJIL 211 (1969).

element, special custom may take precedence over general custom in the same way that a treaty can derogate from customary law. But what if there is a conflict between a universal general principle and a regional general principle? Lammers fails to test his example against such a possible conflict. And if he were to do so, the edifice he erects might collapse, since it would appear that a "general principle" is part of international law precisely because it reflects a deep universal commitment that may not have had the occasion to be translated into customary practice. Such a deep commitment would appear to be contradicted by a "regional principle" to the contrary. And yet there is no logical need to consider a "regional principle" except in those cases where it is in fact contrary to general principle, for otherwise the latter would simply be cited and the former would be rendered otiose.

Seidl-Hohenveldern has some interesting remarks on *The Social Function of Property and Property Protection in Present-day International Law*. He feels that compensation must be paid when a nation expropriates a foreigner's property, although not necessarily full compensation. However, his remarks are discursive and serve at best to highlight some of the prominent contentions that have been made in this field, including the lump sum compensation agreement study of Richard Lillich and Burns Weston.[2]

Three essays in this volume address the problem of enforcing international law. Tammes contributes *Means of Redress in the General International Law of Peace*. His essay is deceptively well organized; it appears to cover most of the forms of sanctions. Yet the lack of an organizing theory means that many ideas may fall between the cracks. The author seems unaware of the critically important contributions to his subject matter of Roger Fisher and Michael Reisman, even though he shows familiarity with many other American authors. Kiss is the author of *Mechanisms of Supervision of International Environmental Rules*, a review of treaty enforcement mechanisms that appears rather obvious. Riphagen weighs in with *Mechanisms of Supervision in the Future Law of the Sea*, an interesting description of enforcement mechanisms contained in the Informal Composite Negotiating Text of the sixth session of the UN Conference on the Law of the Sea.

Henkin contributes an essay entitled *Resolutions of International Organizations in American Courts*. It is—as usual—clear, brief, and authoritative. Somewhat longer and equally scholarly is Alkema's *The Application of Internationally Guaranteed Human Rights in the Municipal Order*, by which "municipal order" he means that of the Netherlands. Purely national impact studies such as these, however, are as likely to cloud as to clarify the international legal picture. One would hope that more scholars would follow the lead of Schreuer in undertaking multinational impact studies of international legislation and resolutions.

Other authors represented in this collection of essays (and a brief indication of their topics) are: Lachs (ICJ's Revised Procedure), Mosler (case law of the European Court of Human Rights), Schermers (international law in the Court

[2] R. Lillich & B. Weston, International Claims: Their Settlement by Lump Sum Agreements (1975). Reviewed by A. Fatouros in 71 AJIL 363–65 (1977).

of Justice of the European Communities), and a translation of the two final chapters of van Panhuys's last work, *Het Recht in de Wereldgemeenschap*.

ANTHONY D'AMATO
Board of Editors

State and Class: A Sociology of International Affairs. By Ralph Pettman. New York: St. Martin's Press, 1980. Pp. 270. Index. $25.

"I am convinced," writes the author at the outset of this discerning but often difficult volume, "that the study of global politics proceeds the wrong way around," *i.e.*, mainly according to general principles adduced from "the flow of diplomatic traffic . . . , the well-springs of foreign policy and the way such policies interact." To explain "the international events that move over and around us" and simultaneously to allay "a growing . . . feeling that the discipline is less than 'relevant'," it is necessary, he contends, "to reach for arguments in terms of the overall social structure of the contemporary world and the fundamental social forces at work there." A Senior Research Fellow in the Department of International Relations at the Australian National University, Pettman strives to locate and give explicit recognition to the "political sociology" of international affairs.

Arguing first and convincingly the existence of a world culture and society, each reinforced and uplifted by "the advent of global norms" in the form of Western-inspired conceptions of individual and collective human rights, Pettman then evolves his central thesis: that "the social structures most characteristic of our age" are those of state and class; that these structures are fundamentally influenced by the "three basic global trends" of industrialization, urbanization, and bureaucratization; ergo, that it is essential to account for these trends, both within and across national frontiers, to approach proper understanding of world affairs, in particular the twin dynamics of global social ordering (international law) and global social change (world conflict). "We need to fasten upon social formations and the development and dissemination of [system-shaping] values," the author writes; "[w]e need . . . a notion not only of [world] *system*, but also of [world] *society*."

In presenting this thesis, Pettman pays uncommon respect to the development theorists, recently emerged political economists, and other "structuralists," as he calls them, "who [variously] apply neo-Marxist/neo-Leninist paradigms to their understanding of world affairs." But never without appropriate qualification. The "structuralist perspective," he observes—and which he sees as usefully highlighting "the uneven spread" of the global wealth (industrial-technological) process by its accent on "the horizontally arranged [socio-economic] hierarchies that run across [national] boundaries"—exaggerates the part played by "the logic of an emerging world capitalist market" and, moreover, fails to account adequately for the balance-of-power influence stressed by the counterpart "pluralist" school. Actually, Pettman is sharply critical of the "pluralist perspective" as well, which he describes as depicting a multitude of formally equal states "ostensibly serving each one's needs [and the wider common interest, as *severally* defined] while bargaining with and balancing out competing claims." This perspective, he asserts, overemphasizes "the way the anarchic nature of the whole constrains the behaviour of the constituent [parts]," and above all is without capacity to explain the modernization of the contemporary world. Accordingly, Pettman tracks a distinctive course of his own, accepting "the task of understanding just who does what to whom and why in a way that employs both perspectives at the same time."

Thus proceeding, Pettman adds usefully to the growing literature which seeks to comprehend our world as a total living organism, consistent with Teilhard de Chardin's observation that "[we] are now at the beginning of the planetisation of Mankind"; and in so doing he helps to redress a critical imbalance in our understanding of how the world works. I offer this opinion, however, in the face of some lamentable weaknesses, both stylistic and substantive: an unnecessarily slow start; a frequently convoluted—hence arduous—syntax; numerous redundancies; occasionally inadequate differentiations between key concepts (*e.g.*, capitalism vs. industrialization/modernization); insufficient empiricism, particularly when it comes to establishing the self-conscious functioning of socioeconomic classes across national boundaries; a substantial neglect of the interplay between state and class, in particular the influence of the latter upon the former. Also, for the readers of this *Journal* especially, one must note a surprising inattention to the variously sympathetic precedents of such international law pioneers as McDougal/Lasswell and Falk. Perhaps most disturbing, however, is the author's tendency to endorse, more or less unqualifiedly, a limited-factor analysis of the world in which we live, as is suggested by his relatively exclusive stress upon state and class and the "pluralist"/"structuralist" paradigms they recommend. In a world dangerously familiar with the powerful forces of race and religion, for example, surely such an orientation, even if assumed mainly for heuristic purposes, should give pause. Still, the book is a rewarding one overall, and inasmuch as the author humbly states that "[n]othing has been concluded," one may hope to hear more from him in the future.

BURNS H. WESTON
Board of Editors

Legal Problems of Codes of Conduct for Multinational Enterprises. Vol. I. Edited by Norbert Horn. Deventer: Kluwer, 1980. Pp. xiv, 509. Index. Dfl.156; $79.

Of the making of books about transnational enterprises there is no end, nor is one likely. Nevertheless, this volume takes its place as a useful contribution to the already abundant literature on or around the subject. Horn indicates in his foreword that the contributions in this volume "are designed to provide, in their entirety, a comprehensive picture of problems with codes of conduct from a legal viewpoint." This may be an overly ambitious aspiration: there are some notable gaps in the volume, mainly (as Samuel Asante has pointed out in the *Harvard International Law Journal*[1]) the small representation of so-called

[1] 22 HARV. INT'L L.J. 255–56 (1981).

Third World points of view. Additionally, the volume tends to gloss over many of the more strident criticisms in the industrialized states themselves, of both transnational enterprise and codes. Nonetheless, it deals with a wide range of issues and does so well.

The book has a first section on the "Normative Nature of Codes of Conduct for Multinational Enterprises," a second describing both some codes and the "Basic Problems and Main Areas of Regulation," and a third on "Implementation and Follow-up Problems of Codes of Conduct." It is topped off with an annex on "Basic Information and Materials on Codes of Conduct," which contains Professor Hans Baade's second contribution to the volume (his first is the lead article in section 1 on *The Legal Effects of Codes of Conduct for MNE's*), a bibliography, and various codes, in completed (OECD and ILO) or draft (UN Commission on TNC's) form.

There is something here for most tastes. The reader interested in the normative nature of various types of international understandings (or sometimes, misunderstandings) will find much meat in Baade's analysis and in what I thought were Ian Brownlie's trenchant and somewhat skeptical comments thereon; and I was impressed with Professor Horn's analysis of codes as an exercise in "an international process of learning and law making"—learning on the job, as it were. The descriptions of code exercises are all useful and often thought-provoking. Considering the statement made in the introduction that the objective was to provide a picture "from a legal point of view," I found refreshing the first lines of the comments of Sten Niklasson, the long-enduring and long-suffering Swedish chairman of the Inter-governmental Working Group on the Code of Conduct of the UN Commission on TNC's, that "these comments . . . are made from a political rather than a legal point of view." Even the attentive reader might find some difficulty in distinguishing clearly between the two approaches, at least in this field of inquiry, where political statements, if reiterated often enough by enough states, may find themselves arguably transformed into normative rules.

The unwillingness of thought to remain in neat boxes is illustrated also by Detlev Vagts's provocative piece in the "Implementation" section on disclosure and the multinational enterprise, which I thought had more than a little to say relevant to the normative aspects of codes, guidelines, and similar efforts. The inability of competent and disinterested auditors to agree even on what an enterprise is worth (as on what a nation's GNP or rate of inflation "really" is) also suggests some difficulties with the formation of norms which presumably assume a reasonable degree of certainty and agreed definition in such areas. Normative consequences may also be considered by the more skeptical as difficult to deduce from some proposed code provisions, such as the admonition that transnational corporations (the phrase used in the United Nations rather than "multinational enterprise") should "recognize and respect the national sovereignty of the countries in which they operate" or, at an even higher level of ambiguity, "the social and cultural objectives" of those countries.[2] Here

[2] *See* UN Commission on Transnational Corporations, Working Paper No. 10, Formulations by the Chairman (Nov. 7, 1979).

normative concept, descriptive analysis, and implementary appraisal merge and overlap in a way which tends to frustrate the neat organizational pattern of the volume. The value of the pieces, which are of a generally high level, remains.

Inevitably, some chapters are already outdated—as this review probably will be when published. Much has happened in the UN exercise since Professor Fatouros wrote his thoughtful and clear analysis; the Transfer of Technology Code, on which Professor Wilner not only writes but lavished much time and thought, now seems to have been abandoned, at least as a consensual understanding, and without regard to its "voluntary" or "binding" nature. And a certain ennui seems to have crept into many of the code efforts and into the forums in which they are discussed. Delegations from the so-called home countries—mainly the developed nations—are more likely to have the participation of officials from Ministries of Foreign Affairs or other similar agencies; the developing nations—which show a rather high rate of absence—are often represented by resident delegations. The reason probably is that the industrialized nations feel that there is still something to lose, and that caution is necessary.

Codes have now occupied center stage for a considerable period of time; and it may be that this is sufficient explanation of a sense of diminished interest, or at least of diminished intensity in the international negotiating process. Fatigue may be part of the reason, but it is likely that the relevance of codes to improvement of the economic and social circumstances of the developing nations is somewhat in doubt. As world capital becomes scarce, as balance-of-payments crises increase in number and intensity, and as the often substantial differences in priorities of those responsible for development decisions and those involved in the politicized discussions at the United Nations become evident, the thought arises that developing countries seem not as intent on achieving a general code of conduct as was once the case. It is quite possible to argue that in a time of economic difficulty, when a principal objective is to attract private foreign investment via TNC's, it is all the more important to have a standard of conduct in place that will regulate the conduct of those entities. In fact, this is not far from the attitude of nations like Mexico or Brazil, which are acutely aware of the importance of capital and technology arriving from abroad, and of the advantages of worldwide marketing and financing systems. But those countries would appear, if actions are the proof, to put their faith in their own legislation, however much they may cooperate in the code negotiations in international forums. Despite isolated instances like that of the WHO code on breast milk substitutes and their marketing, an intensely emotive issue, passion with respect to codes and guidelines seems to have abated, largely because there is little proof that achievement of codes will in fact significantly accelerate progress toward a "New International Economic Order."

This is not to say that there are not valid reasons which give force and importance to the movement toward codes and guidelines. Many of these derive from the perceived and often real injustices of the existing economic system, and the need for measures of rectification, for the good of developed as well as of developing nations. Developing nations, which have maintained a surprising unity on these matters (surprising at least in view of the obvious inequities between the oil haves and the have-nots, and in view of the enormous consequent strains on many a promising nation), are not likely to give up on codes that have, at a minimum, symbolic value and, moreover, provide a target for future negotiations.

Additionally, one very practical reason why the code effort will continue, and would do so even if the industrialized nations were to withdraw from one or another of these exercises, is that it often results in resolutions or decisions. These, like the Charter of Economic Rights and Duties of States, may not be adopted by consensus or regarded by the affected states as declarative or creative of international law. Nevertheless, they may provide what is in effect the law of a relevant organization, and a directive for secretaries-general, commissions, special working groups and the like, as well as an outline for research projects. The significance of the code exercise is thus not ended even when, as was the case with the UNCTAD Transfer of Technology Conference, the code negotiations themselves are adjourned *sine die.*

It is also important that each code which is agreed, however "voluntary," or resolution which is adopted, however short of unanimity it falls, does provide a basis for further discussion. The importance of the OECD "Guidelines," with their insistence on their nonmandatory character, may lie principally in the ability of nations and of organizations like the Trade Unions Advisory Committee to bring specific issues before a group that is mandated by the Guidelines at least to listen and discuss. In this sense, it is not only accurate but important to say of a code, as has often been said about the UN Code of Conduct, that it must be an "evolving" document.

Moreover, though comment on this specific point has been surprisingly scarce, there is likely to be continuing pressure and perhaps reason for discussions of this sort, since the negotiations involving relations between TNC's and nation-states merely reflect an aspect of a broader issue—the relation between any large and powerful corporation, national or transnational, and the state. TNC's, by reason of sheer size and the transnational character of their operations, have often been thought to possess and to exercise a consequent ability to determine national policies and to frustrate national regulation. I have elsewhere suggested that there may be a time dimension to that proposition, and that it may be the TNC, not the nation-state, which is "at bay."[3]

Even so, and maintaining perspective as to the power of the TNC to move mountains and bring down kings (interestingly, spokesmen of both liberal and conservative economic thought, as quoted in the *Washington Post* of Sunday, May 10, 1981—that is, Mark Green and George Gilder—condemned big business as inefficient and praised small enterprise as innovative), one should note that governments of home as well as host countries have been suspicious of the power of corporations. As early as 1933, Berle and Means wrote their classic *The Modern Corporation and Private Property*, which pointed out that the large corporation could and did affect not only the interests of its stockholders but also major societal values. The point has often been taken up, sometimes stridently,[4] sometimes in more restrained terms,[5] and sometimes from the view-

[3] *See* Rubin, *The Multinational Enterprise at Bay,* 68 AJIL 475 (1974).

[4] *See* R. NADER & GREEN, CORPORATE POWER IN AMERICA (1973).

[5] *See* J. K. GALBRAITH, AMERICAN CAPITALISM: THE CONCEPT OF COUNTERVAILING POWER (1952).

point of management worries about efficiency.[6] The point is that corporations were, in their inception, regarded with some suspicion by the states which created them.[7] The utility of the corporate form to economic development has largely accounted for the relaxation of what were originally tightly limited grants of corporate authority, in the charters in which corporations were given their juridical personality. Corporate charters have changed from the original concept of special and narrow grants for a particular purpose, linked to a state interest, to the modern broadly permissive corporation laws. But suspicion remained—and remains—in regard to large corporate enterprise, be it operating nationally or internationally. It is within the memory of many a living person that Mr. Justice Brandeis wrote in *Liggett Co. v. Lee* (288 U.S. 517, 541 (1933)) words which might well have been incorporated into a Group of 77 speech at an UNCTAD session: "Through size, corporations, once merely an efficient tool employed by individuals in the conduct of private business, have become an institution—an institution which has brought such concentration of economic power that the so-called private corporations are sometimes able to dominate the state."

The sentiment has been reflected in the national arena in such proposals as that for Federal Incorporation statutes, a proposal which still has some vigor, though it has been unsuccessful since first propounded in the Democratic platform of 1908.

This is not to suggest that the codes and guidelines that are capably described and analyzed in *Legal Problems of Codes of Conduct for Multinational Enterprises* should be regarded as either a first priority of a decent international economic order or a political necessity of preserving some semblance of North-South dialogue. Too much in most codes is bombast. Too much reflects unreal perceptions. But there is a case for some sets of norms relating to corporate conduct—and, importantly, to the way in which TNC's will be treated by host and home states. And perhaps too much of the opposition to codes reflects a reluctance to recognize the extent of national regulation within industrialized nations themselves and to perceive that the basis for that regulation has its analogue in the international scene.

Within the nation-states, governments have sought to achieve balance, in their own treatment of their own corporations, between the prevention of antisocial conduct and the desirability of encouraging private enterprises and maximizing their contribution to social and economic objectives. There has thus been considerable emphasis, in the international code exercises, on the issue of how states treat corporations, whether national or transnational. This latter aspect of the codes and guidelines—the question of standards of treatment applied to TNC's, as distinct from standards for the conduct of TNC's—has been a major part of the code discussions, whether in the OECD, the ILO, UNCTAD, or in the UN Commission. It receives surprisingly small attention in the volume under review. If, as Asante correctly suggests, the volume contains somewhat too little of developing nation points of view, it also (other than in

[6] *See* P. DRUCKER, THE CONCEPT OF THE CORPORATION (rev. ed. 1964).

[7] *See* Williston, *A History of Business Corporation Law before 1800*, 2 HARV. L. REV. 105 (1888); and Dodd, *The First Half Century of Statutory Regulation of Business in Massachusetts*, HARV. LEGAL ESSAYS 65 (1934).

Guertin's brief comment) has rather little to say about the so-called treatment issue. Fatouros does deal with the issue in his chapter on the UN code and there is some mention elsewhere. But this is not much for a point that has stimulated basic controversy in the UN discussion since the first session of the UN Commission on TNC's—much more controverted and probably important than the issues of definition, or even of legal nature of the code. In fact, were the title of this volume to have been run through a committee of the UN Commission on TNC's, the title could never have been "Codes of Conduct *for* Multinational Enterprises" (emphasis added). The Inter-governmental Working Group itself neatly finesses the question of whether the proposed code is "for" or "about" or "in relation to" TNC's by referring merely to a "Code of Conduct." "For" or "about" what or whom is left for the reader to determine. The issue is thereby postponed, and discussion progresses. Whether the technique will produce a generally acceptable code is still an open question.

SEYMOUR J. RUBIN*
Board of Editors

Legal Imperialism: American Lawyers and Foreign Aid in Latin America. By James A. Gardner. Madison: The University of Wisconsin Press, 1980. Pp. xii, 401. Index. $20.

This is an interesting and useful book, especially to those who believe in the possibility that law and legal method may make a perceptible contribution to economic development in what are now called the "developing countries." It has, to my view, a somewhat misleading title, which promises—or threatens—more than it delivers. The thesis of the book is mainly that American (used throughout to mean from the United States) legal aid, especially in Latin America (the book does refer briefly to experiences in Africa as well), was offered to—perhaps thrust upon—the countries of Latin America in a well-intentioned but mistaken belief that American legal models would contribute to the social and economic development of the nations of that region: that better lawyers would not only be better artisans but better citizens; and that these expectations were not realized. This analysis is to a considerable extent true, though these expectations were mainly those of academics, in or out of universities; but "imperialism," legal or otherwise, is scarcely made of such stuff.

What happened, as the case studies contained in the volume demonstrate, was that a small group of lawyers, mainly teachers, foundation employees, and officials attached to the Agency for International Development, thought that the inculcation of American legal method—particularly, apparently, the so-called Socratic/Langdell method based on analysis and criticism of specific cases—would, if brought into the Latin American system of legal education, produce lawyers who, like American lawyers, would play a major role in social, economic, and political evolution. As Gardner demonstrates, this thought, when

* The writer is U.S. Representative to the UN Commission on Transnational Corporations. The views expressed in this review are entirely his own, and should not be attributed to any official body.

addressed to those who were responsible for and had a stake in Latin American legal education, found no great receptivity and had in the end little demonstrable effect on how aspiring lawyers were, or are, trained in Latin American educational institutions. Anyone familiar with the habits of mind and resistance to change of even United States "pragmatic" legal educators would hardly have been surprised by this result, even had such a person failed to take into account the ferocity with which educators defend their own terrain. As someone has remarked—can it be C. P. Snow?—professors fight for their prestige because they have so little else at stake. Thus, it cannot be astonishing that the American legal "Trojan pony" (a phrase used by one writer and that Gardner reiterates) did not succeed in overcoming Latin American educational resistance to American methodology.

The book, however, is much more modest than its flamboyant title. "Imperialism"—a word suffused with North-South connotations and the smell of battle—seems an extreme description of the professional belief that something could be done to make Latin American legal education more relevant to the needs of the Latin American nations, as they emerged from feudal, largely agrarian societies—a belief that Gardner in fact does not attempt to refute. Perhaps the attempt to infuse Langdell into Latin American law schools was presumptuous as well as foolish—even irrelevant. But it was based on a correct perception of the unreality of much of the Latin American method as well as on the perhaps incorrect assumption that a more pragmatic method would be both acceptable and useful. This is a far cry from "imperialism."

Moreover, the efforts that are cogently described by Gardner were those of a singularly small group of scholars, whose purple prose about the benefits to be derived from "law and development" efforts was more than a little influenced by the fact that it was that prose which earned them the grants that enabled them to carry out these projects. The language of grant proposals (or of bar association or similar orations) is always to be regarded with a certain amount of skepticism. Of more importance is that the failure of these efforts is discussed only in terms of these grants and the projects they supported. More valuable (except perhaps to the grantees) is to know what, if anything, has actually emerged: are Latin American lawyers still the theoreticians who were emerging from the Latin American schools 30 years ago, or are they competent legal technicians, able to cope with the complexities of an increasingly industrialized and increasingly international society? Is the Latin American lawyer able to deal with the intricacies of share issues and bond redemptions and takeovers and licensing agreements, of international trade and of foreign corporations? I would guess that an ample supply of such lawyers does now exist in Latin America (and the Caribbean), and that, trained chiefly in Latin American institutions, they are fully capable of handling the problems of their clients and their societies, and of negotiating effectively on behalf of private or governmental clients, foreign or domestic. If this be true, then the results, however they may have been brought about, are about what was sought.

Gardner effectively demonstrates that many of the projects he describes were based on highly theoretical notions of persons not directly involved in the daily work of an emerging industrial society. The grandiose promises of the grant proposals or of graduation speeches were thus bound to be frustrated. The fact remains that competent and relevant legal services were essential, and that something had to be done to alter the traditional model of the Latin American lawyer, bringing him into the mainstream of societal development. Such a change was effected, probably largely because the need for such persons was evident and the rewards for competence were large; because of increasing interaction between the legal/business systems of Latin America on the one hand, and those of Europe, Japan, and the United States on the other; and partially because of the "legal imperialism" of the earnest pedagogues from the United States. Hence, even with the limited success of the projects described, a large body of Latin American lawyers exists, fully able to deal with intricate and transnational enterprise, with licensing agreements, contracts, concessions, and the intricacies of international sales or arbitration. The idea was right; perhaps the methodology was wrong.

Gardner suggests, from time to time, that the projects failed to develop a lawyer with a social conscience. Considering the minimum level of such conscience among lawyers in general, this should hardly be surprising. Competence and relevance are two ambitious enough aspirations without the additional aspiration to teach a commitment to social justice. And it is of course accurate that competence may be put to the service of repression as well as of justice. That is true in all societies. Some few lawyers may aspire to more. But most are workers of whom excellence in their craft is the best that can be expected. The fault lies not in the method, but in ourselves.

"Law and development," however difficult it may be to define those terms, continue to be a relevant topic. As Latin American societies move into the industrial age, as they have done, they face the same needs as the so-called developed countries for methods of bringing capital, technology, and labor together in a mutually beneficial relationship. The analytic skills that lawyers characteristically acquire, the training in identification of the relevant and clear statement, are continuing requirements. The efforts described by Gardner tried to achieve this training, with some success. His book may make the way more clear for others, and, in the process, help develop that sense of justice and equity which ought to infuse both the teaching and the practice of law.

SEYMOUR J. RUBIN
Board of Editors

La réciprocité en droit international. By Emmanuel Decaux. (Bibliothèque de droit international, vol. LXXXII.) Paris: Librairie génerale de droit et de jurisprudence, 1980. Pp. iii, 374. F.130.

This work emerged from a doctoral dissertation submitted to the University of Paris II in 1978. It attempts to draw an overall picture of reciprocity in (public) international law by tracing its role, first, in the process of creation of international obligations, second, as a condition of the execution of international agreements, and third, with respect to the sanctions of international law. In the course of this *tour d'horizon*, Decaux deals with an impressive number of questions posed by a notion that is pervasive and elusive at the same time. Thus, in the first part of his study (pp. 15–125), the author has something to say on subjects as scattered as unequal treaties, the international law of development (marked by a renunciation of reciprocity in favor of developing countries), the play of reciprocity behind the regime of reservations to multilateral treaties of various types, its facets in the acceptance of the jurisdiction of the International Court of Justice via the optional clause, and the role of reciprocity in the formation of custom and in connection with unilateral acts.

In the second part (pp. 127–219), the author deals with reciprocity as a condition for the application of municipal law, in particular to the treatment of aliens; with reciprocity clauses in bilateral treaties as well as the nondiscrimination clauses in the Vienna Conventions on Diplomatic and Consular Relations; with the famous Article 55 of the French Constitution of 1958; with reciprocity in the mechanism of the most-favored-nation clause; and finally, with the *rebus sic stantibus* situation conceived as a rupture of treaty equilibrium.

In the third part (pp. 221–338), the author discusses retaliation ("*rétorsion*") and the law of reprisals, withdrawal clauses in arms control agreements, Article 60 of the Vienna Convention on the Law of Treaties on remedies in case of breach, and the reduced importance of reciprocity in European Community law and in humanitarian treaties.

Another 10 pages sum up the author's conclusions, followed by an annotated bibliography and a table of cases.

The book is well written, although at some essential points elegance of style and reliance on authorities prevail over originality of thought. It touches, at times verbosely, on most relevant points, but only rarely does it go into the real crux of the matter.

A propos originality of thought, Decaux points out in his bibliography (p. 355) that, as to research on reciprocity in *public* international law proper, "on peut seulement citer celle faite, principalement en langue allemande, par Bruno Simma." The reviewer was astonished therefore to find no discussion at all of his own views on the subject developed in two books and a number of articles. Interestingly enough, this omission did not hinder frequent sensations of déjà vu in the reviewer. In a traditional *Promotion* or *Habilitation* procedure at any university in a German-speaking country, Decaux's method of coping with recent literature by simply ignoring it would be considered an extremely serious flaw. Our French colleagues are notoriously sensitive about the attention paid to French contributions by foreign authors.[1] How about a little more consideration for reciprocity in the academic domain, too?

BRUNO SIMMA
University of Munich

Recueil des Cours de l'Académie de droit international de La Haye, 1978. 3 vols. (Tomes 159, 160, and 161 of the collection.) Alphen aan den Rijn: Sijthoff & Noordhoff. Vol. I, 1979: pp. 463; vol. II, 1979: pp. 436; vol. III, 1980: pp. 442.

The general course in 1978 was taught by Judge Jiménez de Aréchaga (International Court of Justice) under the title, *International Law in the Past*

[1] *Cf.*, *e.g.*, 84 REV. GÉNÉRALE DROIT INT'L PUBLIC 677 (1980).

Third of a Century. It begins with an examination into the sources of obligation: custom, treaties, and general principles, emphasizing doctrinal developments since the Second World War. Fully acknowledging the bias wrought by such an approach in favor of judicial pronouncements at the expense of other evidences of law, Jiménez de Aréchaga concentrates on the doctrinal implications of pertinent decisions of the ICJ. An example is the discussion of Articles 31 and 32 of the Vienna Convention on the Law of Treaties, where he points out that the rejection in Vienna of Professor Myres McDougal's proposal that preparatory work be considered on the same level as the text in treaty interpretation, was consistent with the approach taken by the ICJ in its Advisory Opinion on the *Admission of a State to Membership in the United Nations* ([1948] ICJ *Reports* 57; miscited by obvious oversight to [1950] *id.* at 8 in the Hague *Recueil des Cours*). But there is no mention of the familiar *parole evidence rule* of Anglo-American common law and its civil law counterpart as a deeper reason in doctrine for rejecting the McDougal approach.

The section on general principles focuses primarily on the prohibition of the use of force and is naturally followed by a chapter on collective measures for the maintenance of peace and security and another on the role of the ICJ in settling disputes.

Turning to substantive rules of law, Jiménez de Aréchaga organizes the bulk of the general course around the conception of the state as territorially based, and this leads to an illuminating discussion of the attempt to codify the law of the sea, emphasizing the "common heritage" idea and the evolution of differing opinions that have made the conclusion of UNCLOS III so difficult. A learned outline of the current law of air and outer space follows.

The final chapter, on the law of state responsibility, ends with a discussion of approaches to the vexing question of compensation in the case of nationalization of alien property.

As we have come to expect of Judge Jiménez de Aréchaga, while all of his opinions are clearly stated, many of them are controversial. Two examples might suffice to indicate the flavor of this challenging course. In his discussion of self-defense under Article 51 of the Charter, Jiménez de Aréchaga concludes that the (sole) object of self-defense must be to end the armed attack and that "it would not be permissible for a State, in the course of its defence, to seize and keep the resources and territory of the attacker" (p. 97). But in reaching that conclusion he ignores the words of the Charter: "until the Security Council has taken the measures necessary to maintain international peace and security." It is entirely conceivable that in the case of failure of the Security Council to take the necessary measures the only effective defense involves taking resources (like military equipment) and perhaps even some territory from an implacable enemy. Similarly, in his discussion of expropriation, the assertion that "private ownership of the means of industrial production, is no longer protected by contemporary international law" (p. 298) seems an overstatement. To the extent that property rights are a creature of the municipal law of the situs of the property, private ownership as such has never been protected by international law; to the extent that compensation to an alien property owner in cases of nationalization is sought, questions of amounts of compensation and theoretical bases for reckoning compensation have never been considered settled either in the past or today despite the exaggerated arguments heard on all sides.

The mention of these two examples of what seem advocates' exaggerations by Jiménez de Aréchaga is not a criticism; the time has long passed when a general course in international law could discuss in depth all the issues that must be touched on in a *tour d'horizon*, and it is far more instructive to have firm but debatable conclusions than bland hesitation where the general course touches the most important issues of the day.

An interesting counterpoise to parts of Jiménez de Aréchaga's course is the course by Richard B. Lillich (Virginia), *Duties of States Regarding the Civil Rights of Aliens*. Starting with a recitation of three familiar personal injury claims situations attributable to the act or default of government officials as evidence of the continuing need for a body of international law governing the treatment of aliens, Lillich moves immediately to the protection of private property rights. He seems to accept the historical importance for claimant states' arguments of Vattel's conclusion that "whoever ill-treats a citizen indirectly injures the State, which must protect that citizen," despite the inapplicability of Vattel's social-contract logic to the support of an international law proposition or the refusal by states in most circumstances to acknowledge any duty in municipal law (based on social contract or other theories) to follow with armies the peregrinations of their merchants abroad.[1] Lillich goes on to discuss the Drago doctrine,[2] the Calvo Clause,[3] and the minimum international standard of justice derived from the British approach to the *Don Pacifico* case.[4] The

[1] One strange apparent exception to this refusal is the background paper by David Gantz, while an attorney in the Department of State, saying that "[t]he protection of nationals is not only the right, but the duty of the State" (DIGEST OF UNITED STATES PRACTICE IN INTERNATIONAL LAW 1973, at 334). Six months later the Assistant Legal Adviser for International Claims wrote: "The diplomatic protection afforded by the Government of the United States to its nationals . . . is not a legal right. Such protection, instead is in effect an extra-ordinary legal remedy which is employed by the Department [of State] in its discretion . . ." (*id.* at 333). In the circumstances it is very difficult to understand why the first statement, an internal memorandum by a junior official obviously overruled on the point of law within the Department, was published in a repertory of United States practice.

[2] Lillich at one place, 161 RECUEIL DES COURS 349 (1978 III), attributes the virtual disappearance of forcible self-help to collect contract debts owed to aliens to Convention No. 2 of the 1907 Hague Peace Conference. He does not mention that the second paragraph of Article I of that Convention lifts the prohibition on the use of force in cases in which "the debtor State refuses or neglects" to agree to arbitration of the claim or "fails to submit to the award." Further into the course (*id.* at 358) he mentions the importance of other documents in transforming the Drago doctrine into a rule of positive law.

[3] Lillich apparently believes the common Latin American practice of attempting to place foreign firms on the same legal plane as domestic firms by obtaining a contractual commitment from them not to seek diplomatic intervention but to confine themselves to the remedies available to domestic firms in case of dispute arising under the contract, is legally futile, although it is being revived today in the context of the so-called New International Economic Order (*id.* at 349–53, 368–72). Jiménez de Aréchaga's views are very different. *See id.* at 309–10 (1978 I); and Jiménez de Aréchaga, *International Responsibility*, in SØRENSEN, MANUAL OF PUBLIC INTERNATIONAL LAW 531, 590–93 (1968).

[4] A handy extract of the sizable documentation relating to the *Don Pacifico* case is in L. SOHN & T. BUERGENTHAL, INTERNATIONAL PROTECTION OF HUMAN RIGHTS 40–58 (1973).

course deals at some length with the status as of 1978 of the ILC consideration of a draft code of state responsibility and various other ongoing attempts in the United Nations to formulate human rights provisions in matters other than racial discrimination and self-determination. The bias towards human dignity and the mastery of the legal background and current law-formulating activity are apparent throughout, and on these matters undoubtedly Lillich and Jiménez de Aréchaga share a great deal of common ground. But when Lillich turns again to the "New International Economic Order" and other matters dealing with the international protection of private property, the contrast between his argumentation and Jiménez de Aréchaga's is most illuminating where preferences and value systems on both sides are asserted as universally valid and counter-arguments left unstated. As was the case when the Hague Academy brought D. P. O'Connell and M. Bedjaoui together in similarly complementary courses dealing with state succession and the respect due (or not due) to the private property of aliens as acquired rights,[5] most enlightenment in reading Jiménez de Aréchaga and Lillich comes when the student attempts to discover the unstated reasons for differing evaluations of the same reality. The Academy and the lecturers are to be congratulated.

A course of possible jurisprudential importance, *La Structure de l'ordre juridique international*, was given by Professor Giuseppe Barile (Rome). Building on the conceptions of sociological positivism normally identified with the writings of Gény, Duguit, and Ehrlich, Barile posits the existence of an international community whose unwritten law, analogous to Anglo-American common law, exists in the *conscience juridique* of the members of the international society. Its principles include sovereign equality of states, *pacta sunt servanda*, and state responsibility for international delicts. But this law rests ultimately on the common agreement of states. Thus, Barile finds, reliance on principle in the absence of agreement as to the precise scope of that principle is ineffective to nullify treaties, and *jus cogens* in the sense of some superior law independent of common consent does not exist. On the other hand, unilateral declarations such as those of France which the ICJ found in 1974 to be binding *erga omnes* to exclude further nuclear testing in the atmosphere by France are considered by Barile to be evidence of France's acceptance of a rule, founded in the social conscience of states, as to the inadmissibility of such testing. Thus, without supporting the Court's reasoning, he supports its conclusion in substance. It is possible to disagree with Barile as to his reading of the actual French position and the underlying jurisprudential concepts at play in the *Nuclear Tests* cases, and as to the persuasiveness and utility of his elaborately argued theory of social conscience in general, but the course offers an interesting contribution to the theory of international law.

Guennady P. Zhukov (ICAO) lectured on *Tendances contemporaines du développement du droit spatial international*. After summarizing the terms of the principal treaties, UN General Assembly resolutions, and more or less familiar interpretations of them relating to space activities in general, including liability for injury and assistance to and return of astronauts, Zhukov turns to agencies with purview over telecommunications by satellite: Intersputnik, IN-

[5] 130 Recueil des Cours 95, 457 (1970 II), reviewed in 68 AJIL 545 at 548–50 (1974).

TELSAT, and INMARSAT. His information is detailed, precise, and very current, including brief mentions of various national and regional satellite communications systems not due to be launched until 1982 or later. Turning to television "direct broadcast" satellites, he points out problems of frequency allocation and the even more serious political problems of content control of intrusive foreign broadcasts, but the positions of the various states are not analyzed deeply. Turning to remote sensing, Zhukov disagrees with those writers (naming "S. Lay [*sic*] et H. Taubenfeld") who see no inconsistency between the compilation by some space powers of worldwide resource information through extraordinary current photographic and other remote sensing capabilities and the 1967 Space Treaty and other documents dedicating space to the use of all and upholding the territorial rights of sovereign states, including each state's sovereignty over its natural resources. Zhukov believes the nine-party Moscow Convention of May 19, 1978, binding the USSR, the Eastern European states, Mongolia, and Cuba sets the legal pattern for the future by providing against the use to the prejudice of the state concerned of information concerning natural resources of that state derived from remote sensing by satellite. Finally, the Moon Treaty of December 18, 1979, is analyzed (in a section that must have been added after the 1978 lecture was delivered) as a compromise between the United States as a proponent of immediate exploitation and the USSR as a proponent of safeguards for all mankind against national appropriation of lunar resources (by the United States). There are undoubtedly points at which those familiar with the negotiations would disagree with some interpretations placed by Zhukov on the text and the context.

Several other courses in the 1978 Hague *Recueil des Cours*, while probably of most interest to those specializing in private international law, international organization, trade, or comparative law, deserve special mention here. Judge Franz Matscher (European Court of Human Rights), in a learned course entitled *Étude des règles de compétence judiciaire dans certaines conventions internationales*, discussed how such rules as *res judicata* and *lis pendens* might restrict the jurisdiction of foreign courts. Eric Suy (United Nations) addressed *The Status of Observers in International Organizations*. An aspect of European Community law of increasing importance, the general organization of the Community to handle external relations in light of the *ERTA* case (22/70 of March 31, 1971), was the subject of a course by Professor Jean Boulois (Paris), *La Jurisprudence de la Cour de Justice des Communautés européennes relative aux relations extérieures des Communautés*. Thomas M. Franck (UNITAR) lectured on *Minimum Standards of Public Policy and Order Applicable to Collective International Commodity Negotiations*.

More or less squarely in the private and comparative law area were the General Course on Private International Law, taught in 1978 by Professor Allan Philip (Copenhagen); *Le Renouveau du particularisme en droit international privé* by Professor Juan Antonio Carrillo Salcedo (Madrid); *Le Droit monétaire dans les relations privées internationales* by Professor Philippe Malaurie (Paris II); and *La Solution des problèmes de statut personnel dans le droit des pays arabes et africains* by the late Judge Salah El Dine Tarazi (ICJ).

ALFRED P. RUBIN
Naval War College

Judicial Review of Governmental Action and the Requirement of an Interest to Sue. By P. van Dijk. Alphen aan den Rijn: Sijthoff & Noordhoff, 1980. Pp. lx, 557. Index. Dfl.200; $100.

This book (published as volume XXI of the prestigious *Bibliotheca Visseriana* series) is an English version of a Leiden doctoral dissertation on a topic suggested by Henri Rolin. The author investigates the requirements of standing to sue prescribed by various systems of law that confront a litigant judicially challenging the legality of governmental action. For American lawyers the nature of the problem addressed may be readily grasped by reference to *Flast v. Cohen* (392 U.S. 83 (1968)) and similar cases.

Reviewing the concepts of modern procedural science (*Prozessrechtswissenschaft*) in a manner akin to that utilized in Maarten Bos, *Les Conditions du procès en droit international public* (1957),[1] van Dijk holds that the issue of standing is to be treated as a requirement with respect to the admissibility of the application for judicial relief (*recevabilité, Zulässigkeit*), rather than one with respect to the jurisdiction of the court (*compétence, Zuständigkeit*). In general, he specifies five factors that are needed to confer standing: (1) a prima facie possibility that the court may be able to pass upon the merits of the controversy by applying the law to the concrete facts of the case, *i.e.*, that the application is not patently unmeritorious; (2) that it must *still* be possible for the object of the application to be realized, *i.e.*, that the case has not become moot; (3) that the case is ripe for adjudication, not premature; (4) that the case is appropriate for judicial action, *i.e.*, that administrative remedies have been exhausted, or national remedies in the case of international claims; and (5) that the proceeding does not involve abuse of the right of action as in cases of vexatious or trivial litigation brought for a purpose other than that for which the right of action was granted (*détournement de procédure*).

The same pattern, to a large extent, is found in all the legal systems compared. There are, of course, many variations and these are carefully pointed out. The English, American, French, and German national systems are first reviewed; then the international systems of the European Communities, the European Convention on Human Rights, and the International Court of Justice. The author concludes that in the international sphere there is no present likelihood of extending the right to every member of the public to bring an *actio popularis* merely to vindicate the majesty of law (p. 523). But the European Communities proceedings instituted by Community institutions and member states (unlike those instituted by private parties) are deemed to have been brought for the purpose of maintaining the integrity of the legal order created by the Community Treaties, and hence there is no requirement that the party bringing the action has sustained or is in danger of sustaining a special injury to its particular interests (pp. 252, 258–59).

The author's treatment of the subject is thorough and judicious. The book forms a valuable contribution to the literature on international procedural law.

EDWARD DUMBAULD
U.S. Senior District Judge

[1] Reviewed in 52 AJIL 555–56 (1958).

International Labour Law. By Nicolas Valticos. Deventer: Kluwer, 1979. Pp. 267. Index. Dfl.36.

World Labour Rights and Their Protection. By James Avery Joyce. New York: St. Martin's Press, 1980. Pp. 190. Index. $22.50.

The need to protect the rights of labor has been asserted since the time of the Industrial Revolution. The establishment of the International Labour Organisation in 1918, pursuant to the provisions of the Treaty of Versailles, manifested a growing global concern about workers' rights. It stands as one of the earliest formal recognitions of individual liberties on a worldwide scale. Later, in 1948, the UN General Assembly adopted the Universal Declaration of Human Rights, which acknowledges certain labor rights as basic to the dignity of every human being. The international labor and human rights movements have continued to evolve side by side. Together they reinforce the ability of the world community to penetrate sovereign state boundaries in defense of the individual worker.

Valticos, in *International Labour Law*, and Joyce, in *World Labour Rights and Their Protection*, have traced the scope and development of the international labor movement. Although each author has distinctively shaped and styled his work according to his own purpose, both books make apparent the ever-deepening "global conscience"[1] with regard to the protection of labor.

Professor Valticos's many years of experience with the International Labour Office, culminating with his current post as Assistant Director-General, certainly qualify him as an authority on world labor issues. His expertise is evident in the text of *International Labour Law*, which he originally prepared as a monograph for the *International Encyclopedia for Labour Law and Industrial Relations*. The work has all the textual and structural characteristics of the reference volume it was designed to be. It concisely presents detailed substantive information about the development, content, and practice of international labor law. The author's systematic analysis is essentially objective: he has refrained for the most part from promoting his personal views. His treatment of policy issues is largely restricted to identification of the fundamental purposes of world labor legislation and the principles upon which the structure and operation of the International Labour Organisation (ILO) are based. He also reviews significant policy questions that have been raised over the years and the theories underlying their resolution.[2]

The volume is divided into three parts. An introductory section traces the "historical and general background" of international labor law, its various sources, and the "institutional framework" of the ILO. In part I, Valticos provides a comprehensive, yet concise, catalog of the "content of international

[1] J. JOYCE at 16.

[2] For instance, Valticos objectively describes, *inter alia*, the manner in which the ILO has dealt (1) with the difficulties in separating government from employer and worker representation by states with socialized economies; (2) with disagreements as to its scope and competence; and (3) with the various problems involved in drafting conventions and recommendations to regulate labor matters in states with divergent national conditions and ideologies. *See* in this regard, N. VALTICOS, 30–34, 38–42, 49 and *ff.*

labour law." He examines significant ILO conventions and recommendations as well as the labor rights provisions of other pertinent bilateral and multilateral instruments. Part II describes the "implementation of international labour standards" and includes a discussion of the general obligations of ILO member states, the effect of ratifying conventions, the scope and operation of the supervisory machinery of the ILO and other international organizations, and finally, some of the special ongoing programs and services of the ILO. The book ends on a forward-looking note as Valticos breaks somewhat from his objective style to briefly render his opinion as to the direction the entire international labor law system will likely take in the future.

The volume's extensive documentation and cross-referencing, as well as its selected bibliography, detailed table of contents and index, and system of numbered paragraphs, all ensure its value as an educational and research tool. It is certain to be well utilized, not only by the audience of labor law researchers, employers' organizations, and trade unions for whom it was primarily drafted in its monograph form, but also by the "wider circles" of less specialized readers it was hoped would be reached by publishing it in book form (p. 3).

Valticos has presented his material in such a succinct, well-organized manner that, despite the breadth of its scope and the depth of its detail, the text remains coherent. The precision with which the study is ordered gives it clarity and advances its usefulness as a reference book. Moreover, by so systematically structuring his analysis, Valticos has implicitly illustrated the exact nature of international labor law that has enabled it to give concrete expression to the ideals of the worker protection movement. As an easy-to-read, practical resource manual, Valticos's work makes a significant contribution to that movement.

The book by Joyce plays yet another part in the effort to safeguard the welfare of the world's working class. Joyce's book is a commentary designed to call attention to the "vitally important" relationship among workers, the state, and the developing global framework for protecting the rights of individuals (p. 9). Joyce's attempt is to persuade his readers of the importance of action on all levels—national, international, governmental, and nongovernmental—to improve labor conditions. To do so, he presents general information about many aspects of the current international labor situation.

Joyce limited himself to outlining certain "overriding ideas," leaving it to his readers to further explore the details of those issues which stimulate their interest (p. 15). In theory, such a plan has merit, but the topics he touches upon are so many and so diffuse that, to some extent, this brief work lacks cohesion. Nonetheless, the study is useful as an across-the-board introduction to the kinds of labor abuse occurring around the world and to the methods currently used to protect the rights of workers.

Joyce begins by defining workers' rights within the broader context of human rights. He discusses the United Nations Universal Declaration of Human Rights, which he refers to as the "International Bill of Rights" (p. 19), as well as the two agreements created to implement it—the Covenant on Civil and Political Rights and the Covenant on Economic, Social and Cultural Rights. His apparent purpose in reviewing these human rights documents is to point out the close working relationship between the United Nations and other international institutions with respect to the protection of labor rights (p. 15). He notes in particular that the principles set forth in the UN Declaration have been the foundation of many ILO policies as well as of international agreements regarding labor matters (pp. 19, 25).

The author completes his description of workers' rights in two ensuing chapters devoted to the formalized systems of labor protection developed by the ILO and the European Commission. He then examines the methods used by the United Nations and the ILO—working separately or together—to deal with complaints of specific transgressions against the liberties of individual workers.

Joyce culminates his analysis with a series of nine case studies which he considers the "heart" of his book (p. 13). He recounts actual instances of labor abuse in nine different areas of the world: Chile, Czechoslovakia, Equatorial Guinea, Indonesia, Palestine, the Soviet Union, southern Africa, Tunisia, and Uruguay. In each case he examines the international efforts made to vindicate the rights of the workers involved. This demonstration of the different sorts of injustice suffered by laborers throughout the world cannot fail to achieve Joyce's goal of impressing the reader with the need for continued support for the international labor movement. Throughout each case study, however, Joyce presents a smattering of tangential ideas and issues that cannot all be explored to their logical end. As a consequence, his development of the main point of each study suffers. The book's lack of internal structure is particularly evident in this section. Furthermore, Joyce's failure to adequately document much of the information he imparts will be disturbing to the scholarly reader. He does not supply the references that one would hope for from an author with his background. His justification is the desire for a "smooth running narrative" (p. 9). His goal of producing an easy-to-read, persuasive commentary, however, should not be incompatible with attention to scholarly detail.

The author continues with a discussion of the labor-related activities of nongovernmental organizations, *e.g.*, trade unions, Amnesty International, and other voluntary groups. He finishes with a description of certain proposed international and national remedies for labor rights violations. Appended to the work are the texts of pertinent international agreements and selected ILO conventions, a lengthy list of trade union leaders executed in Chile, and a selected bibliography of ILO publications.

The divergence in the approaches of Valticos and Joyce to an essentially common subject matter is apparent. Valticos's encyclopedic work functions as a valuable reference tool. Joyce's provocative commentary, despite its organizational failings, functions as a general introduction to the grave realities of the world labor situation. As such, the two works complement each other in their mutual attempt to further the progress of the international labor movement.

JOSEPHINE COCKRELL THORNTON
National Labor Relations Board

MARY ST. VILLE
International Law Institute,
Georgetown University Law Center

Humanity in Warfare. By Geoffrey Best. New York: Columbia University Press, 1980. Pp. xi, 400. Index. $25.

British historian Geoffrey Best has furnished us with his thoughtful observations on the history of the idea of moral and legal restraints in the conduct *of* war. His aim is to examine the notions of *jus in bello*, the regulations supposed to govern soldiers; he leaves to others the subject of *jus ad bellum*, the notions of legal and moral restraints on the resort *to* warfare, those regulations supposed to govern statesmen. His work, then, is within the "law of war" genre rather than in the "just war theory" category; or, as Best puts it, "Humanity, not Justice, is its *prime* concern" (p. 5, emphasis in original).

He argues that the idea of trying to limit war's cruelty to both combatants and noncombatants caught on during the Enlightenment and was codified late in the 19th century and early in the 20th in the Geneva and Hague Conventions. By now, he says, "The Geneva Conventions must share celebrity with the Universal Declaration of Human Rights and perhaps the Charter of the United Nations as the most nearly universally known and seemingly accepted statements about what is due to man from man" (p. 3).

Though they may not actually be all that well known in detail to many who are not specialists in this branch of international law, the general provisions of the Conventions are familiar: prisoners deserve consideration, innocent noncombatants deserve immunity from military assault, the rights of neutrals should be respected, particularly barbarous means and weapons should be eschewed, gratuitous destruction should be avoided, and so forth. The task of lawyers and publicists has been to elaborate these notions, the obligation of statesmen and warriors to adhere to the developing code. Geoffrey Best tells the story of these efforts, moving easily back and forth from the materials of intellectual history to the realm of battlefield experience. Unfortunately, in this stylish—if sometimes mannered—narrative, he focuses too narrowly on the European experience, which makes the reader wonder about the alleged universality of the code's acceptance; and he assumes that his reader already knows more European history than it is probably realistic to expect. He also assumes that his reader knows a good deal about the laws of war (which he might usefully have gathered together in an appendix or listing of some sort); so most readers will benefit from a prior reading of another, more introductory text, such as Sydney B. Bailey's *Prohibitions and Restraints in War* (1972).

How about the record of compliance? Alas, of course, it has been uneven at best. The distinction between combatants and noncombatants has been blurred in the 20th century's total wars, ideological wars, and civil wars—all of which encourage the perception that everyone in the other camp is a participant and thus "fair game," no one deserving immunity. Twentieth-century technology has also brought into play weapons that can hardly be used discriminatingly: thermonuclear bombs, missiles, bacteriological agents, even the powerfully lethal gadgetry under the control of an infantry company commander far down the chain of responsibility. Best urges us to marvel that there has been as much compliance as there has been, rather than to dismiss the code cynically as so much wishful thinking overtaken and rendered obsolete in our times.

For, Best insists, the idea of humanity or restraint survives as a standard, a goal, an ideal. As such, it is better than nothing. Even frequently violated, it has nonetheless evidently induced an appreciable amount of restraint, saving many lives and much property. As with our other imperfectly obeyed laws, we ought not to insist naively on high levels of compliance as a requisite for our support. Confounding skeptics and cynics, compliance may well increase too, since it is even in the interest of the military to embrace the code as a tool in its efforts to employ *controlled* violence to accomplish political objectives, while simultaneously trying to limit its losses and protect its people and assets.

JAMES A. STEGENGA
Purdue University

The Laws of Armed Conflicts. A Collection of Conventions, Resolutions and other Documents (2d rev. and completed ed.). Edited by Dietrich Schindler and Jiří Toman. Alphen aan den Rijn and Rockville: Sijthoff & Noordhoff; Geneva: Henry Dunant Institute, 1981. Pp. xxxiv, 933. Index. $105.

This most useful single-volume collection of 80 documents constituting the sources of the codified *jus in bello* has recently been revised and updated.[1] The collection includes all multilateral conventions on the law of armed conflict, whether or not they are or were in force, as well as final acts and resolutions adopted by intergovernmental conferences that drew up the conventions, and resolutions of intergovernmental or nongovernmental organizations in which the law of armed conflict is generally stated. Included are the results of the 1874 Brussels Conference, the 1880 Oxford Manual, and the 1923 Rules of Air Warfare. Except for the U.S. Lieber Code, no national regulations or legislation is included. A unique and highly useful feature of this collection is the inclusion of the full text of all reservations to these conventions.

This collection does not contain any texts concerning the limitation and prohibition of force in international relations (*jus ad bellum*), arms control,[2] or human rights. Apparently, the project to publish a collection of texts on the outlawry of force in international law has been dropped. That is most unfortunate since such a project would fill a notable void. There is no modern collection of documents on the peaceful settlement of disputes or on the *jus ad bellum* and the appearance of such a collection would be significantly useful.

The second edition includes eight new documents representing most of the

[1] The first edition (1973) was noted at 69 AJIL 927 (1975).

[2] The 1925 Geneva Gas Protocol and the 1976 Convention on the Prohibition of Military or Any other Hostile Use of Environmental Modification Techniques (ENMOD) are included because of their provisions prohibiting the *use* of certain weapons, even though they are also considered to be arms control agreements.

developments in the law of armed conflict since the appearance of the first edition in 1973. By far the most important additions are the full texts of the two 1977 Protocols Additional to the 1949 Geneva Conventions for the Protection of War Victims,[3] along with the Final Act of the Diplomatic Conference on Humanitarian Law, which produced those Protocols, and that conference's resolutions. Also added to this new edition are the 1976 Environmental Modification Convention,[4] the 1974 UN General Assembly Resolution 3318 (XXIX) on the Protection of Women and Children in Emergency and Armed Conflict, the 1973 General Assembly Resolution 3103 (XXVIII) on the Basic principles of the legal status of the combatants struggling against colonial and alien domination and racist regimes, and the 1975 resolution of the Institute of International Law on conditions of application of rules, other than humanitarian rules, of armed conflict to hostilities in which UN forces may be engaged.

The notable omission is the 1980 Convention on Prohibitions or Restrictions on the Use of Certain Conventional Weapons Which may be Deemed to be Excessively Injurious or to have Indiscriminate Effects,[5] an omission understandable in light of the professed cut-off date of early 1978. However, some of the lists of signatures, parties, and associated statements are based on replies from the Dutch and Swiss Governments (as depositary) as late as April 8 and October 2, 1980, respectively. Such unevenness is undoubtedly to be attributed to the delays associated with ocean transport of the galleys and page proofs (which were set in the United States, while the authors reside in Switzerland).[6]

The compilation of locations where the texts of the documents are published has been expanded to include five additional secondary sources, including two 19th-century Russian books, in addition to English, French, Spanish, German, and Dutch sources. However, there are no references to Chinese or Arabic sources, the only other official languages of the United Nations not represented in this edition.

Errors of the first edition have been corrected, including the omission of the general provisions of the 1906 Geneva Convention. However, a number of other sources of the texts are still not listed.[7]

On the other hand, the chapters have appropriate cross-references to the 1977 Additional Protocols and the introduction has been usefully expanded to include a summary of the developments in this area of the law since 1972.

Because of the very high cost of this edition, it would be most useful for a

[3] 16 ILM 1391 and 1442 (1977).

[4] Erroneously stated not to be in force. The ENMOD Convention entered into force on Oct. 5, 1978.

[5] 19 ILM 1524–35 (1980); 21 INT'L REV. OF THE RED CROSS 20–32 (1981).

[6] A list of parties to the Geneva Conventions and Additional Protocols, updated quarterly, is available from the Dissemination and Documentation Division of the International Committee of the Red Cross, 17 avenue de la Paix, CH-1211 Geneva, Switzerland.

[7] Such as the Additional Protocols, *supra* note 2, and the Edinburgh Resolution of the Institute of International Law, on the distinction between military objectives and nonmilitary objects in general and particularly the problems associated with weapons of mass destruction; 66 AJIL 470–71 (1972). Schindler and Toman also fail to note the exceptions taken by the United States to portions of this resolution; 67 AJIL 122–25 (1973).

paperback edition to be published. That would certainly further the Red Cross's program of dissemination of the international humanitarian law, and put this most handy book in the reach of the many people around the world who need it.

The introduction states that "the conventions on sea warfare are for the most part outdated, and economic warfare remains to a large extent outside the scope of the laws of war. Finally, the rights and duties between belligerents and third States (neutrals) are highly uncertain." These assertions are certainly true, to the extent that there are no modern codifications or developments of these aspects of the law. However, Additional Protocol I to the 1949 Geneva Conventions has some provisions applicable to war at sea, for example dealing with hospital ships (Article 22), means and methods of warfare (Articles 35–38), and naval shore bombardment (Articles 48–58).[8] These provisions should therefore be reflected in the military manuals currently being written or revised, for example, in Canada, Australia, the United Kingdom, and the United States. Whether there is a need for further codification or development of the law of naval warfare can thus not be properly decided until the influence of the Additional Protocol in this regard is assessed. The same can also be said of the law of neutrality but not of economic warfare. The prospects for early formal changes in either are, however, remote.

J. ASHLEY ROACH
Judge Advocate General's
Corps, U.S. Navy

An International Criminal Court. A Step Toward World Peace: A Documentary History and Analysis. Vol. I: Half a Century of Hope. Vol. II: The Beginning of Wisdom. By Benjamin B. Ferencz. London, Rome, New York: Oceana Publications, Inc., 1980. Vol. I: pp. xvii, 538; vol. II: pp. x, 674. Index. $75 for 2 vols.

There is scant doubt that during war gross violations of human rights affecting both combatants and civilians are needlessly and pervasively committed, more often than not with impunity. This realization underscores the central thesis of the documentary omnibus presently under review: namely, that "there can be no peace without justice, no justice without law and no meaningful law without a court to decide what is just and lawful under any given circumstance"

[8] However, other provisions of Additional Protocol I were explicitly not designed to affect the law of naval warfare. For example, the "existing generally recognized rules of international law applicable to espionage or to the use of flags in the conduct of armed conflict at sea" are not affected by Article 37(1)(d) regarding perfidy or Article 39 regarding emblems of nationality. Also the provisions of part IV providing general protection against effects of hostilities for the civilian population apply to "all attacks from the sea or from the air against objectives on land but do not otherwise affect the rules of international law applicable to armed conflict at sea or in the air"; Additional Protocol I, Art. 49(3).

(p. 1). Accordingly, these volumes set out in broad scope the argument for establishing a court to deal with international crimes.

The first section of each volume—consisting of some one hundred pages—contains a carefully reasoned historical essay that describes various attempts made by international groups and organizations to establish an international criminal court. The bulk of the work, however, is composed of 45 documents which trace and depict the world community's increasing recognition that need for an international criminal court has certainly merited attention and serious concern. Included among these are selections drawn from the Hague Peace Conferences in 1899 and 1907, draft conventions by the League of Nations, relevant documents pertaining to the war crimes trials in Nuremberg and Tokyo following World War II, the evolution of the Genocide Convention, reports by the International Law Commission dealing with international offenses, and the UN conventions on terrorism and against hostage taking. In this regard especially, this compilation should serve most handily as a very utilitarian reference work for interested scholars.

In sum, while the case for establishing an international criminal court is not new (indeed, Ferencz has been an outspoken and ardent champion of such a body for several years), it nevertheless retains great salience precisely because international law *ipso facto* has not been capable of effectively deterring widespread atrocities, whether through war or terrorist activities. Importantly, these volumes add weighty evidence to and make even more compelling the need for creating such an international legal mechanism. The overriding question, however, is clearly whether national governments similarly will come to this realization and adopt such an international adjudicative procedure. Notwithstanding past pessimisms, this reviewer surely, albeit not confidently, hopes that they will do so.

CHRISTOPHER C. JOYNER
The George Washington University

New Directions in the Law of the Sea. Vols. VII and VIII. Compiled and edited by Myron Nordquist, S. Houston Lay, and Kenneth R. Simmonds. *Vols. IX and X.* Compiled and edited by Myron Nordquist and Kenneth R. Simmonds. London, Rome, and New York: Oceana Publications, Inc., 1980. Copublished with the British Institute of International and Comparative Law. Vol. VII: pp. xii, 500; vol. VIII: pp. v, 440; vol. IX: pp. v, 490; vol. X: pp. iv, 495. $40/vol.

When reviewing volumes V and VI of this series, I shared with its editors "the inarticulated premise that the next volume will include the results of the Law of the Sea Conference."[1] Instead of a final volume, we have four more volumes, and the latest achievement of the conference included in vol. X is the revised ICNT of the 1979 eighth session (pp. 134–459).

[1] 72 AJIL 187 (1978).

On the other hand, this reviewer suggested that a partial success or failure of the conference would not result in anarchy, as the practice of states manifested in national legislation and international agreements continued unabated and may eventually contribute to an acceptable regime of the high seas and the deep seabed. With reference to the latter, I suggested that "well-meaning slogans like 'common heritage of mankind' will give way to the usual process of bargaining for securing national or regional interests."[2] The Reagan administration's decision to reexamine the 1980 Draft Convention on the Law of the Sea (Informal Text),[3] and in particular its provisions relating to deep-sea mining, may well become a step in inaugurating this bargaining process. Thus, the cautious statement by the editors that with the adoption of the 1979 ICNT "progress toward an eventual Convention in the future seems now slightly more predictable" (vol. II, p. xi) may well prove too optimistic for the near future in view of the stand taken by the Reagan administration.[4]

The arrangement of documents follows the pattern established in the preceding volumes except for the new part V devoted to materials of the EEC (vol. X, pp. 479–95). In all areas of the law of the sea there has been extensive state practice. The editors note that "claims to an exclusive economic zone (EEZ), in particular, have increased dramatically" since 1977, and that there are "no less than 35 EEZ claims embodied in national legislation, and a further 12 in bilateral agreements" (vol. VI, p. xi). Thus, a radical innovation in the law of the sea has penetrated state practice without or in anticipation of the Convention.

Among the documents the editors call attention especially to the Australia-Papua New Guinea Treaty of December 18, 1978 (vol. VIII, pp. 215–83), which "is precedent-setting in its complexity, dealing with problems of maritime boundary delimitation between opposite and adjacent states in a broad continental shelf area" (vol. VII, pp. xi–xii). With remarkable foresight the editors refer to the U.S.-Canada Treaty to Submit to Binding Dispute Settlement the Delimitation of the Maritime Boundary in the Gulf of Maine and the Agreement on East Coast Fishery Jurisdiction, signed March 29, 1979 (vol. IX, pp. 157–67, 167–213), as "interesting examples of attempted solutions to long-standing and acrimonious fishing and boundary disputes" (vol. VII, p. xii). At this writing the Treaty and Agreement are still "attempted" solutions and the dispute has become, if anything, somewhat more "acrimonious."

Included in the series are two important arbitrations: the *Beagle Channel* arbitration between Argentina and Chile of February 18, 1977 (with the exception of section IV of the Decision entitled "Confirmatory or Corroborative Incidents and Material"), along with the Exchange of Diplomatic Notes between the parties to this arbitration (vol. VII, pp. 220–307, 307–27), and the *United Kingdom-France Arbitration concerning the Delimitation of the Continental Shelf* of June 30, 1977, and the subsequent Decision of March 14,

[2] *Ibid.*

[3] UN Doc. A/CONF.62/DC/WP.2 (1980).

[4] As reported in the *New York Times* of August 25, 1981, at A7, the Law of the Sea Conference at its Geneva session decided to open its next session in New York on March 8, 1982, in order to prepare a treaty to be signed in Caracas (Venezuela) in early September 1982.

1978 (vol. VIII, pp. 283–388, 389–439) from which Judge Waldock's separate and Judge Briggs's dissenting opinions are omitted.

The cumulative table of contents in vol. VI, pp. 887–914, has not been brought up to date. However, there is a useful table of claimed breadths of national jurisdiction with respect to the territorial sea, the exclusive economic zone, and fishery limits (vol. X, pp. 472–77). It appears that 13 states still adhere to the traditional 3-mile limit for their territorial sea. The editors deserve the gratitude of all students of the law of the sea for providing an ample and reliable record of state practice during a particularly dynamic period in the evolution of a branch of international law that has always played a vital role in promoting the peaceful coexistence of states.

These volumes are dedicated to Dr. Robert D. Hodgson, the Geographer of the U.S. Department of State who died prematurely on December 4, 1979. Readers of this *Journal* will want to associate themselves with the tribute paid by the editors to Hodgson:

> As a foremost authority on the geography of the law of the sea, Dr. Hodgson was the trusted advisor to numerous foreign nations who relied on his factual accuracy, fair judgment and impeccable integrity. The international community has lost not only a renowned and irreplaceable scholar, but also a good friend [vol. VII, p. iii].

LEO GROSS
Board of Editors

Traité de Droit Aérien-aéronautique (3d ed.). By Nicolas Mateesco Matte. Montreal: McGill University; Paris: Editions A. Pedone, 1980. Pp. 844.

The third edition of this monumental reference work on international air law differs from the second edition in a number of respects. First, there are approximately one hundred pages of new material dealing primarily with the Hague Convention for the Suppression of Unlawful Seizure of Aircraft, 1970; the Montreal Convention for the Suppression of Unlawful Acts Against the Safety of Civil Aviation, 1971; and additions and modifications to these two treaties as well as to the earlier Tokyo and Warsaw Treaties. Second, the entire section on space law has been eliminated, leaving materials dealing only with aviation and aircraft. Further, there has been an effort to make the materials presented easier to use and understand through a judicious use of additional subtitles.

Otherwise, the text is almost word for word as found in the second edition. Even the conclusions to the second edition are presented as the conclusions to the third edition because, according to the author, they are still current and correct.

While the great value of this volume is its comprehensiveness, if one continues to add on recent developments—even with the elimination of space law—the time is rapidly approaching when it will be impossible to include everything on air law in one volume. Rather than go to two volumes in the fourth edition with the inevitable increase in price, it might be appropriate to look at alternatives. One suggestion would be to separate the textual material from the reproductions of the original treaties and sell the latter separately as a supplemental volume for those who have a need for the exact wording of those documents. This could easily be justified in view of the author's meticulous paragraph-by-paragraph treatment of the various international agreements. Another way to approach the problem would be to eliminate the descriptive material and concentrate on analysis and interpretation, and leave the texts of the treaties and agreements to speak for themselves. This would reduce the work to a more manageable size and at the same time permit the author to put flesh on some of the interesting notions presented in passing in the introduction, such as the statement that the developing international air law is beginning to reflect the transition from the era of supersonic aircraft to that of mass tourist and vacation flights.

In any event, something must be done if the work is to remain the useful tool it is for both the student and the practitioner.

George A. Codding, Jr.
University of Colorado

La Collaboration Internationale en Matière Aéroportuaire. By Guido Rinaldi Baccelli. Montreal: McGill University; Paris: Editions A. Pedone, 1979. Pp. 150.

This book contains some unusual features: an abstract in French and English to conform with thesis requirements at McGill University, and a preface in French and Italian by Giuseppe Fassina, presumably because the author comes from Italy and is intimately involved in the area of civil aviation in that country. The English abstract is obviously a translation from the French version and raises the following questions: How could such a poorly translated and incomprehensible text have been approved by officials in a university that is not lacking in translators? Secondly, could the publishers not have rendered the text readable and meaningful to unilingual anglophones as intended by the very purpose of the abstract?

The study is concerned with international cooperation in airport operations and management, and is divided into two parts. Part 1 is devoted to a general analysis of airports; it examines their juridical status from the standpoint of international law and cooperation and seeks to determine their scope of operation in various municipal systems by examining the issues of ownership (public, private, or mixed), support through state subsidies or user charges, and the extent to which international air transport is facilitated. The account is essentially of a general nature and largely descriptive. Apart from obvious economic and technological developments that have necessitated changes in air and ground operations associated with international air transport, there is little else to support the author's claim that airport operations should now be considered as modern commercial enterprises. Nowhere in the book is this concept defined in such a way as to provide a theoretical framework for the study, nor is the force of the analysis such as to warrant the conclusion. In effect, the reader is left with the impression that whatever has happened to airport operations in recent years has necessarily turned them into modern commercial enterprises.

Part 2 deals with the circumstances in which airport operations may invite civil liability, a matter not yet regulated by international agreement and that is thus covered for the most part by national legislation. The author discusses the nature of responsibility in civilian and common law systems, and suggests, in effect, what must now be considered as a given, that the traditional doctrine of fault as a basis for responsibility, which was sanctioned by the Warsaw Convention of 1929 as amended by the Hague Protocol of 1955, and has now been replaced by the principle of absolute liability, should be extended to airport operations where injury is caused to third parties. This may be the case, as the author points out, where injury to a third party may be attributed to the airport management, the state, or carrier, jointly or individually. In such circumstances, prompt compensation to the injured third party should not be contingent on proof of negligence or the determination as to where ultimate responsibility lies. To this extent, the author seems justified in his plea for increased cooperation in order to evolve uniform rules to govern the basis of responsibility in airport operations. The book should be useful to those seeking general information on airport operations and management.

P-KIVEN TUNTENG
Montreal, Quebec

New Foundations for Asian and Pacific Security. Edited by Joyce E. Larson. New York: National Strategy Information Center, Inc., 1980. Pp. xxx, 260. $8.95.

As the editor of this very useful book for understanding the most intricate and complicated economic, political, and strategic relations in the Asian/Pacific area points out, this region has emerged during the last few years as a crucial arena of great-power rivalry. A new drama is being played in this theater as traditional actors assume startlingly different roles from those they played in the recent past. Besides the United States, the Soviet Union, Japan, and the People's Republic of China, whose interests and ambitions often clash in this region and have led to new or strengthened alignments or relationships, including the Sino-American and Sino-Japanese rapprochements, new actors have emerged to play increasingly important roles. Thus, members of the Association of the South-East Asian Nations (ASEAN), who previously were mere specks in the big-power cosmos, are taking leading parts in the new drama.

This book contains a carefully edited and quite readable version of the addresses, papers, and committee reports of an international conference convened by the National Strategy Information Center (NSIC) and several cosponsoring groups on the subject of the book's title at Pattaya (Thailand) in December 1979. After an insightful "Foreword" on perspectives in war and peace in Asia by Professor Tager (Director of Studies at NSIC), the book is divided into four parts or chapters, each part starting with some specific and pertinent issues and questions formulated by the organizers of the Pattaya Conference to be addressed at the conference: political/military dimensions of security in Southeast Asia, Northeast Asia, economic dimensions of security, and policy proposals and Asian and Pacific security. The conference papers and reports obviously do not go into the details of the various problems raised, but the issues relating, *inter alia*, to the increasing influence of the Soviet Union in the strategic southeast region, the growing military, political, and economic collaboration between the USSR and Vietnam, China's pragmatic foreign policy and new collaboration with the United States for the containment of the Soviet Union, the continuing struggle in Indochina, the predicament of Thailand, Japan's defense posture and the security of Northeast Asia, the tensions on the Korean Peninsula, the threat to East and Southeast Asian sea lanes for commercial shipping, the economic dimensions of security, the growing vitality of ASEAN, the role of Taiwan, and the concept of a Pacific Basin Community are all addressed and discussed by competent scholars in the 22 papers and reports compiled in this book. Among the authors are several statesmen, present or former high government officials, and military leaders from the region. This is indeed a valuable addition to the growing literature on Asia and the Pacific, whose importance has come to be realized only recently in the United States.

R. P. ANAND
East-West Center, Honolulu

Soviet Yearbook of International Law, 1979. Moscow: Izdatel'stvo "Nauka," 1980. Pp. 397. 4 rubles, 80 kopecks.

Are individuals subjects of international law? For decades Soviet texts have said no. In this 1979 *Yearbook* there appears what may be the seeds of change, for a team of Sverdlovsk law professors criticizes the authors of a general text of 1978 for repeating the traditional response. Noting in their book review that the authors say, as usual, that subjects of international law are only collective organizations, the critics say, "in principle a physical person is not excluded from the system of international law," and that "international law protects man, makes secure his fundamental rights and freedoms" (p. 300).

In notable degree this 1979 *Yearbook* focuses on individuals. The noted G. I. Tunkin highlights the impact of Nuremberg, declaring that what the USSR shared in creating as new law has now been accepted by all states and most authors, namely, that individuals who commit crimes against peace are responsible in international law. V. U. Gubin considers the rights of foreigners in the USSR. In long-standing law, confirmed by the 1977 USSR Constitution, they are accorded national treatment, but he emphasizes that to enjoy such treatment they must fulfill obligations identical with those of Soviet citizens, with some exceptions: military service, defense of the USSR, participation in state affairs, and payment of taxes on bachelors and small families. I. P. Blishchenko and N. V. Zhdanov discuss mercenaries and their international law responsibilities, relying on the 1979 OAU Convention and the Angola and Luanda trials. Volunteers who join in the fight for liberation from colonial status cannot be treated as mercenaries.

Clearly, individuals are being recognized increasingly by Soviet authors as a concern of international law, but they are not "subjects." They have obligations to the community of states; states have obligations to them, but the sanctions available to them are strictly limited unless their homeland sponsors their claim, and even then it is not the individual alone who has a right. Tunkin suggests that violations of individuals' rights must be massive, as under the UN Conventions on Genocide and Apartheid, which he sees as extensions of the Nuremberg principles. He leaves for others to develop the rights of individuals as such under the UN Covenants on human rights, which the USSR has ratified. In view of the state of the literature, outsiders would welcome some papers by the Sverdlovsk faculty and like-minded colleagues on just what place individuals now have in international law, and whether they cannot be treated under present circumstances as "subjects" or, at least, on the threshold of being subjects.

As usual, the *Yearbook* contains a wide variety of papers, for the most part on this occasion bearing little relation to each other, but useful in setting forth Soviet views on critical topics. After a lapse of a year, there is published a summary of the 21st (1978) annual meeting of the Soviet International Law Association. Unfortunately, it is much less informative than in the earlier years. The record lists only participants and topics, and adds meaningless phrases such as that there was great interest and broad discussion, but readers are given no hint of positions taken. It would seem that without revealing confidences, more could be reported to give readers who could not attend a clearer impression of the process of formulating positions. Bibliographies and documents are, as usual, valuable research aids, and the English summaries will help many in grasping the portent of the principal papers.

JOHN N. HAZARD
Board of Editors

A Collection of Treaties and other Documents affecting the States of Malaysia 1761–1963. Vols. I and II. Compiled and edited by J. de V. Allen, A. J. Stockwell, and L. R. Wright. London, Rome, New York: Oceana Publications, Inc., 1981. Vol. I: pp. xviii, 504; vol. II: pp. ix, 683. $85.

This compilation is intended to fill the need for a reliable and convenient collection of the documents through which can be traced the evolution of independent Malayan Sultanates into the modern state of Malaysia. Unfortunately, it fails to do so.

The texts reproduced photographically are not the best copies of the original documents; they are typescripts. Thus, the researcher is left to wonder whether the "J. T." Newbold who witnessed the Rembau Treaty of January 9, 1833 (vol. I, p. 272) is the "T. J." Newbold who wrote an important book about the British settlements in the area in 1839. If a simple typing transposition is at fault, what other typing errors have crept through?

The *Consolidated Treaty Series (CTS)* has many of these texts, but there are some disturbing inconsistencies between the two collections. For example, the Treaty of January 28, 1761 between Dalrymple (for the East India Company) and the Sultan of Sulu (vol. II, p. 375) was renewed on November 20,

1761 at a ceremony in Manila unmentioned in this compilation but clearly and briefly adverted to in 42 *CTS* 389–92. Two of the Sulu Treaties in this compilation are not in the *CTS*, but several documents in *CTS* connected with the Sulu transactions are not in the new compilation.

The fact recitation preceding the "Siamese" treaties of 1825 and 1826 is so distorted as to be hopelessly misleading. For example, it is asserted (vol. II, p. 307) that after Burney's Treaty of 1826 "the position of Kelantan and Trengganu remained ambiguous" (a similar assertion is made in vol. I, p. 187). But in his reports to Governor Fullerton in Penang (I(1) *Burney Papers* 177 (1910) and I(3) *id.* at 329), Burney interprets the language of the Treaty he drafted as conceding Thai sovereignty in those Sultanates. He gave that interpretation to the Sultan of Trengganu on August 10, 1826 also, while stopping at Trengganu roadstead en route back to Penang from Bangkok (I(3) *id.* at 367). Despite a later attempt by Burney in internal British correspondence to make the Thai rights appear less substantial, it was partly because the Treaty was clearly intended by its negotiators to affirm Thai sovereignty in Kelantan and Trengganu that Governor Fullerton openly objected to the conclusion of the Treaty; he finally recommended British ratification as "the speediest and least objectionable mode of putting an end to all further negotiation" (I(3) *id.* at 526).

Other assertions, like "the clause underwriting Perak's independence failed to induce the Siamese Government to curb Ligor's advances" (vol. II, p. 307), are even more removed from reality. In the view of Burney, Ligor, as a Thai agent, acted correctly in Perak to counter illegal British actions. Fullerton was ultimately reprimanded by the British Government in India for his disregard of Thai rights in Perak under Burney's Treaty and deprived of most of his military garrison to make his further violation of the Treaty impossible (II(6) *Burney Papers* 205–15).

It may be noteworthy to help explain the biased summaries and choice of texts to be reproduced that Colonial Office records are freely cited, but few Foreign Office records are. For example, it is incomprehensible that in the Kelantan section, which reproduces the Duff Syndicate documents, there are no citations at all to FO 69/224 and 275 containing the original correspondence.

The reviewer is left to wonder how or why a more or less routine job of scholarship could have been so badly mangled.

ALFRED P. RUBIN
Naval War College

BRIEFER NOTICES

De fide et perfidia—Der Treuegedanke in den "Staatsparellelen" des Hugo Grotius aus heutiger Sicht. By Wolfgang Fikentscher. (Munich: Bayerische Akademie der Wissenschaften, Philosophisch-Historische Klasse, 1979. Pp. 152. Bibliography. Index.) This slender volume conveniently presents, with useful commentary, the Latin text (with a German translation) of what Judge van Eysinga in 1941 called the earliest writing of Grotius on international law. This was his treatment of good faith and perfidy (*De fide et perfidia*), the title of chapter 6, Book III of his youthful work *Parallelon rerum publicarum*. The patriotic young Dutch jurist there compared (to the advantage of his own countrymen) the national customs and characteristics of the Greek, Roman, and Dutch peoples. He there, as later in his better known treatises, emphasized the fundamental importance of good faith as the basis of "that law which governs peoples and their rulers."

The work was written in 1601 or 1602 when Grotius was 18 or 19 years old (several years before *De Jure Praedae*, which was written between 1604 and 1606). It was first published (with a Dutch translation) in four volumes (now rare) by the historian Johan Meerman between 1801 and 1803. Another Dutch translation of chapter 6 of Book III by A. Stempels appeared in 1945.

In the present volume the Latin text (and German translation on the opposite pages) occupies 56 pages, while the editor's introduction (in four chapters) fills over 80 pages. The first three chapters deal with the genesis and analysis of the text. The fourth chapter, comprising the last 15 pages of the introduction, ponders the relevance of the Grotian commitment to universal law and a universal church to our world of pluralism and fragmented ideologies. A table lists parallel passages regarding good faith in the *Parallelon, De Jure Praedae*, and the *De Jure Belli ac Pacis*. A list of the titles of the 26 chapters of the *Parallelon* follows, together with a five-page bibliography and an index.

EDWARD DUMBAULD
U.S. Senior District Judge

Droit International Public (2d ed.). By Nguyen Quoc Dinh. 2d ed. prepared by Patrick Daillier and Alain Pellet. (Paris: Librairie Générale de Droit et de Jurisprudence, 1980. Pp. 993. Indexes. Fr.215,30.) It is unusual for a second edition to appear, as this does, just 3 years after the first. The first edition was accompanied by a *Supplément avec mise à jour*, and this edition is meant to incorporate recent developments in a single volume, and, more importantly to give a sense of the place of economics and economic institutions in the contemporary world legal order.

If there was a shortcoming in the first edition, it was the treatment of the place of international organizations dedicated to the solution of economic and monetary problems. Title II of part III of the second edition, "International Economic Relations," corrects the omission. In 50 pages and three chapters it provides a concise introduction to the international economic regime. In particular, the authors present the international economic regime: what it is, how it works, and especially how states and the economic organizations work with each other within that regime. Particular and valuable attention is paid to the activities of the principal financial and monetary organizations, the IMF and the World Bank. A separate section deals with international commercial relations and the GATT.

An entire chapter is devoted to North-South relations, including a rather interesting and controversial concept that the authors term "*le droit du développement*." Without abandoning the idea of the sovereign equality of states, the authors declare that the development needs of certain states call for special rules to deal with the economic inequality of these states. "Dés lors, non réciprocité, préférence et inégalité compensatrice constituent des éléments fondamentaux du droit international du développement" (pp. 745–46).

The work of the late Professor Nguyen Quoc Dinh has been carried on in this second edition by his protégés, Alain Pellet and Patrick Daillier. They have lost none of the verve present in the first edition and have presented their material with a clarity and completeness worthy of their predecessor.

The language is elegant, and the clarity of its presentation and thought-provoking theses will make this book especially valuable to students and to those who must, from time to time, return to basic principles.

F. S. RUDDY
Washington, D.C.

Internationale Konventionen gegen die Folter. St. Galler Expertengespräch 1978. Edited by Alois Riklin. (Bern and Stuttgart: Verlag Paul Haupt, 1979. Pp. 312. DM 38.) In June 1978 experts from eight European states gathered at St. Gallen to discuss the prospects for a draft convention against torture that would have realistic chances of near universal ratification yet lead to the effective elimination of torture. Three draft conventions, those of Sweden, the International Association of Penal Law, and the so-called Swiss Project, formed the basis of the dialogue.

The assembled authorities focused extensively upon the major obstacles to achieving an acceptable draft convention. These included a definition of torture, its status as an international crime, limitation of the convention to acts committed by or on behalf of public officials, optional versus obligatory reporting of violations, and control and enforcement mechanisms.

This volume effectively summarizes the significant viewpoints on the major issues in formulating a convention. While a consensus draft was neither expected nor forthcoming at the sessions, Alois Riklin, in his concluding address to the assemblage, recommended a synthesis of the three draft conventions (whose cornerstone is a two-tiered control mechanism) which commends further serious exploration.

BRUCE M. BOTELHO

Basic Documents on Human Rights (2d ed.). Edited by Ian Brownlie. (Oxford: Clarendon Press; New York: Oxford University Press, 1981. Pp. x, 505. Index. $65, cloth; $34.95, paper.) The second edition of this valuable handbook differs only slightly from the first,[1] except for the omission of the section on "Fundamental Rights in National Legal Systems." This is regrettable because there were rights of subjects or citizens before the rights of man or human rights made their appearance and these national rights were and are independent of human rights. In the section on the United Nations there are new documents on the procedure in the Commission on Human Rights of the Economic and Social Council and the Declaration on Protection from Torture. In the section on European institutions there are included the Final Act of the Helsinki conference and an excerpt from the Judgment of the European Court of Human Rights of April 26, 1979, in the *Sunday Times* case concerning the drug thalidomide, freedom of expression, and contempt of court. The introductions to the nine parts of the book contain useful references to additional documents and brief bibliographies. Although the massive volume *International Protection of Human Rights* and the companion volume of *Basic Documents* by Louis B. Sohn and Thomas Buergenthal appeared in 1973, Brownlie's handbook will still commend itself to many teachers of human rights courses.

LEO GROSS
Board of Editors

[1] Reviewed in 66 AJIL 445–46 (1972).

The Italian Yearbook of International Law. Vol. III, 1977. (Naples: Editoriale Scientifica, s.r.l.; Dobbs Ferry: Oceana Publications, Inc., 1979. Pp. xi, 679. Index.) The third volume of this Italian *Yearbook*, published in English, maintains the high standards of the first two volumes.[1] It contains articles by Italian international law experts, over 300 pages of Italian practice relating to international law (divided into judicial decisions, diplomatic and parliamentary practice, treaties to which Italy is a party, and Italian legislation), a bibliography, and indexes.

The articles deal with a variety of topics such as the origins of the international community, dualism and monism, the Hague Conventions on the Law of Sales and UNCITRAL work in that area, Italian trends in the law of carriage by sea, pollution of the sea from rivers, international codes of conduct for multinational enterprises, oil operations by a belligerent occupant, absence and abstention from voting in international organs, the contribution of Italy at the Conference on Humanitarian Law of Armed Conflict,[2] the U.S.-Italian "Lockheed" agreement, and international aspects of Italian exchange control laws.

Like its predecessors, this volume is most helpful in making the continuing substantial Italian contributions available to those who are not at home in the Italian language. Many scholars and lawyers would welcome similar publications in a number of other languages that are relatively unfamiliar.

WM. W. BISHOP, JR.
Board of Editors

The Caribbean Yearbook of International Relations: 1977. Edited by the Institute of International Relations, University of the West Indies. (Alphen aan den Rijn: Sijthoff & Noordhoff, 1980. Pp. vii, 299. Indexes. Dfl.95; $47.50.) In this, the third *Yearbook* sponsored by the Institute of International Relations in Trinidad and Tobago, social scientists explore many of the issues that highlight academic and political confrontations in the Caribbean and beyond. Its 12 articles, gathered by Leslie F. Manigat and edited by Basil Ince, offer a wide-ranging set of variations on a common theme: the legal and political context for accommodating the aspirations of small countries.

The nation-state's persistence in the face of hostile economic forces is acknowledged by nearly all of its authors. For example, Roy Preiswerk exposes some of the paradoxes of a "statocratic" approach to alleviating world poverty through a "New International Economic Order." Duke E. Pollard surveys the tortuous road to achieving international control over the exploitation of vast seabed resources. The need for coherent policies to finance extraction of valuable mineral wealth is meticulously documented in Dodderidge H. N. Alleyne's study of national petroleum corporations in developing countries.

Traditional issues of international law are not slighted. P. K. Menon traces the controversy over Belize, a dispute which poses anticolonial territorial claims against the sentiments of the people most involved. And A. Thorndyke provides a sympathetic critique of Great Britain's "genuine attempt at decolonisation" in granting Associated Statehood—a patent compromise between autonomy and security—to the smaller islands of the West Indies.

[1] Reviewed in 71 AJIL 836 (1977), and 73 AJIL 329 (1979).

[2] Professor A. Cassese, author of this article, also edited a substantial section of "diplomatic practice" dealing with Italian attitudes at the 1974–1977 conference.

Differing treatments of the "structuralist" and "dependency" explanations of postcolonial history (by Anthony T. Bryan, James A. Caporaso, and Herb Addo) reflect a rich polemical perspective on current events. Why is it, as Walter C. Clemens, Jr., asserts in a brief, concluding review essay, that much of the Caribbean, which is impoverished today, constituted the "richest area of the world" through most of the 18th century? The careful reader will discern a variety of answers to such paradoxes.

WILLIAM J. BRISK
Boston, Massachusetts

Human Rights: Problems, Perspectives, and Texts. Edited by F. E. Dowrick. (Westmead, England: Saxon House, Teakfield Ltd., 1979. Pp. vi, 223. Index. $23. Distributed in USA by Renouf.) A collection of lectures and seminar papers on human rights from disciplines as diverse as political theory, theology, philosophy of science, classics, and geography might seem to hold little of interest to the lawyer *qua* lawyer. Such is not true of this volume. Any student of law inquisitive enough to ponder its origins, besides observing its existing forms, will find an occasional nugget here.

An example is found in the contribution of Colin Warbrick, lecturer in law at the University of Durham, England, where the lectures and papers were delivered in 1978. Just as David Simpson of Amnesty International observes in the final piece "the transfer of the techniques of torture from one country to another," so Warbrick diagnoses a poison seeping across the Irish Sea. Crisis-distorted due process, once clutched at by Westminster to quell problems supposedly unique to Ulster, has found acceptance in legislation applicable to England itself. Acts passed in 1974 and 1976 are described as authorizing police detention for 48 hours (and 5 more days with consent of the Home Secretary) of any suspected terrorist, whether or not connected with events in Northern Ireland.

Warbrick's remedy for the "clear danger of legislation introduced in response to an exceptional threat becoming accepted and acceptable by a process of familiarity" is for "the decision on the existence of any emergency . . . to be reviewable at the international level, though with great attention given to the government's own determination."

So perceptive an insight justifies an international lawyer's journey through the articles constituting this collection, even though much of the material may unsettle any of us who are unaccustomed to seeing "our" subject examined from other perspectives.

JOHN CAREY
Of the New York Bar

Bibliography of International Humanitarian Law. Compiled by Huynh Thi Huong. (Geneva: International Committee of the Red Cross and Henry Dunant Institute, 1980. Pp. xxxix, 389. Analytical table and author index.) Research into the law of armed conflict has until now been particularly difficult for the uninitiated, and tedious for those familiar with this remarkedly complex, specialized, and important area of international law. As part of the "Program of Action of the Red Cross with respect to dissemination of international humanitarian law and of the Principles and Ideals of the Red Cross 1978–1981," the ICRC and the Henry Dunant Institute have published the first comprehensive bibliography of the international humanitarian law applicable in armed conflicts. This volume fills a large void for the researcher in the *jus in bello.*

The bibliography lists over five thousand separate titles of monographs and articles in their original languages, selected from collections of documents, university theses, reviews, and periodicals published in various parts of the world. A majority of the titles are in English, French, Spanish, German, and Italian. There are others in Slavic, Nordic, Arabic, Japanese, and Chinese, with an English or French transliteration of the titles. Also shown are those items where the same text exists in two or more languages.

The book has a logical, detailed analytical table of contents and an author index. With these two tools any researcher should be able to locate quickly the relevant material. As a result, this bibliography should be readily accessible to all who are interested in or in any way responsible for the law of armed conflict, whether as a scholar, teacher, or practitioner.

Nevertheless, this volume does not purport to be complete. It is to be hoped that omissions and new titles in all languages will be brought to the attention of the ICRC or the Henry Dunant Institute for inclusion in a second edition, which will surely be needed in less than a decade.

J. ASHLEY ROACH
Judge Advocate General's Corps, U.S. Navy

BOOKS RECEIVED*

International Law—General

Académie de Droit International. *Recueil des Cours 1980.* Vol. II. (Tome 167 of the collection.) Alphen aan den Rijn: Sijthoff & Noordhoff, 1981. Pp. 450.

Barde, Jacques. *La notion de droits acquis en droit international public.* Paris: Les Publications Universitaires de Paris, 1981. Pp. 349.

Bourne, C. B. (ed.). *The Canadian Yearbook of International Law. Volume XVIII, 1980.* Vancouver: The University of British Columbia Press, 1981. Pp. 425. Index. $32.

Greig, D. W. (ed.). *The Australian Year Book of International Law.* Vol. 7. Canberra: Australian National University, 1981. Pp. xxix, 548. Index. $91.20.

The Indian Year Book of International Affairs, 1980. Vol. XVIII, Part II: *Studies in the History of the Law of Nations* (Grotian Society Papers). Published under the auspices of The Indian Study Group of International Law and Affairs, University of Madras, 1980. Pp. xii, 246. Index. Rs.65.

Jennings, R. Y., and Ian Brownlie (eds.). *The British Year Book of International Law, 1979.* Vol. 50. New York: The Clarendon Press; Oxford University Press, 1981. Pp. ix, 419. Index. $98.

Nagel, Heinrich. *Internationales Zivilprozeßrecht für deutsche Praktiker.* Münster: Aschendorff, 1980. Pp. 753. Index.

Netherlands Yearbook of International Law. Vol. XI: T. M. C. Asser Institute, The Hague. Alphen aan den Rijn and Germantown: Sijthoff & Noordhoff, 1981. Pp. 429. Index. Dfl.150; $75.

Rao, T. S. Rama (ed.). *The Indian Year Book of International Affairs, 1980.* Vol. XVIII, Part I. Published under the auspices of The Indian Study Group of International Law and Affairs, University of Madras, 1980. Pp. vi, 563. Index. Rs.65.

* Mention here neither assures nor precludes later review.

Von Münch, Ingo (ed.). *Festschrift für Hans-Jürgen Schlochauer zum 75. Geburtstag am 28. März 1981*. Berlin, New York: Walter de Gruyter, 1981. Pp. xv, 1023. DM 370; $185.

International Economic Law & Relations

Atwood, James R., and Kingman Brewster. *Antitrust and American Business Abroad* (2d ed.). 2 vols. Colorado Springs: Shepard's/McGraw-Hill, 1981. Vol. I: pp. xxxix, 359; Vol. II: pp. xxxi, 411. Indexes. $120 for 2 vols.

Bokila, Lofumbwa. *Les régimes fiscaux visant à encourager les investissements directs et de portefeuille dans les pays en voie de développement*. Brussels: Etablissements Emile Bruylant, 1981. Pp. 284. Index. BF.1.550.

Bulajić, Milan. *Medunarodno Pravo Ekonomskog Razvoja: Pravni aspekti novog medunarodnog ekonomskog poretka* (International Law on Economic Development: Legal Aspects of the New International Economic Order). Belgrade: Servis Saveza udruženja pravnika Jugoslavije, 1980. Pp. xi, 279.

Dale, Richard. *Anti-Dumping Law in a Liberal Trade Order*. New York: St. Martin's Press, 1980. Pp. xv, 237. Index. $22.50.

D'Herbes, Jean, and Jean Touscoz. *Les Contrats Internationaux de Coopération Industrielle et le Nouvel Ordre Economique International*. Paris: Presses Universitaires de France, 1980. Pp. 350.

Kaye, Harvey, Paul Plaia, Jr., and Michael A. Hertzberg. *International Trade Practice*. 2 vols. Colorado Springs: Shepard's/McGraw-Hill, 1981. Index. $150 for 2 vols.

Nanda, Ved P. (ed.). *The Law of Transnational Business Transactions*. New York: Clark Boardman Company, Ltd., 1981. Index. $75.

Newman, Edwin S., and Eugene M. Wypyski (eds.). *United States International Trade Reports*. Binder I. London, Rome, New York: Oceana Publications, Inc., 1981. $100/binder.

Newton, William H., III. *International Estate Planning*. Colorado Springs: Shepard's/McGraw-Hill, 1981. Index. $75.

The ABC of Copyright. Paris: United Nations Educational, Scientific and Cultural Organization, 1981. Pp. 73. F.20.

Wilson, Donald T. *International Business Transactions in a Nutshell*. St. Paul: West Publishing Co., 1981. Pp. lvii, 393. Index. $7.95.

World Development Report 1981. By The World Bank. New York: Oxford University Press, 1981. Pp. viii, 192. $16, cloth; $6.95, paper.

Law of the Sea & Maritime Law

Brittin, Burdick H. *International Law for Seagoing Officers* (4th ed.). Annapolis: Naval Institute Press, 1981. Pp. xvi, 483. Index. $21.95.

Chen, Frederick Tse-shyang (ed.). *Proceedings of Conference on Deep Seabed Mining and Freedom of the Seas*. Bridgeport: University of Bridgeport School of Law; Westport: United Nations Association of Connecticut, 1981. Pp. viii, 84. $3.50.

Jaenicke, Schanze, and Hauser. *A Joint Venture Agreement for Seabed Mining*. Vol. 5. Deventer: Kluwer; Frankfurt am Main: Alfred Netzber Verlag, 1981. Pp. 127.

Marston, Geoffrey. *The Marginal Seabed: United Kingdom Practice*. New York: The Clarendon Press; Oxford University Press, 1981. Pp. xiii, 316. Index. £18.50; $55.

M'Gonigle, R. Michael, and Mark W. Zacher. *Pollution, Politics, and International Law: Tankers at Sea*. Berkeley, Los Angeles, London: University of California Press, 1981. Pp. xviii, 394. Index. $10.95, paper.

Vitzthum, Wolfgang Graf (ed.). *Aspekte der Seerechtsentwicklung: Die Bundesrepublik Deutschland und die Dritte Seerechtskonferenz der Vereinten Nationen*. Munich: Hochschule der Bundeswehr München, 1980. Pp. vii, 363. DM 10.

Use of Force & Law of War

Adachi, Sumio. *Gendai Senso Hohki Ron* (The Modern Laws of War). Tokyo: Keiseisha Co., Ltd., 1979. Pp. vii, 380. Index. ¥2300.

Hortatos, Constantine. *International Law and Crimes Against the Peace and Security of Mankind.* Athens, 1980. Pp. 222. Index. In Greek.

Dispute Settlement

Arbitration Law in Europe. By the International Chamber of Commerce. Paris: ICC Services, 1981. Pp. 368. $65.

Mani, V. S. *International Adjudication: Procedural Aspects.* (Vol. 4, Developments in International Law series.) The Hague, Boston, London: Martinus Nijhoff Publishers, 1980. Pp. xx, 456. Indexes. Dfl.130; $68.50.

Human Rights

Rights and Responsibilities. International, Social, and Individual Dimensions. Proceedings of a conference sponsored by the Center for Study of the American Experience. Los Angeles: University of Southern California Press, 1980. Pp. 298.

Dupuy, René-Jean (ed.). *The Right to Development at the International Level.* (Workshop at The Hague, 16–18 October 1979.) Alphen aan den Rijn: Sijthoff & Noordhoff, 1980. Pp. xii, 446.

Falk, Richard. *Human Rights and State Sovereignty.* New York and London: Holmes & Meier Publishers, Inc., 1981. Pp. x, 251. Index. $28.50, cloth; $15.75, paper.

The Rule of Law in the Areas Administered by Israel. Israel National Section of the International Commission of Jurists. Tel Aviv: TZATZ, 1981. Pp. 114.

Rumpf, Helmut. *Der internationale Schutz der Menschenrechte und das Interventionsverbot.* Baden-Baden: Nomos Verlagsgesellschaft, 1981. Pp. 106. DM 39.

Vitta, Edoardo, and Valerio Grementieri. *Codice degli Atti Internazionali sui Diritti dell'Uomo.* Milan: Dott. A. Giuffrè Editore, 1981. Pp. vii, 1125. Indexes. L.30.000.

International Criminal Law

Ferencz, Benjamin B. *An International Criminal Court. A Step Toward World Peace: A Documentary History and Analysis. Volume II: The Beginning of Wisdom.* London, Rome, New York: Oceana Publications, Inc., 1980. Pp. x, 674. Index. $75 for 2 vols.

Environment & Natural Resources

Arsanjani, Mahnoush H. *International Regulation of Internal Resources.* Charlottesville: University Press of Virginia, 1981. Pp. 558. Index. $37.50.

Breuer, Georg. *Weather Modification: Prospects and Problems.* New York: Cambridge University Press, 1979. Pp. xiii, 178. Index.

Fawcett, J. E. S., and Audrey Parry. *Law and International Resource Conflicts.* New York: The Clarendon Press; Oxford University Press, 1981. Pp. xiv, 254. Index. $55.

Teclaff, Ludwik A., and Albert E. Utton. *International Groundwater Law.* London, Rome, New York: Oceana Publications, Inc., 1981. Pp. xiv, 490. $50.

Van Lier, Irene H. *Acid Rain and International Law.* Toronto: Bunsel Environmental Consultants; Alphen aan den Rijn: Sijthoff & Noordhoff, 1981. Pp. xxii, 278.

Air & Space Law

Proceedings of the Twenty-Third Colloquium on the Law of Outer Space. International Institute of Space Law of the International Astronautical Federation. New York: American Institute of Aeronautics and Astronautics, 1981. Pp. 287. Index.

Kneifel, J. L. *Fluggesellschaften und Luftverkehrssysteme der sozialistischen Staaten UdSSR, Polen, CSSR, Ungarn, Bulgarien, Rumänien, Kuba, Jugoslawien und der VR China.* Nördlingen: Verlag F. Steinmeier, 1980. Pp. 318. Indexes. DM 98.

——. *Staatliches und internationales Luftverkehrsrecht der sozialistischen Staaten UdSSR, DDR, Polen, CSSR, Ungarn, Bulgarien, Rumänien, Kuba, Jugoslawien und der VR China.* Nördlingen: Verlag F. Steinmeier, 1980. Pp. 220. Indexes. DM 98.

Reijnen, Gijsbertha C. M. *Utilization of Outer Space and International Law*. Amsterdam and New York: Elsevier Scientific Publishing Co., 1981. Pp. xvi, 179. Index. Dfl.150; $63.75.

Rey Caro, Ernesto J. *Los "Delicta Juris Gentium" Contra la Seguridad de la Aviación Civil Internacional*. Córdoba: Universidad Nacional de Córdoba, 1980. Pp. 43.

Wassenbergh, H. A., and H. P. van Fenema (eds.). *International Air Transport in the Eighties*. Deventer: Kluwer, 1981. Pp. ix, 250. Dfl.90.

International Organizations

Ferrari Bravo, Giuliano. *San Francisco. Le Origini del Sistema Coloniale delle Nazioni Unite*. Venice: Marsilio Editori, 1981. Pp. 156.

Jutte, Rudiger, and Annemarie Grosse-Jutte. *The Future of International Organization*. New York: St. Martin's Press, 1981. Pp. 228. Index. $22.50.

Sauvant, Karl P. (ed.). *The Collected Documents of the Group of 77*. Vol. 1. (The Third World Without Superpowers, 2d series.) New York, London, Rome: Oceana Publications, Inc., 1981. Pp. lii, 592. 5 vols. to be published. $50/vol.

Schreuer, Christoph C. *Decisions of International Institutions before Domestic Courts*. London, Rome, New York: Oceana Publications, Inc., 1981. Pp. xiii, 407. Index. $35.

European Community Law

Barack, Boaz. *The application of the competition rules (antitrust law) of the European Economic Community to enterprises and arrangements external to the Common Market*. Deventer: Kluwer, 1981. Pp. xxix, 433. Dfl.90; $45.

Chiti-Batelli, Andrea. *I "Poteri" del Parlamento Europeo*. Milan: Dott. A. Giuffrè Editore, 1981. Pp. 406. Index.

Guy, Diana, and Guy I. F. Leigh. *The EEC and Intellectual Property*. London, Rome, New York: Oceana Publications, Inc., 1981. Pp. xxiv, 375. Index.

Hartley, T. C. *The Foundations of European Community Law: An Introduction to the Constitutional and Administrative Law of the European Community*. Oxford: Clarendon Press; New York: Oxford University Press, 1981. Pp. xxxiv, 551. Index. £20; $49.

Jalles, Isabel. *Implications juridico-constitutionnelles de l'adhésion aux Communautés européennes. Le cas du Portugal*. Brussels: Etablissements Emile Bruylant, 1981. Pp. 309. F.l.378.

Kerse, C. S. *EEC Antitrust Procedure*. London: European Law Centre Ltd., 1981. Pp. xxxvi, 337. Index. $102.

Mangas Martin, Araceli. *El Comité de Representantes Permanentes de las Comunidades Europeas*. Madrid: Centro de Estudios Constitucionales, 1980. Pp. xx, 235. 625 ptas.

Panico, Giuseppe. *La Politica Commerciale Convenzionale della CEE nel sistema commerciale internazionale*. Milan: Dott. A. Giuffrè Editore, 1979. Pp. vii, 372.

Timmermans, C. W. A., and E. L. M. Völker (eds.). *Division of powers between the European Communities and their Member States in the field of external relations*. (Colloquium 30 and 31 May 1980, Amsterdam.) Deventer: Kluwer, 1981. Pp. vi, 149. Dfl.55.

Weber, Ludwig. *Die Zivilluftfahrt im Europäischen Gemeinschaftsrecht*. Berlin, Heidelberg, New York: Springer-Verlag, 1981. Pp. xxviii, 428. Index. DM 114; $51.90.

Private International Law

Njem, Jean-Claude. *Le Régime Juridique et la Nationalisation de Concessions Pétrolières et Autres Concessions d'Immeubles. Une étude de droit international privé au regard des pays en voie de développement*. Stockholm: Almqvist & Wiksell International, 1980. Pp. 295.

Puente Egido, J. *Derecho Internacional Privado Español: Doctrina Legal del Tribunal Supremo*. Barcelona: Editorial Universitaria de Barcelona, 1981. Pp. xxiii, 1456. Index.

U.S. Law of Foreign Relations

Kruglak, Grégory T. *The Politics of United States Decision-Making in United Nations Specialized Agencies: The Case of the International Labor Organization*. Washington: University Press of America, 1980. Pp. ix, 290.

Perkins, John A. *The Prudent Peace: Law as Foreign Policy*. Chicago and London: The University of Chicago Press, 1981. Pp. xvi, 246. Index.

Conflicts & Disputes

Rowles, James. *El conflicto Honduras-El Salvador*. Costa Rica: Ciudad Universitaria Rodrigo Facio, 1980. Pp. 303. Index.

Stone, Julius. *Israel and Palestine: Assault on the Law of Nations*. Baltimore and London: The Johns Hopkins University Press, 1981. Pp. xiii, 223. Index. $17.50.

Arms Control & Disarmament

Barton, John H. *The Politics of Peace: An Evaluation of Arms Control*. Stanford: Stanford University Press, 1981. Pp. 257. Index. $18.50.

Regional & Foreign Law & Relations

Amissah, A. N. E. *The Contribution of the Courts to Government: A West African View*. Oxford: The Clarendon Press; New York: Oxford University Press, 1981. Pp. x, 382. Index. $55.

Asian-African Legal Consultative Committee. *Report of the Seventeenth, Eighteenth and Nineteenth Sessions held in Kuala Lumpur (1976), Baghdad (1977) and Doha (1978)*. New Delhi: The Secretariat of the Committee, 1980. Pp. 170.

Ballard, J. A. (ed.). *Policy-Making in a New State: Papua New Guinea 1972–77*. St. Lucia, London, New York: University of Queensland Press, 1981. Pp. xx, 331. Index. $32.50.

Biedermann, Klaus. *Die Treuhänderschaft des liechtensteinischen Rechts, dargestellt an ihrem Vorbild, dem Trust des Common Law*. Bern: Verlag Stämpfli & Cie AG, 1981. Pp. 580. SW.F.98; DM 108.

Tyler, William G. *The Brazilian Industrial Economy*. Lexington: D.C. Heath and Company, 1981. Pp. xvii, 152. Index. $17.95.

International Relations & Politics

Bilder, Richard B. *Managing the Risks of International Agreement*. Madison: The University of Wisconsin Press, 1981. Pp. xi, 302. Index. $22.50.

Boisson, Philippe. *La Sécurité en Mer*. Dunkerque: Grafic Foto, 1981. Pp. 369. Indexes. F.250.

Cattan, Henry. *Jerusalem*. New York: St. Martin's Press, 1981. Pp. 229. Index. $25.

Gilas, Janusz. *Systemy Normatywne w Stosunkach Miedzynarodowych* (Normative Systems in International Relations). Warsaw: Państwowe Wydawnictwo Naukowe, 1981. Pp. 181. Zl.50.

Meijers, H. *Volkenrechtelijke aspecten van Antilliaanse onafhankelijkheid*. Alphen aan den Rijn: Sijthoff & Noordhoff, 1980. Pp. 682. Index.

IV Jornadas de Profesores de Derecho Internacional y Relaciones Internacionales (4, 5 y 6 de julio de 1979). Granada: Universidad de Granada, 1980. Pp. 271. Index.

Mitchell, C. R. *The Structure of International Conflict*. New York: St. Martin's Press, 1981. Pp. 355. Index. $35.

Sarkesian, Sam C., and William L. Scully (eds.). *U.S. Policy and Low-Intensity Conflict: Potentials for Military Struggles in the 1980s*. New Brunswick and London: Transaction Books, 1981. Pp. viii, 221. Index. $9.95.

Foreign Relations of the United States, 1952–1954, Volume XVI: The Geneva Conference. (Dept. of State Pub. 9167.) Washington: U.S. Govt. Printing Office, 1981. Pp. xxii, 1597. Index.

Treaty Law

Frankowska, Maria. *Umowy międzynarodowe w formie uproszczonej* (International Agreements in Simplified Form). Warsaw: Ossolineum, The Polish Academy of Sciences Press, 1981. Pp. 303. Zl.60.

Kusumowidagdo, Judo Umarto. *Consultation Clauses as Means of Providing for Treaty Obedience: A Study in the Law of Treaties*. Stockholm: Almqvist & Wiksell International, 1981. Pp. 321. Kr.345.

Simon, Denys. *L'Interprétation Judiciaire des Traités d'Organisations Internationales*. Paris: Editions A. Pedone, 1981. Pp. xv, 936.

Scientific, Educational & Cultural Affairs

Journal Institute of Muslim Minority Affairs. Jeddah: King Abdulaziz University, 1980. Pp. 220.

Unesco Yearbook on Peace and Conflict Studies 1980. By the United Nations Educational, Scientific and Cultural Organization. Westport: Greenwood Press, 1981. Pp. xxix, 311. Index. $30.

Miscellaneous

Blanco Gaspar, Vicente. *El Voto Ponderado*. Madrid: Instituto Hispano-Luso-Americano de Derecho Internacional, 1981. Pp. xvi, 228. Index.

Le rôle des capitaux publics dans le financement de l'industrie en Europe occidentale aux XIXe et XXe siècles. (Colloque des 29 et 30 novembre, et ler décembre 1979.) Recueil du Centre d'Etudes Européennes de Waterloo. Brussels: Etablissements Emile Bruylant, 1981. Pp. 214. F.l.145.

Collins, Patrick. *Living In Troubled Lands. The Complete Guide to Personal Security Abroad*. Boulder: Paladin Press, 1981. Pp. 178. $12.95.

Eckstein, Otto. *Core Inflation*. Englewood Cliffs: Prentice-Hall, Inc., 1981. Pp. v, 121. Index. $12.95, cloth; $7.95, paper.

Gardiner, C. Harvey. *Pawns in a Triangle of Hate: The Peruvian Japanese and the United States*. Seattle and London: University of Washington Press, 1981. Pp. x, 222. Index. $25.

INTERNATIONAL LEGAL MATERIALS*

CONTENTS

VOL. XX, NO. 5 (September 1981)

PAGE

JUDICIAL AND SIMILAR PROCEEDINGS

Federal Republic of Germany: Court of Appeals (Munich) Decision with regard to a U.S. Court Request for *Judicial Assistance and the Taking of Evidence* 1025

Inter-American Court of Human Rights: Preliminary Decision on the Application of the Government of Costa Rica with regard to Viviana Gallardo et al. (*Jurisdiction of the Inter-American Court of Human Rights at this Stage*) 1057

Pakistan: Supreme Court Decision in Qureshi *v.* Union of Soviet Socialist Republics (*Sovereign Immunity; U.S.S.R. Trade Representation*) 1060

United Kingdom: House of Lords Judgment in Pioneer Shipping Ltd. *v.* B.T.P. Tioxide Ltd. ("The Nema") (*Appeal of Arbitral Award under the Arbitration Act 1979*)

Introductory Note 1099

Judgment 1105

United States: District Court for the Eastern District of New York Decision in Kunstammlungen zu Weimar *v.* Elicofon (*Restitution of Art Treasures; State Succession*) 1122

TREATIES AND AGREEMENTS

Antigua-Dominica-Grenada-Montserrat-St. Kitts/Nevis-Saint Lucia-Saint Vincent and The Grenadines: Treaty Establishing the *Organization of Eastern Caribbean States* 1166

Egypt-Israel: Protocol Establishing the *Sinai Multinational Force and Observers* 1190

Haiti-United States: Agreement to stop *Clandestine Migration of Residents of Haiti to the United States* 1198

LEGISLATION AND REGULATIONS

Mongolian People's Republic: Law on *Citizenship* 1203

Union of Soviet Socialist Republics:

Law on *Citizenship* 1207

Law on the *Legal Status of Foreign Citizens in the U.S.S.R.* 1211

United Kingdom: *Deep Sea Mining* (Temporary Provisions) Act 1981 1217

United States:

Department of Commerce National Oceanic and Atmospheric Administration Regulations on *Deep Seabed Mining* 1228

Department of Justice Immigration and Naturalization Service Regulations on *Refugee and Asylum Procedures* 1259

Proclamation and Executive Order on *High Seas Interdiction of Illegal Aliens* 1263

OTHER DOCUMENTS

Antarctic Treaty Consultative Meeting: Recommendations adopted at the Eleventh Meeting

On *Antarctic Mineral Resources* 1265

On *Antarctic Marine Living Resources* 1269

Canada-Mexico-United States-Venezuela: Joint Communique on *Caribbean Development* 1271

United States: Department of State Notices concerning *Claims against Iran* 1274

RECENT ACTIONS REGARDING TREATIES TO WHICH THE UNITED STATES IS A PARTY 1277

RECENT ACTIONS REGARDING TREATIES TO WHICH THE UNITED STATES IS NOT A PARTY 1287

NOTICE OF OTHER RECENT DOCUMENTS (not reprinted) 1288

* ILM subscription, $65; concessionary rate to ASIL members, $24. Address orders to ILM, 2223 Massachusetts Ave., NW, Wash., D.C. 20008. Outside U.S., please add $4.50.

The American Society of International Law

2223 Massachusetts Ave., N.W., Washington, D.C. 20008 (202) 265-4313 CABLES "AMINTLAW"

1982 APPLICATION

[ ] REGULAR MEMBERS .... $ 55

[ ] INTERMEDIATE MEMBERS (first 3 years of membership for *those under 30 years of age* at time of application) .... $ 25
Date of Birth ______________

[ ] STUDENT MEMBERS . . . Verification to be completed by a professor or administrative officer of your school: I hereby certify that the applicant is regularly registered in
(school) ______________________________________
for academic year ________ Title ________________
Signature ______________________________________ $ 15

[ ] SPECIAL CATEGORY (persons *not* resident in a member country of the OECD) .... $ 30

[ ] CONTRIBUTING MEMBERS .... $ 75

[ ] SUPPORTING MEMBERS .... $ 150

[ ] ANNUAL PATRON .... $ 500

[ ] LIFE $1,000

($21 of membership fee is allotted to AJIL subscription.)

Please enroll me as a member of the American Society of International Law for the calendar year starting January 1, 19____. My check, money order, UNESCO coupon, or payment in a convertible currency is enclosed $__________. I have checked membership category for which I am eligible.

(Please Print)

Name: ....

Address: ....

City: ....

State (or Country): .... Zip: ....

Member, U.S. Bar? .... State: .... Year: ....

Other Professional Affiliation: ....

Signature: ....

[ ] Please send me ILM at member rate of $24, plus $4.50 if outside U.S.

[ ] Check here if you would like to receive a list of Society publications.

PLEASE MAKE CHECKS PAYABLE TO *The American Society of International Law*. Contributions above obligatory dues, and all dues if membership is related to your work or profession, are tax deductible in the United States.

[ ] *Nonmember* subscription to AJIL (incl. ASIL Proceedings) ... $ 52

Please add $2.50 if you reside outside the U.S.

American Journal of International Law

pril 1982
ol. 76 No. 2

ublished by

merican Society of International Law

PATRONS OF THE SOCIETY

Honorable ARTHUR H. DEAN
Honorable HERMAN PHLEGER
GENEVIEVE E. TILLAR (deceased)
W. ROBERT MORGAN
BRUNSON MACCHESNEY (deceased)
ALONA E. EVANS (deceased)
JOHN N. HAZARD

In Memoriam

DR. JAMES BROWN SCOTT
HENRY C. MORRIS
ARTHUR K. KUHN
ALEXANDER FREEMAN
STANLEY P. SMITH

PATRONAGE, GIFTS AND BEQUESTS

Upon donation to the Society of $5,000 or more by gift or bequest, any member of the Society or individual eligible for membership may be elected a Patron of the Society. Upon donation of at least $5,000 in the name of a deceased person, such person may be elected a Patron posthumously.

Gifts and bequests may be made in the name of the American Society of International Law, Washington, D.C. Such contributions are deductible from federal returns for income, estate and gift tax purposes. The Society is incorporated by Act of Congress approved September 20, 1950 (64 Stat. 869).

MANLEY O. HUDSON MEDAL

The American Society of International Law bestows from time to time without regard to nationality a gold medal to commemorate the life work of Manley O. Hudson. Such awards are made for preeminent scholarship and achievement in international law and in the promotion of the establishment and maintenance of international relations on the basis of law and justice. Medals have been awarded to Manley O. Hudson (1956), Lord McNair (1959), Philip C. Jessup (1964), Charles De Visscher (1966), Paul Guggenheim (1970), Myres S. McDougal (1976), Eduardo Jiménez de Aréchega (1978), Richard Reeve Baxter (1981), and Oscar Schachter (1981).

AMERICAN JOURNAL OF INTERNATIONAL LAW

VOL. 76 April 1982 NO. 2

CONTENTS

		PAGE
The Inter-American Court of Human Rights	*Thomas Buergenthal*	231
Conditioning U.S. Security Assistance on Human Rights Practices	*Stephen B. Cohen*	246
Extraterritorial Jurisdiction at a Crossroads: An Intersection Between Public and Private International Law	*Harold G. Maier*	280
The Torres Strait Treaty: Ocean Boundary Delimitation by Agreement	*H. Burmester*	321
Recent Developments in United Nations Treaty Registration and Publication Practices	*Mala Tabory*	350
Notes and Comments		
The Election of Five Members of the International Court of Justice in 1981	*Shabtai Rosenne*	364
Correspondence		371
Contemporary Practice of the United States Relating to International Law	*Marian Nash Leich*	374
Judicial Decisions	*Monroe Leigh*	385
Current Developments		
The 1981 Session of the UN Sub-Commission on Prevention of Discrimination and Protection of Minorities	*Ton Gardeniers, Hurst Hannum, & Janice Kruger*	405
The Montreal Protocols to the Warsaw Convention on International Carriage by Air	*Marian Nash Leich*	412
A New United Nations Mechanism for Encouraging the Ratification of Human Rights Treaties	*David Weissbrodt*	418
Book Reviews and Notes	*Edited by Leo Gross*	
Butler, William E. (ed.). *International Law in Comparative Perspective*		430
Jiménez de Aréchaga, Eduardo. *El Derecho Internacional Contemporáneo*		431
Puig, Juan Carlos. *Doctrinas Internacionales y Autonomía Latinoamericana*		431
Tabory, Mala. *Multilingualism in International Law and Institutions*		433
Bryan, Greyson. *Taxing Unfair International Trade Practices*		435
Digest of United States Practice in International Law, 1978		437
Lindencrona, Gustaf, and Nils Mattsson. *Arbitration in Taxation*		440
Zagaris, Bruce. *Foreign Inve$tment in the United States*		441
Finger, Seymour Maxwell. *Your Man at the U.N. People, Politics, and Bureaucracy in Making Foreign Policy*		443
Tortora, Manuela. *Institution Spécialisée et Organisation Mondiale: Etude des Relations de l'OIT avec la SDN et l'ONU*		445
Rifaat, Ahmed M. *International Aggression. A Study of the Legal Concept: Its Development and Definition in International Law*		446
Schaefer, Michael. *Die Funktionsfähigkeit des Sicherheitsmechanismus der Vereinten Nationen*		447
Majer, Diemut. *"Fremdvölkische" im Dritten Reich*		448
Krausnick, Helmut, and Hans-Heinrich Wilhelm. *Die Truppe des Weltanschauungskrieges*		448

Ronen, Dov. *The Quest for Self-Determination* 451
Cassese, Antonio, and Edmond Jouve (eds.). *Pour un droit des peuples. Essais sur la Déclaration d'Alger* 451
Melander, Göran, and Peter Nobel (eds.). *International Legal Instruments on Refugees in Africa* 453
Kulikov, R. *O Mezhdunarodno-pravovoi otvetstvennosti za narushenie prav cheloveka* 455
Bothe, Michael (ed.). *Trends in Environmental Policy and Law* 456
Fernández-Shaw, Félix. *La Difusión Internacional de los Programas Audiovisuales* 457
Copyright Protection in the Americas. Binder I 458
Steele, Robert D. (ed.). *The Iran Crisis and International Law* 460
Asian-African Legal Consultative Committee. *Report of the Seventeenth, Eighteenth and Nineteenth Sessions, Held in Kuala Lumpur (1976), Baghdad (1977) and Doha (1978)* 461
Van Panhuys, H. F., W. P. Heere, J. W. Josephus Jitta, Ko Swan Sik, and A. M. Stuyt (eds.). *International Law in the Netherlands.* Vols. II and III 463
Rao, T. S. Rama (ed.). *The Indian Year Book of International Affairs, 1980. Vol. XVIII, Part I* 464
The Indian Year Book of International Affairs, 1980. Vol. XVIII, Part II: Studies in the History of the Law of Nations (Grotian Society Papers) 464
Irwin, Paul. *General Chronological List 1648–1809. Volume I* of *Index-Guide to Treaties. Based on the Consolidated Treaty Series and all other series therein utilised* (Clive Parry, ed.). 466
Foreign Relations of the United States, 1952–1954, Volume XVI: The Geneva Conference 467
Briefer Notices: Labouz, 468; Zarb, 469; Klein, 470; Matte, 471; Waldmann, 472.
Books Received 472
International Legal Materials. Contents, Vol. XX, No. 6 (November 1981) 475

Manuscripts in triplicate may be sent to the Editors-in-Chief of AJIL, Professors Oscar Schachter and Louis Henkin, Columbia University School of Law, New York, N.Y. 10027. Subscriptions, orders for back numbers, correspondence with reference to AJIL and books for review should be sent to the AMERICAN JOURNAL OF INTERNATIONAL LAW (ISSN 0002-9300), 2223 Massachusetts Avenue, N.W., Washington, D.C. 20008.

AJIL is published in January, April, July, and October and is supplied to all members of the American Society of International Law. The annual subscription to nonmembers of ASIL is $52.00, plus $2.50 for all foreign subscriptions (including ASIL Proceedings). Available back numbers of AJIL will be supplied at $11.00 each. ($21 of membership fee is allotted to AJIL subscription.)

EDITORIAL OFFICE:
BOX 44
COLUMBIA UNIVERSITY SCHOOL OF LAW
NEW YORK, N.Y. 10027

BUSINESS OFFICE:
2223 MASSACHUSETTS AVENUE, N.W.
WASHINGTON, D.C. 20008

Second-class postage paid at Washington, D.C. and additional mailing office

Postmaster: If undeliverable, send notice on Form 3579 to: American Journal of International Law 2223 Massachusetts Ave., N.W. Washington, D.C. 20008

Printed by Lancaster Press, Lancaster, Pa. 17604

The American Society of International Law

The American Society of International Law was organized in 1906 "to foster the study of international law and to promote the establishment and maintenance of international relations on the basis of law and justice."

The Society serves as a meeting place and forum for scholars, teachers, officials, lawyers, and others, from some one hundred countries. In April, it holds a three-day Annual Meeting at which current problems of international law are discussed. The Society also sponsors regional meetings outside of Washington in cooperation with other institutions. Salient questions of international law and relations are considered in depth by panels and study groups organized by the Society's Board of Review and Development. Works of scholarship are often published under the Society's auspices in connection with studies sponsored by the Board, many in the Society's series of *Studies in Transnational Legal Policy*.

The Society periodically issues four publications:

The American Journal of International Law, the leading journal in the field of international law, has been published since 1907. The *Proceedings of the American Society of International Law* carries the papers and discussion of the annual meeting of the Society.

International Legal Materials, a bimonthly, is a unique international collection of texts of current official documents, including legislation, treaties, court decisions, and reports. Subscription rates are $24 a year for members of the Society, $65 for others.

The quarterly *Newsletter* provides members with news of the Society and other organizations in the field.

Society membership is open to all persons of whatever nationality and profession who are interested in its objectives. Dues are: regular, $55; special category, $30 for persons *not* resident in a member country of the Organisation for Economic Co-operation and Development; intermediate, $25; student, $15. Membership application form is printed at the back of each issue of AJIL.

THE INTER-AMERICAN COURT OF HUMAN RIGHTS

*By Thomas Buergenthal**

I. Introduction

The Inter-American Court of Human Rights has drafted its Statute, adopted its Rules of Procedure, negotiated its headquarters agreement, and so far dealt with its first case.[1] It is timely, therefore, to describe the Court's institutional framework and to analyze its jurisdiction. A more extensive study, of course, will have to await its developing case law.

The Court was established by the American Convention on Human Rights, which entered into force in 1978; to date the Convention has been ratified by 17 of the 29 member states of the Organization of American States.[2] The Court consists of seven judges, nominated and elected by the states parties to the Convention.[3] The judges must be nationals of an OAS member state, but they need not have the nationality of the states parties to the Convention.[4] The regular term of the judges is 6 years; they may be reelected for one additional term.[5] The judges constituting the first Court were elected in May 1979.[6]

* Of the Board of Editors; Judge, Inter-American Court of Human Rights.

[1] Government of Costa Rica (In the Matter of Viviana Gallardo *et al.*), Inter-American Court of Human Rights, Decision of Nov. 13, 1981, *reprinted in* 20 ILM 1424 (1981). For the Preliminary Ruling in this case, see Decision of July 22, 1981, *reprinted in id.* at 1057.

[2] The American Convention on Human Rights [hereinafter cited as Convention] was *opened for signature* in San José, Costa Rica, on Nov. 22, 1969, and *entered into force* on July 18, 1978. For the official text, see ORGANIZATION OF AMERICAN STATES, HANDBOOK OF EXISTING RULES PERTAINING TO HUMAN RIGHTS [hereinafter cited as HANDBOOK] 27, OEA/Ser.L/V/11.50, doc. 6 (1980). The text as it appears in OAS, OFFICIAL RECORDS, OEA/Ser.K/XVI/1.1, doc. 65, Rev.1, Corr. 2 (1970), is *reprinted in* 9 ILM 673 (1970).

As of January 1982, the following OAS member states had ratified the Convention: Barbados, Bolivia, Colombia, Costa Rica, the Dominican Republic, Ecuador, El Salvador, Grenada, Guatemala, Haiti, Honduras, Jamaica, Mexico, Nicaragua, Panama, Peru, and Venezuela.

On the American Convention in general, see *Symposium: The American Convention on Human Rights*, 30 AM. U.L. REV. 1–187 (1980); Frowein, *The European and the American Conventions on Human Rights—A Comparison*, 1 HUMAN RIGHTS L.J. 44 (1980); L. SOHN & T. BUERGENTHAL, INTERNATIONAL PROTECTION OF HUMAN RIGHTS 1356–74 (1973); Fox, *The American Convention on Human Rights and Prospects for United States Ratification*, 3 HUMAN RIGHTS (ABA) 243 (1973); Buergenthal, *The American Convention on Human Rights: Illusions and Hopes*, 21 BUFFALO L. REV. 121 (1971). For a study of the Court, see Abranches, *The Inter-American Court of Human Rights*, 30 AM. U.L. REV. 79 (1980).

[3] Convention, Art. 52.

[4] *Id.*, Art. 53. On this subject, see Buergenthal, *The American and European Conventions on Human Rights: Similarities and Differences*, 30 AM. U.L. REV. 155, 157–59 (1980).

[5] Convention, Art. 54.

[6] The following were elected in the first election: Thomas Buergenthal (U.S.), Máximo Cisneros (Peru), Huntley Eugene Munroe (Jamaica), César Ordóñez (Colombia), Rodolfo Piza (Costa Rica), Carlos Roberto Reina (Honduras), and M. Rafael Urquía (El Salvador). Judge Urquía resigned shortly after his election and was succeeded by Judge Pedro Nikken of Venezuela, who was elected in October 1979.

The norms governing the exercise of the Court's functions are set out in three instruments. These are, in decreasing hierarchic order, the Convention,[7] the Statute of the Court,[8] and the Rules of Procedure.[9] The Convention provides that the Statute of the Court shall be drafted by the Court and be approved by the OAS General Assembly; it also declares that the Court "shall adopt its own Rules of Procedure."[10] The draft Statute that the Court presented to the General Assembly was extensively amended by the Assembly before it was approved.[11] Among the changes made by the Assembly was the stipulation that member states of the Organization, whether or not parties to the Convention, have the right, in addition to the Court itself, to propose future amendments to the Statute.[12] Since the adoption of the Court's budget is also in the hands of the OAS General Assembly and requires 19 affirmative votes, states not parties to the Convention, potentially at least, have considerable power to affect the functioning of the Court.

The Convention provides that "the Court shall have its seat at the place determined by the States Parties to the Convention in the General Assembly of the Organization."[13] A resolution adopted by the Assembly in 1978 located the permanent seat of the Court in Costa Rica.[14] A two-thirds vote of the states parties would be required to change the permanent seat. But the Court is not required to meet only in Costa Rica, for "it may convene in the territory of any member state . . . when a majority of the Court consider it desirable, and with the prior consent of the state concerned."[15] The specific status of the Court in Costa Rica will be regulated by a headquarters agreement as authorized by the Statute.[16] That agreement was signed on September 10, 1981 by the Court and the Government of Costa Rica; it will enter into force following ratification by the Costa Rican legislature.

II. The Court and its Institutional Context

The draft Statute presented to the OAS General Assembly by the Court in 1979 envisaged a permanent tribunal consisting of full-time judges.[17] This

[7] Convention, Arts. 52–73.

[8] For the text of the Statute [hereinafter cited as Statute], see HANDBOOK, *supra* note 2, at 105, and ANNUAL REPORT OF THE INTER-AMERICAN COURT OF HUMAN RIGHTS TO THE GENERAL ASSEMBLY, 1980 [hereinafter cited as ANNUAL REPORT] 16, OEA/Ser.L/V/111.3, doc. 13, Corr. 1 (1981). The Statute is *reprinted in* 19 ILM 635 (1980).

[9] ANNUAL REPORT, *supra* note 8, at 26, *reprinted in* 20 ILM 1289 (1981).

[10] Convention, Art. 60.

[11] For the text of the draft Statute, see OEA/Ser.P, AG/doc.1112/79 (Oct. 10, 1979). For the report detailing the reasons for some of the changes, see *Informa del Relator de la Primera Comisión—Asuntos Jurídicos y Políticos*, OEA/Ser.P, AG/doc.1198/79 (Oct. 31, 1979).

[12] *See* Statute, Art. 31, which reads as follows: "The present Statute may be amended by the OAS General Assembly, at the initiative of any member state or of the Court itself."

[13] Convention, Art. 58(1).

[14] OAS GA Res. 372 (XIII-0/78), OEA/Ser.P, AG/doc.1020/78, Rev.2, at 97 (1978).

[15] Convention, Art. 58(1).

[16] Statute, Art. 27(1). The Court's power to conclude similar agreements with other governments and entities is spelled out in Articles 27(2), 28, and 29 of the Statute.

[17] *See* Articles 20 and 22 of the draft Statute, *supra* note 11. The Court's draft also contained an alternative possibility, envisaging a system in which the judges would devote 50% of their time to the work of the Court. *See* draft Statute (Alternative), Arts. 21, 22, and 23. The Convention provides that these issues are to be regulated by the Court's Statute. Convention, Art. 72.

proposal was motivated by the Court's concern that a part-time tribunal might give that body an ad hoc image, likely to diminish the prestige and legitimacy it might need to obtain compliance with and respect for its decisions in the Americas. But the General Assembly found this proposal unacceptable, ostensibly at least on the ground that a full-time court would be too expensive and was unjustified until the Court had a substantial case load. The Assembly opted instead for a tribunal composed of part-time judges. It adopted a Statute that leaves the judges free to exercise their respective professions and stipulates merely that certain types of employment, particularly active government service, are incompatible with their judicial functions.[18] As a result, the judges are not on the OAS payroll;[19] they are not required to live in Costa Rica; and they are free to practice law, to teach, and to engage in whatever other occupations they may have in their native countries.

The Court, however, did persuade the General Assembly to include two provisions in the Statute that might facilitate the Court's transformation from a part-time to a full-time tribunal. One of these is Article 16, which requires the judges to "remain at the disposal of the Court" and to "travel to the seat of the Court or to the place where the Court is holding its sessions as often and for as long a time as may be necessary, as established in its Regulations [rules of procedure]." The other provision bearing on this issue is Article 17, which declares that "[t]he emoluments of the President and the judges of the Court shall be set in accordance with the obligations and incompatibilities imposed on them by Articles 16 and 18. . . ." Thus, if the Court's work load consistently required it to stay in session for most of the year, the Court could amend its Rules of Procedure[20] and propose to the General Assembly that it modify Article 18 of the Statute—the provision dealing with incompatibilities—to require judges to discontinue their outside professional activities and to fix a salary for them. The resulting financial burdens for the OAS would be justified only by a dramatic increase in the case load of the Court.[21]

The President of the Court who, together with the Vice President, is elected for a 2-year term and may be reelected, has the obligation to "direct the work of the Court, represent it, regulate the disposition of matters brought before the Court, and preside over its sessions."[22] Article 16 of the Statute provides, moreover, that "the President shall render his services on a permanent basis." This provision has thus far not been interpreted to require the President to reside at the seat of the Court or to suspend the exercise of his profession. A stipulation imposing these requirements was not approved by the General Assembly in 1979, and the budget provided the Court by the OAS has as yet not envisaged a salary for the President or compensation different from that received

[18] Statute, Art. 18.

[19] The judges receive a per diem and an honorarium for each day of service rendered to the Court.

[20] The Court now holds two regular sessions and such special sessions as may be necessary. *See* Statute, Art. 22; Rules of Procedure, *supra* note 9, Arts. 11 and 12.

[21] It is worth noting, in this connection, that a permanent court is not a concept new to the Americas. The Central American Court of Justice, which was established in that region in 1908, required its judges not to exercise any other profession and barred them from holding public office. *See* M. HUDSON, THE PERMANENT COURT OF INTERNATIONAL JUSTICE 1920–1942, at 46 (1943).

[22] Statute, Art. 12.

by the other judges. It is clear, however, that the obligations the Statute imposes on the President, if coupled with a heavy case load, might well necessitate a full-time presidency.

Although the Statute provides that the President and Vice President may be reelected, the Court appears to favor some form of rotation coupled with single terms for both officers. There is also an unwritten preference for geographic balance that is designed to ensure that the President and Vice President are nationals of different regions of the Americas. This approach was reflected in the first two elections. Thus, when a Central American, Judge Rodolfo Piza of Costa Rica, served as the first President, a South American judge, Máximo Cisneros of Peru, was the Vice President. When their terms expired, Judge Carlos Roberto Reina of Honduras became President and Judge Pedro Nikken of Venezuela assumed the Vice Presidency.[23]

The President, the Vice President, and a third judge, who is designated by the President, compose the Permanent Commission.[24] That body acts as the Court's bureau or directorate and "assists and advises the President in the exercise of his functions."[25] In making his designation, the President has sought to ensure that at least one member of the Permanent Commission resides in Costa Rica and that both working languages of the Court—Spanish and English—are represented on it. It may not always be easy, however, to achieve both results, and in the most recent designation, preference was given to making at least one English-speaking judge a member of the Commission.

The Secretariat of the Court is headed by the Secretary—its registrar or chief clerk—who is appointed by the Court for a renewable 5-year term; he may be removed by the Court.[26] Thus, unlike the Inter-American Commission on Human Rights, whose Executive Secretary is appointed and removable by the Secretary General of the OAS,[27] the Court has the power to ensure that its chief administrative officer does not have divided loyalties. All other members of the Court's staff are appointed by the Secretary General of the OAS in consultation with the Secretary of the Court; in practice, the Secretary General has thus far always made the appointments recommended to him by the Secretary of the Court. Moreover, although the staff is subject to the administrative standards of the OAS Secretariat, these may be applied only to the extent that they do not adversely affect "the independence of the Court."[28]

All judicial decisions of the Court must be adopted by the Plenary Court. It does not sit in smaller panels or chambers as does the European Court of Human Rights, for example.[29] Both its small size and the requirement under Article 56 of the Convention that "five judges shall constitute a quorum for

[23] The fact that the first two Presidents of the Court have been Central Americans appears to be a mere coincidence.

[24] Rules of Procedure, *supra* note 9, Art. 6(1).

[25] *Ibid.*

[26] Convention, Art. 58(2); Statute, Art. 14; Rules of Procedure, *supra* note 9, Art. 7(2).

[27] Statute of the Inter-American Commission on Human Rights, Art. 21, HANDBOOK, *supra* note 2, at 95.

[28] Convention, Art. 59.

[29] *See* European Convention on Human Rights, ETS 5, [1953] Gr. Brit. TS No. 71 (Cmd. 8969), Art. 43; A. H. ROBERTSON, HUMAN RIGHTS IN EUROPE 202–03 (2d ed. 1977).

the transaction of business by the Court" would seem to rule out the use of chambers.

The Convention fails to address the problem that would arise if disqualifications, resignations, or the death of a number of judges were to deprive the Court of the required quorum. The Court, however, anticipated this problem by including a provision in the Statute authorizing its President to request that the Permanent Council of the OAS appoint "one or more interim judges who shall serve until such time as they are replaced by elected judges."[30] The task of designating interim judges was assigned to the Permanent Council because it meets on a regular basis throughout the year, whereas the OAS General Assembly holds only one short annual session. The institution of interim or substitute judges, although quite common on the domestic plane, is rare in the case of international tribunals; it might well serve to prevent serious delays in the work of the Inter-American Court.

Interim judges should be distinguished from *ad hoc* judges. The latter are expressly provided for in the American Convention.[31] Besides stipulating that a judge who is a national of a state that is a party to a case before the Court "shall retain his right to hear that case," it declares that if one of the sitting judges is a national of a party to the case, the other state party may designate an *ad hoc* judge. Both states, furthermore, have the right to name *ad hoc* judges if none of the elected judges is their national. Since the *ad hoc* judges must have the same qualifications that the Convention specifies for elected judges, the Court may be deemed to have the power to reject *ad hoc* judges who do not meet these requirements.[32] The Court's Statute assumes that the right to designate *ad hoc* judges is waivable and provides that the right "shall be considered relinquished" if the state fails to name an *ad hoc* judge within 30 days following a written request from the President of the Court.[33]

III. The Court's Jurisdiction

The Inter-American Court of Human Rights has adjudicatory or so-called contentious jurisdiction, that is, jurisdiction to decide disputes involving charges that a state party has violated the human rights guaranteed by the Convention.[34] It also has advisory jurisdiction, which empowers the Court to interpret the Convention and other human rights instruments at the request of OAS member states and various OAS organs.[35]

Adjudicatory Jurisdiction

The Submission of Cases. The Court's power to decide a case referred to it for adjudication is conditioned on the acceptance of its jurisdiction by the states

[30] Statute, Art. 6(3). *See also id.*, Art. 19(4). [31] Convention, Art. 55.

[32] Article 52 of the Convention provides that the judges must meet the following qualifications: they must be "jurists of the highest moral authority"; they must have "recognized competence in the field of human rights"; and they must "possess the qualifications required for the exercise of the highest judicial functions" either in the state of their nationality or the state nominating them. *Cf.* Gross, *The International Court of Justice: Consideration of Requirements for Enhancing its Rôle in the International Legal Order*, 65 AJIL 253, 295–99 (1971).

[33] Statute, Art. 10(4). [34] Convention, Art. 62.

[35] *Id.*, Art. 64. *See further* p. 242 *infra*.

parties to the dispute. A state is not deemed to have accepted the jurisdiction of the Court merely by ratifying the Convention. Acceptance of its jurisdiction is optional under the Convention and requires a separate declaration or a special agreement.[36] That "declaration may be made unconditionally, on condition of reciprocity, for a specific period, or for specific cases."[37] To date, four states parties have deposited the declaration accepting the Court's adjudicatory jurisdiction, namely, Costa Rica, Peru, Venezuela, and Honduras. In addition, of course, all states parties to the Convention may permit the Court at any time, on an *ad hoc* basis, to adjudicate a specific dispute relating to the application of the Convention.

Article 62(3) of the Convention reads as follows:

> The jurisdiction of the Court shall comprise all cases concerning the interpretation and application of the provisions of this Convention that are submitted to it, provided that the States Parties to the case recognize or have recognized such jurisdiction, whether by special declaration pursuant to the preceding paragraphs, or by a special agreement.

This provision needs to be read together with Article 61(1), which declares that "only the States Parties and the Commission shall have the right to submit a case to the Court." Individuals have no standing to do so. Moreover, the states suing and those being sued have to have accepted the jurisdiction of the Court before it may hear the case. Of course, the Commission is free to invite a state that has not accepted the Court's jurisdiction to do so for a specific case, but the state is free to reject the request.[38]

Before the Court may "hear a case, . . . the procedures set forth in Articles 48 to 50 shall have been completed."[39] The procedures referred to are those that govern the disposition by the Commission of cases submitted to it by states or individuals charging violations of the Convention. It is important to note, in this connection, that the American Convention makes the right of individual petition mandatory and the interstate complaint optional.[40] That is, a state that ratifies the Convention is deemed ipso facto to have accepted the right of "any person or group of persons, or any nongovernmental entity legally recognized in one or more OAS member states," to file a petition with the Commission charging a state party with a violation of the Convention.[41] However, before one state party may bring such charges against another state party, both states must have made a separate declaration recognizing "the competence of the Commission to receive and examine" interstate complaints.[42] Thus far, only

[36] Convention, Art. 62(1).

[37] *Id.*, Art. 62(2).

[38] *See*, in this connection, Article 47(3) of the Regulations of the Inter-American Commission on Human Rights [hereinafter cited as Commission Regulations], HANDBOOK, *supra* note 2, at 117, which expressly authorizes the Commission to give that option to states that have not accepted the Court's jurisdiction.

[39] Convention, Art. 61(2).

[40] *Id.*, Arts. 44 and 45; Buergenthal, *supra* note 4, at 159–61; Frowein, *supra* note 2, at 62–63. *See also* Volio, *The Inter-American Commission on Human Rights*, 30 AM. U.L. REV. 65 (1980); Farer & Rowles, *The Inter-American Commission on Human Rights*, in INTERNATIONAL HUMAN RIGHTS LAW AND PRACTICE 47 (J. Tuttle ed. 1978).

[41] Convention, Art. 44. On this subject generally, see Norris, *Bringing Human Rights Petitions Before the Inter-American Commission*, 20 SANTA CLARA L. REV. 733 (1980).

[42] Convention, Art. 45(1) and (2).

four states, Costa Rica, Jamaica, Peru, and Venezuela, have filed that declaration. Parenthetically, it should also be noted that under the American Convention the right of individual petition, besides being mandatory, does not require the petitioner to be a victim of the violation charged.[43]

The procedures set forth in Articles 48 to 50 for dealing with a complaint that is submitted to the Commission envisage a number of litigation stages. The first stage calls for the Commission to determine whether the petition is admissible.[44] At this stage the Commission must decide whether the various preconditions for hearing the case exist.[45] A case that has been ruled admissible proceeds to the second stage. Here the Commission seeks to ascertain the factual allegations by holding hearings, examining documents, and carrying out in-

[43] Article 44 of the Convention does not impose the requirement that the petitioner be a victim of the violation or that he have some other interest in the case. That the Inter-American Commission interprets the Convention as permitting an *actio popularis* petition is readily apparent from its rules of procedure. *See* Commission Regulations, *supra* note 38, Art. 29(6). It might be noted, too, that Article 44 of the Convention speaks of a "violation of this Convention by a State Party" and not merely of a "violation of a human right set forth in this Convention," which is the language found in Article 45, the provision that deals with interstate complaints. Whether this difference in wording means that the scope of the right of individual petition is wider than that of the interstate complaint remains to be seen.

[44] Convention, Art. 48(1)(a).

[45] These preconditions are set out in Articles 46 and 47 of the Convention, which read as follows:

Article 46

1. Admission by the Commission of a petition or communication lodged in accordance with Articles 44 or 45 shall be subject to the following requirements:

a. that the remedies under domestic law have been pursued and exhausted in accordance with generally recognized principles of international law;
b. that the petition or communication is lodged within a period of six months from the date on which the party alleging violation of his rights was notified of the final judgment;
c. that the subject of the petition or communication is not pending in another international proceeding for settlement; and
d. that, in the case of Article 44, the petition contains the name, nationality, profession, domicile, and signature of the person or persons or of the legal representative of the entity lodging the petition.

2. The provisions of paragraphs 1.a and 1.b of this article shall not be applicable when:

a. the domestic legislation of the state concerned does not afford due process of law for the protection of the right or rights that have allegedly been violated;
b. the party alleging violation of his rights has been denied access to the remedies under domestic law or has been prevented from exhausting them; or
c. there has been unwarranted delay in rendering a final judgment under the aforementioned remedies.

Article 47

The Commission shall consider inadmissible any petition or communication submitted under Articles 44 or 45 if:

a. any of the requirements indicated in Article 46 has not been met;
b. the petition or communication does not state facts that tend to establish a violation of the rights guaranteed by this Convention;
c. the statements of the petitioner or of the state indicate that the petition or communication is manifestly groundless or obviously out of order; or
d. the petition or communication is substantially the same as one previously studied by the Commission or by another international organization.

For analysis of these provisions, see Norris, *supra* note 41, at 742–44.

vestigations.[46] At this stage also the Commission explores with the parties the possibilities for reaching a friendly settlement of the dispute.[47] If no friendly settlement is reached, the case proceeds to the third stage.[48] Here the Commission has the duty to draw up "a report setting forth the facts and stating its conclusions."[49] The report is transmitted to "the states concerned"[50] and may be supplemented by "such proposals and recommendations" as the Commission sees fit to make.[51] Within a period of 3 months following the transmittal of the report, the case may be referred to the Court either by the Commission or by the "state concerned."[52]

These then are the procedures that Article 61(2) says must be "completed" before a case is ripe for adjudication by the Court. The application of this requirement raises a number of questions. It might be asked, for example, whether only the states that participated in a given proceeding before the Commission may refer the case to the Court. This question arises when one seeks to determine which states under Article 50(2) of the Convention are "the states concerned" that have the right to receive the Commission's stage-three report. If a state that did not participate in the proceedings requests the report on the ground that one of the individual petitioners is its national, would that state be a "state concerned" and would it be entitled to take the case to the Court?

It is also not clear whether there are any exceptions to the Article 61(2) requirement: for example, does it apply to cases that are referred to the Court by special agreement? State Party *A* and State Party *B* might have a dispute relating to the application of the Convention that does not involve a violation

[46] Convention, Art. 48(1)(d) and (e).

[47] *Id.*, Art. 48(1)(f). The settlement must be made on the basis of "respect for the human rights recognized in this Convention."

[48] Article 49 of the Convention deals with cases in which a friendly settlement has been reached. It reads as follows:

> If a friendly settlement has been reached in accordance with paragraph 1.f of Article 48, the Commission shall draw up a report, which shall be transmitted to the petitioner and to the States Parties to this Convention, and shall then be communicated to the Secretary General of the Organization of American States for publication. This report shall contain a brief statement of the facts and of the solution reached. If any party in the case so requests, the fullest possible information shall be provided to it.

[49] Convention, Art. 50(1). This report must be drawn up within a period of 180 days following the Commission's failure to obtain a friendly settlement. Statute of the Commission, Art. 23(2), HANDBOOK, *supra* note 2, at 95.

[50] Convention, Art. 50(2).

[51] *Id.*, Art. 50(3).

[52] *Id.*, Art. 51(1). If the case is not referred to the Court within the above-mentioned period, the Commission "may, by the vote of an absolute majority of its members, set forth its opinion and conclusions concerning the questions submitted for its consideration." Note the word "may," which suggests that the Commission need not adopt this report. If it fails to do so, the case is presumably silently dropped since the earlier stage-three report, adopted by the Commission pursuant to Article 50 of the Convention, may be transmitted only to the states concerned, which are not at liberty to publish it. *Id.*, Art. 50(2). But if the Commission does adopt the stage-four report and makes appropriate recommendations to the state concerned, it must also prescribe a period of time within which the state is to remedy the situation in question. Once that period has expired, the Commission must "decide by the vote of an absolute majority of its members whether . . . to publish its report." *Id.*, Art. 51.

of any of the human rights that it guarantees. Let us assume that the dispute concerns an alleged breach of the obligation to accord diplomatic immunities to one of the judges.[53] Such a case cannot be referred to the Commission by either state because Article 45 of the Convention provides that the Commission may only deal with interstate complaints charging "a violation of human rights set forth in the Convention." But this type of dispute, it would appear, can be referred to the Court by special agreement between State *A* and State *B*. That it falls within the Court's jurisdiction as a case "concerning the interpretation and application of the Convention"[54] cannot be doubted; neither can the fact that it forms the subject of a valid "special agreement." It would therefore not be unreasonable to argue that in this situation the states may go directly to the Court without submitting the case to the Commission. It is less clear whether the conclusion would be the same if in their special agreement the same states parties sought an adjudication of a dispute involving charges that one of them violated the human rights set out in the Convention.

Another question that remains to be answered is whether the proceedings before the Commission are waivable at the option of a defendant state when the complaining party to the case is an individual. A slightly different issue was recently presented to the Court by the Government of Costa Rica.[55] In this case, even before a private complaint was filed with the Commission, the Government petitioned the Court to determine whether Costa Rica had violated the human rights of a young woman who was murdered by one of her guards in a Costa Rican jail. In submitting the case directly to the Court, the Government of Costa Rica formally claimed the right to waive the proceedings before the Commission. The Court ruled against Costa Rica on that issue and held the case inadmissible. It concluded that the "procedures before the Commission have not been created for the sole benefit of the States, but also in order to allow for the exercise of important individual rights,"[56] and that therefore the power to waive these procedures did not belong to the states alone. The Court emphasized, in this connection, that the right of individuals to file petitions with and to appear before the Commission are important safeguards that enable private parties to play an active role in the investigatory, conciliatory, and quasi-adjudicatory processes by which the Commission exercises its functions. In the Court's view, these safeguards gain added importance because the Convention bars individuals from taking cases to the Court and thus prevents them from playing an equally active role in its proceedings. In assessing the implications of this case, it should be noted that the Court expressly left open the possibility that the proceedings before the Commission might be waivable in situations where (as might be the case with regard to certain interstate complaints) the interests that the Convention seeks to protect would not be significantly impaired by permitting direct access to the tribunal.

Judgments and Preliminary Decisions. The proceedings before the Court in

[53] On the privileges and immunities of the judges, see *id.*, Art. 70.

[54] *Id.*, Art. 62(3).

[55] *See* Government of Costa Rica (In the Matter of Viviana Gallardo *et al.*), Decision of Nov. 13, 1981, *reprinted in* 20 ILM 1424 (1981).

[56] *Id.*, para. 25.

a contentious case terminate with a judgment. By ratifying the Covention, the states parties assumed the obligation "to comply with the judgment of the Court in any case to which they are parties."[57] The Court has the power to enter a declaratory judgment and to award damages.[58] The basic provision on the subject is Article 63(1), which reads as follows:

> If the Court finds that there has been a violation of a right or freedom protected by this Convention, the Court shall rule that the injured party be ensured the enjoyment of his right or freedom that was violated. It shall also rule, if appropriate, that the consequences of the measure or situation that constituted the breach of such right or freedom be remedied and that fair compensation be paid to the injured party.

This provision requires the Court to determine not only whether in the specific case before it there has been a violation of the Convention and what rights the injured party is entitled to enjoy, but also what steps may have to be taken to remedy the violation. As for the power of the Court to award damages, Article 68(2) provides that that part of a "judgment that stipulates compensatory damages may be executed in the country concerned in accordance with domestic procedure governing the execution of judgments against the state." It remains to be seen whether the domestic courts of the states parties will rely on this provision to permit the Court's judgments to be executed as if they were national judgments.

An interesting solution relating to the execution of judgments can be found in the headquarters agreement of September 10, 1981, which the Court concluded with the Government of Costa Rica. Article 27 of that agreement reads as follows: "The decisions of the Court, and in its place those of its President, as soon as they have been communicated to the appropriate administrative or judicial authorities of the Republic, shall have the same effect and executory force as those adopted by Costa Rican courts." The Court plans to include comparable provisions in its agreements with the other states parties. This approach would certainly help to resolve the problems that national courts might otherwise have in deciding what domestic legal effect to accord to the judgments of the Court.

In addition, the Court has the power to grant an extraordinary remedy in the nature of a temporary injunction. This power is spelled out in Article 63(2) of the Convention, which reads as follows:

> In cases of extreme gravity and urgency, and when necessary to avoid irreparable damage to persons, the Court shall adopt such provisional measures as it deems pertinent in matters it has under consideration. With respect to a case not yet submitted to the Court, it may act at the request of the Commission.

As this provision indicates, the temporary injunction is available in two distinct circumstances: for cases already pending before the Court and for cases being dealt with by the Commission that have not yet been referred to the Court for adjudication.

[57] Convention, Art. 68(1).

[58] *Id.*, Arts. 63(1) and 68(2).

Regarding the first category of cases, it would appear that the request for a temporary injunction may be made at any time after the case has been submitted to the Court or even simultaneously with the filing of the case. Of course, the requested relief may only be granted after the Court has determined, if only in a preliminary manner, that the parties are subject to its jurisdiction. Although Article 63(2) does not mention jurisdiction, it is obvious that the Court can only deal with a case, whether it calls for provisional or permanent relief, in which the states parties to the litigation have accepted its jurisdiction. But since jurisdictional issues may at times be extremely complex and intertwined with the merits of the case, the Court should not be required to resolve fully and finally all jurisdictional questions before ordering the requested provisional measures. Having assured itself that such measures are otherwise plainly indicated, and given the need for urgency and the extraordinary character of the relief, the Court might be justified in certain cases to require no more than a prima facie showing of jurisdiction.

The same principle would also appear to apply to the second category of cases, that is, when a preliminary injunction is sought even before the Commission has had a chance to complete its examination of the complaint. Here the Court would obtain jurisdiction only for the purpose of dealing with the request for provisional measures. It would presumably not acquire jurisdiction to decide the case on the merits until the proceedings before the Commission were concluded and the complaint was thereafter referred to it either by the Commission or a state. But even if the case were subsequently not submitted to the Court, the provisional measures should be deemed to remain within its jurisdiction to modify or revoke.

Enforcement of Judgments. The Convention does not establish a formal procedure to enforce the rulings of the Court against recalcitrant states. One provision, however—Article 65—does bear on this subject. It reads:

> To each regular session of the General Assembly of the Organization of American States the Court shall submit, for the Assembly's consideration, a report on its work during the previous year. It shall specify, in particular, the cases in which a state has not complied with its judgments, making any pertinent recommendations.

This provision enables the Court to inform the OAS General Assembly of situations involving noncompliance with its decisions, and it permits the Assembly to discuss the matter and to adopt whatever political measures it deems appropriate. Although Article 65 speaks of "regular sessions" of the Assembly, that does not mean that the matter of noncompliance by a state may not be raised at a special session of that body, either at the request of a member state or following consideration by the OAS Permanent Council. Since the Council acts for the Assembly when it is not in session, the Court would appear to be free to call the Council's attention to cases that might justify emergency measures. This would be true, in particular, in situations involving threats of noncompliance with provisional measures adopted by the Court. Such a situation, in turn, might prompt the Council to convene a special session of the Assembly or to take some other measures it deems appropriate.

Advisory Jurisdiction

Its Scope and Application. The jurisdiction of the Inter-American Court of Human Rights to render advisory opinions is spelled out in Article 64 of the Convention, which reads as follows:

> 1. The member states of the Organization may consult the Court regarding the interpretation of this Convention or of other treaties concerning the protection of human rights in the American states. Within their spheres of competence, the organs listed in Chapter X of the Charter of the Organization of American States, as amended by the Protocol of Buenos Aires, may in like manner consult the Court.
>
> 2. The Court, at the request of a member state of the Organization, may provide that state with opinions regarding the compatibility of any of its domestic laws with the aforesaid international instruments.

An analysis of Article 64 will readily demonstrate that the scope of the advisory power it confers on the Court is more extensive than that enjoyed by any international tribunal in existence today.[59] Thus, first, standing to request an advisory opinion from the Court is not limited to the states parties to the Convention; it extends to any OAS member state. Second, the Court's advisory jurisdiction applies not only to the Convention but also to the interpretation of any other treaty "concerning the protection of human rights in the American states." Third, the right to seek advisory opinions extends to all OAS organs, including the Inter-American Commission on Human Rights and the OAS General Assembly. Finally, all OAS member states may also request opinions from the Court regarding the compatibility of their domestic laws with the Convention or with any of the human rights treaties to which Article 64 refers.

The Court has thus far not received any requests for an advisory opinion. It has therefore not had an opportunity to address the many questions posed by Article 64. For example, it is by no means clear what is meant by "treaties concerning the protection of human rights in the American states." This is not a concept that has an accepted juridical meaning within the inter-American system, and the *travaux préparatoires* of the American Convention do not help explain it. The phrase might refer to human rights treaties concluded exclusively by American states; it might refer to treaties adopted within the framework of the inter-American system; or it might apply to human rights treaties, whether bilateral or multilateral, universal or regional, that include one or more American states among the parties. (The UN Human Rights Covenants are a good example of treaties falling in the latter category.) Equally problematic is the question whether the OAS Charter, which deals with many different subjects, including human rights, is a "treaty concerning the protection of human rights." The answers to these questions are important for they will determine, *inter alia*, whether the Court has the power to interpret a United Nations human rights treaty or the human rights provisions of a bilateral treaty (*e.g.*, one dealing with extradition), or whether its advisory jurisdiction is limited to OAS treaties.

[59] On this subject generally, see Szasz, *Enhancing the Advisory Competence of the World Court*, in 2 THE FUTURE OF THE INTERNATIONAL COURT 499 (L. Gross ed. 1976).

An equally important issue that the Court will have to decide in interpreting Article 64 is whether the American Declaration on the Rights and Duties of Man[60] may be included among "treaties concerning the protection of human rights in the American states." This question is important because the Declaration serves as the normative instrument that the Commission applies in judging the conduct of those OAS member states which have not ratified the Convention.[61] That the Declaration is not a treaty is obvious, but that conclusion alone does not necessarily dispose of the problem because it is now generally accepted that the Protocol of Buenos Aires, which revised the OAS Charter, incorporated the Declaration by reference into the Charter.[62] If this view is sound, it would follow, at the very least, that whenever the Court is called upon to interpret the human rights provisions of the OAS Charter, it is free to look to and draw upon the Declaration.[63] Moreover, if the right of the Commission to judge the conduct of OAS member states by reference to the human rights proclaimed in the Declaration derives from its incorporation into the Charter, it is certainly arguable that the power of the Court to interpret the Declaration independently is the same as its power to interpret the Charter.

To the extent that Article 64(2) permits OAS member states to seek an opinion from the Court regarding the compatibility of their domestic laws with the Convention and with any other "American" human rights treaty, it might have a number of important uses. The provision might be invoked by governments to obtain the Court's opinion on the legality of pending legislation. States considering ratification of the Convention might resort to this procedure to ascertain the Court's views on the need for certain types of reservations. It might also be used by national tribunals when they are called upon to resolve disputes requiring an interpretation of the Convention, or of related domestic legislation, and of the different human rights treaties to which the state is a party. Resort to Article 64 in this context could contribute very significantly to the uniform domestic application of the Convention.[64] This conclusion sug-

[60] The American Declaration on the Rights and Duties of Man was adopted as Resolution XXX by the Ninth International Conference of American States, which was held in Bogotá, Colombia from March 30 to May 2, 1948. The text is *reprinted in* HANDBOOK, *supra* note 2, at 17.

[61] Article 1(2)(b) of the Statute of the Commission declares that in relation to states that have not ratified the Convention "human rights are understood to be . . . the rights set forth in the American Declaration." *See also* Statute of the Commission, Art. 20, and Commission Regulations, Art. 23, HANDBOOK, *supra* note 2, at 95 and 117, respectively, which deal with the right of the Commission to handle petitions directed against these states. *See* Norris, *supra* note 41, at 735–38.

[62] This view, first expounded by Buergenthal, *The Revised OAS Charter and the Protection of Human Rights*, 69 AJIL 828 (1975), has now been accepted by the Inter-American Commission on Human Rights. Case No. 2141 (United States of America), Res. 23/81 of March 6, 1981, OAS/Ser.L/V/11.52, doc. 48, para. 16 (1981).

[63] It remains to be seen what relevance attaches to Article 29(1) of the Convention, which declares that "no provision of this Convention shall be interpreted as . . . excluding or limiting the effect that the American Declaration of the Rights and Duties of Man . . . may have." On the relationship between the Convention and the Declaration, see Buergenthal, *supra* note 2, at 131–34.

[64] Here the Court's advisory jurisdiction could perform a role similar to that performed by the Court of Justice of the European Communities under Article 177 of the EEC Treaty. *See* H. SCHERMERS, JUDICIAL PROTECTION IN THE EUROPEAN COMMUNITIES 288–330 (1976). *See also* Stein, *Lawyers, Judges, and the Making of a Transnational Constitution*, 75 AJIL 1 (1981);

gests the question whether national courts may request an advisory opinion directly from the Inter-American Court or whether they have to go through their governments. The language of Article 64(2) indicates that the request must come from the state, that is, through the government, rather than directly from national tribunals. Consequently, governments might find it useful to establish a domestic procedure to facilitate the transmittal of these requests and to regulate the manner of their presentation to the Court. The matter could also be dealt with by appropriate agreements between the Court and governments, authorizing national tribunals to deal directly with the Court in certain cases.[65]

Finally, the full scope of the Court's power to render advisory opinions remains to be understood and delimited. One issue that might arise in this context may be illustrated by reference to the following hypothetical case: Assume that a complaint has been filed with the Commission against State *X* and that State *X* has not accepted the jurisdiction of the Court. If during the proceedings before the Commission a disagreement arises between State *X* and the Commission regarding the meaning of a provision of the Convention, may the Commission request an advisory opinion from the Court on that legal issue even if State *X* objects? State *X* would presumably argue that this was not a legitimate request for an advisory opinion but a disguised contentious case resorted to by the Commission to get around *X*'s failure to recognize the Court's jurisdiction. The strength of such a contention may well depend on the weight that should be given to the fact that Article 64 imposes no limits on the right to seek advisory opinions; it provides only that the request by OAS organs must be within "their spheres of competence." Although the request in our hypothetical case would appear to be within the Commission's sphere of competence, it remains to be determined whether the existence of an actual dispute in a pending case and the absence of adjudicatory jurisdiction compel a different result.

Efficacy of Advisory Jurisdiction. Resort to the advisory jurisdiction of the Court, whether it be by the Commission, the other OAS organs, or the member states, has a number of advantages that its contentious jurisdiction does not provide. The latter can only be invoked by and against states that have recognized the Court's jurisdiction; no such requirement applies to its advisory jurisdiction. Although the Court's decision in a contentious case is binding, which is of course not true of an advisory opinion, that distinction may not be of great practical significance. Compliance and noncompliance by states with their international obligations depend less on the formal status of a judgment and its abstract enforceability than on the impact of the opinion as a force capable of adding to or detracting from the legitimacy of specific governmental conduct. This latter factor has an important bearing on the perception that

---

Caflisch, *Reference Procedures and the International Court of Justice*, in Gross, *supra* note 59, at 572. *Cf.* Buergenthal, *Interaction of National Law and Modern International Agreements: Some Introductory Observations*, 18 AM. J. COMP. L. 233 (1970); Buergenthal, *International and Regional Human Rights Law and Institutions: Some Examples of Their Interaction*, 12 TEX. INT'L L.J. 321 (1977).

[65] The Court has the power to conclude such agreements. *See* Statute, Art. 27(2).

governments have about the political costs of noncompliance.[66] As a result, states may find it as difficult in some cases to disregard an advisory opinion as a binding decision. At the same time, it is easier for governments to comply with advisory opinions because such rulings do not stigmatize them as violators of human rights, which in turn diminishes the domestic political cost of compliance. The Court may therefore be able to play an important role, even if its contentious jurisdiction is not widely accepted by the states parties, provided that its advisory jurisdiction is resorted to by OAS organs and by the member states.

IV. Conclusion

It is much too early, of course, to tell whether and how well the Inter-American Court of Human Rights will be able to discharge its mission. The answer cannot be divorced from the political climate of the Americas and the attitude of American governments towards human rights in general. But even when that climate is favorable, which it was for a while but may be no longer, much will still depend on the willingness of governments to accept the Court's jurisdiction[67] and on the willingness of the Commission to utilize the Court.

If the Commission were to resort to the Court's advisory and contentious jurisdiction, and do so in a judicious and creative manner, it could play an important role in strengthening the institutional framework and constitutional legitimacy of the entire inter-American human rights system. That the system urgently needs to be reinforced and that it would greatly benefit, particularly now, from juridical reaffirmation of its constitutional legitimacy can hardly be doubted.

The Commission, more than any other OAS organ, has the legal authority and professional competence to lead this effort. Whether it also has the necessary wisdom to do so remains to be seen. It is clear, however, that if the Commission fails to refer cases and requests for advisory opinions to the Court, a great opportunity will have been missed in the struggle to make respect for human rights an integral part of the inter-American political agenda.

[66] *Cf.* R. Fisher, Improving Compliance with International Law 105 (1981).

[67] The fact that only four states have thus far accepted the jurisdiction of the Court should not be seen as a bad omen. After all, it took about 5 years after the European Convention on Human Rights entered into force to obtain the eight acceptances of its jurisdiction, which were a prerequisite for the establishment of the European Court. *See* European Convention on Human Rights, *supra* note 29, Art. 56; A. H. Robertson, *supra* note 29, at 195–96. *Cf.* L. Henkin, How Nations Behave 186–88 (2d ed. 1979).

CONDITIONING U.S. SECURITY ASSISTANCE ON HUMAN RIGHTS PRACTICES

*By Stephen B. Cohen**

INTRODUCTION

> The level of parliament depends on whether it does not merely discuss great issues, but decisively influences them; in other words, its quality depends on whether what happens there matters, or whether parliament is nothing but the unwillingly tolerated rubber stamp of a ruling bureaucracy.
>
> *Max Weber*[1]

In the United States, with its government of separated powers and functions, it is the executive branch, and in particular the Department of State, that bears responsibility for implementing legislation on foreign relations. The success of implementation will depend on political decisions, involving competing national interests, as well as on institutional and personal considerations of the officials concerned. Inevitably, there is a gap between legislation and execution, especially when the Executive is not wholly sympathetic to the law. The gap may even devour legislated policies as the Executive refuses "to take Care that the Laws be faithfully executed,"[2] and bureaucratic and personal considerations distort judgments, exploit the generality and uncertainty of language, and lead to abuse of discretion. A notable instance of this problem has been executive implementation of legislation on international human rights.

The international law of human rights imposes obligations on governments in the exercise of their domestic sovereignty. Under the Universal Declaration, the United Nations Covenants, the European and Inter-American Conventions, and the Helsinki accords, states have defined and agreed to respect certain basic freedoms of persons within their jurisdiction.[3] These obligations suggest a corresponding duty of one government not to support another engaged in serious violations of internationally recognized human rights. In the world of states,

* Associate Professor of Law, Georgetown University Law Center; formerly Deputy Assistant Secretary of State for Human Rights and Security Assistance (1978–1980; *see infra* note 14). This article is based on a study prepared for the International Human Rights Law Group of the Procedural Aspects of International Law Institute, under a grant from the Ford Foundation.

The author is indebted to a number of current and former Department of State officials who reviewed this article. In addition, Richard Bilder, Barry Carter, Joel Handler, Richard Lillich, Michael Seidman, Don Wallace, Edith Weiss, Amy Young-Anawaty, and Karen de Young generously provided comments. Janet Milne gave editorial advice with each new draft. Jeff Turner furnished invaluable research assistance.

[1] M. WEBER, *Parliament and Government in a Reconstructed Germany*, in 2 ECONOMY AND SOCIETY 1392 (1978).

[2] U.S. CONST. art. II, §3.

[3] *See* R. LILLICH & F. NEWMAN, INTERNATIONAL HUMAN RIGHTS: PROBLEMS OF LAW AND POLICY (1979); L. SOHN & T. BUERGENTHAL, INTERNATIONAL PROTECTION OF HUMAN RIGHTS (1973).

the enforcement of international obligations depends on the recognition and implementation of such a duty. While its contours have yet to be articulated under international law, this duty has already been the subject of domestic American statutes that set forth rules for the Executive's conduct of foreign relations with repressive governments. This article examines the legislation—in force since 1973—that conditions a foreign government's eligibility for United States military aid and arms sales on its human rights record.[4]

Congress believed this legislation to be required by American self-interest, as well as supported by principles of international law. The gift of aid and the sale of arms, it is true, can promote important national security objectives of the United States.[5] In addition to enhancing the defense capability of friendly countries, military ties give the United States influence with and access to other governments.[6] Yet governments to which the United States sends military aid and arms are viewed, by their own people and by the world community, as in part sustained and even approved by us. When the government in question is repressive, the perception of American support for it can impose considerable costs for American interests. The government may be overthrown and the supply of American aid and arms deeply resented by its successors.[7] The support of repressive governments also conflicts with traditional American values and damages the international reputation of the United States because of the appearance of complicity in repugnant practices.[8]

The principal (although not exclusive) legislative enactment on human rights and military ties has been section 502B of the Foreign Assistance Act of 1961.[9] The key subsection of this statute, 502B(a)(2), provides a basic rule: military aid is not to be given and arms are not to be sold to "any country, the government of which engages in a consistent pattern of gross violations of internationally recognized human rights."[10] An exception is allowed for cases where "extraordinary circumstances exist which necessitate a continuation of [military aid and

[4] At the same time, Congress also enacted legislation to establish human rights criteria for programs of economic aid. For example, under section 116 of the Foreign Assistance Act of 1961, the President may not provide development assistance "to the government of any country which engages in a consistent pattern of gross violations of internationally recognized human rights." 22 U.S.C. §2151n (Supp. III 1979). For a comprehensive review of all the human rights legislation enacted since 1973, see Weissbrodt, *Human Rights Legislation and U.S. Foreign Policy*, 7 GA. J. INT'L & COMP. L. 231 (1977). For a catalog of all statutes on human rights and foreign policy, see R. LILLICH, U.S. LEGISLATION RELATING HUMAN RIGHTS TO U.S. FOREIGN POLICY (1980) (available from International Human Rights Law Group, Washington, D.C.).

[5] CONGRESSIONAL RESEARCH SERVICE, UNITED STATES ARMS TRANSFER AND SECURITY ASSISTANCE PROGRAMS: PREPARED FOR THE SUBCOMM. ON EUROPE AND THE MIDDLE EAST OF THE HOUSE COMM. ON INTERNATIONAL RELATIONS, 95th Cong., 2d Sess., at xi (Comm. Print 1978) [hereinafter cited as CRS, SECURITY ASSISTANCE STUDY].

[6] *See* UNITED NATIONS ASSOCIATION, UNITED STATES FOREIGN POLICY AND HUMAN RIGHTS 68 (1979); CRS, SECURITY ASSISTANCE STUDY, *supra* note 5, at 6.

[7] *See* Newsom, *Our Arsenal Must Include Our Values*, Wash. Star, April 2, 1981, at A13, cols. 2–3; Whitaker, *Rights and Realpolitik*, N.Y. Times, Feb. 24, 1981, at A19, col. 4; Cohen, *Wrong on Human Rights*, NEW REPUBLIC, March 28, 1981, at 13–14.

[8] *See* Syrkin, *Can a Human Rights Policy Be Consistent?*, in HUMAN RIGHTS AND U.S. FOREIGN POLICY 200, 202, 212 (P. Brown & D. MacLean eds. 1979).

[9] 22 U.S.C. §2304 (Supp. III 1979).

[10] *Id.* subsection (a)(2).

arms sales] and . . . on all the facts it is in the national interest of the United States [to continue such assistance]."[11]

The history of the enactment and implementation of section 502B illuminates the obstacles encountered when Congress tries to influence executive decisions on foreign policy. It is not simply a question of enacting legislation that the Executive implements as a matter of course. A hostile administration may avoid implementation, as during the Nixon and Ford years.[12] Even if high political officials seem sympathetic (as they did during the Carter administration), entrenched bureaucratic interests may actively resist the law, particularly where its subject is human rights and foreign policy. The history also contributes to understanding foreign policy decisions as the product of conflict among bureaucracies with competing interests.[13] The implementation of section 502B

[11] *Id.* subsection (c)(1)(C).

Section 502B contains, in addition to the basic rule, a number of other provisions:

1. Subsection (a)(1) states that "a principal goal of the foreign policy of the United States shall be to promote the increased observance of internationally recognized human rights by all countries."

2. Subsection (a)(2) also prohibits the sale of certain equipment to the police of a government engaged "in a consistent pattern of gross violations of internationally recognized human rights."

3. Subsection (a)(3) directs the President to formulate and conduct programs of military aid and arms sales in a way that "will promote and advance human rights and avoid identification of the United States . . . with governments which deny to their people internationally recognized human rights."

4. Subsection (b) requires the Secretary of State to submit to Congress each year a report on human rights conditions in each country to which the United States proposes to give military aid or sell arms.

5. Subsection (c) establishes a specific procedure by which Congress may reverse an executive decision to provide military aid or sell arms to a particular government.

6. Both subsections (b) and (c) state that, in implementing section 502B, the Secretary of State is to consult with a designated Department of State official, the Assistant Secretary for Human Rights.

7. Subsection (d) defines a number of terms, including the phrase "internationally recognized human rights."

8. Subsection (e) provides that the President may furnish security assistance "to any country with respect to which the President finds that such a significant improvement in its human rights record has occurred as to warrant lifting the prohibition on furnishing such assistance in the national interest of the United States."

9. Subsection (f) requires the President in allocating funds under chapter 22 or the Arms Export Control Act to "take into account significant improvements in the human rights record of recipient countries."

[12] For the best available account of the role of human rights in the foreign policies of the Nixon, Ford, and Carter administrations, see R. Cohen, *Human Rights Decision-Making in the Executive Branch: Some Proposals for a Coordinated Strategy*, in HUMAN RIGHTS AND AMERICAN FOREIGN POLICY 212 (D. Kommers & G. Loescher eds. 1979) [hereinafter cited as R. Cohen, *Human Rights*].

[13] For the two seminal works in this area, see G. ALLISON, ESSENCE OF DECISION (1971); M. HALPERIN, BUREAUCRATIC POLITICS AND FOREIGN POLICY (1974). In explaining policymaking in the bureaucratic process, Allison argues that "what happens is not chosen as a solution to a problem but rather results from compromise, conflict, and confusion of officials with diverse interests and unequal influence." G. ALLISON, *supra*, at 162.

during the Carter years is a story of bureaucratic warfare of the most intense sort. The principal antagonists were the career Foreign Service, with responsibility for the day-to-day management of relations with other countries, and a newly created Department of State Bureau of Human Rights, staffed to a great degree by outsiders. Largely because of the career bureaucracy's resistance to implementation, the Carter record may surprise some readers and also appear to contradict the former President's aggressive public embrace of a human rights oriented foreign policy. It is true that his administration went much further in implementing the statute than its predecessors (who simply disregarded section 502B). But it was considerably more cautious and tentative than may be generally supposed and, at some points, may itself have violated the law.

The article is divided into four parts. Part I discusses the evolution of section 502B and disregard of the statute by the Nixon and Ford administrations. Part II examines the career bureaucracy's resistance to implementation during the Carter administration. Part III analyzes decisions reached during the Carter years, explaining how the statute was interpreted to reduce military aid and arms sales to specific countries.[14] Part IV discusses implications of this study for congressional attempts to influence the Executive's conduct of foreign policy and suggests avenues for further research.

I. The Evolution of Section 502B

Congress enacted legislation on the subject of human rights and military ties for the first time in 1973. From the beginning, the legislation was openly disregarded by the Nixon and Ford administrations, primarily owing to the opposition of Secretary of State Henry Kissinger.[15] Congress responded by

[14] In recounting the implementation of section 502B, this report draws in part on the experience of the author in the Department of State during the Carter administration as one of those responsible for enforcement of section 502B. Although every effort has been made to check his recollections with those of others, the history inevitably reflects his own views and bias. It would not be possible to write on this subject without relying to a significant degree on the personal accounts of those who served in the executive branch. Information that indicates how section 502B was applied to specific questions is, in general, not available to the public. The decisions were made in private within the Department of State, they were rarely publicized by the executive branch, and only on occasion did Congress use its oversight role to elicit detailed explanations of them. The internal Government documents that do furnish a written record will not be publicly available for a number of years, and at any rate, this record is incomplete and to some extent misleading. Some decisions were never recorded at all and the record of others was designed, not to describe accurately the decisions or how they were made, but to place them in the best possible light.

Allison provides a good account of the problem:

> Information about the details of differences in perceptions and priorities within a government on a particular issue is rarely available. Accurate accounts of the bargaining that yielded a resolution of the issue are rarer still. Documents do not capture this kind of information. What the documents do preserve tends to obscure, as much as enlighten. . . . As a master of this style of analysis has stated, "If I were forced to choose between the documents on the one hand, and late, limited, partial interviews with some of the principal participants on the other, I would be forced to discard the documents."

Allison, *supra* note 13, at 181 (quoting Richard Neustadt).

[15] R. Cohen, *Human Rights, supra* note 12, at 220–21; T. Franck & E. Weisband, Foreign Policy by Congress 85 (1979); Congressional Research Service, Human Rights and U.S. Foreign Assistance: Prepared for the Senate Comm. on Foreign Relations, 96th Cong., 1st Sess. 84–85 (Comm. Print 1979) [hereinafter cited as CRS, Human Rights Study].

regularly expanding and amending its initial product in an attempt to tighten the law and thus ensure that human rights concerns would be taken into account in executive branch decisions. During Kissinger's tenure, however, Congress was almost entirely unsuccessful in influencing the Executive to change its behavior. Kissinger's persistent noncompliance with the law was foreshadowed during his confirmation hearings when he explicitly rejected the inclusion of human rights objectives in American foreign policy: "But I do believe that it is dangerous for us to make the domestic policy of countries around the world a direct objective of American foreign policy. . . ."[16]

The absence of discernible impact resulted not only from the Executive's opposition to conditioning military aid and arms sales on human rights factors, but also from the fact that for this entire period the legislation was in a form that made it advisory. The statute became a binding legal requirement only in 1978, when Congress decided that earlier versions had not had a sufficient impact. The following discussion reviews the legislative history that culminated in the 1978 amendments, which left the statute essentially as it is today.

The General Rule

Section 502B was not the first attempt by Congress to legislate on human rights and military relationships. It was preceded by section 32 of the Foreign Assistance Act of 1973, enacted on December 13 of that year.[17] This provision was couched in "sense of the Congress" language. So cast, it expressed a legislative viewpoint that was not legally binding, a form chosen to allow the Executive flexibility in implementation. Section 32 stated: "It is the sense of Congress that the President should deny any . . . military assistance to the government of any foreign country which practices the internment or imprisonment of that country's citizens for political purposes."[18]

In June 1974, 6 months after the enactment of section 32, Robert S. Ingersoll, Assistant Secretary of State for East Asian and Pacific Affairs, testified before the House Foreign Affairs Committee that the Nixon administration had taken no steps to act on the sense of Congress expressed in section 32.[19] A few weeks later, Ingersoll submitted a detailed explanation in which he argued that it was too difficult to define "political prisoner" objectively, expressed doubt that cutting aid was ever an effective or appropriate foreign policy response to human rights violations, and singled out private diplomacy as the preferred means for pursuing human rights concerns.[20]

At about the same time that section 32 was first proposed, Representative Donald Fraser began a parallel effort, which eventually led to enactment of

[16] *Nomination of Henry A. Kissinger: Hearings Before the Senate Comm. on Foreign Relations*, 93d Cong., 1st Sess. 117 (1973).

[17] Foreign Assistance Act of 1973, §32, 87 Stat. 733 (1973).

[18] *Ibid.*

[19] *Fiscal Year 1975 Foreign Assistance Request: Hearings Before the House Comm. on Foreign Affairs*, 93d Cong., 2d Sess. 280–81 (1974).

[20] Letter from Robert S. Ingersoll to the Honorable Thomas E. Morgan (June 27, 1974), *reprinted in id.* at 284–86.

section 502B. During the fall of 1973, the House Subcommittee on International Organizations and Movements, under Fraser's leadership, began a series of extensive hearings on the subject of human rights and foreign policy[21] and, in early 1974, issued a 54-page report emphasizing the existence of a body of international law that recognizes certain basic rights owed by all governments to their citizens.[22] The report further stated that the United States was obligated not only to respect these rights within its own jurisdiction, but also to avoid supporting other governments engaged in violating them.[23] The report concluded, however, that the United States had failed to meet its obligations:

> The human rights factor is not accorded the high priority it deserves in our country's foreign policy. Unfortunately, the prevailing attitude has led the United States into embracing governments which practice torture and unabashedly violate almost every human rights guarantee pronounced by the world community. . . . [C]onsideration for human rights in foreign policy is both morally imperative and practically necessary. . . . The State Department too often has taken the position that human rights is a domestic matter and not a relevant factor in determining bilateral relations. When charges of serious violations of human rights do occur, the most that the Department is likely to do is make private inquiries and low-keyed appeals to the government concerned.[24]

The report made numerous recommendations for change in the conduct of U.S. foreign policy, among which was the idea that military ties should be affected by human rights concerns: "The Department of State should discourage governments which are committing serious violations of human rights through various measures such as . . . withdrawal of military assistance and sales."[25]

In an effort to goad the Executive into taking account of human rights, Fraser proposed and Congress enacted the initial version of section 502B in December 1974.[26] In its first incarnation, section 502B, like section 32, expressed the "sense of Congress" and was therefore merely advisory, rather than binding. It stated:

> It is the sense of the Congress that, except in extraordinary circumstances, the President shall substantially reduce or terminate security assistance to any government which engages in a consistent pattern of gross violations of internationally recognized human rights, including torture or cruel, inhuman, or degrading treatment or punishment; prolonged detention without charges; or other flagrant denials of the right to life, liberty, and the security of the person.[27]

[21] *See generally International Protection of Human Rights, The Work of International Organizations and the Role of U.S. Foreign Policy: Hearings Before the Subcomm. on International Organizations and Movements of the House Comm. on Foreign Affairs*, 93d Cong., 1st Sess. (1974).

[22] *See generally* SUBCOMM. ON INTERNATIONAL ORGANIZATIONS AND MOVEMENTS OF THE HOUSE COMM. ON FOREIGN AFFAIRS, HUMAN RIGHTS IN THE WORLD COMMUNITY: A CALL FOR U.S. LEADERSHIP, 93d Cong., 2d Sess., at 9–11 (Comm. Print 1974) [hereinafter cited as FRASER REPORT].

[23] *See generally* FRASER REPORT, *supra* note 22. at 17–45.

[24] *Id.* at 9–10.

[25] *Id.* at 11.

[26] Foreign Assistance Act of 1974, §46, 88 Stat. 1815 (1974) (current version at 22 U.S.C. §2304 (Supp. III 1979)).

[27] *Ibid.*

The substantive standard of section 502B differed from that of section 32 in three important respects. First, the statute used the term "security assistance" (rather than "military assistance"), and this new term was defined to include sales of arms for cash as well as military aid.[28] Second, it changed the category of relevant human rights violations from "internment or imprisonment" for "political purposes" to "torture," "prolonged detention without charges," and other inhuman treatment.[29] By replacing a status that lacked a precise definition with specific practices, Congress appears to have been responding directly to Ingersoll's complaint that the violations under section 32 had been too difficult to define objectively. Third, it attempted to recognize the need for executive flexibility by providing an "extraordinary circumstances" exception (but at the same time required the President to report to Congress when exceptions were to be made).

It soon became apparent, however, that the Executive, just as it had ignored section 32, intended to give absolutely no effect to the sense of the Congress as expressed in section 502B. In November 1975, the Under Secretary of State for Security Assistance, Carlyle E. Maw, testified that in no case during the preceding year had military aid or arms sales been denied on human rights grounds.[30] At the same time, the administration submitted to Congress a report on executive compliance with section 502B. Instead of providing the information required by the statute, the report attacked the policy enunciated by section 502B and clearly implied that the Executive had no intention of ever refusing military aid or arms sales to any government on human rights grounds.[31]

One month later, frustrated by the blatant refusal of the Executive to implement section 502B, Congress attempted to transform the statute from a statement of its own sentiments into a mandatory requirement.[32] In response to a proposal by Representative Fraser, Congress voted to delete the "sense of the Congress" language and make section 502B legally binding.[33] The House report on the bill emphasized the need to strengthen the statute in order to enforce the will of the Congress:

> Unfortunately, the executive branch response to the existing human rights provision has not been satisfactory. . . . In fact, increased levels of

[28] Under the 1974 version of the statute, security assistance was defined to include "assistance under chapter 2 (military assistance) . . . [and] sales under the Foreign Military Sales Act." Foreign Assistance Act of 1974, §46, 88 Stat. 1816 (1974) (currently codified at 22 U.S.C. §2304(d)(2) (Supp. III 1979)).

[29] *Id.* §46, 88 Stat. 1815 (currently codified at 22 U.S.C. §2304(a)(1) (Supp. III 1979)).

[30] *International Security Assistance Act of 1976: Hearings of the House Comm. on International Relations*, 94th Cong., 1st & 2d Sess. 207–08 (1976) [hereinafter cited as *1976 Act Hearings*].

[31] U.S. DEP'T OF STATE, REPORT TO THE CONGRESS ON THE HUMAN RIGHTS SITUATION IN COUNTRIES RECEIVING U.S. SECURITY ASSISTANCE (1975), *reprinted in Foreign Assistance Authorization Arms Sales Issues: Hearings Before the Subcomm. on Foreign Assistance of the Senate Comm. on Foreign Relations*, 94th Cong., 1st Sess. 377 (1976). Representative Fraser is quoted as having found "the report to be primarily a defense of the State Department's apparent intention not to comply with the law." Gwertzman, *U.S. Blocks Human Rights Data, on Nations Getting Arms*, N.Y. Times, Nov. 19, 1975, at 1, col. 1, 14, col. 4.

[32] *See 1976 Act Hearings, supra* note 30, at 498–500.

[33] 122 CONG. REC. 9587–88 (1976).

> security assistance were requested for a number of countries where serious human rights problems exist.
>
> Consequently, the committee approved the above amendment to Section 502B which makes it binding that the President include human rights considerations in the process in determining levels and kinds of assistance for recipient countries.[34]

President Ford vetoed the foreign aid authorization bill that contained these changes on May 7, 1976. In his veto message, he objected to the transformation of section 502B into a binding directive.[35] Two months later, after a compromise was reached, President Ford signed a revised bill. The sense of the Congress language was replaced by an introduction stating that the section 502B standard was "the policy of the United States."[36] Although the language was weaker than a binding legal requirement, the Senate report indicated that Congress expected the policy to be implemented: "The Committee has taken action in this bill to ensure that human rights considerations are brought to bear on decisions made within the Executive Branch . . . relating to the provision of . . . security assistance."[37]

In January 1977, the Carter administration entered office. Every year for the preceding 4 years, the issue of how human rights concerns should affect military ties had been the subject of congressional action. This time Congress refrained from attempting to strengthen the basic substantive rule of section 502B(a)(2) in order to allow the new Carter administration, publicly committed to renewed emphasis on human rights in foreign policy, an opportunity to implement the legislation as it existed. However, Congress did underline its continuing concern about military ties to repressive governments by providing for the creation of the position of Assistant Secretary of State for Human Rights, with responsibility for participating in decisions on security assistance.[38] In

[34] H. R. REP. NO. 94-848, 94th Cong., 2d Sess. 15 (1976).

[35] President's Message to the Senate Returning S. 2662 Without His Approval, 12 WEEKLY COMP. OF PRES. DOC. 826, 828 (May 7, 1976).

[36] International Security Assistance and Arms Export Act of 1976, §301, 90 Stat. 748 (1976) (current version at 22 U.S.C. §2304 (Supp. III 1979)).

[37] S. REP. NO. 94-876, 94th Cong., 2d Sess. 14-15 (1976).

[38] Foreign Relations Authorization Act, Fiscal Year 1978, §109, 91 Stat. 846 (1977) (current version at 22 U.S.C. §2384 (Supp. III 1979)). The statute provides in part:

> (f)(1) There shall be in the Department of State an Assistant Secretary for Human Rights and Humanitarian Affairs who shall be responsible to the Secretary of State for matters pertaining to human rights . . . in the conduct of foreign policy. The Secretary of State shall carry out his responsibility under section 502B . . . through the Assistant Secretary.
>
> (f)(2) The Assistant Secretary of State for Human Rights and Humanitarian Affairs shall maintain continuous observation and review of all matters pertaining to human rights . . . in the conduct of foreign policy, including—
>
> . . .
>
> (c) making recommendations to the Secretary of State . . . regarding compliance with . . . section [502B].

22 U.S.C. §2384 (f)(1)-(f)(2) (Supp. III 1979). In its report on this legislation, the Senate Foreign Relations Committee explained the rationale for revising the statute:

> Human rights issues . . . have clearly acquired an increased importance in the conduct of

addition, members of the House International Relations Committee indicated that they would watch closely actions taken by the new administration to implement section 502B.[39]

One indication of congressional opinion that the first year of Carter efforts, although substantial, did not go far enough is that in 1978 Congress resumed the process of strengthening section 502B by deleting the prefatory "it is the policy of the United States" language from subsection (a)(2). As a result, it directly states that, absent "extraordinary circumstances," "no security assistance may be provided to any country, the government of which engages in a consistent pattern of gross violations of internationally recognized human rights."[40] The Conference Committee report made it clear that, as a result of the deletion, section 502B(a)(2) was to be a binding requirement that the Executive was obligated to follow as a matter of law:

> [T]he intended effect of this amendment is to substitute for the current policy statement a legal requirement to deny security assistance. . . . [I]t is the intent of the committee of conference to place renewed emphasis on human rights as a major factor that must, as a matter of law, be taken into account in making security assistance decisions.[41]

Country-Specific Legislation

In 1974, when Congress originally enacted section 502B, it also began to pass legislation to limit military aid and arms sales to designated countries. The country-specific legislation was contained in bills authorizing or appropriating funds for military aid, and it named, at various times, Argentina, Brazil, Chile, El Salvador, Guatemala, Paraguay, the Philippines, South Korea, Uruguay, and Zaire.[42] The legislation usually mentioned only military aid and was effective for a single year, although in two cases it expressly prohibited arms sales as well and was of indefinite duration.

Congress has successfully attached country-specific legislation to bills authorizing or appropriating military aid for every fiscal year since 1975.[43] For

---

> U.S. foreign policy, and this provision will serve to give additional stature to the State Department official charged with primary responsibilities in this area. The committee would expect this new Assistant Secretary to be supported by such Deputy Assistant Secretaries and staff as are commensurate with the rank of Assistant Secretary.

S. REP. NO. 95–194, 95th Cong., 1st Sess. 16 (1977), *reprinted in* [1977] U.S. CODE CONG. & AD. NEWS 1625, 1638.

[39] *See Foreign Assistance Legislation for Fiscal Year 1978 (Part 1): Hearings Before the House Comm. on International Relations*, 95th Cong., 1st Sess. 27 (1977) (remarks of Rep. Fraser) (committee expects that, if it refrains from intervening, new administration will not lapse into business-as-usual approach of predecessors); *id.* at 29 (remarks of Rep. Harrington) (administration must support rhetoric with action).

[40] 22 U.S.C §2304(a)(2) (Supp. III 1979).

[41] H. R. REP. NO. 95–1546, 95th Cong., 2d Sess. 27 (1978), *reprinted in* [1978] U.S. CODE CONG. & AD. NEWS 1868, 1874.

[42] On some occasions, Congress has passed amendments that name specific countries. When the amendment does not name targeted countries, Congress reduces the overall aid request by a specific dollar amount and explains in committee reports how the cut is to be applied to specific countries.

[43] In 1976 Congress amended section 502B to establish yet another method for it to reverse executive decisions to "provide security assistance" to a specific country. Under section 502B(c)(1), Congress initiates the reversal by requesting a report from the Secretary of State that indicates the

example, Chile was prohibited from receiving any military aid in fiscal 1975[44] and the amount requested for South Korea was substantially reduced.[45] The legislation for fiscal 1976 contained an indefinite embargo on both military aid and arms sales to Chile.[46] For fiscal 1977, military aid to Uruguay was banned.[47] For fiscal 1978, proposed military aid was eliminated for Argentina, Brazil, El Salvador, Guatemala,[48] Nicaragua, Paraguay,[49] and Uruguay,[50] and reduced for the Philippines.[51] Beginning in fiscal 1979, an indefinite ban was

---

country's human rights practices and whether extraordinary circumstances require a continuation of security assistance to it. Section 502B(c)(4)(A) provides that after receiving the report, "Congress may adopt a joint resolution terminating . . . [or] restricting security assistance for a country."

Curiously, this additional procedure is so cumbersome and ineffective that it has been initiated only rarely and never has it been carried beyond the opening steps. Not once during Carter's term did Congress use section 502B(c) to challenge an executive decision. The procedures were invoked only in 1976 during the last year of the Ford administration. At that time, the House Foreign Affairs Committee requested reports for six countries (Argentina, Haiti, Peru, Iran, Indonesia, and the Philippines), but took no additional steps once the reports were received. Thus, no joint resolution to terminate security assistance has ever been proposed or voted on under section 502B(c)(4). *See* U.S. DEP'T OF STATE, HUMAN RIGHTS AND U.S. POLICY: ARGENTINA, HAITI, INDONESIA, IRAN, PERU, AND THE PHILIPPINES, REPORTS SUBMITTED TO THE HOUSE COMM. ON INTERNATIONAL RELATIONS, 94th Cong., 2d Sess. (Comm. Print 1976) (setting forth congressional requests and State Department's responses).

44 Foreign Assistance Act of 1974, §25, 88 Stat. 1802 (1974).

45 Congress provided that South Korea could receive only $145 million in military aid in fiscal year 1975 unless the President provided a report to Congress "stating that the government of South Korea is making substantial progress in the observance of internationally recognized standards of human rights." *Id.* §26(a). If the President submitted the report, South Korea could receive an additional $20 million in military aid. *Id.* §26(b).

46 International Security Assistance and Arms Export Control Act of 1976, §406, 90 Stat. 758 (1976). At the end of 1981, the embargo was replaced with a directive that no security assistance be provided to Chile unless the President first certifies, *inter alia*, that the Government has made "significant progress in complying with international human rights." International Security Development Cooperation Act of 1981, Pub. L. No. 97–113, §726. A similar provision was enacted for Argentina. *Id.*, §725.

47 Pub. L. No. 94–441, 90 Stat. 1473 (1976).

48 Under the appropriations bill for military aid for fiscal year 1978, Congress prohibited the Executive from providing military sales credits to Argentina, Brazil, El Salvador, Guatemala, and Uruguay. Pub. L. No. 95–148, §503, 91 Stat. 1239 (1977).

49 Under the International Security Assistance Act of 1978, Congress also eliminated military training assistance to Paraguay and Nicaragua, but in doing so it did not name them specifically in the legislation. The conference report explained:

> The Committee of conference agreed (1) to avoid naming specific countries in the statute, and (2) to cut the international military and education training account by $300,000—the exact amount which had been programmed for both Nicaragua and Paraguay.
>
> The elimination of references to specific countries should not be interpreted as approval of the human rights practices in either Nicaragua or Paraguay. This bill already contains a clear and concise prohibition on grant military training to any country which engages in a consistent pattern of gross violations of internationally recognized human rights.

H. R. REP. NO. 95–1546, *supra* note 41, at 31, [1978] U.S. CODE CONG. & AD. NEWS at 1878.

50 *See* note 48 *supra*.

51 Under the appropriations bill for security assistance for fiscal year 1978, Congress appropriated $18.1 million in military aid grants, $1.85 million in military sales credits, and $700,000 in military training funds for the Philippines. Pub. L. No. 95–148, *supra* note 48, §503C. The administration had requested $20 million in military sales credits and $800,000 in military training funds. U.S.

placed on both military aid and arms sales to Argentina.[52] In budgets for fiscal 1980 and 1981, Congress reduced military aid for Zaire.[53] The legislation for fiscal 1981 also eliminated it for Guatemala.[54]

Although usually applicable only to military aid and of limited duration, the country-specific legislation was also a finding by Congress that the Executive had failed to apply section 502B to a government engaged in "gross violations" and that "extraordinary circumstances" would not justify past levels of military aid. The repeated willingness of Congress to legislate on specific countries placed the Executive on notice: unless it began to apply section 502B, Congress might legislate again. While this prospect did not move the Ford and Nixon administrations to alter their practice, it appears to have had significant influence on the Carter administration.

II. Resistance of the Career Bureaucracy Under Carter

The installation of the Carter administration in January 1977 produced a dramatic shift in attitudes of high political officials on the human rights issue.[55] As a presidential candidate, Jimmy Carter had strongly advocated increased emphasis on human rights in American foreign policy and he reaffirmed this position in his inaugural address.[56] Although he did not mention the specific issue of human rights and military ties or indicate his position on implementation of section 502B, his personal call for a human rights oriented foreign policy implied a promise to do considerably more than his predecessors to follow the legislation.

The executive branch, however, did not attempt to conform to the statute's requirements without a fierce internal struggle. Despite the change in attitudes at the highest political level (from opposition to section 502B to endorsement of its underlying principle), the Department of State's career bureaucracy remained implacably hostile and continued to resist implementation. The result was intense bureaucratic warfare between career officials, who resisted implementation, and the office of the newly established Assistant Secretary for Human Rights, which sought adherence to the law.

Dept of State, Congressional Presentation for Security Assistance Program FY 1978, at 4 (1977).

[52] International Security Assistance Act of 1977, §11, 91 Stat. 619–20 (1977), *as amended by* International Security Assistance Act of 1978, §12(c)(1), 92 Stat. 737 (1978). The embargo was repealed at the end of 1981. *See* note 46 *supra*.

[53] Under the International Security Assistance Act of 1979, which provided the security assistance authorization levels for fiscal year 1980, Congress reduced the funds available to Zaire for military sales credit guarantees to $8 million from the $10 million requested by the administration. H. R. Rep. No. 96–495, 96th Cong., 1st Sess. 21 (1979), *reprinted in* [1979] U.S. Code Cong. & Ad. News 1682, 1688. Under the International Security and Development Cooperation Act of 1980, which established the authorization levels for security assistance for fiscal year 1981, Congress further reduced to $6 million the military sales guarantees for Zaire. *See* H. R. Rep. No. 96–1471, 96th Cong., 2d Sess. 42 (1980), *reprinted in* [1980] U.S. Code Cong. & Ad. News 10,881, 10,886.

[54] Morgan, *Panel Rebuffs U.S. Bid To Relax a Rights Sanction*, Wash. Post, March 23, 1979, at A2, col. 3.

[55] *See* Drew, *A Reporter at Large: Human Rights*, New Yorker, July 18, 1977, at 36.

[56] Inaugural Address of President Jimmy Carter, 13 Weekly Comp. of Pres. Doc. 87, 88 (Jan. 24, 1977).

The Attitude of the Career Bureaucracy

The career bureaucracy of the Department of State is the Foreign Service, and the core of the Foreign Service serves in the five regional bureaus for Africa, East Asia, Europe, Latin America, and the Near East. Each bureau has responsibility for managing relations with countries within its region, including issues of military aid and arms sales.

The opposition of the Foreign Service to section 502B was a logical consequence of its conception of its special role or of (what one student of the bureaucracy has labeled) its "organizational essence."[57] The Foreign Service views its primary role or essence as the maintenance of smooth and cordial relations with other governments.[58] It believes that military aid and arms sales are an indispensable means to achieving this goal. When provided, the other government is grateful and more inclined to get along with the United States. When refused, a cordial relationship may be harder to maintain, especially if the other government suspects that the reason for refusal is a judgment that it has mistreated its own citizens.

Keeping other governments happy becomes an end in itself. This phenomenon is often referred to as "clientism" because the Foreign Service views other governments as "clients" with whose interests it identifies, rather than as parties to be dealt with at arm's length according to the national interest of the United States.[59]

The regional bureaus generally make recommendations without rigorously analyzing whether providing security assistance to a particular government will, in fact, serve concrete foreign policy objectives of the United States. Nor is there consideration of whether alternative means might accomplish what is desired. There is rarely exploration of whether the United States might supply economic aid or count on mutual interests to achieve diplomatic goals.

Furthermore, costs are typically excluded from the calculation. The time horizon of the career bureaucracy is short and the possible long-run disadvantage of aiding repressive governments seems alien to its thinking. Even after the examples of Iran and Nicaragua, there is rarely consideration that a particular regime may be overthrown and United States support for it resented by those who follow. Nor is the damage to U.S. standing in the world, or the

[57] *See generally* M. HALPERIN, *supra* note 13, at 28–40.

[58] *See generally* Silberman, *Toward Presidential Control of the State Department*, FOREIGN AFFAIRS, Spring 1979, at 872; Krizay, *Clientitus, Corpulence, and Cloning at State: The Symptomatology of a Sick Department*, POLICY REV., Spring 1978, at 39. Krizay states: "'Good relations' or 'warm relations' are often thought of as an objective to be protected from the threat of domestic interest rather than as an instrument for furthering them." Krizay, *supra*, at 42.

[59] *See* Silberman, *supra* note 58, at 882. Silberman states:

> Inevitably . . . a Foreign Service officer has a tendency toward what is referred to in the State Department as "clientism," a term which suggests overemphasizing the interests of a foreign country (as defined by the governing elite) vis-a-vis the broader interests of the United States. "Good relations" between the host country and the United States (often at our expense) become an end in themselves without sufficient regard to U.S. geopolitical and geostrategic interests.

Ibid. Another author prefers the term "clientitus." *See* Krizay, *supra* note 58, at 43. In Krizay's view, "[c]lientitus is widely recognized as one of the State Department's most unfortunate characteristics. Simply defined, it refers to a tendency to look upon the country or countries within an office's geographic responsibilities as 'clients' deserving special attention." *Ibid.*

conflict with both international legal obligations and traditional American values, weighed in the balance. In effect, the career bureaucracy develops its position by reckoning the national interest in terms of pleasing its "clients," the governments with which it conducts diplomatic relations.[60]

The phenomenon of "clientism" has a number of causes. A Foreign Service officer is typically required to develop personal relations and spend substantial periods of time with high officials of other governments. He tends, therefore, to sympathize and identify with their point of view.[61] If the other government is accused of human rights abuses, he deals with officials who either deny the accusations or explain the excesses as regrettable, but necessary to stem "terrorism" and avoid social chaos. He is much less likely to encounter the victims of repression and hear their point of view.

In addition, the tour of duty in the Foreign Service is usually of 2 to 3 years' duration, after which the officer is rotated to another post. An officer is likely to work on country *A* for 3 years, then switch to country *B*, then to country *C*, and so on. Thus, the short duration reduces the incentive to consider the longer run consequences of decisions.

Moreover, the penalty for questioning established values is heavy.[62] According to one recent Deputy Under Secretary of State:

> Under the present system, the key factor in determining whether an officer will be promoted is the efficiency report written by his immediate supervisor. The knowledge that the good opinion of his supervisor is crucial in determining whether an officer advances at a normal rate or falls behind and is eventually selected out can act as a powerful deterrent to his forthright expression of views on policy matters which may be at variance with views of his supervisor.[63]

Since 1973, when Congress first enacted section 32, the regional bureaus have continually opposed implementation of legislation conditioning security assistance on human rights concerns. They have virtually never initiated a proposal that military aid or arms sales be cut off or reduced on account of a government's human rights performance. Even after the Carter administration

[60] *See* M. HALPERIN, *supra* note 13, at 62. In Halperin's view, "[c]areer officials . . . often develop their position largely by calculating the national interest in terms of organizational interests of the career service to which they belong." *Ibid.*

[61] *See* Silberman, *supra* note 58, at 883. Silberman states: "The other kind of risk typically eschewed by career officers is too vigorous a defense of American interests because such behavior can lead to relative unpopularity with the nation or group of nations in which the officer specializes. . . ." *Ibid.*

[62] *See* M. HALPERIN, *supra* note 13, at 85–86. Halperin states: "The desire for promotion will lead a career official to support the interests of the organization of which he is a member, since he recognizes that promotion will, in large measure, depend on the individual being seen as advancing the interest of his organization." *Ibid.*

[63] W. MACOMBER, DIPLOMACY FOR THE 1970'S: A PROGRAM OF MANAGEMENT REFORM FOR THE DEPARTMENT OF STATE 21–22 (1970). Krizay makes the same point: "The annual Officer Evaluation Report, virtually to the exclusion of all else, determines the officer's career. As a consequence, each officer goes to great lengths to please his superior. . . . A kind of blind loyalty results, reinforcing and exacerbating all the evils of the Department's organization." Krizay, *supra* note 58, at 49.

entered office in 1977, the regional bureaus vigorously fought nearly all attempts to apply section 502B to specific cases. This resistance took a number of different forms. First, they tried to minimize the relevance of section 502B. During the first 2 years, they argued that it could be ignored because it was merely a statement of policy and not legally binding. After it was made legally binding, they argued that the statutory rule was only one of several factors to be weighed in decisions on security assistance.[64]

Second, the career bureaucracy attempted to distort information about human rights conditions in particular countries.[65] The extent of abusive practices was consistently underreported. For example, the Bureau for East Asia persisted in arguing that reports of Indonesian abuses in East Timor were grossly exaggerated and that few abuses had been committed by the Indonesian Army against the Timorese. In fact, an accumulation of reports from reputable sources indicates that a hundred thousand or more Timorese may have died at the hands of the Indonesian military.[66] In the case of Argentina, the Latin American Bureau argued that, at most, hundreds of individuals had been summarily executed by security forces. As the evidence became incontrovertible that the number was actually 6,500 or more, the bureau shifted gears and argued that only Marxist terrorists were the victims.[67] When it was documented that most of the victims were neither Marxists nor terrorists, the bureau maintained that the abuses were the work of local military commanders whom the ruling junta was struggling to control.

As it minimized or concealed negative aspects of a "client's" human rights practices, the career bureaucracy exaggerated positive signs. Improvements were said to have occurred on the basis of insubstantial evidence or self-serving declarations of the government in power. In 1978, for example, the Bureau for the Near East reported that the Shah of Iran was undertaking a major liberalization program, including an end to torture, release of all political pris-

[64] Halperin indicates that, in general, "when . . . legal requirements are not compelling, participants will obey the rules if they feel that the advantages of disobeying or ignoring the rules . . . will in the long run be outweighed by the adverse consequences of having once ignored the rules." M. HALPERIN, *supra* note 13, at 110.

[65] In Halperin's view, "[c]oncern with organizational interests inclines participants to refuse to report or to concede facts. . . ." *Id.* at 144. *See also* CRS, HUMAN RIGHTS STUDY, *supra* note 15, at 92.

[66] Kamm, *The Silent Suffering of East Timor*, N.Y. Times, Feb. 15, 1981, §6, at 35; Kohen, *Invitation to a Massacre in East Timor*, THE NATION, Feb. 7, 1981, at 136.

[67] In its 1979 human rights report, the State Department described attempts to estimate the number killed by Argentine security forces, often referred to as the "disappeared":

> The most carefully recorded and documented list of unexplained disappearances, compiled by the Permanent Assembly for Human Rights in Buenos Aires, contains about 6,500 cases for the period 1976 to 1979. Some estimates, however, run considerably higher. The Mission of the New York City Bar Association . . . considers a figure of 10,000 as more accurate, while Amnesty International asserts that 15–20,000 persons have disappeared.

U.S. DEP'T OF STATE, COUNTRY REPORTS ON HUMAN RIGHTS PRACTICES FOR 1979, REPORT SUBMITTED TO THE SENATE COMM. ON FOREIGN RELATIONS AND THE HOUSE COMM. ON FOREIGN AFFAIRS, 96th Cong., 2d Sess. 239 (Joint Comm. Print 1980). *See generally Human Rights and the Phenomenon of Disappearances: Hearings Before the Subcomm. on International Organizations of the House Comm. on Foreign Affairs,* 96th Cong., 1st Sess. (1979).

oners, and transfer of political authority to an elected parliament.[68] It predicted that this plan would be favorably received by broad segments of the Iranian population.[69] It did not communicate, however, that credible reports of torture persisted, that the secret police continued to arrest political dissidents, that parliamentary elections were rigged and parliamentary powers evanescent, and that Iranians generally regarded the "liberalization" program as a sham.[70] In 1979, the Bureau of African Affairs expressed similar optimism about a decision by Mobutu Sese Seko, President of Zaire, to permit formation of a legislative assembly. While the bureau admitted that the assembly lacked direct political authority, it was still touted as having unlimited powers to debate and question government policies. The bureau neglected to report that Mobutu threatened assembly members who tried to pry into sensitive subjects, such as official corruption, and effectively stopped their inquiries.[71]

Third, the regional bureaus overstated the extent of U.S. interests at stake in particular cases and the damage that could possibly result from failure to approve proposed security assistance. The Latin American Bureau, for example, insisted (albeit unsuccessfully) that failure to provide military aid to Paraguay would seriously undermine a relationship with the Stroessner Government that was important to fighting communism in Latin America. In another case, the Bureau for East Asia warned that, unless military aid to the Philippines was tripled, the United States might lose its military bases there. To support its contention, the bureau cited a threat by President Ferdinand Marcos to terminate an existing base agreement that still had 11 years to run. It failed to report, however, the opinion of a variety of experts that the threat was empty and that Marcos would not risk breaking the legal obligation under an existing treaty.[72]

There were a few exceptions to the pattern of beliefs and behavior described above. Individual Foreign Service officers did attempt on occasion to challenge the wisdom of providing security assistance, although their chances of success were small and such questioning risked damaging their careers.[73] Overall, the

[68] *See* S. Cohen, *Who Lost Iran: Revising Revisionist History,* Wash. Post, Sept. 20, 1980, at D2, cols. 3–4 [hereinafter cited as S. Cohen, *Who Lost Iran*].

[69] *See ibid.*

[70] *Ibid.*

[71] In 1981, the State Department's annual human rights report to Congress noted that the Zairian legislative assembly, which was "[q]uite active during 1979 and early 1980, . . . has since been reined in by the President." U.S. DEP'T OF STATE, COUNTRY REPORTS ON HUMAN RIGHTS PRACTICES: REPORT SUBMITTED TO THE SENATE COMM. ON FOREIGN RELATIONS AND THE HOUSE COMM. ON FOREIGN AFFAIRS, 97th Cong., 1st Sess. 310 (Joint Comm. Print 1981). Instead of merely reining in the assembly members, President Mobutu actually indicated to the members that if they continued to discuss forbidden subjects, he would silence them forever.

[72] As a representative of the Department of State, the author attended a conference of American Philippine scholars held at Eastern Michigan State University in May 1980. At that conference, he interviewed many of these scholars, all of whom expressed great surprise upon learning that some policymakers considered Marcos's threat credible.

[73] In one notable case, career officials in the Bureau for the Near East did question a plan to offer the Pakistani regime of Marshal Zia nearly a half-billion dollars in military aid. They were concerned about the extensive repression practiced by Zia and the resulting disaffection of large numbers of his people. Their sensitivity to the human rights factor had been heightened by the

"clientist" impulse is thus quite strong and for the most part accurately describes the behavior of the career Foreign Service.

The Human Rights Bureau

Given the resistance of the career bureaucracy, concentrated in the regional bureaus, implementation of section 502B during the Carter administration depended on the newly created Bureau of Human Rights, headed by an outsider who was personally committed to the policy of the statute and staffed, to a significant degree, by persons from outside the career bureaucracy. The new bureau began to serve as a counterweight to the "clientism" of the regional bureaus. It took the initiative in insisting that section 502B had to be satisfied before security assistance could be provided, notwithstanding the argument of the career bureaucracy that the statute could be ignored or treated merely as one of several factors. The bureau also developed independent sources of information about human rights conditions in particular countries, which enabled it to challenge the factual reporting of the career bureaucracy.[74] Finally, it attempted to question the national security reasons offered to justify security assistance when the recipient appeared to "engage in gross [human rights] violations."

The creation of a special office for human rights within the Department of State was first recommended by Representative Fraser in 1974.[75] Two years later, Congress created the post of Coordinator for Humanitarian Affairs, with overall responsibility for human rights matters in the Department.[76] However, the Coordinator had a small staff, did not head a separate bureau, and was excluded from decisions on security assistance.[77] In 1977, shortly after Carter took office, Congress directed the designation of the Coordinator as an Assistant Secretary of State, with a specific list of legislated responsibilities, which served to effectuate the earlier Fraser recommendation of a separate bureau for human rights issues.[78] The new Assistant Secretary for Human Rights was provided

---

fall of the Shah of Iran a few months earlier and the intense hostility of Iranians toward the United States for supporting the Shah. These officials did not want to support yet another highly unpopular regime, this time in Pakistan, and produce a repetition of the Iran fiasco. Notwithstanding these qualms, the Carter administration ultimately decided to provide Pakistan with $400 million in economic and military assistance. Oberdorfer, *Pakistan Offered $400 Million Aid*, Wash. Post, Jan. 15, 1980, at A1, col. 1. President Zia, however, dismissed this proposed assistance as "peanuts." Auerbach, *Pakistan Seeking U.S. Guaranties in Formal Treaty, id.*, Jan. 18, 1980, at A1, col. 6 (quoting President Zia).

[74] *Cf.* CRS, HUMAN RIGHTS STUDY, *supra* note 15, at 66 (predisposition of many officials in some regional bureaus to downplay human rights violations has made it important for human rights office to develop its own sources of information).

[75] *See* FRASER REPORT, *supra* note 22, at 13. Additionally, Fraser recommended that a human rights officer be assigned to each regional bureau and that an Assistant Legal Adviser on Human Rights be appointed in the Legal Adviser's Office at the State Department. *Ibid.*

[76] International Security Assistance and Arms Export Control Act of 1976, §301(a), 90 Stat. 750 (1976) (current version at 22 U.S.C. §2384 (Supp. III 1979)).

[77] R. Cohen, *Human Rights, supra* note 12, at 219–20.

[78] *See* note 38 *supra* (describing change in statute and rationale underlying it).

with an enlarged staff and the office was officially recognized as a full-fledged bureau with a status comparable to that of the existing regional bureaus.[79]

This newly strengthened human rights office inserted itself into the established Department of State procedures with vigor. By virtue of section 502B, it was able to claim a right to participate in all decisions on security assistance.[80] When it disagreed with the regional bureaus, which was quite frequent, it insisted that a decision paper—known formally as an action memorandum—be prepared and sent to the Secretary of State for resolution of the issue.

During the first 18 months of the Carter administration, individual proposals for both military aid and arms sales were continually at issue between the regional bureaus and the Bureau of Human Rights and therefore "litigated" through the action memorandum procedure.[81] In some ways, this resembled a judicial process, for it was adversarial in nature, and the action memorandum can be viewed as containing briefs for the position of each side. The action memorandum described each bureau's view of human rights conditions in the country concerned and of U.S. interests said to require approval of the proposed security assistance. The Human Rights Bureau argued its position in the context of section 502B. The bureau cited the statute and emphasized that there were two basic issues for decision: first, whether the proposed recipient was engaged in gross abuses, and second, whether extraordinary circumstances nevertheless required such assistance. The Human Rights Bureau challenged security assistance proposals when it believed the intended recipient was engaged in serious human rights abuses. The concerned regional bureau virtually always disagreed. The action memorandum process thus provided a formal mechanism by which the Human Rights Bureau could attempt to apply section 502B to specific cases.[82]

[79] During the Carter administration, the bureau, which began with a small staff, gradually expanded to about 20 persons, including 3 Deputy Assistant Secretaries and 12 human rights officers. Each human rights officer had primary responsibility for either a region, such as Africa, or a functional area, such as security assistance.

[80] Congress specifically acted to increase the stature of the head of the Human Rights Bureau. *See* S. REP. NO. 95–194, *supra* note 38, at 16, [1977] U.S. CODE CONG. & AD. NEWS at 1638.

[81] *Cf.* CRS, HUMAN RIGHTS STUDY, *supra* note 15, at 2 (regional bureaus often argued against direct use of foreign assistance leverage but were generally opposed by Bureau of Human Rights).

[82] In its efforts, the Bureau of Human Rights was aided by the requirement of section 502B(b) that the Secretary of State submit to Congress each year "a full and complete report . . . with respect to practices regarding the observance of and respect for internationally recognized human rights in each country proposed as a recipient of security assistance." 22 U.S.C. §2304(b) (Supp. III 1979). In theory, the reports provide information concerning human rights practices in foreign countries, upon which Congress can evaluate the extent to which security assistance conforms with section 502B(a)(2). In practice, however, members of Congress have access to information from an array of outside sources on which they rely.

The more important function of the reports was that they forced the career bureaucracy to pay attention to human rights issues and thus mitigated, to a limited degree, its clientist tendencies. Foreign Service officers had to focus on human rights abuses that they might otherwise have chosen to overlook. In the process of gathering information, they sometimes had to speak with political dissidents and victims of repression, which exposed them to other points of view and helped to counteract their tendency to associate only with high officials in power.

The Significance of Bureaucratic Resistance

A recurring theme in modern studies of American government is the unresponsiveness of the bureaucracy to presidential decisions and directives. Presidents Roosevelt, Truman, Eisenhower, Kennedy, and Nixon all remarked on the persistent resistance of career bureaucrats to presidential policies they viewed as misguided. In his book, *Bureaucratic Politics and Foreign Policy,* Morton Halperin wrote:

> [T]hose who are assigned to implement presidential decisions often do not feel obliged to execute their orders. Neither career officials nor political appointees necessarily feel that a presidential decision settles the matter. Participants still have different interests and still see different faces of an issue and have different stakes. They may believe that their conception of what is in the national interest is still correct, and they will resist efforts to do things which they feel are contrary to the national interest or to their own organizational or personal interest even if they have been directed by the President.[83]

The history of section 502B illustrates that the same basic point can be made about congressional directives. The opposition of the career Foreign Service to section 502B recalls comments made over a generation earlier by Franklin Roosevelt about his difficulties with the bureaucracy in general and the Department of State in particular:

> The Treasury is so large and far-flung and ingrained in its practices that I found it impossible to get the action and results I want—even with Henry [Morgenthau] there. But the Treasury is not to be compared with the State Department. You should go through the experience of trying to get any changes in the thinking, policy, and action of the career diplomats, and then you'd know what the problem is.[84]

The bureaucracy is most likely to succeed in resisting legislation when high political officials are hostile to the congressional effort, as Kissinger was during the Nixon and Ford administrations. With the approval of its superiors, the bureaucracy can simply ignore the statute. Even when high political officials are sympathetic to the law, the career bureaucracy may resist implementation and the resistance may produce "political" compromises that only partially implement the law. The "political" compromises that arose during the Carter administration's implementation of section 502B are the subject of the next part of this report.

III. Interpretation and Application of the Statute Under Carter

The public generally identifies the Carter administration with aggressive pursuit of a human rights oriented foreign policy.[85] Some foreign affairs specialists have charged that its "single-minded" approach seriously overemphasized human rights objectives and failed to consider or pursue other im-

[83] M. Halperin, *supra* note 13, at 245.
[84] M. Eccles, Beckoning Frontiers 336 (1951).
[85] *See generally* Drew, *supra* note 55.

portant foreign policy goals, to the detriment of U.S. interests.[86] The general public's impression and the specialists' criticism are attributable, in large measure, to the rhetoric of high administration officials, particularly President Carter himself, who even 2 years into his term declared, "Human rights is the soul of our foreign policy."[87] Moreover, both perceptions suggest that the administration did considerably more than the minimum required by the standards of the law.

Yet a careful examination of actual decisions under section 502B leads to a very different conclusion: that the Carter administration exhibited a remarkable degree of tentativeness and caution, so that its pursuit of human rights goals was anything but "single-minded." Relatively few governments were considered to be "engaged in a consistent pattern of gross [human rights] violations." Security assistance was actually cut off to even fewer, because other U.S. interests were often found to outweigh human rights concerns under the exception for "extraordinary circumstances." Moreover, in some instances, the Carter administration adopted a highly strained reading of the statute which, although not contrary to its literal terms, produced a result contrary to congressional intent. In other cases, the language was simply disregarded, so that decisions violated even the letter of the law.

Fear of Finding

Perhaps the most remarkable evidence of the administration's conservative approach to section 502B was its policy never to determine formally, even in a classified decision, that a particular government was engaged in gross abuses.[88] The primary reason for this policy was the belief that such a determination, even if classified, would inevitably be leaked to the press and become generally known.[89] It was feared that each country named would then consider itself publicly insulted, with consequent damage to our bilateral relationship. In addition, there was concern that once such a finding was revealed, the freedom to alter it might be severely constrained by public political pressures. Any attempt to name a country as a "gross violator" would raise the ire of defense-minded conservatives who did not want military ties cut off. Any attempt to

[86] *See generally* Kirkpatrick, *Dictatorships and Double Standards,* COMMENTARY, Nov. 1979, at 34–45.

[87] Walsh, *Carter Asserts Human Rights Is "Soul of our Foreign Policy,"* Wash. Post, Dec. 7, 1978, at A2, col. 4.

[88] *Cf.* CRS, HUMAN RIGHTS STUDY, *supra* note 15, at 2, 6. The Congressional Research Service concluded that "there was great reluctance formally to identify governments that engaged in consistent patterns of gross violations of . . . human rights. . . . The administration has avoided identifying countries as gross and consistent violators of human rights. . . ." *Ibid.*

[89] Halperin makes this point clear:

> At the top levels of the American government the belief is held that anything of importance . . . will be leaked to the press by some participant unhappy with the drift of presidential decisions. Because this belief is so widely held, it tends to influence significantly the way issues are handled in the executive branch. Often an option under consideration will be rejected on the grounds that it could not be implemented before it was leaked and not successfully implemented unless put into effect before it leaked.

M. HALPERIN, *supra* note 13, at 192–93.

change the finding because a country had improved conditions would be subject to intense scrutiny by human rights partisans to determine whether the supposed improvements were cosmetic or genuine. Thus, maximum flexibility required that no country be formally found to be prohibited from receiving security assistance under section 502B.[90]

In practice, the Secretary of State had to resist pressures both from Congress and within his own Department to make such findings.[91] Administration representatives repeatedly refused congressional requests for a list of governments considered to be engaged in gross abuses, stating that it was administration policy not to draw up such a list.[92] Within the Department, the Secretary of State sought to avoid explaining the reason for decisions on security assistance either in writing or even informally. When he resolved a dispute, he often communicated simply whether the request was approved or disapproved and little more. Particularly in cases of disapproval, the Secretary strenuously avoided ever stating that it was required by section 502B since such a statement would have meant that the government in question was considered to be engaged "in a consistent pattern of gross violations of human rights."

The Development of a Body of Precedents

Because of the administration's policy of not making explicit findings under section 502B, the legal basis for particular outcomes was rarely made clear to the contesting bureaus.[93] It was often difficult to say in a particular case exactly why the Secretary of State believed that section 502B did or did not apply. If security assistance was approved, it might have been because the government was found not to be engaged in gross abuses; or that it was, but fit within the extraordinary circumstances exception; or that some other consideration, not explicitly mentioned in section 502B, was read into the statute and had determined the outcome. If security assistance was disapproved, it was never formally stated that this was because the proposed recipient was considered to be a gross violator under section 502B.

[90] The Congressional Research Service concluded: "Specificity with respect to principles guiding human rights initiatives . . . has been seen by some as threatening to unduly limit flexibility in application of policy. Indeed, strong arguments can be made for the benefits of vagueness in policy definition where policy evolution and change seem likely." CRS, HUMAN RIGHTS STUDY, *supra* note 15, at 49.

[91] *Cf. ibid.* (explicit identification of specific countries strongly resisted at high levels within Department of State).

[92] In 1978 Congress acquiesced in this practice of refusing to make *public* such a list. The conference report on the 1978 legislation transforming section 502B into a binding legal requirement also explained that Congress did not "intend to require the executive branch to publicly identify those countries which it considers to be consistent violators." H.R. REP. NO. 95-1546, *supra* note 41, at 27, [1978] U.S. CODE CONG. & AD. NEWS at 1874.

[93] The Congressional Research Service concluded on the basis of extensive interviews with Carter administration officials that "each case . . . seemed to be reviewed on its own merit, and individual decisions did not seem to produce principles on which subsequent cases could be decided." CRS, HUMAN RIGHTS STUDY, *supra* note 15, at 2. It further noted that "[t]he case-by-case approach followed by the Administration, combined with the reluctance to articulate—indeed, apparently even to formulate—principles of sufficient specificity to guide individual decisions, contributed to congressional concern." *Id.* at 3.

Owing to this lack of clear direction and the persistence with which both the Human Rights Bureau and the regional bureaus pursued their respective objectives, a considerable volume of action memorandums on security assistance issues were produced during the first half of the Carter administration. After the initial period, however, when a body of precedents was created, the amount of "litigation" began to decrease[94] as contesting bureaus inferred by the pattern of outcomes how the Secretary of State was interpreting section 502B.[95] The major issues of interpretation are discussed below. The three key questions were:

(1) When was a foreign government considered to be engaged "in a consistent pattern of gross violations of internationally recognized human rights"?

(2) What U.S. interests constituted "extraordinary circumstances"?

(3) What was encompassed by the category "security assistance"?

1. Gross Violations. The threshold issue under section 502B is whether a particular government "engages in a consistent pattern of gross violations of internationally recognized human rights." At the outset, it is necessary to explain that the issue never arose with respect to many governments that appear to have practiced gross abuses. The question whether section 502B might apply to them was never raised because they were never seriously considered for security assistance for a variety of reasons other than human rights. For example, Communist countries (the Soviet Union and its Warsaw Pact neighbors, and Cambodia, China, and Vietnam) and Soviet client states (such as Afghanistan, Cuba, Ethiopia, Iraq, Libya, and South Yemen) were barred for national security reasons.[96] In addition, a number of countries (for example, Chile[97] and South Africa[98]) were already prohibited by other legal requirements from receiving security assistance.

After these countries were eliminated, approximately 70 remained that were

[94] By the end of 1978, in the view of the Congressional Research Service, "[o]ur interviews suggest that the most intense period of bureaucratic conflict over human rights has now passed and that ways have recently been sought for reducing the amount of time and attention required for managing human rights decisions." *Id.* at 67.

[95] In the view of the Congressional Research Service, "these patterns have evolved out of a continuing—and often highly contentious—set of incremental policy struggles between competing elements of the foreign policy decisionmaking structure." *Id.* at 66.

[96] In addition, there is a statutory bar. Except in exceptional circumstances, the President may not provide Communist countries with security assistance. 22 U.S.C. §2370(f) (1976).

[97] International Security Assistance and Arms Export Control Act of 1976, §406, 90 Stat. 758, *as amended by* International Security Assistance Act of 1978, §§10(b)(5), 12(c)(5), 92 Stat. 735, 737 (1978).

[98] Under General Assembly Resolution 2624, the United Nations called upon its member nations to implement fully the provisions of Security Council Resolution 282 in light of the apartheid practices of the Government of South Africa. GA Res. 2624 (XXV) (1970). Under Resolution 282, the Security Council called upon the member states of the General Assembly fully to embargo the supplying of arms, spare parts, and any forms of military assistance to the Government of South Africa. SC Res. 282, 25 UN SCOR at 12, UN Doc. S/INF/25 (1970). The United States had already instituted such an embargo, prior to 1970. In 1963, President John F. Kennedy announced that the United States unilaterally would not sell arms to South Africa as long as it practiced apartheid. A. SCHLESINGER, JR., A THOUSAND DAYS 583 (1965).

seriously considered for military aid and arms sales. A narrow reading of the "gross violations" language was adopted, so that, in the end, only about 12 of the 70 were thought to fall within it. While in some respects the narrow reading was consistent with the congressional purpose, in others it appeared to subvert the intended meaning of the statute. The narrow reading was derived from the way that the four basic elements of the category were interpreted. First, there must be violations of "internationally recognized human rights." Second, the violations must be "gross." Third, the frequency of violations must result in a "consistent pattern." Fourth, the government itself must be engaged, which is to say, responsible for the violations.

A definition of internationally recognized human rights is contained in section 502B itself. According to subsection (d)(1), this term "*includes* torture or cruel, inhuman, or degrading treatment or punishment, prolonged detention without charges and trial, and other flagrant denial of the right to life, liberty, or the security of the person" (emphasis added).[99] The use of the word "includes" suggests that the list of abusive practices in the statute is not meant to be all-encompassing. The formulation is open-ended and holds out the distinct possibility that violations other than those listed might trigger the termination of security assistance. However, the statute's sponsor, Representative Fraser, opposed this view, and the legislative history contains strong evidence that Congress wanted the quoted language to be interpreted narrowly rather than expansively. In 1974, when section 502B was first enacted, Representative Gross (R., Iowa) offered an amendment (which was defeated) to expand the coverage to all human rights generally.[100] The rejection of the Gross amendment implied that Congress intended to focus only on one narrow, albeit very important, category of human rights abuses involving torture, arbitrary imprisonment, and cruel and inhuman punishment.

The Carter administration followed Fraser's interpretation. In its decisions on security assistance, it was careful to go no further than required by the abuses specifically listed in subsection (d)(1). A government was considered to fall within it only when it practiced arbitrary imprisonment, torture, or summary execution of relatively large numbers of its own people. That a government was authoritarian, denied basic civil and political liberties, or failed to promote basic economic and social rights was not, by itself, enough to invoke the statutory prohibition on military ties.

The second element, that the violations must be "gross," was read to mean that they must be significant in their impact. For example, although arbitrary imprisonment is one of the listed violations, detention without charges for several

[99] 22 U.S.C. §2304(d)(1) (Supp. III 1979) (emphasis added). Under the International Security and Development Cooperation Act of 1980, Pub. L. No. 96–533, §701(b), 94 Stat. 3156 (1980), Congress added a clause on "disappearances" because "[d]isappeared persons currently constitute one of the most serious gross violations of human rights and of the principle of the Universal Declaration of Human Rights." H.R. REP. NO. 96–884 (pt. 1), 96th Cong., 2d Sess. 54 (1980), *reprinted in* [1981] U.S. CODE CONG. & AD. NEWS 10,815, 10,870.

[100] Under Representative Gross' amendment, security assistance could not be provided or defense articles sold to a country until "the President certifies to the Congress that such country is satisfactorily observing internationally recognized standards of human rights with respect to its citizens." 120 CONG. REC. 39,135 (1974). The House of Representatives rejected the amendment by voice vote. *Id.* at 39,137.

days was not considered "gross" because of the relatively brief period of confinement.

Third, the element of a "consistent pattern" was held to mean that abuses had to be significant in number and recurrent. Isolated instances of torture or summary execution, while certainly gross abuses, would not trigger termination of security assistance under section 502B. For example, the reported imprisonment and torture of several dozen labor leaders in Tunisia was considered not to be sufficient by itself to constitute a "consistent pattern." This reading of "consistent pattern" is not unreasonable, given Representative Fraser's concern that the statute not reach too broadly. However, an additional gloss was put on this language that seems at odds with the congressional purpose.

Even when gross abuses were significant in number and recurrent, the "pattern" was occasionally held not to be "consistent," if steps were taken to stop some abuses. Perhaps the most dramatic example of the use of this interpretation to avoid a section 502B problem is the case of Indonesia. At the beginning of 1977, its Government appeared to be engaged in gross abuses on two fronts. In Indonesia proper, it was holding thirty thousand prisoners, in detention since the 1966 civil war, on suspicion of Communist sympathies.[101] At the same time, it was annexing East Timor and in the process of exterminating perhaps one hundred thousand or more civilian inhabitants of that island.[102] The adoption and implementation of a plan for freeing the thirty thousand prisoners within 3 years was considered sufficient to "break" the consistent pattern, notwithstanding evidence of continuing gross abuses on a large scale in East Timor.

Ordinarily, the fourth element, that the government itself engage in or be responsible for the violations, was not an issue if the other criteria were already met. In most instances, governments did not deny responsibility but sought to justify the abuses to U.S. officials on grounds of national security, fighting terrorism, anticommunism, and the like. Absent such an admission, however, the word "engages" was read to require "approval" by the highest ranking officials of the government in question, even if they lacked effective control over the military forces committing the abuses.

For example, in 1980 the Department of State argued that the Government of El Salvador was not one that "engages" in admittedly gross abuses committed with the approval of military commanders, because of evidence that the five-person ruling junta may not have approved.[103] This reading of the word "engages" was highly disingenuous, because any security assistance provided to the Government of El Salvador would have been delivered to the military

[101] U.S. DEP'T OF STATE, REPORT ON HUMAN RIGHTS PRACTICES IN COUNTRIES RECEIVING U.S. AID: REPORT SUBMITTED TO THE SENATE COMM. ON FOREIGN RELATIONS AND THE HOUSE COMM. ON FOREIGN AFFAIRS, 95th Cong., 2d Sess. 360–63 (Joint Comm. Print 1979).

[102] *See supra* note 66.

[103] In response to a specific congressional inquiry, the Department of State asserted that the new Government in El Salvador was attempting to curb human rights violations by the military. *See* Letter from J. Brian Atwood, Assistant Secretary for Congressional Relations, to the Honorable Matthew F. McHugh (Oct. 22, 1980) (copy on file with the author). For a critique of this position, see Americans for Democratic Action, Security Assistance and El Salvador: What the Law Says (unpub., copy available from Americans for Democratic Action, Washington, D.C.).

commanders and their forces. Therefore, for purposes of the statute, they should have been considered as the "government" that "engages" whether or not the formal, but powerless, political authorities had approved their practices.

Which governments were considered to be engaged "in gross violations"? While the Carter administration never formally determined, privately or publicly, that any government was a "gross violator" under section 502B, this question was directly addressed in action memorandums and departmental meetings before decisions on security assistance were made by the Secretary of State. Thus, whether governments did or did not fit within the category was constantly in the forefront of the decision maker's mind. He was aware that it was contrary to section 502B to approve security assistance to a "gross violator," absent extraordinary circumstances. His decisions on a case-by-case basis formed a pattern reflecting his assessment of human rights practices of particular governments; one can infer from this pattern which countries were implicitly regarded as falling within the "gross violator" category.

The approximately 70 countries seriously considered for military aid and arms sales were divided into three basic categories. The first included a significant number of functioning democracies with good records of respect for basic human rights. As a result, such governments were thought not to raise a serious human rights question under section 502B. Among them were the Governments of Western Europe, Australia, New Zealand, and Japan, and a number of Third World Governments, including Botswana, Colombia, Costa Rica, Kenya, and Venezuela. A second category comprised governments that were authoritarian and, on occasion, might engage in the gross abuses described in subsection (d)(1). When the practices of such governments were closely examined, the frequency of abuses was considered too low to constitute a "consistent pattern." Among the countries in this group were Morocco, Singapore, Taiwan, Tunisia, and Thailand. The third category consisted of governments practicing torture, arbitrary detention, or summary execution on a significant scale that were therefore considered to be engaged in gross violations under the statute. Although no formal "hit" list of countries in the third category was ever prepared, it could easily have been inferred from the pattern of decisions on specific security assistance issues raised in action memorandums.[104] By the middle of Carter's term, the implied list would have looked more or less as follows:

Latin America:	Argentina, Bolivia, El Salvador, Guatemala, Haiti, Nicaragua, Paraguay, Uruguay
East Asia:	the Philippines, South Korea
The Middle East:	Iran
Africa:	Zaire

Changed circumstances in particular countries caused the implied list to be modified at certain points. For example, Bolivia was not on the list when elected

[104] *Cf.* CRS, HUMAN RIGHTS STUDY, *supra* note 15, at 39 (most officials seem to agree that countries such as Korea, the Philippines, and Iran have violated certain internationally recognized human rights); *id.* at 58–59 (governmental policies of widespread killings and torture are widely seen as repugnant; such conditions have existed in Chile, Argentina, Uruguay, and Nicaragua at times during past 5 years).

civilian Governments were in power in 1977 and 1979, but was on it following military coups in 1978 and 1980.[105] Nicaragua was on it when Anastasio Somoza was in power and off it for at least the initial period following the revolution. As noted, the administration argued in 1980 that the new Government of El Salvador could not be considered responsible for military abuses.

2. Extraordinary Circumstances. The Carter administration always gave considerable weight to arguments that other U.S. interests might require continuation of security assistance, even when the government in question was thought to be a "gross violator." Thus, the charge that its pursuit of human rights was "single-minded" and to the exclusion of other interests was far wide of the mark. If anything, the administration gave excessive credence to claims that some specific foreign policy objective would and could be promoted only if security assistance were provided, and often failed to subject such claims to rigorous analysis.

The administration did require some showing of a substantial and specific interest before the exception for extraordinary circumstances was available. A mere desire for cordial relations, without more, was never held sufficient to constitute "extraordinary circumstances." However, once a specific interest of some substantiality was cited, the exception was usually invoked. Because of the liberal use made of the exception for "extraordinary circumstances," the number of countries subject to a section 502B cutoff was quite modest. In the end, human rights concerns resulted in the termination of security assistance to only eight countries, all in Latin America: Argentina, Bolivia, El Salvador, Guatemala, Haiti, Nicaragua, Paraguay, and Uruguay.

Extraordinary circumstances were found for all of the other countries considered to be gross violators. Thus, Indonesia (although technically not on the list) was a key member of ASEAN (the pro-Western association of Southeast Asian countries) and important to countering Soviet and Vietnamese influence in the region. Iran was judged critical because it shared a long border with the Soviet Union, was a major supplier of oil to the West, and defended our strategic interests in the Persian Gulf. Military ties with South Korea were deemed essential to deterring the threat of an invasion from the north. Military bases in the Philippines were judged critical to the United States and a security assistance relationship essential to keeping the bases. Finally, Zaire, the third largest country by area in Africa, was the source of nearly all the West's cobalt, a material crucial to the performance of high-performance jet engines.[106]

[105] *See* 80 DEP'T STATE BULL., No. 2042, Sept. 1980, at 71 (statement of Edmund S. Muskie, Secretary of State) (United States terminating military assistance to emphasize concern about recent coup d'état in Bolivia).

[106] Early on, Secretary of State Vance announced that the administration would continue to provide security assistance to South Korea, the Philippines, and Indonesia, despite section 502B, for reasons of national security. Gwertzman, *U.S. Cuts Foreign Aid in Rights Violations; South Korea Exempt,* N.Y. Times, Feb. 25, 1977, at A1, col. 6.

After Ronald Reagan won the presidential election in November 1980, the Human Rights Bureau compiled a report on the statutory human rights provisions and the policies and procedures under which they had been implemented during the Carter administration. In the security assistance section, the report stated: "Military assistance including weapons sales is denied to countries whose governments torture, summarily execute, and/or arbitrarily imprison appreciable numbers of their citizens, unless national security interests nonetheless dictate such assistance. *Examples of the latter exceptions: Indonesia, the Philippines, South Korea and Zaire.*" U.S. Dep't of State, Project Legacy, Tab F, at 3 (1981) (emphasis added) (copy on file with the author).

No claims of similar magnitude were made for United States interests in Latin American countries on the list. None supplied a critical resource, shared a border with the Soviets, or acted as a special surrogate to defend U.S. interests in the entire region. The Latin American Bureau did argue that Argentina fit within the exception, asserting that the need to cooperate in policing sea lanes of the South Atlantic to counter a Soviet naval threat constituted "extraordinary circumstances." This position, however, was rejected because the threat was not viewed as extraordinary and, in any case, alternative means existed to counter it.[107]

In all the cases where a substantial interest was found, the administration assumed, mostly without question, that arms sales and military aid would automatically help secure it. In no case did the administration seriously consider that such approval might actually make the interest less attainable, particularly over the longer run. For example, during 1977 and 1978, the United States approved the sale of billions of dollars of sophisticated weaponry to Iran under the Shah. The enormous cost of these arms fed the Iranian belief that the country's oil wealth was being wasted to benefit U.S. defense companies, which reinforced anti-American feelings in Iran.[108] Similarly, in 1978, the U.S. Government signed an agreement tripling military aid to the Philippines in order to make more secure its military bases there. But the net effect of this action was probably to make the bases less secure because it associated the United States with the unpopular, ineffective, and corrupt Marcos dictatorship.[109]

Why the failure to ask what seems to be an obvious question: whether security assistance might, in some cases, not promote or even make it harder to achieve desired objectives? On one level, the explanation is the lack of an adequate bureaucratic mechanism for raising the issue. The career bureaucracy, given its "clientist" perspective, was hardly likely to ask whether a program of military aid or arms sales might cause more harm than good and virtually never did. The Bureau of Human Rights was simply not equipped to do so. With a professional staff of only about 20, it had its hands full simply trying to collect and present information about human rights practices. Raising this other issue would have required detailed knowledge about the internal political dynamics of other countries and the bureau generally lacked sufficient independent data to challenge the regional bureaus. Moreover, on those occasions when it tried (as, for example, in the case of arms sales to Iran), it was viewed by the Secretary of State as going beyond the area of its mandate. While the bureau could be expected to have detailed knowledge about human rights abuses, judgments about national security were to be left to the experts in the regional bureaus who knew best.

At another level, the failure to consider such issues assumes a fundamental conflict between the pursuit of morality (human rights) and the pursuit of self-interest (national security). Such a dichotomy is implicit in the term *Realpolitik*, which connotes the idea that moral goals have no place in a rationally self-interested foreign policy. Whether one accepts or rejects the dichotomy depends

[107] *Cf.* Anderson, *Argentina Is No Ally,* N.Y. Times, Aug. 2, 1980, at A21, cols. 1–3.

[108] *See generally* S. Cohen, *Who Lost Iran, supra* note 68.

[109] *See generally* S. Cohen, *Keeping An Unpopular Despot at Arm's Length,* Wash. Post, Feb. 22, 1981, at C4, cols. 1–6.

largely on one's political and moral values. It is noteworthy, however, that the drafters of section 502B firmly rejected it. The 1974 Fraser subcommittee report stated, "consideration for human rights in foreign policy is both morally imperative and *practically necessary*."[110] This view is reflected in the language of the section 502B exception. Not only must "extraordinary circumstances" exist, but in addition it must be found that providing security assistance is, "on all the facts," in the national interest.[111] This latter phrase suggests the kind of inquiry that should be made before invoking the exception and that the Carter administration failed to make.

3. Security Assistance. Even when a government was considered to be a "gross violator" and there were no "extraordinary circumstances," the termination of security assistance by the Carter administration was at times less than complete. Special exceptions to the general rule of subsection (a)(2) were created, most notably for the sale of certain military items to "gross violators" when it was believed that approval might induce human rights progress. These exceptions were not set out in the statute and therefore went beyond the letter of the law. Moreover, in at least one instance, involving Argentina, the exceptions were abused in a way that seriously undermined the purpose of section 502B. The exceptions arose in the course of interpreting the term "security assistance," which includes both the gift of military aid and the sale of arms.[112] Because each involves somewhat different considerations, they are discussed separately below.

The Carter administration's first application of section 502B to military aid marked a sharp departure from the Nixon-Ford policies of ignoring the statute altogether. Shortly after taking office, Secretary of State Vance expressed support for the principle that human rights concerns should affect decisions on security assistance. He also announced that, under section 502B, the budget for fiscal year 1978 would include no military aid for Ethiopia or Uruguay and that amounts for Argentina would fall by 50 percent.[113]

At the same time, the administration did propose military aid for a number of other governments that appeared to be engaged in gross violations and not to qualify for the extraordinary circumstances exception—among them, El Salvador, Guatemala, Nicaragua, and Paraguay. However, most of the funds requested and authorized for these Latin American Governments in the budget for fiscal year 1978 were never disbursed. Moreover, beginning with the fiscal

[110] FRASER REPORT, *supra* note 22, at 9 (emphasis added).

[111] *See* 22 U.S.C. §2304(c)(1)(C)(ii) (Supp. III 1979).

[112] Under 22 U.S.C. §2304(d)(2) (Supp. III 1979), security assistance is defined to include grant military aid "sales of defense articles or services, extensions of credits . . . , and guarantees of loans under the Arms Export Control Act."

[113] *See Foreign Assistance Legislation for Fiscal Year 1978 (Part 1): Hearings Before the House Comm. on International Relations*, 95th Cong., 1st Sess. 1–34 (testimony of Cyrus Vance, Secretary of State); Oberdorfer, *In Rights Push, Vance Asks Cuts in 3 Nations' Aid,* Wash. Post, Feb. 25, 1977, at A6, col. 4. In response, Argentina's military Government denounced the Carter administration's decision to reduce the military aid package. De Onis, *Argentina Says Carter Interferes,* N.Y. Times, March 1, 1977, at A6, col. 1. The Government of Argentina ultimately decided to reject the proposed military assistance. De Onis, *Argentina and Uruguay Reject U.S. Assistance Linked to Human Rights, id.,* March 2, 1977, at A10, col. 5.

year 1979 and continuing through fiscal year 1981, essentially no military aid was provided for Governments on the implied "hit" list of Latin American countries engaged in gross violations for which no extraordinary circumstances were found to exist.[114] Exceptions to this rule were made on a few occasions. Military aid was requested for Bolivia when its Government seemed to be making progress in curbing human rights abuses, but later the administration refused to disburse the aid funds after a military coup led to a dramatic increase in violations.[115] In addition, a small amount of military aid destined for Haiti was justified as intended for the purchase of air-sea rescue equipment.

More troubling was a decision to request a quarter of a million dollars in military training funds for Guatemala in the fiscal year 1981. In the few years preceding submission of the budget, Guatemalan military forces were believed to have killed over five thousand people, including leaders of the moderate political opposition.[116] The Secretary of State's decision to go ahead with the aid package, notwithstanding these facts, probably reflected his own view that military training generally should not be reduced for human rights reasons, as well as a desire not to refuse the newly appointed head of the Latin American Bureau who had fought hard for the aid. Yet the decision seemed to be clearly contrary to section 502B. Certainly, Congress held this view, as both House and Senate committees voted overwhelmingly for country-specific legislation to remove the Guatemala package from the 1981 military aid budget.[117]

The arms sales component of security assistance is defined by subsection (d)(2) as including all sales of "defense items" under the Arms Export Control Act, and the term "defense items" is given a broad scope by the Act.[118] It includes not only weapons such as tanks, guns, jet fighters, and naval warships, but also a host of support and auxiliary equipment such as communications equipment, unarmed military transports, and radars.[119] Moreover, any services provided in connection with such equipment are also covered.[120]

The Carter administration did not automatically terminate all sales of defense items when a government was considered to be engaged in "gross violations" and "extraordinary circumstances" were not found. It adopted instead a "flexible" approach and broke up the panoply of defense items subject to the Arms

[114] Each year prior to Congress's consideration of the authorization and appropriation bills for military aid for the upcoming fiscal year, the Department of State submits to Congress a "Congressional Presentation Document," which details the administration's request for military aid grants and military sales credits. To review the Carter administration's requests in fiscal years 1978 through 1981, see U.S. DEP'T OF STATE, CONGRESSIONAL PRESENTATION FOR SECURITY ASSISTANCE PROGRAM FY 1978 (1977); CONGRESSIONAL PRESENTATION FOR . . . FY 1979 (1978); CONGRESSIONAL PRESENTATION FOR . . . FY 1980 (1979); CONGRESSIONAL PRESENTATION FOR . . . FY 1981 (1980).

[115] *See* note 105 *supra*.

[116] Hoge, *Repression Increases in Guatemala as U.S. Is Seeking to Improve Ties,* N.Y. Times, May 3, 1981, at 1, cols. 2–3. *See also* Hoge, *Guatemala Keeps a Step Ahead of Rights Gunmen,* N.Y. Times, May 4, 1981, at 2, col. 2.

[117] Morgan, *Panel Rebuffs U.S. Bid to Relax a Rights Sanction,* Wash. Post, March 23, 1979, at A2, col. 3.

[118] *See* 22 U.S.C. §2794(3) (1976).

[119] *Id.* §2794(3)(A)–(B).

[120] *Id.* §2794(4) and (7).

Export Control Act (and therefore section 502B) into a number of subcategories:

(1) New weapons: tanks, artillery, fighters and bombers, and naval warships;

(2) Spare parts for previously acquired weapons;

(3) Support equipment: trucks, unarmed aircraft and ships, radios, and radars; and

(4) Safety-related items: ambulance aircraft and air-sea rescue equipment.

New weapons were consistently withheld, whenever requested. On the other hand, safety-related items were almost never denied, and spare parts and support equipment were approved for sale on numerous occasions.[121] These exceptions, of course, are contrary to the literal language of section 502B, and the regional bureaus advocating approval felt it necessary to construct a legal rationale for this position. The exception for safety-related items was justified in terms of the underlying purpose of the statute, that is, the protection of basic human rights. To disapprove the sale of equipment devoted to rescuing lives, it was argued, would defeat the basic goals of the statute. Items in the two middle categories (spare parts for weapons and support equipment) were approved on the basis of a different, but related, consideration: that a sale of defense items was on occasion needed to encourage another government to improve human rights conditions, and that spare parts and support equipment (as contrasted with new weapons) were an acceptable means of providing an inducement. In effect, section 502B was read to mean that Congress was concerned most about actual weapons and would be willing to permit the sale of other items when it was reasonable to suppose that it would lead to human rights improvements.

While the exception for safety-related items appears reasonable because of the direct connection with saving lives, that for spare parts and support items is fraught with danger. Such items are as critical to military performance as weapons themselves. Moreover, spare parts and support equipment typically make up a large part of a military's total acquisitions. Thus, to continue to approve such items is to continue a significant military supply relationship between the United States and the recipient. This danger may be acceptable if there are definite advantages to be gained in terms of human rights improvements. The risk, however, is that exceptions will be granted on the basis of unrealistic hopes that improvements will follow. If that turns out to be the case, then making these exceptions could undermine the purposes of section 502B.

The inducement rationale was invoked to justify spares and support items for five Latin American countries: Argentina, El Salvador, Guatemala, Para-

[121] *See* U.S. Dep't of State, A Review of U.S. Human Rights Policy and Application of Laws Affecting Security and Economic Assistance in Latin America (unpub. document on file with the author). The Assistant Secretary of State for Human Rights and Humanitarian Affairs, Patricia Derian, also confirmed this decision in a speech at Dade Community College in Miami, Florida, on Oct. 7, 1980.

guay, and Uruguay.[122] While in no case was there clear evidence that making exceptions helped induce a government to improve human rights conditions, it also appears that, for the latter four countries, approvals did little harm, perhaps because relatively small dollar amounts were involved.[123] However, in the case of Argentina the exception appears to have been abused. Argentina was considered to be one of the most serious human rights violators in the non-Communist world because of the torture and summary execution of thousands of political dissidents and other "undesirables" by government security forces.[124]

During 1977 and 1978, Argentina submitted requests to purchase about $200 million in defense items from the United States. The Latin American Bureau argued that approval of spares and support items was justified under section 502B as not involving new weapons and as an inducement for Argentina to improve human rights conditions. The Bureau of Human Rights was opposed on the grounds that section 502B contained no exception for spare parts and support items and that, in any case, approval was unlikely to have the desired effect. The Secretary of State found the former's arguments persuasive and approved the sale of nearly $120 million in weapons.[125]

It now appears that the approval of spares and support items was based on unrealistic hopes and did not elicit steps to curb abuses in Argentina. Human rights violations continued at a high level throughout the period during which these items were sold.[126] The dollar value of U.S. arms sales to Argentina in 1978 was actually higher than in any prior year.[127] Consequently, the Argentine Government may have believed the American executive branch to be deeply divided over whether security assistance to Argentina should be affected by its human rights practices, and this belief may have substantially reduced the impact of American human rights pressures on Argentina during 1977 and most of 1978. The level of abuses there began to decline only after a statutory embargo on all security assistance, enacted by Congress, went into effect on October 1, 1978.[128] Thus, the numerous exceptions for spare parts and support equipment before that date were not only of doubtful legality, but also undermined the basic purpose of the legislation.

[122] *See* note 121 *supra.*

[123] To review the levels of arms sold to Argentina, El Salvador, Guatemala, Paraguay, and Uruguay, see DEFENSE SECURITY ASSISTANCE AGENCY, DEP'T OF DEFENSE, FOREIGN MILITARY SALES AND ASSISTANCE FACTS 1980, at 6, 34 [hereinafter cited as MILITARY SALES AND ASSISTANCE FACTS].

[124] *See* note 67 *supra.*

[125] De Young & Krause, *Our Mixed Signals on Human Rights in Argentina,* Wash. Post, Oct. 29, 1978, at C1 and 2, cols. 4-5, 1-2.

[126] *See supra* note 67.

[127] MILITARY SALES AND ASSISTANCE FACTS, *supra* note 123, at 6, 34.

[128] *See* text accompanying and note 52, *supra.* In its initial draft, the embargo legislation was to have become effective 1 year earlier, on Oct. 1, 1977. The congressional sponsors agreed to defer the effective date for 1 year after the Department of State complained that a statutory ban (which could be changed only by new congressional action) would destroy its ability to respond quickly to changed conditions. The Department promised, in return, that no arms sales would be approved in the interim unless Argentina first demonstrated significant human rights progress. The approval of a large volume of sales during the year before the cut-off date, without any such progress, violated this explicit understanding between the Executive and members of Congress.

The Congressional Response

It should be obvious from the record that the Carter administration did much more than its predecessors to implement section 502B. The procedural requirements that the statute be applied to decisions on providing security assistance and that the Human Rights Bureau be involved were carried out in a reasonable manner. Human rights concerns were given a hearing at nearly all stages in the process of providing military aid and selling arms and the Bureau of Human Rights was afforded a reasonably full opportunity to make its views known through action memorandums. Sales of new weapons were banned to eight Latin American countries. In addition, the same countries, with a few exceptions, received little or no military aid for fiscal years 1978 through 1981. The decision to withhold military aid and weapons on human rights grounds, even from this small number of governments, was a radical departure from the practice of past administrations.

Yet, if the standard of comparison is not the practice of prior administrations, but instead the substantive rule of section 502B, the record of implementation appears much more modest. The Carter administration exhibited considerable flexibility in applying the law to actual decisions, and at some points its decisions appear to have been contrary to the substantive rule. After a few positive steps, a "pattern" of abuse was held to be no longer "consistent" even if widespread torture, arbitrary imprisonment, and summary execution continued. Liberal and uncritical use was made by the Executive of the exception for "extraordinary circumstances," so that security assistance was actually terminated only to a limited number of countries, all in Latin America. Especially troublesome were the reading of the term "defense items" to create an exception for spares and support items, not provided for in the statute, and the abuse of that exception in the case of Argentina.

During 1977 and 1978, members of Congress, particularly on the House International Relations Committee, expressed unhappiness over the administration's performance in the implementation of section 502B. Some complained about the exceptions made under subsection (a)(2) for spares and support items. Others felt that there had been excessive use of the exception for "extraordinary circumstances" and specifically mentioned the administration's failure to reduce military aid for the Philippines, South Korea, and Zaire.[129] In part because so many exceptions were being made, in 1978 Congress eliminated the introductory phrase, "it is the policy of the United States," in order to transform section 502B(a)(2) into a binding legal requirement.[130] Surprisingly, however, the strengthening of the basic rule on military aid and arms sales had no impact on the Carter administration. There was no diminution in the scope of exceptions either for "extraordinary circumstances" or for spares and support items. The change in the substantive law alone was apparently not enough to influence the Executive to alter its behavior.

[129] *See, e.g., Human Rights in the Philippines, Recent Developments: Hearings Before the Subcomm. on International Organizations of the House Comm. on International Relations*, 95th Cong., 2d Sess. (1978).

[130] *See* International Security Assistance Act of 1978, §6(a), 92 Stat. 731 (1978).

IV. Conclusions

What are the lessons to be drawn for implementation by the Executive when Congress attempts to legislate foreign policy? The history of section 502B is a case study of executive frustration of congressionally mandated foreign policy and underlines the need, particularly with this kind of legislation, for clearer directives, less discretion, and more assiduous congressional oversight. While these observations emerge from experience in the human rights area, they are relevant to other congressional attempts to influence the Executive's conduct of foreign policy. They are especially apt when congressional objectives may require decisions that displease particular governments and that will therefore be resisted by the Foreign Service bureaucracy whose paramount interest is maintaining cordial relations. For example, conclusions about the effectiveness of legislation conditioning security assistance on human rights practices are likely to be highly relevant to legislation conditioning nuclear exports on practices with respect to nuclear proliferation.

Congress has the most decisive impact when its directives allow the Executive no discretion at all, as in the country-specific legislation stating precisely which governments are to be denied military aid and arms sales on human rights grounds. On the other hand, whenever the statute permits any exercise of discretion at all, the career Foreign Service is likely to use it to attempt to thwart congressional objectives.

Precision in a statute, of course, is a matter of degree and some provisions allow considerably more discretion than others. No one should be surprised at the bureaucracy's lack of enthusiasm for implementing a vaguely worded general directive. Given its "clientist" impulse, the Foreign Service can be expected, for example, to ignore a statutory directive that the United States "disassociate itself from governments that violate internationally recognized human rights." In such a provision, the means of disassociation are unspecified and left to the diplomat to choose. Disassociation, moreover, is set forth as only one foreign policy goal, which presumably may give way to other objectives when, in the judgment of the bureaucracy, the national interest so requires.

But compared to such a hypothetical statute, section 502B is a model of precision. The means for achieving disassociation are particularized both by the clear, unambiguous definition of security assistance and by the requirement that it be denied in specific cases. The disassociation objective is ranked relative to other foreign policy goals, and it is to be paramount whenever the other government "engages in a consistent pattern of gross violations" and "extraordinary circumstances" are absent. While both these phrases do have considerable elasticity, it should also be clear that the arbitrary imprisonment, summary execution, and torture of thousands of people amount to a "consistent pattern" and that a mere desire for cordial relations without more is not "extraordinary" by any reasonable standard. Yet the Foreign Service consistently argued the contrary and resisted attempts to apply section 502B to deny military aid or arms sales in nearly every instance when its application was urged. In other words, giving the Foreign Service any discretion at all is to invite its abuse.

There are, perhaps, some drawbacks to statutes that deny all discretion, such as the country-specific legislation. Once such a provision is enacted, the Executive lacks the flexibility to respond quickly to changed conditions.[131] While Congress has a legitimate role to play in setting basic foreign policy goals, it may be less well equipped to make day-to-day decisions about how best to fulfill those goals in specific cases. Its members, by and large, are not specialists in foreign affairs, and they generally lack the detailed knowledge and expertise required to make careful assessments of human rights practices and United States interests or to balance the benefits and costs of providing military aid or selling arms to a particular government.[132]

For these reasons, a general rule that sets forth basic goals may be preferable to country-specific legislation. Yet the history of section 502B suggests that the creation or tightening of a general rule will produce, by itself, little change in executive behavior. Special implementing mechanisms are required if a substantive rule is to have a direct influence on decisions. Because the career bureaucracy can be expected to abuse the discretion allowed by a general rule, a countervailing center of bureaucratic influence is essential to implementation.

When Congress does provide an implementing mechanism, implementation will still be highly dependent on the attitudes of high political officials. If they are hostile, even a general rule written with a high degree of precision will probably have little impact on executive decisions. The career Foreign Service will exert no influence on political appointees to implement the law, and the Bureau of Human Rights can be effectively neutralized. The Assistant Secretary is a presidential appointee, and a hostile administration can either select someone to fill the position who will not push for implementation or simply leave the post vacant. In such a case, country-specific legislation is the only effective means for Congress directly to influence specific decisions on military aid and arms sales.

Even when a hostile administration disregards section 502B, the statute may serve as an affirmation by Congress that disassociation from repressive governments is a desirable goal of U.S. foreign policy. It reinforces the idea that military ties with such governments can impose considerable costs and should not be pursued unless they are the only available means of securing especially important national interests. Its existence legitimates efforts by Congress to enact legislation that prohibits military aid and arms sales to specific countries. It may also focus the attention of journalists, scholars, and the interested public on executive decisions that would otherwise escape scrutiny.

This examination of attempts by Congress to require the Executive to withhold military aid and arms sales on human rights grounds suggests another important issue: whether withholding is an effective instrument for enforcing adherence to international human rights law. A definitive answer to this question is far from easy to obtain. It may be difficult to determine whether a government has taken positive steps to improve human rights conditions. Changes that are merely "cosmetic" must be distinguished from those which

[131] T. Franck & E. Weisband, *supra* note 15, at 32–33.
[132] *Ibid.*

indicate real improvement. When positive changes do occur, it may be difficult to say whether U.S. actions or other factors were decisive. But the fact that positive changes are lacking does not mean that U.S. actions have been ineffective. Although a targeted government may not have altered current practices, it may be deterred from worse violations. Moreover, regimes other than the immediate target may be influenced by the risk of being denied United States security assistance if they engage in repression. While the impact of withholding security assistance on human rights practices is beyond the scope of this article, it is the logical next question for scholars interested in international human rights.

EXTRATERRITORIAL JURISDICTION AT A CROSSROADS: AN INTERSECTION BETWEEN PUBLIC AND PRIVATE INTERNATIONAL LAW

*By Harold G. Maier**

I. Introduction

Historically, public international law and private international law have been treated as two different legal systems that function more or less independently. Public international law regulates activity among human beings operating in groups called nation-states, while private international law regulates the activities of smaller subgroups or of individuals as they interact with each other. Since the public international legal system coordinates the interaction of collective human interests through decentralized mechanisms and private international law coordinates the interaction of individual or subgroup interests primarily through centralized mechanisms, these coordinating functions are usually carried out in different forums, each appropriate to the task. The differences between the processes by which sanctions for violation of community norms are applied in the two systems and the differences in the nature of the units making up the communities that establish those norms tend to obscure the fact that both the public and the private international systems coordinate human behavior, and that thus the values that inform both systems must necessarily be the same.

Conceptual separation of the two systems makes it possible for a single legal theory simultaneously to encompass two apparently conflicting propositions—that only the will of the sovereign state makes law and that the sovereign state is legally limited in its freedom by collective community will—without having to resolve the logical inconsistency. That form of mental legerdemain is relatively harmless and, in fact, has considerable functional utility (as long as it is recognized for what it is) for conceptualizing many international issues. Such intellectual sleight of hand, however, becomes counterproductive when a decision maker must identify the limits on a sovereign's freedom to give effect to its own legislated social policies in its own courts over persons over whom it has de facto power. Decision makers in these cases stand at an intersection between public and private international law. The remainder of this discussion focuses on the nature and utility of the road maps currently available to help identify the paths that cross there and suggests some alterations in the cartography to provide more accurate guidance for the traveler. Those guides include the doctrine of comity, the current *Restatement*s of conflicts and foreign relations law, the tentative drafts for revision of the foreign relations *Restatement*, and an independent line of Supreme Court cases decided since the late 1950's. An

* Professor of Law and Director of Transnational Legal Studies, Vanderbilt University. The research for this article was supported in part by a grant from Vanderbilt University School of Law.

examination of these guides indicates that they fail to focus the decision maker's attention on the importance of making decisions that will serve not only the interest of his own sovereign, or the competing interests of two or more sovereigns having contact with the transaction to be regulated, but the needs of the international system of states as well.

II. Comity

The earliest road map to this intersection is found in the original concept of comity. The doctrine of comity is not a rule of public international law, but the term characterizes many of those same functional elements that define a system of international legal order. In Anglo-American law the extension of comity to another nation is viewed as a unilateral decision of the forum, not as an act required by a rule of the public international system.[1] This emphasis on the voluntary nature of the doctrine has led to its use to describe an amorphous never-never land whose borders are marked by fuzzy lines of politics, courtesy, and good faith.[2] Like the concept of public policy in the conflict of laws, the label "comity" in modern times has sometimes come to serve as a substitute for analysis.[3] The comity principle was originally developed to explain how a sovereign state, absolutely powerful within its own territory, could give recognition or effect in its courts to another nation's laws without diminishing or denying its own sovereignty. The doctrine is also one of local restraint, limiting the application of sovereign power to extraterritorial events and persons. This second manifestation represents the role played by the doctrine in transnational regulatory cases.[4]

1

> I would like to emphasize the importance of separating international law and comity for the purpose of analysis of the pending legislation. Comity is discretionary; international law is obligatory. Comity enjoins forbearance in the exercise of legitimate jurisdiction when another sovereign also has legitimate jurisdiction under international law. However, comity does not come into play at all unless a nation has a legitimate basis in international law for asserting jurisdiction in the first place.

Energy Antimonopoly Act of 1979 (Part 1): Hearings Before the Senate Comm. on the Judiciary, 96th Cong., 1st Sess. 779 (1979) (statement of Monroe Leigh). *See* Lorenzen, *Story's Commentaries on the Conflict-of-Laws—One Hundred Years Later*, 48 HARV. L. REV. 15, 35–36 (1934). For a discussion of this proposition in a broader context, see Nussbaum, *Rise and Decline of the Law-of-Nations Doctrine in the Conflict of Laws*, 42 COLUM. L. REV. 191 (1942).

2

> Comity is a recognition which one nation extends within its own territory to the legislative, executive, or judicial acts of another. It is not a rule of law, but one of practice, covenience, and expediency. Although more than mere courtesy and accommodation, comity does not achieve the focus of an imperative or obligation. Rather, it is a nation's expression of understanding which demonstrates due regard both to international duty and convenience and to the rights of persons protected by its own laws.

Somportex Ltd. v. Philadelphia Chewing Gum Corp., 453 F.2d 435, 440 (3d Cir. 1971).

3 *Cf.* Paulsen & Sovern, *"Public Policy" in the Conflict of Laws*, 56 COLUM. L. REV. 969, 1016 (1956).

4 Although the term "comity" has ancient roots, its earliest uses in Roman jurisprudence did not reflect those territorial principles that support the modern rules of conflict of laws. *See* M. WOLFE, PRIVATE INTERNATIONAL LAW 19–20 (2d ed. 1950); Yntema, *The Comity Doctrine*, 65 MICH. L. REV. 9 (1966); Lorenzen, *Huber's de Conflictu Legum*, 13 ILL. L. REV. 375, 375–77

The Dutch scholar, Ulrich Huber, set out to reconcile the fact and theory of national territorial authority with the needs of a developing international trading system in which persons and commerce moved across state lines.[5] Huber summarized his analysis in three now well-known axioms:

> 1. The laws of every sovereign authority have force within the boundaries of its state, and bind all subject to it, but not beyond.
>
> 2. Those are held to be subject to a sovereign authority who are found within its boundaries, whether they be there permanently or temporarily.
>
> 3. Those who exercise sovereign authority so act from comity, that the laws of every nation having been applied within its own boundaries should retain their effect everywhere so far as they do not prejudice the powers or rights of another state, or its subjects.[6]

These axioms are practically, rather than theoretically, oriented. Taken together, they state that acts of foreign sovereigns should, when appropriate, be given effect within another state's territory and that courts of all nations should indulge a presumption against the extraterritorial impact of law. The third axiom emphasizes the practical necessity for the forum to recognize appropriate foreign rules to facilitate international economic intercourse. Huber wrote:

> Although the laws of one country can have no direct force in another country, yet nothing could be more inconvenient to the commerce and general intercourse of nations than that transactions valid by the law of one place should be rendered of no effect elsewhere owing to a difference in law.[7]

The principle of comity entered Anglo-American jurisprudence principally through scholarly writings and judicial decisions about choice of law that were strongly influenced by Huber's writings. Although British courts had begun to develop choice-of-law principles before they received the comity doctrine, the theories of Huber and his Dutch contemporaries provided a convenient rationale to support the development of private international law principles in Great

---

(1918). The use of the term to describe a theory for accommodating conflicting legal policies of territorial sovereigns was developed by scholars in 17th-century Holland to resolve conflicts between the laws of the various Dutch provinces. Davies, *The Influence of Huber's de Conflictu Legum on English Private International Law*, 18 BRIT. Y.B. INT'L L. 49, 52 (1937); Yntema, *supra*, at 20; Lorenzen, *supra*, at 16–17.

[5] Yntema, *supra* note 4, at 26. Huber's approach should be distinguished from that of the statutists who reasoned a priori from a conceptual classification of statutes as real, personal, or mixed to determine the extent of their extraterritorial recognition. *Id.* at 21–25.

[6] Translated in Davies, *supra* note 4, at 56–67. A translation of the entire *De conflictu legum* is found in an appendix to this article. *Id.* at 64–78.

[7] *Id.* at 59. It has been argued that Huber's theory included the requirement that the forum recognize a customary *jus gentium* from which private international law principles could be derived. Yntema, *supra* note 4, at 28–30. Whether or not he viewed international custom as the authoritative source of private international law rules, it is clear that Huber's basic principles represent a recognition that mutual tolerance and limited claim are essential functional components of a dynamic international economic and political order in a territorially divided world. In this sense, Huber's attitude parallels that found in section 403, Tentative Draft No. 2, *Restatement of Foreign Relations Law (Revised)*, discussed *infra* at page 300. *See generally* Lowenfeld, *Public Law in the International Arena: Conflict of Laws, International Law, and Some Suggestions for Their Interaction*, 163 RECUEIL DES COURS 315 (1979 II).

Britain.[8] British conflict-of-laws doctrine was introduced into United States case law as part of British common law.[9] Joseph Story, in both his judicial opinions and his great treatise on conflicts,[10] adopted a local law interpretation of Huber's three maxims that emphasized the importance of considering the international implications of choice-of-law decisions.[11]

These international considerations fall into two general categories. One category bears on the maintenance of amicable external relations with other nation-states and stresses the importance of extending courtesy to other sovereigns and reciprocal recognition of national governmental interests. This category suggests that comity is a standard for external political conduct.[12] The second category relates to the forum state's self-interest in making choice-of-law decisions that will further the development of an effectively functioning international system. Such a system would foster the growth of transnational commercial and social intercourse.

It is the comity of the first category that represents modern American judicial and scholarly usage and is reflected in many of the more recent transnational regulation cases.[13] This use of the term to describe the judicial branch's role in international political relations obscures the utility of Story's other use of the term "comity" to describe a helpful analytical approach in transnational cases.[14] In their political form, comity and reciprocity are to be determined on a case-by-case basis in the light of political perceptions, not principled legal analysis. It is that view of the doctrine that prevails in American courts today.[15]

Story's second use of the term "comity" treats it as a legal principle rather than a political one. This second usage suggests the need for just choices of law to encourage transnational commercial and social intercourse in a system that assumes mutual restraint by both sovereign states and private parties in ex-

[8] Nygh, *The Territorial Origins of English Law*, 2 TASMANIAN L. REV. 28, 40 (1968). Lord Mansfield endorsed Huber's version of the comity doctrine in Robinson v. Bland, 2 Bur. 1077, 1 W.Bl. 234, 259 (1760), a case involving the enforcement of a foreign gambling contract, and in Holman v. Johnson, (1775) 1 Cowp. 341, a case concerning the applicability of British customs laws to a French sales contract. Mansfield's view stressed the needs of commercial practicality and justice to the parties in international commerce. *Id.* at 343.

[9] *See* Nadelmann, *Joseph Story's Contribution to American Conflicts Law: A Comment*, 5 AM. J. LEGIS. HIST. 230 (1961).

[10] J. STORY, COMMENTARIES ON THE CONFLICT OF LAWS (Bigelow ed. 1883) [hereinafter cited as Story's COMMENTARIES].

[11] *Id.* at 32.

[12] *Id.* at section 7, 33–38.

[13] *See* text at note 73 *infra*.

[14] The tendency to treat comity as a political concept rather than as a tool for legal analysis is attributable to the opinion in Hilton v. Guyot, 159 U.S. 113 (1895), where the Supreme Court refused to enforce a French judgment because France would review a U.S. judgment *de novo*. The reciprocity principle adopted by the court was based on a political concept of comity that differed significantly from the concept of reciprocal interaction found in Huber's comity principle and in Story's second use of the term. The reciprocity principle as applied in Hilton can be logically justified only as requiring a political determination designed to discourage specified conduct by a foreign government. *See* Maier, *The Bases and Range of Federal Common Law in Private International Matters*, 5 VAND. J. TRANSNAT'L L. 133, 155–56 (1971).

[15] Professor Kurt Nadelmann called this "the internationalist approach with a safety valve." Nadelmann, *Introduction* to Yntema, *supra* note 4, 65 MICH. L. REV. 1, 6 n.42 (1966).

ercising power, and it emphasizes principles of justice and practicality as policies for determining applicable law. This aspect of Story's view of the role of comity, like Huber's, was pragmatic. Story wrote:

> The true foundation on which the administration of international law must rest is, that the rules which are to govern are those which arise from mutual interest and utility, from a sense of the inconvenience which would result from a contrary doctrine, and from a sort of moral necessity to do justice, in order that justice may be done to us in return.[16]

Thus, early United States conflicts doctrine clearly recognized that choice-of-law decisions must reflect the values of the general governmental system as well as the interests of the individual litigants by including principles of practical utility as part of their theoretical base. Comity, as used by Story in this second context, described an appropriate judicial approach for arriving at private international law decisions. It is clear that he did not view the comity doctrine as one designed to substitute political evaluations by the courts for normal common law methods for resolving conflicts issues.[17]

In the late 19th and early 20th centuries, Professor Joseph Henry Beale replaced Story as the leading influence on choice-of-law thinking in the United States. Correct principle under Beale's theory required the forum to give effect to any right that had "vested" within the territory of a foreign sovereign. Beale rejected the role of the forum as ultimate policymaker in private international cases. He wrote:

> The doctrine of comity seems to mean only that in certain cases the sovereign is not prevented by any principle of international law, but only by

[16] Story's COMMENTARIES, at 33. This pragmatic position should be distinguished from another view of comity, held by many continental writers, that rules of private international law were dictated by a *jus gentium* whose content could be derived by analysis of first principles. *See* Yntema, *supra* note 4, at 21–25. It was this continental view of comity that was attacked by Samuel Livermore some 6 years before Story's treatise was published. S. LIVERMORE, DISSERTATIONS ON THE QUESTIONS WHICH ARISE FROM THE CONTRARIETY OF THE POSITIVE LAW OF DIFFERENT STATES AND NATIONS (1828). Although Livermore argued in support of the statutist classifications of laws as real, personal, and mixed to guide choice of law, he, like Story, also endorsed the pragmatic necessity of developing choice-of-law principles that would serve the interests of effective international commercial and social interaction. *Id.* at 28.

[17] That this was Story's intention was made clear by the fact that his entire treatise is based on the opinions and results in many conflict-of-laws cases, as well as on a survey of the writings of the civilian and common law scholars in the field, not a priori reasoning. Nadelmann indicates that Story mentions more than five hundred judicial decisions from common law courts in the first edition of the *Commentaries*, Nadelmann, *supra* note 9, at 237; and approximately seven hundred in the second edition, Nadelmann, *Bicentennial Observations on the Second Edition of Joseph Story's Commentaries on the Conflict of Laws*, 28 AM. J. COMP. L. 67 (1980). Much of the treatise is devoted to stating specific choice-of-law rules for application to various types of legal subject matter.

Story's use of the term "comity" to characterize the legal relationship between private international decision making and the needs of the international system was not understood by continental scholars. The pragmatic elements of this use of the comity doctrine together with Story's emphasis on the freedom of the forum to create choice-of-law policy and his occasional references to the need for international courtesy (*see, e.g.*, Story's COMMENTARIES, section 618), suggested to some continental commentators that Story was advocating resort to a political rather than a legal approach to the resolution of private international law problems. Lorenzen, *supra* note 1, at 35.

> his own choice, from establishing any rule he pleases for the conflict of laws. In other words, it is an enabling principle rather than one which in any particular case would determine the actual rule of law.[18]

This rejection of a comity principle that was descriptive of the functional law formation process in favor of an analytical framework that viewed law solely as the result of a sovereign command seriously hindered the development of appropriate judicial methods for describing the intersection between public and private international law.[19] Beale's successors in influence on the development of U.S. conflict of laws, especially Professor Walter Wheeler Cook, reasoned that if law consisted principally of the decisions of courts, then the only rights that could be recognized in the forum were rights created by the forum.[20] Thus, Cook's "local law theory" laid the groundwork for the return of the principal functional and pragmatic elements of the comity doctrine—albeit shorn of its historic label—to United States private international cases. A modern reexamination of these elements by national decision makers to identify global policies to be served in transnational regulatory cases would create a more accurate and complete conceptual framework within which issues of extraterritorial jurisdiction could be analyzed. The theoretical and functional beginnings for such a development are found in the existing American Law Institute *Restatements* and in modern judicial decisions seeking to reconcile governmental and private interests in transnational cases.

III. The American Law Institute's Restatements

The Restatement (Second) of Conflicts

Ideally, the intersection between public and private international law might be described in a single restatement devoted to the law applicable in domestic courts to transnational events or transactions. Neither the *Restatement (Second) of Conflict of Laws*[21] nor the *Restatement (Second) of Foreign Relations Law*

[18] 3 J. H. Beale, A Treatise on the Conflict of Laws 1965 (1935). Beale did not, however, believe that the forum was controlled in its choice of law by public international law. *See* 1 *id.*, §5.1. Rather, restraints on the forum's freedom to create choice-of-law principles were grounded in Beale's strict Austinian conception of the nature of law. Cheatham, *American Theories of Conflict of Laws: Their Role and Utility,* 58 Harv. L. Rev. 361, 379–85 (1944). Beale treated comity merely as descriptive of the duty to give effect to vested rights and rejected the attempt in Hilton v. Guyot, 159 U.S. 113 (1895), to equate comity with reciprocity. 1 J. H. Beale, *supra*, §6.1.

[19] Beale recognized a vague relationship between the two bodies of law but made no effort to articulate the nature and extent of their interaction. On the question of extraterritorial jurisdiction, he wrote:

> [F]or surely it is not a proper function of the Law of Nations to determine the punishability of an individual for an act done abroad. On the other hand, it is pointed out that the interests concerned are solely individual, and should be determined by that branch of international law which concerns individual rights.

1 J. H. Beale, *supra* note 18, §1.9, at 43.

[20] Cook, *The Logical and Legal Bases of the Conflict of Laws* (1924), *reprinted in* AALS, Selected Readings on Conflict of Laws 71 (1956).

[21] Restatement (Second) of Conflict of Laws (1971) [hereinafter cited as Restatement (Second) of Conflicts].

of the United States[22] effectively identifies the interrelationship between the private and public conceptual constructs. In fact, barring one or two cross-references, one could almost conclude that each of the two works was written without regard to the existence of the other. It is somewhat ironic that it is the *Restatement (Second) of Conflicts*, not the *Restatement (Second) of Foreign Relations Law*, that contains specific reference to the needs of the international system as one of the desiderata to be considered in determining the reach of lawmaking and law-applying authority.[23]

Section 6 is the heart of the *Restatement*'s analytical framework. After making it clear that a court is required to follow clear statutory directions by its own legislature about choice of law, the section lists the now familiar seven factors to be considered in choosing the applicable rule. Those factors are headed by "the needs of the interstate and international system."[24] Although the *Restatement* denies that the factors are set forth in any particular order of priority,[25] the comments to the section stress the primary importance of systemic considerations:

> Probably the most important function of choice-of-law rules is to make the interstate and international systems work well. Choice-of-law rules, among other things, should seek to further harmonious relations between states and to facilitate commercial intercourse between them. In formulating rules of choice of law, a state should have regard for the needs and policies of other states and of the community of states. Rules of choice of law formulated with regard for such needs and policies are likely to commend themselves to other states and to be adopted by these states. Adoption of the same choice-of-law rules by many states will further the needs of the interstate and international systems and likewise the values of certainty, predictability and uniformity of result.[26]

If there is a single unifying theme that runs throughout the *Restatement (Second) of Conflicts*, it is that conflict-of-laws rules differ in purpose from other legal rules. Rather than representing policy decisions about the rights and

[22] RESTATEMENT (SECOND) OF FOREIGN RELATIONS LAW OF THE UNITED STATES (1965) [hereinafter cited as RESTATEMENT (SECOND) OF FOREIGN RELATIONS LAW].

[23] In many respects, the *Restatement (Second) of Conflicts* is a refined and modernized version of the functionally important elements of Story's comity doctrine. The format and approach taken by the *Restatement* directly parallel the organization and approach of Story's *Commentaries*. Like Story and the legal theory of comity, the *Restatement* in its recommendations depends almost exclusively upon territorial relationships for initial guidance in choice-of-law decisions. *See* Reese, *American Trends in Private International Law: Academic and Judicial Manipulation of Choice of Law Rules in Tort Cases*, 33 VAND. L. REV. 717, 733–34 (1980). Like the *Commentaries*, the *Restatement* begins with a statement of the more general values to be served in choice-of-law cases and then sets forth specific rules that reflect these values, drawn in large measure from the results in decided cases. The thrust of Story's second category of comity considerations is revitalized in the elements of section 6 of the *Restatement (Second) of Conflict of Laws*.

[24] Additional factors listed are the relevant policies of the forum; the relevant policies of other concerned states and the relative interests of those states in the determination of particular issues; the protection of justified expectations; the basic policies underlying the particular field of law; certainty, predictability, and uniformity of result; and ease in the determination and application of the law to be applied.

[25] RESTATEMENT (SECOND) OF CONFLICTS §6, Comment *c*.

[26] *Id.*, §6, Comment *d*.

duties of those subject to a legal system, conflict-of-laws rules are policy decisions about how the system's component parts interact with each other.[27] Despite this fact, direct consideration by decision makers of the interests of the interstate or international system, as distinguished from the other, more specific elements of section 6, is relatively rare.[28] The *Restatement* does not clearly identify these interests and they have not been adequately articulated in the literature.

There is a current trend in scholarly and judicial writings to borrow the analytical techniques developed by U.S. courts to deal with more traditional choice-of-law cases[29] for use in analyzing transnational regulatory problems.[30] This notion clearly stems from a recognition that judicial decisions in regulatory cases should avoid the public international/private international distinction in order to free courts to identify and articulate more accurately the true bases of their decisions. The model most often referred to is one of governmental interests balancing, built upon the elements of section 6 of the *Restatement (Second) of Conflicts* and found in various forms in conflict-of-laws theories developed by other writers.[31] A wholesale and uncritical borrowing of this approach for use in transnational regulation cases would be inappropriate, impractical, and misleading.

In purely intranational cases, courts need not consider the impact of choice-of-law decisions on the shape and structure of the federal system except in the context of constitutional law. The needs of the interstate system are protected by federal constitutional provisions, especially the full faith and credit clause[32] and the negative implications of the commerce clause.[33] The due process clause prohibits egregiously unreasonable or unfair choices of law.[34] Since require-

[27] Maier, *Coordination of Laws in a National Federal State: An Analysis of the Writings of Elliott Evans Cheatham*, 26 VAND. L. REV. 209, 242–47 (1973).

[28] Reese, *Legislative Jurisdiction*, 78 COLUM. L. REV. 1587, 1593 (1978).

[29] In one sense, of course, all decisions about whether the forum's law will govern a given event or specified parties is a choice-of-law decision. The principal distinction is that in nonregulatory choice-of-law cases the court will apply the law of a foreign jurisdiction if it finds that that jurisdiction has a greater interest in the transaction than the forum. In the regulatory cases, if the forum's local law is inapplicable, the case is dismissed. Rarely will the court attempt to apply the regulatory system of a foreign nation.

[30] *See, e.g.*, Lowenfeld, *supra* note 7, at 328–29; Mannington Mills v. Congoleum Corp., 595 F.2d 1287, 1297–98 (3d Cir. 1979); United States v. Vetco, Inc., 644 F.2d 1324, 1330 (9th Cir. 1981).

[31] There is a technical distinction between governmental interests analysis, generally associated with the late Professor Brainerd Currie, and other types of analysis designed to indicate which rule should govern a given issue. Generally, however, all modern choice-of-law methods seek to identify the state whose law is most appropriately applied, and that determination always involves answering the question, which body politic ought to influence most strongly the result in the case? In this sense, then, all modern choice-of-law methods involve some attempt to identify and weigh the interests of various political subdivisions having contact with a transaction or occurrence. For a description of the various approaches, see Reese, *supra* note 23; Westbrook, *A Survey and Evaluation of Competing Choice-of-Law Theories: The Case for Eclecticism*, 40 MO. L. REV. 407 (1972).

[32] *See, e.g.*, Order of United Commercial Travelers v. Wolfe, 331 U.S. 586 (1947). *See also* Allstate Ins. Co. v. Hague, 449 U.S. 302, 321 (1981) (Stevens, J., concurring).

[33] *See, e.g.*, Bibb v. Navajo Freight Lines, Inc., 359 U.S. 520 (1959); Raymond Motor Transportation, Inc. v. Rice, 434 U.S. 429 (1978).

[34] Home Insurance Co. v. Dick, 281 U.S. 397 (1930).

ments of full faith and credit to sister state laws are minimal,[35] except in the special areas of enforcement of sister state judgments,[36] and since interference with interstate commerce is clearly prohibited by the commerce clause, courts usually find it unnecessary to consider the interests of states in maintaining a viable system of national federalism[37] apart from the constitutional limitations on state activity. The presence of this constitutional safety net encourages a cavalier attitude by state courts toward the appropriate role of system interests in formulating interstate choice-of-law policy. Courts applying the methods of the *Restatement* in interstate cases focus on the interests of the states involved and balance those interests without reference to system needs. The assumption appears to be that if the law of the state with the greatest governmental interest is applied, the interests of the general system will automatically be served.[38]

When the needs of the interstate system are considered directly in domestic choice-of-law cases, the analysis is superficial at best. Some courts and commentators emphasize the danger that one political subdivision may become angry with another, which raises the unrealistic specter of civil conflict brought on by an inappropriate choice of law by a sister state.[39] Under this view, the needs of the system play a political role. Treating the preservation of good political relations between states as the principal relevant system interest suggests that the court is umpiring a competition and that the best interests of each state are always served by the application of its own substantive rule. This approach obscures the forum's role as a coordinator of conflicting policies and its duty to consider system values of fairness, predictability, and smooth interaction independently of the states' substantive interests as reflected in the relevant local law rules.[40]

Theoretically, opinions in transnational choice-of-law cases ought to be a rich source of analysis of international system needs. The absence of readily identifiable international constitutional protections and the fact that domestic

[35] Wells v. Simonds Abrasive Co., 345 U.S. 514 (1953); Carroll v. Lanza, 349 U.S. 408 (1955).

[36] Milwaukee County v. M. E. White Co., 296 U.S. 268 (1935).

[37] The term "national federalism" is used to suggest the overriding importance of maintaining a viable national state while preserving values of local self-government appropriate to the political philosophy that supports the constitutional allocations of power. *See generally* Maier, *supra* note 27.

[38] This same assumption operates in most transnational choice-of-law cases but without even the limited protection afforded to the system in interstate cases by the full faith and credit clause. *See, e.g.*, Babcock v. Jackson, 12 N.Y.2d 473, 240 N.Y.S.2d 743, 191 N.E.2d 279 (1963); Intercontinental Hotels Corp. (Puerto Rico) v. Golden, 15 N.Y.2d 9, 254 N.Y.S.2d 527, 203 N.E.2d 210 (1964).

[39] *See, e.g.*, Conklin v. Horner, 38 Wis.2d 468, 157 N.W.2d 579, 584 (1968); Clark v. Clark, 107 N.H. 351, 354, 222 A.2d 205, 209 (1966); R. LEFLAR, AMERICAN CONFLICTS LAW 208 (3d ed. 1977).

[40] *See* Cheatham, *Conflict of Law: Some Developments and Some Questions*, 25 ARK. L. REV. 9, 9–11 (1971); Cheatham & Maier, *Private International Law and its Sources*, 22 VAND. L. REV. 27, 97–98 (1968); Cheatham, *Some Developments in Conflict of Laws*, 17 *id.* at 193 (1963).

As one writer puts it, identification of the policies supporting a rule of law "focuses not on the motive or intentions of the legislature but on community purposes or goals as disclosed by the problems that evoked the rule, its function in the network of existing community arrangements, and the beneficial consequences to the community of its implementation." Ratner, *Choice of Law: Interest Analysis and Cost Contribution*, 47 S. CAL. L. REV. 817, 819 (1974).

courts are themselves participating in the international constitutive process when they decide these cases suggest that analysis of system needs would be essential to the effective resolution of transnational choice-of-law issues. Such an approach would seem required by the diversity of political and social values in the international community and the lack of an authoritative decision maker to protect the system in an ultimate review and evaluation of municipal assertions of authority.

Despite these differences in the interstate and international systems, courts in the United States have not distinguished between them in transnational choice-of-law cases. Some of the most important U.S. conflict-of-laws decisions involve contacts in both the United States and the foreign country,[41] and courts have usually not treated the foreign element as having special significance.[42] This lack of special attention to international system needs probably stems from the fact that the courts are always considering the rights and duties of private parties to each other, and the interests of governments are not directly engaged.[43] Thus, transnational choice-of-law cases in fact provide little special insight into the role played by systemic considerations in resolving transnational issues. Direct discussion of system needs, if it occurs at all, is usually in terms of maintaining amicable international relations, which directly parallels the approach in interstate choice-of-law cases.

The transnational regulatory cases are another matter. These cases directly involve the interests of the nation-states because the regulations embody legislative decisions about the structure and goals of society. The application of these regulatory policies to foreign events or persons may result in a direct clash between sovereigns when the governmental value judgments of one are held to have impact within the territorial boundaries of another. A government always has a direct interest in the outcome of a regulatory case, even when the governmental viewpoint is represented by a citizen-prosecutor seeking private recovery.[44] Thus, transnational regulatory cases always decide the correlative rights of governments. In this sense they are distinguishable from nonregulatory choice-of-law cases in which the issue is which of two or more conflicting governmental policies shall be applied to private persons, none of whom functionally serves as a government surrogate. When conflicting regulations are involved, or even when a regulation of the forum does not conflict directly with positive foreign governmental policy, international political conflict can result

[41] *See* Babcock v. Jackson, 12 N.Y.2d 473, 240 N.Y.S.2d 743, 191 N.E.2d 279 (1963); Auten v. Auten, 308 N.Y. 155, 124 N.E.2d 99 (1954); Neumeier v. Kuehner, 31 N.Y.2d 121, 335 N.Y.S.2d 64, 286 N.E.2d 454 (1972).

[42] The *Restatement (Second) of Conflicts*, section 10 points out that there may be special factors in an international case that indicate a different result from that which would be reached in a purely domestic decision.

[43] Courts in the United States have been quite successful in avoiding conscious or unconscious parochialism. *See* Cheatham & Maier, *supra* note 40, at 42–43; Du Bois, *The Significance in Conflict of Laws of the Distinction between Interstate and International Transactions*, 17 MINN. L. REV. 361, 380 (1932).

[44] Private rights to recover are provided in the United States, for example, under both the securities statutes and regulations and the antitrust laws to encourage persons to serve as surrogates for government prosecutors by bringing private suits for violations.

from the forum's application of the value judgments represented by the regulation in question to foreign events or persons.[45] Such conflict brings with it injury to the international system by replacing international cooperation and accommodation with intergovernmental confrontation.

A second distinction between regulatory cases and ordinary choice-of-law cases is that the forum will normally not apply the regulation of a foreign government. If the foreign regulation appropriately applies to the case before the court, the action will usually be dismissed. This is true not only because of the practical difficulty of importing a foreign regulatory system, but also because of the traditional attitude that one nation will not become another's political agent by giving effect to foreign governmental rights, barring special local statutory direction to do otherwise.[46] In international regulatory cases, then, the foreign government can normally expect the regulation of the forum to be applied or the case to be dismissed. Thus, the forum's action will likely not reflect the foreign nation's local law interests represented by its regulatory scheme.

The *Restatement (Second) of Conflicts* provides only general guidance toward a solution to this problem. Section 9 of the *Restatement* permits a court to apply its local law to an issue "when such application . . . would be reasonable in the light of the relationship of the state and of other states to the person, thing or occurrence involved."[47] Thus, section 9 addresses the role of municipal states and of nations vis-à-vis each other, but does not emphasize the need to consider the unit's interest in preserving an effective system, except to the extent that the general requirement of reasonableness accomplishes that end. Section 9 does not explicitly incorporate the principles of section 6 as do some of the other sections.[48]

Thus, the conflicts *Restatement* does not make clear the importance of international system considerations in determining the results in regulatory cases. Rather, the *Restatement (Second) of Conflicts* is quite explicit that issues raised by the application of regulatory legislation to foreign events or persons are primarily the concern of the *Restatement (Second) of Foreign Relations Law of the United States*.[49] Consequently, the only description of international system

[45] Hacking, *The Increasing Extraterritorial Impact of U.S. Laws: A Cause for Concern Amongst Friends of America*, 1 NW. J. INT'L L. & BUS. 1 (1979). The most recent flap over the extraterritorial application of U.S. antitrust laws is described in E. Gordon, *Extraterritorial Application of United States Economic Laws: Britain Draws the Line*, 14 INT'L LAW. 151 (1980).

[46] *See* H. STEINER & D. VAGTS, TRANSNATIONAL LEGAL PROBLEMS 932–34 (1976).

[47] RESTATEMENT (SECOND) OF CONFLICTS §9.

[48] *See, e.g., id.*, §§145, 149, 154, 188.

[49] *Id.*, §9, Comments *f* and *h* refer to both the nationality and territoriality principles. *See also* §53, Comments *d* and *e*. These references are virtually the only recognition in the conflicts *Restatement* that international system needs are a relevant consideration in determining the territorial scope of U.S. regulatory legislation.

The scholarly and judicial efforts devoted to demonstrating that public international law does not dictate the content of choice-of-law rules (*see, e.g.*, Nussbaum, *Rise and Decline of the Law of Nations Doctrine in the Conflict of Laws*, 42 COLUM. L. REV. 197–99 (1942)) may have obscured the relationship between the principles of choice of law and the international legal limitations on the assertion of jurisdiction in regulatory cases. It would be quite appropriate for the conflicts needs by the American Law Institute to assist the courts in determining the appropriate scope of United States regulatory legislation is found in the *Restatement (Second) of Foreign Relations Law.*

In the regulatory cases, the *Restatement (Second) of Conflicts* and the *Restatement (Second) of Foreign Relations Law* combine with statutory construction maxims to encourage an analytical approach that discourages overt consideration of the effect of an assertion of jurisdiction to prescribe or enforce in light of the needs of the transnational legal system. Courts in the United States are not free to give effect to international legal requirements in the face of a clear congressional direction to do otherwise.[50] Thus, whenever Congress acts within its broad constitutional powers and clearly intends that the statute in question shall be applied in the situation before the court, the court must apply the legislation even though that application would violate international law. This proposition is recognized and affirmed in both the *Restatement (Second) of Conflicts*[51] and the *Restatement (Second) of Foreign Relations Law.*[52] Since Congress has not usually considered the transnational reach of legislation couched in broad terms but aimed primarily at domestic needs,[53] U.S. courts regularly presume that Congress intended that a regulation apply within the limits of international law.[54] Those international legal principles are found by the courts in the *Restatement (Second) of Foreign Relations Law.*

The Restatement (Second) of Foreign Relations Law

General Provisions. The *Restatement (Second) of Foreign Relations Law* "represents the opinion of The American Law Institute as to the rules that an international tribunal would apply if charged with deciding a controversy in accordance with international law."[55] All the *Restatement* rules purport to be rules of international, not municipal, law unless otherwise indicated.[56]

The *Restatement* distinguishes two types of jurisdiction that a state may exercise. Jurisdiction to prescribe is "the capacity of a state under international law to make a rule of law." Jurisdiction to enforce is the "capacity of a state under international law to enforce a rule of law" by the act of any governmental branch.[57] In order to enforce any legal rule, both jurisdiction to prescribe and

---

Restatement to recognize that no decision in private international law can be made without having an impact on the structure of the international legal climate and to state principles that would take that impact into account. This could clearly be done without implying that choice-of-law rules are dictated by the consent of nations. *See* McDougal, *The Impact of International Law upon National Law: A Policy Oriented Perspective*, in M. McDOUGAL ET AL., STUDIES IN WORLD PUBLIC ORDER 157, 185 (1960).

[50] The Over-the-Top, 5 F.2d 838 (D. Conn. 1925); RESTATEMENT (SECOND) OF CONFLICTS §6(1) and Comment *b*; Cheatham & Reese, *Choice of Applicable Law*, 52 COLUM. L. REV. 959, 961 (1952).

[51] RESTATEMENT (SECOND) OF CONFLICTS §9, Comment *b*.

[52] RESTATEMENT (SECOND) OF FOREIGN RELATIONS LAW §3, Comment *j*.

[53] RESTATEMENT (SECOND) OF CONFLICTS §6(2), Comment *c*.

[54] The *Charming Betsy*, 6 U.S. (2 Cranch) 64, 118 (1802).

[55] RESTATEMENT (SECOND) OF FOREIGN RELATIONS LAW, Preface, at xii.

[56] *Id.*, §2(2).

[57] *Id.*, §6.

jurisdiction to enforce that rule in the particular situation must exist.[58] Either prescription or enforcement of a rule without adequate jurisdiction violates international law.[59]

Under the principles of the foreign relations *Restatement*, a state is free to adopt whatever choice-of-law rules it chooses, as long as it does not act arbitrarily.[60] A state may not, however, by means of its choice-of-law rules, confer upon itself jurisdiction to prescribe and enforce rules of law that it would otherwise lack. This distinction is of special importance in transnational regulatory cases. A party's appearance before a forum does not make the local law rules of that forum automatically applicable at the forum's discretion.[61] Conversely, a forum is not required to give effect to another state's prescription even if that state has jurisdiction to prescribe under international law. The international jurisdiction rules state the permissible scope of state action. They are not supranational prescriptions requiring the application of another state's regulation.[62] The rules thus indicate when state action would violate the public international legal rights of other states but do not indicate when exercise of

[58] *Id.*, §7. This distinction between jurisdiction to enforce and jurisdiction to prescribe is not entirely satisfactory because the categories sometimes overlap. For example, if a court issues a subpoena *duces tecum* to a corporate party, ordering that corporation to require its wholly owned foreign subsidiary to produce documents whose production would violate the laws of the country in which the papers are located, it is not clear whether the issuance of the subpoena is an exercise of jurisdiction to enforce or jurisdiction to prescribe. Some U.S. courts have distinguished the issuance of the subpoena from the issuance of a contempt order to enforce it, holding that although the subpoena may be a valid exercise of jurisdiction to prescribe a rule of conduct for the domestic corporate party, issuance of a contempt citation against that party for its foreign subsidiary's failure to produce the documents amounts to enforcing the subpoena in a foreign country and therefore violates international jurisdictional rules. *See, e.g.*, First Nat'l City Bank v. Internal Revenue Service, 271 F.2d 616 (2d Cir. 1959); *In re* Application of Chase Manhattan Bank, 297 F.2d 611 (2d Cir. 1962). Other courts have held that the power to issue the subpoena carries with it the power to issue the contempt citation and that the latter action is controlled solely by judicial discretion, not by international jurisdictional requirements. *See, e.g.*, State of Ohio v. Arthur Anderson & Co., 570 F.2d 1370 (10th Cir. 1978); *In re* Westinghouse Electric Corp. Uranium Contracts Litigation, 563 F.2d 992 (10th Cir. 1977). At least one court has held that issuance of the subpoena is the exercise of enforcement jurisdiction but that jurisdiction to enforce the subpoena depends upon jurisdiction to prescribe the underlying cause of action in connection with which the evidence is sought. *See* FTC v. Compagnie de Saint-Gobain-Pont-à-Mousson, 636 F.2d 1300 (D.C. Cir. 1980).

[59] RESTATEMENT (SECOND) OF FOREIGN RELATIONS LAW §8. Although cases involving jurisdiction to regulate normally arise in the context of an attempt to enforce those regulations, even bare prescription may raise international legal issues. In some instances the prescription of a rule without jurisdiction to do so may adversely affect foreign states by forcing their nationals to consider the rule's potential applicability when planning their activities. *Id.*, Comment *b*; Mann, *The Doctrine of Jurisdiction in International Law*, 111 RECUEIL DES COURS 1, 38 (1964 I).

[60] RESTATEMENT (SECOND) OF FOREIGN RELATIONS LAW §9.

[61] *Id.*, §9(2)(b).

[62] This distinction between jurisdiction to enforce and jurisdiction to prescribe is familiar in U.S. interstate conflict-of-laws cases. The fact that a state can apply its own rule without violating due process does not mean that some other state must necessarily give that rule full faith and credit in its own courts. Conversely, the fact that a state may apply the rule from some other jurisdiction without violating due process does not mean that the full faith and credit clause requires the application of that rule. *Cf.* Kirgis, *The Roles of Due Process and Full Faith and Credit in Choice of Law*, 52 CORNELL L. REV. 94 (1976).

jurisdiction would serve the interests of the international system as well as the interests of the state whose regulation is being applied. Conversely, the rules do not provide guidance about how the forum's assertion or refusal of jurisdiction to prescribe or enforce relates to the need to preserve or improve a legal climate conducive to effective transnational economic and social interaction.

The jurisdictional rules of the *Restatement* are based primarily on the nationality and territoriality principles of public international law.[63] Under these principles states may have concurrent jurisdiction to prescribe or enforce rules of law for the same facts or parties.[64] International law does not forbid the exercise of such concurrent jurisdiction.[65] Therefore, acting in those situations where Congress has not indicated the intended scope of the legislation in question, United States courts have created a jurisprudence of judicial restraint, based on the provisions of section 40 of the *Restatement*, to resolve jurisdictional conflicts of this kind.

The principal function of section 40 is to provide international legal sanctions for the exercise of judicial restraint, which permits courts to justify their decisions not as judicial legislation but rather as being consonant with the presumed intent of Congress to act in accordance with international legal principles. Section 40 provides:

> Where two states have jurisdiction to prescribe and enforce rules of law and the rules they may prescribe require inconsistent conduct upon the part of a person, each state is required by international law to consider, in good faith, moderating the exercise of its enforcement jurisdiction, in the light of such factors as
>
> (a) vital national interests of each of the states,
> (b) the extent and the nature of the hardship that inconsistent enforcement actions would impose upon the person,
> (c) the extent to which the required conduct is to take place in the territory of the other state,
> (d) the nationality of the person, and
> (e) the extent to which enforcement by action of either state can reasonably be expected to achieve compliance with the rule prescribed by that state.

[63] Under the *Restatement*, a state always has jurisdiction to regulate the conduct of its own nationals wherever that conduct may occur. RESTATEMENT (SECOND) OF FOREIGN RELATIONS LAW §30(a). Furthermore, a state may regulate all conduct that takes place within its borders and exercise jurisdiction over any conduct outside its territory that causes substantial and directly foreseeable effects within its borders if the conduct and effects are generally recognized by other nations as elements of a crime or tort. *Id.*, §§17–18. The *Restatement* also adopts the protective principle that permits a nation to exercise jurisdiction over events occurring abroad to protect "its security as a state" if the conduct in question is generally regarded as a crime by the world community. *Id.*, §33. Since actions abroad that have effects within the United States are covered by sections 17 and 18 and all nationals are subject to U.S. jurisdiction under section 30(a), the protective principle appears to have relevance only when foreigners act outside the United States with intent to injure U.S. security interests but without achieving any effect within this country. These principles are virtually identical to those adopted in the Harvard Research in International Law, 29 AJIL, Supp. 435, 445 (1935), which, in turn, relied heavily on the opinion in the S.S. *Lotus* case, [1927] PCIJ, ser. A., No. 10.

[64] RESTATEMENT (SECOND) OF FOREIGN RELATIONS LAW §37.

[65] *Id.*, §39.

Unlike the requirements specified in the other jurisdictional sections of the *Restatement (Second) of Foreign Relations Law*, those in section 40 are not firmly grounded in either international custom or convention.[66] The requirement that the various factors listed be considered in good faith in determining whether enforcement jurisdiction should be exercised merely endorses the truism that reciprocal tolerance is an element of the international legal process. In effect, the section incorporates a rule of reason, with reasonableness determined largely by the forum's perception of the relative state interests involved and fairness to the parties of enforcing the rules in question.[67]

The reporter for the *Restatement (Second) of Foreign Relations Law* finds a parallel between section 40 and ordinary U.S. choice-of-law doctrine. Referring to section 53 of the original *Restatement of Conflicts*, he writes:

> The parallel between conflict of laws doctrine and the present Section is clear. In both cases the question is not one of lack of jurisdiction but of the desirability of exercising power in a hardship situation (from the standpoint of the person concerned) or of international difficulty or tension (from the standpoint of the states concerned).[68]

[66] Metzger, *The Restatement of Foreign Relations Law of the United States: Bases and Conflicts of Jurisdiction*, 41 N.Y.U. L. REV. 7, 18–20 (1966).

[67] Unlike the situation in U.S. municipal law, the reasonableness concept inherent in section 40 is not relevant to whether prescriptive or enforcement jurisdiction exists ab initio. Professor Willis Reese suggests that in determining whether a state in the United States can exercise either judicial or legislative jurisdiction, the general criteria of fairness to the parties and the relationship of the assertion of jurisdiction to the federal system's needs should apply. *See* Reese, *supra* note 28. Reese argues that two sets of general policies should be considered to serve systemic needs. One set of policies requires essential fairness to the parties. Among the considerations that give rise to fairness issues are whether the parties have *relied* on a specific rule of law or legal system in creating their relationships or planning their actions and whether the parties had legitimate expectations that certain functional results would flow from their relationships. Legislative jurisdiction should not exist when its exercise would defeat either of these expectations. The second set of policies addresses whether jurisdiction is consistent with the needs of the system's political units. The most important systemic value, Reese argues, is that a state should not "without good reason apply its law in disregard of the substantial interests of some other state or states." *Id.* at 1608. In any event, a state usually has legislative jurisdiction if its own interests would be served by the application of its law. *See also* Reese, *Limitations on Extraterritorial Application of Law*, 4 DALHOUSIE L. REV. 589 (1978).

Under section 40, these same elements are considered in determining whether already existing jurisdiction should be exercised, not whether the decision maker has jurisdiction to prescribe or enforce the rule in question. If one examines section 40 of the *Restatement* in light of Professor Reese's categories, it becomes clear that subsection (b) and, to some degree, subsection (c) primarily reflect considerations that Reese would characterize as issues of fairness to the parties. Subsections (a), (c), and (d) clearly fall within the category of systemic considerations. The states' territorial concerns and the nationality of the persons involved reflect state interests that are directly related to assumptions of sovereign authority and responsibility inherent in the international system. Enforcement within the territory of another state raises considerations directly related to the international system's structure. Subsection (e) reflects practical considerations. There is no need for a state to attempt an enforcement that would not accomplish its policy goals, regardless of its jurisdictional authority. Other methods of achieving the same result may well be more reasonable. *See* RESTATEMENT (SECOND) OF FOREIGN RELATIONS LAW §40, Comment *e*, at 119. *Cf.* Lowenfeld, *supra* note 7, at 326–27.

[68] RESTATEMENT (SECOND) OF FOREIGN RELATIONS LAW §40, Reporter's Note 2, at 120–21.

This distinction is significant. United States courts are charged with determining whether the exercise of enforcement jurisdiction is reasonable without addressing the relationship between that exercise and existing or developing rules of international law. Section 40 requires only a determination whether it would be wise to enforce a municipal rule, given the existence of a recognized international authority to apply it.[69] By taking this approach, section 40 indicates that the reasonableness of exercising jurisdiction in a given case is juridically separable from the question whether the power to prescribe or enforce exists. Whether to enforce a rule is treated as a political, not a legal, issue. Thus, section 40 embodies the segment of Story's comity concept that emphasizes the political importance of avoiding international confrontation.[70] Under section 40, the needs of the system, the relative interests of the states involved, and issues of fairness to the parties are not accorded the special force that would flow from their characterization as legal rather than policy considerations.[71] By its terms, the factors listed need be considered only as a matter of international cooperation and courtesy. The section invokes judicial discretion to solve a problem of international politics, not legal analysis to resolve an issue of transnational law.

Like section 6 of the *Restatement (Second) of Conflicts*,[72] section 40 of the *Restatement (Second) of Foreign Relations Law* is unabashedly territorial in its assumptions. This emphasis on territoriality leads U.S. courts to focus on the laws, policies, and interests of the sovereigns whose legal regimes are potentially involved, and not to consider whether the adoption of a proposed jurisdictional approach would facilitate transnational commercial interaction if generally applied by the world community. Thus, section 40 does not enable a court to create a conceptual framework within which the question of how best to coordinate sovereign policies can be effectively addressed. This omission of any global frame of reference has left the courts with only an injunction to "act reasonably" as a guide. Recent decisions reflect a case-by-case approach in which the courts conglomerate territorial contacts and diplomatic considerations into decisions that reflect systemic values only accidentally, if at all.

Section 40 Applied. Courts in recent U.S. cases have overtly considered the interests of other nations relative to those of the United States in determining whether jurisdiction to prescribe or to enforce U.S. regulatory legislation exists. In these cases courts have taken an important step toward more accurate and sophisticated analysis by beginning to recognize a relationship between legal and political considerations in dealing with transnational issues. Basing their analyses on section 40 of the *Restatement (Second) of Foreign Relations Law*, the courts, after determining whether jurisdiction exists under the territorial or nationality principles, have resolved concurrent jurisdiction by exercising

[69] *Cf.* RESTATEMENT (SECOND) OF CONFLICTS §9, Comment *b*, distinguishing the court's authority to apply a given legal rule from the question whether the legislature intended that the rule apply to the persons or events in the case.

[70] RESTATEMENT (SECOND) OF FOREIGN RELATIONS LAW §40, Reporter's Note 2, at 120–21.

[71] *See* G. Williams, *International Law and the Controversy Concerning the Word "Law"*, 22 BRIT. Y.B. INT'L L. 146, 153 (1945).

[72] *See* Reese, *supra* note 23, at 733.

"voluntary restraint" when the regulatory interests of foreign nations having contact with the transaction or occurrence are great or when those of the United States are minimal. In doing so, they have adopted Story's second use of the term "comity" to characterize the rationale supporting judicial restraint.

The trend toward this approach is most evident in certain antitrust cases. After establishing that sufficient contact exists between the United States and the facts of the case to permit the application of U.S. antitrust rules, the courts require a balancing of the interests of the United States and the foreign countries involved to determine the propriety of exercising jurisdiction. In *Timberlane Lumber Co. v. Bank of America*,[73] the court sought to identify the point where "the interests of the United States are too weak and the foreign harmony incentive for restraint too strong to justify an extraterritorial assertion of jurisdiction," and identified these considerations with "international comity and fairness."[74] In *Mannington Mills v. Congoleum Corp.*,[75] the court ordered that the interests of the United States be balanced against those of each of 26 foreign countries to determine whether the foreign interest in providing patent protection to the defendant was greater than the U.S. interest in permitting competitive trade in the patented product by non-patent holders. The court based its decision on considerations of "foreign policy, reciprocity, comity, and limitations of judicial power."[76]

Considerations of "international comity" were paramount in both *In re Uranium Antitrust Litigation, Westinghouse Electric Corp. v. Rio Algom*[77] and *Zenith Radio Corp. v. Matsushita Electric Industrial Co., Ltd.*[78] In each of these cases, the court treated the wisdom of exercising jurisdiction as being different from whether jurisdiction existed under international law. The courts required an evaluation of the contacts and comity considerations but provided no guidance as to which contacts should be given greatest weight under the facts of each case or what values, other than general reasonableness, might be served by giving greater emphasis to some considerations than to others.

This same distinction between the existence of jurisdictional power and the wisdom of exercising it and a similar failure to articulate the systemic values served by each decision appear in the recent production-of-documents cases. Typically in these cases, a U.S. court has personal jurisdiction over a party in control of documents or other evidence located abroad whose production would violate the law of the country that is the situs of the evidence. One line of cases decided since the publication of the *Restatement (Second) of Foreign Relations Law* weighs the interests of the United States in producing the evidence against the interest of the foreign government in prohibiting its production. When production would violate the criminal laws of the situs, U.S. courts will not

[73] 549 F.2d 597 (9th Cir. 1976).

[74] *Id.* at 613. The court drew up a list of several elements to be considered to determine the reasonableness of exercising jurisdiction. *Id.* at 614, esp. n.31.

[75] 595 F.2d 1287 (3d Cir. 1979).

[76] *Id.* at 1296. The court expanded the list of contacts and political considerations adopted in *Timberlane*. *Id.* at 1298.

[77] 617 F.2d 1248 (7th Cir. 1980).

[78] 494 F.Supp. 1161 (E.D. Pa. 1980).

order it, not only because to do so would be unfair to the party charged but because the enforcement of such an order would exacerbate relations between nations.[79]

Courts distinguish those cases in which there would be no violation of foreign criminal prohibitions by balancing the interests of the United States and the foreign government and finding that U.S. interests are paramount.[80] However, one court found that balancing interests to determine the enforceability of a production order was unworkable; such balancing involved political determinations that were inappropriate for a court because they inevitably would require it to evaluate economic and social policies of a foreign country.[81] At least one court ruled that the balancing of interests in such cases was more appropriately carried out in international negotiations, and thus recognized the international character of the decision-making process involved.[82] By contrast, in *United States v. Vetco, Inc.*,[83] the court found that the Swiss criminal law interests in prohibiting production of documents were outweighed by the interests of the United States in receiving those documents to help determine federal tax liability. The court rejected the defendants' request that the Internal Revenue Service be required to negotiate with the Swiss authorities before a contempt citation for failure to produce the documents would issue. The courts in these cases have not produced an effective synthesis of relevant values to characterize the interrelationship between international legal power and wise national policy.

The court in *United States v. Mitchell*,[84] a case involving transnational environmental regulation, emphasized the distinction between balancing national interests in a judicial setting and balancing those same interests as part of an international negotiation process. In that case, the court found that a moratorium on the taking of dolphins under the Marine Mammal Protection Act of 1972[85] could not be applied to create criminal liability for a U.S. citizen who captured dolphins in Bahamian waters under a license from the Bahamian Government. The court couched its opinion in terms of congressional intent, but an important element in finding lack of such intent was the court's determination that the balancing of Bahamian against United States interests was

[79] Note, *Foreign Nondisclosure Laws and Domestic Discovery Orders in Antitrust Litigation*, 88 YALE L.J. 612 (1979); Note, *Discovery of Documents Located Abroad in U.S. Antitrust Litigation: Recent Developments in the Law Concerning the Foreign Illegality Excuse for Non-Production*, 14 VA. J. INT'L L. 747 (1974). Pre-*Restatement* cases are discussed in Note, *Limitations on the Federal Judicial Power to Compel Acts Violating Foreign Law*, 63 COLUM. L. REV. 1441 (1963).

[80] In United States v. First Nat'l City Bank & William T. Loveland, 396 F.2d 287 (2d Cir. 1968), and State of Ohio v. Arthur Andersen, 570 F.2d 1370 (10th Cir. 1978), there was no showing that any foreign criminal prohibition would in fact be violated. In United States v. Field, 532 F.2d 404 (5th Cir. 1976), the evidence sought was oral testimony about foreign banking records from a witness already before the court.

[81] FTC v. Compagnie de Saint-Gobain-Pont-à-Mousson, 636 F.2d 1300 (D.C. Cir. 1980).

[82] Westinghouse Electric Corp. v. Rio Algom Ltd., 480 F.Supp. 1138, 1148 (N.D. Ill. 1979).

[83] 644 F.2d 1324 (9th Cir. 1981), *as amended* Oct. 22, 1981, *cert. denied*, 50 U.S.L.W. 3465 (1981).

[84] 553 F.2d 996 (5th Cir. 1977).

[85] 16 U.S.C. §1362(13) (1976).

most appropriately carried out by negotiation.[86] It was clear that the court recognized the relationship between the jurisdictional determination that it was asked to make and the need to maintain effective relationships between nations by giving effect to legitimate community expectations. It did not, however, attempt to synthesize these two considerations into a process for judicially resolving future jurisdictional conflicts.

Most cases arising under the securities regulation statutes do not raise the kind of direct conflict between governmental policies found in the antitrust and production-of-documents cases. Most of the transnational securities cases concern the applicability of the antifraud provisions of the securities regulations to securities sales occurring outside the United States or to fraudulent securities sales to U.S. citizens where the fraudulent acts occur in foreign countries. Prescriptive jurisdiction in these cases is found to exist when either the conduct leading to the fraudulent sale or the effect of the sale occurs within U.S. territory.

The opinions in these cases do not deal with section 40 elements, but the courts consider a number of different governmental interests related to the conduct and effects tests of sections 17 and 18 to determine whether the securities laws' antifraud provisions apply.[87] The United States interests protected include maintaining reliable securities exchanges,[88] protecting persons in the United States from fraud perpetrated abroad,[89] restraint in the exercise of jurisdiction to conserve court time and judicial energy,[90] protecting the reliability of the United States as a situs for elements of securities transactions by preventing anyone from planning or perpetrating fraudulent acts in the country,[91] protecting the general moral climate in the United States by punishing fraud perpetrated here,[92] and protecting purchasers and sellers in whom the United States had a governmental interest.[93] All these policies support the use of the conduct and effects tests employed in these cases. The courts also recognize and seek to nurture a systemic interest in encouraging a worldwide climate in which securities defrauders will be prosecuted under the laws of many nations, thus improving the reliability of transnational securities transactions and serving the

[86] 553 F.2d at 1002.

[87] Section 40 has greater relevance to attempts to extend registration requirements and other regulatory measures to foreign broker dealers or foreign issuers, but there is a paucity of case law on this subject. For a review of the issues involved and an examination of the relationship to the antifraud cases, see Hacker & Rotunda, *The Extraterritorial Regulation of Foreign Business Under the U.S. Securities Laws,* 59 N.C. L. REV. 643 (1981). *See also Report on Proposed SEC Rules,* 21 REC. N.Y.C. B.A. 240 (1966).

[88] Schoenbaum v. Firstbrook, 405 F.2d 200 (2d Cir. 1968), *on rehearing*, 405 F.2d 215 (2d Cir. 1968).

[89] SEC v. Kasser, 548 F.2d 109 (3d Cir. 1977); Bersch v. Drexel Firestone, 519 F.2d 974 (2d Cir. 1975); Travis v. Anthes Imperial Ltd., 437 F.2d 515 (8th Cir. 1973); Leaseco Data Processing Equipment Corp. v. Maxwell, 468 F.2d 1326 (2d Cir. 1972).

[90] Des Brisay v. Goldfield Corp., 549 F.2d 133 (9th Cir. 1977); Bersch v. Drexel Firestone, 519 F.2d 974 (2d Cir. 1975).

[91] Continental Grain (Australia) v. Pacific Oilseeds, Inc., 592 F.2d 409 (8th Cir. 1979); United States v. Cook, 573 F.2d 281 (5th Cir. 1978); SEC. v. Kasser, 548 F.2d 109 (3d Cir. 1977).

[92] Continental Grain (Australia) v. Pacific Oilseeds, Inc., 592 F.2d 409 (8th Cir. 1979).

[93] Bersch v. Drexel Firestone, 519 F.2d 974 (2d Cir. 1975).

general system goals of protecting persons from fraudulent acts regardless of their nationality or where the acts take place.[94]

The opinions in these regulatory cases have not yet correctly synthesized the apparent competition between legal and political considerations into a coherent analytical framework within which community expectations about the permissible scope of prescriptive and enforcement jurisdiction can be consistently articulated in common situations. These cases separate the question whether jurisdiction exists from the question whether, once found to exist, it should be exercised. To separate the existence of authority from the wisdom of applying it in this way suggests that the international system legitimizes the exercise of power to resolve concurrent jurisdiction without regard to the relative interests of the states involved. Such an assumption is not only unrealistic but denies the nature of the demand-response-accommodation process that is the essence of the international legal system. For a domestic court to take the position that considerations of relative national interests are irrelevant to the question whether legitimate authority to prescribe or enforce exists reinforces a perception that the court operates outside the international law formation process and should view itself as playing principally a political role in determining whether or not effective power should be exercised. The authority-restraint distinction frees the court from weighing its decision in the light of its impact on the international law formation process and insulates it from the need to evaluate the impact of the assertion of jurisdiction on the development of reciprocal expectations about the legitimacy of the exercise of power in similar situations by other potential regulators in the international community. These cases, therefore, do not accurately describe the intersection between public and private international law and leave the analyst in a political never-never land in which a rule of international law can be said to exist even though it does not reflect legitimate interests of the international community.

This false distinction between authority and restraint creates difficulties much greater than those suggested by a mere dispute over verbal formula. Since courts in these cases are always operating under legislative language that on its face suggests that the statute is applicable to the foreign events or persons involved, there is some anomaly in a court's finding that a regulation may be applied without violating international jurisdictional standards but that the congressional command will not be followed if the *court* determines that as a matter of policy the regulation is inappropriately applied. The tendency in these cases is toward finding U.S. statutes applicable, and the authority-restraint distinction makes it difficult for the courts adequately to assess and articulate the relationship between the decision in the case at hand and the development of an international consensus about the legality of applying national power to foreign events or persons in the type of situation at issue. Furthermore, this judicial approach suggests that Congress should regard itself as being free of international legal constraints when drafting legislation, as long as it can identify an appropriate effect upon United States commerce, within the context of the

[94] SEC v. Kasser, 548 F.2d 109 (3d Cir. 1977); Bersch v. Drexel Firestone, 519 F.2d 974 (2d Cir. 1975).

theory of objective territoriality. Since, in many instances, such an effect is equivalent to the effect on foreign commerce required to create congressional power under the U.S. Constitution, the authority-restraint distinction in the existing case law implies greater congressional freedom than the international community will in fact tolerate.

Tentative Draft No. 2 of the *Restatement of Foreign Relations Law (Revised)* seeks to build on the instinctive recognition in these cases of a relationship between international law and wise national politics by creating a coherent format for inquiry into jurisdictional problems so as to reflect accurately the process by which the exercise of national power is legitimized in the international community. By eliminating the distinction between authority and wise policy the Tentative Draft takes a significant step toward obliterating the inappropriate distinction between the policies influencing the public international law of nations and those influencing private international choice of law in jurisdictional cases.

IV. The Proposed Revisions to the Restatement

Tentative Draft No. 2 of the *Restatement of Foreign Relations Law (Revised)*[95] avoids the fallacious distinction between authority and wisdom implicit in section 40 of the *Restatement (Second)* and developed in judicial opinions in extraterritorial regulatory cases. While adopting the principles of territoriality and nationality and the protective principles from the earlier *Restatement*, the Tentative Draft No. 2 makes it clear that the presence of these connecting elements does not in all instances establish jurisdiction to prescribe a rule of law. The draft points out that nations in fact temper assertions of jurisdiction based on these factors with considerations of reasonableness.[96] Therefore, under this draft, whether jurisdiction exists ab initio is not determined by mechanical analysis of factual contacts but by judicial evaluation of the propriety of the exercise of power.[97] Stated conversely, the unifying theme of the Tentative Draft's provisions is that mere factual connection will not legitimize the exercise of power if, in the light of other factors, such an exercise is unreasonable. Factors to be considered in determining the element of reasonableness are set forth in section 403:

> §403. Limitations on Jurisdiction to Prescribe
>
> (1) Although one of the bases for jurisdiction under §402 is present, a state may not apply law to the conduct, relations, status, or interests of persons or things having connections with another state or states when the exercise of such jurisdiction is unreasonable.
>
> (2) Whether the exercise of jurisdiction is unreasonable is judged by evaluating all the relevant factors, including:
>
> (a) The extent to which the activity (i) takes place within the regulating

[95] Restatement of Foreign Relations Law of the United States (Revised), Tent. Draft No. 2 (1981) [hereinafter cited as Tent. Draft No. 2]. This draft is summarized in 75 AJIL 987 (1981).

[96] *Id.*, ch. 1, Jurisdiction, Introductory Note, at 89–93.

[97] *Id.*, §403, Reporter's Note 10.

state, or (ii) has substantial, direct, and foreseeable effect upon or in the regulating state;

(b) the links such as nationality, residence, or economic activity, between the regulating state and the persons principally responsible for the activity to be regulated, or between that state and those whom the law or regulation is designed to protect;

(c) the character of the activity to be regulated, the importance of regulation to the regulating state, the extent to which other states regulate such activities, and the degree to which the desirability of such regulation is generally accepted;

(d) the existence of justified expectations that might be protected or hurt by the regulation in question;

(e) the importance of regulation to the international political, legal or economic system;

(f) the extent to which such regulation is consistent with the traditions of the international system;

(g) the extent to which another state may have an interest in regulating the activity;

(h) the likelihood of conflict with regulation by other states.

(3) An exercise of jurisdiction which is not unreasonable according to the criteria indicated in Subsection (2) may nevertheless be unreasonable if it requires a person to take action that would violate a regulation of another state which is not unreasonable under those criteria. Preference between conflicting exercises of jurisdiction is determined by evaluating the respective interests of the regulating states in light of the factors listed in Subsection (2).

(4) Under the law of the United States:

(a) a statute, regulation or rule is to be construed as exercising jurisdiction and applying law only to the extent permissible under §402 and this section, unless such construction is not fairly possible; but

(b) where Congress has made clear its purpose to exercise jurisdiction which may be beyond the limits permitted by international law, such exercise of jurisdiction, if within the constitutional authority of Congress, is effective as law in the United States.

An important advance made by this draft over section 40 is that the Tentative Draft recognizes the ultimate truth that the existence of international legal rules must necessarily depend upon their reasonableness. In a consensual legal system, the legitimacy of the exercise of power cannot be established in any other way. The approach recommended in section 403 points up to the court engaged in fashioning a decision about jurisdiction in a transnational regulatory case the important fact that in deciding the case, it is incrementally contributing to the development of the reasonableness standard in the international community and thus is playing a role in the formation of an international legal norm. To accomplish this result fully, the Tentative Draft, when reformulated, must explicitly include in its recommended considerations a direction to the court to carry out what Professor Myres McDougal has called "the final task": "appraising the impact of the claim to competence and the counterclaim to . . . lack of jurisdiction upon the common interests of the community."[98]

[98] M. McDougal, H. Lasswell, & I. Vlasic, Law and Public Order in Space 748 (1963).

Section 403(2) lists relevant factors to consider in determining whether jurisdiction is reasonable, including elements drawn from section 6 of the *Restatement (Second) of Conflicts* and from section 40 of the *Restatement (Second) of Foreign Relations Law.* Subsections 403(2)(a) and (b) suggest a qualitative evaluation of physical or social connections between the regulating state and the parties or events to be regulated. A reasonable application of the regulation therefore requires something more than a technical *de minimis* connection between the parties or events and the regulating state. Subsection 403(2)(d) calls to the decision maker's attention the parties' interest in preserving a regularized decision-making system that will permit them to realize expectations justified by their legitimate assumptions about the system. Subsections 403(2)(c), (g), and (h) emphasize the importance of evaluating the interests of all states potentially involved and determining whether these interests may be represented by conflicting regulations. Subsections 403(2)(e) and (f) are as close as the draft comes to reflecting the injunction of section 6 of the *Restatement (Second) of Conflicts* that the international system's needs must be given paramount importance in developing methods of choosing law. These subsections stress, however, the relationship of the regulation's substance to the international milieu, not the propriety of asserting jurisdictional power in light of the needs of the system as a whole.

The use made of section 403 in later sections that address specific subject areas makes it clear that section 403 is designed to play the same role in Tentative Draft No. 2 that section 6 plays in the *Restatement (Second) of Conflict of Laws.* Both sections establish pervasive general principles reflected in later, more specific sections. For example, subsections 415, 416, and 418 deal with antitrust, securities regulations, and enforcement of U.S. law abroad through control over local parents or subsidiaries, respectively. These specialized sections reflect the application of traditional principles of nationality and territoriality, including the conduct and effects tests, developed in United States case law. Each of the sections incorporates the principle of reasonableness solely by reference to section 403(2). Section 403 does not attempt to set forth rules or to list exhaustively the various elements to be considered in determining whether an assertion of jurisdiction is reasonable.[99] Rather it, like section 6, establishes a process by which cases about jurisdiction can be decided.

Because the factors to be considered are eclectic and do not necessarily suggest similar results when all are taken into account in the same case, section 403 needs to provide additional guidance to decision makers for resolving problems of extraterritoriality. Recent comments by Professor Willis Reese about section 6 of the conflicts *Restatement* need to borne in mind when considering section 403 as well. Reese wrote:

> Section 6 has both strengths and attendant weaknesses. Its strengths are that it lists the principal values that are of importance in choice of law. Its weaknesses stem directly from these strengths. In all but the simplest cases, the values stated are likely to point in different directions such that the court will be required to determine which values are of greatest importance for the purpose at hand. In other words, section 6 is eclectic in

[99] Tent. Draft No. 2, §403, Comment *b*.

> that it places emphasis upon a number of policies or values. . . . [I]t cannot be denied that the prinicipal weakness of the *Restatement* is the relatively little guidance that it affords. Properly viewed, it is a transitional document.[100]

Above all, it is essential that section 403 provide a general context in which the relevance of the various elements mentioned can be viewed. Reasonableness is a relative term. To be fully effective in accomplishing its purpose, section 403 must make it explicit that jurisdiction depends upon reasonableness measured not only in the light of the interests of other nations having direct connection with the case, but also measured in the light of the needs of the international system with special reference to the importance of maintaining jurisdictional rules that will support, ease, and encourage international economic and social intercourse.

Tentative Draft No. 2 places too much emphasis on the need to arbitrate between conflicting municipal interests[101] and not nearly enough emphasis on the role of the court or other decision maker as a facilitator of transnational interaction whose task should be to decide so as to coordinate the exercise of national power to serve the needs of all states for an effectively functioning legal system. No matter how incisive the interests analysis engaged in before a decision is rendered, the result will reflect the local law interests of only that state whose regulation is finally applied. If none but conflicting municipal interests are considered, the court is reduced to the role of a referee in a zero-sum game. Only if the principles that support the final result reflect the systemic as well as the local law interests of the states involved will the ultimate decision adequately contribute to the maximization of benefit for all states and thus to a true "balancing" of national interests. One can readily envision a situation in which a state's short-term local law interest would be served by application of its domestic regulation to a foreign event or person, but its long-term interest in an effective system would be better served by a more restrictive jurisdictional claim. This important aspect of the interest-balancing process should be explicitly recognized by any new restatement of foreign relations law. Such recognition would provide a framework within which the role of the municipal decision maker could be conceptually related to the needs of the public international legal system to permit that decision maker to address public transnational needs in the context of private international law decisions.

V. The Needs of the International System

The functional intersection between public and private international law in transnational regulatory and related cases is recognized by a group of United States Supreme Court cases decided since the mid-1950's. The Court makes it clear that only by reaching decisions that reflect the needs of the international system will United States courts also arrive at results reflecting important U.S. interests in the development of a legal regime within which transnational intercourse can take place effectively. A key element in these cases is the rec-

[100] Reese, *supra* note 23, at 733–34.

[101] *See, e.g.*, Tent. Draft No. 2, §403, Reporter's Notes 5 and 6.

ognition that one nation should not seek to impose its own values on others because it is essential to the development of the international legal system that it permit each participant to maximize its own values without coercion from abroad while coordinating concurrent prescriptive and enforcement authority to this end.[102] That coordination can occur only if municipal courts recognize that they as well as the national executive and legislature participate in the process of reciprocal tolerance and limited response that energizes the international law formation process.[103]

Lauritzen v. Larsen[104] is the first of this group of cases. The Court ruled that the Jones Act, a maritime workman's compensation statute, was inapplicable to a Danish seaman employed in New York on board a vessel engaged in international commerce owned and registered in Denmark. By its terms, the Jones Act applied to "every seaman." The Court pointed out that Congress had used this all-inclusive language with the understanding that United States courts would read it to accommodate and reconcile U.S. interests with those of foreign countries in the light of existing international legal principles.[105] Justice Jackson's opinion examined both the role of choice-of-law rules in the transnational commercial system and the contacts in the case that might identify the applicable national law. He pointed out that national courts regularly do not exploit contacts that might otherwise justify the application of local law. Rather, they apply in these cases a more universal maritime rule that "has the force of law, not from extraterritorial reach of national laws, nor from abdication of its sovereign powers by any nation, but from *acceptance by common consent of civilized communities of rules designed to foster amicable and workable commercial relations*."[106]

Jackson's emphasis is on the functional role of judicial decision making in the international system. He did not emphasize the needs of individual nation-states whose contacts with the case may give rise to narrowly nationalistic interests. Instead, he described the nations' interest in maintaining a smoothly functioning international legal regime:

> [International law] aims at stability and order through usages which considerations of comity, reciprocity and long-range interest have developed to define the domain which each nation will claim as its own. Maritime law, like our municipal law, has attempted to avoid or resolve conflicts between competing laws by ascertaining and valuing points of contact between the transaction and the states or governments whose competing laws are involved. The criteria appear to be arrived at from weighing of the significance of one or more connecting factors between the shipping transaction regulated and the national interest served by the assertion of authority. . . . [I]n dealing with international commerce we cannot be unmindful of the necessity for mutual forbearance if retaliations are to be avoided; nor should we forget that any contact which we hold sufficient

[102] *See* McDougal, *supra* note 49, at 209.

[103] *See* McDougal, *The Hydrogen Bomb Tests and the International Law of the Sea,* 49 AJIL 356, 358 (1955).

[104] 345 U.S. 571 (1953).

[105] *Id.* at 577; *see* Windward Shipping v. American Radio Ass'n, 415 U.S. 104 (1973).

[106] 345 U.S. at 582 (emphasis added).

> to warrant application of our law to a foreign transaction will logically be as strong a warrant for a foreign country to apply its law to an American transaction.[107]

Each choice-influencing factor was evaluated in terms of its utility as the basis for a choice-of-law rule that would aid the smooth functioning of the international commercial and maritime system. The Court considered seven such factors and evaluated the choice-of-law rule suggested by each factor. It rejected the place of the wrongful act, the place of the signing of the employment contract, and the automatic application of forum law because use of any of these connections would create an unworkable system by subjecting shipboard activities to a multiplicity of laws. A foreign forum's inaccessibility to the plaintiff was relevant to making a just choice of law, but the Court did not balance Danish and U.S. interests in the plaintiff's welfare to reach the result. Only when rejecting the allegiance of the injured party and the allegiance of the shipowner as controlling contacts did the Court suggest that the weight of national interest might turn the scale in a different setting. The Court adopted the ship's registration as the controlling contact because use of the law of the flag offered the greatest certainty and predictability for regulating shipboard activities.[108] The Court refused even to consider whether U.S. interests would be advanced if by applying the Jones Act to foreign ships and seamen their operating costs would increase. The Court said that such an argument was more properly presented to Congress because it is the political branches, not the judiciary, that are concerned with determining "which law does whom the greater or lesser good."[109] To apply the Jones Act in the case "would bring [the United States] into conflict with the maritime world."[110] Although *Lauritzen* is sometimes characterized as supporting a balancing-of-interests approach for determining applicable law,[111] in fact the Court emphasized throughout the opinion the pragmatic importance of selecting choice-influencing factors that, if generally applied, would encourage the development of a practical and just legal regime to govern maritime commerce.

The *Lauritzen* rationale was reiterated in *Romero v. International Terminal Operating Co.*[112] In that case the Jones Act was not applied to a claim brought by a Spanish seaman on a Spanish flag vessel owned by a Spanish corporation for an injury in a U.S. port. The Court reemphasized the considerations of practicality and fairness to the parties and the nations that were controlling in *Lauritzen*:

> [W]e must apply those principles of choice of law that are consonant with the needs of a general federal maritime law and with due recognition of our *self-regarding respect for the relevant interests of foreign nations* in the

[107] *Ibid.*

[108] *Id.* at 583–92. The Court's suggestion that it arrived at its decision by adding up relevant contacts seems to be purely makeweight. *See id.* at 592. Such a rationale does not comport with the thrust of the bulk of the opinion and would ignore the very policies that Justice Jackson emphasizes in the opinion's earlier portions.

[109] *Id.* at 593.

[110] *Id.* at 592.

[111] *See, e.g.*, McCulloch v. Sociedad Nacional de Marineros, 372 U.S. 10, 19 n.9 (1963).

[112] 358 U.S. 354 (1959).

> regulation of maritime commerce as part of the legitimate concern of the international community. . . . The controlling considerations are the *interacting interests* of the United States and of foreign countries, and in assessing them we must move with the circumspection appropriate when this Court is adjudicating issues inevitably entangled in the conduct of our international relations.[113]

The opinion made it clear that it was not the relative weight of U.S. and Spanish interests in providing for the injured seaman's recovery that determined the applicable law but rather the paramount interest of the United States in maintaining a reciprocally fair system for transnational interaction.[114] The Court wrote:

> [The place-of-injury rule] does not fit the accommodations that become relevant in fair and prudent regard for the interests of foreign nations in the regulation of their own ships and their own nationals, and *the effect upon our interests of our treatment of the legitimate interests of foreign nations.*[115]

Adopting the place-of-injury rule would be "disruptive of international commerce."[116]

The United States interests potentially affected by "treatment of the legitimate interests of foreign nations" were clearly not the limited local law policies of the Jones Act. Rather, United States interests would be endangered by failure to recognize legitimate foreign concern for maintaining an international system that gives due protection to its members' expectations. Those expectations are protected if each state uses an analytical approach that emphasizes reciprocal state interaction to resolve issues of concurrent jurisdiction.[117] The Court in *Lauritzen* and *Romero* clearly recognized that accommodation and compromise of competing claims reflect more than courteous political exchange. They are the dynamic of international law creation. The legitimacy of international legal rules and consequently their binding force depend on the effective functioning of this dynamic. States' jurisdictional decisions should be designed to contribute to the maintenance and development of a reliable and fair system in which specific substantive sovereign rights are capable of subordination to more general national systemic interests.

Eight years before *Lauritzen*, Judge Learned Hand stressed the importance

[113] *Id.* at 383 (emphasis added).

[114] *Compare* Currie, *The Silver Oar and All That*, 27 U. CHI. L. REV. 1, 74 (1959).

[115] 358 U.S. at 384 (emphasis added). [116] *Ibid.*

[117] The *Lauritzen* rationale was substantially perverted in Hellenic Lines, Ltd. v. Rhoditis, 398 U.S. 306 (1970), where the Supreme Court, in an opinion by Justice Douglas, weighed contacts to find that a Greek seaman injured in the port of New Orleans on board a Greek flag vessel owned by a Greek corporation could recover under the Jones Act because the corporation's controlling shareholder was a United States domiciliary and the ship made regular runs between Greece and the United States. The Court's reasoning in *Rhoditis* does not weaken the validity of the *Lauritzen* rationale for application in the regulatory cases. The majority in *Rhoditis* was clearly concerned with effectuating the compensatory policies of the Jones Act. It made no effort to analyze the potential effect of the choice-of-law decision on the international maritime system. The significant contacts analysis from *Rhoditis* was adopted in Antypas v. Cia. Maritima San Basilio, S.A., 541 F.2d 307 (2d Cir. 1976), also a Jones Act case.

of attending to the needs of the international system in regulatory cases. In *United States v. Aluminum Co. of America*,[118] Hand pointed out that general words such as those in the antitrust acts should not be interpreted "without regard to the limitations customarily observed by nations upon the exercise of their powers." The limitations referred to were those "generally . . . fixed by the 'Conflict of Laws.'"[119] He described this intersection between the custom of nations and private international rules as a manifestation of the objective territoriality principle and made it clear that functional considerations were important in determining whether jurisdiction should be asserted. Rejecting the proposition that the antitrust laws would prohibit acts outside United States borders that only had an unintended effect on United States commerce, he wrote:

> Almost any limitations on the supply of goods in Europe, for example, or in Latin America, may have repercussions in the United States if there is trade between the two. Yet when one considers the international complications likely to arise from an effort in this country to treat such agreements as unlawful, it is safe to assume that Congress certainly did not intend the Act to cover them.[120]

By "international complications," Hand could not have meant short-term political repercussions that might arise from the application of U.S. antitrust laws to foreign events in this case. By the time of the decision, the cartel had been out of existence for several years and the intervening events of World War II had certainly erased any remaining possibility of an adverse effect on United States foreign political relations from the application of United States law. Therefore, it is clear that Hand inferred congressional restraint from the proposition that to assert jurisdiction based only on the unintended effect of a foreign transaction on United States trade would create a precedent that would adversely affect the international trading system. Hand went on to say that these same practical considerations led him to reject jurisdiction based solely on intent to affect United States trade.[121] Thus, he limited his holding to the "intended effects" test for which *Alcoa* traditionally stands.

In a series of decisions about the applicability of the National Labor Relations Act to foreign crews on foreign flag vessels, the Supreme Court subordinated short-term substantive advantages for U.S. workers that might flow from the application of the NLRA to these maritime contracts to the nation's interest in restraining the assertion of jurisdiction in hope of nurturing a legal regime that would permit the effective operation of international maritime commerce. In these cases the Court did not describe the role of systemic considerations in its rationale as clearly as it had in *Lauritzen*. The reasons for restraint are sometimes articulated in terms of possible adverse political reaction, sometimes in terms of presumed congressional intent, and sometimes in terms of possible adverse economic consequences. In every case, however, the Court recognized that any claim of competence would legitimize similar reciprocal claims by other maritime nations. Although the Court focused on specific instances of

[118] 148 F.2d 416 (2d Cir. 1945).

[119] *Id.* at 443.

[120] *Ibid.*

[121] *Id.* at 443–44.

possible retaliation in support of its holdings, it seems clear that the recognition runs throughout these cases that an inappropriate assertion of jurisdiction would also have a more general adverse impact on the transnational legal regime.

In *Benz v. Compania Naviera Hildago*,[122] the Court refused to apply the NLRA when a ship of Liberian registry with a foreign crew was picketed in a U.S. port in support of the crew's wildcat strike. The Court stressed the disruptive effect that the application of United States law to wholly foreign parties would have on the international maritime system and found that Congress would not have intended such a result.

In *McCulloch v. Sociedad Nacional de Marineros de Honduras*,[123] the United Fruit Company owned a Honduran corporation that owned several cargo ships operating between the United States and Honduras. The ships flew the Honduran flag and their crews of Honduran nationals were represented by a Honduran labor union. When the National Maritime Union, an American labor organization, petitioned the National Labor Relations Board for a representation election, the NLRB ordered the election because the substantial U.S. contacts in the case outweighed those of Honduras. The Supreme Court upheld an injunction against the NLRB to prevent it from enforcing its election order. In doing so, it made it clear that the short-term political importance of the case justified judicial intervention to review the NLRB's election order.[124] The Court, however, broadened the scope of its rationale to include considerations that would apply to other future cases, pointing out that an application of the NLRA under these circumstances would "invite retaliatory action from other nations as well as Honduras."[125] The Court implied that to apply the NLRA in this case would violate international law.[126] Thus, in the Court's view, it was not solely United States-Honduran relations that would be injured by the NLRB's action but the general maritime legal regime as well.

Explicitly rejecting the balancing-of-interests approach adopted by the Board, the Court wrote:

> [T]o follow such a suggested procedure to the ultimate might require that the Board inquire into the internal discipline and order of all foreign vessels calling at American ports. Such activity would raise considerable disturbance not only in the field of maritime law but in our international relations as well. In addition, enforcement of Board orders would project the courts into application of the sanctions of the Act to foreign-flag ships on a purely *ad hoc* weighing of contacts basis. This would inevitably lead to embarrassment in foreign affairs and be entirely infeasible in actual practice.[127]

In *Windward Shipping v. American Radio Association*,[128] the Court put both *Benz* and *McCulloch* in context when it refused to apply the NLRA in a suit to enjoin United States unions from picketing against low wages paid to foreign crews on foreign-owned vessels that had come to U.S. ports. The Court wrote that the NLRA was not intended to "erase long standing principles

[122] 353 U.S. 138 (1957).

[123] 372 U.S. 10 (1963).

[124] *Id.* at 16–17.

[125] *Id.* at 21.

[126] *Ibid. McCulloch* was decisive in Incres Steamship Co. v. International Maritime Workers Union, 372 U.S. 24 (1963), a similar case decided the same day.

[127] 372 U.S. at 19.

[128] 415 U.S. 104 (1974).

of *comity and accommodation* in international maritime trade. . . . We are even more reluctant to attribute to Congress an intention to *disrupt this comprehensive body of law* [international maritime law] by construction of an Act unrelated to maritime commerce and directed solely at American labor relations."[129] Explicitly adopting the principles of *Lauritzen*,[130] the Court emphasized the serious economic consequences to international commerce that might flow from applying the NLRA, noted the possibility of retaliation by foreign governments, and found irrelevant the argument that applying the Act would advance U.S. interests by removing a competitive advantage held by foreign shipowners who paid lower wages.[131]

The modern application of the sovereign immunity and act of state doctrines gives primacy to the international commercial system's needs even at the expense of short-term detriment to more limited United States interests. Although the cases in these areas focus on separation of executive and judicial powers, a key policy consideration informing these decisions is whether the ultimate resolution of each case will serve to develop principles that will encourage effective transnational commercial and political intercourse. During the 1940's, courts in sovereign immunity cases rationalized the controlling effect granted to executive recommendations in separation-of-powers terms by recognizing the paramount role of the executive branch as the spokesman for the nation in the international sphere. The executive branch alone was capable of playing the appropriate role in the demand-response-accommodation process to preserve and develop an effective system of transnational interaction.[132]

The "Tate letter" of 1952[133] made it clear that systemic interests were appropriately reflected in the sovereign immunity doctrine. The adoption of the restrictive theory of sovereign immunity was stimulated both by its acceptance by other nations and by the need to provide effective legal recourse within the transnational commercial system for private parties doing business with foreign governments.[134] Judicial recognition of this doctrine suggests that sovereign accountability in commercial affairs is essential to effective transnational economic intercourse.[135] The Court of Appeals for the Second Circuit stated in 1964:

> The purpose of the restrictive theory of sovereign immunity is to try to accommodate the interest of individuals doing business with foreign governments in having their legal rights determined by the courts, with the interest of foreign governments in being free to perform certain political acts without undergoing the embarrassment or hindrance of defending the propriety of such acts before foreign courts.[136]

[129] *Id.* at 112–13 (emphasis added). [130] *Id.* at 113 n.13.

[131] *Cf.* text at note 109.

[132] Republic of Mexico v. Hoffman, 324 U.S. 30 (1945); *Ex parte* Peru, 318 U.S. 578 (1943); Maier, *Sovereign Immunity and Act of State: Correlative or Conflicting Policies?*, 35 U. CIN. L. REV. 556 (1966).

[133] Letter from Acting Legal Adviser Jack B. Tate to Acting Attorney General Philip B. Perlman, May 19, 1952, 26 DEP'T STATE BULL. 984 (1952).

[134] *Ibid.*

[135] *See* National City Bank v. Republic of China, 348 U.S. 356 (1955).

[136] Victory Transport Inc. v. Comisaria General, 336 F.2d 354, 360 (2d Cir. 1964), *cert. denied*, 381 U.S. 934 (1965).

It is not the interests of individual sovereigns that are balanced against each other but the importance to all nations of maintaining an effective transnational commercial system that is balanced against more immediate national benefits.[137] Public and private international policies meet in the restrictive theory, much as they did in Huber's third maxim and for many of the same reasons.[138]

International system considerations support modern decisions involving the act of state doctrine. The policy of preventing judicial interference with the executive branch's conduct of foreign affairs reflects the Supreme Court's awareness that where direct confrontations between sovereigns arise, compromise and accommodation of national interests are best worked out through international negotiations and diplomacy, not through unilateral judicial analysis and decision. In *Banco Nacional de Cuba v. Sabbatino*,[139] the Court permitted the Cuban Government to recover property expropriated in Cuba without compensation to its U.S. owners when that property was found in this country. The disagreement between Justice White, the single dissenting Justice, and the majority turned, in large part, on which decision would best serve the needs of the international system.

The majority grounded its decision on the constitutional relationship between the executive branch and the judiciary in the conduct of foreign affairs. Its rationale emphasized that the international system could not function effectively if domestic courts took it upon themselves to determine the validity of expropriations of foreign property by foreign sovereigns. The Court pointed out that judicial examination of the validity of such takings would exacerbate international relations. The act of state doctrine was not required either by international law or by the inherent nature of sovereign authority.[140] Therefore, the doctrine's content and application were determined by judicial perceptions of policies arising "out of the basic relationships between branches of government in a system of separation of powers."[141] The interests of both the United States and the "community of nations as a whole in the international sphere" would be best served by leaving the process of compromising conflicting interests to the executive branch.[142] In the special circumstances of the case, judicial determination of the Cuban expropriation's validity under international law would not contribute to the effective development of the international system because whether compensation was required was in serious dispute.[143]

Leaving the duty of articulating international legal principles to the executive branch enabled a process that would more accurately reflect the functional

[137] Section 1602 of the Foreign Sovereign Immunities Act of 1976, 28 U.S.C. §§1330, 1602–1611, attempts to regularize the process for determining immunity and to eliminate ad hoc political determinations by the State Department in which immunity issues were resolved on a case-by-case basis. Under the Act, immunity is determined by the judiciary. The substance of this congressional mandate was prepared by the Department of State. The procedures and rules laid down in the Act are to operate until a multinational agreement can create an international system reflecting the comparative interests of world community members in a single codified accommodation. Letter of Transmittal from Secretary of State William Rogers and Attorney General Richard Kleindienst to the Speaker of the House of Representatives, Jan. 16, 1973 (copy in author's files).

[138] *See* text at note 5 *supra*.

[139] 376 U.S. 398 (1963).

[140] *Id.* at 421.

[141] *Id.* at 423.

[142] *Ibid.*

[143] *Id.* at 428.

assumptions on which the international system is built. The Court reasoned that since the Executive acts both as an interpreter of generally accepted rules and as an advocate of international community standards it believes to be desirable, it is better fitted than the judiciary to demand, respond, and compromise to develop appropriate international legal principles about compensation requirements.[144] A judicial practice of adjudicating the validity of foreign governmental takings would injure the transnational commercial system by rendering titles in transnational commerce uncertain and might well alter the flow of international trade.[145] In sum, judicial abstention provided the best hope of "progress toward the goal of establishing the rule of law among nations."[146] The Court refused to adopt a rule that forum law would automatically govern in act of state cases because system interests were served by presuming the foreign transaction valid.[147]

Justice White, dissenting, also emphasized the importance of applying the act of state doctrine in the light of international system needs:

> The reasons that underlie the deference afforded to foreign acts affecting property in the acting country are several; such deference reflects an effort to maintain a certain stability and predictability in transnational transactions, to avoid friction between nations, to encourage settlement of these disputes through diplomatic means and to avoid interference with the executive control of foreign relations.[148]

He concluded that judicial abstention would not serve these goals:

> The achievement of a minimum amount of stability and predictability in international commercial transactions is not assured by a rule of nonreviewability which permits any act of a foreign state regardless of its validity under international law, to pass muster in the courts of other states. The very act of a foreign state against aliens which contravenes rules of international law, the purpose of which is to support and foster an order upon which people can rely, is at odds with the achievement of stability and predictability in international transactions.[149]

In these passages White makes it clear that his concern, like that of the majority, is focused on the long-term impact of the Court's decision on the development of a stable and effective international regime to serve both public and private participants. Thus, the entire Court agreed that international system considerations were paramount to short-term United States interests in this case. The disagreement was over how those system interests might best be served.

This same theme is reflected in the most recent act of state decision by the Supreme Court, *Alfred Dunhill of London, Inc. v. The Republic of Cuba*.[150] In this case, the Cuban Government had placed several expropriated cigar-manufacturing corporations in a form of operating receivership. Dunhill had made payments to the Cuban corporations for goods purchased both before and after the confiscation and sued to recover funds paid for cigars shipped after the expropriation because it believed this money was due to the cigar companies'

[144] *Id.* at 430–33.
[145] *Id.* at 433.
[146] *Id.* at 437.
[147] *Id.* at 438.
[148] *Id.* at 447 (White, J., dissenting).
[149] *Id.* at 459 (White, J., dissenting).
[150] 425 U.S. 682 (1976).

former owners, not the now Cuban-controlled corporations. The Cuban Government argued in the lower courts that it owed Dunhill nothing. On appeal, the Cubans claimed that their assertion of no liability below amounted to an act of state and that the Court was bound, under the *Sabbatino* doctrine, to accept the Cuban Government's position without further inquiry. The Supreme Court rejected this argument and emphasized that the same international system considerations that supported the restrictive theory of sovereign immunity were relevant in *Dunhill*. The Court wrote:

> The potential injury to private businessmen—and ultimately to international trade itself—from a system in which some of the participants in the international market are not subject to the rule of law has therefore increased correspondingly. . . . In their commercial capacities, foreign governments do not exercise power peculiar to sovereigns. Instead, they exercise only those powers that can also be exercised by private citizens. . . . There may be little codification or consensus as to the rules of international law concerning exercises of governmental powers. . . . However, more discernible rules of international law have emerged with regard to the commercial dealings of private parties in the international market. The restrictive approach to sovereign immunity suggests that these established rules should be applied to the commercial transactions of sovereign states. . . . For all the reasons which led the Executive Branch to adopt the restrictive theory of sovereign immunity, we hold that the mere assertion of sovereignty as a defense to a claim arising out of purely commercial acts by a foreign sovereign is no more effective if given the label "Act of State" than if it is given the label "sovereign immunity."[151]

Although this portion of the opinion was joined by only three Justices in addition to Justice White, its author, the Justices who refused to join did so because they believed that a different approach was more likely to serve international system interests. The dissenting Justices took the position that the balancing of interests required to resolve the issue was best carried out by the executive branch by negotiation rather than by a general judicial rule creating a commercial act exception to the act of state doctrine.[152]

The most striking deference to the needs of the international system by the Supreme Court is found in the choice-of-forum cases. *The Bremen v. Zapata Off-Shore Co.*[153] is a case in which the role of maritime law as a unifying element in transnational commercial transactions was forcefully recalled by the Court to enforce a choice-of-forum clause in an international towage contract. When an oil-drilling rig was damaged on the high seas while under tow by the defendant, plaintiff sued in a Florida federal court. The Supreme Court ordered the suit dismissed because the parties had agreed in the towage contract that "any dispute arising must be treated before the London Court of Justice."[154] The Court gave effect to the forum selection clause because enforcement

[151] *Id.* at 703–05.

[152] *Id.* at 725–28. The Department of State in an amicus brief had supported a commercial act exception to the act of state doctrine similar to the commercial act exception in the Tate letter for sovereign immunity cases. *See also* Letter from Monroe Leigh, Legal Adviser, to the Solicitor General, Nov. 26, 1975, *id.* at 706–11.

[153] 407 U.S. 1 (1971).

[154] *Id.* at 2.

would support the development of an effective international system to facilitate the flow of international commerce and serve the needs of transnational businessmen. The Court wrote:

> For at least two decades we have witnessed an expansion of overseas commercial activities by business enterprises based in the United States. . . . The expansion of American business and industry will hardly be encouraged if, notwithstanding solemn contracts, we insist on a parochial concept that all disputes must be resolved under our laws and in our courts. . . . [I]n an era of expanding world trade and commerce, the absolute aspects of the doctrine of the *Carbon Black* case [denying effect to a forum selection clause] have little place and would be a heavy hand indeed on the future development of international commercial dealings by Americans. We cannot have trade and commerce in world markets and international waters exclusively on our terms, governed by our laws, and resolved in our courts.[155]

Justice Douglas's dissent makes it clear that the Court explicitly evaluated all competing interests in the light of the long-term importance to this country of supporting an effective international commercial system.[156] Douglas objected to the enforcement of the forum selection clause because it was likely that the London court would give effect to the exculpatory clauses in the towage contract, contrary to the U.S. policy reflected in the Limitation of Liability Act[157] and U.S. judicial decisions holding that such exculpatory clauses would be of no effect. By rejecting an effort to resolve the case solely by weighing the competing interests of the United States, Great Britain, and Germany in the transactions in question, the majority clearly recognized that U.S. interests in encouraging predictability in the international trading system were controlling in a transnational commercial setting.

The rationale of *The Bremen* was logically applied in a nonadmiralty case, *Scherk v. Alberto-Culver*.[158] In that case, Alberto-Culver, a Delaware corporation with its principal office in Illinois, agreed to purchase three corporations located in Germany and Liechtenstein from Scherk, a German citizen, who warranted that various trademarks owned by these corporations were unencumbered. A clause in the contract provided that disputes would be settled by arbitration in accordance with the rules of the International Chamber of Commerce in Paris under the laws of the state of Illinois.[159] Alberto-Culver sought to rescind the sale when it discovered that the trademarks were encumbered. When Scherk refused, Alberto-Culver filed suit for damages in a federal court in Illinois, asserting fraudulent misrepresentation in violation of section 10(b) of the Securities Exchange Act of 1934[160] and of rule 10(b)-5.[161] Scherk moved to dismiss the action for want of jurisdiction or to stay it pending the arbitration required by the contract, a motion that was denied by the district court, which

[155] *Id.* at 8–9.

[156] *Id.* at 20–24 (Douglas, J., dissenting).

[157] 46 U.S.C. §185.

[158] 417 U.S. 506 (1974); *see* Maier, *The Three Faces of Zapata: Maritime Law, Federal Common Law, Federal Courts Law*, 6 VAND. J. TRANSNAT'L L. 387, 390–97 (1973).

[159] 417 U.S. at 508 n.1.

[160] 48 Stat. 881 (1934), *as amended*, 15 U.S.C.A. §§78a–78hh.

[161] 17 C.F.R. §240.10b-5.

enjoined Scherk from proceeding with the Paris arbitration. The court of appeals affirmed.

The Supreme Court of the United States, relying heavily on the reasoning in *The Bremen*, ruled that the arbitration clause must be given effect and the case dismissed. The Court distinguished *Wilko v. Swan*,[162] a purely domestic case relied on in the courts below, because *Scherk* involved an international business transaction. Recognition and enforcement of the arbitration clause was essential to the preservation and development of a predictable system in which transnational commercial transactions could take place. The Court wrote:

> [U]ncertainty will almost inevitably exist with respect to any contract touching two or more countries, each with its own substantive laws and conflict-of-laws rules. A contractual provision specifying in advance the forum in which disputes shall be litigated and the law to be applied is, therefore, an almost indispensable precondition to achievement of the orderliness and predictability essential to any international business transaction. . . . A parochial refusal by the courts of one country to enforce an international arbitration agreement would not only frustrate these purposes, but would invite unseemly and mutually destructive jockeying by the parties to secure tactical litigation advantages. In the present case, for example, it is not inconceivable that . . . Scherk . . . might have sought an order in France or some other country enjoining Alberto-Culver from proceeding with its litigation in the United States. Whatever recognition the courts of this country might ultimately have granted to the order of the foreign court, the dicey atmosphere of such a legal no-man's-land would surely damage the fabric of international commerce and trade, and imperil the willingness and ability of businessmen to enter into international commercial agreements.[163]

The Court made it clear that it was the U.S. interest in encouraging effective transnational commercial intercourse that took primacy over the interests represented by the securities laws. As pointed out by the four dissenting Justices, the majority's position flew directly in the face of a provision in the 1934 Act that made agreements to arbitrate liabilities under section 10 void and inoperative. The majority rejected the dissent's argument that Congress intended "American standards of fairness" to govern transactions of this kind. To take this position "demeans the standards of justice elsewhere in the world, and unnecessarily exalts the primacy of United States law over the laws of other countries."[164] The majority insisted on a global view of United States interests in a case where a narrow weighing of the competing governmental interests involved would likely have reached an opposite result.

Although elements of local law interest balancing or references to short-term political issues are found in some of these cases, one central theme is clear and compelling. The Court repeatedly recognizes that any decision applying mu-

[162] 346 U.S. 427 (1953). [163] 417 U.S. at 516–17.

[164] *Id.* at 517 n.11. Agreements to arbitrate will probably not be given effect to prevent private actions in U.S. courts under the antitrust laws. *See, e.g.*, Applied Digital Technology v. Continental Casualty Co., 576 F.2d 116 (7th Cir. 1978); Hunt v. Mobil Oil Corp., 410 F.Supp. 10 (S.D.N.Y. 1975), *aff'd*, 550 F.2d 58 (2d Cir. 1976), *cert. denied*, 434 U.S. 984 (1977).

nicipal law to a transnational transaction will create legitimate reciprocal expectations about the applicability of foreign law to activities with similar relationships to foreign forums. This realization signals restraint in applying United States legislation to persons or events subject to the Court's power. In each case, the U.S. interest in contributing to the development of an effective international regime was given preference over U.S. local law interests reflected in the rule in question. While recognizing an important need to prevent international discord and political recrimination, the Court repeatedly emphasized the correlative principle that decisions about applicable law should be made under legal principles that facilitate accommodation rather than confrontation between interested nations, both in the instant case and in the future.

In several instances, the Court suggested that the judiciary was an inappropriate branch of government to balance United States interests against those of foreign governments when this task could be better undertaken by the Executive in diplomatic exchange or international negotiation. In every instance the court weighed the immediate interest of the United States in applying its own local law against its national interest in contributing to the development of an effective international system reflecting pragmatic functional values. Those systemic values mentioned include preservation of stability and order through decisions contributing to predictability for business planners in determining the applicable law, adoption of law selection principles that consistently identify which nation's policies are likely to be applied in similar cases regardless of forum, maintenance of a high regard for the principle of territorial sovereignty to identify the governmental unit that is accountable to its fellows for conduct carried on within its borders, deference to the need to facilitate the flow of goods and persons in transnational commercial intercourse, and continued concern for fairness to parties by respecting their legitimate expectations and thus encouraging useful transnational activity.

Some of the passages quoted are more comprehensive than others in their reference to systemic principles. Taken together, however, they make it clear that the Supreme Court recognizes the principle that assertions of jurisdictional power should be made with the understanding that they are part of a process of interaction and that the wisdom of each assertion should be weighed with that in mind. In none of these cases did the Court narrowly balance political or commercial interests of the states directly involved without reference to the relevance of the decision to the needs of the international system as a whole.

Professor Arthur von Mehren has defined a just legal system as one containing two principal elements:

> This conception of justice assumes that preferred values and purposes can be determined where disagreement exists or is possible. Until these preferences are authoritatively established, the justice of any given rule or institution is not formally established. A further implication is that legal rules and institutions must be known, or at least knowable, by the individuals for whose activities these rules or institutions have significance. Information must be available about the rules and institutions operative and, to the extent that the consequences of present action lie in a more or less remote future, the legal order must provide for stability and continuity. The imperatives of equal treatment, stability, and continuity re-

quire that rules be uniformly administered and that institutions operate in a coherent manner.[165]

These elements are clearly to be encouraged in a coordinated transnational system. The lack of agreed-upon values and purposes in the international community as well as the lack of a single authoritative decision maker suggest that elements related to the structure and function of the system itself must be given special attention by national courts if their decisions in regulatory cases are to serve system needs. As one writer has put it:

> Jackson's approach and the approach followed by other courts since the end of World War II, suggest that any single contact or territorially oriented nexus is at once too narrow and too broad a basis for jurisdiction. Rather an assumption of prescriptive competence by a state requires an analysis of wider considerations stemming both from the legitimate interests of the nations concerned as well as the demands of the international order.[166]

To this end, the important systemic values identified by the Supreme Court, especially those relating to the need for predictability in jurisdictional principles, should be given explicit endorsement and articulation in any new draft of section 403 of the *Restatement of Foreign Relations Law.*

VI. Conclusion

Every attempt to describe the results of the law formation process in black letter rules both codifies existing practice and has important implications for future law development. Writing a restatement in any legal area requires a series of choices among sometimes subtly varying formulations. Each choice creates a slightly different dynamic for legal evolution. In this sense, any restatement of a subject matter is a crossroads in law development. In fields like foreign relations law and conflict of laws, the importance of a restatement is enhanced because issues in these fields arise less frequently for adjudication than do purely local law issues and the courts are more likely to rely on *Restatement* formulations than on relatively sparse judicial precedent. Also, the complex and abstract nature of the issues involved makes it difficult for courts to engage in meaningful policy analysis working from primary sources alone.[167]

Common social and political assumptions tend to harmonize decisions in purely domestic cases in the United States. Also, the constitutional standards of due process and full faith and credit and the unifying effect of the commerce clause prevent serious deviations from basic standards in purely intranational decisions. The situation is different in transnational cases. Societal and political assumptions may differ radically between nations. Competing regulatory regimes may be very dissimilar, both in their social purposes and in their enforcement procedures. It is for this reason that it is difficult to transpose prin-

[165] A von Mehren, *Choice of Law and the Problem of Justice*, 41 L. & Contemp. Prob. 27, 28 (1977).

[166] Collins, *Traffic in the Traffickers: Extradition and the Controlled Substances Import and Export Act of 1970*, 83 Yale L.J. 706, 722–23 (1974).

[167] *See* Maier, *supra* note 27, at 246–47.

ciples and practices developed to resolve purely domestic jurisdictional conflicts to the transnational setting. Tentative Draft No. 2 recognizes this difficulty. Referring to the provisions of section 6 of the *Restatement (Second) of Conflict of Laws*, the draft comments:

> Those principles, however, were designed to guide the choice of law to be applied by a court, and were developed in the context of conflicts between laws of the States of the United States; this Restatement addresses the limitations imposed by international law on the policy of nation-states, and international considerations may call for different evaluations and formulations, in a number of respects.[168]

The sections of the Tentative Draft No. 2 dealing with international standards governing the exercise of jurisdiction fail to make clear *how* those different evaluations and formulations are to be arrived at, and what values should influence U.S. courts in contributing to the legitimization of international jurisdictional norms. Failure to articulate these values in terms of international system needs will seriously weaken the effectiveness of the *Restatement* in stimulating the development of a more rational system of international jurisdictional norms by means of domestic judicial decisions.

There is a necessary difference in perception between courts' deciding jurisdictional issues in transnational cases and their balancing interests of states of the United States. Unilateral attempts to balance national interests in transnational cases can result, at best, in a pale reflection of the true weight and complexity of the competing interests involved. A unilateral decision maker cannot simulate intellectually the international process of demand, response, and compromise whose result reflects the vector of the various competing forces operative in the international law formation process. These complexities encourage the so-called homing tendency of the courts in ordinary choice-of-law cases.[169] In transnational regulatory cases, this tendency is likely to be even stronger. The interests and values of a foreign state are necessarily more difficult for a municipal court to perceive and weigh than those social convictions shared by the court as decision maker and its own legislature or executive. For a court to balance objectively the United States interest in applying U.S. antitrust laws to foreign activity against a foreign state's interest in permitting anticompetitive activity to achieve rationalization of production is difficult at best.[170] Similarly, a court is unlikely to perceive foreign interests in protecting business documents as being especially important when compared to U.S. interests in perusing those documents to assist in tax collection.[171] The result of such interest balancing will usually reflect an understandable bias in favor of the forum's policy, grounded in unsophisticated analysis, overt chauvinism, or erroneous perceptions of a constitutional duty to advance legislative policies described in broad language but designed primarily for use in a domestic context.

[168] Tent. Draft No. 2, ch. I, Introductory Note, at 88.

[169] *See, e.g.*, Akehurst, *Jurisdiction in International Law*, 46 BRIT. Y.B. INT'L L. 145, 185–86 (1973).

[170] *See, e.g.*, Westinghouse Electric Corp. v. Rio Algom, 480 F.Supp. 1138, 1148 (N.D. Ill. 1979), discussed in text at note 82.

[171] *See, e.g.*, United States v. Vetco, 644 F.2d 1324, 1333 (9th Cir. 1981), discussed in text at note 83.

I do not suggest that United States courts are the purveyors of a conscious parochialism. On the contrary, the development of a weighing approach to resolve conflicting exercises of concurrent jurisdiction results from a felt need for a legal doctrine that will carry with it the sanctions and regularity of law, while reflecting appropriate concern for legitimate national sensitivities and interests. The Supreme Court opinions discussed above recognize, however, that merely weighing or otherwise evaluating the interests of the states involved solely in terms of competing local law policies will not appropriately accommodate those national interests in the context of the entire community's needs or in light of each state's interest in a smoothly functioning community system. These needs must be considered in the light of effective principles of transnational organization, not solely in terms of whether a given decision may create short-term disharmony between the nations involved. A revision of the Tentative Draft should emphasize the importance of evaluating all results derived from the elements in section 403 to find out whether reaching that same result in similar cases in this and other forums will encourage decisions directed to creating a workable international rule that will serve the interests of all public and private participants in international affairs. In transnational regulatory cases the needs of the international system must be overtly considered in determining the territorial scope to be accorded congressional acts in all instances where Congress has not clearly directed otherwise. Without a clear direction in a new *Restatement* to consider these needs as well as the competing local law interests of the states involved, domestic courts will be less likely to fulfill their role as contributors to a smoothly functioning system of private and governmental interaction.

In its current form, the Tentative Draft gives no such direction. It identifies the contacts that are considered relevant to determine whether an appropriate nexus exists between the regulating state and the events and parties in question, but it does not articulate the values that should inform the weighing of these contacts under the reasonableness standard. The identification of the relevant factors listed in section 403 is useful, but it is essential that something more than a vague standard of reasonableness be articulated to supply the context in which they are to be evaluated. Directing a general search for reason and fairness is in no meaningful sense a rule of law,[172] nor even an effective description of an analytical method likely to lead to one. The elements listed in section 403 are important because they are among those that are appropriately considered in an analytical process designed to arrive at results that will reflect the shared expectations of the world community. It must not be forgotten that section 403, as well as most of the remainder of the *Restatement*, purports to restate *international* law. It is essential that international community values be paramount in the national decision maker's attention as he makes jurisdictional claims.

As presently cast, section 403 treats the court as an umpire to resolve a competition between states, not as a coordinator of legitimate, but conflicting, governmental claims. Such coordination will arise only from decisions designed

[172] *Compare* Lowenfeld, *supra* note 7, at 329.

to develop shared expectations whose legitimacy is determined by the extent to which they embody community values and thus contribute to transnational interaction energized by mutual respect and reciprocal restraint. Decisions that articulate and apply systemic values tend to encourage reciprocal treatment by other states' decision makers in like situations. Whether such decisions are taken to reflect state recognition of an *opinio juris* that international law permits or prohibits the jurisdictional claim or whether they are viewed merely as wise judicial policy formulations is largely irrelevant. The repetition of similar decisions based on clear value choices would contribute to the growth of transnational expectations about legitimate limits on the exercise of power. Conversely, an ad hoc weighing of often contradictory elements in the light of a general rubric to be subjectively reasonable can only contribute to greater rather than lesser conflict in situations of concurrent jurisdiction. Any judicial decision that fails to consider the needs of the international system in light of shared community values must necessarily fall short of achieving an effective coordination of national laws and concurrent national claims to jurisdictional power. Exclusive focus upon competing national interests identified principally by means of territorial connections on the assumption that such a focus will automatically reflect the broader interests of the international community will not alone contribute to the development of a more effective set of legal norms representing community values.

It is essential that the black letter rules of the new *Restatement* specifically direct the courts, where there is not a clearly contrary legislative command, to give important consideration to the needs of the international system when determining whether U.S. regulatory jurisdiction exists. The relevant basic values to guide this analysis are found in those Supreme Court cases that have emphasized the importance of considering international system needs and in the legal principle of comity as articulated by Huber and Story. These sources make it clear that the needs of the system, in addition to those overriding considerations of justice and fairness that should inform and guide all law, are best served by deference to the values of predictability, courtesy, and reciprocity that guarantee respect for the legitimate expectations of other governments and, thus, ensure reciprocal respect for our own.[173]

Perhaps the most important result encouraged by focusing on system needs is the increased likelihood of developing predictability in the system. Predictability is an element of reasonableness and is essential to achieving justice.[174] Although it is possible that, in a very broad sense, "our aim is reasonableness, not certainty,"[175] the needs of the states and their subjects in the international community will not be well served unless the value of predictability is given high priority.

It is unfortunate that, in borrowing from the elements of section 6 of the *Restatement (Second) of Conflicts*, section 403 did not include among the

[173] *Cf.* Tent. Draft No. 2, §403, Reporter's Note 6; R. FALK, THE ROLE OF DOMESTIC COURTS IN THE INTERNATIONAL LEGAL ORDER 36 (1964); Ongman, *"Be No Longer a Chaos": Constructing a Normative Theory of the Sherman Act's Extraterritorial Jurisdictional Scope*, 71 NW. L. REV. 733, 761–62 (1977); 35 ALI, PROC. 433 (1958) (comments by Sir Hartley Shawcross).

[174] *See Maier, supra* note 27, at 252–56.

[175] Lowenfeld, *supra* note 7, at 329.

important elements to be considered the values of certainty, predictability, and uniformity of result and the desirability of ease in determining which of two or more concurrent jurisdictional claims is legitimate. An unruly reasonableness disserves the principle of practical utility, and thus fails to encourage consideration of an important element of justice. The *Restatement* must emphasize that the U.S. and thus the community's interest in developing and maintaining an effective international system is as important as the local law interests embodied in the substance of the regulations in question. The American Law Institute's endorsement of the proposition that analysis of the needs of the international system in making jurisdictional determinations is a relevant judicial task would expand the legal horizons of United States forums beyond the narrow substantive policies of the various local regulations.[176] Such an approach in the new *Restatement* would make it clear to U.S. and foreign courts that in these cases they sit as transnational courts participating in a transnational lawmaking process.[177] The policies that energize their decisions should reflect transnational considerations that include both public and private values to serve the needs of the public and private entities that operate across national lines. If the *Restatement* can channel judicial activity along this proper path, it will have marked out a road leading to decisions designed to be "convenient to commerce and general intercourse of nations,"[178] and accurately mapped an important intersection between public and private international law.

[176] Professor Lowenfeld specifically includes system needs in his list of elements to be considered in making transnational jurisdictional decisions. *See id.* at 328–29.

[177] *See* P. JESSUP, TRANSNATIONAL LAW 5 (1956).

[178] U. HUBER, DE CONFLICTU LEGUM, translated in Davies, *supra* note 4, at 59.

THE TORRES STRAIT TREATY: OCEAN BOUNDARY DELIMITATION BY AGREEMENT

*By H. Burmester**

Introduction

The delimitation of maritime boundaries is one of the major areas of ocean law where disputes between countries occur with frequency and where the development of governing principles of law remains difficult. At the Law of the Sea Conference, delimitation of the continental shelf and economic zones between states with opposite or adjacent coasts was one of the last issues to be resolved.[1] Major judicial and arbitral decisions, such as the *North Sea Continental Shelf* cases[2] before the International Court of Justice and the *Anglo-French Continental Shelf* arbitration,[3] have gone some way to developing a body of relevant law to assist states in the solution of their maritime boundary problems. These decisions have clarified some of the relevant factors that states should take into account, but major boundary problems remain. On the Aegean Sea, Greece and Turkey have still not reached any solution;[4] relations between Canada and the United States have been severely strained by their slow progress on maritime boundary issues;[5] Libya and Tunisia have referred their conti-

* Faculty of Law, Australian National University. The author was formerly an officer of the Australian Attorney-General's Department and a member of the Australian negotiating team for the Torres Strait Treaty.

[1] Arts. 74(1) and 83(1) of the Draft Convention on the Law of the Sea (Aug. 1981), UN Doc. A/CONF.62/L.78. Oxman points out that the agreed texts were not considered satisfactory by many states. Oxman, *The Third United Nations Conference on the Law of the Sea: The Tenth Session (1981)*, 76 AJIL 1, 14–15 (1982).

Further citations in this article to the Draft Convention will refer to the Informal Text of August 1980, UN Doc. A/CONF.62/WP.10/Rev.3, *reprinted in* 19 ILM 1126 (1980).

[2] [1969] ICJ Rep. 3.

[3] The United Kingdom of Great Britain and Northern Ireland and the French Republic Delimitation of the Continental Shelf Decision of 30 June 1977, Cmnd. 7348 (1978), *reprinted in* 18 ILM 397 (1979). For brief notes on the case, see Colson, *The United Kingdom-France Continental Shelf Arbitration*, 72 AJIL 95 (1978) and 73 *id.* at 112 (1979). A further discussion appears in Bowett, *The Arbitration Between the United Kingdom and France Concerning the Continental Shelf Boundary in the English Channel and South-Western Approaches*, 49 Brit. Y.B. Int'l L. 1 (1978).

[4] An attempt by Greece to bring the matter before the International Court of Justice failed. Aegean Sea Continental Shelf Case (Greece v. Turkey) (Jurisdiction), [1978] ICJ Rep. 3. For a summary, see 73 AJIL 493 (1979).

[5] The Treaty Between the Government of the United States of America and the Government of Canada to Submit to Binding Dispute Settlement the Delimitation of the Maritime Boundary in the Gulf of Maine Area was signed on March 29, 1979. It was linked with the Agreement on East Coast Fishery Resources, which ran into major opposition in Congress and was withdrawn in March 1981 by President Reagan. However, both countries have now ratified the Treaty as amended and the boundary dispute is being submitted to a Chamber of the ICJ. The Treaty and Agreement, in S. Exec. Docs. U and V, respectively, 96th Cong., 1st Sess. (1979), are *reprinted*

nental shelf dispute to the International Court of Justice.[6]

The signing in December 1978 by Australia and Papua New Guinea of the Treaty concerning Sovereignty and Maritime Boundaries in the area between the two Countries, including the area known as Torres Strait, and Related Matters thus represents a significant achievement.[7] Not only does the Treaty indicate that direct negotiation can successfully resolve complex maritime boundary disputes, but it also contains several novel and significant features that may point the way to solutions elsewhere. Among the novel features are separate seabed and fisheries jurisdiction lines, establishment of a Protected Zone, and complex arrangements regarding the sharing of the catch of commercial fisheries. Although the Treaty delimits a stretch of approximately 1200 miles, from the Coral Sea in the east to the Arafura Sea in the west, the most significant aspects of the Treaty relate to the Torres Strait area itself and this article will be primarily concerned with that area.

The Torres Strait area is a unique expanse located between Cape York at the northern extremity of Australia and the southern coast of Papua New Guinea. The area consists of a considerable number of islands, some large and inhabited, others amounting to no more than small rocks and uninhabited cays. They are all Australian, with the exception of one or two small islands close to the Papua New Guinea coast. The Australian islands include the three major inhabited islands of Boigu, Dauan, and Saibai, literally only a few hundred yards off the Papua New Guinea coast. Apart from the islands, the area is full of reefs and shoals; navigation by large vessels is largely confined to the North East Channel, which runs through the central Strait area. These geographical features complicated the maritime delimitation problem.

As well as the special geographical features of the area, one of the major factors that had to be taken into account in devising solutions to the maritime delimitation problem was the need to protect the livelihood and life style of the local inhabitants. The Papua New Guineans of the immediately adjacent area and the Torres Strait islanders are ethnically distinct. The islanders are themselves distinct from the Australian aboriginal people. The local inhabitants still engage in many traditional activities which the Treaty has sought to protect.[8]

The Treaty reflects the realization that a maritime boundary dispute is often

---

in 9 NEW DIRECTIONS IN THE LAW OF THE SEA 157–210 (M. Nordquist & K. Simmons eds. 1980). *See* Rhee, *The Application of Equitable Principles to Resolve the United States-Canada Dispute over East Coast Fishery Resources,* 21 HARV. INT'L L.J. 667 (1980); McRae, *Adjudication of the Maritime Boundary in the Gulf of Maine,* 17 CAN. Y.B. INT'L L. 292 (1979); Rhee, *Equitable Solutions to the Maritime Boundary Dispute Between the United States and Canada in the Gulf of Maine,* 75 AJIL 590 (1981); Feldman & Colson, *The Maritime Boundaries of the United States, id.* at 729.

[6] At the time of writing, no decision had yet been given in this case. *See* Case Concerning the Continental Shelf (Tunisia/Libyan Arab Jamahiriya), [1979] ICJ REP. 3, for the order setting the procedure and time limits for the hearing of the case.

[7] For the text, see 18 ILM 291 (1979). The treaty is subject to ratification.

[8] For the most detailed study on the socioeconomic conditions of the area, see the Torres Strait Islanders series published by the Research School of Pacific Studies, Australian National University, 1974–1975, particularly vol. I, H. DUNCAN, SOCIO-ECONOMIC CONDITIONS IN THE TORRES STRAIT; vol. V, THE BORDER AND ASSOCIATED PROBLEMS (E. K. Fisk ed.), and vol. VI, E. K. FISK, POLICY OPTIONS IN THE TORRES STRAIT.

not a one-issue problem. In the present case, by treating separately (1) the people, (2) maritime jurisdiction, (3) the islands, (4) fisheries resources, and (5) navigation, and devising solutions to each, the parties were able to reach agreement on what the author considers a just and equitable solution to a complex problem. Such solutions are more likely to result from agreement between the parties concerned than from judicial or arbitral decisions. While such an approach may lead to complexity (in this case a treaty of 32 articles and 9 annexes), it also ensures that each matter is dealt with in the light of its unique characteristics. Too often, maritime delimitation disputes are seen simply as a process of drawing a single line on a map. Through failure to have proper regard to all the surrounding circumstances, negotiations often become protracted and fruitless and no durable solution results. The solution negotiated in the Torres Strait Treaty points to the fact that ocean issues will be settled in the most satisfactory manner once jurisdictional and conceptual approaches are abandoned and functional solutions sought. This has proved apparent in the Law of the Sea Conference itself, particularly when it comes to navigation and pollution.

This article will review the Treaty provisions in relation to each of the five issues mentioned above. Certain provisions in the Treaty may not be readily understood at first glance; in addition to them, this article also seeks to explain some of the novel features.

In considering the provisions of the Treaty, one must keep in mind the unique background to its negotiation: that it was negotiated between a developed country and its former dependent territory, which had recently gained independence. Negotiation of the boundary was one of the major steps in the disengagement of Papua New Guinea from its former dependent relationship, and conclusion of the Treaty had, as a result, added symbolic significance. This special relationship between the two countries colored their respective aims. For Papua New Guinea it was important to obtain a single, all-purpose boundary that, apart from maritime jurisdiction, removed what was seen as a historic anomaly: Australian territory extended to within several hundred yards of the Papua New Guinean coast. Whatever the legal merits, Papua New Guinea also based its claim on moral grounds. Any proposal that maintained Australian influence or control throughout the Strait was seen as suspect because Papua New Guinea understandably feared that Australia would be able, through its weight in the bilateral relationship, to continue to exercise a disproportionate influence. While this view may have appealed initially to some Australians, Australia's perception of the issues involved in the negotiations was quite different. There were a number of significant political and constitutional constraints on the Australian Government, arising largely from its federal structure. But more significantly, Australia was concerned to protect the rights and livelihood of the traditional inhabitants of the Torres Strait. The fact that Australian territory extended up to the Papua New Guinean coast was not seen as an anomaly but as a historical fact. From the Australian perspective, the human element of the problem was therefore very important. To Papua New Guinea, the human element was much less significant. All groups of Papua New Guineans generally follow a traditional way of life, and to single out traditional inhabitants of a particular area for special treatment could well be perceived as undesirable and unjustified. Facilitation of cross-border movement is one thing; establishment of special rights for one particular group is another.[9]

Despite the very different aims and perceptions of the two countries, they were able to incorporate some significant compromises in the Treaty. In return for special provisions on resources, Papua New Guinea was prepared to go along with Australian proposals designed to meet the special needs of the local inhabitants. Taken as a whole, the Treaty represents a creative approach to maritime delimitation that equitably takes account of the various interrelated issues.

Historical Background

The history of the establishment of the "border" between Queensland and Papua is relevant to the problem of devising a maritime boundary suitable for present conditions. In 1859 Queensland was established as a colony separate from New South Wales. Due to uncertainties as to which islands off its coast formed part of the colony, in 1872 all islands within 60 miles of the coast were brought under the jurisdiction of Queensland. This still left the northern islands of the Torres Strait outside the jurisdiction of Queensland. At the time, Papua had still not been annexed to the British Empire or established as a Protectorate. This was not to happen until 1884. Concern that the northern islands might fall into foreign hands led to a further proclamation in 1879 that brought into force Letters Patent describing the islands to be annexed as

> certain islands in Torres Straits and lying between the Continent of Australia and Island of New Guinea, that is to say all islands included within a line drawn from Sandy Cape . . . thence from Bramble Cays in a line west by south (south seventy-nine degrees west) true; embracing Warrior Reef, Saibai, and Tuan Islands, thence diverging in a north westerly direction so as to embrace the group known as Talbot Islands; thence to and embracing the Deliverance Islands. . . .

This imprecise definition was to lead to problems in determining whether certain features were or were not part of Queensland. Several efforts were made between 1885 and 1920 to move the boundary further south.[10] It was recognized that once Papua became a British possession there was no need for the Queensland boundary to include the islands hugging the Papuan coast. The proposals to redraw the boundary foundered, however, because successive Queensland governments did not agree to the various proposals made by the colonial and local administrative authorities. By the 1970's, the 1879 line was firmly entrenched. What then became important was to determine its precise location.

[9] The author is indebted to G. Dabb, a member of the Papua New Guinean negotiating team, for a valuable exchange of views on the different perceptions of the two countries.

[10] For a more detailed description of the historical background, see P. VAN DER VEUR, SEARCH FOR NEW GUINEA'S BOUNDARIES, ch. 3 (1966). *See also* JOINT FOREIGN AFFAIRS AND DEFENCE COMMITTEE, THE TORRES STRAIT BOUNDARY, [Australian] Parliamentary Paper 416/1976, App. IX, which reproduces many of the documents and correspondence relating to the alteration of the boundary in 1879.

An examination of the original documents, charts, and associated documents led Australia to conclude that the small islands of Kawa, Mata Kawa, and Kussa lying close to the Papua New Guinean coast were in fact part of Papua New Guinea and not included within the islands annexed by the 1879 proclamation.[11] While this came as a surprise to many Australians who were used to seeing the islands included as part of Queensland on most maps, the original documents clearly demonstrate that the 1879 line did not, in fact, embrace these islands.[12]

In addition to the problem of its actual location, the 1879 line came to be seen as a "border" in the same way as a land boundary. The line described in the 1879 Proclamation, however, is clearly only one that indicates the islands annexed to Queensland. At the time, the concept of sea or seabed boundaries, even for territorial seas, was not at all developed and the line was not intended to serve such a purpose. It was to have essentially the same status as the line designated in the 1867 Alaska cession agreement between Russia and the United States.[13] That agreement indicated the territory and adjacent islands to be ceded by reference to geographical limits defined in part by a line running across the Bering Sea and passing through certain designated points.[14] The dispute between the United States and Canada over the status for purposes of maritime boundary delimitation of the line A–B drawn by the Alaskan Boundary Tribunal, from Cape Muzon to the entrance to Portland Canal in the Dixon Entrance, also appears to involve questions similar to those raised by the 1879 line.[15]

The true position is that the 1879 line did not in any sense represent a maritime boundary. The position was complicated, however, by the fact that Australian legislation concerning offshore petroleum and sedentary species had used the 1879 line as a convenient administrative division between Queensland and Papua for purposes of jurisdiction over both living and nonliving seabed resources. While such an arrangement may have been satisfactory while Papua remained an Australian territory, it was not an appropriate basis on which to divide the area between two independent nations.[16] Because of the way that the 1879 line had been drawn, a number of anomalies also existed. For instance,

[11] The detailed reasoning and documentation that led to this conclusion are contained in a document entitled *Status of the Islands of Kawa, Mata Kawa and Kussa,* tabled in the Australian Parliament. The document is reproduced as an Annex to JOINT FOREIGN AFFAIRS AND DEFENCE COMMITTEE, THE TORRES STRAIT TREATY, [Australian] Parliamentary Paper 101/1979.

[12] This view is not universally shared. *See* the remarks of J. Griffin, *Territorial Implications in the Torres Strait,* in THE TORRES STRAIT TREATY 92–137 (P. Boyce & M. White eds., 1981).

[13] 15 Stat. 539, TS No. 301, 11 Bevans 1216.

[14] The U.S. State Department apparently takes the view that the 1867 line defines the boundary between the continental shelves of the United States and the USSR. *See* Feldman & Colson, *supra* note 5, at 751–53.

[15] Bourne & McRae, *Maritime Jurisdiction in the Dixon Entrance: The Alaska Boundary Re-examined,* 14 CAN. Y.B. INT'L L. 175 (1976).

[16] Papua New Guinea became independent on Sept. 16, 1975. In May 1976, the Foreign Ministers of Papua New Guinea and Australia publicly stated that the line "does not represent the Australian view of the appropriate permanent location of the seabed boundary," 47 AUSTL. FOREIGN AFF. REC. 336 (1976).

the line as drawn in Australian legislation did not accord a territorial sea of 3 miles to Bramble Cay. Australia was not prepared in the negotiations to forgo such a right or to regard itself as estopped from arguing that it had the right to a full territorial sea around Bramble Cay.

While the true status of the 1879 line was recognized early on in the official negotiations, the popular confusion over the matter did cause problems. The islanders and the state of Queensland, in particular, adopted the slogan "Border No Change" and saw any suggestion that maritime areas south of the 1879 line be given up to Papua New Guinea as an unnecessary concession by Australia. This reaction eventually abated, however, as the true state of affairs was gradually conveyed to the interested parties. It also lost much of its bite once it became clear that no Australian land territory was to be relinquished and that special arrangements to protect the livelihood of the local inhabitants would be included in any Treaty.

Nevertheless, the discussion and problems inspired by the 1879 line did highlight how accidents of history often play a significant role not just in land boundary delimitation, but also in maritime boundary delimitation.

History of the Negotiations

While Papua remained an Australian territory and New Guinea a United Nations Trust Territory, little consideration was given to the need for an international maritime boundary between them and Australia. As the prospect of independence for the territories increased in the early 1970's, attention began to be directed to the problem of the boundaries of the likely new state. In 1971 Australia negotiated an agreement with Indonesia that put on a secure basis the continental shelf boundary between Indonesia and Papua New Guinea,[17] but at the time of its independence on September 16, 1975, the maritime boundary between Papua New Guinea and Australia remained unsolved.

Negotiations had commenced as early as 1973. In a joint statement on January 17, 1973 by the newly elected Prime Minister of Australia, Gough Whitlam, and the Chief Minister of Papua New Guinea, Australia indicated that it was willing to negotiate relocation of the border but that it was reluctant to be party to any settlement not accepted by the islanders.[18] It was recognized that the state government of Queensland would also need to be consulted. Negotiations continued for the next few years with little public interest, other than occasional newspaper headlines of disputes between the Australian and Queensland governments, the latter seeing itself as guardian of the islanders' interests.[19] The new Australian Government elected in December 1975 moved quickly to advance negotiations. In June 1976 certain fundamental points were

[17] Agreement between Australia and Indonesia establishing Certain Seabed Boundaries, May 18, 1971, in UNITED NATIONS, NATIONAL LEGISLATION AND TREATIES RELATING TO THE LAW OF THE SEA, UN Doc. ST/LEG/SER.B/18, at 433 (1976), *reprinted in* 10 ILM 830 (1971).

[18] 44 AUSTL. FOREIGN AFF. REC. 41 (1973).

[19] A detailed description of the negotiations with Papua New Guinea, and between the Australian and Queensland governments, up to October 1975 appears in a statement to the Australian House of Representatives by Mr. Whitlam on Oct. 9, 1975, *reproduced in* 46 *id.* at 586 (1975).

agreed at the Foreign Minister level:[20]

> A seabed boundary would be delimited between Australia and Papua New Guinea. It would run through the protected zone which would be established in the Torres Strait. Papua New Guinea agreed that the seabed boundary would lie to the north of all Australian inhabited islands except Boigu, Dauan and Saibai. Australia accepted that the seabed boundary would be drawn in a location more southerly than the line at present applying under Australian legislation for offshore petroleum administration purposes.
>
> Papua New Guinea had accepted that Australia would retain all Australian inhabited islands. It had been agreed that the Australian territorial sea around the islands of Boigu, Dauan and Saibai, which would lie to the north of the seabed boundary, would be three miles, and that there would be a line delimiting the territorial seas between these islands and Papua New Guinea.
>
> A zone would be established in the Torres Strait to protect and preserve the traditional way of life and livelihood of the Torres Strait Islanders and the residents of the adjacent coast of Papua New Guinea, including fishing and freedom of movement throughout such a zone, both north and south of the seabed boundary.

It is of interest that at this time there was only agreement on negotiation of a seabed boundary. Reference was also made to Australian retention of all *in*habited islands, but no mention was made about the future of the uninhabited islands. Certainly, the attitude of Papua New Guinea at the time was that it was negotiating "an all purpose international boundary" in which each nation would have "full sovereignty," and that the new boundary line would be "on top of the water, under the sea and up in the sky."[21]

It became apparent by the end of 1976 that the two countries were seriously deadlocked. Both sides wanted a comprehensive settlement, but Australia was not prepared to allow the seabed line, which by this stage had been provisionally agreed, to become an all-purpose line, cutting off completely the Australian islands north of the line. This opposition was a reflection in part of increasing agitation by the islanders and the state government of Queensland not to "sell out" the islanders' interests. Nor was Australia prepared to contemplate the transfer of uninhabited islands. Any transfer of territory would create constitutional difficulties.[22]

In February 1977, the two parties decided to defer further negotiations for the immediate future, although they agreed to continue trying to resolve the issues through bilateral negotiations.[23] In addition to having reached an impasse,

[20] 47 *id.* at 336 (1976).

[21] JOINT FOREIGN AFFAIRS AND DEFENCE COMMITTEE, *supra* note 10, at 11–12.

[22] Section 123 of the Australian Constitution requires the consent of the Parliament of a state, and the approval of the majority of the electors of a state, before the limits of a state can be increased, diminished, or otherwise altered. Any cession of islands forming part of the state of Queensland would therefore be subject to this provision, and the necessary approvals were unlikely to be forthcoming.

[23] Text of joint communiqué by Prime Ministers of Australia and Papua New Guinea, Feb. 11, 1977, 48 AUSTL. FOREIGN AFF. REC. 88 (1977).

both Governments faced elections in 1977. At this time, moreover, Papua New Guinea enacted its National Seas legislation, which extended its territorial sea from 3 to 12 miles and provided for a 200-mile zone of offshore seas.[24] Consequently, Australia and Papua New Guinea needed to reach agreement on interim arrangements to take account of the proposed establishment of 200-mile fishing or economic zones.[25]

In early 1978, negotiations were resumed and rapid progress was made. It was then that Australia announced its finding that the three uninhabited small islands of Kawa, Mata Kawa, and Kussa just off the Papua New Guinean coast were not among the Torres Strait islands annexed to Queensland.[26] In May 1978, a detailed outline of the elements agreed between the two countries was made public.[27] For the first time, the delimitation of a separate fisheries resources line was recognized as a basis for a settlement, together with provisions for sharing the catch and freedom of navigation. Throughout the remainder of 1978, officials held detailed negotiations to translate the principles agreed by the Foreign Ministers into treaty provisions. Finally, on December 18, 1978, the Treaty was signed by the Prime Ministers and Foreign Ministers of the two countries. The Treaty has still not been ratified, not because of any change of heart by either side, but essentially because of difficulties met in implementing certain of the complex treaty provisions in domestic legislation.

The above brief outline shows that the final result only occurred after a breakdown in the negotiations. The rigid and single-focus approach of the initial round of negotiations, where attention was given primarily to drawing a single maritime boundary, did not lead to productive solutions. It was only after the adoption of an imaginative, broadly focused approach that a solution acceptable to all the parties concerned—not just governments but the people themselves—was achieved. The Treaty represents an *agreed* solution that was reached without the assistance of any third party. While the possibility of referring the dispute to the International Court of Justice was mentioned from time to time in the press, both sides appreciated that no tribunal or court would be able to provide a comprehensive solution that dealt satisfactorily with the whole complex of issues involved. That the negotiations were successful is testimony to the fact that a developing country and a developed country can

[24] The legislation consisted principally of the National Seas Act (No. 7 of 1977). It established a territorial sea of 12 miles, provided for declaration of archipelagic baselines, and created offshore seas extending 200 miles from the baselines. Five other specific resource-related laws were enacted. *See* Krueger & Nordquist, *The Evolution of the 200-Mile Exclusive Economic Zone: State Practice in the Pacific Basin*, 19 VA. J. INT'L L. 322, 353–55 (1979). Papua New Guinea has not yet established archipelagic baselines; the legislation is merely enabling in this respect.

[25] It was not until March 1978 that the National Seas legislation was actually proclaimed. By then Australia and Papua New Guinea had been able to work out suitable interim arrangements, which ensured as little overlap in jurisdiction as possible. *See* the statement by the Australian Foreign Minister, March 31, 1978, 49 AUSTL. FOREIGN AFF. REC. 152 (1978). It was November 1979 before Australia declared its own 200-mile fishing zone, at which time special interim arrangements in relation to the exercise of jurisdiction in the Torres Strait area were introduced. COMMONWEALTH OF AUSTRALIA GAZETTE S225 (Nov. 2, 1979).

[26] *Supra* note 11 and accompanying text.

[27] 49 AUSTL. FOREIGN AFF. REC. 242 (1978).

sit down and arrive at equitable solutions to problems concerning allocation of maritime resources. That the agreement contains so many novel and imaginative solutions says much for the ability of negotiation, if approached by both sides with an open mind and goodwill, to produce solutions to difficult problems. It is to the special features of the Treaty that this article will now turn.

Special Features of the Treaty

The People

As mentioned, the Torres Strait islanders are ethnically distinct from the Papua New Guineans of the immediately adjacent coastal area. At the time of the last Australian census for which there are figures (1971), there were 9,663 enumerated islanders. Of these about 16 percent lived on the main islands directly appurtenant to Cape York, the northern extremity of the Australian mainland. These islands include Thursday Island, the most heavily populated of the islands and the administrative center for the region. In this group of islands the islanders generally live as part of the general community. About 2,500 others, or less than 25 percent, live in the "reserve" islands scattered throughout the Strait, including Boigu, Dauan, and Saibai just off the Papuan coast. It is on these reserve islands that the traditional way of life of the islanders continues. In 1971 almost 60 percent of the islander population lived outside the Torres Strait region in other parts of Australia. The islanders are Australian citizens and form part of the population of the state of Queensland. No treaty could ignore their rights.[28]

Economic activity in the region is limited, but includes pearling and fishing. However, the pearling industry has suffered in recent years so that commercial fishing, particularly for barramundi and crayfish, holds the major economic potential for the area in the immediate future.

The people of coastal Papua to whom the Torres Strait is significant live mostly around the delta of the Fly River and on associated islands, including the large island of Daru, the administrative headquarters of the Western Province, which is located in the northeast corner of the Strait. Economically, they are not as well off as the Australian islanders and receive no pension or social security income. Unlike most of the islanders, they depend for a small cash income on fishing, particularly for barramundi and crayfish. The northern Warrior Reefs are a highly regarded fishing ground and Daru is being developed as a center for the processing and handling of much of the catch.[29]

In the past, there was freedom of movement between the islands and the coast of Papua New Guinea. Traditional activities were pursued without concern for the niceties of international boundaries or customs and immigration formalities. During the negotiations, the islanders made very clear to the Aus-

[28] For a detailed account of the islanders' way of life, see H. Duncan, *supra* note 8; Joint Foreign Affairs and Defence Committee, *supra* note 10, at 22–34.

[29] The study by Duncan, *supra* note 8, highlights the lack of interest by many of the islanders in earning cash income, because of an alternative source of income from public money. This is clearly not the attitude of Papua New Guineans, who are seeking to develop commercial fishing.

tralian Government their concern that traditional practices and freedom of movement be allowed to continue. The islanders insisted that "traditional boundaries" in fact existed between their areas and areas belonging to the inhabitants of Papua New Guinea.[30] These boundaries were similar to, but not identical with, the 1879 line referred to above. At the time of the negotiations, it was apparent that the use of the Strait by islanders and coastal Papuans involved considerable movement of both groups through the area. While not great in numbers, the islanders and coastal Papua New Guineans who lived in the Strait or its vicinity depended largely on its resources for their livelihood. Their traditional way of life was closely linked to the special features of the area.

In order to meet many of the concerns of the inhabitants and in recognition of the special environmental vulnerability of the area, the two Governments agreed in the Treaty to a number of special provisions designed to protect the area and its traditional inhabitants. Basically, this was done by establishing a Protected Zone, "comprising all the land, sea, airspace, seabed and subsoil" within a defined area,[31] which essentially comprises the whole of the central Torres Strait area, including the islands and reefs at the eastern and western entrances to the Strait.[32] The zone does not include the major administrative center of Thursday Island and its associated islands, nor does it include Daru, a similar Papua New Guinean administrative center.

The principal purpose of the parties in establishing the zone and "in determining its northern, southern, eastern and western boundaries" was stated to be "to protect the traditional way of life and livelihood of the traditional inhabitants including their traditional fishing and free movement."[33] A further purpose was to protect and preserve the marine environment and indigenous fauna and flora in the Protected Zone and its vicinity.[34] By referring to the determination of the boundaries of the zone, the parties attempted to acknowledge in some way that regard had been had to the representations by the islanders concerning the location of their traditional boundaries. Within the zone free movement and the performance of "lawful traditional activities" are to be permitted.[35]

The establishment of precise boundaries of the zone obviously could create difficulties if a particular activity happened to extend a little beyond the designated boundary. In order to avoid difficulties that may arise from the unavoidable rigidity of lines on maps, provision is made to extend the various rights conferred in the zone to areas "in the vicinity of" the zone. This term is not defined, other than as describing "an area the outer limits of which might vary according to the context in which the expression is used."[36] Its lack of certainty may cause difficulties in law enforcement, but without such a provision necessary flexibility would have been lost.

[30] *See* the islanders' views in a memorandum prepared by Island Chairmen in September 1975, JOINT FOREIGN AFFAIRS AND DEFENCE COMMITTEE, *supra* note 10, at 40.

[31] Art. 10(1).

[32] Annex 9 to the Treaty gives the detailed description.

[33] Art. 10(3).

[34] Art. 10(4).

[35] Art. 11.

[36] Art. 1(3).

The Treaty defines "traditional inhabitants" broadly. One of the criteria is that the islanders or Papua New Guineans concerned "maintain traditional customary associations with areas or features in or in the vicinity of the Protected Zone in relation to their subsistence or livelihood or social, cultural or religious activities."[37] "Traditional activities" is also defined broadly, and it is provided that in applying the definition, except to activities of a commercial nature, "traditional" shall be interpreted liberally and in the light of prevailing custom.[38] Similarly, the definition of "traditional fishing" concentrates on the purpose of fishing, rather than on the manner, and thus seeks to avoid problems caused by the use of new technology.[39]

As well as free movement and performance of traditional activities, each party agrees to allow, on a reciprocal basis, the pursuit by traditional inhabitants of the other customary rights of access to and usage of areas of land, seabed, seas, estuaries, and coastal tidal areas that are in or in the vicinity of the Protected Zone.[40] Within the zone each party also agrees to take legislative and other measures to protect and preserve the marine environment.[41] Moreover, provision is made for the environmental assessment of any activity that may cause pollution or other damage to the marine environment[42] and for the protection of indigenous species of fauna and flora.[43] In a further effort to protect the islanders and their environment, the parties agreed to a moratorium for a minimum of 10 years on the mining and drilling of the seabed and subsoil of the Protected Zone for purposes of exploration or exploitation of mineral resources.[44]

The freedoms indicated above that are to apply in the Protected Zone obviously could cause problems if abused. Immigration, customs, quarantine, and health formalities therefore continue to apply to the traditional inhabitants, except in cases of temporary stay for the performance of traditional activities.[45] Each party reserves its right to limit free movement to control abuses involving illegal entry or evasion of justice and to apply immigration, customs, health, and quarantine measures to meet problems that may arise such as outbreaks of disease.[46] Adequate control of quarantine and illegal immigration were of particular concern to Australia.

Finally, in order to ensure the effective working of the zone, liaison arrangements[47] and a Joint Advisory Council consisting of representatives of the national Governments, regional governments, and traditional inhabitants are established.[48] The council is only advisory and cannot adopt or implement measures of its own in the area. Management and administration in the zone remain with the respective governments.

This extensive description of the arrangements for the special Protected Zone has been provided because they represent an important component of the Treaty. They indicate that the needs of inhabitants of an area subject to maritime

[37] Art. 1(1).

[38] *Ibid.*

[39] *Ibid.*

[40] Art. 12.

[41] Art. 13(1) and (2).

[42] Art. 13(5).

[43] Art. 14.

[44] Art. 15.

[45] Art. 16.

[46] Art. 16(3).

[47] Art. 18.

[48] Art. 19.

delimitation can be dealt with in special ways, at the same time that the actual delimitation issues are treated separately. The accommodation of the special needs and interests of the inhabitants by the imposition of a Protected Zone over the main area in dispute made possible the actual delimitation of the area in a way that would probably not otherwise have been acceptable to either Government. If the delimitation had been approached in the traditional way of seeking only to draw a single maritime boundary, it is unlikely that an agreement acceptable to those whose interests would be most directly affected could have been reached. As it is, the local inhabitants have accepted the agreement secure in the knowledge that their traditional life style is protected and will not be seriously jeopardized by delimitation lines dividing up the area.[49]

Even before Papua New Guinea became independent, the concept of a protected zone was in the air. In 1974 the Parliament of the state of Queensland passed a resolution urging the establishment of an international marine park in the area.[50] At the same time, the Australian Government was working on proposals for an environmentally protected area.[51] Throughout the negotiations, there was a willingness by both sides to consider special provisions that would effectively protect the interests of the islanders, although they were essentially devised to meet Australian concerns. The solution that emerged is unique in comparison with measures adopted by other states to secure protection of special areas.

International commissions to advise on the use and management of particular areas of water are not new in international law. For example, the Convention on Fishing and Conservation of the Living Resources in the Baltic Sea establishes an international body to "keep under review the living resources" and to make recommendations to be implemented by the member states.[52] Similarly, Canada and the United States have used an International Joint Commission to regulate the quality of the water in the Great Lakes.[53] These international arrangements differ, however, from the Torres Strait Treaty, in which an area is actually given a special status—regardless of the jurisdictional rights of particular states—certain rights are conferred on its inhabitants, and Governments have obliged themselves to manage it with a view to protecting both the local inhabitants' rights and the environment. Although the special status and rights in the zone are directly created by the Treaty, it is left to each Government to ensure that they are given effect.[54] To this extent, the jurisdictional division of the area remains significant.

[49] Extensive consultations were held with the local inhabitants, including several visits to the area by Australian Government ministers.

[50] On April 2, 1974. For the text, see JOINT COMMITTEE ON FOREIGN AFFAIRS AND DEFENCE, *supra* note 10, at 77.

[51] *See* the statement by Mr. Whitlam in October 1975, *supra* note 19.

[52] Art. IX, UN Doc. A/C.1/1035 (1973), *reproduced in* 12 ILM 1291 (1973).

[53] Treaty Relating to Boundary Waters of Canada and the United States, Jan. 11, 1909, 36 Stat. 2448, TS No. 548, 12 Bevans 319; Agreement on Great Lakes Water Quality, April 15, 1972, 23 UST 301, 24 UST 2268, TIAS Nos. 7312, 7747, *reprinted in* 11 ILM 694 (1972); Agreement on Great Lakes Water Quality, Nov. 22, 1978, 30 UST 1383, TIAS No. 9257.

[54] As mentioned above, the Joint Advisory Council has no executive or management powers under the Treaty.

Maritime Jurisdiction

The Treaty does not treat delimitation in respect of maritime jurisdiction as raising a single question. Instead, it establishes separate lines for seabed and fisheries jurisdiction and makes special provision for residual jurisdiction. While for the most part the two lines that define the respective limits of the seabed and fisheries jurisdiction of the two parties are identical, in the Torres Strait area itself they diverge. This is significant. It constitutes a clear precedent for the separate treatment of the seabed and superjacent waters for delimitation purposes.

The Treaty describes a line that divides the area of seabed and subsoil over which Australia and Papua New Guinea are to have "seabed jurisdiction."[55] The definition in Article 1 states that "seabed jurisdiction" is "sovereign rights over the continental shelf in accordance with international law, and includes jurisdiction over low-tide elevations, and the right to exercise such jurisdiction in respect of those elevations, in accordance with international law." It is of interest to note the special reference to low-tide elevations, to which further reference will be made below.[56]

The seabed line runs from a point in the west on the previously agreed Indonesia/Australia continental shelf boundary,[57] through the center of Torres Strait, and then out into the Coral Sea in the east. The line eventually ends at a point that is equidistant not only from Australian and Papua New Guinean base points (Mellish Reef and Pocklington Reef, respectively) but also from a base point that the Solomon Islands is expected to use in subsequent maritime delimitations with Australia and Papua New Guinea. It should be noted that, because of the geomorphological configuration of the area, the seabed line extends more than 200 nautical miles from the base points. The fisheries jurisdiction line, by contrast, terminates at a different point.[58] The western portion of the line essentially represents a median line between the Australian and Papua New Guinean coasts. The eastern portion is a median line in part, but in the area where the small Coral Sea islands become relevant, the line is a modified median that neither gives full weight to the islands nor completely ignores their influence. The line in this area seems consistent with those described in other delimitation agreements involving islands that distort a mainland-to-mainland median line.[59] (See map 1.)

In the Torres Strait itself, the seabed line passes to the south of a number of Australian islands, which have only a 3-mile territorial sea around them. These include the three inhabited islands of Boigu, Saibai, and Dauan. A

[55] Art. 4(1).

[56] *Infra* p. 339.

[57] *Supra* note 17.

[58] It terminates at the point where the 200-mile zones cease to overlap.

[59] *See* Karl, *Islands and the Delimitation of the Continental Shelf: A Framework for Analysis,* 71 AJIL 642 (1977). R. D. Hodgson in 1973 suggested a special regime might be considered to protect the interests of masked coastal states such as Papua New Guinea: *Islands and Special Circumstances,* in LAW OF THE SEA: THE EMERGING REGIME OF THE OCEANS 137, 173 (J. K. Gamble & G. Pontecorvo eds., 1973). *See also* the comprehensive analysis of state practice in C. R. SYMMONS, THE MARITIME ZONES OF ISLANDS IN INTERNATIONAL LAW, ch. IV (1979).

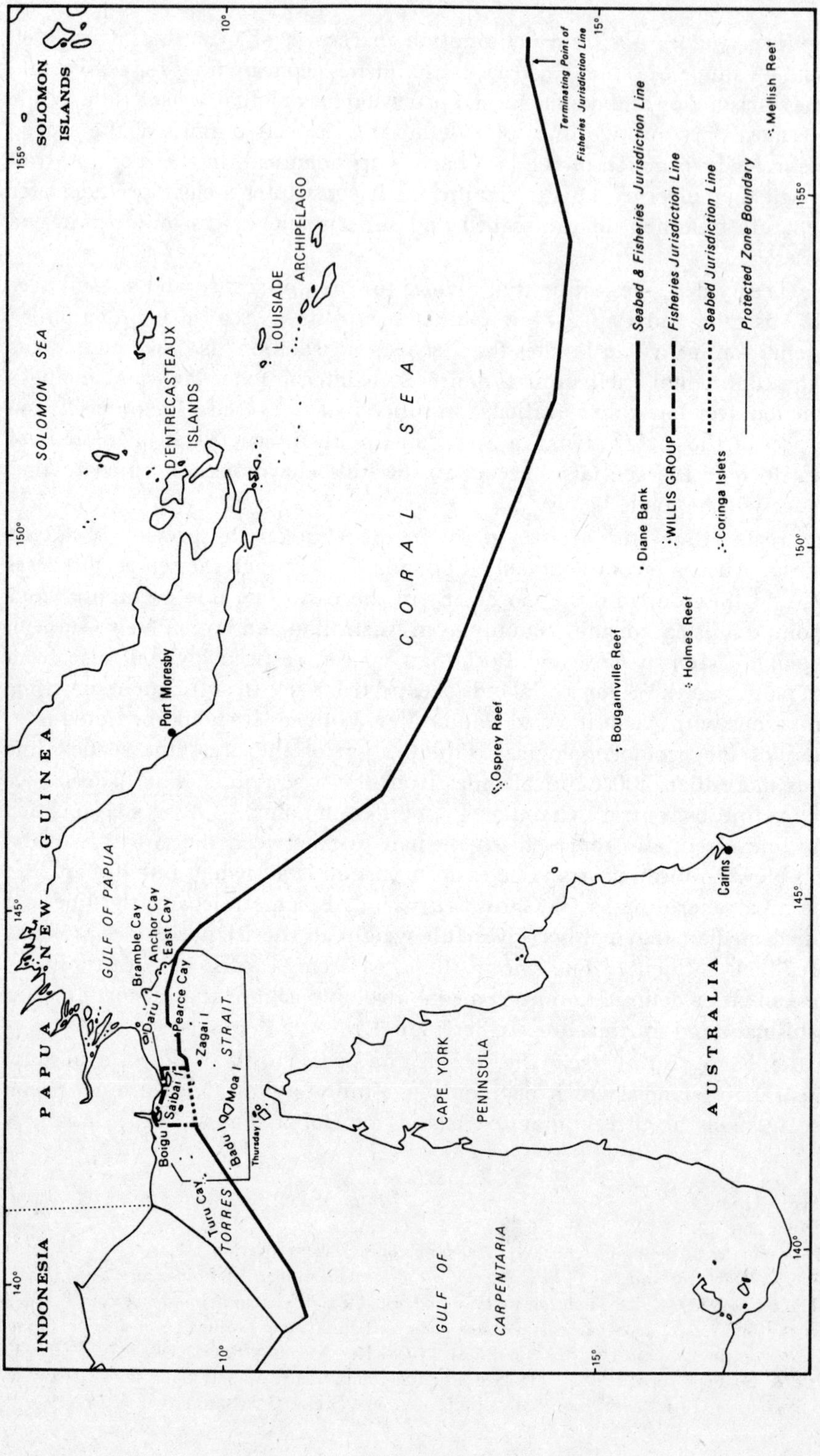

MAP 1
DELIMITATION LINES AGREED IN THE TORRES STRAIT TREATY

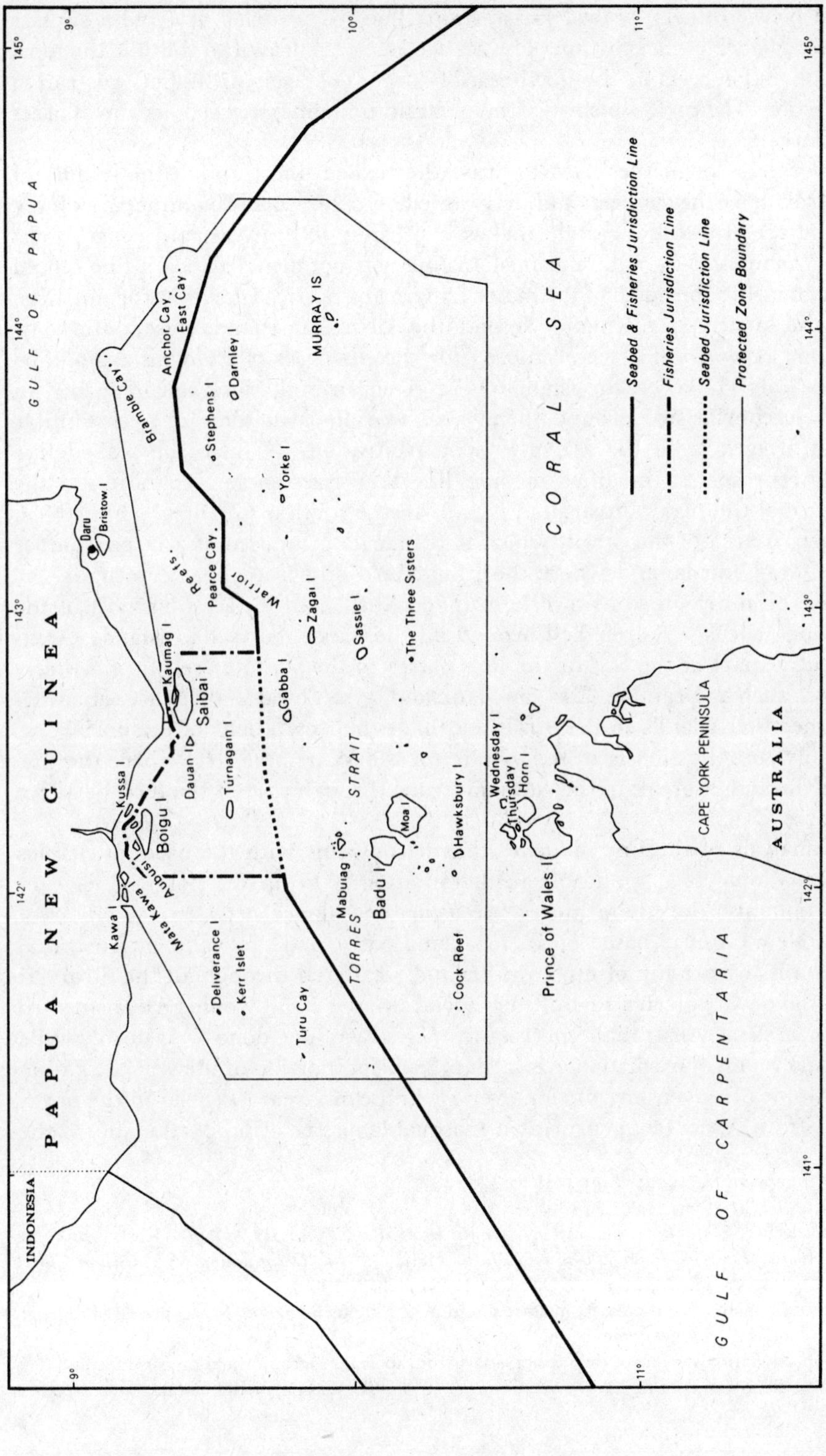

MAP 2
CENTRAL TORRES STRAIT AREA

number of Australian enclaves are thus created in areas otherwise falling within Papua New Guinean seabed jurisdiction. The parties tried to avoid a similar result for fisheries jurisdiction. The seabed line was drawn so that for the most part the major reefs to the northeast of Cape York remain under Australian jurisdiction. (Map 2 illustrates the delimitation lines agreed in the Torres Strait area.)

The precise principles used to draw the seabed line through the middle of the Strait have never been publicly stated. However, an examination of the maps attached to the Treaty[60] makes it possible to draw certain conclusions. First, a mainland-to-mainland median line was not drawn. Such a line would have run just to the north of the major fringing or portico islands at the northern tip of the Australian mainland. Second, the Australian islands close to the coast of Papua New Guinea were ignored for the purposes of charting a modified median line. However, the islands were given an individual belt of seabed (a 3-mile territorial sea) around them.[61] The result is in some respects similar to that arrived at in the *Anglo-French* arbitration.[62] Third, the seabed line largely represents a modified median line that gives some recognition to the influence of the major Australian islands in the south of the Strait. Fourth, in the eastern area of the Strait, which is primarily composed of a large number of reefs and shoals, and where the islands are numerous but very small, the line has been drawn so as to retain under Australian jurisdiction most of the reefs and at least a 3-mile belt around all the major Australian islands. As in the central part of the Strait, the line passes to the south of certain northerly features, such as Bramble, East, and Anchor Cays. These features are separated from the other islands in the Strait and have their own belts of territorial sea. The only complication is in the vicinity of the Warrior Reefs, where the line passes through a break in the reefs and runs through part of the territorial sea of Pearce Cay.

An analysis of the line indicates that it conforms with the basic principles of international law applicable to delimitation.[63] From the point of view of proportionality, the line achieves a reasonable balance between the rights of Papua New Guinea, based on its mainland coast, and the rights of Australia, based on its ownership of numerous islands scattered throughout the Strait. If every island were given a 12-mile territorial sea, the Strait would be transformed into an area of Australian sovereignty. This was not done.[64] Instead, while Australia retains jurisdiction over a significant proportion of the seabed, Papua New Guinea is given jurisdiction over a significant area of seabed in the north of the Strait. Apart from ensuring a reasonable degree of proportionality,[65] the

[60] The maps are *reproduced in* 18 ILM 325, 327 (1979).

[61] *Infra* p. 342.

[62] *Supra* note 3.

[63] *See* Blecher, *Equitable Delimitation of Continental Shelf,* 73 AJIL 60 (1979); Karl, *supra* note 59; Symmons, *The Canadian 200-mile Fishery Limit and the Delimitation of Maritime Zones around St. Pierre and Miquelon,* 12 OTTAWA L. REV. 145 (1980).

[64] Australia from 1967 did assert jurisdiction in a 12-mile fishing zone. It was prepared to forgo this in the final Treaty settlement.

[65] Proportionality was one of the factors, apart from special geographic and physical factors, that the International Court in the *North Sea Continental Shelf* cases said should be taken into account. [1969] ICJ REP. at 54.

line is essentially a modified median line. The reasons for its modification are not difficult to perceive. The geographical characteristics of the area made a pure median line inappropriate. Other circumstances that were regarded as relevant, such as security considerations, the distribution of the natural resources, and the use of the area by inhabitants of the two countries, are primarily taken care of in special provisions on the particular issue and not in the seabed delimitation itself. From the point of view of the development of the international law of delimitation, the actual location of the seabed jurisdiction line therefore sets no new precedents. It is the special features associated with the drawing of the line that may bear on the further development of international law.

During the negotiations, it was proposed that a seabed line not be drawn through the central Torres Strait area at all. Advocates of this course, particularly some of the traditional inhabitants, argued that the establishment of a protected zone in which mineral exploitation would be prohibited, or limited for a number of years, would remove the need to draw a seabed line through the area.[66] This argument did not prevail. The two Governments considered it necessary to avoid any possibility of future disagreement at a time when a solution might be more difficult to reach. To leave a gap in the seabed line was seen as leaving open for future dispute one of the basic issues in the maritime delimitation. For similar reasons, joint control or management of seabed mineral resources in the area was also seen as an unsatisfactory solution.[67]

As mentioned, the separate fisheries jurisdiction line is identical with the seabed jurisdiction line, except in the central Torres Strait where it diverges to embrace the Australian islands just off the coast of Papua New Guinea.[68] The northern limit of the line in this area of divergence represents in part the territorial sea delimitation line between certain Australian islands and the Papua New Guinean coast.[69] The eastern and western limits of the area of divergence are lines running south along the meridians of longitude from the respective eastern and western limits of the territorial sea of the Australian islands of Saibai and Boigu. The divergence was made in recognition of the importance of the living resources of the area to the inhabitants of the Australian islands and in order to avoid establishing Australian-inhabited enclaves north of a general all-purpose maritime boundary between Australia and Papua New Guinea. Such a result would have given the islanders the clear sense that they were cut off from Australia, and perhaps vulnerable to the wishes of Papua New Guinea. The same considerations did not apply to the uninhabited islands of Bramble Cay, Anchor Cay, and East Cay or to Deliverance Island, Kerr Islet, and Turu Cay. They became enclaves north of the fisheries and seabed lines, and they have 3-mile territorial seas. The southern part of the territorial

[66] JOINT FOREIGN AFFAIRS AND DEFENCE COMMITTEE, *supra* note 9, at 40.

[67] *Contrast* the Agreement between Japan and the Republic of Korea Concerning Joint Development of the Southern Part of the Continental Shelf Adjacent to the Two Countries, Jan. 30, 1974, *reproduced in* 2 S. ODA, THE INTERNATIONAL LAW OF OCEAN DEVELOPMENT 95 (1975).

[68] Art. 4(2). Fisheries jurisdiction is defined in Article 1 as "sovereign rights for the purpose of exploring and exploiting, conserving and managing fisheries resources other than sedentary species."

[69] Art. 3(1) and Ann. 1 to the Treaty.

sea of Pearce Cay is crossed by the seabed and fisheries jurisdiction lines. It is therefore not an enclave, even though the island itself lies north of the lines.

The seabed and fisheries jurisdiction lines do not apply to maritime jurisdiction in respect of all relevant matters, such as pollution or marine scientific research. The Draft Law of the Sea Convention[70] recognizes, however, that the jurisdiction of a state in its economic zone extends to such matters. In the Treaty, the parties dealt with this problem by making special provision for "residual jurisdiction," which is defined as:

> (a) jurisdiction over the area other than seabed jurisdiction or fisheries jurisdiction, including jurisdiction other than seabed jurisdiction or fisheries jurisdiction insofar as it relates to *inter alia*:
>
> (i) the preservation of the marine environment;
> (ii) marine scientific research; and
> (iii) the production of energy from the water, currents and winds; and
>
> (b) seabed and fisheries jurisdiction to the extent that the exercise of such jurisdiction is not directly related to the exploration or exploitation of resources or to the prohibition of, or refusal to authorise, activities subject to that jurisdiction.[71]

Special provision is made for the exercise of this jurisdiction in the "top hat" area, where the seabed and fisheries jurisdiction lines diverge.[72] Outside this area, no special provision is made. It may be assumed, therefore, that when full economic zones are established,[73] full jurisdiction over residual matters will be exercised by each party, outside the "top hat" area, as if the seabed and fisheries jurisdiction line represented an economic zone delimitation line. This would be in accord with developing international law, as reflected in Article 56 of the Draft Law of the Sea Convention.[74]

In the "top hat" area where jurisdiction is divided, the exercise of jurisdiction over pollution, for instance, is closely related to the particular resources for which protection is sought. Where the seabed and fisheries lines diverge, Australia will obviously have an interest in the prevention of pollution affecting fisheries resources, while Papua New Guinea will have an interest in pollution related to seabed resources. Thus, the parties agreed in this area that "(a) neither Party shall exercise residual jurisdiction without the concurrence of the other Party; and (b) the Parties shall consult with a view to reaching agreement on the most effective method of application of measures involving the exercise of residual jurisdiction."[75]

Interestingly, the definition of "residual jurisdiction" consists of two elements,[76] one of which is jurisdiction other than seabed or fisheries jurisdiction.

[70] Art. 56, *supra* note 1.

[71] Art. 4(4).

[72] Art. 4(3).

[73] Papua New Guinea under its National Seas legislation, *supra* note 24, established a 200-mile zone of offshore seas. It has not, however, legislated to control matters such as scientific research or pollution. Australia has to date only established a 200-mile fishing zone.

[74] Article 56 sets out the matters over which a coastal state has sovereign rights or jurisdiction. Article 59 recognizes that Article 56 may not be exhaustive and provides for resolution of conflicts that may arise in respect of unattributed rights or jurisdiction.

[75] Art. 4(3).

[76] *Supra* note 71.

This element includes jurisdiction with regard to preservation of the marine environment and control of marine scientific research. It also includes jurisdiction with regard to the "production of energy from the water, currents and winds." Unlike Article 56(1)(a) of the Draft Law of the Sea Convention,[77] which gives the coastal state sovereign rights over this activity when it is engaged in "for the economic exploitation or exploration of the zone," the Treaty treats the production of energy as a matter of residual jurisdiction that does not form part of fisheries or seabed jurisdiction.

As for the second element of residual jurisdiction, matters may fall within it that appear at first glance to be included within seabed or fisheries jurisdiction, if the exercise of such jurisdiction is "not directly related to the exploration or exploitation of resources or to the prohibition of, or refusal to authorise, activities subject to that jurisdiction." Essentially, therefore, any exercise of jurisdiction not directly related to the control of seabed or fisheries resources falls within the definition of residual jurisdiction.

If one takes the jurisdiction of a state over artificial islands, installations, or structures as an example, one can see how the definition works. Article 60 of the Draft Law of the Sea Convention recognizes the exclusive jurisdiction of a coastal state in its economic zone over such islands and over certain installations and structures.[78] Article 80 extends this jurisdiction to areas of continental shelf.[79] However, the definitions of "seabed jurisdiction" and "fisheries jurisdiction" in the Treaty, when read with that of "residual jurisdiction," only confer jurisdiction over these matters on a state to the extent that they relate to the exploration and exploitation of the seabed or fisheries resources. Thus, the jurisdiction of Australia and Papua New Guinea over artificial islands in the area of divergence only extends to artificial islands that are directly related to the exploration or exploitation of the particular resources over which the individual state has jurisdiction. A similar result obtains for installations and structures, although Article 60 would not, in any event, confer jurisdiction on a coastal state over every such installation and structure.

The reference to "jurisdiction over low-tide elevations" in the definition of "seabed jurisdiction"[80] appears to preclude any argument that a low-tide elevation is an artificial island and thus subject to the provisions on residual jurisdiction. The inclusion of this reference was also intended to prevent the argument from being raised, in areas outside the area of divided jurisdiction, that the jurisdiction of the party entitled to exercise seabed jurisdiction did not run in respect of these features. Because the area is full of low-tide elevations of one kind or another, it was thought desirable to put the matter beyond doubt.

Although the Treaty demonstrates the feasibility of separate maritime delimitation lines for separate purposes such as fisheries and seabed resources, if states do so agree, it is clear that they must also determine how to deal with

[77] *Supra* note 1.

[78] *Ibid.* Article 60 only confers jurisdiction over installations and structures for the purposes provided for in Article 56 and other economic purposes or if they may interfere with the exercise of the rights of the coastal state in the zone.

[79] *Ibid.* Article 80 applies Article 60 *mutatis mutandis* to the continental shelf.

[80] *Supra* p. 333.

matters of residual jurisdiction in areas of divergence. In the Torres Strait Treaty, the parties essentially left this question for future resolution by mutual agreement, but they defined "residual jurisdiction" broadly so that it encompasses jurisdiction over any matter not directly related to resource exploration and exploitation. Consequently, they have forgone certain rights that otherwise, in the light of developments in international law, would be within their jurisdiction by virtue of their sovereign rights over an area for resource purposes. The fact that the two parties agreed in this particular case to these special arrangements reflects their belief that to a large extent the exercise of jurisdiction over matters such as artificial islands in this particular area may be some time off. It also reflects their judgment that it is not possible to deal with matters such as pollution or scientific research divorced from the activity to which they relate, whether it be seabed resource extraction or something else. With goodwill on both sides, there seems no reason why the novel provisions on residual jurisdiction should not work. The solution reached belies the suggestion of some[81] that a single maritime boundary "will invariably be adopted" by states and reinforces the thesis of this article that one should not approach delimitation issues with a focus on a single objective.[82]

In fact, Australia may well conclude another maritime delimitation agreement that provides for separate seabed and fisheries jurisdiction lines. This agreement would be with Indonesia in the Timor Sea area.[83] Negotiations are still under way, but on an interim basis the outer limit of the Australian fishing zone does not extend in certain areas as far as the seabed line negotiated in 1972.[84]

Before leaving the question of maritime jurisdiction, reference should be made to Article 9 of the Treaty, which deals with wrecks. Jurisdiction over wrecks of vessels or aircraft on the seabed is acknowledged to belong to the party who has seabed jurisdiction over the area where the wreck is located. There is provision for the parties to consult if a wreck of historical or special significance to one party is found in an area under the jurisdiction of the other. This provision reflects the parties' concern to protect historic objects found at sea, a concern that is given further recognition in Article 303 of the Draft

[81] *E.g.*, McRae, *supra* note 5, at 301.

[82] An interesting argument is made by Professor Lumb that, in order to avoid different delimitation lines, it may be possible in some circumstances for fisheries zones to be delimited by lines other than median lines. This writer is not attracted by the argument. Lumb, *The Delimitation of Maritime Boundaries in the Timor Sea,* 7 AUSTL. Y.B. INT'L L. 72, 84–86 (1981).

[83] Negotiations between Australia and Indonesia are being conducted to fill the "gap" opposite East Timor in the seabed line negotiated by Australia and Indonesia in 1972. At the time, East Timor was a Portuguese colony and no separate agreement was reached in relation to this area. Negotiations are also being held to reach agreement on a delimitation line for fisheries purposes.

[84] When Australia established a 200-mile fishing zone in 1979, the interim delimitation line established between Australia and Indonesia was a median line drawn from the most favorable base points, including a number of small islands. COMMONWEALTH OF AUSTRALIA GAZETTE, *supra* note 25, at S225. In the Timor Sea area, however, it does not extend in places as far as the seabed line negotiated in 1972. *See* Agreement between Australia and Indonesia establishing certain Seabed Boundaries in the Area of the Timor and Arafura Seas, supplementary to the Agreement of 18 May 1971, Oct. 9, 1972, in NATIONAL LEGISLATION AND TREATIES RELATING TO THE LAW OF THE SEA, *supra* note 17, at 441, *reprinted in* 11 ILM 1272 (1972) and 12 *id.* at 357 (1973).

Convention on the Law of the Sea.[85] While Article 303 refrains from indicating the basis for jurisdiction over archaeological and historical objects,[86] Article 9 clearly asserts that jurisdiction over such objects appertains to the coastal state on whose continental shelf the objects are located. Australia has asserted such jurisdiction in the past.[87]

The Islands

As often happens when islands are involved, sovereignty over certain islands in Torres Strait became an issue in dispute that affected the delimitation of maritime areas. The Treaty, however, deals fully with this issue. Article 2, paragraph 1 provides that Papua New Guinea recognizes the sovereignty of Australia over more than a dozen named islands north of the seabed line, and all islands lying between the mainland of the two countries and south of the seabed jurisdiction line. Paragraph 2 of Article 2 states that no island over which Australia has sovereignty other than those specified in the list lies north of the seabed line.

The Torres Strait area is full of reefs and shoals and low-tide elevations. Its character is such that islands may develop over time. Moreover, there was room for argument during the negotiations over whether certain features actually amounted to islands under international law.[88] Certain of the features over which Papua New Guinea accepted Australian sovereignty, such as Pearce Cay and East Cay, are in fact minuscule, consisting of only a few rocks or small sand cays.[89] In these circumstances, paragraph 2 of Article 2 is designed to prevent Australia from arguing that any other features north of the seabed line amount to islands under its sovereignty. This provision is reinforced by Article 2(3)(b),[90] which as drafted is ambiguous about the position of future features

[85] *Supra* note 1.

[86] Article 303 was first adopted at the resumed ninth session in August 1980. It recognizes that states have the duty to protect archaeological objects and objects of historical origin found at sea. It then provides that in order to control traffic in such objects the coastal state may, in exercising its rights in relation to the contiguous zone, presume that their removal from the seabed from the area of the contiguous zone would result in an infringement within its territory or territorial sea of the regulations of the coastal state that apply to the contiguous zone. This most unusual provision represents a compromise that was forced on a largely apathetic conference. From a legal point of view, it represents a peculiar addition to the contiguous zone regime. Owing largely to the efforts of Australia, the article goes on to provide that it is without prejudice to other international agreements and rules of international law regarding the protection of archaeological objects. For further discussion of Article 303, see Oxman, *The Third United Nations Conference on the Law of the Sea: The Ninth Session (1980)*, 75 AJIL 211, 239–41 (1981). For archaeological and historical objects found in the Area beyond national jurisdiction, see the Draft Convention, Art. 149.

[87] Historic Shipwrecks Act, 1976.

[88] The generally accepted definition of an island at international law is "a naturally-formed area of land, surrounded by water, which is above water at high tide." Geneva Convention on the Territorial Sea and the Contiguous Zone, 15 UST 1606, TIAS No. 5639, 516 UNTS 205, Art. 10.

[89] An examination of Annex 4 to the Treaty, which illustrates the territorial sea around certain of the islands, indicates the tiny features that were categorized as islands.

[90] Article 2(3)(b) provides that Australia recognizes the sovereignty of Papua New Guinea over "(b) all the other islands that lie between the mainlands of the two countries and north of the [seabed] line . . ., other than the islands specified in subparagraph 1(a) of this Article." *See*

that may emerge. Papua New Guinea probably regards the provision as ambulatory in nature. It is not clear that Australia does.

The other significant provision relating to sovereignty over islands is paragraph 3 of Article 2, in which Australia recognizes Papua New Guinean sovereignty over the islands of Kawa, Mata Kawa, and Kussa. As already mentioned, it was only in 1978 that Australia discovered that the islands were not historically part of its territory. Although at that time the Government was accused of "researching away" the islands, a well-detailed and documented case was presented for public scrutiny.[91]

Early in the negotiations, Papua New Guinea sought the transfer to it of all uninhabited islands in the northern part of the Strait. This demand was strongly opposed by the Australian Government and various interests in Australia, including the Torres Strait islanders and the state government of Queensland. The discovery of a sound historical basis for saying that certain islands never formed part of Australia therefore enabled Australia to appear to be giving Papua New Guinea something in return for the latter's acceptance of Australian sovereignty over all other islands. Once the question of sovereignty over islands could be settled amicably, the basis for drawing lines of maritime jurisdiction became clearer.

The Treaty contains another significant provision on islands, the agreement by both parties to limit their territorial seas. Australia has to date only claimed a 3-mile territorial sea around its territory.[92] Papua New Guinea in 1977 established a 12-mile territorial sea.[93] Under Article 3, Australia agreed to limit the territorial sea around its islands north of the seabed line to 3 miles. For the northernmost islands, it was necessary to delimit the northern part of their territorial sea with that of the Papua New Guinean mainland.[94] The delimitation of other parts of the territorial sea of those islands and of that of other Australian islands north of the seabed line is described specifically in an annex to the Treaty.[95] The outer limits of the territorial seas consist of a series of intersecting arcs of circles having a radius of 3 miles and drawn from specified points. This method was adopted rather than defining baselines because of the unstable nature of many of the islands' foreshores and the difficulty of actually ascertaining the low-water mark around them. The problem is acute in many cases because the islands are surrounded by mangroves. Thus, the Treaty specifically provides that around these islands the "territorial seas shall not be enlarged or reduced, even if there were to be any change in the configuration of a coastline or a different result from any further survey."[96]

Papua New Guinea for its part agreed not to extend its territorial sea into certain areas. These include the agreed areas of Australian territorial sea to the north of the seabed line, the agreed area of Australian fisheries jurisdiction

---

Dingley, *Eruptions in International Law: Emerging Volcanic Islands and the Law of Territorial Acquisition*, 11 CORNELL INT'L L.J. 121 (1978).

[91] *Supra* note 11.

[92] It did, however, claim a 12-mile fishing zone in 1967.

[93] *Supra* note 24.

[94] Art. 3(1).

[95] Ann. 3 to the Treaty. The limits are shown on maps forming Annex 4.

[96] Art. 3(2).

north of the seabed line, and the area south of the agreed seabed line.[97] Nor is it to intrude into these areas with archipelagic baselines or archipelagic waters. In the absence of such a provision, a 12-mile Papua New Guinean territorial sea could seriously intrude into areas that had otherwise been agreed to be subject to Australian jurisdiction.

It may be argued that Australia could legally have claimed a continental shelf around the islands greater than the 3 miles to which it agreed. Certainly, the *Anglo-French* arbitration[98] suggests that enclaves on the continental shelf of another state are entitled to at least 12 nautical miles of their own shelf, particularly as the 12-mile limit of territorial sea is becoming generally accepted in international law.[99] But just as with the Aegean Sea, the consequence here of a general claim to a 12-mile territorial sea around all islands needs to be kept in mind. Such a claim would effectively have turned the Torres Strait area into a sea of Australian jurisdiction extending up to within a mile or so of the Papua New Guinean mainland. (This was in fact largely the case under the 12-mile fishing zone established by Australia in 1967.) Such a result was not seen as satisfactory or equitable by either side. The agreement by Australia to limit its territorial sea should be seen as part of the overall settlement under which Australian interests were largely protected. A protected zone safeguards the interests of the inhabitants, and the fisheries enforcement provisions enable Australia to exercise jurisdiction over its nationals no matter where an alleged offense occurs. Australian retention of sovereignty over large territorial seas in the northernmost part of the Strait was thus seen as unnecessary.

On the other hand, throughout the negotiations Papua New Guinea sought to gain Australian agreement to proposals that would give it some control over the uninhabited islands, even if transfer of sovereignty was not possible. Australia, however, was not prepared to forgo the right to a territorial sea around the small uninhabited islands. Australia could argue, with the support of good authority, that every piece of territory gives rise to an appurtenant territorial sea and that it is not appropriate for territory not to be accorded its normal appurtenant maritime rights up to at least 3 miles.[100] Nevertheless, Australia did agree to special provisions on fisheries within the territorial sea around

[97] Art. 3(6)(b).

[98] *Supra* note 3.

[99] *See* the discussion in Symmons, *supra* note 63.

[100] International lawyers appear divided over whether a solution by which a state would renounce any territorial sea around certain territory is possible. In the *Fisheries* case between Norway and the United Kingdom, Lord McNair, in his dissenting opinion, said:

> To every State whose land territory is at any place washed by the sea, international law attaches a corresponding portion of maritime territory consisting of what the law calls territorial waters. . . . International law does not say to a State: "You are entitled to claim territorial waters if you want them." No maritime State can refuse them. . . . The possession of this territory is not optional, not dependent upon the will of the State, but compulsory.

[1951] ICJ REP. 116, 160. This view of the inseparability of territorial sea from land is supported by J. H. W. Verzijl because "as a general rule" the territorial sea has "no independent existence as an element of the national territory severed from the coast which it borders." 3 J. VERZIJL, INTERNATIONAL LAW IN HISTORICAL PERSPECTIVE 54–55 (1970). This view is also supported in 1 L. OPPENHEIM, INTERNATIONAL LAW 463 (8th ed. H. Lauterpacht, 1955).

islands,[101] including additional rights for Papua New Guinean fishermen in the territorial seas of uninhabited islands north of the seabed line.

Fisheries Resources

Within the Protected Zone, the parties established a special regime for the conservation and management of "Protected Zone commercial fisheries."[102] These are defined as

> fisheries resources of present or potential commercial significance within the Protected Zone and, where a stock of such resources belongs substantially to the Protected Zone but extends into an area outside but near it, the part of that stock found in that area within such limits as are agreed from time to time by the responsible authorities of the Parties.[103]

Fisheries resources means "all living natural resources of the sea and seabed, including all swimming and sedentary species."[104] Thus, within the Protected Zone the parties have dispensed with distinctions between sedentary and other species. For management purposes, division of jurisdiction on the basis of lines of seabed or fisheries jurisdiction is largely disregarded in favor of a regime that seeks to manage the living resources as a whole, even though their actual allocation is determined by reference to jurisdictional rights. The fisheries regime in the Protected Zone has two major aspects: first, the sharing of the resources, and second, the enforcement of conservation measures.

Article 23 sets out detailed provisions for the sharing of the total allowable catch of a particular Protected Zone commercial fishery. The total allowable catch is determined jointly by the parties. In general, in areas under the jurisdiction of one state, that state is entitled to 75 percent and the other state to 25 percent of the allowable catch. This applies in areas both of territorial sea and of fisheries jurisdiction. However, the catch in the territorial sea around *uninhabited* Australian islands north of the seabed line is to be shared 50:50. Special provision is also made to give Papua New Guinea sole entitlement to the allowable catch of the barramundi fishery near its coast in areas outside the territorial sea of Australian islands. This provision reflects the special economic significance of this fishery to the local inhabitants, as well as its biological association with Papua New Guinea. The special barramundi entitlement is disregarded in calculating the total allowable catch to which the more general sharing formula is applied.

This view is not supported, however, by G. Schwarzenberger, who says that it is "not easy to see why a coastal State should contravene international law if it relinquished its claims to a part or the whole of its territorial sea." 1 G. SCHWARZENBERGER, INTERNATIONAL LAW 324 (3d ed. 1957). He does not consider that the argument that a state has duties, as well as rights, in the territorial sea requires that jurisdiction over the territorial sea be regarded as compulsory. He says, however, that "so long as, for *any* purposes, [a state] claims the right of jurisdiction over its territorial sea, it is clear that it is subject to *all* the duties which international law imposes on a State which claims such rights." *Id.* at 325. *See also* I. BROWNLIE, PRINCIPLES OF PUBLIC INTERNATIONAL LAW 124 (2d ed. 1973).

[101] *See* "Fisheries Resources" *infra.*

[102] Arts. 20–28.

[103] Art. 1.

[104] *Ibid.*

Any provision for the sharing of resources raises complex problems. How, for instance, is the share to be calculated? The Treaty provides for sharing both in respect of each individual commercial fishery and in respect of the overall catch of Protected Zone commercial fisheries. Thus, the catch of barramundi, crayfish, skipjack, tuna, and prawns are each to be shared in the agreed proportions. The Treaty provides that this apportionment should normally be made in terms of weight or volume. To take account of particular concerns or distribution patterns, shares may be varied by agreement in subsidiary arrangements,[105] but the overall apportionment of all the Protected Zone commercial fisheries is to be maintained in the proportions agreed in the Treaty. For this purpose, regard is to be had to the relative value of the individual fisheries. The parties are to base such a calculation on an agreed common value for the production of each individual fishery, based on the value of the raw product at the processing facility. This provision is designed to overcome problems that could arise if the value of the processed product were taken into account, which might well vary among the different markets where the product might be sold.[106]

Apart from the general sharing provisions, there is a transitional clause designed to ensure that in the 5-year period after the entry into force of the Treaty the existing level of catch taken by each party will not be reduced, provided that it remains within the allowable catch. But there is provision for the catch to be progressively adjusted during the second 5-year period to reach the level to which each party is normally entitled.[107]

It is too early to assess whether the provisions on sharing the catch will work effectively. In part, it will be difficult to obtain sufficient information on how much, and where, a particular fishery has been exploited. No subsidiary arrangements have yet been concluded, but they may provide a way to overcome such thorny problems as how to determine precisely what proportion of fish were taken in the territorial sea or elsewhere. While the special treatment for sharing purposes given to fish caught in the territorial sea of the uninhabited Australian islands can be seen as justifiable politically, in terms of practical implementation it may give rise to problems. Nevertheless, the provisions in the Treaty do appear to contain sufficient flexibility to ensure that the spirit of the agreement is complied with even if its finer points are disregarded in practice.

The other significant fishery matter for which the Treaty makes special provision is the enforcement of fisheries laws. The detailed implementation of these provisions within the framework of the ordinary criminal law system of the two countries has already caused considerable difficulty. In short, the Treaty envisages the issuance of licenses by each country to permit commercial fishing in Protected Zone commercial fisheries. These licenses can extend to any such fishery and are not confined to areas under the jurisdiction of the issuing state. At the request of the issuing party, the other party is obliged to endorse such

[105] Art. 23(7). Article 22 provides for the parties, where appropriate, to negotiate subsidiary conservation and management arrangements.

[106] The parties may agree on a point other than the processing facility, but prior to any enhancement of the value through processing or further transportation or marketing. Art. 23(6).

[107] Art. 24.

licenses authorizing the holder to fish in areas under that other party's jurisdiction. Persons so authorized to fish in waters under the jurisdiction of the other party are to comply with the relevant fisheries laws and regulations of that other party, except that they shall be exempt from licensing fees, levies, and other charges.[108] This avoids the need for fishermen to pay two license fees. Fishing by third states is subject to consultation between the two parties, and vessels under the control of nationals of a third state shall not be licensed to exploit Protected Zone commercial fisheries without the concurrence of authorities of both parties.[109]

Just as licenses are applicable throughout the zone, so each state is to apply its fisheries laws to the unauthorized use of vessels of its nationality to fish in Protected Zone commercial fisheries.[110] Within areas under its jurisdiction, each party is primarily responsible for investigation of suspected offenses. Corrective action, including the prosecution of an alleged offender, will normally be the responsibility of the state of nationality rather than the state in whose jurisdiction the offense was committed. The latter state is entitled to investigate the alleged offense and to detain the alleged offender and his vessel. If it appears, however, that the offense was committed in the course of traditional fishing or by a person or vessel licensed by the other party to fish in the zone, then the detaining party shall either release the alleged offender and his vessel or hand them over to authorities of the first party in accordance with arrangements that will avoid undue expense or inconvenience. Thus, the Treaty provides essentially for enforcement on the basis of nationality, although the state in whose area of jurisdiction an alleged offense occurs may investigate and obtain evidence, and the other party is to facilitate the admission of that evidence in its courts.[111]

As with the sharing arrangements, it is not yet possible to say whether these provisions will work. It is understood that difficulties have arisen in trying to translate these general principles into specific provisions of domestic law. In particular, the handing over of suspects without the normal use of extradition procedures raises problems.

The concept of national jurisdiction for enforcement purposes throughout a particular maritime area is not a new feature of fishery management regimes. The Treaty of 1973 between Argentina and Uruguay concerning the La Plata River[112] provided for a zone within which each party would have jurisdiction over its own vessels. Under that Treaty, the authorities of one party may seize a vessel of the other party when caught in violation of the relevant fishing or pollution laws, and the violating vessel is then to be placed at the disposal of the authorities of the other party. Similarly, in the 1977 Reciprocal Fisheries Agreement between Canada and the United States,[113] provision was made for flag state enforcement in "boundary regions" beyond the zones of either party.

[108] Art. 25.
[109] Art. 26.
[110] Art. 28.
[111] *Ibid.*
[112] Nov. 19, 1973, *reprinted in* 13 ILM 251 (1975).
[113] Feb. 24, 1977, 28 UST 5571, TIAS No. 8648, *reprinted in* 16 ILM 590 (1977). The Agreement was temporary and is no longer in force.

There was no provision, however, for the investigation or detention of vessels of the other party or for the handing over of such vessels to that party.

The inclusion of special enforcement provisions in the Torres Strait Treaty is a further reflection of the parties' desire largely to ignore the jurisdictional delimitation provisions within the Protected Zone and to manage it as an entity. The special provisions on enforcement were mainly sought by Australia, which wished to avoid the bringing of islanders before courts in Papua New Guinea. This concern arose not so much out of a belief that the system of justice in Papua New Guinea was inadequate, but out of a desire to ensure so far as possible that Australian citizens who lived and worked in the Protected Zone did not find themselves suddenly subject to Papua New Guinean jurisdiction because a seabed or fisheries line had arbitrarily been drawn through the Strait. As with so many of the other Treaty provisions, acceptance of a special regime for fisheries enabled the actual maritime delimitation lines to be drawn where they in fact were. Without special provisions to protect the source of the islanders' livelihood, fishing, it is unlikely that they would have found either a fisheries jurisdiction or a seabed jurisdiction line acceptable. The problem of ensuring the livelihood of fishermen in the Georges Bank area off Canada and the United States has thwarted the conclusion of the proposed treaties for that area.[114] Although the fisheries treaty contained elaborate provisions for the sharing of catch, it was perceived by U.S. fishermen as an inadequate protection of their livelihood.

Because there was a moratorium on seabed mining and, in any event, nonliving resources were seen as contributing marginally to the value of the area, no special provisions were made for the sharing of seabed nonliving resources.[115]

Navigation

Torres Strait is a major international shipping route. The route itself passes just to the north of Thursday Island at the northern tip of mainland Australia and then turns northeast through what is called the Great North East Channel. The eastern entrance of the shipping route lies between Bramble and Anchor Cays. Navigation by large vessels in the rest of the Strait is hazardous and, in many cases, impossible owing to the large number of reefs and sand bars. Through the Channel itself pilotage is strongly advised and is used in nearly every case.

Since Australia has sovereignty over all the islands in the Strait, the security and control of the shipping route lies clearly with Australia. Still, there is a right of innocent passage through the territorial seas of the islands.[116] Furthermore, the Strait qualifies under the definition in the Draft Law of the Sea Convention as an international strait through which a right of transit passage would exist.[117] Nevertheless, Papua New Guinea, if it was to gain no control

[114] *Supra* note 5, especially Colson & Feldman, at 754–60.

[115] The only provision made was the inclusion of the normal common deposit article providing for consultation and equitable sharing of the proceeds of a single accumulation extending across the seabed jurisdiction line. *See* Art. 6.

[116] Territorial Sea Convention, *supra* note 88, Art. 14.

[117] *Supra* note 1, Arts. 37 and 38.

over territory in the Strait, understandably wanted the Treaty to include some guarantees of its navigational and other rights through the area.

This concern was met by the special provisions on navigation by vessels and aircraft within the Protected Zone.[118] In and over the waters of the zone north of the seabed jurisdiction line, and south of that line but beyond the limits of the territorial sea, each party accords high seas freedoms of navigation and overflight to vessels and aircraft of the other party. These freedoms, however, are subject to the requirement that each party take action to ensure that its vessels or aircraft comply with certain measures. These include observance of international regulations for the prevention and reduction of pollution from ships and compliance with the immigration, customs, and fiscal laws of the other party. The freedom of navigation obviously does not extend to vessels engaged in exploration or exploitation of resources. Civil aircraft are also given the rights of overflight and transit in Australian island territory north of the seabed line. This applies to both scheduled and nonscheduled services. The result of these provisions is that Papua New Guinean coastal trading vessels can move freely between points on the southern coast, without facing restrictions that might otherwise have been caused by the existence of territorial seas around the numerous Australian islands. Similarly, aircraft can fly from Daru to points on the southern coast of Papua New Guinea without the need for approvals and compliance with other formalities that could normally be expected to arise from any need to enter Australian airspace.

Apart from its concern about the movement of local traffic, Papua New Guinea wished to be assured that overseas commerce and foreign shipping destined for or leaving from its ports would not be denied access to the Strait. Consequently, a guaranteed right of passage through routes used for international navigation is also given.[119] The right is to be no more restrictive than the regime of transit passage through straits used for international navigation described in Articles 34 through 44 of the Informal Composite Negotiating Text of the Third United Nations Conference on the Law of the Sea.[120] These articles appear in the Draft Law of the Sea Convention in similar form.[121] There is provision for the parties to agree on another regime of passage if the mentioned provisions are revised, are not included in a law of the sea convention, or fail to become generally accepted principles of international law. This provision indicates the growing acceptance of the work of the Law of the Sea Conference as already reflecting in many of its parts sound principles of law suitable for bilateral adoption by states.

As with the other features of the Treaty, the navigation provisions were designed to allay special concerns. Because of their inclusion, it was no longer so important for navigation and security purposes that Australian territorial sea or seabed jurisdiction continue to extend in places right up to the Papua

[118] Art. 7.

[119] Art. 7(6).

[120] 8 THIRD UNITED NATIONS CONFERENCE ON THE LAW OF THE SEA, OFFICIAL RECORDS, UN Doc. A/CONF.62/WP.10 and Add.1 (1977), *reprinted in* 16 ILM 1108 (1977), issued at the conclusion of the sixth session of the Law of the Sea Conference.

[121] *Supra* note 1, Arts. 34–44.

New Guinean coast. Nor was it so important for Papua New Guinea to gain control of some Australian islands.

Conclusion

The above outline of the special provisions of the Torres Strait Treaty is intended to indicate the many complex issues that had to be dealt with. Although the Treaty is primarily a delimitation agreement, it was only possible to arrive at a solution on maritime boundaries by tackling all the other related issues. The author would suggest that only in this way can complex delimitation issues be resolved. Although the quest for solutions led to some significant and novel provisions such as those on residual jurisdiction, in its results the Treaty is consistent with the general principles of international law on delimitation.

The recent agreements between Canada and the United States reflect a similar attempt to resolve a complex delimitation situation. While fisheries were treated separately and a comprehensive solution to that particular issue was devised,[122] it was largely divorced from other aspects of the delimitation problem. By asking an international tribunal to draw a "single maritime boundary,"[123] the parties have significantly limited their room to negotiate and to fashion creative solutions.

It is hoped that the successful conclusion by agreement of the Torres Strait Treaty will serve as a valuable precedent for other negotiators in other parts of the world, faced with similarly complex problems. While the Law of the Sea Conference debates the issue of delimitation interminably, Australia and Papua New Guinea have shown what can be achieved by agreement.

[122] Agreement on East Coast Fishery Resources, *supra* note 5. The Agreement contains complex management and sharing arrangements for individual fishing stocks.

[123] Agreement to Submit to Binding Dispute Settlement the Delimitation of the Maritime Boundary in the Gulf of Maine Area, *supra* note 5, Art. II.

RECENT DEVELOPMENTS IN UNITED NATIONS TREATY REGISTRATION AND PUBLICATION PRACTICES

*By Mala Tabory**

The framework for the systematic registration and publication of international agreements on an intergovernmental level was set in Article 18 of the League of Nations Covenant, and later in Article 102 of the United Nations Charter.[1] The purpose of treaty registration and publication is to give effect to the principle and policy of "open covenants"—enunciated as the first of President Wilson's Fourteen Points—in lieu of secret diplomacy.[2] In addition, these procedures serve to record "contemporary trends in substantive international law" for the benefit of judicial and government practitioners, scholars, and specialists in various fields.[3]

The United Nations has devoted considerable effort to the implementation of Article 102 by developing a set of Regulations to put into operation the

* Faculty of Law, Tel Aviv University, Israel. The author acknowledges the support of the Leonard Davis Institute for International Relations in the preparation of this paper.

[1] Charter Article 102(1) provides that "[e]very treaty and every international agreement entered into by any Member of the United Nations . . . shall as soon as possible be registered with the Secretariat and published by it."

Before the League of Nations, the systematic publication of treaties was undertaken voluntarily as a matter of private enterprise. *See* resolutions of 1885, 1891, and 1892 of the Institute of International Law.

On treaty registration and publication generally, see, *inter alia*: Harvard Research in International Law, Draft Convention on the Law of Treaties, 29 AJIL, Supp. 657, 912 (1935); Eagleton, *The Handling of Treaties by the Secretariat of the United Nations, Report of the Committee to Study Legal Problems of the United Nations*, 45 ASIL, PROC. 139 (1951); UNITED NATIONS, LAWS AND PRACTICES CONCERNING THE CONCLUSION OF TREATIES 184–85, UN Doc. ST/LEG/SER.B/3 (1953), references; Rosenne, *United Nations Treaty Practice*, 86 RECUEIL DES COURS 281, 426 (1954 II); Boudet, *Enregistrement des accords internationaux*, 64 REV. GÉNÉRALE DROIT INT'L PUBLIC 596 (1960); A. D. MCNAIR, THE LAW OF TREATIES, ch. 10 (1961); Myslil, *Registrace a publikace mezinárodních smluv*, 103 PRAVNÍK (Czech.) 949 (1964); L. GOODRICH, E. HAMBRO, & A. SIMONS, CHARTER OF THE UNITED NATIONS 610 (3d rev. ed. 1969); Conforti, *Sulla registrazione degli accordi internazionali presso le Nazioni Unite*, in STUDI IN MEMORIA DI ENRICO GUICCIARDI 491 (1975); Aiueva, *Registratsiia mezhdunarodnykh dogovorov v mezhdunarodnykh organizatsiiakh*, 21 PRAVOVEDENIE (USSR) (No. 1) 105 (1977). *See also* Vienna Convention on the Law of Treaties, UN Doc. A/CONF.39/27 (1969), Arts. 77(1)(g) and 80, and discussion on the registration of treaties in the International Law Commission, 1962–1966, and in the Vienna Conference.

[2] Jan. 8, 1918, *reprinted in* 1 FOREIGN RELATIONS OF THE UNITED STATES, 1918, Supp. I, at 12. *Also* letter to Secretary of State Lansing, March 12, 1918. *See* 1 D. H. MILLER, THE DRAFTING OF THE COVENANT 19 & n.1 (1928); Hudson, *The Registration and Publication of Treaties*, 19 AJIL 273, 273 & n.4 (1925).

[3] Lillich, *The Obligation to Register Treaties and International Agreements with the United Nations*, 65 AJIL 771 (1971).

registration and publication functions.[4] During the first three decades of the United Nations, Article 12 of the Regulations provided that the Secretariat should publish every treaty or international agreement registered, or filed and recorded, in the original language or languages, as well as in English and French translation.

The Treaty Section of the Office of Legal Affairs in the UN Secretariat carries out the functions of registration and publication of treaties and international agreements. The procedure for treaty registration with the United Nations involves the following sequence of operations: the verification of the treaty; the establishment of a registration file and preparation of the entry to appear in the Register of Agreements and in the *Monthly Statement*; the legal decision to register; the coding by computer of treaty-related data and the verification of computer tests; the printing of the *Monthly Statement*; and the dispatch of a registration certificate.[5]

The procedure relating to treaty publication includes translation into the required languages,[6] the technical preparation of the manuscripts for publication, and printing and binding the volumes of the *Treaty Series*. Although registration (or filing and recording) and publication are two distinct phases, they are part of a "continuous and interdependent process."[7]

It is important to note that the UN General Assembly and the Secretariat have refrained from defining what constitutes a "treaty or international agreement" subject to registration under Article 102 of the Charter or to filing and recording under the Regulations. The terms "treaties" and "registration" are

[4] The Regulations adopted by the UN General Assembly in 1946 closely follow the Regulations first approved in 1920 by the League of Nations Council to give effect to Article 18 of the Covenant: The Registration and Publication of Treaties as Prescribed under Article 18 of the Covenant of the League of Nations: Memorandum Approved by the Council of the League of Nations, 1 LEAGUE OF NATIONS O.J. 154 (1920), *reproduced in* 1 LNTS 8 and UN Doc. A/C.6/51 (1946). Regulations to Give Effect to Article 102 of the Charter of the United Nations, adopted by the General Assembly as Res. 97 (I), Dec. 14, 1946 [hereinafter cited as GA Regulations] (text in 1 UNTS xx), slightly amended by GA Res. 364B (IV), Dec. 1, 1949, and 482 (V), Dec. 12, 1950, amended text *in* 76 UNTS xviii, and 5 UNITED NATIONS, REPERTORY OF PRACTICE OF UNITED NATIONS ORGANS [hereinafter cited as REPERTORY] 283 (1955).

[5] UN Doc. A/C.6/33/5/Add.1, Ann. I, paras. 1–4 (1978); GA Regulations, *supra* note 4, Arts. 7, 8, 11, and 13.

[6] The Treaty Section receives many international agreements concluded in languages other than English and French, which are the official languages of the Secretariat. In such cases, the registered agreements are translated into those languages by the Translation Services. A treaty appears in the *UNTS* in all its authentic languages, as well as in English and French. *E.g.*, the Agreement on Collaboration in Health Services between Czechoslovakia and Sudan, 1970, which is authentic in Czech, Arabic, and English, appears in the *UNTS* in those three languages, followed by a translation in French (764 UNTS 107). The *UNTS* also includes any official translations required by the formal clauses of a treaty (*e.g.*, in Arabic, German, Italian, and Japanese for the 1973 Convention on the Prevention of Pollution from Ships; *see* UN Doc. A/C.6/33/5/Add.1, Ann. I, para. 14 (1978)). As stated at the beginning of every volume of the *UNTS*, "Unless otherwise indicated, the translations of the original texts of treaties, etc., published in this *Series* have been made by the Secretariat of the United Nations." On several occasions the General Assembly has urged states to provide the Secretary-General, where possible, with translations in English and/ or French for the purpose of publication (GA Res. 482 (V), para. 2 (1950); GA Res. 1092 (XI), para. 3 (1957)).

[7] UN Doc. A/C.6/33/5/Add.1, Ann. I, para. 4 (1978).

used throughout this paper to refer to any instruments registered or filed and recorded.[8]

I. Practical Problems of Registration

Concurrent with the rise in the number of independent states and intergovernmental organizations, and the growing complexity and widening scope of agreements between them, there has been an increase in the number of treaties submitted to the United Nations for registration. Given the continual cumulative growth in the number of past registrations, each new treaty registered requires more research to determine whether it meets the criteria for registration, whether it has ever been registered before, and whether related treaties that might be referred to in the text have already been registered. These factors add geometrically to the time necessary for processing the registration. (The processes related to the Secretary-General's depositary functions and the administrative deposit of agreements concluded by the United Nations also involve research, often on material still awaiting registration and therefore difficult to provide, and this augments the Secretariat's burden.[9])

Ideally, documents submitted for registration should be recorded by the Secretariat on the day of receipt. In fact, however, by July 1977 there was a 20-month delay in processing documents received for registration, and a 2-year delay in publishing the *Monthly Statement*.[10] The reason was that registration under the system originally employed by the Treaty Section, involving the recording of millions of data items manually (on index cards), was a dull, time-consuming task, and consequently also risked being unreliable. Also exacting were the preparation of Certificates of Registration for all newly registered agreements and the issuance of the *Monthly Statement* (a provisional document) and the Register of Agreements. All these functions were manually handled by the Treaty Section. As for the publication of treaties, while 1 year is considered a reasonable time lapse between the registration of a treaty and its

[8] On various aspects of what these terms encompass and the distinction between them, see Doc. 933, IV/2/42(2), 13 UNCIO Docs. 705 (1945); 5 Repertory, *supra* note 4, at 292–96; 2 *id.*, Supp. No. 1, at 398–403 (1958); 4 *id.*, Supp. No. 3, at 191, para. 4, and 195–96, paras. 7–13 (1973); Note by the Secretariat, UN Doc. ST/LEG/SER.A/. . . , [Monthly] Statement of Treaties and International Agreements registered or filed and recorded with the Secretariat during [Month] (statement also appears in abbreviated form in all volumes of the UNTS from vol. 212); UN Circular Note No. 213, Oct. 9, 1979, Ann. II, at 1. *See also* Schachter, *The Development of International Law Through the Legal Opinions of the United Nations Secretariat*, 25 Brit. Y.B. Int'l L. 91, 128 (1948); H. Kelsen, The Law of the United Nations 697–98 (1950); Brandon, *Analysis of the Terms "Treaty" and "International Agreement" for Purposes of Registration under Article 102 of the United Nations Charter*, 47 AJIL 49 (1953); Rosenne, *supra* note 1, at 288; 3 G. Schwarzenberger, International Law 439 (3d ed. 1957); R. Higgins, The Development of International Law Through the Political Organs of the United Nations 256 *ff.*, 329–31 (1963).

[9] UN Doc. A/C.5/1566, paras. 6, 9, and 17 (1973).

[10] Article 13 of the GA Regulations provides that the Secretariat publish a statement every month of the treaties and international agreements registered, or filed and recorded, during the previous month. UN Doc. A/32/214, paras. 18–21 (1977); GA Res. 32/144, 6th preambular para. (1977). By October 1978 there was a 29-month delay in the *Monthly Statement*; UN Doc. A/33/258, para. 4 (1978).

publication in the *UN Treaty Series*, by July 1977 the interval had reached 5 years on the average.

Legally, the delays involved in registering and publishing treaties do not affect the date of registration because the day of receipt by the Secretariat of the treaty in question is considered the official date of registration, regardless of when the actual registration is carried out.[11] Nevertheless, such delays fail to implement fully the Charter provision to register treaties "as soon as possible." In practice, the delays prevent the realization of immediate and full benefit from the registration and publication of treaties.

II. Measures for Reducing Delays

In considering the problems involved in the registration and publication of treaties and the production of the *Treaty Series*, the General Assembly's Sixth Committee concluded that the Treaty Section should attempt to reduce the cost and backlog in publishing the *Treaty Series*, while still respecting the Regulations.[12] The General Assembly subsequently recommended stopgap measures, which included temporarily deferring the publication of certain categories of treaties so as to reduce the interval between registration and publication of the remaining categories.[13]

The main efforts and innovations undertaken by the United Nations to cope more efficiently with the registration (or filing and recording) and publication of treaties have been directed toward (1) computerization, (2) selectivity in publication, and (3) cooperation with governments and other international organizations.

Computerization

The tedious nature and large volume of the Treaty Section's work made its manual operation unwieldy.[14] The question of computerizing UN treaty material was first formally raised in 1973. It was proposed that a computerized file be established to replace the card system used for indexing registers, working files, and other lists previously maintained in the Treaty Section. The computerized data would include basic descriptive information on all treaties and subsequent actions, duly classified and indexed. The programming would make possible the inclusion of additional information as it became available.

The automated system would enable the Treaty Section to execute its functions efficiently, to integrate new data, and to make available for any purpose information concerning over 30 thousand treaties registered since 1946 and several thousand others registered earlier with the League of Nations. The preparation of the *Monthly Statement* would be facilitated, as would be the

[11] GA Regulations, *supra* note 4, Art. 6.

[12] 26th and 27th Sess. UN Doc. A/C.5/1566, para. 2 (1973). For earlier, unsuccessful efforts to adopt measures to effect economy and reduce delays, see 2 Repertory, *supra* note 4, Supp. No. 1, at 403, para. 24, and 406–09, paras. 37–49.

[13] GA Res. 32/144, 32 GAOR, Supp. (No. 45) 210 (1977); *see* UN Doc. A/32/214, paras. 29–34 (1977). The problems of delays were further considered by the General Assembly at the 33d and 34th sessions.

[14] UN Doc. A/C.5/1566, para. 21 (1973).

issuing of registration certificates and notifications of deposit. All treaty-related information stored by the Secretariat would be included in the system. The computer would be connected to a printer capable of automatically producing manuscripts of various documents normally issued by the Secretariat, as well as reports and statistics. The use of the same data base by all Treaty Section staff members to record and retrieve information would bring about standardized, integrated procedures and simplified operations. In addition, double registrations, which sometimes occurred, would be made less likely. The system would be able rapidly to provide information such as whether a treaty could be registered or filed and recorded, or whether this had been previously undertaken, and what subsequent actions had been taken with respect to any given treaty.

Aside from expediting the bureaucratic registration of treaties, computerization would expand indexing capability to include more subject categories, and thus make it possible to search for new types of information. For example, earlier agreements that might serve as a basis for translating a new treaty on a similar subject could be rapidly located to assist in the development of a consistent and standardized terminology by the Treaty Section and the Translation Service. In fact, the computer could be used to help carry out all research required for the registration, translation, and publication of treaties, for answering outside inquiries, and for executing complex research projects involving large quantities of data and based on multifaceted criteria.

In the long run, computerization would also permit a reduction in the staff required for information retrieval and research and to program the requests. Thus, better service would be obtained at reduced costs.[15]

In 1974 the Secretariat began to develop the automated United Nations Treaty Information System[16] (which has become known by the acronym SIONUT, for Système informatisé de l'Organisation des Nations Unies pour les traités). The system became fully operational in 1978. Since then, SIONUT has been used by the Treaty Section as planned in every phase of its work, *i.e.*, data storage, research, and production of the *Monthly Statement*, registration certificates, and lists of treaties.

Despite some problems,[17] computerization enabled the Registration Group of the Treaty Section, by August 31, 1980, to work on files received the same month. By that time the backlog of work had been totally eliminated. There was a 10-month delay in the work of the legal officer responsible for the final checking of the registration procedure. As for the publication of the *Monthly Statement*, it was envisaged that the delay would be entirely eliminated by 1982.[18]

[15] *Id.*, paras. 23–38.

[16] Approved at GA 28th sess., GA Res. 3195A (XXVIII), 28 GAOR, Supp. (No. 30) 125 (1973). *See* 28 GAOR, C.6 (1456th mtg.), paras. 1–4 (1973); UN Doc. A/C.6/L.1004 (1974).

[17] By October 1979, outstanding problems included making the use of SIONUT easily accessible to parties outside the United Nations, such as governments and organizations; completing the verification of certain old (post-1945) data; and computerizing the data relating to treaties registered with the League of Nations Secretariat. UN Doc. A/34/466, paras. 19–20 (1979).

[18] UN Docs. A/35/423, para. 4 (1980); A/34/466, para. 14 (1979); A/36/570, paras. 7–8 (1981); A/C.5/36/25 (1981); A/36/7/Add.5 (1981).

During 1980, the Secretariat continued to improve SIONUT by broadening existing programs, especially the research program which is a primary function of the system. A new program was developed that would make it possible to make lists of agreements by parties available to outside users. Also, work was begun on the computerization of the data relating to agreements registered with the League of Nations Secretariat. Indexers preparing the Cumulative Indexes to the *Treaty Series* will have direct access to SIONUT services. Thus, in several ways SIONUT promises to improve the administrative operation connected with registration procedures.[19]

Selectivity in Publication

In December 1977, as stated, to alleviate the problem of delays in publishing the *Treaty Series*, the General Assembly decided to postpone the publication of certain categories of treaties until no more than a 1-year interval between registration and publication could be obtained.[20] The treaties whose publication was to be postponed were texts of limited interest or those already published either in the *Treaty Series* or elsewhere by the international organizations that had concluded them. The postponement of these categories would less adversely affect the objectives of Article 102 of the Charter than would a delay in publishing other treaties.

Under the procedure envisaged, the agreements involved would continue to be registered in the order in which they were received by the Secretariat, but the *Treaty Series* under the assigned registration number would list only information about the title, parties, entry into force, and registration, followed by a note stating that the text itself would be published in a later volume. An advantage of this system was that it would be possible subsequently to publish a series of similar agreements together in consecutive volumes. While not reducing the overall backlog in the publication of the *Treaty Series*, this practice would make available more promptly those agreements which are of particular importance in the context of Article 102 of the Charter. While there seemed to the Secretary-General to be no legal contradiction with the Regulations, he nevertheless sought and obtained the approval of the General Assembly before implementing this solution.[21]

The temporary postponement in publishing certain treaties only marginally reduced the backlog in the publication of the *Treaty Series* (from 276 to 217 volumes). In addition, the instruments omitted would eventually have to be published. Thus, a more far-reaching and permanent solution was required. The recommended solution entailed the decision to refrain from publishing the complete text of certain treaties.

[19] UN Docs. A/35/423, paras. 8–10 (1980); A/36/570, para. 23 (1981).

[20] These included treaties concluded by international organizations (primarily the United Nations and the specialized agencies such as the World Bank and the International Development Association), those dealing with specific development projects, and conference and seminar agreements that expire long before their publication in the *Treaty Series*, but not agreements containing general provisions applicable to specific projects. GA Res. 32/144, op. para. 3 (1977). *See* UN Doc. A/32/214, paras. 29–34 (1977).

[21] UN Doc. A/32/214, paras. 30–33 (1977).

In 1978 the UN Legal Counsel, Eric Suy, suggested that it might be desirable to consider amending the Regulations to give the word "publishing" an interpretation more consistent with actual conditions, without affecting the completeness of the UN compilation of treaties. The Secretariat proposed that in the absence of a precise definition of the term "publication" as employed in Article 102 of the Charter, this term could be interpreted as applying to limited publication, provided the latter was undertaken by the Secretariat. Limited publication would make it possible to take into account the increase in the number of treaties, especially those of a nonpolitical nature.[22]

Despite the fact that the word "published" had generally been interpreted by the General Assembly as meaning "published *in extenso* in the *Treaty Series*,"[23] a system of partial publication had once been used in the *UN Treaty Series* to avoid reproducing a long series of almost identical agreements.[24] On other occasions, the reproduction of certain annexes, which were not essential to the understanding of the main treaty document, was omitted.[25] Likewise, while the same broad interpretation had also been accepted as regards Article 18 of the League of Nations Covenant, several important multilateral treaties registered with the League's Secretariat were not published in its *Treaty Series* "owing to the publicity which they had already obtained."[26]

Consequently, at its 33d session, the General Assembly amended Article 12 of the Regulations to give the Secretariat the option of not publishing *in extenso* certain bilateral treaties[27] belonging to one of the following categories: (1) assistance and cooperation agreements of limited scope concerning financial, commercial, administrative, or technical matters; (2) agreements relating to the organization of conferences, seminars, or meetings; and (3) agreements that are to be published otherwise than in the *Treaty Series* by the UN Secretariat or by a specialized or related agency. This limited publication system was initiated in 1979.[28]

One problem of this arrangement was that the decision whether a treaty is included in the category of "assistance and co-operation agreements of limited scope" might lend itself to subjective considerations and leave too much discretion to the Secretariat. The Secretariat conceded that the determination of which treaties fall in this category does involve some discretion on its part. While it did not seem possible to define this category any further without losing

[22] UN Doc. A/C.6/33/SR.20, para. 7, at para. 8 (1978). Note by the Secretariat, dated Nov. 21, 1978, addressed to the Working Group [of the Sixth Committee], *in* UN Doc. A/C.6/33/5/Add.1, Ann. II, para. 3 (1978).

[23] UN Doc. A/C.6/33/5/Add.1, Ann. II, para. 5 (1978).

[24] 65 UNTS 3.

[25] 52 UNTS 211 n.2.

[26] *See* Treaty of Trianon, 1920, No. 152, 6 LNTS 188 n.1; *see also* Nos. 34–39, 74–80.

[27] Art. 12 as amended by GA Res. 33/141A (1978), 33 GAOR, Supp. (No. 45) 222–23. At the 33d session, pursuant to the Report of the Secretary-General, UN Doc. A/33/258 (1978), the question of treaty registration was referred to the 6th Committee, which for its consideration reconstituted the Informal Working Group it had set up in 1977. The proposals of the Informal Working Group (UN Doc. A/C.6/33/5 & Add.1 & Corr. 2 (1978)) were adopted by the 6th Committee (UN Doc. A/33/466 (1978)) and became Res. 33/141.

[28] UN Doc. A/34/466, paras. 3 and 4 (1979).

its practical advantages, the Secretariat felt that if it were given the latitude to exercise its judgment, it could satisfactorily decide on the selection of those treaties not to be published.[29]

Nevertheless, Article 12 of the Regulations, as amended, contains the following procedures to minimize the drawbacks of limited publication in the *Treaty Series* and to curb the Secretariat's discretion in this regard: the Secretariat will, upon request, make available to any state, intergovernmental organization, or private person (against payment by the latter) a copy of any treaty not published *in extenso*. More significantly, the *Monthly Statements* will indicate which treaties the Secretariat is considering not publishing,[30] which will facilitate control by the General Assembly and the states concerned.[31] Such control could be manifested by the decision to publish *in extenso* a treaty that had been omitted in the past since all such omissions are not irreversible. So that control can be exercised, the format of the *Treaty Series* will permit the publication as an annex at any time of the full text of any treaty not published initially.[32]

On the other hand, the Secretariat did not consider it possible to publish an analytical summary of the treaties not published, "since such a task would entail the risk of publishing a subjective version that might lead to misinterpretation by third parties."[33]

The attitudes and practice in the United Nations regarding the Secretariat's discretion to determine what constitutes a treaty have not effectively changed over the years. In the absence of a firm definition, a wide construction was initially adopted. Most representatives at the San Francisco meetings establishing the United Nations agreed that no restrictions should be placed on the nature of the instruments subject to registration, and by implication that almost any treaty could have political significance.[34] The Regulations formulated by the General Assembly call for the registration of every treaty and every international agreement "whatever its form and descriptive name" (Article 1). In an early session of the General Assembly, it was agreed that even commercial and technical international agreements were subject to registration.[35] The General Assembly reiterated the principle of full registration, for example in 1950, when it requested that the Secretary-General continue "to publish all treaties

[29] UN Doc. A/C.6/33/5/Add.1, Ann. II, para. 10 (1978).

[30] Art. 12(3), amended GA Regulations, *supra* note 27. The *Statement of Treaties and International Agreements* registered or filed and recorded with the Secretariat during each month, *supra* note 8, opens with a note by the Secretariat including the revised Article 12(2) and (3) of the Regulations. The treaties not to be published *in extenso* that were registered or filed and recorded with the Secretariat after Jan. 1, 1977 are identified in the *Monthly Statements* themselves by an asterisk preceding the title. For a list of the agreements registered or filed and recorded with the Secretariat during the period from Feb. 23, 1973 to Dec. 31, 1976 not to be published *in extenso* that could not be identified in the *Monthly Statements* because they had already been published or sent for printing, see UN Doc. A/35/423, Ann. II (1980).

[31] *See* UN Doc. A/C.6/33/5/Add.1, para. 9 (1978).

[32] *Id.*, Ann. II, paras. 11–14.

[33] *Id.*, para. 15.

[34] *See* R. RUSSELL, A HISTORY OF THE UNITED NATIONS CHARTER: THE ROLE OF THE UNITED STATES 1940–1945, at 329 & n.10, 925 (1958); Doc. IV/2/A/3, 13 UNCIO Docs. 787 (1945).

[35] 2 GAOR, C.6 (54th mtg.) 112, 117 (1947); *see* Schachter, *supra* note 8, at 132 & n.1.

and international agreements in their full and unabridged form, including all annexes."[36] Efforts to define categories of treaties whose technical, specialized, or temporary nature might place them outside the scope of Article 102 of the Charter were largely unsuccessful, and the matter was left to gradual development through practice.[37]

The Secretariat has interpreted the provisions of Article 102 broadly; without exception, it has resolved doubtful cases in favor of registration. Thus, it apparently did not reject any treaties submitted to it for registration or filing and recording, including many agreements of a financial and commercial nature that under League of Nations practice would not have seemed to some states to be subject to registration. Likewise, it registered agreements with temporary effect and some that had already been carried out.[38]

In contrast, the above-mentioned decision to waive or delay *in extenso* publication of certain categories of treaties restricts the scope of the agreements to be published. The new measures, however, do not directly cancel out or negate the earlier attitude regarding the scope and definition of treaties. As amended, the Regulations provide an administrative means of coping with the plethora of international instruments involved by identifying certain categories of treaties that continue to require registration and remain subject to publication, but that for practical reasons (*e.g.*, duplicate instruments already published) have secondary priority as regards publication. The basic consideration of publicity for all agreements, which underlies Article 102 of the Charter and which was given effect in the Regulations, has been modified to grant priority to "prompt publicity" for the more important treaties. Presumably, a delay of several years in publishing a treaty defeats part of the purpose that publicity was intended to achieve. The amended Regulations thus seek to conform with the spirit rather than the letter of Article 102 of the Charter, even at the expense of forgoing publication in full of all treaties.

As of January 1981, the backlog in the publication of the *Treaty Series* (275 volumes) was not yet under control. In order to remedy the situation, the General Assembly at its 35th session adopted a 9-year recovery plan to diminish the backlog gradually and eliminate it altogether by December 1988.[39] It is expected that agreements will then be published within 1 year of the date of registration.

Cooperation with International Organizations

Efforts by the United Nations to deal with the registration and publication of treaties have been focused primarily on intraorganizational procedures. Another aspect of selectivity on the part of the UN Secretariat that might com-

[36] GA Res. 482 (V), para. 5 (1950). It provided, however, that for annexes he may use discretion in employing less expensive methods of reproduction. *See* 5 REPERTORY, *supra* note 4, at 312, para. 101 & n.100, and 311, paras. 96–99.

[37] 5 REPERTORY, *supra* note 4, at 292–96, paras. 18–31, especially 31.

[38] Schachter, *supra* note 8, at 131 & nn.2–5.

[39] *See* UN Docs. A/36/570, paras. 9–11 and 17 (1981); A/35/423, para. 5 (1980); A/33/258, paras. 20, 23(c–d) (1978). The backlog was expected to decrease by 10 volumes in 1981, 20 volumes in 1982, 30 volumes in 1983, and 40 volumes each year after that until 1988.

plement intraorganizational processes is cooperation in publication with other intergovernmental organizations. The stopgap measures initiated by the Secretary-General discussed above consisted of the postponement of publication of certain agreements, primarily those normally registered by specialized agencies (*e.g.*, the International Bank for Reconstruction and Development and the International Development Association), some of which were voluminous.[40] In 1978 the Secretary-General consulted with a number of international organizations—*inter alia*, the World Bank—in order to explore the possibility of pooling their resources with those of the United Nations to assist in the earliest possible publication of the *Treaty Series*.[41]

The UN Secretariat decided to undertake a systematic survey of the practices of states and international organizations in the field of treaties to evaluate international activities, available resources, and new methods in this area. To this end, the Secretariat in 1979 sent general questionnaires to governments and international organizations regarding their treaty-related activities. It was hoped that this information would help achieve better coordination among the respondents. The Secretariat's evaluation of the questionnaires is expected to yield concrete proposals to the General Assembly for further revising the Regulations and for enabling the international community to make the best possible use of SIONUT.[42] A sufficiently large number of responses were expected to reach the Treaty Section to permit the Secretariat to formulate an accurate assessment of international practice and of the requirements of the international community as regards treaties and the development of the SIONUT programs by the 37th session or later.[43]

It might indeed be envisaged that the secretariats of international organi-

[40] UN Doc. A/32/214, paras. 29, 34 & n.8 (1977).

[41] GA Res. 32/144, paras. 2 and 4 (1977), *reiterated in* GA Res. 33/141B, paras. 3–4 (1978). UN Doc. A/33/258, paras. 15 and 23(d) (1978).

[42] Questionnaire regarding activities in the field of international agreements, UN Circular Note No. 213, Oct. 9, 1979, Ann. I. UN Doc. A/34/466, paras. 6 and 23 (1979). *See* GA Res. 34/149, paras. 3–4, 34 GAOR, Supp. (No. 46) 248 (1979).

[43] UN Docs. A/35/423, paras. 7 and 13 (1980); A/36/570, paras. 18–21 (1981).

Under domestic law, it is often required that treaties be promulgated or officially published. On state practice regarding treaty registration and publication, see, *inter alia*, for the United States: DEP'T OF STATE, FOREIGN AFFAIRS MANUAL, Circular 175 Procedure, secs. 720.2(h), 724, 725, 746.3 and references therein; L. SUMMERS, THE INTERNATIONAL LAW OF PEACE 222–24 (1972). For Canada: J.-G. CASTEL, INTERNATIONAL LAW CHIEFLY AS INTERPRETED AND APPLIED IN CANADA 945 (1976). For China: H. CHIU, THE PEOPLE'S REPUBLIC OF CHINA AND THE LAW OF TREATIES 44 (1972). For France: [le Roy *et al.*] *La Publication des engagements internationaux de la France*, 8 ANNUAIRE FRANÇAIS DE DROIT INTERNATIONAL 888 (1962). For Israel: Ha'aretz (Tel Aviv daily newspaper), Sept. 4, 1975, at 3. For the United Kingdom: A. D. MCNAIR, *supra* note 1, at 190. For the USSR: Butler, *On the Definition and Publication of Treaties Under Soviet Law*, 10 ISRAEL Y.B. ON HUMAN RIGHTS 224 (1980).

On the registration and publication procedure in intergovernmental organizations, see generally 5 REPERTORY, *supra* note 4, at 301–02, paras. 55–57. Also for the IAEA: P. SZASZ, THE LAW OF THE INTERNATIONAL ATOMIC ENERGY AGENCY 915–20 (1970). For ICAO: Chicago Aviation Convention, 1944, Art. 83, 15 UNTS 295. For the ILO: 15 UNTS 35, Art. 20; 26 UNTS 323. For the Pan-American Union (now the OAS): Hudson, *Registration of Treaties by the Pan-American Union*, 38 AJIL 98 (1944); 14 M. WHITEMAN, DIGEST OF INTERNATIONAL LAW 126 (1970).

zations and specialized agencies or other related agencies, including the International Atomic Energy Agency and probably any new authority to be established by the Third United Nations Conference on the Law of the Sea, that engage in treaty registration might "pool" their work and resources with the United Nations for mutual benefit and in order to avoid duplication. For example, the Organization of American States systematically publishes the text of treaties in which the OAS participates (and other treaties occasionally) in its *Treaty Series*. The *OAS Treaty Series* reproduces all authentic texts of the agreements which coincide with the Organization's official and working languages (English, Spanish, Portuguese, and French). The OAS General Secretariat systematically informs the UN Secretariat about the signing of international agreements and subsequent action thereto for purposes of registration or filing and recording under Article 102 of the UN Charter. With the help of computerized tapes, it would be unnecessary for both organizations to undertake the technical aspect of preparing the same instruments for publication.

III. Conclusion

The *UN Treaty Series* continues to constitute an important tool for the functioning of foreign ministries, especially in developing countries.[44] The effective use of SIONUT can be expected to bring benefits—in terms of accuracy of the information and savings in manpower, costs, and storage facilities—to the United Nations, the treaty sections of individual states, and other users of treaty materials. At the same time, the survey of the practice of intergovernmental organizations and states, particularly those with the means and technical ability to publish treaties more speedily than the United Nations, might indicate types of agreements—multilateral as well as bilateral—on which the United Nations might cooperate. Advantage might be taken of publication efforts by other bodies to spare the Secretariat from duplicating their work. Such cooperation could be advanced by coordinating computer software packages, which would facilitate the transfer of computerized information by international organizations and governments.

While the possibility of computerizing the texts of reservations and declarations is being studied, computerization of the texts of treaties themselves, which is theoretically possible with modifications of the existing programs, is regrettably not envisaged at present.[45] Considerable benefit could be derived from the computerized exchange of texts between the United Nations and states and intergovernmental organizations. As a result of such cooperation, the United Nations might in many cases be able to reproduce a document as submitted and thus avoid the prepublication stages of preparing the *Treaty Series*. The format of the *Treaty Series* would then be similar to that of *International Legal Materials*, which indicates the source of the documents reproduced, and the UN Secretariat could supply the translations and editorial work where necessary. Eventually, it might be possible for the United Nations to require that

[44] UN Doc. A/C.6/33/5/Add.1, para. 9 (1978).
[45] UN Circular Note No. 213, Oct. 9, 1979, Ann. II, at 7.

treaty texts be submitted according to a predetermined standard format to facilitate such a procedure.

The possibility of reproducing treaties directly as submitted will be considerably enhanced as the ability to transfer documents to computer storage through visual scanning of the texts—thus bypassing various time-consuming stages—becomes technologically and economically feasible. In fact, future developments in international telecommunications may enable the viewing of texts stored in one central UN memory bank almost instantaneously at terminals throughout the world. Progress in the use of satellites for international communications indicates that this is a realistic possibility. Furthermore, the time may come when not only specific texts could be viewed (and locally reproduced as necessary), but also a search could be made of all instruments in any given index category. In effect, a personal index according to the user's needs could be ordered from the computer. In the long run, such developments may render conventional publication processes obsolete.

For the present, the backlog in the publication of treaties limits one of the purposes of the registration and publication of treaties, namely, publicity about the exact contents of treaties. Such a publication backlog may conceivably have legal implications in situations concerning the application of successive treaties relating to the same subject matter (Article 30 of the 1969 Vienna Convention on the Law of Treaties) and the termination of the operation of a treaty implied by the conclusion of a later treaty (Article 59 of the Convention) where the parties are unaware of an earlier treaty.

Throughout the quest for ways to eliminate the backlog, the purpose of the Regulations, as originally formulated to implement Article 102 of the Charter, cannot be separated from the changes introduced. Specifically, if one of the purposes of registered and public documents is to ensure open diplomacy, then selective publication, however carefully defined and regulated, arguably works against it. This criticism, however, is somewhat offset by the publication of basic information concerning the status of the agreements not published and by the availability of the treaty texts, or identical texts previously published, from other sources.

The procedure of amending the formal Regulations to reflect contemporary practice, and of adjusting the practice to cope realistically with the increasing demands of modern international intercourse, is salutary. This is so insofar as the original purpose of the Regulations is maintained. The amendment procedure was initiated with the decision to limit partially the *in extenso* publication of bilateral treaties. The further modification of the Regulations, which for the most part have been kept intact for over 30 years, to incorporate up-to-date solutions to unresolved or new problems is to be encouraged.

During the early sessions, the Secretary-General reported to the General Assembly on the registration and publication of treaties, and these reports were followed by debates. Some authorities find the suppression of this practice in 1950 regrettable, for the debates kept the issue under review and had the psychological effect of reminding members of the obligations under Article 102 of the Charter.[46] This writer would suggest that the renewed interest in the

[46] *E.g.*, Rosenne, *supra* note 1, at 429.

past decade in improving the registration and publication operations—which includes the computerization of the entire process and the attention required on the part of the Secretariat and the Fifth and Sixth Committees of the General Assembly to implement this method—has adequately replaced the previous reporting practice.

Despite the revisions of the registration and publication procedures outlined above, there is room for further improvement. In practical terms, the text of a treaty in all its authentic versions usually remains unavailable, or difficult to obtain, for several years following its adoption, either because it has not yet entered into force or because it has not yet been published. In this connection, a suggestion was raised before the General Assembly in 1978 that a system be established for the publication of major multilateral agreements in all their authentic texts, even prior to their coming into force. This would be achieved by issuing them in a single brochure in all their authentic versions.[47] This proposal was inspired by statements made in the League of Nations in 1920, that the registration and publication of a treaty as soon as the text has been decided upon, even prior to its ratification and entry into force, would be useful.[48] The proposal takes into account the fact that currently at least six languages are employed in the United Nations, and even more in some specialized agencies.[49]

To a limited extent, the annual volumes of the *United Nations Juridical Yearbook* fulfill this function. The *Yearbook* contains the texts of some treaties relating to international law concluded during the year of reference, in order to publicize these treaties even prior to their entry into force and to reduce the problems caused by the delay in their publication (following entry into force and registration) in the *UN Treaty Series*. For example, the Vienna Convention on the Law of Treaties of May 23, 1969, which entered into force only on January 27, 1980 and will not be published in the *Treaty Series* for some time, appeared in the 1969 *Yearbook*. However, this is a limited effort, restricted to the most significant international law treaties and extracts from agreements dealing with the legal status of the United Nations and related intergovernmental organizations. It is confined to the texts in the four languages in which the *Yearbook* is published (English, French, Russian, and Spanish), as opposed to all the authentic texts of the treaty in question in addition to English and French.[50]

The UN Secretariat also issues certified true copies of multilateral agreements for the use of governments and international organizations. Occasionally, an agreement may also be reproduced as a document of the General Assembly, the Security Council, or another organ, or it may be published for the general information of the public at large by the Department of Public Information or other Secretariat services.

[47] Ambassador Shabtai Rosenne, UN Doc. A/33/PV.89 (1978); *see* Questionnaire, UN Circular Note No. 213, Oct. 9, 1979, Ann. I, para. 5.06 and Ann. II, para. 5.06.

[48] 1 LNTS 11, para. 5.

[49] *See* M. TABORY, MULTILINGUALISM IN INTERNATIONAL LAW AND INSTITUTIONS, chs. I–II (1980).

[50] UN Doc. A/C.6/33/5/Add.1, Ann. I, paras. 10–14 (1978).

The suggestion to extend such preregistration publication on a systematic basis may place an added burden on the UN Secretariat, which is seeking measures to cope with its present responsibilities or to reduce them. It would be valuable, however, especially as concerns major international instruments, such as the future Convention on the Law of the Sea, which become indispensable to practitioners and scholars from the time of their adoption.

The key to further developments in treaty registration and publication probably lies in the realm of computerization. Like many other institutions, the Treaty Section resorted to computerization only when it became absolutely necessary for its efficient functioning. The possibilities offered by automation, including word-processing machines, are continually expanding. It is conceivable that before long the technology developed will easily overcome those delays in the publication process that are purely mechanical. It may further be envisioned that the advantages of automation at the United Nations will offer worldwide benefits, as the information computerized at UN headquarters may be made available directly to terminals at foreign ministries, major libraries, and research centers.

Finally, in the absence of enforceable legal sanctions to encourage states to register their agreements,[51] it remains for states and for intergovernmental and scholarly organizations to support the registration of treaties on a voluntary basis for the common benefit of the international community, as was urged in the pages of this *Journal* in an editorial comment.[52] This is the prerequisite for deriving full benefit from the administrative and technical measures undertaken by the United Nations to achieve comprehensive and up-to-date registration and publication of treaties.

[51] *See, inter alia*, 5 REPERTORY, *supra* note 4, at 297–98, paras. 35–40; A. D. MCNAIR, *supra* note 1, at 185–90; L. GOODRICH, E. HAMBRO, & A. SIMONS, *supra* note 1, at 613–14; R. HIGGINS, *supra* note 8, at 334–36.

[52] Lillich, *supra* note 3.

NOTES AND COMMENTS

THE ELECTION OF FIVE MEMBERS OF THE INTERNATIONAL COURT OF JUSTICE IN 1981

The terms of office of five Members of the International Court of Justice—Judges Sir Humphrey Waldock, President of the Court (United Kingdom), Isaac Forster (Senegal), André Gros (France), Nagendra Singh (India), and José María Ruda (Argentina)—expired on February 5, 1982. Following practice, an election to fill those vacancies was held during the 36th session of the United Nations General Assembly (September–December 1981). On January 21, 1981, the Secretary-General brought the forthcoming election to the attention of the states parties to the Statute and requested nominations of candidates from their national groups by August 15. On that very day, August 15, Sir Humphrey Waldock died. The occasional vacancy thus created in the Court would exist either until a successor was elected for the remainder of his term, or until February 5, 1982, if no occasional election was held. In this connection, Article 5 of the Statute provides that the Secretary-General's invitation to the national groups should be sent out at least 3 months before the date of the election. For the regular partial election, as seen, there was no difficulty in meeting that requirement. However, even if the Secretary-General had dispatched the invitations on the very day he received the notification of the occasional vacancy, August 17, 1981, that election could not have been held before the end of November and in the very closing days of the normal session of the General Assembly—which would have been after the date usually reserved for the election of Members of the Court, the second half of October or early November.

Questions that arose during the election of 1981 related to the following aspects: (a) the issue of the occasional election; (b) the designation of the agenda item; (c) the nominations; and (d) the conduct of the election.

(a) The Issue of the Occasional Election

In accordance with Article 14 of the Statute, the Secretary-General duly advised the President of the Security Council of the vacancy occasioned by the death of Sir Humphrey. At the same time, he pointed out that Sir Humphrey had died closer to the end of his term of office than any other Member in the history of the present Court and that the regular election would probably be held before the casual election, which would fill the same seat for only a few weeks. Consequently, he suggested that the Security Council which, under Article 14 of the Statute, is to fix the date for casual elections, might wish to consider whether it should insist that one be held in the circumstances. The Secretary-General delayed sending the invitations required by Article 14 of the

Statute pending the decision of the Council.[1] On August 25, the President of the Security Council informed the Secretary-General:

> On the basis of consultations with the members of the Security Council . . . the Council considers that, as the vacancy which has arisen . . . will be filled through the regular election procedure as from 6 February 1982, no purpose would be served by invoking the procedures of the Statute of the Court relating to the filling of a casual vacancy for the remainder of Sir Humphrey's term of office. Those procedures are applicable in cases where otherwise a considerable delay would elapse in filling a vacancy. No such delay is involved in this instance, as the seat will be filled as from 6 February 1982.[2]

It was requested that the Secretary-General bring that communication to the attention of the General Assembly "in connexion with item 15(*c*) of the provisional agenda."[3]

This is an important new interpretation of the Statute, and in the particular circumstances of the case it can be welcomed. It is true that the Court sat on the merits of the *Tunisia/Libya Continental Shelf* case with one vacancy in its ranks together with one absence of a Member for personal reasons and, following the death of Judge El-Erian before the termination of the case, decided it with an even number of judges; and that both in this case and generally (as will be seen) it worked under the presidency of the Vice-President as Acting President. But if an occasional election had been held, the new judge would not in fact have been able to take part in the decision in that case, since he would have become a Member of the Court after the termination of the oral proceedings.[4] The only possible disadvantage that could have resulted from the decision of the Security Council would have related to the precedence of the Member selected in the occasional election. Had he also been chosen in the regular election, his precedence would have dated from the time of the occasional election (and not from February 6, 1982 and from his seniority in age at that date), following Article 3 of the Rules of Court of 1978. In the present instance, the consequences of both eventualities would have been identical.

We would go further. It is a cardinal principle of interpretation that a treaty should be interpreted in good faith and not lead to a result that would be manifestly absurd or unreasonable.[5] The interpretation by the Secretary-General and by the Security Council of the provisions of the Statute on the filling

[1] On the procedure for filling occasional vacancies, see our Note, *The 1981 Occasional Elections to Fill Two Vacancies on the International Court of Justice,* 75 AJIL 349 (1981).

[2] UN Doc. A/36/451-S/14645 (Aug. 26, 1981).

[3] For the provisional agenda, see UN Doc. A/36/50 (July 17, 1981), subsequently adopted as such, UN Doc. A/36/251 (Sept. 18, 1981). Item 15 was entitled "Elections to fill vacancies in principal organs" and subitems (*a*) and (*b*) referred respectively to the Security Council and ECOSOC.

[4] *Cf.* the case of Judge Ammoun, elected to the Court on Nov. 16, 1965 to fill an occasional vacancy, who did not take part in the second decision in the *South West Africa* cases, the hearings having terminated during that November. ICJ Pleadings, 8 South West Africa cases 100 (1966).

[5] *Cf.* Arts. 31 and 32, Vienna Convention on the Law of Treaties, UN Doc. A/CONF.39/27 (1969), *reprinted in* 63 AJIL 875 (1969), 8 ILM 679 (1969).

of casual vacancies in this case may be held up as an illustration of an interpretation meeting this condition.

As mentioned, Sir Humphrey was President of the Court at the date of his death, and his term of office would have come to an end on February 5, 1982. By Article 14 of the Rules of Court, if a vacancy in the presidency or the vice-presidency occurs before the current term is due to expire, "the Court shall decide whether or not the vacancy shall be filled during the remainder of the term." It appears that the Court decided not to fill that vacancy, and in consequence all the President's functions for the remainder of the term were exercised by the Vice-President, Judge Taslim Elias, as Acting President.[6]

A further tragedy befell the Court with the death on December 12, 1981 of Judge Abdullah El-Erian (Egypt), whose term of office would have expired on February 5, 1988. On December 21, 1981, the Security Council, at its 2321st meeting, adopted Resolution 499 (1981), by which it decided that the election to fill this casual vacancy would be held during the resumed 36th session of the General Assembly (which had suspended its session on December 18, on the understanding that the casual election would be one of the items to be taken up when the session resumed).[7]

(b) The Designation of the Agenda Item

As noted, the election of five Members of the International Court of Justice appeared in the provisional agenda and later in the agenda of the 36th session of the General Assembly as subitem (*c*) of a composite agenda item entitled "Elections to fill vacancies in principal organs." Up to the last regular election in 1978, the item of the election of five Members of the Court had always appeared as a separate agenda item. The introduction of a composite agenda item referring to elections to fill vacancies in principal organs occurred during the 34th session of the General Assembly,[8] and at the time it attracted no comment. It was first applied to elections to fill occasional vacancies in the Court during the 35th session, and this was the first instance of its application to a regular election. It is understood that this rearrangement is merely designed to reduce the aggregate number of items listed on the agenda of the General Assembly (an optical illusion!), regarded by many as unnecessarily overgrown, and that it is not intended to effect any coalescence of those listed as subitems. If there is any interaction between different items and subitems on the agenda, that is the product of external factors and is not related to the way they are enumerated on the formal agenda of the General Assembly.

Nevertheless, the inclusion of the election of Members of the Court—individuals, not states—in this particular composite agenda item, which relates to the election of states to collegiate principal organs, is to be deprecated. It carries

[6] In addition to the *Tunisia/Libya Continental Shelf* case, other pending cases at the end of December included *Application for Review of Judgement No. 273 of the United Nations Administrative Tribunal* (advisory opinion) and the *Delimitation of the Gulf of Maine* case (Canada/United States of America).

[7] UN Docs. S/14799 (Dec. 17, 1981); S/14806 (Dec. 21, 1981); S/PV.2321, at 2 (prov.) (Dec. 21, 1981); A/36/PV.105, at 73 (prov.) (Dec. 18, 1981).

[8] UN Doc. A/34/251, item 15 (1979).

with it the danger, for the elections of the Members of the Court at least, that the political factor which inevitably characterizes this election will be enhanced. Indeed, in 1981 an interconnection of a political character was at one time perceived among the election of the nonpermanent members of the Security Council, the election of five Members of the International Court of Justice, and the appointment of the Secretary-General, to which is to be added the election to the International Law Commission, itself enlarged during the session from 25 to 34 members. This full interconnection was broken by several events, but above all by the difficulties that arose over the recommendation by the Security Council concerning the appointment of the Secretary-General, and the decision embodied in General Assembly Resolution 36/39 of November 18, 1981 (mostly negotiated earlier) to enlarge the International Law Commission. These events effectively isolated the election of Members of the Court from the other elections (they probably had a greater impact on the election of the members of the enlarged Commission).

In our comment on the occasional elections held in January 1981, cited in note 1 above, we objected to the inclusion of the election of Members of the Court—whether a regular or an occasional election—in any such composite agenda item; we accepted it only for those particular occasional elections as a means of avoiding procedural complications inherent in introducing new items on the agenda of the General Assembly after its session had begun.[9] Considering that its Members are all elected in their individual capacity and that the "General Assembly" in which the elections are held is not the same as the United Nations General Assembly, but is enlarged by the participation of states that are parties to the Statute without being members of the United Nations (at present three in number), we continue to believe that the dignity and independent status of the Court require that all elections of its Members be maintained as a separate item on the agenda of the General Assembly, and not as a subitem of some other composite item made up of unlikes.

This question does not arise in the Security Council.

(c) The Nominations

Sixteen persons were originally nominated for the five vacancies,[10] but after withdrawals their number was reduced to thirteen.[11]

It is understood that several national groups originally purported to submit more than four candidates, apparently on the basis of a reinterpretation of the last sentence of Article 5, paragraph 2 of the Statute. By that provision, "In no case may the number of candidates nominated by a group be more than double the number of seats to be filled." The first sentence of that paragraph

[9] Rosenne, note 1 *supra*, at 357. Those two elections were designated as two sub-subitems of one subitem.

[10] UN Doc. A/36/302-S/14502 (Sept. 14, 1981). For the curricula vitae of the candidates, see Doc. A/36/303-S/14503 and Corrs. 1 and 2 (Sept. 22, 1981).

[11] UN Doc. A/36/302/Rev.1-S/14502/Rev.1 (Nov. 4, 1981). This revised list was issued at the specific request of the General Assembly at its 43d meeting on Nov. 2, 1981. UN Doc. A/36/PV.43, at 43 (prov.) (1981). Such reissue is not unprecedented, and it greatly facilitates the conduct of the elections.

states that "[n]o group may nominate more than four persons. . . ." It had always been understood, on the basis of the original *travaux préparatoires*, that the rule was that laid down in the first sentence of Article 5, applicable to general elections (in the present Court, the election of 1946) and to the triennial regular election of five Members of the Court, and that the second sentence constituted an exception applicable only to occasional elections. That was the interpretation applied during the period of the Permanent Court[12] and hitherto consistently as regards the present Court. The attempted reinterpretation could result in entitling each national group to nominate up to ten candidates for each regular triennial partial election—a consequence that would be as disastrous as it would be absurd and unmanageable. It is therefore satisfactory to record that the national groups concerned agreed not to submit more than four candidates for the five vacancies.

In this connection, one should note that if a plurality of occasional elections occurs simultaneously, as was the case in January 1981, each vacancy is treated individually and becomes a separate subitem, or now sub-subitem, on the agenda. Thus, if there are more than two occasional vacancies, the number of nominations by each national group for occasional elections may exceed four, provided that it does not make more than two nominations for each individual vacancy.

(d) The Conduct of the Election

Following the customary agreement between the regional groups, the election was held on November 5, 1981, in the 2306th meeting of the Security Council and the 48th meeting of the (enlarged) General Assembly at its 36th session; these two electoral organs met independently of one another, in accordance with Article 8 of the Statute.

In the Security Council, where the absolute majority required was 8, four ballots were necessary. On the first, it was announced by the President (Ambassador Taïeb Slim, Tunisia) that Guy Ladreit de Lacharrière (France) and Robert Y. Jennings (United Kingdom) received the required majority, 11 and 10, respectively. On the second ballot, Kéba Mbaye (Senegal) and Nagendra Singh (India) received the required majority of 11 and 8, respectively. On the third ballot, no candidate received the required majority. On the fourth, José María Ruda (Argentina) received the required majority, 9.

In the enlarged General Assembly, the required absolute majority was 80 from a total of 156 members of the United Nations (two new members were admitted earlier in the session) and three nonmembers, parties to the Statute. Three ballots were required. On the first ballot, de Lacharrière (127), Jennings (107), and Mbaye (95) received the required majority. On the second ballot, Nagendra Singh (88), and on the third, Ruda (80) received the required majority. The election was thus completed in one afternoon.

It will be noted that this election produced no change in the nationalities of

[12] *See* INSTITUT FÜR AUSLÄNDISCHES ÖFFENTLICHES RECHT UND VÖLKERRECHT, STATUT ET RÈGLEMENT DE LA COUR PERMANENTE DE JUSTICE INTERNATIONALE: ELÉMENTS D'INTERPRÉTATION 31, 59 (ed. Schenk von Stauffenberg, 1934); M. HUDSON, THE PERMANENT COURT OF INTERNATIONAL JUSTICE, 1920–1942, at 155 (1943).

the Members of the Court. On the other hand, two of the retiring judges were reelected. The national groups of the permanent members of the Security Council appeared to have insisted on rotation of their nominees.[13]

In a triennial partial election of five Members of the Court, there are today 75 disponible votes in the Security Council if all its 15 members are present (as was the case). It was known in the General Assembly that the full tally of the votes announced by the President of the Security Council after the first ballot only accounted for 61 votes since, unlike the Council of the League of Nations, the Security Council has always convened for the election of Members of the Court in open meetings, following decisions of the Preparatory Commission of the United Nations.[14] In the instant case, this figure was widely thought to have indicated an exceptionally large number of abstentions, not entirely unexpected in view of the proximity of the election of the 34 members of the International Law Commission (with some intermixture of candidates for the two organs) and the complications beginning to emerge over the upcoming deadlock in the Security Council about its nomination of the Secretary-General (a position for which nationals of several of the candidates for the Court, and for the Commission, were waiting in the wings). However, a reexamination of the ballot papers after the meeting of the Security Council disclosed the omission of 14 votes from the count and that the correct outcome of the first ballot would have given the required majority to de Lacharrière (14), Jennings (12), Mbaye (10), and Nagendra Singh (9).[15]

At the 2321st meeting of the Security Council, held on December 21, 1981, the President (Ambassador Olara Otunnu, Uganda) made the following statement:

> As President of the Security Council I wish to make the following statement on behalf of the Council:
>
> The President of the Security Council has been informed by the Secretariat that following the 2306th meeting of the Security Council, on 5 November 1981, devoted to the election of five members of the International Court of Justice, a further examination of the ballots established that an error had inadvertently been made in the tally of votes on the first ballot.
>
> As the final result of the voting would have remained the same, the Security Council confirms that the result of the balloting announced at the conclusion of the 2306th meeting remains valid.

The representative of Mexico then made a statement, which partly lifted the veil on that announcement. His statement included the following:

> My delegation particularly thanks you [the President] for the care that you have shown in dealing with this matter. My Government's request that the Council take a decision on it was motivated solely by a concern to safeguard the prestige of this body and to see that its actions were reliable and worthy of respect.

[13] Professor Jennings was nominated by the national group of the United Kingdom before the death of Sir Humphrey Waldock.

[14] On this aspect, see our 1 THE LAW AND PRACTICE OF THE INTERNATIONAL COURT 181 n.2 (1965).

[15] From inquiries made by the present writer through colleagues who participated in the election in the Security Council.

> In principle, we agree that the mistake did not in any way affect the final outcome of the voting. But we feel that only the Council has the competence to confirm or ratify the validity of its decisions. That has now been done through a statement by the President, endorsed by all the members, which is without doubt a healthy precedent which will help to enhance our authority.[16]

While this Note was in the press, it was learned that the Security Council has decided to adopt a new procedure for counting the votes, to avoid a recurrence of this type of inadvertent error.

A minor procedural incident occurred at the 2306th meeting of the Security Council. After the fourth ballot, the President, following practice, asked the Council "to remain in session until the President of the General Assembly has informed the Council of the results of the voting in the General Assembly." The provisional record of that meeting does not indicate what time the request was made, and it is simply followed by an announcement of the results of the voting in the General Assembly. That took some time. After the first ballot, the General Assembly formally suspended the meeting at 3:30 P.M. and resumed at 4:25 P.M. After the second ballot, it formally suspended the meeting at 4:35 P.M. and resumed at 5:00 P.M. After the third ballot, it formally suspended the meeting at 5:20 P.M. and resumed at 5:40 P.M. On the other hand, only a few minutes are required to count the votes in the Security Council, where the ballot papers were removed from the ballot box by the President and their contents read out by him in the presence of his colleagues. The meeting of the General Assembly, which had been called to order at 3:10 P.M., rose at 5:45 P.M., and that of the Security Council, called to order at 3:20 P.M., at 5:50 P.M. There was obviously a long interval between the announcement of the result of the fourth ballot in the Security Council and the completion of the third ballot in the General Assembly, and the record indicates that several members of the Security Council were away from their seats when its President announced the result of the election. These included the representatives of the USSR, the United Kingdom, and the Philippines, and it was requested that the President's announcement in such circumstances not constitute a precedent. The President explained that he did not think that there was any precedent, since the Security Council was in session and members were supposed to be in their places when he made his statement. "This statement was a formality, since we have all been following what has been happening there and here. I am sure this creates no precedent, and it will not do so if members of the Council remain in their places during the meetings."[17]

Sed quaere?

Courtesy would seem to require a more flexible approach in the future, perhaps through an attempt to make the relevant suspensions and resumptions of the meetings of the Security Council coincide with those of the General Assembly.

SHABTAI ROSENNE*

[16] UN Doc. S/PV.2321, at 3 and 4 (prov.) (1981).

[17] UN Doc. S/PV.2306, at 36 (prov.) (1981).

* Honorary member, American Society of International Law; member, Institute of International Law; Ambassador-at-Large and member of the Israel delegation to the 36th session of the General Assembly. The views expressed in this note are the personal views of the writer only.

CORRESPONDENCE

The *American Journal of International Law* welcomes short communications from its readers. It reserves the right to determine which letters shall be published and to edit any letters printed.

TO THE EDITORS-IN-CHIEF:

January 10, 1982

Judge Jessup's Editorial Comment on *Intervention in the International Court* (75 AJIL 903 (1981)) highlights the broader implications of the Court's Judgment of April 14, 1981 in the *Case Concerning the Continental Shelf (Tunisia/Libyan Arab Jamahiriya), Application of Malta for Permission to Intervene.* May I be allowed to add the following observations:

1. The opening sentence of the Comment states that this was the first time that the Court "ruled upon the right of a third state to intervene in a case to which two other states are parties." To be more precise, this was the first time that the Court ruled on a request to intervene under Article 62 of the Statute. This article does not grant an inherent *right* of intervention—at least not in the sense of Article 63—but gives the Court discretion to allow a state to intervene; a state may prove that it has a legal interest but the Court may still refuse its request on other grounds. The two types of intervention are in fact distinguished later on in the Comment (p. 904).

2. For Jessup, paragraph (*c*) of the 1978 Rules is very important (p. 903). It is indeed unfortunate that we must await a future pronouncement on the jurisdictional link issue, especially since it was one of the principal bones of contention among the litigants. However, paragraph (*c*) must be put in its proper perspective and its importance in intervention proceedings must not be overestimated. Although the rule in its present form is a direct consequence of the problems identified in the *Nuclear Tests* cases (1974), that does not mean that this rule has become a sine qua non condition for the application of Article 62 of the Statute. The Rules of Court are subordinate to the Statute. The insistence on the necessity of a jurisdictional link arises from a failure to distinguish the nature of jurisdiction on the merits from the incidental jurisdiction of the Court. Unlike the action on the merits, incidental jurisdiction, of which intervention forms a part, is independent of the consent of the original parties to the proceedings and arises from express provisions of the Statute.

3. Jessup makes an interesting reference to advisory opinions, in which cases states are free to submit their views without having to prove an interest of a legal nature (p. 905). The *Tunisia/Libya* proceedings, while contentious in nature, were rather special since the Court was not asked to decide a concrete delimitation dispute, but to render its judgment on "what principles and rules of international law may be applied for the delimitation of the area of the continental shelf appertaining to Libya and Tunisia respectively." This wording brings the case closer to a request for an advisory opinion and Jessup may be inferring by analogy that the rules applicable to advisory opinions, rather than the more stringent requirements for intervention, could have been applied to Malta's request to intervene. Given the circumstances of this particular case, this line of reasoning could well have been adopted by the Court. However, one would hesitate to apply the analogy on a more general basis as Judge Jessup seems to be doing when he quotes with approval the statement that "a more active participation by third states . . . could make the Court more relevant in international litigation." While it is desirable that states should

interest themselves in the Court, the consensual nature of its jurisdiction would not seem to permit it to develop into a forum for submitting views.

4. As Jessup rightly states, the central point of the Court's decision is "the identification of the type of legal interest which must be demonstrated under Article 62." For the Court, a legal interest is one that is directly in issue in the proceedings as between the parties or as between the applicant and either of the parties (paras. 19 and 22 of the judgment); it excludes an interest simply in the Court's pronouncement in a case regarding the applicable general principles and rules of international law (para. 30). Prima facie, these two principles are mutually exclusive; however, when applied to the *Tunisia/Libya* proceedings they would not seem to disqualify Malta's request. The Court readily agreed that Malta's was more than a general interest in abstracto in international legal principles and that Malta had a specific legal interest in the subject matter of the proceedings. This subject matter consisted exactly of an examination of the international legal principles to be applied in an eventual delimitation; so there seems to be no reason why Malta's intervention could not have had as its object the presentation of its views on the principles and rules of international law at issue in the principal proceedings. In the words of Oda J. (para. 19), "more cannot be demanded of Malta than of Tunisia and Libya."

It is unlikely that the possibility of interventions will discourage states from seeking access to the Court since this possibility has always existed. It is more likely that its restrictive interpretation of legal interest will dissuade potential intervenors from applying to participate in future proceedings. We might therefore have to wait a considerable time before a future decision throws some light on the issue of jurisdictional link.

TANIA LICARI

TO THE EDITORS-IN-CHIEF

Joe C. Barrett (1897–1980)

In American transnational relations, Joe Barrett, "small-town lawyer from Arkansas," as he liked to identify himself, was the right man at the right time for a giant step forward in the protection of our interests abroad. Concern about unnecessary conflicts in interstate legal relationships made him a very active member of the National Conference of Commissioners on Uniform State Laws and led to the presidency of the conference. The work on interstate uniformity convinced him that the United States policy of abstaining from participation in international unification of law activities because the subject matter had traditionally been dealt with by state legislatures merely resulted in leaving both federal and state interests unprotected.

When the International Institute for the Unification of Private Law invited Commissioners on Uniform State Laws to attend a conference to be held in Barcelona in the early fall of 1956, Joe Barrett decided to go on his own and see what was happening in the rest of the world regarding uniformity of law. From Barcelona he proceeded to The Hague where the second postwar session of the Hague Conference on Private International Law was taking place. An understanding had been reached that the national organization in the United States, which had expressed interest in the work of the Hague Conference, would send observers to this meeting and Joe Barrett was one of this small group.

He served again as an observer at the next session of the Hague Conference in 1960. The Commissioners on Uniform State Laws at this stage appointed a committee with Barrett as its Chairman to evaluate the need for American participation in international unification of law work. The Commission's report played a major role in the decision of the U.S. Government to seek passage of the congressional joint resolution of 1963 authorizing membership in the Institute and the Hague Conference.

Barrett's work in the Conference of Commissioners resulted in his becoming a leading authority on the problems of federal states as they may arise on the international level. For example, under his leadership as President of the Conference, work was carried on in tandem with the counterpart Canadian Commission, which resulted in the Uniform Foreign Money-Judgments Recognition Act. His experience and judgment were of great value to the United States in the course of his service as member of the Advisory Committee on Private International Law of the Secretary of State and as a delegate to numerous international conferences regarding the unification of private international law.

PHILIP W. AMRAM
RICHARD D. KEARNEY
KURT NADELMANN
WILLIS L. M. REESE

CONTEMPORARY PRACTICE OF THE UNITED STATES RELATING TO INTERNATIONAL LAW

MARIAN NASH LEICH*

The material in this section is arranged according to the system employed in the annual *Digest of United States Practice in International Law*, published by the Department of State.

ALIENS

(U.S. *Digest*, Ch. 3, §3)

Illegal Haitian Migrants

In an exchange of notes dated September 23, 1981, between the American Ambassador at Port-au-Prince, Haiti, Ernest H. Preeg, and the Haitian Minister of Foreign Affairs, Edouard Francisque, the two countries agreed upon measures to establish a cooperative program of interdiction and selective return to Haiti of certain Haitian migrants and vessels involved in the illegal transport of persons from Haiti to the United States.

The substantive portion of Embassy Note No. 277, a French translation of which was incorporated in the Ministry of Foreign Affairs reply Note No. SG/CG:20008, follows:

> I have the honor to refer to the mutual concern of the Governments of the United States and of the Republic of Haiti to stop the clandestine migration of numerous residents of Haiti to the United States and to the mutual desire of our two countries to cooperate to stop such illegal migration.
>
> The United States Government confirms the understandings discussed by representatives of our two governments for the establishment of a cooperative program of interdiction and selective return to Haiti of certain Haitian migrants and vessels involved in illegal transport of persons coming from Haiti.
>
> Having regard to the need for international cooperation regarding law enforcement measures taken with respect to vessels on the high seas and the international obligations mandated in the Protocol Relating to the Status of Refugees, done at New York, 31 January 1967, the United States Government confirms with the Government of the Republic of Haiti its understanding of the following points of agreement:
>
> Upon boarding a Haitian flag vessel, in accordance with this agreement, the authorities of the United States Government may address inquiries, examine documents and take such measures as are necessary to establish the registry, condition and destination of the vessel and the status of those on board the vessel. When these measures suggest that an offense against United States immigration laws or appropriate Haitian laws has been or is being committed, the Government of the Republic of Haiti consents to

* Office of the Legal Adviser, Department of State.

the detention on the high seas by the United States Coast Guard of the vessels and persons found on board.

The Government of Haiti agrees to permit upon prior notification the return of detained vessels and persons to a Haitian port, or if circumstances permit, the United States Government will release such vessels and migrants on the high seas to representatives of the Government of the Republic of Haiti.

The Government of the Republic of Haiti also agrees in the case of a U.S. flag vessel, outbound from Haiti, and engaged in such illegal trafficking, to permit, upon prior notification, the return to a Haitian port of that vessel and those aboard.

In any case where a Haitian flag vessel is detained, the authorities of the United States Government shall promptly inform the authorities of the Government of the Republic of Haiti of the action taken and shall keep them fully informed of any subsequent developments.

The Government of the Republic of Haiti agrees, to the extent permitted by Haitian law, to prosecute illegal traffickers of Haitian migrants who do not have requisite permission to enter the country of the vessel's destination and to confiscate Haitian vessels or stateless vessels involved in such trafficking. The United States Government likewise agrees, to the extent permitted by United States law, to prosecute traffickers of United States nationality and to confiscate United States vessels engaged in such trafficking.

The Government of the United States agrees to the presence of a representative of the Navy of the Republic of Haiti as liaison aboard any United States vessel engaged in the implementation of this cooperative program.

The United States Government appreciates the assurances which it has received from the Government of the Republic of Haiti that Haitians returned to their country and who are not traffickers will not be subject to prosecution for illegal departure.

It is understood that under these arrangements the United States Government does not intend to return to Haiti any Haitian migrants whom the United States authorities determine to qualify for refugee status.

In furtherance of this cooperative undertaking the United States Government formally requests the Government of the Republic of Haiti's consent to the boarding by the authorities of the United States Government of private Haitian flag vessels [where] such authorities have reason to believe that the vessels may be involved in the irregular carriage of passengers outbound from Haiti.

I have the honor to propose that, if the foregoing is acceptable to the Government of the Republic of Haiti, this note and Your Excellency's confirmatory reply constitute an agreement between the United States Government and the Government of the Republic of Haiti which shall enter into force on the date of your reply and shall continue in force until six months from the date either government gives notice to the other of its intention to terminate the agreement.[1]

[1] Dept. of State Files L/T.

By Proclamation 4865, "High Seas Interdiction of Illegal Aliens,"[2] dated September 29, 1981, President Ronald Reagan declared that the continuing migration of persons to the United States in violation of U.S. laws is a serious national problem, detrimental to the interests of the United States, and that the continuing illegal migration by sea of large numbers of undocumented aliens into the southeastern United States is a particularly difficult aspect of the problem. The President proclaimed, therefore, that the entry of undocumented aliens from the high seas was suspended and would be prevented by the interdiction of certain vessels carrying such aliens.

On the same date, the President issued Executive Order 12324 to carry out the suspension and interdiction of entry that he had proclaimed. It read:

> By the authority vested in me as President by the Constitution and statutes of the United States of America, including Sections 212(f) and 215(a)(1) of the Immigration and Nationality Act, as amended (8 U.S.C. 1182(f) and 1185(a)(1)), in view of the continuing problem of migrants coming to the United States, by sea, without necessary entry documents, and in order to carry out the suspension and interdiction of such entry which have concurrently been proclaimed, it is hereby ordered as follows:
>
> Section 1. The Secretary of State shall undertake to enter into, on behalf of the United States, cooperative arrangements with appropriate foreign governments for the purpose of preventing illegal migration to the United States by sea.
>
> Sec. 2. (a) The Secretary of the Department in which the Coast Guard is operating shall issue appropriate instructions to the Coast Guard in order to enforce the suspension of the entry of undocumented aliens and the interdiction of any defined vessel carrying such aliens.
>
> (b) Those instructions shall apply to any of the following defined vessels:
>
> (1) Vessels of the United States, meaning any vessel documented under the laws of the United States, or numbered as provided by the Federal Boat Safety Act of 1971, as amended (46 U.S.C. 1451 *et seq.*), or owned in whole or in part by the United States, a citizen of the United States, or a corporation incorporated under the laws of the United States or any State, Territory, District, Commonwealth, or possession thereof, unless the vessel has been granted nationality by a foreign nation in accord with Article 5 of the Convention on the High Seas of 1958 (U.S. TIAS 5200; 13 UST 2312).
> (2) Vessels without nationality or vessels assimilated to vessels without nationality in accordance with paragraph (2) of Article 6 of the Convention on the High Seas of 1958 (U.S. TIAS 5200; 13 UST 2312).
> (3) Vessels of foreign nations with whom we have arrangements authorizing the United States to stop and board such vessels.
>
> (c) Those instructions to the Coast Guard shall include appropriate directives providing for the Coast Guard:
>
> (1) To stop and board defined vessels, when there is reason to believe that such vessels are engaged in the irregular transportation of persons or violations of United States law or the law of a country with which the United States has an arrangement authorizing such action.

[2] For the text of Proc. 4865, see 46 Fed. Reg. 48,107 (1981).

(2) To make inquiries of those on board, examine documents and take such actions as are necessary to establish the registry, condition and destination of the vessel and the status of those on board the vessel.

(3) To return the vessel and its passengers to the country from which it came, when there is reason to believe that an offense is being committed against the United States immigration laws, or appropriate laws of a foreign country with which we have an arrangement to assist; provided, however, that no person who is a refugee will be returned without his consent.

(d) These actions, pursuant to this Section, are authorized to be undertaken only outside the territorial waters of the United States.

Sec. 3. The Attorney General shall, in consultation with the Secretary of State and the Secretary of the Department in which the Coast Guard is operating, take whatever steps are necessary to ensure the fair enforcement of our laws relating to immigration (including effective implementation of this Executive Order) and the strict observance of our international obligations concerning those who genuinely flee persecution in their homeland.[3]

Treaties and Other International Agreements

(U.S. *Digest*, Ch. 5, §5)

Executive Agreements—Transmission to Congress

On April 27, 1981, the Department of State issued new regulations, in final form, effective July 13, 1981, to implement the Case-Zablocki Act[1] on coordinating international agreements of the United States with the Secretary of State and reporting them to the Congress. The text of the regulations is in Title 22, *Code of Federal Regulations*, pt. 181, "Coordination and Reporting of International Agreements."[2]

Jurisdiction

(U.S. *Digest*, Ch. 6, §5)

U.S.-U.K. Agreement on Vessels Trafficking in Drugs

In an exchange of notes on November 13, 1981, between Edward J. Streator, the American Chargé d'Affaires *ad interim* at London, and Lord Carrington, Secretary of State for Foreign and Commonwealth Affairs, the United States and the United Kingdom concluded an Agreement to Facilitate the Interdiction by the United States of Vessels of the United Kingdom Which Are Suspected of Being Engaged in Trafficking in Drugs, with a Related Letter. The effect of the Agreement is to obviate the necessity of requesting individual authorizations from the United Kingdom for U.S. enforcement authorities to board, search, and seize British flag vessels on the high seas and to arrest their crews.

Under the Agreement, the United Kingdom agreed not to object to the boarding by U.S. authorities (primarily, the U.S. Coast Guard) of private vessels

[3] *Id.* at 48,108–09, *reprinted in* 81 Dept. State Bull., No. 2057, Dec. 1981, at 62.

[1] 1 U.S.C. §112b.

[2] *See* 46 Fed. Reg. 35,917–21 (1981).

under the British flag outside the limits of the territorial sea and contiguous zone of the United States and within specified areas in any case in which the U.S. authorities reasonably believe that the vessel has on board a cargo of drugs for importation into the United States in violation of U.S. laws. The specified areas comprise the Gulf of Mexico, the Caribbean Sea, that portion of the Atlantic Ocean west of longitude 55° west and south of latitude 30° north, and all other areas within 150 miles of the Atlantic coast of the United States.

On boarding the vessel, U.S. authorities may address inquiries to those on board, examine the ship's papers, and take such other measures as are necessary to establish the place of registration of the vessel. If these measures suggest that an offense against U.S. laws relating to the importation of narcotic drugs is being committed, the United Kingdom agreed not to object to a search of the vessel by U.S. authorities.

If U.S. authorities then believe that an offense against such U.S. laws is being committed, the United Kingdom agreed not to object to seizure of the vessel (and the arrest of its crew) and its being taken into a U.S. port.

Under the fourth paragraph of the Agreement, within 14 days of the vessel's entry into port the United Kingdom may object to continued exercise of U.S. jurisdiction for purposes of U.S. laws relating to the importation of narcotics, whereupon the U.S. Government is required to release the vessel without charge. The United States may not institute forfeiture proceedings before the end of the 14-day period.

Under the fifth paragraph of the Agreement, the United Kingdom may object within 30 days of the vessel's entry into port to prosecution of any UK national found on board, whereupon the U.S. Government must release the person. The United Kingdom agreed that it would not otherwise object to prosecution of any person found on board the vessel.

The United States is required to inform United Kingdom authorities promptly of any boarding of a vessel under the British flag and to keep them fully informed of subsequent developments. If any loss or injury results from any U.S. action in contravention of the arrangements or of any improper or unreasonable U.S. action pursuant to them, representatives of the two Governments shall meet at the request of either to decide any question relating to compensation. They shall meet in any case from time to time to review the working of the arrangements.

The Agreement entered into force immediately, and may be terminated by either Government on one month's notice, but will continue to remain effective in respect of proceedings based on action taken during its validity.

The Related Letter, also dated November 13, 1981, was from an official of the Maritime, Aviation and Environment Department of the Foreign and Commonwealth Office to an American Embassy official, and set out the following interpretations:

> With regard to the reference in paragraph 1 of the Note to "Private vessels under the British flag", the Government of the United Kingdom understand that term as referring in this context to private vessels registered in the United Kingdom or in any territory for whose international relations the Government of the United Kingdom are responsible.

> With regard to paragraph 5 of the Note, the Government of the United Kingdom consider that all persons on board a British vessel should in principle enjoy equal treatment under the law. In agreeing not to object to prosecution by the United States of anyone other than a United Kingdom national the Government of the United Kingdom act on the understanding that questions relating to the prosecution of the nationals of other States are of primary concern to their State of nationality.
>
> The Government of the United Kingdom do not consider that this Exchange of Notes should be regarded as setting a precedent for the conclusion of any further agreement affecting the freedom of passage of British ships on the high seas.

The Department of State submitted background information on the Agreement to the Senate Committee on Foreign Relations and to the House Committee on Foreign Affairs on January 18, 1982, in fulfillment of a longtime procedure adopted at congressional request (and to be codified at Title 22, *Code of Federal Regulations*, §181.7(c) (1982)). The background information read in part:

> In 1974 the U.S. began a maritime narcotics interdiction program on the high seas, aimed at blunting the enormous flow of seaborne narcotics destined for the U.S. These illicit shipments were (and are) originating in the Caribbean Islands and South America, and are bound for the Atlantic and Gulf Coasts of the United States. In response to the needs of this program, the Department of State, working with concerned foreign governments, developed a procedure by which informal case-by-case agreements concerning boarding, search, and seizure of foreign flag vessels suspected of narcotics trafficking on the high seas could be arranged with the flag state of origin of the suspected vessel. This program has been quite successful in obtaining permission from most governments to board, search, and if carrying narcotics, to seize their vessels on the high seas.
>
> The U.K. became involved in this program from time to time because of the fact that ships homeported in U.K. Caribbean Dependency States are registered in Britain, and fly the British flag. Crews of these vessels are seldom "British"—usually being third country nationals (mostly Colombian).
>
> . . . .
>
> The legal authority for this Agreement is contained in: Article II of the Constitution; the Comprehensive Drug Abuse Prevention and Control Act of 1970, as amended, 22 U.S.C. §2291(a) and 21 U.S.C. §881; the Tariff Act of 1930 as amended, 19 U.S.C. §§1581(h) and 1587(a); 49 U.S.C. §782; and 10 U.S.C. §2734(a) and (d).[1]

Economic Sanctions

(U.S. *Digest*, Ch. 10, §12)

U.S. Measures Against Polish Government and Soviet Union

In a statement delivered on nationwide television on December 23, 1981, President Ronald Reagan called upon the Polish Government to honor its

[1] Dept. of State Files L/T.

commitments under the UN Charter, the Helsinki accords, and the Gdansk agreement of August 31, 1980 with the leaders of the Solidarity movement. He emphasized that, if the outrages in Poland did not cease, the United States could not and would not conduct "business as usual" with the perpetrators and those who aided and abetted them. The President stated in part:

> The United States is taking immediate action to suspend major elements of our economic relationships with the Polish Government.
>
> We have halted the renewal of the Export-Import Bank's line of export credit insurance to the Polish Government.
>
> We will suspend Polish civil aviation privileges in the United States.
>
> We are suspending the right of Poland's fishing fleet to operate in American waters.
>
> . . . .
>
> These actions are not directed against the Polish people. They are a warning to the Government of Poland that free men cannot and will not stand idly by in the face of brutal repression.
>
> . . . .
>
> The Soviet Union, through its threats and pressures, deserves a major share of blame for the developments in Poland. So I have also sent a letter to President Brezhnev urging him to permit the restoration of basic rights in Poland as provided for in the Helsinki Final Act. In it, I informed him that, if this repression continues, the United States will have no choice but to take further concrete political and economic measures affecting our relationship.[1]

Action to implement the President's decisions in regard to Poland consisted, *inter alia*, of cessation of credit guarantees for the export of $200 million worth of agricultural commodities, which the Polish Government had requested on November 18, 1981, as the most urgently needed portion of a total of $740 million worth of agricultural commodities for which it had requested credit assistance on October 18, 1981. Action was similarly postponed on the remaining $540 million. In addition, the Department of Agriculture suspended the unshipped 887-ton balance of a 60,000-ton dairy commodity sale for zlotys to the Polish Government.

In regard to Polish fishing, the decision adopted was to withhold any fishing allocations for calendar year 1982.

In regard to aviation, the Department of State informed the Polish Chargé d'Affaires on December 24, 1981, that steps were being taken to suspend Poland's civil aviation privileges immediately;[2] and on December 26, 1981, Under Secretary of State Walter J. Stoessel informed Acting Chairman Elizabeth Bailey of the Civil Aeronautics Board that the operation of the U.S.-Polish Air Transport Agreement of 1972 should be regarded as suspended until further notice, and that the President requested the Board to take appropriate action to suspend the operating authority of the designated Polish airline until further notice.[3]

[1] 17 WEEKLY COMP. OF PRES. DOC. 1406 (Dec. 28, 1981).

[2] Dept. of State File No. P82 0007–1089. [3] *Id.*, No. P82 0007–1149.

The Civil Aeronautics Board issued a show-cause order to LOT[4] on December 26, 1981, and an order suspending permit[5] on December 29, 1981, that, subject to the President's disapproval, suspended the foreign air carrier permit issued to LOT in 1980[6] until further order of the Board.

In the show-cause order, the Board, noting the "recent upheavals" in Poland and also the President's address of December 23, stated in part:

> Under section 102[a](5) of the [Federal Aviation] Act [of 1958, as amended, 49 U.S.C. §1302(a)(5)], the Board must consider the foreign policy and defense needs of the United States in assessing the public interest. In the circumstances of this case, we are plainly obligated to give the President's assessment of the pertinent decisional criteria great deference. To the extent that the Executive Branch has already taken the necessary steps to suspend the Agreement, it would appear that LOT's permit has ceased to be effective. . . .

In its finalizing order (order suspending permit), the Board stated in part:

> On December 28, LOT timely filed comments in response to the Board's Order urging that it not be made effective because allegedly unlawful and inconsistent with the U.S.-Poland bilateral Air Transport Services Agreement. In addition a comment was filed by American Travel Abroad, Inc. (AMTA), as the largest U.S. tour operator to Poland, urging that any suspension be as brief as possible and that additional action be taken to minimize the inconvenience to the traveling public.
>
> We reject LOT's arguments and we are finalizing the suspension proposed in Order 81–12–155. . . .
>
> LOT first argues that the President has not taken any action which is effective to suspend the U.S.-Poland Air Transport Services Agreement. However, in response to our inquiry, the Department of State has advised us to the contrary. In these circumstances we are constrained to follow the advice of the State Department, considering its responsibility and expertise with regard to that issue.
>
> LOT further asserts that the terms of the Air Transport Services Agreement do not permit its suspension or termination. Specifically it argues that the Agreement is by its terms effective to March 31, 1982, and otherwise requires a one-year notification for termination.
>
> Obviously, the President's action is of the most extraordinary nature, brought about by exceedingly serious world events. Clearly, under such circumstances, there resides in the President and the Executive Branch of the U.S. Government ample authority to suspend application of an Executive Agreement between the United States and a foreign country, whether or not such suspension is provided for under the specific terms of the Agreement. This is a political question which is clearly one for the President. That the President has made such a decision is reflected in his public television speech of December 23, as confirmed by the letters of the Department of State attached to this Order.[7]

[4] In re foreign air carrier permit of POLSKIE LINIE LOTNICZE (LOT), Docket 40339, Order No. 81–12–155.

[5] Order No. 81–12–171.

[6] By Order No. 80–6–111.

[7] The Board's footnote to these letters is omitted here.

Subsequently, on December 29, 1981, the President announced that the repression in Poland was continuing and President Brezhnev's response to his letter had made clear the Soviet Union's lack of understanding of the seriousness of U.S. concern and of its own obligations under both the Helsinki Final Act and the UN Charter. President Reagan had therefore decided to take the following immediate measures with regard to the Soviet Union:

> —All AEROFLOT service to the United States will be suspended.
>
> —The Soviet Purchasing Commission is being closed.
>
> —The issuance or renewal of licenses for the export to the USSR of electronic equipment, computers, and other high-technology materials is being suspended.
>
> —Negotiations on a new long-term grains agreement are being postponed.
>
> —Negotiations on a new US-Soviet maritime agreement are being suspended, and a new regime of port-access controls will be put into effect for all Soviet ships when the current agreement expires on December 31.
>
> —Licenses for an expanded list of oil and gas equipment will be required for its export to the Soviet Union. Issuance of such licenses will be suspended. This includes pipe layers.
>
> —US-Soviet exchange agreements coming up for renewal in the near future, including the agreements on energy and science and technology, will not be renewed. There will be a complete review of all other US-Soviet exchange agreements.

Following the President's announcement, the United States Government formally notified the Soviet Government of the suspension of AEROFLOT's flights, by a letter from Secretary of State Haig to Soviet Foreign Minister Gromyko, dated December 29, 1981, as well as by a diplomatic note handed to a First Secretary of the Soviet Embassy at Washington.

The Civil Aeronautics Board issued a show-cause order to AEROFLOT[8] on December 30, 1981, and a finalizing order[9] on January 4, 1982, effective January 5, 1982, that, subject to disapproval of the President pursuant to section 801(a) of the Federal Aviation Act of 1958, as amended, withdrew the air transportation privileges contained in AEROFLOT's foreign air carrier permit until further order of the Board.

The Board's show-cause order read in part:[10]

> Aeroflot Soviet Airlines holds a foreign air carrier permit issued under section 402 of the Federal Aviation Act of 1958, as amended, which authorizes up to two roundtrips per week between Moscow and New York/Washington, D.C.[a] The authority granted by that permit is specifically made subject to "all applicable provisions of any treaty, convention, or

[8] In re foreign air carrier permit of General Department of International Air Services (AEROFLOT Soviet Airlines), Docket 40351, Order No. 81-12-178.

[9] Order No. 82-1-6.

[10] Footnotes to the excerpted portions of the order are as follows:

[a] Order 74-3-137, decided March 15, 1974, served April 1, 1974.

agreement affecting international air transportation now in effect or that may become effective during the period this permit remains in effect, to which the United States and the U.S.S.R. shall be parties."

The United States and the Soviet Union are parties to a bilateral civil aviation agreement.[b] One critical feature of this bilateral is that the service that may be operated by designated carriers shall be approved by both contracting parties. There have been a series of intergovernmental agreements to determine service levels. The last of these was permitted to expire on March 31, 1979 on the assumption that a mutually acceptable pattern of service between the countries would be established in further negotiations. Those negotiations never occurred, and it is unlikely that they will take place in the near future. Consequently, in the absence of an agreement establishing schedules, frequency, and capacity, Aeroflot has been operating flights to and from the United States in recent years at the discretion of the United States Government; and we have permitted Aeroflot to continue special services to the United States despite the fact that no U.S. carrier served the Soviet Union.

. . . .

Under section 402(f)(1) of the Act, the Board may alter, amend, or cancel foreign air carrier permits "whenever it finds such action to be in the public interest." Under section 102(a)(5) of the Act, the Board must consider the foreign policy and defense needs of the United States in assessing the public interest.[c] In the circumstances of this case, we have weighed the merits of the request in light of section 102 and all other statutory criteria, and have tentatively concluded that the considerations raised by the Department are of overriding importance here. In reaching this conclusion, we share the Department's assessment that the curtailment of Aeroflot's service to the United States does not conflict with our aviation agreement with the Soviet Union, especially since there is presently no guaranteed level of service under the agreement. Against this background, we have tentatively decided to withdraw the operating privileges previously granted to Aeroflot under its permit. Our action shall be effective on receipt of advice from the President that he does not intend to disapprove the Board's implementing order under section 801 of the Act. It is our present intent that this action be final not later than January 5, 1982, and shall continue until further order of the Board. Because of this schedule, we must require interested persons to file responsive pleadings on or before 9 a.m., January 4, 1982.

On December 30, 1981, the Department of State called in the Soviet Trade Representative and the Deputy Chairman of the Soviet Purchasing Commission to inform them that the Commission was to cease doing business on or before a specified date and to hand them a note to the Soviet Embassy confirming the notification. (The United States considered the Soviet Embassy responsible for ensuring cessation of all the Commission's operations and departure of all its Soviet national personnel, dependents, and other accompanying persons.)

In regard to maritime matters, the Department discussed with Soviet maritime attachés on December 17, 1981, the policy that would govern Soviet access

[b] The United States-U.S.S.R. Civil Air Transport Agreement of 1966, as amended.

[c] See Order 81–12–155, proposing to suspend the foreign air carrier permit of Polskie Linie Lotnicze (LOT).

to U.S. ports after December 31. On December 17, the Coast Guard notified U.S. shipping agents involved in Soviet maritime trade as follows:

> 1. The US/USSR bilateral maritime trade agreement will expire on 31 December 1981. Therefore, port calls beginning on or after 1 January 1982 for Soviet flag merchant vessels desiring entry into any U.S. port will be considered under fourteen-day request criteria *vice* four-day notice criteria. Port entry applications must be submitted by the vessel's agent to commandant, U.S. Coast Guard . . . fourteen days prior to the day of entry, excluding the day of receipt.
>
> 2. . . . Four-day notices for entry to the 40 ports specified in the maritime agreement will continue to be honored for port calls beginning on or before 31 December 1981. . . .[11]

Subsequent to the President's announcement of Poland-related sanctions on December 29, 1981, the Department informed Soviet Embassy officials on December 30 that a stricter regime would govern Soviet flag vessel access to U.S. ports. Press guidance of that date stated that there would be a presumption of U.S. approval for the time being of port requests by Soviet ships involved in strictly or overwhelmingly bilateral trade, but that there would be a presumption of U.S. denial of port requests by Soviet passenger vessels and ships involved in cross-trading (carriage by a carrier operating in a specific trade and not flying the flag of the exporting or importing nation in that trade).[12]

On December 30, 1981, the Office of Export Administration, International Trade Administration, Department of Commerce imposed interim regulations to implement the President's decisions, effective immediately.

The existing requirement for foreign policy purposes of a validated export license for export to the Soviet Union (including Estonia, Latvia, and Lithuania) and also to Afghanistan of specified oil and gas exploration and production equipment, and technical data related to oil and gas exploration and production, was expanded, through amendments to Title 15, *Code of Federal Regulations*, parts 379, 385, and 399, to include commodities and technical data for transmission (including transportation) or refinement of petroleum or natural gas for energy usage, excluding petrochemical feedstocks.[13]

The commodities and technical data covered by the new controls are also subject to an amendment to the General Orders (15 C.F.R., pt. 390) under the Export Administration Regulations, that suspended, effective December 30, 1981, all licensing for exports to the Soviet Union.[14]

[11] Dept. of State File No. P82 0008–2129.

[12] Dept. of State Files, EUR/SOV.

[13] 47 Fed. Reg. 141–44 (1982).

[14] *Id.* at 145.

JUDICIAL DECISIONS

MONROE LEIGH

Act of state doctrine—liability of U.S. banks for deposits in foreign branches—choice of law—day of breach rather than day of judgment controls currency conversion

VISHIPCO LINE v. CHASE MANHATTAN BANK, N.A. 660 F.2d 854.
U.S. Court of Appeals, 2d Cir., September 29, 1981.

Plaintiffs, ten Vietnamese corporations and a Vietnamese citizen, maintained piastre demand deposit accounts at the Saigon branch of Chase Manhattan Bank (Chase) until 1975, when Chase closed the branch to escape the Communist insurgents. Shortly after the fall of Saigon, the new Communist regime announced the confiscation of all industrial and commercial establishments and banks. Chase subsequently refused to honor the depositors' demands for payment from Chase's home office in New York, and the depositors brought a diversity action for breach of contract in federal district court.

The general rule in U.S. banking law is that the home office is ultimately liable for deposits in its foreign branches, but the law of the jurisdiction in which the branch is located controls that liability. Consequently, Chase interposed a number of defenses based on Vietnamese law. In particular, Chase argued (1) that the plaintiff corporations had no standing to sue because the confiscation decree had deprived them of their legal identities; and (2) that the Vietnamese Government had succeeded to ownership of the bank deposits. The district court (per Carter, J.) agreed with both contentions and, in addition, reasoned that the act of state doctrine precluded judicial examination of the legality of the confiscation decree. It accordingly entered judgment for Chase.

The U.S. Court of Appeals for the Second Circuit reversed. In a unanimous opinion, the court (per Mansfield, J.) held that Vietnamese law governed Chase's defenses.[1] It found, however, that the evidence was "wholly insufficient" to support the district court's finding that the Vietnamese Government had assumed the corporate mantle of the plaintiff corporations and thus extinguished their capacity to sue. To make that showing, more was required than mere confiscation of the corporate assets: "it must be found that the government stepped into the shoes of the corporate plaintiffs by formally assuming their assets and liabilities, thus replacing the former management."[2] In the view of the court, a government that confiscates abandoned assets "is no more the successor in interest to the departed corporation than a bank robber is to a bank victimized by him."[3]

[1] Even though the New York choice-of-law rule provides that the entire case be governed by foreign law, the court of appeals considered that rule discretionary and applied New York law to the parties' underlying obligation in the absence of any contrary contention by the parties. 660 F.2d 854, 860.

[2] *Id.* at 861. [3] *Ibid.*

Nor was the act of state doctrine a barrier to plaintiffs' recovery. The act of state doctrine does not require U.S. courts to give effect to foreign acts of state as to property located outside the acting state's territorial jurisdiction. The court of appeals reasoned that when Chase closed its branch, the situs of Chase's debt was no longer in Vietnam and the Vietnamese confiscation decree was therefore powerless to discharge Chase of its liability.

Chase's final defense was that the plaintiffs should still recover nothing even if the home office were ultimately liable because the obligation (payable in the now worthless Vietnamese piastre) must be converted prior to payment into U.S. dollars at the rate of exchange prevailing on the day of judgment. Such a "judgment day" rule is consistently followed by the federal courts in non-diversity cases and in many other jurisdictions.[4] In this diversity case, however, the court of appeals considered itself bound to apply New York law, which utilizes the currency conversion rule as of the date of breach.

In view of the marked increase in the volume of business conducted by foreign branches of U.S. banks, the court of appeals decision is likely to arouse considerable interest. The result reached by the court is ultimately based on the rationale that U.S. banks that choose to operate abroad through branches rather than through subsidiaries "reassure foreign depositors that their deposits will be safer with them than they would be in a locally incorporated bank."[5] In the Second Circuit's view, fairness dictates that the parent assume liability for deposits it is unable to return abroad, for whatever reason. Such a view is consistent with the general principle that the home office is ultimately liable for the obligations of its branches.

The court's actual holding, however, rests on highly technical grounds involving choice of law, the situs of the debt, and the effect of the particular act of the foreign state. Moreover, even with victory on all these points, the depositors here would have recovered nothing but for the fact that New York is one of relatively few jurisdictions following the "breach day" currency conversion rule. Thus, even if a subsequent court shares the Second Circuit's strong orientation in favor of the foreign depositor, all of these obstacles to recovery will remain, and the outcome will turn on the circumstances of the particular case.

Aliens—deportation—Refugee Act of 1980—standard of review—substantial evidence test

McMULLEN v. IMMIGRATION & NATURALIZATION SERVICE. 658 F.2d 1312. U.S. Court of Appeals, 9th Cir., October 13, 1981.

The Immigration and Naturalization Service (INS) sought to deport to the Republic of Ireland Peter McMullen, an alien and former member of the Provisional Irish Republican Army (PIRA), for entering the United States illegally. McMullen resisted deportation, relying on section 243(h) of the Ref-

[4] *See* Deutsche Bank Filiale Nurnberg v. Humphrey, 272 U.S. 517 (1926). A similar rule, reversing the traditional British practice, was adopted by the House of Lords in a controversial decision, Milangos v. George Frank (Textiles) Ltd., [1975] 3 All E.R. 801.

[5] 660 F.2d at 863.

ugee Act of 1980 (8 U.S.C. §1253(h) (Supp. 1 1981)), which prohibits the Attorney General from deporting any alien "if the Attorney General determines that such alien's life or freedom would be threatened in such country on account of race, religion, nationality, membership in a particular social group, or political opinion." McMullen contended that because he had refused to carry out a PIRA execution and had subsequently cooperated with investigators from the United States and Scotland Yard, he was considered a traitor by the PIRA and would be executed if returned to Ireland. The immigration judge agreed with McMullen and held that if he were deported, he would be persecuted by the PIRA for his political beliefs.[1] The Board of Immigration Appeals (the Board) disagreed, concluding that McMullen had not shown sufficient likelihood of persecution. The U.S. Court of Appeals for the Ninth Circuit reversed the Board and granted McMullen's petition for review on the ground that the Board's decision was not supported by substantial evidence.

In reaching its conclusion, the court of appeals posed two essential issues: (1) What is the appropriate standard of review of a Board of Immigration Appeals finding of no likelihood of persecution under the Refugee Act of 1980?[2] and (2) Was the Board's finding that McMullen did not show a likelihood of persecution supported by the evidence when evaluated under the appropriate standard of review?

Regarding the first issue, the court concluded that a finding of no likelihood of persecution by the Board must be supported by substantial evidence in the record. To this end, the court contrasted the former statute, which granted the Attorney General absolute discretion to decide whether or not to withhold deportation,[3] with the new language of section 243(h). The court noted that under the former statute, decisions by the Attorney General were granted extreme deference by the courts, subject only to a finding of a lack of due process or an abuse of discretion. The INS argued that the abuse-of-discretion standard remained applicable and that the court should therefore defer to the Board's no-likelihood-of-persecution finding. McMullen, on the other hand, argued that the new mandatory language of section 243(h) justified replacing the abuse-of-discretion standard with a substantial evidence standard. The court of appeals agreed with McMullen; it found that "[t]he role of the reviewing court necessarily changes when the charge to the agency changes from one of discretion to an imperative."[4] Accordingly, the court held, because the new section 243(h) removes the absolute discretion formerly vested in the Board, "[a] factual determination is now required, and the Board must withhold deportation if certain facts exist."[5]

[1] *In re* Extradition of McMullen, No. 3–78–1099 MG (C.D. Cal. 1979), 74 AJIL 434 (1980). The Government conceded that persecution within the meaning of section 243(h) includes persecution by nongovernmental groups, such as the PIRA, where it is shown that the government of the proposed country of deportation is unwilling or unable to control such groups.

[2] The court noted that because the relevant statute was significantly amended in 1980, this question is one of first impression.

[3] *See* Immigration and Nationality Act, 7 U.S.C. §1253(h), 66 Stat. 212 (1952).

[4] 658 F.2d 1312, 1316.

[5] *Ibid.* In reaching this decision, the court also relied on general standards of administrative law; it noted that "[a]gency findings arising from public, record-producing proceedings are normally

Having determined the appropriate standard of review, the court turned to whether the Board's finding of no likelihood of persecution was supported in the instant case by substantial evidence. On the basis of a careful review of the record, the court concluded that it was not. Conceding that the burden of proof is on the alien to show a likelihood of persecution, the court found that McMullen's testimony and extensive supporting documentation demonstrated that he had resigned from the PIRA without permission, that he had refused to carry out its orders, that the PIRA systematically tortures and murders traitors, that the PIRA considered McMullen a traitor for cooperating with the U.S. Government and Scotland Yard, and that the Republic of Ireland is unable to control the PIRA.

The INS, which submitted no evidence of its own contradicting McMullen's claims, argued simply that McMullen's testimony was inherently unbelievable because a petitioner in a deportation case is motivated to lie in his own interests. In rejecting this argument, the court attached considerable weight to the fact that the immigration judge, who heard McMullen testify and observed his demeanor, found McMullen's testimony credible. The court also refused to ignore as self-serving McMullen's documentary evidence, such as letters from his family in Ireland. Noting as a general matter the limited availability to an alien of evidence for a deportation hearing, the court concluded that "[i]f McMullen, a well known former PIRA member with an extensively documented claim of probable persecution, failed to present sufficient proof, then it appears close to impossible for anyone in McMullen's position to make out a §243(h) case."[6]

The decision in this case may be compared profitably with *United States v. Mackin* (668 F.2d 122 (2d Cir. 1981), summarized at p. 391 *infra*), which involved the "political offense" exception to a U.S. extradition treaty. While the two cases concern statutes and remedies that will in most cases be mutually exclusive, the inherent issues presented—the effect of an alien's political beliefs on removal from the United States and the respective roles of the Executive and the judiciary in the decision-making process—are not dissimilar. Regarding deportation, as *McMullen* makes clear, the issue of executive intervention has been resolved by statute: under the Refugee Act of 1980 the Attorney General's opinion is no longer relevant. Regarding extradition, however, there is no such statute, although legislation addressing the issue of executive intervention has recently been introduced before Congress.[7] While the extradition issue would appear to be somewhat more complex than the related deportation issue, it can at least be concluded that, on the evidence of *McMullen*, the deportation legislation has achieved laudable results.

---

subject to the substantial-evidence standard of review." *Ibid. See* Citizens to Preserve Overton Park, Inc. v. Volpe, 401 U.S. 402, 414 (1971).

[6] 658 F.2d at 1319. *Cf.* UNITED NATIONS HIGH COMMISSIONER FOR REFUGEES HANDBOOK ON PROCEDURE AND CRITERIA FOR DETERMINING REFUGEE STATUS ¶196, at 47 (1979) (noting that refugees fleeing political persecution are often limited in the evidence they can submit to support their claims).

[7] S. 1639, 97th Cong., 1st Sess. (1981).

Antidumping—settlement of claim—statutory authority—constitutionality

COMMITTEE TO PRESERVE AMERICAN COLOR TELEVISION (a.k.a. COMPACT), ET AL. v. UNITED STATES. 527 F.Supp. 341.
U.S. Court of International Trade, November 18, 1981.

Plaintiffs, the Committee to Preserve American Color Television (COMPACT) and the Imports Committee, Tube Division, Electronic Industries Association, challenged the validity of certain settlement agreements into which the United States had entered with importers of Japanese television sets. These agreements settled all claims for antidumping duties levied on imported television sets from July 1, 1973 to March 31, 1979. The Government's action was taken pursuant to section 617 of the Tariff Act of 1930, as amended, which authorizes the Secretary of the Treasury to compromise claims arising under the customs laws of the United States. The U.S. Court of International Trade held that the Government's settlement of the claims for the antidumping duties was lawful.

At issue in the case was the proper interpretation of sections 616, 617, and 618 of the Tariff Act of 1930, as amended. Section 616 (19 U.S.C. §1616), entitled "Compromise of Claims," states in relevant part:

> It shall not be lawful for any officer of the United States to compromise or abate any claim of the United States arising under the customs laws for any fine, penalty, or forfeiture, and any such officer who compromises or abates any such claim or attempts to make such compromise or attempts to relieve any persons, vessel, vehicle, merchandise, or baggage from any such fine, penalty, or forfeiture shall be guilty of a felony. . . : Provided, that the Secretary of the Treasury shall have power to remit or mitigate any such fine, penalty, or forfeiture, or to compromise the same in the manner provided by law.[1]

Section 617 (19 U.S.C. §1617) states in relevant part:

> Upon a report by a customs officer, United States Attorney, or any special attorney, having charge of any claim arising under the customs laws . . . the Secretary of the Treasury is authorized to compromise such claim, if such action shall be recommended by the General Counsel for the Department of the Treasury.[2]

Section 618 (19 U.S.C. §1618), entitled "Remission or Mitigation of Penalties," states in relevant part:

> Whenever any person interested in any vessel, vehicle, merchandise, or baggage seized under the provisions of this Act, or who has incurred . . . any fine or penalty thereunder, files . . . a petition for the remission or mitigation of such fine, penalty, or forfeiture, the Secretary of the Treasury, or the Secretary of Commerce . . . may remit or mitigate the same upon such terms and conditions as he deems reasonable and just. . . .

[1] In 1948, section 616 was repealed, although the substance of this section was retained in 18 U.S.C. §1915.

[2] The responsibilities of the Secretary of the Treasury, insofar as they relate to the settlement of claims for antidumping duties, were subsequently transferred to the Secretary of Commerce pursuant to Reorg. Plan No. 3 of 1979, §5(a)(1)(C), 44 Fed. Reg. 69,273 (1979).

Plaintiffs contended that the settlement agreements were not authorized by section 617 and were therefore *ultra vires*, illegal, and void. They argued that when read in conjunction with sections 616 and 618 and viewed in the context of relevant legislative history, section 617 only authorized the Secretary to settle claims for fines, penalties, or forfeitures arising under U.S. customs laws but not claims for antidumping duties. Alternatively, plaintiffs claimed that the agreements in question deprived them of a property interest without due process of law insofar as the settlements preempted an administrative determination of antidumping duties as required by section 751 of the Tariff Act of 1930, as added by the Trade Agreement Act of 1979 (19 U.S.C. §1675).

In upholding the settlement agreements, the court first examined the language of section 617 and found that by its express terms it authorized the Secretary to compromise any claim arising under U.S. customs laws. Relying on the "plain language" of the statute, the court concluded that "[t]here is no doubt that a claim for dumping duties is a 'claim arising under the customs laws.' "[3]

The court also noted that sections 616 and 617 were enacted into law at the same time by the same Congress. Section 616 specifically authorized the compromise of claims for "any fine, penalty or forfeiture"; yet section 617 referred to *any* claim arising under the customs laws without reference to this limiting phrase. The court concluded that "the failure to include that same phrase in section 617 can only mean that section 617, unlike section 616, is not limited in scope."[4]

The court next traced the statutory history of these provisions and observed that while the language of sections 616 and 618 originated in certain provisions of the Act of June 22, 1864 (18 Stat. 189), the language of section 617 first appeared in the Tariff Act of 1922. On this basis, the court rejected the plaintiffs' claim that section 617 was inextricably linked with sections 616 and 618 and instead concluded that section 617 should be read independently.

Plaintiffs' final contention was that the settlement agreements violated their rights to an administrative review of antidumping duties as required by section 751 of the Tariff Act of 1930[5] and that by settling the claim without a hearing, the Government had denied them a property interest without due process of law. In rejecting this argument, the court relied on *Zenith Radio Corp. v. United States* (509 F.Supp. 1282, 1287–88 (Ct. Int'l Tr. 1981)), which held that section 617 and section 751 are separate and distinct statutes. Thus, the court held, "even assuming a property interest was acquired under section 751 it was a contingent one since it remained subject to an exercise of the authority under section 617."[6] Accordingly, since section 617 did not require the Secretary to grant a hearing prior to the settlement, any property interest that plaintiffs

[3] 527 F.Supp. 341, 343.

[4] *Id.* at 345.

[5] Section 751 (19 U.S.C. §1675) requires the Secretary to conduct a periodic review and determination of antidumping duties and provides that "[w]henever the administering authority or the Commission conducts a review under this section it shall, upon the request of any interested party, hold a hearing . . . in connection with that review."

[6] 527 F.Supp. at 350.

may have acquired under section 751 was subject to compromise without a hearing.

The ultimate question not addressed in this case is whether the outstanding antidumping order confers a protected property interest upon the plaintiffs. The hearing requirement of section 751 may suggest an affirmative answer. On the other hand, a domestic manufacturer who initiates a successful antidumping proceeding has no right to damages and does not share in the antidumping duties collected.

Extradition Treaty—executive versus judicial determination of the political offense exception—nonappealability of magistrate's extradition determination

UNITED STATES v. MACKIN. 668 F.2d 122.
U.S. Court of Appeals, 2d Cir., December 23, 1981.

The Government of the United Kingdom of Great Britain and Northern Ireland sought the extradition of a member of the Provisional Irish Republican Army, Desmond Mackin, pursuant to Article VIII of the Extradition Treaty between the United States and the United Kingdom.[1] The request for extradition was based upon Mackin's indictment in Northern Ireland on charges of attempted murder of a British plainclothes soldier. A U.S. magistrate denied the request for extradition on the ground that the offense for which extradition was sought was of a "political character" within the meaning of the Extradition Treaty, which provides that extradition shall be denied if "the offense for which extradition is requested is regarded by the requested Party as one of a political character."[2] The magistrate concluded that Mackin had been part of a political uprising in the area where the offense was committed and that the offense was committed in connection with the uprising. The United States appealed from the magistrate's decision and, in the alternative, sought mandamus to order her to grant the request on the ground that the magistrate had no authority to interpret the "political offense" clause of the Treaty and should have referred that question to the executive branch. Mackin challenged the court's power to entertain the appeal and contended that mandamus should be denied because interpretation of the Treaty was a proper question for the judicial branch. The Court of Appeals for the Second Circuit (per Friendly, J.) dismissed the Government's appeal for lack of jurisdiction.

Addressing first the power of the court to entertain the appeal, the court traced the principle of nonappealability of extradition decisions to *In re Metzger* (46 U.S. (5 How.) 175 (1847)). In that case the Supreme Court held that it lacked power to review an extradition order issued by a district court judge exercising a "special authority" from which the law provided no avenue of appeal. The Second Circuit rejected the Government's argument that subsequent enactments and amendments of the extradition laws manifested a congressional intent to alter the Supreme Court's decision and render decisions on extradition appealable. The court concluded that the clear weight of judicial

[1] 28 UST 227, TIAS No. 8468.

[2] *Id.*, Art. V(1)(c)(i).

authority and the alternative means available for challenging an extradition order—the writ of habeas corpus and the refiling of the extradition request—underscored the view that such orders are nonappealable. Moreover, recent public statements by members of Congress and representatives of the Departments of Justice and State had reiterated this view.[3] Finally, the court held, section 2291 to Title 28, which authorizes appeals to the courts of appeals, encompasses only "final decisions of the district courts of the United States." The decision of a magistrate, however, is not a final decision of a district court.[4] Accordingly, the magistrate's decision was nonappealable.

Turning to the Government's petition for mandamus, the court noted that in certain circumstances courts have power to hear mandamus petitions even though appellate jurisdiction does not exist. In every instance, however, mandamus is reserved for "exceptional cases" in which intervention is necessitated by "usurpation of power, clear abuse of discretion and the presence of an issue of first impression."[5] The only issue of that quality raised by the present case was whether the magistrate exceeded her jurisdiction by deciding, without consulting the Executive, that the crime for which Mackin's extradition was sought fell within the political offense exception to the Treaty.

The Government argued that the plain language of the political offense exception delegated the decision-making power in extradition cases to the executive branch. Noting that the Seventh Circuit recently rejected a similar argument in a case involving the Extradition Treaty between the United States and Israel,[6] the Second Circuit rejected the Government's textual argument and supporting theories of policy and analogy. This rejection of the argument that the Executive has sole discretion to decide whether a crime is a political offense comports with the general rule that the courts have authority to interpret a treaty when they are called on to apply it (see *Baker v. Carr*, 369 U.S. 186, 211–13 (1962)).

The magistrate's decision in *Mackin* has been sharply criticized on public policy grounds for defining political offenses in a way that would allow international terrorists to seek shelter in the United States.[7] To counteract this result, the State Department is currently asking Congress to enact legislation that would confine requests for extradition to federal district courts, permit appeals from district court decisions on extradition requests, and empower the Secretary of State to determine whether extradition should be refused on political offense grounds.

[3] *See, e.g.*, 127 CONG. REC. S9952 (daily ed. Sept. 18, 1981) (remarks of Sen. Thurmond); *id.* at S9953 (remarks of Sec'y Haig); *The Extradition Act of 1981: Hearings Before the Senate Comm. on the Judiciary*, 97th Cong., 1st Sess. (1981) (testimony of Michael Abbell, Office of International Affairs, Criminal Division, Dep't of Justice).

[4] Pursuant to 28 U.S.C. §3184, extradition proceedings are conducted by "any justice or judge of the United States, or any magistrate authorized to do so by the courts of the United States or any judge of a court of record of general jurisdiction of any state."

[5] 668 F.2d 122, 131 (quoting American Express Warehousing, Ltd. v. Transamerica Ins. Co., 380 F.2d 277, 283 (2d Cir. 1967)).

[6] Abu Eain v. Wilkes, 641 F.2d 504 (7th Cir. 1981), 75 AJIL 662 (1981).

[7] *See, e.g.*, N.Y. Times, Dec. 29, 1981, at A14 (editorial).

Foreign Sovereign Immunities Act—no jury trial in action brought against a foreign state

REX v. CIA. PERVANA DE VAPORES, S.A. 660 F.2d 61.
U.S. Court of Appeals, 3d Cir., September 17, 1981.

Plaintiff, an injured longshoreman, brought an action to recover for personal injuries suffered while unloading cargo from a ship. The defendant is a Peruvian corporation, the shares of which are wholly owned by the Government of Peru. Included in plaintiff's claim for relief was a request for jury trial. The district court granted this request[1] and certified its decision for immediate appeal. By a vote of two to one, the Court of Appeals for the Third Circuit reversed.

The Third Circuit agreed with the Courts of Appeal for the Second and Fourth Circuits that the applicable jurisdictional statute supports denial of the jury demand.[2] Section 1330(a) of the Foreign Sovereign Immunities Act of 1976 (28 U.S.C. §§1330, 1602–1611) (FSIA) provides that the district courts "shall have original jurisdiction . . . of any nonjury civil action against a foreign state as defined in section 1603(a)."[3] Thus, the sole basis for federal subject matter jurisdiction over foreign states and their instrumentalities expressly precludes jury trials. The Third Circuit followed the reasoning of the Second Circuit in rejecting the argument that an action could be maintained against a state-owned corporation, although not against the state itself, under section 1332(a)(2) of the FSIA, which authorizes suits between "citizens of a State and citizens or subjects of a foreign state" and imposes no restrictions on jury trial. In addition, the Third Circuit rejected the reasoning of the district court that the plaintiff's action, which was based upon the Longshoremen's and Harbor Workers' Compensation Act (33 U.S.C. §905(b)), created a foundation for federal question jurisdiction under 28 U.S.C. §1331.

Addressing the potential conflict between the Seventh Amendment[4] and the FSIA, the Third Circuit concurred with the conclusions of the Second and Fourth Circuits, although it "arrive[d] by a slightly different route."[5] While the other circuits had reasoned that the Seventh Amendment applies only to *actions* recognized at common law in 1791, the Third Circuit eschewed "this static approach to a vital constitutional guarantee."[6] Rather than viewing "common law as frozen in 1791,"[7] the court concluded that the proper inquiry is "whether [the] action is in the nature of a legal *remedy* similar to a suit at common law."[8] A review of the sovereign immunity doctrine persuaded the court that "[h]istory . . . conclusively demonstrates that actions against foreign sovereigns have never existed at common law."[9] Thus, in enacting the FSIA

[1] Rex v. Cia. Pervana de Vapores, S.A., 493 F.Supp. 459 (E.D. Pa. 1980).

[2] *See* Williams v. The Shipping Corp. of India, 653 F.2d 875 (4th Cir. 1981); Ruggiero v. Compania Peruana de Vapores, *et al.*, 639 F.2d 872 (2d Cir. 1981), 75 AJIL 664 (1981).

[3] Under the FSIA, corporations owned by a foreign state are considered foreign states. 28 U.S.C. §1603 (1976).

[4] The Seventh Amendment states in relevant part: "In Suits at common law, where the value in controversy shall exceed twenty dollars, the right of trial by jury shall be preserved. . . ."

[5] 660 F.2d 61, 63.

[6] *Id.* at 66.

[7] *Ibid.*

[8] *Id.* at 67 (emphasis added).

[9] *Id.* at 68.

Congress could not have created "a cause of action in the nature of a common law remedy."[10]

The Third Circuit's decision is significant for several reasons. Together with the Second and Fourth Circuits, it formulates a unanimous rule among the appellate courts that have examined the issue against jury trials in actions under the FSIA. The Third Circuit's decision also comports with decisions of the Supreme Court emphasizing that the right to jury trial extends to all actions involving rights and remedies similar to those enforced at common law.[11]

As Judge Sloviter pointed out in dissent, however, the majority's analysis "looks to the nature of the defendant rather than to the nature of plaintiff's claim or rights."[12] Judge Sloviter argued that Congress could not extinguish the right to jury trial by defining a "foreign state" to include a state-owned corporation. She was unconvinced by the majority's reliance upon the historic immunity accorded to foreign states and the analogy to the sovereign immunity of the United States. Thus, Judge Sloviter would have held that the FSIA is unconstitutional insofar as it prohibits jury trials in actions against corporations controlled by foreign states.

Forum non conveniens—alien tort—balancing test

PIPER AIRCRAFT CO. v. REYNO; HARTZELL PROPELLER, INC. v. REYNO. 102 S.Ct. 252.
U.S. Supreme Court, December 8, 1981.

These cases arose out of the crash of a small commercial aircraft in the Scottish highlands in which the pilot and passengers were killed. At the time of the crash, the plane was subject to Scottish air traffic control. The airplane was registered in Great Britain and was owned and operated by companies organized in the United Kingdom. The decedents were Scottish subjects and residents, as were their heirs and next of kin. The investigation of the accident was conducted by British authorities, and at the time of trial the wreckage of the plane was located in a hangar in England. The airplane and its propellers were manufactured in the United States by petitioners Piper Aircraft Co. (Piper) and Hartzell Propeller, Inc. (Hartzell).

Respondent Reyno, administratrix of the estates of the passengers, brought wrongful death actions against Piper and Hartzell in the United States District Court for the Middle District of Pennsylvania claiming negligence and strict liability.[1] Respondent, who was not related to and did not know any of the decedents or their survivors, freely admitted that the actions against Piper and Hartzell were filed in the United States because U.S. laws regarding liability, capacity to sue, and damages were more favorable to her position than were Scottish laws. Scottish law does not recognize strict liability in tort and does

[10] *Id.* at 69.

[11] *See, e.g.*, Pernell v. Southall Realty, 416 U.S. 363, 375 (1974); Curtis v. Loether, 415 U.S. 189, 193–94 (1974); Parsons v. Bedford, 28 U.S. (3 Pet.) 433, 446–47 (1830).

[12] 660 F.2d at 70.

[1] These suits were initially brought in the Superior Court of California. On petitioner's motion, they were removed to the United States District Court for the Central District of California and subsequently transferred to Pennsylvania.

not allow wrongful death actions unless brought by a decedent's relatives, who themselves may sue only for loss of support and society. Petitioners moved to dismiss on the ground of *forum non conveniens*, and the district court granted the motion, observing that Piper and Hartzell had both consented to submit to the jurisdiction of the Scottish courts and to waive any statute of limitations defense that might have been available.

The United States Court of Appeals for the Third Circuit reversed. It held that the district court had abused its discretion in granting dismissal and that, in any event, dismissal is automatically barred whenever the law of an alternative forum is less favorable to a plaintiff than the law of the chosen forum.

The Supreme Court granted *certiorari* to consider

> whether, in an action in federal district court brought by foreign plaintiffs against American defendants, the plaintiffs may defeat a motion to dismiss on the ground of *forum non conveniens* merely by showing that the substantive law that would be applied if the case were litigated in district court is more favorable to them than the law that would be applied by the courts of their own nation.[2]

The Supreme Court (per Marshall, J.) reversed the decision of the court of appeals, holding that the district court had not abused its discretion in granting dismissal.

The Supreme Court stated that the district court had applied the appropriate test for a *forum non conveniens* analysis, *i.e.*, the balancing test set forth in the companion cases of *Gulf Oil Corp. v. Gilbert* (330 U.S. 501 (1947)) and *Koster v. Lumbermen's Mutual Casualty Co.* (330 U.S. 518 (1947)). The Court observed that the *Gilbert* Court began with the proposition that ordinarily a plaintiff's choice of forum should not be disturbed, but that dismissal on the ground of *forum non conveniens* lies within the sound discretion of the trial court when an alternative forum has jurisdiction to hear the case, when plaintiff's choice imposes a heavy burden on either defendant or the court, and when plaintiff cannot offer any specific reasons demonstrating the convenience of his choice. To aid in performing the balancing test, *Gilbert* set forth a list of "private interest factors" pertaining to the convenience of the litigants and "public interest factors" pertaining to the convenience of the forum.[3]

The Court expressly approved the district court's distinction between resident or citizen plaintiffs and foreign plaintiffs. In this regard, the Court held, the central purpose of any *forum non conveniens* analysis is "to ensure that the trial is convenient"; and such convenience can be assumed when a plaintiff has chosen the home forum. Such an assumption is "much less reasonable," how-

[2] 102 S.Ct. 252, 261 n.12.

[3] The private interest factors outlined by the *Gilbert* Court include the "relative ease of access to sources of proof; availability of compulsory process for attendance of unwilling, and the cost of obtaining the attendance of willing, witnesses; possibility of view of premises, if view would be appropriate to the action; and all other practical problems that make trial of a case easy, expeditious, and inexpensive." Public interest factors include burden on the court's calendar; the local interest in having localized controversies decided at home; the interest in having a diversity action decided in a forum that is at home with the law that governs; the avoidance of unnecessary conflicts of law, or the application of foreign law; and the unfairness of burdening citizens in unrelated forums with jury duty. 330 U.S. at 508–09.

ever, when plaintiffs (or as here, the real parties in interest) are foreign.[4] With this distinction in mind, the Court concluded that the district court's application of the private and public interest factors outlined in *Gilbert* was reasonable: fewer evidentiary problems would be encountered if the trial were held in Scotland; a Scottish forum would permit impleading of potential third-party defendants; a trial in Scotland would avoid the situation of requiring a U.S. jury to interpret and apply unfamiliar foreign law; and Scotland's greater interest in the outcome of the litigation pointed to Scotland as the appropriate place for trial.

In approving the district court's analysis, the Court expressly rejected the Third Circuit's position that dismissal is automatically barred if a change in forum would mean application of a law less favorable to plaintiff than that of the chosen forum. The Court held that unless a foreign alternative forum offers a remedy so inadequate as to be no remedy at all, the possibility of a change in substantive law should not be given conclusive or even substantial weight in the *forum non conveniens* analysis. Otherwise, the Court reasoned, dismissal might be barred even though trial in the chosen forum was plainly inconvenient, which would render the doctrine of *forum non conveniens* a nullity. Finally, the Court noted in passing that an opposite result would substantially increase the flow into American courts of foreign plaintiffs against American manufacturers.

In reaffirming that less deference is to be paid to the choice of U.S. courts by foreign plaintiffs, the Court substantially lightened defendants' threshold burden in making the *forum non conveniens* argument under the *Gilbert* test. Thus, although the Supreme Court's reasoning in these cases does not depend solely upon the fact that the real parties in interest were foreign, this decision will nevertheless make it more difficult in practice for foreigners to sue U.S. manufacturers for accidents that occur outside this country. The decision can also be expected to reduce the burden on American courts from procedurally complex and costly suits that may have relatively little connection with the United States.

European Community Case Note

European Community law—conflicts between Community law and treaty obligations of member states—standing of individual fisherman to invoke Article 234 in defense

ATTORNEY GENERAL v. BURGOA. Case No. 812/79, [1980] ECR 2787.
Court of Justice of the European Communities, October 14, 1980.

The Court of Justice of the European Communities was asked to rule on four questions of Community law certified to it by the Circuit Court of Cork County, Ireland. These questions arose as a result of prosecution by Irish officials of a Spanish fisherman seized in July 1978, 20 miles off the coast of Cork, and charged with fishing illegally in Ireland's coastal waters. The ques-

[4] 102 S.Ct. at 265–66.

tions certified to the Court dealt primarily with issues concerning possible conflicts between Irish domestic law and European Community (EC) law, most notably Article 234 of the Treaty of Rome (298 UNTS 11). Article 234 states in relevant part: "The rights and obligations arising from the agreements concluded before the entry into force of this Treaty between one or more Member States on the one hand, and one or more third countries on the other, shall not be affected by the provisions of this Treaty."

Traditionally, Ireland had claimed a fishery zone of only 12 miles; it excluded foreigners completely from the first 6 miles, and regulated their activities in the 6–12-mile zone. This 12-mile fishing limit was recognized by Ireland when it, along with many other Western European nations, including Spain, agreed to the London Fisheries Convention of 1964, which contained an identical formula.

In 1977, however, increased concern over conservation of marine resources led many countries, including Ireland and all other EC member nations, to redefine their fishing limits to extend to 200 miles. In the same year, pending the conclusion of outline agreements between the EC and certain other nations, the EC formulated a series of interim regulations to govern fishing in the waters of member states by citizens of nonmember nations. The EC regime applicable to Spanish fishermen at the time of the seizure in question was Regulation No. 341/78, which established a system of licenses and quotas.

At trial in Ireland, Burgoa, the master of the seized vessel, claimed that prosecution under the Irish Fisheries (Amendment) Act of 1978, which imposed penalties for unauthorized fishing in Irish waters, would violate the concept of the primacy of EC law over Irish law. The court held the trial in abeyance and sought the opinion of the EC tribunal through certified questions as to whether a conflict existed.

The questions certified to the EC Court of Justice were: (1) Does Article 234 of the Treaty of Rome create rights and obligations for the institutions or member states of the European Communities? (2) Does Article 234, or any other rule of Community law, maintain or uphold rights of the beneficiaries of treaties to which Article 234 applies, which national courts of the member states must uphold? (3) Is the 1964 London Fisheries Convention a treaty of the kind to which Article 234 applies? and (4) Would a conviction of the defendant under the Irish penal statute in the proceedings in Ireland be contrary to EC law?

Burgoa contended that Article 234 prevented member states and Community institutions from taking any action that would impair obligations entered into by a member state prior to joining the EC. Accordingly, he argued that Article 234 protected his rights as a "traditional fisherman" under the London Fisheries Convention to fish beyond the 6-mile limit. Alternatively, Burgoa argued that because the Irish penal statute under which he was being prosecuted conflicted with the EC's system of fishery regulation, it must therefore be void.

The Court held that EC law created no impediment to the resumption of Burgoa's prosecution in Ireland. Addressing the certified questions in turn, the Court held, first, that Article 234 must be interpreted to mean that application of the EC Treaty does not affect obligations of member states to nonmember countries established prior to the member's joining the EC and that Community institutions are bound not to impede the performance of those obligations. The Court concluded, however, that the purpose of Article 234 is only to protect member states from being forced to abandon previous commitments by application of inconsistent Community law. It creates, in effect, rights that the member states can assert against the Community.

Second, the Court held that Article 234 is not intended to protect third-party interests and that it therefore does not create rights that individuals from nonmember nations can assert. Thus, EC law does not compel member state courts to uphold the rights of individuals, nor does it adversely affect those rights.

Third, the Court held that the London Fisheries Convention of 1964 is an agreement to which Article 234 would apply. However, the Court's response to the first two questions indicated that an individual claimant like Burgoa could not invoke Article 234 as a basis for avoiding a lawsuit; only an EC member state could do so.

Fourth, the Court held that the EC's licensing scheme set forth in its Regulation No. 341/78 would only prevent Irish prosecution if the purpose of the Irish penal statute were inconsistent with the purpose of the regulation. In this case the Court held that both the Irish statute and the EC regulation were intended to promote conservation of resources in Community waters. The regulation did not, by its nature, preempt the enactment of enforcement legislation by member states. Since there was no showing that the Spanish vessel had obtained the license required by the EC regulation, enforcement of the Irish penal statute was entirely consistent with the Community's regulatory scheme.

The significance of the Court's ruling in this case lies in its narrow interpretation of Article 234, specifically, that Article 234 only applies to regulations between member states and the EC as a whole and that it creates no rights for individuals from nonmember states.[1] The Court's ruling appears sound when the ramifications of a contrary result are taken into consideration. If the Court were to entertain individual claims under Article 234, it would be placed in the difficult position of determining the purposes and effects of the national laws of its member states in every case where an Article 234 defense was asserted by a private party.[2]

[1] The Court does not include an illustration of the proper application of Article 234. The opinion suggests, however, that Article 234 might be raised by one EC member against another. Thus, for example, had France complained to the Court of Justice that Ireland had allowed Burgoa to fish without a license in Ireland's protected waters in violation of Regulation No. 341/78, it would appear from the Court's ruling that Ireland could then have invoked Article 234 as a defense by contending that the Community regulation wrongfully impaired Ireland's obligations to Spain as a result of the London Fisheries Convention. On the other hand, under the facts of the present case, Burgoa could not claim Article 234 protection but was forced to seek a defense in Irish domestic law.

[2] Thus, in the instant case, the Court would have had to ascertain whether, under Irish law, Ireland maintained obligations to Spain as a result of the London Fisheries Convention of 1964 or whether those obligations had been nullified by the subsequent extension of the fishery zone to 200 miles.

United Kingdom Case Notes

Act of state doctrine in Great Britain—nonjusticiability of sovereign transactions—territorial dispute over offshore oil concession

Buttes Gas & Oil Co. v. Hammer and Others. [1981] 3 W.L.R. 787. House of Lords, October 29, 1981.

In this case, the House of Lords resolved a 10-year-old dispute between two American oil firms, Buttes Gas and Oil Co. and Occidental Petroleum Corp., involving their rights to exploit a discovery of oil in the Arabian Gulf. At the heart of the dispute were the competing claims of two neighboring Arab emirates, Sharjah and Umm al Qaiwain (UAQ), and the State of Iran to an oil-rich deposit lying 9 miles from the island of Abu Musa, which is located in the Arabian Gulf some 40 miles south of Sharjah and UAQ. The emirates were, at the relevant times, sovereign states in separate treaty relations with the United Kingdom, which was responsible for their foreign relations.

In 1969, oil concessions in the offshore seabeds of Sharjah and UAQ were obtained by Buttes and Occidental, respectively. Each company subsequently claimed the right to exploit the oil deposit lying off Abu Musa, Occidental by virtue of a map attached to its concession, and Buttes by virtue of a decree made in September 1969 by the Ruler of Sharjah declaring that the territorial sea of the emirate (including Abu Musa, to which it claimed title) was extended from 3 to 12 miles. Buttes contended that it had no knowledge of Occidental's map; and Occidental claimed that Sharjah's decree was in fact made in March or April of 1970 and that it was fraudulently backdated to a period prior to Occidental's concession so as to give Buttes the color of right to the disputed area. In May 1970, the United Kingdom, hoping for a settlement among the competing states, recommended to the Ruler of UAQ that Occidental not be permitted to operate in the disputed area for 3 months. Occidental, however, sent a drilling platform toward the location, which was turned back by the British Navy. Following this show of force, the Ruler of UAQ ordered Occidental not to operate within 12 miles of Abu Musa.

The instant case was triggered when Dr. Armand Hammer, chairman of Occidental, openly accused Buttes of colluding with the Ruler of Sharjah to backdate the decree of 1969/1970. Buttes sued Occidental for slander, and Occidental counterclaimed for damages of over $4 million, charging that Buttes and the Ruler of Sharjah fraudulently conspired to cheat and defraud Occidental and to cause Her Majesty's Government to act unlawfully to Occidental's injury. In its defense, Buttes sought an order that the court should not exercise jurisdiction because the actions on which Occidental based its claims were acts of state of the Governments of Sharjah, UAQ, Iran, and the United Kingdom. In 1974 the Court of Appeal (per Lord Denning, M.R.) refused Buttes's request on the ground that although the scope of the act of state doctrine was ill-defined in English law, it did not extend as widely as in the United States where the courts had refused to entertain a similar action between the same parties.[1] After

[1] *See, e.g.*, Occidental Petroleum Corp. v. Buttes Gas & Oil Co., 331 F.Supp. 92 (C.D. Cal. 1971), 65 AJIL 815 (1971).

6 more years of legal skirmishing, the present case reached the House of Lords, which reversed the lower court and held that the merits of the case were nonjusticiable.[2]

Buttes contended, first, that the English courts will not try an action that would require them to pronounce, directly or indirectly, on rights in immovable property situated abroad. To this, Occidental argued that questions relating to foreign territory may be decided by English courts where those decisions are collateral to the main question. The Court agreed with Occidental that the English courts have in the past and without difficulty decided questions depending upon the ascertainment of foreign boundaries. The Court also agreed that there may be other cases where a question relating to foreign territory, and even to the title thereof, may be capable of determination either as a matter of fact or as a question incidental to the main issue. But here the Court held, "the question of title to the location . . . is at the heart of the case. It is essential to Occidental's claim . . . to establish that before the intervention of Buttes and Sharjah it had a right with some degree of legal validity over the sea-bed at the location. . . ." This question could not be decided simply as an issue of fact upon evidence: "it calls, on the contrary, for adjudication upon the validity, meaning and effect of transactions of sovereign states."[3]

The Court next considered Occidental's contention that what might otherwise have been a nonjusticiable question had become justiciable through the actions of Her Majesty's Government, *i.e.*, that because the United Kingdom had set its seal of approval on the relevant dispositions of Sharjah and UAQ up to 1971, there would be no potential breach of comity or possibility of embarrassing the United Kingdom in its foreign relations if the Court were to pass upon them. The Court disposed of this argument on factual grounds, by showing through an analysis of relevant documents that the United Kingdom did not approve or disapprove of the acts of Sharjah and UAQ, but rather regarded them as issues of international law.

Turning to the "generally confused topic" of act of state, the Court began by segregating that version of the doctrine illustrated by cases concerned with the applicability and examinability of "foreign municipal legislation within its own territory." As to this, Occidental contended, first, that foreign legislation can be called in question where it is seen to be contrary to international law or public policy and, second, that foreign legislation need only be recognized within the limits of the authority of the state concerned. The Court found neither of these arguments persuasive. As to the first, the Court admitted that the attack on Sharjah's decree was not upon its validity under the law of Sharjah, but rather upon its efficacy in international law; however, the Court concluded that it is one thing to assert that effect will not be given to foreign municipal law if it is *contrary* to public policy or international law, "and quite another to claim that the courts may examine the validity, under international law, or some doctrine of public policy, of . . . acts operating in the area of transactions between states."[4] As to the second argument, the Court held that

[2] Lord Wilberforce wrote the opinion of the unanimous Court, which included Lord Fraser of Tullybelton, Lord Russell of Killowen, Lord Keith of Kinkel, and Lord Bridge of Harwich.

[3] [1981] 3 W.L.R. 787, 800.

[4] *Id.* at 804.

to attack the decree of Sharjah purportedly extending its territorial waters on the ground that the decree was extraterritorial was circular and therefore unpersuasive.

Finally, the Court addressed what it deemed to be the essential question: whether, *apart* from the particular rules thus far discussed, there exists in English law "a more general principle" that the courts will not adjudicate upon the transactions of foreign sovereign states. "[I]t seems desirable," the Court went on, "to consider this principle, if existing, not as a variety of 'act of state' but one for judicial restraint or abstention." Against this notion, Occidental argued that although there may be traces of such a general principle, it has now been crystallized into particular rules within which Buttes must bring its case or fail. However, the Court concluded that

> there is, and for long has been, such a general principle, starting in English law, adopted and generalised in the law of the U.S.A. which is effective and compelling in English courts. This principle is not one of discretion, but is inherent in the very nature of the judicial process.[5]

After tracing the history of this principle from *Blad's* case ((1673–4) 3 Swans. 602) through *Banco Nacional de Cuba v. Sabbatino* (376 U.S. 398 (1964)), the Court turned its attention to the American cases that have barred Occidental's claims on the basis of act of state. As to these, the Court admitted that in the American cases emphasis was laid upon the foreign relations aspect of the matter, whereas there was no indication in the present case that Her Majesty's Government would be embarrassed by the Court's inquiry into the relevant issues. The Court concluded, however, that "the ultimate question what issues are capable, and what are incapable, of judicial determination must be answered in closely similar terms in whatever country they arise, depending, as they must, upon an appreciation of the nature and limits of the judicial function."[6] Thus, if the proceeding before the Court were to continue, it would inevitably involve such issues as which state had sovereignty over Abu Musa, the width of the territorial waters of the island, the boundary of the continental shelf between Sharjah, UAQ, and Iran, and the motives of the Ruler of Sharjah in making the decree of 1969/1970. These and similar issues, the Court held,

> have only to be stated to compel the conclusion that these are not issues upon which a municipal court can pass. Leaving aside all possibility of embarrassment in our foreign relations . . . there are . . . no judicial or manageable standards by which to judge these issues . . . the court would be in a judicial no-man's land: the court would be asked to review transactions in which four sovereign states were involved, which they had brought to a precarious settlement, after diplomacy and the use of force, and to say that at least part of these were "unlawful" under international law.[7]

For these reasons, the Court concluded that the counterclaim "cannot succeed without bringing to trial non-justiciable issues," and, accordingly, it refused to entertain Occidental's appeal.[8]

[5] *Ibid.*

[6] *Id.* at 809.

[7] *Id.* at 810.

[8] Buttes also invoked the doctrine of sovereign immunity insofar as it excludes actions concerning property which is in the ownership, possession, or control of a foreign state, or in which a foreign

The full significance of this case cannot be accurately assessed at this time. Heretofore, the British act of state doctrine has been regarded as more limited in scope than its American counterpart.[9] However, ensuing decisions in the United Kingdom may indeed treat Lord Wilberforce's opinion in this case as having greatly expanded the concept of judicial restraint by creating a "sovereign transactions" corollary to the British act of state doctrine, the limits of which can be determined only on a case-by-case basis in the future.

Sovereign immunity—restrictive theory

MARBLE ISLANDS v. I CONGRESO DEL PARTIDO. [1981] 3 W.L.R. 328. House of Lords, July 16, 1981.

Actions against a vessel (*I Congreso*) owned by the Republic of Cuba, which was "constructed, found and arrested" within the United Kingdom, to secure payment of claims arising against the Cuban State Shipping Agency (Mambisa) for the illegal conversion of two cargoes of sugar. The claimants were the Chilean owners of two cargoes of sugar on board two sister ships. The vessels were chartered by Mambisa to Cubazucar, another Cuban Government entity which had contracted to deliver the cargoes of sugar to purchasers in Chile.

The claimant cargo owners alleged that on September 11, 1973 the *Playa Larga*, a vessel owned by the Government of Cuba through Mambisa, was in the process of unloading sugar in Valparaiso harbor when the coup d'état that brought the Pinochet Government into power took place. At the time of the coup Mambisa, on instructions of the Government, ordered the *Playa Larga* to leave Chile, which she did immediately without obtaining port clearance or finishing unloading, and in doing so carried away certain unloading equipment and tackle belonging to other parties. The *Playa Larga* met at sea her sister ship, the *Marble Islands*, prior to the latter's arrival in Chilean territorial waters, and thereafter both, under orders of Mambisa, proceeded to Peru. The *Marble Islands*, unlike the *Playa Larga*, was owned at the time of the coup d'état by a Liechtenstein corporation and flew the Somali flag.

In harbor in Peru, the agents of the cargo owners requested the discharge of the sugar, which had been paid for, but both masters refused. Thereafter, the *Playa Larga* left Peru and returned to Cuba where the balance of her cargo was sold by Mambisa. The *Marble Islands* also left Peru intending to return to Cuba but was arrested at the Panama Canal on the application of the cargo owners. However, she broke arrest and sailed westward across the Pacific to North Vietnam. In the course of her passage her ownership and flag were transferred to the Republic of Cuba. Upon arrival in Haiphong the cargo of the *Marble Islands* was sold by the master to yet another Cuban state enterprise (Alimport). Thereafter Alimport, on instructions of the Government of Cuba, donated the cargo of sugar to the people of North Vietnam.

---

state claims an interest. The Court, however, dismissed this contention summarily, declaring that the doctrine "does not . . . apply since there is no attack direct or indirect upon any property of any of the relevant sovereigns, nor are any of them impleaded directly or indirectly." *Id.* at 799.

[9] *Cf. In re* Claim by Helbert Wagg & Co. Ltd., [1956] 1 Ch. 323; The *Rose Mary*, [1953] 1 W.L.R. 246.

On these facts the courts of the United Kingdom were called upon to determine whether the acts of conversion with respect to the cargo of each of these two vessels were governmental acts, in which case the defense of sovereign immunity would bar adjudication on the merits; or commercial transactions, in which case the Government of Cuba would not be entitled to rely on the plea of sovereign immunity.

With respect to the *Playa Larga*, all the Law Lords agreed that the defense of sovereign immunity was not available to defeat the claim of the cargo owners. However, their Lordships were divided with respect to the *Marble Islands*. Lord Wilberforce delivered an opinion, in which Lord Edmund-Davies concurred, holding that Cuba was entitled to invoke the defense of sovereign immunity. In their view, "The acts of the Republic of Cuba were and remained in their nature purely governmental."[1]

Lord Diplock and two other members of the Court were of the view that neither claim was subject to the defense of sovereign immunity, for reasons more fully stated below. Accordingly, the House of Lords rejected the plea of sovereign immunity with respect to both actions.

This judgment is significant for several reasons:

> (1) All the Law Lords agreed that the restrictive theory of sovereign immunity was a part of the law of England even before the enactment of the British State Immunity Act, 1978, which in fact entered into force after the occurrences giving rise to the present claims and was not retroactive in legal effect.
>
> (2) All the Law Lords agreed that the adoption of the restrictive theory of immunity in British law, which had first been declared for cases arising in rem in *The Philippine Admiral* ([1977] A.C. 373), was applicable also in cases arising in personam.
>
> (3) All the Law Lords agreed that the critical issue was to determine and apply, on the complicated facts in these two appeals, the distinction between sovereign acts and commercial acts. They differed in this application.

It was strongly argued by counsel for the cargo owners that the Court should adopt the principle "once a trader, always a trader." If this principle had been accepted, the outcome would have been easy, since obviously both charters commenced as commercial transactions. However, Lord Wilberforce expressly rejected this contention and Lord Diplock, writing for the majority, did not express an opinion. Lord Wilberforce concluded that the restrictive theory should apply with respect to the *Playa Larga*, but the Cuban Government's actions after it purchased the *Marble Islands* from its private owners made that situation different. The intervention of the Government to direct the transfer of the cargo of the *Marble Islands* to the people of North Vietnam constituted a sovereign act and should be protected from judicial inquiry by the doctrine of sovereign immunity.

Lord Diplock, while agreeing with Lord Wilberforce with respect to the *Playa Larga*, differed as to the *Marble Islands*. In both cases the ships had

[1] [1981] 3 W.L.R. 328, 345.

indeed been controlled by the policy of the Government of Cuba, first in abandoning the mission of delivering sugar to Chile, and later in disposing of the sugar cargoes. However, in the case of the *Marble Islands*, Lord Diplock took the position that the relevant transaction, *i.e.*, the discharge and sale of the cargo to Alimport, was "deliberately treated by the Cuban government as being effected under private law and not in the exercise of any sovereign powers."[2] He held, therefore, that the Cuban Government was not entitled to interpose the defense of sovereign immunity. Lord Keith and Lord Bridge joined in this view. Accordingly, the plea of sovereign immunity was disallowed.

This case is the first in which a court of final resort in the United Kingdom has grappled in detail with the difficult task of defining the line of demarcation between sovereign and commercial acts. (It has not yet been done in the United States.) The rejection of the principle "once a trader, always a trader" indicates that in the United Kingdom the courts will probably approach the task of definition on a case-by-case basis. It remains to be seen whether they will set guidelines that prevent foreign sovereigns from devising "forms" of sovereign action in order to throw the mantle of immunity over state trading agencies engaged in commercial activities.

[2] *Id.* at 348.

CURRENT DEVELOPMENTS

The 1981 Session of the UN Sub-Commission on Prevention of Discrimination and Protection of Minorities

The 34th annual session of the Sub-Commission on Prevention of Discrimination and Protection of Minorities, a subsidiary body of the UN Commission on Human Rights, was held in Geneva from August 17 to September 11, 1981.[1] The 26 expert members of the Sub-Commission serve in a personal capacity and are elected for 3-year terms by the Commission on the nomination of governments. The most recent elections were held in March 1981 and saw the reelection of 13 former Sub-Commission members. There was an increase in the number of sub-Saharan African members, with a concomitant decrease in Asian and Middle Eastern members.

Criticism of the Sub-Commission at the March 1981 session of the Commission cast its shadow on the 1981 session of the Sub-Commission and resulted in a somewhat less activist session than might have been expected. For example, a 1980 request by the Sub-Commission to the Commission for general authorization to conduct on-site investigations (with the consent of the country concerned) was not resubmitted by the 1981 Sub-Commission;[2] similarly, an earlier request for an impartial information-gathering service also was dropped;[3] and, while there is still a desire among the Sub-Commission's members for some kind of emergency UN mechanism to consider human rights violations, the Sub-Commission recommended the creation of a new UN High Commissioner for Human Rights rather than directly offering its own expertise.[4]

While the Sub-Commission may have been somewhat more subservient to the Commission than in past years, it did make important progress in the area of its greatest successes, the drafting of legal norms and the adoption of recommendations to improve enforcement of international human rights law.

Other highlights of the 1981 session, in addition to the discussions on the relationship between the Sub-Commission and the Commission, included:

- discussions on the rights of indigenous populations and the adoption of resolutions calling for an annual working group and preparation of draft principles on the rights of indigenous populations;
- discussions of violations of human rights in specific countries under

[1] For an analysis of the Sub-Commission's 1980 session and a brief discussion of its structure, see Hannum, *Human Rights and the United Nations: Progress at the 1980 Session of the U.N. Sub-Commission on Prevention of Discrimination and Protection of Minorities*, 3 Human Rights Q. 1 (1981), and Current Developments Note, 75 AJIL 172 (1981).

[2] Res. 22 (XXXIII), UN Doc. E/CN.4/1413, E/CN.4/Sub.2/459 [hereinafter cited as 1980 Report], at 78 (1980).

[3] Res. 19 (XXXIII), 1980 Report at 76.

[4] Res. 12 (XXXIV), UN Doc. E/CN.4/Sub.2/495 [hereinafter cited as 1981 Report], at 86 (1981).

the confidential "1503 procedure" and public debates under ECOSOC Resolution 1235;

• contributions of various Sub-Commission working groups, most notably the Working Group on Slavery;

• recommendations on potential international guidelines concerning the exploitation of child labor; and

• decisions to start or continue studies on the right of conscientious objection to military service, the rights of the mentally ill, the independence of judges and lawyers, and states of siege or emergency.

Relationship with the Commission

Although the Commission has, on many occasions, encouraged the Sub-Commission to assume more responsibility and to broaden the scope of its activities, at the Commission's 1981 session several members strongly criticized the Sub-Commission for exceeding its terms of reference.[5] The strongest attack came from Brazil, which criticized the Sub-Commission for taking actions without obtaining authorization from the Commission and for pursuing measures that lie outside the scope of activity entrusted to it.[6]

The discussion of the Sub-Commission's role and competence resulted in the adoption of a resolution by the Commission which, to anyone who had followed the discussions, was surprisingly moderate in tone. The resolution, *inter alia*, invited the Sub-Commission to take note of the comments and suggestions made by members of the Commission and noted that the use of alternates to represent expert members "might not on occasion be in keeping with the character of that body."[7]

In anticipation of a discussion by the Sub-Commission of its mandate and its relationship to its parent bodies, the UN Secretariat prepared an unofficial document on the role and competence of the Sub-Commission.[8] Despite its unofficial character, this document did dispel some of the confusion among Sub-Commission members about the merits of the Commission's criticisms.

On the other hand, several Sub-Commission members believed that a continued hierarchical relationship with the Commission would be disadvantageous to the work of the Sub-Commission, and they suggested that the Commission was too political a body to act on certain recommendations of the Sub-Commission. One suggestion was to change the status of the Sub-Commission to a "Committee of Experts on Human Rights," which would report directly to ECOSOC and only communicate its recommendations and reports to the Com-

[5] *See* statements by Brazil, UN Doc. E/CN.4/SR.1592, at 5 (1981); Syria, Uruguay, Argentina, and the Soviet Union, UN Doc. E/CN.4/SR.1593, at 2, 7, 11, and 13 (1981); Poland, India, and Cuba, UN Doc. E/CN.4/SR.1594, at 3, 6, and 10 (1981); and France, UN Doc. E/CN.4/SR.1595, at 4 (1981).

[6] Statement by Brazil, *supra* note 5.

[7] Commission Res. 17 (XXXVII), 37 UN ESCOR, Supp. (No. 5) 219, UN Doc. E/CN.4/1475 (1981).This admonition was evidently ignored, as no fewer than ten alternates replaced Sub-Commission members at one time or another during the 1981 session.

[8] UN Division of Human Rights, The Role and Competence of the Sub-Commission on Prevention of Discrimination and Protection of Minorities (informal paper on file with the International Human Rights Law Group, Washington, D.C., June 15, 1981).

mission.[9] This suggestion will be discussed further at next year's Sub-Commission session under a new agenda item on the status of the Sub-Commission and its relationship with other UN bodies.[10]

Rights of Indigenous Populations

The decision to develop international guidelines and to establish a forum to consider the rights of indigenous populations was undoubtedly one of the most important developments of the Sub-Commission's 1981 session.[11] The issue was first raised by the Director of the Division of Human Rights in his impressive opening speech,[12] and it remained a primary topic of concern throughout the session. In addition, the Sub-Commission finally had before it the first part of the decade-old Study of the Problem of Discrimination against Indigenous Populations, which offered it an obvious factual basis for action.

The Sub-Commission took two important steps to attempt to redress earlier failures to act. First, it requested that the Commission and ECOSOC approve the establishment of a working group on indigenous populations, which would meet prior to each Sub-Commission session to review and discuss material received from governments and NGO's and make recommendations to the full Sub-Commission, much in the way the Working Group on Slavery operates.[13] This request was approved by the Commission on Human Rights in March 1982 and will now be forwarded to ECOSOC.

In a related resolution, the Sub-Commission enlarged the task of its special rapporteur, José R. Martínez-Cobo, and asked that he include in his final report "a text containing draft principles relating to the rights of indigenous populations."[14] If the study is finally completed by the next session, the draft principles could become the first important topic to be discussed by the new working group on indigenous populations.

Violations of Human Rights

Although the entire agenda of the Sub-Commission is, in a sense, concerned with human rights violations, three items have become the focus for discussions of specific allegations of violations. These three items are the confidential communications procedure under ECOSOC Resolution 1503; the question of violations of human rights and fundamental freedoms in all countries, which is considered publicly under the provisions of ECOSOC Resolution 1235 (XLII) and Commission Resolution 8 (XXIII); and the human rights of persons subject to any form of detention or imprisonment.

Fewer countries were recommended for consideration by the Commission

[9] *See* remarks of Ahmed Khalifa, UN Doc. E/CN.4/Sub.2/SR.896, at 5 (1981). The Commission for Social Development and the Commission on the Status of Women were cited as existing examples of independent expert bodies.

[10] Dec. 2 (XXXIV), 1981 Report at 95.

[11] *See* UN Docs. E/CN.4/Sub.2/SR.905–09 (1981).

[12] The entire text is set forth in UN Press Release HR/1080, Aug. 17, 1981.

[13] Res. 2 (XXXIV), 1981 Report at 76.

[14] Res. 3 (XXXIV), *id.* at 77.

under the Resolution 1503 communications procedure than at last year's session, and all those forwarded to the Commission—Afghanistan, Argentina, the German Democratic Republic, Haiti, Paraguay, Uruguay, and Venezuela—had previously been considered by the Sub-Commission.[15] Information on the human rights situations in Bolivia, Chile, El Salvador, and Guatemala will continue to be reported by the special rapporteurs or other mechanisms established for those countries.

The wide-ranging public debate on the general question of violations under ECOSOC Resolution 1235 included country-specific allegations by both Sub-Commission members and representatives of NGO's, which continues a trend that now encounters little opposition.[16] The issue of self-determination in Afghanistan, Angola, Kampuchea, and Namibia was of particular concern at this year's session, and frequent reference was made to the persecution of the Baha'is in Iran[17] (often accompanied by a defense of Islam as a religion of peace and compassion). Alleged violations of human rights were noted in Argentina, Bolivia, Brazil, Chile, Czechoslovakia, El Salvador, Equatorial Guinea, Guatemala, Israel, Morocco, Northern Ireland, Paraguay, the Philippines, South Korea, the Soviet Union, Sri Lanka, Tunisia, the United States, Uruguay, and Zaire.[18] Asbjørn Eide updated a 1980 report on Kampuchea, with recommendations for UN supervision of elections, withdrawal of foreign troops, and the repatriation of refugees.[19] Government observers from 32 countries were present, and many accused of violations requested the right to reply. Several interventions were reminiscent in spirit of the more political atmosphere of the General Assembly, such as the allegations of Vietnam's "venomous imperialism" made by the observer from China.[20]

In keeping with its efforts to avoid criticism from its parent body for exceeding its mandate, the Sub-Commission asked the Secretary-General to communicate its concern to the Chairman of the Commission (rather than directly to the country concerned) over the fate of three black South Africans condemned to death. As a result of this request, the Chairman (coincidentally from Brazil, one of the nations most critical of the Sub-Commission) sent a telegram to the Minister of Foreign Affairs of South Africa, appealing for clemency on humanitarian grounds.[21]

Resolutions adopted under the "gross violations" item were kept carefully within even a narrow view of the Sub-Commission's mandate, and they included reference to, *inter alia*, persecution of the Baha'is in Iran,[22] Israeli occupation of territories in the Middle East and Israeli bombing raids,[23] El Salvador

[15] This is not necessarily a complete or definitive list but has been compiled on the basis of information available at the time of writing.

[16] *But see* statements of Halima Warzazi and Louis Joinet concerning criticism of one's own country. UN Doc. E/CN.4/Sub.2/SR.903, paras. 46, 51, and 52 (1981).

[17] *See* especially the statements of Khalifa and Syed Masud, UN Press Release HR/1099, Aug. 31, 1981, and Warzazi, UN Doc. E/CN.4/Sub.2/SR.904, para. 7 (1981).

[18] *See* UN Press Releases HR/1099, 1100, and 1101, Aug, 31, 1981; 1981 Report at 26.

[19] UN Doc. E/CN.4/Sub.2/L.780 (1981). *See* UN Docs. E/CN.4/Sub.2/487 and Add.1 (1981) for the Kampuchean replies.

[20] Authors' notes, Aug. 31, 1981.

[21] *See* 1981 Report at 25.

[22] Res. 8 (XXXIV), *id.* at 80.

[23] Res. 9 (XXXIV), *id.* at 81.

(noting, after much debate, the need for all political forces to participate in a peaceful settlement of the conflict),[24] and withdrawal of foreign troops and respect for the right of self-determination in Afghanistan[25] and Kampuchea.[26] The Sub-Commission also resolved to seek further information on the right to leave one's country.[27]

The discussion of the rights of detainees and prisoners unfortunately added little to the present depressing state of knowledge on the ill-treatment often suffered by such persons.[28] The Sub-Commission's sessional Working Group on Detention did refer specifically to continuing violations of human rights through summary execution, especially of political prisoners; the misuse of statements or confessions made by detainees; disappearances; and the practice of incommunicado detention.[29] With respect to the last issue, several members of the working group stated that "nothing could justify such detention, and even if there were exceptional cases in which a justification could be found, such detention should in no circumstances exceed 24 hours."[30]

A preliminary report by Erica-Irene Daes on principles for the protection of persons detained on the ground of mental illness was considered under the item on detainees as well as that relating to scientific and technological developments.[31] While noting that the problem of the treatment of mental patients was universal, Daes underscored that the guidelines to be presented in her 1982 final report would seek, in particular, to provide guarantees to prevent the involuntary admission to and detention in mental hospitals of persons exercising their human rights.[32]

Widespread violations of human rights are common in situations of states of siege or martial law, and one of the most important progress reports (along with that relating to detention on grounds of mental illness) was that of Nicole Questiaux on the implications for human rights of states of siege or emergency. Questiaux's excellent oral report was subsequently issued as a written document,[33] and it identified seven principles that should serve as minimum standards in an alleged emergency situation:

> —proclamation: the emergency must be officially declared;
> —notification: if a state is party to a relevant international instrument, specific notification of the justification for and extent of any derogation must be given to the appropriate body;
> —exceptional nature of threat: the threat must be imminent and endanger the very existence of the state;
> —proportionality: any measures taken must be only those that are strictly required by the exigencies of the emergency situation;

[24] Res. 10 (XXXIV), *id.* at 83.

[25] Res. 11 (XXXIV), *id.* at 84.

[26] Res. 13 (XXXIV), *id.* at 86.

[27] Res. 7 (XXXIV), *id.* at 80.

[28] *See* UN Doc. E/CN.4/Sub.2/471 (1981) for a non-country-specific summary of information submitted by NGO's.

[29] UN Doc. E/CN.4/Sub.2/L.774, *reproduced in* 1981 Report at 34.

[30] 1981 Report at 35.

[31] UN Doc. E/CN.4/Sub.2/474 (1981); *see* 1981 Report at 37–39.

[32] Draft guidelines were suggested by the International Association of Penal Law and the International Commission of Jurists in UN Doc. E/CN.4/Sub.2/NGO/85 (1981).

[33] UN Doc. E/CN.4/Sub.2/490 (1981).

—nondiscrimination: emergency measures cannot discriminate on the ground of race, color, sex, language, religion, or social origin;

—inalienability of rights: certain fundamental rights such as the right to life and freedom from torture cannot be derogated from under any circumstances; and

—compatibility with other obligations under international law: this includes such basic norms as the right to self-determination and the prohibition against the use of force, as well as norms for the protection of the individual.

Slavery and Slavery-like Practices; Exploitation of Child Labor

The activities of the Working Group on Slavery caused heated debate in the full Sub-Commission, perhaps a measure of the working group's effectiveness.[34] In response to a report by the Anti-Slavery Society for Human Rights and the attention of the working group, Mauritania invited Sub-Commission experts to conduct an on-site investigation of the human rights situation in that country.[35] Government responses also were received from Guatemala in reference to a 1980 Anti-Slavery Society report;[36] Thailand, concerning the sale of children;[37] Ethiopia, regarding slavery in Humera;[38] Greece;[39] India;[40] Italy;[41] Spain, regarding child labor;[42] and the Dominican Republic, regarding migrant workers.[43]

The resolution adopted by the Sub-Commission on the Slavery Working Group's report recommended, *inter alia*, that the Commission (not the Sub-Commission itself) send a delegation to Mauritania to ascertain that country's needs; ask the UN Department of Public Information to increase public awareness of the problem of slavery and slavery-like practices; and transmit, through the Secretary-General, information provided by NGO's and the working group's report to the countries concerned "for information and such observations as they may wish to make."[44]

A worldwide media campaign to stimulate public awareness of the exploitation of child labor was proposed in a major study by Abdelwahab Bouhdiba.[45] Among the strategies envisaged were an international training program for factory inspectors and enforcement procedures to be coordinated with efforts by UNESCO, INTERPOL, and the UN Human Rights Division.

[34] The working group's report is contained in UN Doc. E/CN.4/Sub.2/486 (1981); summaries of the debates may be found in UN Docs. E/CN.4/Sub.2/SR.908–11 (1981).

[35] *See* UN Doc. E/CN.4/Sub.2/SR.909, paras. 59–60 (1981); and, for the text of the telegram from Mauritania to the Director of the Human Rights Division, UN Doc. E/CN.4/Sub.2/489 (1981).

[36] UN Doc. E/CN.4/Sub.2/460 (1981).

[37] UN Doc. E/CN.4/Sub.2/461 (1981).

[38] *See* UN Doc. E/CN.4/Sub.2/SR.909, paras. 61–62 (1981).

[39] *Id.*, paras. 55–58.

[40] UN Doc. E/CN.4/Sub.2/AC.2/36 (1981).

[41] UN Doc. E/CN.4/Sub.2/AC.2/47 (1981).

[42] UN Doc. E/CN.4/Sub.2/AC.2/37 (1981).

[43] UN Doc. E/CN.4/Sub.2/AC.2/44 (1981).

[44] Res. 16 (XXXIV), 1981 Report at 89, para. 6.

[45] UN Doc. E/CN.4/Sub.2/479 (1981). The Sub-Commission's resolution on this topic provides for consideration of a "concrete programme of action" at its next session. Res. 18 (XXXIV), 1981 Report at 90.

Future Work of the Sub-Commission

A number of final reports will be presented at the 1982 session, and several progress reports were delivered at this session, including a draft report by Abu Sayeed Chowdhury on discrimination in the administration of criminal justice;[46] L. M. Singhvi's brief progress report on his Study on the Independence of the Judiciary, Jurors, and Assessors and the Independence of Lawyers;[47] and a draft report by Raúl Ferrero on the New International Economic Order and the Promotion of Human Rights, which stressed the interdependence of economic rights and civil and political rights.[48] The 1982 session will consider a study on the status of the individual in contemporary international law and a report on conscientious objection to military service.

Observations

The 1981 session of the Sub-Commission is somewhat difficult to evaluate, as inaction on some issues was balanced by important initiatives on others. There were two major influences throughout the session: concern over the Commission's criticism in March 1981 of the overly independent attitude demonstrated by the Sub-Commission in recent years, and the fact that one-half of the Sub-Commission's members were newly elected at that same Commission session. The newly elected members, in particular, seemed understandably confused as to the extent of autonomy that the Sub-Commission does or should enjoy.

The change in style that resulted from this confusion and criticism is vividly demonstrated by comparing the 1980 and 1981 resolutions on Afghanistan adopted by the Sub-Commission. The 1980 resolution directly "calls upon those States responsible" for violating the right to self-determination "to cease all acts of suppression against the peoples concerned."[49] The 1981 resolution, after expressing satisfaction at Commission and General Assembly resolutions calling for the withdrawal of foreign troops, "calls on . . . invites . . . further invites . . . requests . . . [and] recommends" to the Commission that it take various actions; there is no direct appeal to any country.[50]

It is certainly possible that concern over the formal addressees of the resolutions exalts form over substance, as the expression of the Sub-Commission's opinions is equally apparent whether it draws the attention of the Commission to a situation or whether it directly addresses the state in question. Nevertheless, the refusal of the Sub-Commission even to send information to governments for comment seems to be an overly sensitive and potentially damaging limitation on the competence of the Sub-Commission to consider factual matters clearly within its mandate.

The willingness of many members to raise specific allegations of human rights violations during debate on the public agenda item on gross violations and the criticism by some members of the excessive confidentiality of the 1503

[46] UN Doc. E/CN.4/Sub.2/L.766 (1981).

[47] UN Doc. E/CN.4/Sub.2/481 (1981).

[48] UN Doc. E/CN.4/Sub.2/477 (1981).

[49] Res. 26 (XXXIII), 1980 Report at 83.

[50] Res. 11 (XXXIV), 1981 Report at 84.

procedure tend to counter any interpretation that this Sub-Commission is less actively concerned with human rights than the one that served from 1978 to 1980. Welcome energy and expertise were brought to the Sub-Commission by new members such as Marc Bossuyt, Asbjørn Eide, Jonas Foli, and L. C. Mubanga-Chipoya. In addition, the Sub-Commission did initiate a major new program through its request for a presessional working group on indigenous populations. It also became the first UN body to propose formally the establishment of a UN High Commissioner for Human Rights, although that action apparently had little impact on the General Assembly's subsequent consideration of the issue. The Sub-Commission's continued support of the Commission's Working Group on Enforced or Involuntary Disappearances was also welcome.

The primary question to be answered after the 1980 session of the Sub-Commission was whether or not its parent bodies—the Commission and ECOSOC—would grant it the increased role it seemed to be seeking. The answer from the Commission in 1981 was clear and negative. The Sub-Commission must therefore identify those areas definitely within its mandate in which it can continue to work and at least place moral pressure on the Commission to respond to urgent crises and other important human rights issues.

On the whole, the successes of the 1981 session seem to outweigh its disappointments. Seemingly minor matters such as the appearance of Sweden and Syria before the Sub-Commission's Working Group on Encouragement of the Ratification of Human Rights Instruments or the prompt reaction of the Chairman of the Commission to the Sub-Commission's request that he send a telegram to South Africa provide valuable precedents for future action. In the imperfect world of human rights and the at least equally imperfect world of the United Nations, most members of the Sub-Commission seem honestly to be seeking more effective measures to implement existing human rights norms.

TON GARDENIERS, HURST HANNUM, AND JANICE KRUGER*

THE MONTREAL PROTOCOLS TO THE WARSAW CONVENTION ON INTERNATIONAL CARRIAGE BY AIR

On November 10, 1981, the Senate Committee on Foreign Relations voted by 16 to 1 to report favorably to the Senate for advice and consent to ratification, with three provisos, Montreal Protocols 3 and 4 to Amend the Convention for the Unification of Certain Rules Relating to International Carriage by Air (the Warsaw Convention).[1] By ratifying the Protocols, the United States, which

* This article was prepared for the International Human Rights Law Group by the authors, who represented the Procedural Aspects of International Law Institute/International Human Rights Law Group at the 1981 session of the Sub-Commission. A more detailed analysis of the Sub-Commission's session will appear in the August 1982 issue of *Human Rights Quarterly*.

[1] TS No. 876, 137 LNTS 11.

For President Ford's letter, dated Jan. 14, 1977, transmitting Protocols 3 and 4 to the Senate for advice and consent to ratification, see S. EXEC. DOC. B, 95th Cong., 1st Sess. (1977). The Department of State's report to the President on the Protocols, dated Dec. 23, 1976, is at *ibid.*

at present is party only to the Warsaw Convention itself and not to any of the subsequent Protocols revising it (The Hague, 1955, and Guatemala City, 1971), would adopt the newest versions of the Warsaw rules. Without the Protocols, liability for death of or injuries to passengers in international air transportation to, from, or having a stopping place within the United States is governed by the Warsaw Convention and by the special Montreal Agreement among the principal U.S. and foreign international air carriers of 1966.[2] Under the Montreal Agreement, the carriers waived certain Warsaw Convention defenses and agreed to accept liability for passenger injury or death up to $75,000. However, Article 25 of the Convention, which permits plaintiffs who can establish "wilful misconduct" by the carrier to break the $75,000 liability limit, continues in full force.

Portions of the report of the Senate Committee on Foreign Relations follow:

MONTREAL PROTOCOL 3

This Protocol amends the Guatemala City Protocol. The following provisions are included in the Guatemala City Protocol:

An unbreakable airline liability limit of approximately $120,000, regardless of fault, in the case of passenger death or injury, [and] $1,000 per passenger baggage liability limit;

A settlement inducement clause designed to force airlines to settle a claim within six months by subjecting them to added costs (including attorney fees) if in a subsequent trial a court awards more than the airline's offer;

Facilitation of suits against foreign airlines in the U.S. by permitting an action in the domicile of the passenger if the airline has an "establishment" there;

Recognition of the right of each participating nation to establish a supplemental compensation plan to operate within its territories.

In accordance with this latter provision the Civil Aeronautics Board in July 1977 approved a Supplemental Compensation Plan along the following lines:

(1) An additional $200,000 of available recovery for loss of life—increasing the total to $320,000—and unlimited medical coverage; and

(2) A $2.00 per ticket surcharge to provide for a compensation fund to pay supplemental recoveries (the surcharge to be adjusted and probably reduced over time).

MONTREAL PROTOCOL NO. 4

This Protocol amends and updates the cargo provisions of the Warsaw Convention, as amended [at The] Hague. By ratifying Montreal Protocol No. 4, the United States would adopt the most recent rules with respect to cargo documentation and liability limits in cargo cases. The Protocol sets a limit of 17 SDRs (about $21) per kilogram in the case of cargo.

. . . .

[2] 49 U.S.C. §1502, Agreement CAB 18900.

Committee Comments

The Committee agrees with the position taken by the Ford, Carter and Reagan administrations in support of U.S. ratification of Montreal Protocols No. 3 and 4. We support ratification with the understanding that a Supplemental Compensation Plan will be in place to increase the recoveries available to U.S. citizens.

The Montreal Protocols are the result of decades of effort by the United States to improve the existing Warsaw treaty system. The United States has been a party to that system since 1934; limitations on airline liability are therefore not a new concept, but a fact of life in international aviation for many years. The purpose of this arrangement has been to provide a uniform international system of rules and practices for the protection of travelers and shippers. It would bring airlines around the world up to at least a minimum level of compensation for loss of life, insure quick and reliable recoveries (in most cases within six months), and promote greater efficiency in the handling of cargo and baggage.

The Committee is concerned that the failure to follow through on the Montreal Protocols, which were the result of long and difficult efforts by the United States, might not only undercut our influence within the International Civil Aviation Organization and other forums, but would actually spell the end of the Warsaw Convention. That treaty is seriously outdated at the present time, and without the ratification of these modernizing amendments and the continued vigorous leadership of the United States, it is doubtful that the Warsaw regime will survive. The result could be a lengthy period of confusion during which the rules of jurisdiction and the standards for liability are completely unpredictable.

The Committee is well aware that the trade-off for participating in the Warsaw system, as amended by the Protocols, is the agreement to an absolute ceiling on the liability of airlines to each accident victim. If the limit set by the Protocol of approximately $120,000 (the estimated current value of 100,000 SDRs, or Special Drawing Rights) was absolute and could not be supplemented by a domestic compensation plan, the level would clearly be unacceptable. Even with an additional $200,000 possible recovery as allowed under Article 35A of Protocol 3, it will be desirable to seek continued increases in the agreed limit to keep pace with inflation and other circumstances.

However, on balance, the Committee believes that the special features of international civil aviation do justify the continued participation of the United States in a system of limited liability so long as it operates to ensure swift, sure and sufficient compensation when supplemented by a domestic compensation plan which substantially increases the recoveries for U.S. citizens. In effect, the Senate would be approving a three-tiered system under which the airlines would be liable for the first $120,000 per passenger, the supplemental plan would provide an additional $200,000 of coverage, and the individual would be expected to provide for recoveries beyond $320,000 by private insurance. The $320,000 limit should be sufficient to cover the large majority of Americans who fly abroad and do so more quickly and reliably with less litigation and related expenses. The fact that this approach has been endorsed overwhelmingly by the American Bar Association, an organization not generally supportive of no-fault liability systems, is indicative of the strength of the arguments for it.

The Committee was not persuaded by the principal arguments made against the Protocols.

The first is that the level of recoveries allowable under the proposed system, roughly $320,000 per person, is so low that it cannot be justified. Data provided to the Committee relating to the five most recent domestic airline accidents (in which the Warsaw limits do not apply) shows that 85 percent of the settlements in these cases are less than the level under consideration here. Therefore, the vast majority of Americans would be covered at such a level. However, it should also be noted that in some of these cases the settlements have taken years, with a considerable percentage of the recoveries going to attorneys' fees. For example, a $400,000 recovery in which the trial attorney receives 25 percent or more of the total would be a recovery to the claimant well below the total available under the proposed system. Attorneys' fees of 33 percent and even 40 percent are not uncommon in suits of this kind. Individuals who could expect much larger recoveries would be on notice to insure themselves for higher amounts without passing that cost on to all passengers and without incurring the large percentage cost which normally goes to trial attorneys.

The second point raised against the Protocols is the suggestion that unlimited liability coverage for international air carriers can be purchased for less than the $2.00 surcharge under the previously proposed Supplemental Compensation Plan, even though the latter would provide coverage limited to $200,000. The Committee is simply not convinced that this is the case. We have been told by experts in the insurance industry that unlimited insurance for international carriers would probably cost much more than the price paid for domestic travel. In any case, that would be a question to be considered by the CAB in reviewing the cost of a supplemental plan.

The third argument is that the Senate should take no action until the Civil Aeronautics Board has once again reviewed the supplemental compensation plan which it approved four years ago. We are dealing, in some respects, with a chicken-and-egg problem here. The CAB has taken no further action on the proposed plan since 1977 because it had no reason to think that the Senate would be approving the Montreal Protocols. It would certainly be expected to do so once the Senate takes positive action. The Committee also believes that the CAB, subject to a further judgment by the President, is the appropriate body to judge the factors relating to the cost and structure of a supplemental plan, once the Senate has made the larger decision to support continued U.S. participation in a limited liability system with a supplemental plan in the range of the one previously approved. If anything, the CAB may recommend higher levels of coverage, once it has reviewed the intervening data and heard expert testimony and public arguments. Ultimately, the President himself will make the final judgment on entry into force of the Protocols for the United States. But he would also be the judge, once they are in force, as to whether they continue to be adequate over time. In other words, failure to take positive action in the Senate at this time would simply be a decision in itself against U.S. participation in the proposed system, a decision which the Committee does not think is in the best interests of the vast majority of Americans who fly abroad.

> Therefore, the Committee recommends that the Senate approve the proposed resolution of ratification and report the Montreal Protocols favorably to the Senate for advice and consent.[3]

The Committee's favorable recommendation for advice and consent to the Montreal Protocols was accompanied by three provisos regarding further presidential action, the first of which applied prior to U.S. ratification, as a precondition, and the second and third of which were to become operative following the Protocols' entry into force for the United States.

The first proviso forbade deposit of U.S. instruments of ratification until the President had determined that "a satisfactory supplemental compensation plan, as reviewed and approved by the Civil Aeronautics Board or its appropriate successor, will be in operation for the United States."

The second proviso required the President to give notice of U.S. denunciation of the Protocols if he determined that such a plan, "as periodically reviewed by the Civil Aeronautics Board in light of new economic or other relevant circumstances," was not in operation for the United States, or that the best interests of U.S. airline passengers were no longer served by continuing adherence to the Protocols.

The third proviso required the United States Government to "continue actively to seek to negotiate higher limits on the liability of carriers than those provided under these Protocols."[4]

The Committee on Foreign Relations had held hearings on the Montreal Protocols on July 26, 1977, but in the face of opposition from certain groups, including the American Trial Lawyers Association and the Aerospace Industries Association, had taken no further action upon them. On September 29, 1981, the Committee again heard testimony on the Protocols. Following that hearing, Senator Nancy Landon Kassebaum asked the Department of State to furnish answers to questions about the Protocols raised by the Association of Trial Lawyers of America. The Department replied by a letter from Assistant Secretary of State Richard Fairbanks dated November 9, 1981, setting out the Association's questions and the Department's answers. Portions of the letter follow:

> *Question 1:*
>
> At the [July] 26, 1977 hearings, DOS [the Department of State], DOT [the Department of Transportation], and the CAB [Civil Aeronautics Board] agreed that Montreal Protocols 3 and 4 were inextricably tied to a Supplemental Compensation Plan which was approved by the Civil Aeronautics Board and designed to enable victims of international aviation disasters to recover provable damages up to approximately $317,000.
>
> I understand that the Supplemental Compensation Plan has been the subject of an appeal filed in the United States Court of Appeals for the District of Columbia in 1977 and that to date the Civil Aeronautics Board has routinely postponed filing its "record" in the matter on the ground that it is reconsidering the Supplemental Compensation Plan and exploring

[3] S. EXEC. REP. NO. 97-45, 97th Cong., 1st Sess. 4-7 (1981).
[4] *Id.* at 7-8.

other alternatives to it. Is it not premature for the Committee to consider Montreal Protocols 3 and 4 when the Supplemental Compensation Plan which was to be an "integral" part of the package is in such an unsettled state?

Answer:

We do not believe that it is premature for the Senate to consider the Protocols pending any further refinement of the supplemental compensation plan.

It will be in order to review the supplemental compensation plan prior to the entry into force of the Protocols for the U.S. in order to ensure that the plan is adequate and appropriate to protect the interests of American claimants. However, this determination will turn on the circumstances at the time the Protocols enter into force. Most major aviation countries are awaiting the Senate's decision on advice and consent to ratification before acting themselves on the Protocols. Thus, even after the Senate's decision, considerable time may elapse before the Protocols can be brought into force.

Accordingly, further detailed proceedings concerning the supplemental compensation plan as a precondition for Senate action could substantially delay the day when the Protocols can be brought into force because other nations await our lead. The results of the review could also be outdated and need further revision by the time the Protocols enter into force.

Question 3:

Attorneys for both the airlines and aviation accident victims claim that it is the limited liability system spawned by the Warsaw Convention which Montreal Protocols 3 and 4 amend which impedes the speedy settlement of claims since extraordinary measures must be taken to obtain full and fair compensation for aviation accident victims. In any event, the hearings of 1977 on the Protocols produced testimony that settlement of claims today frequently is accomplished within months of an aviation disaster. What real evidence is there that the Warsaw Convention system as modified by the Protocols would promote early settlement of cases?

Answer:

One cannot guarantee that the Protocols and supplemental compensation plan will speed settlements in all cases. However, claimants will no longer be engaged in extensive litigation over the question of willful carrier misconduct. All they must do is prove the actual extent of their damages. This can only help to make recovery swifter than in present circumstances where willful carrier misconduct would be asserted by claimants and contested by carriers. Moreover, the Protocols include a "settlement inducement clause" permitting a court to impose attorneys' fees on a carrier, over and above the carrier's liability limit, if the carrier has not offered, within six months of the date the claim was filed, an amount at least equal to the ultimate recovery. This provides a clear incentive for speedy settlement.

Question 5:

Would the abolition of the limited liability system that presently prevails in international aviation have any meaningful effect or impact upon the well-organized uniform rules adopted and promulgated by the International Civil Aviation Organization (ICAO)?

Answer:

Ratification of the Protocols will not directly affect current ICAO standards and recommended practices. However, we believe that U.S. repudiation of the Montreal Protocols—which were largely the product of U.S. urging and leadership—would impair U.S. credibility, influence, and authority in future international aviation negotiations in ICAO and elsewhere.[5]

MARIAN NASH LEICH*

A NEW UNITED NATIONS MECHANISM FOR ENCOURAGING THE RATIFICATION OF HUMAN RIGHTS TREATIES

Introduction

The ratification of international human rights treaties is critical to the worldwide observance of human rights and fundamental freedoms. The United Nations General Assembly and Commission on Human Rights have repeatedly emphasized the importance of ratification and have frequently encouraged states to ratify the relevant international instruments. Despite these efforts, acceptance of human rights treaties has been uneven; a considerable number of states have failed to ratify.

Recognizing that a regular mechanism for encouraging ratification would be more effective than general exhortations, the Sub-Commission on Prevention of Discrimination and Protection of Minorities, a subsidiary body of the Commission on Human Rights, established in 1979 a sessional working group to consider ways and means of encouraging acceptance of human rights treaties. The procedures of the Working Group on the Encouragement of Universal Acceptance of Human Rights Instruments were modeled on the highly successful methods used by the International Labour Organisation to encourage its members to accede to labor standards. In 1980 and 1981, the working group began by systematically considering the written explanations of governments as to impediments they had encountered in ratifying human rights treaties and by receiving representatives from several countries to discuss these difficulties.

This Note will discuss the rationale for the establishment of the working group, the group's accomplishments thus far, and recent debate concerning its authority. Finally, suggestions will be made for future objectives on which the group may profitably focus.

Importance and Appropriateness of Encouraging Ratification

In keeping with its mandate to promote universal respect for human rights, the General Assembly has promulgated over 35 standard-setting treaties, which set forth obligations to be undertaken by ratifying countries for ensuring the

[5] Dept. of State File No. P82 006–0592.

* Office of the Legal Adviser, Department of State.

observance of human rights.[1] The General Assembly acknowledged in its often cited Resolution 32/130 (1977) that

> [i]t is of paramount importance for the promotion of human rights and fundamental freedoms that member States undertake specific obligations through accession to or ratification of international instruments in this field; consequently the standard setting work within the United Nations system in the field of human rights and the universal acceptance and implementation of the relevant international instruments should be encouraged.[2]

Recognition of the importance of encouraging ratification of international human rights treaties is not new to the United Nations. The General Assembly and the Commission on Human Rights have urged member states to accept these instruments on numerous occasions.[3] But despite the frequency and eloquence of the general exhortations to ratify, ratifications continue to be made at only a moderate pace.[4] Clearly, the goals of widespread ratification and implementation of human rights treaties cannot be met by relying on general resolutions requesting ratification.

Establishment of the Working Group

At its 32d session in 1979, the Sub-Commission on Prevention of Discrimination and Protection of Minorities adopted Resolution 1B (XXXII), which established the Working Group on the Encouragement of Universal Acceptance of Human Rights Instruments.[5] The Sub-Commission gave the working group a threefold mandate: (1) to make requests, through the Secretary-General, to governments that had not yet ratified the principal instruments that they inform the Sub-Commission of circumstances or difficulties preventing ratification or

[1] *See* Human Rights: A Compilation of International Instruments, UN Doc. ST/HR/Rev.1 (1978).

[2] GA Res. 32/130, 32 UN GAOR, Supp. (No. 45) 150, UN Doc. A/32/45 (1977).

[3] *See, e.g.*, urging ratification of the International Convention on the Elimination of All Forms of Racial Discrimination: GA Res. 3225, 29 UN GAOR, Supp. (No. 31) 86, UN Doc. A/9631 (1974); GA Res. 34/28, 34 UN GAOR, Supp. (No. 46) 166, UN Doc. A/34/46 (1979); urging ratification of the Human Rights Covenants and Optional Protocol to the Civil and Political Covenant: GA Res. 3270, 29 UN GAOR, Supp. (No. 31) 90, UN Doc. A/9631 (1974); GA Res. 34/45, 34 UN GAOR, Supp. (No. 46) 169, UN Doc. A/34/46 (1979); urging ratification of the International Convention on the Suppression and Punishment of the Crime of Apartheid, Human Rights Comm'n Res. 6, 37 UN ESCOR, Supp. (No. 5) 201, UN Doc. E/CN.4/1475 (1981).

[4] UNITED NATIONS, MULTILATERAL TREATIES IN RESPECT OF WHICH THE SECRETARY-GENERAL PERFORMS DEPOSITARY FUNCTIONS: LIST OF SIGNATURES, RATIFICATIONS, ACCESSIONS, ETC. AS AT 31 DECEMBER 1979, UN Doc. ST/LEG/SER.D/13, at 111 (1980); updated through June 15, 1981, by UN Doc. E/CN.4/Sub.2/463 (1981).

[5] Report of the Sub-Commission on Prevention of Discrimination and Protection of Minorities on its Thirty-second Session, Res. 1B, UN Doc. E/CN.4/1350 (1979); *see* UN Doc. E/CN.4/Sub.2/L.716 (1979). Eight nongovernmental organizations submitted a statement to the Sub-Commission supporting the establishment of the working group and stressing the need for improved methods of encouraging ratification of human rights treaties. UN Doc. E/CN.4/Sub.2/NGO/80 and Add.1 (1979). The resolution was adopted by a vote of 17 to 2 with two abstentions. José Martínez Cobo of Ecuador and Dumitru Ceausu of Romania voted against the resolution. Mario Amadeo of Argentina and Hicri Fisek of Turkey abstained.

adherence; (2) to examine replies and, if necessary for further clarification, to invite representatives from such governments for discussions with the working group; and (3) to consider what assistance the United Nations might offer to enable them to ratify as soon as possible. The working group was to accomplish its purposes during regular Sub-Commission sessions, which would avoid the expense of presessional meetings. It was to direct its attention to certain human rights instruments enumerated in the resolution[6] and to such other instruments as might be designated by the Sub-Commission.

Pursuant to Resolution 1B (XXXII) of the Sub-Commission, the Secretary-General in December 1979 asked governments that had not ratified the treaties to forward the specified explanatory information.[7] Through the report on its 32d session, the Sub-Commission in the spring of 1980 informed the Commission on Human Rights of the creation of the sessional working group.[8] The Commission offered no objection, taking note of the Sub-Commission's report without a vote.[9]

The Working Group on the Encouragement of Universal Acceptance of Human Rights Instruments held its first meetings during the 33d session of the Sub-Commission in the fall of 1980. During the interim, 20 countries had responded to the Secretary-General's initial request for information. The group examined the replies and representatives of Australia, France, and the Netherlands appeared before it with oral clarifications of their countries' positions.[10]

These representatives explained the remaining obstacles to ratification in their respective countries. A common difficulty was the question of extraterritorial criminal responsibility arising from the Convention against Apartheid.[11] The group ended the session with plans to discuss the designation of additional instruments for attention at the next session. The Sub-Commission took note of the working group's report without resolution, decided to allot more time to future sessions, and requested that the Secretary-General make a study of the issue of extraterritorial criminal responsibility.[12]

[6] The International Covenant on Economic, Social and Cultural Rights; the International Covenant on Civil and Political Rights; the Optional Protocol to the International Covenant on Civil and Political Rights; the International Convention on the Elimination of All Forms of Racial Discrimination; the Convention on Prevention and Punishment of the Crime of Genocide; the International Convention on the Suppression and Punishment of the Crime of Apartheid; the Slavery Convention; the Protocol amending the Slavery Convention signed in Geneva on September 26, 1976; and the Supplementary Convention on the Abolition of Slavery, the Slave Trade and the Institutions and Practices similar to Slavery.

[7] Note Verbale by the Secretary-General, UN Ref. No. G/SO 234 (17-4) (1979).

[8] Report of the Sub-Commission, *supra* note 5, considered at the Commission's 1559th to 1563d meetings.

[9] Human Rights Comm'n Dec. No. 7, 36 UN ESCOR, Supp. (No. 3) 202, UN Doc. E/CN.4/1408 (1980).

[10] Report of the sessional Working Group on the Encouragement of Universal Acceptance of Human Rights Instruments, UN Doc. E/CN.4/Sub.2/453 (1980).

[11] *See* Note by the Secretary-General containing a summary of information submitted by Governments, UN Doc. E/CN.4/Sub.2/452 and Adds.1, 2 (1980).

[12] Report of the Sub-Commission on Prevention of Discrimination and Protection of Minorities on its Thirty-third Session, UN Doc. E/CN.4/1413, at 84–85 (1980).

Scope of Authority Questioned at the 1981 Human Rights Commission

In February and March 1981, the Commission on Human Rights held its 37th session in Geneva; the report of the Sub-Commission received close attention and was the subject of considerable debate.[13] The representative from Brazil, Jardim Gagliardi, criticized the Sub-Commission's work in some instances as beyond its terms of reference.[14] In particular, he assailed the Sub-Commission for communicating directly with member states and for adopting resolutions and recommendations with budgetary effects that had not first been submitted for authorization by the Commission and ECOSOC.

After some debate, the Commission finally adopted a resolution reaffirming the Sub-Commission's significant role. Although the Commission referred to the debate surrounding the issue of competence, it only invited the Sub-Commission to take note and to bear in mind its tasks.[15] Thus, the Commission did not take steps to delimit or redefine the Sub-Commission's terms of reference. The working group on treaty ratification was not even mentioned in the resolution. Also at the 37th session, the Commission considered the Draft Medium-Term Plan for the Human Rights Programme for the Period 1984–1989, which was submitted for comment by the Secretary-General.[16] In setting out the general orientation of the program, the drafters "expected that useful contributions to the further ratification of international instruments will be made by the Sub-Commission's Working Group on the ratification of international standards in the field of human rights."[17]

The Working Group Meets Again

In August and September 1981, the working group and the Sub-Commission considered the questions raised in February and March by several Commission members. Members of the Sub-Commission supported its right to communicate directly with member states on human rights issues, as it had done for many years without objection. At the same time, the working group met for six sessions, carefully continued its country-by-country review of governmental replies, discussed the adequacy of the replies from the point of view of completeness and substance, and reconfirmed its authority to discuss replies directly with governments by inviting Sweden and Syria to participate in its deliberations.[18] Neither Sweden nor Syria interposed any objections.

Based upon the recommendations of the working group, the Sub-Commission adopted a resolution by a vote of 20 in favor, none against, and only the Soviet

[13] 37 UN ESCOR, Supp. (No. 5) 160, UN Doc. E/CN.4/1475 (1981).

[14] *See* UN Doc. E/CN.4/SR.1592, at 5–10 (1981).

[15] Human Rights Comm'n Res. 17, 37 UN ESCOR, Supp. (No. 5) 219, UN Doc. E/CN.4/1475 (1981); *see* UN Doc. E/CN.4/SR.1635, at 8-11 (1981).

[16] Note by the Secretary-General, Review of the Draft Medium-Term Plan for the Period 1984–1989, UN Doc. E/CN.4/1424, Annex (1980).

[17] *Id.* at 3. The Human Rights Commission took note of the plan. Human Rights Comm'n Dec. No. 9, 37 UN ESCOR, Supp. (No. 5) 246, UN Doc. E/CN.4/1475 (1981).

[18] Report of the sessional Working Group on the Encouragement of Universal Acceptance of Human Rights Instruments, UN Doc. E/CN.4/Sub.2/L.785 (1981).

expert abstaining, that continued the efforts of the working group by asking the Secretary-General to renew in 1981 the requests of 1979 and 1980 for governments to explain their difficulties in ratifying the principal human rights treaties.[19] The Sub-Commission sought to make the Secretary-General's inquiry even more pointed by individualizing the notes verbales to governments, that is, by drawing attention to those specific treaties each government had not yet ratified. The United States, for example, has signed but not ratified many of the principal human rights treaties.[20] The Sub-Commission's resolution also requested that the Secretary-General invite the Governments of the Philippines, Rwanda, Iran, the Solomon Islands, and Suriname to supply additional information because the working group was not satisfied with the previous responses from those countries. The Sub-Commission resisted efforts to expand the mandate of the working group to include other human rights treaties, but decided to reconsider this issue at its next session.[21]

All in all, the working group continued its work with the support of the Sub-Commission. Several states, including Australia which had appeared before the working group in 1980, had ratified the human rights instruments by 1981. While the working group has not yet generated substantive discussion of the general problems raised by ratification, which one might expect in the future, it has begun to establish itself as a relatively innovative institution for achieving the ratification, and thus ultimately the implementation, of human rights standards.

Legitimacy of the Working Group

The Brazilian delegate to the 1981 Human Rights Commission called into question the very heart of the working group's mandate: the mechanism of soliciting information from nonratifying states. This challenge to the Sub-Commission's competence presents two issues. First, does the Sub-Commission specifically have the authority, within its terms of reference, to encourage ratification by requesting information directly from governments regarding reasons for failure to ratify? The second, broader question is: should an international

[19] Draft Report of the Sub-Commission on Prevention of Discrimination and Protection of Minorities to the Commission on Human Rights on its Thirty-fourth Session, Res. 19, UN Doc. E/CN.4/Sub.2/(XXXIV)/CRP.2, at 113 (1981); *see also* UN Doc. E/CN.4/Sub.2/L.790 (1981) (draft resolution submitted by five members of the Sub-Commission: Marc Bossuyt of Belgium, Ibrahim Jimeta of Nigeria, Louis Joinet of France, Syed Masud of India, and Ivan Toševski of Yugoslavia; Julio Oyhanarte of Argentina was the only member of the working group who did not join in sponsoring the resolution).

[20] *See* Weissbrodt, *United States Ratification of the Human Rights Covenants*, 63 MINN. L. REV. 35, 35–37 (1978).

[21] In 1981 the working group discussed the possibility of adding three more treaties to its mandate: the International Convention Against the Taking of Hostages, the Convention on the Elimination of All Forms of Discrimination Against Women, and the Convention for the Suppression of the Traffic in Persons and of the Exploitation of the Prostitution of Others. *See* UN Doc. E/CN.4/Sub.2/L.785, at 3 (1981); UN Doc. E/CN.4/Sub.2/NGO/87 (1981) (recommendation of several nongovernmental organizations that the Convention on the Elimination of All Forms of Discrimination Against Women be included within the working group's purview). The working group, however, resisted the addition of these new instruments in the belief that it should concentrate its efforts to be effective.

organization involve itself in encouraging ratification of its treaties, once adopted, and if so, to what extent?

As to the first issue, Mr. Gagliardi of Brazil asserted that direct communication with states is outside the Sub-Commission's competence. However, its terms of reference of 1948, which were expanded in 1949, seem to contemplate the receipt of information from governments by mandating that the Sub-Commission is to "undertake studies" in regard to human rights and to perform other functions delegated by ECOSOC and the Human Rights Commission.[22]

The Sub-Commission's request for information from member states follows a very common practice of the Sub-Commission in particular, and of the United Nations in general. The Sub-Commission has long studied human rights issues by means of inquiries to governments. For example, in preparing his Study of Discrimination in Education, Charles D. Ammoun, who was special rapporteur of the Sub-Commission, was supported by a note verbale of April 13, 1954, from the Secretary-General to member governments requesting assistance.[23] Such inquiries to governments have become a standard practice.[24]

The working group's invitation to several states for oral presentations, however, provides a greater opportunity for encouraging ratification and is a substantial innovation in the Sub-Commission's practice. Within the human rights field, only the Human Rights Committee organized under the UN Covenant on Civil and Political Rights and the Racial Committee under the International Convention on the Elimination of All Forms of Racial Discrimination have regularly pursued this approach.[25] Nevertheless, the Sub-Commission's working group does not violate the Sub-Commission's rules or terms of reference by inviting state representatives to discuss treaty ratification. Rule 69 of the Rules of Procedure of the Functional Commissions of the Economic and Social Council specifically provides authority for the Sub-Commission to "invite any State to participate in its deliberations on any matter of particular concern to that State."[26] Hence, the Economic and Social Council has long authorized the Sub-Commission to pursue the approach it adopted for the working group on discussions of treaty ratification.

As to the second, broader question: on the one hand, Gagliardi argued that once an international organization has adopted a treaty and opened it for

[22] 9 UN ESCOR, Supp. (No. 10) 6, UN Doc. E/CN.4/350 (1949).

[23] Ammoun, Study of Discrimination in Education, UN Doc. E/CN.4/Sub.2/181/Rev.1, at 177 (1957).

[24] *See, e.g.*, Krishnaswami, Study of Discrimination in the Matter of Religious Rights and Practices, UN Doc. E/CN.4/Sub.2/200/Rev.1, at 76 (1960); Santa Cruz, Study of Discrimination in the Matter of Political Rights, UN Doc. E/CN.4/Sub.2/213/Rev.1, at 100–01 (1962); Santa Cruz, Racial Discrimination, UN Doc. E/CN.4/Sub.2/307/Rev.1, at 314 (1971).

[25] *See, e.g.,* Buergenthal, *Implementing the Racial Convention,* 12 TEX. INT'L L.J. 187, 194 (1977); Fischer, *Reporting Under the Covenant on Civil and Political Rights: The First Five Years of the Human Rights Committee,* 76 AJIL 142 (1982).

[26] UNITED NATIONS, RULES OF PROCEDURE OF THE FUNCTIONAL COMMISSIONS OF THE ECONOMIC AND SOCIAL COUNCIL, rule 69(2), at 17 (1977) [hereinafter cited as FUNCTIONAL RULES]; UN JURIDICAL Y.B., UN Doc. ST/LEG/SER.C/6, at 204 (1968). While there was some criticism at the Human Rights Commission of the Sub-Commission for directly addressing governments, such criticism was not focused on the working group.

acceptance, the organization has no authority to take steps to encourage its entry into force.[27] On the other hand, international organizations exist to promote certain goals that in principle all members share. In pursuit of those goals, organizations adopt conventions and treaties in accordance with Charter authority. Encouraging the acceptance of those instruments is simply further promotion of the goals of the organization. As noted above, United Nations bodies have often encouraged states to ratify instruments. The effect of such encouragement is not to interfere with a government's sovereign determination to ratify or not to ratify, but to urge governments to exercise that discretion.[28]

Responding to the criticisms of the Sub-Commission, the Director of the UN Human Rights Division[29] noted that the 1962 advisory opinion of the International Court of Justice in regard to *Certain Expenses of the United Nations*[30] provides some guidance about the authority of the Sub-Commission to encourage ratification of human rights treaties and to communicate directly with governments. In determining whether peacekeeping expenses were improperly incurred by the United Nations, the Court was asked first to consider whether the peacekeeping activity was improper or unauthorized by the Charter. The Court responded that "each organ [of the United Nations] must, in the first place at least, determine its own jurisdiction."[31] This reasoning could support the Sub-Commission, as it determines its own jurisdiction to promote human rights.[32] The establishment of the working group represents the Sub-Commission's effort to organize its work as efficiently as possible. Such an internal procedural affair has always been within the competence of the Sub-Commission.[33]

The experience of other international organizations confirms the propriety and efficacy of these techniques. Since 1919, the International Labour Organisation has operated a successful reporting mechanism to encourage ratification of its conventions.[34] The working group's approach follows the ILO model in

[27] UN Doc. E/CN.4/SR.1592, at 9 (1981).

[28] Such was the conclusion of the United Nations Institute for Training and Research (UNITAR) in its analysis of the reporting approach as a method for encouraging ratification of treaties. O. SCHACHTER, M. NAWAZ, & J. FRIED, TOWARD WIDER ACCEPTANCE OF UN TREATIES 52 (1971) [hereinafter cited as UNITAR study]; *see also* I. DETTER, LAW MAKING BY INTERNATIONAL ORGANIZATIONS 168–70 (1965).

[29] UN Doc. E/CN.4/SR.1595, at 8 and 9 (1981); *see* United Nations Division of Human Rights, The Role and Competence of the Sub-Commission on Prevention of Discrimination and Protection of Minorities 20 (internal unpub. memo, June 15, 1981).

[30] Advisory Opinion on Certain Expenses of the United Nations, [1962] ICJ REP. 151.

[31] *Id.* at 168.

[32] The ICJ in its advisory opinion, however, was discussing the legal authority of the principal organs of the United Nations: the General Assembly, the Security Council, and the Secretary-General. There is some doubt that such broad self-interpretation of mandate would apply to the Sub-Commission. At least, the parent organs of the Sub-Commission, that is, the Commission on Human Rights and the Economic and Social Council, possess the authority to alter the mandate of the Sub-Commission. However, under its present broad mandate, with no express limits on its right to promote human rights, and with a long, uncriticized practice of pursuing similar activities, the Sub-Commission might well be entitled, in accordance with the reasoning of the ICJ advisory opinion, to interpret its own mandate—at least in the first instance.

[33] *See* FUNCTIONAL RULES, *supra* note 26, rules 21 and 24, at 6–7.

[34] ILO CONST. Art. 19, para. 5.

which member states report on their ratification of ILO conventions and recommendations. The reports, or the failure of members to report, are examined by a group of independent experts, the International Labour Committee of Experts on the Application of Conventions and Recommendations.[35] Supplementing the formal reporting procedures, informal discussions between ILO staff and government representatives during sessions of the International Labour Conference have been perhaps the most effective means of resolving technical difficulties that impede ratification.[36]

In 1930 the League of Nations adopted a similar procedure for encouraging ratification of League conventions.[37] The League's reporting procedure and the attention it focused on the importance of ratification resulted in a large increase in ratifications.[38] Historical records do not explain why the League's system of reporting on the status of ratifications was not immediately incorporated into UN practice, if not the Charter.[39] The Economic and Social Council was given the authority to "make arrangements with the members of the United Nations and with the specialized agencies to obtain reports on the steps taken to give effect to its own recommendations and to recommendations on matters falling within its competence made by the General Assembly."[40] In practice, ECOSOC has frequently obtained reports from governments regarding actions taken on individual resolutions and on groups of recommendations.[41]

[35] Such reports are included in the INTERNATIONAL LABOUR CONFERENCE, REPORTS OF THE COMMITTEE OF EXPERTS ON THE APPLICATION OF CONVENTIONS AND RECOMMENDATIONS, Report III, pt. 3.

[36] The ILO system has been successful. As of January 1, 1981, the 152 member states of the ILO had reported over 4,856 ratifications of the then existing 153 ILO conventions. ILO, Chart of Ratifications of International Labour Conventions (Jan. 1, 1981). *See also* E. LANDY, THE EFFECTIVENESS OF INTERNATIONAL SUPERVISION 203–04 (1966).

[37] Resolution of Oct. 3, 1930, LEAGUE OF NATIONS O.J., Spec. Supp. 83, at 12 (1930); for discussion on the resolution, see *id.*, Spec. Supp. 84, at 213–17 (1930); *see also* Resolution of Sept. 23, 1926, *id.*, Spec. Supp. 43, at 27 (1926).

In addition to the ILO and League of Nations systems of reporting, constitutional provisions of some UN specialized agencies authorize similar procedures. WHO CONST., 14 UNTS 185, Art. 20; UNESCO CONST., 4 UNTS 275, Art. VIII; *see* Ago, *La Codification du droit international et les problèmes de sa réalisation,* in RECUEIL D'ÉTUDES DE DROIT INTERNATIONAL EN HOMMAGE À PAUL GUGGENHEIM 93, 117 (1968); *see also* another precursor of the working group: Final Act of the International Conference on Human Rights, Teheran, 22 April to 13 May 1968, UN Doc. A/CONF.32/41, at 19, 48 (1968).

[38] *See* F. WILCOX, THE RATIFICATION OF INTERNATIONAL CONVENTIONS 133 (1935).

[39] This statement is based on such sources as the UNCIO Docs. (1945); UNITED NATIONS, REPORT OF THE PREPARATORY COMMISSION OF THE UNITED NATIONS, UN Doc. PC/20 (1945); COMMENTARY ON THE REPORT OF THE PREPARATORY COMMISSION OF THE UNITED NATIONS, CMD. NO. 6734 (1946). *See also* R. RUSSELL, A HISTORY OF THE UNITED NATIONS CHARTER (1958); L. GOODRICH, E. HAMBRO, & A. SIMONS, CHARTER OF THE UNITED NATIONS, COMMENTARY AND DOCUMENTS (3d and rev. ed. 1969); N. BENTIVICH & A. MARTIN, A COMMENTARY ON THE CHARTER OF THE UNITED NATIONS (1950); J. ROBINSON, HUMAN RIGHTS AND FUNDAMENTAL FREEDOMS IN THE CHARTER OF THE UNITED NATIONS (1946); J. CAMARA, THE RATIFICATION OF INTERNATIONAL TREATIES (1949); Q. WRIGHT, INTERNATIONAL LAW AND THE UNITED NATIONS (1960); K. HOLLOWAY, MODERN TRENDS IN TREATY LAW (1967).

[40] UN CHARTER, Art. 64, para. 1.

[41] ECOSOC regularly reports to the General Assembly under UN Charter Article 15(2) on the implementation of recommendations by member governments.

A 1971 study by the United Nations Institute for Training and Research entitled *Toward Wider Acceptance of U.N. Treaties* found that it would be within the competence of the United Nations to institute procedures similar to those of the ILO.[42] The UNITAR study suggested the establishment of a committee of experts that would systematically review states' positions on treaty ratification. In the field of human rights, the Sub-Commission's Working Group on Universal Acceptance of Human Rights Instruments is just such a body.

Problems of Ratification to be Considered by the Working Group

The sessional Working Group on Universal Acceptance of Human Rights Instruments has just begun its efforts and it may be too soon to assess what contribution it may ultimately make to encouraging treaty ratification. Nevertheless, based upon the initial governmental replies to the working group's inquiries about impediments to ratification and the working group's early sessions, several observations and suggestions may be offered with a view toward maximizing the success of the group. First, following the example of the ILO,[43] the group should focus its attention on certain particularly important treaties. Even the nine treaties that were identified in its authorizing resolution may be too many for the group to consider efficiently during the few days available for meetings. The working group might address one or two treaties at a time to achieve the greatest effect upon ratifications, for example, by beginning with the two Covenants, which are the central human rights instruments, and then proceeding to the other instruments.

Second, the working group might delineate or concentrate on one or two issues that frequently delay or prevent ratification. It could explore those issues in detail and identify measures the United Nations might take to assist states in overcoming their problems. Such an issue was the question of extraterritorial criminal responsibility raised by the Apartheid Convention, which, as mentioned above, troubled many governments[44] and prompted the working group at its first sessions to request a study of that issue.[45]

Several other problems deserve study and attention by the working group. For example, Australia's reply mentioned the problem of federalism,[46] and the Senate hearings that discuss this impediment to ratification of the Covenants were incorporated by reference in the U.S. response.[47] The working group could determine the extent of this problem and could consult with federal states like Australia and Canada, which have apparently overcome such difficulties in ratifying some of the principal treaties. Indeed, the group might convene a

[42] UNITAR study, *supra* note 28, at 16.

[43] *See, e.g.*, ILO GB Doc. 208/SC/1/6 (1978).

[44] Including those of Australia, the Federal Republic of Germany, the Netherlands, New Zealand, and Sweden. *See* UN Doc. E/CN.4/Sub.2/452, at 3, 6, 9, and 12 (1980); UN Doc. E/CN.4/Sub.2/452/Add.4, at 1–2 (1981).

[45] *See* text at note 12 *supra*.

[46] UN Doc. E/CN.4/Sub.2/452, at 3 (1980).

[47] *Id.*, Add.2; *International Human Rights Treaties: Hearings Before the Senate Comm. on Foreign Relations*, 96th Cong., 1st Sess. 26 (1979) (testimony of Roberts B. Owen, Legal Adviser, Dep't of State).

discussion at which those countries could offer advice to others encountering similar impediments to ratification, and thus foster a valuable dialogue among countries. Specifically, Canada could explain how it has been able to overcome provincial objections to ratification of the Covenants and the Optional Protocol to the Civil and Political Covenant. Such a presentation might prove useful to Australia, which has ratified the Covenants and is still considering the Optional Protocol, and to the United States. While the U.S. Departments of Justice and State have attempted to protect state prerogatives regarding the human rights treaties, they have not generally consulted state officials, as apparently have Australia and Canada. Perhaps such consultation will clarify which objections states actually have and which might be overcome.

The working group at its 1981 session found many other problems of ratification in the governmental replies, but it has not yet fully considered them. For example, governments gave the following reasons for not ratifying the Optional Protocol to the International Covenant on Civil and Political Rights: (1) that the title included the word "optional"; (2) that individuals would be entitled to file complaints against states; and (3) that the procedure in the Protocol overlapped with regional human rights structures.[48] With regard to the Slavery Convention, one government expressed concern over the compulsory jurisdiction of the International Court of Justice.[49] In addition, the working group's 1981 report had this to say about the International Convention on the Suppression and Punishment of the Crime of Apartheid:

> [I]t was noted that the reasons often given by States for not having become parties to it were that: (a) such States had already become parties to the International Convention on Elimination of All Forms of Racial Discrimination; (b) in their view, the definition of the crime of *apartheid* itself was rather vague; (c) the Convention established extra-territorial criminal jurisdiction for the crime of *apartheid;* and (d) there was incompatibility between the obligations imposed by the Convention and domestic legislation. Incompatibility with domestic legislation was evoked by States as a reason for not adhering to several other instruments as well.[50]

A third possible approach that the working group might consider is suggested by the UNITAR study of 1971, which demonstrated that some impediments to treaty ratification are not substantive.[51] An extreme example emerged in the replies to the working group of Rwanda and the United Republic of Cameroon, who explained that they lacked the texts of several human rights instruments.[52] The Secretary-General promptly supplied the texts.

A number of states, including Belgium, the Dominican Republic, Ethiopia, Iran, Italy, Luxembourg, Mexico, Morocco, Rwanda, Spain, Suriname, the United States, and Venezuela, indicated that various treaties had been under

[48] UN Doc. E/CN.4/Sub.2/452/Add.3, at 5 (India), 8 (Ukrainian Soviet Socialist Republic), and 8–9 (USSR) (1981).

[49] *Id.* at 8–9 (USSR).

[50] UN Doc. E/CN.4/Sub.2/L.785, at 5–6 (1981).

[51] UNITAR study, *supra* note 28, at 9.

[52] UN Doc. E/CN.4/Sub.2/452, at 11 and 13 (1980).

consideration by administrative or legislative bodies for some period.[53] The UNITAR study found that treaty ratifications were often delayed by such nonsubstantive matters as inefficient bureaucratic coordination, administrative lethargy, the drafting of implementing legislation, and a lack of trained personnel to consider ratification issues.[54] The working group might ask these countries whether technical assistance or some of UNITAR's ideas for coordinated administrative consideration of treaties might be helpful to them.

Moreover, some of the governments that were considering the treaties assured the working group that they would complete the ratification process "in the near future" or in a short time.[55] Hence, after an appropriate interval, the group might inquire of Ethiopia, Iran, Mexico, and the Solomon Islands, for example, whether they had made any progress or might need assistance.

A fourth approach that the working group might consider derives from the experience of the ILO.[56] Certain UN staff members could be assigned responsibility for offering technical assistance identified by the working group as necessary for speedy ratification. Papua New Guinea indicated in its reply that the Covenants may conflict with customs and laws of that country.[57] Perhaps technical assistance and a knowledge of the way the Covenants have been applied in countries with similar problems might aid the Government of Papua New Guinea in achieving ratification.

Finally, the Director of the Human Rights Division and his staff could follow the example of the ILO by holding informal meetings with governmental representatives on the difficulties of obtaining acceptance of human rights treaties, using the working group's material as a basis for discussion. In addition, in the course of receiving governmental delegations during the sessions of the General Assembly, the Secretary-General could initiate discussions about ratification of the principal human rights instruments.

Conclusion

The new Working Group on Universal Acceptance of Human Rights Instruments has the potential of encouraging greater ratification of human rights treaties, if questions about its competence raised at the 37th session of the Human Rights Commission do not impede its efforts.

[53] *Id.* at 4, 8, 9, and 11; *id.*, Add.2; *id.*, Add.3, at 3, 5, 6, 7, and 10 (1981).

[54] UNITAR study, *supra* note 28, at 81–92.

[55] UN Doc. E/CN.4/Sub.2/452, at 4, 8, and 11 (1980).

[56] *See, e.g.*, discussion of the Report of the Committee on the Application of Conventions and Recommendations, comments of Mrs. Makabir, Employers' delegate from Trinidad and Tobago and Vice-Chairman of the committee, 66 ILC, PROC. 42/7, 42/8 (1980):

> The ILO is to be commended on the extent to which it gives assistance to countries, particularly developing countries. . . . An impressive system of direct contacts, missions, national and international seminars, fellowships and other means of assistance has been developed over the years, which has been of great help to developing countries. . . . The progress which has been achieved as a result is a tribute to the efficacy of this assistance.

See also id. at 42/13 (remarks of Mr. Isacsson, Government delegate from Sweden); *id.* at 42/20 (remarks of Mr. Haase, Government delegate from the Federal Republic of Germany).

[57] UN Doc. E/CN.4/Sub.2/452/Add.3, at 6 (1981).

A specific grant of authority to solicit governmental reports and appearances would be clearly preferable to the current implied authority. If doubt remains about the competence of the Sub-Commission to assign such tasks to its sessional working group, ECOSOC and/or the General Assembly should give the necessary authorization. Indeed, a resolution by one of those bodies would endow the working group with an incontestable mandate, higher visibility, and consequent increased effectiveness. Without such a resolution, however, the working group would still be able to pursue significant United Nations objectives while remaining within its mandate. It can continue to encourage the communication of difficulties encountered by states in the ratification process and to determine what assistance can be given. The group's approach combines previously tested reporting techniques with an innovative method for open discussion of human rights treaty ratifications. The present mandate of the Sub-Commission certainly encompasses such efforts.

The working group's efforts to study and communicate problems commonly encountered in the ratification of human rights instruments, and to provide states with assistance, should make it possible to increase the number of states parties to human rights treaties. Other organizations such as the International Committee of the Red Cross and the UN High Commissioner for Refugees might also consider such methods for encouraging ratification of their respective treaties. The ILO and now the Working Group on Encouragement of Universal Acceptance of Human Rights Instruments could provide valuable models for other international organizations concerned with the implementation of a variety of important standards.

DAVID WEISSBRODT*

* Professor of Law, University of Minnesota. The author is very grateful for the assistance of Patricia A. Moses in preparing this article.

BOOK REVIEWS AND NOTES

EDITED BY LEO GROSS

International Law in Comparative Perspective. Edited by William E. Butler. Alphen aan den Rijn: Sijthoff & Noordhoff, 1980. Pp. vii, 315. Selective Bibliography. Index. Dfl.85; $42.50.

This superb collection, with a skillful introduction by Professor Butler that makes the job of reviewing easier, deserves the attention of all who have been remiss in heeding fully the utility of comparative law and the comparative method in relation to international law—which is to say, I suspect, the majority of us. Composed of essays from the last 40 years ("a reflection on the state of the literature," Butler usefully notes (p. 1), "and not the editorial policy followed in selecting materials for inclusion"), it convincingly demonstrates Butler's central thesis that "whatever one's understanding of the nature of the international system, comparison has now become an essential handmaiden for illuminating essential aspects of its structure and operation and its relationship to other legal orders, either existing or ideal models, past or present" (p. 8). As Butler ably summarizes,

> the comparative method has been found useful in identifying trends in the emergence of general principles of international law (and the same would hold true for regional or subsystems of international law), as a means of filling gaps in or interpreting international treaties and even customary international law, of evaluating state practice as a constituent element in the formation of customary rules of international law, of exploring parallels between rules of municipal law and international law and the possibility that the former may comprise part of the latter, as a means of probing and clarifying the underlying ideologies, values, legal institutions, and cultures of states in order to better comprehend the international legal system, avert misunderstandings and misconceptions, and lay the groundwork for a more viable world order, of elaborating, exploring, and developing the law of international institutions, of assisting international tribunals, of codifying international law and developing individual branches of international law, of clarifying goals and values held by policymakers whose actions and decisions affect international law, of assessing compliance by states with international law, to mention only some of the principal uses observed or advocated by the contribution [*sic*] to this volume [p. 5].

The "deep skepticism" about the interrelation of comparative and international law of an earlier generation of scholars, such as Sir Hersch Lauterpacht and the late H. C. Gutteridge (whose classic essay on *Comparative Law and the Law of Nations* begins the collection), is thus put effectively to rest.

The book is divided into five principal parts—"The Comparative Method in International Law"; "Municipal Legal Systems and the International Legal Order"; "Comparative Policy Studies and International Law"; "International Legal History in Comparative Perspective"; "The Role of Comparison in International Organizations"—and it embraces contributions from a healthy diversity of jurisprudential and cultural perspectives. Besides those of Gutteridge and Butler himself, the writings of Kiss, Bothe, and Ress, Dutoit, Baskin, and Fel'dman, Tille and Shvekov, Haraszti, Rajski, L. C. Green, A. T. von Mehren, McDougal, Schwarzenberger, Connelly, Mankiewicz, and Valticos are found; and among these are several essays from the Tenth International Congress of Comparative Law held at Budapest in August 1978, reported to be the first "international gathering" to consider the interrelation of comparative and international law. However, except for several references in the concluding (and helpful) selective bibliography, the book inexplicably disregards the views of "Third World" publicists on the subject. Its preeminently Euro-American (East-West, socialist-nonsocialist) emphasis, one hopes, is due to factors other than deliberate neglect or inadvertent oversight. On the other hand, this weakness in no way detracts from the book's clear and convincing message, *i.e.*, that "[t]he concern . . . is not *whether* to use comparison, but *how*, *when*, and *where*" (p. 5).

In sum, Professor Butler has put together an admirable collection that should have definitive influence among comparative and international lawyers in the years to come. In any event, this reviewer agrees completely with Butler that "[t]he day is upon us when international legal training must include an adequate dosage of comparative legal study appropriately fashioned to serve international law in the best possible manner" (p. 8).

BURNS H. WESTON
Board of Editors

El Derecho Internacional Contemporáneo. By Eduardo Jiménez de Aréchaga. Madrid: Editorial Tecnos, 1980. Pp. 379. Indexes.

Doctrinas Internacionales y Autonomía Latinoamericana. By Juan Carlos Puig. Caracas: Universidad Simón Bolívar, 1980. Pp. 316. Indexes.

Professor of international law, member of the United Nations International Law Commission from 1961 to 1969, Judge of the International Court of Justice from 1970 to 1979, and its President for 3 years from 1976 to 1979, Eduardo Jiménez de Aréchaga is the quintessential international lawyer: a scholar, practitioner, and judge of genuinely cosmopolitan outlook and experience.

El Derecho Internacional Contemporáneo, the Spanish edition of the General Course in Public International Law delivered at the Hague Academy in 1978, is a lucid, informed, and well-documented presentation of some of the major areas of international law as we turn the corner into the last two decades of the 20th century.

The overarching theme of these lectures is that international law has undergone substantial transformations between 1945 and 1978 and that whatever deficiencies remain, and they are many, the past third of a century has seen significant developments: the outlawry of war and the use or threat of force, the full emergence of international organizations, the recognition of the principle of self-determination, and the acceptance of the concept of *jus cogens*, to name but a few. This view of international law is optimistic, perhaps too optimistic, in the light of recent events that have underscored the fragility of basic Charter principles of nonaggression and peaceful settlement of disputes. Furthermore, the ability of international organizations to deal constructively with pressing political, economic, and social problems is increasingly suspect.

The author does not examine every aspect of international law but has chosen to concentrate on those areas where it is possible to observe the "transformations" in international law. The book is divided into 10 chapters dealing with custom (ch. I), the law of treaties (chs. II–III), general principles of international law governing the conduct of states (ch. IV), collective measures for the maintenance of peace and security (ch. V), the peaceful settlement of disputes and the International Court of Justice (ch. VI), subjects of international law—the state and its territory, the law of the sea, air, and outer space (chs. VII–IX)—and international responsibility (ch. X).

To all of these subjects, Judge Jiménez de Aréchaga brings a wealth of experience and erudition. In view of his tenure on the International Law Commission and the International Court of Justice, the chapters dealing with custom as a source of international law, the law of treaties and the peaceful settlement of disputes, and the International Court of Justice are of particular interest. The views expressed are always judicious. On the proposition that resolutions of the UN General Assembly constitute a new and autonomous source of international law, for example, he finds that this is not in harmony either with the Charter or the Statute of the Court. Rather, citing Castañeda with approval, he is of the view that while General Assembly resolutions do not create law, they may authoritatively prove its existence. The chapter on custom is particularly interesting in its analysis of the jurisprudence of the International Court of Justice beginning with the 1969 judgment in the *North Sea Continental Shelf* cases. The Court, in the author's view, has taken an innovative approach to custom without falling into the extremes of legal heterodoxy.

Finally, particular mention must be made of the chapter dealing with international responsibility. This is an area of uncodified international law in which Jiménez de Aréchaga has made a significant contribution in his earlier work and which is here updated to include such instruments as the Charter of Economic Rights and Duties of States and the most recent reports of the International Law Commission.

The professional background of Juan Carlos Puig is similar to that of Jiménez de Aréchaga. Puig has had a distinguished career as both a teacher and a practitioner. In this latter capacity he has served as his country's Foreign Minister and has participated in the formulation and negotiation of Argentina's river basin policy. At the present time, Puig is a member of the faculty of the Simón Bolívar University in Venezuela, one of the newest universities in Latin America and one that has rapidly acquired an excellent reputation. The volume is published by the Institute of Advanced Studies of that university.

The body of Puig's published work indicates a steady progression from an examination and analysis of traditional international law towards a more sociological and political science orientation. His recent works, *La política de poder en América Latina* (1973) and *Derecho de la comunidad internacional*

(1975), are clearly stepping stones in the evolution of an analysis of the role and function of contemporary international law culminating in the present volume. The two books reviewed here are asymmetrical: while *El Derecho Internacional Contemporáneo* is concerned to present a positivistic view of international law with its reliance on the practice of states and judicial decisions, *Doctrinas Internacionales y Autonomía Latinoamericana* is concerned less with what international law is or may be than with the discrepancies that exist between normative international law and the sociological or political reality. It is the author's not inconsiderable objective to achieve a synthesis of the normative and sociological approaches in a new theory, "la teoría trialista," which integrates the normative approach with social reality and justice in a manner that will satisfy the expectations of Latin American and developing countries in general. In the final analysis, however, there is little that is new in the theory presented by Puig; it appears to be a somewhat updated and slightly broader version of regional international law theories, in particular the so-called American international law popularized by Alvarez at the beginning of the century. If the results of Puig's analysis are less than novel, this book nevertheless demonstrates that the Latin American school is alive and well.

RALPH ZACKLIN
United Nations

Multilingualism in International Law and Institutions. By Mala Tabory. Alphen aan den Rijn: Sijthoff and Noordhoff, 1980. Pp. xx, 284. Index. Dfl.65; $32.50.

At a time when the use of one language is rapidly giving way to plurilingualism in international relations, it is appropriate to review and reflect on the impact of this new method of international communication on the development of the international legal order. Mala Tabory has undertaken this task in a most admirable way and provided us not only with a quite exhaustive, informative description of present practices and problems relating to the formulation, adoption, and interpretation of international legal texts in different language versions, but also with a thoughtful evaluation and useful suggestions for future directions in this field.

In Tabory's own words, language is the tool of the legal workshop. In her book she not only focuses on the problems created by multilingual texts as an end product, but also takes us on a guided tour of the workshop, showing us how the tool is used and the end product is shaped. It is this detailed exposure of the technical aspects of the creation of multilingual texts and the attention to the need to deal with multilingual problems at the drafting stage, rather than through techniques of interpretation at the time of application of a legal text, that make this study an original and very valuable contribution. The first and major part of the book is therefore devoted to the preparation of multilingual texts. It opens with a comprehensive survey of linguistic practices in official international affairs and describes the rules governing the use of different languages in various international organizations and conferences. A review of the rules and practices in the organs and bodies of the United Nations, as well as of the specialized and related agencies, reveals confusing diversity in the modalities of the implementation of sexilingualism in the UN system and points to the decreasing value of distinguishing between "official" and "working" languages. The diversity in international practice is further accentuated by a description of the situation in other international organizations, including European international institutions and other regional organizations, as well as in international codification conferences. Against this background, Tabory proceeds with a detailed description of the actual procedures for preparing authentic multilingual documents. This chapter includes the drafting and translating processes in the UN system and in the European Community, as well as the special procedures followed for the adoption of multilingual conventions. Brief attention is also given to the bilateral practice of one state.

Tabory then turns to the general problems of translating. One major recommendation stands out here and is of particular importance to legal draftsmen used to working in a unilingual legal system: drafters should anticipate and take into consideration the difficulties that may arise in the subsequent translation and phrase the original version accordingly. Stylistic beauty in a particular language may have to be sacrificed for the sake of a truly uniform multilingual text.

The second part of Tabory's study considers the problems of reconciling different language versions of treaties and other international texts in the course of their implementation, *i.e.*, after the harm of producing linguistic divergences has been done. She takes a critical look at the provisions relating to multilingual texts in the 1969 Vienna Convention on the Law of Treaties (Article 33 relating to interpretation and Article 79(3) relating to correction) before discussing some major problems of multilingual interpretation. Among the latter, she deals with such questions as possible distinctions in the status of different authentic versions, the right to rely on only one version or the obligation to consult several versions, the existence of a hierarchical order in the rules of interpretation, and the interpretation of UN resolutions and other documents of international organizations as compared to international treaties. Tabory's study confirms the absence of sufficiently firm guidelines to overcome the problems of multilingual interpretation and the author indicates areas in which future study and clarification would be useful.

Notwithstanding the increasing complexities and difficulties involved in multilingual drafting and interpretation, Tabory has to admit, in her conclusions, that only a relatively small number of linguistic discrepancies of significant practical or legal consequence have been recorded. She sees this as an encouraging development made possible not only by improved translation techniques, but also by diplomatic efforts to avoid conflicts resulting from linguistic discrepancies. There is, nevertheless, room for improvement in drafting, as well as in interpretation, and Tabory's suggestions in this respect deserve to be implemented. These proposals are not made without an awareness of the political considerations involved in the use of different languages in international legal affairs, to which Tabory also gives sufficient attention throughout her book.

An impressive amount of information on existing practices and extensive references to relevant documents and other literature make this study a useful reference work on the subject of the preparation and interpretation of multilingual legal texts. The review of the multilateral treaty-making process to be undertaken in the UN General Assembly should benefit from Tabory's excellent study, but there should be many other beneficiaries as well. The book is required reading for any lawyer or diplomat who has to participate in the legislative or quasi-legislative activities of international organizations or conferences.

RAYMOND SOMMEREYNS
United Nations Secretariat

Taxing Unfair International Trade Practices. By Greyson Bryan. Lexington: D. C. Heath and Company, 1980. Pp. xxii, 370. Index.

One of the most perplexing and complex areas of international trade law is the subject of "unfair trade practices" such as dumping or subsidies. Dumping is the export sale of goods to a foreign market at a price below that charged in the home market. Subsidies are grants or benefits usually supplied by governments to producers of goods, sometimes only for goods exported, other times irrespective of exporting activity. For almost a century there has been a view that dumping and subsidization in connection with goods flowing in international trade are "unfair" practices that should be prohibited by international agreement, or that importing governments should be allowed to respond to such practices by imposing "antidumping duties" or "countervailing duties" on the imports affected. In recent decades, some major trading nations, particularly the United States, have turned increasingly to these responses in their international trade relations. These practices have been the source of so much friction and ill will between nations that international negotiations have been necessary to attempt to frame rules that could help bring peace. The Tokyo Round of multilateral trade negotiations completed two important treaty "codes" in 1979 to deal respectively with dumping and subsidies, and the rules of these codes were introduced into U.S. law by the Trade Agreements Act of 1979. A growing segment of the legal profession finds that it must master the intricate rules dealing with these subjects. Frequently, as in the recent steel cases, the issues become front-page material.

In these circumstances, it would seem that the publication of a book dealing with antidumping and countervailing duties should be a welcome contribution to lawyers, scholars, and government officials. Despite the somewhat misleading title, this book, by Greyson Bryan of Harvard Law School, takes up these two subjects, each in a separate part of the book. Because each part was designed to stand alone for the reader interested only in that part, the book contains extensive passages that are printed verbatim in both parts. Yet the author has imposed an intelligent overall structure on each subject, and takes up the details of the U.S. legal rules that apply. As an aid to finding sources, and as a nondefinitive explanation of the rules, the book is therefore useful. There are also intelligent discussions of the economic policies relating to the two subjects.

Unfortunately, however, this book is a flawed, albeit ambitious, effort. There are a number of statements that are either wrong or seriously misleading, which raises doubts in the reader's mind about other material in the book.

The author evidences a lack of understanding about the legal nature of international agreements. He writes that the General Agreement on Tariffs and Trade, and the two Tokyo Round agreements on antidumping and countervailing duties, are "non-self-executing executive agreements" and not treaties. "Accordingly," he writes, "implementing legislation must be passed by Congress before they become binding upon the United States" (p. xvi). Elsewhere the author states (p. 260), "Since GATT is a non-self-executing executive agreement, it does not have the force of law," and (p. 22) "[s]ince the 1967 Code [on antidumping] expressly requires that the signatories implement its provisions . . . it is a non-self-executing agreement and, as such, it is not binding upon the United States." These propositions overlook the well-accepted doctrine that an international agreement can be binding in international law even though not directly applicable as part of municipal law.[1] Furthermore, executive agreements *can* sometimes be binding, and even self-executing, without approval of either the Congress or the Senate, as the Supreme Court taught us in the 1937 *Belmont* case,[2] although for other reasons most of the Tokyo Round agreements were not.

In addition, the GATT, in virtually all cases addressing the issue in U.S. federal and state courts, has been deemed to be directly applicable to U.S. law (albeit for reasons that courts do not always correctly specify).[3] These are not merely technical errors, "without prejudice." The relationship of international agreements (those mentioned above are all most certainly "binding") to U.S. municipal law is both subtle and pregnant, particularly in the light of the stated preference of courts to choose among alternative interpretations of domestic law so as to avoid breaching an international obligation.[4]

Unfortunately, the misstatements and errors in the book are not confined to the problems outlined above. The author surmises (pp. 63–4) that the 1979 Act "appears to codify the de minimis rule" of dumping injury. This flies in the face of a stiffening of the statutory language, some ambiguous legislative history, and an explicit statement in the House committee report on the bill that the use of the term "de minimis" was "specifically rejected by the Committee."[5]

Another example of the troublesome lack of precision in the book occurs at page 23, where the author says, "the 1979 [antidumping] code imposes antidumping duties only to the extent that they are necessary to alleviate injury in the import market." In fact, this code does *not impose* antidumping duties at all. It merely *permits* nations themselves to impose such duties in certain

[1] *See, e.g.,* L. HENKIN, FOREIGN AFFAIRS AND THE CONSTITUTION, chs. V and VI (1972).

[2] *See id.* at 177, 184.

[3] *See, e.g.,* Jackson, *GATT in U.S. Domestic Law*, 66 MICH. L.R. 249 (1967).

[4] RESTATEMENT (2D) OF FOREIGN RELATIONS LAW OF THE UNITED STATES §145, Comment *b* (1965).

[5] H.R. REP. NO. 96-317, 96th Cong., 1st Sess. 46 (1979).

described circumstances. Furthermore, the language in the code addressing this point reads, "The amount of the anti-dumping duty must not exceed the margin of dumping" (Art. 8, para. 3). Neither of the provisions cited by the author for his proposition supports it, and he fails to cite the clause quoted above. The question whether to limit duties to an amount needed to alleviate injury was an important negotiating issue in the Tokyo Round, both in the Antidumping Code and in the Subsidies Code. U.S. negotiators knew well that Congress would not tolerate such a provision, and they did not accept any mandatory language in either code that would prevent the United States from imposing duties to the full extent of the dumping *margin* or amount of the subsidy, as the case might be. In general, contrary to the author's apparent view (pp. 22–3), the U.S. executive and legislative branches believed that the 1979 Trade Agreements Act was not inconsistent with any U.S. international obligations from the Tokyo Round agreements. That viewpoint may be challengeable, but not for any of the reasons asserted in this book.

It is unfortunate that such a timely, needed, and ambitious book fails to achieve its goals. But perhaps it is at least partly a commentary on the complexity and subtlety of the subject matter undertaken, that this is so.

JOHN H. JACKSON
Board of Editors

Digest of United States Practice in International Law, 1978. By Marian Nash Leich. Dept of State Pub. No. 9162. Washington: U.S. Govt. Printing Office, 1980. Pp. xxii, 1802. Index. $19.

The sixth annual *Digest of United States Practice in International Law* covering the year 1978 is again a masterful compilation of written materials reflecting the legal aspects and repercussions of the conduct of foreign relations by the United States. Following the pattern initiated by the editor of the first volume of the series, Arthur Rovine, Marian Nash Leich, who had the responsibility for the present tome, collected, edited, and arranged a staggering array of texts of international agreements, actions in international organizations, diplomatic correspondence, presidential documents, reports to Congress, testimony before congressional committees, international arbitral awards, decisions of domestic courts, amicus briefs of the Department in domestic litigation, interdepartmental memorandums, departmental replies to congressional, interagency, or private inquiries, and even press releases or speeches of departmental officers. As a result of the new editor's industry the present volume is three times longer than that for 1973. Luckily, a carefully prepared index, itself filling 89 printed pages, helps the reader to find the way to the materials that are to be consulted.

Undoubtedly one of the main causes for the bulk of the tome is the attention given to the ever-growing number and types of issues of international law arising in litigation before domestic courts or administrative tribunals and the Department of State's involvement in such suits, either because the Government is a party or acts as amicus curiae. These cases cover a broad spectrum of questions ranging from attacks on the constitutionality of the Panama Canal

Treaties[1] to proceedings involving the status of individuals, especially expatriates[2] and aliens.[3] A few of these cases involved allegedly illegal activities of alien officials of international organizations or functionaries of foreign missions.[4]

The period covered by this volume constituted the second year of the operation of the Foreign Sovereign Immunities Act and brought a substantial number of decisions applying the statute.[5] The case law revealed that the draftsmanship of the Act, intertwining grants of personal and subject matter jurisdiction, posed difficult questions, sometimes of constitutional dimensions, and produced difficult tasks for the courts. Moreover, the interrelation between the congressional

[1] Edwards v. Carter, 445 F.Supp. 1979 (D.D.C. 1978), *aff'd*, 580 F.2d 1055 (D.C. Cir. 1978), *cert. denied*, 436 U.S. 907 (1978), *rehearing denied*, 580 F.2d 1055 (D.C. Cir. 1978), [1978] DIGEST at 665–73; Mease v. Heinz, 80 F.R.D. 119 (E.D. Pa. 1978), [1978] DIGEST at 698; Smith v. Eagleton, 455 F.Supp. 403 (W.D. Mo. 1978), [1978] DIGEST at 697.

[2] Of general interest is the case of *Matter of Davis* in which the Board of Immigration Appeals affirmed the decision of an immigration judge, holding that a former citizen of the United States, who had formally renounced his nationality pursuant to section 401(f) of the Nationality Act of 1940 to become a "world citizen," was excludable as an immigrant without visa pursuant to 8 U.S.C. §1182(a)20, Interim Decision 2650, 16 B.I.A. 514, [1978] DIGEST at 242–47, *aff'd*, Davis v. District Director, Immigration, etc. 481 F.Supp. 1178 (D.D.C. 1979). The standard of proof required to find voluntary expatriation by a person having dual nationality at birth and the constitutionality of 8 U.S.C. §1481(c) were at issue in Terrazas v. Vance, 577 F.2d 7 (7th Cir. 1978), [1978] DIGEST at 239–42. The holding in that case, which faulted the statutory standard on constitutional grounds, subsequently was reversed by the Supreme Court in Vance v. Terrazas, 444 U.S. 252, *rehearing denied*, 445 U.S. 920 (1980), and resulted ultimately in a finding of expatriation, Terrazas v. Muskie, 494 F.Supp. 1017 (N.D. Ill. 1980), *aff'd*, 653 F.2d 285 (7th Cir. 1981).

[3] Noteworthy among these cases were those involving the right to tuition-free schooling of children having the status of undocumented aliens and those of entrants seeking asylum. The first category is represented by Doe v. Plyler, 458 F.Supp. 569 (E.D. Tex. 1978), [1978] DIGEST at 288–98, *aff'd*, 628 F.2d 448 (1980), *prob. juris. noted*, 101 S.Ct. 2044, *argued* 12/1/81, 50 U.S.L.W. 3457 (1981). For a companion case, see *In re* Alien Children Education Litigation, 501 F.Supp. 544 (S.D. Tex. 1980), *C. A. stay dissolved*, 448 U.S. 1327 (1980), *aff'd*, 50 U.S.L.W. 3098, *prob. juris. noted*, 101 S.Ct. 2044, *argued* 50 U.S.L.W. 3457 (1981). Judge Seals in the companion case discussed at length the international law aspects, 501 F.Supp. 544 at 589–96. The second category is represented by Sannon v. United States, 460 F.Supp. 458 (S.D. Fla. 1978), [1978] DIGEST at 355–64, a decision which subsequently was ordered to be vacated and replaced by dismissal as moot, 631 F.2d 1247 (5th Cir. 1980). For a companion case, see Haitian Refugee Center v. Civiletti, 503 F.Supp. 442 (S.D. Fla. 1978), *app. pending sub nom.* Smith v. Haitian Refugee Center.

[4] United States v. Enger, 472 F.Supp. 490 (N.N.J. 1978), [1978] DIGEST at 93–107; United States v. Humphrey & Truong, 456 F.Supp. 51 (E.D. Va. 1978), [1978] DIGEST at 123–24, *aff'd sub nom.* United States v. Truong Dinh Hung, 629 F.2d 908 (4th Cir. 1980), cc. Chagnon v. Bell, 642 F.2d 1248 (D.C. Cir. 1980). For the final disposition of the case against Humphrey and Truong Dinh Hung, see 50 U.S.L.W. 3547 (*cert. denied*) and Washington Post, Jan. 26, 1982.

[5] [1978] DIGEST at 883–914, containing excerpts from United Euram Corporation v. Union of Soviet Socialist Republics, 461 F.Supp. 609 (S.D.N.Y. 1978); Yessenin-Volpin v. Novosti Press Agency, 443 F.Supp. 849 (S.D.N.Y. 1978); Outboard Marine Corp. v. Pezetel, 461 F.Supp. 384 (D. Del. 1978); Gray v. Permanent Mission of the People's Republic of the Congo to the United Nations, 443 F.Supp. 816 (S.D.N.Y. 1978), *aff'd*, 581 F.2d 1044 (2d Cir. 1978); 40 D 6262 Realty Corp. v. United Arab Emirates, 447 F.Supp. 710 (S.D.N.Y. 1978); Jet Line Services, Inc. v. M/V. Marsa El Hariga et al., 462 F.Supp. 1165 (D. Md. 1978); Ipitrade Int'l v. Federal Republic of Nigeria, 465 F.Supp. 824 (D.D.C. 1978); Carey v. National Oil Corp., 453 F.Supp. 1097 (S.D.N.Y. 1978), *aff'd*, 592 F.2d 673 (2d Cir. 1979); Upton v. Empire of Iran, 459 F.Supp. 264 (D.D.C. 1978), *aff'd*, 607 F.2d 494 (D.C. Cir. 1979).

grant of subject matter jurisdiction under the FSIA and the mandate of abstention pursuant to the judge-made act of state doctrine created additional analytical and policy problems reflected in a series of cases.[6] An illustrative example of that type was *National American Corp. v. Federal Republic of Nigeria & Central Bank of Nigeria*,[7] which was one segment of the worldwide web of litigation in the wake of the notorious cement flood, precipitated by the improvident purchase program of Nigeria.[8] Another chunk of case law is collected under the heading "Jurisdiction over Vessels"[9] and focuses on the extraterritorial applicability and enforceability on the high seas of U.S. legislation against the importation of narcotics.

The amount of space consumed by the inclusion of a vast quantity of sometimes lengthy excerpts from judicial decisions is a legitimate cause for concern. Yet, it seems to be justified, because these excerpts reveal so clearly the impact of domestic judicial control over important aspects of the conduct of foreign affairs. Moreover, they often furnish the occasion for showing to what extent and in what way the Government has participated in the proceedings by way of amicus briefs or suggestions and, also, for presenting the legislative and diplomatic repercussions of important decisions. Thus, the report of the case of *Pfizer, Inc. v. Government of India et al.*[10] is accompanied[11] by materials on proposed legislation overturning the result of that case and on the Department of State's opposition to the measure on the ground that it might conflict with foreign policy interests, including the spirit of important treaty obligations.[12]

The year 1978 witnessed a climax of endeavors of the Government of the United States to strengthen its peaceful relations in different parts of the world. In particular it saw the final conclusion of the Panama Canal Treaties,[13] which raised difficult procedural and substantive questions in respect to the Senate's action giving advice and consent,[14] and the normalization of relations with the People's Republic of China[15] with the attendant readjustment of relations with Taiwan.[16] It also brought the Camp David accords,[17] constituting a milestone

[6] In addition to the case cited *infra* note 7, see Outboard Marine Corp. v. Pezetel, *supra* note 5, and Letelier v. Chile, 488 F.Supp. 665 (D.D.C. 1980), 502 F.Supp. 259 (D.D.C. 1980).

[7] 448 F.Supp. 622 (S.D.N.Y. 1978), *aff'd*, 597 F.2d 314 (2d Cir. 1979), [1978] DIGEST at 914–19.

[8] *See* the detailed factual discussion in Texas Trading v. Federal Republic of Nigeria, 647 F.2d 300 (2d Cir. 1981), and especially the list of foreign cases, *id.* at n.15.

[9] [1978] DIGEST at 827–50, including United States v. Cadena, 585 F.2d 1252 (5th Cir. 1978). The holding of the court of appeals with respect to foreign flag vessels in United States v. Postal, 589 F.2d 862 (5th Cir. 1979), and United States v. Williams, 617 F.2d 1062 (5th Cir. 1980), is criticized in my Editorial Comment, 74 AJIL 892 (1980).

[10] 434 U.S. 308 (1978), [1978] DIGEST at 804.

[11] [1978] DIGEST at 811.

[12] The text of the German note (Dept. of State File No. P82 0010–1873) and the concerns of the Department about the compatibility of the proposed legislation with treaty obligations unfortunately are not included in the excerpt from the testimony.

[13] [1978] DIGEST at 1027–70, 1682–83. *See also* pp. 655–73, 697–700 (constitutionality); pp. 700–04 (effect on third parties); pp. 674–77 (exchange of ratifications).

[14] *Id.* at 689–94, 729–34, and 1053–56.

[15] *Id.* at 70–72, 734.

[16] *Id.* at 73–75, 734–65.

[17] *Id.* at 1541–60. For the text of the Peace Treaty of March 26, 1979, see DEPT. STATE BULL., No. 2026, May 1979, at 3–15.

in the mediation efforts of the United States to restore peace between Egypt and Israel as well as in the Near East in general. Necessarily, these events are reflected in a substantial increase in the size of the volume.

The *Digest* is the most telling testimony to the importance of legal questions in the conduct of foreign affairs by the United States, and to the contribution of the courts, as well as of the Executive, to the maintenance of legality and an orderly adjustment of international law to the changing needs of the international community. The editor deserves the gratitude and plaudits of practitioners and scholars in the field for her painstaking and intelligent labors in assembling and organizing an indispensable source of materials.

STEFAN A. RIESENFELD
Board of Editors

Arbitration in Taxation. By Gustaf Lindencrona and Nils Mattsson. Deventer: Kluwer, 1981. Pp. 92. Dfl.45.

The existence of a comprehensive double taxation treaty between two states does not in fact eliminate the possibility of double taxation. Such an effect can arise from conflicting interpretations of the provisions of the treaty, *e.g.*, concerning certain operative terms such as royalty or dividends. In other instances, the taxpayer may be deemed to be a resident for tax purposes in both states. Still another cause of double taxation is the adjustment of transfer prices between related enterprises in the contracting states. The tax treaties regularly contain a mechanism for the resolution of such cases, referred to as the mutual agreement procedure, which essentially implies that the highest tax authorities of the two states shall attempt to reach agreement on such mutually consistent tax measures as would eliminate the double taxation.

The present work by two prominent Swedish professors of fiscal law is the result of a commission by the Tax Section of the World Association of Lawyers of World Peace Through Law to investigate and propose methods for the solution of international tax controversies of the nature indicated above. Their proposal was adopted at the association's Ninth Conference in 1979.

The study examines in detail the imperfections of the mutual agreement procedure, principally the absence of an ultimate remedy in case of failure to achieve an agreement, but also certain complications of a legal nature such as the relationship between an agreement and judgments of the national tax courts. In addition, the study discusses previous work on the subject, such as the efforts of the OECD to further refine the provisions of its model double tax convention and the proposal in 1976 by the Commission of the European Communities for a directive on arbitration procedures to eliminate double taxation resulting from adjustment of the profits of related enterprises, as well as the work and recommendations of the International Fiscal Association.

On the basis of their findings, the authors suggest arbitration as the preferable conflict-solving mechanism. Having examined the function of various well-known commercial and other arbitral institutions, among them the Court of Arbitration of the International Chamber of Commerce, the Arbitration Institute of the Stockholm Chamber of Commerce, and the International Centre for Settlement of Investment Disputes, for comparative purposes, they consider ad hoc arbitration less suitable and instead propose the creation of a permanent arbitration institute to which all disputes that cannot be solved in the mutual agreement procedure could be referred by either state (but not by the taxpayer concerned) under a tax treaty. Each case would be heard and decided by an arbitral commission composed of three members, of which each state party would appoint one; the chairman would be designated by the two parties jointly. Any award would be final and binding on the states. The institute itself would primarily have coordinating and administrative functions.

In order to gain the widest possible acceptance, it is proposed that the institute be given the status of an autonomous institution under the auspices of the United Nations. The authors recommend Stockholm as the location of the institute, on account of Sweden's policy of nonalignment.

The study ends with an exhaustive analysis of such incidental aspects as procedural matters, publication of the awards, and the position of the taxpayer in the context of an arbitration. In a concluding section, the authors advocate an international tax court as the ultimate goal in the efforts to create a permanent body competent to settle international tax disputes.

The study represents a commendable effort to analyze the rather complex issues involved in the mutual agreement procedure under existing treaties and to propose a way finally to resolve disputes between the contracting states. Nevertheless, realization of the proposed solution would require a substantial amount of international preparatory work, including the renegotiation of a large number of tax conventions. One may regret the omission from the study of any information on the frequency of application of the mutual agreement procedures and their duration, the types of tax issues involved, and similar data, which (though available in other sources) would have enabled the nonexpert reader fully to appreciate the need for a reform of the mutual agreement procedure.

HANS M. CARLSTEN
Wetter & Wetter Advokatbyrå, Stockholm

Foreign Inve$tment in the United States. By Bruce Zagaris. New York: Praeger Publishers, 1980. Pp. x, 323. Index.

When I was growing up in the foreign policy establishment in the early 1960's, the big slogan for development was foreign investment. The gap between the capital needs of the LDC's (as they were then called) and the availability of capital was going to be eliminated by private investors, *i.e.*, large corporations, mostly based in the United States, that would combine their capital, management, and technology for benefit of both host and home country.[1] Then came

[1] *See, e.g.*, R. MIKESELL & ALLEN, ECONOMIC POLICIES TOWARD LESS DEVELOPED COUNTRIES, REP. PREPARED FOR THE SUBCOMM. ON FOREIGN ECON. POLICY OF THE JOINT ECON. COMM., 87th Cong., 1st Sess. (1961); FOREIGN AID THROUGH PRIVATE INITIATIVE, REP. OF THE ADVISORY COMM. ON PRIVATE ENTERPRISE IN FOREIGN AID (THE WATSON COMM. REP.) (1965).

a series of shocks—expropriations in Cuba, South America, and Asia and Africa as well; attacks, sometimes justified, often exaggerated, on the business practices of the "multi's"; the rise to wealth of Arab petroleum exporters; the fall in the relative value of the dollar and the realization that international investment is a two-way street. As such American firms as Gimbels, A & P, and American Motors fell under foreign ownership or control, sentiments that the United States was used to hearing from Brazil and Chile and Mexico (and lately from Canada) were coming from Ohio and Indiana and Texas. Not that there was pressure in the United States for expropriation—that has not been the (North) American way. But perhaps some restraints—disincentives, screening committees, or licensing boards—would be a good idea. More than one member of Congress thought the Foreign Investment Review Act adopted in 1974 by Canada might be a good idea for the United States. Just as these lines were written, there was new excitement in the United States about purchase by the Government of Kuwait of an American oil drilling and engineering company, Santa Fe International, which had a subsidiary that designed nuclear power plants.

My own view, consistent, I think, with that prevailing in Washington, is that if one believes in a relatively open international economy, with free flow of capital, goods, and services, one should not in principle restrain international investment—coming in or going out. We have come to realize that corporate shares, or indeed dollars, pounds, and yen, are assets in many ways like steel, textiles, or automobiles; and that the whole world is better off to the extent there is one grand market, not a series of protected regions or sectors. On the other hand, I suspect that the concern reflected in recent American legislation, such as the Foreign Investment Study Act of 1974,[2] the International Investment Survey Act of 1976,[3] and the Agricultural Foreign Investment Disclosure Act of 1978,[4] as well as President Ford's executive order creating the Committee on Foreign Investment in the United States,[5] will give Americans a somewhat greater understanding of the apprehensions and ambivalence felt in Latin America, in Canada, and in Europe about investment originating in the United States.

The discussion deserves to be continued and it is hard to quarrel with the proponents of the legislation mentioned, who say we need a more systematic data base. I had hoped, when I saw the title of the book sent to me for review, for a thoughtful analysis of the by now mounting information,[6] and discussion of investment in the United States, in the context of our international economic

[2] Pub. L. No. 93–479, 88 Stat. 1450 (1974).

[3] Pub. L. No. 94–476, 90 Stat. 2059 (1976), 22 U.S.C. §§3101–08.

[4] Pub. L. No. 95–460, 92 Stat. 1263 (1978), 7 U.S.C. §§3501–08.

[5] Exec. Order No. 11,851, 40 Fed. Reg. 20,263 (1975), *reproduced in* 3 C.F.R. 990 (1971–1975 comp.).

[6] *See* U.S. DEPT. OF COMMERCE, FOREIGN DIRECT INVESTMENT IN THE UNITED STATES, REPORT OF THE SECRETARY OF COMMERCE IN COMPLIANCE WITH THE FOREIGN INVESTMENT STUDY ACT OF 1974 (9 vols. 1976); U.S. DEPT. OF THE TREASURY, FOREIGN PORTFOLIO INVESTMENT IN THE UNITED STATES: RESULT OF THE BENCHMARK SURVEY DONE UNDER THE FOREIGN INVESTMENT STUDY ACT (2 vols. 1976); as well as periodic updates in the Department of Commerce monthly publication, SURVEY OF CURRENT BUSINESS.

policy, the problems of employment and technology, and (if it exists) an industrial policy. I am sorry to say I was wholly disappointed, and no one who looks for what I did should bother with this book.

What the book does do is to give a rather primitive overview of some of the legislation relevant to a foreign investor, particularly the investor interested in real estate or natural resources.[7] But there is no treatment of securities regulation, of banking (perhaps the most active area of foreign acquisitions), or of antitrust. The emphasis is on taxation, though there are excursions into restrictions by states on alien ownership of land, and there is a brief (and embarrassingly thin) attempt at a historical introduction to foreign investment in the United States. It is hard to write about taxation without being either too complicated or too simple. My impression is that the author errs throughout in the latter direction.

In short, foreign investment in the United States is still a subject looking for the right author. It hasn't found him, in my judgment, in Mr. Zagaris.[8]

ANDREAS F. LOWENFELD
Board of Editors

Your Man at the U.N. People, Politics, and Bureaucracy in Making Foreign Policy. By Seymour Maxwell Finger. New York and London: New York University Press, 1980. Pp. xx, 320. Index. $26.50.

In this book former Ambassador Maxwell Finger has given us a valuable and sensitive picture of the working of the U.S. Mission to the United Nations, with special attention to the principal U.S. Representatives. The author is at his best, quite naturally, in discussing those Representatives with whom he was closely associated: Henry Cabot Lodge, Adlai Stevenson, Arthur Goldberg, George Ball, Russell Wiggins, Charles Yost, and George Bush.

The author is preoccupied with the relationship between our Representatives to the United Nations and the Presidents under whom they served. Inevitably, this leads him to consider a certain tension which is supposed to exist between our Mission in New York and the Department of State in Washington. Intimate involvement with UN matters in three administrations leads this reviewer to the impression that this tension is more apparent in New York than in Washington. At each session of the UN General Assembly there are more than a hundred items on the agenda. The cumulative agenda of the UN Security Council, published annually by the Secretary-General, shows well over a hundred items. Almost every aspect of U.S. foreign policy comes before some organ of the United Nations in some form. U.S. policy on these matters cannot

[7] The book is full of paragraphs such as the following:

> A real estate broker is an individual who not only finds property, but also negotiates on behalf of one or more of the parties. In most states an individual is not authorized to act as a real estate broker without a license from the state in which he or she does business. A broker often employs a salesperson, who in many states is also required to be licensed [p. 16].

[8] I may be getting stuffy, but I must say I was put off right at the start by the book's title, which is printed *Foreign Inve$tment in the United States*.

be made by the Mission in New York. It is in Washington that one draws upon the total resources of the U.S. Government, receives a massive flow of information, has ready access to other departments and agencies directly involved in the issues at hand, can keep in touch with the leadership and important committees of Congress, and can take into account dozens of secondary and tertiary questions involved in important foreign policy issues. If the head of the U.S. Mission in New York wishes to participate actively and realistically in the making of policy, he or she must spend considerable time in Washington as a participant in the complex processes through which policy is made in the most complicated constitutional and political system to be found anywhere in the world. It is not enough for our Representative to the United Nations to send telegrams to Washington or to make judgments based upon the passing parliamentary situations which occur in the United Nations itself. Communication works best when our Representative to the United Nations can be present for interdepartmental discussions, meetings of the National Security Council, and meetings of the Cabinet. Another reason for frequent visits to Washington by our Representative is the need to educate Washington about the United Nations, the importance of the discussions which occur there, and our stake in the outcome of its deliberations.

It should be noted that the work of our Mission to the United Nations is burdensome. With 157 members the simple process of keeping in touch with other delegations is a strenuous task. The Permanent Representatives of all these members, including the smallest countries, are not satisfied to be in touch with some relatively junior member of our delegation; as a matter of prestige, they expect to be in touch with the head of our Mission. The consequent demands on the time and energy of our "Man at the U.N." are formidable.

When a President sets about to recruit a major public figure to head our Mission to the United Nations, he will try to be as persuasive as possible. When President Truman asked Secretary of State Edward Stettinius to move from his Cabinet position in Washington to the post in New York, he described the UN appointment as the most important appointment at his disposal. This reviewer was present with President-elect John F. Kennedy when he telephoned Adlai Stevenson to get him to take the UN post. Kennedy described the position to Stevenson in the most glowing terms and, if one were to take his word at that moment literally, one would wonder if there were any foreign policy role left for the President or for the Secretary of State.

Two necessities must coexist: one, our Mission to the United Nations must receive its instructions through a steady flow of instructions from the Department of State; on the other hand, our principal Representative to the United Nations must always have, if he needs it, direct access to the President himself, just as does every other American ambassador. If there is a certain tension built into these two requirements, it can only be overcome by a close and personal working relationship between a Secretary of State and the head of our Mission in New York.

Ambassador Finger speculates about the ideal for our "Man at the U.N."—reminiscent of Sir Harold Nicolson's famous chapter on "The Ideal Diplomatist." This reviewer has a very simple formula for the ideal person: someone with the forensic skills of an Adlai Stevenson and with the negotiating skills of an Arthur Goldberg.

DEAN RUSK
University of Georgia School of Law

Institution Spécialisée et Organisation Mondiale: Etude des Relations de l'OIT avec la SDN et l'ONU. By Manuela Tortora. Brussels: Etablissements Emile Bruylant, 1980. Pp. xii, 519. Index. F.2,600.

This reviewer's initial reaction, when confronted with yet another study of the International Labour Organisation, was to wonder whether there could be anything more to be said about an organization that has been in existence for more than 60 years and that, for very good reasons, has attracted a good deal of attention not only from scholars but also from its own officials. Works by Jenks, Morse, Wolf, and Valticos all spring to mind. In addition, the ILO must be the only specialized agency to have commissioned its own history, the results of which are to be found in Alcock's *History of the International Labour Organisation*, published in 1971 as a contribution to the Organisation's 50th anniversary celebrations.

It is surprising then to discover that until now there has been no comprehensive study made of the relations between the ILO and the League of Nations and the United Nations, in other words between the specialized agency of which the ILO is the prototype and the central political organization. This gap in the literature has been filled by Manuela Tortora whose study, which originated as a doctoral thesis at the Institut Universitaire de Hautes Etudes Internationales in Geneva, demonstrates a rare mastery of subject matter and maturity of judgment. This is a notable addition to the excellent series published by Bruylant under the general title Organisation Internationale et Relations Internationales.

In the view of the author the notion of a specialized agency rests on three basic assumptions: the separability of the technical and political fields; the existence of separate, definable functional activities; and the establishment of some degree of coordination between the functional and the political bodies. The theoretical formulation of the concept of a specialized agency may therefore be expressed as two complementary and interrelated ideas: a division of labor and coordination between the technical activities carried out by the functional agencies and the maintenance of peace, which is the task of the political organization.

Tortora has wisely chosen to follow a chronological order. Part 1 examines the relations between the ILO and the League of Nations, while part 2 places the ILO in the context of the UN system. The relationship between the ILO and the League was a difficult one, stemming in part from the financial dependence of the ILO on the League, administrative problems involving common services, and the differences in membership which developed as a result of the breakdown in the principle of common membership. The personalities of the chief administrative officers also contributed to these difficulties. The survival of the ILO after World War II and the demise of the League resulted in a considerably strengthened ILO vis-à-vis the United Nations. The ILO not only expanded its own role and activities but naturally took the lead in coordinating the activities of the specialized agencies. An agreement concluded between the ILO and the United Nations in 1946 established the autonomy of the ILO within the UN system and made detailed provision for the bilateral relationship of the two organizations. The coordination aspects of this agreement became a model for the other specialized agencies.

As far as the division of labor is concerned, the years since 1946 have brought the ILO a steady broadening of its activities, particularly in the area of technical assistance, and a politicization induced by the tripartite structure of the membership, the ideology of the Organisation, and the very nature of its activities—not to mention the personalities of two of its most recent Director-Generals, David Morse and C. W. Jenks. The author concludes that the notion of coordination has expanded as it has become increasingly difficult to distinguish between the political and the technical. In carrying out this study of the ILO, the author has, in fact, produced the definitive work on functionalism and coordination. This brilliant debut is accompanied by a 40-page bibliography and an index.

RALPH ZACKLIN
United Nations

International Aggression. A Study of the Legal Concept: Its Development and Definition in International Law. By Ahmed M. Rifaat. Stockholm: Almqvist & Wiksell International; Atlantic Highlands, N.J.: Humanities Press Inc., 1979. Pp. xxiv, 355. Index. Sw.kr. 137; $45.

As long as international aggression continues, books will be written about it. One of the more recent contributions is the dissertation of a lecturer in law from the Police Academy at Cairo who completed his doctoral studies in Stockholm. Dr. Rifaat set out "to present to the non-specialist reader having general knowledge of international law, a correlated historical background of the evolution of international aggression (*i.e.,* both aggressive war and aggression) from medieval times to the present" (p. xiv). His book should be of interest to those who seek to know more about a subject that remains in the forefront of international concern.

Rifaat's three-part study follows a logical historical sequence as it traces the concept of aggression prior to 1919, to the period between the world wars, and then to contemporary international law. In his *tour d'horizon* he touches such interesting points as the doctrine of "just war" as deduced from verses of the Holy Koran: "Those who believe, and suffer exile and strive with might and main, in God's cause, with their goods and their persons, have the highest rank in the sight of God: They are the people who will achieve (salvation)" (p. 8). Ancient doctrines thus offer insights into the inspiration underlying some contemporary perceptions regarding the legality of violent behavior.

The author outlines the concept of aggression as seen from the vantage point of such different regional organizations as the North Atlantic Treaty Organization, the Warsaw Treaty Organization, and the League of Arab States. He points to the need for centralized armed forces to make collective security more effective. He touches upon UN debates regarding aggression in Korea, Suez, the Congo, and the Middle East, and the consensus definition of aggression.

Not all of Rifaat's observations will go unchallenged. That "aggressive war was completely and unconditionally prohibited" (p. 60) by the Pact of Paris, that "war was in principle prohibited by the Covenant" (p. 180), that England and France must share German guilt for World War II (pp. 175–76), and that the Nuremberg tribunals were imposing victors' vengeance and ex post facto law are conclusions that are not universally shared. His characterization of military occupation as "continuous aggression," "twofold aggression," "aggression exceeding defence," "permanent aggression," and "continuous aggression of utmost gravity" (p. 271) goes beyond anything considered or accepted in the UN consensus definition of aggression.

Rifaat concludes that state aggression is criminal and that states should be liable to make reparation, while guilty individuals, regardless of rank, should face penal sanctions. He recommends the establishment of international criminal courts with compulsory jurisdiction and power to deal with crimes against peace and humanity. He argues that it would be easier to create such courts on a regional basis among states with common traditions and interests. Drawing upon work already done by the United Nations, he submits a draft statute for his proposed international regional criminal court. Rifaat thus joins many others who look to an international system where codification, court, and enforcement will help to maintain a more tranquil social order. Although some of his facts and some of his views are questionable, the general thrust of Rifaat's book is in the right direction. Welcome aboard!

BENJAMIN B. FERENCZ
Of the New York Bar

Die Funktionsfähigkeit des Sicherheitsmechanismus der Vereinten Nationen. (Vol. 77 in the series Beiträge zum ausländischen öffentlichen Recht und Völkerrecht.) By Michael Schaefer. Berlin, Heidelberg, New York: Springer-Verlag, 1981. Pp. xxi, 471. Index. DM 105; $62.

New books on the United Nations are always welcome, and Schaefer's study of "the functional effectiveness of the security mechanism of the United Nations" is no exception. While scholars familiar with the English-language literature treating the United Nations will find little new of substance in this recent contribution (indeed, it draws heavily from such literature), the author nevertheless offers a competent and thorough political/legal examination of the Organization's peace responsibilities in theory and practice.

The book is divided into three analytical sections. Part I examines the linkages of the United Nations to the League of Nations, the concept of peace found in the UN Charter, and the UN machinery that comprises the "security mechanism." A central problem has always been that "peace" is not clearly defined in the Charter, and as the author notes, one finds differing interpretations of peace within the Charter itself. The "security mechanism" involves primarily the Security Council, General Assembly, and Secretary-General, but in a broader sense various other secondary bodies are also part of the peace process.

In part II the author is concerned with probing the UN "security mechanism" in practice. He presents a series of case studies in historical, legal, and political detail. The studies include Indonesia (1947–1949), Czechoslovakia (1948 and 1968), Korea (1950–1952), the Congo (1960–1962), and the Mideast conflicts (1956, 1967, and 1973). The purpose of these studies is to provide empirical data for judging in part III the UN peacekeeping mechanism in a series of different contexts and for testing several theses relevant to effective peacekeeping.

The conclusion, not surprisingly, is that UN peacekeeping has not worked in practice as originally envisaged by the Charter. Peacekeeping has been hampered by such features of modern politics as Big Power disagreement, the emergence of new nations, and East-West/North-South divisions. The familiar path of the changing peacekeeping functions of UN organs and the evolution of the Charter are retraced, after which the author notes: "The original concept of collective coercive measures such as military action to deter and counter military aggression is giving way more and more to a new system for a collective assertion of international obligations (such as the right to self-determination, human rights)" (p. 448).

Although the UN "security mechanism" has remained relatively undeveloped, the "best way" of making if more effective, Schaefer believes, is to "strengthen the policy-formation and decision-making mechanisms in the Security Council" (p. 449). He recommends, *inter alia*, restructuring the Security Council to reflect emerging political patterns and to provide for a balanced participation of all world regions within a system of permanent, semi-permanent, and nonpermanent members. The lingering problems, however, of national sovereignty and Big Power distaste for artificial UN voting majorities remain. While the author has not solved the problem of "peace," his work at least reminds us of "where we stand."

FOREST L. GRIEVES
University of Montana
Universität des Saarlandes

"Fremdvölkische" im Dritten Reich. By Diemut Majer. (Vol. 28, Schriften des Bundesarchivs.) Boppard am Rhein: Harald Boldt Verlag, 1981. Pp. 1024. Index. DM 96.

Die Truppe des Weltanschauungskrieges. By Helmut Krausnick and Hans-Heinrich Wilhelm. (Vol. 22, Quellen und Darstellungen zur Zeitgeschichte.) Stuttgart: Deutsche Verlags-Anstalt, 1981. Pp. 688. Index.

Hans Frank, a former President of the Law Academy and Society of International Law of Germany, before being hanged at Nuremberg in 1946 for the enslavement of one million Poles and the murder of three million Jews, prophesied: "A thousand years will pass and still this guilt of Germany will not have been erased." During the early postwar years, most Germans found it difficult to come to grips with their past. The succeeding generation is now trying to comprehend the enormous perversion of law that took place in the Third Reich. Two recent books, based on doctoral dissertations, offer a scholarly illumination of the Hitler racial program. The titles, drawn from Nazi terminology, are practically untranslatable, but these comprehensive works contain new information and insights that are worthy of widespread attention and appreciation.

Fremdvölkische—"ethnic foreigners"—in the Third Reich, a study of over one thousand pages and some four thousand comprehensive footnotes, is the product of 10 years of effort by Diemut Majer. She sets the scene by reviewing the structure of Germany under National Socialism: absolute authority vested in the *Führer*, and a Nazi Party hierarchy superior to the regular administrative apparatus of the state. Repudiating the ideal that "all men are created equal," Nazi doctrine taught that the German Aryan was a superior being. Those not of German race or blood, such as Slavs, blacks, Gypsies, or Jews, were fit only for slavery or death. Dr. Majer scoured German records and reached into hitherto inaccessible archives in Poland to ascertain how the German legal and judicial system, which had a tradition of respect for law, responded to the Nazi program of genocidal racial discrimination. Her principal focus was on the annexed and occupied territories of eastern Poland, including a region governed by Hans Frank, the distinguished German jurist turned Lieutenant General and mass murderer of the Nazi Security Service.

The acts of persecution within Germany that heralded the Nazi rise to power were promptly reinforced by an imprimatur of legality. Race and ideology became the basis for special laws to protect "German blood and honor." Majer notes that the obedient German mind accepted as just and justified whatever was printed in the German civil code. In occupied Poland, German practices set the precedents. Governor-General Frank considered his domain as a colony to be exploited to the maximum for German benefit. Penal law and criminal ordinances prohibiting all forms of opposition to German rule became the principal tool for enforcing Nazi policies. Failure to comply with vague and broadly formulated police decrees, many of which are cited by Majer, could be punished by incarceration in a concentration camp or death. Judges, fearing admonition for failure to follow the Nazi Party line, soon learned to interpret the law in ways that supported the Nazi objectives. Police brutality was considered beyond their jurisdiction as German judges came to regard as their legal duty the carrying out of racial policies against the non-Aryan "ethnic foreigners." It becomes apparent from Majer's documented account that the blindfolded goddess of justice did not choose to see the massive injustice that surrounded her.

Majer concludes that the Hitler regime proved most efficient in getting the German judiciary to bend justice in order to support the political objectives of Nazi ideology. The grant of almost unlimited discretion to local authorities in occupied territories made it easier for those prepared to employ illegal means to prevail over those who might have felt bound by traditional legal restraints. She fears that the same abuses can occur in any dictatorship and argues that a safeguarding agency, such as the Constitutional Court of the Federal Republic of Germany, with which she was associated, can provide greater protection in the future. Perhaps she is looking toward East Germany, where no such court exists and where the German Democratic Republic condemns Nazism while pretending never to have had any connection with it.

Majer's study is comprehensive and well written. Its objectivity is reflected in the many citations and it is rounded out by an extensive bibliography, photographs, a map, and an index. It is a significant supplement to the existing literature.

Die Truppe des Weltanschauungskrieges (The Troops of the Ideological War) describes murderous activities that did not seek to cloak the face of cruelty with the mask of law. Helmut Krausnick, who recently celebrated his 75th birthday, is a German historian and former Director of the Munich-based Institute for Contemporary History. His coauthor, Hans-Heinrich Wilhelm, was born shortly before the end of World War II. Their book describes the activities of *Einsatzgruppen*—special police "action groups"—whose assignment was to follow the German armies into Poland and Russia and, after the fighting had ceased, to eliminate all those who might pose a threat to the present or future security of the Third Reich. Among the targets of these extermination squads, totaling some three thousand men, were the nobility, the intellectuals, and the clergy; those considered racially inferior, such as Gypsies or Jews, were marked for immediate death. Typical was the massacre at Babi Yar, near Kiev, where "[i]n two days on 29 and 30 September 1941, according to the official report of the competent unit, not less than 33,771 Jews were shot. Over a hundred trucks were needed to transport their clothing, which was made available to the National Socialist People's Welfare Agency" (p. 15, translation by reviewer). During the first 9 months, the *Einsatzgruppen* managed to murder at least 750,000 Jews, and with the help of other units the total soon exceeded 2.2 million.

Krausnick presents an overall view showing how and when the *Einsatzgruppen* were organized, the nature of their mission, and how they operated from 1938 to 1942 in cooperation with the regular German Army and other administrative agencies in the occupied areas. The details of their activities are culled from about three thousand pages of daily "Situation Reports" sent from the eastern front to headquarters of the Security Service in Berlin. In the second part of the book, Wilhelm concentrates on the activities of one of the four major *Einsatzgruppen*. He considers the background and personalities of the commando leaders and notes that, contrary to popular belief, they were not the criminal types normally associated with the image of concentration camp guards. They were high-ranking police officials; many were jurists or other professionals. Several of the mass murderers flaunted a "Dr." title before their names and one of the most ruthless, Dr. Dr. Rasch, even boasted two doctorates. He was one of those who argued that it would be more efficient not to shoot Jews if they were physically fit; they could be worked to death (p. 628). His career, like Frank's, ended on the gallows at Nuremberg.

In a concluding analysis, Wilhelm seeks to determine when the decision to annihilate the Jews was made. Uncertainty remains regarding the precise genesis of the extermination plan, but there is no doubt that Hitler desired the elimination of the Jews and that no questions would be asked about the methods used. The ideological war against innocent and defenseless people would not have been possible, finds Wilhelm, without strong direction from Hitler and the cooperation and support of the police, the army, and a host of others. The book is thoroughly persuasive, carefully documented, and supported by a comprehensive bibliography of the related German literature.

These two outstanding German studies give added weight and confirmation to revelations made during the prosecution of the "Justice Case" and the *Einsatzgruppen* Case" at the Nuremberg proceedings subsequent to the trial before the International Military Tribunal. Unfortunately, the German authorities have not yet agreed to publish the complete texts of the "Situation Reports" from the eastern front. They are among the most damning chronicles of racial cruelty ever recorded and would help to persuade whatever doubters may still exist regarding the enormity of Nazi crimes. After all, as Martin Broszat, a noted German expert on the Holocaust, says in his introduction to the Krausnick/Wilhelm book, "The theme still concerns us all."

BENJAMIN B. FERENCZ
Former Executive Counsel,
Nuremberg War Crimes Trials

The Quest for Self-Determination. By Dov Ronen. New Haven and London: Yale University Press, 1979. Pp. xiv, 144. Index. $15.

Pour un droit des peuples. Essais sur la Déclaration d'Alger. Edited by Antonio Cassese and Edmond Jouve. Paris: Berger-Levrault, 1978. Pp. 220.

Both Dov Ronen and editors Antonio Cassese and Edmond Jouve treat self-determination, but each book has a different approach. Ronen is concerned to explain the inner motives for achieving self-determination, while Cassese and Jouve have extended their examination of the classical doctrine of self-determination and human rights for all groups to include protection against colonialism and economic exploitation.

Ronen in his scholarly book finds that self-determination is the attempt to be "free" or to be "free from" others perceived as oppressors. The idea of self-determination, according to the author, is a "positive human condition" for a "good life" or self-fulfillment. People asking for self-determination refer not to the legal term but to the idea of an "inalienable right" to freedom from "them." Colonial peoples expect that the end of foreign rule will bring an improvement in the quality of their lives, including a higher standard of living. The author stresses that in his opinion the term "self" in self-determination refers to the individual, not to any aggregation of human beings. It is the individual, not the group, that desires through self-determination to acquire a chance for a better life independent from outside pressure or interference.

Historically, self-determination, the author says, may be based on the following concepts: (1) national identity, as developed by the French Revolution;

(2) national minority rights, as perceived by Wilson; and (3) Marx's proposed classless homogeneous society, which is viewed as an expression of freedom from oppression. Finally, former colonial units, irrespective of size or economic viability, are entitled to, and many have recently achieved, political independence. Moreover, some ethnic groups, such as the Scots, Eritreans, and Bangladeshi, who are different culturally, linguistically, or by religion from other groups in their societies, have asked for self-determination and have created new political or military movements or new states. The author admits that, based on these criteria, hundreds of new states could be created unless the demand for self-determination can be satisfied without secession.

Obviously, such a process would gradually give new content to the legal principle of territorial integrity. Existing states that mostly follow a policy of integration by applying the principles of equal rights would be threatened with a loss of territory, a decline in their economic base, and even dissolution. Without a doubt, in some cases the striving for self-determination will lead to the formation of new states and to secessions, but in many instances, autonomy or devolution might be a preferable approach in order to retain the existing states as a unit.

With some justification, the author tries to explain disintegration on the state level and integration on the international level as not necessarily contradictory. They are developments based on the assertion of individuals and groups on the national level and the attempt to create larger economic or perhaps strategic units on the international level.

Pour un droit des peuples is a collection of essays based on the Algiers Declaration composed by an International Conference of Jurists in July 1976; it is more a political than a legal document. The conference, a continuation of the Russell II Court, was sponsored by the Government of Algeria and was called on the suggestion of the court's former president, Senator Lelio Basso. The Declaration attempts to extend existing legal norms in order to give rights not only to individuals and states, but also to the "people." The Declaration includes references to most of the human rights and self-determination, as established by UN declarations, conventions, and resolutions. However, it extends the accepted protections to include protection from imperialism, "which continues to dominate a part of the world"; and it gives the people the right to control their resources and even compensation for past injustices. Moreover, it specifies the rights of the people to protection of their environment and culture. In case of exploitation, the people should resist by political means and, in extremis, by force.

The Declaration, which is essentially interpreted but not critically discussed by the contributors to the book, is a possible avenue for future development of international law, but it would need the general support of states, and particularly the major states, in order to become an accepted norm of international law.

FRANZ B. GROSS
University of New Haven

International Legal Instruments on Refugees in Africa. Edited by Göran Melander and Peter Nobel. Uppsala: Scandinavian Institute of African Studies, 1979. Pp. xix, 397. Index.

The Scandinavian Institute of African Studies has produced a valuable series of monographs on African problems including topics of interest to international lawyers such as *African Boundary Problems* (1969), *Scandinavian Development Agreements with African Countries* (1971), and *Land-Locked Countries of Africa* (1973). The latest in this series, however, *International Legal Instruments on Refugees in Africa*, is no credit to that record. Its shortcomings appear to be so egregious as to require comment.

Africa harbors more refugees than any other continent and their miseries have evoked worldwide concern. The states of that continent for years have been particularly active in supporting international legislation in this field. The volume under review might therefore have served a useful purpose. However, it is dismally short of achieving that objective.

The editors have posed the problems against the broader perspective of space and time by commencing with the European legislation of the League of Nations period. What they have failed to reveal is the basic point that today the African states have contributed substantially more to international agreements in this field than the other members of the Third World. For example, but one Asian and only five Latin American states have become parties to the basic UN Convention of July 28, 1951[1] on the status of refugees and the Protocol of January 31, 1967,[2] whereas 30 African states have done so. This point is obscured by the extraordinary failure (with but 13 exceptions out of 95 entries) to indicate which states are parties to the various agreements (presented mostly in the form of excerpts) and which states had voted for or against particular resolutions of the UN General Assembly or other international organizations. Given the frail legal force of General Assembly resolutions, it is important to know how individual members voted on refugee issues. Where no negative votes were recorded, abstentions acquire great significance. Without such indications, the resolutions fall into a legal-political void. There is, in addition, no identification of any states that have enacted domestic legislation in implementation of the various international agreements and resolutions.

Equally disturbing are the gaps that this collection reveals. First of all, the pervasive problems involving generally the admission and the expulsion of aliens have been largely ignored and statelessness as such is reflected only in the two Conventions of 1954 and 1961 (pp. 90 and 102).[3] There is nothing on the so-called Nansen passports and the Statutes of the Nansen International Office for Refugees.[4] The editors evidently assumed that agreements on European refugees are relevant in the African context, but while they included an excerpt on the arrangement modifying the Convention of July 5, 1922 concerning

[1] 189 UNTS 150. [2] TIAS No. 6577.

[3] The trend-setting protocols on statelessness produced by the Hague Conference of 1930 (*see* 5 M. HUDSON, INTERNATIONAL LEGISLATION 381 *ff.* (1936)) are absent.

[4] *Id.* at 872.

Russian and Armenian refugees, no text of that basic agreement is provided nor of the related agreements with the Refugee Settlement Commission accepted by Great Britain, France, and Italy in 1923 and 1924. Likewise, there is nothing on the equally significant agreements on the contemporaneous problems involving Latvian, Greek, and Bulgarian refugees (Agreements of August 3, 1921, September 29, 1923, and September 8, 1926). An excerpt appears from the Convention of February 10, 1938 concerning refugees from Germany but nothing on the underlying Agreement of July 4, 1936. While a useful compilation is provided of resolutions of ECOSOC and the OAU as well as the Addis Ababa Conference of 1967 and the Geneva Conferences of 1975 and 1977 (pp. 302–92), the problems relative to refugees from Namibia including agreements with Uganda, Kenya, Ethiopia, Tanzania, and Botswana have been left aside. Ignored as well is the European Agreement on the Abolition of Visas for Refugees, No. 31 of April 20, 1959 of the Council of Europe. Nor is the collection of resolutions of the UN General Assembly on refugees complete. Missing are Resolutions 2198 (XXI) of December 6, 1966, 2325 (XXII) of December 16, 1967 (para. 5), 2678 (XXV) of December 9, 1970 (para. 12), 31/35 of November 30, 1976 (para. 4), and Security Council Resolution 190 of July 29, 1970 (para. 10).

One might question whether these missing materials might not have more appropriately taken the place of some 60 pages less directly concerned with refugees in Africa such as the London Agreement of 1945 on War Crimes, the Convention for the Amelioration of the Condition of Wounded, Sick and Shipwrecked Members of Armed Forces at Sea, and the Convention on the Prevention and Punishment of Crimes against Internationally Protected Persons, including Diplomatic Agents (pp. 182–242). The volume has been further expanded by the publishing of all entries in both French and English—today, as distinguished from the League of Nations period, a waste of high printing costs that the Scandinavian Institute of African Studies might have spared the Swedish International Development Authority, which supported the production.

The collection contains no discussion of the literature in the field such as Paul Weis's *The International Protection of Refugees* (48 AJIL 193 (1954)); Atle Grahl-Madsen's *The Status of Refugees in International Law,* vol. I (1966); *The Rights of Refugees*, an extensive analysis and report on refugees undertaken by the Asian-African Legal Consultative Committee and published in 1967; and Issa Ben Yacine Diallo's *Les Réfugiés en Afrique* (1974), to mention but some of the more recent publications in the field. Nor have the editors sought as background to explore the underlying causes for the eruption of refugee catastrophes in Africa, which would justify a study of the sort the editors have undertaken, and for the reactions of the African states as revealed in international legal instruments.

Having chosen to open this compilation with documents from the League of Nations, the editors could have profited from the model established at that period by Hudson's volumes on *International Legislation* which, except for the duplicative publication of both French and English texts common at that time, might have led them to avoid some of the shortcomings indicated above. One would also have thought that the collaboration of two editors might have ensured against the occurrence of the more notable failings. Professor Widstrand's expression of hope "that this collection will prove its value in the development of the protection and rights of African refugees" (p. iv) may possibly prove to have been generously optimistic.

JOHN H. SPENCER

O Mezhdunarodno-pravovoi otvetstvennosti za narushenie prav cheloveka (On International-Legal Responsibility for Violation of Human Rights). By R. Kulikov. Moscow: Mezhdunarodnye Otnoshenia, 1979. Pp. 96.

The aim of this booklet, printed in 25 thousand copies, is, evidently, to inform Soviet readers when violations of human rights are connected with responsibility under international law, and when they are not, and thus remain totally within the realm of the respective national law.

Its whole reasoning strictly follows official Soviet doctrine. Accordingly, pertinent international legal responsibility is limited to two basic situations: to cases of criminal violations of human rights, and to gross, large-scale violations of them. The first type of situation is illustrated by apartheid in South Africa. In the second category, it is the Chilean case that is mostly referred to, though there is also reference to the Northern Ireland problem, as illustrated by the *Ireland v. The United Kingdom of Great Britain and Northern Ireland* case, terminated by the judgment of the European Court of Human Rights of January 18, 1978. What is more, in a sweeping generalization on page 71, one reads that situations in which there are large-scale violations of human rights are marked by the characteristics inherent "in the whole system of capitalist exploitation and deprivation of the broad working masses of elementary social and economic rights."

Nothing of this kind exists, according to the author, in the USSR—quite the reverse. However, as is known by every reader of the world press, and especially of such highly specialized periodicals as the *USSR News Brief—Human Rights*, published simultaneously in English and French and extremely conscientiously edited by Cronid Lubarski, gross violations of human rights take place there every day. This goes on quite apart from the elements of genocide in the high season of the Gulag era.

The clear task of the author is to impress upon the readers the allegation, repeated a dozen times, that individual cases of violation of human rights are exclusively within the national jurisdiction of each country. What follows is that individuals may not lodge pertinent complaints with UN bodies, and that the latter should not deal with them, as this would be tantamount to interference in the internal affairs of states.

Generally speaking, what is inconvenient is simply not mentioned—*e.g.*, the existence of the Optional Protocol to the International Covenant on Civil and Political Rights, or the European Social Charter. The (West) European system of human rights protection is presented in such a way as to make it look almost pointless for the individual; but when the author deems it convenient, he does not hesitate to refer to it, *e.g.*, to the *Lawless* case (pp. 59–60). On page 4, readers are misinformed that the International Covenants came into force in 1966.

A final word: In August 1980, striking Polish workers demanded, among other things, the publication, in a mass edition, of the texts of the International Covenants. This was contained in the "social contract" signed in Szczecin, and 50 thousand copies of a pertinent brochure were, in fact, printed in October 1980. There is a real hunger for the full texts of the Covenants in the USSR. If any genuine concern existed for the promotion of the knowledge of international human rights, the printing of these texts would be much more appropriate than publications such as the one here reviewed.

RICHARD SZAWLOWSKI
Vancouver, British Columbia

Trends in Environmental Policy and Law. Edited by Michael Bothe, Project Coordinator. Gland, Switzerland: International Union for Conservation of Nature and Natural Resources, 1980. Pp. xxi, 404. $27.50.

Beginning with the question, How can we conserve our environment?, the authors of the 19 short essays in this volume attempt to identify trends in the use of particular tools to protect the environment. The authors represent a truly international collection of expertise; all but three of the essays, however, are in English.

Twelve of the essays are comparative in their analysis, according to Bothe, while only seven purport to address the international dimensions of environmental conservation. The comparative materials are outstanding and provide decision makers and academics alike with a wealth of information concerning constitutional, legislative, and regulatory attempts to protect the environment. Based mostly on experiences under legal systems of the developed world, but including some references to Third World attempts to conserve the environment, these essays offer jurisprudential and policy analysis of such central issues as the relationship of property rights and individual liberty to environmental strategy, the relative merits of the "polluter pays" and "common burden" methods of cost apportionment, and the utility of environmental impact assessments, public participation, and civil and criminal liability for protecting the environment. Nearly all of the comparative essays are accompanied by extensive notation, and thus the reader is provided with data, analysis, and useful bibliographical references. For those who believe that both decision makers and academics on the national and international levels can benefit from the knowledge accumulated in the various national experiments with different mechanisms for protection of the environment, this book is a treasure house.

On the whole, the seven essays that purport to address the international dimensions of environmental protection are not of the same high quality as the comparative works. In most of them the authors either busy themselves counting the number of environmental doctrinal angels on the head of a pin or only superficially deal with international issues while remaining primarily in the comparative genre. Typical of the latter category are the essay by de Klemm,

La Protection des zones d'intérêt écologique, nearly two-thirds of which is purely comparative, and the essay by Alexandre Kiss, which devotes only one of its 15 pages to international considerations. Notable for its absence is any discussion of the possible juridical utility of Karel Vasak's intriguing notion that there is a third-generation international human right, a so-called solidarity right to a clean environment.[1]

Two of the international essays, however, are deserving of note. Peter Sand's seven-page effort, *The Creation of Transnational Rules for Environmental Protection*, sets forth a brief, though coherent, review and analysis of what he denominates "eco-standards," "eco-permits," and "eco-audits," which reminds us of the myriad of nondramatic international mechanisms that serve daily to make this planet a bit more habitable. P.-M. Dupuy's *International Liability for Transfrontier Pollution* focuses on the variety of regimes for compensating transfrontier pollution victims. His work is thought-provoking in its treatment of past and present efforts to provide channels for legal relief to such victims and in its proposals for improvement of public and private international mechanisms for compensation. Also noteworthy are Dupuy's warning regarding the limited usefulness of the doctrine of international liability and his emphasis on the need to prevent pollution rather than merely compensate its victims.

While reading the international essays in this book, one is struck by the possibility that the lack of depth marking most of them may well be a reflection of the lack of recent major improvements in the ways that the international legal regime addresses environmental problems. In nearly all of them, so much of the analysis derives from the work of the 1972 UN Stockholm Conference on the Human Environment, to the exclusion of other sources, that one suspects the conference has been the only international environmental show in town. Perhaps the greatest contribution of this book to international lawyers is the message one derives from comparing the wealth of national experience presented in the comparative essays with the relative paucity of international experience revealed in the international essays: international law, public and private, has not yet begun to address our planet's environmental concerns with anything near the attention deserved and required.

MARTIN FEINRIDER
Nova University Law Center

La Difusión Internacional de los Programas Audiovisuales. By Félix Fernández-Shaw. Madrid: Editorial Tecnos, 1980. Pp. 348. Indexes.

A videotape of an international football match played in Germany may be barred from rebroadcast in Sweden because it has too many commercials. A tape of a radio broadcast originating in Spain may be unusable in Argentina because it contains phrases which, perfectly innocuous in their native Castilian, are to the Argentine ear gross obscenities. A motion picture made in France

[1] *See* Vasak, *Pour les Droits de l'homme de la troisième génération: les droits de solidarité*, in INTERNATIONAL INSTITUTE OF HUMAN RIGHTS, SUMMARY OF LECTURES—TENTH STUDY SESSION (1979).

may be unsalable in the Middle East because it shows people eating with their left hands, or in Asia because it is printed on 70-mm film. The broadcast in Great Britain of a phonograph record made in the United States may create an obligation to pay royalties to the composer, the lyricist, the arranger, the vocalist, or all of them.

Anyone who proposes launching an audiovisual production—motion picture, phonograph record, video-cassette, audiotape—on the international market must face at the outset the fact that the business bristles with problems. These are technical, cultural, linguistic, commercial, and—not the least—legal. None of them can be played by ear, and none of them can wait until the product is in the can before it is resolved. The technical, cultural, and economic aspects must be addressed by the experts in those fields, while the legal issues may depend on local customs law and practice, on other municipal laws, on any of a host of multilateral and bilateral international agreements, or on global conventions. Looming large, of course, are the questions of international copyright protection and the various treaties dealing with authors' rights; a considerable segment of the work under review is devoted to their discussion.

In the end, the responsibility rests on authors, producers, and media executives to know their markets and confront all these hurdles before production begins. In their work they may call upon the good offices of several international organizations, as well as nongovernmental national and international associations of professionals in the various audiovisual media.

Fernández-Shaw has devoted his career to the international aspects of the audiovisual media, finding time as well to serve his Government as Ambassador to Syria. His present work originated as a university dissertation, and portions of it do indeed smell of the lamp; but it is more than a doctoral thesis: it is at once a law book, a technical manual, an index of treaties, and a handbook of tips for authors and producers. Its sobriety is relieved by the occasional sprightly phrase, which rescues it from the tedium of a mere chart of the rocks and shoals of international audiovisual program marketing.

MALCOLM T. DUNGAN
Of the California Bar

Copyright Protection in the Americas. Binder I. Organization of American States. General Secretariat. Dobbs Ferry: Oceana Publications, Inc., 1979. $75 per binder.

The Organization of American States has recently issued an updated edition of its collection of copyright statutes and conventions in force in the American states. This work was first published in 1943; subsequent editions were published in 1950 and 1962, and in 1967 a supplement to the third edition appeared. In the 12 years between publication of that supplement and the present edition, many changes were made in the copyright legislation included in the earlier editions and several new states joined the OAS; both factors warranted preparation of an updated version.

The material included in *Copyright Protection in the Americas* is organized into three parts. Part 1 is devoted to summaries of the constitutional, statutory, and regulatory provisions relating to copyright in force in the OAS member states. Part 2 will consist of a historical and analytical treatment of the inter-American and universal copyright treaties, and part 3 will contain the texts of these treaties. Binder I includes part 1 only; parts 2 and 3 will appear in a second binder to be published at a later date.

The summaries of the national legislation included in Binder I are valuable source material for any legal practitioner or scholar interested in the protection of copyrights in the Americas. There is one entry for each of the 25 OAS member states and each entry follows a uniform format. The basic constitutional and legislative provisions pertaining to copyright for each state, as well as its copyright office, are listed. The copyright protection afforded in each of the states is then summarized, with sections devoted to general provisions, persons and works protected, duration of copyright, infringement, authors' associations, registration formalities, and protection of foreign works. For many, of course, this latter section on protection of foreign works will be of greatest interest. This section is subdivided into a description of any relevant national legislation and lists of bilateral and multilateral treaties to which the state is a party. In addition to the entries for the OAS member states there is also an appendix that summarizes the copyright legislation in force in the United Kingdom. This has been included because of its relevance to copyright protection in the English-speaking countries of the Caribbean. Each of the national entries appears in both English and Spanish.

The uniformity of format in each of the national entries is both the strength and a weakness of *Copyright Protection in the Americas.* It permits the reader to compare easily the relevant provisions of various nations' copyright laws. However, by virtue of including summaries rather than translations, the OAS has interposed the authors of those summaries between interested researchers and the actual legislative provisions themselves. One more layer of judgment—what to include or exclude, how to summarize complex provisions accurately—is added, and that much more chance of imprecision or error is created. Since the OAS has decided to include the actual texts of regional and universal copyright treaties in Binder II, perhaps it should consider including the texts of the legislative provisions as well. Together with the summaries already available, their inclusion would make *Copyright Protection in the Americas* a nearly perfect research tool.

A word concerning the geographical coverage of this work is in order. Obviously, the OAS is only concerned with copyright protection in its member states. But there are several American states that are not members of the OAS—Canada and Cuba, for example—and summaries of their copyright protection will not be found in this volume.

The principal substantive change in Binder I from earlier editions was the inclusion of summaries of copyright legislation in the five nations that joined the OAS after this work was last supplemented in 1967. A major change in format was also incorporated: the work is published in looseleaf binders, which permits more frequent updating of its contents.

Binder I of *Copyright Protection in the Americas* is a valuable reference and with frequent updatings by the OAS should remain so for a long time to come.

MICHAEL A. NEWCITY
Singapore

The Iran Crisis and International Law. Proceedings of the John Bassett Moore Society of International Law. Edited by Robert D. Steele. Charlottesville: John Bassett Moore Society of International Law, 1981. Pp. xvii, 237.

The 2-day symposium whose proceedings are reported in this volume could not have been more timely. The papers were delivered on October 31 and November 1, 1981, in the full heat of negotiations and other actions to resolve the crisis. A presidential election campaign was under way. The election came only a few days later; 7 weeks after the symposium the Iran hostage agreements and other governmental actions were announced.[1] Although the specific outcome of the crisis was not predicted by the symposium, the book is a useful addition to the literature of the Iranian revolution and its international ramifications. The *Dames & Moore* case[2] and the sputtering Iran-Iraq conflict demonstrate that the last chapters of this story may be years in the writing.

The symposium presented four panel discussions, followed by comments and questions from the floor, plus a luncheon address by Professor John Norton Moore. The book also includes a foreword by Professor Rouhollah K. Ramazani, a preface by the editor, updating documents, and biographies of discussants.

Panel I commented on the *Hostages* case and other public international law issues. Dean Emeritus Hardy Cross Dillard, former Member of the International Court of Justice, gave insights on the composition of the Court, the problem of objectivity and impartiality on the Court, and enforceability of its judgments. Professor Leo Gross discussed preliminary objections issues, and Professor Stephen Schwebel, now a Member of the Court, addressed the merits of the case. Professor Richard Lillich concluded with remarks on the impact on the case of the law of treatment of aliens and human rights, and the rescue attempt. He also commented on the state of the law of forcible self-help for the protection of foreign nationals.

The second panel addressed commercial aspects of the crisis, focusing on the assets freeze. Jack Goldklang, U.S. Justice Department, related the history of the U.S. International Emergency Economic Powers Act and its role in the freeze. John Pritchard, an attorney working in banking litigation, discussed private claimants' roles in the crisis. Charles Brower, also in private practice, addressed issues involving the U.S. Foreign Sovereign Immunities Act. Stanley

[1] The January 19, 1981 agreements with Iran, presidential executive orders concerned with the crisis, and the opinion of the U.S. Attorney General on the January 19 agreements and executive orders, are *reproduced in* appendixes to *The Iran Crisis.* Texts of the agreements are also *reprinted in* 75 AJIL 418 (1981) and 20 ILM 223 (1981); executive orders are *reprinted in* 74 AJIL 428 (1980); *id.* at 668; 75 *id.* at 430–31 (1981); 18 ILM 1549 (1979); 20 *id.* at 282 (1981); *id.* at 412.

[2] Dames & Moore v. Regan, 101 S.Ct. 2972 (1981), 20 ILM 897 (1981), *noted,* 75 AJIL 954 (1981).

Sommerfield, then Director of the U.S. Treasury Department Office of Foreign Assets Control, gave the background to the blocking of Iranian assets.

Moore spoke on foreign policy aspects of the oil crisis at the luncheon; he suggested four initiatives for defusing the continuing problem: (1) filling the U.S. strategic petroleum reserve; (2) de-linking the Arab-Israeli conflict from oil policy; (3) accelerating the consumer nation agreement on impact limits; and (4) a producer-consumer accord for oil.

Panel III, moderated by Professor Christopher Joyner, presented the Iranian legal perspective. Professor Majid Khadduri summarized aspects of Islamic law and religion. Leonard Boudin, counsel for the central bank of Iran, discussed the freeze order and current litigation. John Westberg, an attorney with extensive diplomatic and practical experience in Tehran, outlined basic Iranian attitudes about law and the development and structure of the Iranian legal system.

The final panel, also moderated by Joyner, focused on the Iran-Iraq dispute. Former U.S. Ambassador Richard Parker discussed the conflict's impact on American foreign policy. Khadduri summarized the treaty law background, and Professor John Vafai explored the impact of ethnic conflict in Iran on the war.

The book was probably produced on a slim budget. It was reproduced from typed copy, the binding is inadequate (the review copy already has loose pages that require stapling), and there are a few proofreading errors. Nevertheless, the symposium is a valuable commentary on a crisis that already has a growing bibliography. It revealed attitudes and positions of the chief actors, although representatives of some participants spoke personally and not for their principals, at a critical time. Second, the papers offer useful background for all who examine the Iran crisis in retrospect—sociological and economic information for the lawyers, and an explanation of legal aspects for those in foreign relations or diplomatic history. Finally, the symposium is a tribute to its sponsor, the John Bassett Moore Society, and its student editorial board, for conceiving, organizing, and coordinating the event, and publishing its proceedings.

GEORGE K. WALKER
Wake Forest University

Asian-African Legal Consultative Committee. *Report of the Seventeenth, Eighteenth and Nineteenth Sessions, Held in Kuala Lumpur (1976), Baghdad (1977) and Doha (1978)*. New Delhi: Secretariat of the Committee, 1980. Pp. 170.

Possibly reflecting the expanded role of the Group of 77, the work of the Asian-African Legal Consultative Committee appears to be diminishing in initiative and scope. Reports of the sessions have become briefer;[1] the volume under review covers three annual sessions in only 170 pages. In consequence, the views of individual delegations are no longer revealed and the summaries of the discussions take on a faceless and flavorless character.

[1] 71 AJIL 583 (1977).

For the most part, the last three sessions have accentuated trends noted at previous occasions. Nevertheless, the latest developments have sharpened issues and set in relief conflicts and contradictions. One pervasive contradiction has emerged in the discussions on the law of the sea.[2] These last sessions reaffirmed the principle enunciated in UN General Assembly Resolution 2750B (XXV) with respect to landlocked countries, namely, that the resources of the seabed and ocean floor beyond national jurisdiction "are the common heritage of mankind." At the same time, they reveal a further development of the trend to restrict access to that "common heritage" by landlocked states (pp. 54–6). In this context, but three states (Jordan, Nepal, and Uganda) of those participating in these sessions are landlocked. With regard to environmental law,[3] Principles 21 and 22 of the Stockholm Conference of 1972 adumbrating the concept of strict liability for the polluter—"the polluter pays"[4] (p. 88)—appear to give way to the need of developing countries to undertake industrialization with limited liability (p. 90).

Several points are to be noted on the recurring subject of international trade.[5] The F.A.S. contract remains the model to be adopted for the agricultural products of the developing countries (p. 128). In turn, the law of the contract should likewise be that of the exporter rather than that of the importer or any agreed choice of law. This view is carried further by the consensus that contract disputes should be arbitrated in accordance with UNCITRAL rules,[6] not by "compulsory arbitration under the auspices of a trading association in the West as provided for in the standard contracts currently in use" (p. 129). To that end, six regional arbitration centers, three in Asia and three in Africa should be established (p. 149). In the case of Africa, there should be panels of African arbitrators. One might doubt, however, whether importers would rush to accept that formula. Somewhat more realistically, the discussions revealed opposition to recognition of the defense of sovereign immunity in arbitration agreements (p. 148).

A fresh topic for the sessions was the Vienna Convention on Succession of States in Respect of Treaties.[7] The "clean slate" and the "opting in" formulas (Arts. 15–19) were, understandably, readily accepted, as were Articles 11 and 12 concerning succession to boundaries, servitudes, and other dispositive agreements, save for treaty provisions establishing foreign military bases (Art. 12(3)). Following an attitude adopted at the Third and Tenth Sessions,[8] the Committee continued to evince distrust of the International Court of Justice as a forum for resolving disputes over the interpretation of international agreements (p. 70).

Particularly significant is the work of the Committee on Refugees and Asylum which, since the 1966 session in Bangkok,[9] has devoted much study and dis-

[2] 69 *id.* at 472 (1975); 70 *id.* at 198 (1976); 74 *id.* at 488 (1980).

[3] 74 *id.* at 488 (1980).

[4] 11 ILM 1420 (1972).

[5] 67 AJIL 181 (1973); 69 *id.* at 472 (1975); and 71 *id.* at 583 (1977).

[6] 15 ILM 702 (1976).

[7] UN Doc. A/CONF.80/31 (1978), 17 ILM 1488 (1978), and 72 AJIL 971 (1978).

[8] 56 AJIL 575 (1962); 67 *id.* at 181 (1973).

[9] 63 *id.* at 368 (1969); 67 *id.* at 180 (1973); and 70 *id.* at 198 (1976).

cussion to these problems.[10] The trend during the last three sessions was to expand the areas of protection for refugees. Objection was voiced (p. 117) to the deletion from the early Bellagio and Geneva drafts on asylum[11] of the provision that "asylum shall not be refused by a Contracting State solely on the ground that it could be sought from another State." Likewise, the requirement of "well-founded fear" of persecution or punishment as a basis for granting asylum was held (pp. 117–18) to have led to abuse under the 1951 Convention on the Status of Refugees (Article IA(2)),[12] and it was therefore suggested that the offending phrase should be replaced by "has reasonable grounds to believe that he would be subjected to" (pp. 117–18). Further objection was raised to the exclusion from the drafts of the earlier provision that "[n]o person shall be extradited to a State to the territory of which he may not be returned by virtue of [the principle of *non-refoulement*]" (p. 119) and, significantly, to exclusion of a requirement that an asylee should be entitled in the country of asylum to an "equal protection of the laws" guarantee (pp. 119–20). At a time when the problems of refugees have assumed almost overwhelming dimensions and urgency, the continuing contributions of the Asian-African Legal Consultative Committee in this field are to be especially commended.

JOHN H. SPENCER

International Law in the Netherlands. Vols. II and III. Edited by H. F. van Panhuys, W. P. Heere, J. W. Josephus Jitta, Ko Swan Sik, and A. M. Stuyt. Alphen aan den Rijn: Sijthoff & Noordhoff; Dobbs Ferry: Oceana Publications, Inc. Vol. II, 1979: pp. xx, 388. Index. Dfl.70; $35. Vol. III, 1980: pp. xxix, 469. Index. Dfl.75; $37.50.

As stated in the review of the first volume,[1] this series aims to treat various standard topics in international law with specific reference to Dutch materials; hence the omission of some topics for which such materials are not available. The work is sponsored by an international law research and documentation center maintained by eight Dutch universities. Seventeen Dutch scholars, from academic or official life, are contributors to the present volumes.

The topics treated in volume II are international organizations and associations such as Benelux and the European Communities, criminal matters (including supranational criminal law and Dutch extradition law), and disarmament and peaceful settlement of disputes. Volume III deals with persons (nationality and fundamental human rights), self-determination, protection of foreign investments, official privileges and immunities, war and neutrality, and the relation between international law and municipal law.

The quality of scholarship is high throughout, and the utilization of Dutch sources is illuminating. Statements of Dutch representatives at UN gatherings

[10] *Cf.* THE RIGHTS OF REFUGEES: BACKGROUND MATERIALS (1967), 409 pages published by the Committee.

[11] 27 UN GAOR, Supp. (No. 12A) (1972) and UN Doc. A/10177 (1975).

[12] 189 UNTS 150.

[1] 73 AJIL 739 (1979).

illustrate the development of Dutch views, and the ministries' practice of accompanying draft legislation or treaties submitted to Parliament with an explanatory memorandum (*memorie van toelichting*) likewise furnishes a rich source of expository materials. Characteristic of Dutch efforts has been the attempt to include in treaties on particular subjects a provision for judicial settlement of disputes regarding interpretation and application of the treaty, and to establish institutionalized agencies for fact-finding (somewhat reminiscent of the Bryan treaties) (vol. II, pp. 304–07), which would not only facilitate settlement of disputes but tend to prevent disputes by enabling governments to adopt more enlightened policies by virtue of better information regarding existing conditions.

First Amendment buffs may find fruitful suggestions in a proposed amendment to the Dutch Constitution protecting "freedom of philosophy of life (*levensovertuiging*)" in addition to freedom of religion. Another amendment would recognize "distribution of prosperity" as an aim of governmental policy (vol. III, p. 121). The concluding chapter on judicial application of international law in the Dutch internal order is somewhat esoteric but highly interesting.

EDWARD DUMBAULD
Senior U.S. District Judge

The Indian Year Book of International Affairs, 1980. Vol. XVIII, Part I. Edited by T. S. Rama Rao. Published under the auspices of The Indian Study Group of International Law and Affairs, University of Madras, 1980. Pp. vi, 563. Index. Rs.65.

The Indian Year Book of International Affairs, 1980. Vol. XVIII, Part II: Studies in the History of the Law of Nations (Grotian Society Papers). Published under the auspices of The Indian Study Group of International Law and Affairs, University of Madras, 1980. Pp. xii, 246. Index. Rs.65.

The current volume of the *Year Book* appears in two parts. Part I contains 14 articles on international law and politics and comparative law, 20 decisions of Indian courts in private international law, and 17 book reviews. Part II is devoted exclusively to the *Grotian Society Papers* on "Studies in the History of the Law of Nations" and also forms vol. IV of these *Papers*.

As with previous volumes of the *Year Book*, the present one contains works by Indian and non-Indian scholars covering a wide range of issues at the international, regional, and local levels. International lawyers and students of world politics will find a crisp analysis of the tensions between the role of the United Nations and that of regional organizations in the maintenance of peace and security in the article on *Regionalist Challenge and Universalist Response* by Dr. Rafiu Akindele (University of Ife, Nigeria). The shift away from reliance on the United Nations in peace and security matters has occurred, according to Akindele, not merely because of the political and institutional realities (use of the veto, in particular) of the United Nations, but also because transformations within regional organizations have invited greater resort to them.

Professor Rahmatullah Khan (Nehru University, Delhi) has analyzed the impediments to the development of large- and small-scale fisheries in his article on *Indian Ocean Fisheries Development and Management Strategies.* Other articles on international law are *The Search for Peace: A Historical Approach* by Henry Strakosch (Sydney University), *The Employment of Diplomatic Protection as an Alternative Remedy to Individual Action* by W. Paul Gormley (Research Center, Hague Academy), *The ICJ Judgement in the Fisheries Jurisdiction Case—A Critique* by S. Rama Rao (University of Madras), and *Changing Directions in Maritime Zone: A Survey* by S. K. Duba (University of Delhi).

In his article, *Sovereign Immunity in the Conflict of Laws—Some Recent Trends*, Professor C. G. Raghavan (Nagpur University) examines the practice of Afro-Asian states, finding that although these states have politically preferred the restrictive approach, their municipal courts have not yet moved away from the traditional theory of absolute sovereign immunity. Other articles in the fields of comparative and private international law are *Democracy and the Theory of Law* by M. Anantha Narayanan (former chief justice, Madras High Court), *Legitimacy, Legitimation and Adoption Under Indian Private International Law* by R. Murali (University of Madras), and *Marriage in Indian Conflict of Laws: Some Recent Developments*, by T. S. Rama Rao, editor of the *Year Book*.

Articles on "International Affairs" include *Rise of Communism in Malaya (1930–1948)* by V. Suryanarayan (University of Madras), *India's Nuclear Test: Politics and Opinion* by S. C. Tiwari (University of Jabalpur), *A General Overview of International Aviation Policies* by S. Bhatt (Airport Officer, Delhi), and *World Population: International Problems and Remedial Programmes* by B. S. Sehgal (University of Jammu).

The eight essays constituting vol. IV of the *Grotian Society Papers* underscore the importance of historical studies, both for a better understanding of contemporary issues and for challenging myths that creep into the theory and practice of international law. In his analysis of *The Role of German Treaty Making in the Partition of Africa*, Professor Alexandrowicz makes two important points. First, that the agreements between the German Protector and indigenous rulers in Northwest, Southwest, and East Africa clearly establish that the European scramble for territory in Africa was in reality a scramble for *titles* to territory—a situation understandable only if the territory, far from being *terra nullius*, actually was ruled by sovereign political entities that were subjects of international law. Second, he debunks the view that the African Protectorate was a phantom institution by showing that in all cases German and African rule coexisted for a significant time and that the absorption of the African territories came at a later stage. Ironically, it was Southwest Africa that enjoyed the longest period of such coexistence—20 years—followed by 10 years of German colonial rule until World War I. Alexandrowicz concludes that colonial rule constituted only a brief episode in African political history and that precolonial African history is a valid antecedent for modern international law, a conclusion identical to that derived by him from his previous studies of European colonies in Asia.

Professor Rubin's well-documented article, *Is War Still Legal*?, demonstrates that moral impulses to refrain from inflicting injury on other humans and destroying property have led to nominal legal obligations for states but that, in a bow to *Realpolitik*, these obligations do not significantly hamper the military activities of states. Professor Fawcett's essay on *The Judicial Use of History* finds that the PCIJ and the ICJ have frequently been injudicious in selecting and admitting historical evidence. Professor Seidl-Hohenveldern's article, *Confiscation of Corporations and of Shareholders' Rights in the Conflict of Law*, uses a 16th-century dispute between the municipality of Frankfurt and the counts of Hanau to examine problems raised by the attempted extraterritorial application of acts of state interfering with the personality, management, and assets of juridical persons. The interests involved and the resolutions attempted have not changed over time, he concludes.

Other essays in the *Papers* include *Legal Problems of the Channel Tunnel Scheme: 1868–1883* by Geoffrey Marston (Cambridge University), *The Law of Piracy* by J. W. Boulton, *International Law as a Science (The Place of Doctrine in the History of its Sources)* by J. A. Carty, and *The Legal Position of Tibet* by T. S. Rama Rao.

FARROKH JHABVALA
Florida International University

Index-Guide to Treaties. Based on the Consolidated Treaty Series and all other series therein utilised. Edited by Clive Parry. *Volume I: General Chronological List 1648–1809.* By Paul Irwin. Projected at 4–6 vols. Dobbs Ferry: Oceana Publications, Inc., 1979. Pp. xxxvi, 555. $75 per vol.

This volume provides guidance to modern treaties from the peace settlements of Münster and Osnabrück through 1808, the texts of which are incorporated into the *Consolidated Treaty Series (CTS)*, which is expected to consist of approximately two hundred volumes covering the period from 1648 to 1918. This collection of treaty texts and indexes constitutes a massive but convenient resource which, supplemented by the *League of Nations* and *United Nations Treaty Series*, is of enormous reference value to students of international law and relations.

This volume presents a handy listing of treaties, agreements, conventions, concordats, and other international instruments spanning a century and a half. Individual entries give a formal or unofficial descriptive treaty title, date and place of signature, and names of signatories. It is to be supplemented by special chronologies of colonial and postal-telegraphic agreements, and an overall index to parties.

The primary purpose of this volume is to provide specific guidance to the texts of treaties contained in the *CTS*, together with textual sources and other materials used in compiling it. The language(s) in which the treaty text is given in the sources cited is also indicated. Some entries contain supplementary notes concerning subsidiary instruments, accessions, subsequent developments, and disputes over the identity of the parties or the date or place of signature.

The compiler furnishes a 26-page table of abbreviations and bibliography of the sources cited in the *CTS*, such as "B.S.P." (*British and Foreign State*

Papers) and "Archives dipl." (*Archives diplomatiques, Recueil de diplomatie et d'histoire*). The American sources include Davenport's *European Treaties* . . . (4 vols.), Elliot's *American Diplomatic Code* . . . (2 vols.), Malloy's *Treaties . . . and Agreements* . . . (2 vols.), and Miller's *Treaties and Other International Acts* . . . (8 vols.). But other American compilations—such as the *Statutes at Large* (through 1951) and *Treaties and Other International Agreements of the United States of America, 1776–1949* (13 vols.)—are not cited.

The parties to the treaties listed are primarily European states and principalities, but also include Barbary Coast nations, the Papacy, royal families, and the British East India Company. Most of the treaties are bipartite. Their principal subjects embrace alliances, armistices, commercial relations, peace settlements, and territorial dispositions. Some deal with claims or consular, extradition, maritime, navigation, and neutrality affairs. The 30 treaties to which the United States became a party pertain largely to peacemaking, amity, commerce, and friendship, but also include the Franco-American Alliance (1778) and the Louisiana Purchase (1803).

ELMER PLISCHKE
University of Maryland, Emeritus
Gettysburg College, Adjunct Professor
American Enterprise Institute, Adjunct Scholar

Foreign Relations of the United States, 1952–1954, Volume XVI: The Geneva Conference. (Dept. of State Pub. 9167.) Washington: U.S. Govt. Printing Office, 1981. Pp. xxii, 1597. Index.

Reminiscent of the *Foreign Relations* volumes on the World War II summit conclaves and postwar ministerial meetings, this volume provides the basic, comprehensive, official documentary record of U.S. foreign policy for the multipartite meetings on Korea and Indochina convened in Geneva in 1954. This was a two-in-one conference, concerned with Korean unification from April 26 to June 15, and termination of hostilities in Indochina from May 8 to July 21. Aside from the United States, the principal participants were France, the People's Republic of China, the USSR, and the United Kingdom. Fourteen other countries attended the sessions on Korea, including ANZUS, NATO, and SEATO nations, as well as the two Koreas. The sessions on Indochina involved the five major powers, plus Cambodia, Laos, and the two Vietnams.

This compilation is the second to be published in a series of 16 volumes planned for the years 1952–1954—previous *Foreign Relations* volumes pertained to single years, except for the Lansing papers (1914–1920) and special volumes of documents on Japan (1931–1941) and the Soviet Union (1933–1939). Typically, this is an anthology of diplomatic communications and memoranda, together with occasional explanatory and cross-reference editorial notes. However, it also contains such conference papers as negotiating draft proposals, policy proposals, minutes of meetings, and reports, as well as agreements (with annexes), declarations and, in the case of Indochina, cease-fires for Cambodia, Laos, and Vietnam. Many of the issues raised involve important legal questions.

Although the two sets of meetings overlap in time, their documentation is presented in separate parts—Korea, pp. 1–394, and Indochina, pp. 395–1568. Both parts present materials arranged in major functional sections, consisting of topical subsegments, with documents arranged chronologically thereunder. Both introductory sections deal with commentary on sources and the methods of presenting materials, lists of papers prepared for the meetings, schedules of plenary sessions, and lists of participants. The second section of each conference compilation consists of preconference materials, including U.S. position papers, and commentary on American preparations, administrative and procedural questions, and related considerations.

The third section, on conference proceedings, focuses on delegation proposals, plenary and other sessions, functional issues, and the conclusions of the negotiations. For Indochina this is followed by a separate section presenting documents prepared by the conference international secretariat—such as draft armistice agreements and arrangements for political and legal settlements. The final sections of both series provide postconference documents, including views on the results of the conference, legal analyses, an Allied report to the United Nations on Korea, and arrangements concerning the International Control Commission for Indochina.

Those desiring a concise yet inclusive documentary record of this important multipartite conference on two festering Far Eastern issues of the 1950's will welcome this volume. It evidences the traditional high standards of selectivity, coverage, organization, and style that the community of scholars has come to expect of the *Foreign Relations* series. Its use is facilitated by a list of abbreviations and symbols, a list of persons involved in the conference with their official titles, and a comprehensive subject/person index.

ELMER PLISCHKE
University of Maryland, Emeritus
Gettysburg College, Adjunct Professor
American Enterprise Institute, Adjunct Scholar

BRIEFER NOTICES

L'Organisation des Nations Unies et la Corée. Recherches sur la fiction en droit international public. By Marie-Françoise Labouz. (Paris: Publications Universitaires de Paris, 1980. Pp. 382. Annotated bibliography and index.) This study, originally a doctoral thesis, is noteworthy for the completeness of coverage in its three parts: "The UN and the Division of Korea"; "The UN and Armed Intervention in Korea"; and "The UN and Attempts to Settle the Korean Question." The author deals with the legal issues in the problem of Korean relations with the United Nations Organization, from the time of the Allied occupation of the peninsula in 1945 to the removal of the Korean item from the agenda of the General Assembly through dissolution of the UN Commission on the Unification and Rehabilitation of Korea in 1973, by consensus, and the subsequent attempt to promote final settlement of the dispute in 1975 (Resolution 3390A and B, Nov. 18, 1975).

Besides the more obvious juridical questions, the study covers such infrequently considered issues as the application of humanitarian law to the military conflict and the prisoners of war in Korea, the replacement of the armistice accord by a peace treaty, the liquidation of the UN Command, and the ultimate admission of Korea, last of the postwar "divided states," to the Organization. Labouz's coverage is matched by the extensiveness of her documentation and of her references to other literature on the questions concerned.

The study is noteworthy, finally, for the author's rigorous theoretical examination of the idea of legal fiction, as distinct from political fiction and violation of law, from the viewpoint of its utilization in the numerous issues raised. The book makes salutary reading for American students of the Korean-UN problem.

RUTH B. RUSSELL

Les Institutions Spécialisées du Système des Nations Unies et leurs Membres. By Antoine H. Zarb. (Paris: Editions A. Pedone, 1980. Pp. xvi, 598.) Books that undertake to examine the constitutional and internal workings of international organizations in a systematic manner have become something of an endangered species. The sheer mass of documentation and the constantly shifting structure of organizational frameworks are a daunting prospect for all but the most knowledgeable and persistent researcher. In these circumstances, the tendency is to examine either particular problems or particular organizations rather than to survey the system as a whole. All students of international organizations are, therefore, indebted to Zarb for this volume, which combines an encyclopedic knowledge of the history and constitutions of the specialized agencies with the insights of a practitioner. The book is written in an engagingly familiar prose style that will render it accessible even to those for whom French is a second language.

This book is not an examination of the work of the specialized agencies but of their constitutions as functioning legal instruments. The focus, as the title indicates, is the member state, its rights and obligations. The first part of the book consists of a brief account of the origins, purposes, and structures of the specialized agencies of the UN system and the International Atomic Energy Agency (IAEA), including the most recent additions to the family, the World Intellectual Property Organization (WIPO) and the International Fund for Agricultural Development (IFAD). While this part is largely descriptive in nature, it is extremely useful to have all of this material gathered together in a form that is readily usable. This is followed by a slim second part in which the author sets out the particularities of the specialized agencies as reflected in their constitutive instruments, name, logo, emblem and flag, and their choice of headquarters.

The first two parts serve essentially as an introduction to the third and fourth parts of the book, in which Zarb examines the legal status of the specialized agencies, including that of representatives and officials, their legal personality and capacity, and the questions of coordination (part III) and membership (part IV). Parts III and IV account for two-thirds of the nearly six hundred-page volume. The comprehensiveness of treatment is impressive, for while certain topics are familiar, *e.g.*, the legal status of the specialized agencies, representatives, and international officials, more highly specialized topics are also covered. There are excellent chapters dealing with legal personality and capacity (part III, ch. IV) and coordination (part III, ch. V).

Part IV deals with membership in the specialized agencies, its rights, obligations, and sanctions. The question of membership, both admission and expulsion, has been one of the most controversial aspects of the constitutional law of international organizations in recent years. It is to be regretted, therefore, that Zarb, no doubt for reasons of methodology, has omitted a detailed analysis of such questions as the expulsion of South Africa and the admission of Namibia.

Abundant footnotes and a well-organized and selected bibliography complete this excellent volume, which is destined to be a standard reference work for years to come.

RALPH ZACKLIN
United Nations

Statusverträge im Völkerrecht. Rechtsfragen territorialer Sonderregime. By Eckart Klein. (Berlin, Heidelberg, New York: Springer-Verlag, 1980. Pp. xiv, 395. Index. DM 86; $50.80.) Klein's volume deals with a relatively obscure, but interesting, aspect of the law of treaties. His definition is more explicit than Sir Humphrey Waldock's ("treaties providing for objective régimes"): the term *Statusverträge* means "treaties intended to define the status of a State, of a territory, or of an international waterway as constituting a generally binding régime" (earlier terms were "international settlement" or "international arrangement").

According to Klein, these elements have to be present in a status treaty: (1) the treaty order instituted must relate to territory; (2) the parties to the treaty must intend a settlement in the general interest; (3) the intention of the parties to the treaty must be to create an objective regime in the sense that the territory in question acquires a legal status respected by all states; (4) the parties to the treaty must possess a territorial competence relative to the settlement intended, a competence not possessed by third states, and other states possessing such competence must have agreed to the proposed settlement (p. 23).

At various points in the volume, three leading opinions/decisions/judgments are analyzed on the existence of status treaties: the advisory opinion of the Committee of Jurists (League of Nations) on the legal aspects of the Aaland Islands question (1920), the judgment of the PCIJ in the *Wimbledon* case (1923), and the array of advisory opinions and judgments of the ICJ concerning South West Africa/Namibia (1950–1971).

The legal competence of the states concluding a status agreement concerning a given territory does not, of course, by itself imply an obligation of third parties to respect the newly created regime. The power of the treaty parties to settle matters with effect *erga omnes* is to be regarded as a competence that is attributed to them by third states (pp. 209 *ff.*).

The key factor in establishing whether an "objective régime" valid *erga omnes* does exist, is whether or not a general interest is served. And the parties to the treaty must intend to create a regime binding on third parties (pp. 67 *ff.*). A fairly recent example of such intent is supplied by Article X of the Antarctic Treaty. A *Statusvertrag* therefore represents an exception to the general rule that treaties cannot validly impose obligations on nonparty states. In Lauterpacht's phrasing, a treaty "intended to make an 'international settlement' would seem to be a case of unanimous implied consent."[1]

[1] 1 L. OPPENHEIM, INTERNATIONAL LAW 833 n.1 (7th ed. Lauterpacht 1953).

Klein's volume is extremely well done and fully documented, with copious footnotes and a bibliography of some 750 items. It makes stimulating reading: the author delves into numerous court decisions and into related issues, such as conflicting *Statusverträge*, the question of *rebus sic stantibus* as touching on the subject under consideration, the effect of war on status treaties, and neutralization arrangements. The one drawback to Klein's work is the language problem, inasmuch as the appended English summary (pp. 350–59) cannot convey the outstanding coverage of the subject matter in this work.

GERHARD VON GLAHN, *Emeritus*
University of Minnesota-Duluth

Space Policy and Programmes Today and Tomorrow. The Vanishing Duopole. By Nicolas Mateesco Matte. (Montreal: Institute and Centre of Air and Space Law, McGill University, 1980. Pp. 183.) The author is the Director of the Institute and Centre of Air and Space Law, McGill University, and has written extensively in the field of space law. This short book is intended as an overview of various national space policies still in the transitional stage. The author's major emphasis is on the past policies and programs of the USSR (referred to as practical and earth-oriented) and those of the United States (called hesitant and shortsighted). Matte's view is that the lack of a coherent U.S. policy was due to the changing goals of five different Presidents over the past 25 years. He regards the Outer Space Treaty of 1967 as of little practical utility, which was why it was "denounced from the moment of signature" (p. 22). The author does not elaborate on who denounced it or why and seems to overlook the many advantages of that Treaty. Matte also finds the same "emptiness" in the Astronaut Agreement of 1968 (p. 43). Most space lawyers would not agree since that treaty provides the basis for international cooperation in space rescue and salvage operations.

The first part of the book is devoted to the two decades from 1961 to 1979. Matte believes that the United States suffered from a leadership crisis during the first half of that period (1961–1969), while the continuity of leadership in the Soviet Union permitted it to establish long-range goals. During the second half (1969–1979), he believes there was a period of transition as the space duopoly of the USSR and the United States began to give way to greater multistate and regional participation. In the first part of the book, some of the activities in space of Japan, Canada, developing countries, and the European Space Agency are mentioned.

In the second part, Matte identifies specific problem areas where greater international cooperation and an enhanced rule of law are required. These include the role of private enterprise, the transfer of technology from industrial to developing states, the control of military activity, and environmental safeguards. The annexes contain some of the major space pronouncements by four U.S. Presidents and the leaders of the USSR. While the book contains the author's checklist of problems requiring international solution, it is written more from a political perspective than from an economic, technological, or legal standpoint. It will be of value to readers wishing to supplement the author's two well-known treatises on space law, *Aerospace Law* (1969 and 1977).

HAMILTON DESAUSSURE
The University of Akron School of Law

Regulating International Business through Codes of Conduct. By Raymond J. Waldmann. (Washington and London: American Enterprise Institute for Public Policy Research, 1980. Pp. 139. $5.25.) Codes of conduct are a relatively recent phenomenon, but they are quickly assuming an important role in the regulatory framework that governs the growing, yet increasingly fragile, international trade system. Moreover, these codes both arise out of, and form an integral part of, the often sharp dialogue between the industrialized nations and the Third World. Recent debate over the proposed Code on Restrictive Business Practices (1980) and the flap over the Code on Breastmilk Substitutes (1981) have focused attention on the critical issues of the nature of the codes themselves and the questions they address.

This brief volume seeks to explore this uncharted legal territory. The author first sketches the political, legal, and economic context with particular emphasis upon the legal status of codes and the clash between the positions of the two main protagonists, the Group of 77 and Group B. He then focuses upon two major examples: the Andean Investment Code and the OECD Code for Multinational Enterprises. Later chapters deal with draft proposals such as the UNCTAD Codes for Liner Conferences and Technology Transfer. Having highlighted the numerous problems surrounding the subject, Waldmann concludes with a discussion of policy options available to the United States.

Despite some unnecessary political rhetoric, the book presents an excellent and quite balanced overview. If it leaves many questions unanswered, that is perhaps because of the novelty of the subject. The author redeems any shortcomings not only by establishing a firm foundation for further study of the problems he outlines, but also by providing both an appendix containing the subject codes and a truly superb bibliography to aid in the task.

JOHN R. LACEY
Hartford, Connecticut

BOOKS RECEIVED*

International Law—General

Asociación Argentina de Derecho Internacional. *El Derecho Internacional en los Congresos Ordinarios.* Córdoba, 1981. Pp. 362.

Bernhardt, Rudolf (ed.). *Encyclopedia of Public International Law. Instalment 1: Settlement of Disputes.* Published under the auspices of the Max Planck Institute for Comparative Public Law and International Law. Amsterdam: North-Holland Publishing Company, 1981. Pp. xiii, 209.

Corriente Córdoba, José A. (ed.), with Enrique Rubio Torrano and Pedro Lozano Bartolozzi. *Anuario de Derecho Internacional.* Vol. IV, 1977–1978. Pamplona: Ediciones Universidad de Navarra, S.A., 1981. Pp. xii, 683.

Degenhardt, Henry W. (comp.). *Treaties and Alliances of the World* (3d ed.). Detroit: Gale Research Co., 1981. Pp. ix, 409. Index. $70.

Annuaire Français de Droit International. Vol. XXVI, 1980. Paris: Editions du Centre National de la Recherche Scientifique, 1981. Pp. 1316.

Kroneck, Friedrich J., and Thomas Oppermann (eds.). *Im Dienste Deutschlands und des Rechtes: Festschrift für Wilhelm G. Grewe zum 70. Geburtstag am 16. Oktober 1981.* Baden-Baden: Nomos Verlagsgesellschaft, 1981. Pp. 660. DM 189.

* Mention here neither assures nor precludes later review.

Von Wahlendorf, H. A. Schwarz-Liebermann. *The Forms of Action at International Law*. Published by author. Pp. iii, 55.

International Economic Law & Relations

Campbell, Dennis (ed.). *Legal Aspects of Joint Ventures in Eastern Europe*. Deventer: Kluwer, 1981. Pp. 133. Index. Dfl.96; $48.

Canenbley, Cornelis (ed.). *Enforcing Antitrust against Foreign Enterprises*. Deventer: Kluwer, 1981. Pp. xiii, 125. Dfl.74; $37.

Fischer, Peter (ed./annotator), with Thomas W. Wälde. *A Collection of International Concessions and Related Instruments*. Vol. I. London, Rome, New York: Oceana Publications, Inc., 1981. Pp. vi, 505. Index. $50.

Olson, Robert K. *U.S. Foreign Policy and the New International Economic Order: Negotiating Global Problems, 1974–1981*. Boulder: Westview Press; London: Frances Pinter Ltd., 1981. Pp. xviii, 168. Index. $22.50.

Schachter, Oscar, and Robert Hellawell. *Competition in International Business*. New York: Columbia University Press, 1981. Pp. 441. Index. $35.

Law of the Sea & Maritime Law

Amato, Luciano, Tecla Faranda, Tullio Scovazzi, and Tullio Treves. *La Legislazione Italiana sul Diritto del Mare*. Milan: Dott. A. Giuffrè Editore, 1981. Pp. li, 290. Index. L.16.000.

Anand, Ram Prakash (ed.). *Law of the Sea: Caracas and Beyond. Developments in International Law, 3*. New Delhi: Radiant Publishers; The Hague: Martinus Nijhoff Publishers, 1980. Pp. viii, 399. Index. Dfl.110; $58.

Dupuy, René-Jean. *L'Océan Partagé*. Paris: Editions A. Pedone, 1979. Pp. viii, 291.

Hill, Christopher. *Maritime Law*. London, Rome, New York: Oceana Publications, Inc.; London: Pitman Books Limited, 1981. Pp. xxi, 394. Index. $37.50.

Use of Force & Law of War

O'Brien, William V. *The Conduct of Just and Limited War*. New York: Praeger Publishers, 1981. Pp. xii, 495. Index.

Smith, Myron J., Jr. *The Secret Wars: A Guide to Sources in English. Vol. II: Intelligence, Propaganda and Psychological Warfare, Covert Operations, 1945–1980*. Santa Barbara: ABC-Clio, Inc., 1981. Pp. lxxxii, 389. Index. $67.50.

Human Rights

Hevener, Natalie Kaufman (ed.). *The Dynamics of Human Rights in U.S. Foreign Policy*. New Brunswick and London: Transaction Books, 1981. Pp. ix, 374. Index. $19.95.

Lillich, Richard B. (ed.). *The Family in International Law: Some Emerging Problems* (Third Sokol Colloquium). Charlottesville: The Michie Company, 1981. Pp. xii, 164. Index. $17.50.

International Criminal Law

Lillich, Richard B. (ed.). *International Aspects of Criminal Law: Enforcing United States Law in the World Community* (Fourth Sokol Colloquium). Charlottesville: The Michie Company, 1981. Pp. ix, 245. Index. $19.50.

Environment & Natural Resources

Katō, Ichirō, Nobuo Kumamoto, and William H. Matthews (eds.). *Environmental Law and Policy in the Pacific Basin Area*. Tokyo: University of Tokyo Press, 1981. Pp. ix, 229. Index. ¥5400.

Air & Space Law

Mankiewicz, René H. *The Liability Regime of the International Air Carrier*. Deventer: Kluwer, 1981. Pp. xxvii, 259. Index. Dfl.108; $54.

Seara Vázquez, Modesto. *Derecho y Política en el Espacio Cósmico*. México: Universidad Nacional Autónoma de México, 1981. Pp. 171.

International Organizations

Halderman, John W. *The Political Role of the United Nations: Advancing the World Community*. New York: Praeger Publishers, 1981. Pp. xii, 217. Index. $24.95.

Higgins, Rosalyn. *United Nations Peacekeeping. Documents and Commentary. Vol. IV: Europe 1946–1979*. Issued under the auspices of the Royal Institute of International Affairs. New York and Oxford: Oxford University Press, 1981. Pp. xii, 419. Index. $89; £40.

Kunig, Philip. *Das völkerrechtliche Nichteinmischungsprinzip: Zur Praxis der Organisation der afrikanischen Einheit (OAS) und des afrikanischen Staatenverkehrs*. Baden-Baden: Nomos Verlagsgesellschaft, 1981. Pp. 449. DM 77.

Landskron, William A. (comp./ed.). *Annual Review of United Nations Affairs, 1980*. Dobbs Ferry: Oceana Publications, Inc., 1981. Pp. ix, 491. Index. $27.50.

Sybesma-Knol, R. G. *The Status of Observers in the United Nations*. Brussels: Vrije Universiteit Brussel, 1981. Pp. xi, 484. Index.

European Community Law

Lasok, Dominik, and Panayotis Soldatos (eds.). *Les Communautés Européennes en Fonctionnement* (The European Communities in Action). Brussels: Etablissements Emile Bruylant, 1981. Pp. 604. BF.2.500.

Parry, Anthony, and James Dinnage. *Parry and Hardy: EEC Law* (2d ed.). London, Rome, New York: Oceana Publications, Inc.; London: Sweet and Maxwell, 1981. Pp. lvi, 531. Index. $50.

Arms Control & Disarmament

Laszlo, Ervin, and Donald Keys (eds.). *Disarmament: The Human Factor*. (Proceedings of a Colloquium on the Societal Context for Disarmament, sponsored by UNITAR and Planetary Citizens, held at the United Nations, New York, 1978.) New York: Pergamon Press Inc., 1981. Pp. x, 164. Index. $12.50.

Comparative Law & Foreign Law

Butler, William E. (ed.). *Anglo-Polish Legal Essays*. Dobbs Ferry: Transnational Publishers, Inc., 1982. Pp. xiv, 258. Index. $19.50.

Orban, Edmond, Gérard Bergeron, Edward McWhinney, and Gérald-A. Beaudoin. *Mécanismes pour une nouvelle Constitution*. Ottawa: Editions de l'Université d'Ottawa, 1981. Pp. x, 146. Index.

Péteri, Zoltán, and Vanda Lamm (eds.). *General Reports to the 10th International Congress of Comparative Law*. Budapest: Akadémiai Kiadó, 1981. Pp. 1048. $75.

International Relations & Politics

Chiu, Hungdah. *Agreements of the People's Republic of China: A Calendar of Events 1966–1980*. New York: Praeger Publishers, 1981. Pp. xvii, 329. Index.

Anuario Mexicano de Relaciones Internacionales, 1980. Mexico: Universidad Nacional Autónoma de México, 1981. Pp. 1087. Indexes.

Zartman, I. William, and Maureen R. Berman. *The Practical Negotiator*. New Haven and London: Yale University Press, 1982. Pp. xiii, 250. Index. $20.

Miscellaneous

Godson, Roy (ed.). *Intelligence Requirements for the 1980's: Covert Action*. Washington: National Strategy Information Center, Inc., 1981. Pp. ix, 243. $7.50.

Gomi, Yuji. *Guide to Japanese Taxes 1981–82*. Tokyo: Zaikei Shōhō Sha, 1981. Pp. 282. Index. Dfl.60.

Wilkins, William J. *The Sword and the Gavel*. Seattle: The Writing Works, 1981. Pp. vii, 328. Index. $14.95.

INTERNATIONAL LEGAL MATERIALS*

CONTENTS

VOL. XX, NO. 6 (November 1981)

PAGE

LEGISLATION AND REGULATIONS

Inter-American Court of Human Rights: *Rules of Procedure* 1289

International Energy Agency: Dispute Settlement Center *Rules of Procedure for Arbitration* 1307

Switzerland: Law on *International Judicial Assistance in Criminal Matters* 1339

Union of Soviet Socialist Republics: Statute on the *All-Union Maritime Satellite Communications Association* 1365

TREATIES AND AGREEMENTS

Canada-United States: Treaty on *Gulf of Maine Boundary Dispute Settlement* 1371

Council of Europe: European Agreement on *Transfer of Responsibility for Refugees* 1391

France-United States: Exchange of Notes on *Legal Cooperation in the Field of Child Custody* 1401

Hague Conference on Private International Law: 1961 Convention *Abolishing the Requirement of Legalisation for Foreign Public Documents* 1405

Israel-United States: Memorandum of Understanding on *Strategic Cooperation* 1420

JUDICIAL AND SIMILAR PROCEEDINGS

Inter-American Court of Human Rights: Decision on the Application of the Government of Costa Rica with regard to Viviana Gallardo et al. (*Jurisdiction of the Inter-American Court of Human Rights; Referral to the Inter-American Commission on Human Rights*) 1424

United States: Brief Submitted to the Court of Appeals for the District of Columbia Circuit in Maritime International Nominees Establishment *v.* Guinea (*Foreign Sovereign Immunities Act; ICSID Arbitration; Waiver of Immunity*) 1436

OTHER DOCUMENTS

International Monetary Fund and World Bank 36th Annual Meetings:

Interim Committee Communique on *Problems of Inflation and the World Economic Outlook* 1488

Development Committee Communique on *Economic Problems and Adequate Financing* 1490

Group of Ten Communique on *Strengthened Surveillance* 1493

Group of 24 Communique on *Worsening Economic Outlook and Debt Service Burden* 1493

United Nations:

General Assembly Resolution on the *Situation in Kampuchea* 1499

International Conference on Kampuchea Declaration on *Kampuchea* 1503

United States:

Notices concerning the *Claims against Iran* 1506

Announcement of *Policy concerning Conventional Arms Transfers* 1508

RECENT ACTIONS REGARDING TREATIES TO WHICH THE UNITED STATES IS A PARTY 1510

RECENT ACTIONS REGARDING TREATIES TO WHICH THE UNITED STATES IS NOT A PARTY 1516

NOTICE OF OTHER RECENT DOCUMENTS (not reprinted) 1518

INDEX TO VOLUME XX 1519

* ILM subscription, $65; concessionary rate to ASIL members, $24. Address orders to ILM, 2223 Massachusetts Ave., NW, Wash., D.C. 20008. Outside U.S., please add $4.50.

THE COMMISSION
OF THE EUROPEAN COMMUNITIES

is pleased to announce the publication

ANNUAL SUPPLEMENT 1978
Vol. 8—Tome I and II

COLLECTION OF THE AGREEMENTS CONCLUDED BY THE EUROPEAN COMMUNITIES

This major work of reference brings together the full texts of agreements made by the European Communities with non-member States or with other bodies governed by international law, particularly international organizations, and of the Community Acts concluding those agreements.

"Agreements" in this context means agreements governed by international law whether contained in a single instrument or two or more related instruments, and whatever particular titles they may have.

The scale of their economic and commercial capacity has made the European Communities an important partner on the world scene. This work bears witness also to the outward looking attitude of the Institutions, and the breadth and diversity of the external activity of the Communities in the areas covered by the treaties establishing them.

The Collection comprises five basic volumes containing the texts of all the agreements in force at 31 December 1975, amendments made to those texts before that date being referred to in the footnotes or given after the text of the agreement concerned.

The work is kept up to date by annual supplements.

Contents

Volume 1 **Bilateral agreements EEC-Europe 1958–1975** covering agreements with Austria, Malta, Spain, Portugal.
1977 1,048 pp.

Volume 2 **Bilateral agreements EEC-Europe 1958–1975** (continued) covering agreements with Finland, Norway, Sweden, Iceland.
1977 776 pp.

Volume 3 **Bilateral agreements EEC-Europe 1958–1975** (continued) covering agreements with Switzerland, Greece, Yugoslavia, Turkey, Cyprus.
1978 880 pp.

Volume 4 **Bilateral agreements EEC-Asia, EEC-Africa, EEC-America 1958–1975**
1978 1,008 pp.

Volume 5 **Bilateral agreements EAEC, ECSC: Multilateral agreements EEC, EAEC, ECSC 1952–1975** with index to Volumes 1–5
1979 970 pp.

Volume 6 **Annual Supplement 1976**
1979 1,606 pp.

Volume 7 **Annual Supplement 1977**
1980 1,525 pp.

Volume 8 **Annual Supplement 1978**
1981 ±3,500 pp.

Published in: Danish, Dutch, English, French, German, Italian.

Price (excluding VAT) in Luxembourg:

Vols. 1 to 5	BFR	10.000	UKL	157	USD 276	
Basic Vol. (1–5) each	BFR	2.000	UKL	31,40	USD 55.20	
Vol. 6 (Ann. Suppl.)	BFR	2.000	UKL	31,00	USD 68.00	
Vol. 7 (Ann. Suppl.)	BFR	2.500	UKL	37,80	USD 85.50	
Vol. 8 (Ann. Suppl.)	BFR	3.300	UKL	43	USD 94	IRL 55

OFFICE FOR OFFICIAL PUBLICATIONS OF THE EUROPEAN COMMUNITIES
L-2985 Luxembourg

CHINESE YEARBOOK OF INTERNATIONAL LAW AND AFFAIRS 1981 VOL. 1

Edited by Hungdah Chiu

Table of Contents

Foreword	Yi-ting Chang
Articles	
Hungdah Chiu	The International Law of Recognition and Multi-system Nations—With Special Reference to Chinese (Mainland-Taiwan) Case
Ralph N. Clough	Taiwan's International Status
Lyushun Shen	The Taiwan Issue in Peking's Foreign Relations in the 1970's: A Systematic Review
Ying-jeou Ma	Foreign Investment in the Troubled Waters of the East China Sea
Recent Development	
David Simon	Legal Development in U.S.-ROC Trade from January 1, 1979 through June 1, 1981
Jyh-pin Fa	The Development of Human Rights in the Republic of China: 1971–1981
Hungdah Chiu	Excerpts of Important Foreign Policy Statements of the Republic of China, January 1, 1979 to October 30, 1981

Contemporary Practice and Judicial Decisions of the Republic of China Relating to International Law

Book Review and Article Summary

List of Bilateral Treaties/Agreements Concluded by the Republic of China, January 1, 1979 to December 31, 1980

List and Selected Text of Bilateral Official, Semi-Official or Unofficial Agreements Concluded between the Republic of China and Countries Without Diplomatic Relations, January 1, 1979 to October 31, 1981

Republic of China's Diplomatic and Consular Missions Abroad

Republic of China's Official, Semi-Official or Unofficial Missions Abroad

Foreign Diplomatic, Consular, Semi-Official or Unofficial Missions in the Republic of China

Statistics in Brief of the Republic of China, 1971–1980

Bibliography on Selected Academic Articles Published in the Republic of China Relating to International Law, Relations and Foreign Policy, January 1, 1979 to December 31, 1980

Index

Published by the Occasional Papers/Reprints Series in Contemporary Asian Studies, Inc. for the Chinese Society of International Law—Chinese (Taiwan) Branch of International Law Association, 1982.

ISBN : 0-942128-93-X

MULTI-SYSTEM NATIONS AND INTERNATIONAL LAW THE INTERNATIONAL STATUS OF GERMANY, KOREA, AND CHINA

Edited by Hungdah Chiu and Robert L. Downen

TABLE OF CONTENTS

Foreword	Ray S. Cline
Introduction	John Norton Moore
Chapter I	
Assessing the International Status of Partitioned Nations: Theories and Findings	Ray E. Johnston
Comments by Hungdah Chiu	
Chapter II	
The International Law of Recognition and Multi-system Nations—with Special Reference to Chinese (Mainland-Taiwan) Case	Hungdah Chiu
Chapter III	
The Unification and Division of Multi-system Nations: A Comparative Analysis of Basic Concepts, Issues and Approaches	Yung Wei
Chapter IV	
Multi-system Nations and International Law, with Special Reference to Dutch Practice	Swan Sik Ko
Comments by Hungdah Chiu	
Chapter V	
The Case of Germany	Gottfried-Karl Kindermann
Comments by Jürgen Domes	
Chapter VI	
Divided Nations and International Law, the Case of the Two Koreas	Nam Yearl Chai
Comments by Seung Hwan Kim and Se Jin Kim	
Chapter VII	
Taiwan's International Status	Ralph N. Clough
Chapter VIII	
Divided Nations and International Law: The Case of Taiwan	Aleth Manin
Chapter IX	
Recognition Policy with respect to Multi-system States: The Case of China	Morton A. Kaplan
Chapter X	
Overall Evaluation	Robert Sutter, Yung Wei, Stephen Guest, and Swan Sik Ko

Appendices

1. Divided Nations and International Law: Political Reality and Legal Practice	Yung Wei
2. Basic Facts Concerning Two Chinas, Two Koreas, and Two Germanys	Hungdah Chiu
Index	203 pp. U.S. $5.00

The American Society of International Law

2223 Massachusetts Ave., N.W., Washington, D.C. 20008 (202) 265-4313 CABLES "AMINTLAW"

1982 APPLICATION

[ ] REGULAR MEMBERS . . . . $ 55

[ ] INTERMEDIATE MEMBERS (first 3 years of membership for *those under 30 years of age* at time of application) . . . . $ 25
Date of Birth ____________

[ ] STUDENT MEMBERS . . . Verification to be completed by a professor or administrative officer of your school: I hereby certify that the applicant is regularly registered in
(school) ____________________________
for academic year __________ Title ______________
Signature ____________________________ $ 15

[ ] SPECIAL CATEGORY (persons *not* resident in a member country of the OECD) . . . . $ 30

[ ] CONTRIBUTING MEMBERS . . . . $ 75

[ ] SUPPORTING MEMBERS . . . . $ 150

[ ] ANNUAL PATRON . . . . $ 500

[ ] LIFE $1,000

($21 of membership fee is allotted to AJIL subscription.)

Please enroll me as a member of the American Society of International Law for the calendar year starting January 1, 19____. My check, money order, UNESCO coupon, or payment in a convertible currency is enclosed $__________. I have checked membership category for which I am eligible.

(Please Print)

Name: . . . .

Address: . . . .

City: . . . .

State (or Country): . . . . Zip: . . . .

Member, U.S. Bar? . . . . State: . . . . Year: . . . .

Other Professional Affiliation: . . . .

Signature: . . . .

[ ] Please send me ILM at member rate of $24, plus $4.50 if outside U.S.

[ ] Check here if you would like to receive a list of Society publications.

PLEASE MAKE CHECKS PAYABLE TO *The American Society of International Law*. Contributions above obligatory dues, and all dues if membership is related to your work or profession, are tax deductible in the United States.

[ ] *Nonmember* subscription to AJIL (incl. ASIL Proceedings) . . . $ 52

Please add $2.50 if you reside outside the U.S.

American Journal of International Law

July 1982
Vol. 76 No. 3

Published by

American Society of International Law

PATRONS OF THE SOCIETY

Honorable ARTHUR H. DEAN
Honorable HERMAN PHLEGER
GENEVIEVE E. TILLAR (deceased)
W. ROBERT MORGAN
BRUNSON MACCHESNEY (deceased)
ALONA E. EVANS (deceased)
JOHN N. HAZARD
Honorable JOHN R. STEVENSON
ARTHUR R. ALBRECHT

In Memoriam

DR. JAMES BROWN SCOTT
HENRY C. MORRIS
ARTHUR K. KUHN
ALEXANDER FREEMAN
STANLEY P. SMITH

PATRONAGE, GIFTS AND BEQUESTS

Upon donation to the Society of $5,000 or more by gift or bequest, any member of the Society or individual eligible for membership may be elected a Patron of the Society. Upon donation of at least $5,000 in the name of a deceased person, such person may be elected a Patron posthumously.

Gifts and bequests may be made in the name of the American Society of International Law, Washington, D.C. Such contributions are deductible from federal returns for income, estate and gift tax purposes. The Society is incorporated by Act of Congress approved September 20, 1950 (64 Stat. 869).

MANLEY O. HUDSON MEDAL

The American Society of International Law bestows from time to time without regard to nationality a gold medal to commemorate the life work of Manley O. Hudson. Such awards are made for preeminent scholarship and achievement in international law and in the promotion of the establishment and maintenance of international relations on the basis of law and justice. Medals have been awarded to Manley O. Hudson (1956), Lord McNair (1959), Philip C. Jessup (1964), Charles De Visscher (1966), Paul Guggenheim (1970), Myres S. McDougal (1976), Eduardo Jiménez de Aréchega (1978), Richard Reeve Baxter (1981), Oscar Schachter (1981), and Hardy Cross Dillard (1982).

Second-class postage paid at Washington, D.C. and additional mailing office

Postmaster: If undeliverable, send notice on Form 3579 to: American Journal of International Law 2223 Massachusetts Ave., N.W. Washington, D.C. 20008

Printed by Lancaster Press, Lancaster, Pa. 17604

AMERICAN JOURNAL OF INTERNATIONAL LAW

VOL. 76 July 1982 NO. 3

CONTENTS

PAGE

The Grotian Vision of World Order *Cornelius F. Murphy, Jr.* 477

Contempt, Crisis, and the Court: The World Court and the Hostage Rescue Attempt *Ted L. Stein* 499

The Egyptian-Israeli Peace Treaty and Access to the Gulf of Aqaba: A New Legal Regime *Mohamed ElBaradei* 532

Sea Boundary Delimitation Between States Before World War II *Sang-Myon Rhee* 555

Editorial Comments

Critical Defense Zones and International Law: The Reagan Codicil *W. Michael Reisman* 589

A Turnabout in Extraterritoriality *Detlev F. Vagts* 591

The Falklands (Malvinas), International Law, and the OAS *Seymour J. Rubin* 594

Hardy Cross Dillard (1902–1982) *Oscar Schachter* 595

Notes and Comments

Large-Scale Migrations of Asylum Seekers *David A. Martin* 598

The Francis Deák Prize 610

Contemporary Practice of the United States Relating to International Law *Marian Nash Leich* 611

Judicial Decisions *Monroe Leigh* 616

Current Developments

The Codification and Progressive Development of International Law: A UNITAR Study of the Role and Use of the International Law Commission *Thomas M. Franck & Mohamed ElBaradei* 630

The 1981 U.S.-Czechoslovak Claims Settlement Agreement: An Epilogue to Postwar Nationalization and Expropriation Disputes *Vratislav Pechota* 639

Restatement of the Foreign Relations Law of the United States (Revised): Tentative Draft No. 3 *Louis Henkin* 653

Book Reviews and Notes *Edited by Leo Gross*

Bilder, Richard B. *Managing the Risks of International Agreement* 658

McWhinney, Edward. *Conflict and Compromise* 658

Mani, V. S. *International Adjudication: Procedural Aspects* 660

Bassiouni, M. Cherif. *International Criminal Law: A Draft International Criminal Code* 661

Geertz, Clifford. *Negara, The Theater State in Nineteenth-Century Bali* 663

Lillich, Richard B. (ed.). *U.S. Ratification of the Human Rights Treaties. With or Without Reservations?* 666

Newberg, Paula R. (ed.). *The Politics of Human Rights* 667

Nanda, Ved P., James R. Scarritt, and George W. Shepherd, Jr. (eds.). *Global Human Rights: Public Policies, Comparative Measures, and NGO Strategies* 668

Calogeropoulos-Stratis, Aristidis S. *Droit humanitaire et Droits de l'homme—La protection de la personne en période de conflit armé* 669
Goodwin-Gill, Guy S. *International Law and the Movement of Persons Between States* 670
Levin, D. B. *Mezhdunarodnoe Pravo, Vneshniaia Politika i Diplomatiia* 672
Sonnenfeld, Renata (ed.). *Odpowiedzialność Państwa w Prawie Międzynarodowym* 673
Frankowska, Maria. *Umowy Międzynarodowe w Formie Uproszczonej* 673
Gilas, Janusz. *Systemy Normatywne w Stosunkach Międzynarodowych* 674
Frenzke, Dietrich. *Die Rechtsnatur des Sowjetblocks: Eine juristische Entschleierung* 674
Fawcett, J. E. S., and Audrey Parry. *Law and International Resource Conflicts* 675
Arsanjani, Mahnoush H. *International Regulation of Internal Resources* 675
Bizec, René-François, and Yves Daudet (eds.). *UN Code de Conduite pour le Transfert de Technologie* 678
Grewlich, Klaus W. *Transnational Enterprises in a New International System* 679
Crosswell, Carol McCormick. *Legal and Financial Aspects of International Business* 682
Akinsanya, Adeoye A. *The Expropriation of Multinational Property in the Third World* 683
Timmermans, C. W. A., and E. L. M. Völker (eds.). *Division of powers between the European Communities and their Member States in the field of external relations* 684
Ress, Georg (ed.). *Souveränitätsverständnis in den Europäischen Gemeinschaften* 686
Les Travailleurs Etrangers et le Droit International 687
Breuer, Georg. *Weather Modification: Prospects and Problems* 688
Van Lier, Irene H. *Acid Rain and International Law* 689
Apollis, Gilbert. *L'Emprise Maritime de l'Etat Côtier* 690
Ferrero Costa, Eduardo. *El Nuevo Derecho del Mar: El Perú y las 200 Millas* 691
Teclaff, Ludwik A., and Albert E. Utton. *International Groundwater Law* 692
Wassenbergh, H. A., and H. P. van Fenema (eds.). *International Air Transport in the Eighties* 693
Pambou Tchivounda, Guillaume. *La Conférence au Sommet: Contribution à l'Etude des Institutions des Relations Internationales* 695
Blanco Gaspar, Vicente. *El Voto Ponderado* 695
Cattan, Henry. *Jerusalem* 696
Willamette Law Review. Vol. 17, no. 1 697
Dinstein, Yoram (ed.). *Israel Yearbook on Human Rights. Vol. 10* 698
Netherlands Yearbook of International Law. Vol. XI, 1980 699
Bourne, C. B. (ed.). *The Canadian Yearbook of International Law. Vols. XVII, 1979* and *XVIII, 1980* 700
Greig, D. W. (ed.). *The Australian Year Book of International Law*. Vol. 7 701
Briefer Notices: Brittin, 702; Lerner, 703; Reijnen, 703; Barton, 704; Meijers, 705; Israel National Section of the International Commission of Jurists, 705; *South African Yearbook of International Law, Volume 5, 1979*, 706; Hsiung and Kim (eds.), 707; Matte, 707.
Books Received 708

OFFICIAL DOCUMENTS

Argentina-United Kingdom: UN Security Council Resolution 502 (1982) 712
International Legal Materials. Contents, Vol. XXI, No. 1 (January 1982) and No. 2 (March 1982) 713

The American Society of International Law

The American Society of International Law was organized in 1906 "to foster the study of international law and to promote the establishment and maintenance of international relations on the basis of law and justice."

The Society serves as a meeting place and forum for scholars, teachers, officials, lawyers, and others, from some one hundred countries. In April, it holds a three-day Annual Meeting at which current problems of international law are discussed. The Society also sponsors regional meetings outside of Washington in cooperation with other institutions. Salient questions of international law and relations are considered in depth by panels and study groups organized by the Society's Board of Review and Development. Works of scholarship are often published under the Society's auspices in connection with studies sponsored by the Board, many in the Society's series of *Studies in Transnational Legal Policy*.

The Society periodically issues four publications:

The American Journal of International Law, the leading journal in the field of international law, has been published since 1907. The *Proceedings of the American Society of International Law* carries the papers and discussion of the annual meeting of the Society.

International Legal Materials, a bimonthly, is a unique international collection of texts of current official documents, including legislation, treaties, court decisions, and reports. Subscription rates are $24 a year for members of the Society, $65 for others.

The quarterly *Newsletter* provides members with news of the Society and other organizations in the field.

Society membership is open to all persons of whatever nationality and profession who are interested in its objectives. Dues are: regular, $55; special category, $30 for persons *not* resident in a member country of the Organisation for Economic Co-operation and Development; intermediate, $25; student, $15. Membership application form is printed at the back of each issue of AJIL.

THE GROTIAN VISION OF WORLD ORDER

*By Cornelius F. Murphy, Jr.**

I.

At the beginning of the 14th century, the great poet Dante published an imaginative proposal for world order. His experience had led him to believe that the multiplicity of cities, states, and kingdoms was the source of great discord and strife. They were depriving mankind of that tranquility which was necessary for the full development of its intellectual powers. There was a need for a single impartial ruler who, standing above the contentiousness of lesser governments, could bring about a regime of universal justice and peace. In the *De monarchia* the holder of universal authority was to be the Roman emperor. The genius of the Romans devised the most effective forms of government that the world had ever known. As the Roman Catholic Church had universal authority in matters spiritual, the Holy Roman emperor should exercise a supreme, global authority to which all the various kingdoms and republics would be politically subordinate.[1]

As Europe became separated into distinct nationalities, the need for an international power became increasingly evident. Differences in language, custom, and institutions accelerated the antagonisms between the various peoples of the continent. Some superior authority was needed to contain the warfare which had become increasingly destructive and threatened the peace of the Christian community. For a time, the papacy aspired to exercise the office of supreme arbiter. The sacredness of the position commanded respect as the power of excommunication inspired fear. Belonging to no one nation, the Holy Father was exempt, in principle, from the biases and selfishness generated by the particularities of blood and geographic position. Yet, however beneficial the conciliatory intervention of individual popes, the general authority of the office was gradually disappearing. Because of the Avignon experience the papacy had shown partiality towards French kings. And as it pursued its temporal power, its position became more deeply entangled with Italian politics.[2]

There were additional factors that were inimical to religious control of political strife. Throughout the 14th and 15th centuries a mood of anticlericalism was growing in Europe, a revulsion against both the arrogance of the higher prelates and the vices and ignorance of the minor clergy. Expectations of temporal authority shifted to the Roman emperor. As the heir of those who had shaped the legal principles of Europe, and the only sovereign possessed of an

* Professor of Law, Duquesne University School of Law.

[1] DANTE, DE MONARCHIA (On World Government) (Liberal Arts ed. 1949). *See also Dante and World Empire*, in THE SOCIAL AND POLITICAL IDEAS OF SOME GREAT MEDIEVAL THINKERS, ch. V (F. J. C. Hearnshaw ed. 1923); F. HINSLEY, POWER AND THE PURSUIT OF PEACE 14–19 (1963). According to Hinsley, *De monarchia* was not published until the 16th century. It was placed on the *Index* in 1554.

[2] J. BRYCE, THE HOLY ROMAN EMPIRE (1904).

inviolate title, the emperor was the ideal of a perfect monarch to whom the preservation of peace could be entrusted.

But Dante's vision was not to be realized. The political position of the emperors might have improved in light of the general aversion to papal authority, but they were unable to capitalize on the opportunity. Except for the gathering of the Council of Constance (1414–1418) by Sigismund, the emperors did not fulfill a truly international role. Their influence was not much greater than that of other princes and their actual resources were less than those of the kings of France and England.[3]

The growth of nationalism and the internal political consolidation of nations intensified in the 15th century. They were sparked by forces much stronger than the vague appeals to Catholic unity symbolized by the Holy Roman emperor. Throughout Europe the power of feudal lords was being broken. The duty of personal loyalty of vassal to lord was being transformed into bonds of allegiance of subject to monarch in a nation-state. Machiavelli's *Prince*, written early in the 16th century, justified the state as a self-sufficient, nonmoral entity. Later in the same century Jean Bodin, reflecting the realities of power in France, made sovereign power and unity of government the essence of the state.[4]

Under these circumstances, the empire could not sustain itself as an international power supreme among Christian states. Since the crowning of Otto the Great in Rome, the offices of German king and Roman emperor had been united in one person. As the rulers of the other European powers, both great and small, repudiated imperial control, the emperor was left with a contracted sphere of influence. Germany became the realm of his international jurisdiction.[5] The tension that had characterized relations between the supreme authority of the emperor and that of the nation-states of Europe was now transferred to a struggle between the emperor and the German princes. With the Reformation, Germany would become a central theater in the drama of religious conflict that would destroy the pretensions of the emperor to supranational authority.

The consolidation of power within the separate nation-states had intensified the quarrels among the European family of nations. Yet in spite of periodic wars there was a residual sense of unity engendered by a common religious faith. The Reformation shattered this precarious concord. In addition to its theological importance, the Reformation was also a rebellion of the states against the Church. The Church was the last remaining obstacle to the determination of the European princes to have supreme authority within their territories.

The antagonisms generated by the religious divisions of the Reformation emerged in the armed conflict of the Thirty Years War. In the Peace of Westphalia (1648) the war would be concluded with the full recognition of the sovereignty of all the princes, both Catholic and Protestant, within their respective domains. Lutherans and Calvinists would be declared free from all jurisdiction of the Pope or any Catholic prelate. And the Holy Roman emperor

[3] *Id.*, chs. XV–XVIII.

[4] *Ibid. See also* J. BRIERLY, THE LAW OF NATIONS, ch. I (6th ed. 1963).

[5] J. BRYCE, *supra* note 2, ch. XX; Schaefer, *The Medieval Empire Made Germany a Nation*, in THE HOLY ROMAN EMPIRE IN THE MIDDLE AGES 17 (R. E. Herzstein ed. 1966).

would be bound not to interfere with the administration of the independent states. He would, in effect, be stripped of all important public and transnational authority.[6]

The rising power of separate nation-states impressed upon the minds of thoughtful Europeans the necessity of creating a new form of general order that would encompass both Europe and the wider expanse of the newly discovered worlds beyond. The rising spirit of adventure and commerce meant that the degree of interaction among sovereigns would be intensified. There was a fear that the relations between states would be uncontrolled and uninspired by any unifying ideals. In theory and practice, absolute independence was replacing the modalities of a common life. As the authority of the Holy Roman emperor rapidly declined, it was futile to revive Dante's vision of global order.

The need for a new harmony was perceived by the Jesuit theologian Suárez, lecturing and writing in Coimbra at the beginning of the 17th century. He acknowledged the divisions both within the Christian republic and throughout the known world. But in the *jus gentium*, or law of nations, he saw the possibilities of a common interest. Though each sovereignty was a self-sufficient commonwealth, each was also a member of a *universum*: the human race. Humanly speaking, sovereign independence is not absolute. Mutual assistance and reciprocal need can never be eliminated, and some law is needed to guide and regulate such intercourse. This *jus gentium* has a rational basis, because the human race, even though divided into many different peoples and kingdoms,

> always preserves a certain unity, not only as a species, but also a moral and political unity (as it were) enjoined by the natural precept of mutual love and mercy; a precept which applies to all, even to strangers of every nation.
>
> Therefore, although a given sovereign state, commonwealth, or kingdom may constitute a perfect community in itself, consisting of its own members, nevertheless, each one of these states is also, in a certain sense, and viewed in relation to the human race, a member of that universal society; for these states when standing alone are never so self-sufficient that they do not require some mutual assistance, association, and intercourse, at times for their own greater welfare and advantage, but at other times because also of some moral necessity or need. This fact is made manifest by actual usage.[7]

The *De legibus* of Suárez was published in 1619. In the new century there was a more pressing need for an articulated order. The armed clashes between sovereign princes and the revulsion aroused by the savagery of the wars of religion made it imperative that the modern, as well as the medieval, world

[6] J. BRYCE, *supra* note 2, ch. XX; Gross, *The Peace of Westphalia, 1648–1948*, 42 AJIL 20 (1948). *See also* Falk, *A New Paradigm for International Legal Studies: Prospects and Proposal*, 84 YALE L.J. 969, 980–87 (1975). The text of the Treaty of Westphalia appears in 1 MAJOR PEACE TREATIES OF MODERN HISTORY 7 (F. L. Israel ed. 1967).

[7] F. SUÁREZ, DE LEGIBUS AC DEO LEGISLATORE, bk. II, ch. XIX, para. 9, in 2 SUÁREZ, SELECTIONS FROM THREE WORKS (Carnegie Endowment trans. 1944). *See also Francisco Suarez*, in THE SOCIAL AND POLITICAL IDEAS OF SOME GREAT THINKERS OF THE SIXTEENTH AND SEVENTEENTH CENTURIES, ch. 4 (F. J. C. Hearnshaw ed. 1926).

establish some means of controlling violence. The ideal of a world state was lost. In its place were numerous states possessing various degrees of power, but all committed to the new ideal of sovereign independence. If the separate state, accountable to no distinct higher authority, should become the highest form of human community, all possibilities of international justice would be lost. Some systematic constraints had to be devised that would take account of the fundamental facts but also invoke deeper standards. There must be an appeal to basic principles that could elicit the submission of a sovereign will and reconcile the spirit of national independence with the goals of justice and peace.

In 1625, while in exile in Paris, the Dutch humanist Huig de Groot, or Grotius, published his treatise *De jure belli ac pacis*. A devout man of letters, Grotius was deeply moved by the horrors of the religious wars. Having written on the laws of prize and freedom of the seas, he now constructed a general theory of law that he hoped would bring order out of the chaos of international conflict.

Grotius sought to strike a middle ground between the polar views on the legitimacy of warfare then prevalent in Europe. At one extreme were the pacifists, of which Erasmus was the most notable example. They believed that the use of arms could not be reconciled with a Christian conscience. At the other were those who maintained that all wars commenced by sovereign will were lawful and that the practices of warfare were not subject to moral restraint. Grotius distinguished righteous from unrighteous wars and imposed limits upon the violence of belligerents. He was determined to demonstrate that justice would not be silenced by the clash of arms.

In warfare unwritten laws were in force between enemies. The laws were those of nature and of nations, and the precepts of Judeo-Christian charity. The dictates of right reason expressed the moral sense of rational human nature and indicated the presence of moral turpitude or the necessity of action. Grotius sought to give the principles of natural law a human, as well as a divine, authority. Perceived instinctively, they were also proclaimed by general agreement among the best minds and confirmed by the practices of civilized nations. These common dictates of conscience constituted the *jus naturale*.[8] They were supplemented by various forms of volitional law, which he classified as the *jus*

[8] 2 H. GROTIUS, DE JURE BELLI AC PACIS, bk. I, ch. I, pt. X (Carnegie Endowment trans. 1925) [hereinafter cited as DE JURE BELLI AC PACIS]. The influence of Suárez upon Grotius has been a matter of scholarly dispute. *See, e.g.*, 2 F. SUÁREZ, SELECTIONS, *supra* note 7, *Introduction*.

For general studies of Grotius, see E. DUMBAULD, THE LIFE AND LEGAL WRITINGS OF HUGO GROTIUS (1969); GREAT THINKERS OF THE SIXTEENTH AND SEVENTEENTH CENTURIES, *supra* note 7, ch. VI; T. HOLLAND, STUDIES IN INTERNATIONAL LAW (1898); T. WALKER, A HISTORY OF THE LAW OF NATIONS 278–336 (1899); J. WESTLAKE, CHAPTERS ON THE PRINCIPLES OF INTERNATIONAL LAW, ch. III (1894); J. BRIERLY, *supra* note 4, at 29–35; A. NUSSBAUM, A CONCISE HISTORY OF THE LAW OF NATIONS, ch. IV (1947); H. LAUTERPACHT, *The Grotian Tradition in International Law*, 23 BRIT. Y.B. INT'L L. 1 (1946), *reprinted in* 2 INTERNATIONAL LAW, COLLECTED PAPERS (E. Lauterpacht ed. 1975); Del Vecchio, *Grotius and the Foundations of International Law*, 37 N.Y.U.L. REV. 260 (1962); van Vollenhoven, *Grotius and the Study of Law*, 19 AJIL 1 (1925); Balogh, *The Traditional Element in Grotius' Conception of International Law*, 7 N.Y.U.L.Q. 261 (1929); C. S. EDWARDS, HUGO GROTIUS, THE MIRACLE OF HOLLAND (1981); Bull, *The Grotian Conception of International Society*, in DIPLOMATIC INVESTIGATIONS, ch. 3 (H. Butterfield & M. Wight eds. 1966).

voluntarium. Of paramount importance was the *jus gentium*. The product of human need and will, it manifested a sense of right and justice common to all nations and embodied principles that were independent of state boundaries.

For Grotius, the *jus gentium* did not have the breadth of meaning that it had for either the Roman jurists or the Spanish theologians. In the *De jure belli ac pacis* it only comprised the regulative institutions prevailing between states. As it applied to these public relations between states, the law of nations expressed the will of international society. It created obligations and conferred permissions within the limits of reason. But there were higher duties. The volitional divine law, expressed in Revelation, created the supreme obligations of humility, long-suffering, and love.[9] Like the great Spanish writers before him, Grotius denied the absolute right of rulers to engage in war. Right reason prohibits all use of force that takes away what rightly belongs to others. Yet recourse to arms might be legitimate; wars could be begun for just cause. The redress of wrongs was a principle of natural law. Since between states there is no common superior, each must protect what it conscientiously believes to be its natural rights even to the extent of inflicting punishment upon a wrong-doer. If undertaken by lawful authority and for proper reasons, warfare constitutes an enforcement of law and right. And it has a pacific purpose. If conducted according to moral precepts, it will lead to peace as its ultimate goal.[10] In spite of these concessions to violence, Grotius's work reflected a deep personal aversion to war. He had an intense desire greatly to restrict its occasions and its scope.

Wars undertaken for purposes of expediency were unjust. Defense of life and defense of property were just causes, but they were strictly construed. Anticipatory self-defense was forbidden. Complete security in this life is impossible; to suggest that the possibility of attack confers a right to attack offends natural equity and that faith in Providence which is assumed by all believers.[11] Further, if the cause of war is unjust, all acts arising from it are immoral, even, he insisted, if hostilities are commenced in a lawful way.

As for the individual called to take up arms, Grotius generally commended submission to authority. Nevertheless, the demands of conscience take precedence over legal commands. If ordered to go to war, one must not serve if the cause is clearly unjust. Where the cause is doubtful, the subject should refrain, for disobedience in such cases is a lesser evil than slaughter of the innocent.[12]

The conduct of war posed the greatest difficulties for this great Dutch hu-

[9] De jure belli ac pacis, bk. I, ch. I, pt. XV (Carnegie trans. 1925). The text of the *Prolegomena*, which appears in the Carnegie translation, is *reprinted in Grotius: Law of War and Peace*, 35 AJIL 205 (1941). *See also* Reeves, *The First Edition of Grotius' De Jure Belli Ac Pacis, 1625*, 19 *id.* at 12 (1925); and *Grotius' De Jure Belli Ac Pacis: A Bibliographic Account*, *id.* at 251.

[10] De jure belli ac pacis, bk. I, chs. II–IV; bk. II, ch. I. *Compare* F. Suárez, *On Charity*, Disputation XIII, in 2 Selections, *supra* note 7, at 799; F. Vitoria, *De jure belli*, in De Indis et de jure belli (1696) (Carnegie trans. 1917). *But see* Bull, *supra* note 8. Bull criticizes the enforcement thesis of the Grotian tradition, which assumes that a consensus can be reached within international society as to the justice of a particular war. Bull argues that the Grotian ideal is unworkable and impedes the operation of positive rules that limit the scope of war.

[11] De jure belli ac pacis, bk. II, ch. I, pt. XVII.

[12] *Id.*, bk. I, ch. IV, pt. I.3; Bk. II, ch. XXVI, pt. III.

manist. Moral justice would allow the intentional killing of others only as a just penalty or if necessary to protect life and property. And there was a general duty to avoid injury to the innocent. But the customs of warfare, which Grotius considered to be part of the *jus gentium*, conferred a general right to inflict harm upon one's enemies. The law of nations had no means of determining the justice of a particular war or the amount of fair restitution. The killing of combatants, even those who had surrendered, was permissible under the law of nations. Capture of property without limit and enslavement of defeated populations were also allowed. Here the appeal to divine law was critical. It provided the *temperamentum* that could reduce the cruelty endemic to the conduct of war.[13]

By nature one is compelled to do to the enemy whatever is necessary to conclude a just war. Yet Christian principle forbids the doing of more harm than what, in good conscience, is likely to produce good. In vindicating right, we may be obliged to refrain from insisting upon what we are entitled to by the law of nature. Even natural law is modified by the superior norm of love of one's neighbor.[14]

De jure belli ac pacis commended itself to the conscience of the age.[15] It restated the wisdom of the ancients and applied it to the unprecedented circumstances of the world of the Renaissance and Reformation. It was not original. Other jurists, such as Gentilis and Ayala, had covered much of the same ground. But Grotius showed that the totality of international relations could be systematically subject to law. He recognized the separateness and independence of states and appealed to a superstructure of legal and moral principles that should hold sway over the will of all mankind. By striking an integral combination of natural, human, and divine laws, Grotius extended the vision of the great jurist-theologians who preceded him. Like Suárez and Vitoria, Grotius contemplated the universe as subject to the reign of jurisprudence.

Yet the work was not an academic treatise. It had a didactic purpose. Grotius's aim was to touch the minds and hearts of men, especially rulers. The *De jure* is permeated with appeals to honor and to the noblest religious and moral sentiments.[16] In this sense it was not successful, as the slaughter of the religious wars continued after its publication.[17] But the approach, which emphasizes the

[13] *Id.*, bk. III, chs. IV and XI, pt. XI.

[14] *Id.*, bk. II, ch. I, pt. VIII. *Compare* bk. I, ch. II, pt. VIII.

[15] In 1623 Emeric Crucé published a pamphlet entitled *Le Nouveau Cynée*, an impassioned attempt to persuade the princes of his time of the folly of war. He wrote:

> The distances that separate domiciles cannot lessen in any way the ties created by blood, nor can they take away the basic similarity in men's nature which is the true foundation of friendship and human society. Why should I, a Frenchman, wish to harm an Englishman, a Spaniard, or an Indian? I cannot when I consider that they are men as I am, and that just as they, I am subject to error and sin, and that all nations are joined by a natural and insoluble bond. This tie means that one man cannot call another an alien unless he follows the common, deeply-rooted prejudice passed down from generation to generation.

E. CRUCÉ, THE NEW CINEAS 36–37 (C. F. & E. R. Farrell trans. 1971).

[16] *See, e.g.*, DE JURE BELLI AC PACIS, bk. III, ch. XXV; bk. I, ch. II, pt. VIII; bk. III, ch. IV, pt. XIX.

[17] *E.g.*, the Sack of Magdeburg in 1631 when 24,000 inhabitants were slaughtered. *See* H. Lauterpacht, *supra* note 8, at 14.

personal responsibility of those holding sovereign power, gives the work a permanent value. Grotius emphatically rejected the "reason of state" motivations for war and insisted that supreme temporal authority could be exercised with justice. Rulers should not take account only of persons entrusted to their care; their foreign policy must consider the interests of the whole human race.

The emerging states of the 16th and 17th centuries were the creatures of personal rule. State policy, in a dynastic system, was the policy of a ruling prince. The mystical, impersonal, and irresponsible state had yet to make its appearance. The obligations of international law could be addressed directly to a personal monarch. A majority of the rulers to whom Grotius appealed possessed supreme authority within the various states and kingdoms[18] that were then dividing among themselves the territory of Europe. Never again would they submit to a higher political authority. This insubmissive determination was reinforced by Grotius. He refuted the pretensions of universal rule made on behalf of the Holy Roman Empire and advised his readers to disregard the fantasies of Dante.[19]

II.

The identity of states and individuals is one mark of the Grotian system. The sociability of individuals is another. What distinguishes man is a desire for social life. He has a need to live in a way that is "peaceful and organized according to the measure of his intelligence with those of his own kind."[20] Endowed with a capacity for goodness and altruism, he can understand the essential moral principles derived from a rational social nature. This capacity of human nature makes the precepts of right reason the ultimate source of law. It would prove to be the weakest part of Grotius's theory.

The premise of an *appetitus socialis* was vulnerable. It was out of touch with changing conceptions of human nature, which were beginning to appear in the moral and political philosophy of the 17th century. When more fully understood by empirical and psychological observation, man seemed to be governed more by his passions than by his reason. The consolidations of state power throughout Europe were providing fresh reflections upon the origins of government and the relationships between the individual and sovereign power. Hypotheses of an original state of nature were plentiful and a liberal spirit was abroad. The individual was becoming the focal point of speculative thought. And, contrary to the Grotian assumptions, he was seen as selfish and asocial.

Hobbes's philosophy affirmed these changing conceptions of human nature.[21] In a state of nature there exist only separate individuals, among whom there is no natural tendency to live in society. Apart from political institutions, every

[18] Some international capacity, such as the power of making alliances, was conferred upon more than 300 members of the Holy Roman Empire. A. NUSSBAUM, *supra* note 8, at 115; Falk, *supra* note 6, at 985.

[19] DE JURE BELLI AC PACIS, bk. II, ch. XXII, pts. XIII–XIV.

[20] Grotius, *Prolegomena*, *supra* note 9, para. 6.

[21] Hobbes lived from 1588 to 1679. *Elementa philosophica de cive* was published in 1642 and republished in 1647. *Leviathan* was published in 1651. For a summary of Hobbes's influence upon international theory, see E. DICKINSON, THE EQUALITY OF STATES IN INTERNATIONAL LAW, ch. III (1920).

man is endowed with an equal natural right of self-preservation. It includes the right to do what is necessary to preserve life and to be the sole arbiter of what, in fact, is necessary to expand one's liberty. Hobbes drew a critical distinction between natural law and natural right. The former contained restraints necessary to make life secure. The latter implied liberty. There was a natural equality. By the law of nature every person must be accounted equal to every other.

The state of nature was a state of war. To overcome this chaos men entered, by way of covenant, into a society in which they conferred upon a sovereign power all of the rights necessary to assure peace. This sovereign mortal god or Leviathan possessed supreme and unlimited power. He enforced the covenant, protected individuals from mutual injury, and defended them from foreign invasion. So far as subjects were concerned, the will of the state was the source and criteria of right. Sovereign judgment was for them the law of God, the law of nature, and the law of nations.

Like Grotius, Hobbes believed that states, when instituted, assumed the personal qualities of men. But the conclusions Hobbes drew from the common premise were radically different. Grotius hoped that princes and statesmen would be guided in their actions by the principles of natural law and Christian love. Admittedly, there were no temporal sanctions. Yet those who denied justice would suffer inner torments, while obedience would bring peace of conscience. For Hobbes states were, with respect to each other, in a condition analogous to what prevails among individuals in a state of nature. The law of nations and the law of nature were the same. The laws that dictate to men what they ought to do and avoid with regard to one another are addressed to sovereign princes in their mutual relations. Above all, each sovereign has the same right, in protecting the safety of his people, that a particular man has in protecting the safety of his own body.[22]

Hobbes devoted passing attention to international relations. But his ideas endangered the entire Grotian vision of world order. It was a challenge that would shape much of the literature of international law for the remainder of the 17th century. Its influence can be seen most clearly in the philosophy of Spinoza.

Spinoza's views on international morality provided a more distinctive application of the Hobbesian thesis. He agreed that men, by nature, seek their own self-preservation and an unlimited extension of their liberty and power. But Spinoza's conception had deeper philosophical roots. The tendency to self-preservation is a characteristic of all beings. The power of self-maintenance is the actual essence of a particular thing. The greater its power of self-preservation in the face of external influences, the greater its reality and individual nature. From this philosophical premise Spinoza concluded that men necessarily seek to preserve their life and magnify their power and liberty. With logical rigor he applied this insight to all phases of human existence.[23]

[22] T. HOBBES, LEVIATHAN, ch. XXX; and ELEMENTA PHILOSOPHICA DE CIVE, ch. XIV.

[23] S. HAMPSHIRE, SPINOZA (1952). *See also Spinoza*, in GREAT THINKERS OF THE SIXTEENTH AND SEVENTEENTH CENTURIES, *supra* note 7, ch. IX.

Like Hobbes, Spinoza saw the natural condition of men as one of endless conflict. He also agreed that to avoid a war of all against all it was necessary for individuals to vest superior power and coercion in one man or group. And, like Hobbes, he saw power rather than some moral ideal as the fundamental concept in the study of societies. The expressions "good" and "bad" did not refer to intrinsic properties. They were objects of desire, revealing only the pleasures and aversions of the human subject.[24]

For Spinoza there was no natural law or covenant upholding a political compact. One's own safety and happiness are the ultimate measure of conduct. The sovereign serves the individual's interest so long as he is sovereign in fact and actually wields the power necessary to hold the community together. These general ideas were used to comprehend the relations between the individual and the supreme political authority within the nation-state. They were then applied *more geometrico*, to international relations.

Formation of sovereign states did not terminate the state of nature. It simply transferred it to a higher plane. Commonwealths are enemies by nature. If one wishes to attack another, it may do so. To wage war by right, all that is necessary is the will to do so. However, there need not be a permanent state of hostilities. Agreements to act in concert for the purposes of each may be formed. But they remain in force only so long as the fear of loss or hope of gain remains. Each, as a party to an alliance, has the full right to break the treaty whenever it wishes. It cannot be accused of treachery. Each, as an equal, is subject to the universal urge to self-preservation. It is entitled to exist on the basis of its own resources as soon as circumstances permit. Moreover, in international relations each sovereign submits to no higher law than the safety of his realm. Each state has an equal right to look after itself.[25]

It is difficult to imagine a more devastating attack upon the whole Grotian system of international law. Where objective moral principles were foundational, they are now nonexistent. Power replaces righteousness. The painful effort to determine the concrete conditions under which war may justly be waged is abandoned.[26] And good faith in the upholding of agreements, which was crucial to the Grotian vision of peace, falls under the weight of self-preservation.

It would be intolerable if the emerging society of independent sovereign states, now sanctified by the Treaty of Westphalia, was to be governed by power relations. Constant tensions and conflict were incompatible with the hope for universal peace inspired by the conclusion of the religious wars. The challenge to the new world order raised by new philosophical principles had to be met at a level of reflective thought. The task would involve taking account of the insights of the state of nature theorists while remaining faithful to the supremely moral outlook of *De jure belli ac pacis*. That responsibility fell to a great German Lutheran jurist, Samuel Pufendorf.

The changing currents of political thought had brought the natural conditions

[24] S. HAMPSHIRE, *supra* note 23, ch. 4.

[25] B. SPINOZA, A TREATISE ON POLITICS, ch. III (1677). H. Lauterpacht, *Spinoza and International Law*, 8 BRIT. Y.B. INT'L L. 89 (1927).

[26] *Compare* DE JURE BELLI AC PACIS, bk. II, chs. XXII–XXIV.

of human existence into a new prominence. Affirmations of individual liberty and natural equality were attracting great attention; the asocial implications of the new theories were profoundly disturbing. The chaotic coloring of the notions of a natural state and the artificial character of government were threatening to established views of national, as well as international, order. In 1672 Baron Pufendorf published *De jure naturae et gentium*.[27] He sought to preserve the principles of the Grotian system by giving its basic norms a more secure foundation than had been provided in the work of the Dutch humanist. From this vantage point, Pufendorf would strive to incorporate the positive features of Hobbesian thought into a universal system of jurisprudence. He would reject Grotius's compromises with human wisdom, express more clearly the obligations of natural law, and then rigorously apply its principles to the domain of international relations.

De jure naturae begins with a careful, systematic treatment of basic ethical issues: the origin of moral ideas, the formation of conscience, the understanding of moral principles, the freedom of the will, and the nature of moral obligation.[28] These abstract principles of correct conduct needed to be fixed upon unshakable foundations. In defining the *jus voluntarium* of divine law, Grotius had emphasized the counsels of Christian perfection. Hobbes had grounded obligations upon agreement. Neither approach was satisfactory. A rule of moral action must have the power, without compulsion, to influence the will of a rational agent reflecting upon the consequences, for good or ill, of his conduct. This is possible only if the norm appeals to free choice in circumstances where the subject perceives the rule as the command of a superior.[29]

Natural liberty is the fundamental datum. The moral laws which direct that freedom must have a transcendent origin. The precepts of natural law are deduced from human reason. Man has the power to understand, in light of his condition, that if he wishes to be happy he must order his life by the natural law.[30] But the dictates of reason cannot be autonomous. They cannot have the force of law unless we presuppose the existence of God and his Providence.[31]

[27] *De jure naturae* was preceded by *Elementorum jurisprudentiae universalis* (The Elements of Universal Jurisprudence) in 1660 and followed by *De officio hominis et civis* (The Duty of Man and Citizen) in 1673.

[28] S. PUFENDORF, DE JURE NATURAE ET GENTIUM, bk. I (Carnegie trans. 1934) [hereinafter cited as DE JURE NATURAE]. *Compare* ELEMENTORUM JURISPRUDENTIAE *passim* (Carnegie trans. 1931).

[29] DE JURE NATURAE, bk. I, ch. VI. *Compare* ELEMENTORUM JURISPRUDENTIAE, Definition XIV. Unlike Grotius, Pufendorf did not admit of a *jus voluntarium divinum* regulating international behavior. *Natural law*, which is common to all men, is derived from the interaction of reason and will. *Civil law* refers to the rules imposed in a single state. Moral theology concerns the dictates given to Christians in Holy Scripture. Following the Lutheran tradition, natural law, directed to the external conduct of man, makes man a worthy member of human society. The precepts of moral theology, directed at the heart, train the citizen of the heavenly city who is only a sojourner on earth. *See* DE OFFICIO HOMINIS ET CIVIS, Greeting (Carnegie trans. 1927) [hereinafter cited as DE OFFICIO].

[30] DE JURE NATURAE, bk. II, ch. I, paras. 3–8; bk. II, ch. III, paras. 13–15.

[31]

> [W]e cannot agree with Grotius, when he says in his Prolegomena that natural laws "will have some place, even if we should grant—what can only be done with the greatest impiety—that there is no God, or that He does not concern Himself with the affairs of men" [*Prole-*

In the Grotian system, the precepts of natural law were intimately bound up with the idea of man as a social being. The presumed sociability was mocked by Hobbes and Spinoza. The genius of Pufendorf lies in his ability to grant the premises of the state of nature theory and turn them to his advantage. The inclination to social life is now a consequence of the instinct towards self-preservation. The individual cannot exist without the help of his fellow man. Yet it must be conceded that he is "malicious, petulant, and easily irritated," as well as inclined to do injury to others. There is, naturally, only one solution:

> For such an animal to live and enjoy the good things that in this world attend his condition, it is necessary that he be sociable, that is, be willing to join himself with others like him, and conduct himself towards them in such a way that, far from having any cause to do him harm, they may feel that there is reason to preserve and increase his good fortune. . . . And so it will be a fundamental law of nature, that "Every man, so far as in him lies, should cultivate and preserve toward others a sociable attitude, which is peaceful and agreeable at all times to the nature and end of the human race." . . . [B]y a sociable attitude we mean an attitude of each man towards every other man, by which each is understood to be bound to the other by kindness, peace, and love, and therefore by a mutual obligation.[32]

Societies are not introduced to temper an inherent anarchy. They appear because they are essential to the full preservation of individual human existence.

According to Pufendorf, the error of Hobbes—and Spinoza[33]—lies in their inability fully to grasp the essential distinction between man and other animals. The distinguishing feature is reason, by which Pufendorf meant the power to discern the good rather than the faculty of logical thought. The lower animals' actions are determined by desire and passion. They are not constrained by an inward moral sense. Man's dignity, by contrast, lies in a voluntary conformity to rule. Unfettered liberty, free of all restraints, can be attributed only to God. Such a lawless liberty is inappropriate for man because it is not compatible with his nature. His supreme dignity lies in the possession of an immortal soul whose operations are manifest in intellect, judgment, and moral choice.[34]

The natural liberty of man is affirmed, but as conditioned by reason and restrained by natural law. Equality is also accepted by Pufendorf. All are naturally equal, endowed with a sense of self-esteem which is rooted in human dignity. Natural law requires that each man should treat another as his equal by nature, as much a man as he is himself. But, if measured by moral reason, equality should not be a cause of fear and discord. The weak should not envy the strong and those who excel should not disdain the less fortunate.[35]

> *gomena*, para. 11]. For if some man should devise such an impious and idiotic theory, and imagine that mankind had sprung from itself, then the dictates of reason could in no possible way have the force of law, since law necessarily supposes a superior.

DE JURE NATURAE, bk. II, ch. III, para. 19. *Compare* the study of Grotius by Professor Edwards, *supra* note 8. The thesis of that work is that Grotius was not a secularist but rather retained theological presuppositions in his work.

[32] *Id.*, bk. II, ch. III, para. 15.

[33] *Id.*, bk. II, ch. II.

[34] *Id.*, bk. II, ch. III, paras. 3–8.

[35] *Id.*, bk. III, ch. II.

Hobbes's opinion that the law of nature and the law of nations were the same was accepted by Pufendorf. He also accepted the assumption that separate states, having no common political superior, stood in the same relation to each other as men in a state of nature.[36] He hoped that here, as with the premises of natural liberty and equality, he could transform the assumptions of the new political theories in the light of moral perception. In doing so, however, Pufendorf would weaken one of the essential elements of the Grotian jurisprudential system.

Like the scholastic jurists, Grotius had included the *jus gentium* in his universal theory of law. The great Dutch reformer, however, had restricted its scope. Suárez carefully distinguished the *jus naturale* from the *jus gentium*, giving each a legitimacy within its respective sphere of reference. Both were differentiated from the *jus civile*. The *jus gentium* was an independent source of law that manifests the jural authority of mankind.[37] It included the law common to all nations as well as those public rules which prevail between states. Grotius discarded the former and sought to preserve the latter under the category of *jus voluntarium*.[38] Under Pufendorf, both the broad and the more restricted *jus gentium* were excluded from the definition of law.

The so-called law of nations does not exist because it does not bind in conscience. Neither the customs of nations nor the practices of states establish obligatory norms because they do not proceed from a superior. Practices that conform to the requirements of rational nature are binding as precepts of natural law. Law only arises through the principles that can be derived from universal reason.[39] In the civil laws of separate nations those elements which are universal belong to natural law. The rest are unique to each separate legal system. Law, strictly so-called, consists only of natural law at one extreme and *jus civile*, or civil law, at the other.

The law of nations was eliminated in order to make international relations more securely subject to laws whose ethical appeal would be compelling. The difficulties experienced by Grotius in admitting the validity of barbarous customs as part of the law of nations could be avoided. By extending the scope of the precepts of right reason in the context of a systematic moral treatise, Pufendorf hoped both to avoid the anarchy implicit in the state of nature and to assert the superiority of the rules of natural law over the principles derived from purely human sources.

The examples that the German jurist used to illustrate his thesis would startle the modern reader. With respect to the law of ambassadors, envoys by the law of nature are inviolable. The rules are derived by simple deduction from an obvious axiom. Natural law requires the pursuit of peace. By necessary inference it provides for the safety of those without whom the end cannot be secured. The ambassador is immune from the jurisdiction of the receiving state with respect to the business of his sovereign. But natural law only protects the envoy with respect to his peaceful pursuits. If an ambassador resides at a foreign

[36] *Id.*, bk. II, ch. III.

[37] F. SUÁREZ, DE LEGIBUS, *supra* note 7, bk. II, chs. XVII–XX.

[38] *See* DE JURE BELLI AC PACIS, bk. I, ch. I, pt. XIV.

[39] DE JURE NATURAE, bk. II, ch. III, para. 23.

court primarily to obtain the secrets of the other state, all other privileges may be withdrawn at the discretion of his host. In such circumstances there is no breach of law, provided the sovereign prince is willing to see his own ambassador similarly treated.[40]

The law of nations becomes superfluous once it is seen that institutions that previous writers classified under *jus gentium* actually belong to natural law. This perception arises from an elevated understanding of the structure of international relations. Hobbes and Spinoza assumed that the state of mutual conflict between individuals, which is relieved by the establishment of sovereign states, is then transferred to the relations between sovereigns. For Pufendorf, the natural state of men, even apart from their submission to civil law within commonwealths, is one of peace rather than war.[41] Where reason rather than passion controls the actions of princes, a universal measure of judgment is operative. It reveals the general rules of living with others. Man is, admittedly, divided. But he knows that submission to his immediate anxious desires leads to his destruction and the ruin of those under his care. The long-range view, encouraged by reflective reason, brings peace and security as well as personal respect.[42]

The inclination towards peace moves an individual subject to obey his sovereign's commands.[43] It also guides that same sovereign in his international behavior. Obeying only the commands of his Creator, he knows that he should not harm another prince who is not injuring him or interfere with his possessions. And his reason tells him he should faithfully perform whatever agreements he has made with another head of state. The supremacy of the moral law guarantees the observance of these rules of right reason. Treaties of peace are unnecessary. They add nothing to the obligations of natural law nor do they make the performance of these universal duties more certain. A civilized man, having reverence for God, does not make agreements that require any more than what the law of nature already requires.[44]

Pufendorf's *De jure naturae et gentium* makes a heroic effort to sustain the Grotian vision of universal peace against the threats implicit in changing conceptions of human nature. There is a constant appeal to the higher powers of reason and will, which are designed by divine plan to control the passions and desires of our lower nature. But this Lutheran jurist was fully aware of man's depravity. From entirely different premises, his ideas about the conduct of human affairs in an unorganized international society were painfully similar to the conclusions reached by Hobbes and Spinoza.

Greed and lust for power move the hearts of men. Even the gentle teachings of Christ cannot eliminate the evil, oppression, and treachery that so often rent the fabric of human order. What was said of the Romans and Carthaginians could be applied to all nations: Between them there is "either war, preparation for war, or unsettled peace." Peace is natural. However, since it is moral, it belongs to what ought to be. Without precautions it does not guarantee the

[40] *Ibid.*

[41] *Id.*, bk. II, ch. II, para. 9. *See* the discussion in E. DICKINSON, *supra* note 21, at 75–81.

[42] DE JURE NATURAE, bk. II, ch. II.

[43] DE OFFICIO, bk. II, ch. XVIII.

[44] DE JURE NATURAE, bk. II, ch. II, para. 11. *But see* DE OFFICIO, chs. XVI and XVII.

security of states. Repose enjoyed amidst ambitious and powerful neighbors is extremely dangerous. If peace is desired, Pufendorf counsels, it is best to be prepared for war.[45]

A more sober estimate of reality had begun to temper the post-Grotian idealism. And state of nature speculation had an even deeper influence. While he sought to contradict the view that relations between nations were inherently hostile, Pufendorf retained the essential structural dichotomies assumed by Hobbes and Spinoza. In their mutual relations sovereigns assume the position of individuals in a state of nature. Like individuals, they are bound by natural law. But individuals who have become members of a civil society submit to lawful authority. This greatly restricts their natural liberties. The same cannot be said of sovereigns who confront each other, as equals, on the plane of international relations.

The absence of a common superior enhances the dignity of each sovereign.[46] But it also qualifies the self-enforcement of moral principles. This is obvious in Pufendorf's treatment of questions of legitimate violence. Fear of a foreign prince is not a just cause of war. One must be morally certain that the other intends injury. However, if just cause exists, and efforts at peaceful settlement fail, one must seriously weigh any increase in the adversary's power. The law of nature imposes mutual duties of peace. But if peace is broken, the injured state can use force against the aggression to any degree it thinks desirable.

Such a natural right exists for sovereigns even though it is no longer possessed by individuals living within a state. This contrast led Pufendorf to some alarming conclusions. If the injury is slight, the sovereign may use whatever degree of violence necessary to assure security against future aggression. And rules of proportionality do not apply. They only are relevant to the judgments of civil tribunals where punishment is imposed by a superior upon a subject.[47]

Grotius had rejected anticipatory self-defense. The possibility of attack could not justify the use of force. If insecurity was the cause, trust in Divine Providence was the remedy.[48] But if the aggressive intent is clear, Pufendorf asked, must the potential victims passively await their fate? The first duty of natural law is that man should direct his attention to himself. He will fulfill his duties towards others more readily if he first attends to his own preservation and development.[49] From this principle Pufendorf reasoned that one is not obliged to await another's attack.

[45] DE JURE NATURAE, bk. II, ch. II, para. 12.

[46]

> Government, indeed, is a natural thing, and it was nature's intention that men should set up governments among themselves. But it was no less the purpose of nature that he who holds supreme authority over other men should be free from any interference on their part, and should thereby enjoy natural liberty; unless, indeed, we choose to admit into the same order something superior even to what is supreme. And for this reason it is in accordance with nature that the man who has no master should govern himself and his actions by the dictates of his own reason.

Id., bk. II, ch. II, para. 4. *See also* E. DICKINSON, *supra* note 21, ch. III.

[47] DE JURE NATURAE, bk. VIII, ch. VI, paras. 3–7. *Compare* bk. II, ch. V, paras. 4–8. There is some slight qualification in DE OFFICIO, bk. II, ch. XVI, para. 12.

[48] DE JURE BELLI AC PACIS, bk. II, ch. I, pts. XVI–XVII.

[49] DE JURE NATURAE, bk. II, ch. IV.

The aggressor is the one who first conceives a plan to harm another, as well as the one who actually employs violence. Within states, innocent defense is greatly limited. Those who live in states cannot attack one who intends to injure them. The potential aggressor must be brought before the common sovereign and made to give a bond of peace. Between *sovereigns* it is different. Innocence may appeal to Providence, but the prince who takes insufficient precautions should not expect divine intervention. The wise statesman thinks of war even in times of peace. He is entitled to take defensive measures against those who are preparing to do him harm.[50]

Similar conclusions were reached with respect to agreements with adversaries. Good faith performance of treaties was a central theme in the Grotian theory and it called for the performance of pacts with enemies.[51] But, according to Pufendorf, if the hostilities were caused by the adversary's injustice, the injured party could inflict harm without limit. It is confusing to demand that a sovereign keep faith with an enemy who has not renounced his unlawful aims. To the degree that such agreements are observed, they have their justification in utility and necessity. They are not moral obligations.[52]

Pufendorf had an aversion to treaties promising peace and friendship since these duties were imposed by the higher principles of natural law. If a treaty of peace is to have any meaning, the underlying dispute must be resolved. Grotius had sought to resolve the difficult question whether imposed peace treaties, accepted for fear of further devastation, created any permanent duties of performance. His conclusion was that under the law of nations such treaties were valid if the war had been formally declared on both sides. He qualified his judgment by an appeal to higher standards of personal conduct. A prince who has extorted a promise from a defeated adversary in an unjust war cannot retain what he has received because to do so would violate the honor and duty of a good man.[53]

The validity of treaties imposed by military superiority has always been a major concern of Western legal thought. The conclusions reached by Grotius have been generally followed, if reluctantly, by other international scholars. Interests of general stability would seem to preclude revision even if the victor engaged in the war for unlawful reasons.[54] Pufendorf's disagreement on this point was prophetic, especially when one considers the fate of the Treaty of Versailles at the conclusion of the First World War.

The appeal to honor is plainly useless because Grotius insisted that restitution must be consensual. Pufendorf argued that if the war was unjust, the vanquished—assuming he had, before defeat, sought settlement by peaceful means—could forcibly seek restitution as soon as he recovered sufficient military power to do so.[55]

[50] *Id.*, bk. II, ch. V, para. 6.

[51] De jure belli ac pacis, bk. II, chs. XI–XV; bk. III, chs. XI–XX.

[52] De jure naturae, bk. VIII, ch. VII.

[53] De jure belli ac pacis, bk. III, ch. XIX, pt. XI.

[54] J. Brierly, *Some Considerations on the Obsolescence of Treaties*, in The Basis of Obligation in International Law 115 (H. Lauterpacht & C. H. M. Waldock eds. 1958).

[55] De jure naturae, bk. VIII, ch. VIII.

III.

The Grotian vision of world order assumed the legitimacy of the emerging society of independent states and kingdoms. The hope was that the field of international relations could be regulated by universal principles. At one level, Pufendorf reinforced and elevated that vision. The duties of sovereigns were clarified by a systematic ethic. Expectations of compliance were enhanced by an unequivocal attribution of moral commands to a sovereign God. And Pufendorf gave the Grotian vision a deeper existential foundation. Responding imaginatively to state of nature theories, he made coherent connections between transcendent norms and the natural liberty of states. But the Grotian principles, though widely acclaimed, proved incapable of bringing order and stability to the destructive rivalries inherent in the nation-state system. Force, rather than the virtues and moderation of rulers, became the measure of international behavior.[56]

The 17th-century theories of international law grounded their principles upon the power of reason, morality, and natural law. Their subsequent impotence can be traced to several factors. For one, the spiritual and cultural consequences of the Reformation had created a milieu that was unreceptive to appeals for intellectual or ethical uniformity. Grotius's attempt to replace religious unity with a solidarity based upon reason and the general heritage of the West could not take root in such an environment. By emphasizing the divine origins of natural law, Pufendorf gave global jurisprudence a theological stature. But such higher speculation can have a formative influence upon human affairs only if the underlying religious principles are widely shared. In the Europe of the 17th century, the Lutheran jurist could not expect to command the general respect achieved by a Spanish jurist writing in an earlier era. Indeed, the theological gloss was inimical to the spirit of the age. Grotius, sensing the rise of secularism, had appealed to the general culture of Europe as a confirmation of his principles of law and ethics. Pufendorf rejected the *jus gentium* because he believed that there could not be a positive law of nations among equals. In so doing, he implicitly denied those same states the dignity of participating in a law-creating process. And his concessions to human depravity weakened the fragile authority of transcendent principles.

In Grotian and post-Grotian thought, law was grounded upon human sociability.[57] This characteristic distinguished man from other species. It provided the individual, and the state, with an opportunity to accommodate self-preservation and independence with the need for cooperation and mutual support. The coercive power of the absolute monarchs might reconcile sociability and order within the nation-state. It was more problematic whether such a principle

[56] *See* the description of the climate in the 18th century in F. RUDDY, INTERNATIONAL LAW IN THE ENLIGHTENMENT, ch. 2 (1975).

[57] In the 18th century Jean Barbeyrac translated Pufendorf's *De jure naturae et gentium* and the *De jure belli ac pacis* into French, with notes and cross-references. Barbeyrac was then translated into English and appended to English editions of the two classics. There was no doubt of Barbeyrac's preference for Pufendorf, and his attitude tended to discredit Grotius and spread the ideas of the German jurist. E. DICKINSON, *supra* note 21, at 83–84. Over time, the theories of Pufendorf and Grotius were understood as being mutually antagonistic.

could establish harmony upon the plane of interstate relations. Any attempt to establish a general order upon a societal principle implies that in cases of conflict the right of others, or the general interest, will prevail over the ambitions of an individual member. The state, as a collective moral person, was expected to discern the dictates of right reason as they are derived from the condition of mankind formed into a world society. But in post-Grotian thought the naturalism of Pufendorf was tipping the balance in favor of the individual interest conceived as the right of self-preservation. Furthermore, the basic identification between the state as an artificial person and the natural man, in the circumstances of that time, necessarily weakened the ideal of a society of nations.

Naturalist theory assumed that, cognizant of the hazards of life in a state of nature, the individual, if civilized, had become a member of an organized commonwealth. The relationship between commonwealths, by contrast, was one of natural liberty. And this was appropriate. All kingdoms were by their own nature free and independent. They had equal rights and none had legitimate superiority over another. Social organization was therefore unnecessary. The Holy Roman Empire was an abomination. And a league to enforce universal peace was unnecessary since, according to Pufendorf, it would add nothing to obligations already imposed upon states by the natural law.

The emergence of a multiplicity of states established some kind of society among them. It was too close to natural liberty and equality to create a predominate sense of mutual need and interdependence. Dante's vision of a world state was thoroughly discredited. The ideal of social unity envisioned by Suárez was rapidly disappearing from the European imagination. The alleged society had no reality apart from that of its members.

The separate states of the Westphalian system stood in relation to each other as individuals in a state of nature. Why did the jurists of the 17th century not perceive a parallel need for organized existence? It was assumed that upon the formation of nation-states the state of nature was simply transferred to the plane of international relations. The individual person, possessed of natural liberty, could grasp the necessity of entering a civil society to relieve the perils of isolated existence. Why was there not a similar imperative for states who were in parity with natural man? The simple answer is that the historical conditions of that century were inhospitable to such speculation. The Treaty of Westphalia had ratified the independence of states and had broken the bonds of submission to all higher authority. But the resistance to international organization was based upon deeper reasons, which implicate the intellectual outlook of that critical period of global history.

The Renaissance and the Reformation had drawn liberally upon classical learning in an attempt to understand, and justify, the changing culture and political conditions of Europe. The philosophers and jurists who sought to explain the profound innovations they had experienced were selective in their recourse to antiquity. Individualism and independence required modifications of traditional ideas concerning man and society. This was particularly true of matters of political theory.

The insubmissiveness of the age demanded adjustments in traditional ideas of hierarchical power. Dante's vision of world order assumed that the discord among states and kingdoms required the establishment of a supreme political authority that could impartially administer a world government. The common good of the universal community would then take precedence over the disparate interests of separate commonwealths. Hoping to end papal interference in secular affairs, he envisioned the Church as possessing universal authority in matters spiritual, while the Holy Roman emperor would exercise supreme power in matters of temporal peace and prosperity.[58] The *De monarchia*, in its essential preference for the Roman tradition, was the reflection of a particular culture. But it was also a manifestation of wider philosophical principles. It was an extension of the Aristotelian view of human nature.

For Aristotle man was a political animal. The impulse to form political societies is a natural tendency, born of the desire for fulfillment. The first relationship is the family; the first society, the village. The development continues:

> When several villages are united in a single complete community, large enough to be nearly or quite self-sufficing, the state comes into existence, originating in the bare needs of life, and continuing in existence for the sake of a good life. And therefore, if the earlier forms of society are natural, so is the state, for it is the end of them, and the nature of a thing is its end. For what each thing is when fully developed, we call its nature, whether we are speaking of a man, a horse, or a family. Besides, the final cause and end of a thing is the best, and to be self-sufficing is the end and the best.
>
> Hence it is evident that the state is a creation of nature, and that man is by nature a political animal. And he who by nature and not by mere accident is without a state, is either a bad man or above humanity; he is like the
>
> "Tribeless, lawless, hearthless one,"
>
> whom Homer denounces—the natural outcast is forthwith a lover of war; he may be compared to an isolated piece at draughts.[59]

Aristotle appears to consecrate the state as the highest good. But the deeper meaning is that any particular form of political organization is a variable, human need the constant. Man wishes not only to live but to live well. The tendency to form political communities is inherently dynamic. It involves indeterminate transitions from one form of political organization to another as the requirements of unity, peace, and development are transformed by historical circumstances. Changes are motivated by an awareness that an existing form of government is inadequate to the complete realization of human needs.

Dante's vision is compatible with the Aristotelian political philosophy. The poet's intuition is of a need to move, on the universal plane, from the existing state system to a more adequate form of political organization. Between the

[58] DANTE, DE MONARCHIA, bk. III. Pope Boniface VIII in the bull *Unam Sanctum* (1302) had claimed absolute sovereignty, subject to divine law, over all of Christendom. It was provoked by the attempt of the French King, Philip IV, to tax the French clergy without prior papal consent. *See* Falk, *supra* note 6, at 981.

[59] ARISTOTLE, POLITICS, bk. I, ch. 2.

14th and 17th centuries, political reflection, if it had remained in touch with ancient wisdom, might have given a theoretical explanation for the necessity of world government. The decline of the Holy Roman Empire and the rising power of the nation-states made such a transition, as a practical matter, virtually impossible. But speculative thought was also moving in different directions.

John of Paris, in his *De potentale regia et papali*, written at the beginning of the 14th century, took the same themes upon which Dante was meditating and reached quite different conclusions. Dante attributed supreme world authority to the Roman emperor and absolute spiritual authority to the Church. John of Paris argued that the Church requires universality but political authority does not. He assumed that a natural instinct gives rise to civil society. But men are diverse in interest. Their dispersal into separate states and kingdoms is also natural because it reflects such diversity. They are self-sufficient as well as independent communities. There is no need for them to be subordinate to a higher political authority.[60]

The struggle against papal supremacy was of special importance to France. In the same century Pierre Du Bois, a French *avocat royal*, published *De recuperatione Terre Sancte*. It was a plea for general peace amongst Christians in order that they unite for a crusade to recover the Holy Land. But the real intention was French domination. Du Bois proposed transferring the temporal power of the papacy to France and uniting the whole world under the rule of the king of France.[61]

Claims were made on behalf of national independence against both papal supremacy and the universal authority of the emperor. Before the Reformation, some critics of the emperor sought to reduce his political supremacy in a manner consistent with the general theory of a universal Christian society. Bartolus of Sassoferrato wrote that any assertion that the emperor was not the monarch of the entire world would be heretical. Yet, insisting upon the de facto independence of Italian city-states, he would attribute only a vague spiritual authority to the emperor.[62]

By the 16th century jurists and theologians were denying, with greater frequency, all claims to universal power, whether made on behalf of the papacy or the emperor.[63] In these historical circumstances, deeper reflection upon the political requirements of mankind could not be pursued in the cosmopolitan spirit of the Greek philosophers. A growing national consciousness and consolidation of territorial power were making the notion of state self-sufficiency a compelling ideal. The case of Suárez is, in this regard, particularly instructive. An ardent and loyal Catholic, he defended spiritual authority against monar-

[60] G. SABINE, A HISTORY OF POLITICAL THEORY, ch. XIV (3d ed. 1961).

[61] *Pierre Du Bois and the Domination of France*, in SOCIAL AND POLITICAL IDEAS OF SOME GREAT MEDIEVAL THINKERS, *supra* note 1.

[62] *See* Gross, *supra* note 6, at 30–31.

[63] When the Emperor Charles V was Charles I of Spain, Vitoria held that the emperor is not the lord of the whole world and that the Pope did not have universal civil authority. According to the Spanish jurist, the Pope had the right to pass judgment upon the conflicting claims of Christian sovereigns where war is imminent. DE INDIS, *supra* note 10, sec. II. Soto reached similar conclusions, as did Suárez. *See* B. HAMILTON, POLITICAL THOUGHT IN 16TH CENTURY SPAIN (1963).

chical absolutism. But he was also favored by Philip II, and his philosophy of law made full deference to the nation-state as a supreme political authority.

For Suárez, civil authority resided in the people as a community. Kings rule by consent. When the power is transferred to the king, he becomes the vicar of God and must be obeyed by the populace. Monarchical power, unless it lapses into tyranny, is internally absolute. The power is superior to the kingdom that confers it. Does the sovereign owe allegiance to any higher temporal authority? The Christian republic was in theory a hierarchical society; it had joint supreme rulers with different spheres of competence, the Pope and the emperor. In fact, by the latter half of the 16th century most of Europe had made effective claim to independence. The empire was a chimera and no effective authority was exercised beyond the emperor's ancestral territory. The Christian society was breaking up and being replaced by a series of strong nation-states.

Suárez dealt with these changing realities as a jurist. He qualified the self-sufficiency of states by affirming the existence of a world society. All are bound to observe the *jus gentium*, the positive unwritten human law established by the customs of nearly all nations. Closely related to natural law, its precepts are in accord with nature. Their reasonableness elicits consent. And their establishment by common usage creates a general obligation. But the power of kings could not be subject to any higher *coercive* law. No civil laws are established that universally bind all men. There is no legislative power with jurisdiction over the whole world:

> For the power in question does not reside in the whole community of mankind, since the whole of mankind does not constitute one single commonwealth or kingdom. Nor does that power reside in any one individual, since such an individual would have to receive it from the hands of men, and this is inconceivable, inasmuch as men have never agreed to confer it [thus], nor to establish one sole head over themselves. Furthermore, not even by title of war, whether justly or unjustly, has there at any time been a prince who made himself temporal sovereign over the whole world. This assertion is clearly borne out by history. And therefore, the ordinary course of human nature points to the conclusion that a human legislative power of universal character and world-wide extent does not exist and has never existed, nor is it morally possible that it should have done so.[64]

The conclusion reflects the commanding influence that the idea of national sovereignty held over the imaginations of philosophers. The self-sufficient nation-state, which recognizes no higher temporal power, is the irreducible datum. This independence, while not subject to political authority, is, in the mind of

[64] F. SUÁREZ, DE LEGIBUS, *supra* note 7, bk. III, ch. IV, para. 7. On the *jus gentium*, see *id.*, bk. II, ch. XIX, para. 6.

The claim has been made that the two conceptions—that of self-sufficiency on the one hand, and membership in a wider community on the other—are fundamentally irreconcilable. J. BRIERLY, *Suárez's Vision of a World Community*, in THE BASIS OF OBLIGATION, *supra* note 54, at 358, 362. This criticism would seem to reflect, albeit unconsciously, the conception of law derived from modern legal positivism. The Spanish jurist-theologian accepted the *jus gentium* as law even though not the command of a superior. A more telling criticism would be that Suárez's conception is incomplete or insufficient.

Suárez, under the reign of a conception of law conceived as an embodiment of eternal justice. Universal jurisprudence fills the vacuum left by the absence of universal jurisdiction.[65]

The same ideal sustained the international vision of Grotius. There was no perceived need for a political conception of international relations. The genius of Aristotle was acknowledged, but now an instinct for society or sociableness replaced the Aristotelian notion of a natural impetus towards political life.

The mutual relations engendered by sociability are measured and guided by the law of nature. Expediency is the cause of the nation-state and its internal order of positive laws.[66] The establishment of states has created some form of society among their members. As with the natural state of individuals, the law necessary to regulate the mutual relations of these self-sufficient political communities is the natural law:

> [T]he natural state of nations with regard to one another is a state of social life and peace. This society is also one of equality and independence, which establishes an equality of right among them, and pledges them to have the same regard and respect for one another. Hence the general principle of the law of nations is nothing more than the general law of sociability, which obliges nations having intercourse with one another to the practice of the same duties as those to which individuals are naturally subject. . . .[67]

The new world society that was appearing as a result of the Westphalia settlement was based on the absolute sovereignty of its constituent members. It was accompanied by the vision of an order generated by the highest principles of reason and charity. Before the close of the 17th century, the inadequacy of the ideal had become apparent. Efforts were made to establish an international authority. Some aimed at a European political system with a revived position for the emperor. But, in the main, they were inspired by the exigencies of

65

> The Spanish mind . . . contemplates the universe as subject to the reign of jurisprudence . . . Suarez' treatise . . . lifts jurisprudence from being the science of individual litigation into a philosophy of the universe. This was the atmosphere in which International Law grew up, and without which it was impossible that it should have grown up.

J. N. FIGGIS, STUDIES OF POLITICAL THOUGHT FROM GERSON TO GROTIUS 188–89 (1907).

66 "[I]n the first instance men joined themselves together to form a civil society not by command of God, but of their own free will, being influenced by their experience of the weakness of isolated households against attack. From this origin, the civil power is derived. . . ." DE JURE BELLI AC PACIS, bk. I, ch. IV, pt. VII.3.

> [I]t is not enough to say that man is by Nature herself drawn into civil society, so that without it he cannot and will not live. For surely it is evident that man is an animal of the kind that loves itself and its interest to the utmost degree. When, therefore, he voluntarily seeks civil society, it must be that he has had regard to some utility which he will derive from it for himself. And though, outside of society with his kind, man would have been much the most miserable of creatures, still the natural desires and necessities of man could have been abundantly satisfied through the first communities, and the duties performed out of humanity or by agreement. Hence it cannot at once be inferred from man's sociability that his nature does tend exactly to civil society.

S. PUFENDORF, DE OFFICIO, bk. II, ch. V, para. 2.

67 Burlamaqui, *Principes du droit naturel, quoted in* E. DICKINSON, *supra* note 21, at 88.

practical politics rather than reflective thought.[68] Meanwhile, the imperative need for specific rules to regulate interstate conflict was clearly perceived. In such decentralized circumstances, the lacunae could only be filled by reasserting the authority of the customary law of nations and the legitimacy of law creation through state practice.[69]

Within the fragile structure of sociability, legal positivism was both necessary and inevitable. In one sense, it supplemented the higher authority of natural law. There also was a common bond between the positivists and the natural law theorists. The positivists believed that the potential chaos of interstate relations could be subject to legal rules. Grotius sought to establish juridical relations among nations without the institution of political authority. Subsequent visions of world order would prove to be variations on these themes.

[68] *See, e.g.,* the appraisal of Sully's *Grand Design* in F. HINSLEY, *supra* note 1, at 25–32.

[69] J. WESTLAKE, *supra* note 8, ch. IV. The gaps were being filled by jurists such as Bynkershoek, who hoped to ground a common law of nations upon reason and custom. *See* his QUAESTIONUM JURIS PUBLICI (Carnegie trans. 1930). And *see* the reaction to Pufendorf in S. RACHEL, DE JURE NATURAE ET GENTIUM DISSERTATIONES (1676) (Carnegie trans. 1916).

CONTEMPT, CRISIS, AND THE COURT: THE WORLD COURT AND THE HOSTAGE RESCUE ATTEMPT

*By Ted L. Stein**

The "*Hostages*" case was surely one of the most remarkable ever to be presented to the World Court for a decision.[1] And among its remarkable features, none is more striking than that prior to delivery of the Court's Judgment the United States attempted to rescue the hostages by force. This attempt to accomplish by force what the United States had sought to achieve through the judicial process raised profound issues regarding the relationship between the use of force and adjudication, the purpose and effect of interim measures of protection, and the role of the Court in the contemporary international order. This article will analyze these issues in the light of the Court's treatment of the rescue attempt.

I. The Court's Response

The Court's response to the rescue attempt is contained in the final two paragraphs of its opinion.[2] Considering that it could not "let pass without comment the incursion into the territory of Iran made by United States military units,"[3] the Court made a series of interrelated observations. First, the Court conceded the "understandable preoccupations" of the United States for the safety of the hostages and acknowledged the "understandable feelings of frustration"[4] at their continued detention, notwithstanding two resolutions of the United Nations Security Council[5] and the Court's own Order requiring their

* Assistant Professor of Law, University of Washington School of Law. While a member of the staff of the Office of the Legal Adviser, U.S. Department of State, the author participated in the preparation and presentation of the United States case before the International Court of Justice in the *Hostages* case. The views expressed here are the author's own and not necessarily those of the Department of State.

The author wishes to acknowledge the contributions of his colleagues William T. Burke, John O. Haley, Robert Berring, Stewart Jay, and Thomas C. Armitage who read an earlier version of this manuscript and provided many helpful suggestions.

[1] Judge Morozov, writing from a perspective admittedly somewhat distant from the author's, commented: "*The situation in which the Court has carried on its judicial deliberations in the current case has no precedent in the whole history of the administration of international justice either before this Court, or before any international judicial institution.*" Case Concerning United States Diplomatic and Consular Staff in Tehran (United States of America v. Iran), [1980] ICJ Rep. 3, 53 (Morozov, J., dissenting) (emphasis in original). The decision is *reprinted in* 74 AJIL 746 (1980), 19 ILM 553 (1980).

[2] *Id.*, paras. 93 and 94. Earlier in the opinion (para. 32), the Court had summarized the facts of the rescue mission based on information provided by the United States in response to the Court's request. *Id.*, para. 32.

[3] *Id.*, para. 93.

[4] *Ibid.*

[5] In Resolution 457, adopted on Dec. 4, 1979, the Council "[u]rgently" called upon Iran "to release immediately the personnel of the Embassy of the United States of America being held in Teheran, to provide them protection and to allow them to leave the country." The Council reiterated this call in paragraph 3 of Resolution 461 of Dec. 31, 1979.

release.[6] This expression of sympathy was coupled with an express disavowal of any finding that the rescue attempt was unlawful. As the Court carefully noted, "neither the question of the legality of the operation of 24 April 1980, under the Charter of the United Nations and under general international law, nor any possible question of responsibility flowing from it, is before the Court."[7] In sum, the Court was not prepared to say that the operation was either morally blameworthy or legally impermissible.[8]

[6] In paragraph 47(1)(A)(ii) of its Order of Dec. 15, 1979, the Court indicated that pending a final decision in the case, the

> Government of the Islamic Republic of Iran should ensure the immediate release, without any exception, of all persons of United States nationality who are or have been held in the Embassy of the United States of America or in the Ministry of Foreign Affairs in Tehran, or who have been held as hostages elsewhere, and afford full protection to all such persons, in accordance with the treaties in force between the two States, and with general international law.

[1979] ICJ REP. 7, para. 47(1)(A)(ii). The Order is *reprinted in* 74 AJIL 266 (1980), 19 ILM 139 (1980).

[7] [1980] ICJ REP. 3, para. 94. The Court thus left to another day, a day that one suspects will never come, a definitive statement of its views regarding the law governing the use of force in defense of the lives of nationals abroad. The question has long been the subject of sharp controversy, both among states and learned commentators. The authorities are exhaustively canvassed in Dr. Brownlie's classic work, I. BROWNLIE, INTERNATIONAL LAW AND THE USE OF FORCE BY STATES 289–301 (1963), and have more recently been reviewed in connection with the Entebbe and *Mayaguez* affairs; *see, e.g.*, Friedlander, *Mayaguez in Retrospect: Humanitarian Intervention or Showing the Flag*, 22 ST. LOUIS U.L.J. 601 (1979); Murphy, *State Self-Help and Problems of Public International Law*, in LEGAL ASPECTS OF INTERNATIONAL TERRORISM 553 (A. Evan & J. Murphy eds. 1978); Paust, *Entebbe and Self-Help: The Israeli Response to Terrorism*, 2 FLETCHER F. 86 (1978); Paust, *The Seizure and Recovery of the Mayaguez*, 85 YALE L.J. 774, 800–02 (1976). Notably, the President of the Court, Sir Humphrey Waldock, had in his 1952 lectures at the Hague Academy opined that the use of force in defense of the lives of nationals abroad was permissible in carefully defined circumstances. Waldock, *The Regulation of the Use of Force by Individual States in International Law*, 81 RECUEIL DES COURS 455, 467, 503 (1952 II). Ironically, Sir Humphrey's example of a situation justifying the use of force, suggested by the Abadan oil incident, was the complete breakdown of law and order in Iran resulting in an imminent threat of death or serious injury to foreign nationals. *Id.* at 503.

[8] As noted above, the Court in the *Hostages* case did not make any finding as to the lawfulness per se of the rescue attempt; however, certain aspects of the May 24 Judgment contain tantalizing suggestions that the category of "armed attacks" under Article 51 of the UN Charter extends well beyond major armed assaults. At two points in the Judgment, the Court termed the takeover of the Embassy an "armed attack." [1980] ICJ REP. 3, paras. 57 and 91. It is possible, of course, that the Court used this phrase in a purely descriptive sense; at other points in the Judgment, the Court referred simply to an "attack" (*e.g.*, paras. 17, 24, and 25) or "assault" (para. 18). Still, the Court could hardly have been unaware of the significance of the phrase "armed attack." The Court, in fact, had taken specific note of the assertion by the United States, in its report to the Security Council on the rescue attempt, that the mission had been carried out "in exercise of its inherent right of self-defence with the aim of extricating American nationals who have been and remain the victims of the Iranian armed attack on our Embassy." *Id.*, para. 32.

The significance of the Court's repeated choice of phrase is underlined by the contrary position urged by Judge Morozov:

> I consider that, without any prejudice to the above-mentioned exclusive competence of the Security Council, the Court, from a purely legal point of view, could have drawn attention to the undeniable legal fact that Article 51 of the Charter, establishing the right of self-defence, may be invoked only "if an armed attack occurs against a Member of the United Nations".

The decision to attempt the rescue did not, however, escape strong censure:

> When, as previously recalled, this case had become ready for hearing on 19 February 1980, the United States Agent requested the Court, owing to the delicate stage of certain negotiations, to defer setting a date for the hearings. Subsequently, on 11 March, the Agent informed the Court of the United States Government's anxiety to obtain an early judgment on the merits of the case. The hearings were accordingly held on 18, 19 and 20 March, and the Court was in course of preparing the present judgment adjudicating upon the claims of the United States against Iran when the operation of 24 April 1980 took place. The Court therefore feels bound to observe that an operation undertaken in those circumstances, from whatever motive, is of a kind calculated to undermine respect for the judicial process in international relations; and to recall that in paragraph 47, 1 B, of its Order of 15 December 1979 the Court had indicated that no action was to be taken by either party which might aggravate the tension between the two countries.[9]

This critical passage will occupy our attention for much of this article. At present, however, it suffices to note that the Court voiced two grounds of objection to the rescue mission. First, the mission was action "of a kind calculated to undermine respect for the judicial process in international relations," a characterization that the Court linked to the fact that in March the United States had asked for expedition in the Court's proceedings after having earlier sought deferral of the oral argument. Second, the Court implied that attempting to rescue the hostages by force was incompatible with its Order for interim measures.

This two-pronged censure was not accompanied by any further sanction against the United States. Referring to the lawfulness of the operation, the Court stated:

> [T]his question can have no bearing on the evaluation of the conduct of the Iranian Government over six months earlier, on 4 November 1979, which is the subject-matter of the United States' Application. It follows that the findings reached by the Court in this Judgment are not affected by that operation.[10]

The reasoning that supports this conclusion is not at all self-evident. Both temporally and conceptually the "findings" of the Court went far beyond merely

---

> It should have added that in the documentation officially presented by the United States to the Court in response to its request relating to the events of 24–25 April 1980 there is no evidence that any armed attack had occurred against the United States.

Id. at 56–57 (Morožov, J., dissenting). Judge Tarazi appears to have held a similar view. *Id.* at 64–65 (Tarazi, J., dissenting).

If, indeed, the Court's references to "armed attack" were studied rather than casual, operations such as the rescue mission are lawful not because the right of self-defense under the UN Charter is coextensive with the preexisting customary law right of self-defense, which extended beyond defense against "armed attack" (*see, e.g.*, D. BOWETT, SELF-DEFENSE IN INTERNATIONAL LAW 185–86 (1958); M. MCDOUGAL & F. FELICIANO, LAW AND MINIMUM WORLD PUBLIC ORDER: THE LEGAL REGULATION OF INTERNATIONAL COERCION 232–41 (1961)), but because the right of self-defense against armed attack has arisen.

[9] [1980] ICJ REP. 3, para. 93.

[10] *Id.*, para. 94.

evaluating the conduct of the Iranian Government on November 4, 6 months prior to the rescue attempt.[11] First, the Court characterized Iran's violation as a continuing one extending up to the very date of the Judgment.[12] More importantly, the Court's findings included a grant of affirmative relief to the United States,[13] as well as a declaration that the United States was entitled to reparations from Iran.[14] The conclusion that the rescue attempt could not "affect" the evaluation of Iran's conduct on November 4 was hardly startling. But that conclusion is a far cry from the Court's second conclusion, *i.e.*, that the rescue attempt, already characterized by the Court in sharply critical terms, was irrelevant to the right of the United States to judicial relief. Certainly, it is difficult to concur with the Court's assertion that the second conclusion "follows" from the first.

Judge Morozov and Judge Tarazi, in separate dissenting opinions, focused on precisely the question whether the conduct of the United States ought to have affected its rights before the Court. Judge Morozov, referring to the 1955 Treaty of Amity, Economic Relations and Consular Rights under which the United States had made certain claims,[15] asserted that "the United States of America, according to commonly recognized principles of international law, has now deprived itself of any right to refer to the Treaty of 1955 in its relations with the Islamic Republic of Iran."[16] Dealing specifically with the question

[11] This is true whether the reference to the Court's "findings" is understood to relate solely to the operative paragraph of the Judgment or to portions of the reasoning as well.

For a discussion of the related question whether the "decision" of a tribunal for purposes of a request for interpretation includes both the *dispositif* and key elements of the tribunal's reasoning, see Delimitation of the Continental Shelf, Decision of 14 March 1978 (Interpretation of the Decision of 30 June 1977) (UK-France), 54 ILR 139, 166–71, 18 ILM 462 (1979).

[12] [1980] ICJ REP. 3, para. 95(1). The Court had not hesitated in the body of its opinion to evaluate Iran's conduct subsequent to the Nov. 4 takeover, and indeed subsequent to the date on which the Application was filed. *See, e.g., id.*, paras. 74 and 75.

[13] In operative subparagraphs 3 and 4 of the *dispositif*, the Court unanimously decided that the Government of Iran must "terminate the unlawful detention" of the hostages and "entrust them to the protecting Power"; ensure that they "have the necessary means of leaving Iranian territory"; place the "premises, property, archives and documents" of the U.S. Embassy and Consulates in Iran in the hands of the Protecting Power; and not subject any member of the U.S. diplomatic or consular staff to "any form of judicial proceedings or to participat[ion] in them as a witness." *Id.*, para. 95.

[14] *Id.*, para. 95(5). Judges Morozov, Tarazi, and Lachs dissented from this finding. The basis for Judge Morozov's and Judge Tarazi's dissents is discussed *infra* in text at notes 15–21. Judge Lachs felt that subparagraph 5 was redundant in view of subparagraph 2, which declared that Iran's international responsibility had been engaged by its violations of obligations owed to the United States. *Id.* at 47 (Lachs, J., sep. op.).

[15] Aug. 15, 1955, 8 UST 899, TIAS No. 3853. The most important of the claims made under the Treaty was that Iran had violated its obligation under Art. II(4) to afford U.S. nationals in Iran "the most constant protection and security" and to assure them reasonable and humane treatment while in custody. The applicability of the Treaty was of particular importance in respect of the two hostages not entitled to immunity under the Vienna Conventions. The Court upheld the claims of the United States under the Treaty. [1980] ICJ REP. 3, paras. 50–54, 67, 77, 80, and 90.

[16] *Id.* at 52 (Morozov, J., dissenting). Judge Morozov did not specify the "commonly recognized principles of international law" to which he referred. These principles evidently were not "commonly recognized" even by the majority of the Court. In an apparent reply to Judge Morozov, the majority stated:

of reparations, Judge Morozov admitted that under general international law, "some violations of freely accepted international obligations may be followed by a duty to make compensation for the resultant damage."[17] Nonetheless,

> taking into account the extraordinary circumstances which occurred during the period of judicial deliberation on the case, when the Applicant itself committed many actions which caused enormous damage to the Islamic Republic of Iran, the Applicant has forfeited the legal right as well as the moral right to expect the Court to uphold any claim for reparation.[18]

It should be emphasized that for Judge Morozov the rescue attempt was only the most egregious of a series of objectionable United States actions. These other actions included freezing Iranian assets, prohibiting trade with Iran, making an inventory of Iranian assets and U.S. claims, and preparing legislation to facilitate the processing and payment of such claims, including the claims of the hostages and their families.[19] In Judge Morozov's view, these actions were a bar to an award of reparations.

Judge Tarazi's position was more nuanced, but he, too, considered the United States to have prejudiced its right to reparations from Iran. Judge Tarazi could not agree with a finding that the Government of Iran was internationally responsible unless the Court also found "that the Government of the United States of America, by reason of its conduct both before and after the institution of proceedings, has equally incurred responsibility."[20] For Judge Tarazi, as

---

> The point has also been raised whether, having regard to certain counter-measures taken by the United States vis-à-vis Iran, it is open to the United States to rely on the Treaty of Amity, Economic Relations, and Consular Rights in the present proceedings. However, all the measures in question were taken by the United States after the seizure of its Embassy by an armed group and subsequent detention of its diplomatic and consular staff as hostages. They were measures taken in response to what the United States believed to be grave and manifest violations of international law by Iran, including violations of the 1955 Treaty itself. In any event, any alleged violation of the Treaty by either party could not have the effect of precluding that party from invoking the provisions of the Treaty concerning pacific settlement of disputes.

Id., para. 53. The holding that Iran's obligations survived the imposition of sanctions by the United States is one of general importance in the law governing self-help and judicial remedies for responses to breaches of conventional obligations. *See generally* Damrosch, *Retaliation or Arbitration—or Both? The 1978 United States-France Aviation Dispute*, 74 AJIL 785 (1980).

[17] [1980] ICJ REP., at 53 (Morozov, J., dissenting).

[18] *Ibid.*

[19] It appears that Judge Morozov was under the misapprehension that such legislation had in fact been introduced. *See id.* at 54. In fact, no legislation on claims and the disposition of Iranian assets was ever introduced, although considerable staff work had been done by the time of the Court's May 24 Judgment.

[20] *Id.* at 65 (Tarazi, J., dissenting). Judge Tarazi stated an additional condition on his assent to a finding that Iran was internationally responsible. For Judge Tarazi, any finding of responsibility had to be "relative not absolute," *ibid.*, which meant taking into account the entire history of U.S.-Iran relations during the regime of the Shah. *Id.* at 60–63.

The Court did consider the relevance of this history to the case. The Court held first that allegations of improper U.S. interference in Iranian affairs could not be accepted without proof, *id.*, para. 82; and second that proof of such interference would not in any case constitute a defense to the claims made by the United States in the case, *id.*, paras. 83–89. It is important to note, however, that the Court did not entirely exclude the possibility that "some of the circumstances alleged, if duly established, may later be found to have some relevance in determining the confor Judge Morozov, the rescue attempt was but one of several seriously objectionable measures taken by the United States after the onset of the crisis.[21] As we shall see, it is a point of some significance in understanding the majority's approach to the rescue mission that the majority, unlike Judges Morozov and Tarazi, sharply distinguished between the rescue attempt and other U.S. actions during the crisis.

It is apparent from this summary that the Court's response to the rescue mission embodies a number of interesting and provocative judgments. First, the Court found an operation that it was not prepared to condemn as either immoral or illegal nonetheless incompatible with respect for the judicial process. This suggests that the notion of respect for judicial process constitutes an independent perspective from which to criticize the conduct of a litigant. The Court, however, neither elaborated this notion nor explained in what respect or respects the rescue mission was objectionable. Second, as an additional basis of objection to the mission the Court cited the duties of the United States under the Order of December 15, 1979, a citation itself worthy of note. The duty of the United States to refrain from any action that might aggravate tensions apparently survived Iran's blatant disregard of the Order. The Court thus appears to have rejected the view that there is an implied condition of reciprocity in every interim measures order. Third, the fact that the Court simultaneously implied that the rescue attempt violated the interim measures Order and refused to question the legality of the rescue attempt raises the question whether an interim measures order may bar what is *ex hypothesi* an otherwise lawful exercise of the right of self-defense, and whether the use of force *pendente lite* is necessarily unlawful. Finally, the Court's refusal to penalize the United States for undertaking the rescue mission raises the question whether an international tribunal, and more particularly the Court, may employ a readily available method of vindicating its authority, *i.e.*, withholding relief from a litigant guilty of improper conduct. In the remainder of this article we shall explore these three sets of issues: namely, the source and content of the concept of "respect for the judicial process in international relations"; the relationship among interim measures, the use of force, and the judicial settlement of disputes; and the availability of sanctions for conduct incompatible with the duties of a litigant before the Court.

II. An International Law of Contempt of Court?

Lawyers trained in the Anglo-American system can perhaps be forgiven if their instantaneous reaction to the Court's characterization of the rescue mission is to conclude that the United States had been found guilty of a contempt of court. Indeed, the Court's choice of phrase, "an operation . . . of a kind calculated to undermine respect for the judicial process in international relations," is a nearly verbatim transposition to the international plane of textbook defi-

---

sequences of the responsibility incurred by the Iranian State with respect to that conduct [the seizure of the Embassy and detention of the hostages], although they could not be considered to alter its unlawful character." *Id.*, para. 89. Apparently this concession did not go far enough to satisfy Judge Tarazi's insistence that international responsibility must be viewed in relative terms.

[21] *Id.* at 63–65 (Tarazi, J., dissenting).

nitions of contempt. Oswald's classic treatment of the law of contempt, for example, contains the following definition: "To speak generally, contempt of court may be said to be constituted by any conduct that tends to bring the authority and administration of the law into disrespect or disregard. . . ."[22] More recently, the House of Lords defined contempt in similar terms, tying this definition to the functions of judicial authority in a well-ordered society:

> The provision of such a system for the administration of justice by courts of law and the maintenance of public confidence in it, are essential if citizens are to live together in peaceful association with one another. "Contempt of court" is a generic term descriptive of conduct in relation to particular proceedings in a court of law which tends to undermine that system or to inhibit citizens from availing themselves of it for the settlement of their disputes.[23]

The resonance between the Court's treatment of the rescue attempt and the classical notion of contempt is amplified by the tone of offended judicial dignity that may be discerned in the Court's opinion. The reference to the alternating requests for delay and dispatch in the proceedings perhaps expresses a sense that the United States had trifled with the Court. And the parallel to contempt is further reinforced by the Court's implication that the rescue mission violated the Order of December 15.

This passage of the opinion in the *Hostages* case suggests that the Court may be developing a body of law whose function is akin to the function of contempt of court in Anglo-American law, *i.e.*, the protection of the judicial process itself from harm caused by the actions of litigants and others involved in the process. Prior decisions of the Court provide further evidence of such a development.

An incident during the *Nuclear Tests* case[24] provides perhaps the best illustration of this. Prior to the official announcement of the interim measures Order in that case, the Prime Minister of Australia correctly predicted the outcome of the deliberations, including the exact division of the Court.[25] The Court conducted an investigation to determine whether there had been a leak and, if so, its source. In its resolution formally closing the investigation of the episode, the Court noted that it had "above all been mindful of the need to protect the integrity of the international judicial process as well as the dignity of the principal judicial organ of the United Nations."[26] The Court strongly disapproved of any statements anticipating its decision in a pending case and reiterated "its view that any making, circulation or publication of such statements is incompatible with the fundamental principles governing the good

[22] J. OSWALD, CONTEMPT OF COURT 6 (3d ed. 1910). American sources also use language closely paralleling the Court's. *See generally* 17 AM. JUR. 2D, *Contempt*, §3 (1964) ("Generally speaking, he whose conduct tends to bring the authority and administration of the law into disrespect or disregard . . . is guilty of contempt").

[23] Attorney-General v. Times Newspaper, Ltd., [1974] A.C. 273, 307 (Diplock, L.J.).

[24] Nuclear Tests Case (Australia v. France), [1973] ICJ REP. 99.

[25] The history of the episode and of the Court's efforts to determine the source of the leak, if there was one, is recounted in a resolution adopted by the Court on March 21, 1974. [1973–74] Y.B. ICJ 127. Additional material may be found in the Comments by the President, 2 Nuclear Tests Cases, ICJ Pleadings 406–08 (1978), and in the opinions by Judge Lachs, [1974] ICJ REP. 253, 273 (Lachs, J., dec.), and Judge Gros, *id.* at 293–96 (Gros, J., dissenting).

[26] Resolution of March 21, 1974, *supra* note 25, para. 4.

administration of justice."[27] President Lachs likewise referred to the "good administration of justice and respect for the Court" in justifying the secrecy of judicial deliberations.[28] He declared that the Australian Prime Minister's statement and related press reports "exceeded what is legally admissible in relation to a case *sub judice*."[29]

Judge Gros went a step further: "The statement in question concerned a decision of the Court and could lead to a belief that persons privy to its deliberations had violated their obligation to keep it secret, with all the consequences that supposition would have entailed if confirmed."[30] Judge Gros could not accept the Court's decision to act, in his view, "as if a saddened silence were the only remedy and the sole solution."[31]

In the *Barcelona Traction* case, there is another instance of the Court's concern that a party's conduct might undermine respect for the international judicial process. In that case, the Court indicated considerable discomfort with the protraction of the proceedings and felt compelled to point out that their length had resulted from the very long time limits, and then the extension of those limits, requested by the parties.[32] The Court nonetheless was "convinced of the fact that it is in the interest of the authority and proper functioning of international justice for cases to be decided without unwarranted delay."[33]

The Court's concern with the possibility that the conduct of a litigant might reflect badly on the process of international justice appears as early as the *Corfu Channel* case.[34] It will be recalled that in defense of its minesweeping operation in the Corfu Channel, the United Kingdom had pointed to the need to preserve the mines as evidence in the proceedings on its claim against Albania.[35] In a famous passage most often studied for the light it sheds on legal restraints on the use of force, the Court responded to and rejected the argument. In concluding its condemnation of intervention by force the Court added, "Intervention is perhaps still less admissible in the particular form it would take here; for, from the nature of things, it would be reserved for the most powerful States, and might easily lead to perverting the administration of international justice itself."[36] Underlying this statement is the conviction that it would be intolerable were proceedings before the Court, an institution designed to promote the peaceful settlement of disputes, to provide a positive incentive for the use of force by powerful states against weak ones. The result would be not only

[27] *Id.*, para. 5.

[28] [1974] ICJ REP. at 273 (Lachs, J., dec.).

[29] *Ibid.*

[30] *Id.* at 295 (Gros, J., dissenting).

[31] *Id.* at 296.

[32] Barcelona Traction, Light & Power Co., Ltd., [1970] *id.* at 3, 30–31. Judge Fitzmaurice's separate opinion makes plain that the Court was responding to the charge that its proceedings were unduly slow and cumbersome. While Judge Fitzmaurice understood that counsel often needed extended periods to prepare a case, "[s]trong objection exists however when the blame . . . is publicly ascribed to the supposed dilatoriness or procrastination of the Court itself . . . in evident ignorance or else heedlessness, of the true facts." *Id.* at 113 (Fitzmaurice, J., sep. op.). Interesting in light of our present inquiry is Judge Fitzmaurice's express recognition of the relationship between such charges and respect for the Court: "Nor is this by any means the only way in which the Court has been misrepresented in a manner detrimental to the dignity and good order of its functioning as an independent judicial institution." *Ibid.*

[33] *Id.* at 31.

[34] [1949] ICJ REP. 4.

[35] *Id.* at 34.

[36] *Id.* at 35.

disorder, but systematic bias in the decisions of the Court. Thus, a litigant who used force to secure evidence in a case both would have used force unlawfully and would have "pervert[ed] the administration of . . . justice itself."

It appears, then, that the Court's reference in the *Hostages* case to "respect for the judicial process" as a standard of assessment is no new departure. While the catchwords have varied from case to case, the concern seems a constant one. The possibility that a litigant's conduct would reflect adversely on the process of international adjudication itself has always been recognized.

The development of an international concept paralleling contempt of court should not raise any serious problem under Article 38(1)(c) of the Court's Statute referring to "general principles of law recognized by civilized nations." Although it is often asserted that contempt of court is a creature unique to the common law,[37] and indeed "simply does not belong to the world of ideas of a Latin lawyer,"[38] the unique features of the common law concept are matters of degree, form, and procedure.[39] For example, although the use of imprisonment as a means of coercing compliance with court orders is unusual in civil law systems, it is not unknown.[40] Even in those countries which eschew imprisonment, disobedience to court orders is not treated as a matter of indifference,[41] and this is the truly significant point. The problem of the effectiveness of judicial decisions is recognized and addressed in all municipal systems.

[37] *See* Pekelis, *Legal Techniques and Political Ideologies: A Comparative Study*, 41 MICH. L. REV. 665, 667–77 (1943). In the proceedings before the European Court of Human Rights in the *Sunday Times* case, the United Kingdom argued that because the institution of contempt of court was peculiar to the common law countries, the proper scope of international review by the European Court was quite narrow. The European Court, while rejecting the conclusion drawn by the United Kingdom, did not contest the validity of the premise that the institution of contempt "has no equivalent in many other Member States of the Council of Europe." Sunday Times Case, 58 ILR 491, 531 (Eur. Ct. Human Rights 1979). The joint dissenting opinion, signed by nine judges, agreed that contempt is "peculiar to the legal traditions of the common-law countries." *Id.* at 540.

[38] Pekelis, *supra* note 37, at 668.

[39] *See, e.g.*, Newman, *The General Principles of Equity*, in EQUITY IN THE WORLD'S LEGAL SYSTEMS: A COMPARATIVE STUDY 589, 612 (R. Newman ed. 1973); Szladits, *The Concept of Specific Performance in Civil Law*, 4 AM. J. COMP. L. 208, 218–20, 228 (1955).

[40] Professor Dawson notes the absence in France of body attachment as a means of coercing compliance with court orders, but demonstrates that the situation is not at all the same in Germany. Dawson, *Specific Performance in France and Germany*, 57 MICH. L. REV. 495, 516, 533–38 (1959). It is important to keep this distinction in mind, for it suggests that the peculiarity of even the civil contempt notion is exaggerated by emphasis on the French system. *Cf.* Pekelis, *supra* note 37, at 666 (noting that he is focusing on law in the Latin countries of Europe).

[41] The tortured historical development of the *astreinte* in France illustrates this in a perverse way. Despite resistance from the highest French courts and from writers of authority, the lower courts, responding to a continuing felt need for a frankly coercive sanction, made several attempts to use the *astreinte* for this purpose. *See* Dawson, *supra* note 40, at 512–25. More recently, the coercive use of the *astreinte* has apparently been accepted as legitimate even by the Cour de Cassation; nevertheless, some scholars retain doubts about its legality. *See* P. HERZOG, CIVIL PROCEDURE IN FRANCE 561, 563–64 (1967).

In many countries, failure to comply with court orders is itself a penal offense. *See, e.g.*, the West German Penal Code, §137; the Italian Penal Code, Arts. 334 and 388; the Norwegian Penal Code, Arts. 343 and 344; the Polish Criminal Code, Arts. 258 and 259; the Romanian Penal Code, Art. 271; the Swedish Penal Code, ch. 17, §13; and the Turkish Criminal Code, §309 (trans. in 4, 23, 3, 19, 20, 17, and 9 AMERICAN SERIES OF FOREIGN PENAL CODES, respectively (1961–78)).

Interestingly, it is not only modern systems that have reinforced the authority of judicial decisions

Moving away from the use of contempt sanctions to coerce compliance with court orders, we find that here, too, the difference between common law and civil law systems is easily overstated. Conduct that is punishable as a contempt of court may be punishable as an ordinary penal offense in many civil law jurisdictions. Thus, a recent survey of the English law of contempt cited as examples of contempt the following, *inter alia*: publishing material prejudicial to a fair criminal or civil proceeding; "scandalizing the court" by impugning the integrity or honesty of judge or jury; interfering with witnesses, parties, judges, juries, or court officers; and violating the duties of court officers.[42] Under the French Penal Code, the same kinds of conduct are recognized as penal offenses.[43] The most egregious kinds of conduct, *e.g.*, perjury, bribery, intimidation of the tribunal, seem to be universally condemned.[44] And even less outrageous conduct tending to undermine respect for judicial decisions is widely condemned. For example, the French Penal Code provides generally in Article 226:

> Any person who publicly, by acts, words or writings, seeks to discredit a judicial act or decision, under conditions of a nature to injure the authority of the courts or their independence, shall be punished by imprisonment of from one to six months and a fine from 500 F to 20,000 F, or of only one of these two penalties.[45]

---

by attaching criminal penalties to noncompliance. *See Deuteronomy* 17:8–13; and for comment on this passage, A. SCHREIBER, JEWISH LAW AND DECISION-MAKING: A STUDY THROUGH TIME 53 (1979).

[42] G. BORRIE & N. LOWE, THE LAW OF CONTEMPT 35–129, 153–74, 205–52 (1973). I refer here only to so-called "constructive" or "indirect" contempts not occurring in the presence of the judge. For a discussion of direct contempt, see *id.* at 5–34.

The American law of contempt is reviewed by Dobbs, *Contempt of Court: A Survey*, 56 CORN. L. REV. 183 (1971). Professor Dobbs offers a similar catalog of circumstances where American courts have held persons in contempt. *Id.* at 185–219.

[43] C. PEN. Art. 227 (prejudgment publications designed to exert pressure on witnesses or judges); *id.* Art. 222 (words, writings, or drawings tending to impugn honor or dignity of judges or jurors); *id.* Art. 223 (gestures or threats to judge or juror in performance or because of performance of duties); *id.* Art. 365 (subordination of perjury); *id.* Art 224 (gestures, threats, or drawings aimed at ministerial officers, commandants, or agents of the public force in performance of or because of performance of duty).

[44] The following are offered as examples without any pretense to exhaustiveness or to system: the Argentine Penal Code, Arts. 237, 257, and 275–276; the Austrian Penal Act, §§104, 105, 199, and 312; the Greek Penal Code, Arts. 167, 224, 228, and 237; the Greenland Criminal Code, §§16, 17, 27, 31–32, and 35–36; the South Korean Criminal Code, Arts. 129–133, 136, 152, and 154; the Norwegian Penal Code, §§111–114, 127, 128, and 163–167; the Polish Penal Code, Arts. 233, 235, 239, 241, 247, and 253; and the Turkish Criminal Code, Arts. 211–214, 216–217, 219–221, 232, 233, 255, 286–287, 290, and 291 (trans. in 6, 12, 18, 16, 2, 3, 19, and 9 AMERICAN SERIES OF FOREIGN PENAL CODES, respectively (1960–73)).

Even in common law systems, some serious interferences with the judicial process may be punishable only as an ordinary offense, but not as contempt. Thus, in federal court in the United States perjury alone will not constitute a contempt. *See In re* Michael, 326 U.S. 224 (1945). But perjury is, of course, punishable and that fact, rather than the procedure by which punishment is imposed, is critical for present purposes.

[45] C. PEN. Art. 227. The translation follows FRENCH LAW: CONSTITUTION AND SELECTIVE LEGISLATION 8–25 (H. DeVries, N. Galston, & R. Loening eds., 1981).

Similar provisions can be found in the penal codes of many other representative jurisdictions.[46]

The point is that the common law is not alone in expressing concern for maintaining "respect for the judicial process." Nor is it alone in providing sanctions for conduct that undermines respect for that process. Nor, finally, is the common law at all unusual in identifying certain kinds of conduct as intolerable. It appears that any legal system providing for the judicial settlement of disputes must treat as a matter of serious concern any conduct which tends to obstruct, deflect, or frustrate that process. No system designed to reach an impartial judgment in accordance with law, on the basis of accurately determined facts, can tolerate the forgery of documents, the subornation of perjury, the bribery of witnesses, the corruption of the tribunal, or the intimidation of witnesses or the tribunal. International tribunals are no exception to this rule; when confronted with such conduct, they have uniformly considered it objectionable.[47] But even less extreme conduct, *e.g.*, pressuring a party by means of threats of adverse publicity to compromise his legal rights or destroying property that is the subject matter of litigation, can be objectionable. For all such conduct undermines respect for the judicial process in the way that is most significant: it undermines confidence in that process as a fair, reliable, and effective means of settling disputes in accordance with law.

It is to this common concern of all legal systems that the Court appealed in the *Hostages* case. The Court's phraseology, bringing so forcibly to mind the notion of contempt of court, is not a parochial reference to the peculiar features of that legal institution. It constitutes, instead, international judicial recognition of the fact that the law of contempt reflects universal concerns about the requirements of a functioning adjudicatory process. In consequence, if in the future we find the Court drawing upon the law of contempt for analogies to suggest what kind of conduct "undermine[s] respect for the judicial process in international relations," we should not be surprised. But the law of contempt does not, strictly speaking, supply the test of a litigant's conduct. The test, as suggested above, must be whether the conduct in question tends to undermine confidence in the judicial process as a method of settling international disputes impartially, reliably, and effectively.

It follows that a litigant before an international tribunal is obligated to refrain from conduct incompatible with the proper functioning of the judicial process. This general obligation results directly from the decision to seek judicial relief.[48] It is but an emanation from the duty to exercise the right to judicial or arbitral relief in good faith.[49] More concretely, it means that a litigant is subject to a

[46] In addition to the statutes cited in note 41 *supra* pertaining to noncompliance with judicial orders, a number of countries penalize conduct disrespectful to the authority of the judiciary. *See* the Argentine Penal Code, Art. 244; the Italian Penal Code, Art. 342; the Romanian Criminal Code, Art. 239; and the Turkish Criminal Code, Art. 268 (trans. in 6, 23, 20, and 9 AMERICAN SERIES OF FOREIGN PENAL CODES, respectively (1963–78)).

[47] *See* text *infra* at notes 48–52.

[48] *See* Ungarisches Erdgas A.G. v. Etat roumain, 5 Trib. Arb. Mixtes 951, 955 (1925).

[49] *See* Friedman Case, U.S.-German Mixed Claims Comm'n, Consol. Ed. of Dec. & Opin. 607, 613 (1925); E. DUMBAULD, INTERIM MEASURES OF PROTECTION IN INTERNATIONAL CONTROVERSIES 182 (1932); *cf.* K. CARLSTON, THE PROCESS OF INTERNATIONAL ARBITRATION 53–61 (1946) (party's right to a tribunal free from corruption and to proceedings free from fraud).

number of specific obligations relating to evidentiary matters,[50] the independence of the tribunal,[51] and the efficient conduct of judicial business.[52]

Among the most basic of these obligations is the obligation to refrain from any action that prejudges the merits of the case or prevents execution of the decision of the tribunal. As Elihu Root declared in 1929 during the discussions of amendments to the Statute and Rules of the Permanent Court, "The parties to a case, when they submitted their controversy to the Court, might be regarded as having come under an obligation not to destroy the subject matter of the controversy or in any way to anticipate the judgment of the Court by action of their own."[53] Indeed, the Permanent Court considered this obligation one of the primary sources of the Court's power under Article 41 of the Statute to indicate provisional measures. That power, said the Court, was but an application of

> the principle universally accepted by international tribunals . . . that the Parties to a case must abstain from any measure capable of exercising a prejudicial effect in regard to the execution of the decision to be given and, in general, not allow any step of any kind to be taken which might aggravate or extend the dispute.[54]

The duty to refrain from measures anticipating the outcome of the case and the duty to refrain from measures prejudicing execution of the decision are closely related, but nonetheless distinct. Looked at from one perspective, the two duties are mirror images. A litigant state may not take measures prejudicing execution for the very reason that it might lose the case; if victory were absolutely certain, there would be no harm in taking such measures. But because success is never absolutely certain, good faith requires a state to avoid taking action anticipating a decision in its favor and impairing its ability to comply with a judgment against it. And here we return to the problem of respect for the judicial process: a judgment that cannot be executed is one that detracts from

[50] A litigant may not, therefore, rely on falsified documents or tamper with witnesses before the tribunal, conduct that the commentators are unanimous in considering a basis for nullity of the award. *See* W. REISMAN, NULLITY AND REVISION: THE REVIEW AND ENFORCEMENT OF INTERNATIONAL JUDGMENTS AND AWARDS 37, 483, 494–95 (1971); B. CHENG, GENERAL PRINCIPLES OF LAW 158–60 (1953); K. CARLSTON, *supra* note 49, at 57–61. Nor may a litigant withhold from the tribunal reasonably available evidence relevant to decision of the case. *See* D. SANDIFER, EVIDENCE BEFORE INTERNATIONAL TRIBUNALS 112–18, 147–62 (rev. ed. 1975); C. JENKS, THE PROSPECTS OF INTERNATIONAL ADJUDICATION 424–25 (1964); W. REISMAN, *supra*, at 593–603. The Corfu Channel Case, [1949] ICJ REP. at 35, suggests, in addition, that a litigant may not gather evidence by improper means, in particular by the use of force.

[51] A litigant may not corrupt a member of the tribunal, *see* K. CARLSTON, *supra* note 49, at 53–57; violate the secrecy of judicial deliberations, *see* the discussion of the episode in the *Nuclear Tests* cases in text at notes 24–31 *supra*; or induce a court functionary to violate his duties to the court, *ibid.*; *see especially* [1974] ICJ REP. 253, 295 (Gros, J., dissenting).

[52] *Cf.* Barcelona Traction, Light & Power Co., Ltd., [1970] ICJ REP. at 31 (suggesting that the Court would not tolerate deliberately dilatory tactics).

[53] Comm. of Jurists on the Statute of the Permanent Court of International Justice, League of Nations Doc. C.166.M.66.1929.V, at 64 (minutes of the session held at Geneva, March 11–19, 1929).

[54] Electricity Co. of Sofia & Bulgaria, [1939] PCIJ, ser. A/B, No. 79, at 199. *Cf.* Nuclear Tests Case, [1973] ICJ REP. at 106 (no action to be taken which could "prejudice the rights of the other Party in respect of the carrying out of whatever decision the Court may render in the case"); Fisheries Jurisdiction Case, [1972] ICJ REP. 12, 17 (same).

the reputation of the tribunal as an effective means of resolving disputes. As Dumbauld put it: "Impossibility of executing the judgment is only one species of prejudice; but stands out by reason of the fact that it not only injures the aggrieved party but offends against the dignity of the court and renders ridiculous the authors of the judicial proceeding."[55]

The obligation to avoid measures anticipating the decision has another and broader aspect, which results directly from the exceptional character of international jurisdiction in the international legal order. The decision to submit a dispute to judicial resolution manifests a preference for an outcome reached through the judicial method over an outcome dependent on the use each state is able to make of power to support its view of its rights.[56] The international legal order is generally tolerant of unilateral nonforcible coercion as a means of compelling another state to recognize one's rights. It is likewise tolerant of self-help measures as a means of either obtaining reparation for injuries believed to have been done or bringing about directly an end to the violation of rights. As a general rule, therefore, in the absence of arbitral or judicial remedies, each state is free to take nonforcible action of either sort against its opponent based on its own appreciation of the legal merits.[57] However, subject to certain qualifications discussed below, once judicial proceedings are under way, it is incompatible with the implied preference for an outcome determined by law to employ coercion or self-help premised on one's own view of the rights and wrongs of the controversy.[58] Although coercive measures designed to affect the adversary's course of conduct ordinarily will not in fact prejudice one's ability to comply with an adverse decision, such measures are nonetheless prohibited because they are premised on the party's subjective assessment of the situation rather than the tribunal's. They are impermissible precisely because to the

[55] E. Dumbauld, *supra* note 49, at 28 n.l.

[56] As one of the leading students of the Court has said:

> The principal objective of the political function of adjudication, and hence of the Court as the institution for that purpose, is to meet the desire for completely non-political treatment of a matter, and its solution on the basis of law. A reference to the Court by a State or the States concerned is evidence of their conclusion, as a matter of political choice, that judicial settlement would be the most appropriate manner of overcoming the difficulty facing them.

1 S. Rosenne, The Law and Practice of The International Court 91 (1965).

[57] The International Law Commission in its study of state responsibility has recently reaffirmed the existence in customary international law of a right to take reprisals not involving the use of force. [1979] 2 Y.B. Int'l L. Comm'n 115, UN Doc. A/CN.4/SER.A/1979/Add.1, pt. 2. The commentary to Article 30 of the Commission's draft articles contains a wealth of source material on the question of reprisals. *Id.* at 115–22.

[58] Dumbauld properly related the restraints on the right to take reprisals to the tribunal's authority to indicate interim measures of protection:

> The law does not always speak with such a clear voice that *bona fide* differences of opinion are rendered impossible. Until it has been approved and established by a judicial decision having force of *res judicata*, no party is obliged to accept his opponent's view of the law as correct. Is he free to act upon his own view as correct, or must he act upon the assumption that his opponent may possibly be right? The former alternative applies in the absence of provisions authorizing interim protection; the latter if the law has introduced such remedies.

E. Dumbauld, *supra* note 49, at 28 (footnote omitted). For further development of the relation between interim measures of protection and the obligation to refrain from coercive measures *pendente lite*, see text *infra* at notes 84–90.

extent they are effective, they frustrate the promise of an outcome based upon law rather than power. Whether measures of self-help will impede the ability to comply with an adverse judgment depends on the particular circumstances; even if they do not have this effect, they too are impermissible, for they are designed to bring about the termination of the conflict without regard to the impartial determination the parties agreed to seek when they assented to the tribunal's jurisdiction.

III. THE RESCUE MISSION AND RESPECT FOR THE JUDICIAL PROCESS

As we have just seen, the test of a litigant's conduct is whether the conduct in question undermines respect for the judicial process as an impartial, reliable, and effective means of settling disputes according to law. The task that next arises is to examine against this standard the validity of the Court's objection to the rescue mission itself.

One factor in explaining the Court's criticism may have been the conviction that the success of the rescue mission would have prejudiced the ability of the United States to comply with a judgment in some respects adverse to it. The possibility of such a judgment cannot, as we have seen, be entirely disregarded by any litigant. Even in the context of the *Hostages* case, in which the U.S. position was overwhelmingly strong, the possibility of a partially adverse judgment was not entirely hypothetical. For example, there was some possibility that the Court would require the United States to make available as witnesses or parties in Iranian judicial proceedings the two hostages not entitled to diplomatic immunity.[59] The rescue mission might have prejudiced the ability of the United States to comply with this judgment. The Court might reasonably have taken the view that the commitment of lives, resources, and national prestige involved in extricating the hostages by force would as a practical matter preclude compliance by the United States with such a directive.[60]

More importantly, the Court probably considered the rescue mission incompatible with the basic premise of resort to judicial remedies, the commitment to seek an outcome according to law rather than power. Under no obligation to initiate judicial proceedings or to continue them in the face of Iranian obduracy, the United States freely chose to do both. And in so choosing, the United States affirmed its intention to seek the release of the hostages through means compatible with the judicial process.

All of the three judges who wrote separate or dissenting opinions rested their objections to the rescue mission in part on this basic incompatibility. Judge

[59] Under subparagraph 4, the Court decided that "no member of the United States diplomatic and consular staff may be kept in Iran to be subjected to any form of judicial proceedings or to participate in them as a witness." [1980] ICJ REP. 3, para. 95. No similar exemption for other U.S. nationals was provided.

[60] It is true, of course, that the United States would have been reluctant to comply with such a directive even had the hostages initially been released in response to the Court's interim measures Order. Still, the United States would have found it significantly more difficult to comply with a decision requiring return of some of the hostages if their release from captivity had been accomplished by military rather than judicial means. Had the hostages initially been released in response to the Court's Order, a pattern of compliance with authoritative decisions would have been created which the United States would have been very reluctant to upset.

Tarazi, who gave the matter the most extended treatment,[61] was quite explicit on this point. He derived from the principle that the Court's jurisdiction is based upon and limited by the consent of states two "essential consequences":

> (*a*) any State is free to ignore the possibility of the judicial solution of a dispute, either by omitting to refer it to the International Court of Justice, or by refusing to submit to the Court's jurisdiction, to the extent that the circumstances of the case enable it so to refuse;
> (*b*) however, once a State presents itself before the Court as an applicant and requests it to direct the respondent State to submit to the law, the option it possessed before the institution of proceedings disappears. The whole dossier of the dispute at issue is taken in hand by the Court. The applicant State must refrain from taking any decisions on the planes of either domestic or international law which could have the effect of impeding the proper administration of justice.[62]

These principles led Judge Tarazi to condemn several of the nonmilitary measures taken by the United States; he concluded that they impermissibly anticipated a favorable judgment and might prejudice the possibility of complying with an unfavorable one.[63] It was the rescue attempt, however, that was "the gravest encroachment upon the Court's exercise of its power to declare the law in respect of the dispute laid before it. . . . I must say that it was not conducive to facilitating the judicial settlement of the dispute."[64] Judge Lachs, balancing his criticism of Iran's failure to appear and present its case, likewise stated that "the Applicant, having instituted proceedings, is precluded from taking unilateral action, military or otherwise, as if no case is pending."[65] Judge Morozov recalled that the "invasion" of Iran took place

> in a period of judicial deliberation, and was directed (at least according to the explanation given by the United States) not toward the settlement of the dispute in a peaceful way, for example, by negotiations or similar means (which could take place in parallel with judicial proceedings), but *by force*.[66]

[61] [1980] ICJ REP. at 63–65 (Tarazi, J., dissenting).

[62] *Id.* at 63.

[63] In particular, he took exception to legislation to compensate the hostages from Iranian assets, which he felt "constituted an encroachment on the functions of the Court, for until the Court has ruled upon the principle of reparation the applicant State is not entitled to consider that its submissions, or part of them, have already been accepted and recognized as well founded." *Id.* at 64. Such legislation also raised the possibility of a conflict between the requirements of domestic law and the Court's ultimate judgment, a conflict that would prejudice the ability of the United States to comply with the judgment. *Ibid.*

The problem to which Judge Tarazi referred was recognized by lawyers working on the draft legislation. The legislation could have been structured to avoid any such conflict, for example, by giving the President a purely discretionary authority to vest Iranian assets for a variety of purposes including satisfying an actual award of reparations by the Court. While the President had authority under the International Emergency Economic Powers Act, 50 U.S.C. §§1701–1706 (Supp. II 1978), to block Iranian assets, new legislation would have been necessary to authorize vesting for any purpose. *See* Dames & Moore v. Regan, 101 S.Ct. 2972, 2983 n.5 (1981).

[64] [1980] ICJ REP. at 64 (Tarazi, J., dissenting).

[65] *Id.* at 48 (Lachs, J., sep op.).

[66] *Id.* at 56 (Morozov, J., dissenting). Judge Morozov also objected to the claims legislation, complaining that the United States was acting "as judge in its own cause" in making arrangements to compensate the hostages. *Id.* at 54.

It is this same incompatibility between seeking judicial relief and resorting to force that perhaps explains the Court's otherwise puzzling emphasis on the U.S. request for delay in the scheduling of oral argument.[67] By deciding on March 11, 1980 to go forward with oral argument, the United States impliedly represented that judicial proceedings would be permitted to run their course before action was taken premised on the belief that a favorable judgment would have little practical effect on the release of the hostages. That representation required the United States to give Iran a chance to react to the final judgment that the United States was seeking.

To be sure, an applicant before the Court need not believe in its heart of hearts that a judgment in its favor will be respected.[68] It is indeed quite legitimate to pursue judicial remedies in the full anticipation that compliance will not be forthcoming.[69] Nonetheless, to take action premised on the futility of judicial relief in advance of judgment contributes to undermining respect for the effectiveness of the Court. It adds to the impact of the respondent's actual disregard of the judgment, a demonstration of the applicant's own conviction that such disregard is certain. By emphasizing that the proceedings had been

[67] The United States left no doubt in its oral presentation to the Court that American reluctance to go forward with the case in February was motivated by the desire to avoid taking any action that might prejudice the success of the Secretary-General's Commission of Inquiry whose activities, it was hoped, would lead to a resolution of the crisis. Once the Commission effectively had ceased to function, there was no further need to delay the proceedings before the Court, and the United States therefore urged the Court to proceed with maximum expedition. (The official text of the oral argument has not as yet been published by the Court. However, an excerpted version containing the whole presentation by Roberts B. Owen, United States Agent, and a summary of the presentation by Stephen Schwebel, Deputy Agent, has been published by the Department of State. *U.S. Presses Case in World Court on American Hostages in Iran*, DEP'T STATE BULL., No. 2038, May 1980, at 36 [hereinafter cited as Oral Argument Excerpt]. Owen's statement linking the request for deferral to the Commission's efforts may be found in *id.* at 56, 59–60.)

The Court did not take exception either to the activities of the Commission or to the change in U.S. preferences consequent upon its failure. To the contrary, both in its conduct of the case and in the text of its Judgment, the Court amply and properly took account of the possibility that alternative processes of dispute settlement could parallel proceedings in the Court. The Court held that neither the fact that the Security Council was actively seized of the hostage problem, nor that the Secretary-General was employing his good offices with a view towards its resolution, nor even that a special Commission of Inquiry had been established, affected either its competence or the admissibility of proceedings. [1980] ICJ REP. 3, paras. 40–44.

[68] The UN Charter itself envisions the possibility of noncompliance by providing for Security Council enforcement of judgments of the Court. UN CHARTER art. 94(2). The record of noncompliance with decisions of the Court, including disregard of interim measures orders and advisory opinions, is reviewed in Janis, *The Role of the International Court in the Hostages Crisis*, 13 CONN. L. REV. 263, 283–84 (1981).

[69] In fact, the United States had a number of legitimate objectives in pursuing the case long after it became apparent that Iran would not comply with an adverse decision. Chief among these was judicial affirmation of the importance and continued vitality of the norms of diplomatic intercourse. Other objectives were also significant. For example, the United States sought to obtain a binding decision that the Treaty of Amity continues in force, a point of some potential importance in eventual proceedings before an international claims tribunal. Finally, the Court's Judgment was a necessary step in establishing an unassailable basis for compensating the hostages or their families from Iranian assets. For a detailed analysis of the objectives the United States was pursuing in the Court, see Gordon & Youngblood, *The Role of the International Court in the Hostages Crisis—A Rejoinder*, 13 CONN. L. REV. 429 (1981).

delayed at the request of the United States itself, the Court made clear that, if on April 24 the United States found it necessary to take action incompatible with the simultaneous pursuit of judicial remedies, that necessity arose to some extent from the U.S. Government's own desire for an extension of the proceedings. In other words, the fact that the rescue mission occurred *pendente lite* rather than subsequent to judgment was due at least in part to the preferences of the United States rather than to the inherent pace of international adjudication.[70]

IV. Power and Law: Force as a Special Case

We have just seen that a principal basis of the Court's objection to the rescue mission was its apparent incompatibility with the premise of resort to judicial remedies, and that this commitment to an outcome determined by law rather than power was renewed by the United States when it continued to pursue judicial remedies even after Iran's disregard of the interim measures Order.

However, this explanation of the Court's objection to the rescue mission leaves one end still loose. The majority, unlike Judges Lachs, Morozov, and Tarazi, did not criticize the nonmilitary measures taken by the United States against Iran. Yet, with respect to both timing and substance, these nonmilitary measures seem quite similar to the rescue mission. Some of these measures were imposed between the date of the interim measures Order and rendition of the judgment.[71] All were attempts to achieve by coercion, though not by force, the same object the United States was pursuing in the Court. If, as earlier suggested, coercive measures of all kinds are incompatible with resort to the judicial process, these nonmilitary measures ought to have been condemned by the Court as well. But far from condemning them, the Court, to use Judge Morozov's phrase, accepted these actions as "some kind of normal countermeasures."[72]

[70] The Court's Judgment might well have been delivered before the rescue mission had it not been for the delay requested by the United States.

[71] Steps taken by the United States subsequent to the oral proceedings included breaking off diplomatic relations with Iran, prohibiting exports to Iran, preparing an inventory of blocked Iranian assets and a census of outstanding claims with a view to legislation to facilitate processing and payment of such claims, restricting payments to Iran, and prohibiting travel to Iran. 16 Weekly Comp. of Pres. Doc. 611–12 (April 14, 1980). The Court took note of these measures. [1980] ICJ Rep. 3, para. 31.

[72] [1980] ICJ Rep. at 52 (Morozov, J., dissenting). The passage in the majority opinion that appears to have inspired this characterization is found in paragraph 53 of the opinion. *Id.*, para. 53.

The distinction between responsive measures lawful in themselves ("retorsion") and measures lawful only as responses to prior violations of legal right ("reprisal") is neither relevant nor helpful in the present context. The point made in the text is that pursuit of judicial remedies excludes efforts to resolve the dispute by the use of power. Whether the particular employment of power would be lawful or unlawful in any other context is not of great consequence.

The United States had considerable difficulty determining how to characterize some of its own actions during the crisis. The assets freeze, probably the most severe deprivation visited upon Iran, was initially justified as a protective measure taken in response to Iran's threat to repudiate its obligations to U.S. nationals and withdraw its assets from U.S. financial institutions. Subsequently, the freeze was justified as a response to Iran's unlawful detention of the hostages. In oral argument

The distinction implicitly drawn by the Court, and rejected by Judges Lachs, Morozov, and Tarazi, requires us to look more closely at the basis of the duty to refrain from measures of coercion or self-help *pendente lite.* In this inquiry, we are greatly assisted by plenary consideration of this duty in the recent arbitral decision on the 1978 U.S.-France aviation dispute.[73] The tribunal in that case considered the question whether "countermeasures," *i.e.*, reprisals or sanctions, are permissible when a case is *sub judice.* It held:

> To the extent that the tribunal has the necessary means to achieve the objectives justifying the countermeasures, it must be admitted that the right of the Parties to initiate such measures disappears. In other words, the power of the tribunal to decide on interim measures of protection . . . leads to the disappearance of the power to initiate countermeasures and may lead to an elimination of existing countermeasures to the extent that the tribunal so provides as an interim measure of protection.[74]

The tribunal distinguished this situation from that obtaining in the period prior to the establishment of the tribunal when countermeasures are generally permissible.[75] The rule as articulated by the tribunal is in sum that countermeasures are generally permissible in the period before judicial remedies are available, but that the existence of effective judicial remedies leads to the disappearance of the right to impose countermeasures.

The relationship between this rule and the obligations implicit in resort to judicial remedies should be apparent. Countermeasures are but one species of measures anticipating the outcome of arbitral or judicial proceedings. They are based on a state's own appreciation of its legal situation vis-à-vis another state and are intended to bring about an outcome in accordance with that appreciation.[76] They are permissible before the tribunal is in a position to order interim measures of protection because no state is obliged to permit irreparable prejudice to its rights during the period between the institution of proceedings and final judgment.

Preserving those same rights during this period is the very purpose of interim measures of protection.[77] When the tribunal is able to protect a party's rights from irreparable harm *pendente lite* by an indication of provisional measures,

---

to the Court, the United States invented a new category to describe the assets freeze, "a justified, prudent, and proportional measure of restraint in the circumstances." Oral Argument Excerpt, *supra* note 67, at 56.

For a general and thorough consideration of legal issues related to the assets freeze, see Edwards, *Extraterritorial Application of the U.S. Iranian Assets Control Regulations*, 75 AJIL 870 (1981).

[73] Case concerning the Air Services Agreement of 27 March 1946 (United States v. France), 54 ILR 304, 336–41 (1978). Damrosch, *supra* note 16, discusses the case in depth.

[74] Case concerning the Air Services Agreement of 27 March 1946 (United States v. France), 54 ILR at 340–41.

[75] *Ibid.*

[76] *Id.* at 337. *See* E. DUMBAULD, *supra* note 49, at 28, *quoted at* note 58 *supra*; *see also* [1979] 2 Y.B. INT'L L. COMM'N 115–22, *supra* note 57.

[77] Statute of the International Court of Justice, Art. 41(1); Nuclear Tests Case, [1973] ICJ REP. at 103 (para. 20) (Art. 41 intended "to preserve the respective rights of the Parties pending the decision of the Court, and presupposes that irreparable prejudice should not be caused to rights which are the subject of dispute in judicial proceedings"); Fisheries Jurisdiction Case (United Kingdom v. Iceland), [1972] ICJ REP. 12, 16. *See generally* E. DUMBAULD, *supra* note 49, at 4–7.

the justification for countermeasures "disappears."[78] Replacing the party's authority to apply countermeasures with the tribunal's authority to indicate interim measures of protection represents an advance from the perspective of world order; an interim measures order substitutes an impartial judicial determination for a coerced outcome based on one party's view of its own rights.

The *Hostages* case teaches, however, that when such a judicial determination has been flouted by the addressee of the order, the right to initiate new nonforcible countermeasures revives.[79] A state simply cannot be expected in such a situation to permit irreparable prejudice to its rights any more than it can in the period prior to constitution of the tribunal. In fact, a prohibition on countermeasures even in the face of disregard of an interim measures order would impose so grossly unfair a burden on an applicant state that resort to judicial remedies would itself be discouraged.

We must therefore modify our earlier suggestion that all coercive measures intended to bring about the resolution of a dispute are barred *pendente lite*. Measures not involving the use of force are permissible when judicial remedies have been employed and have proved unavailing.

But the use of force is different. In the first place, it is by now axiomatic that the use of force as a means of reprisal or sanction is forbidden in contemporary international law.[80] As a result, the right to institute nonforcible measures of reprisal or sanction has no correlate involving the use of force. Never having existed, a right to take forcible reprisals cannot revive upon the disregard of an interim measures order. Therefore, the rescue mission cannot be justified in the same terms as the various nonmilitary measures taken by the United States.

The fact that the rescue mission cannot be justified as a measure of reprisal or sanction does not, of course, establish its objectionable character.[81] To establish this, and to understand properly the Court's criticism of the mission, we must examine the relationship between restraints on the use of force and the functioning of international judicial machinery.

This relationship can best be appreciated by means of a brief historical

[78] Case concerning the Air Services Agreement of 27 March 1946 (United States v. France), 54 ILR at 340.

[79] To this limited extent, the Court must be understood as endorsing the view that there is an implied condition of reciprocity in every interim measures order. The United States had urged this view in a series of presentations to the Court. *See World Court Rules on American Hostages*, DEP'T STATE BULL., No. 2035, Feb. 1980, at 40, 48 (in oral argument on interim measures request); *see also* Oral Argument Excerpt, *supra* note 67, at 56. But the Court's citation of its interim measures Order as one basis for condemning the rescue mission shows that some U.S. obligations survived Iran's blatant disregard of the Order.

[80] The Declaration on Principles of International Law concerning Friendly Relations and Co-operation among States in Accordance with the Charter of the United Nations makes this uncharacteristically plain: "States have a duty to refrain from acts of reprisal involving the use of force." GA Res. 2625, 25 UN GAOR, Supp. (No. 28) 121, 122, UN Doc. A/8028 (1970). Even authorities supporting recognition of a general right of reprisal are careful to exclude forcible reprisals. *See, e.g.*, [1979] 2 Y.B. INT'L L. COMM'N 118, *supra* note 57 (collecting authorities); Case concerning the Air Services Agreement of 27 March 1946 (United States v. France), 54 ILR at 337.

[81] The Court carefully avoided characterizing the rescue mission as an unlawful use of force. *See* text at note 7 *supra*.

review. The effort to "outlaw war" and the effort to establish machinery for the judicial settlement of disputes have proceeded in parallel at least from the days of the Hague Peace Conferences at the turn of the century. And from the very beginning, the two efforts were critically linked in treaties whose characteristic feature was to restrain the use of force *pendente lite*. This linkage may be observed in the 1902 Treaty of Corinto,[82] in the 1907 Hague Convention respecting the Limitation of Force for the Recovery of Contract Debts,[83] and in the "cooling-off" provisions of the "Bryan Treaties" concluded in 1913–1914 by the United States and various other countries.[84]

The Covenant of the League of Nations marked the culmination of this stage of development. The Covenant provided for the establishment of the Permanent Court of International Justice and imposed general obligations to settle disputes by arbitration or other peaceful means.[85] The members of the League pledged not to "resort to war" during the pendency of arbitral proceedings and for a period of 3 months thereafter.[86] They also agreed not to resort to war against any member of the League that complied with an arbitral decision.[87] Under the structure established in the Covenant, then, the right to resort to war was suspended during the pendency of arbitral proceedings. The obligation to arbitrate disputes and machinery for this purpose were thus linked directly to an obligation to refrain from the use of force *pendente lite*.

Against the background of the Covenant and similar instruments, it was but a short step to the conclusion that there existed under customary international law an obligation to refrain from the use of force during the pendency of arbitral or judicial proceedings. Dumbauld, for example, took the position that

> resort to war for the solution of a dispute referred to arbitration is repugnant to the obligations which the parties have assumed. An agreement to arbitrate would be nugatory if, after deciding that a dispute shall be settled by arbitration, parties remained free to settle it by war. Acts of

[82] Convention of Peace and Arbitration, Jan. 20, 1902, Costa Rica-El Salvador-Honduras-Nicaragua, Art. 11, 190 Parry's TS 357. Under the Treaty the parties were obligated to refrain from a variety of military measures while arbitral proceedings were in progress in order to avoid impeding settlement of the dispute by those means. E. DUMBAULD, *supra* note 49, at 93–95, discusses the Treaty of Corinto and the limited experience under it.

[83] *Signed* Oct. 18, 1907, 36 Stat. 2241, TS No. 537, 205 Parry's TS 250. Force could not be used against a state that agreed to arbitration of questions relating to its debt, until and unless the state refused to honor the arbitral award. *See* I. BROWNLIE, *supra* note 7, at 24, 225–26.

[84] Pending the report of a commission of inquiry, declaration of war or initiation of hostilities was forbidden. *See, e.g.*, Treaty for the Advancement of Peace, Jan. 22, 1914, United States-Bolivia, 38 Stat. 1868, TS No. 606; Treaty for the Advancement of Peace, July 24, 1914, United States-Brazil, 39 Stat. 1698, TS No. 627; Treaty for the Settlement of Disputes, Oct. 13, 1914, United States-Sweden, 38 Stat. 1872, TS No. 607 (barring any "act of force"). *See* E. DUMBAULD, *supra* note 49, at 99–101; I. BROWNLIE, *supra* note 7, at 23, for consideration of the "Bryan Treaties."

[85] LEAGUE OF NATIONS COVENANT art. 12, para. 1, *reprinted in* 1 M. HUDSON, INTERNATIONAL LEGISLATION 1 (1931) (disputes likely "to lead to a rupture" to be submitted to arbitration or inquiry by League Council); *id.* art. 13, para. 1 (obligation to submit to arbitration all disputes recognized to be "suitable for arbitration").

[86] *Id.* art. 12, para. 1.

[87] *Id.* art. 13, para. 4.

> hostility are certainly inconsistent with the expressed desire for peaceful solution of the controversy.
>
> . . . .
>
> It should be emphasized that the obligation not to resort to war in question here is entirely independent of legal limitations on warmaking as such. It is not war *per se* which is illegal here; it is failure to live up to the promise to arbitrate.[88]

The basic incompatibility between force and judicial redress thus gained legal recognition.

This is not to say, however, that the use of force in self-defense *pendente lite* became unlawful. Statements such as that just quoted and the treaty provisions on which they are based must be read against the background of the then prevailing law respecting the use of force generally. As demonstrated by Brownlie and others, the Covenant and other instruments concluded prior to the Kellogg-Briand Treaty were intended to restrict the previously unrestricted right to use force in the enforcement of rights, *i.e.*, as a measure of self-help, sanction, or reprisal.[89] By prohibiting the use of force pending the outcome of arbitral proceedings, the Covenant restricted the lawful use of force in the enforcement of rights to cases where the underlying right had been judicially recognized. There was as yet no question of restricting the use of force to cases of self-defense or community authorization.[90] Nor was there any question of restricting the exercise of the right of self-defense itself.[91] In other words, the Covenant's restraints on the use of force *pendente lite* were restraints on the

[88] E. DUMBAULD, *supra* note 49, at 182–83.

[89] *See* I. BROWNLIE, *supra* note 7, at 48, 56, 58, 68. As Professor Brownlie explains:

> The essence of the Covenant . . . was the obligation to use peaceful means of settling disputes, resort to war being conditional on failure of the procedures for peaceful settlement for which provision was made. . . . The Covenant therefore must be interpreted as a creature of its time and on the assumption that a right to go to war recognized by the customary law still existed.

Id. at 56.

Efforts prior to the Kellogg-Briand Treaty to strengthen the League's peace machinery were likewise premised on the lawfulness of force as a means of enforcing rights. The abortive Draft Treaty of Mutual Assistance, for example, declared aggressive war an international crime, but provided specifically that a war waged by a victorious party in a case before the Permanent Court or an arbitral tribunal was not aggressive war. As Brownlie states, such a provision "is in harmony with the Covenant in that it assumes the legality of war as a means of settlement." *Id.* at 68.

For additional consideration of the circumstances under which resort to war was permissible within the framework of the Covenant, see Waldock, *supra* note 7, at 471.

See also E. NANTWI, THE ENFORCEMENT OF INTERNATIONAL JUDICIAL DECISIONS AND ARBITRAL AWARDS IN PUBLIC INTERNATIONAL LAW 123–26 (1966).

[90] After Kellogg-Briand, the right to resort to force no longer turned on the merits of the underlying controversy or indeed on the outcome of judicial consideration of the controversy. *See* I. BROWNLIE, *supra* note 7, at 89–90.

[91] Even the Kellogg-Briand Treaty did not restrict the right to self-defense, a point made crystal clear by Secretary Kellogg's famous explanatory note to the governments of 14 countries invited to become parties to the Treaty. The text of the note is reproduced in J. SHOTWELL, WAR AS AN INSTRUMENT OF NATIONAL POLICY 296–303 (1929), and is discussed in the same work at 172–76.

use of force in the enforcement of rights, not in the exercise of the right of self-defense. Under the Covenant and similar instruments, the use of force in the enforcement of rights *pendente lite* became an unlawful use of force; the use of force in self-defense, even *pendente lite*, did not.

Nor did the United Nations Charter change the law in this respect. Article 51 of the Charter provides that "nothing" in the Charter impairs the inherent right of individual or collective self-defense. That sweeping negation is broad enough to comprehend not only the obligations growing out of Article 2(4) on the use of force, but also those arising from Articles 2(3) and 33 on the peaceful settlement of disputes, Article 94 on the International Court of Justice, and Article 41 of the Court's Statute on interim measures of protection. As Rosenne points out in connection with Article 91 of the Charter, which establishes that the Statute of the Court is an integral part of the Charter, "those portions of the Charter which are of general application to the Organization as a whole, and to each one of its organs individually, are applicable also to the Court."[92] It follows that neither general obligations derived from the submission of the case to the Court nor specific obligations embodied in an interim measures order can deprive a party of the right to self-defense. The otherwise lawful use of force in self-defense does not become an unlawful use of force simply because it occurs while a case is *sub judice*.

The contrary conclusion would price international adjudication out of the market in peace-threatening situations, precisely those in which resort to available judicial remedies should be encouraged. In a crisis, political leaders often feel impelled to "do something" to relieve pressures for military action against an adversary; on several occasions, including perhaps the hostage crisis itself, "doing something" has meant filing a case in the Court.[93] And if cases brought

[92] 1 S. ROSENNE, *supra* note 56, at 68.

[93] *See* T. ELIAS, NEW HORIZONS IN INTERNATIONAL LAW 139 (1979) (citing Greece's Application to the Court in the *Aegean Sea Continental Shelf* case as an example); 1 S. ROSENNE, *supra* note 56, at 16. The Pakistani Application in the *Trial of Pakistani Prisoners of War* case may have been similarly motivated.

In the hostage crisis itself, the pressures in favor of using force had become quite strong by the time the U.S. Application was filed on Nov. 29. The President himself had hinted darkly at the possibility that force would be used. On Nov. 20, in response to new reports that the hostages would be put on trial, the White House stated that the "United States is seeking a peaceful solution to this problem through the U.N. and every other available channel," but that "other remedies . . . explicitly recognized in the Charter of the United Nations" were available. According to Smith, *Putting the Hostages' Lives First*, N.Y. Times Magazine, May 18, 1981, at 76, 83, on that same day the United States threatened through Swiss intermediaries to mine or blockade Iranian harbors if the hostages were mistreated. On Nov. 28, the President held a news conference to discuss the situation in Iran. When asked about its effects on the credibility of the U.S. military deterrent and the possibility of war, the President emphasized both that the United States had the "full support of our allies" and that he was committed to seeking the hostages' release through peaceful means. He added, however, that the United States had other "options" available to it if diplomacy proved unavailing.

Both the White House statement and the transcript of the news conference are included in Appendix B to the Memorial of the United States. The Memorial, which contains a wealth of primary source material on the development of the crisis through early January 1980, has not yet been published by the Court, but is available from the Government Printing Office. CASE CONCERNING UNITED STATES DIPLOMATIC AND CONSULAR STAFF IN TEHRAN (UNITED STATES v. IRAN), MEMORIAL OF THE GOVERNMENT OF THE UNITED STATES (1980).

under such circumstances have not typically demonstrated the Court's effectiveness in conventional terms, the decision to file suit may provide breathing space sufficient to negotiate a settlement or at least sufficient to let passions cool. Moreover, the possibility cannot be discounted entirely that both sides will see in proceedings before the Court a path away from the precipice.[94] These are benefits not lightly to be discarded in the name of a rule of doubtful formal validity. The use of force in self-defense thus remains lawful even during the course of judicial proceedings.

Emphasis on the lawfulness of the use of force must not, however, be permitted to obscure a basic truth that was given recognition in the League Covenant and similar instruments and that underlies their provisions restraining the use of force *pendente lite*. Judicial machinery was made available so that resort to force would be unnecessary. But equally, resort to force was barred so that judicial machinery could function effectively. In other words, only one of the purposes of restraints on the use of force *pendente lite* was to reduce the incidence of force in international life. A second, and equally basic, purpose was to ensure the maintenance of conditions under which the judicial process could function effectively to settle the dispute.[95]

The fulfillment of that second purpose is independent of the lawfulness of the use of force itself. Indeed, this is the premise of the Court's apparent distinction in the *Hostages* case between unlawful actions and actions incompatible with respect for the judicial process.[96] The use of force, even the lawful use of force, is a uniquely disorderly means of resolving an international controversy. It disrupts efforts to resolve the dispute by judicial or other pacific means. Even under a colorable or indeed a valid claim of self-defense, it heightens antagonisms, inflames passions, and generates new conflict. The use of force is the classic example of action that, in the words of the Court's interim measures Order, "may aggravate the tension between the two countries or render the existing dispute more difficult of solution."[97] Consequently, the Court's treatment of the rescue mission rests on the distinction between situations where the right to use force does not exist and those where the right exists but its exercise would adversely affect the political environment and thus would cloud the prospects for successful adjudication of the controversy.

It is here, in fact, that the two elements of the Court's criticism of the rescue

[94] The availability of a far less prestigious forum for airing Iranian grievances, the ad hoc Commission of Inquiry, nearly resulted in resolution of the crisis. *See* Smith, *supra* note 93, at 88–91.

[95] The point is made expressly by Dumbauld, commenting on the Court's power to forbid "invasion" *pendente lite*:

> As shown by the last example, the Court may forbid acts of self-help and hostilities to the extent that such conduct interferes with the Court's functioning or jeopardizes execution of its task. Preservation of peace as such is not the task of the Court, but of the League of Nations. The Court may forbid only such fighting as impedes its own functioning.

E. DUMBAULD, *supra* note 49, at 167.

[96] [1980] ICJ REP. 3, para. 93.

[97] [1979] ICJ REP. 7, para. 47(1)(B).

For assessments of the impact of the rescue attempt, see Kifner, *How a Sit-in Turned into a Siege*, N.Y. Times Magazine, May 18, 1981, at 70–73; Smith, *supra* note 93, at 96–98.

attempt become linked. A common theme unites the apparently separate conclusions that the mission undermined "respect for the judicial process in international relations" and that it violated the general provision of the interim measures Order. As we have seen, every litigant is under a duty to conduct itself throughout a case in such a manner that the judicial process can function reliably, impartially, and effectively. Because the use of force *pendente lite* impairs the prospects for judicial resolution of the controversy, it is incompatible with this duty regardless of its lawfulness *vel non*. And because the requirements of the judicial process itself are the touchstones of the determination that a use of force is improper though not unlawful, the Court has a special claim to competence to evaluate such conduct. For the same reason, the appropriate question to be asked by the Court is not whether the use of force is unlawful, but instead whether the interference with the judicial process in the particular case merits withholding judicial remedies from the offending party.

We must note one highly significant limitation on the position that the use of force must always be regarded as incompatible with the obligations of a litigant before the Court. An interim measures order is directed to actions that make the "existing dispute" more difficult to resolve, actions that "aggravate the tensions" resulting from the situation as it is at the time the interim measures order is issued. The use of force in self-defense to respond to a threat not existing at the time the order was issued, is not covered. A state would therefore not be in violation of an interim measures order in a case involving title to disputed territory it had occupied at the outset of the case if it were to respond with force to an invasion of the territory by the opposing state. Similarly, a state that used force to protect its fishing vessels from forcible acts of interference on the high seas beginning or intensifying subsequent to an interim measures order would not thereby violate the order.[98] In neither case would the defensive use of force disappoint expectations of restraint legitimately raised by the decision to pursue judicial remedies, expectations premised on a different factual context. In contrast, where the exigency allegedly justifying the resort to force existed at the outset of the proceedings and had not changed in quality or degree, the use of force would aggravate the "existing situation" with which the order was concerned. In the *Hostages* case, the United States made no effort

[98] The example is drawn from the *Fisheries Jurisdiction* case. Despite the Court's interim measures Order requiring Iceland to refrain from enforcing its fishing regulations, Icelandic gunboats began a campaign of harassment of British fishing vessels that included cutting their trawl lines. As Icelandic harassment intensified and came to include the firing of rifles or cannons, the United Kingdom determined it was necessary to introduce British naval vessels in a "purely defensive role" in the waters claimed by Iceland, but covered by the Court's Order. Memorial on the Merits of the United Kingdom, 1 Fisheries Jurisdiction Case, ICJ Pleadings 286 (1975). The Government of Iceland took a different view, referring in a letter addressed to the Court to "the tension which has been provoked by the presence of British armed vessels within the fifty-mile limit." Fisheries Jurisdiction Case, [1974] ICJ REP. 3, 18.

The Court did not criticize the measures taken by the United Kingdom to protect its fishing vessels from acts of interference. In its only comment on compliance with the interim measures Order, the Court noted that the United Kingdom's compliance with the catch limitation features of the Order was unquestioned. *Id.* at 16–17. In contrast, the Court noted Iceland's disregard of the provision barring enforcement of its fishery regulations. *Id.* at 17. The Court's refusal to criticize the intervention of the British Navy is strong support for the proposition stated in the text.

to demonstrate to the Court that the rescue mission was undertaken in response to a new or more imminent peril to the hostages' lives.[99]

As explained at length above, the United States did not by seeking judicial relief limit its freedom to act. It did, however, limit its freedom to act without offense to the Court. A scrupulous regard for the Court and its processes would have led the United States either to terminate proceedings once Iran's attitude became unmistakably clear or to forgo a military solution.

V. The Problem of Sanctions

We saw earlier that the very fact that a state has elected to pursue available judicial remedies imposes certain obligations upon it. In general, a state is required to conduct itself in relation to the case and the matter in dispute in such a manner as to avoid bringing into question the reliability, impartiality, or effectiveness of the international judicial process. Conduct not conforming to this norm tends "to undermine respect for the judicial process in international relations" and may, moreover, be incompatible with provisions of an interim measures order.

The question that remains is whether an international tribunal, and the International Court of Justice in particular, may, in subsequent proceedings in the case, itself impose sanctions on a litigant whose conduct fails to meet this standard. The idea has an instinctive appeal: a litigant whose conduct is incompatible with the proper functioning of the judicial process ought not to be able to use that process for its own ends. Certainly, no other class of sanctions lies as much within the actual power of the tribunal itself to administer; the court's decision to impose a special burden on the delinquent state in subsequent proceedings or to deny it relief is entirely self-executing.[100] No other actor can claim a competence equal to the court's in assessing the gravity of the harm caused by the litigant's improper conduct. And though other sanctions may also be proper in a given case, their availability hardly seems a basis for denying generally the tribunal's authority to impose penalties of its own.[101]

[99] None of the documentation submitted to the Court suggested the existence of a new threat to the hostages; indeed, the U.S. assertion that the mission had been carried out "in exercise of its inherent right of self-defence with the aim of extricating American nationals who have been and remain the victims of the Iranian armed attack on our Embassy," [1980] ICJ Rep. 3, para. 32, tends to negate the existence of a new threat to the hostages.

[100] *Cf.* 1 S. Rosenne, *supra* note 56, at 124–25 (enforcement of interlocutory orders with the exception of interim measures orders).

[101] Thus, the failure of a judgment-debtor to comply with a judgment of the International Court of Justice may expose it to sanctions at a number of different levels. The prevailing party may be entitled to seek to coerce compliance with the judgment by nonforcible sanctions and to execute the judgment by nonforcible means of self-help, *e.g.*, the seizure of assets to satisfy a damages award. *See* 1 S. Rosenne, *supra* note 56, at 133–48; E. Nantwi, *supra* note 89, at 120–47; Schachter, *The Enforcement of International Judicial and Arbitral Decisions*, 54 AJIL 1, 16–17 (1960). The same failure to comply may expose the recalcitrant party to sanctions by the Security Council. UN Charter art. 94(2). Finally, the failure to comply with the judgment may be made a bar to the institution of proceedings for revision before the Court. Statute of the International Court of Justice, Art. 61(3). Thus, the refusal to comply with a final judgment may result in sanctions imposed by the prevailing party, the Security Council, and the Court itself.

In fact, there can be no serious question of the authority of international tribunals to attach serious consequences to the violations of certain duties. One well-known example of judicial enforcement of the duties of litigants relates to evidentiary matters. As we saw earlier, a litigant before an international tribunal is obligated to make available to the tribunal all relevant information reasonably accessible to it.[102] The failure to produce such evidence can have a variety of consequences. Where the information is presumptively in the hands of the party who fails to produce it, adverse inferences as to the facts may be drawn by the tribunal.[103] The tribunal's authority to draw such adverse inferences need not be specified in the *compromis*, rules of procedure, or other constitutive instrument. It is inherent.[104] In addition to this inherent authority, some international tribunals have been granted express authority to respond to failures to produce relevant documents or material. For example, the Anglo-German Mixed Arbitral Tribunal established after the First World War was empowered to "make such order as it thinks fit" in the event of noncompliance by a party or government agent with a request for the production of documents, books, or other objects.[105] This provision presumably empowered the tribunal to impose a variety of sanctions in cases of nonproduction, although we cannot be sure since no cases seem to have arisen under it. Perhaps with such a provision in mind, Professor Sandifer suggests that a default judgment might be entered against a nondisclosing party.[106]

Article 49 of the Statute of the International Court of Justice deals with a related problem. It authorizes the Court to take "formal note" of any refusal to produce documents or explanations it has requested. At the very least, Article 49 empowers the Court to employ the sanction of judicial censure, a sanction whose seriousness should not be underestimated. A state's primary object in proceedings before the Court may be to garner the political benefit of demonstrating that its position is based on legal right, that it (and not the other party) is "law-abiding," and that the other party's actions are the ones that challenge the established order of things. In a context where rectitude is the primary value at stake, censure by the Court is a significant sanction.

Moreover, it is by no means clear that Article 49 limits the Court to taking note of the refusal. Respected scholars have suggested that the very purpose

[102] *See* sources cited at note 50 *supra*.

[103] *See* Parker Claim, Op. of the Comm'n 35, 37, 40 (1926), 4 R. Int'l Arb. Awards 35, 37–40; Kling Claim, Op. of the Comm'n 36, 44–46 (1930), *id.* at 575, 582–84. *See generally* D. SANDIFER, *supra* note 50, at 147–54.

[104] D. SANDIFER, *supra* note 50, at 460. The support for this position is drawn primarily from the jurisprudence of the U.S.-Mexican claims commissions of the 1920's. It should be observed, however, that Article VIII(4) of the Rules of Procedure of the U.S.-Mexican General Claims Commission and the corresponding article of the rules for the U.S-Mexican Special Claims Commission empowered the tribunal to "take note" of a refusal to permit the inspection of documents and records. The rules are reproduced in A. FELLER, THE MEXICAN CLAIMS COMMISSIONS 365 (General Claims Commission), 408 (Special Claims Commission) (1935).

[105] Anglo-German Mixed Arbitral Tribunal Rules of Procedure, Art. 25, 1 Trib. Arb. Mixtes 109, 115–16. The authority of the U.S.-Mexican claims commissions to "take note" of refusals to permit document inspection may also be cited in this regard. *See* note 104 *supra*.

[106] D. SANDIFER, *supra* note 50, at 112.

of "taking note" is to establish the predicate for other sanctions. Professor Reisman, conceding that it is "difficult to say precisely what 'take note' signifies," adds that, "if it is to mean anything, it must be that the tribunal will apply any of a variety of sanctions, as it deems the circumstances merit."[107] Among the sanctions he considers within the power of the Court under Article 49 are levying costs against the withholding party, shifting the burden of proof, or ultimately giving judgment by default.[108] Professor Sandifer appears to share this view, but correctly notes that the Court has been very cautious about exercising whatever power is implicit in Article 49, including even the power to draw inferences adverse to the nonproducing party.[109] In the *Corfu Channel* case, the only instance to date of an unambiguous refusal to produce a requested document, the Court concluded that no inference adverse to the United Kingdom should be drawn.[110]

Another unambiguous authorization for judicial enforcement of a litigant's duties appears in Article 61 of the Court's Statute. Paragraph 3 of that article permits the Court to "require previous compliance with the terms of the judgment before it admits proceedings in revision."[111] The provision is frankly coercive in design. The remedy of revision may be made unavailable to a state that fails to perform the most basic implied obligation of all, *i.e.*, to carry out a judgment in good faith. Once compliance has been obtained, the proceedings may go forward.[112] Although the Court has not had occasion to consider the possible application of Article 61(3), it is strikingly analogous to the rule in

[107] W. REISMAN, *supra* note 50, at 599.

[108] *Id.* at 603. He adds that "on review, a claim of non-disclosure, if upheld, could result in nullification of the award upon demonstration of the materiality of the suppressed material." *Ibid.*

[109] D. SANDIFER, *supra* note 50, at 460.

[110] [1949] ICJ REP. at 32. Whether the Court's decision rested on the conclusion that the United Kingdom's claim of "naval secrecy" constituted a valid claim of privilege, or on the Court's guess as to the probable content of the document, or instead on a combination of the two together is unclear. W. REISMAN, *supra* note 50, at 601.

Interestingly, in the *Hostages* case itself, the United States sought to invoke a kind of privilege resting on the privacy interests of the hostages' families. At an early stage, the Court sought the names of the hostages; the United States justified its refusal to provide this information by a desire to protect the hostages' families from publicity and possible harassment. Despite this policy of the U.S. Government, the names of the hostages ultimately became general knowledge and the United States supplied a list to the Court. No sanction was imposed by the Court for the delay, perhaps in recognition of the validity of the U.S. concern.

The privacy rationale was also invoked in another context. The United States offered to the Court for its *in camera* inspection sworn, signed, affidavits of 6 of the 13 hostages who had been released on Nov. 20, 1979. Oral Argument Excerpt, *supra* note 67, at 49. The Court did not agree to an *in camera* procedure, but did allow the United States to submit the affidavits with the names deleted. The Court apparently relied upon these affidavits in assessing the facts. [1980] ICJ REP. 3, paras. 11 and 23.

[111] This article constitutes an exception to the general rule stated by Rosenne that noncompliance with final judgments "does not normally enable the Court to impose any sanction *vis-à-vis* the recalcitrant State, either in that or in any other case." 1 S. ROSENNE, *supra* note 56, at 125–26.

[112] The legislative history of Article 61(3) is rather sparse, but tends to confirm that its purpose was to provide the Court with a means of assuring compliance with its judgments. Permanent Court of International Justice, Advisory Comm. of Jurists, Procès-Verbaux of the Proceedings of the Committee (June 16th–July 24th, 1920) 744–45.

common law countries that "a contemnor may not be heard."[113] For so long as the suitor places himself above the law and refuses to comply with a court order, ordinary judicial remedies for correction of a judgment will be unavailable to him.[114]

The authority of a tribunal to enforce obedience to interim measures orders is more problematic. A few international tribunals have been authorized expressly to punish disobedience to their orders. The Anglo-Austrian, Anglo-Belgian, and Anglo-Hungarian Mixed Arbitral Tribunals are cases in point. The rules of procedure of each of these tribunals provided in Articles 74 and 75 for the imposition of sanctions upon a party disobeying an order of the tribunal. The range of permissible sanctions extended to dismissal of the claim or entry of judgment by default.[115] This power does not seem to have been relied upon by any of the three tribunals.[116] Nor was the provision of such a power widely imitated.[117] Although it would be clearly improper on the basis of this record to conclude that such a power is inherent, it would be equally erroneous to assert that such a power is unknown in international law.

Turning to the International Court of Justice itself, we find that the early history of the Statute and Rules of Court contains some support for the view that the Court lacks the authority to enforce its interim measures orders. During the discussions of the Advisory Committee of Jurists on the Statute of the Permanent Court, Mr. Fernandes urged that interim measures orders "be supported by effective penalties" to be imposed at the discretion of the Court.[118] This suggestion was opposed, and the discussion then focused on the need to provide a link between the Court and the Council of the League of Nations.[119] Subsequently, during the drafting of the original Rules of Procedure of the Permanent Court, the Court's Committee on Procedure opined that "as the Court had no power to enforce decisions with regard to interim measures,"

[113] For a general consideration of this rule in England, see G. BORRIE & N. LOWE, *supra* note 42, at 367–69; Dobbs, *supra* note 42, at 278–282, considers the same rule in the United States. The authors make clear that this sanction is an extreme one that is used sparingly.

[114] The leading judicial authorities for the rule in England as well as in the United States both uphold the denial of a right to appeal to a party who has not complied with a lower court order. *See* Hadkinson v. Hadkinson, [1952] All E.R. 567; National Union of Marine Cooks & Stewards v. Arnold, 348 U.S. 37 (1954).

[115] *See* 1 Trib. Arb. Mixtes 633, 650, 666.

[116] E. DUMBAULD, *supra* note 49, at 129–44, reviews the jurisprudence of all the mixed arbitral tribunals in regard to interim measures. He reports no case considering the problem of noncompliance. The present author's own review failed to turn up any such case either.

[117] Interestingly enough, no parallel rule appears in the Rules of Procedure of the Anglo-German Mixed Arbitral Tribunal, 1 Trib. Arb. Mixtes 109, or in the rules of procedure for tribunals established by pairs of continental countries, even when one of the pair was also a participant in one of the above-mentioned tribunals with the United Kingdom; *see, e.g.*, Rules of Procedure of the Austrian-Serbo-Croat-Slovene Mixed Arbitral Tribunal, *id.* at 698; Rules of Procedure of the Bulgarian-Belgian Mixed Arbitral Tribunal, *id.* at 231. This pattern suggests that the sanction for disobedience provision was a British invention that did not find favor with the continental countries. The comparison presents a rather neat example of differing attitudes to contempt of court.

[118] PCIJ, Procès-Verbaux, *supra* note 112, at 588.

[119] *Ibid.*

there was no need to develop special procedures for the indication of such measures.[120] The Committee's express premise, rather than its conclusion, is what interests us.

The persuasive force of this evidence, however, is diminished by a consideration of its context. Assertions that the Court lacked power to "enforce" its orders seem principally to refer to the absence of an executive arm attached to the Court, an impression confirmed by the emphasis placed in these discussions on the link between the Court and the League Council.[121]

Indeed, contemporaneous evidence indicates that the eminent jurists who drafted the Court's original Rules of Procedure believed that the Court possessed the authority under the Statute to enforce interim measures orders. The original version of Article 57 of the Rules gave the Court authority to "place on record" any refusal by a party to comply with an order of the Court.[122] The legislative history of this provision indicates that the Court was authorized to employ a range of sanctions comparable to those available under the "take note" language of Article 49 of the Statute.[123] Mr. Nyholm in fact asserted without contradiction that the Court could take noncompliance into account in its final judgment.[124] In the only direct response to Nyholm's assertion, Lord Finlay agreed and added, "In such a case damages should be stipulated in the judgment."[125] The adoption of Article 57 and the discussion surrounding it thus are strong support for the conclusion that the Court is empowered under the Statute to impose some sanctions for disobedience to its interim measures orders.[126]

The Court's jurisprudence with regard to interim measures orders tends to confirm this conclusion, at least to the extent of permitting the Court to censure

[120] PCIJ, ser. D, No. 2, at 302.

[121] PCIJ, Procès-Verbaux, *supra* note 112, at 588, 736.

[122] The complete text of the relevant portion of Article 57 was as follows: "Any refusal by the parties to conform to the suggestions of the Court or of the President, with regard to such measures, shall be placed on record." PCIJ, ser. D, No. 1, at 56.

[123] The provision in question appears to have been drawn from Article 105 of a draft by Nyholm, which empowered the Court to "attach due legal weight to the fact [of noncompliance] when deciding the principal question at issue." *Id.*, No. 2, at 377.

[124] *Id.* at 77.

[125] *Ibid.* During the *Fisheries Jurisdiction* case, the United Kingdom sought an award of damages for Iceland's harassment of British fishing vessels in the period subsequent to the Court's interim measures Order. Memorial of the United Kingdom, *supra* note 98, at 375–78. The submission does not appear to have been based on the view that violation of the interim measures Order itself constituted an independent basis for the award of damages; instead, the position was that Iceland's acts interfered with the right of UK nationals to fish freely on the high seas. *Id.* at 377–78. Following the negotiation of a *modus vivendi*, the United Kingdom withdrew this submission, Argument of Rt. Hon. Samuel Silkin, *id.* at 446–47, 472, and the Court consequently had no occasion to pass upon it.

[126] The text of Article 57 remained unaltered through the 1926 revision of the Rules. PCIJ, ser. D, No. 1, at 56. In the 1931 revision of the Rules, the clause under discussion was deleted from Article 57. *Id.*, No. 1 (2d ed.), at 42. The principal motive for the change was to avoid featuring so prominently in the text of the Rules the possibility of noncompliance with an order of the Court. *See id.*, No. 2 (Add. 2), at 187, 198–99. Then-Professor Hudson applauded the deletion: "fortunately, this hint of disobedience has now disappeared from the rules." Hudson, *The Amended Rules of the Permanent Court of International Justice*, 25 AJIL 427, 435 (1931).

a disobedient litigant. In three of the four cases in which an interim measures order has been disregarded, the Court has made specific mention of that fact.[127] However, more severe sanctions against respondent states, in particular entry of judgment, may be precluded by the terms of Article 53 of the Court's Statute. In cases where the respondent fails to appear, Article 53 requires the Court to satisfy itself that the contentions of the applicant are well-founded in fact and law before giving judgment in its favor. Since each time that the Court has noted a respondent state's failure to comply with an interim measures order, Article 53 has been applicable,[128] the Court may well have been prohibited from imposing more severe sanctions.

Caution in imposing severe sanctions against respondents also finds support in two other special characteristics of interim measures orders. First, the Court will not require a definitive showing on jurisdiction as a predicate for the indication of provisional measures; it is enough to show prima facie that jurisdiction exists.[129] This rule, though now settled, has long been controversial;[130] there may be considerable hardship in requiring a state that has not submitted to the jurisdiction of the Court to maintain what may be a quite onerous temporary regime. The hardship would be far greater, of course, if final judgment on the merits of the controversy could be rendered against that same state for failing to comply with the interim measures decree. Permitting the Court to impose severe sanctions for noncompliance with an interim measures order thus would make it very possible for a final judgment on the merits to be rendered against a state when it is not subject to the Court's jurisdiction. When to all of these problems are added the lingering doubts that interim measures orders are binding at all,[131] the Court's cautious attitude toward imposing on respondents sanctions more severe than censure appears amply justified.

Applicants, however, stand in a different position in relation to the Court. They come to it seeking its aid, professing their commitment to its processes, and asserting the binding force of the provisional orders they seek. Sanctions more serious than censure do not therefore raise the same problems as if they

[127] Case concerning United States Diplomatic and Consular Staff in Tehran, [1980] ICJ REP. 3, paras. 75 and 93; Nuclear Tests Case, [1974] ICJ REP. at 258–59 (para. 19); Fisheries Jurisdiction Case, *id.* at 16–17 (paras. 33–34). The tone adopted by the Court in these cases varies widely; in the *Hostages* case, the Court sharply censured Iran for its disobedience, while in the *Nuclear Tests* case the Court merely reported the Australian complaint that the Order had been violated.

In the fourth case involving noncompliance with an interim measures order, the Court made no mention of the fact of noncompliance. Anglo-Iranian Oil Co., [1952] ICJ REP. 93.

[128] Case concerning United States Diplomatic and Consular Staff in Tehran, [1980] ICJ REP. 3, para. 11; Nuclear Tests Case, [1974] ICJ REP. at 257 (para. 15); Fisheries Jurisdiction Case, *id.* at 8–10 (paras. 14–18).

[129] Case concerning United States Diplomatic and Consular Staff in Tehran, [1979] ICJ REP. at 13 (para. 15); Nuclear Tests Case, [1973] ICJ REP. at 101 (para. 13); Fisheries Jurisdiction Case, [1972] ICJ REP. at 15–16 (paras. 15–17).

[130] For a thorough consideration of the doctrine, see Mendelson, *Interim Measures of Protection in Cases of Contested Jurisdiction,* 46 BRIT. Y.B. INT'L L. 259 (1972–73); *see also* Goldsworthy, *Interim Measures of Protection in the International Court of Justice,* 68 AJIL 258, 262–68 (1974).

[131] *See generally* Goldsworthy, *supra* note 130, at 273–74.

were imposed on respondents. In domestic law, the parallel distinction is made: sanctions for noncompliance with court orders are more generally available against the party seeking relief than against the party from whom relief is sought.[132] An analogy to the equitable doctrine of unclean hands suggests itself as well. "Bad," even though not unlawful, conduct may be a bar to obtaining equitable relief. Although the conduct in question might not be actionable in itself, it operates as a bar to affirmative relief in favor of the offending party.[133] A doctrine similar to "unclean hands" appears to be recognized in international law.[134] And Article 61(3) manifests the acceptance of an analogous principle in the Statute of the Court itself; as we have seen, a state that fails to comply with a final judgment may be denied the right to institute proceedings for revision.[135] The raw material necessary to fashion a distinction between applicants and respondents appears to be available. We would suggest that the Court does have the authority to impose sanctions more severe than censure on an applicant state in violation of its duties under an interim measures order.

In deciding whether that authority should be exercised, however, two factors, in addition to the gravity of the applicant's offense, are appropriately taken into

[132] *See* Dobbs, *supra* note 42, at 279. *See also* Kirchner v. Kirchner, 5 N.J. Super. 341, 344, 69 A.2d 30, 31 (1949). The point is clearly made in a decision of the California Supreme Court:

> A defendant is always under compulsion. The plaintiff is always seeking affirmative relief at the hands of the court. The defendant is merely contesting plaintiff's right to such relief. While, therefore, it is improper, under such circumstances, to deprive a defendant of the right to make his showing as to the matter urged against him, and, by striking out his answer, to compel him to submit to a judgment without a hearing upon the merits, the case of a plaintiff is far different. He is seeking the court's aid, and it is manifestly just and proper that, in invoking that aid, he should submit himself to all legitimate orders and processes.

O'Neill v. Thomas Day Co., 92 P. 856, 859 (1907).

[133] A leading treatise on equity jurisprudence concludes an extended discussion of the "unclean hands" doctrine with the following statement:

> Misconduct which will bar relief in a court of equity need not necessarily be of such a nature as to be punishable as a crime or to constitute the basis of legal action. Under the maxim, any willful act in regard to the matter in litigation, which would be condemned and pronounced wrongful by honest and fair-minded men, will be sufficient to make the hands of the applicant unclean.

2 POMEROY'S EQUITY JURISPRUDENCE §404 (5th ed. Symons 1941).

[134] The maxim that "he who comes into equity must come with clean hands" was relied upon expressly in the Medea Case, 3 J. MOORE, HISTORY AND DIGEST OF INTERNATIONAL ARBITRATIONS TO WHICH THE UNITED STATES HAS BEEN A PARTY 2731, 2739 (1898), and in Judge Hudson's famous concurring opinion in the Diversion of Water from the Meuse, [1937] PCIJ, ser. A/B, No. 70, at 77. *See* C. JENKS, *supra* note 50, at 412–13. On many more occasions, international tribunals have applied the rule that a party may not profit by his own wrong. *See* B. CHENG, *supra* note 50, at 149–58. This rule is related to, but admittedly somewhat distinct from, the "unclean hands" doctrine in that it bears directly on the foundation of the plaintiff's right, rather than merely on the availability of a remedy.

The decision in the *Barcelona Traction* case did not reject the contention that the "unclean hands" doctrine is part of international law. The Court merely rejected the contention that unlawful action by Barcelona Traction could provide a legal justification for unlawful action by Spanish authorities. Barcelona Traction, Light & Power Co., Ltd., [1970] ICJ REP. at 51.

[135] *See supra* text at notes 110–113.

account. First, it is proper to compare the conduct of the two parties. In domestic law, the plaintiff's "unclean hands" are no bar to relief unless the parties are *in pari delicto*.[136] An analogous rule should be applied on the international plane. Although it may not be necessary to insist that the parties be *in pari delicto* in order to justify the imposition of some sanctions by the Court, severe sanctions still should not ordinarily be imposed on the applicant where the respondent has acted in a contumacious manner. Where the respondent has already demonstrated its intention to frustrate the judicial process as a method of dispute resolution, the damage done to that process by the applicant's conduct is less than in cases where the process has been respected by the respondent.

Second, and here again the analogy to domestic law may be drawn, sanctions may be imposed more readily when their purpose is to coerce compliance with an order rather than to punish disobedience.[137] The distinction between coercive and penal sanctions also draws support from the fact that on the international plane the clearest authority for the judicial enforcement of a litigant's duties, Article 61(3) of the Statute, is patently coercive in design. Thus, where an interim measures order requires the applicant to take a particular course of action, *e.g.*, post security, withdraw troops from disputed territory, judicial relief appropriately may be withheld pending compliance.[138] In contrast, the purely penal use of sanctions other than censure should be rare. The imposition of such sanctions is particularly questionable in cases where the applicant's principal object in the proceedings is judicial validation. In such a case, sharp censure may be a serious sanction, depriving the applicant of much of the benefit of a judgment in its favor.

If these standards are applied to the rescue attempt, the Court's decision not to penalize the United States by denying it relief seems a proper exercise of discretion. To be sure, the rescue attempt constituted a serious failure to abide by the terms of the interim measures Order and a serious breach of the commitment to resolution of the crisis by orderly processes. However, by the time the rescue mission was undertaken, Iran's own disregard of the interim measures Order and its own contempt of the Court had made clear that the proceedings were not going to "resolve" the dispute, in the sense of eliminating the cause of friction between the two countries. In this situation, Iran's attitude and not that of the United States was chiefly responsible for the destruction of the political conditions necessary to make the international judicial process effective. Second, denying the United States relief, whether in part or in whole, would have been a pure penalty rather than a coercive device to gain compliance with the terms of the Order. In the circumstances of the particular case, moreover, the object of the United States in pursuing judicial remedies, once Iran's disregard of the Court had become manifest, was to obtain judicial affirmation of the correctness of the U.S. position. The sharp rebuke delivered by the Court diminished the political value of the Court's Judgment in favor of the United

[136] 2 POMEROY'S EQUITY JURISPRUDENCE, *supra* note 133, at §403.

[137] *See* Dobbs, *supra* note 42, at 279.

[138] E. DUMBAULD, *supra* note 49, at 173 ("Compliance with previous orders of the Court may well be made the condition of invoking its aid").

States; by adding its criticism of the mission to that of others, the Court in particular made it more difficult for the United States to present itself to the Security Council as the defender of law and law-abiding behavior. In partial consequence, the United States did not press for a Security Council resolution calling on Iran to comply with the May 24 Judgment.

VI. Conclusion

The international judicial process is premised on a set of expectations of reliability, impartiality, and effectiveness, each of which implies corresponding obligations for the states participating in the process. To assure reliability, states are forbidden to introduce false or doctored evidence. For the same reason, they are required to produce relevant evidence reasonably available to them. To safeguard impartiality, states are forbidden to corrupt the tribunal or any of its members. And to assure the effectiveness of the process as a means of resolving disputes and producing outcomes in accordance with law, states may not take action that prevents the execution of a judgment, anticipates it, or destroys the political conditions necessary for resolution of the dispute by judicial means. If international adjudication is to play a useful role in international affairs, these obligations must be respected. International courts and tribunals must be willing to use the authority they possess to enforce these duties.

Even in the best of circumstances, circumstances where there exists a current and coincident political agreement to settle a dispute judicially, these obligations will be under some strain. In such circumstances, however, the jointly perceived interest in judicial settlement will serve to cement those obligations essential to the success of the process. But in circumstances where an old agreement, though legally binding, no longer represents a current consensus on the way to resolve the dispute, the strains can become enormous. In a crisis, unilateral resort to the judicial process becomes one element of an overall effort, often haphazard and improvised, to win, to bend the adversary to one's own will. And though this use of judicial remedies is legitimate (for courts are designed to enforce rights as well as to settle disputes), there is a grave risk that in a crisis a frustrated litigant will take action incompatible with the minimal expectations surrounding the judicial process. In such a case, the role of the tribunal becomes even more important and more difficult. Unless the tribunal retains its perspective as a guardian of the expectations accompanying adjudication, it becomes a mere instrument in the hands of one of the parties, to the ultimate detriment of the international judicial process itself. Unless the tribunal's guardianship is sensitive to the particular circumstances of each case, inequitable results equally detrimental to the process will be reached. In the *Hostages* case, the International Court of Justice managed this difficult role very well indeed.

THE EGYPTIAN-ISRAELI PEACE TREATY AND ACCESS TO THE GULF OF AQABA: A NEW LEGAL REGIME

*By Mohamed ElBaradei**

The Gulf of Aqaba is a long, narrow body of water on the eastern side of the Sinai Peninsula. The western shore is Egyptian, the eastern shore is Saudi Arabian, and the head of the Gulf is Israeli and Jordanian territory. The islands of Tiran and Sanafir front the entrance and have been under Egyptian occupation since 1950. Saudi Arabia, however, maintains the claim that the two islands are Saudi Arabian territory. The length of the Gulf is about 96 miles; the breadth at the entrance to the Gulf is 5¾ miles; at its widest the Gulf measures 14½ miles. The entrance to the Gulf is through the Strait of Tiran (about 3 miles wide), between Tiran Island and the Egyptian coast. There are two passages in the Strait; Enterprise Passage and Grafton Passage, 1,300 and 950 yards wide, respectively. Enterprise Passage, which lies close to the Sinai Peninsula coast, is the principal navigation channel into the Gulf, and the only channel that can be navigated safely by vessels of substantial size. On the coastline, Egypt and Saudi Arabia each have over 100 miles of territory; also Jordanian territory encompasses about 3½ miles and the territory of Israel about 6 miles.

Both Egypt and Saudi Arabia claim 12 miles of territorial sea. The combined claims would mean, in fact, that neither Israel nor Jordan could reach the Red Sea without traversing the territorial sea of either Egypt or Saudi Arabia, even excluding the Strait of Tiran, which is within the territorial sea of Egypt and must be crossed.[1] This distinguishes the Gulf of Aqaba from many other gulfs and inland seas surrounded by more than one state, such as the Arab/Persian Gulf, where a stretch of the high seas exists within the gulf or the inland sea. Further, unlike the vast majority of gulfs and inland seas surrounded by more than one state, the Gulf is characterized by the fact that some of the coastal states are not situated at its entrance. This exceptional characteristic of the Gulf is shared with only three of the bays and estuaries, namely, the Tana Lagoon, the Gulf of Fonseca, and the Chetumal Bay.[2]

* Special Fellow, United Nations Institute for Training and Research (UNITAR); Adjunct Associate Professor, New York University School of Law. The views expressed herein are personal views and do not necessarily reflect the position of UNITAR or any other entity.

[1] *See* Kennedy, A Brief Geographical and Hydrographical Study of Bays and Estuaries the Coasts of Which Belong to Different States, 1 UNITED NATIONS CONFERENCE ON THE LAW OF THE SEA, OFFICIAL RECORDS 198, 208–09 (1958) [hereinafter cited as UNCLOS I, OFF. REC.]; Salek, *A Consideration of the Legal Status of the Gulf of Aqaba*, 52 AJIL 660 (1958); Melmaid, *Legal Status of the Gulf of Aqaba*, 53 *id.* at 412 (1959).

[2] M. STROHL, THE INTERNATIONAL LAW OF BAYS 375 (1963). In the first case, communication with the high seas is of very limited nature and is only possible during a certain period of the year. In the other two cases, navigation is guaranteed for all coastal states by either a judicial decision

Israel has maintained that all ships bound for the Israeli port of Eilat have a right of unrestricted passage through the Strait and the Gulf. On the other hand, Egypt and the rest of the Arab states held the view that such right of passage did not exist on the ground that a state of belligerency existed between them and Israel; that the Gulf was a *mare clausum*, which fell under the regime of historic waters; and that the Israeli title over the Gulf was not valid. Egypt, therefore, continued in the early 1950's to subject such passage to its authorization, search, and seizure. This was regarded by Israel to be an illicit blockade.[3] In the aftermath of the Israeli military action against Egypt in 1956, a United Nations peacekeeping force was stationed near the entrance to the Gulf and continued to observe and control the coastline of the Sinai Peninsula, from the northern end of the Gulf to the Strait of Tiran. After the withdrawal of UNEF in May 1967, Egypt reasserted its right to subject passage in the Gulf of Aqaba to its authorization, visit, and search.[4] Shortly, however, the 1967 Arab-Israeli War broke out; one of its results was the occupation of the entire Sinai Peninsula by Israel, and its control over navigation through the Strait of Tiran and the Egyptian territorial sea of the Gulf of Aqaba. This situation ended in April 1982 upon the withdrawal of Israel from Sinai in accordance with the provisions of the Egyptian-Israeli Peace Treaty.[5]

Access to the Gulf is now governed by Article V(2) of that Treaty, which declares that "[t]he Parties consider the Strait of Tiran and the Gulf of Aqaba to be international waterways open to all nations for unimpeded and non-suspendable freedom of navigation and overflight."[6]

For legal purposes, the Gulf of Aqaba and the Strait of Tiran at its entrance are considered to be an inland sea. Inland seas can be divided into two categories:

(Gulf of Fonseca) or agreement between them. *See* L. BOUCHEZ, THE REGIME OF BAYS IN INTERNATIONAL LAW 138–40, 158–59, 209–13 (1963).

[3] On the question of the legal status of the Gulf of Aqaba and the Strait of Tiran, see generally L. BLOOMFIELD, EGYPT, ISRAEL AND THE GULF OF AQABA IN INTERNATIONAL LAW (1957); P. PORTER, THE GULF OF AQABA: AN INTERNATIONAL WATERWAY; ITS SIGNIFICANCE TO INTERNATIONAL TRADE (1957); Eckert, *The Strait of Tiran: Innocent Passage or an Endless War?*, 22 U. MIAMI L. REV. 873 (1968); Gross, *The Geneva Conference on the Law of the Sea and the Right of Innocent Passage through the Gulf of Aqaba,* 53 AJIL 564 (1959); Hammad, *The Right of Innocent Passage in the Gulf of Aqaba,* 15 REV. EGYPTIENNE DROIT INT'L 118 (1959); Hashem, *Rationale of the Theory of Historic Bays with Special Reference to the International Status of the Gulf of Aqaba,* 25 *id.* at 1 (1969); Johnson, *Some Legal Problems of International Waterways with Particular Reference to the Strait of Tiran and the Suez Canal,* 31 MOD. L. REV. 153 (1968); Salek, *supra* note 1; Lapidoth, *Le Passage par le détroit de Tiran*, 73 REV. GÉNÉRALE DROIT INT'L PUBLIC 30 (1969); Murti, *The Legal Status of the Gulf of Aqaba,* 7 INDIAN J. INT'L L. 201 (1967).

[4] On the role of the United Nations Emergency Force, see 1 R. HIGGINS, UNITED NATIONS PEACEKEEPING 1946–1967, at 221–526 (1969). For Egypt's reassertion of its right to restrict passage through the Gulf of Aqaba, see 22 UN SCOR (1341st–1346th mtgs.), UN Docs. S/PV.1341–1346 (1967).

[5] "Israel will complete withdrawal of all its armed forces and civilians from the Sinai not later than three years from the date of exchange of instruments of ratification of this Treaty." Treaty of Peace, Egypt-Israel, Mar. 26, 1979, Ann. 1, Art. I, *reprinted in* 18 ILM 362 (1979) [hereinafter cited as Treaty of Peace].

[6] *Id.*, Art. V(2).

(1) landlocked seas, and (2) inland seas connected with the high seas by means of a strait. "From the geographical point of view, the difference between bays and inland seas of the second category, is that the bay itself is directly connected with the high seas, while between the inland sea and the high seas, a strait or arm of the sea is situated."[7] A contextual understanding and evaluation of the regime established by the Peace Treaty would therefore require an inquiry into customary and treaty law relevant to inland seas and straits at their entrances, including the particular legislative history of the Gulf of Aqaba.

I. The Regime of Inland Seas in International Law

The Period Prior to the Hague Codification Conference

The changing political, technical, and economic conditions in the first half of the 19th century—England supreme at sea after 1805; the commencement of the steam age; the need for raw materials and markets in the new industrial states—led to a shift in the predominant principle underlying the development of the law of the sea. Freedom of navigation and communication overshadowed security considerations as the guiding principle in the development of the law of the sea.[8]

The principle of freedom of navigation affected the development of the law in many respects: the extravagant exclusive claims over large areas of the sea almost disappeared;[9] the cannon range, considered equivalent to 3 miles, became the generally accepted extent of the territorial sea;[10] and the right of innocent passage through the territorial sea became an established rule of customary international law.[11]

The right of innocent passage through the territorial sea was assumed in state practice to apply a fortiori to that part of the territorial sea which constituted a strait connecting two parts of the high seas.[12] The statements of some of the commentators in the 19th century went so far as to suggest that innocent passage was first established with respect to the latter part of the territorial sea, and later extended to other parts.[13]

[7] L. Bouchez, *supra* note 2, at 20.

[8] *See* 1 I. Bruel, International Straits 54–55 (1947); M. McDougal & W. Burke, The Public Order of the Oceans 197 (1962).

[9] *See* J. Colombos, The International Law of the Sea §72 (6th rev. ed. 1967); W. Hall, A Treatise on International Law 185–87 (8th ed. Higgins 1924).

[10] *See* R. Phillimore, Commentaries Upon International Law §§197–98 (3d ed. 1879); T. Twiss, The Law of Nations Considered as Independent Political Communities §179 (2d rev. ed. 1884); H. Wheaton, Elements of International Law 225 (3d ed. 1846).

[11] 3 G. Gidel, Le Droit international public de la mer 195 (1932–34). By the end of the 19th century the right seemed to be firmly established in the practice of states. "[E]n temps de paix, s'opposer au passage, au transit d'un navire ami, constituerait une atteinte aux convenances internationales." H. Bonfils, Manuel de droit international public 284 (4th ed. P. Fauchille 1905).

[12] I. Bruel, *supra* note 8, at 102.

[13] *Compare* Wheaton's statement that the exclusive claim of the coastal state over territorial straits "is controlled by the *right* of other nations to communicate with the sea thus connected," H. Wheaton, *supra* note 10, at 229 (emphasis added), *with* his statement that claims over other parts of territorial seas have been "sometimes extended to exclude other nations from the innocent

The particular importance of straits for the freedom of communication was stressed at the beginning of the 19th century[14] and continued to be highlighted and emphasized. This was manifested in efforts to draft a convention applicable to all straits in order to ensure freedom of navigation therein,[15] and lay behind proposals to internationalize "tous les détroits et les canaux indispensables au commerce international et à assurer leur inviolabilité par une police international."[16] It also led some publicists to voice the opinion that straits connecting two parts of the high seas should be treated as part of the high seas they connected.[17]

The importance of straits for communication was defined primarily in terms of their geographical functions: "It is the relation which the channel of communication bears to navigation generally as a means of access to the seas thus connected which, rather than any other circumstances, is decisive of the equities of foreign maritime States."[18]

A distinction thus continued to be made between straits connecting two parts of the high seas and those connecting part of the high seas with an inland sea. With respect to straits leading to inland seas where both the strait and the inland sea were surrounded by the territory of one state, and the strait was entirely within the territorial sea of that state, the widely held view was to apply the rules of bays by way of analogy. Such inland seas were considered "closed seas" subject in their entirety, irrespective of their width, to the exclusive jurisdiction of the coastal state; foreign navigation could be excluded from these "internal waters."

---

use of the waters washing the shores of a particular state, in peace and war. . . . This exclusive claim is *sanctioned* both by usage and convention, and must be considered as forming part of the positive law of nations," *id.* at 239 (emphasis added).

[14] "Les détroits sont des passages pour communiquer d'une mer à l'autre; si l'usage des mers, domaine commun de l'humanité, est libre, la communication entre elles doit l'être également, ou autrement la liberté de ces mêmes mers ne serait qu'une chimère." G. DE RYNEVAL, INSTITUTIONS DE DROIT DE LA NATURE DES GENS, bk. 2, ch. 9, §7 (1803).

[15] *See* the draft convention on the Régime des détroits et des canaux maritimes, [1914] ANNUAIRE DE L'UNION INTERPARLEMENTAIRE 142. *See also* the proposal for a general straits convention prepared by Laun for the Conference of Neutrals held in Stockholm in 1916, *reprinted in* I. BRUEL, *supra* note 8, App. 2, at 238.

[16] Schücking, *Le Développement du Pacte de la Société des Nations*, 20 RECUEIL DES COURS 353, 447 (1927 V).

[17] "Straits which connect two parts of the high seas are considered—irrespective of their width, and of the territorial sovereignty—as part of the high seas and therefore free for the international community." K. GAREIS, INSTITUTIONEN DES VÖLKERRECHTS 86 (2d ed. 1901) (trans. by author). *See also* M. MOYE, LE DROIT DE GENS MODERNE 269–70 (2d ed. 1928); L. HAUTEFEUILLE, DES DROITS ET DES DEVOIRS DES NATIONS NEUTRES EN TEMPS DE GUERRE MARITIME 97–99 (2d ed. 1858). The majority of commentators, however, were cognizant of the diversity of interests involved. And while the importance of straits for freedom of communication led to the commentators' conclusion that straits should not be closed, the security interests of coastal states led to their other conclusion that straits are part of the territorial sea of the coastal states and that freedom of navigation is limited only to passage which is innocent. *See* 1 P. COBBETT, LEADING CASES OF INTERNATIONAL LAW 153 (4th ed. 1922); Harvard Research in International Law, Territorial Waters, Arts. 8–12, 23 AJIL Supp. (1929) [hereinafter cited as Harvard Research].

[18] 1 C. HYDE, INTERNATIONAL LAW CHIEFLY AS INTERPRETED AND APPLIED BY THE UNITED STATES 279 (1922).

> If the strait leads through a single country into an inland sea lying entirely within the same country as was formerly the case of the Bosphorus leading through the Turkish land on both sides into the Black Sea, entirely surrounded by Turkish land until Russia gained a footing in its coast . . . nothing is presented but an extreme instance of a bay the entrance to which is less than twice the width of the littoral sea. The rule that the inner part of such a bay, no matter how widely extended, belongs to the country in which it lies must be applied. It will be within the right of that country to exclude foreign navigation from its internal waters, and consequently from the strait which leads to them.[19]

On the other hand, once the strait or the inland sea was bordered by more than one state, it was widely held that the inland sea and the strait at its entrance could not be subject to the exclusive sovereignty of coastal states or the regime of internal waters, but should be opened to foreign navigation and

[19] 1 J. WESTLAKE, INTERNATIONAL LAW 193 (1904–13). *See also* 1 L. OPPENHEIM, INTERNATIONAL LAW §195 (4th ed. McNair 1928); A. HERSHEY, THE ESSENTIALS OF INTERNATIONAL LAW AND ORGANIZATION §198 (1927). The Strait of Kertch leading to the Sea of Azov, both surrounded by Russian territory, has often been cited as an application of this rule. Some commentators made a distinction between inland seas in terms of their width:

> When a body of inland waters, whatever its extent, and whether called a sea or bay or by any other name, communicates directly with the ocean, then the question of whether it falls within the category of "territorial waters" would seem to depend primarily on whether it is by its local configuration appurtenant to the land; and possibly also on whether it is bounded by the territory of more than one state. The former is probably the dominant consideration.

P. COBBETT, *supra* note 17, at 249. (It should be noted that the term "territorial waters" was used by Cobbett to denote "internal waters" where no right of passage exists.) Other commentators such as Fiore and Fauchille recognized only a territorial sea belt within the inland sea irrespective of its width or the number of coastal states bordering it. *See* P. FIORE, INTERNATIONAL LAW CODIFIED 186 (1918); 1 P. FAUCHILLE, TRAITÉ DE DROIT INTERNATIONAL PUBLIC, pt. 2, at 211 (8th ed. 1921–26).

The question of passage through the Strait of Canso leading to the Gulf of St. Lawrence was the subject of controversy between the United States and Great Britain. The British Government submitted the question to the legal officers of the Crown, who answered as follows:

> By the treaty of 1818 it is agreed that American citizens should have the liberty of fishing in the Gulf of St. Lawrence, within certain defined limits, in common with British subjects; and such treaty does not contain any words negativing the right to navigate the passage of the Gut of Canso, and therefore it may be conceded that such right of navigation is not taken away by that convention; but we have now attentively considered the course of navigation to the Gulf by Cape Breton, and likewise the capacity and situation of the passage of Canso, *and of the British dominions on either side*, and we are of opinion that, independently of treaty, no foreign country has the right to use or navigate the passage of Canso. . . .

1 J. MOORE, A DIGEST OF INTERNATIONAL LAW 790 (1906) (emphasis added). The question remained controversial for nearly a century owing to the disagreement between the United States and the United Kingdom on the legal status of the Gulf of St. Lawrence, which was considered by the former to be part of the high seas, and by the latter to be part of the British territory. The issue was settled by the Permanent Court of Arbitration in 1910, which recommended that the parties conclude an agreement to the effect that "[i]n every bay not hereinafter specifically provided for the limits of exclusion shall be drawn three miles seaward from a straight line across the bay in the part nearest the entrance at the first point where the width does not exceed ten miles." The North Atlantic Coast Fisheries case, Hague Ct. Rep. (Scott) 141, 188 (Perm. Ct. Arb. 1916). This recommendation was accepted and an agreement to this effect was concluded by representatives of Great Britain and the United States on July 20, 1912. 4 M. WHITEMAN, DIGEST OF INTERNATIONAL LAW 215–16 (1965).

subject to the right of innocent passage: "Les mers intérieures au sense large sont libres; le seul fait que le littoral appartient à plusieurs Etats donne la liberté: même l'Etat auquel appartiennent les deux bords du détroit ne peut fermer le passage."[20] The rationale behind the rule was explained as the need to guarantee freedom of navigation for all coastal states:

> En écartant la construction d'une ligne transversale dans le cas de pluralité de riverains, on ne laisse au-devant des territoires respectifs des Etats riverains et de leurs laisses de basse mer qu'une bande de mer "territoriale" (et non pas d'eaux intérieures): or il est de la nature juridique de la mer territoriale de comporter le droit de "passage inoffensif". La liberté des communications maritimes avec la mer ouverte des Etats riverains de la baie se trouve ainsi juridiquement assurée. Telle est la raison, simple et décisive, encore que non exposée par les auteurs, pour laquelle il y a lieu d'écarter la détermination de la mer territoriale à l'aide d'une ligne transversale tirée en travers de la baie, lorsque plusieurs Etats sont riverains de cette baie.[21]

In the case of the Bay of Fundy, Umpire Bates, appointed under the Anglo-American Claims Convention of 1853 in consequence of the seizure of the U.S. vessel *Washington*, decided that the Bay of Fundy was not a British bay as claimed by the United Kingdom:

> The Bay of Fundy is from 65 to 75 miles wide and 130 to 140 miles long. It has several bays on its coasts. Thus the word bay, as applied to this great body of water, has the same meaning as that applied to the Bay of Biscay, the Bay of Bengal, over which no nation can have right to assume sovereignty. One of the headlands of the Bay of Fundy is in the United States, and ships bound to Passamaquoddy must sail through a large space of it. The islands of Grand Menan (British) and Little Menan (American) are situated nearly on a line from headland to headland. These islands, as represented in all geographies, are situated in the Atlantic Ocean. The conclusion is, therefore, in my mind irresistible that the Bay of Fundy is not a British bay, nor a bay within the meaning of the word as used in the treaties of 1783 and 1818.[22]

The fact that the bay was surrounded by more than one state was regarded to be the determining factor in that decision:

> La sentence arbitrale du 23 décembre 1854 relative à la baie de Fundy a considéré que cette baie était une mer libre non pas seulement parce que son entrée avait une largeur de 65 à 75 milles, mais encore et surtout parce que ses côtés n'appartenaient pas tous au même Etat, l'un de ses caps étant situé sur le territoire des Etats-Unis et l'autre sur celui de la Grande-Bretagne.[23]

This rule was upheld even under the "historic bay" doctrine. In the *Gulf of Fonseca* case, decided on March 9, 1917, the Central American Court of Justice held that the gulf, surrounded by the territory of Honduras, Nicaragua, and El Salvador, "is an historic bay possessed by the characteristics of a closed

[20] 1 E. Nys, Le Droit international 448 (1904).

[21] G. Gidel, *supra* note 11, at 595–96.

[22] 4 J. Moore, History and Digest of International Arbitrations to Which the United States Has Been a Party 4344 (1898).

[23] P. Fauchille, *supra* note 19, at 384.

sea."[24] The Court, nonetheless, expressly recognized the existence of a right of innocent passage for merchant ships.[25]

The view was maintained, however, that coastal states could agree to consider the waters of small bays and inland seas as internal waters subject to their exclusive sovereignty, provided that freedom of access was guaranteed to all of them:

> When the geographical relationship of a bay to the adjacent or enveloping land is such that the sovereign of the latter, if a single State, might not unlawfully claim the waters as part of its territory, it is not apparent why a like privilege should be denied to two or more States to which such land belongs, at least if they are so agreed, and accept as between themselves a division of the waters concerned. No requirement of international law as such deprives them of that privilege, notwithstanding the deposition of some who would leave little room for its application.[26]

But that privilege was not to be applicable to large inland seas such as the Black Sea:

> In this particular case the magnitude of the water area involved, its connection with the ocean, its importance as a means of access to certain countries adjacent to it, and the resulting general interest of maritime powers that it be dealt with as the high seas, have combined to justify the insistent demand that the Black Sea be not partitioned among the surrounding States. . . .[27]

The Hague Codification Conference

Despite the lack of success of the Hague Codification Conference in codifying customary international law, its preparatory work, deliberations, and provisional rules provide insight into the views and practice of states at the time.

Inland seas and straits at their entrances were regarded in the Bases of Discussion of the Hague Conference to be subject to the same rules applicable to bays. "[W]here a strait is merely a channel of communication with an inland sea, the rules regarding bays apply to such strait and sea."[28] And the observation

[24] Republic of El Salvador v. Republic of Nicaragua, trans. in 11 AJIL 674, 693 (1917).

[25] Despite the Court's holding that the gulf is a closed sea, entirely owned by the riparian states, it nonetheless considered the waters outside the coastal belt of each state as a "zone of maritime inspection" where a right of innocent passage existed. *See id.* at 714–15. Commenting on this decision Gidel stated: "L'arrêt de la Cour de Justice Centre-Américaine . . . n'attribue pas aux eaux de ce golfe le caractère d'eaux intérieures comme l'exigerait ce caractère de baie historique, mais le caractère d'eaux territoriales. C'est là une anomalie tout à fait notable dans le système logique des baies historiques." G. GIDEL, *supra* note 11, at 627. For the concept of historic waters and historic bays and the different theories for the acquisition of historic titles, see Y. BLUM, HISTORIC TITLES IN INTERNATIONAL LAW (1965); Historic Bays, Memorandum by the Secretariat of the United Nations, 1 UNCLOS I, OFF. REC. 1–38.

[26] C. HYDE, *supra* note 18, at 475 (2d ed. 1945). *See also* P. JESSUP, THE LAW OF TERRITORIAL WATERS AND MARITIME JURISDICTION 476 (1927); ASIL, Project No. 10 (National Domain), Art. 6, 20 AJIL Supp. 319 (1926); Harvard Research, Art. 6 and commentary, *supra* note 17, at 274–75.

[27] C. HYDE, *supra* note 18, at 484 (2d ed. 1945).

[28] Bases of Discussion for the Conference for the Codification of International Law Drawn up by the Preparatory Committee, Basis of Discussion No. 17, League of Nations Doc. C.74.M.39.1929.V.2, at 60 [hereinafter cited as Bases of Discussion].

on the rule added that "it will then be necessary to take into consideration whether there is only one or several coastal States as well as the breadth of the strait and the existence of any usage varying the ordinary rule."[29]

This view was confirmed during the deliberations of the conference. An observation to one of the articles formulated by the conference again stated that "as regards such straits [connecting part of the high seas with an inland sea], the rules concerning bays, and where necessary islands, will continue to be applicable."[30]

The rules formulated in the Bases of Discussion with respect to bays were a reflection of the view of the majority of states participating in the conference.[31] Bays surrounded by one coastal state were regarded as falling within that state's exclusive authority if they did not exceed 10 miles in width or by usage were under the exclusive authority of the coastal state.[32] On the other hand, bays surrounded by more than one coastal state were regarded as being subject to the regime of territorial waters irrespective of their width. "If two or more States touch the coast of a bay or estuary of which the opening does not exceed ten miles, the territorial waters of each coastal State are measured from the line of low water mark along the coast."[33]

The Second Sub-Committee of the conference adopted rules for bays surrounded by one state.[34] It did not, however, for unknown reasons, formulate rules with regard to bays surrounded by more than one state. A passage in the committee's report nonetheless suggests that it was the committee's view that such bays should be subject to the regime of territorial waters, and to a right of innocent passage.[35] The failure to formulate rules for inland seas and bays surrounded by more than one state was explained as due to the Second Sub-Committee's attempt to formulate general legal definitions for these sea areas:

[29] *Ibid.* The assimilation of the regime of inland seas to that of bays was in conformity with the views of the majority of states as expressed in their replies to the questionnaire of the Preparatory Committee of the Conference. *See id.* at 66 (Denmark); *id.* at 55 (Germany); *id.* at 57 (India); *id.* at 58 (New Zealand and Norway); *id.* at 55 (South Africa); *id.* at 58–59 (Sweden); *id.* at 57 (United Kingdom).

[30] 1 Acts of the Conference for the Codification of International Law, Plenary Meetings, Ann. 10 (Report of the Second Committee: Territorial Sea, App. 2), at 134, League of Nations Doc. C.351.M.145.1930.V [hereinafter cited as Report of the Second Committee].

[31] *See* Bases of Discussion, *supra* note 28, at 39–45.

[32] *Id.* at 45, Bases of Discussion Nos. 7, 8.

[33] *Ibid.,* Basis of Discussion No. 9. The majority of states regarded bays surrounded by more than one state as subject to the regime of territorial waters. *See id.* at 39 (Australia); *ibid.* (Germany); *id.* at 42 (India); *ibid.* (Japan); *id.* at 43 (the Netherlands); *ibid.* (New Zealand); *id.* at 42–43 (United Kingdom). *But see* Denmark, Sweden, and the United States who expressed the view that bays surrounded by more than one state could be subject to the regime of internal waters. *Id.* at 40 (Denmark); *id.* at 44 (Sweden); Report of the Second Committee, *supra* note 30, at 132 (United States).

[34] Report of the Second Committee, *supra* note 30, at 131.

[35]

> Just as the case of bays which lie within the territory of more than one coastal State, it has been thought better not to draw up any rules regarding the drawing of the line of demarcation between the respective *territorial* seas in straits lying within the territory of more than one coastal State and of a width less than the breadth of the two belts of territorial sea.

Report of the Second Committee, *supra* note 30, at 134 (emphasis added).

> The problems raised . . . involved questions of facts upon which purely juristic conclusions, taking the form of generalized statements, are practically impossible. One would have to enter into centuries-old antinomies of nationalism and realism to uncover all of the difficulties of conception and definition involved in such matters as these.[36]

The legal regime applicable to inland seas and bays surrounded by more than one state was thus left undecided at the end of the Hague Conference. But despite the inconclusive outcome of the conference, its deliberations revealed a clear distinction between the legal regimes applicable to bays and inland seas surrounded by one state and those surrounded by more than one state.[37]

The Work of the International Law Commission

At its third session, the ILC decided to initiate its work on the "Regime of the Territorial Sea."[38] The ILC draft articles completed at the eighth session did not contain any rules on inland seas. The Commission merely repeated, in one of its comments, the prevailing doctrine: "Where such stretches of water communicate with the high seas by a strait or arm of the sea, they are considered as 'internal seas' if the coasts, including those of the waterway giving access to the high seas, belong to a single State. If it is not the case they are considered as high seas."[39] The Commission added: "These rules may, however, be modified for historical reasons or by international arrangement."[40]

[36] Reeves, *Codification of the Law of Territorial Waters*, 24 AJIL 486, 498 (1930).

[37] It should be noted that straits connecting two parts of the high seas were regarded during the conference deliberations as a special category of straits subject to a nonsuspendable right of innocent passage applicable to merchant vessels and warships. The rule adopted by the Second Sub-Committee states: "Under no pretext whatever may the passage even of warships through straits used for international navigation between two parts of the high sea be interfered with." Report of the Second Committee, *supra* note 30, at 134. The identification of straits connecting two parts of the high seas as a special category of straits was confirmed by the International Court of Justice in the *Corfu Channel* case:

> It is, in the opinion of the Court, generally recognized and in accordance with international custom that States in time of peace have a right to send their warships through straits used for international navigation between two parts of the high seas without the previous authorization of a coastal State, provided that the passage is *innocent.* Unless otherwise prescribed in an international convention, there is no right for a coastal State to prohibit such passage through straits in time of peace.

Corfu Channel Case, [1949] ICJ REP. 3, 28. It should be noted further that the geographical function of straits subject to the above-mentioned right of passage was regarded by the Court as the decisive criterion. This is clear in the authoritative French text: "Le critère décisif paraît plutôt devoir être tiré de la situation géographique du Détroit, en tant que ce dernier met en communication deux parties de haute mer, ainsi que du fait que le Détroit est utilisé aux fins de la navigation international." *Ibid. See also* C. ROUSSEAU, DROIT INTERNATIONAL PUBLIC 446 (1953).

[38] Report of the International Law Commission on its third session, [1951] 2 Y.B. INT'L L. COMM'N 123, 140, UN Doc. A/CN.4/SER.A/1951 (1957). The Commission considered the subject during its fourth, sixth, seventh, and eighth sessions; at the end of the latter, it drew up its final report consisting of 25 articles. Report of the International Law Commission covering the work of its eighth session, [1956] 2 Y.B. INT'L L. COMM'N 253, 254–59, 265–77, UN Doc. A/CN.4/SER.A/1956/Add.1 (1956).

[39] ILC 8th session report, *supra* note 38, at 277–78.

[40] *Id.* at 278.

The ILC draft articles also did not contain any rules with respect to bays surrounded by more than one coastal state. However, the legal regime applicable to this category of bays and inland seas was discussed by the Commission in connection with Israel's comments on the proposed rule for passage through straits connecting two parts of the high seas:

> [T]he correct manner of looking at the question is to regard the principle of freedom of navigation as predominant, and the exercise of any rights of sovereignty, including those classified by the Commission as rights of protection, as an exception from the predominant right and interest of the international community. What this means is that where access to a given port—whether an existing one or one which at some future date a State may wish to establish—is only possible by traversing a strait (in the geographical sense), then it is quite immaterial whether that strait is or is not within the waters classed as the territorial sea of one or more of the littoral States, or what is the legal nature (gulf, bay, high seas) of the waters on which the harbour is situated. In such circumstances, the right of passage for the ships of all nations, and quite regardless of their cargo, is and must remain absolutely unqualified, and the littoral State or States have no right whatsoever, so long as the matter is not regulated by Convention, to hinder, hamper, impede or suspend the free passage of those ships. The same rule is also true as regards warships.[41]

But the ILC special rapporteur, who stated that Israel "appeared to have in mind the Gulf of Aqaba,"[42] expressed the view that the situation of the Gulf of Aqaba is "exceptional—possibly unique."[43]

This view was shared by the majority of the Commission, who argued that the case in question was exceptional and not a matter on which the ILC should enunciate a general rule. The problem was compared to that of a bay where the right of access could be based on international agreement or long usage. The regime of passage through straits, according to this view, cannot apply. To forbid under any circumstances the suspension of passage through a strait leading to a gulf would be unfair to the coastal state(s) concerned. And if a state saw fit to establish a port at a point that could only be reached through the territorial sea of other states, it must accept the consequences.

On the other hand, some members of the Commission argued that since a state setting up an installation on a river has a certain right vis-à-vis the control of the flow of that river upstream, it would seem that a state has a right to establish a port such as that envisaged and vessels should have normal access to it.[44] At the end of the discussion, however, the Commission decided that "the question raised by the Israeli Government related to an exceptional case

[41] *Id.* at 55–56. The Israeli comments were made in connection with the rule adopted by the Commission, in reliance on the ICJ decision in the *Corfu Channel* case, to govern straits connecting two parts of the high seas. "There must be no suspension of the innocent passage of foreign vessels through straits normally used for international navigation between two parts of the high seas." Report of the International Law Commission covering the work of its seventh session, [1955] 2 Y.B. INT'L L. COMM'N 19, 39, UN Doc. A/CN.4/SER.A/1955/Add.1 (1960).

[42] Summary record of the 336th meeting (June 13, 1956), [1956] 1 Y.B. INT'L L. COMM'N 202, UN Doc. A/CN.4/SER.A/1956 (1956).

[43] *Ibid.*

[44] For a summary of the discussion, see *id.* at 202–03.

which did not lend itself to the formation of a general rule."[45] The Commission further assimilated the case to that of bays:

> The question was asked what would be the legal position of straits forming part of the territorial sea of one or more States and constituting the sole means of access to a port of another State. The Commission considers that this case could be assimilated to that of a bay whose inner part and entrance from the high seas belong to different States. As the Commission felt bound to confine itself to proposing rules applicable to bays, wholly belonging to a single coastal State, it also reserved consideration of the above-mentioned case.[46]

The reason given for not formulating rules applicable to bays surrounded by more than one state was the Commission's lack of "sufficient data at its disposal concerning the number of cases involved or the regulations at present applicable to them."[47] This reason is not unlike the one said to be behind the Hague Codification Conference's inability to formulate a general regime for this category of bays and inland seas.

The First United Nations Conference on the Law of the Sea

During the deliberations at the 1958 Geneva Conference on the Law of the Sea,[48] an amendment was introduced to expand the legal regime applicable to straits connecting two parts of the high seas so as to include straits at the entrance of inland seas surrounded by more than one state. According to that amendment, not only should straits connecting two parts of the high seas be subject to a nonsuspendable right of passage, but also straits "used for international navigation between a part of the high seas [and] the territorial waters of a foreign State."[49] The expansion of the concept of straits was considered by the sponsors of the amendment to be based on the fact that passage should not be suspended in waters that are essential to maritime communications. The United Kingdom's delegate stated: "The main purpose of any maritime voyage was, after all, to arrive at the port of destination."[50] The delegate of the Netherlands added: "It was insufficient to declare the high seas open to traffic without also guaranteeing the right of entry into seaports. If the right of access to ports was to be assured to land-locked States, *a fortiori* it should be guaranteed to the maritime countries."[51]

[45] *Id.* at 203.

[46] ILC 8th session report, *supra* note 38, at 273. Bays surrounded by one state were considered to be internal waters if their width did not exceed 15 miles. *Id.* at 268–69.

[47] *Id.* at 269.

[48] The conference was held in Geneva from Feb. 24 to April 28, 1958, and was attended by 85 states. It adopted four Conventions dealing with: (1) the Territorial Sea and the Contiguous Zone, 516 UNTS 205; (2) the High Seas, 450 UNTS 82; (3) Fishing and Conservation of the Living Resources of the High Seas, 559 UNTS 285; and (4) the Continental Shelf, 499 UNTS 311. *See* 2 UNCLOS I, OFF. REC. at 132–43.

[49] 3 UNCLOS I, OFF. REC. at 231.

[50] *Id.* at 79.

[51] *Id.* at 88. On the question of access to ports, see C. HYDE, *supra* note 18, at 581–82 (2d ed. 1945). It should be noted that access of landlocked states to the internal waters of other states, as provided in Art. 3 of the Geneva Convention on the High Seas, 13 UST 2312, TIAS No. 5200, 450 UNTS 82, was made dependent upon agreement with the coastal state.

Strong objections were raised, however, to the proposed amendment. In the words of the delegate of Saudi Arabia: "International law provided for the right of innocent passage through straits connecting two parts of the high seas; it did not provide for such a right in the case of straits linking the open sea with an internal sea or with the territorial sea of a particular State."[52] After recalling the definition of straits in the *Corfu Channel* case and the comments of the ILC in this regard, he concluded that "the amended text no longer dealt with general principles of international law, but had been carefully tailored to promote the claims of one State."[53]

The amendment was adopted in the First Committee of the conference by a majority of one vote.[54] During the consideration of the text in the Plenary, a motion was submitted by the delegate of Egypt for a separate vote to oppose "paragraph 4 as adopted by the First Committee, and [vote] in favour of the International Law Commission's draft, which in no way constituted an infringement on the freedom of navigation."[55] The arguments introduced in the committee were repeated. The delegate of Denmark opposed the motion: "The principle of freedom of navigation was indivisible, and when vessels crossed a portion of the high seas on their way to a port, it was irrelevant whether or not they had to pass through the territorial sea of another State."[56] By contrast, the Saudi delegate supported the motion: "The subject the conference was now considering was the passage through straits connecting two parts of the high seas, and the principle of freedom of navigation in those circumstances should be applied in accordance with established principles of international law."[57]

The motion was defeated by a very narrow margin and the article as amended was adopted.[58] Straits subject to a nonsuspendable right of innocent passage were thus defined in the 1958 Geneva Convention on the Territorial Sea and the Contiguous Zone as "straits which are used for international navigation between one part of the high seas and another part of the high seas or the territorial sea of a foreign State."[59]

Sørensen, the Danish delegate to the conference, explained the motivation for the amendment and the atmosphere surrounding the vote:

> [W]hat was in everybody's mind, without being officially stated, was the Strait of Tiran at the entrance to the Gulf of Aqaba, giving access from the Red Sea to Israel's port of Eilath. A decision on the abstract question, which had been left open by ILC, would therefore also involve an expression of opinion as to the legality of Egyptian measures amounting to a blockade of this port. In this specific context, the vote became a test not only of attitudes toward the principle of free maritime communications but also of attitudes toward the Arab-Israel conflict.[60]

[52] 3 UNCLOS I, OFF. REC. at 93.

[53] *Id.* at 96. *See also* the statement of the delegate of Indonesia, *id.* at 93–94.

[54] The result of the vote was 31 in favor to 30 against, with 10 abstentions. *Id.* at 100.

[55] 2 UNCLOS I, OFF. REC. at 65. [56] *Ibid.*

[57] *Ibid.*

[58] The motion was defeated by 34 votes to 32, with 6 abstentions. And Art. 17, which contained the amended provision, was adopted by 62 votes to 1, with 9 abstentions. *Ibid.*

[59] *Id.* at 134.

[60] M. SØRENSEN, LAW OF THE SEA 236 (Int'l Conciliation No. 520, 1958). *See also* Dean, *The Geneva Conference on the Law of the Sea: What Was Accomplished*, 52 AJIL 607, 621 (1958).

But despite the decision of the conference to apply the straits regime to those straits at the entrance to inland seas surrounded by more than one state, no similar attempt was made to establish a regime for the inland seas themselves. Verzijl, the Dutch delegate to the conference, provided the explanation: "All problems concerning pluristatal bays were deliberately eliminated [from the proceedings] because it was deemed impossible to reach any measure of consensus with regard to the legal status of this type of inlet from the sea from the point of view of territorial sovereignty."[61]

The abstention by the ILC and the conference from enunciating a legal regime for bays, gulfs, and inland seas surrounded by more than one state was considered a reflection of the lack of uniformity in the practice of states. "[I]t is impossible to derive generally applicable criteria from the practice of States as to the claims of coastal States to bays surrounded by two or more States."[62]

This diversity was ascribed to the important role of the geographical position of the coastal states, and to the fact that the main function of the bay or inland sea (*e.g.*, navigation, economic exploitation, defense) varied from one to another.[63] The conclusion, therefore, was that the regime of such sea areas continued to be "extremely uncertain"[64] since "[i]t is possible that such bays or other inlets also constitute inland State territory, either *pro diviso* or *pro indiviso* (as an area under co-sovereignty), but they may equally well be either territorial sea or even part of the open sea. There is no general imperative rule in existence. . . ."[65]

Equally, the extension by the conference of the legal regime of straits to those at the entrance to inland seas has proven to be of no practical utility. None of the Arab coastal states on the Gulf of Aqaba, for which the provision was intended, acceded to the Territorial Sea Convention. The restriction of coastal competence to suspend passage when deemed essential for security considerations or to require authorization for passage of warships was dissatisfying to the Arab coastal states. But it was the conviction that a regime had been

[61] 3 J. Verzijl, International Law in Historical Perspective 27 (1968–72). The result, according to Verzijl, was that

> no legal solution of any kind was reached either as regards the closing line of such bays towards the high seas, or as regards their possible legal status of either themselves forming part of the high seas, or, alternatively, of being subject to a co-imperium of the riparian States, or as regards the frontier delimitation between the latter inside the bay concerned, should it neither belong to the high seas nor fall under their co-sovereignty.

Id. at 28. Verzijl uses the term "inlets from the sea" to mean:

> a variety of widely differing aqueous formations which have one feature in common, namely, that they are all situated on the inner side of the general coastline, base-line of the territorial sea, and are in open communication with the sea, whatever denomination is applied to them: bays, gulfs, fiords, seas, haffs, firths, lagoons, limans, estuaries, and so on.

Id. at 27; *see also* M. Strohl, *supra* note 2, at 375.

[62] L. Bouchez, *supra* note 2, at 170.

[63] For the complexities of the issues involved in the formulation of a regime applicable to bays and inland seas surrounded by more than one state, and the practice of states in this respect, see *id.* at 116–98; J. Verzijl, *supra* note 61, at 590–610; M. Strohl, *supra* note 2, at 371–97.

[64] J. Verzijl, *supra* note 61, at 294.

[65] *Ibid.* Verzijl further stated that "the only rule in force is that there is no general rule and that all depends on the particular features of the case in question." *Id.* at 592.

"imposed" in the absence of an equal and simultaneous resolution of other relevant political and legal issues involved in the Arab-Israeli conflict that led all Arab states to refrain from becoming parties to the Convention.[66] This has rendered the provision ineffectual because of the widely held view that it was not part of customary international law and could only be binding upon ratification.[67]

The result was the continuation of the uncertainty surrounding the regime of gulfs and inland seas surrounded by more than one state and, more specifically, the continuation of the dispute over the legal regime applicable to the Gulf of Aqaba.[68]

Security Council Resolutions 242 and 338

In the aftermath of the 1967 Arab-Israeli War, the Security Council adopted Resolution 242, which set forth the principles for the establishment of a just and lasting peace in the Middle East.[69] Paragraph 2(a) of that resolution affirmed "the necessity . . . [f]or guaranteeing freedom of navigation through international waterways in the area."[70] By Resolution 338 of October 22, 1973, the Council again called upon the parties concerned "to start immediately the implementation of Security Council resolution 242 (1967) in all of its parts."[71]

It is not clear which article of the Charter the Council based its action upon. This is due to the Council's approach to its role in peaceful settlement, which

[66] Tunisia, the only Arab state that signed the Convention, made a reservation to the effect that it "does not consider itself bound by the provisions of article 16, paragraph 4 of this Convention." UNITED NATIONS, MULTILATERAL TREATIES IN RESPECT OF WHICH THE SECRETARY-GENERAL PERFORMS DEPOSITARY FUNCTIONS, UN Doc. ST/LEG/SER.D/5, at 373 (1972).

[67] Dean, *supra* note 60, at 623; Fitzmaurice, *Some Results of the Geneva Conference on the Law of the Sea*, 8 INT'L & COMP. L.Q. 73, 79, 100–02 (1959); Gross, *supra* note 3, at 293–94. *But see* Lapidoth, *supra* note 3, at 38–40. It should be noted that even if the Arab coastal states were to have become party to the Convention, the Geneva provision could have been of no practical significance. Passage through the Gulf could possibly have been interdicted without an apparent violation of the Geneva provision, which merely regulates access to the Strait at the entrance of the Gulf, while remaining completely silent on the legal regime applicable to the Gulf itself. Verzijl, whose delegation was one of the sponsors of the Geneva provision, states:

> The only subject that was discussed and resolved [with respect to the legal status of pluristatal bays] was the right of innocent passage from the high seas into such pluristatal bays—and *vice versa*—through the territorial sea of one or more States which dominate their entrance, and even that only in the somewhat disguised formula of a general principle . . . a provision which in its final words clearly covers situations such as that of the Gulf of Aqaba.

J. VERZIJL, *supra* note 61, at 27–28. He failed, however, to explain how the question of passage through the entrance to the Gulf could be separated from the larger question of access to the Gulf itself, especially in view of his statement that the legal regime of gulfs and inland seas surrounded by more than one state is extremely uncertain and that in the particular case of the Gulf of Aqaba, "it is uncertain what exactly is the legal regime of the Gulf from the point of view of territorial sovereignty." *Id.* at 602.

[68] *See* text accompanying note 4 *supra*.

[69] 22 UN SCOR, Res. & Dec. 8, UN Doc. S/INF/22/Rev.2 (1967), *reprinted in* 17 ILM at 1469.

[70] *Ibid.*

[71] 27 UN SCOR, Res. & Dec. 10, UN Doc. S/INF/129 (1973), *reprinted in* 17 ILM at 1470.

is often based on its general powers and responsibilities rather than on specific Charter provisions.[72]

The language of the resolution, however, suggests that its intention was to provide the general principles that should constitute the basis for peaceful settlement rather than to prescribe the detailed implementation of these principles or the specific terms of the settlement, a process that was left to negotiations among the parties.[73] The term "freedom of navigation" should thus be understood as a reference to the general principle that should underlie the regimes of passage "through international waterways in the area," rather than as an indication of the applicability of the high seas freedom of navigation to these waterways. The use of the word "through," which suggests that the term is used merely in connection with the regime of passage and not as a reference to the traditional high seas freedom, is supportive of that conclusion.

The term "international waterways," which is derived from the language of the International Court of Justice in the *Corfu Channel* case,[74] could be understood to mean waterways used for international navigation, *i.e.*, between two states other than the coastal state, in contradistinction to waterways used exclusively for local navigation and leading to internal waters of the coastal state.

Moore has written that "the Security Council has dealt specifically with the issue [Tiran] in Resolutions 242 and 338. . . . These actions . . . are binding on all members of the United Nations, and thus override both the Territorial Sea Convention and UNCLOS Article 45(1)(b) for the Strait of Tiran. . . ."[75] This view, however, begs the question, for it is not settled that the Council action is of a binding legal nature in the sense of Article 25 of the Charter. In fact, the prevailing view is that the Charter does not impose any obligation on members to accept and carry out recommendations that the Security Council might make for the pacific settlement of disputes, under Articles 36 or 37 of the Charter.[76] If Security Council Resolutions 242 and 338 are binding on Israel and Egypt, it is because of their specific acceptance by these two states as a basis for the establishment of peace in the Middle East.[77] But the binding nature of these resolutions remains limited to those parties that have accepted them.

[72] L. GOODRICH, E. HAMBRO, & A. SIMONS, CHARTER OF THE UNITED NATIONS 259 (3d rev. ed. 1969).

[73] *See, e.g.*, paragraph 3 of Resolution 242, which requested that the UN Secretary-General designate a special representative "in order to promote agreement and assist efforts to achieve a peaceful and *accepted* settlement in accordance with the provisions and principles of the resolution." 22 UN SCOR, Res. & Dec. 8, *supra* note 69 (emphasis added).

[74] [1949] ICJ REP. at 29. "[T]he Court has arrived at the conclusion that the North Corfu Channel should be considered as belonging to the class of international highways through which passage cannot be prohibited by a coastal State in time of peace." *Ibid.*

[75] Moore, *The Regime of Straits and the Third United Nations Conference on the Law of the Sea,* 74 AJIL 77, 113 (1980) (footnote omitted).

[76] L. GOODRICH, E. HAMBRO, & A. SIMONS, *supra* note 72, at 208–09.

[77] *See, e.g.*, preambular paragraph 1 of the Treaty of Peace in which Egypt and Israel expressed their conviction "of the urgent necessity of the establishment of a just, comprehensive and lasting peace in the Middle East in accordance with Security Council Resolutions 242 and 338." Treaty of Peace, *supra* note 5.

Second, it is equally questionable that a binding action by the Council, in the form of general principles, would automatically override relevant international law norms or exclude the need for an agreement among the parties on the interpretation and application of these general principles in conjunction with international law norms in existence. The Egyptian-Israeli Peace Treaty seems to have accepted this latter view by making a distinction, for the purpose of applying the principle of freedom of navigation to "international waterways in the area," between the regime of the Suez Canal and that of the Gulf of Aqaba.[78] This distinction was made primarily because in the case of the former, the principle of freedom of navigation had to be interpreted closely together and in conformity with the specific treaty law of the 1888 Constantinople Convention, while in the case of the latter, it had to be construed on the basis of a set of imprecise customary norms and practices.

Nevertheless, the emphasis laid down by the Security Council on the principle of freedom of navigation was particularly instructive in the case of the Gulf of Aqaba because of the past claims of exclusive use by some of the Gulf states. The affirmation of the principle of freedom of navigation was therefore an explicit support of the often expressed view that gulfs and inland seas surrounded by more than one state should always, in time of peace, be subject to a right of access by all coastal states.

The Third United Nations Conference on the Law of the Sea

In the Draft Convention drawn up at the Third United Nations Conference on the Law of the Sea (UNCLOS III),[79] straits "used for international navigation between one area of the high seas or an exclusive economic zone and another area of the high seas or an exclusive economic zone"[80] are recognized as subject to a new regime of transit passage in order to restrict coastal competence over passage and secure submerged passage of submarines and overflight of aircraft. The right has been defined as "the exercise . . . of the freedom of navigation and overflight solely for the purpose of continuous and expeditious transit of the strait."[81]

[78] *Id.*, Art. 5.

[79] The Third United Nations Conference on the Law of the Sea was convened in 1973 by a General Assembly resolution that defined the mandate of the conference to be the adoption of a "convention dealing with all matters relating to the Law of the Sea." GA Res. 3067, 28 UN GAOR, Supp. (No. 30) 13, UN Doc. A/9030 (1973).

[80] Draft Convention on the Law of the Sea, UN Doc. A/CONF.62/L.78, Art. 37 (1981) [hereinafter cited as Draft Convention].

[81] *Id.*, Art. 38(2). Two major issues were at stake in the negotiation of the regime of straits: (1) the rights of submerged passage by submarines and overflight by airplanes regarding straits falling within the territorial sea of coastal states, a right that does not exist under the concept of innocent passage in customary international law; and (2) the discretionary competence of coastal states under the concept of innocent passage to exclude passage on the ground that it is not innocent. It was because of these two issues, perceived to be of vital strategic importance to the two major maritime powers, that the novel concept of transit passage was introduced by the United States and the Soviet Union. Both of them made it clear that a satisfactory solution to the question of straits is a key to a new law of the sea treaty. *See* Burke, *Submerged Passage Through Straits: Interpretation of the Proposed Law of the Sea Treaty Text*, 52 WASH. L. REV. 193 (1977).

Straits at the entrance of inland seas, however, are exempted from the new regime owing to their marginal importance to navigation.[82] Article 45(1) of the Draft Convention states: "The régime of innocent passage . . . shall apply in straits used for international navigation . . . [b]etween an area of the high seas or an exclusive economic zone and the territorial sea of a foreign State."[83]

Unfortunately, however, the Draft Convention has maintained the incongruous separation, initiated at the 1958 Geneva Conference, between the regime of straits at the entrance to inland seas and that of the inland seas themselves. This is more unfortunate in view of the fact that the UNCLOS Draft Convention contains a separate part on the question of inland seas.

Part IX of the Draft Convention is entitled "Enclosed or Semi-Enclosed Seas" and is composed of two articles. The first defines enclosed or semi-enclosed seas as "a gulf, basin, or sea surrounded by two or more States and connected to the open seas by a narrow outlet or consisting entirely or primarily of the territorial seas and exclusive economic zones of two or more coastal States."[84] The second article recommends that states bordering on such seas cooperate in the exercise of their rights and duties under the Convention, especially with regard to living resources, the marine environment, and the conduct of scientific research.[85]

No mention, however, is made of any special regime applicable to these sea areas, loosely defined to include large stretches of the open sea (*e.g.*, the Mediterranean Sea), as well as small bays and inland seas (*e.g.*, the Gulf of Aqaba). Proposals that the general rules included in the Draft Convention be applied to inland seas "in a manner consistent with the special characteristics of these seas and the needs and interests of their coastal States"[86] did not achieve the necessary consensus. This could be regarded as a rejection of the view expressed by some publicists that coastal states could, through agreement, close bays or inland seas to foreign navigation.[87]

[82] *See, e.g.*, the statement of the Soviet Union's delegate: "The regime covering straits used for international navigation should not be extended to straits linking the high seas with the territorial sea of any state. Navigation in straits of that kind, such as the Straits of Tiran . . . should be governed by the rules for innocent passage." Sub-Committee II of the Committee on the Peaceful Uses of the Sea-bed and the Ocean Floor Beyond the Limits of National Jurisdiction, UN Doc. A/AC.138/SC.II/SR.58, at 125 (1973).

[83] Draft Convention, *supra* note 80, Art. 45. This article was regarded as applicable to the Head Harbor Passage, the Strait of Georgia, and the Gulf of Honduras besides the Strait of Tiran. *See* Moore, *supra* note 75, at 112.

[84] Draft Convention, *supra* note 80, Art. 122. [85] *Id.*, Art. 123.

[86] Draft Articles on Enclosed and Semi-Enclosed Seas, 3 THIRD UNITED NATIONS CONFERENCE ON THE LAW OF THE SEA, OFFICIAL RECORDS 237, UN Doc. 62/C.2/L.72 (1975).

[87] *See* Verzijl's statement that an agreement *inter se* between coastal states to close a bay or an inland sea by drawing a straight baseline, while guaranteeing one another freedom of access,

> would certainly be valid and could not be challenged by third States which desire to have free access to the bay contrary to the common decision of the adjacent States. The general rule, enunciated by Gidel with a view to protecting the interests of one or more less favourably situated riparian States, would therefore seem to need qualification to the effect that it ceases to operate when the riparian States themselves collectively agree on a closing line, on the understanding that this line does not exceed the length of twenty-four miles, just as in the case of a unistatal bay.

J. VERZIJL, *supra* note 61, at 595.

The abstention by the conference from enunciating a special regime for any of these sea areas could further be construed as an indication of the intention of the participants to subject inland seas and similar sea inlets surrounded by more than one state, irrespective of their width, to the general norms and regimes set out in the Draft Convention. Territorial sea would therefore be measured from the low-water line along the coast and a right of innocent passage would exist.[88]

Nevertheless, the unfortunate inclusion under a single definition of such disparate sea areas as the Mediterranean Sea and the Gulf of Aqaba has contributed to the conference's inability to deal with the specific problem of certain gulfs and inland seas, where access to some of the coastal states could only be effected by passage through the territorial sea of some other coastal states. The result was an anomalous situation: passage through a strait at the entrance of an inland sea with the above characteristics would be subject to a nonsuspendable right of innocent passage, while passage through the inland sea itself would be subject to a right of innocent passage that could be temporarily suspended.[89] Undoubtedly, this duality of norms is not rationally justified if the intention was to safeguard freedom of access at all times to all coastal states. A proper approach would have been for the UNCLOS III Draft Convention to enjoin against the suspension of passage in both the inland sea and the strait at its entrance.[90]

II. The Regime Established by the Egyptian-Israeli Peace Treaty

The general approach adopted in the Peace Treaty with regard to access to the Gulf of Aqaba is a sound one. It recognizes the politico-legal nature of the dispute and rightly addresses it as an inseparable element of the Arab-Israeli conflict. It also acknowledges the imprecise nature of the existing general international law norms and correctly embarks on the establishment, through bilateral agreement, of a new regime.

The first sentence of Article V(2) of the Peace Treaty is declaratory in character: "The Parties consider the Strait of Tiran and the Gulf of Aqaba to be international waterways, open to all nations for unimpeded and nonsuspendable freedom of navigation and overflight."[91] The preliminary determi-

[88] Draft Convention, *supra* note 80, Art. 5.

[89] *Compare* Art. 25(3) *with* Art. 45(2), *id.*

[90] The necessity for such a norm is not limited to cases such as the Gulf of Aqaba where the inland sea falls in its entirety within the territorial sea of coastal states; it extends to other cases such as the Arab/Persian Gulf where there are large areas of high seas. In the latter case, passage in certain areas of the gulf has to be effected, because of navigational requirements, through the territorial sea of Iranian islands. No agreement, however, existed during the UNCLOS informal negotiations on the nature of such passage. While some states expressed the view that passage under these circumstances should be subject to the regime of transit passage applicable to the strait at the entrance of the gulf, others maintained that such passage should be subject to the regime of innocent passage applicable in the territorial sea, which could be subject to suspension; *see ibid.*

[91] Treaty of Peace, *supra* note 5. The language of the Peace Treaty dealing with the regime of the Gulf of Aqaba is based on the similar language of the Framework for the Conclusion of a Peace Treaty Between Egypt and Israel, dated Sept. 17, 1978: "the Strait of Tiran and the Gulf of Aqaba are international waterways to be open to all nations for unimpeded and nonsuspendable freedom of navigation and overflight." Camp David Agreements, *reprinted in* 17 ILM 1463, 1470 (1978).

nation that the Gulf and the Strait are "international waterways" is in conformity with paragraph 2(a) of Security Council Resolution 242 of 1967,[92] which implicitly requires the identification by the parties of "international waterways in the area," subject to the principle of freedom of navigation.

The stipulation that navigation should not be subject to suspension is similar to Article 16(4) of the 1958 Territorial Sea Convention and Article 45(2) of the UNCLOS III Draft Convention,[93] both intended to apply to the Strait of Tiran. The Peace Treaty, however, extends the provision to the Gulf as well, and thus remedies a serious loophole in both instruments.

But the Peace Treaty goes beyond the long established regime of innocent passage in the territorial sea,[94] a regime that has been regarded as equally applicable to the Strait of Tiran under both the Geneva Convention and the UNCLOS III Draft Convention. The Peace Treaty instead uses the term "freedom of navigation and overflight," which is usually associated with the high seas and which is regarded to be "comprehensive in intention including movement, observation, inspection, maneuvers, tests, and so forth, carried out above, on, and below the surface."[95]

The departure from the application of the regime of innocent passage to sea areas that fall within the territorial sea finds a precedent in the UNCLOS III Draft Convention. This is in connection with the regime of transit passage applicable to a certain category of straits.[96] There, the term "freedom of navigation and overflight" is also used.[97] But the reading of the term in its context makes clear that it is used, as in the case of Security Council Resolution 242 of 1967, to refer to the general principle underlying the newly established right of transit passage rather than to indicate the applicability of the high seas freedom of navigation. The duties of passing ships and aircraft during passage and the correlative coastal rights are specified in detail in the UNCLOS III Draft Convention in a manner indicative of the distinction between "transit passage" and "freedom of navigation."[98] Reisman aptly formulated this conclusion: "Since the major differences between innocent passage and freedom of navigation are the conditions and right of qualification of the coastal state with regard to the former, 'transit passage' seems more a species of innocent passage than a high seas freedom."[99]

[92] *See* text accompanying note 70 *supra.*

[93] Convention on the Territorial Sea and the Contiguous Zone, *supra* note 48, 15 UST 1606, TIAS No. 5639, 516 UNTS 205; Draft Convention, *supra* note 80.

[94] Convention on the Territorial Sea and the Contiguous Zone, *supra* note 48, Arts. 14–23; Draft Convention, *supra* note 80, Arts. 17–32, 45.

[95] Reisman, *The Regime of Straits and International Security: An Appraisal of International Lawmaking*, 74 AJIL 48, 57 (1980). *See also* Burke, *supra* note 81, at 201.

[96] Draft Convention, *supra* note 80, Arts. 34–44.

[97]

> Transit passage means the exercise in accordance with this Part of the freedom of navigation and overflight solely for the purpose of continuous and expeditious transit of the strait between one area of the high seas or an exclusive economic zone and another area of the high seas or an exclusive economic zone.

Draft Convention, *supra* note 80, Art. 38(2).

[98] Draft Convention, *supra* note 80, Arts. 39–43.

[99] Reisman, *supra* note 95, at 70.

In the Peace Treaty, however, there is no mention of any duties on the part of passing ships and aircraft or of the extent of coastal competence and rights. This could lead to the interpretation that the parties' intention was to subject the Gulf to a comprehensive and unqualified freedom of navigation and overflight.[100] But a careful reading of the Treaty and its annexes refutes this interpretation. First, it is clear that the parties continue to regard the Strait and the Gulf as part of the territorial sea and not as part of the high seas.[101] The exercise of freedom of navigation and overflight is therefore limited by, and has to be reconciled with, the exercise of certain competence and rights in the territorial sea. Reference to such competence has in fact been made in relation to the performance of "normal police functions" in the territorial sea of the Gulf.[102] Second, it was agreed by the parties that, for security considerations, their permissible naval and aerial military activities in some parts of their territorial sea, including that of the Gulf, would be restricted.[103] It does not therefore seem plausible, in such a security-conscious agreement, that the intention was to create rights for third states that exceed the rights of the parties themselves or to subject the Gulf to the high seas freedom of navigation and overflight, which includes such security-risking activities as the conduct of military maneuvers and the carrying out of research and survey activities.

The above could suggest that what the parties in fact intended was to establish a regime that goes beyond the regime of innocent passage prescribed by the Geneva Convention and the UNCLOS III Draft Convention for the Strait of Tiran,[104] but that falls short of the freedom of navigation and overflight applicable in the high seas. The objective of the parties thus seemed to be the establishment of a regime analogous in content to the UNCLOS regime of transit passage, which firmly assures the right of the international community to freedom of communication while preserving coastal states' rights of protection and self-preservation. If this interpretation is correct, then a clarification of the duties of passing ships and aircraft as well as of coastal rights and competence is required. Such clarification could even be pressing in light of the fact that the Peace Treaty assigns to a third party, the United Nations forces or its alternative multinational force, the task of "[e]nsuring the freedom of navigation through the Strait of Tiran in accordance with Article V of the Treaty of Peace."[105]

[100] *Cf.* Reisman's interpretation of the language of the Camp David Framework for a Peace Treaty, *supra* note 95, at 76.

[101] *See* Treaty of Peace, *supra* note 5, Ann. 1, Art. IV(3).

[102] "Egyptian civil police equipped with light boats, lightly armed, shall perform normal police functions within the territorial waters of Zone C." *Ibid.* Zone C is bounded by the international boundary and the Gulf of Aqaba on the east. *Id.*, Ann. 1, Art. II(1)(C).

[103] *Id.*, Ann. 1, Arts. III, IV.

[104] The intention of the parties to establish a regime for the Gulf that goes beyond the regime of innocent passage is confirmed by Article VIII of Annex III: *"Without prejudice to the provisions of Article V of the Treaty of Peace* each Party recognizes the right of the vessels of the other Party to innocent passage through its territorial sea in accordance with the rules of international law." *Id.*, Ann. III, Art. VIII (emphasis added).

[105] *Id.*, Ann. I, Art. VI(2)(d). The parties agreed to ask the United Nations to provide forces and observers to supervise the implementation of Annex I to the Treaty concerning Israeli withdrawal and security arrangements, and to employ their best efforts to prevent any violation of its

The new regime is binding on the parties and, subject to Article 103 of the UN Charter,[106] overrides between them all conflicting customary and multilateral treaty norms that are not *jus cogens*.[107] The regime, however, is characterized by its bilateral character and the absence from the agreement of the two other coastal states bordering the Gulf, Saudi Arabia and Jordan. The obligation established by the Peace Treaty to open the Gulf to all nations for freedom of navigation and overflight could thus only bind them upon their express acceptance.[108] This is because the regime is a new one and not a codification of customary law.

In the absence of such acceptance, a diversity of legal norms would continue to be applicable. That part of the Gulf constituting the territorial sea of Egypt and Israel would be subject to the regime established by the Peace Treaty, while the other part, which falls within the territorial sea of Saudi Arabia and Jordan, would continue to be subject to general international law norms. However, the operational significance of the new regime would not be affected since access to Israel through the Strait of Tiran and the Gulf of Aqaba could be gained by passage solely through or over the Egyptian and Israeli territorial sea.[109] This would also be the case even if the claims of Saudi Arabia with regard to the two islands at the entrance of the Strait were to be maintained.[110] And the Treaty is clear regarding the intention of the parties to subject their relations to the new regime irrespective of the acceptance of that regime by other coastal states: "The Parties will respect each other's right to navigation and overflight for access to either country through the Strait of Tiran and the Gulf of Aqaba."[111] Nevertheless, it is to be hoped that all the Gulf states will

---

terms. *Id.*, Ann. I, Art. VI(1). In identical letters accompanying the Peace Treaty, and addressed to the President of Egypt and the Prime Minister of Israel, the President of the United States indicated that if the UN Security Council failed to establish and maintain the arrangements called for in the Peace Treaty, "the President will be prepared to take those steps necessary to ensure the establishment and maintenance of an acceptable alternative multinational force." *Id.*, Letters Accompanying the Peace Treaty, 79 DEP'T STATE BULL., No. 2026, May 1979, at 14, 15. In view of the Security Council disagreement on the establishment of a UN force, a Multinational Force has been assembled to undertake the tasks assigned in the Peace Treaty to UN forces and observers.

[106] "In the event of a conflict between the obligations of the Members of the United Nations under the present Charter and their obligations under any other international agreement, their obligations under the present Charter shall prevail." UN CHARTER art. 103. *See also* Treaty of Peace, *supra* note 5, Art. VI(5).

[107] Vienna Convention on the Law of Treaties, UN Doc. A/CONF.39/27 (1969), Art. 53, *reprinted in* 8 ILM 679 (1969), 63 AJIL 875 (1969).

[108] "An obligation arises for a third State from a provision of a treaty if the parties to the treaty intend the provision to be the means of establishing the obligation and the third State expressly accepts that obligation in writing," Vienna Convention on the Law of Treaties, *supra* note 107, Art. 35.

[109] *See* text accompanying note 1 *supra.*

[110] This is due to the geographical location of the main navigational channel in the Strait of Tiran, *supra* note 1, which makes it almost certain that it would continue to be part of Egypt's territorial sea under any delimitation agreement.

[111] Treaty of Peace, *supra* note 5, Art. V(2), 2d sentence. *See also* Agreed Minutes to Art. V: "The second sentence of paragraph 2 of Article V shall not be construed as limiting the first sentence of that paragraph. The foregoing is not to be construed as contravening the second sentence of paragraph 2 of Article V. . . ." 18 ILM at 392.

find it possible to agree on a unified regime for the Gulf, which would ensure the uniformity of legal norms applicable to such a small body of water.

The Treaty also establishes a right for all nations to use the Gulf and the Strait for "freedom of navigation and overflight."[112] Such a right for third states, which is more inclusive in nature and scope than existing customary and multilateral treaty rights, could be exercised upon the assent of a third state, which is presumed so long as the contrary is not indicated.[113] A state exercising this right, however, shall comply with the pertinent conditions provided for in the Treaty or established in conformity with it.[114] These conditions, however, could not diminish or detract from any acquired customary or multilateral treaty rights.

But a third state would not be able to claim this newly established right with respect to the part of the Gulf that falls within the territorial sea of Saudi Arabia and Jordan. In this situation, general customary and multilateral treaty law will continue to be applicable. The rights and obligations of these two coastal states and third states will remain subject to the regime of innocent passage with its broad coastal competence, passage duties, and overflight limitation.

Appraisal and Conclusion

Access to bays and inland seas and similar small sea areas that are surrounded by more than one state has been subject to numerous legal regimes in the practice of states. This is because of the divergence in the principal function of these sea areas as well as the varied geographical locations of the coastal states. These variations in functions and features have led to the lack of a consistent body of law to govern their legal status, including the question of access. It has also led to the view that no attempt to formulate general norms should be made: "The guiding principle in solving the problem of bays enclosed by more than one State had to consist not in the development of generally applicable rules, but in the application of special regulations in accordance with the prevailing circumstances."[115]

Certain general norms should, however, provide guidelines to these special regulations and act as their underpinning. Gulfs and inland seas surrounded by more than one state are sometimes important and in certain cases essential for freedom of communication between coastal states and the high seas. This should result in the recognition of a right of passage between all coastal states and the high seas, a right that could be exercised irrespective of the legal nature of the sea area (bay, gulf, inland sea, etc.) through which passage is effected and that could not be suspended or impeded. The importance of such a right has often been expressed, although it has never materialized into precise general norms. The regime established in the Egyptian-Israeli Peace Treaty could thus be regarded as an important contribution towards the affirmation of this right in the practice of states.

[112] Treaty of Peace, Art. V(2), 1st sentence.

[113] *See* Vienna Convention on the Law of Treaties, *supra* note 107, Art. 36(1).

[114] *Id.*, Art. 36(2).

[115] L. Bouchez, *supra* note 2, at 117.

Equally, these sea areas, because of their intimate relation to the land mass, are often important for coastal protection and defense. This should result in the recognition as well of a coastal right of protection and self-preservation that would not hamper the exercise of uninterrupted passage. It is this latter right that is not clearly spelled out in the Peace Treaty. This is due, it is suggested, to the psychological importance that has been attached to the question of access to the Gulf in the matrix of the Arab-Israeli conflict. The use of the term "freedom of navigation and overflight" without qualifying conditions is an attestation to that fact. This usage, however, as mentioned, could give rise to the adverse interpretation that the term was used in its high seas context, which connotes a broad range of military activities and operational practices. This seemingly unintended interpretation, if not checked, could have unwarranted implications. One such implication could be the claim by third states that the new regime establishes a right for submarines and other naval ships and aircraft to hover freely in the Gulf and/or to conduct research and survey activities.

It is suggested, therefore, that the Peace Treaty be supplemented to reflect what is believed to be the true intention of the parties, *i.e.*, the establishment of a regime of access to the Gulf that ensures the unimpeded and nonsuspendable right of passage for all states while protecting coastal states against possible abuse and interference. This could be effected through a detailed regulation of the duties of passing ships and aircraft, as well as of the permissible coastal rights and competence. Such regulations might be similar in content to those in the UNCLOS III Draft Convention regarding transit passage.[116] The regulations should, however, *inter alia*, affirm the basic principles that "freedom of navigation and overflight" is solely limited to the requirements of passage; that passing ships and aircraft are obliged to refrain from any activities that could adversely affect coastal interests; and that coastal states are entitled to adopt laws and regulations for the protection of their security, economic, and other recognized interests. Enactment of these regulations would affirm the coastal states' right of protection and guard against potential conflicts, to the benefit of the coastal states and of the international community.

[116] *See* Draft Convention, *supra* note 80, Arts. 34–44.

SEA BOUNDARY DELIMITATION BETWEEN STATES BEFORE WORLD WAR II

*By Sang-Myon Rhee**

Despite the increasing significance of customary law in the delimitation of sea boundaries between states, the principles that evolved during the three centuries prior to World War II have generally been ignored. Although a comprehensive study in this field is needed, the studies that exist begin either with the Truman Proclamation of 1945 or the discussions of the International Law Commission in the early 1950's. The Commission itself declared that there was no law on the matter and attempted to legislate rules in the interest of the progressive development of international law. This hasty and ambitious attempt left a gap between the conventional law and customary law, which later resulted in many disputes.

The importance of customary law is underscored by the draft provisions on delimitation of the economic zone and the continental shelf adopted in 1981 at the Third United Nations Conference on the Law of the Sea. These provisions state that "[t]he delimitation of the exclusive economic zone [continental shelf] between States with opposite or adjacent coasts shall be effected by agreement on the basis of international law, as referred to in article 38 of the Statute of the International Court of Justice, in order to achieve an equitable solution."[1]

This article will examine the development of principles on the delimitation of sea boundaries between the establishment of a modern international society of equal sovereign states after the Treaty of Westphalia in 1648 and the inception of the continental shelf doctrine in 1945. Particular attention will be given to analyzing the competing principles on delimitation that emerged during the period.

I. Early Efforts to Establish Principles

Sea boundary problems would come to a head with the establishment of a definite territorial sea in the 18th and 19th centuries. However, belts of their coastal waters had long been regarded as owned by coastal states, though there was no agreement on the precise limits. Even that staunch advocate of freedom of the seas, Hugo Grotius (1583–1645), recognized the possibility of appropriating a territorial sea; he cautiously stated that a portion of the sea might be divided by analogy with the principle regarding the delimitation of international rivers, that "in doubtful cases . . . sovereignty extends to the middle

* Professor of Law, Seoul National University. This article was written when the author was a research fellow at Harvard Law School. The author acknowledges his gratitude to the late Richard R. Baxter, Leo Gross, M. J. Peterson, Louis B. Sohn, Arthur T. von Mehren, and others for their help. The views expressed herein are the author's own.

[1] *See* Draft Convention on the Law of the Sea, UN Doc. A/CONF.62/L.78 (1981), Arts. 74(1) and 83(1).

of the river" (in dubio . . . imperia ad medietatem fluminis utrinque pertingunt).[2] The doctrine of the middle line was based on the fundamental principle of sovereign equality. But his concept of the dividing line was ambiguous; he was not sure whether sovereignty should extend to the middle on the surface of the water or to the middle of the channel.[3]

It was Samuel Pufendorf (1632–1694) who first proposed principles regarding sea boundaries in his masterpiece *De jure naturae et gentium* (1672). His strong background in mathematics and geometry helped him to devise well-organized principles regarding sea boundary delimitation that are worthy of close examination even today: "[S]i autem diversi populi fretum, aut sinum accolant, eorum imperia pro latitudine terrarum ad medium usque ejusdem pertinere intelligentur; nisi . . . per conventionem indivisim id imperium contra exteros exercere, ipso autem promiscue inter se isto aequore uti placuerit. . . ." ([I]f several people live upon a strait or bay, their several dominions are understood to extend straight out from their territories to its centre, unless . . . by convention they decide to exercise that dominion as a unity against foreigners but to use those waters promiscuously among themselves. . . .)[4] Pufendorf's proposal to delimit sea boundaries equally, unless the states agree to exclude foreigners and share the waters among themselves, appears to be logically sound, but it raised questions. The clause "eorum imperia pro latitudine terrarum ad medium usque ejusdem pertinere intelligentur" was translated in an English edition published in 1703 by Oxford University as "the sovereignty of each shall be conceived to reach into the middle of the water from every part of their respective shore."[5] Of course, it is impossible to delimit the sea boundary geometrically "from every part of their respective shore," but this apparently represents the ideal of equal division. However, in the French edition of 1712, translated by Barbeyrac, the clause reads: "l'empire de chacun s'étend jusqu'au milieu, à proportion de la largeur de leurs Terres."[6] The French edition well represents the true meaning of the original Latin text. Thus, the correct English translation should have been that "the sovereignty of each shall extend into the middle in proportion to the breadth of its land."

The method of delimitation proposed by Pufendorf is composed of dual principles, *i.e.*, equality and proportionality. From the context it appears that equality is qualified by proportionality. But on a closer look, one could conclude that proportionality guides the whole principle of equal delimitation. The notion of proportionality seems to be more deeply rooted in history than the theory of equal delimitation. Proportionality was created as a bulwark against the impractical and illogical claim that the whole body of rivers, lakes, or arms of the sea could be used by one coastal state to the total exclusion of the other.

[2] 1 H. GROTIUS, DE JURE BELLI AC PACIS, bk. II, ch. III, pt. XVIII (Carnegie Endowment ed. of 1646, 1913).

[3] Grotius also stated that "si exaruisset flumen, imperii terminus maneret medietas alvei, qui proxime fuisset." He did not clearly distinguish between "ad medietatem fluminis" and "medietas alvei." *See id.*, pt. XVII.

[4] S. PUFENDORF, DE JURE NATURAE ET GENTIUM, bk. IV, ch. V, §8 (Carnegie Endowment ed. of 1688, 1934).

[5] S. PUFENDORF, OF THE LAW OF NATURE AND NATIONS, bk. IV, ch. V, §8 (Oxford 1703).

[6] S. PUFENDORF, LE DROIT DE LA NATURE ET DES GENS, bk. IV, ch. V, §8 (1712).

The theory was based on the general principle of law that lakes and other running water should be a natural part of and give access to the land.[7]

This notion was invoked by Austria in the 18th century in its claim against the Republic of Venice over a part of Lake Garda. When Austria acquired a portion of the shore of the lake, it challenged the Venetian claim over all its waters, which was based on historical rights. The dispute became acute in 1756 when the parties were negotiating a treaty to delimit the boundary. Austria argued that "rivers as well as lakes (except in case of public agreement) are a part of the continents which they nourish and they become divided in proportion to frontages."[8] The Austrian claim was supported by the general principle of law that legal values increase in direct proportion to the extension of the subject.[9]

The notion of proportionality had deep roots in European law. The Italian Civil Code of 1865 provided that if a river or stream formed a new bed or abandoned its former one, the owners should divide it along the middle of the bed itself, following the length of the frontage of their respective properties.[10] If there were islands and accretions on both sides of the median line, the median was to be the boundary; but if there were islands and accretions only on one side of the line, the boundary between the adjacent owners was to be marked by perpendicular lines drawn from the median line to the extremities of their frontage on the bank.[11] Similarly, the Austrian Civil Code of 1811 provided that if an island was formed in the middle of a body of water, the owners of the properties situated along its two banks had the exclusive right to appropriate it in two equal shares or to divide it between them in proportion to the length of their parcels of land on the shore.[12]

The principle of proportionality was applied in many instances to the delimitation of lake boundaries between states. For instance, the Supreme Court of the Holy Roman Empire in 1526 settled the dispute over Lake Sant' Andrea between the two families of Arco and Castelbarco in accordance with the principle of proportionality.[13] Lake Geneva was divided in the same manner among the five riparians by the Treaty of Lausanne of October 30, 1564.[14] Vittorio Adami, writing over three centuries later, explained how it was possible to achieve such a proportional division as follows:

> The fixing of boundary lines on lakes, whose waters wash the shores of two or more States, depends upon the shape and the area of the water surface.
>
> . . . In the case where portions of both banks belong to the same State, if the boundary marks on the two opposite banks are placed vis à vis, the

[7] *See* H. GROTIUS, *supra* note 2, at bk. II, ch. II, pt. IV; *id.*, ch. III, pt. VII.

[8] V. ADAMI, I CONFINI DI STATO NELLA LEGISLAZIONE INTERNAZIONALE 41 (1919), translated as NATIONAL FRONTIERS IN RELATION TO INTERNATIONAL LAW 40 (trans. T. T. Behrens 1927) [hereinafter pages in translation cited in brackets].

[9] *Id.* at 44 [42].

[10] CODICE CIVIL ITALIANO, Art. 461 (1865).

[11] *Id.*, Art. 458.

[12] DAS ALLGEMEINE BÜRGERLICHE GESETZBUCH FÜR DAS KAISERTUM OESTERREICH, Art. 407 (1811).

[13] V. ADAMI, *supra* note 8, at 42 [40].

[14] *Ibid.*

> lake boundary line is the line joining the two boundary marks; if, on the contrary, the two marks are not opposite one another, the boundary line starting from one of the marks, crosses the surface of the water in a direction perpendicular to the coast, till it joins the median line of the lake, then following this line, it continues till it meets the other perpendicular starting from the opposite shore.[15]

These rudimentary methods may not be geometrically accurate in implementing the principle of proportionality, but they do represent a resourceful attempt by various means to achieve an equitable solution.

These early ideas of delimitation, which were developed for rivers and lakes, were not widely applied to the delimitation of maritime boundaries between states. Until the 19th century, there was no compelling need for such delimitation because the regime of the territorial sea was not fully established. The first sea boundaries were drawn in narrow straits and arms of the sea. For instance, in 1661 Norway and Sweden established a fjord boundary in the Bay of Christiana by connecting certain median points between the two coasts. The sea boundary started at a median point between the outermost islands of Koster and Tisler and ran to the terminus of the land boundary. The states did not dare to establish a lateral territorial sea boundary from the median point, which would have extended further oceanward.[16]

Gradually, however, coastal states became more interested in establishing the outer limits of their territorial seas than in dividing relatively small areas between them. Bynkershoek's suggestion in 1702 that "the control of the lands ends where the power of weapons ends" (potestatem terrae finiri, ubi finitur armorum vis)[17] received support, for example, from Vattel in 1758,[18] and in 1782 the limit was concretely defined as 3 miles by Galiani in accordance with the contemporary range of cannon.[19] After its introduction into Anglo-American jurisprudence in the early 1800's[20] and its use in the Anglo-American Treaty of October 20, 1818,[21] the 3-mile rule became increasingly prevalent.[22]

Nevertheless, the "cannon shot" rule seems to have inhibited the development of flexible ideas for equitable solutions by encouraging some writers to adhere to the strict rule of the median line. Georg F. von Martens, for example, while referring to the "cannon shot" rule as customary for coastal waters, endorsed

[15] *Id.* at 39 [38].

[16] For the text of the Treaty, see Recueil des traités de la Norvège 580–84 (1907). *See also* Strupp, *Der Streitfall zwischen Schweden und Norwegen*, in 2 DAS WERK VOM HAAG, DIE GERICHTLICHEN ENTSCHEIDUNGEN 62–64 (ed. W. Schücking 1917).

[17] C. VAN BYNKERSHOEK, DE DOMINIO MARIS, ch. II, at 365 (1744).

[18] *See* 1 EMMERICH DE VATTEL, LE DROIT DES GENS OU PRINCIPES DE LA LOI NATURELLE, bk. I, ch. XXIII, at 250–51 (1758).

[19] *See* F. GALIANI, DE' DOVERI DE' PRINCIPI NEUTRALI VERSO I PRINCIPI GUERREGIANTI, E DI QUESTI VERSO NEUTRALI 432 (1782).

[20] *See, e.g.*, The *Twee Gebroeders*, 165 Eng. Rep. 422 (Adm. 1800) (per Sir W. Scott); The *Twee Gebroeders*, *id.* at 485 (Adm. 1801) (per Sir W. Scott); The *Anna*, *id.* at 809 (Adm. 1805) (per Sir W. Scott); The *Brig Anne*, 1 Gallison (U.S. Circuit Ct. Rep.) 62 (1812) (per Story, J.).

[21] *See* TS No. 112.

[22] *See, e.g.*, T. W. FULTON, THE SOVEREIGNTY OF THE SEA 576 *et seq.* (1911).

the median line for lakes, rivers, and straits.[23] This idea was similar to the traditional notion that sovereignty should extend to and end at the middle. The "cannon shot" rule, designed to measure the outer limit of the territorial sea, was not adequate as a general theory for the delimitation of sea boundaries between states.

II. Competing Principles of Delimitation

With the general adoption of the regime of the territorial sea in the early 19th century, attention began to focus on the problem of delimiting boundaries in the coastal waters between opposite and adjacent states. Adding a territorial sea to states' domains raised two new problems. First, many of the bays, straits, and other arms of the sea bordered by different states on opposite shores were less than twice as wide as the breadth of the territorial sea. In such cases, these bodies of water were subject to division between the states fronting them. Second, the newly acquired territorial sea extending from the terminus of the land boundary was also to be divided, but there were no established rules for such delimitation between adjacent states. Naturally, the distinction between opposite and adjacent situations is not absolute, for bays and gulfs can be both opposite from and adjacent to one another to varying degrees. But it is useful to begin with the distinction because it has been used in practice.[24]

Opposite States: Median Line v. Thalweg

Sea boundary problems between opposite states were generally regarded as less difficult to resolve than those between adjacent states, for it was plausible to imagine that the sovereignty of each would meet in the middle. The situation of adjacent states, however, was altogether different. It is therefore not surprising that most of the sea boundaries created in the earlier part of the 19th century were agreed upon by opposite states. The maritime frontier between Finland and Sweden, established by the Peace Treaty of September 17, 1809, traversed the middle of the Gulf of Bothnia and the Aaland Sea, where it bisected the rock called the Märket and then entered the Baltic Sea, after passing between certain listed Finnish and Swedish islands.[25] In the United States, New Jersey and New York agreed to divide Raritan Bay through the middle in the interstate compact of September 16, 1833.[26] Since the signing

[23] G. F. von Martens, The Law of Nations, bk. IV, ch. IV, sec. 4 (4th ed. trans. Wm. Cobbett, 1829). *See also* by the same author: 1 Précis du droit des gens moderne de l'Europe, bk. II, ch. 1, sec. 40 (1801); Einleitung in das positive europäische Völkerrecht, bk. II, ch. I, sec. 34 (1796); 1 Primae lineae iuris gentium europaearum practici, bk. IV, ch. IV, secs. 109–10 (1785).

[24] Most of the writers who proposed principles or rules on delimitation before World War II distinguished opposite and adjacent situations. The International Law Commission also recommended slightly different rules for each situation to the 1958 Geneva Conference on the Law of the Sea. [1955] 1 Y.B. Int'l L. Comm'n 253; [1956] *id.* at 300.

[25] *See* Addendum 1, UN Doc. A/CN.4/71/Add.1, at 2, to the Information and Observations Submitted by Governments Regarding the Question of the Delimitation of the Territorial Sea of Two Adjacent States, UN Doc. A/CN.4/71 (1953).

[26] 4 Stat. 708, 11 Martens Nouveau Recueil 713 [hereinafter cited as MNR].

of the Treaty of Nanking of August 29, 1842, which ceded Hong Kong to the British, the boundary with China has been assumed to be the middle of the strait between the mainland and the island of Hong Kong, even though the Treaty did not specify a line.[27] In the Treaty of June 15, 1846 between the United Kingdom and the United States, the water boundary in the Pacific border region passed through the middle of the Strait of Juan de Fuca and the channel separating the continent from Vancouver Island.[28] Japan and Russia agreed on January 26, 1855 that their frontier should pass between the islands of Ituprup and Urup, but specified no further details.[29]

Scholars began to pay attention to this neglected issue in the middle of the 19th century. In 1861 Travers Twiss endorsed the principles suggested by Samuel Pufendorf in 1672 by recommending the median line principle as a general rule and "the central deep-water line" as a supplementary rule; but he asserted at the same time that "the right of *innocent use* of the entire bay or strait for the purposes of navigation or passage may be common to both Nations."[30] In 1868, Johann Caspar Bluntschli emphasized the duty to accept either a line or a common zone between states without proposing any specific rule, even though he was firmly convinced that the thalweg principle should be applicable to navigable rivers and the median line principle to lakes. The purpose of the common zone was presumably to preserve equal access and the right of navigation in straits and other channels where the 3-mile zones overlapped.[31] In 1872 David Dudley Field suggested a combined principle in an international code he proposed to the International Law Association:

> The limits of national territory, bounded by a river or other stream, or by a strait, sound, or arm of the sea, the other shore of which is the territory of another nation, extend outward to a point equidistant from the territory of the nation occupying the opposite shore; or if there be a stream or navigable channel, to the thread of the stream, that is to say, to the mid-channel; or, if there be several channels, to the middle of the principal one.[32]

His idea is quite pragmatic because of the special equitable consideration he gave to the mutual interest in navigation by suggesting that the riparian states share the channel or stream of navigation.

The proposals of all three scholars involve dual principles. Twiss referred to a "central line" or a "central deep water line," Bluntschli to a "line" or a "common zone," and Field to a line connecting "equidistant points" or the "thread of the stream." They had in mind, on the one hand, an equal division of the surface of the water, and on the other, equal access to and sharing of the navigable waters—the paramount interest. As a result of the invention of

[27] 3 G. GIDEL, LE DROIT INTERNATIONAL PUBLIC DE LA MER 748 (1934).

[28] 34 BRIT. FOREIGN & ST. PAPERS 14 [hereinafter cited as BFSP].

[29] 57 *id.* at 1054; for the Japanese and Russian texts, see 1 Kyo joyaku isan (Old Collection of Treaties) 521 (1945).

[30] T. TWISS, THE LAW OF NATIONS 251 (1861).

[31] *See* J. BLUNTSCHLI, DAS MODERNE VÖLKERRECHT DER CIVILISIRTEN STATEN ALS RECHTSBUCH DARGESTELLT, Art. 303 (1868).

[32] *See* D. FIELD, OUTLINES OF AN INTERNATIONAL CODE 16 (1872).

steamships and the increase in tonnage of vessels, mutual preservation of equal rights of navigation in the deep-water channel or thalweg was essential to coriparian states. For this practical reason, the thalweg principle, which had emerged only in the early 19th century, soon challenged the traditional middle line principle.[33] It prevailed to such an extent in navigable waters that numerous provisions for a median line in previous agreements were often misinterpreted as the "middle of the stream," the "middle of the channel," the "center of the main channel," and so on.[34]

This confusion over the competing principles, the median line and the thalweg, emerged in a dispute between the United Kingdom and the United States about unclear provisions in the Treaty of June 15, 1846, relating to the location of "the channel which separates the continent from Vancouver's Island."[35] The principle of division was clearly stipulated in the Treaty as "through the middle of the said channel, and of Fuca's Strait, to the Pacific Ocean," but the parties differed over the choice of the channel in the coastal archipelagoes. They submitted the dispute to the German Emperor, William I, who ruled on October 21, 1871 in favor of the U.S. position that the boundary should be the middle of the Haro Channel.[36] On March 10, 1873, a Protocol on the water boundary was signed in Washington, D.C., by the two parties.[37] The line was ultimately fixed by connecting median points with many straight lines and one curved line. The parties applied the median line principle flexibly by ignoring rocks and taking navigational routes into consideration.

A similar dispute later arose between the two countries over an unclear description of the boundary in the Portland Channel area between Alaska and British Columbia. The crucial issue was which of two channels in the area was the Portland Channel, which would be the maritime boundary between the two countries. Because the eastern channel was deeper and wider than the western channel, the United States asserted that the boundary should be the eastern channel passing Pearse and Wales Islands and British Columbia. The United Kingdom contended that the thalweg principle should be applicable to navigable rivers but not to maritime channels. It also claimed that historical

[33] The thalweg principle was first adopted for the Rhine by the Peace Treaty of Luneville of Feb. 9, 1801. *See* 7 Martens Recueil de Traités 296 [hereinafter cited as MRT]. *See also* N. Kercea, Die Staatsgrenze in den Staatflüssen, *passim* (1916); 3 J. Verzijl, International Law in Historical Perspective 537 *et seq.* (1970) [hereinafter cited as J. Verzijl, International Law]. The term "thalweg" is a German word composed of two separate words, "Thal," a valley, and "Weg," way, meaning the middle, the deepest or most navigable channel. Since this term had no English equivalent, it was often translated as "fairway," "main channel," "middle of the channel," or "middle of the main stream."

[34] *E.g.*, the phrase in the Peace Treaty between Great Britain, France, and Spain that was concluded in 1763, "a line drawn along the middle of the river Mississippi from its source to the river Iberville," was later interpreted by the U.S. Supreme Court in Iowa v. Illinois, 147 U.S. 1, 8 (1892), *quoted in* Louisiana v. Mississippi, 202 U.S. 1, 50 (1906), as meaning "along the middle of the channel of the river Mississippi."

[35] *See* note 28 *supra* and accompanying text.

[36] *See* 1 J. B. Moore, History and Digest of the International Arbitrations to Which the United States Has Been a Party 230 (1898).

[37] *See* 1 Papers Relating to the Foreign Relations of the United States, 1873, at XXV.

factors strongly favored selection of the western channel as the boundary. On January 24, 1903, the parties agreed to submit the case to an ad hoc arbitration tribunal composed of three jurists from each country. On October 20 of that year, the majority held that the Portland Channel was the western channel between Wales Island and Sitklan Island, which was known as Tongas Channel.[38] The American contention based on the thalweg principle was not sustained. The parties did not dispute that the boundary in the selected channel should be a median line. The tribunal drew the boundary without difficulty along the middle of the channel on the map attached to the award. It was a curved line, passing midway between the two shores. The arbitrators generally ignored small islands and divided the channel roughly in half.[39]

Thus, although the median line principle was recognized as a general rule of law in these two cases, it was very flexibly applied in practice. The U.S. Supreme Court in *Louisiana v. Mississippi* (1906), however, found the thalweg appropriate for navigable waters. The Court stated that "where there is no necessary track of navigation, the line of demarcation is drawn in the middle, . . . but whenever there is a deep water sailing channel therein . . . the rule of the thalweg applies."[40] In this case, the Court did not apply the general rule of the median line, which was not claimed by either party, but the principle of the thalweg or main channel of navigation, as claimed by Louisiana. In stressing equal access to and preservation of the main channel for mutual navigation, the Court also took into account the parties' interests in the disputed oyster bed and certain geological aspects of the channel, *i.e.*, that "[o]n the Mississippi side the islands and shores are of sea sand formation while those on the Louisiana side are alluvial."[41] The Court rejected the historical line claimed by Mississippi and found that Louisiana had stronger historical rights to title over the maritime area on its side of the thalweg.[42]

Equitable delimitation was thus sometimes achieved by the flexible application of the median line principle and sometimes by application of the rule of the main channel of navigation to preserve equal rights of navigation. In some rare cases, states preferred to establish a common zone instead of dividing the area concerned. For instance, France and Spain agreed on March 30, 1879 to establish a common zone in the Bay of Figuier. First, the parties established a bay closing line, which was subsequently divided into three equal parts. The two points on the bay closing line were then connected to the land boundary terminus, which divided the water surface of the bay into three parts: the middle part was to be a common zone, while the other two would naturally belong to each riparian state.[43] Likewise, the narrow Bay of Atlaman at the southern boundary of Eastern Roumelia was left to the common use of Turkey and

[38] TRIBUNAL, ALASKA BOUNDARY PROTOCOLS, ORAL ARGUMENTS, WITH INDEX, AWARD OF THE TRIBUNAL, AND OPINIONS OF ITS MEMBERS, *passim* (1903). *See also* 98 BFSP 152; 96 *id.* at 84; 12 *id.* at 38. For comments, see, *e.g.*, 202 U.S. at 53. *See also* T. HODGINS, THE ALASKAN BOUNDARY TRIBUNAL AND INTERNATIONAL LAW 7 (1904).

[39] *See* ATLAS OF AWARD, ALASKAN BOUNDARY TRIBUNAL (Washington, D.C. 1904).

[40] 202 U.S. at 50.

[41] *Id.* at 23.

[42] *Id.* at 26.

[43] 70 BFSP 176–79; 4 Martens Nouveau Recueil Général, 2d ser., at 364 [hereinafter cited as MNRG 2d].

Roumelia by the 1879 Act of the European Commission.[44] In general, such condominium arrangements are probably not long lasting; most of those established in the period studied were terminated after serving certain purposes.[45]

Instead of sharing the interests at stake by establishing common zones, states generally preferred to divide the area concerned through negotiation. In the boundary delimitation in Chetumal Bay between British Honduras (Belize) and Mexico on July 8, 1893, the bay was roughly divided in half by five straight-line segments connected by right angles.[46] The first segment passed midway through the strait of Boca Bacalar Chica and the last one ended at the mouth of the River Hondo, where the boundary then followed the deepest channel. On June 27, 1900, France and Spain established a negotiated boundary in the Western Bay (Baie de l'Ouest) between Mauritania and Spanish Sahara based on certain median points, and a negotiated boundary in the Gulf of Guinea based on the exterior thalweg of the Muni River.[47] In order to obviate any future dispute, the parties described the boundary in a precise manner by using geographical coordinates of longitude and latitude.

In the fjord area in the Gulf of Christiana between Norway and Sweden, the median line boundary established on March 15, 1904 was composed of a series of broken straight-line segments, connecting 18 selected midpoints.[48] The United Kingdom and the United States adopted a similar method in the Boundary Agreement of May 21, 1910 regarding the Passamaquoddy Bay. The median line principle had originally been agreed upon in the Boundary Treaty of April 11, 1908. The boundary starts at a point in the mouth of the St. Croix River and continues in a southwesterly direction generally following several midpoints between the U.S. coast of Maine and the Canadian Deer and Campobello Islands to a fixed point in the Grand Manan Channel. The segments of the boundary were plotted on the basis of azimuth and distance. Essentially, the boundary was a negotiated line that deviated from a strict median line because historical fishing rights and the mutual convenience of navigation were taken into account.[49]

Despite the variety of methods used in practice, the median line principle was respected as a general rule for the delimitation of narrow straits by numerous scholars, such as David Dudley Field, Imbart Latour, John Bassett Moore, and Travers Twiss.[50] Scholarly bodies followed this trend. In 1894, the Institute of International Law recommended the median line principle for the delimitation of narrow straits.[51] This proposal was accepted in toto by the International Law Association in Brussels in 1895.[52] Thus, the median line principle survived as a general rule applicable to the territorial sea between

[44] 70 BFSP 1293.

[45] 3 J. VERZIJL, INTERNATIONAL LAW 538 *et seq.*

[46] 85 BFSP 58–60.

[47] 32 MNRG 2d at 59–61.

[48] *See* the Grisbadarna arbitration, *reprinted in* 4 AJIL 226, 227–28 (1910).

[49] TS No. 497.

[50] D. FIELD, *supra* note 32, at 16; J. IMBART LATOUR, LA MER TERRITORIALE 64 (1889); 1 J. B. MOORE, *supra* note 36, at 658; F. PERELS, MANUEL DE DROIT MARITIME INTERNATIONAL 46 (1884); T. TWISS, *supra* note 30, at 251.

[51] INSTITUT DE DROIT INTERNATIONAL, 13 ANNUAIRE 330 (1894).

[52] INTERNATIONAL LAW ASSOCIATION, REPORT OF THE 17TH CONFERENCE HELD AT BRUSSELS IN 1895, at 105 (1896).

opposite states despite frequent challenges by the thalweg. Few writers or scholarly bodies endorsed the thalweg principle as a general rule, for it was thought to be applicable only to those straits and channels where the thalweg was easily identifiable and where the preservation of equal access and the right of navigation was paramount.

Adjacent States: Perpendicular Line and Median Line

The issues involved in the delimitation of lateral territorial sea boundaries were virtually ignored before the middle of the 19th century. In some cases, a lateral territorial sea boundary was thought to be unnecessary. For instance, in 1845 the Netherlands rejected a Belgian proposal to extend the land boundary in the diked River Zwin into the North Sea.[53] This negative attitude left the boundary uncertain.

The thalweg principle might be applicable in those bays and estuaries where the thalweg is identifiable, but that can often be extremely difficult. However, the thalweg cannot serve as a general method of delimitation of the territorial sea because it gradually disappears at a short distance from the coast. If the land boundary terminates at a place where there is no thalweg, application of the thalweg principle is naturally out of the question.

In *Louisiana v. Mississippi*, the United States Supreme Court lamented the lack of any legal precedents for the delimitation of sea boundaries between adjacent states:

> The attempt to extend the rule beyond the estuaries of the river into the open sea, that is, into the open waters of the Gulf of Mexico, cannot be supported either by reason or authority. Not by reason, because the wide expanse of water, unconfined between banks, utterly fails to serve as a boundary; not by authority, because there is no precedent for such an extension of the rule in any work on international law.
>
> Whenever it is necessary for two contiguous States to run a water boundary through an archipelago of islands off their coasts it is only possible to do so by convention, as international law provides no rule upon the subject.[54]

However, since the middle of the 19th century, several noteworthy precedents had been established, and they all followed similar patterns.

Some of the early agreements, however, suffered from vagueness. For example, the Treaty of Guadalupe Hidalgo of February 2, 1848 between Mexico and the United States stated this about lateral sea boundaries: "The boundary line between the two Republics shall commence in the Gulf of Mexico, three leagues from land, opposite the mouth of the Rio Grande. . . ." Neither the location of the terminus of the sea boundary nor the direction of the line was mentioned. The sea boundary in the Pacific area was to extend "one marine league due south of the southernmost point of the Port of San Diego."[55] The Boundary Treaty of September 27, 1882 between Mexico and Guatemala stated that the boundary started at a point in the sea 3 leagues from the mouth of

[53] *See* G. GIDEL, *supra* note 27, at 765.

[54] 202 U.S. at 29.

[55] 9 Stat. 922, TS No. 207.

the River Suchiate, without indicating the direction of the line or the exact starting point.[56] A similar method was suggested for delimiting the Canal Zone between Panama and the United States on November 18, 1903, but it was later elaborated upon in the Boundary Convention of September 2, 1914. According to the original agreement, the Canal Zone would extend 3 miles following the latitude from the mean low-water mark into the Caribbean Sea and the Pacific Ocean.[57]

In establishing a territorial sea boundary in the Bay of Figuier in 1879, France and Spain first closed the bay by a transverse line of about 3 kilometers connecting the extreme point of Cape Higuera and the Pointe du Tombeau, and then chose the meridian passing through the middle of that line as their territorial sea boundary.[58] The meridian method was also adopted in 1885 by Portugal and Spain in delimiting the territorial waters of the estuary of the Rio Guadiana. However, a dispute arose later over the location of the meridian because of the fluctuations of the delta. On March 27, 1893, Portugal and Spain settled the problem by placing the boundary midway between the two claimed meridians.[59]

The method of delimitation following latitude or meridian is simple and convenient, if the coast runs straight along a latitude or longitude. A line perpendicular to the coast may also be drawn if the coast is more or less straight. For instance, a draft convention on the delimitation of waters for fishing in the Bay of Mentone between France and Italy was concluded early in 1892; it has never been ratified.[60] According to Adami, the traditional boundary was made conspicuously visible from the sea by two large triangular markers fixed on the coast along a line perpendicular to the shore that passed through the boundary at the water's edge, so that the sea boundary could be identified as a straight line extending to the outer limit of the territorial sea.[61]

Delimitation of the territorial sea between adjacent states was long neglected by international lawyers. It was first dealt with in September 1908 by Deszö Dârday at the Twenty-fifth Conference of the International Law Association in Budapest. Dârday found that there were some "open questions" regarding possible methods, one of which was an extension of the land boundary, and the other, the straight line perpendicular to the coast where the dry-land boundary abuts upon the sea. He seemed to prefer the latter, but he was not satisfied with this method as a general rule because it would not be applicable where the land boundary terminates at the tip of a promontory or at the deep corner of a bay. To rectify any inequities deriving from these circumstances, Dârday suggested the use of the median line principle, which had already been proposed as a rule of delimitation in narrow straits between states.[62]

[56] 73 BFSP 272.

[57] 33 Stat. 2234, TS No. 431; 38 Stat. 1893, TS No. 610.

[58] *See* note 43 *supra*.

[59] 14 MNRG 2d at 77; 22 *id.* at 414.

[60] For the text, see 22 *id.* at 291–93. *See also* Addendum 2, at 2, to Information and Observations Submitted by Governments, *supra* note 25 (France).

[61] V. ADAMI, note 8 *supra*, at 53 [50].

[62] INTERNATIONAL LAW ASSOCIATION, REPORT OF THE 25TH CONFERENCE HELD AT BUDAPEST, SEPTEMBER 21ST–26TH, 1908, at 546–48 (1909).

III. Consolidation of the Principles

The Grisbadarna Case

On October 23, 1909, the Permanent Court of Arbitration at The Hague became the first international tribunal to make a ruling on the delimitation of territorial waters between states. In its arbitral award of that date on the territorial sea boundary dispute between Norway and Sweden, the tribunal considered the principles of delimitation developed since the mid-17th century.[63]

The Treaty of 1661 had set the maritime frontier between Norway (then united with Denmark) and Sweden roughly in the middle of the waters between the two countries, with its terminus between the Norwegian island of Tisler and the Swedish island of Koster.[64] Between the end of the Napoleonic Wars in 1815, when Denmark ceded Norway to Sweden, and the close of the 19th century, the question of the boundary had no practical significance. However, when the joint kingdom moved towards peaceful separation, the boundary question again took on weight because the delimitation would also determine possession of the rich lobster grounds on the bank of Grisbadarna.

Norwegian and Swedish commissioners, relying on the median line principle used in the 1661 fjord boundary, jointly proposed on August 18, 1897 a boundary line composed of straight-line segments connecting midpoints labeled I to XVIII. The joint proposal was approved by a royal resolution on March 15, 1904. However, the parties disagreed about how to divide the area beyond point XVIII mainly because of overlapping interests in the Grisbadarna bank, which was approximately midway between the two countries (see map 1). In a special agreement of March 14, 1908, Norway and Sweden decided to submit the case to a tribunal of the newly established Permanent Court of Arbitration in The Hague.[65] They requested that it "decide whether the boundary line is to be considered, either wholly or in part, as being fixed by the boundary treaty of

[63] *See* for the Grisbadarna Case (Norway v. Sweden), BUREAU INTERNATIONAL DE LA COUR PERMANENTE D'ARBITRAGE, RECUEIL DES COMPTES RENDUS DE LA VISITE DES LIEUX ET DES PROTOCOLES DES SÉANCES DU TRIBUNAL ARBITRAL, CONSTITUÉ EN VERTU DE LA CONVENTION DU 14 MARS 1908, POUR JUGER LA QUESTION DE LA DÉLIMITATION D'UNE CERTAINE PARTIE DE LA FRONTIÈRE MARITIME ENTRE LA NORVÈGE ET LA SUÈDE 1 (1909); the award is *reprinted in* Hague Ct. Rep. (Scott) 487 (Perm. Ct. Arb. 1909), 11 R. Int'l Arb. Awards 155, translated into English in Hague Ct. Rep. (Scott) 121, 4 AJIL 226 (1910), G. G. WILSON, THE HAGUE ARBITRATION CASES 102 (1915). For commentaries, see Editorial Comment, 4 AJIL 186 (1910); François, *La Cour permanente d'Arbitrage, son origine, sa jurisprudence, son avenir*, 87 RECUEIL DES COURS 498 (1955 I); Hammarskjöld, *Determinazione di frontiera*, 5 RIVISTA DI DIRITTO INTERNAZIONALE 121 (1910); Note, 17 REV. GÉNÉRALE DROIT INT'L PUBLIC 177 (1910); Strupp, *supra* note 16, at 47.

[64] In the Peace Treaty of Roskilde of Feb. 26, 1658, the King of Denmark, then the King of Norway, ceded the Norwegian province of Bohuslan to Sweden, and this decision was later confirmed by the Treaty of Copenhagen of March 27, 1660. The results of the delimitation process between the commissioners of the two parties were stipulated in the Treaty of Oct. 26, 1661, together with an attached map. The original text was in Danish and Swedish. For the text, see note 16 *supra*; *see also* Strupp, *supra* note 16, at 62. For background information, see, *e.g.*, Hammarskjöld, *supra* note 63, at 121.

[65] By virtue of the *compromis* of March 14, 1908 between Norway and Sweden, 102 BFSP 731, 2 MNRG 3d at 761, the tribunal of arbitration was composed of three members: Beichmann (Norway), Hammarskjöld (Sweden), and Leoff, the presiding judge (the Netherlands).

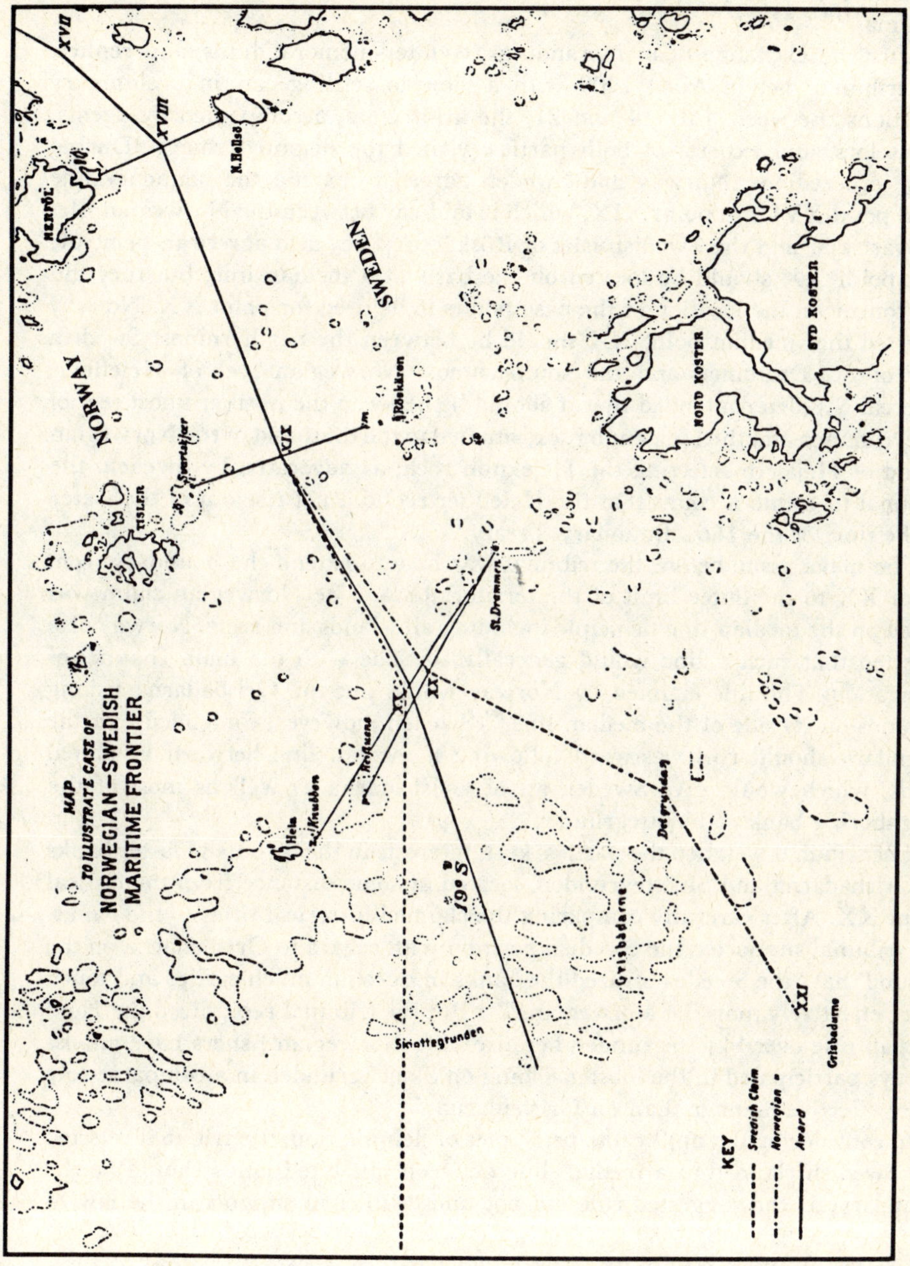

MAP 1

THE GRISBADARNA ARBITRATION

SOURCE: adapted from G. G. WILSON, THE HAGUE ARBITRATION CASES 133 (1915).

1661 together with the map thereto annexed, and in what manner the line thus established should be placed," and that it "fix this boundary line, taking into account the circumstances of fact and the principles of international law," "as far as the boundary line shall not be considered as fixed by said treaty and said map."[66]

After the exchange of memorandums, counter-memorandums, and replies, the tribunal met in April 1909 with a view to settling certain preliminary questions. Between July 14 and 21, the arbitrators, accompanied by agents, counselors, and experts of both parties, visited the disputed zone.[67] During these proceedings, Norway and Sweden agreed to extend the boundary line from point XVIII to point XIX, which is midway between the Norwegian islet of Svartskjär and the Swedish islet of Röskären. They also agreed in principle that point XX should be located on the basis of a median line, but they did not concur on the location of the base points to be used for point XX. Norway asserted that median point XX should be between the northernmost Swedish reef of St. Drammen and the southernmost Norwegian reef of Heiefluer, whereas Sweden contended that it should be between the northernmost reef of St. Drammen and the Hejeknub rock, situated to the southeast of the Norwegian island of Heja. In selecting the Hejeknub rock, as advocated by Sweden, the tribunal took into account that the Heiefluer reef did not rise out of the water at the time of the 1661 Boundary Treaty.[68]

The major issue before the tribunal was how to extend the boundary from point XX to the outer limit of the territorial sea. The Norwegian claim was based on the median line principle including all islands and reefs. Norway also asserted that such a line would generally coincide with the main channel of navigation. The line claimed by Norway would put the Grisbadarna fishing grounds on its side of the median line.[69] Sweden, however, contended that the boundary should run westward following a median line between inhabited lands, which would give Sweden all of Grisbadarna as well as most of the neighboring bank of Skjöttegrunden.[70]

The tribunal weighed the parties' keen interests in the disputed lobster banks of Grisbadarna and Skjöttegrunden, located at some distance from the critical point XX. After carefully comparing the claimed historical titles to the banks, the tribunal supported the Swedish position with regard to Grisbadarna on the ground that "the Swedes utilized the banks in question much earlier and much more effectively than the Norwegians."[71] But the tribunal recognized the Norwegian title over Skjöttegrunden because "the Norwegian fishers have almost always participated in the lobster fishing on Skjöttegrunden in a comparatively more effective manner than on Grisbadarna."[72]

In considering the applicable principles of delimitation, the tribunal rejected the Swedish claim that a median line between inhabited lands should be the boundary, as the suggested rule did not find "sufficient support in the law of

[66] *See* the *compromis*, *id.*, Art. III; for the English translation, see 4 AJIL at 226–27.
[67] Hammarskjöld, *supra* note 63, at 121; *see also* Strupp, *supra* note 16, at 76.
[68] 4 AJIL at 230.
[69] *See* Strupp, *supra* note 16, at 78.
[70] *Ibid.*
[71] 4 AJIL at 234.
[72] *Id.* at 235.

nations in force in the seventeenth century."[73] The tribunal also rejected the Norwegian claim that a median line between islands should be applied because it had been used to determine the boundary in the "inner" agreed area. The arbitrators believed that different rules should be applied beyond the "inner" area. The islands beyond this area should be disregarded because they were not mentioned in either the 1661 Boundary Treaty or the accompanying map and because the 1661 boundary was drawn from the sea to the land, not from the land to the sea.[74] The tribunal also rejected the Norwegian alternative argument for the main channel or thalweg principle because that rule had never been followed in the present case.[75]

After rejecting the two major principles advanced by the parties, the tribunal declared the applicable principle to be as follows:

> [W]e shall be acting much more in accord with the ideas of the seventeenth century and with the notions of law prevailing at that time if we admit that the automatic division of the territory in question must have taken place according to the general direction of the land territory of which the maritime territory constituted an appurtenance, and if we consequently apply this same rule at the present time in order to arrive at a just and lawful determination of the boundary. . . .
>
> . . . [C]onsequently, the automatic dividing line of 1658 should be determined (or, what is exactly the same thing expressed in other words) the delimitation should be made today by tracing a line perpendicularly to the general direction of the coast, while taking into account the necessity of indicating the boundary in a clear and unmistakable manner, thus facilitating its observation by the interested parties as far as possible.[76]

The general direction of the coast, as determined by the expert and "conscientious survey" of the members of the tribunal, swerves about 20 degrees westward from due north, and therefore the line should run westward to about 20 degrees to the south. Unfortunately, however, such a line would have crossed the important Grisbadarna bank, and thus proved unsuitable. In order to remedy the problem, the tribunal tilted the line to 19 degrees south instead of 20 degrees; it based this remedy on equitable considerations supported by "all of several circumstances of fact." The principal circumstances were that "lobster fishing in the shoals of Grisbadarna has been carried on for a much longer time, to a much larger extent, and by [a] much larger number of fishers [who were] subjects of Sweden than . . . subjects of Norway" and that Sweden had performed various executive acts "owing to her conviction that these regions were Swedish," whereas Norway had shown "much less solicitude" in this regard.[77]

The tribunal's declaration that "in accord with the ideas of the seventeenth century and with the notions of law prevailing at that time . . . the delimitation should be made today by tracing a line perpendicularly to the general direction of the coast" later became a target of criticism, because the tribunal gave little information about the historical background. In questioning the reasoning of the ruling, Arnold Raestad argued that the first attempts to determine bound-

[73] *Id.* at 232.
[74] *Id.* at 231.
[75] *See* Strupp, note 16 *supra.*
[76] 4 AJIL at 232.
[77] *Id.* at 233.

aries between adjacent maritime territories by drawing a perpendicular line occurred in the second half of the 19th century.[78] Karl Strupp maintained that because no such rule existed in the 1660's, the tribunal had decided the case mainly on a factual basis.[79] In the view of Gilbert Gidel, the tribunal did not need to decide whether a line perpendicular to the general direction of the coast was considered as a rule of international law at the time when the land boundary was determined.[80] Indeed, the tribunal did not present sufficient evidence of legal acceptance of the principle of delimitation by a line perpendicular to the general direction of the coast.

The reasoning of the award was probably based on the general principles of law regarding division of rivers and lakes prevailing in Europe in the 17th century, as well as on doctrinal suggestions by contemporary scholars such as Pufendorf. According to Adami's history of the general principles of law governing delimitation of lakes between adjacent states, the boundary line starting from the land boundary terminus would cross the surface of the water "in a direction perpendicular to the coast, till it joins the median line of the lake."[81] Pufendorf did not directly mention any perpendicular line, but his principle of proportionality did not purport to achieve delimitation by mathematical calculation of the "length" (longitudino) of the coastline, but rather by the "breadth" (latitudino) of the general direction of the coast.[82] Once the breadth of the general direction of the coast is determined between two adjacent states, it is a matter of course that equal division can be made by a line perpendicular to the general direction of the coast.

In theory, the line perpendicular to the general direction of the coast looks simple and convenient, but in practice it is extremely difficult to determine the general direction. Despite the limited applicability of the perpendicular line without any objective method of determining the general direction of the coast, its ideal of dividing the territorial sea into two equitable parts in consideration of the general direction of the coast is notable. When it can be found, the line perpendicular to the general direction of the coast would be useful not only in determining whether a given median line is equitable, but also in modifying an inequitable one.

Although the tribunal rejected both the Norwegian claim involving strict application of a median line including all islands and the Swedish assertion of a median line between inhabited lands ignoring islands, it did not reject the median line principle as such. The tribunal did recognize its applicability in the "inner area," where the states are opposite. In the "outer area," where they are adjacent, and where any further application of the median line would produce inequities, the tribunal declared *ex propio motu* that the boundary should be a line perpendicular to the general direction of the coast. Thus, the tribunal arrived at an equitable decision by the concurrent usage of the two principles.

The significance of the *Grisbadarna* ruling is that it was based upon the

[78] A. RAESTAD, KONGENS STRØMME 361 (1912).

[79] *See* Strupp, *supra* note 16, at 124.

[80] G. GIDEL, *supra* note 27, at 769.

[81] V. ADAMI, *supra* note 8, at [38].

[82] *See* S. PUFENDORF, *supra* note 4, bk. IV, ch. V, §8.

notion of an equitable solution. The tribunal had the competence to make an equitable determination, as it was charged in the *compromis* with "taking into account the circumstances of fact and the principles of international law."[83] Although the tribunal did not state that it was applying equity as a matter of law, its application of the principle of a line perpendicular to the general direction of the coast as *lex proprio motu* resulted from the equitable consideration of the "circumstances of fact," and was firmly based on the conviction that the decision must be equitable. Furthermore, considering the unsuitable "circumstance of fact" that such a line would cut across the Grisbadarna bank, the tribunal decided on an equitable remedy and tilted the line by a degree, so that the boundary would pass midway between Grisbadarna and Skjöttegrunde. The tribunal's equitable consideration of the "circumstances of fact" and its concurrent application of the median line principle in the "inner area" and the perpendicular line principle in the "outer area" together with an equitable remedy deserve much attention even today.

The Beagle Channel Controversy

The choice between the two competing principles, the median line and the thalweg, figured prominently in the territorial and sea boundary disputes between Argentina and Chile in the Beagle Channel. The Beagle Channel is a narrow seaway with an average breadth of 3 to 3.5 miles and a total length of 120 to 150 miles. The Boundary Treaty of 1881 had described the delimitation of the eastern mouth of the strait so vaguely that both the maritime boundary and jurisdiction over the islands of Picton, Lennox, and Nueva were disputed in the late 19th century. Argentina, basing its position on the thalweg principle, maintained that the channel should be the western one through Picton and Richmond Channels. From the Chilean point of view, which favored the median line principle, the mouth of the channel should be Moat Bay between Tierra del Fuego in the north and Picton and Nueva in the south. To settle these territorial and maritime boundary disputes, Argentina and Chile signed a general Treaty of Arbitration on May 28, 1902.[84] Subsequently, on June 28, 1915, a Protocol for arbitration was signed, but it was never ratified.[85] De-

[83] *See* note 66 *supra* and accompanying text. [84] 95 BFSP 759–61.

[85] In the Protocol signed in 1915, the British Government was nominated as arbitrator in accordance with the 1902 general Treaty of Arbitration. In the second Protocol of 1938, the parties selected Homer S. Cummings, the Attorney General of the United States. In the third Protocol signed in 1960, the parties decided to submit the case to the International Court of Justice. None of these Protocols were ratified for various reasons.

On July 22, 1971, Argentina and Chile signed a *compromiso* under which the British Government was appointed as arbitrator. The court of arbitration, set up by the British Government, was composed of five judges from among members of the International Court of Justice, who had been selected by both parties. Three written pleadings were submitted to the Court in 1973, 1974, and 1975, respectively. There were two consecutive rounds of oral pleadings in the fall of 1976. On February 18, 1977, the Court unanimously adopted its decision, giving the three disputed islands to Chile. This award was delivered to the parties on May 2, 1977. On January 25, 1978, Argentina declared that the decision was null and void for various reasons, including the argument that "the drawing of the maritime boundary carried out by the Court on the Chart annexed to the Award suffers from inexactitudes and technical errors that render it totally untrustworthy." *See* Declaration spite the failure of the attempt to settle the disputes by arbitration at that time, both parties advanced significant legal arguments.

At the Twenty-first Conference of the International Law Association in Buenos Aires in 1922, Segundo R. Storni of Argentina presented draft articles of an international convention concerning territorial waters. In Article 8 on the delimitation of the territorial waters of international straits, he proposed that, "without specifying the particular rules to be applied, the delimitation of jurisdiction should be subject to an agreement to be made between the riparian states concerned" because "[t]he median line of a strait does not necessarily always represent an equitable jurisdictional boundary."[86] Storni did not suggest any specific principles to serve as underpinnings for the negotiations. He emphasized the possibility of resolving disputes by flexible negotiation, presumably having in mind that the "thalweg principle" was better for Argentina than the median line principle. The Argentinian, Dr. E. S. Zeballos, had already expressed his country's disapproval of the median line and preference for the thalweg in delimiting the Beagle Channel in *La Prensa* of Buenos Aires in 1915.[87]

Storni's assertion that the delimitation of straits between states should be decided by agreement was sharply criticized by Guillermo Guerra of Chile at the Twenty-third Conference of the International Law Association held at Stockholm in 1924.[88] After attacking the idea of condominium, which had been suggested by Bluntschli in 1868, Guerra argued that the thalweg principle should not be applied to straits. First of all, he doubted the validity of the thalweg principle for delimiting sea boundaries, citing Bluntschli's point that "the frontier line should be the middle of the lake because there is no thalweg in the lake."[89] He maintained that "the thalweg principle may be applicable only in rivers where the water flows by gravity, not in the sea where the surface of the water is horizontal and does not move by gravitation." He even joked that "the thalweg is to the river, what the crater is to the volcano."[90] The main point of his argument, however, was that the principle should not be applied to the Beagle Channel because the thalweg not only would be difficult to determine, but also would zigzag and thus result in an impractical line.

Guerra's argument was also based on the arbitral decision of 1903 on the

---

of Nullity, attached to the Note Delivered by the Ministry of Foreign Affairs of Argentina to the Ambassador of Chile, Jan. 25, 1978, *reprinted in* RELACIONES CHILENO-ARGENTINAS: LA CONTROVERSIA DEL CANAL BEAGLE, ALGUNOS DOCUMENTOS INFORMATIVOS 133, 139 (1978), translated into English in 17 ILM 739 (1978). *See generally* RELACIONES CHILENO-ARGENTINAS, *supra*, at II–XII.

[86] *See* Storni, *La Mer territoriale*, in 2 INTERNATIONAL LAW ASSOCIATION, REPORT OF THE 31ST CONFERENCE HELD AT BUENOS AIRES, 24TH AUGUST–30TH AUGUST, 1922, at 99 (1923).

[87] *See* J. GUERRA, EAUX TERRITORIALES DANS LES DÉTROITS PEU LARGES; MEMORANDUM PRÉSENTÉ À L'INTERNATIONAL LAW ASSOCIATION (CONFÉRENCE DE STOCKHOLM, 1924) 18 (1924).

[88] *Id., passim.*

[89] *See* J. BLUNTSCHLI, *supra* note 31, Art. 301.

[90] *See* J. GUERRA, *supra* note 87, at 20, 27; *see also* Guerra, *Les Eaux territoriales dans les détroits, spécialement dans les détroits peu larges*, 31 REV. GÉNÉRALE DROIT INT'L PUBLIC 232, 245 *et seq.* (1924).

Portland Channel. He found similarities between the Portland Channel and Beagle Channel disputes; the parties involved were at odds over the islands at the mouths of the straits and over the competing principles of the median line and the thalweg. He asserted that the thalweg doctrine was in no way applicable to the Beagle Channel since it had been rejected in the *Portland Channel* decision. He maintained further that the applicable principle should be a median line drawn on the surface of the waters without taking into account their depth, since the United Kingdom and the United States had recognized the median line principle for the delimitation of the Portland Channel.[91]

Thereafter, Argentinians no longer actively endorsed the thalweg principle.[92] Ten years after the debate, the then authority on the law of the sea, Gilbert Gidel, observed that the theory of the line of the deepest water seemed to be impossible to accept as a general criterion for delimitation in narrow straits. According to Gidel, if it were applied to the Beagle Channel, the thalweg would have capricious and uneven results. He admitted that in exceptional cases it could be used as a corrective to evident inequities caused by application of the median line principle, which was regarded as a general rule of law applicable in the absence of contrary agreements and exceptional physical conditions.[93]

[91] *See* J. GUERRA, *supra* note 87, at 24–25, and Guerra, *supra* note 90, at 250–51.

[92] In the 1973 Memorial to the ad hoc court of arbitration in Geneva, Argentina changed its earlier position, and in principle adopted the median line, equidistant between opposite coasts. The Memorial synthesized the "consistent and authoritative guide-lines" from a significant number of bilateral treaties and opinions of writers at the time of the controversial Boundary Treaty of 1881 as follows:

> (a) Division of maritime jurisdictions (territorial waters) is achieved normally by means of the median line, equidistant from two opposite coasts. This solution simply expresses an incontestable general principle: the equality of states.
>
> (b) The rule governing the use of waters for navigation also arises from the same general principle. Thus where the rigorous application of a median line would deprive one or other of the two states of the use of waters necessary for navigation, there must be a deviation from the median line rule.

Memorial of the Argentine Republic I (Text), Argentine-Chilean Arbitration concerning the Region of the Beagle Channel 436 (1973).

Argentina requested that the Court decide that "the boundary-line between the respective maritime jurisdictions of the Argentine Republic and of the Republic of Chile from meridian 68°37′38.5″W. of Greenwich runs along the median line of the Beagle Channel, deviating from that line only where inflexions are necessary so that each country may always navigate in waters of its own." *Id.* at 445.

Since the parties agreed on the median line principle, the Court explained the tracing of the boundary line as follows:

> The Boundary-Line itself is the resultant of construction lines drawn between opposite, shore to shore, points, sometimes to or from straight baselines. It is in principle a median line, adjusted in certain relatively unimportant respects for reasons of local configuration or of better navigability for the Parties. Over the whole course, account has been taken of sandbanks, siltings etc. which would make a strict median-line unfair, as in the case of certain islets or rocks.

REPUBLIC OF CHILE, CONTROVERSY CONCERNING THE BEAGLE CHANNEL REGION, AWARD (Bilingual edition with additional notes and documents), para. 110, at 182, and Ann. IV, para. 4, at 350 (1977); the award is *reprinted* in English *in* 17 ILM 634 (1978).

[93] G. GIDEL, *supra* note 27, at 755–59.

Attempts at Codification

There were several attempts to establish principles and rules for the delimitation of territorial sea boundaries during the 1920's. Individual scholars and private associations put forward a number of proposals. When the League of Nations Committee of Experts for the Progressive Development of International Law included the territorial sea in its project for the 1930 Hague Codification Conference, most observers expected the issue of delimitation to be crucial and to receive systematic treatment.[94]

In 1925, the Finnish jurist Björksten presented a comprehensive analysis of the differences between opposite and adjacent situations. He thought there were three types of possible situations: the opposite, the adjacent, and the mixed, comprising aspects of the first two types in varying degrees. Regarding the opposite situation, he recommended the median line as a "presumptive sea boundary," with the possibility of agreement on the thalweg in special circumstances. Regarding the adjacent situation, however, he envisaged several ways of determining the sea boundary: following the direction of the land boundary, the meridian, or latitude, or a line perpendicular to the coast. Here, he also allowed for supplementary exceptions, such as a local median line between coastal islands and the thalweg or mid-channel line where common navigation is involved.[95]

In 1926, the International Law Association of Japan presented draft rules for the delimitation of straits, and bays or gulfs between states:

> In the case of bays and gulfs the coasts of which belong to two or more States, the littoral waters follow the trend of the coasts according to the general rule. In those portions of such bays and gulfs where the distance between the two coasts does not amount to six marine miles, the dividing line between the respective littoral waters shall in principle be the middle line measured from the two coasts.
>
> In the case of straits the coasts of which belong to two or more different States, the littoral waters follow the trend of the coasts according to the general rule; but in case the distance between the two shores does not amount to six marine miles, the dividing line between respective littoral waters shall in principle be the middle line measured from the two coasts.[96]

The proposal seems to have been intended to cover both opposite and adjacent situations, but it did not address the possibility of locating lateral sea boundaries in places other than bays, gulfs, and straits. The middle or median line principle was recommended "in principle" for bodies less than 6 miles wide, which left open the possibility that agreements might deviate from the rule.

The Harvard Research of 1929 distinguished the territorial sea boundary

[94] *See generally* Report to the Council of the League of Nations on the Questions Which Appear Ripe for International Regulation by the Committee of Experts for the Progressive Codification of International Law, League of Nations Doc. C.196.M.70.1927.V.1, at 7 *et seq.*

[95] S. R. Björksten, Das Wassergebiet Finnlands in völkerrechtlicher Hinsicht 93–98 (1925).

[96] 25 Kokusaihō Gaikō Zasshi (Journal of International Law and Diplomacy) 599, 608–09, 635–36 (1926).

issues relating to straits from those relating to bays, among which the adjacent situation was included. As for straits, it was provided that "[i]n the absence of special agreement to the contrary, where two or more states border upon a strait, the territorial waters of each state extend to the middle of the strait in those parts where the width does not exceed six miles."[97] The Harvard Research made no attempt to deal with "the tracing of boundary lines in the waters of a bay by the extension of the land boundaries," but it envisaged that in light of the award in the *Grisbadarna* case in 1909, "[t]he principle of division of adjacent waters by lines perpendicular to the general trend of the coast in practice makes an equable division of the territorial waters, though of course historical, vested, and other rights and conditions may be considered."[98]

In 1925, the Committee of Experts for the Progressive Codification of International Law charged a subcommittee, composed of Walther Schücking, Barbosa de Magalhaes, and George Wickersham, with the preparation of a report relating to questions of territorial waters. Subsequently, in 1927 Walther Schücking, rapporteur of the subcommittee, prepared a detailed memorandum with draft articles, in which he recommended that "[s]traits not exceeding 12 miles in width whose shores belong to different States shall form part of the territorial sea as far as the middle line."[99] After wondering whether the boundary between adjacent states should be the prolongation of the land frontier toward the sea or a line perpendicular to the coast where the land boundary terminates, he observed that in the case of existing states the boundary should be settled on the basis of historical considerations. In the event of a political change in the coastal frontier, "it would be advisable to establish special rules in each case having regard to the special geographical circumstances" in the area concerned. However, he also recommended that "[i]t would be better to arrange for the conclusion of a special agreement between the States concerned, or for the settlement of the matter by arbitration or an ordinary tribunal, than to lay down an immutable principle."[100]

De Magalhaes, while concurring on the importance of settlement by a special agreement or by a third-party decision, criticized Schücking's ideas on basing settlements on historical factors and the establishment of special rules, and proposed the following draft article concerning general principles for the delimitation of the territorial sea boundaries between adjacent states:

> The limit between the territorial waters of a State and those of another contiguous State is constituted by a line drawn perpendicular to the coast from the point at which the frontier between the two States meets that coast. When the frontier between two contiguous States is formed by a river which touches both of them and is common to both where it reaches

[97] Draft Convention on Territorial Waters, Text and Comment, 23 AJIL, Spec. Supp. 281 (1929).

[98] *Id.* at 275.

[99] Memorandum by Mr. Schücking, in Report of the Sub-Committee of the Committee of Experts for the Progressive Codification of International Law, League of Nations Doc. C.44.M.21.1926.V.10, at 33, *reprinted in* Report to the Council of the League of Nations, *supra* note 94, at 59 [hereinafter pages in reprinted report cited in brackets].

[100] *Id.* at 16 [42].

> the coast, the line of demarcation between the territorial waters of the two States is formed by the line of the *exterior thalweg* of the river as far as it can be traced, and thereafter by a line perpendicular to the coast as far as the outer limit of the territorial waters.[101]

Wickersham recognized the general applicability of the principle of thalweg or middle of the navigable channel, but he was not willing to accept de Magalhaes's proposal for the exterior thalweg, contending that there was no authority for it.[102]

Because of these divergent views, delimitation of the territorial sea boundary between adjacent states was excluded from the draft proposal. The subcommittee merely proposed the median line principle for the delimitation of straits.[103] The draft articles were distributed to governments for comments. Out of 27 governments that responded, 13 commented favorably on adoption of the median line principle. Among the latter, Japan suggested the insertion of the proviso "as a rule," and Sweden proposed that the boundary "should, failing any provision to the contrary in a convention or in the absence of any other special reason, follow the median line."[104] The other 14 governments did not comment at all on the proposed median line principle and did not propose any alternative principles. Thus, the median line proposal was provided with the proviso "in principle" in Basis of Discussion No. 16 on territorial waters, prepared in 1929 by the Preparatory Committee for the Codification Conference of 1930.[105]

Contrary to the Preparatory Committee's expectation that its proposal would be readily accepted, it became one of the most controversial issues before the Second Sub-Committee of the Second Committee of the Codification Conference. The Swedish delegation proposed deleting the phrase "in principle" on the ground that it could arouse misunderstanding and differences in interpretation.[106] This change was supported by Yugoslavia, but the Norwegian delegate expressed doubt about the need for any general rule on delimitation in straits and proposed, instead, settlement by special agreement.[107]

The issue was further studied in the Legal Sub-Committee. There the rapporteur also suggested solution by common agreement between states. Finding this wording too vague, the Danish and Swedish delegations jointly proposed that "[the line of demarcation] . . . is that which results from agreements

[101] Observations by Mr. de Magalhaes, *id.* at 40 [65–66].

[102] Observations by Mr. Wickersham, *id.* at 46 [71].

[103] Draft Convention Amended by Mr. Schücking in Consequence of the Discussion in the Committee of Experts, *id.* at 47 [72].

[104] The 13 states that expressly supported the median line principle were Australia, Denmark, Estonia, Germany, Great Britain, India, Italy, Japan, the Netherlands, New Zealand, Romania, South Africa, and Sweden. *See* General Observations Submitted by Certain Governments, in Bases of Discussion for the Conference for the Codification of International Law Drawn up by the Preparatory Committee, League of Nations Doc. C.74.M.39.1929.V.2, at 10–59.

[105] *Id.* at 59–60.

[106] Minutes of the Second Committee (Territorial Waters), in 3 Acts of the Conference for the Codification of International Law, League of Nations Doc. C.351(b).M.145(b).1930.V.16, at 116–17.

[107] *Id.* at 17.

concluded or to be concluded, or, failing this, by other rules of international law."[108]

Because of the deep disagreement over principles, the subcommittee could not settle on an acceptable rule despite the further study in the Legal Sub-Committee. The Second Sub-Committee ultimately thought it better not to draw up any rules on delimitation of straits between states, and merely referred to those it had drawn up for bays bordered by more than one state.[109] Thus, just as the issue of delimitation of the territorial sea between adjacent states was deleted in 1926 from the draft proposal by the subcommittee of the Committee of Experts, the problem of delimitation in straits was removed from the final draft by the Second Committee of the 1930 Hague Conference. Despite its increasing importance, the issue of delimitation of the territorial sea between states was not considered sufficiently ripe for codification, as there existed no uniform principle of delimitation.

Crystallization of Principles and Rules

Several lateral sea boundaries established between adjacent states in the latter part of the 19th century and the early 20th century were delimited following latitude or longitude. In the *Grisbadarna* arbitration, as has been seen, the tribunal declared *ex proprio motu* that a line perpendicular to the general direction of the coast should be the boundary. This *Grisbadarna* principle was generally used in 1913 by the Italian authorities in Libya in their proposal to the French authorities for delimiting the sea boundary in Tunis at Ras Ajdir. The Italian proposal was tacitly accepted by the French authorities in Tunisia.[110] It appears that the perpendicular line method was an outgrowth of the method of delimitation by longitude or latitude. In most cases the perpendicular line was drawn along longitude or latitude, and not necessarily at a right angle to the general direction of the coast. Thus, in 1914 Panama and the United States agreed to extend the Canal Zone by 3 miles along the latitude from the mean low-water mark into the Caribbean Sea and the Pacific Ocean, notwithstanding the geographical irregularities.[111] States generally chose to use this simple and convenient method because there was no objective way to determine the general direction of the coast, but this inherent difficulty militated against wide application of the perpendicular line.

Two years after the *Grisbadarna* arbitration, Pasquale Fiore attempted to establish a general rule of "common agreement" rooted in the median line principle. He suggested using the median line to delimit narrow seas between

[108] The proposals by the rapporteur and the Danish and Swedish delegations in the Legal Sub-Committee were not printed in the Acts of the Conference. The French text cited by G. GIDEL, *supra* note 27, at 758 & n.1, reads: "[la ligne de démarcation] . . . est celle qui résulte des accords conclus ou à conclure, soit, à leur défaut, des autres règles du droit international."

[109] *See* Draft Reports on the Work of the Second Sub-Committee, 3 Acts of the Conference, *supra* note 106, Ann. III, at 208. *See also* Compromise-Proposal of the French Delegation, *id.* at 220.

[110] *See* Case Concerning the Continental Shelf (Tunisia/Libyan Arab Jamahiriya), [1982] ICJ REP. 3, paras. 92–95.

[111] *See* text and sources cited at note 57 *supra*.

opposite states and the territorial sea facing river mouths between states where the opposite and adjacent situations mix. Although he did not mention a general rule for adjacent states, it appears that he believed that most disputes could be settled with reference to the median line principle. However, he did not intend that it be applied strictly; rather, in cases where the median line would create "an unreasonable and harsh rigorism," it should be modified or avoided on the basis of "considerations of equity."[112]

Since the early 20th century when the median line principle and the thalweg were clearly distinguished, they have scarcely been regarded as mutually exclusive rules, but as ones that might supplement each other. For instance, in the Declarations of September 28, 1912 between France and Germany relating to the delimitation of the boundary between the French possessions of Dahomey and the Sudan, and the German territory of Togo, the thalweg principle was employed from the designated terminus of the river boundary up to a point in the lagoon where the thalweg was identifiable, from which point the boundary followed the seaward median line.[113] On the same day, the parties agreed to delimit Mondah Bay between French Equatorial Africa and the Cameroon. Here the thalweg principle was also respected in a similarly restricted way; it was to supplement the median line boundary only when the unstable estuary of the River Massolié was situated south of the designated end of the median line boundary.[114]

After World War I, the median line was more precisely drawn by connecting geographical coordinates between opposite states. For instance, in the maritime delimitation between Finland and Sweden in the Aaland Islands Convention of October 20, 1921 among ten European powers, the boundary was drawn by connecting selected median points with geographical coordinates up to a tenth of a minute.[115] On February 24, 1925, the United Kingdom and the United States delimited a segment of sea boundary 2,383 meters long by extending a line connecting two mid-distance points in the middle of Grand Manan Channel to the high seas in order to complete the territorial sea boundary between Maine and New Brunswick. Contrary to their earlier assumption, the parties found that the terminus of the boundary line specified by the previous Treaty of May 21, 1910 at the middle of the Channel was less than 3 miles from both the Canadian shore of Grand Manan Island and the U.S. coast of Maine.[116]

The thalweg principle was employed in some cases where the preservation of equal rights in navigation was of prime interest. For instance, the route of the principal channel of navigation was firmly recognized as an international sea boundary in Flensburger Föhrder in the Treaty of July 5, 1920 between the Principal Allied and Associated Powers, and Denmark.[117] The thalweg

[112] P. FIORE, LE DROIT INTERNATIONAL CODIFIÉ ET SA SANCTION JURIDIQUE 502 (1911), translated as INTERNATIONAL LAW CODIFIED AND ITS LEGAL SANCTION 419–20 (trans. E. M. Borchard 1918).

[113] 106 BFSP 1001.

[114] *Id.* at 974.

[115] 114 *id.* at 421.

[116] 35 Stat. 2003, TS No. 497; 36 Stat. 2477, TS No. 551; 44 Stat. 2102, TS No. 720.

[117] 2 LNTS 241.

principle was also applied in the Agreement of October 28, 1922 between Finland and Russia,[118] and in the territorial sea boundary Agreement of October 19, 1927 between Johore and Singapore.[119] Nevertheless, there were few jurists who would endorse the thalweg principle as a general rule of law in the delimitation of territorial sea boundaries between opposite states.

Between adjacent states, although the *Grisbadarna* principle was not prevalent, it was applied in a few cases, particularly where the coast at the boundary terminus was rather straight. Albania and Yugoslavia signed a Protocol of Delimitation in July 1926, providing that "the boundary [between Albania and Yugoslavia] starting from the limit of the territorial waters in the Adriatic Sea follows first a straight line perpendicular to the general direction of the coast and ends up at the mouth of the principal arm of the Boyana."[120] At the request of the Preparatory Committee of the Hague Codification Conference, the Belgian Government, in a letter of December 19, 1928, stated its policy to be that "[t]he boundary between the contiguous territorial seas of two neighboring countries should lie along a line perpendicular to the coast, at the end of the land frontier."[121] Later, the French Government affirmed this view and explained that "[n]o interests are injured by this delimitation, since the adjacent French and Belgian coasts are straight and the frontier is perpendicular to the coast."[122]

Since most coastlines were irregular with indented coastal formations and scattered islands, many states continued to have doubts about the general applicability of the perpendicular line. The development of technical means of delimitation infused states with the desire to determine "every inch" of their territorial sea. The median line principle appealed to this desire for precise delimitation, for no other principle had such certitude in application. The Finnish-Norwegian frontier Convention of April 28, 1924 provided a detailed description of the "equal distance" method:

> From the point where the channel ends in the Arctic Ocean beyond the mouth of the Jakobselv (Vuoremajoki) the dividing line between the territorial waters of the two Contracting States shall be drawn in such a way that any point on the said line shall be situated at an equal distance from the coasts of the two States, measured from the nearest point on the mainland, islands, islets or reefs which is not perpetually submerged.[123]

This appears to be a developed concept of the median line. Owing to the rather straight coastal formation overall, the "equal distance" line generally coincided with the line perpendicular to the general direction of the coast.

[118] 19 *id.* at 183, 194.

[119] Straits Settlements and Johore Territorial Waters (Agreement) Act, 1928, 18 & 19 Geo. 5, c. 23, Art. 1.

[120] This is the author's translation from the French text. *See* Protocole de délimitation de la frontière serbe-croate-slovène-albanaise (July 1926), *quoted in* P. LAPRADELLE, LA FRONTIÈRE 216 & n.1 (1928); *see also* G. GIDEL, *supra* note 27, at 768 & n.1.

[121] Belgian letter of Dec. 19, 1928, *reprinted in* Bases of Discussion, *supra* note 104.

[122] French letter of Aug. 2, 1953, *reprinted in* Addendum 2, at 1, to Information and Observations Submitted by Governments, *supra* note 25.

[123] 30 LNTS 49, 61.

After the Hague Codification Conference, where the median line principle was seriously considered as a general rule for the delimitation of narrow straits between states, the median line was frequently used. For instance, Italy and Turkey, settling disputes regarding sovereignty over certain islets off the Anatolian coast, delimited the territorial sea boundary on January 4, 1932 in accordance with the median line principle.[124] On January 30, 1932, Denmark and Sweden delimited their territorial sea boundary in seven straight-line segments drawn on the basis of the median line principle.[125] Boundaries were precisely described using geographical coordinates up to seconds. A similar method was followed in the Protocol of February 22, 1932 on the delimitation of the territorial sea between Denmark and Norway.[126]

A few years after the Hague Conference, Gilbert Gidel attempted to synthesize the divergent views. According to him, the boundary in narrow straits must be drawn

> according to the median line: (1) except when other agreements are made between the interested states, and (2) except when the geographic configuration is such that the use of the median line system would lead to an excessive disproportion in the participation of the riparian states in the various uses to which the body of water under consideration naturally lends itself.[127]

As for adjacent states, Gidel concluded that both in practice and in doctrine the general rule was "the median line perpendicular to the general direction of the coast." He believed that if necessitated by special circumstances, the median line could be adjusted so as to represent the general direction of the coast.[128]

A similar view was taken at that time by the American Institute of International Law in its codification project on the territorial sea. Regarding opposite states, the Institute proposed that "if the shores of the strait or of the inland sea belong to more than one state, the waters of the strait are divided among them by a navigable median line parallel to their shores, unless there is a special agreement among them." Between adjacent states, according to the Institute, "the territorial sea is divided by a straight line perpendicular to the spot where the said frontier terminates."[129]

IV. Developments After the Hague Conference

The New Equidistance Method

Despite the efforts of states to draw the median line boundary as fairly as possible, there was no uniform method of demarcation. From the outset, the median line was an unclear term. It was often confused with the thalweg and other similar terms.[130] Nevertheless, because sovereign rights can best be pro-

[124] 135 BFSP 629. [125] *Id.* at 474.

[126] *See* Information and Observations Submitted by Governments, *supra* note 25, at 9.

[127] This is the author's translation from the French text. *See* G. Gidel, *supra* note 27, at 768–71.

[128] *Ibid.*

[129] *See* American Institute of International Law, Codification of Public International Law, Project on the Territorial Sea, Arts. V, XIV (1933).

[130] *See* note 34 *supra* and accompanying text.

tected by a division of the area concerned as equally as possible, it is not surprising that the vague median line concept eventually evolved into a precise one.[131]

For most of its history, the median line was seen as a sort of point of convergence to be approached as nearly as possible, but probably not attained exactly, because it was regarded as virtually impossible to trace a mathematical line between irregular coasts. This meant that any sea boundary agreement stipulating the median line principle should have been accompanied by a map. Otherwise, several interpretations were possible.

In its report on the location of the median water boundary line between the United States and Canada in Lake Erie, the International Waterways Commission stated in 1913 that the median line principle implied three possibilities:

> —A line being at all points equally distant from each shore;
>
> —A line following the general lines of the shores and dividing the surface water area as nearly as practicable into two equal parts;
>
> —A line along the mid-channel dividing the navigable portion of the lake, and being at all points equally distant from the shoal water on each shore.[132]

The first possibility is what might be called "the landsman's or the shoreline viewpoint" (see figure 1). S. Whittemore Boggs described this concept as follows: "Suppose that one might start with one of the shores of the lake and from successive points draw lines to the nearest point on the opposite shore; the line connecting the mid-points of each of these lines might be regarded as the median line of the lake." He correctly contended that "this concept is quite impossible, even from one shore, and . . . the result from the opposite shore would be quite dissimilar."[133] Despite its obvious defects, this method of designating the median point has been widely used. Each state would establish a sort of middle line by just connecting certain midpoints from its own shore. Because the result obtained from one shore is generally different from that obtained from the other, this method has caused frequent disputes.

The second possibility derives from the fact that the median line should leave one-half of the area on each side. But any number of lines may be drawn to that effect. Such a definition implies no specific method of delimitation. Still, this concept may be suitable for testing whether a specific line has been drawn in an equitable way, so that rectifications can be made if necessary.

The third possibility has been widely used in rivers and in some straits where navigation is of prime importance. The mid-channel rule rests upon "equitable considerations" and is intended to guarantee to each riparian state "equality of access" and the "right of navigation."[134] However, the mid-channel is generally imprecise and not easily identifiable in many cases.

In 1934 the German jurist Fritz Münch tried to define the term "*Mittellinie*"

[131] Wisconsin v. Michigan, 295 U.S. 455, 462 (1935).

[132] COMPILED REPORTS OF THE INTERNATIONAL WATERWAYS COMMISSION, 1905–1913, at 578 (Ottawa 1913).

[133] Boggs, *Problems of Water-Boundary Definition: Median Line and International Boundaries Through Territorial Waters*, 27 GEOGRAPHICAL REV. 445, 447–48 (1937).

[134] Wisconsin v. Michigan, 295 U.S. at 461.

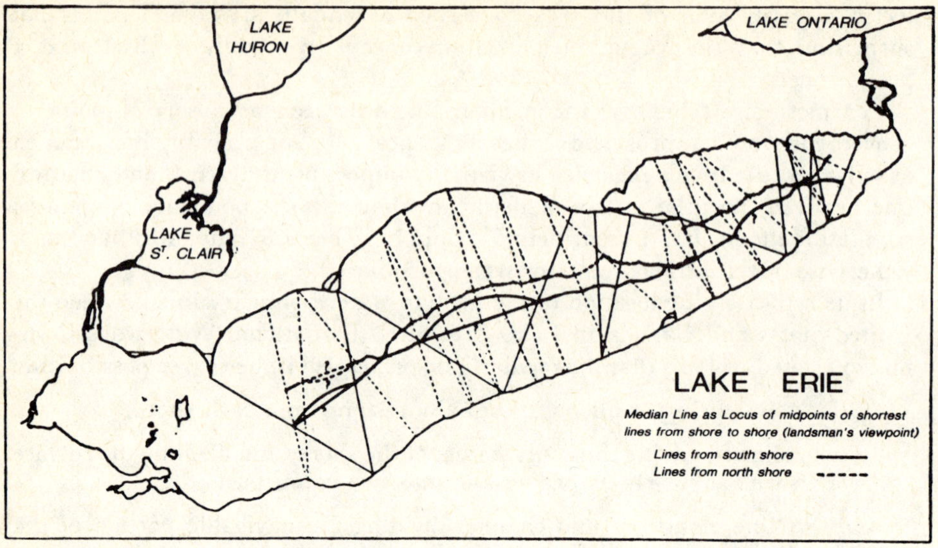

FIGURE 1

S. W. BOGGS'S CRITICISM OF THE MEDIAN LINE DRAWN FROM A LANDSMAN'S VIEWPOINT

The median line is the locus of the midpoints of all lines drawn from points on one shore to the nearest point on the opposite shore. The line differs as it is drawn from the north or the south shore, the two versions only occasionally being coincident.

SOURCE: adapted from S. W. BOGGS, INTERNATIONAL BOUNDARIES 181 (1940).

or median line in a new perspective, and also proposed a new method of drawing it:

> "Median line" in the strict sense of the words relates to cases in which neighbors lie either completely or partially opposite one another, in straits, archipelagos, and bays; the perpendicular line is the median line of straight coasts, where every point of the perpendicular line is equally distant from the coasts of neighboring states.[135]

Convinced that delimitation by median line is possible not only between opposite states but also between adjacent states, Münch boldly attempted to find a true median line "from the point of view of a vessel in navigation, not from that of the landsman or the shoreline."[136] Between opposite states, he suggested drawing a median line equidistant from each base point by drawing many midway lines between base points. But his method proved to be erroneous, because on his hypothetical and sketchy map every island was only a point. He therefore failed to prove the general applicability of his method to real situations. For adjacent states, he believed that a median line could be composed of broken median-line segments drawn perpendicularly, first, to the local coast in a bay; second, to the hypothetical line between the starting point of the sea boundary

[135] This is the author's translation from the German text. *See* F. MÜNCH, DIE TECHNISCHEN FRAGEN DES KÜSTENMEERS 156 (1934).

[136] This correct approach by Münch to the median line principle probably influenced Boggs. *See* Boggs, *supra* note 133, at 447.

and the outer edge of the bay; and third, to the general trend of the coast. His initial idea to draw the lateral median line so as to divide the area as equally as possible is praiseworthy, but by using his own hypothetical and sketchy map, he again failed to prove the general applicability of his method.[137]

Soon after the publication of Münch's technical study, Gilbert Gidel severely criticized its technical errors, though he did not suggest a better way of drawing a median line.[138] Gidel firmly supported the median line principle as a general rule for straits, yet he was hesitant to approve its general applicability to the territorial sea between adjacent states, for he believed in the equally convincing principle of a line perpendicular to the general direction of the coast. He subsequently arrived at a compromise, namely, "the median line perpendicular to the general direction of the coast."[139]

A new method of plotting the median line was invented in 1936 by S. Whittemore Boggs, Special Adviser on Geography in the U.S. Department of State (see figure 2).[140] When Col. Lawrence Martin was studying the Michigan-Wisconsin water boundary question, he invited Boggs to make a strict delimitation of the median line in Lake Michigan. Boggs later wrote that the equidistance technique he then developed was used by the U.S. Supreme Court in preparing its decree of March 16, 1936 regarding *Wisconsin v. Michigan*.[141] The decree corrected the boundary description for the Green Bay section of Lake Michigan enunciated by the Court in its decree of November 22, 1926.[142]

Boggs defined his new concept as "the line every point of which is equidistant from the nearest point or points on opposite shores."[143] He correctly asserted that "only one such line can be drawn, and this is therefore a precise definition," and argued that "indication of the boundary on published charts is not essential, though it is desirable."[144] As to the method of plotting it on a chart, he stated:

> The median line, being equally distant from opposite shores, follows a straight line that is equally distant from two projecting points on the two shores until a third point that is equally distant is reached; then it usually proceeds in relation to one of the first two points and the new point. Each such straight line lies on the perpendicular that bisects the line connecting the two nearest points on opposite shores; in fact, the median line consists of a series of such straight lines, each of which is extended until it intersects the next.[145]

[137] F. MÜNCH, *supra* note 135, at 162–63.

[138] *See* G. GIDEL, *supra* note 27, at 770–71 n.3.

[139] *Id.* at 768.

[140] *See* Boggs, *supra* note 133, at 447.

[141] Boggs, *Delimitation of Seaward Areas Under National Jurisdiction*, 45 AJIL 240, 258 n.30 (1951); *see also* Wisconsin v. Michigan, 295 U.S. at 462; Wisconsin v. Michigan, 297 U.S. 547 (1936).

[142] Michigan v. Wisconsin, 272 U.S. 398 (1926).

[143] *See* Boggs, *supra* note 133, at 448.

[144] *Id.* at 448–49.

[145] In laying down such a line on the chart, according to Boggs,

> it is necessary to discover points which lie on the line by trial and error but as regards any point in the lake, in order to find on which side of the median-line boundary it lies, it is necessary only to swing a compass from that point on the chart to opposite shores of the lake or river in order to ascertain which shore is the nearer and, therefore, on which side of the boundary the point is situated.

Id. at 449.

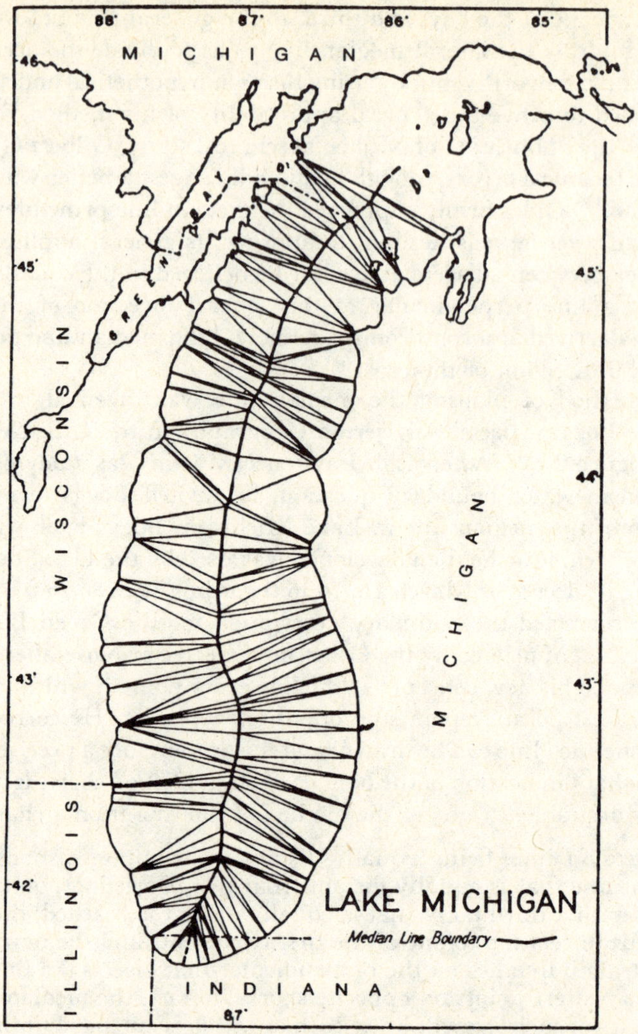

FIGURE 2

S. W. BOGGS'S EQUIDISTANCE LINE

The drawing shows the line all points of which are equidistant from the nearest points on opposite shores. The Michigan-Wisconsin boundary in Green Bay and to the middle of Lake Michigan, according to the decree of the United States Supreme Court of March 16, 1936, is also shown (as a broken line).

SOURCE: adapted from S. W. BOGGS, INTERNATIONAL BOUNDARIES 185 (1940).

It is to be noted that this method was suggested only for opposite states; for adjacent states, Boggs stuck to the straight-line method of dividing the territorial sea. But he rejected the two means advanced by his predecessors, the straight extension of the land boundary and a straight line perpendicular to the coast, and instead devised a new one of his own: a straight line drawn from the land boundary terminus to the equidistant intersection point on the outer limit of the territorial sea. If both states have the same breadth of territorial sea, such a line can easily be drawn (with a compass) from each side as if the other did not exist. Despite the apparent simplicity of this method, it may result in an inequitable delimitation, depending upon the particular geographical and other special circumstances. Such inequities may be minor when the breadth of the territorial sea is 3 miles, but the broader the territorial sea, the greater the inequities that may arise.

Nevertheless, by exposing the inconsistencies inherent in the two methods previously suggested—extension of the land boundary and a line perpendicular to the general trend of the coast—Boggs did make an important contribution. He pointed out that the former method usually results in a boundary that is accidental in direction, whereas the latter is faulty because it is not always feasible to determine the general trend of the coast. In addition, he proved both methods to be unsatisfactory because they usually leave a zone of water that does not belong to either state even though it is within the limits of the territorial seas.[146] He did not explain why he would not use the equidistance line instead of the straight line connecting the land boundary terminus and the equidistant intersection point, but such a line does not run counter to the equidistance principle because it is in fact a simplified or straightened-out equidistance line.

Equitable Considerations

From the very first disputes between states over the establishment of sea boundaries in the modern era, attempts have been made to divide or share interests equally and fairly. The median line principle has often been used in light of the fundamental notion that the sovereignty of each shall be conceived of as extending to the middle. The median line principle, which later developed into the equidistance principle, does not always produce an equal division of the maritime space to be delimited between states. In the interest of attaining the goal of equal division, equitable considerations have been closely and inherently associated with the equidistance principle.

In some cases, condominium arrangements have been established in order to share interests instead of dividing them. Despite the notion that friendly neighbors ought to be able to share maritime interests harmoniously, neither reason nor authority encourages the belief that condominium arrangements will be permanent. The foundation of maritime jurisdiction is the seaward extension of land domain, which is held individually by states. A sea boundary simply marks off the individual domain of each state, which includes both the body of water marked off and the appurtenant maritime interests. Condominium has not received much support among scholars, and has been established only in a few cases. However, it is one way of solving disputes in cases where mere division would not provide convenience and efficiency in the use of the sea, and where interests in the sea could be exploited more equitably and effectively than by dividing them in terms of maritime space.

In the overwhelming majority of cases, disputes between opposite and adjacent states have been resolved by establishing boundaries. From the outset,

[146] *Id.* at 452–55.

principles for sea boundaries were closely associated with the ideal of equitable division. Pufendorf suggested, for example, that between opposite states the median line be drawn so that the sovereignty of each would be "in proportion to the breadth of its land."[147] The *Grisbadarna* principle that between adjacent states the lateral territorial sea boundary should be a line perpendicular to the general direction of the coast was also based upon the equitable consideration of circumstances relating to both sides of the boundary.[148] Another reflection of Pufendorf's equitable guideline is found in Gidel's idea of "a median line perpendicular to the coast."[149]

This ideal of equal and fair division has been enriched and amplified by other principles and equitable considerations. The thalweg or main channel principle, for example, has been used to guarantee access to and navigation in the waterway to each riparian state, in the sense that equal division of the surface of the water is far less significant than the mutual ability to navigate along the thalweg, where large vessels can travel.[150]

Historic title and other vested rights have been respected at sea as well as on land,[151] and have taken precedence over the median or equidistance line principle, as well as over all other rules. Historic title was considered, for instance, in the delimitation of the territorial sea boundary between Canada and the United States in the Passamaquoddy Bay; but in other cases, such as the "Wielingen" controversy between Belgium and the Netherlands,[152] and the "Ems-Dollard" affair between Germany and the Netherlands,[153] it became a main obstacle to establishing a boundary.

The question of islands was not so significant in the early modern period. The fate of islands was often decided by the location of the thalweg, or sometimes

[147] *See* notes 4–6 *supra* and accompanying text.

[148] 4 AJIL at 232.

[149] G. GIDEL, *supra* note 27, at 768–71.

[150] Louisiana v. Mississippi, 202 U.S. at 23, 49.

[151] *Id.* at 26.

[152] The traditional water boundary between Belgium and the Netherlands follows first the direction of the land boundary—which is hardly at all different from the perpendicular line in the general direction of the coast—until it reaches the Wielingen, the principal channel of navigation of the River Scheldt. Sovereign rights in the whole "Wielingen" have been claimed by the Netherlands on historic grounds. The Netherlands asserted that the boundary line should be pushed off to some distance in a westerly direction parallel to the Belgian coast, because the Wielingen forms a principal navigational channel parallel to the coast, while Belgium maintained that the boundary between the contiguous territorial seas of two neighboring countries should lie along a line perpendicular to the coast. *See* Information and Observations Submitted by Governments, *supra* note 25, at 7, 11; *see also, e.g.*, H. DE HOON, L'ESCAUT ET SON EMBOUCHURE: LE DIFFÉREND DES WIELINGEN (1927); de Visscher & Ganshof, *Le Différend des Wielingen*, REV. DROIT INT'L & LEGIS. COMP., 3d ser., No. 1, at 293, 328 (1920).

[153] It is ironic that the Netherlands, while on the one hand asserting historic rights in the Wielingen against Belgium, on the other hand had to deny a historic claim to the mouth of the River Ems by Germany. The water boundary line between Germany and the Netherlands follows a straight line in a direction indicated by Article 41 of the Treaty of Meppen of 1824. From the point where the line ends, the Netherlands asserted that the boundary line should follow the thalweg of the principal navigation channel and outflow of the River Ems into the open sea, while Germany claimed most of the estuaries on the basis of historic title except for the area in the Dollard that had been previously agreed upon. *See* Information and Observations Submitted by Governments, *supra* note 25, at 11.

by the median line. Pufendorf's aforementioned guideline implies that certain islands may be ignored in order to achieve an equal and fair division. The *Grisbadarna* principle of delimitation by a straight line perpendicular to the general direction of the coast also implies ignoring islands unless they are considered as part of that general direction.[154]

Supporters of the median line principle like Guerra were well aware that strict insistence on the median line would often produce inequitable results; he once remarked that just as tyranny is better than anarchy, so the median line principle is better than "no rule."[155] Münch, the initiator of the technical study of the equidistance line method, was hesitant to apply it as a strict rule and suggested methods for straightening out the inconvenient zigzag line produced by scattered islands and coastal indentations:

> In every deviation from the median line, *i.e.*, by applying the thalweg principle or by simplifying the boundary upon demarcation, the boundary should not zigzag between the sinuosities of the nearest base points on either side. It seems also that when the neighboring countries on the same mainland are adjacent to one another, and there is an island off the coast of one country which shifts the outer limit of the territorial sea, this ought not to influence the lateral boundary.[156]

Even though Boggs invented the equidistance method, he devoted much thought to simplifying the equidistance line in order to obtain an equitable and convenient boundary. Between opposite states, where he considered the equidistance line method more applicable, he suggested straightening out zigzags in the line by trading areas. Between adjacent states, as has been seen, he suggested drawing a straight line from the land boundary terminus to the equidistant point on the outer limit of the territorial sea.[157]

CONCLUSION

The fundamental principle of sea boundary delimitation between states has been that delimitation between equal states should be based on principles and rules of international law. The general guideline for an equitable delimitation was that the powers of equal sovereigns equally reach out and abut in the middle of the waters. The median line drawn by connecting certain midpoints

[154] Boggs noted the difficulties in determining how to treat islands when delimiting the territorial sea between states in accordance with the median or equidistance line principle. He separated coasts into three categories: first, the general trend of the coast, as mentioned in the *Grisbadarna* award; second, straight lines drawn from point to point along the coast and from outer points of the most seaward islands, like the Norwegian straight baseline system; third, lines drawn from each of the nearest base points from which the median or equidistance line is calculated. The last one was proposed by the United States at the Codification Conference of International Law in 1930, on the grounds that it is the only one that can meet the interest of navigators, and that only one median line can be drawn from such base points. However, Boggs later observed that "historic waters" and "skjaergard" should be exceptions to the American position. *See* Boggs, *Delimitation of the Territorial Sea*, 24 AJIL 541, 543, 544, 555 (1930).

[155] *See* J. GUERRA, *supra* note 87, at 27.

[156] This is the author's translation from the German text. *See* F. MÜNCH, *supra* note 135, at 165.

[157] *See* Boggs, *supra* note 133, at 455–56.

was generally believed to be the one that met the principle of equality. But the median line does not always guarantee an equitable delimitation owing to scattered islands and other irregular coastal formations. Various efforts were made to find a way to chart an equitable median line, by ignoring small islands or by taking account of other equitable considerations. In many cases the median line was replaced by some other convenient line: between opposite states, sometimes the thalweg was used where the preservation of equal access and navigational rights was the prime interest; between adjacent states, most of the lateral boundaries followed latitudes, longitudes, or some other azimuth perpendicular to the general direction of the coast.

There was no geometric method for constructing the median line; often the exact demarcation of the median line was not even called for. It was only after World War I, as states came to be sensitive about every nook and corner of their territorial sea, that the need for accurate delimitation gained momentum. Many scholars and institutions responded by offering proposals on delimitation, and some of them attempted to develop a geometric method for plotting the median line. In 1936, S. Whittemore Boggs finally developed the equidistance method, which consisted of a "line every point of which is equidistant from the nearest point or points on opposite shores." He proved that only one such line is possible in any maritime area.

The equidistance method, primarily proposed for the delimitation of lakes between coriparians, was also suggested for the delimitation of sea boundaries between opposite states, but it was not recommended as a general rule of delimitation between adjacent states at that time. Few scholars, including Boggs, were convinced of its general applicability between adjacent states. In fact, few lateral boundaries were delimited in accordance with the equidistance method. Any small island or any minor coastal projection could cause the equidistance line to swerve, which would result in inequities because of the progressively distorting effect. Indeed, there is no basis to suppose that the equidistance method should have been adopted as a general rule of delimitation between adjacent states.

The aim of delimitation has always been to find a mutually acceptable boundary, based on principles and rules that would provide an equitable result. The principles developed for the "marginal seas" before World War II can be utilized nowadays to delimit boundaries in the territorial sea and other zones of extended national jurisdiction. Although the stakes have increased as states' interests in the seas have multiplied, coastal geographical circumstances, which are generally decisive in delimitation, remain almost the same. Further investigation into customary principles of delimitation should be undertaken so as to supplement the vague provisions in the conventional law.

EDITORIAL COMMENTS

CRITICAL DEFENSE ZONES AND INTERNATIONAL LAW: THE REAGAN CODICIL

Conflicts may erupt from mistakes and misperceptions. Because of the increasing speed, total destructiveness, and irrevocability of the contemporary instruments of violence, minimum world order requires that states communicate to their adversaries, clearly and in advance, exactly which parts of the planet they deem indispensable to their own security and, hence, which expansive political or military changes initiated by or enuring to the benefit of an adversary will be unacceptable and likely to lead to war. These processes of communication are complex. Not all that is demanded is deemed reasonable. Not all that is demanded wins acceptance. The areas referred to in such communications may be reciprocally accepted as critical defense zones or CDZ's. In the past, failure to indicate such zones unequivocally may have contributed to the eruption of conflict.

Since World War II, explicit as well as tacit communication of critical defense zones has been fairly routine. The Soviet Union has insisted on Eastern Europe as a defense zone. Without explicitly conceding the propriety of the claim, the Western states have, in effect, complied with the demand. Even at moments of opportunity, such as the Hungarian uprising of 1956 and the Czech "spring" of 1968, the West exploited the events for propaganda value, but refrained from adventures or overt support. This part of the so-called Brezhnev doctrine[1] has been accepted in practice. Conversely, the Monroe Doctrine[2] and corollaries such as the Selden Resolution[3] may be viewed as the clearest communication to adversaries that expansions of power and changes in alliance pattern in the designated zones will be opposed by force.[4] Smaller states have also communicated critical zone messages to their adversaries with deterrent effect.

CDZ's are not tantamount to proprietorship. Unlike spheres of influence in some earlier periods, they do not import an option *erga omnes* to annex territory in the zone at some future time. Yet unquestionably, they attenuate the political discretion of elites in the states within the zone and limit the self-determination

[1] Kovalev, *Sovereignty and the Internationalist Obligations of Socialist Countries*, Pravda, Sept. 26, 1968, trans. in 20 CURRENT DIG. SOVIET PRESS [hereinafter cited as CDSP], No. 39, Sept. 26, 1968, at 10–12, and in N.Y. Times, Sept. 17, 1968. The document is now popularly attributed to Brezhnev. *See also* B. MEISSNER, THE BREZHNEV DOCTRINE (East Europe Monographs, No. 2, 1970).

[2] Monroe Doctrine, Annual Message to Congress of Dec. 2, 1823 (Seventh Annual Message) from the President, in 2 J. D. RICHARDSON, A COMPILATION OF THE MESSAGES AND PAPERS OF THE PRESIDENTS, sec. 787.

[3] Selden Resolution: Sense of the House of Representatives Relative to International Communism in the Western Hemisphere, H.R. Res. 560, 89th Cong., 1st Sess., 111 CONG. REC. 24,347 (1965).

[4] For a regional equivalent, see Organization of American States, Eighth Meeting of Consultation of Ministers of Foreign Affairs, Serving as Organ of Consultation in Application of the Inter-American Treaty of Reciprocal Assistance, documents *reprinted in* 56 AJIL 601, 604–08 (1962).

options of the rank and file there. In this respect, they are offensive to such basic policies of contemporary international law as self-determination and political independence of states, even though they resonate positively with urgent demands for the maintenance of global minimum order.

Indignant protests of CDZ's can achieve little more than a self-stimulated exhilaration of righteousness. A more realistic approach can temper their rigor by acknowledging their potential contribution to minimum order, while insisting that a state averring a CDZ claim no more than necessary for its own minimum security. From the standpoint of the state declaring a CDZ, *complete* control of both internal public order and external alignments would promise the greatest efficiency. Such a regime also poses the gravest violation of other international constitutive norms. The critical point in a viable system is that CDZ's should operate with as much fidelity as possible to other basic international norms. Unlawful behavior by a major power in a critical zone would involve substantial interventions in the internal public order of states there. In particular, attempts to suppress genuinely indigenous efforts at self-government, change of government, or amelioration of public order systems with greater conformity to international norms would appear to be doubtful extensions of the CDZ doctrine.

Appraised in terms of these standards, current demands by the Soviet Union to change aspects of public order *within* Poland must be deemed unlawful.[5]

The so-called Carter doctrine of January 1980 would appear to be a lawful exercise of the critical zone practice. Following Soviet aggression in Afghanistan, President Carter declared: "An attempt by any outside force to gain control of the Persian Gulf region will be regarded as an assault on the vital interests of the United States of America, and such an assault will be repelled by any means necessary, including military force."[6] The lawfulness of the Carter doctrine derives from its promised defense of governments from *external* aggression as well as its CDZ communication. It is not a disguised technique of intervention in the internal affairs of states within the zone.

On October 1, 1981, President Reagan issued statements that the White House promptly characterized as "The Reagan Codicil to the Carter Doctrine." In response to a question, the President said, ". . . Saudi Arabia we will not permit to be an Iran." In clarification, the President added that "in Iran I think the United States has to take some responsibility for what happened."[7] Immediately afterwards, a White House aide explained to the *New York Times* that "the President was now pledging to support the Saudi monarchy against

[5] *See* 33 CDSP, No. 41, Nov. 11, 1981, at 8; 33 CDSP, No. 40, Nov. 4, 1981, at 6; *id.* at 8; 33 CDSP, No. 39, Oct. 28, 1981, at 13; 33 CDSP, No. 38, Oct. 21, 1981, at 8; 33 CDSP, No. 37, Oct. 14, 1981, at 1; 33 CDSP, No. 34, Sept. 23, 1981, at 8; *id.* at 22; 33 CDSP, No. 31, Sept. 2, 1981, at 19; 33 CDSP, No. 30, Aug. 26, 1981, at 14; 33 CDSP, No. 25, July 22, 1981, at 7; 33 CDSP, No. 22, July 1, 1981, at 1; 33 CDSP, No. 21, June 24, 1981, at 15; *id.* at 16; 33 CDSP, No. 20, June 17, 1981, at 10; 33 CDSP, No. 17, May 27, 1981, at 1; 33 CDSP, No. 12, April 22, 1981, at 19; 33 CDSP, No. 11, April 15, 1981, at 19; 33 CDSP, No. 10, April 8, 1981, at 19; 33 CDSP, No. 5, March 4, 1981, at 5; 33 CDSP, No. 1, Feb. 4, 1981, at 11.

[6] 16 WEEKLY COMP. OF PRES. DOC. 197 (Jan. 23, 1980).

[7] Transcript of President's News Conference on Foreign and Domestic Matters, N.Y. Times, Oct. 2, 1981, at A26.

internal as well as external threats."[8] That sense was confirmed some 2 weeks later in remarks made by the President to a luncheon meeting of media editors.[9]

The Reagan codicil, thus, is qualitatively different from the Carter doctrine and other lawful applications of CDZ; it purports to extend the conception of CDZ from one of concern with external alignments and alliances of states in regions critical to national defense to a prerogative of active intervention and suppression of popularly demanded internal change in favor of a particular local elite. Legally, it is a most dubious expansion of CDZ. Politically, it is in the melancholy tradition of King Canute.

W. MICHAEL REISMAN

A TURNABOUT IN EXTRATERRITORIALITY

The standard pattern in international maneuvers over extraterritoriality has been for the United States to step off by taking action that seems to project its legislative or investigative powers beyond its borders. One or more European states respond with protests, now fairly standardized, that the United States has gone too far; sometimes they go further and pass legislation designed to thwart the original move. Various further sidesteps and glides follow until the relationship comes to rest at some sort of halfway point.[1] Two recent episodes find the roles rather neatly reversed. In each the Commission of the European Communities led off with proposals, voices in the United States spoke up to say that the action was extraterritorial and improper, and the consequent maneuvers are now in progress. Partly because the sources for these two affairs are scattered, it seems useful to present a summary version at this time, though no resolution has been achieved and no lessons can yet be drawn about their effect on the field of jurisdiction in international law.

The first episode was touched off by the European Commission's proposal of rules that, if adopted, would impose compulsory disclosure of data on American-based concerns with subsidiaries in Europe. The centerpiece is the "Vredeling Proposal," named after the Commissioner from the Netherlands

[8] Smith, *Reagan and the Saudis*, *id.* at 1, 4–5.

[9] Remarks by Reagan to Editors, *id.*, Oct. 18, 1981, at 38, col. 1.

[1] For collections of materials on these U.S. challenges and foreign responses on extraterritoriality, see L. EBB, INTERNATIONAL BUSINESS: REGULATION AND PROTECTION 583–612 (1964); H. STEINER & D. VAGTS, TRANSNATIONAL LEGAL PROBLEMS 1014–47 (2d ed. 1976). This is not to assert that the United States has never before been in the position of opposing extraterritorial measures by foreign states. *See* Steiner, *International Boycotts and Domestic Order: American Involvement in the Arab-Israeli Conflict*, 54 TEX. L. REV. 1355, 1395–1402 (1976) (discussion of extraterritoriality aspect of Arab boycott of Israel and its role in the U.S. response); J. B. MOORE, REPORT ON EXTRATERRITORIAL CRIME AND THE CUTTING CASE (U.S. Dep't of State 1887) (protest over Mexican libel conviction of El Paso editor). For an attempt to restate international law rules on extraterritoriality, see RESTATEMENT OF THE FOREIGN RELATIONS LAW OF THE UNITED STATES (REVISED), Tent. Draft No. 2, §§402–04, 415–18 (1981); see also Maier, *Extraterritorial Jurisdiction at a Crossroads: An Intersection Between Public and Private International Law*, 76 AJIL 280 (1982).

who fathered it.[2] It builds upon existing rules in the laws of states of the Community and in the Community's jurisprudence that are designed to fortify the position of labor in dealing with management about such issues as plant closings and reassignments of functions between divisions or affiliates. Under the Vredeling plan the management of a "dominant" (parent) organization located outside the Community would have to furnish each of its subsidiaries in the Community with 40 days' advance notice of certain decisions. The decisions listed relate to the closure or transfer of an establishment, substantial changes in its activities, major modifications of firm organization, and cooperation (joint venture) agreements with other firms. The outreach of these rules is not clear, but possibly a transfer by a firm of activities from Brazil to the United States might be held to have a "substantial effect" on its European employees and the news would therefore have to be passed on to their representatives.[3]

The other proposed directives, designated Nos. 7 and 9 in a series of rulings designed to make company law more uniform in the Community, apply to groups of affiliated companies.[4] They would impose some duties on non-European parent corporations. On the whole those burdens are not specially onerous, but some do raise theoretical problems of extraterritoriality, such as one requiring the publication of consolidated financial statements that in effect would reveal non-European activities. Although most such U.S.-based firms provide the data pursuant to requirements of the Securities and Exchange Commission, they resist the principle that a host state could make such demands.

American business organizations have vocally protested these developments. A bill that proposed to enact the "Protection of Confidential Business Information Act" (shades of the Protection of Trading Interests Act of the United Kingdom![5]) was introduced into both Houses of Congress in 1981.[6] Its preamble declares that the imposition of obligations to disclose such secrets "is inconsistent with international law and comity." The Securities and Exchange Commission would be authorized to issue protective orders. Violations of such an order would be subject to a civil penalty, and any fine or penalty imposed by a foreign state for a nondisclosure ordered by the Commission would be unenforceable in U.S. courts and, indeed, could be recovered from the foreign state by a suit in this country.

[2] 23 O.J. EUR. COMM. (No. C 297) 3 (1980).

[3] For an argument that such actions would have to be notified, see Kirkland, *Multinationals—Bad News Brewing*, FORTUNE, Dec. 14, 1981, at 142, 144.

[4] 22 O.J. EUR. COMM. (No. C 14) 2 (1979) (7th directive); the 9th directive has not as yet been published, though it has evidently been circulated informally for comments. Both are based on Article 54(3)(g) of the Treaty of Rome. *See generally* E. STEIN, HARMONIZATION OF EUROPEAN COMPANY LAWS (1971).

[5] The British Act and its purposes are discussed in Lowe, *Blocking Extraterritorial Jurisdiction: The British Protection of Trading Interests Act, 1980*, 75 AJIL 257 (1981). A similar French law is treated in Herzog, *The 1980 French Law on Documents and Information*, *id.* at 382.

[6] H.R. 4339, 97th Cong., 1st Sess. (1981), and S. 1592, 97th Cong., 1st Sess. (1981). A bill with somewhat similar objectives that would amend the Trade Act of 1974 to authorize the President to respond to foreign practices that discriminate against U.S. foreign investment is H.R. 4407, 97th Cong., 1st Sess. (1981).

The other branch of the controversy involves proceedings brought by the Commission against International Business Machines. As is well known, IBM has been subject to a wide-front assault in the U.S. courts by private litigants and the Department of Justice.[7] It has succeeded in fending off all its adversaries. The central issues in the Commission's attempt are the counterparts of those in the American suits. In effect, it charges that IBM takes various steps, when it develops a new computer, to make it difficult for competitors to design peripheral equipment that can be made "plug-compatible" with the IBM product. In particular, it is said, IBM does not disclose sufficient details, at the time it announces new machines, to allow competitors to develop their new offerings in time to match IBM's peripheral equipment. IBM staged an unusual counteroffensive by appealing to the Court of Justice in Luxembourg, but the Court rejected it as premature.[8] In March of this year, newspapers reported that the Assistant Attorney General in charge of the Antitrust Division was conveying to his European counterparts the U.S. view that an ultimate Commission order directed at IBM would result in extraterritorial effects upon the U.S. economy.[9]

What developments might one expect from all of this? It is difficult to choose at this point between two plausible scenarios. One is that, given the harshness of the economic winds blowing around the industrial world, states will draw apart over policies on direct investment and such related matters as employment. They will then seize all plausible gambits for putting their interests ahead of those of other states. Controversies will abound between home country and host country states over who has the right to control multinationals stretched between them. Observers see a somewhat similar happening in trade matters despite the apparent gains of the Tokyo Round.[10]

The more cheerful version stresses that the states of the industrial world have much to lose from destructive and shortsighted attempts to gain such advantage. As the balance of foreign direct investment holdings between the United States and Europe moves towards equilibrium,[11] neither side will have that much to gain from insistence on the universal primacy of jurisdiction of the home (or of the host) country. In such a climate sensible rules could be worked out. These could either allocate jurisdiction along agreed-upon neutral standards or pool the responsibility in some joint agency. Different problematic

[7] The history of the Government's case is reported as United States v. International Business Machs. Corp., 69 Civ. 200, 4 TRADE REG. REP. (CCH), Case No. 2039. For decisions in private cases, see, *e.g.*, Telex Corp. v. International Business Machs. Corp., 510 F.2d 894 (10th Cir.), *cert. dismissed*, 423 U.S. 802 (1975); *In re* IBM Peripheral EDP Devices Antitrust Litig., 481 F.Supp. 965 (N.D. Cal. 1979).

[8] International Business Machs. Corp. v. Commission, Case No. 60/81, Nov. 11, 1981, COMMON MKT. REP. (CCH) ¶8708. Technically, the procedure attempted was a suit to declare void the acts of the Commission initiating a proceeding and the statement of objections about IBM's practices. In addition to extraterritorial grounds, IBM relied upon procedural irregularities by the Commission.

[9] Wall St. J., March 31, 1982, at 1, col. 6.

[10] *E.g.*, Schott, *Can World Trade Be Governed?*, CHALLENGE, March/April 1982, at 43.

[11] This point is elaborated in the forthcoming volume, C. WALLACE, THE MULTINATIONAL ENTERPRISE: LEGAL CONTROLS: TECHNIQUES OF INDUSTRIALIZED HOST STATES AND THE PROSPECTS FOR INTERNATIONAL CONTROLS.

subject matters might lend themselves better to one than to the other remedy. Thus, one might expect an allocation of inextricably international antitrust decisions to the state with primary economic concern, but look to some combination of regulatory authorities and professional accountants to get acceptable uniform international rules on minimum disclosure practices.

DETLEV F. VAGTS

THE FALKLANDS (MALVINAS), INTERNATIONAL LAW, AND THE OAS

An African saying is that when elephants fight, it is the grass that suffers. A consequence of the resolution adopted by the Organization of American States Ministers of Foreign Affairs on April 28, 1982 may well be serious damage to at least one of the principal organs of the OAS, the Inter-American Juridical Committee. The OAS resolution of April 28 cited, as a principal justification, a January 16, 1976 declaration of the Juridical Committee that Argentina "has an undeniable right of sovereignty over the Malvinas Islands." Fortunately or otherwise, the plain fact is that the Juridical Committee had—and has—no authority to make any such declaration in regard to a territorial dispute.

Articles 105 through 111 of the Charter of the OAS establish and define the duties of the Juridical Committee. That body consists of 11 jurists, elected in their individual capacities for 4-year terms by the General Assembly of the OAS. The committee under Article 105 is to act as a consultative body for the OAS in "juridical matters," and it is charged to promote the progressive development and codification of international law, with special reference to integration of the developing nations of the region and to harmonization of national laws. Aside from a mandate (Article 109) to establish cooperative relationships among universities, centers of learning, and the like, those are its sole authorities. The committee has no authority to act as a judicial, as distinguished from a juridical, body. That is, it can discuss and issue opinions on matters of general principle—but not on any type of specific dispute. It has no authority to pass on any specific disputes, perhaps least of all on the many territorial disputes that exist either among the American Republics or between any of those Republics and any other state. Nor does the committee have any procedures for hearing arguments or evidence in regard to conflicting claims.

The January 1976 resolution in regard to the Malvinas Islands—or Falklands—was adopted by 7 of the 11 members of the committee, on the basis of an entirely *ex parte* presentation. On a similar basis, the committee had earlier undertaken to pronounce itself in favor of Panamanian claims to the Canal Zone. Later, in 1979, a resolution adopted by a bare majority—6 of the 11 members—ventured into yet another territorial dispute, this time with regard to Guatemalan claims to Belize. I have been a member of the Inter-American Juridical Committee since 1974, but was not present during either the Canal Zone or the Falklands discussion. I was present for the Belize discussion. At that time, I filed an opinion objecting to the Belize resolution, and stating what

I believe to be obvious, that in all three cases—and any other attempts to intrude in disputes between states—the committee acted with no authority, and that its opinions in all three cases were entirely void. Individual members are of course free to say, as individuals, whatever they wish. But as a collective body, and as an organ of the OAS, the committee is without jurisdiction, and its opinions on such matters, as a collectivity, are entitled to no weight whatsoever.

When the Belize resolution was discussed in the OAS, there was general approval of my views on the jurisdiction of the committee, perhaps because territorial claims there involved not only Guatemala and the United Kingdom (not to speak of the inhabitants of Belize), but also Mexico. It is unfortunate that the Ministers of Foreign Affairs decided nonetheless to rely on an obviously invalid declaration re the Falkland Islands of the Inter-American Juridical Committee. It would be sad indeed if there were not better justifications for a call for the cessation of hostilities. And it exacerbates matters that no mention was made of the rights and interests of the inhabitants of the islands, despite the fact that the Belize resolution explicitly referred to such rights.

This action by the Ministers is particularly unfortunate because it inevitably calls into question the willingness of the OAS to adhere to its own Charter. The Juridical Committee is considered to be one of the principal organs of the OAS. But, as I stated in my 1979 opinion, its willingness "to take positions in specific and controverted cases, rather than confining itself to discussion of principles, jeopardizes the status of the Committee and inevitably gives rise to question as to its role in the Inter-American system."

SEYMOUR J. RUBIN*

HARDY CROSS DILLARD (1902–1982)

Hardy Cross Dillard, a member of the Editorial Board of this *Journal* since 1955, died on May 12, 1982, in his eightieth year. He was an inspiring figure in our profession, a wise and beloved colleague and friend. His illustrious and varied career—as a law school teacher and dean, military officer, leader of the bar, scholar, and writer—culminated in his service as a Judge of the International Court of Justice in the years 1970–1979. On April 23, 1982, he was awarded the Manley O. Hudson Gold Medal by the American Society of International Law for his outstanding services to international law and for promoting international relations on the basis of law and justice.

Judge Dillard brought to his judicial role the wide learning and humanistic concerns that graced his writing and teaching. The individual opinions he wrote on the Court are evidence of his sensitivity to the fundamental dilemmas faced by international law generally. Perhaps more than any other judge in recent times, Judge Dillard looked beyond the field of international law for understanding of the issues presented to the Court. He drew upon his knowledge of contract and property law for felicitous analogy; he turned to moral philos-

* These views are the personal views of the author.

ophy to reveal underlying assumptions; he reminded us of socio-historical forces and of the human drives that moved governments and institutions. Remarkably, he did this without pedantry and in a graceful, unpretentious manner.

We must turn to his lectures, addresses, and occasional essays to get the full flavor of Hardy Dillard's play of mind. His interest was largely in the imponderables of law and human aspirations, but there was nothing ponderous in his discourse. With wit and humor, he illustrated the abstract with anecdotes, stories, actual cases culled from a vast repertory. Poker games, sporting events, Southern folklore, lawyers' tales, wordplay figured prominently in his discourse. Interspersed were observations of Aristotle, Santayana, Whitehead, contemporary logicians and linguistic analysts. Only the dullest could fail to be stimulated.

Hardy Dillard's distinctive flavor—especially his "Dillard" stories—reflect his Southern background and education. He was born in New Orleans; his father was a professor of classical languages. Surely much of Hardy Dillard's fascination with language and humanistic ideas may be attributed to an early and continuing exposure to classical learning. His father was not an "ivory tower" classicist. He took an active part in efforts to overcome the handicaps imposed on the black population of the South, especially in regard to university education. (Dillard University in New Orleans is named for him, a tribute to his work for black education.) Hardy Dillard continued in that tradition, opposing segregation and advocating the complete removal of racial barriers in education and elsewhere. As a member of the Commission to Revise the Constitution of Virginia (in 1968) he had a gratifying opportunity to give effect to these views.

Hardy Dillard's education included (atypically for international lawyers) a BS degree of the Military Academy at West Point, a factor of some importance in his later career. West Point was followed by law studies in Charlottesville (LLB 1927), two years of practice in New York City, and then membership on the faculty of the University of Virginia Law School. He remained on that faculty for about 40 years (with time out in World War II) and served as its dean from 1963 to 1968. In World War II his West Point background, his teaching, and his international legal knowledge made him a natural choice to direct the training of military government officers. By the end of the war, he had the rank of colonel and several military awards including the Legion of Merit (Oak-Leaf Cluster). He rounded out his military career as Director of Studies at the National War College (1946–1947). Later he served as a legal adviser to the High Commissioner in Germany (1950) and as an adviser to the Air Force Academy (1966–1970).

He began his teaching of international law in 1929 and continued with it throughout his teaching career. He also taught other subjects: jurisprudence, contracts, constitutional law, and comparative law. His knowledge of these fields gave him insights into international law that probably would not have occurred to the more specialized international lawyer. His published writing on international law increased markedly in the 1950's,[1] often in connection

[1] A selected bibliography of his writings up to 1968 may be found in the *Virginia Journal of International Law* for April 1968.

with "distinguished lectureships" in various universities, here and abroad. The lectures given by him at the Hague Academy of International Law in 1957, under the title of *Some Aspects of Law and Diplomacy*,[2] gave him an opportunity to range broadly over the field. They are "vintage Dillard" and remain pertinent today. Elected to the Editorial Board of the *Journal* in 1955, he took an increasingly active role in *Journal* affairs and in the American Society of International Law. (He served as President of the Society in 1962–1963.) One of his principal interests in the Society was the inauguration of the ambitious program of studies placed under the aegis of an interdisciplinary Board of Review and Development. During the formative period of this program, Professor Dillard did much to ensure that a strong-minded group, divided over methodology and political stands, adjusted their differences so that a coherent plan of work would emerge. The aims of that program were close to his heart because they fitted well into his conception of international law. That conception was summed up by him not long ago in the following sentence: "[I]nternational law should be realistic, creative, and axiologically oriented; it should take account of social psychology, sociology, economics, and politics, and it should furnish a functional critique in terms of social ends rather than in terms of the norms themselves."[3] He went on to add that the social ends served by law must not be "chimerical ends subjectively appraised, but realizable ends objectively assessed."[4] He appreciated that this was an ideal and that subjective preferences could not be entirely eliminated in the creation or application of law. Yet he felt it important that a line be maintained between legal and political decisions, for otherwise the law becomes "subservient to whatever those in authority say is good."[5] The problem of demarcation was one he often returned to, always conscious of the limits of law but convinced of its essential value in counteracting arbitrary and irrational political action.

A final word needs to be said about his contribution to this *Journal*. His articles and comments speak for themselves. But at least equally significant was his behind-the-scenes role, especially in evaluating and commenting on manuscripts submitted for publication. He welcomed that role; even when seriously ill he requested that manuscripts be sent to him. He read them with care and often did his own research so as to comment more effectively. His primary aim was to improve the quality of the submissions and he took pleasure, as well as pains, in performing that task. Many contributors, though they are not aware of it, owe him much, as do our readers. To Hardy Dillard, international lawyers were all part of a common collegial enterprise. He valued diverse views and he bestowed praise widely and generously. He will long be remembered for his encouragement, for his penetrating questions, and for the light he shed on the perplexities of our discipline.

OSCAR SCHACHTER

[2] 91 RECUEIL DES COURS 447 (1957 I), also published separately by A. W. Sijthoff (Leiden 1957).

[3] Book Review, 18 VA. J. INT'L L. 181, 190–91 (1977).

[4] *Id.* at 191.

[5] *Id.* at 189. *See also* Dillard, *The Policy-Oriented Approach to Law*, 40 VA. Q. REV. 627 (1964).

NOTES AND COMMENTS

Large-Scale Migrations of Asylum Seekers

The formidable problems posed by massive movements of asylum seekers have drawn increasing international attention. Such problems, one should remember, are not new, even though some of the recent debate tends to treat them as though they were.[1] The basic charter of modern refugee law, the United Nations Convention relating to the Status of Refugees,[2] was meant in significant measure to deal with the large-scale movements of World War II. Hundreds of thousands of homeless people, still in need of protection and secure resettlement, remained dispersed throughout Europe when the treaty was drafted in 1951.[3] Starting in 1956, over two hundred thousand left Hungary precipitously, largely bound for distant resettlement. And perhaps ten million people fled into India in 1971 from what was then East Pakistan; most returned after the birth of Bangladesh. Other examples during this period, particularly in Africa, could be called to mind.[4]

Nevertheless, since 1975, when the Indochina exodus began, developments have seemed somehow to pose more acutely the problems associated with large-scale influx. As Malaysia, Thailand, Somalia, Pakistan, the United States, and others have found themselves the direct recipients of sudden large movements, all in a short span of years, international concern has mounted to new levels. Perhaps this reaction reflects in part the enhanced drama of exodus by small boats. Perhaps it stems from the expanded reach and greater impact of the modern media. It may also be explained by a keener public awareness that the world grows ever more crowded, and a resultant greater resistance to those who migrate. Beyond these factors, some of the recent migrations did exhibit a disturbing new characteristic: deliberate involvement of the government in forcing out large numbers of its citizens. Whatever the reason, the massive movements of recent years have evoked new efforts to deal with their causes, and they have inspired the international community to reconsider its basic approaches to protection and assistance and the legal framework for such action.

I. Source States: Root Causes

The Office of the UN High Commissioner for Refugees (UNHCR) repeatedly stresses that its role "is non-political and strictly humanitarian."[5] This

[1] *See generally* C. Keely, Refugee Policy: The Case for a Development-Oriented Strategy 14–25 (1981).

[2] 1951 Convention relating to the Status of Refugees, *entered into force* Apr. 22, 1954, 189 UNTS 137.

[3] *See* Sadruddin Aga Khan, *Legal Problems Relating to Refugees and Displaced Persons*, 149 Recueil des Cours 287, 301 (1976 I); L. Holborn, Refugees: A Problem of Our Time 36–43, 57–64 (1975).

[4] *See* Sadruddin Aga Khan, *supra* note 3, at 301–09.

[5] This particular comment appears in the statement submitted by UNHCR to the Secretary-General's compilation titled International Co-operation to Avert New Flows of Refugees, Report

declaration vastly understates the adroit political maneuvering the UNHCR has undertaken and must continue in order to fulfill its humanitarian mission: assuring assistance and legal protection to the world's displaced. But the slogan, inaccurate as it is, probably facilitates the political work that remains, *sub silentio*, in UNHCR's field of action. Governments undergoing the stresses provoked by refugee flows doubtless find it easier to cooperate in what can be billed as a purely humanitarian effort. Moreover, the slogan accurately reflects certain genuine limits on UNHCR's role, limits observed as the necessary price of UNHCR's relative insulation from many of the political controversies that have riven the United Nations. The Office generally steers wide of assessing blame for refugee flows or tracing root causes to human rights abuses, aggression, or other misbehavior of governments. At the level of formal pronouncements, refugee flows simply exist, and UNHCR functions to assure that the individuals swept up in them receive care and protection.

Although this basic delimitation of UNHCR's function evolved for sound reasons, the resulting UN institutional structure bears certain real disadvantages. None of the other UN organs theoretically responsible for the more controversial political aspects of refugee affairs carries any focused responsibility at all comparable to the mandate of the High Commissioner. As a result, when large numbers of refugees cross a border, the international limelight too often fastens on the receiving countries; their actions are subjected to minutely critical scrutiny, while the sending countries, the real sources of the problems, remain happily in the shadows.

Canada launched the first of the recent efforts to redress this imbalance. It charted its course carefully, believing that a lengthy process of world education on the causes of massive refugee flows, probably extending over several years, would be necessary. Otherwise, Canada feared a rush of support by Third World countries for resolutions hastily assigning all blame to the familiar UN villains of colonialism, Zionism, and apartheid.

Recognizing that massive exoduses often result from human rights abuses, Canada chose the UN Commission on Human Rights as its forum. In early 1980, at Canada's urging, the Commission adopted a resolution that called on source countries to cooperate "in helping to prevent and eliminate conditions which may precipitate such exoduses." The resolution further urged the Secretary-General to take a more active political role aimed at alleviating the human rights problems underlying the flight, and it asked him to prepare a summary of "findings and recommendations" on this subject for the next session of the Commission.[6]

---

by the Secretary-General, 36 UN GAOR (Agenda Item 66) at 43, UN Doc. A/36/582 (1981). The Statute of the Office of the United Nations High Commissioner For Refugees, GA Res. 428 (V), Annex, para. 2, 5 UN GAOR Supp. (No. 20) at 46, UN Doc. A/1775 (1950), explicitly provides that the work of the High Commissioner shall be "of an entirely non-political character." *See* L. HOLBORN, *supra* note 3, at 89–90 (discussing this provision in the Statute).

[6] Commission on Human Rights, Res. 30, 36 UN ESCOR Supp. (No. 3) at 191, UN Doc. E/1980/13, E/CN.4/1408 (1980). The General Assembly later endorsed this approach and requested that the Commission on Human Rights provide further recommendations after receiving the Secretary-General's report. GA Res. 35/196 (Dec. 15, 1980).

The Secretary-General submitted a cautious three-page document as his report. Noting that root causes of massive exoduses "are often very complex," the Secretary-General asserted that he does indeed take suitable measures to alleviate such situations, including references to human rights denials where appropriate. But he warned that public disclosure of the details of these efforts might only prejudice future attempts. In any event, his report carefully avoided any descent into such details.[7]

At its 1981 session, the Commission therefore looked elsewhere for steps to continue this initiative. It adopted a resolution asking the Secretary-General to appoint a special rapporteur to study the question of human rights and massive exoduses.[8] When Prince Sadruddin Aga Khan, a former High Commissioner for Refugees and a respected international figure, was named as the rapporteur, hopes soared in some quarters that the report would spell out in detail the human rights abuses that have helped launch massive migrations and would open clear avenues for effective and creative dealing with root causes.

The rapporteur's study did not fulfill those hopes.[9] Hard-hitting, country-specific findings of human rights abuses probably could not be expected of a diplomat engaged in his own campaign for the post of Secretary-General (although, of course, it was not known at the time of appointment that the Prince would be a candidate). In any event, as the report itself suggests, the world's relative inaction on root causes stems less from a lack of creativity about what to do than from a lack of political will to do it.[10]

The report's treatment of core human rights issues is disappointing. A rather perfunctory section moves article by article through the Universal Declaration of Human Rights, only to confirm, unsurprisingly, that violation of those rights indeed may play a role in massive exoduses. This discussion proceeds in abstract terms and does not address specific situations. Later sections of the report are devoted to a broader description of various "push" and "pull" factors that lead to massive migrations. The approach in the latter sections, emphasizing impersonal forces and factors, is almost clinical. Certainly, many such factors lie beyond the reach of deliberately crafted changes. But reading the report, one almost loses the sense that human decisions contribute to the persecution, suffering, or privation that drives people out, and that humans therefore have some obligation to strive to redress the situation.[11]

Some of the momentum for attention to root causes derived from dissatisfaction with the July 1979 Geneva conference convened to consider the refugee crisis in Southeast Asia. The agenda for that meeting was oriented almost exclusively toward "humanitarian" issues of relief and resettlement, and attempts were made to thwart statements condemning Vietnam for causing the outflow. *See* Alvarez, *United Nations Meeting on Refugees and Displaced Persons in South-East Asia*, 21 HARV. INT'L L.J. 290 (1980).

[7] Question of the Violation of Human Rights and Fundamental Freedoms in any Part of the World, with Particular Reference to Colonial and Other Dependent Countries and Territories, Report of the Secretary-General, Commission on Human Rights, UN Doc. E/CN.4/1440 (1981).

[8] Commission on Human Rights, Res. 29, 37 UN ESCOR Supp. (No. 5) at 230, UN Doc. E/1981/25, E/CN.4/1475 (1981).

[9] Study on Human Rights and Massive Exoduses, Report by Special Rapporteur, Commission on Human Rights, UN Doc. E/CN.4/1503 (1981).

[10] *Id.* at (i).

[11] The original report contained three lengthy annexes describing mass exoduses over the last

The ultimate recommendations of the report, although modest, may contain the seeds of useful undertakings. They emphasize the need to assure a coordinated approach to both the country of origin and the country of asylum whenever a mass exodus seems likely or is under way. To this end the report recommends, in general terms, a UN early-warning system to detect incipient mass exoduses, and the appointment of a Special Representative for Humanitarian Questions as the central figure for both monitoring and mediation. Such a representative, the report suggests, could be assisted by a corps of "humanitarian observers" who, by establishing a presence in the affected region, might help ease tensions and perhaps contribute to earlier resolution of the crisis.[12]

Meantime, a separate initiative, spearheaded by the Federal Republic of Germany and addressed to the same set of problems, had been launched in the General Assembly. Germany's approach was more legalistic than Canada's, devoting considerable attention to the development of general international principles that might define more clearly the responsibilities of source countries.[13] Some supporters of the Canadian initiative felt misgivings about this proposal. They feared it might upset the measured pace of the educational effort they considered necessary. And a two-track approach, one in the General Assembly and one in the Commission, might only blunt the impact of each.

Despite these worries, the General Assembly adopted a German-sponsored resolution in late 1980. It expressed concern about the suffering and burdens caused by flows of refugees, and it invited member states and UN organs to submit comments and suggestions on "international co-operation to avert new flows of refugees and to facilitate the return of those refugees who wish to return."[14] As with the resolutions of the Human Rights Commission, the drafters chose their language carefully, to indicate that the quest is to remove the causes underlying such migration, rather than simply to bottle up the migrants. Nevertheless, some concern lingers that, whatever the original intention, the effect of the two initiatives will be to give countries new justifications for thwarting their citizens' basic right to leave.[15]

---

decade and also more general patterns of international migration during that period. Singled out for detailed attention were four case studies: Afghanistan, Ethiopia, Indochina, and Mexico. (The report acknowledges that the fourth such situation, the steadier flow of persons from Mexico to the United States, is not "a mass exodus of the classical type," but states that this study was included to round out the picture; such a flow "constitutes an increasingly familiar dimension to the over-all context of mass exodus." *Id.*, Ann. II, at 38.) These annexes provoked objections, both from some of the source countries depicted and from those who felt the source countries' actions had been treated too generously. Ultimately, a compromise was reached. The special rapporteur's report was sanitized by removing the offending annexes and all references to them. It was then "reissued for technical reasons," as the accepted euphemism describes it. UN Doc. E/CN.4/1503* (1981). (The original report, including the annexes, had been made widely available. It bears this same UN document number, minus the asterisk.)

[12] *Id.*, Recommendations at (i)–(ii). The report also contains general suggestions for improved provision of immediate relief aid and longer term development assistance. *Id.* at 44–50.

[13] *See* International Co-operation to Avert New Flows of Refugees, *supra* note 5, at 18–25 (submission by Federal Republic of Germany setting forth 10 principles as recommended "general guidelines for the conduct of States").

[14] GA Res. 35/124 (Dec. 11, 1980).

[15] A significant piece is missing from the "right to leave any country, including [one's] own,"

Over 30 states took up the General Assembly's invitation and tendered preliminary suggestions, though many of them noted the political difficulty of the undertaking and several went further to voice skepticism about its likely fruits. These comments were collected by the Secretary-General and submitted to the General Assembly's 36th session in late 1981.[16] The General Assembly took note of the comments and, overriding some resistance to the creation of another UN body, established a group of 17 governmental experts to develop recommendations on appropriate means for international cooperation to avert new massive flows of refugees. The group was specifically directed to take account of the special rapporteur's report to the Commission on Human Rights, expected within a few weeks.[17]

In light of this development, the Human Rights Commission's action in 1982 essentially marked the end to the two-track approach to the issue. The Commission thanked the special rapporteur for his report, urged him to continue discussions on his recommendations, and stressed that he should remain available for consultations with the group of governmental experts. In this way it seemed to suggest that the most important future action on this issue will take place in that separate venue, although "human rights violations and mass exoduses" will remain on the Commission's agenda.[18]

This new phase of attention to root causes may seem to have produced rather little in the way of concrete results. Certainly, it has spawned no breakthrough ideas holding clear promise of averting new flows, nor has it suggested how direct action on root causes could avoid the political deadlocks that block much UN action. The Canadian and German initiatives, however, have kept alive the fledgling recognition of institutional inadequacy in confronting countries

---

outlined in Article 13(2) of the Universal Declaration of Human Rights. That right means little unless one has somewhere else to go, yet the Declaration announces no corresponding right to enter anyone else's country. *See* H. LAUTERPACHT, INTERNATIONAL LAW AND HUMAN RIGHTS 349 (1950). A similar, but more subtle, gap appears in Article 14, which speaks of a right "to seek and to enjoy in other countries asylum from persecution." An earlier draft of this article recited a right to seek "and to be granted" asylum. The wording was changed because several nations feared the breach the original version implied in the traditional and jealously guarded prerogative of nations to control the entry of aliens. The right to seek and enjoy asylum therefore amounts to a right against the country of origin, not a claim against another state that the refugee might hope to enter. *See id.* at 421–23; Weis, *Recent Developments in the Law of Territorial Asylum*, 1 HUMAN RIGHTS J. 378 (1968). The desire of states to maintain control over entry likewise explains the dimensions of Article 13.

Since 1948, when the Declaration was adopted, a series of ad hoc resettlement efforts has succeeded, in general, in finding new homes for those who have chosen to leave or to seek asylum. As a result, the international community generally has escaped confronting too starkly the inevitable clash between control over entry and the expansive promise seemingly held out by Articles 13 and 14. Recurrent mass exoduses, accompanied by increasing resistance to resettlement, may strip the world of the luxury of this inattention. The resulting awareness is unlikely to lead to greater receptiveness to entry and relocation. A more mature realism about the scope of the right to leave or the right to seek asylum is perhaps the most to be hoped for. The real issue is whether any stiffer insistence that persons stay within their own borders will be accompanied by vigorous efforts to improve human rights observance in the would-be migrant's home country or instead will reflect simply a rather selfish retreat into stricter policing of national boundaries.

[16] International Co-operation to Avert New Flows of Refugees, *supra* note 5.

[17] GA Res. 36/148 (Dec. 16, 1981).

[18] Commission on Human Rights, Res. No. 1982/32 (March 11, 1982).

that are the sources of refugee flows. They have opened a new dimension to international concern about human rights abuses—a dimension that underscores the legitimacy of international action in the human rights field by calling attention to the tangible and intractable problems that may be visited on other states if abuses continue. And the initiatives have fostered a few tentative rounds of experimentation in trying to redress the institutional inadequacies. That experimentation is painfully far from success, but it deserves to be continued.

II. Receiving States: Protection and Assistance

The other half of the large-scale influx picture involves the practices of receiving states. Although these have not suffered from the same institutional inattention, some observers have suggested that the world has not adequately adjusted the individual-focused, European-centered approach of earlier years to deal with the massive influxes now experienced. Australia has taken the lead in pressing this issue. It urged the Executive Committee of the High Commissioner's Programme (Ex. Comm.), at its 1979 and 1980 meetings, to recognize and elaborate a concept of "temporary refuge" as a kind of intermediate level of protection appropriate to large-scale influxes.[19]

Australia's main argument ran as follows: When people are fleeing their home country in massive numbers, the indispensable first step in achieving a humane solution is their admission to another nation. Receiving nations are often reluctant to allow admission, however, both because they feel overwhelmed if forced to cope alone with the influx, and because they may understand that admission is tantamount to a grant of "asylum" in the strongest sense. "Asylum," Australia noted, has been used in different and potentially confusing ways. Sometimes it implies any form of protection, however rudimentary, even if the asylum seekers are confined indefinitely in bleak refugee camps.[20] In the stronger usage, it seems to denote the stage of rights and liberties appropriate to a durable solution[21]—perhaps the full array of protections, including free movement and rights to employment, guaranteed by the UN Convention and Protocol[22] to refugees lawfully in the country of refuge. This confusion, in the view of Australia's representatives, may have contributed to the failure of nearly all Asian nations to adhere to the Convention and Protocol.[23] In any event,

[19] Australia was not necessarily calling for a new treaty. The failure of the 1977 conference convened to prepare a convention on territorial asylum will probably deter new treaty-drafting efforts in this field for many years to come. *See generally* A. GRAHL-MADSEN, TERRITORIAL ASYLUM (1980). Australia instead meant its proposal primarily to precipitate explicit recognition, clarification, and improvement of existing practices—practices that are consistent with existing treaties but not extensively addressed therein.

[20] *See, e.g.*, 43 INSTITUT DE DROIT INTERNATIONAL, ANNUAIRE 376 (1950). *See generally* 2 A. GRAHL-MADSEN, THE STATUS OF REFUGEES IN INTERNATIONAL LAW 3–6 (1972).

[21] *See, e.g.*, Arts. 1(1) and 2 of Draft Convention on Territorial Asylum, prepared by Carnegie Endowment Working Group, Jan. 15, 1972, *reprinted in* A. GRAHL-MADSEN, *supra* note 19, at 174; Refugees Without an Asylum Country, Concl. 15 (XXX), 30 Ex. Comm. of UNHCR, paras. (a) and (c), 34 UN GAOR Supp. (No. 12), UN Doc. A/34/12/Add.1 (1979).

[22] 1951 Convention relating to the Status of Refugees, *supra* note 2; 1967 Protocol relating to the Status of Refugees, *entered into force* Oct. 4, 1967, 19 UST 6223, TIAS No. 6577, 606 UNTS 267.

[23] Some progress has been made on this score since Australia voiced these concerns. Japan and the Philippines became parties to both the 1951 Convention and the 1967 Protocol in 1981.

both clarification of the receiving state's immediate obligations and improved practices to encourage international help are sorely needed.

Clear elaboration of a "temporary refuge" concept would serve both ends, Australia argued. The term itself has appeared, although somewhat erratically, in resolutions of the Ex. Comm. since 1977. For example, reacting to refusals by Southeast Asian nations to allow refugee boats to land, the Ex. Comm. in 1979 called for more liberal admission policies and stressed that in large-scale influxes, "persons seeking asylum should always receive at least temporary refuge."[24]

Though the terminology may be relatively new, Australia pointed out, the phrase certainly does not describe a new reality. Persons involved in such massive flows of asylum seekers almost always enter a receiving state outside the ordinary lawful channels. Article 31(2) of the UN Convention, governing treatment of refugees unlawfully in the country of refuge, specifically recognizes that restrictions on the movements of such entrants may be permissible. The article's only limitation on confinement is a cryptic one: the restrictions must be deemed "necessary." Moreover, Article 31(2) envisages that in some circumstances such refugees' movements may remain restricted indefinitely (until they are able to move on to another country) and their presence in the receiving country will not be regularized.[25] Nevertheless, they will still enjoy the most important protection, for they are shielded against return to the state that threatens persecution, under the *non-refoulement* guarantee of Article 33.

Australia proposed that the term "temporary refuge" be used consistently and exclusively to describe this more limited form of protection extended in accordance with Article 31. Other similar phrases that have appeared occasionally—including "temporary asylum"[26] and "provisional asylum"[27]—should be avoided as confusing. As a corollary, Australia urged that the term "asylum" be applied only when the broader array of protections and rights appropriate to a durable solution has been achieved. Such clarity of usage, Australia sug-

[24] Refugees Without an Asylum Country, *supra* note 21, at para. (f) (1979 resolution). The term's first appearance in an Ex. Comm. resolution is contained in Asylum, Concl. 5 (XXVIII), 28 Ex. Comm. of UNHCR, 32 UN GAOR Supp. (No. 12), UN Doc. A/32/12/Add.1 (1977). (This usage is new. Formerly, "temporary refuge" denoted instead limited protection given in diplomatic facilities against, *e.g.*, mob violence. *See* 2 A. GRAHL-MADSEN, *supra* note 20, at 6; 75 AJIL 142 (1981).)

[25] 1951 Convention, *supra* note 2, Art. 31(2). This is not to deny that Article 31 is chiefly devoted to setting forth *protections* required even for refugees unlawfully in the country of refuge, principally protection against the imposition of penalties for illegal presence, provided that the refugee comes directly from a country where persecution was threatened and presents himself promptly to the authorities of the receiving state. *Id.*, Art. 31(1). Nevertheless, even while protecting against penalties of that sort, the article plainly countenances significant restrictions. Other articles of the Convention underscore the permissibility of such restrictions because their protections apply only to refugees "lawfully in" or "lawfully staying in" the country of refuge. *See, e.g.*, Arts. 17, 18, 19 (gainful employment), Arts. 23, 24 (public relief and social security), and Art. 26 (freedom of movement).

[26] *See, e.g.*, General, Concl. 11 (XXIX), 29 Ex. Comm. of UNHCR, 33 UN GAOR Supp. (No. 12), UN Doc. A/33/12/Add.1 (1978); General, Concl. 14 (XXX), 30 Ex. Comm. of UNHCR, 34 UN GAOR Supp. (No. 12), UN Doc. A/34/12/Add.1 (1979).

[27] *See* Art. 3(3) of 1967 Declaration on Territorial Asylum, GA Res. 2312, 22 UN GAOR Supp. (No. 16) at 81, UN Doc. A/6716 (1967), *reprinted in* A. GRAHL-MADSEN, *supra* note 19, at 161.

gested, would reassure states receiving massive influxes that admission is not necessarily tantamount to asylum. Admission in such circumstances implies only the lesser, but nonetheless significant, protections of "temporary refuge." Australia was not calling, however, for mere acquiescence in the most restrictive practices of states that have set up primitive refugee camps. Instead, the international community should flesh out the skeleton of Article 31 by specifying appropriate minimum standards of treatment to be accorded those given temporary refuge.

The other problem remains: the need for international assistance. But Australia saw in "temporary refuge" some contribution toward a solution to this problem as well. A nation's choice to extend only temporary refuge, it argued, would serve as a signal to the international community that the receiving country urgently needs assistance. In this sense, the concept of temporary refuge could provide a way "to link admission of refugees with international solidarity."[28]

At both the 1979 and 1980 Ex. Comm. meetings, the proposal met with a decidedly mixed response. Skeptics feared that elaboration of a new concept would only erode protections already available to asylum seekers under existing treaties and international practice. If temporary refuge were seen too readily as a less burdensome response than full refugee status, receiving states would be tempted to afford only the lesser protections. They might also seize on the practice of temporary refuge as a way of absolving themselves of responsibility for any part in a durable solution.

Faced with a marked division of opinion at the 1980 session, the Ex. Comm. temporized. The resolution noted the "extensive practice" of temporary refuge during large-scale influxes, but balanced that observation with a reference to the practice's "exceptional character." The Ex. Comm. further affirmed the need "to define the nature, function and implications of the grant of temporary refuge," and it asked the High Commissioner to convene a group of experts "to examine temporary refuge in all its aspects within the framework of the problems raised by large-scale influx."[29]

Fourteen government officials and legal scholars met in Geneva in April 1981 in response to the High Commissioner's call. The remarkable aspect of the group's "Conclusions," carefully considered line by line during the final two days of the meetings, consists in their studious avoidance of the term "temporary refuge."[30] Instead, circumlocutions like "asylum on a temporary basis" appear throughout. The group of experts proved even more resistant than the Ex. Comm.'s members toward giving any blessing to what might be seen as a firm new legal concept or status clearly separate from full refugee status.

Two main strands of resistance to the Australian proposal ran through the deliberations. The first, pressed especially by several European members of the

[28] Memorandum, Australian Views on the International Protection of Refugees: Temporary Refuge and International Solidarity (presented at the Ex. Comm. meeting, Geneva, Oct. 1980, mimeo).

[29] Temporary Refuge, Concl. 19 (XXXI), 31 Ex. Comm. of UNHCR, 35 UN GAOR Supp. (No. 12A), UN Doc. A/35/12/Add.1 (1980).

[30] UNHCR, Report on the Meeting of the Expert Group on Temporary Refuge in Situations of Large-Scale Influx, UN Doc. EC/SCP/16, paras. 37–43 (1981).

group, lay in a renewed concern over the erosion of existing protections. Australia had described temporary refuge as a link between admission and international solidarity. That linkage, some feared, might work in reverse. The receiving state might invoke the failure of international support to justify terminating the refuge (which, after all, is labeled "temporary") and returning the asylum seekers to the country they had fled. Temporary refuge might therefore weaken the paramount commitment to *non-refoulement*. Plainly, Australia had not intended such a result, but it was seen as a genuine danger. The second strand of opposition appeared principally in the interventions of African members of the group. Pointing to the broad definition of "refugee" in the OAU refugee treaty[31] and to many African nations' impressive record of receptivity to large populations of refugees, they suggested that the drive for temporary refuge reflected only a regional problem affecting Southeast Asia. A new universal concept was not needed to redress a regional difficulty. Against this combined resistance, the Australian proposal for terminological clarity made no headway.

Ironically, however, even as the group of experts voiced its doubts and avoided Australia's preferred terminology, its formal Conclusions reveal a basic acceptance of the practice for which Australia sought recognition. The final document readily acknowledges that first-asylum countries may be overwhelmed, unable to provide the full measure of a durable solution within their own borders. It therefore emphasizes the need for international burden sharing, and it offers general suggestions for improvement in the international machinery available to render emergency assistance. It reaffirms, as well, the importance of the involvement of the UNHCR, both in coordinating assistance and in fulfilling its traditional role of protection.

The most important part of the Conclusions probably consists of a lengthy list of standards outlining the minimum acceptable treatment of individuals who are part of massive influxes.[32] Article 31(2) of the UN Convention, the Conclusions note, "contains provisions regarding the treatment of refugees who entered a country without authorization." Because that article does not cover all aspects of the treatment of such individuals, however, additional elaboration is necessary.

The itemized list of standards, although lengthy, contains no real surprises. Some of the standards simply reaffirm those provisions of the UN Convention that apply to all refugees, even those not lawfully present in the country of refuge—such as protection against discrimination based on race, religion, or nationality; a right of free access to courts of law; and permission to transfer certain assets. Other guidelines are drawn from broadly accepted human rights standards, rooted in the Universal Declaration of Human Rights: family unity should be respected; asylum seekers should not be subjected to cruel, inhuman,

[31] Art. I, 1969 Organization of African Unity Convention Governing the Specific Aspects of Refugee Problems in Africa, *entered into force* June 20, 1974, 691 UNTS 14.

[32] UNHCR Report, *supra* note 30, para. 41. The group built on an earlier list of standards compiled by a group assembled to address refugee problems in Asia. *See* International Institute of Humanitarian Law, Report of the Working Group on Current Problems in the International Protection of Refugees and Displaced Persons in Asia (San Remo, Jan. 1981), para. 44.

or degrading treatment; they should receive the basic necessities of life, including food, shelter, and basic sanitary and health facilities. Still other standards are distilled from recent humane practices in refugee camps: for example, the sending and receiving of mail should be allowed; where possible, there should be arrangements to record births, deaths, and marriages.

At its meeting in October 1981, the Ex. Comm. adopted the group's Conclusions with only two changes meriting comment here.[33] First, it strengthened the hortatory passages calling for improved international cooperation and burden sharing. Second, rather than perpetuate the expert group's use of the potentially confusing phrases "asylum on a durable basis," and "asylum on a temporary basis," the Ex. Comm. chose to substitute the notion of "admission" for "asylum." The Ex. Comm.'s version states that if a receiving state "is unable to *admit* them [asylum seekers] on a durable basis, it should always *admit* them at least on a temporary basis" and provide protection in accordance with the principles spelled out in the statement.[34] This change may well achieve added terminological clarity. Clarity is purchased, however, not as Australia had hoped, by limiting the application of the term "asylum," but by refraining altogether from descriptive use of that potent word, a word long associated with humanitarian protection.

One important issue probably drew inadequate attention from both the Ex. Comm. and the group of experts, although it received more extensive treatment at a later meeting in San Remo, Italy, described below. That issue is the problem of definition: who is entitled to claim protection and aid when asylum seekers arrive in large numbers?

The UN Convention and Protocol provide one potential answer, in their familiar but rather narrow definition of "refugee." In essence, a person qualifies as a refugee under these instruments if he is outside his country of origin and has a well-founded fear of persecution based on race, religion, nationality, membership in a particular social group, or political opinion, if he were to return.[35] This definition, however, leaves out many persons commonly thought of as refugees. For example, it does not cover most of those who flee the scene of an armed conflict, and armed conflict is a conspicuous source of many influxes that reach massive proportions. Similarly, the doubts have grown in recent years as to whether those now fleeing Vietnam fit the Convention definition or instead are "economic migrants," although the international community generally persists in responding to these persons as refugees. The same question has bedeviled the U.S. response to arriving Cubans and Haitians.

Whatever the merits of those particular debates, the United Nations has increasingly sensed a need to free at least a portion of the international response possible through the UNHCR from the narrow confines of the Convention definition. Successive resolutions of the General Assembly therefore have approved an expansion of the High Commissioner's responsibility to include a

[33] Executive Committee of the High Commissioner's Programme, Report on the Thirty-second Session of the Executive Committee of the High Commissioner's Programme, UN Doc. A/AC.96/601 (1981).

[34] *Id.* at 16 (emphasis added).

[35] 1951 Convention, *supra* note 2, Art. I(A)(2).

wider category of "displaced persons."[36] In parallel fashion, a growing body of opinion holds that the UN definition is obsolescent and should be replaced by a definition like the one contained in the OAU treaty. The OAU definition explicitly includes not only Convention refugees but also those who flee war, invasion, or civil strife.[37]

The Conclusions of the Geneva group of experts reflect the influence of this body of opinion—but in an oblique way that permitted the group to avoid addressing the definitional issue directly. An early paragraph (accepted without change by the Ex. Comm.) states that asylum seekers in large-scale influx situations may include both those escaping persecution and those fleeing war or civil disturbance.[38] Framed as a description, this passage is unassailable, and so the wording went largely unchallenged. But the key question is not the character of those who *seek* asylum; it is the character of those who have an internationally recognized *entitlement* to asylum (or protection or admission).

The San Remo meeting, a round table of 29 participants convened by the International Institute of Humanitarian Law,[39] led to a more searching discussion of this critical issue because some of the participants there questioned the wisdom of too sweeping an endorsement of the OAU definition.[40] It is indeed hard, they acknowledged, to quarrel with this broader definition for purposes of UNHCR involvement and the immediate emergency response. There simply is no time to do the individualized screening commonly necessary to apply the Convention definition, and in any event that definition does not mark the bounds of need for humanitarian action.

But adoption of the broader definition, without further qualification of the context in which it is to apply, would carry more profound implications. Under Article 33 of the Convention, a state's obligation not to expel or return (the *non-refoulement* obligation) protects only those who are "refugees," as defined in the Convention. For an asylum seeker, meeting the definition therefore means not only immediate protection, but also in most cases an entitlement to stay in the country of refuge indefinitely. Indefinite stay unavoidably results whenever third-country resettlement cannot be secured and no political change in the country of origin removes the threat of persecution. Nothing in current ex-

[36] *See, e.g.*, GA Res. 3143, 28 UN GAOR Supp. (No. 30) at 89, UN Doc. A/9030 (1973); GA Res. 68, 32 UN GAOR Supp. (No. 45) at 140, UN Doc. A/32/45 (1977); GA Res. 26, 33 UN GAOR Supp. (No. 45) at 139, UN Doc. A/32/45 (1978). *See also* ESC Res. 2011, 61 UN ESCOR Supp. (No. 1) at 2, UN Doc. E/5889 (1976) (commending UNHCR efforts on behalf of refugees, displaced persons, and "victims of man-made disasters"). For a general description of this evolution, see Sadruddin Aga Khan, *supra* note 3, at 301–10.

[37] 1969 OAU Convention, *supra* note 31, Art. I(1) and (2).

[38] UNHCR Report, *supra* note 30, para. 37.

[39] The meeting was officially titled Round Table on the Problems Arising from Large Numbers of Asylum Seekers, and it considered many other issues relating to protection and assistance. This group did not shrink from use of the term "temporary refuge," and its report gave a mild boost to usage of the term "asylum" in the sense of a durable solution. *See* International Institute of Humanitarian Law, Report of the Round Table on the Problems Arising from Large Numbers of Asylum Seekers (San Remo, June 1981), para. 10.

[40] Questions of this sort are also being raised elsewhere. *See, e.g.*, International Co-operation to Avert New Flows of Refugees, *supra* note 5, at 10 (comments submitted by Belgium); Ex. Comm. Report, *supra* note 33, para. 48.

perience suggests that either third-country resettlement or voluntary repatriation has become easier to achieve. As government leaders come to feel more acutely their own nation's vulnerability to large-scale influxes, and as they perceive growing resistance in third countries to sustaining high levels of resettlement, they are hardly clamoring for ways to narrow the range of their possible responses. In this nervous climate, it was argued, few states are likely to surrender in advance the ultimate option of returning to the home country large categories of persons not meeting the Convention definition.[41] Yet that is exactly what unqualified adoption of the OAU definition asks them to do.

One need not endorse this new restrictiveness, the round table's doubters pointed out, to acknowledge that it may rest on legitimate concerns. Receiving states are caught on the horns of a difficult dilemma, torn between an impulse toward humanitarian response and a feeling that hospitality only invites the flow to continue until it may become unmanageable. No definition can ever hope to resolve that tension completely. But no one wishing to have a genuine impact on states' practices can afford to ignore these palpable concerns. An unrealistic approach to the definition of "refugee," it was argued, might only render national leaders deaf to the otherwise sound humanitarian recommendations being advanced for dealing with large-scale influxes.

Ultimately, these doubts did not prevail. The final report of the San Remo round table contains a general endorsement of the broader definition as a basis for both assistance and protection in response to large-scale influxes.[42] A faint reflection of the doubters' concerns, however, appears in a later paragraph acknowledging obliquely that some asylum seekers might not be recognized as refugees.[43]

The overall problems provoked by large-scale influxes are sufficiently daunting, and the dilemma of receiving states is sufficiently intractable, that assuredly none of these meetings has spoken the last word on the legal framework for response. One may hope that the genuine difficulties implicit in any widening of the definition of "refugee" will command closer attention as the debate continues.

DAVID A. MARTIN*

[41] On the contrary, it may prove difficult to retain full protection even for the entire group of persons who do meet the Convention definition. For example, there are serious efforts under way in the United States to recant the Convention definition and protect only an even narrower category: those for whom the grounds for a fear of persecution existed *before* they left their home countries. *See* S. 776, 97th Cong., 1st Sess. §5, 127 CONG. REC. 2578 (1981) (introduced by Sen. Huddleston, with 7 cosponsors).

[42] Report of the Round Table, *supra* note 39, para. 8.

[43] *Id.*, para. 12.

* Assistant Professor of Law, University of Virginia. The author was a member of the Geneva group of experts and a participant in the San Remo round table. An earlier and considerably different version of this Note was submitted as a working paper for a UN Symposium on the Fundamental Human Rights of Refugees held in Tokyo in December 1981.

THE FRANCIS DEÁK PRIZE

The Board of Editors of the *American Journal of International Law* announces with pleasure the award of the Deák Prize for 1982 to Barry Buzan for his article, *Negotiating by Consensus: Developments in Technique at the United Nations Conference on the Law of the Sea*, which appeared in the April 1981 issue at page 324. The Deák Prize honors the memory of the late Francis Deák by recognizing especially meritorious contributions to the *Journal* by its younger authors.

The Board of Editors extends its congratulations to Dr. Buzan and its appreciation to Mr. Philip Cohen, President of Oceana Publications, Inc., through whose generosity an award is made to the recipients of the prize.

CONTEMPORARY PRACTICE OF THE UNITED STATES RELATING TO INTERNATIONAL LAW

MARIAN NASH LEICH*

The material in this section is arranged according to the system employed in the annual *Digest of United States Practice in International Law*, published by the Department of State.

EDUCATIONAL AND CULTURAL AFFAIRS

(U.S. *Digest*, Ch. 12, §2)

Illicit Import, Export, and Transfer of Cultural Property

A letter from Powell A. Moore, Assistant Secretary of State for Congressional Relations, to Senator Robert J. Dole, Chairman of the Senate Committee on Finance, dated March 9, 1982, set out the Department of State's report on S. 1723, a bill to implement the UN Convention on the Means of Prohibiting and Preventing the Illicit Import, Export and Transfer of Ownership of Cultural Property.

The proposed legislation was the successor to a bill originally submitted by the Department to the 94th Congress on July 31, 1975, a revised version of which was introduced in the 95th Congress as H.R. 5643 and was passed by the House of Representatives in 1977. (H.R. 5643 was subsequently considered by the Senate Committee on Finance but not reported out.) H.R. 5643, as it passed the House, was reintroduced in 1979 in the 96th Congress as H.R. 3403, and hearings were held. Reintroduced again in 1981 as S. 1723, the new legislative bill reflects changes following the 1979 hearings.

The Department of State supported S. 1723 with two suggested amendments.[1] The major portion of Assistant Secretary Moore's letter follows:

> As the Committee is aware, the Convention was adopted by the Sixteenth General Conference of UNESCO in 1970 by a vote of 77 to 1. The Senate gave its advice and consent to U.S. ratification of the Convention on August 11, 1972, but the deposit of the instrument of ratification is being held until the passage of implementing legislation. To date 45 countries have become parties to the Convention.
>
> The legislation is important to our foreign relations, including our international cultural relations. The expanding worldwide trade in objects of archaeological and ethnological interest has led to wholesale depredations in some countries, resulting in the mutilation of ceremonial centers and archaeological complexes of ancient civilizations and the removal of stone

* Office of the Legal Adviser, Department of State.

[1] The suggested amendments were intended (1) to clarify the authority of customs authorities to seize an item already admitted upon the basis of apparently satisfactory evidence, should it later be ascertained that the item would not have been admitted, had the correct facts been known; and (2) to require a setting out of "facts," rather than "belief," as a basis for certain required statements.

sculptures and reliefs. In addition, art objects have been stolen in increasing quantities from museums, churches and collections. The governments which have been victimized have been disturbed at the outflow of these objects to foreign lands, and the appearance in the United States of objects has often given rise to outcries and urgent requests for return by other countries. The United States considers that on grounds of principle, good foreign relations, and concern for the preservation of the cultural heritage of mankind, it should render assistance in these situations.

Under the Convention each party agrees to cooperate in a number of important respects to help protect the cultural heritage of other states. The most significant part of the Convention is Article 9, under which parties agree "to participate in a concerted international effort to determine and carry out" necessary corrective measures in cases in which a state's cultural patrimony is in jeopardy from pillage of archaeological or ethnological materials. Another important provision, Article 7(b) of the Convention, requires parties to prohibit the import of cultural property stolen from museums, or religious or public monuments or similar institutions and to take appropriate steps to recover and return such cultural property.

The legislation now before the Committee, as was the case with the Government bill submitted on July 31, 1975, focuses on these two main aspects of the Convention. Section 2 of the legislation deals with the pillage of archaeological or ethnological materials and provides that if the President has made certain significant determinations, and has considered the advice of a committee of experts, negotiations may be undertaken of agreements with other governments to restrict the importation of objects of archaeological or ethnological interest subject to or threatened by pillage. The agreements will define the objects to be protected. However, no agreement may enter into force with respect to the United States until the President determines that other nations having significant import trade in the archaeological and ethnological material have implemented, as part of a concerted international effort, import restrictions comparable to those of the United States. Once the United States has entered into the agreement, the United States would then issue regulations precluding entry of the objects in question into the United States.

Section 7 of the legislation would prohibit the importation into the United States of objects stolen from museums or religious or public monuments or similar institutions of another country and sets up procedures for seizure and judicial forfeiture of such objects and for their return to the countries from which they have been stolen.

As was true of the original Government bill, this legislation and the Convention it implements do not have retroactive effect, do not modify any state law regarding title to cultural property, and do not preempt any other remedies available under federal or state law.

S. 1723 is improved over the legislation originally submitted to the Congress in 1975. The legislation reflects accommodations made to views expressed by members of the archaeological, ethnological and museum communities as well as by the dealers in art objects, in hearings and meetings, when the bill was under consideration in the House in previous sessions.

In the light of the primary role of the International Communication Agency in the international cultural field, the bill is worded so that the

Director of the International Communication Agency has been substituted for the Secretary of State in Sections 4 and 5(e) of the bill, thereby assigning to the Director the responsibilities described therein. An amendment to this provision may be necessary if, as expected, the name of the International Communication Agency is changed back to the United States Information Agency.

In conclusion, the Department considers that the legislation before the Committee is long overdue, and the Department urges its expeditious consideration and early passage.[2]

Regional Peacekeeping

(U.S. *Digest*, Ch. 14, §5)

The Sinai Multinational Force and Observers

In identical letters dated March 19, 1982, to Thomas P. O'Neill, Jr., Speaker of the House, and Senator Strom Thurmond, President pro Tempore of the Senate, President Ronald Reagan reported deployment to the Sinai of U.S. military personnel and equipment as part of the Sinai Multinational Force and Observers, to carry out responsibilities in implementation of the 1979 Treaty of Peace between Egypt and Israel. The text of the President's letter follows:

> On December 29, 1981 I signed into law Public Law 97–132, a Joint Resolution authorizing the participation of the United States in the Multinational Force and Observers (MFO) which will assist in the implementation of the 1979 Treaty of Peace between Egypt and Israel. The U.S. military personnel and equipment which the United States will contribute to the MFO are now in the process of deployment to the Sinai. In accordance with my desire that the Congress be fully informed on this matter, and consistent with Section 4(a)(2) of the War Powers Resolution, I am hereby providing a report on the deployment and mission of these members of the U.S. Armed Forces.
>
> As you know, the 1979 Treaty of Peace between Egypt and Israel terminated the existing state of war between those countries, provided for the complete withdrawal from the Sinai of Israeli armed forces and civilians within three years after the date of the Treaty's entry into force (that is, by April 25, 1982), and provided for the establishment of normal friendly relations. To assist in assuring compliance with the terms of Annex I to the Treaty, so as to enhance the mutual confidence of the parties in the security of the Sinai border area, the Treaty calls for the establishment of a peacekeeping force and observers to be deployed prior to the final Israeli withdrawal. Although the Treaty called on the parties to request the United Nations to provide the peacekeeping force and observers, it was also recognized during the negotiations that it might not be possible to reach agreement in the United Nations for this purpose. For this reason, President Carter assured Israel and Egypt in separate letters that "if the Security Council fails to establish and maintain the arrangements called for in the Treaty, the President will be prepared to take those steps necessary to ensure the establishment and maintenance of an acceptable alternative multinational force."

[2] Dept. of State File No. P82 0042–2194.

In fact, it proved impossible to secure U.N. action. As a result, Egypt and Israel, with the participation of the United States, entered into negotiations for the creation of an alternative multinational force and observers. These negotiations resulted in the signing on August 3, 1981 by Egypt and Israel of a Protocol for that purpose. The Protocol established the MFO and provided in effect that the MFO would have the same functions and responsibilities as those provided in the 1979 Treaty for the planned U.N. force. Included are: the operation of checkpoints, reconnaissance patrols, and observation posts; verification of the implementation of Annex I of the Peace Treaty; and ensuring freedom of navigation through the Strait of Tiran in accordance with Article V of the Peace Treaty. By means of an exchange of letters with Egypt and Israel dated August 3, 1981, the United States agreed, subject to Congressional authorization and appropriations, to contribute an infantry battalion, a logistics support unit and civilian observers to the MFO, as well as a specified portion of the annual costs of the MFO. The U.S. military personnel to be contributed comprise less than half of the anticipated total MFO military complement of approximately 2,500 personnel.

In Public Law 97–132, the Multinational Force and Observers Participation Resolution, Congress affirmed that it considered the establishment of the MFO to be an essential stage in the development of a comprehensive settlement in the Middle East. The President was authorized to assign, under such terms and conditions as he might determine, members of United States Armed Forces to participate in the MFO, provided that these personnel perform only the functions and responsibilities specified in the 1979 Treaty and the 1981 Protocol, and that their number not exceed 1,200 at any one time.

In accordance with the 1981 Egypt-Israel Protocol, the MFO must be in place by 1300 hours on March 20, 1982, and will assume its functions at 1300 hours on April 25, 1982. Accordingly, the movement of U.S. personnel and equipment for deployment to the Sinai is currently under way. On February 26 five unarmed UH–1H helicopters (which will provide air transportation in the Sinai for MFO personnel), together with their crews and support personnel, arrived at Tel Aviv; on March 2 approximately 88 logistics personnel arrived at Tel Aviv; on March 17, the first infantry troops of the First Battalion, 505th Infantry, 82nd Airborne Division arrived in the Southern Sinai; and by March 18 a total of 808 infantry troops, together with their equipment, will have arrived. These troops will be equipped with standard light infantry weapons, including M–16 automatic rifles, M–60 machine guns, M203 grenade launchers and Dragon anti-tank missiles.

The duration of this involvement of U.S. forces in the Sinai will depend, of course, on the strengthening of mutual confidence between Egypt and Israel. The U.S. contribution to the MFO is not limited to any specific period; however, each country which contributes military forces to the MFO retains a right of withdrawal upon adequate prior notification to the MFO Director-General. U.S. participation in future years will, of course, be subject to the Congressional authorization and appropriations process.

I want to emphasize that there is no intention or expectation that these members of the U.S. Armed Forces will become involved in hostilities.

Egypt and Israel are at peace, and we expect them to remain at peace. No hostilities are occurring in the area and we have no expectation of hostilities. MFO forces will carry combat equipment appropriate for their peacekeeping missions, to meet the expectations of the parties as reflected in the 1981 Protocol and related documents, and as a prudent precaution for the safety of MFO personnel.

The deployment of U.S. forces to the Sinai for this purpose is being undertaken pursuant to Public Law 97–132 of December 29, 1981, and pursuant to the President's constitutional authority with respect to the conduct of foreign relations and as Commander-in-Chief of U.S. Armed Forces.[1]

[1] 18 WEEKLY COMP. OF PRES. DOC. 349–50 (March 29, 1982), 128 CONG. REC. S2513 (daily ed. March 22, 1982). *See also* 76 AJIL 181 (1982).

JUDICIAL DECISIONS

MONROE LEIGH

Aliens—equal protection—state requirement of citizenship for public employment

CABELL v. CHAVEZ-SALIDO. 102 S.Ct. 735.
U.S. Supreme Court, January 12, 1982.

José Chavez-Salido and other lawfully resident aliens were denied jobs as deputy probation officers with the Los Angeles County Probation Department because they failed to meet the citizenship requirement of section 1031(a) of the California Government Code for "public officers or employees declared by law to be peace officers."[1] The aliens brought suit in the United States District Court for the Central District of California challenging the constitutionality of the citizenship requirement under the equal protection clause of the Fourteenth Amendment. The district court found the citizenship requirement to be unconstitutional both on its face and as applied. The Supreme Court, in a five to four decision, reversed.[2]

Justice White, writing for the majority, held that where a statute, such as the one in question, deals with a matter resting firmly within a state's constitutional prerogatives and constitutional responsibility for its own government, a strict scrutiny test need not be applied. Whether a restriction on legally resident aliens serves political rather than economic goals is to be evaluated, said the Court, under the two-step analysis set forth in *Sugarman v. Dougall.*[3] First, the classification must not be substantially overinclusive or underinclusive, but must be sufficiently tailored to the government's claim that it serves legitimate political ends.[4] Second, even if so tailored, the classification may only be applied to persons who "participate directly in the formulation, execution, or review of broad public policy [and hence] perform functions that go to the heart of representative government."[5]

Applying this analysis, the Court concluded, first, that the California classification was sufficiently tailored to the state's sovereign powers to withstand

[1] California Government Code §1031(a) requires "public officers or employees declared by law to be peace officers" to be citizens of the United States. Section 830 of the California Penal Code declares that deputy probation officers shall be classified as peace officers.

[2] A three-judge court was properly convened, and appeal directly to the U.S. Supreme Court was available under the jurisdictional statute in effect at the time. 22 U.S.C. §§2281, 2284 (1976). The availability of three-judge courts has since been limited. Pub. L. No. 94–381, 90 Stat. 1119.

[3] 413 U.S. 634 (1973). *Sugarman* invalidated a New York statute that barred lawfully resident aliens from the competitive civil service on the ground that the statute was facially inconsistent with the equal protection clause of the Fourteenth Amendment.

[4] Because the statute in *Sugarman* indiscriminately included certain menial jobs and omitted other important political functions, the Court held that the classification was too imprecise to be deemed a proper exercise of the state's power to define its political community.

[5] 102 S.Ct. 735, 740 (quoting 413 U.S. at 647).

a facial challenge. Under the California Penal Code, peace officers are responsible for enforcing substantive areas of the law, have the power to make arrests, and receive training in the use of firearms. These powers, the Court reasoned, brought the classification in line with *Foley v. Connelie* (435 U.S. 291 (1978), 72 AJIL 923 (1978)), which upheld a New York statute requiring state troopers to be U.S. citizens.

The Court also held that the statute was constitutional as applied. The Court noted that deputy probation officers have the power to arrest, to supervise probation, to decide whether to institute judicial proceedings against juvenile offenders, and, moreover, have substantial discretion which must be exercised in the first instance without supervision. Thus, the Court concluded, these officers "sufficiently partake of the sovereign's power to exercise coercive force over the individual that they may be limited to citizens."[6]

Justice Blackmun, writing for the dissent, took issue with the majority's interpretation and application of *Sugarman* and *Foley*. First, Blackmun reasoned that the California statute should be examined under a stricter level of scrutiny, the application of which would render the California statute invalid on its face. As in *Sugarman*, Blackmun argued, the California legislature made no attempt to tailor the statute to positions where citizenship might arguably be relevant. Further, the history of the statute indicated that the California legislature had never made a reasoned judgment to exclude aliens from each individual peace officer position. Indeed, Blackmun noted, California counties apparently may appoint aliens to the positions of *chief* probation officer if the best interests of the county will be served.[7] Thus, the dissent concluded, the California requirement failed to meet *Sugarman*'s mandate that "the means the State employs . . . be precisely drawn in light of the acknowledged purpose."[8]

Second, the dissent found the statute to be unconstitutional as applied. As the Court had held in *Foley*, the state may exclude aliens from jobs involving the execution of public policy only when they constitute "one of the basic functions of government" and "fulfil[l] a most fundamental obligation of government to its constituency."[9] The dissent charged that the majority erred in holding that the position of deputy probation officer met this test, observing that deputy probation officers do not exercise a degree of discretion similar to that of policemen, judges, and jurors.

Cabell v. Chavez-Salido represents yet another example of the Burger Court's deference to state laws and practices. In reviewing the citizenship restriction in question, the Court was particularly reluctant to probe beyond the face of the statute to consider the sufficiency of the legislature's rationale. Instead, the Court was willing to defer to the state's perception of its sovereign function. Although this deference may be appropriate in certain cases, it is troubling to see the Court defer to a state's judgment at the potential expense of an individual's constitutional rights.

[6] 102 S.Ct. at 743.

[7] *Id.* at 750 (Blackmun, J., dissenting).

[8] *Id.* at 747 (Blackmun, J., dissenting, quoting 413 U.S. at 643).

[9] *Id.* at 748 (Blackmun, J., dissenting, quoting 435 U.S. at 297). *See also* Ambach v. Norwick, 441 U.S. 68 (1979), 73 AJIL 683 (1979).

Extradition—forcible abduction as a constitutional defense to federal jurisdiction—the "Ker-Frisbie" standard

UNITED STATES v. CORDERO. 668 F.2d 32.
U.S. Court of Appeals, 1st Cir., December 14, 1981.

In 1978, an undercover agent for the U.S. Drug Enforcement Administration, posing as a cocaine buyer in Panama, identified Josephine Cordero and William Sorren to Panamanian authorities as alleged drug dealers planning to smuggle cocaine from Colombia into Puerto Rico. The Panamanians arrested and jailed the defendants and later sent them by air to Venezuela. From Venezuela, the defendants were sent to Puerto Rico, where they were tried and convicted in the United States District Court for the District of Puerto Rico for conspiracy to import cocaine and for the use of interstate communications facilities in furtherance of that conspiracy.[1] The defendants appealed their convictions to the United States Court of Appeals for the First Circuit claiming, *inter alia*, that the trial court lacked jurisdiction. The court of appeals affirmed the convictions.

Defendants' jurisdictional attack was two-pronged. First, they argued that a federal district court has no jurisdiction over the person of any defendant whose return from refuge abroad is accomplished other than in accordance with the terms of an extradition treaty between the United States and the refuge state. In rejecting this contention, the court reasoned that treaties of extradition are made for the benefit of the governments concerned. Under international law, it is the contracting foreign government, not the defendant, that would have the right to complain about a violation. Thus, when the refuge state voluntarily releases a criminal defendant to the United States in a manner other than that which is described in the applicable extradition treaty, the federal court's jurisdiction over the defendant's person is unaffected.

> Extradition treaties normally consist of commitments between governments to the effect that each *will return* those accused of certain crimes at the request of the other. . . . Nothing in the treaty prevents a sovereign nation from deporting foreign nationals for other reasons and in other ways should it wish to do so.[2]

In this case, the court held, Panama and Venezuela initiated the deportations themselves; therefore, the manner in which the defendants were deported had no bearing on the federal court's jurisdiction.

As their second argument, the defendants asserted that the United States had obtained jurisdiction over their persons through an unreasonable invasion of their constitutional rights. The court disagreed, noting that, at most, the evidence showed that Panamanian and Venezuelan officials had mistreated the defendants while in custody. There was no evidence that the United States or any of its agents had engaged in, or were responsible for, any improper conduct. Accordingly, Panama and Venezuela bore full responsibility for any mistreatment alleged by defendants.

[1] Comprehensive Drug Abuse Prevention and Control Act of 1970, §§403(b), 1002, 1013, 21 U.S.C. §§843(b), 952, 953 (1976).

[2] 668 F.2d 32, 37.

In this regard, the court held that the defendants' appeal was controlled by the line of cases including *Ker v. Illinois* (119 U.S. 436 (1886)) and *Frisbie v. Collins* (342 U.S. 519 (1952)), which established the rule that obtaining jurisdiction over a defendant through forcible abduction, without more, will not defeat a federal court's jurisdiction. The court distinguished this case from *United States v. Toscanino* (500 F.2d 267 (2d Cir. 1974), 69 AJIL 406 (1975)), in which the Second Circuit held that federal courts do not have the power to try a defendant who has been forcibly abducted into a court's jurisdiction when such abduction included a deliberate, unnecessary, and unreasonable invasion by the U.S. Government of the defendant's constitutional rights. Observing that the only alleged mistreatment of the defendants occurred at the hands of Panamanian and Venezuelan officials, the court found no grounds for applying *Toscanino*, reasoning that a federal court's refusal to try prisoners held in the inhumane custody of foreign nations would not improve conditions of detention of those nations, but would merely afford a safe haven for fugitives.

Federal Kidnapping Act—foreign commerce jurisdiction—high seas jurisdiction

UNITED STATES v. MCRARY. 665 F.2d 674.
U.S. Court of Appeals, 5th Cir., January 11, 1982.

In 1974, Clifford McRary arranged to be transported on a sport fishing vessel from Key West, Florida to the Dry Tortugas. Approximately 8.5 miles off the Florida coast, McRary hijacked the vessel and forced the crew at gunpoint to transport him to Cuba. After conviction for violation of Cuban law and serving a prison term in Cuba, McRary returned to the United States, where he was arrested and charged with kidnapping in violation of the Federal Kidnapping Act (18 U.S.C. §1201 (1976 & Supp. IV 1980)).[1] That statute provides, in pertinent part:

> (a) Whoever unlawfully seizes, confines, inveigles, decoys, kidnaps, abducts, or carries away and holds for ransom or reward or otherwise any person, except in the case of a minor by the parent thereof, when:
>
> (1) the person is wilfully transported in interstate or foreign commerce; [or]
>
> (2) any such act against the person is done within the special maritime and territorial jurisdiction of the United States;
>
> . . .
>
> shall be punished by imprisonment for any term of years or for life.

The indictment charged that McRary unlawfully caused the captain and first mate of the vessel to be "transported in foreign commerce" in violation of section 1201(a)(1). At trial, McRary objected to the Government's contention that federal jurisdiction was based on transportation in foreign commerce and requested that the jury be instructed in the language of section 1201(a)(2) (high seas jurisdiction).[2] Apparently on the basis of testimony that Florida territory

[1] For a summary of earlier proceedings in this case, see 74 AJIL 939 (1980).

[2] The term "special maritime and territorial jurisdiction" as used in §1201(a)(2) is defined in 18 U.S.C. §7 (1976) to include any vessel on the high seas owned in whole or in part by a United States citizen. *See* 665 F.2d 674, 676 n.2.

extended 10.5 miles out to sea, the trial court declined to instruct the jury on high seas jurisdiction, and McRary was thereupon convicted of kidnapping in "foreign commerce." The U.S. Court of Appeals for the Fifth Circuit (per Henderson, J.) reversed on the ground that the judge's instructions to the jury were erroneous.

The appeals court held that jurisdiction in this case could not be predicated on transportation in foreign commerce. It interpreted the foreign commerce provision of section 1201(a)(1) to require both a forced departure from U.S. territory and a subsequent involuntary entry into a foreign state. The court concluded that the first of these two conditions was lacking because, contrary to the belief of the trial court, the territorial jurisdiction of the United States extends only 3 miles from its shores.[3] Thus, the court reasoned, since the kidnapping took place 8.5 miles from the Florida shore, it occurred on the high seas and not within U.S. territory.[4]

In support of its position that jurisdiction under section 1201(a)(1) exists only when there has been a forced departure from U.S. territory, the court observed that Congress clearly intended interstate or foreign commerce to require transportation from one state to another state or to a foreign country.[5] The court noted that the word "commerce" was "consistently preceded in the statute by 'interstate or foreign' without any hint that 'commerce' should have separate meanings for each."[6] In addition, the court observed that Congress had separately provided for kidnapping on the high seas by enacting section 1201(a)(2), which invokes federal jurisdiction on the high seas provided that the vessel in question is owned in whole or in part by U.S. citizens.[7] The court reasoned that this proviso would be undercut if it adopted the Government's argument, as

> the United States would be extending its jurisdiction to include acts committed in international waters even if there were no connection between the vessel and the United States. Such an expansion of domestic jurisdiction to vessels on the high seas with no attachment to the sovereign would be a clear violation of international law.[8]

Under the Fifth Circuit's holding, foreign commerce jurisdiction under section 1201(a)(1) may be defeated by kidnappers who are clever enough to wait until they are more than 3 miles beyond U.S. shores before producing their guns. Yet, as the court itself observes, the Federal Kidnapping Act was intended

[3] *See, e.g.*, United States v. Louisiana, 363 U.S. 1 (1960); 4 M. WHITEMAN, DIGEST OF INTERNATIONAL LAW 1–14 (1965).

[4] A further ground for the court's reversal was its finding that neither the failure to instruct the jury on high seas jurisdiction nor the denial to allege such jurisdiction in the indictment was harmless error.

[5] The court also relied on United States v. McInnis, 601 F.2d 1319 (5th Cir. 1979), in which the Fifth Circuit held that foreign commerce jurisdiction is not applicable when kidnappers contrive a plan in the United States to entice their victim into a foreign country so that he may be abducted there. As the court noted, however, *McInnis* did not present the precise issue confronted in *McRary*, where a kidnapping had already taken place before the victim entered the foreign state.

[6] 665 F.2d at 678.

[7] *See* note 1 *supra*.

[8] 665 F.2d at 678 (citing Geneva Convention on the High Seas, Apr. 29, 1958, 450 UNTS 82, TIAS No. 5200, 13 UST 2312, Arts. 2, 5, 6; United States v. Rodgers, 150 U.S. 249 (1893)).

"to prevent kidnappers from evading capture by moving from one jurisdiction to another."[9] The court's analysis does not provide compelling justification for this ironic result. While the statute in issue supports the court's holding that transportation from a state to a foreign country is necessary to foreign commerce jurisdiction, that fact alone does not compel the conclusion that the kidnapping must occur within U.S. territory. Moreover, even if the court were correct in holding that an unlawful act must occur within U.S. territory, its reading of section 1201(a)(1) seems overly restrictive. The statute expressly provides for jurisdiction in cases where a person transported in foreign commerce has been "inveigled" or "decoyed," as well as kidnapped. If these terms are to be given effect, they should certainly apply to the circumstances of this case.

Nor is the court's conclusion justified by the existence of high seas jurisdiction under section 1201(a)(2). In the present case, the application of this section would apparently have led to the affirmance of McRary's conviction by virtue of the U.S. registry of the hijacked vessel.[10] However, it would appear that under the court's holding a hijacker could escape liability under both parts of section 1201(a) if the vessel in question was not owned in whole or in part by U.S. citizens and if the hijacker waited to commandeer the vessel until after crossing the 3-mile territorial limit.

Foreign Agents Registration Act—scope of registration requirement for agents of foreign principals

ATTORNEY GENERAL v. IRISH NORTHERN AID COMMITTEE. 668 F.2d 159. U.S. Court of Appeals, 2d Cir., January 5, 1982.

In 1971, responding to a threatened enforcement action by the Attorney General, the Irish Northern Aid Committee (INAC) registered as the agent of a foreign principal under the Foreign Agents Registration Act (FARA) (22 U.S.C. §611(c)(1) (1976)).[1] INAC named as its foreign principal the Northern Aid Committee of Belfast, Ireland. INAC thereafter filed semi-annual registration statements with the Department of Justice. However, alleged deficiencies in its statements caused the Attorney General to order INAC to produce its books and records for inspection.[2] When INAC refused, the Attorney General brought an action in federal district court to enjoin INAC from violating various

[9] 665 F.2d at 677.

[10] In this regard, the court observed: "We agree with the government that under the evidence presented at the trial a jury could have found high seas jurisdiction." *Id.* at 680 n.10. It is unclear from the decision why McRary himself "submitted a request to instruct the jury in the language of 18 U.S.C. §1201(a)(2)," *id.* at 676, when the Government's failure to obtain such an instruction apparently saved McRary from being convicted under that section.

[1] Section 611(c)(1) defines the term "agent of a foreign principal" as:

> any person who acts as an agent, representative, employee, or servant, or any person who acts in any other capacity at the order, request, or under the direction or control, of a foreign principal or of a person any of whose activities are directly or indirectly supervised, directed, controlled, financed, or subsidized in whole or in major part by a foreign principal. . . .

[2] Attorney Gen. v. Irish N. Aid Comm., 346 F.Supp. 1384 (S.D.N.Y.), *aff'd mem.*, 465 F.2d 1405 (2d Cir.), *cert. denied*, 409 U.S. 1080 (1972).

provisions of FARA, claiming that INAC's registration statements were inaccurate and incomplete, primarily because INAC had failed to identify the Irish Republican Army (IRA) as its foreign principal.[3] INAC challenged the determination of the district court that it was an "agent of a foreign principal" as defined in FARA and that its foreign principal was the IRA. The district court granted the Attorney General summary judgment. On appeal, the Court of Appeals for the Second Circuit affirmed per curiam the district court's decision, adopting Judge Haight's "comprehensive opinion."

The Second Circuit chose to add to the district court's opinion in order "to express a note of caution concerning the statute's coverage of those who act at the 'request' of a foreign principal."[4] The district court had concluded that agency is established under FARA if the defendant is shown to be a "representative" of the IRA or acts at its "request." On appeal, INAC argued that the agency relationship must meet the standard of the *Restatement (Second) of Agency*, which focuses on "control" of the agent by the principal. The Second Circuit rejected this argument and concluded that in determining agency for the purposes of FARA the question "is not whether the agent can impose liability upon his principal but whether the relationship warrants registration by the agent to carry out the informative purposes of the Act."[5]

While acknowledging that FARA mandates registration by a person who undertakes certain acts at the "request" of a foreign principal, the Second Circuit warned that "this word is not to be understood in its most precatory sense. Such an interpretation," the court reasoned, "would sweep within the statute's scope many forms of conduct that Congress did not intend to regulate."[6] Noting the difficulty of interpreting the term "request," the court observed that the "surrounding circumstances" normally will indicate whether a "request" by a foreign principal triggers the reporting requirements of FARA. For instance, a finding of agency relationship is more likely when a foreign principal asks specified individuals to do specific acts than when a foreign principal simply issues a plea to members of a large religious, racial, or ethnic group for contributions or generalized political support.

The Second Circuit's opinion is consonant with current realities of foreign-domestic contacts. As the court of appeals pointed out, a broad interpretation of the term "request" could render all Americans who sent aid to earthquake victims in Italy "agents" of the Italian Government. The decision also comports with the clear expression of congressional intent in subjecting agents of foreign principals to the requirement of FARA. The House report accompanying the 1966 amendments to FARA states:

> Under existing law it is possible . . . to find an agency relationship (and thus the possibility of registration) of persons who are not, in fact, agents of foreign principals but whose acts may incidentally be of benefit to foreign interests. . . . This may have been desirable when the Foreign

[3] Attorney Gen. v. Irish N. Aid Comm., No. 77 Civ. 708-CSH (S.D.N.Y. May 1, 1981).

[4] 668 F.2d 159, 160–61.

[5] *Id.* at 161.

[6] *Ibid.*

Agents Registration Act was amended in 1942, but does not appear warranted in present circumstances.[7]

The decision thus hews closely to the fundamental purpose of FARA, which is to protect the integrity of the decision-making processes of the United States Government through public disclosure of foreign involvement in domestic affairs.

International Organizations Immunities Act—Foreign Sovereign Immunities Act—restrictive immunity—commercial activity

TUCK v. PAN AMERICAN HEALTH ORGANIZATION. 668 F.2d 547.
U.S. Court of Appeals, D.C. Cir., November 13, 1981.

Ronald Tuck, a Washington attorney, had contracted to provide legal services to the Pan American Health Organization's (PAHO) Staff Association. PAHO is an international organization that was integrated into the World Health Organization as its regional office in 1949. The Staff Association is a voluntary association formed by PAHO employees. Tuck filed suit in the United States District Court for the District of Columbia against PAHO and its Director, Dr. Hector Acuna, for interference with his contract of services, alleging both common law and constitutional violations. The district court dismissed the suit for failure to state a claim because of an absence of "state action." The Court of Appeals for the District of Columbia (per Edwards, J.) affirmed the dismissal of all counts against PAHO and Dr. Acuna in his official capacity and reversed dismissal of the common law claims against Dr. Acuna in his individual capacity. Unlike the district court, however, the court of appeals based its decision for dismissal on the ground that the defendants enjoyed immunity from such suit.

After disposing of the threshold jurisdictional issue, the court of appeals determined that the defendants were in most respects immune from suit. Citing *Broadbent v. Organization of American States* (628 F.2d 27 (D.C. Cir. 1980)), the court held that it need not decide whether the International Organizations Immunities Act of 1945 (IOIA) (22 U.S.C. §288a(b) (1976)), when read in light of the Foreign Sovereign Immunities Act (FSIA) (28 U.S.C. §§1604, 1605 (1976)), granted PAHO absolute or restrictive immunity. Tuck had alleged that PAHO engaged in the business of leasing commercial and residential property in the District of Columbia, which amounted to "commercial activity" within the meaning of the FSIA. The court, however, found no nexus between such activity and PAHO's supervision of its civil service personnel, which was the action of which Tuck complained. Thus, the court concluded that PAHO was immune from suit even under the less expansive restrictive immunity standard. For this reason it was unnecessary to decide whether the absolute immunity standard should be applied.

The court also found that IOIA expressly provided immunity to Dr. Acuna as to acts relating to his functions as PAHO's Director. The court recognized,

[7] H.R. REP. NO. 1470, 89th Cong., 2d Sess. 4, *reprinted in* [1966] U.S. CODE CONG. & AD. NEWS 2397, 2401.

however, that the IOIA would not automatically insulate Dr. Acuna from suit in his individual capacity and remanded the case for a determination with regard to Dr. Acuna's personal liability.

Treaties—military law—individual rights under treaties—constitutional rights of U.S. military personnel abroad

UNITED STATES v. WHITING. 12 M.J. 253.
U.S. Court of Military Appeals, January 18, 1982.

Kurt L. Whiting, a sergeant in the United States Air Force stationed in West Germany, was convicted by general court-martial for, *inter alia*, stealing mail matter and the unauthorized possession of classified documents. The evidence against Whiting was obtained after the U.S. base commander authorized a search of Whiting's off-base apartment without the consent of West German authorities. The Air Force Court of Military Review reversed the conviction, concluding that certain evidence should have been excluded since it was obtained in violation of the U.S. Government's obligations under the Agreement Between the Parties to the North Atlantic Treaty Regarding the Status of Their Forces, June 19, 1951 (4 UST 1792, TIAS No. 2846), and the supplementary agreement (hereinafter collectively referred to as the NATO Agreements). Upon a certified question from the Judge Advocate General, the U.S. Court of Military Appeals reversed the decision of the Air Force Court of Military Review and held that the NATO Agreements did not confer upon Whiting any rights to object to the admission of evidence because it was obtained by an unreasonable search and seizure.

The Court of Military Appeals (per Everett, C.J.) reviewed the language of Article VII of the NATO Agreement, which provides certain procedural safeguards for American military personnel who are tried in foreign courts. These safeguards include prompt and speedy trial, the right to confront accusers, and the right to counsel. Article VII also imposes an obligation on the United States and Germany to render mutual assistance in the investigation and collection of evidence needed to prosecute offenses committed by U.S. servicemen abroad.[1]

Based on the language of Article VII and the supplementary agreement, the Court concluded that

> nothing therein . . . purports to confer upon individuals any specific rights with respect to searches and seizures. Instead the obligations are placed

[1] Art. VII(2)(a) of the NATO Agreement states:

> The military authorities of the sending State shall have the right to exercise exclusive jurisdiction over persons subject to the military law of that State with respect to offences, including offences relating to its security, punishable by the law of the sending State, but not by the law of the receiving State.

Article VII(6)(a) states in relevant part: "The authorities of the receiving and sending States shall assist each other in the carrying out of all necessary investigations into offences, and in the collection and production of evidence, including the seizure and, in proper cases, the handing over of objects connected with an offence."

> on the contracting parties to assist one another in certain law enforcement activities, and the performance of those obligations is exclusively within the province of the Executive and Legislative Branches.[2]

Therefore, the court held, Whiting could not rely on an alleged violation of the NATO Agreements (*i.e.*, the base commander's failure to obtain West German authorization for the search) as a basis for excluding the evidence.

Judge Cook concurred, failing to see any "encroachment on an individual's expectation of privacy by the failure of military authorities to effect liaison with authorities of the host nation before execution of a valid military authorization to search."[3] He relied upon Military Rule of Evidence 315(c)(4)(B), which states that where a treaty or other agreement requires concurrence from the host country before conducting a search, noncompliance does not render the search unlawful.

Judge Fletcher dissented and criticized the majority for failing to apply the requirements of the U.S. Constitution. He observed that the absence of a specific right to challenge the search under the NATO Agreements "does not abrogate [Whiting's] right under the fourth amendment to object in an American court-martial to unreasonable search and seizure by our government."[4] In Judge Fletcher's opinion the military police had not complied with orderly procedures under the Manual for Courts-Martial and had therefore violated Whiting's Fourth Amendment rights.

Whether a treaty, in addition to establishing the rights and duties of the signatory governments, also confers rights on individuals will depend upon its language and the interpretation thereof. It is also a question of interpretation as to whether a treaty creates rights or obligations of a "self-executing" character.[5] A self-executing treaty is enforceable in U.S. courts without statutory implementation.[6]

The NATO Agreements in force between the United States and West Germany and examined by the court in this case contain no prohibition against unreasonable searches and seizures. Moreover, the U.S. obligation, if any, under the Agreements to obtain West German consent to a search would appear to be for the benefit of the German Government, in deference to its sovereignty, and not for the benefit of U.S. servicemen abroad. Thus, as far as Whiting's specific claim is concerned, the majority properly concluded that the NATO Agreements did not confer on Whiting individual rights enforceable in U.S. courts.[7]

The majority, however, did not consider Whiting's constitutional rights, the application of which might have led to a contrary result. There is evidence, for example, that the history of the NATO Agreement itself supports the appli-

[2] 12 M.J. 253, 255.

[3] *Id.* at 257.

[4] *Id.* at 259.

[5] *See generally* 14 M. WHITEMAN, DIGEST OF INTERNATIONAL LAW 302–05 (1970); L. HENKIN, FOREIGN AFFAIRS AND THE CONSTITUTION 158 (1972).

[6] *See, e.g.*, Hopson v. Kreps, 622 F.2d 1375, 1380 (9th Cir. 1980).

[7] *See, e.g.*, Pauling v. McElroy, 164 F.Supp. 390 (D.D.C. 1958), *aff'd*, 278 F.2d 262 (D.C. Cir. 1960).

cation of the Fourth Amendment to U.S. servicemen abroad. When the Senate gave its advice and consent to the NATO Agreement, it expressed grave concern over the prospect of American personnel being subject to foreign criminal justice. It passed a resolution expressing the sense of the Senate that if an American subject to U.S. military jurisdiction is tried by a foreign court, the U.S. commanding officer will be obligated to determine whether applicable foreign laws provided procedural safeguards comparable to those contained in the U.S. Constitution. If there is a danger that the individual would not be protected because of the absence of such safeguards, the commanding officer is obligated to request a waiver of host country criminal jurisdiction. (*See* 4 UST 1792, 1828, TIAS No. 2846.) The Senate's concern that servicemen appearing before *foreign* tribunals receive benefits comparable to those of the Constitution arguably implies that servicemen are also intended to enjoy such benefits, including freedom from unreasonable searches and seizures, in the administration of criminal justice by U.S. military authorities.

American jurisprudence provides general support for this conclusion. In *Reid v. Covert* (354 U.S. 1 (1957)), the Supreme Court held that Congress could not, in a capital case in time of peace, subject wives of American military personnel to court-martial jurisdiction and thereby deny them the right to be tried by a jury or indicted by a grand jury. The plurality opinion in *Reid* stated that "[w]hen the Government reaches out to punish a citizen who is abroad, the shield which the Bill of Rights and other parts of the Constitution provide to protect his life and liberty should not be stripped away just because he happens to be in another land."[8]

Since *Reid,* several courts have refused to apply the exclusionary rule—*i.e.,* the rule excluding as evidence the fruits of an unlawful search—to unreasonable searches and seizures by *foreign* officials, absent U.S. involvement in the search.[9] These decisions rest on the theory that since the exclusionary rule is a judicially created mechanism to deter improper searches by U.S. law enforcement authorities, it has no application to improper searches by foreign officials. By implication, the Fourth Amendment and the exclusionary rule do apply to unreasonable searches carried out by U.S. military police abroad.[10] Moreover, the Court of Military Appeals has elsewhere indicated that it will apply the exclusionary rule to evidence obtained from an unreasonable search, regardless of whether the search was conducted by foreign police acting alone or with American police assistance.[11]

[8] 354 U.S. 1, 6 (1957).

[9] *See, e.g.,* Stonehill v. United States, 405 F.2d 738 (9th Cir. 1968), *cert. denied,* 395 U.S. 960 (1969).

[10] *Cf.* Byars v. United States, 273 U.S. 28, 33 (1927).

[11] *See* United States v. Jordan, 1 M.J. 334, 338 (C.M.A. 1976).

United Kingdom Case Note

Banking—letter of credit—unenforceability based on IMF Agreement and the demands of international comity

United City Merchants (Investments) Ltd. v. Royal Bank of Canada. [1981] 3 W.L.R. 242.
Court of Appeal (Civil Division), March 13, 1981.

In this appeal, challenging dismissal of an action for payment under a confirmed irrevocable letter of credit, the English Court of Appeal held that the credit in question was an "exchange contract" contrary to the exchange control regulations of Peru and therefore partially unenforceable under the International Monetary Fund (IMF) Agreement, April 30, 1976 (29 UST 2203, TIAS No. 8937). The court also found the credit to be wholly unenforceable because of fraud.

Plaintiffs were Glass Fibres and Equipments Ltd. (Glass Fibres) of England, party to an underlying contract, and United City Merchants (Investments) Ltd. (UCM), as assignee of Glass Fibres. Glass Fibres had contracted for the sale of equipment to defendant Vitro Refuerzos S.A. (Vitro), a Peruvian corporation. Vitro had arranged payment by an irrevocable letter of credit through codefendant Banco Continental S.A. (Banco) of Lima, and the credit was confirmed by codefendant Royal Bank of Canada (Royal Bank).[1]

In 1975, Glass Fibres and Vitro agreed upon $256,043 as the sale price of the equipment. Shipment was to be made from London to Peru on or before December 15, 1976, and payment was to be made by Royal Bank's London branch by sight drafts against clean bills of lading on or before December 31, 1976. In July 1976, Glass Fibres assigned its rights and benefits under the letter of credit to UCM. Upon Vitro's request, Glass Fibres increased the machinery's purchase price with the understanding that the balance would serve for further purchases. Vitro requested that Glass Fibres deposit the money in excess of the original purchase price in the Miami account of a company closely associated with Vitro. Had the transaction been completed, "$331,043 would have found its way to the account" in Miami, to be held beneficially for Vitro.[2] The letter of credit thus became a vehicle for Vitro to exchange Peruvian sols for United States dollars.

The machinery was shipped to Peru one day later than the date agreed upon by the parties. UCM thereafter presented documents to defendants for payment, but the documents were rejected. Vitro did not take delivery of any of the equipment.

At the time of these transactions, both England and Peru were signatories

[1] So came about four contracts: (1) the contract between Glass Fibres and Vitro—on its face a contract for the sale and purchase of goods; (2) a contract between Vitro and Banco . . . for the opening of an irrevocable transferable letter of credit in favour of Glass Fibres for account of Vitro . . . ; (3) a contract between Banco and the defendants [Royal Bank] in March 1976 by which the defendants agreed to confirm the letter of credit, which Banco opened; (4) the contract between the defendants as confirming bankers and Glass Fibres as beneficiaries of the letter of credit of March 30, 1976, which is the contract sued on.

[1981] 3 W.L.R. 242, 249.

[2] *Id.* at 250.

to the IMF Agreement. The law in Peru prohibited most Peruvian corporations (including Vitro) from maintaining or establishing deposits in a foreign currency, whether in Peru or abroad, and the violation of this rule constituted fraud against the state.[3] The overvaluation of imports and obligations to be paid for in a foreign currency in contravention of the provisions of Peru's foreign exchange certificates system was also fraud against the state.[4]

When plaintiffs sued on the contract between Royal Bank as the confirming banker and Glass Fibres as beneficiary of the letter of credit, nonpayment was defended on two grounds: an IMF defense, and a fraud defense. First, defendants argued that the transaction was in violation of Peru's exchange control regulations and therefore unenforceable in England by reason of the Bretton Woods Agreement Order-in-Council 1946, which gave the force of law to Article VIII, section 2(b) of the IMF Agreement. Article VIII, section 2(b) states: "Exchange contracts which involve the currency of any member and which are contrary to the exchange control regulations of that member maintained or imposed consistently with this Agreement shall be unenforceable in the territories of any member."

In an extensive opinion authored by Lord Justice Stephenson, whose conclusions two other justices largely shared, the Court of Appeal first examined the question whether the letter of credit was an "exchange contract" within the meaning of Article VIII, section 2(b) of the IMF Agreement. The court rejected a broad definition of exchange contracts, *i.e.*, "contracts which in any way affect a country's exchange resources,"[5] and instead adopted a definition that included only contracts to exchange the currency of one country for the currency of another. Thus, the court held, unless a letter of credit can be shown to be a disguised agreement to exchange currencies, it will be considered no more than an agreement to pay dollars against documents.

Plaintiffs argued that banks' contractual obligations would be seriously undermined if the court were to uphold the defendants' refusal to honor the letter of credit. They contended that the court should not look beyond the face of the letter to its object and ultimate outcome, or to other contracts associated with it, including possible exchange contracts. The court agreed that "[c]redits, by their nature, are separate transactions from the sales or other contracts on which they may be based and banks are in no way concerned with or bound by such contracts."[6] In the present case, however, the court went further and examined the context of the overall transaction of which the letter of credit formed a part. It did not feel bound to close its eyes to the object of the contract and "fall over backwards to avoid complying with the demands of international comity."[7] While international commerce calls for enforcement of letters of credit, the court observed, international comity requires judicial enforcement of the IMF Agreement.

In this instance, the court found the letter of credit to be an unenforceable exchange contract. Stephenson reasoned that the integral function played by

[3] Decree Law 18,275 of May 15, 1970, Arts. 1 and 18, *quoted in* 3 W.L.R. at 250.

[4] Decree Law 18,891 of June 17, 1971, Art. 7, *quoted in* 3 W.L.R. at 250.

[5] 3 W.L.R. at 251 (quoting F. Mann, The Legal Aspect of Money 441 (3d ed. 1971)).

[6] 3 W.L.R. at 252.

[7] *Id.* at 258.

the letter of credit in carrying out the underlying sales contract tainted it with the same vice that infected the agreement between Vitro and Glass Fibres. Glass Fibres' overpayment and the special disposition of U.S. dollars in Miami betrayed the "wolf of an unenforceable exchange contract in the sheep's clothing of an enforceable sale contract."[8] Thus, the credit contracts, although ostensibly made for other purposes, were rendered unenforceable to the extent that they had as their ultimate object the exchange of currencies.

As to the defendants' second answer, the court held that under the circumstances fraud was a complete defense. The trial court had found that defendants were entitled to withhold payment because they were presented with a bill of lading that, although it conformed on its face with the terms of the credit, was falsely made by the person who issued it. Unchallenged findings established that the loading broker's employee fraudulently altered the date on the bills of lading and falsely attested that the goods were "actually on board" when in fact they were not. This employee was not plaintiffs' agent, and plaintiffs had no knowledge of his actions. The Court of Appeal held, however, that even though plaintiffs may have been innocent of the fraud, "[b]anks trust beneficiaries to present honest documents."[9] The same result, the court observed, could be expected under section 5–114(2) of the Uniform Commercial Code in the United States.

The decision in this case is noteworthy in two respects. First, despite the fact that the seller was innocent of fraud, the court attributed to the seller the actions of one who was not his agent. Second, and more significant, was the court's willingness to look behind the letter of credit to the underlying transaction and find that a violation of Article VIII, section 2(b) of the IMF Agreement presented an adequate defense to nonpayment. It can certainly be argued that this result properly recognizes the importance of a sovereign's international agreements without unduly burdening international trade.

[8] *Id.* at 251–52.

[9] *Id.* at 264.

> [I]f beneficiaries go to others (as they have to) for the documents they present, it is important to all concerned that those documents should accord, not merely with the requirements of the credit but with the facts, and if they do not because of the intention of anyone concerned with them to deceive, I see good reason for the choice between two innocent parties putting the loss upon the beneficiary, not the bank or its customer.

Id. at 264–65.

CURRENT DEVELOPMENTS

The Codification and Progressive Development of International Law: A UNITAR Study of the Role and Use of the International Law Commission

A recent 16-month study by UNITAR (the United Nations Institute for Training and Research), carried out by the undersigned and another,[1] asserts that the International Law Commission "is no longer playing the central role in the law-making process that it could and should play."[2] With such iconoclastic conclusions, the report instantly became the subject of heated debate in UN corridors in New York and Geneva and, to a lesser extent, on the floor of the Sixth Committee of the General Assembly.

While the Chairman of the Commission stoutly defended its work before the General Assembly's Sixth Committee, pointing out that the ILC "was constantly seeking to improve its working methods,"[3] others expressed doubts. Ambassador Rosenne, a leading authority on the subject, noted that a "certain malaise existed about the Commission, its work, its methods of work, its programme, its relations with the General Assembly through the Sixth Committee, its role with regard to the implementation of Article 13 of the Charter and many other matters."[4] A British delegate to the Sixth Committee noted diplomatically that "it had occasionally been argued that in recent years it had allowed itself to concentrate unduly on topics of peripheral interest to the international community."[5] Some of the Sixth Committee's commentators endorsed UNITAR's criticisms and various of its proposed remedies,[6] while others criticized the criticism.[7]

This dissonance is as it should be, since the primary purpose of UNITAR in preparing the study was to provoke reconsideration of the Commission's place within the UN system: its role, procedures, and institutional infrastructure. Such reconsideration stirs important political, as well as legal, sensitivities. The remainder of this Note will summarize the UNITAR study and its findings.

The ILC's mandate is derived from a 1947 General Assembly resolution[8] that established the Commission and approved its statute. The General Assembly acted pursuant to Article 13(1)(a) of the UN Charter, which empowers it to "make recommendations for the purpose of: (a) promoting international co-operation in the political field and encouraging the progressive development

[1] M. ElBaradei, Thomas M. Franck, R. Trachtenberg, The International Law Commission: The Need for a New Direction (UNITAR, 1981) [hereinafter cited as UNITAR].

[2] *Id.* at 3.

[3] Mr. Thiam, UN Doc. A/C.6/36/SR.36, at 8 (1981).

[4] *Id.* at 9.

[5] Sir Ian Sinclair (UK), UN Doc. A/C.6/36/SR.40, at 5 (1981).

[6] Mr. Maynard (the Bahamas), UN Doc. A/C.6/36/SR.51, at 5 (1981); Mr. El-Banbawi (Egypt), UN Doc. A/C.6/36/SR.41, at 11 (1981).

[7] Mr. Stavropoulos (Greece), UN Doc. A/C.6/36/SR.50, at 5 (1981).

[8] GA Res. 174 (II), 2 UN GAOR (123d plen. mtg.) (Nov. 21, 1947).

of international law and its codification." The statute echoes that the Commission's task is "the promotion of the progressive development of international law and its codification."[9] Progressive development was defined as "the preparation of draft conventions on subjects which have not yet been regulated by international law or in regard to which the law has not yet been sufficiently developed in the practice of States."[10] Codification was to be "the more precise formulation and systemization of rules of international law in fields where there already has been extensive state practice, precedent or doctrine."[11]

Although the ILC's statute recognizes the role of other official intergovernmental bodies engaged in codification and progressive development, the Commission rightfully claims pride of place as the intended principal legislative-drafting organ of the United Nations system, much as the International Court of Justice is the premier adjudicative organ.[12] The ILC is also the only drafting body with versatile jurisdiction over *any* subject in the field of international law.[13] Indeed, during its first two decades the Commission did succeed in producing draft conventions directed to a wide selection of the important legal issues of the day, including the law of the seas (1958), diplomatic relations (1961), consular relations (1963), and the law of treaties (1969). These were essential building blocks in the development of the postwar international legal system; and the system did not then seriously consider employing any other master mason.

The UNITAR study observes, however, that the ILC is now in danger of losing its preeminence because it has failed, in various ways, to accommodate itself to the inevitable concomitants of earthshaking changes in the community it serves. The emergence of a Third World majority in the state system has wholly altered the system's agenda: its priorities and its *a prioris*. In the words of the study, the "Third World is not interested only in the codification and adaption of existing international law; rather it is emphasizing the need for the dynamic evolution of international law and its extension to new activities. The Commission has not adequately responded to these major changes in circumstances."[14] The report charges that the Commission has eschewed new topics of interest to the Third World: for example, the elaboration of economic rights and duties pertaining to development and trade. The reason often advanced by ILC members, that these topics are not yet "ripened" by sufficient state practice to warrant codification, merely confirms the Third World's concern that the Commission is neglecting its duty to engage in the "progressive development,"[15] precisely, of topics that may not yet be ready for codification.

[9] Statute of the International Law Commission, Art. I, para. 1.

[10] *Id.*, Art. XV.

[11] *Id.*, Art. XVII.

[12] "The work done by the [International] Court [of Justice], at the judicial level, and that done by the Commission, at the legislative level, are complementary and make those bodies, respectively, the principal judicial and legal organs of the United Nations system." [1974] 2 Y.B. INT'L L. COMM'N, pt. 1, at 310, para. 208, UN Doc. A/CN.4/SER.A/1974.

[13] Review of the Multilateral Treaty-Making Process: Observations of the International Law Commission, UN Doc. A/35/312/Add.2, para. 11 (1980).

[14] UNITAR at 5.

[15] For a discussion of the distinction between progressive development and codification, see S. Rosenne, *The International Law Commission, 1949–59*, 36 BRIT. Y.B. INT'L L. 104, 158 (1960).

It is not widely appreciated that, to the Third World states, "progressive development" is the neglected and scorned—by the Western as well as the Communist world—halfway house along the path a principle takes in its tortuous and uncertain ascent from "ought" to "is."

One consequence of all this is that many topics that the General Assembly might have assigned to the ILC have been handed, instead, to a proliferating gaggle of ad hoc bodies. The UNITAR report traces the beginning of this diffusionary tendency to the creation of the Committee on the Peaceful Uses of Outer Space. That circumvention of the ILC resulted in the conclusion of the 1967 Treaty on Principles Governing the Activities of States in the Exploration and Use of Outer Space, Including the Moon and other Celestial Bodies.[16] In the UNITAR study's view:

> [I]t was the Commission's declining to assert its competence over the developing law of outer space that set the stage for the proliferation of more *ad hoc* bodies. Once launched, the tendency expanded to include even some of the areas which had customarily been considered to be within the domain of the Commission. Two examples are the creation of the committee on the peaceful uses of the sea-bed and the ocean floor beyond the limits of national jurisdiction, and the establishment of the *Ad Hoc* Committee on the Drafting of an International Convention against the Taking of Hostages.[17]

Perhaps even more germane is the decision of the General Assembly in 1980 to entrust UNITAR, not the ILC, with the task of examining evidence of the emergence of legal principles applicable to economic relations between developed and developing states,[18] an exercise in "progressive development" that involves research into treaties, state practice, and international conduct, leading to a draft restatement of evolving principles rather than to any legal codification.

While the UNITAR report cites the arguments of both those ILC members who do, and those who do not, wish to see the Commission deal also with questions where the law may be partially unsettled and political considerations abound,[19] it accepts the view urged by the UN Secretary-General as early as 1971,[20] that the Commission's long-term program of work should take into account the changing priorities of the international community, rather than confine itself to "safe" questions of little interest such as the codification of law applicable to the diplomatic bag and courier (which is currently on its agenda).

[16] For the creation of the Ad Hoc Committee, see the discussion in 13 UN GAOR (982d–989th mtgs.), UN Docs. A/C.1/SR.982–89 (1958). *See also* GA Res. 1348 (XIII), 13 UN GAOR Supp. (No. 18) 5, UN Doc. A/4090 (1958); M. LACHS, THE LAW OF OUTER SPACE (1972).

[17] UNITAR at 6. For the creation of the Sea-bed Committee, see GA Res. 2467A (XXIII), 23 UN GAOR Supp. (No. 18) 15, UN Doc. A/7218 (1968); GA Res. 2750 (XXV), 25 UN GAOR Supp. (No. 28) 25, UN Doc. A/8028 (1970). The final report of the Sea-bed Committee is at 28 UN GAOR Supp. (No. 21), UN Doc. A/9021 (1973). For the Ad Hoc Committee on Hostages, see the discussion at 31 UN GAOR (54th, 64th, 69th, and 70th mtgs.), UN Docs. A/C.6/SR.54, 64, 69, and 70 (1977).

[18] GA Res. 35/166 (Dec. 15, 1980). For the discussion leading up to this resolution, see 35 UN GAOR, C.6 (68th–75th mtgs.), UN Docs. A/C.6/SR.68–75 (1980).

[19] UNITAR at 8–10.

[20] UN Doc. A/CN.4/245 (1971), *reprinted in* [1971] 2 Y.B. INT'L L. COMM'N, pt. 2, at 1–100, UN Doc. A/CN.4/SER.A/1971.

Why has this not happened? The study suggests that some of the fault lies with the Commission's membership, some with the structure of the Commission and its supporting bureaucracy, and some with the community of states as represented in the General Assembly's Sixth Committee. The UNITAR authors think that the ILC's problems have now become so entrenched that each of these causes must be addressed before the Commission can be expected to change direction. Unless some reforms are made, the ILC will merely replicate the UN system's wanton penchant for addressing institutional inadequacy and obsolescence by institutional replication and functional fragmentation—by setting up new little principalities to do the neglected tasks of the old without actually abolishing the latter. Naturally, it follows from this that the old and the new will become primarily engaged in *inter se* territorial disputes of arcane and unseemly futility.

Must legal draftsmanship stagger down this well-trodden, but dead, path? With the signposts so unambiguous, why has the ILC not recharted its own path? Inevitably, the members of the Commission disagree as to the direction its work should take. A significant number sided with Professor Paul Reuter: "Unless, of course, it was asked to do otherwise, the Commission would do better to choose less urgent topics, which might be of less direct concern to peoples and nations—which [are] more in need of peace and food than of legal texts—but were ripe for codification."[21] Others feel that, since the Commission is not a negotiating body of plenipotentiaries, its members are ill-suited to venture into areas where governments may disagree.[22] These members cite the rejection of the Commission's draft on arbitral procedures as an instance of the fate that befalls works of the Commission that get ahead of the nations' will to agree.[23] According to the UNITAR study, even if these views are not those of a majority, the "outcome of these cleavages among the members is that the Commission tends to follow the lead of those least interested in expanding the scope of Commission activities to the new areas of international law."[24] Collegiality and the Commission's preference for consensus allow "a minority of

[21] [1973] 1 Y.B. INT'L L. COMM'N 161, para. 31, UN Doc. A/CN.4/SER.A/1973 (statement of P. Reuter).

[22] Some members who hold this view give the Commission's work on the definition of aggression as an example of the inadvisability of taking up topics that are politically controversial. After deliberations, the Commission found itself hopelessly split concerning the correct approach to the problem. It reported to the Sixth Committee its decision to abandon efforts to formulate a definition. According to some observers, the Commission's failure in this instance caused it to be skeptical about taking on projects of a primarily political nature. For the results of the Commission's discussions and the reactions of the Sixth Committee, see respectively, Report of the International Law Commission covering the work of its third session, 6 UN GAOR Supp. (No. 9) 8–10, UN Doc. A/1858 (1951), and 6 UN GAOR, C.6 (278th–295th mtgs.), UN Docs. A/C.6/SR.278–95 (1951).

[23] *See* Rosenne, *supra* note 15, at 150–51. Rosenne gives three reasons for the General Assembly's rejection of the draft on arbitral procedure: (1) the boldness of the Commission's approach in basing the draft on a concept of judicial instead of diplomatic arbitration, (2) a feeling that the draft relied too heavily on progressive development, and (3) the fact that the political climate of the United Nations was not ready for a further extension of the judicial settlement of disputes in the place of diplomacy.

[24] UNITAR at 12.

members opposed to the inclusion of a particular topic . . . to prevent the Commission from taking up such topics."[25]

Other members of the Commission freely concede that its agenda has, in this way, become a veritable *What's What* of drafting trivia, a parody of the world's urgent agenda. Currently before the Commission are codifications of law pertaining to succession of states in respect of matters other than treaties, state responsibility, treaties concluded between states and international organizations or between two or more international organizations, nonnavigational uses of international watercourses, the status of the diplomatic courier and diplomatic bag not accompanied by diplomatic courier, relations between states and international organizations (second part of the topic), jurisdictional immunities of states and their property, and international liability for injurious consequences arising out of acts not prohibited by international law. "With the exception of the topic of non-navigational uses of international watercourses," the UNITAR study concludes, "the Commission has maintained its previous basic commitment to the codification of topics of traditional international law."[26]

Inherent resistance to change, particularly by members from some developed countries, is compounded by absenteeism, especially among members from developing countries who tend to double as senior officials of their national governments or regional organizations. An agenda of esoterica breeds absenteeism and vice versa. And as the Commission's work becomes less and less relevant, its membership, perversely, becomes the more prestigious. This is not illogical, for very important and busy international legal luminaries are willing and able to grace a commission that is engaged in codifying the immunities of the diplomatic bag—since it does not excessively tax the conscience or endanger the national interest to miss most of the meetings on such a topic—while they would be less likely to seek election if the topics were of sufficient importance to warrant their serious and continuous attention. Noting a "seven hat problem," the UNITAR study reports:

> [M]any of these members find it hard to fulfill their responsibilities of attendance at Commission meetings because of conflicting professional commitments. In some cases, on the present Commission, members have been absent for the vast majority of meetings. Such poor attendance is lamentable and prevents the Commission from functioning up to its potential.[27]

And it inevitably reinforces the urge towards the trivial.

The procedures and bureaucratic infrastructure of the ILC do not promote self-reform. An example is the slow rate of progress on the topics being prepared for codification. The UNITAR study finds that the average time between the ILC's initial investigation of a topic and the production of final draft articles is 7 to 10 years. State responsibility has been on its agenda for over 25 years. "Except for specific, circumscribed subjects," the UNITAR study says, "the Commission, as a part-time body, cannot possibly cope on a regular basis with urgent demands of the General Assembly."[28]

Such slow progress is virtually inevitable, given the Commission's penury.

[25] *Ibid.*

[26] UNITAR at 13.

[27] *Id.* at 29.

[28] *Id.* at 15–16.

As early as 1951, the ILC recommended to the General Assembly that it become a full-time operation[29] and was turned down, in part because of the cost. Almost certainly, the same response would obtain today. Yet the present fiscal arrangement pays members a per diem barely sufficient to cover their stay in Geneva during the annual 12-week session of the Commission. All but those on pension or of great personal wealth must therefore be expected to hold full-time posts elsewhere, which are likely to interfere with regular attendance at the Commission's session. The special rapporteurs receive a small additional payment that does not remotely compensate for the time they ought to spend on their topics between sessions in order to set a fast pace for the rest of the Commission.

These problems are not assuaged by the Commission's staff, which is drawn from the Codification Division of the UN Secretariat's Office of Legal Affairs. Since the division has many responsibilities, only five members can be spared on a relatively full-time basis to serve the ILC.

So little research support can be provided by the division that the special rapporteurs must look elsewhere for the help essential to their task. Those who come from foreign offices or universities able to provide a research base are thus much better positioned than others—primarily from developing countries—who can expect no such help. This may account, in part, for the relative paucity of rapporteurs from Third World countries.

Another share of the overall responsibility for the ILC's quandary rests with the Sixth Committee of the General Assembly, which reviews the Commission's work and may assign it topics. As the UNITAR study points out, this "oversight" function is less effective than it might be were not so many members of the ILC also their countries' representatives on the committee. Except for a certain few members considered beyond the pale, the United Nations is surprisingly like a club. The membership hates unpleasantness and any criticism of what is being done is usually smothered under a bale of circumlocution. This clubbiness is particularly evident when the Sixth Committee of the General Assembly, consisting in part of the members of the ILC, is given the role of overseeing the performance of the Commission.

A study of the Commission's lapse raises many chicken-or-egg questions, which are probably of little prescriptive value. It is too late, for example, to ask whether the Sixth Committee does not assign important new topics to the ILC because it perceives the Commission as essentially unwilling and unable to deal with them, or whether the failure of the Sixth Committee to challenge (or trust) the Commission with important issues is responsible for the ILC's *immobilisme*. Whatever their origins, two effects seem to have become welded into a *circulo inextricabilis*. The UNITAR study finds that the

> majority of United Nations members is thus unwilling to entrust important issues to the Commission. This is in part a reaction to the Commission's self-perception, and in part a result of factors external to the Commission. The reluctance of the Third World nations to entrust their most sensitive

[29] Report of the International Law Commission to the General Assembly, [1951] 2 Y.B. INT'L L. COMM'N 137–39, UN Doc. A/CN.4/SER.A/1951/Add.1.

> and urgent concerns to the International Law Commission stems from a perception that the Commission is wedded in some fundamental way to a relatively static concept of international law. This perception has been a logical implication of, and has been reenforced by, the Commission's own understanding of its role.

However, the "attitude of the Third World to the International Law Commission [also] partially developed as an extension of its attitude towards the legal organs of the U.N. as a whole [since the] decision of the International Court of Justice in the 1966 South West Africa case. . . ."[30] There is a feeling that legal institutions are unlikely to be sympathetic to the aspirations of those who seek to change the status quo, which breeds a reticence toward them. Moreover, these feelings have been reinforced "by the perceived lack of influence of the members from the developing countries" on the Commission.[31] UNITAR's study attributes this to their being relatively inexperienced and overcommitted to other responsibilities, as well as to their lack of research staff support. Until these perceived deficiencies are corrected, even the Third World countries that most desire the progressive development of law in areas of special concern are unlikely to refer those concerns to a body in which they see themselves as playing with an insuperable handicap.

The UNITAR study concludes by considering a series of proposals for reform which are meant to address these three linked components of the Commission's condition: its membership, its procedures and bureaucratic infrastructure, and its oversight by the Sixth Committee. The study lays out a range of options, rejects some, and endorses others.

As to membership, the report reconsiders the case for a full-time Commission and, while admitting its advantages, rejects it primarily because it would be too expensive and, to a lesser extent, because the Commission might thereby lose the valuable services of senior officials and scholars unwilling to abandon all other responsibilities. Instead, the report proposes a compromise: a part-time Commission as at present, but with full-time rapporteurs.[32]

Under the prevailing system, the study finds, special rapporteurs who must also hold full-time posts elsewhere are overworked and find it difficult to spend the time needed to prepare their topics.

> As a result, many of the reports, which are supposed to be delivered to Commission members in advance of the annual session, are not finished until the session has already commenced. Members are thus unable to study the reports of the special rapporteurs at length before being asked to comment upon them.[33]

Full-time rapporteurships would alleviate that inadequacy and would also make it easier for Third World members to serve as special rapporteurs by making it possible for them to afford a leave of absence from competing commitments.

Changes in the procedures and infrastructure of the Commission include a proposal for abandoning the present practice of keeping items on a long-

[30] UNITAR at 14. For the South West Africa case, see [1966] ICJ REP. 6.
[31] *Ibid.*
[32] *Id.* at 20.
[33] *Ibid.*

term program of work until they are completed. The report proposes a 5-year agenda, coinciding with the term of office of the commissioners and composed of items that could be completed during the period.[34] Each 5-year cycle would be "zero based" in the sense that uncompleted items would not automatically be carried over.

Further to accelerate the ILC's working schedule, the study urges more use of topical chambers composed of a special rapporteur and a maximum of four other members. Such chambers could meet for one or two intensive weeks, between regular sessions of the full Commission, and would then report to the next plenary meeting. The use of multiple rapporteurs where a subject lends itself to subdivision is also urged.

In particular, the UNITAR report proposes improvements in the research services provided to the ILC.[35] At a minimum, the Codification Division must be able to augment the personnel available to assist rapporteurs. In the opinion of the UNITAR authors, however, the overall problem of restoring credibility and cohesion to the process of progressive development and codification of law requires a system-wide response, particularly as this process has already become so fragmented through *ad hoc-ery* and institutional proliferation. They therefore propose the establishment of a UN legal research center, which could serve a number of functions. It would provide an enhanced research potential for the ILC, but also for the many other specialized and ad hoc bodies within the UN system, which currently develop their own—often inadequate—research staff or must do without. Such coordinate research, aside from providing better service with a more rational marshaling of resources, would also create a functional network linking those involved in many currently unrelated, overlapping, and sometimes contradictory efforts at research and drafting. It could also provide a pool of technical, nonlegal expertise that would augment the capacity of the ILC to deal with the complex interdisciplinary problems that are so often high on the system's agenda, but are now thought to be beyond the ILC's narrow base of expertise.[36] "There is no reason," the study says, "why a body like the International Law Commission cannot handle any legal topic regardless of its technical, scientific, or inter-disciplinary complexity,"[37] providing it is properly staffed.

The present tendency, of course, is strenuously in the opposite direction. The system required experts to support the decade-long Conference on the Law of the Sea, so a legal staff was assembled to develop an expertise exclusively on this subject. If and when those negotiations produce an Authority to administer the Area beyond national jurisdiction, some of these lawyers will form a new legal research staff. So proliferation occurs, unless a conscious effort is made to reverse the trend. Inexorably, the UN system will become a series of closed, unrelated legal research clusters: an uneconomic and inflexible use of a scarce and costly resource. There is no reason, for example, why the talents of a sea lawyer, whenever temporarily underutilized by the sea Authority, should not be redeployed to encompass research on the nonnavigational uses of rivers for the ILC.

[34] *Id.* at 24.

[35] *Id.* at 30.

[36] *Id.* at 30–32.

[37] *Id.* at 31.

A final recommendation directed to reform of the ILC's modus operandi calls for greater variety in the form of its product. Having too long focused virtually exclusively on codification—producing draft articles for international conventions—the Commission should consider other kinds of output, including "model rules,"[38] restatements, and analyses of emerging trends in state and interstate practice. This could accelerate the disposition of topics. "State responsibility" could perhaps finally be laid to rest if it were agreed to issue the product as a restatement of principles rather than as a draft treaty for which nations no longer seem to be calling with discernible urgency. The prospect of working on "progressive development" could also be improved if the ILC did not have to cap each research project with a treaty.[39] "Progressive development" is almost a contradiction of the treaty form, since it implies some movement in the direction of, rather than a final arrival at, lawmaking.

If such reforms, or a significant portion of them, or other viable options could be instituted, the Commission might again be eligible to serve as the principal instrument of legislative research and drafting in the UN system. It would then be up to the system to make proper use of it. This requires, above all, the cooperation of the General Assembly's Sixth Committee. The committee must provide the political guidance as to what topics are urgent and deserve priority in the ILC's 5-year agenda. And, if the Commission is to work in areas that involve political sensitivity, the Sixth Committee, as an organ of plenipotentiaries, will have an essential role in reviewing and guiding the ongoing drafting process. This role cannot be discharged, as at present, by formal set-piece speeches of verbal back patting. The members of the committee must challenge and guide the work of the Commission by providing detailed critiques of its work-in-progress. Such critiques could also compensate for the tendency of most states simply not to respond to the questionnaires sent them periodically by the ILC in an effort to elicit specific "feedback." In the words of the UNITAR study: "If the Commission is to take a bolder approach to the development of the law, the Sixth Committee must provide the parameters in which the Commission can work, by detailing the limits of political feasibility."[40] While the UNITAR study does not say so, it would undoubtedly help if members of the ILC were not placed in the embarrassing position of reviewing their own work as members of the Sixth Committee.

The UNITAR study is by no means intended as an attack on the ILC. Given

[38] "Model rules" have been used only once. *See* the Model Rules on Arbitral Procedure, [1958] 2 Y.B. INT'L L. COMM'N 80–88, UN Doc. A/CN.4/SER.A/1958. During the consideration of the topic of nonnavigational uses of international watercourses, some members suggested that the Commission should produce a framework agreement that could be used by two or more states desiring to regulate the uses of a common watercourse. *See* [1979] 2 Y.B. INT'L L. COMM'N, pt. 2, at 166, UN Doc. A/CN. 4/SER.A/1979. At the 1980 session of the Commission, it was decided to concentrate on drafting a set of articles containing basic rules applicable to international watercourses generally. These articles would be designed to complement more detailed arrangements for particular international watercourses to be negotiated by the states concerned. *See* Report of the International Law Commission on the work of its 32d session, 35 UN GAOR Supp. (No. 10), UN Doc. A/35/10 (1980).

[39] UNITAR at 26–27.

[40] *Id.* at 26.

the extraordinary change in the international agenda and the paucity of means at its disposal, the Commission has functioned remarkably well. Nevertheless, the UNITAR study concludes, it is

> gradually drifting from the centre of the international law-making process. As it completes the basic work of the codification of the fundamental areas of international law, the Commission will find itself with largely marginal topics on its agenda. Because the Commission has proved to be an efficacious and highly competent part of the law-making process this diminution in status is regrettable. At the same time, there is a growing incoherence in the U.N. legislative system as a whole. The lack of coordination among the proliferating *ad hoc* law-making bodies is becoming an increasing problem. Returning the International Law Commission to its former importance may help to alleviate this problem to some extent by placing a strong actor at the centre. Of course, other steps must be taken as well.[41]

The report does not say so, but it implies that if the tendency towards legal fragmentation is not arrested, the system may soon have no further significant use for the ILC, in which case it should be retired.

THOMAS M. FRANCK & MOHAMED ELBARADEI*

THE 1981 U.S.-CZECHOSLOVAK CLAIMS SETTLEMENT AGREEMENT: AN EPILOGUE TO POSTWAR NATIONALIZATION AND EXPROPRIATION DISPUTES

I. THE AGREEMENT

After 35 years of on-again, off-again negotiations, on November 6, 1981, the United States and Czechoslovakia initialed an Agreement on the Settlement of Certain Outstanding Claims and Financial Issues.[1] Congress approved the Agreement in a bill passed on December 16, 1981, which the President signed into law 2 weeks later.[2] Procedural arrangements required for the implementation of the Agreement were completed in January 1982,[3] and in mid-February the basic reciprocal undertakings of the parties were performed.

The Agreement is conspicuous in several respects. It is the last in the series of U.S. claims settlements reached with the socialist countries of Central and Eastern Europe since the Second World War.[4] For Czechoslovakia the settle-

[41] *Id.* at 17.

* Of the Board of Editors, and Member, Professional Staff, the United Nations Institute for Training and Research, respectively. The views expressed herein are those of the authors and not necessarily those of UNITAR.

[1] 21 ILM 371 (1982).

[2] Czechoslovakian Claims Settlement Act of 1981, 95 Stat. 1675, Pub. L. No. 97-127 (1981), *reprinted in* 21 ILM at 414 [hereinafter cited as the 1981 Act].

[3] On Jan. 29, 1982, American, British, and Czechoslovak representatives signed a protocol in Prague providing for the modalities of the return to Czechoslovakia of the monetary gold held in the West.

[4] The settlements included agreements with Bulgaria (July 2, 1963), Hungary (May 29, 1956 and March 6, 1973), Poland (July 16, 1960), Romania (March 30, 1960), and Yugoslavia (July

ment closes an era in which pending foreign claims often hampered the development of normal relations with Western countries.[5] Finally, because it provides more than 100 percent of the principal of certified U.S. claims, the Agreement is unprecedented in the history of postwar claims negotiations and constitutes probably the most favorable settlement ever negotiated by the United States Government on behalf of its citizens.[6]

Under the Agreement, Czechoslovakia recognized the validity of claims of U.S. nationals whose properties, rights, and interests in Czechoslovakia had been affected by nationalization, expropriation, and other measures involving takings of foreign property by the Czechoslovak Government between 1945 and the date of the Agreement; and it agreed to pay $81.5 million immediately in settlement to be distributed to the claimants.[7] For its part, the United States Government consented to the return to Czechoslovakia of the remainder of its share of Nazi-looted monetary gold recovered by Allied armies at the close of the Second World War. The gold, which was in the custody of the American-British-French Tripartite Commission, was held partly in the United States (8.2 metric tons) and partly in Great Britain (10.2 metric tons). The United States had withheld its consent to the return of this gold pending resolution of the claims issue.[8]

In addition, the Agreement resolved several other outstanding issues:

(1) Czechoslovakia agreed to pay the United States $2.87 million immediately, and a further $2 million within the next 2 years, for surplus

---

19, 1948 and Nov. 5, 1964). *See also* Rode, *The American-Polish Claims Settlement Agreement of March 30, 1960,* 55 AJIL 452 (1961); Christenson, *U.S.-Rumanian Claims Settlement Agreement of March 30, 1960, id.* at 617; Lillich, *The United States-Bulgarian Claims Settlement Agreement of 1963,* 58 *id.* at 686 (1964); Sipkov, *United States-Bulgarian Claims Settlement Agreement of July 2, 1963,* 4 VA. J. INT'L L. 187 (1964); Peselj, *The New Yugoslav-American Claims Agreement,* 59 AJIL 362 (1965); Sutton, *American Claims Against Yugoslavia,* 3 INT'L LAW. 262 (1969); 2 R. LILLICH & B. WESTON, INTERNATIONAL CLAIMS: THEIR SETTLEMENT BY LUMP SUM AGREEMENTS (1975).

[5] Czechoslovakia has concluded claims settlement agreements with the following Western countries: Austria (Dec. 19, 1974), Belgium/Luxembourg (Sept. 30, 1952), Canada (April 18, 1973), Denmark (Dec. 23, 1958), France (June 2, 1950), Iceland (Nov. 24, 1947), Great Britain (Sept. 28, 1949 and Dec. 16, 1981), the Netherlands (June 11, 1964), Norway (June 9, 1954), Sweden (Dec. 22, 1956), and Switzerland (Dec. 22, 1949). In addition, Czechoslovakia concluded a number of treaties with socialist countries, providing for a mutual waiver of claims and obligations arising out of one another's nationalization programs. *See* Drucker, *Compensation Treaties Between Communist States,* 10 INT'L & COMP. L.Q. 238 and 904 (1961).

[6] Past U.S. foreign claims settlements typically have netted claimants only about 40 cents on the dollar of the principal amount of their claims, and no payment of interest. Under the 1981 Agreement, full compensation, plus some interest, will be paid.

[7] Arts. 1, 2, 3, 4, and 8. Article 1 is so drafted as to emphasize that the above sum and further amounts due to the United States under the Agreement are in full settlement and discharge of all the *mutual* claims of the parties.

[8] Arts. 5 and 6. The gold issue was the major leverage of the United States in the negotiations, especially after the dramatic increase in world gold prices of the last several years; the current value of the 18.4 metric tons of gold released to Czechoslovakia is about $250 million.

The principal transaction under the Agreement, the transfer of the gold to Czechoslovakia in exchange for the cash payment of the settlement, was effected in the manner set forth in an annex to the Agreement and involved intermediary countries, principally the United Kingdom, and banks.

equipment it had purchased in 1946 from the U.S. Third Army but had never paid for.[9]

(2) Czechoslovakia also agreed to release about $1 million in U.S. bank accounts in Czechoslovakia that had been frozen.[10]

(3) Czechoslovakia's counterclaim of $16 million was effectively abandoned. The counterclaim had been made in response to the U.S. Government's confiscation of a steel mill purchased in the United States by Czechoslovakia in 1947, but never delivered.[11]

(4) The United States agreed to release its blocking control over Czechoslovak properties, rights, and interests in the United States and not to obstruct in any way their transfer to Czechoslovakia.[12]

One outstanding issue that was not resolved by the Agreement concerned defaulted prewar Czechoslovak bonds. However, the Czechoslovak Government agreed to negotiate with the representatives of the American bondholders and, if no agreement was reached within 6 months, to discuss the matter with the U.S. Government at the diplomatic level.[13]

The Issue of Nationalization

Postwar nationalization in Czechoslovakia was effected in two stages: first, in 1945, when President Beneš signed decrees on nationalization of mines, certain industrial enterprises, banks, and insurance companies;[14] second, in and after 1948, when the Communist Party under Klement Gottwald ousted from the Government its democratic coalition partners and decreed sweeping nationalization and expropriation of private property.[15]

The legislation enacted in the first phase acknowledged the obligation to pay compensation for nationalized property, except in the case of property owned by German or Hungarian public and private corporations, persons of German or Hungarian nationality, and persons irrespective of nationality who had engaged before and during the war in activities detrimental to Czechoslovak statehood. An important provision stated that if compensation was refused to a legal person, natural persons that had a capital interest in the property and did not belong to the category of collaborators, traitors, and the like named in the exclusion, were to be recompensed in proportion to their shares. No distinction between Czechoslovak nationals and aliens was made. Compensation proceedings were governed by administrative law, and claims were decided by

[9] Art. 10.

[10] Art. 9.

[11] There is no direct reference in the Agreement to this particular counterclaim. The claim is covered by the general clause of Article 1(2); *see* note 7 *supra*. The steel mill was seized by the U.S. Government in 1948 and later sold to Argentina for $9 million.

[12] Art. 11.

[13] *See* the Letter of Czechoslovakia attached to the Agreement, 21 ILM at 395.

[14] Nos. 100–103/1945, Collection of Laws and Regulations of the Czechoslovak Republic. *See also* Oatman, *The Nationalization Program in Czechoslovakia,* 15 DEP'T STATE BULL. 1027 (1946); and Rado, *Czechoslovak Nationalization Decrees: Some International Aspects*, 41 AJIL 795 (1947).

[15] Nos. 114, 115, 117, 118, 120, 122–126, 171/1948, Collection of Laws and Regulations of the Czechoslovak Republic.

administrative, not judicial, tribunals. The Government announced that it would negotiate compensation for nationalized enterprises in which foreign capital was invested directly with the governments of the owners, and in November 1946 it concluded an Agreement on Commercial Policy and Compensation Claims with the United States. Under the Agreement, nationals of each country were assured "adequate and effective compensation" by the Government of the other for properties it had nationalized or requisitioned.[16]

The laws enacted during the second stage did not, in principle, deny compensation for nationalization: they even stipulated the basis for determining the amount of compensation payable. However, as could have been expected, the post-1948 Government did not subscribe to the view that prompt, adequate, and effective compensation was the norm of international law. The right to nationalize all private property was regarded as a sovereign right, and state sovereignty was deemed to empower the Government to determine the terms and conditions of compensation, if any, to be provided for foreign-owned property.[17]

It was on this issue that a fundamental dispute arose between the United States and Czechoslovakia. It should be noted, however, that the United States Government never questioned the right of Czechoslovakia to nationalize private assets under its jurisdiction; the only disputed question was the amount of compensation.[18]

By its nature, the 1981 U.S.-Czechoslovak Agreement is a global settlement that covers all U.S. claims arising out of the nationalization and expropriation programs of the Czechoslovak Government after 1945; it does not deal with each individual claim separately.[19] It is broadly based on the international standard set forth in the United Nations resolution of December 14, 1962 on permanent sovereignty over natural resources,[20] but it is so drafted as to be without prejudice to either side's view of the applicable international law.

It has been maintained that the global settlements following the postwar nationalizations in the East European countries are "negotiated compromises and as such do not constitute a departure from the traditional international law principle";[21] yet, while they have created no new law common to the West and the East, their prevalence in the settlement practice cannot fail to undermine

[16] 61 Stat. 2431, TIAS No. 1569, 7 UNTS 119.

[17] R. Bystrický, Základy mezinárodního práva soukromého (Fundamentals of International Private Law) 222 (1958).

[18] Negotiations on the amount of the compensation had been held intermittently since 1949 and had twice reached *ad referendum* agreements: in 1963 the U.S. Government was prepared to settle for less than 20% of the principal amount of its claim, and in 1974 for about 40%. The 1974 draft agreement further provided that the $20.5 million settlement would be payable in installments over a period of 12 years, without interest. Needless to say, the terms of the 1981 Agreement are a considerable improvement.

[19] On the problem of global settlements, see generally R. Lillich & B. Weston, *supra* note 4; Domke, *Foreign Nationalizations*, 55 AJIL 585 (1961); Yates, *Postwar Belgian International Claims: Their Settlement by Lump Sum Agreements*, 13 Va. J. Int'l L. 554 (1973); Seidl-Hohenveldern, *Austrian Practice on Lump Sum Compensation by Treaty*, 70 AJIL 763 (1976).

[20] GA Res. 1803 (XVII), 17 UN GAOR Supp. (No. 17) 15, UN Doc. A/5217, *reprinted in* 57 AJIL 710 (1963), 2 ILM 223 (1963).

[21] Mr. John Stevenson in 54 ASIL, Proc. 112 (1960).

each side's case concerning the content of relevant international rules. Several scores of such global settlements have been reached through negotiation and compromise; it would surely be wrong to dismiss them as diplomatic decisions that are addressed to private pecuniary claims and have no legal effect beyond the unique circumstances giving rise to them. In the absence of other precedents, it is difficult to see how international customary law could preserve the classical doctrine of responsibility for nationalization predicated on the existence of an unlawful act, or, on the other hand, how it could create a universal norm recognizing the right of the nationalizing state to determine unilaterally the conditions under which property is taken from foreigners and whether or not compensation should be paid. Common sense and justice require a reappraisal of the doctrines unsustained by practice, so as to enable international law to play its proper role in facilitating rationality in decisions.

The Issue of the Monetary Gold

While compensation for nationalized properties was the primary aim of the American negotiators, the recovery of monetary gold was the main Czechoslovak concern. For peculiar reasons, the question was not entirely financial; both history and emotion, including memories of the Munich betrayal, were involved. The Czechoslovak monetary gold was at the center of a major political and legal row in 1939 when, shortly after the occupation of Prague by Hitler, the Bank for International Settlements in Basel, Switzerland, rashly acceded to the request of directors of the Prague National Bank, acting under duress, that all deposited Czechoslovak treasury gold be moved from Basel to the account of the German Reichsbank at the Bank of England in London.[22] When the news leaked a few weeks later, both the Basel-based bank and the Bank of England were accused in the British Parliament and in the press of collaboration with the Germans; quite naturally, the Czechoslovak government-in-exile and every Czechoslovak Government in power since the war have held that the gold was wrongfully transferred to the German Reichsbank. After the 1939 transfer, the gold never left London. The British Government froze the account when war broke out, and the gold coins and bullion were held as a German asset until 1946 when they came under the control of the Tripartite Commission.

The powers and functions of the Tripartite Commission for the Restitution of Monetary Gold[23] included the duty to adjudicate upon any claim made by any country to a share of the gold found in Germany by the Allied forces, to determine the amount of the share if such a claim was admitted, and to carry out distribution. All decisions were by unanimous agreement of the members; when the Commission was in doubt about or unable to deal with a matter, it

[22] *See* Schwarzenberger, *The Bank for International Settlements and the Czech Gold Assets Held by the Bank of England*, 3 MOD. L. REV. 150 (1939); E. TÁBORSKÝ, THE CZECHOSLOVAK CAUSE IN INTERNATIONAL LAW 49–61 (1944).

[23] The Commission was established in 1946 to implement part III of the Agreement on Reparation signed in Paris on Jan. 14, 1946 by 18 nations, including Czechoslovakia. Under part III, the gold recovered by the Allied forces was to be divided among the countries from which it had been wrongfully taken according to each country's proven losses. For the articles establishing the Tripartite Commission, see 15 DEP'T STATE BULL. 565 (1946).

was referred to the Governments of the United States, Great Britain, and France for joint instructions, which served to preserve the rule of unanimity.

Czechoslovakia's share of the gold was determined by the Commission and a portion of it was transferred to Czechoslovakia in 1948. Further transfers were halted because the United States, the United Kingdom, and France refused to sign the decrees of release. When its claims were settled, France withdrew its opposition, and the United Kingdom also made known its willingness to release the gold. The United States, however, moved in the opposite direction. In 1974 U.S. consent was expressly linked by statute to the conclusion of a claims agreement satisfactory to Congress, and in 1980 Congress attempted to enact legislation providing for unilateral action by the United States with regard to that portion of the Czechoslovak share held by the Federal Reserve Bank.

These U.S. actions called into play certain fundamental legal issues, to which the discussion now turns.

(1) The Question of Ownership. It was asserted that the gold involved could not be considered to be Czechoslovak property and that Czechoslovakia could not acquire title to it until its final allocation and delivery to Czechoslovakia.[24] It is probably arguable that until the adjudication of the Czechoslovak claim by the Tripartite Commission and its determination of the amount of the Czechoslovak share, there was nothing to which Czechoslovakia could claim property rights (although its Government repeatedly rejected this argument during the negotiations by pointing out that the share deposited at the Bank of England was physically identical with the gold wrongfully transferred to Germany). But once this determination was made and the depositary institutions so notified, the title of property could be disputed only at the expense of inconsistency with the Commission's own decisions.

The precedent in question involved monetary gold deposited at two Italian institutions in Rome in the name of the Bank of Albania and seized by the Germans in September 1943. After the war the Italian Government stated that 88.5 percent of the share capital of the Bank of Albania had been the property of the Italian state, and it submitted a claim under the Paris Agreement on Reparation. The Albanian Government had submitted a similar claim to the Tripartite Commission. On November 17, 1950, the Commission referred the matter to the Governments of the United States, the United Kingdom, and France, which appointed an arbitrator (Professor Georges Sauser-Hall) to advise them on the question of ownership. The arbitrator determined that the gold "belonged to Albania, within the meaning of Part III of the Paris Act of January 14, 1946."[25] In anticipation of such a determination, the Three Powers had agreed to deliver the gold not to Albania itself, but to the United Kingdom in partial satisfaction of the earlier Judgment of the International Court of Justice in the *Corfu Channel* case of 1949.[26] Such a decision would have been inconceivable without the prior establishment of title by the arbitrator.

[24] *See Settlement of Claims Against Czechoslovakia: Hearing Before the Subcomms. on Europe and the Middle East and on International Economic Policy and Trade of the House Comm. on Foreign Affairs,* 96th Cong., 2d Sess. 28 (1980) (Legal Opinion of the Dep't of State and the Dep't of the Treasury).

[25] *See* [1954] ICJ, Pleadings, Case of the Monetary Gold Removed from Rome in 1943, at 10.

[26] Washington Statement of April 25, 1951, *quoted in* [1954] ICJ REP. 19, 21.

In the Czechoslovak case, title was established by the Tripartite Commission itself in 1947, when the 24 tons of gold clearly became the property of Czechoslovakia. In fact, approximately 6 out of the 24 tons were delivered to Czechoslovakia shortly thereafter. The position of the United Kingdom and the United States, in whose custody the undelivered portions remained after the Second World War, is best thought of as analogous to that of custodian-trustees.

(2) The Right of the United States to Dispose of the Gold. The Paris Agreement is silent on whether a member of the Tripartite Commission may withhold consent. But the right seems to derive from the consensual procedure used by the Commission in making its decisions and to apply especially to matters on which the Commission feels unable to act. The Paris Agreement does not provide for remedies, and as the *Monetary Gold* case demonstrates, no remedies are readily available unless the Three Powers extend an ad hoc offer to the aggrieved party to bring its case before an international tribunal.[27] Like other kinds of veto power, the right to withhold consent to an arrangement made under the Paris Agreement is practically unlimited; perhaps the only legal defense against it is the doctrine of the abuse of rights: "There is no legal right, however well established, which could not, in some circumstances, be refused recognition on the ground that it has been abused."[28] However, aside from the impracticability of invoking it outside a judicial context, the doctrine is clearly inapplicable where the exercise of the right, though causing damage to another state, is in response to an abuse of rights by that state.[29] The absence of objective international procedures for dispute settlement plainly makes it inappropriate to appraise the right to withhold consent on the basis of legal criteria and, instead, makes it subject to political considerations.

A related issue arose in 1980 when the U.S. House of Representatives considered requiring the United States Government, failing an agreement with Czechoslovakia within a reasonable time, to seize the gold allocated to Czechoslovakia by the Tripartite Commission, and to sell it and invest the proceeds for income with which to pay the claimants.[30] Some proponents of this solution referred to the Albanian gold ultimately delivered to Great Britain in partial settlement of the *Corfu* damages.[31] Earlier, a class action had been brought in the U.S. federal courts on behalf of the United States citizens whose property in Czechoslovakia had been nationalized. The primary purpose of the action was to have the gold held in New York used to satisfy the unpaid portion of the awards granted under the Czechoslovakian Claims Program by the U.S. Foreign Claims Commission. The action also sought to have Czechoslovakia's share of the gold in England transferred to the United States and made available to satisfy the awards.[32]

[27] [1954] ICJ REP. at 29.

[28] H. LAUTERPACHT, THE DEVELOPMENT OF INTERNATIONAL LAW BY THE INTERNATIONAL COURT 164 (1958).

[29] For example, the Austrian Constitutional Court determined, in a decision of Sept. 27, 1967, that vesting of certain Czechoslovak assets in Austria for the purpose of inducing that Government to conclude a claims settlement agreement was justifiable in terms of a legitimate public purpose. *See* 97 J. DROIT INT'L 340 (1970).

[30] H.R. 7338, 96th Cong., 2d Sess. (1980).

[31] *House Hearing, supra* note 24, at 122.

[32] Logan v. Secretary of State, 553 F.2d 107 (D.C. Cir. 1976).

In both instances, the administration took the position that the gold was not a conventional asset and that its unilateral seizure by the United States, while a negotiated settlement of U.S. claims was still possible and being pursued, would be contrary to international law. The Department of State asserted that it "recognizes and allows the immunity of the gold from the jurisdiction of the U.S. courts for the purpose of attachment, suit or other legal process in the action."[33] The Department of the Treasury further pointed out that "[d]omestic legislation which would require the Treasury Department to seize and sell the gold in the United States is certain to be controversial and could affect the willingness of foreign central banks to hold assets in this country."[34]

The British and French Governments made clear their opposition to the proposed U.S. legislation. The British Government asserted that the proposed sale of the

> gold held by the Federal Reserve Bank, if carried out, would be illegal under the terms of the Paris Agreement. . . . Since the gold is held in the name of the three governments on the Tripartite Commission Her Majesty's Government would regard any attempt by one party to the Paris Agreement to dispose of the gold without the consent of the other two parties as in disregard of its trustee obligations to the other signatories of the Paris Agreement.[35]

According to the French Government, the Three Powers in that Agreement clearly set forth the principle of immunity regarding the gold in their custody; the United States therefore had "no claim" on the portion in the Federal Reserve Bank. "The mere fact that the United States Congress could claim its own competence to legislate on that issue would constitute a serious breach of the universally recognized norms of international law. It is out of the question for France to admit that domestic law overrules international commitments."[36]

The Albanian gold case substantially differed as regards international law. First, there was unanimity among the Governments of the United States, the United Kingdom, and France that the gold should be delivered to Great Britain; that agreement was duly executed and, in accordance with international due process, enabled both Albania and Italy to contest the decision before the International Court of Justice.[37] Second, the action was taken not in pursuance of a unilateral claim but in order to enforce and execute an earlier decision of the International Court; the Three Powers therefore acted within the limits of an internationally adjudicated claim.[38] In the case of the Czechoslovak gold

[33] *House Hearing, supra* note 24, at 180 (letter from Deputy Legal Adviser, Dep't of State, to Attorney General).

[34] *Id.* at 21 (statement of Assistant General Counsel for International Affairs, Dep't of the Treasury). A detailed argument is at p. 28 *ff.*

[35] *Id.* at 24.

[36] *Ibid.*

[37] Albania did not avail itself of the opportunity and made no application to the Court. Italy instituted proceedings against the United States, the United Kingdom, and France, but the Court found that the matter upon which it had been asked to adjudicate was in fact concerned with a claim of Italy against Albania. Without Albania's consent, the Court ruled that it had no jurisdiction in the case.

[38] *See* Corfu Channel Case (Merits), [1949] ICJ REP. 12, and (Compensation), *id.* at 244.

there was neither an agreement among the Three Powers nor any international decision to implement.

The Most-Favored-Nation Clause

From the beginning, the Czechoslovak Government emphasized that the question of compensation depended partly upon the advantages granted to Czechoslovak export trade because its membership in the General Agreement on Tariffs and Trade (GATT) had not brought it most-favored-nation status. The 1974 tentative agreement was linked to possible most-favored-nation treatment for Czechoslovakia. However, the new claims settlement Agreement involves no such linkage. Although it does remove one obstacle to more normal political and economic relations between the two countries, U.S. negotiators made clear that they considered claims an issue unrelated to trade, and that any agreement on claims would involve no commitment by the United States to offer most-favored-nation status or any other trade concessions.[39]

The human rights situation in Czechoslovakia obviously loomed in the background. The repressive measures taken by the Government against its citizens hampered the negotiations, particularly in light of the need for congressional approval of any agreement reached.

II. THE IMPLEMENTING LEGISLATION

The Role of Congress Before 1981

In 1958, at the request of the administration, Congress enacted legislation[40] establishing a procedure for American citizens to file claims with the U.S. Foreign Claims Settlement Commission for the losses they had sustained from the nationalization of their property in Czechoslovakia. The Commission adjudicated 2,630 claims against Czechoslovakia in the amount of $72 million, plus $41 million in interest, by 1962. Under congressional authorization, approximately $8.5 million worth of the adjudicated claims were satisfied from the proceeds of the sale of the Czechoslovak steel mill equipment.

On two occasions, however, namely in 1963 and in 1974, Congress was responsible for the repudiation by the U.S. Government of tentative settlements with Czechoslovakia. Information regarding the 1974 arrangement reached Congress during its deliberations on the Trade Act of 1974; Congress promptly secured its control over the matter by inserting a new section 408 into the Act calling for the renegotiation of the arrangement and its submission to Congress as part of any agreement made with Czechoslovakia. It further stipulated that none of the gold in question could be released without congressional approval.[41]

Congress did not oppose the previous settlements and issue this injunction in 1974 solely out of concern over the Czechoslovak nationalization case. As

[39] H.R. REP. NO. 97-385, 97th Cong., 1st Sess. 9 (1981).

[40] Title IV of the International Claims Settlement Act of 1949, as amended, Pub. L. No. 85-604, 72 Stat. 527 (codified at 22 U.S.C.A. §1621 *et seq.*).

[41] 19 U.S.C. §2438.

a supporting Senate report put it:

> One-sided agreements of this nature are especially dangerous to the United States and its citizens at this particular time in history when nations in various parts of the world are threatening to expropriate or nationalize U.S. properties worth billions of dollars, while other nations have already taken valuable U.S. holdings without the payment of just compensation. The United States simply cannot afford to proclaim in the face of this trend that expropriations of U.S. properties will quickly be forgotten if the taking nation ultimately offers a mere pittance in return.[42]

The time when these words were uttered was one of heightened sensitivity on all sides. In 1974 the emerging concept of a "New International Economic Order" was given normative expression in the Charter of Economic Rights and Duties of States by the UN General Assembly.[43] Clearly, the proposed Czechoslovak settlement touched off a protective reaction in Congress, which not only perceived the immediate inconvenience to some 26 hundred individual claimants, but also grasped the long-term implications as justification for a new international principle.[44] The view that only partial compensation is due for nationalization of foreign property would have received additional confirmation in the U.S.-Czechoslovak agreement.

The role assumed by Congress was not limited to monitoring the developments and reserving its approval for a final agreement: it also functioned as a spur to the negotiating process. When a stall developed and prospects for an early settlement receded, congressional determination to assure payment to the restive claimants intensified and led to a legislative proposal to liquidate the Czechoslovak gold so that they could be paid if a satisfactory negotiated settlement could not be reached promptly.[45]

The Czechoslovakian Claims Settlement Act of 1981

The U.S.-Czechoslovak Agreeement of November 6, 1981 provides that the U.S. Government will have exclusive competence to distribute the compensation received, in accordance with its legislation.[46] The Czechoslovakian Claims Settlement Act of 1981, passed on December 16, 1981, constitutes the implementing legislation. In addition to giving the congressional approval required under section 408(b) of the Trade Act of 1974, it authorizes the Foreign Claims Settlement Commission to reconsider certain U.S. claims against Czechoslovakia and provides for the distribution and disbursement to U.S. claimants by the Treasury of the funds received under the Agreement.

[42] *See* S. REP. NO. 93–1298, 93d Cong., 2d Sess. (1974).

[43] GA Res. 3281 (XXIX), 29 UN GAOR Supp. (No. 31) 50, UN Doc. A/9631 (1974), *reprinted in* 69 AJIL 484 (1975), 14 ILM 251 (1975).

[44] On the principle enunciated in Article 2(2)(c) of the Charter, see, *e.g.*, García-Amador, *The Proposed New International Economic Order: A New Approach to the Law Governing Nationalization and Compensation*, 12 LAW. AMERICAS 1 (1980); Weston, *The Charter of the Economic Rights and Duties of States and the Deprivation of Foreign-Owned Wealth*, 75 AJIL 437 (1981).

[45] H.R. 7338, *supra* note 30, and S. 754, 97th Cong., 1st Sess. (1981). However, as everybody seemed to recognize that agreement would be preferable, action on the bill was not pressed and it was reported without recommendation. S. REP. NO. 97–211, 97th Cong., 1st Sess. 3 (1981).

[46] Art. 3.

The net sum of $81.5 million, minus a small sum for expenses incurred by the Department of the Treasury and the U.S. Foreign Claims Settlement Commission, is to be divided among three separate accounts in the Czechoslovakian Claims Fund established by section 402(b) of the International Claims Settlement Act of 1949:

> (1) An account of $74.55 million, to be available for payments on the unpaid balance of awards certified by the Foreign Claims Settlement Commission pursuant to section 410 of the International Claims Settlement Act of 1949;[47]
>
> (2) An account of $1.5 million, to be available for payment of such *new* claims as may arise from the taking of property between August 8, 1958[48] and the date on which the Agreement entered into force;[49] and
>
> (3) An account of $5.4 million, to be available for *ex gratia* payments of previously denied claims of the so-called Beneš group of claimants.[50]

Nationality and Ownership. The policy of the United States has been to espouse claims that have been "continuously owned" by its nationals from the date of the injury to the date the claim is presented.[51] This principle is reiterated in the Agreement.[52] The Czechoslovakian Claims Settlement Act, however, departs from this principle in one important respect: it sets aside a portion of the settlement for persons who were not U.S. citizens when their property was nationalized. These claimants, who are referred to as the "Beneš" group, include persons (1) whose property was expropriated by the pre-February 1948 Government of President Beneš on or after January 1, 1945 and before January 26, 1948; (2) who had become U.S. nationals by February 26, 1948; and (3) whose previous claims were denied by the U.S. Foreign Claims Settlement Commission solely on the ground that "such property was not owned by a person who was a national of the United States on the date of such nationalization or taking."[53] The Commission is directed to redetermine the validity and the amount of any such claim that had been denied.

The idea to compensate these former Czechoslovak citizens and other persons, to whom the compensation promised in 1945 had never been made, first appeared during congressional consideration of the bill that contemplated liquidating the Czechoslovak gold. However, it was tempered by the reaction of the Department of State:

> Under well-established principles of international law, to which the United States adheres, the United States cannot espouse claims against

[47] Section 4(b)(1) of the 1981 Act.

[48] The date that Congress approved Title IV ("Claims Against Czechoslovakia") of the International Claims Settlement Act of 1949, *supra* note 40.

[49] Section 4(b)(2) of the 1981 Act. These are not nationalization claims, as no nationalization took place in Czechoslovakia between 1958 and 1981.

[50] Section 4(b)(3) of the 1981 Act.

[51] For the policy with regard to claims against Czechoslovakia, see §405 of the International Claims Settlement Act of 1949, as amended, *supra* note 40. Under section 401 of the Act, a "national of the United States" is defined to be either a natural person who is a citizen or who owes permanent allegiance to the United States, or a legal person organized under U.S. law if more than a 50% interest is owned by nationals of the United States. It does not include aliens.

[52] Art. 2.

[53] Section 6(b) of the 1981 Act.

> foreign governments for injuries inflicted upon persons who were not U.S. citizens at the time of the injury. . . . [T]he United States view [is] that, under international law, the date of taking is fixed by the date of the expropriation decree and/or the date of physical seizure, and not by a subsequent date of repudiation of an undertaking to provide compensation.
>
> Deviation from the established legal principles cited above would create a precedent with implications beyond this immediate case. It could open a broad range of new and marginal claims for the U.S. Government to pursue, without support under international law. At the same time, it could erode our ability to espouse legitimate claims of U.S. citizens in the face of worthless undertakings by a foreign government to provide future compensation.[54]

Despite this warning, when the time came to implement the negotiated settlement, Congress decided that payment had been denied to this group of claimants on grounds that were "faulty and inconsistent with the intent of Congress in enacting the 1958 law calling for the adjudication of claims against Czechoslovakia."[55] The fact that payment will be made *ex gratia*, as a matter of equity, may be psychologically important but seems to be irrelevant as a matter of law. That was probably why it was deemed advisable to create the legal fiction of "deferred" taking of property, which would make it possible to hold that injury was inflicted upon the claimants after they became U.S. nationals. The reasoning behind this legal construction appears in the report of the House Committee on Foreign Affairs:

> These claimants—the so-called "Beneš" claimants—were U.S. nationals by February 26, 1948, when the Communists took power in Czechoslovakia. Action, however, had been taken against some or all of their properties by the previous government of Eduard Beneš, albeit with public promises by that government of fair and just compensation. . . . The committee believes . . . that actions against property accompanied by promise of compensation should not, in this case, have been treated as takings, and that, in fact, the properties of these claimants were taken by the Communist government when that government took power and repudiated the promises of compensation made by the Beneš government.[56]

The position adopted by Congress refers to equality of lawful rights of the person and to protection in preserving these lawful rights when the person changes his nationality. Even though Congress did not intend to innovate insofar as international law was concerned,[57] it helped raise the question of basic fairness in the dogma of nationality of claims.

The establishment of an international law of human rights, which depends substantially on intercession by other states in behalf of the rights even of a state's own nationals, and the fact that the rights of individuals are generally

[54] S. REP. NO. 97-211, *supra* note 45, at 5 (letter of Assistant Secretary of State for Congressional Affairs).

[55] H.R. REP. NO. 97-385, *supra* note 39, at 10.

[56] *Ibid.*

[57] Quite to the contrary: on the doctrinal plane it reaffirmed, in a face-saving clause inserted in section 6(2)(B) of the 1981 Act, the previous principle and practice of the United States, and added that "[i]n making payments under this section, the Congress does not establish any precedent for future claims payments."

becoming less dependent on nationality make it necessary to reexamine certain assumptions underpinning the dogma of nationality. Even though property rights have lost much of their sanctity, the right of an individual not to be arbitrarily deprived of his property is a human right recognized in the Universal Declaration. In addition, since some countries take unnecessarily harsh measures toward their former citizens,[58] it would be unfair to deny those persons protection by their new homeland.[59]

The principle of nationality of claims was never regarded as absolute,[60] and some have even doubted its reasonableness.[61] Sir Hersch Lauterpacht wondered what position the International Court of Justice would adopt if it were faced with the problem in a concrete situation. He concluded that there was

> no warrant for the assumption that the Court will invariably respect the claim of a sovereign State not to be made accountable for the infliction of an injury upon an individual, in a manner contrary to international law, except at the instance of the State of which that individual is a national at the time of the occurrence of the injury and of the institution of the proceedings before the court.[62]

Consequently, the exception to the rule of nationality of claims made in favor of the "Beneš" group of claimants is not in conflict with international law, and no legal fiction of the sort created by the congressional committee was needed to justify its adoption.

Dual Nationality. Under the terms of the United States-Czechoslovak Naturalization Treaty of July 16, 1928, "nationals of Czechoslovakia who have been or shall be naturalized in the territories of the United States shall be held by Czechoslovakia to have lost their former nationality and to be nationals of

[58] *Compare, e.g.*, the recent practice of the Czechoslovak authorities with regard to property rights of Czechoslovak citizens who apply and are granted permission to emigrate from Czechoslovakia. Such persons are obliged to file with the local authorities a declaration renouncing all their property rights and interests in Czechoslovakia. Persons who have left the country without official permission are criminally prosecuted under section 109 of the Penal Code and, if convicted, are sentenced *in absentia* and their properties confiscated. In this way, the Czechoslovak authorities seek to prevent the espousal of claims of former citizens by their new country of residence.

[59] Such protection is routinely extended to claims arising from certain material interests, such as social security or alimony payments. The 1981 Act requires in section 12 that the Secretary of State conduct a review analyzing the equity and reciprocity of the social security payments made to residents of each country by the other. The review should recommend ways to achieve greater equity for the residents of both countries and possible U.S. actions to correct the inequities.

[60] In the case of the Railway Line Panevezys-Saldutiskis, [1939] PCIJ, ser. A/B, No. 76, at 16, the Permanent Court of International Justice recognized that the rule of nationality of claims was subject to exceptions; and in the Reparation for Injuries case, [1949] ICJ REP. 174, 180, the International Court of Justice denied the applicability of the rule in the case before it and stated that there were important exceptions to the rule.

[61] *See* the dissenting opinion of Judge van Eysinga in the *Railway Line Panevezys-Saldutiskis* case, especially his observation on the "doubtful reasonableness" of a rule "which would entail that, when a change of sovereignty takes place, the new State or the State which has increased its territory would not be able to espouse any claim of any of its new nationals in regard to injury suffered before the change of nationality." [1939] PCIJ, ser. A/B, No. 76, at 35. This observation can be applied, *mutatis mutandis*, when a person has changed his nationality not as a result of the change of territorial sovereignty but because of voluntary or forced emigration.

[62] H. LAUTERPACHT, *supra* note 28, at 352.

the United States." However, there is an exception to this rule: "The foregoing provisions of this Article shall not be applicable to a national of either country who obtains naturalization in the other while his country is at war."[63] It is only in connection with this exception that a conflict of nationality may arise.

Technically, the state of war between Czechoslovakia and Germany during the Second World War was terminated by the unilateral declaration of the President of the Czechoslovak Republic of February 3, 1955. When it began is a matter of some controversy. On December 16, 1941, President Beneš, then in exile, proclaimed that Czechoslovakia was in a state of war with all countries at war with the United Kingdom, the Soviet Union, and the United States, and that the state of war with Germany had begun the moment that the German Government had committed acts of violence against the security, independence, and territorial integrity of the Czechoslovak Republic. Subsequently, the specific date was variously interpreted as September 17, 1938 (the day of the first incursions of irregular troops organized by Nazi Germany), September 29, 1938 (the day the Munich settlement was imposed upon Czechoslovakia), and March 15, 1939 (the day the German armies completed the occupation of the country).[64]

As could be expected, the Czechoslovak negotiators asserted that, for the purpose of determining eligibility for compensation, those persons that were naturalized in the United States between September 17, 1938 and February 3, 1955 could not be held to have lost their former nationality and were therefore dual nationals. As such, they were not to be included in the negotiated settlement. However, the date of termination of war for the above purpose was later agreed to coincide with the cessation of hostilities in the European theater on May 8, 1945. As a consequence, the number of claims presented in behalf of American citizens thought to have dual nationality dwindled appreciably.

Although no formal agreement has been reached on this particular problem, Czechoslovakia seems to accept the view that personal status is determined by dominant nationality.[65]

CONCLUDING OBSERVATIONS

It has been the theory of international law that when a state takes up a case of its national by resorting to international protection on his behalf, that state is actually asserting its own right. The espousing state therefore has the right to dispose of the claim, can compromise it, and can accept a settlement providing less than full compensation to its national.[66] And strictly, international law does not require the espousing state to pay the recovery over to its nationals.

[63] TS No. 804, 96 LNTS 2208, Art. 1.

[64] *See* Kopal, *Počátek válečného stavu mezi Československem a Německem* (The Commencement of the State of War Between Czechoslovakia and Germany), 13 ČASOPIS PRO MEZINÁRODNÍ PRÁVO (Prague) 135 (1969).

[65] *See generally* Rode, *Dual Nationals and the Doctrine of Dominant Nationality,* 53 AJIL 139 (1959).

[66] *See* Kunz, *The Nottebohm Judgment,* 54 *id.* at 561 (1960). U.S. practice has been to pay the claimants. *See* note 6.

This theory is reflected in the U.S.-Czechoslovak Agreement of November 6, 1981. As from the settlement date,[67] the Czechoslovak Government is released from all obligations to the United States or to its nationals relating to properties, rights, or interests affected by Czechoslovak measures of nationalization, expropriation, disposition, or other taking that arose prior to the date of the Agreement.[68] The U.S. Government undertook not to pursue or present any such claims to the Czechoslovak Government, and the latter agreed to refer any such claims presented directly to it to the former.[69] The question arises whether these terms apply to unsatisfied portions of claims made by the "Beneš" group. Although they were designated by Congress as beneficiaries of the lump sum settlement, their claims remain outside its scope as defined by Article 2 of the Agreement. This ambiguity, however, is more apparent than real. If such claims were ever presented to the Czechoslovak Government, it could not be prevented from referring them to the United States, and once before the U.S. Government, they would become inadmissible for having been satisfied already, albeit only partially.[70]

VRATISLAV PECHOTA

RESTATEMENT OF THE FOREIGN RELATIONS LAW OF THE UNITED STATES (REVISED): TENTATIVE DRAFT NO. 3

On May 19, 1982, the reporters presented to the American Law Institute Tentative Draft No. 3 of the *Restatement of the Foreign Relations Law of the United States* (*Revised*).[1]

Tentative Draft No. 3 includes:

Part IV. Jurisdiction (continued), §§401, 419–420, 431–433

Part V. The Law of the Sea, §§501–502, 511–517, 521–522

Part VII. The Protection of Persons (Natural and Juridical), §§701–703, 711–713, 721–722

The second segment of Part IV (Jurisdiction), which is included in Tentative Draft No. 3, includes an amended version of section 401 which had been laid over the previous year.[2] In presenting the amended version the reporters reiterated their conclusion that the limitations that international law imposes on different aspects of a state's jurisdiction can best be understood under three headings: jurisdiction to prescribe, to adjudicate, to enforce. Comment *a* explains

[67] The "settlement date" is defined by Art. 7 of the Agreement; it is Feb. 20, 1982.

[68] Art. 8(1).

[69] Art. 8(2).

[70] Under Article 4(2) of the Agreement, the U.S. Government undertook to furnish to the Czechoslovak Government the names of claimants who receive awards and copies of the decisions and awards.

[1] Tentative Draft No. 1 was considered by the Institute in June 1980, and Tentative Draft No. 2 in May 1981. *See* 74 AJIL 954 (1980), 75 AJIL 987 (1981).

[2] *See* 75 AJIL at 989.

that these are not presented as three discrete conceptual categories, since adjudication can be seen largely as a means of law enforcement. But the three headings identify different aspects of the exercise of authority by a state, which, because they employ different means and have different consequences, have led to different principles of limitation under international law. In particular, while Tentative Draft No. 2 had presented the principles of limitation applicable to adjudication (whether or not used for what is commonly seen as law enforcement), sections 431–433, in this Tentative Draft, set forth limitations on enforcement other than through the courts, including limitations both on administrative action and on police action in foreign countries.

Sections 419–420 present additional United States applications illustrating the principles of jurisdiction to prescribe set forth in sections 402–403, Tentative Draft No. 2.[3] These sections are applications in particular of section 403(3), which addressed the problem that arises when two states having jurisdiction to prescribe with respect to a person issue contradictory demands. Under section 419, prohibitions by the state in whose territory the act is to be carried out ordinarily prevail over orders of other states.

Section 420 applies that principle to requests for disclosure of information. It requires that an order to produce documents and information located abroad be issued by a court, not merely by a private party or by a U.S. agency as is possible under the Federal Rules of Civil Procedure and comparable State rules. Section 420 also requires that a request for production of documents or information located abroad meet a more stringent test of direct relevancy, necessity, and materiality than is required for comparable requests for documents or information located in the United States. If disclosure of information located outside the United States is prohibited by a law of the state in which the information is located, the person to whom the order is directed may be required to make a good faith effort to secure permission from the foreign authorities to make the information available. The court may not ordinarily impose sanctions on the person except in cases of deliberate concealment or removal of the information, or of failure to make a good faith effort to obtain permission to make it available.

Section 431 deals with jurisdiction to enforce law through executive, administrative, or police actions, including such measures as placing someone on a blacklist or restraining the transfer of assets. The Tentative Draft states that such measures, too, may be employed to enforce law against persons located outside the territory of the enforcing state only where the state has jurisdiction to prescribe, and if the person is given notice and a fair opportunity to be heard. Enforcement measures must be reasonably related to the violation and proportional to its gravity.

Sections 432–433 set forth the limitations on the means that a state may use outside its territory to enforce its laws. International law forbids the exercise of enforcement functions in a foreign state without its consent, and if a person is abducted from another state without its consent, the other state may demand that the individual be returned. But if return is not demanded, the Tentative

[3] *Id.* at 989–90.

Draft accepts *male captus, bene detentus* as the general rule under both international law and the law of the United States.[4]

In Part V, the reporters set forth

> so much of the Law of the Sea as seems desirable to include in this Restatement and which it seems safe to restate at this time. As the tentative table of contents indicates, we plan an additional chapter on the Resources of the High Seas but that, we have concluded, had better wait at least until the final outcome of the UN Law of the Sea Conference. The materials here presented rely heavily on the Draft Convention that has emerged from the Third Law of the Sea Conference, since, as regards the subjects we deal with, the Draft Convention largely reflects principles of customary law and previous conventions to which the United States is party [p. xxiv].

The Tentative Draft (§511), then, accepts as customary law a 12-mile territorial sea, an extended continental shelf, and a 200-mile exclusive economic zone, as well as a special status for archipelagic states (§511, Comment *g*). The draft is more tentative as to the principles of delimitation of the exclusive economic zone (or the continental shelf), which remained highly controversial, and their final articulation still uncertain, when the Tentative Draft was published.

When Part V was considered at the annual session of the Institute, the reporters indicated that the text would have to be looked at again in the light of developments, including the position taken by the United States during the final stages of the UN Conference on the Law of the Sea and after the conference was completed.

Part VII, Protection of Persons (Natural and Juridical) "looks substantially different from the treatment of those matters in the previous Restatement. It includes the international law of Human Rights, which has developed considerably in the past decades" (p. xxiv). Particularly noteworthy is section 702, which sets forth as customary international law of human rights:

> A state violates international law if, as a matter of state policy, it practices, encourages or condones
>
> (a) genocide,
> (b) slavery or slave trade,
> (c) the murder or causing the disappearance of individuals,
> (d) torture or other cruel, inhuman or degrading treatment or punishment,
> (e) prolonged arbitrary detention,
> (f) systematic racial discrimination, or
> (g) consistent patterns of gross violations of internationally recognized human rights.

[4] *See* Ker v. Illinois, 119 U.S. 436 (1886); Frisbie v. Collins, 342 U.S. 519, 522 (1952). Section 433(3) of the Tentative Draft states that under the law of the United States, a person apprehended in a foreign state, whether by foreign or by U.S. officials, and delivered to the United States, may be prosecuted in the United States, but finds an exception where the person "was treated in such outrageous and reprehensible manner as to shock the conscience of civilized society." *Compare* United States v. Toscanino, 500 F.2d 267 (2d Cir. 1974); *see* Tentative Draft No. 3, §433, Comment *c* and Reporters' Note 3.

Section 703 sets forth the remedies for violation of human rights. It takes the position that a state party to an international human rights agreement has, as against any other state party violating the agreement, the remedies generally available for violation of an international agreement, as well as any special remedies provided by the particular agreement (§703(1)). Any state may pursue international remedies against any other state for a violation of the customary international law of human rights (§703(2)). As to "humanitarian intervention" by one state in the territory of another where human rights were violated, Comment *e* states:

> It is generally accepted that a state may act to rescue victims or potential victims in an action strictly limited to the purpose, in circumstances not likely to involve disproportionate destruction of life or property in the state where the rescue takes place. Whether a state may intervene with military force in the territory of another state without its consent, not to rescue the victims but to prevent, terminate or suppress human rights violations, is not agreed or authoritatively determined. Such intervention might be acceptable if taken pursuant to resolution of a UN body or of a regional organization such as the Organization of American States.

Private remedies for human rights violations are available only where provided by international agreement or under a state's municipal law. The reporters cite (Note 7) the individual remedy found in *Filartiga v. Peña-Irala*[5] for a victim of torture in Paraguay against the alleged torturer, under 28 U.S.C., section 1350, giving the U.S. federal courts jurisdiction of a "civil action by an alien for a tort only, committed in violation of the law of nations."

Sections 711–713 deal with state responsibility for injury to nationals of other states. In presenting these sections the reporters noted that the relevant law, especially as it relates to economic injury, is in some disarray, but the Tentative Draft does not differ from the previous *Restatement* in major respects on substantive issues (although the subject is presented differently and treated in briefer compass, in accordance with the overall plan of the revised *Restatement*). The reporters noted the turbulent history of that law and the vigorous attack on it, particularly the effort to have questions of compensation for expropriation governed by national law alone. They conclude, however, that expropriation of alien properties continues to be governed by international law and that international law requires, *inter alia*, that there be "just compensation." The reporters note that it has been and continues to be the U.S. position that just compensation means "prompt, adequate and effective compensation."

Tentative Draft No. 3 takes "an intermediate position" on the significance of an "internationalization clause" in a concession contract between a state and a private investor. According to the draft, if such a clause incorporates by reference the principles of international law or common principles, they are to be applied, but the clause does not convert the contract into an international agreement governed by the law of international agreements as reflected in the Vienna Convention on the Law of Treaties. That state would have a basis for claim under international law principles of responsibility for injury to foreign nationals if there were "discriminatory or other arbitrary repudiation" of the

[5] 630 F.2d 876 (2d Cir. 1980).

contract, or if, the contract being breached, the private party were not "given an adequate forum to determine the claim of breach or is not compensated for any breach determined to have occurred" (§712(2) and Comment *h*).

Tentative Draft No. 3 also includes sections 721–722, which restate selected principles of constitutional law particularly relevant to the foreign relations of the United States. Section 722 declares that while the Constitution expressly limits certain benefits to citizens, the safeguards of the Bill of Rights and of the Thirteenth and Fourteenth Amendments are enjoyed by aliens equally with citizens, generally even by temporary or undocumented aliens, although the equal protection of the laws does not preclude some distinctions between citizens and aliens, or between categories of aliens. The Institute did not have time to consider those sections at its annual meeting and they will presumably be presented again as part of Tentative Draft No. 4 in spring 1983.

The reporters indicated that they hoped to present in 1983 the rest of Part IV (Jurisdiction and Judgments), Part VI (The Law of the Environment), and an installment of Part VIII (Selected Law of International Economic Relations). A Tentative Comprehensive Table of Contents of the entire project, including both the materials already presented and those projected, appears at the front of Tentative Draft No. 3 (pp. xii–xxi).

LOUIS HENKIN

BOOK REVIEWS AND NOTES

EDITED BY LEO GROSS

Managing the Risks of International Agreement. By Richard B. Bilder. Madison: The University of Wisconsin Press, 1981. Pp. xi, 302. Index. $22.50.

Professor Bilder's concise analysis, systematization, and appraisal of risk reduction in *concluding* international agreements is a sign of the times and a valuable contribution to legal craftsmanship. Understandably, the author safeguards himself by seven instructive caveats.

Against the background of the writer's varied diplomatic and legal experiences, the sections in the book on nonbinding arrangements, equivocal agreements, and rewards for full performance acquire an authenticity of their own. Conversely, frank admissions such as that of the primarily Western responsibility for the metalegal character of the Helsinki Final Act can but enhance confidence in the academic integrity of Bilder's study.

With few adaptations, the book is likely to suit détente—and cold war—managers anywhere as a reliable manual for their trainee-negotiators. In due course, these products of the Wisconsin master are likely to find that their protective efforts will result in their own neutralization and, in all probability, some contraction of consensual engagements.

Bilder attempts to counteract negative effects of the legal techniques expounded by pointing to five ways towards more effective and constructive risk management. Yet, what appears to be needed beyond this is a complementary work, which none would be better qualified to write than the author of the book under review, on managing the risks of international *non*agreement.

Admittedly, such a work would have to be addressed to higher echelons than foreign service legal departments: the top-class mandarins concerned with major policy decisions. Across the ages, the relevant issues appear to have changed but little and can be condensed into three questions of stark simplicity:

(1) Are the risks of nonagreement preferable to those of agreement?

(2) Are there weighty reasons against departing from the well-tried working principles of formal and substantive reciprocity?

(3) Is a contracting party powerful and self-confident enough to leave to its potential partner the risk of going back on its consensual undertakings?

G. SCHWARZENBERGER
London

Conflict and Compromise. By Edward McWhinney. New York: Holmes & Meier Publishers, Inc., 1981. Pp. 160. Index. $17.50, cloth; $8.50, paper.

In this concise and readable book, Professor McWhinney captures the broad currents of change that have transformed the international arena in the postwar era. Using an interdisciplinary approach, he shows that this transformation has brought with it new political and economic challenges and created new tensions which, if not resolved, are likely to lead to serious conflict in the interstate system. His point of departure is the question whether international law has kept pace with these changes and whether it has a role to play today in the prevention of international conflict and in the very process of change in the world order.

The book first examines four "revolutions" that have marked the course of recent history: the fall of colonialism, the rise of socialism, the development of modern economic thought, and the dramatic advances in science and technology. These revolutions, it is argued, have had a profound impact on the international community, not simply by increasing drastically the number and diversity of nations, but by creating new possibilities and expectations which the "old" international community did not know. Economic theoreticians, we are reminded, have raised the hope that new nations may skip some of the long and tortuous stages through which Europe, and to a lesser extent the United States, had to go to reach an industrialized state.

But while these revolutions were taking place, a corresponding revolution in international law, the book suggests, did not occur. Because of the "narrowness of [its] original ideological basis," international law has not been able to "encompass all the main competing, social and economic systems of the present day." It has not developed that "necessary symbiosis between positive law and social change that we regard as axiomatic for our own internal law system." The result is a mistrust of international law by developing nations who see it as part of a system designed to preserve the economic and political status quo.

The rest of the book examines cursorily major issues of world relations such as the nature of the UN Charter, the role of the World Court, détente, disarmament, international technical cooperation, and the movement toward a "New International Economic Order." While insightful, this sweeping approach fails to generate an appropriate synthesis. Legal questions posed at the beginning are not integrated into the analysis and the various issues discussed are left largely unconnected.

The final chapter ends with a list of what the author identifies as key "antinomies" or competing choices which we face for forging the future direction of the world community. These are on the whole familiar themes (*e.g.*, the bilateral vs. the multilateral approach), and are unaided by significant analysis.

One entry on the list of antinomies is the "choice" between judicial methods of settling disputes and "other modes of dispute settlement favouring diplomatic and more consciously political methods." Though he poses them as mutually exclusive, McWhinney seems aware that both are possible and necessary. In his able discussion on détente, he notes that the initial step-by-step diplomatic approach served as the basis for eventual legal arrangements. For this he gives credit to Western lawyers and university professors who "refused to be constrained by traditional official positions" and who insisted that success was possible only by "eschewing [the] bitter and largely futile debate over political ideology and concentrating on current tensions in Soviet-Western relations together with the immediate range of practical solutions."

For the general reader and for students who want to get some sense of the general contours of the world system, *Conflict and Compromise* should prove instructive. The panoramic view of international relations is perceptive and marked by good judgment. But although sensitive to change, the book neither inspires change nor offers guidance as to how it may be brought about. How can international law be updated to "capture the dynamics of the world revolution of our time" and deal effectively with the pressing problems facing us today? A more pluralistically based international law is no doubt desirable, but it will promote justice and world order no better than the "old" international law without more guidance than we are given here.

ROGER FISHER
Board of Editors

International Adjudication: Procedural Aspects. By V. S. Mani. The Hague, Boston, London: Martinus Nijhoff Publishers, 1980. Pp. xx, 456. Indexes. Dfl.130; $68.50.

Anyone who is interested in or involved with international adjudication would do well to have this excellent volume at his or her right hand. Its unique feature is that it focuses almost exclusively on international procedure—procedure before ad hoc international arbitral tribunals as well as procedure before the International Court of Justice.

Procedural law assumes a much greater significance in international law than it does in municipal law (or at least in municipal adjudication), where the right of the parties as to choice and composition of a tribunal is restricted and where parties may be compelled to submit to a tribunal. According to the author, "it is almost impossible to bring two disputant States before an international tribunal if the tribunal cannot command their confidence."

In order to command the confidence of the parties, a tribunal's rules of procedure must be seen to be upholding two fundamental procedural rights, "*audi, alteram partem*" (the right of all parties to be heard) and "equality of the parties." These two procedural norms are really two sides of the same coin. They both ensure that neither party is given a procedural advantage over the other and "instil confidence in the minds of litigant States on the efficiency and impartiality of [the tribunal's] mechanism." These two procedural norms serve other important functions as well. They "tend to serve the sovereign sensibilities of States." They "facilitate effective conduct of adjudication enabling the tribunal to gather adequate material information concerning the dispute and [to] adjudicate the controverted claims." Finally, "they ensure effective participation by the disputant parties in the communicative process" (p. 15).

Mani considers the fundamental procedural norms as "general principles of law recognized by civilized nations." He then takes the reader through a variety of topics: initiation of proceedings, written proceedings, oral arguments, presentation of evidence, intervention, and interim measures of protection. In each of these areas he raises and solves a number of practical questions that he relates back to fundamental procedural norms. The book is not a practice manual, but a scholarly treatment of the subject and all the better for it.

Despite the considerable practical value of the work, a number of cautions and criticisms are in order. The work undervalues the role of the application in unilaterally instituted proceedings. It is treated as one species of *acte introductif*. In Mani's view, "the main object of the document instituting proceedings is to activate the jurisdictional facilities of a tribunal with respect to a particular disputed situation" (p. 88).

Actually, the application plays an important role in framing the issues to be put before the Court. Failure to pay sufficient attention to the drafting of the application can have a prejudicial effect on the applicant's case. In the *Polish Agrarian Reform and the German Minority* case,[1] for instance, the Permanent Court of International Justice denied the Applicant's request for interim measures on the ground that the measures requested, injunctive relief from future injury, were inconsistent with the Application, which merely requested declaratory relief with respect to acts already committed.

The author would also have performed a service if he had attempted to clear up what must be a source of confusion surrounding the word "pleadings." To the common lawyer the word relates to the *acte introductif* and formal reply. It does not refer to the detailed argumentation contained in a brief or other submission, which would be the common law parallel to the "memorial." Nor does it refer to oral argument.

The book purports to examine the procedure of international arbitral tribunals and the procedure of permanent tribunals such as the International Court of Justice and the Court of Justice of the European Communities. A reader with a special interest in the latter Court will find only scattered references to it, and the study does not even mention such tribunals as the European Court of Human Rights. The author's perceptions are undoubtedly valid for those tribunals, but they are primarily based on an examination of the International Court of Justice.

Last, despite the considerable scholarship displayed by the author, there are some gaps. It is somewhat surprising that a book dealing with international arbitration does not contain a single reference to J. Gillis Wetter's five-volume work on the subject.[2] Likewise, the chapter on interim protection overlooks important articles by M. H. Mendelson,[3] J. B. Merrills,[4] and others.

JEROME B. ELKIND
The University of Auckland

International Criminal Law: A Draft International Criminal Code. By M. Cherif Bassiouni. Alphen aan den Rijn: Sijthoff and Noordhoff, 1980. Pp. xxxv, 250. Dfl.100; $50.

The assassinations of King Alexander of Yugoslavia and Prime Minister Barthou of France created interest in the need to regulate international terrorism and concomitantly in the desirability of a court with jurisdiction over offenses

[1] [1933] PCIJ, ser. A/B, No. 58, at 175.

[2] THE INTERNATIONAL ARBITRAL PROCESS: PUBLIC AND PRIVATE (1979).

[3] *Interim Measures of Protection in Cases of Contested Jurisdiction*, 46 BRIT. Y.B. INT'L L. 259 (1972–1973).

[4] *Interim Measures of Protection and the Substantive Jurisdiction of the International Court*, 36 CAMBRIDGE L.J. 86 (1977).

described as crimes by international law. The efforts of the League of Nations to this end were frustrated by the resistance of states to accepting the draft conventions prepared under the League's auspices, and it was not until the war crimes trials consequent upon World War II that the problem of an international criminal law again became of interest. Originally, it appeared that international crimes would be restricted to those against peace and security, but the sudden upsurge in terrorist acts beginning in the 1960's created an interest in an international criminal law that was wider in scope and that would apply to individual actors. Bassiouni has for some years been a prolific writer in this field and since 1974 he has been Secretary-General of the International Association of Penal Law, as well as Dean of the Association's International Institute of Higher Studies in Criminal Sciences. In this latter capacity he has prepared a draft of an International Criminal Code which, in a revised form, has been submitted to the United Nations. The present book provides the text of this Draft Code.

The volume is divided into two sections. In the general part is to be found a short survey of the history, scope, and content of international criminal law, while the remaining two hundred or so pages comprise the text of the Draft Code together with a 70-page bibliography. The Code itself not only consists of a list and definition of crimes, but also embodies an "enforcement part" that imposes obligations upon states and gives the Code a practical significance. The Code reflects the postwar origins of interest in international criminal law, since it opens with wrongs that are war-related: aggression, war crimes, and the unlawful use of weapons, genocide, and crimes against humanity. It is interesting to note that although there is a section concerned with defenses, there is no reference to the issue of superior orders. The new interest in the political aspect of international criminal law is represented by the crime of apartheid, yet Geneva Protocol I of 1977, which makes this a grave breach of the law of armed conflict, is not mentioned. Traditional offenses *contra jure gentium* appear in the form of slavery and piracy, and such generally recognized offenses as unlawful use of the mails, drug offenses, falsification and counterfeiting, interference with submarine cables, and the traffic in obscene publications reflect the views of the 19th century and the League era. In addition, the Code lists such new international crimes as torture (unfortunately, the commentary was written too early to include any reference to the *Filartiga* decision), aerial hijackings and the like, hostage taking, offenses against internationally protected persons, theft of national and archaeological treasures (a problem of special significance for the United Kingdom as an ex-imperial power), and bribery of public officials. In addition, one offense is included that was originally of concern principally in regard to the law of armed conflict, but that has now assumed more general significance, namely, unlawful medical experimentation. In this connection, perhaps even more important than the definition of the offense is the carefully circumscribed explanation of the defense of consent.

Although it is generally accepted that for an international criminal code to be truly effective there must be an international tribunal possessed of criminal competence, the prospects for such a tribunal are somewhat remote. However, Bassiouni in the enforcement part to his Code obligates the contracting parties to cooperate with an international criminal jurisdiction without giving any outline of a statute for such a tribunal. Instead, he bases his projections on the principle *aut dedere aut judicare* and provides a detailed outline for judicial cooperation among the parties. Finally, there is an appendix "for an international criminal court direct enforcement model." This concerns the activities of an international criminal court, its procedure and jurisdiction, but does not indicate how the tribunal is to be established.

If it were likely that states would be prepared to move towards the adoption of an international criminal code and to accept jurisdiction by some type of international criminal tribunal, there is little doubt that the proposals put forward by Bassiouni and his colleagues could serve as a useful basis for such developments.

L. C. GREEN
University of Alberta

Negara, The Theater State in Nineteenth-Century Bali. By Clifford Geertz. Princeton: Princeton University Press, 1980. Pp. xii, 295. Index. $18.50, cloth; $5.95, paper.

What can we of the international legal community possibly learn from classical Bali? One answer comes easily. Bali, a remote and exotic place, must have exhibited a primitive order, somehow, suggestively, comparable to the international legal order. Geertz's *Negara* invites such comparison without substantiating the analogy as framed: neither order is primitive in the usual sense of the word.

It is, of course, one of the frequent, apparently contagious assertions of international theory, obtaining the status of irreducible wisdom, that the law among nations is a species of primitive law. Primitive legal orders have long histories of autonomy, few subjects (whose demands on the order are furthermore modest and well defined), high levels of regard for rules, and low levels of institutionalization. All these family features get summed up as decentralization—synoptic statement, master concept, all-purpose explanation, incantation. The deficiency of this view is that decentralization is made possible, but not demanded, by an order's autonomy and small size. Beyond this, orders may vary considerably in complexity and formality without appreciably shedding their decentralized character. In other words, centralization is a particular kind of institutionalization that makes a legal order a "modern" one possessing modalities for making and enforcing rules *in their appearance* external to, and poised above, the subjects of the order. Legal orders may take other forms of institutionalization, acquiring an intricacy and formality quite unlike that of the primitive model, but equally unlike the modern one. Such orders may develop as they do because they are not as isolated or as penetrated, as small or as big, as narrow or as broad in scope as available models posit. International law would seem to be one of these intermediate orders, neither fish nor fowl by the usual reckoning, and thus inadequately understood by the usual comparative procedure, *i.e.*, comparing it with primitive orders on the one hand, and modern orders on the other.

These remarks are intended to suggest that international law theory needs a new model for the purposes of comparison. Such a model cannot be just of itself or of its earlier states of development, if the comparison is to have any independent meaning, but must be adduced from the experiences of other legal orders which, from the vantage point of existing models, appear equally intractable. Judging from Geertz's *Negara*, the decentralized state system and complex legal order of 19th-century Bali may be an exceptional candidate for model building. Geertz, already renowned for anthropological studies of Bali, emphasizes the ceremonial dimensions of political order on the island at a time when it was organized into seven principal kingdoms, each with less than one hundred thousand residents. Ancient ties of blood among rulers counted only for rank. Dutch control was nominal and outside influences inconsequential. Deftly using abundant ethnographic materials, Geertz depicts the incessant politics of ruling class culture, the organization of rice growing, trade, religious practice, and public ceremony. Everywhere we find extensive demonstrations of power and position, fractious and often violent behavior nonetheless rule-bound to an extraordinary degree—conflict almost always arising from alleged violations of rules and incompatible interpretations of obligation—and a remarkably stable order, indeed, one that structurally and institutionally has been unchanged for centuries despite, or because of, the extremely fluid quality of the island's politics.

Stability of the system and political flux are occasioned by a "myth of the exemplary," a peculiar transcendence of sovereignty as centralized control in the idea that rule exemplifies a "supernatural order, 'the timeless Indic world of the gods' upon which men should, in strict proportion to their status, seek to pattern their lives" (p. 13). Politics is jockeying over status and success is being confirmed in one's status by having to do nothing. Manifest control is thus *inversely* related to position, for exercising power derogates from the presumption that one's status makes such an activity unnecessary. If we make allowances for the exaggerated quality of these features of Balinese political life, we can easily see their correspondence with features of international life today: Status depends on having power but not using it; politics uses up capabilities and requires much ceremonial display without changing anything very much; actors with high status identify themselves as exemplars of some mythic order of their own making and find themselves accordingly inhibited in what they can do; perennial conflict coexists with, indeed, reinforces, rule-oriented behavior, while the superfluity of rules and their connection to status and exemplary considerations present numerous opportunities for conflict. Bali as a model points up signal features of our own global order, which is exactly what a model should do. These very features are obscured to us otherwise because we are conditioned to look for other things by other models.

Geertz means to correct some of the undue emphasis in Western political theory on coercive control as the defining quality of the state—"[i]mpressed with command, we see little else"—by restoring "our sense of the ordering force of display, regard and drama" (p. 121). What he seeks to do for the theory of the state is a fortiori appropriate to the system of states and becomes an even more telling critique of international theory because, like Bali after all, centralization of coercive potential is not even an ostensible condition of the order. And what Geertz's reconstruction of 19th-century Bali shows us about the international order generally, it does more specifically for its legal properties.

Law as we understand it was hardly the exclusive source of the complex order of Bali but was certainly one of its more visible elements, whether in treaty or customary form. Consider treaties,

> written treaties contracted among various of the major powers of the island. These treaties were hardly the most crucial element in that complex of symbols which maintained at least the vision and promise of overall order, if not very much of its substance. Nor were the treaties so terribly binding as documents, as directed toward such politically central issues as to provide a structural backbone for a genuine "international" polity. They were as purely ceremonial, in their juridical way, as were politesse, gift exchange, and cosmopolitan worship [p. 41].

Now contrast this with the role of customary law at the less exalted level of rice cultivation, and of daily life in general.

> Here, rather as with the treaties between states already discussed, the main framework for . . . case-by-case adjustment was a very highly developed, almost obsessively specific collection of customary practices—established precedents which, though there was no superordinate political body to enforce them, had nonetheless the force of law, if only because they provided a dictionary of legitimate, agreed-upon grievances. . . . The number of these "customary laws" was extremely great, and their content varied widely from place to place. . . . The Balinese seem rarely to have been faced with a situation without an applicable "law," or at least some sort of rule from which they could plausibly draw an analogy [p. 83].

We ought not to be misled by easy linguistic parallels. The correspondence between treaty law and customary law in the Balinese and international orders, respectively, is not exact. By examining the differences, we lay bare two generic kinds of law worked into these intricately institutionalized, ceremonially inclined, but substantially decentralized orders. The first kind, represented in Bali by treaties and in the international order by some of the grander multilateral treaties, General Assembly declarations, agreements like the Helsinki Final Act, judgments of the World Court, and conceivably some unilateral actions labeled doctrines, seem to reflect symbolic, but deeply normative concerns. They look like rules, but they cannot be enforced. The point is precisely that they are not supposed to work as enforceable rules, only as reinforcements of the order in its general proportions. As such, they are an indispensable but almost uniformly overlooked adjunct to high politics—they are lawyerly artifacts revealing the ceremonial arrangements within which high politics takes on meaning for its celebrants.

The other kind of law is customary on Bali. In the international order it consists of customary rules, most treaties, codificatory texts, international administrative regulations, and the lion's share of the material written by or passing through the hands of lawyers in foreign ministries and, of course, many other government ministries with specialized foreign affairs to discharge. What all these rules have in common is that they are almost invisible to outsiders.

Their complexity and specificity defy the kind of general statement that the conventional model of law from Austin on requires. These rules are formalized operating procedures found wherever bureaucracies function. Enforcement is neither possible nor needed. They serve as a dictionary, to use Geertz's apt word, too great ever to be assembled in one place, for the daily life of the contemporary order.

Geertz's book, for all its intrinsic value, may have an additional worth which even its author could not have anticipated. It grants us who gaze perhaps too steadfastly at the international legal order an undeniable exotic model of law and order, which may nonetheless be closer to global reality than any of the models we currently use, to frame our vision and organize our thoughts.

N. G. ONUF
The American University
School of International Service

U.S. Ratification of the Human Rights Treaties. With or Without Reservations? Edited by Richard B. Lillich. Charlottesville: University Press of Virginia, 1981. Pp. viii, 203. $12.95.

These are the edited proceedings of a conference held on January 18, 1979 under the auspices of the International Human Rights Law Group in Washington, D.C. It followed upon transmittal by President Carter to the Senate for its advice and consent on February 23, 1978 of four human rights treaties: the Covenant on Civil and Political Rights; the Covenant on Economic, Social and Cultural Rights; the Convention on the Elimination of All Forms of Racial Discrimination; and the American Convention on Human Rights. Until that date, few imagined the United States would actually sign these conventions. The failure of the Senate to ratify the still pending Genocide Convention more than 30 years after its signing afforded few reasons for optimism as to these later treaties.

The President's message recommended ratification of the four conventions only with the addition of several dozen reservations, declarations, understandings, and statements (collectively "reservations"). The essays in this book deal essentially with the issue of the correctness and wisdom of these reservations. Lillich and Henkin are most concerned about the declaration accompanying each convention that purports to make them non-self-executing and thus unenforceable in U.S. courts in the absence of legislation. Other reservations are viewed by the authors as superfluous, violative of international law, or just downright "churlish." Henkin calls on the Senate to ratify without most of these reservations.

The exchange among the participants in the conference on the non-self-executing reservation is instructive. Arthur Rovine notes that other countries that have become parties, such as Finland, Denmark, Canada, Italy, and Austria, have all used reservations to make the treaties compatible with domestic law. Failure to take a similar approach in the U.S. Senate would doom the treaties, or serve to rekindle a Bricker-type amendment to the Constitution. Much as one can resonate to Henkin's urgings, Rovine's prognosis is likely to prevail in fact.

The appendix contains the messages of transmittal to the Senate and the text of the four conventions.

In light of the comments by Assistant Secretary for Human Rights and Humanitarian Affairs Abrams that little value should be attached to treaties dealing with economic and social rights, and in the face of strong opposition to any human rights treaties by Senators as influential with the Reagan administration as Jesse Helms, this volume takes on a hollow quality such as attaches to a fleeting memory. Regrettably, it seems that for the next few years at least, this book will afford only an academic interest to the reader.

RITA E. HAUSER
Of the New York Bar

The Politics of Human Rights. Edited by Paula R. Newberg. New York and London: New York University Press, 1981. Pp. ix, 287. Index. $22.50, cloth; $9, paper.

This book is a series of essays. Most of them were written initially as background material for a U.S.-United Nations Association Policy Panel on human rights in American foreign policy, whose report appeared in December 1979. The essays have been revised for this publication and several new papers have been added.

Unlike other volumes on the subject, which are often tied to specific episodes in the conduct of American foreign policy, this book attempts to articulate a theoretical framework that transcends any particular period of time. Thus, the opening essays by Dankwart Rustow and Richard Falk place the contemporary framework of human rights in an appropriate historic context: they trace the concept of individual rights as a means of protecting a citizen against abuses by his own government to the transference of these same rights as a standard for judging the activities of other governments in interstate relations.

Tracy Strong raises serious questions about the efficacy of American policies to protect foreign individuals, as distinct from measures intended to alter the social fabric of another state that is conducive to persistent violations of rights. Perhaps the two approaches are harmonious; too often, however, harsh criticism of a state that is a violator of rights produces few systemic changes, whatever the fate of particular individuals. Although the Polish dilemma was not yet on the world scene at the time of the writing of these essays, one may well query whether Western encouragement of Solidarity and harsh criticism of Poland at the Madrid conference will in the end have served to aid Poles desirous of a greater measure of human freedom, more than a policy oriented toward liberalization of trade, exchanges, and cooperative relations in general with the Polish Government. These are not easy questions. The collected essays offer an excellent counterpoint to this type of dilemma facing American policy makers, whose support for the human rights of individuals is laudable, but for whom practical considerations of *Realpolitik* limit the range of appropriate responses.

Domestic politics and ideological commitments also color the nature of America's response to human rights violators, especially if the violator is a

Communist state. It is not yet clear whether the typical range of responses in these situations has influenced the violators to moderate their policies.

The essay on social justice and political equality by Joseph Elder, based on an examination of land tenure policies and rural development in South Asia, is pregnant with insight for the major policy questions posed today in Central America. Here the implications of basic human needs, which many would distinguish from rights, come into focus. U.S. support of governments that ignore those basic human needs can clearly be read as a failure to promote human rights considerations. The persistent inattention to these needs produces rank injustices and almost always violations of the personal integrity of the individual who seeks to redress the wrongs.

The book concludes with a statistical analysis for implementing human rights policy that is a fascinating attempt at quantification. The authors concede that any such analysis may well be flawed by the inability to collect and to assess accurately the basic data on violations. Arguments always abound as to whether atrocities were committed, by whom, and on what scale, as is amply demonstrated by the current debate over alleged massacres in Nicaragua and El Salvador. Data collecting by an unimpeachable authority is perhaps the most important issue to be addressed by the human rights community. Private, rather than governmental or international organization, sources are needed to respond to this task if credibility is to be maintained. The authors urge the U.S. Government to collect quantitative data. But human rights data are not the same as the economic or military statistics to which the authors refer. Subjective evaluations are required in many instances. The best one can hope for is U.S. partial funding of independent private bodies in the field; in the current political climate, alas, this is not likely to occur.

RITA E. HAUSER
Of the New York Bar

Global Human Rights: Public Policies, Comparative Measures, and NGO Strategies. Edited by Ved P. Nanda, James R. Scarritt, and George W. Shepherd, Jr. Boulder: Westview Press, 1981. Pp. xi, 318. Index.

This volume addresses the issues related to the definition and implementation of human rights at the national, regional, and international level. The contributors accept the political difficulties inherent in contemporary efforts to formulate policies that incorporate and advance universally established human rights standards but believe it is necessary and possible to contribute to those efforts through the identification of problem areas, refinement of monitoring procedures, and analysis of a wider range of political, legal, and economic options for citizens and governments.

The work is divided into three sections. The first, public policies, reviews U.S. foreign policy developments under the Carter administration, noting the pitfalls and shortcomings while maintaining that, on balance, the effort was beneficial to the international human rights movement. The papers cover economic, military, and diplomatic policies of both the executive and the legislative branches. In addition to three general appraisals, there are papers on food aid, arms transfers, immigration, and a good regional study, that of U.S. policy toward Latin America.

The second section addresses the very difficult but desirable objective of measuring human rights performance. Here the various authors identify the problems and inherent limitations, offer possible designs and models for measurement and cross-cultural comparison, and provide two examples of applications of these techniques. In a highly normative area such as this one, quantitative studies must be analyzed with special attention to the sources of the data being employed. When ideological biases are minimized and the normative nature of any conclusions conceded, efforts like those presented here may provide useful information for policy makers as well as scholars.

The third and most valuable section is that on nongovernmental strategies. Too little attention has been paid to this particular area of human rights action, despite the international recognition of Amnesty International and increased public transnational involvement in these organizations. The contributors discuss the special role of nongovernmental organizations in the entire process of defining human rights, developing international standards, focusing attention on violations, and working to reduce abuses and expand protection. There is also an article on nongovernmental efforts to assess human rights practices and a case study of the southern Africa project of the Lawyers' Committee for Civil Rights Under Law.

This book, especially section three, makes a valuable contribution to the human rights literature, and will be of interest to scholars of international relations and international law.

NATALIE K. HEVENER
University of South Carolina

Droit humanitaire et Droits de l'homme—La protection de la personne en période de conflit armé. By Aristidis S. Calogeropoulos-Stratis. Geneva: Institut Universitaire de Hautes Etudes Internationales, 1980. Pp. 257.

This volume, the seventh in a collection of works on international law, provides a juridical analysis of the relationship between general human rights law and humanitarian law governing armed conflict. While reflecting that, in varying circumstances, these two complex legal regimes appear either to reinforce or to contradict one another, Calogeropoulos-Stratis emphasizes the importance of reconciling these regimes in a practical manner so that the individual will be effectively protected in times of armed conflict. The study examines the principal legal agreements relating to these regimes, in particular the 1950 European Convention on Human Rights, the third and fourth Geneva Conventions of 1949, and Geneva Protocols I and II of 1977.

The volume is divided into four parts, each followed by specific conclusions. Part I addresses the historical evolution of general human rights law and humanitarian law; a chapter examining the origin of the protection of the individual is followed by one on the rapprochement between these two regimes. Part II addresses conditions of application, with a chapter on the application of humanitarian law followed by one on the application of general human rights law in times of armed conflict. Part III examines the applicable law itself, and consideration is given to a minimum standard of the rights of the individual. The final part describes the implementation of the law, with a chapter on the application of humanitarian law followed by one on the application of general human rights law. The volume ends with general conclusions derived from the study.

The author rejects opposing theories which would either deny any interpenetration of the two regimes, or regard them as a single operating whole, in favor of a synthesized theory. This approach recognizes the distinctness of the two legal regimes without deeming them incompatible, and suggests that in times of armed conflict it would be both legally admissible and practicable to apply their distinct mechanisms for the protection of the individual. Calogeropoulos-Stratis emphasizes the rapprochement of these regimes in certain domains, even though each system remains fundamentally autonomous, and he stresses that certain fundamental rights of the individual (regarded as being identical in both regimes) may be viewed as establishing a minimum standard of protection from which there can be no derogation. He suggests that recent developments in humanitarian law embodied in the 1977 Geneva Protocols have drawn the two regimes more closely together by recognizing a series of fundamental guarantees inspired by general human rights law, and extending the category of protected persons.

The author further suggests that the rapprochement of these regimes places the problem of protecting the individual in a new dimension. While they are applied under totally independent conditions and confront substantial difficulties in implementation, the independent nature of their implementation could function positively to enhance the protection of the individual in times of armed conflict.

This work is an important contribution to the neglected relationship between general human rights law and humanitarian law governing armed conflict and, as such, will be of considerable interest to scholars and practitioners.

RICHARD KENNEDY GUELFF
Of the District of Columbia Bar

International Law and the Movement of Persons Between States. By Guy S. Goodwin-Gill. Oxford: Clarendon Press, 1978.* Pp. xxvii, 324. Index. $34.95.

This well-organized and tightly written book, by a legal adviser in the Office of the UN High Commissioner for Refugees, focuses upon selected aspects of the treatment of aliens in contemporary international law, specifically their right to enter a foreign state and the conditions under which that state can expel them. While acknowledging that states still possess wide discretion in regard to aliens, the author takes as his central thesis that such discretion "is clearly limited and confined by established and emergent rules and standards of international law" (p. v). "Further amelioration of the position of the alien,"

* The *Journal* regrets that publication of this review was delayed by faulty mail service.

he predicts, "will, most probably, be accomplished through the medium of bi- and multilateral treaties" (p. 86).

Under traditional international law, states possessed an absolute right, in the absence of a treaty, to exclude aliens; similarly, they also possessed a broad right to expel them, although, as the *Ben Tillet* case suggests, they may be liable "for any hardship or loss thus inflicted beyond what is inevitable in the fact of expulsion."[1] Over the years a network of bilateral treaties has limited the discretion of states in matters of entry and exclusion, as have such multilateral treaties as the Treaty of Rome, calling for the free movement of persons within the EEC. This growing body of treaty law eventually may contribute to a new set of customary international law norms substantially restricting the existing sovereign rights of states, but in the author's opinion that day has yet to arrive. Admirably refusing to let the wish become the parent of the thought, he correctly concludes that "except in those areas in which treaties or peremptory norms operate, such as that of non-discrimination, it is not easy to bring matters of entry and exclusion within the bounds of [customary] international law" (p. 94).

With respect to expulsion, the author initially suggests that under customary international law an expelling state enjoys "a fairly wide margin of appreciation" (*cf.* p. 262), although he subsequently concludes somewhat unconvincingly that it now imposes "significant limitations upon the discretionary power to expel aliens" (p. 308). In any event, as in the case of entry and exclusion, he sees progressive development coming via the treaty route: hence his cautious observation that "[i]t may be that the most effective confinement of the discretionary power of expulsion can be achieved by way of the regional treaty-based organization such as the E.E.C." (p. 309).

Throughout his discussion of exclusion and expulsion, the author informs his analysis and evaluation with constant references to international human rights norms, including ones found in the 1951 Refugees Convention, the 1954 Convention on Stateless Persons, and, most frequently, the European Convention on Human Rights. He also takes note of the UN Covenants on Civil and Political Rights and Economic, Social and Cultural Rights, pointing out that they arguably reflect or crystallize existing or emerging norms of customary international law (pp. 67, 73). By using international human rights norms to reformulate the traditional international law governing the treatment of aliens, the author adopts the approach first taken by García-Amador in his 1961 Draft Convention on State Responsibility[2] and further developed by this reviewer in his 1978 Hague lectures.[3] Baroness Elles's Draft Declaration on the Human Rights of Non-Citizens,[4] now pending before the UN General Assembly, also takes the same approach and, in its Article 7 covering expulsion, provides further support for the author's thesis.

[1] 2 A. McNair, International Law Opinions 109 (1956).

[2] García-Amador, Sixth Report on State Responsibility, UN Doc. A/CN.4/134 and Add. 1 (1961), *reprinted in* [1961] 2 Y.B. Int'l L. Comm'n 1, 46, UN Doc. A/CN.4/SER.A/1961/Add.1.

[3] Lillich, *Duties of States Regarding the Civil Rights of Aliens*, 161 Recueil des Cours 329 (1978 III).

[4] Elles, International Provisions Protecting the Human Rights of Non-Citizens, UN Doc. E/CN.4/Sub.2/392/Rev.1, at 53 (1980).

As stated at the outset, the author has organized and written his book in admirable fashion. Starting with the near absolute rights of states under traditional international law, he convincingly describes the process by which their arbitrary discretion in matters of exclusion and expulsion has been chipped away, a process that has accelerated with the emergence and recognition of international human rights norms in recent years. The author suggests no master plan for the future—continued acceleration of the existing process via the treaty route is his principal recommendation—but his careful appraisal of the current state of the law and his cautious predictions about its future development mark him as an enlightened positivist from whom further high-quality contributions can be expected in the future.

RICHARD B. LILLICH
University of Virginia
School of Law

Mezhdunarodnoe Pravo, Vneshniaia Politika i Diplomatiia (International Law, Foreign Policy and Diplomacy). By D. B. Levin. Moscow: Mezhdunarodnye Otnosheniia, 1981. Pp. 143. 60 kopecks.

How has resumption of cold war polemics influenced Soviet international lawyers? D. B. Levin's monograph suggests that it has sent them back to the rhetoric of the predétente period: "The socialist state's policy conforms totally to the principles of international law which have a generally democratic character. In contrast the foreign policy of capitalist states with its tendency to violate the peace and independence of peoples, contradicts these principles and distorts them" (p. 6). U.S. policy, notably its economic boycott of the USSR and its sanctions declared because of Soviet military assistance to Afghanistan, are seen as violations of law (UN Charter Art. 2(4)), while Soviet actions are described as serving exclusively the aims of defense authorized under the Soviet-Afghan Treaty and UN Charter Article 51 (p. 14).

Western international lawyers will grieve to find the rhetoric of decades past revived by Soviet legal scholars. This renewal should cause no surprise, for as Levin says, law is in Soviet eyes an instrument of policy, and Soviet policy is now clearly hostile to Western positions. There is a bright spot, however, for Levin explains that although Soviet diplomacy holds to deeply felt principles, it is ready to compromise, if necessary, so long as the compromise does no violence to principles (p. 18). He expects the West to compromise too, out of fear of popular reaction expressed in parliamentary elections and street demonstrations. He holds that the Soviet leadership is justified in stimulating such reaction in playing its role as "vanguard of peaceful social progress" (p. 23).

Although recognizing a close link between policy and law, Levin explains that they are not the same, for "international law has an independent existence; it is composed of general international law norms regulating relations between states regardless of whether their observance corresponds to subsequent changes of interests and desires of individual states" (p. 32). To bring law and policy into accord after a change in the latter, Levin favors renegotiation of the treaty creating the norm, rather than reinterpretation of the treaty by a tribunal. In so saying, Levin reexpresses the traditional Soviet distaste for tribunals, which cannot be controlled as can diplomatic conferences (p. 98).

In his discussion of sources of law, Levin repeats a familiar Soviet position that no norm is to be recognized generally, regardless of how many states support it, unless representatives of both capitalist and socialist camps are numbered among the proponents (p. 37). He also favors the role played by informal organizations such as peace associations and Pugwash conferences in the development of law. Levin reminds his readers that "peaceful coexistence" does not preclude ideological struggle (p. 45).

The matter of sovereignty receives its customary attention. Levin claims priority for Soviet diplomacy in extending respect for sovereignty to all peoples, in implementation of Soviet hostility to colonialism, and he lists as proof of this fact early Soviet treaties with the Baltic and Islamic neighbors of the USSR. For Westerners who might question whether there has been continuing respect for sovereignty more recently in these areas, Levin has a ready answer: Communist states give special attention to the fostering of sovereignty when a state is on the road to socialism (p. 60). Leonid Brezhnev is quoted to the effect that if domestic or foreign forces hostile to socialism try to turn a people back to capitalism, it is a problem for all socialist countries. In short, it is evident that self-determination is to be encouraged only when it leads in one sociopolitical direction.

General and complete disarmament is again espoused, as it always is by Soviet diplomats, but Levin links it with maintenance of the principle of "equality of safety" for both sides. He argues that the United States and NATO are violating the equality rule in rearmament (p. 91). Westerners may wish that some supreme authority were available to determine when equality exists. Being doubtful that such a person or institution is to be found, this reviewer remains pessimistic after reading this book that the rule of law can be expected to triumph over the rule of force. The Soviet messianic spirit as the "vanguard of peaceful social progress" stimulates the fears of Western policy makers, and when the West organizes to contain the powers who see themselves in the vanguard, this organization is seen in turn by the East as proof of aggressive intent.

JOHN N. HAZARD
Board of Editors

Odpowiedzialność Państwa w Prawie Międzynarodowym (State Responsibility according to International Law). Edited by Renata Sonnenfeld. Warsaw: Polski Instytut Spraw Międzynarodowych, 1980. Pp. 340, including an English summary of contents (pp. 326–40).

Umowy Międzynarodowe w Formie Uproszczonej (International Agreements in a Simplified Form). By Maria Frankowska. Warsaw: Polska Akademia Nauk, Instytut Państwa i Prawa, 1981. Pp. 304, including an English summary of contents (pp. 293–304). Zl.60.

Systemy Normatywne w Stosunkach Międzynarodowych (Normative Systems in International Relations). By Janusz Gilas. Warsaw: Państwowe Wydawnictwo Naukowe, 1981. Pp. 182, including an English summary of contents (pp. 181–82). Zl.50.

Of these three scholarly studies, the one edited by Renata Sonnenfeld is the most interesting. It pays due attention to the fact that scientific-technological progress has extended the state's pecuniary responsibility for damages to another state to cases where no international obligation has been violated: in such cases, involving activities on the seabed and in outer space and the use of nuclear energy, the responsibility is founded on the theory of the risk involved.

Particularly interesting is the chapter by Henryk de Fiumel on state responsibility in the mutual relations of the members of the Council of Mutual Economic Assistance (COMECON in Western parlance). This responsibility arises when a state either invalidates a contract by a domestic enterprise with an enterprise of another member state or prevents the implementation of such a contract, and a member state has suffered damages in consequence. The author rejects the prevailing "socialist" doctrine, which confines the responsibility in such cases to the defaulting enterprise, and he imputes it to the state itself. He also recommends the conclusion of a multilateral convention on the mutual responsibility of the COMECON member states and the establishment of a court of arbitration for the settlement of disputes that might arise over implementation of the convention.

The other chapters of this book deal with state responsibility resulting from exploration of seabed resources, among others, and for pollution of international maritime areas; with the responsibility resulting from use of inland waters and the atmosphere, if this proves to be harmful to another state (for instance, to another riparian state); with responsibility for activities in outer space if they lead to contamination of outer space; with responsibility for nuclear damage inflicted by one state on another; with responsibility for damages caused to cultural property, not only during a war but also in peacetime if a state allows the importation of cultural objects from another state that forbids such exports.

Frankowska's book discusses international agreements concluded in a simplified form such as the so-called executive agreements of the United States. She believes that the lack of a requirement that they be ratified to enter into force is the best criterion for distinguishing them from treaties. She takes note of the rapid growth of such agreements, especially since the Second World War, and of the interesting fact that they are frequently on the same subjects as treaties requiring ratification.

Gilas's book analyzes the interplay in international relations of moral, political, and comity norms of behavior with international law. It is the least interesting book of the three.

W. W. KULSKI
Duke University

Die Rechtsnatur des Sowjetblocks: Eine juristische Entschleierung. By Dietrich Frenzke. Berlin: Berlin Verlag, 1981. Pp. 256. Indexes. DM 30.

Here is a daring exposé of the true legal nature of the Soviet bloc. Uncompromisingly applying the principles of classical international law and rejecting all deviations from the scriptures in the guise of anomalies, occasional exceptions, and so forth, the author proceeds to measure relations within the community headed by the USSR by these precise standards. Focusing on the criterion that resort to physical force is sanctioned in this intramural setting, he decides that the terms of the association do not square with the peremptory norms of the modern international legal code, nor do they yet fulfill the requirements of a constitutional law system either. He then proclaims that the "family" repertory staged by the USSR and its partners represents a special mix or blend combining international and constitutional law features.

This approach concentrates on literary and doctrinal artifacts and slights empirical evidence. The indictment is dogmatic and betrays both a definite set of a priori assumptions about the Soviet and East European record and a strong dislike for local policies. The analysis eschews any attempt at evenhandedness: Soviet legal pronouncements are contrasted with Moscow's political performance and found wanting, which is fine, but the official rhetoric of other states is spared the same acid test and is accepted at face value, which enables Frenzke to draw invidious comparisons between the good guys and the bad guys. Singling out the "use of force" yardstick obscures the multifaceted visage of the so-called Socialist Commonwealth, misses the nuances in the status of the individual members vis-à-vis the USSR, overlooks the differences between the rules observed in the quieter sectors of economic, cultural, and scientific interaction and the more stringent controls imposed in pursuit of the premier objectives of maintenance of political and military "unity." Even the conclusion is oddly perverse, for by abandoning the fairly safe signposts of international law practice for the *terra incognita* of some *sui generis* concoction filling the interstices between international law and constitutional law, he tosses away the only viable scale for appraising Soviet behavior in the world arena and holding the USSR accountable for violating consensual prescriptions. Recognize somebody's excuse that he is marching to a different drummer and you really have no grounds left for criticizing the drill.

George Ginsburgs
Rutgers University Law School, Camden

Law and International Resource Conflicts. By J. E. S. Fawcett and Audrey Parry. New York: The Clarendon Press; Oxford University Press, 1981. Pp. xiv, 254. Index. $55.

International Regulation of Internal Resources. By Mahnoush H. Arsanjani. Charlottesville: University Press of Virginia, 1981. Pp. 558. Index. $37.50.

These two books come at a time of heightened awareness of international resource questions, and each in its own way advances our thinking in regard to international law and institutions for managing the resources and resolving conflicts arising out of the competition for scarce and valuable resources.

Fawcett and Parry examine the prevention and resolution of particular types of resource conflict, including foreign investment, management of commodity trade, marine resources, oil, nuclear materials, and outer space. Although they note the primitive nature of the international legislative process and the general inadequacy of international institutions, they are reasonably optimistic about the development of international law in regard to international resource conflicts. They cite the codification of the law of the sea in one or more international conventions and the Outer Space Treaty of 1967 as examples of the development of international law through codification, and they go on to observe that "the UN general assembly is also beginning to acquire the character of a primitive legislature—UNCLOS and UNCTAD are in effect 'committees of the whole.'" They identify three principles that have wide acceptance in international law: "equitable sharing of resources, environmental responsibility and fair competition." They conclude that "the vast widening of human activities leading to the breaking down of frontiers, pressures on common resources, and conflict, revealed in the surveys of marine resources, nuclear materials, and earth satellite uses are leading to an extended adoption of international regimes."

Dr. Arsanjani examines international resources law and institutions from the point of view of balancing the interests of the international community as a whole rather than those of the individual nation-states. She first discusses the development of international institutions and law over global resources such as the oceans, international rivers, airspace and outer space, and climate and weather.

She then examines the less traditional concept of international competence over resources located within the internal boundaries of nation-states, which are customarily subject to the exclusive jurisdiction or sovereignty of those nation-states. She notes that "the rising demands for the shared use of resources located within the territorial boundaries of particular states have increased the number and variety of agreements purporting to confer rights to such resources." In this category she discusses the historical practice of use by individual nations of international servitudes, licenses, or leases to obtain rights to resources in other states, such as mineral resources, rights of transit over land, or transit through water in the territory of another nation. She cites the Suez Canal and the Panama Canal as examples of the assertion by the international community of some jurisdiction over resources located within the territory of an individual nation.

She then goes on to a much newer and more controversial topic, that of global conservation, planning, and development of resources. Even though particular resources like energy or food may be located within the national boundaries of sovereign nations and even though these resources have traditionally been under the exclusive control of those individual states, Arsanjani argues that because the entire global community has an interest in the prudent use of these resources, the international community must have a strong role in their planning, development, and conservation. She says that

> one cannot simply rely on past experience and the intelligence of the human mind to take care of all crises in due time . . . therefore, a deliberate effort should be made to understand the nature and interrelationships of these crises and, through global planning and collective action, to begin to solve them.

She rejects the marketplace as the sole determinant in the planning and allocation of these resources. She says "[t]here is no doubt that cost and benefit analysis should be taken into account in conservation planning, but since conservation is a decision made for the production and just distribution of all values, the question of efficiency should not be permitted to jeopardize this basic policy."

She reviews fishing resources, food resources, and nonrenewable resources such as hydrocarbons and concludes that "conservation now reflects a demand for a series of collective, urgent, coordinated, comprehensive, and continuous actions for the protection and survival of the human race and its civilization in a world of scarce resources." She endorses, therefore, the establishment of an "International Resources Organization" (IRO). "The function of the IRO will be the implementation of a global conservation policy through providing information and recommendations to the national and regional institutions or commissions for resource development." She would call upon the IRO to "conduct comprehensive scientific investigations on the development of new resources and substitution of new resources for future generations."

Although she notes a substantial growth in international institutions, as do Fawcett and Parry, she concludes that there is much to be done in the development of international law and institutions; she particularly recognizes the need to develop bilateral and regional efforts because "to expect international conventions to formulate detailed recommendations to solve all global and regional environmental problems is naive."

In regard to pollution control or, as she designates it, "regulation of injurious use," she posits that, "given the contemporary level of development of science and technology, where the possibility for doing irreversible damage to the vital interest of countries through injurious use of shareable resources has increased substantially, there is need for fast and effective preventive processes to protect the vital interest of these communities." Pollution abatement measures, she says, should not be limited "to injurious use of the oceans, but also the atmosphere, land masses, and other kinds of incidents affecting resources." However, she does not go so far as to advocate that international organizations venture upon the land base of nations to dictate directly such policies as land use and waste disposal policies. She simply says that "bi-lateral and regional agreements are preferable methods of improving and implementing abatement measures in ways that protect the exclusive and inclusive interest of the smaller and larger communities."

Thus, Arsanjani addresses some of the most difficult issues in the international regulation of natural resources, that is, those resources which are internal to the national boundaries of individual nations, and in so doing she, along with Fawcett and Parry, contributes to our understanding of management, use, and development of scarce natural resources. The two books are useful in different ways and deserve the attention of scholars and policy makers, as we prepare to enter the 21st century and an age of increased competition for essential resources.

ALBERT E. UTTON
The University of New Mexico School of Law

UN Code de Conduite pour le Transfert de Technologie. Under the direction of René-François Bizec and Yves Daudet. Paris: Economica, 1980. Pp. 217.

This book derives its special flavor from the fact that it was written by 10 different authors. All of them are experts in international licensing or have been involved in one way or another in the negotiations for the Transfer of Technology Code. The research was conducted with the support of the Center of International and Community Studies and Research in Aix-en-Provence, which is attached to the University Aix-Marseille III. It is especially significant that the French delegation permitted the authors to use the notes and materials it had used in the negotiations.

René-François Bizec outlines in the first part of the book the concept of the proposed Code. France is, of course, given as an example, but detailed supplementary statistics are provided about the size and extent of technology transfers of all industrialized nations. Third World countries, in raising demands for "de-globalization," including restrictions on multinational corporations, will have to appreciate that certain limitations may hinder international law in resolving issues of this kind. Perhaps this is one reason why the Code, for now, seems to have been abandoned.

André Marelle, in the following chapter, reviews the evolution of the Code from 1961 to 1979. The objectives of the Code are discussed in chapter IV by Professor Daudet, together with Bernard Temy. The delicate problem of negotiating with the various blocs of nations is analyzed. In chapter V, Dr. Martine Hiancé and Bernard Nicolaieff probe into the controversial area of restrictive commercial practices in connection with technology transfers. Jacques Gaudin in chapter VI addresses the question of guaranties in international licensing agreements.

In chapter VII, Pierre Lassé deals with the effects of the Code on multinational enterprises. This area is at the center of controversies between industrialized nations and developing nations and their vigorous supporters from the socialist countries. In 1977, for instance, 80 percent of all royalties received by the United States were received by multinational enterprises. Under the proposed "prohibition against restrictive practices," these firms would be deprived of any protection of their intellectual property vis-à-vis their own subsidiaries in foreign countries. While under U.S. antitrust laws and European Community laws, limitations already exist on price fixing, for example, the Code lists restrictive practices reaching far beyond currently applicable international rules.

In chapter VIII, the law of the European Community is contrasted with the rules of the proposed Code. This chapter was prepared by Professor Bonassies and contains many references to the leading cases regarding licensing of technology.

The book constitutes an interesting commentary on the proposed Code, presenting the French and, notably, the European points of view. The outline of the proposed Code in the annex should help make this book useful to the international practitioner, corporate counsel, and scholar alike.

EBERHARD H. RÖHM
Of the New York Bar

Transnational Enterprises in a New International System. By Klaus W. Grewlich. Alphen aan den Rijn: Sijthoff & Noordhoff, 1980. Pp. x, 229. Index. Dfl.85; $42.50.

Current international economic uncertainties and related energy concerns, emphasizing the extent of interdependence of national economies over the international spectrum, have further intensified the interest in activities and control of multinational enterprises (MNE's)[1] in recent years. It is clear, as the author points out, that "[t]he world-wide operations of [MNE's] are an important aspect of international economic interdependence" (p. 5) and that "their role profoundly affects the whole spectrum of international economic relations" (p. 1). This is attested to by a burgeoning literature on the subject as well as by the spate of committees, commissions, conferences, groups of experts, etc., dedicated to the subject in all its aspects within the major international and regional bodies and governmental and nongovernmental organizations. It is therefore refreshing to find a book with as sensible and balanced an approach as the one here reviewed.

The author recognizes that "the undifferentiated radical bias of certain quarters against [MNE's] in general is unjustified," that it has sometimes been too ideological, ignoring important evidence and facts. He believes the truth of the matter lies somewhere between the two extremes, and he takes care to present, to contrast, and to balance the interests of the developing and developed worlds. While concentrating somewhat more on the former, he does so without losing his perspective of the whole.

Grewlich's own introductory assessment establishes this balanced approach from the outset by juxtaposing the recognized benefits to the host of MNE investment with the simultaneous potential for tensions and conflict that can, in certain circumstances, be generated by MNE activities. Moreover, Grewlich sees tensions as resulting not only from MNE activities directly but also from the developing countries' own paradoxical feelings, which lead them to desire foreign investment for the stimulus it gives to their economic development, while motivating them to strive for a large degree of local control. This dilemma, Grewlich points out, has often led to tensions among the developing (host) countries, the MNE's, and the industrialized (home) countries. The author emphasizes not only that the recognized positive contributions of the MNE fail to mitigate such tensions, but that "the source of tension is never solely—and probably in many cases even not primarily—economic" (p. 85). He sees the tensions as, rather, political in nature.

Grewlich submits that one way to avoid resultant clashes (some other main causes of which are enumerated in the study) would be to establish an agreed-upon set of standards of behavior which, to be effective, must be based on a clear understanding of three particular "areas of concern," which he enumerates. It is his declared purpose to deal in his study with these three areas of concern, namely:

> (i) the present—real and perceived—role of [MNE's] in national economies and international economic relations; (ii) the existing governmental and

[1] While Grewlich refers to these entities as "transnational" ("TNE's"), conforming to UN terminology, the reviewer takes the liberty of using the term most widely adopted in legal circles to identify those enterprises described in this work.

> intergovernmental policies designed to establish a framework for [MNE] operations; (iii) notably, the conditions for an optimum contribution which [MNE's] can possibly make to world development in the context of an emerging new international economic system [p. 2].

Again reflecting his efforts to shun polarization is his choice of the term "new international economic *system*" as opposed to either "New International Economic *Order*" or "new international economic *dis*order," as it has sometimes been called by its opponents.

Additionally, the author sees the process toward establishing a new international economic system as having not only political and economic components, but also an important ideological aspect. Accordingly, in his efforts to examine existing national and international approaches, he sets out to deal as well with the "underlying philosophy and the policy objectives" of a proposed worldwide framework of standards. In pursuit of this objective, Grewlich provides the reader with a schema of the provisions to be contained in the envisaged framework, offering substantive proposals designed to exemplify the basic philosophy. One objective of the standards, for example, would be

> to maintain the necessary degree of economic liberalism and entrepreneurial freedom . . . based on a philosophy which rewards, develops, and reinforces the essential virtues of a free enterprise system, such as investment, innovation, and the will to take a personal economic risk, as these are the basic conditions for sustained economic growth and development [p. 176].

The author's proposed system is aimed at being "responsive to the particular needs of developing countries, while preserving the vital force of economic liberalism and the essential virtues of a free enterprise system" (p. 204). If the latter does not accompany the former, Grewlich predicts, there will inevitably be a decline in productivity detrimental to the "South" even more than to the "North."

Although Grewlich's proposals tend to reiterate a number of the provisions already found in the various codes and guidelines currently in existence or under formulation, the author rightly points out that any set of standards must contain both rights and obligations for all parties concerned and must reflect an equitable balance of interests of these parties. This is the only realistic way of assuring universal support, without which such standards are clearly void of practical effect.

Despite the primary emphasis placed on the development of standards for direct investment in "a new international economic system" and on the "basic philosophical choices" that the author deems necessary for establishing a balanced set of standards, he does not overlook the indispensable role of individual nation-states in regulating MNE activity, nor does he neglect to foresee the potential ill effects of overregulation or of failure to pursue collective efforts in international forums leading to an equitable solution on the global level.

One disappointment to the legally oriented reader is that, while the author is a lawyer, it is difficult to see the work as a legal treatise. As a political and socioeconomic statement, it is an unusually realistic assessment; but legal practitioners and academics are left with no hard law,[2] nor is the content enlivened with any elucidating examples drawn from case law[3] or relevant legislative measures aimed at MNE operations. This could be attributed to the fact that the author has delineated the issue not as a legal one, nor even as primarily a sociological or economic one but, rather, as political, requiring political solutions. "What the developing countries really demand," writes Grewlich, "is not merely an increased participation in economic benefits but a fundamental redistribution of political power" (p. 153).

For readers already immersed in the literature, official documents, and legislation surrounding the MNE phenomenon, there are few surprises. By the author's own admission, "[t]he really new and significant is not generally separated from mere repetition and synthesis of existing knowledge; there is still a lack of basic research and frontier thinking" (p. 15). While this could apply in large part to Grewlich's own work, the study certainly can be said to represent a careful, comprehensive, and ordered analysis of the current trends and developments—and the realities of present-day MNE-government relations and control balance—stripped of the emotional excesses that characterized much of the early literature in this field and that tended to produce distortions.

While a few points along the way might be argued,[4] the work is a significant contribution to the already massive literature on the subject, owing to its logical and systematic analysis of the MNE issue at its current stage of development and its notable achievement of a substantially realistic and balanced approach. Based as it is on the fundamental idea that "[t]he major objective of policy makers and executives should . . . be to create conditions in which, as far as possible, the positive aspects prevail for all parties" (p. 68) and that, "in general, the promotion of direct investment in developing countries is a rational means to achieve higher welfare levels (indifference curves) in a certain group of developing countries as well as in the developed countries" (p. 62), Grewlich's work should be of interest to those in all of the above categories.

CYNTHIA DAY WALLACE
International Law Institute
Georgetown University Law Center

[2] Some legally oriented discussion is provided by the author's well-formulated and cogent discussion of the legal aspects of the instruments postulating a new international economic order in ch. 6, but even this discussion inevitably remains in the realm of "soft law."

[3] There is one parenthetical allusion to the *Badger* case on p. 116.

[4] *E.g.*: (a) The author's statement that "control is usually determined on the basis of ownership" (p. 26), citing 25% or more of the voting stock as a basic criterion of controlling ownership, would be considered by many as outdated. (b) If universal agreement on any of the currently formulated or in-draft proposals for international codes or guidelines has still not been achieved, it is difficult to conceive that a new set of standards will find a more positive response or elicit the desired global consensus. (c) It may regrettably prove overly optimistic to think that the U.S. Foreign Corrupt Practices Act of 1977 will, after "short-term disadvantages," in the long run "help to ensure the survival of liberalism by renouncing the unacceptable face of capitalism and by enhancing the integrity and credibility of the liberal Western economic system" (p. 180), since the activities forbidden under this Act are, in many instances, initiated not by the MNE's, but rather by the host governments, some of whom see this as a normal way of doing business. (d) The study repeatedly emphasizes (*e.g.*, pp. 153, 174, and 204) that it is the role and even the moral duty of

Legal and Financial Aspects of International Business. By Carol McCormick Crosswell. New York, Rome, and London: Oceana Publications, Inc., 1980. Pp. ix, 350. Index. $40.

The book under review is a survey of problems often encountered in international business. The following topics are discussed: (1) the selection of suitable markets; (2) the choice of corporate form; (3) different local incorporation requirements; (4) antitrust considerations in the United States and abroad; (5) taxation and tax incentives; (6) sources of capital, insurance, and financial devices; (7) international dispute settlement; and (8) evaluation of political climates.

Crosswell handles this unusually broad range of subjects by discussing them separately in independent chapters, but does not attempt to cross-reference into a single analysis each area of inquiry. While this is a useful approach for newcomers to the field who could benefit from an overview, the book fails to provide the reader with a sense of how to balance antitrust considerations with tax considerations, or how to determine whether advantageous financing incentives outweigh the dangers of political uncertainty. Still, the book is useful for the reader who has isolated a particular problem area, *e.g.*, securing financing, and needs an overview of the sources that could be tapped.

A few significant subjects are not discussed, including import duties, export controls, and antidumping laws. The impact of import duties on the profitability of exports should be considered before relocating overseas for export to the United States or elsewhere. Moreover, while the author discusses licensing arrangements in great detail, there is no discussion of U.S. laws or any other nation's laws restricting the export of services and technical data. Finally, while the antitrust laws and their extraterritorial application are considered, Crosswell makes only minor mention of the antidumping laws and the restrictions they impose upon pricing products in international trade. Inclusion of these subjects would substantially improve the usefulness of the book.

A multi-volume treatise is needed to consider every country and its environment for investment. A single volume would present an uneven depth of analysis for many of the countries discussed. To overcome this flaw, the author has chosen to consider several countries in depth as representative of particular topics, *i.e.*, Ireland, for a discussion of local investment incentives; the Cayman Islands, Bermuda, and the Netherlands Antilles, for a discussion of tax havens; and Brazil, for a discussion of investment in South America. While numerous brief overviews of the European nations are used to discuss the benefits and burdens associated with each country, the detailed analyses are more helpful to the reader in learning to examine international investment problems. Notably, however, there is little analysis and discussion of investment in the Middle East, Africa, and Asia.

The book would be substantially improved if the author focused on developing

---

the West to take the initiative in developing the "new international economic system," since it was the West that created the "old" system. It could be argued that this ignores the fact that it is precisely owing to the developing world's disillusionment with the "old" system that these countries have launched their own initiative to create the "new order." They are not likely to trust the West to develop a "new order" favorable to their interests.

nations as well as on Western Europe, the United States, and a few South and Central American nations. It also would be improved if chapters were reviewed and in some instances combined or reorganized to eliminate occasional repetition in the areas of international finance and taxation. On balance, however, it is not often that one finds discussion of such a variety of issues gathered so concisely in a single volume. The author is to be commended.

STEPHAN M. MINIKES
Of the District of Columbia and New York Bars
BRUCE A. LEICHER
Of the District of Columbia Bar

The Expropriation of Multinational Property in the Third World. By Adeoye A. Akinsanya. New York: Praeger Publishers, 1980. Pp. xi, 386. Index.

In a thoroughly researched work, the author, a Nigerian political scientist, examines the views of capital-importing and capital-exporting states on international legal rules governing the expropriation of alien property, examines the motivation for such expropriations, and analyzes the future of private foreign investment in the developing world. The book contains an analysis and summary of the rules governing expropriation of alien enterprises. The generally accepted tenet that a state has the inherent sovereign right to expropriate foreign-owned property located within its territory for reasons of public utility, security, or national interest is set out.

With respect to the most controversial aspect of expropriation, the quantum of compensation, divergent views held by developed, developing, and socialist nations are explained. The author asserts that this divergence has led to the emergence of negotiated lump sum compensation agreements as a rule of customary international law. Accepting the view that UN General Assembly resolutions may acquire the character of rules of customary international law, the author posits that expropriating states are free to determine the amount of any compensation and that disputes relating to such an amount should be settled according to municipal, rather than international, law.

Many developed-country readers will disagree with the author's contention that no compensation is due as a result of the imposition of various administrative and legislative measures, such as taxation and various monetary or fiscal regulations, no matter how onerous or arbitrary these measures may be. Acceptance of this proposition would be seen as sanctioning various governmental actions that may have the effect of "creeping" expropriations.

Again relying on the authority of various UN resolutions, the author asserts that the Calvo Doctrine, negating the right of nationals of capital-exporting states to claim diplomatic protection, is emerging as a rule of customary international law. Given that adherents of the Calvo Doctrine have been primarily confined to Latin America and that even certain Latin American nations apply the doctrine with some flexibility, the author's conclusion seems as yet unwarranted.

Motivations behind expropriation of alien property include a fear and dislike of multinational corporations, which, with inflexible policies, contribute to local underdevelopment by draining off natural resources. There is also a fear of multinational interference in domestic politics and disappointment in the low rate of multinational reinvestment in the local economy. However, given the need of many developing countries for private capital, technology, and management skills, the author concludes that developing countries and multinational investors must reach an accommodation. Counseling restraint on the behalf of capital-exporting states, he sees political and economic sanctions in response to expropriations as not being effective generally in ensuring compensation settlements.

Like many writings on the subject, the work does not squarely address the issue of when governmental action rises to the level of an expropriation. In a world where more and more expropriations are of the "creeping" nature, the author focuses on the less thorny issue of outright expropriation.

The reader will be struck by some notable redundancies and inaccuracies in the presentation of material. Nevertheless, the author has painstakingly researched a broad subject matter so as to provide a reference work of utility with respect to Third World views on state responsibility for foreign private investment.

LEO PHILLIPS, JR.
Overseas Private Investment Corporation

Division of powers between the European Communities and their Member States in the field of external relations. (Colloquium 30 and 31 May 1980, Amsterdam.) Edited by C. W. A. Timmermans and E. L. M. Völker. Deventer: Kluwer, 1981. Pp. vi, 149. Dfl.55; $27.

This is a first-rate work. It is difficult to choose a topic for a colloquium that is precise and intellectually engaging. It is even harder to find the right participants, to ensure that the written contributions do not drown out the spoken comments, and to produce a printed version that keeps something of the immediacy of the meeting itself. The organizers of this colloquium, the European Institute of the University of Amsterdam and the Section for European and Economic Law of the University of Groningen, are to be congratulated for their efforts. The contents of the volume can best be conveyed by the titles of the papers. The first part consists of *The Competence of the EEC* (Professor Bleckmann), *Division of External Powers between Community and Member States in the field of harmonization of National Law—A Case Study* (Professor Timmermans), and *The Division of External Relations Power between the European Economic Community and the Member States in the Case-Law of the Court of Justice* (Mr. Barav), with written comments by Professor Seidl-Hohenveldern (the position as seen by third states) and Mr. Justice Pescatore (a view from the Court), followed by a general discussion. The second part contains two more policy-oriented papers, *Some comments on the practice* (Mr. Bourgeois) and *The effects of the main cases of the Court of Justice in the field of external competences on the conduct of Member States* (Mr. Burrows), written contributions by Professor Jacobs, Mr. Gosses, Professor Simmonds, and Mr. Völker, and a final general discussion.

This is not a work for persons beginning to study the legal structure of the external relations of the European Community. To derive full benefit the reader will need already to know the relevant articles of the Treaty and to have a good grasp of the "*grands arrêts*": the *ERTA* and *Kramer* cases, Opinions 1/75 (the *Local costs* case), 1/76 (*Rhine Laying up fund* case), and 1/78 (*International Rubber Agreement* case), and Ruling 1/78 (Euratom: IAEA physical protection convention). While the reader will not emerge at the end with a textbooklike set of conclusions, the book provides, especially through the general discussions which involved some 30 selected participants, a display of virtually all the arguments that have so far been used, and all their intricacies, concerning the distribution of powers between the Community and its member states in the field of external relations. It is not the task of a review to recall each point made, but some that may be mentioned as illustrations are how mixed agreements involving participation in international organizations will work in practice; whether the Court was correct in the *International Rubber Agreement* Opinion to deal with the financial issues as it did; the exact delimitation between, and implications of, the *ERTA* case and Opinion 1/76; and the way in which sanctions were adopted over Iran (and, one may add, more recently in the case of the USSR).

The work is thus centered on case law and terms under which treaties have been entered into. This is "hard law," to use an expression employed in the book, indeed the foundation upon which the Community rests in this sphere. This is surely right; the European Community exists because of a treaty and not, say as a state does, because people in the street identify with that country. But the external relations of the European Community are a larger and more comprehensive process than a legal analysis suggests. It is not merely that law and politics come very close together here, but that for the member states of the European Community it is very difficult in practice for them to have separate external policies. Just as a major part of the work of the foreign ministries of the member states now consists of dealings concerning the internal workings of the Community, so externally joint action has become inescapable. The question is, what policy is to be followed, and here evidently opinions differ, with the need for individual member states to adjust their positions. It is not merely a question of the loss of clear-cut independent foreign policy options—it has always been necessary to adapt these to gain the support of others and to achieve objectives—but of the implications within the Community that are the principal issues, whether the subject concerns textile imports, export credits, or energy policy. The difficulty becomes one, in short, of providing political legitimacy for the line chosen, insofar as this involves a sacrifice of national interest for one or another member state in the sector concerned. But unless agreement is reached, the results are likely to be small and short-lived. The first thing a third state wishes to know when approached by a member state is whether the view advanced or suggestion made is backed by the others. If the answer is no, the third state can pick and choose; if the answer is yes, the third state must take notice. At the broader, political level, there is no real division of powers between the Community and its member states, as is pointed out by Mr. Wellenstein and Mr. Brinkhorst, the two participants with the most experience of actual practice, but it is the Community that provides the central core and structure for this process.

MICHAEL HARDY
Brussels

Souveränitätsverständnis in den Europäischen Gemeinschaften. Edited by Georg Ress. Baden-Baden: Nomos Verlagsgesellschaft, 1980. Pp. 226. DM 46.

This ninth volume of the Schriftenreihe des Arbeitskreises Europäische Integration e.V. (series of the European Integration Society) consists of three papers on "Europäische Direktwahlen und staatliches Souveränitätsverständnis" (European direct elections and the concept of state sovereignty) and two papers on "Auswärtige Befugnisse der Europäischen Gemeinschaften und nationale auswärtige Gewalt" (external powers of the European Communities and national foreign affairs). The first three deal with the aspects of international law and European Community law involved in the decision of the European Council of Ministers of September 20, 1976 on the direct election of the European Parliament (M. Hilf), the French attitude towards that election (J.-P. Jacqué), and national and European concepts of sovereignty (A. Bleckmann). The latter papers concentrate on the relationship between the powers of the European Communities in external affairs and those of the member states (H. Krück) as well as upon legal problems involved in defining the treaty-making power of the European Communities and the member states (M. Dauses).

The greater part of the book is devoted to the direct election of the European Parliament, which was the main reason that the Europe Institute of the University of Saarland held an international colloquium in 1978 chaired by the editor of the book, Georg Ress. In discussing national constitutions, Jacqué makes a distinction between a constitutional limitation of the sovereignty of member states in favor of the Community and an unconstitutional transfer of sovereignty to the latter (pp. 81–84). Bleckmann states that by now the European Communities already have a substantial amount of (internal and external) sovereignty (pp. 56–62). According to Hilf, the direct election of the European Parliament may reinforce the legitimization of the powers of the European Communities and affect, in that manner, the relationship between the sovereignty of the Community and that of the member states (pp. 29–30). In his introduction Ress argues that although the idea of a dual sovereignty (both for member states and for the Community) would not be acceptable permanently, it would be during a transition period (p. 18).

The papers, theses, and interventions appear to reflect a dissatisfaction over the question of (dual) sovereignty. This might be caused by a certain lack of understanding that from the point of view of international law, sovereignty is not itself a right, nor is it a criterion for statehood (J. Crawford, *The Creation of States in International Law* (1979), pp. 26–27[1]). Apart from that, the book

[1] Reviewed by G. Zaphiriou in 74 AJIL 737–38 (1980).

makes a useful contribution to a better understanding of the European Community as an international legal phenomenon. As such, it is one of the relatively few efforts to cross the boundary between European Community law and international law.

P. J. I. M. DE WAART
Free University, Amsterdam

Les Travailleurs Etrangers et le Droit International. (Colloque de Clermont-Ferrand pour la Société Française pour le Droit International, les 25, 26 et 27 mai 1978.) Paris: Editions A. Pedone, 1979. Pp. vii, 445.

This study publishes in book form the contributions to the 11th colloquium of the French Society of International Law in May 1978, which devoted its attention to the increasing political, economic, and legal implications of migrant workers in Europe. The book is divided into three parts: international migrations (part I), the socioeconomic situation of the migrant worker (part II), and the legal status of the migrant workers in public (international) law (part III). The arrangement of the presentations in parts II and III calls for some comment: the contributions in part II on the legal order and the status of the migrant workers (Mr. Flory), the status of the migrant worker in the European Community in the light of its jurisprudence (Mr. Chevalier), and the European Convention on the Legal Status of Migrant Workers (Mr. Golsong) are primarily of a legal nature and should have been placed in part III; whereas the issue of transfer of funds of migrant workers (part III) affects first and foremost the socioeconomic situation of the migrant workers. The study on international regulations concerning clandestine trafficking (part I) fails to mention two reports prepared by Mrs. Halima Warzazi at the request of the United Nations Sub-Commission on Prevention of Discrimination and the Protection of Minorities on "Exploitation of labour through illicit and clandestine trafficking" (UN Docs. E/CN.4/Sub.2/351 (1972) and E/CN.4/Sub.2/L.629 (1975)).

The participants focused primarily on the status of migrant workers from countries belonging to the European Economic Community and the Council of Europe. Special attention was also given to achievements of the International Labour Organisation in this field. Several speakers correctly distinguished the difference in application between EEC and ILO conventions and the Council of Europe's Convention on the Legal Status of Migrant Workers (No. 93, 1977). While the EEC and ILO conventions are legal acts of the respective organizations, the Council of Europe's Convention cannot be conceived as such without the additional provisions of the Convention itself (Art. 33).

A common denominator of the colloquium was that regional standard setting (European Community and Council of Europe) through bilateral and multilateral agreements is preferable to international standard setting, because it affords the beneficiaries of the norms (*i.e.*, the migrant workers) better recourse to legal remedies. Although the special nature of the phenomenon of "migrant workers," having more private international law aspects than public international law aspects, does indeed call for a regional solution by the countries concerned, one should not forget that the situation of migrant workers bears upon two fundamental issues: the status of the individual in international law and whether norms and their sanctions shall be set nationally or internationally. Those issues are not resolved by this colloquium on the migrant worker, but light is shed upon the practical difficulties encountered when implementing theoretical norms.

J. VAN AGGELEN
Human Rights Division
United Nations, Geneva

Weather Modification: Prospects and Problems. By Georg Breuer. New York: Cambridge University Press, 1979. Pp. xiii, 178. Index.

Scientists have been trying to develop techniques to increase rainfall, moderate hurricanes, dissipate lightning, and modify other weather phenomena. What are their prospects? What problems would they create if they succeeded? How should we handle these problems? Breuer has written a comprehensive, readable book that addresses these questions. Originally published in German in 1976 as *Wetter Nach Wunsch?*, the book is particularly noteworthy as one of the few publications to discuss knowledgeably the whole range of issues associated with weather modification.

The book is divided into three parts. In part I Breuer reviews the scientific theories underlying the development of weather modification technology and discusses the difficulty in evaluating the results of particular attempts to alter rainfall or other weather phenomena. He astutely points to the large gap between the slow advance of scientific theory and the rapid application of the infant technology. In part II Breuer reviews the methods developed thus far to modify weather. His treatment of the material in both parts is refined and lucid.

In part III the author highlights the social, economic, ecological, and legal aspects of weather modification. While he provides an excellent review of many of the issues, his discussion of the international aspects of hurricane modification, a topic of current concern, is surprisingly narrow and does not address the problems associated with developing a program acceptable to other countries. In the final section Breuer offers his own policy proposal: a world weather authority, under the auspices of the World Meteorological Organization, to manage all weather modification operations that could have effects outside a country's border. This is reminiscent of the proposal by the World Peace Through Law Center in 1971. While Breuer acknowledges the utopian character of his proposal in view of the nationalism of states, he sees little hope for the use of weather modification unless it is supervised by a world authority. Unfortunately, he does not systematically identify the critical problems that he believes are raised by successful weather modification technology and that necessitate a world authority, nor does he explain how his proposed world weather authority would respond to these problems.

Nevertheless, the author has given us an informed and well-written overview of the broad range of scientific, technical, and social problems associated with weather modification that should be read by anyone interested in this specific field and in the more general issues raised by the development of new technologies affecting the common resources of states.

EDITH BROWN WEISS
Georgetown University Law Center

Acid Rain and International Law. By Irene H. van Lier. Toronto: Bunsel Environmental Consultants; Alphen aan den Rijn: Sijthoff & Noordhoff, 1981. Pp. xxii, 278.

This survey of the scientific, economic, and international law considerations relevant to the acid rain problem is a useful and timely work. Although it focuses on the situation in North America, it has a full discussion of the problem as perceived in Europe.

Acid rain, formally defined as rain with a pH level of 5.6 or less, affects broad areas of the United States, although its effects are most pronounced in the East. Sulphur and nitrogen compounds, principally from fossil fuel combustion of power plants and automobiles, chemically combine with moisture in the atmosphere to form acids. These substances travel long distances and finally fall to earth in the form of rain or dry fallout. There is as yet a great deal of uncertainty about the effects of this precipitation, but it is established that it results in a gradual acidification of streams and lakes, resulting in the death of fish populations. Acid rain also erodes buildings and eats at the metal in water pipes and waste, which adds lead and other metals to drinking water with consequences to health not yet fully understood. Beyond this, it may also be responsible for declines in crop and forest productivity.[1]

The *Trail Smelter* arbitration decision of 1941 dealing with short-range transborder air pollution by sulphur dioxide (SO_2) fumes originating in Canada and causing damage in the United States articulated the principle that

> no State has the right to use or permit the use of its territory in such a manner as to cause injury by fumes in or to the territory of another or the properties or persons therein, when the case is of serious consequence and the injury is established by clear and convincing evidence.[2]

The environmental principles of the 1972 Stockholm Declaration on the Human Environment[3] (particularly Principles 6 and 21) reflect similar international law principles on good neighborliness and the duty of states to exercise due diligence to prevent the pollution of areas beyond their jurisdiction. The problem of applying international law principles to acid rain, however, is that its causes are still uncertain, the sources of the relevant pollution are hard to identify, and the damages are only beginning to become clear.

[1] For a graphic illustration of the proverb "[o]ne picture is worth a thousand words," see the magnificently illustrated article, LaBastille, *Acid Rain, How Great a Menace?*, NAT'L GEOGRAPHIC, Nov. 1981, at 652.

[2] 3 R. Int'l Arb. Awards 1905, 1963–65 (1941).

[3] UN Doc. A/CONF.48/14/Rev.1, at 3–5 (1973).

It seems likely that problems such as acid rain will exert a strong stimulus to the formation of new international agreements to deal with transborder pollution. The UN Economic Commission for Europe in 1979 adopted a Convention on Long-Range Transboundary Air Pollution,[4] which contains a general commitment "to limit and, as far as possible, gradually reduce and prevent air pollution including long-range transboundary air pollution" by use of "the best available technology which is economically feasible."

The United States and Canada signed a Memorandum of Intent concerning Transboundary Air Pollution in August 1980.[5] This Memorandum commits the two Governments "to develop a bilateral agreement which will reflect and further the development of effective domestic control programs and other measures to combat transboundary air pollution." Canada estimates that one-half of the acid rain in Canada comes from the United States. U.S. spokesmen point out that American emission controls are much more stringent than Canada's and that Canadian pollution also drifts to the United States. How to mandate further controls when their cost effectiveness is unclear remains a problem.

Van Lier's book is a balanced and workmanlike assembly of the legal, scientific, economic, and institutional background information on a significant problem that is likely to generate interesting developments in international law.

TIMOTHY ATKESON
Of the District of Columbia Bar

L'Emprise Maritime de l'Etat Côtier. By Gilbert Apollis. Paris: Editions A. Pedone, 1981. Pp. 293. F.128,40.

This book is essentially a study of the development of national control by coastal states of the maritime areas adjacent to their coasts. For readers of French this is as good an introduction to the problem as this reviewer has seen. Its inclusion in international law libraries is highly recommended.

The book is divided into four parts. The first section is a basic introduction, which includes a definition of the concepts "emprise maritime" and "Etat côtier," and a discussion of limitations on control and the legitimation of national control over contiguous maritime areas by coastal states. The modern formulation of such control dates from the Truman Proclamation of 1945.

The second portion of the work is concerned with validation of the legal process of extension of coastal state control. The initial chapter of this section deals with the concept of adjacency as the theoretical foundation for an extension of coastal state control. This is followed by an extensive discussion in the second chapter of the fact that such extensions are unilateral acts by states, the validity of which has an international aspect.

The third division of *L'Emprise Maritime de l'Etat Côtier* deals with the problem of justification of national authority exercised by the coastal state. As the author correctly indicates, nationalization of marine resources has been justified primarily on the basis of economics for over 30 years, but within an international political context. States have clearly recognized development of

[4] 18 ILM 1442 (1979).

[5] 20 ILM 690 (1981).

resources within adjacent marine areas as being within their vital national interests. This is especially true of developing countries in the context of a new international law of the sea. The author includes extensive discussions of the exclusive economic zone as an instrument of national development policy and permanent sovereignty over natural resources. The fourth section deals with coastal state protection of the marine environment, based on the precedents of neutrality and national security.

The author completes his study with a chapter of general conclusions. Coastal state expansion of maritime jurisdiction is not a phenomenon of our epoch but was also endemic to the international system of the 18th and 19th centuries. National practice has always been the primary source of the international law of the sea. A considerably larger number of states is presently exercising maritime ambitions, both in the creation of coastal zones and in the formulation of international norms. States of the Third World are not solely responsible for the expansion of claims to adjacent coastal waters. Developed states have contributed through claims to defense and security zones. Developing states did contribute the concept of exclusive fishing zones. Developed states have actually been the primary beneficiaries of coastal state expansion owing to both geographic advantage and technological development.

J. A. VOSBURGH
University of Arizona

El Nuevo Derecho del Mar: El Perú y las 200 Millas. By Eduardo Ferrero Costa. Lima: Pontificia Universidad Católica del Perú, 1979. Pp. 456. Indexes.

The eminent international legal scholar Ferrero Costa has written a complete analysis of the Peruvian claim to a 200-mile territorial sea. Peru remains one of the hard-core territorialists at the Third United Nations Conference on the Law of the Sea, and the book is a defense of the claim to a 200-mile territorial sea or marine sovereignty zone. A review of the "old international law," which prevailed up to the beginning of UNCLOS III, discloses that it was the tool of the chief maritime powers of the 19th and 20th centuries, the United States and Great Britain, who simply promulgated the law without consultation with other nations. The 3-mile territorial limit, therefore, was the result of unilateral action that was not in the best interests of all states. The Truman Proclamation of 1945 is regarded as the key factor in the subsequent actions of Latin American states in extending their own jurisdiction beyond the 3-mile limit. Peru did so in 1947 with an extension to 200 miles of its sovereignty claim.

The book traces some of the important developments in the evolution of a changing attitude towards the law of the sea in Latin America such as the Declaration of Santiago by Chile, Ecuador, and Peru, the activities of the Inter-American Council of Jurists, the Principles of Mexico of 1956, and the 1970 Declarations of Montevideo and Lima. In the view of Ferrero Costa, a clear consensus emerged in Latin America in support of the right of each country to determine its own territorial limit and resource zone. The United States is clearly the opponent of this Latin American consensus. One problem with this section of the book is that the author continually refers to a consensus when it is highly unlikely that one existed or exists. For example, the Principles of Mexico, which proposed the right of the coastal state to determine for itself its territorial zone, were passed as a preparatory study by a vote of 11 to 9, hardly an overwhelming consensus. And Peru is decidedly in the minority at UNCLOS in its current claim of a 200-mile territorial sea.

The second half of the book develops the logic for Peru's claim and rests primarily on the assumption that waters off the coast of Peru constitute a unified and indivisible ecological system entitling Peru to its wealth. The scientific evidence for such a claim is not conclusive. Other arguments are also employed, one a bit stretched, such as the fact that there is no other country off the coast of Peru for a long distance, so what difference does it make if 200 miles are claimed? Under the "new international law" there is absolute equality of all states and the resources of the seas are to be used to help the developing states. If so, one is hard pressed to understand why the anchoveta catch off Peru, a truly important harvest, is used to feed animals in the developed zone. The catch is entirely by Peruvian vessels and one wonders why this valuable product is not used directly to help the population of Peru. The book is an excellent presentation of the Group of 77's position on the resources of the sea, but this reviewer remains unconvinced that Peru is entitled to the claim of a 200-mile territorial sea; a 200-mile exclusive economic zone, yes, but not a sovereign zone.

C. RICHARD BATH
The University of Texas at El Paso

International Groundwater Law. By Ludwik A. Teclaff and Albert E. Utton. London, Rome, New York: Oceana Publications, Inc., 1981. Pp. xiv, 490. $50.

This book is composed of two parts: the first, 188 pages in length, consists of eight studies, three-quarters of them by different authors; the second is a collection of treaties, interstate compacts, municipal law, proposals of a national and international character, and some EEC documents. Since the first study is the only item that has not been previously published elsewhere, the book is really a collection of materials on the subject of groundwater from the international law aspect.

The theme of the book can be stated shortly. It is that the demand for fresh water increases while its supply decreases, and this has led, and will continue to lead, to increasing extraction of groundwater with unknown and probably dire consequences for the future, in particular, irreversible pollution of the groundwater. This is lamentable, for the quantity and quality of groundwater, both national and international, are seriously threatened. Unfortunately, as the eight studies show again and again, international law dealing with groundwater hardly exists; when all of the documents in this book are winnowed, hardly a few grains of law are left.

The various authors are unanimous in the remedies they propose. They stress the need for rational management, the first principle of which is that all fresh water resources should be treated in an integrated fashion. Implicit in this proposition is the need for joint institutions to study the water resources in question, to plan their optimum and equitable utilization, to monitor compliance with plans, and perhaps even to participate in their enforcement. Concerning substantive rules, it is asserted persuasively that the legal principles governing surface water apply to groundwater.

This "precious, baffling resource we call groundwater," to use the words of one of the authors, presents a challenge to lawyers; the law must catch up and keep pace with the exploitation of this resource so that the water can be rationally utilized and prudently conserved. This book provides a timely guide for those who would meet this challenge.

C. B. BOURNE
The University of British Columbia

International Air Transport in the Eighties. Edited by H. A. Wassenbergh and H. P. van Fenema. Deventer: Kluwer, 1981. Pp. ix, 250. Dfl.90.

This book seeks to determine the direction of regulation of international air transport in this decade. The outcome of the ongoing battle between deregulation and protectionism is the major factor affecting the direction of such regulation. To help analyze the likely results of this battle the editors have divided this book into two parts: the first consists of the texts of papers presented at the first Netherlands Colloquium on International Air Transport held near The Hague in 1980; and the second presents an approach to regulation of air transport through the presentation of a draft plurilateral treaty. The papers cover a wide range of topics including policy aspects of international aviation, the economics of national airlines and the air transport industry in general, and the financial and pricing aspects of international air transport.

The main strength of this book is the diversity of the points of view expressed. Unfortunately, its biggest weakness derives from the same diversity. Although the choice of speakers at the colloquium is impressive, too many of the papers speak as if there were no one else discussing the issues. Perhaps the nature of a collection of presented papers precludes discussion, but one would hope that just the opposite would be true. A forum such as the Netherlands colloquium is the perfect opportunity to generate discussion, as opposed to mere speechmaking. Unfortunately, with few exceptions the authors of the papers do not analyze the issues involved, but rather lecture the reader on their own points of view. Those who favor deregulation seem to have little understanding of the nationalistic (and frequently the economic) need for protection of national airlines. Those favoring protectionism seem unwilling to address the issues of consumer convenience and fare economies which may be achieved by deregulation.[1] Moreover, the tone of the papers suggests that the opposing arguments are so far politicized as to hamper the chances for successful compromise, a dogmatic entrenchment reminiscent of North/South debates.

[1] *See* Raben, *Deregulation: A Critical Interrogation,* in INTERNATIONAL AIR TRANSPORT IN THE EIGHTIES 13, 13 (H. Wassenbergh and H. van Fenema eds. 1981). Of the papers presented, Director-General Raben's critical analysis of deregulation is probably the most realistic assessment of the situation today.

The most disconcerting aspect of this book is the apparent inability of almost all of the authors to analyze the economic viability of their approaches. While the relevance of economic considerations is more obvious to those pursuing the goal of deregulation, such considerations are equally relevant to an analysis of protectionism. Neither side seems to have come to terms with the fact that severe financial restraints can hamper the ability of airlines to respond to changes in the nature and costs of their businesses. The recent failure of Laker Airways and the distressing financial situation of many of the U.S. airlines[2] highlight the importance of analyzing the financial consequences of any approach to air transport regulation.

Notwithstanding the general lack of a true discussion of the issues raised by deregulation and protectionism, several of the papers are informative and incisive. Professor Lowenfeld's discussion of U.S. deregulation and the contrasting conditions in the rest of the world provides a basis for evaluating his conclusion that deregulation will continue to spread. Similarly, the two papers on financing in the air transport industry hint at the very real danger that the airlines will be unable to finance the replaning of their fleets. As these papers point out, nearly $137 billion will be required in the 1980's to allow the airlines to modernize their fleets.[3] The sources of this money are not obvious.

Part II of this book provides an approach to the general issue of regulation of air transport on an international basis by presenting a draft Plurilateral Air Transport Agreement.[4] The draft Agreement is meant to provide some (but not complete) uniformity of regulation. This uniformity would be in contrast to the widely varying degrees of regulation that have arisen as a result of the negotiation of bilateral agreements.

The discussions of the draft Agreement make it clear that the Agreement is intended to have substantive import. Its real value, however, arises more from the procedural approach it advocates than from any substantive modifications that it may produce. Certainly the air transport industry is so international in character as to suggest that bilateral agreements are an inefficient way to regulate, but in order for procedure to be substantively effective the procedures must be widely accepted. While the draft Agreement provides an approach to the problems caused by bilateralism, the failure to assess reasonably the likelihood of its acceptance leaves the reader wondering about its ultimate value.

This book is informative and timely. Its failure to provide the reader with sufficient analysis of the arguments advanced detracts from its overall value. Since the book tends to be technical and at the same time not an exhaustive treatment of the subject, its usefulness to any but those involved in the study of the regulation of international air transport is limited.

FREDERIC A. EUSTIS, III
Of the New York Bar

[2] *See, e.g.,* Wall St. J., Jan. 26, 1982, at 6, col. 1; *id.*, Feb. 26, 1982, at 12, col. 1.

[3] Oort, *Financing of the U.S. Airline Industry in the 80's,* in INTERNATIONAL AIR TRANSPORT IN THE EIGHTIES 113, 116 (H. Wassenbergh and H. van Fenema eds. 1981).

[4] The explanations of the draft treaty and portions of the first papers would have benefited from an explanation of the terms used. Most readers who are not specialists in aviation law will not understand much of the industry terminology used to describe, for example, the kinds of rights that are typically exchanged by treaty.

La Conférence au Sommet: Contribution à l'Etude des Institutions des Relations Internationales. By Guillaume Pambou Tchivounda. Paris: Librairie Générale de Droit et de Jurisprudence, 1980. Pp. 452. Indexes. F.195.

This book is a comprehensive study of summit conferences. There can be no doubt that such conferences have become a major aspect of modern international diplomacy, and this book is a useful contribution to understanding the phenomenon. The author's approach is descriptive and analytical.

He gives three reasons for the prevalence of summit conferences, especially in the period since World War II: (1) the personalization of power among all states in the head of government; (2) the increasingly multidimensional character of international relations, which creates multiple and inexorable links among various domestic and international issues; and (3) changes in transportation and communication systems that make it possible for heads of government to meet easily.

In the period since World War II, not only has there been an increasing number of summit conferences, but they have become key bodies of such international organizations as the Central African Customs and Economic Union and the Organization of African Unity. They are a regular feature of the European Communities and, since the early days of the energy crisis, a principal mechanism for efforts to coordinate the macroeconomic policies of the seven most important market economies. All of these developments are described in detail in the book, and there are several useful listings of various types of summit conferences.

The author believes that summit conferences have several advantages. These are mostly associated with having individuals with the capacity to commit their states meet face to face. The problems and disadvantages of the summit conferences stem from the same feature. Given the authority of the individuals involved, public expectations may be roused that cannot be met. Because the individuals are busy, they have little time to devote to the issues. The prominence of the individuals makes secrecy difficult to maintain.

The author concludes that summit conferences have become more frequent, institutionalized, and generalized, and he predicts that these trends will continue. These conclusions are unexceptional, but the book is full of useful detail. Readers may wish, however, that the analysis had been more extensive and far-reaching.

HAROLD K. JACOBSON
Board of Editors

El Voto Ponderado. By Vicente Blanco Gaspar. Madrid: Instituto Hispano-Luso-Americano de Derecho Internacional, 1981. Pp. xvi, 228. Index.

This is a book about weighted voting as applied in international organizations. Such voting is often to be found in economic bodies that have an important financial impact on their member states.

Blanco Gaspar, who teaches at the University of Alcalá de Henares and is a legal adviser in the Spanish Ministry of Foreign Affairs, has undertaken a detailed analysis of the use of weighted voting in international organizations and describes the plans of over one hundred authors that have dealt with this subject. In so doing, the author has reviewed the practice of the United Nations and specialized agencies. He has placed special emphasis on organizations that have an institutionalized system of weighted voting such as the World Bank and the European Community organizations, which constitute the clearest living examples of the use of the system.

The author also discusses the question of proportional representation and uses certain characteristics of national constitutions in order to apply them on the international level where a greater integration of world order is being sought. The best and most advanced example of proportional representation on the non-national level is the European Parliament. But even it does not have total proportional representation.

The book is an encyclopedic referencc to the subject of weighted voting, which is today a reality on the international scene. The doctrinal bases for arriving at this point of development involve reconsideration of the significance of sovereignty, and this converts the pages devoted to this aspect of the subject matter of the book into an interesting study of the movement of international organization towards supranationality. In this regard, the author concludes that the mediation of interests by weighted voting and direct representation would change the character of states as subjects of rights and duties in a new legal order.

Detailed footnotes and an extensive bibliography complete the contents of a very useful book.

GERALD F. FITZGERALD, Q.C.
Ottawa, Canada

Jerusalem. By Henry Cattan. New York: St. Martin's Press, 1981. Pp. 229. Index. $25.

The author of this book is a very distinguished jurist who is a barrister-at-law, was a member of the Palestine Bar, and taught at the Jerusalem Law School. He has written several books on the Palestine problem, with which he is very familiar.

In the present book Cattan discusses the history of Jerusalem from its beginnings to the recent past. He analyzes the various Security Council and General Assembly resolutions bearing on the city's status, including General Assembly Resolution 181 (II) which established Jerusalem as a *corpus separatum* under an international regime with the Trusteeship Council as the administering authority. The author maintains that this resolution is binding upon the Israelis but not upon the Palestinians since they possessed sovereignty over Palestine after its detachment from Turkey at the end of World War I (p. 107). He then deals in some detail with the nonrecognition by the international community of the Israeli annexation of the modern sector of the city and, in 1967, of the Old City. In a postscript the author deals with the Israeli Knesset's approval of a bill on July 30, 1980 making a "complete and united Jerusalem" (including the Old City) the capital of Israel and with the rejection of this action by the Security Council.

Cattan is very critical of U.S. support of Israel as well as of the Camp David Agreements and the Egyptian-Israeli Peace Treaty. He does not mention the Saudi peace plan announced by Prince (now King) Fahd on August 8, 1981, which called for Israeli withdrawal from all Arab territory occupied in 1967, including Jerusalem, for guarantees of freedom of worship in the holy places, and for the creation of an Arab state with Jerusalem as its capital. The plan was unacceptable to the more radical Arab states and Israel.

The author himself proposes as an interim solution the establishment of "conservatory and protective measures" in implementation of the UN resolutions. These would include evacuation by Israel of the *corpus separatum*, withdrawal of Israeli settlers, and annulment of Israeli colonization and judaization of the city. A tripartite Communal Council with equal Moslem, Christian, and Jewish representation would administer the city pending a final solution. In case of the expected stiff Israeli resistance to these proposals, the author advocates the use of force.

The book is well organized and shows the author's thorough knowledge of the problem of Jerusalem and its legal ramifications. However, it also shows the large gap still separating the positions of the Israelis and the Palestinians. It should be of interest to all who in one capacity or another are concerned with the problem of Jerusalem and Palestine as a whole.

HERBERT J. LIEBESNY
Arlington, Virginia

Willamette Law Review. Vol. 17, no. 1. Symposium issue on International Law and Foreign Policy in the 1980s. Salem: Willamette University College of Law, 1980. Pp. 301. $5.

The articles in this symposium issue are all taken from contributions of participants in the Law Professors' Workshop on National Security and Foreign Policy Issues in the 1980's, cosponsored by the Willamette University College of Law. There are three main categories of contributions to the issue, the first providing general treatments of the topic of international law and foreign policy, followed by pieces addressing selected current issues and those concerned with geographical studies.

Most interesting and valuable are the contributions to the general theme, especially the essay by the late Hardy Cross Dillard, which interrelates law and policy with an emphasis on the World Court, and the invaluable overview of current international law problems by Thomas Franck. In addition, the last article written by Alona Evans, concerning terrorism, contains some excellent insights into the problem of combating terrorists and some extremely useful proposals for international legal action.

Other pieces are less satisfying and some rather polemic. Perhaps because of the national security portion of the workshop title, an overriding concern with the Soviet Union is manifest, as well as renewed attention to dominoes and how they fall. Uneven quality is a problem with almost all symposia and conferences and this one is no exception. In addition, geographical area studies tend to run the risk of being overtaken by current events, as in the case of

Central America. It is nevertheless clear that the three pieces mentioned above would alone justify the addition of this volume to any international law library, while other contributions are certainly interesting and thought-provoking.

Overall, the impression remains that the title of the issue would be better written as "International Law *or* Foreign Policy." Most of the articles are clearly positioned to advocate one view or the other, with the foreign policy contributors manifesting at best indifference to international law. One states bluntly that "[i]llegality has importance only in terms of political costs." Such a view is apparent in several pieces and no doubt represents a perspective of which international lawyers should be reminded from time to time. The book thus usefully demonstrates to its readers how far even U.S. policy makers appear to be from accepting an international order based on the rule of law.

DINAH SHELTON
University of Santa Clara

Israel Yearbook on Human Rights. Vol. 10. Edited by Yoram Dinstein. Tel Aviv: Faculty of Law, Tel Aviv University, 1980. Pp. 406. Indexes.

The current, 10th, volume of the *Israel Yearbook on Human Rights* for the main part lacks the specific Israeli emphasis of some of its predecessors. Apart from the 15 or so pages devoted to judgments of the Supreme Court of Israel relating to the administered (occupied) territories, there is little that is of specific Israeli significance. As a result, this volume is of wider general significance in the field of human rights than has been true of some of the earlier volumes.

Four papers are concerned with aspects of armed conflict. One by the present reviewer puts forward the contention that there is perhaps more protection for human rights in time of armed conflict than there is in time of peace. Another, by the editor, on the law of war at sea is probably of more historical than current significance. Historians will probably be interested in Dr. Lador-Lederer's paper on Jews as prisoners of war, which points out that those captured on the western front received better treatment than their colleagues from the east. The final paper in this general section is concerned with the psychology of genocide (Professor Charny).

The papers on human rights *per se* are divided into two sections, the first in a "general" and the other in a "specific" context. The general papers are contributed by Dr. Rosenne who provides a detailed account of the adoption of the 1979 Hostages Convention; by Dr. Weis, formerly of the Legal Department of the High Commissioner for Refugees, who deals briefly with "refugees in orbit," that is to say, those who have no country of asylum; and by Dr. Tabory, whose paper on language rights as human rights might more properly have been in the "specific" section and is the longest in the volume. As to specific issues, Professor Konvitz looks at the *Bakke* case in considering whether the U.S. Constitution is colorblind; Professor Friedland is concerned with Canadian legal perspectives in the field of national security, while Dr. Bracha examines somewhat similar issues in Israel. In addition, there are two unrelated papers, one by Professor Butler on the definition and publication of treaties under Soviet law, and another of purely historical significance by Dr.

Namdar on the role of the majority and the right of the minority in the process of communal enactment in the Balkan Jewish communities in the 16th century. In view of the relatively narrow readership that this would reach if printed in a journal devoted to legal history, a case can probably be made for its inclusion in the *Yearbook*.

Many democratic countries are now considering whether they should adopt a bill of rights. This issue has been settled for Canada by the inclusion of a Charter of Rights in the new Constitution, but it is still of serious import in the United Kingdom, particularly insofar as English courts have to face issues arising under the European Convention. In this connection, Lord Lloyd of Hampstead's piece on the controversy regarding a bill of rights is of topical interest.

For those interested in human rights and the law regarding their protection, volume 10 of the *Israel Yearbook* should prove attractive.

L. C. GREEN
University of Alberta

Netherlands Yearbook of International Law. Vol. XI, 1980. T. M. C. Asser Institute, The Hague. Alphen aan den Rijn and Germantown: Sijthoff & Noordhoff, 1981. Pp. 429. Index. Dfl.80; $40.

The familiar format of this useful publication is maintained in the present volume. In addition to leading articles and notes, it contains summaries of Dutch state practice, treaties, domestic legislation with international impact, and judicial decisions, and a bibliography of books and articles written during the period covered. The articles deal with the legal status of aliens under agreements between member states of the Council of Europe; legal and nonlegal norms; the Final Act of Helsinki (a nonlegal agreement); and the *Iran Hostages* case before the International Court of Justice. An interesting aspect of state practice is the inclusion of sports in all Dutch international cultural exchange treaties since 1966 (p. 257).

On the issue of sovereign immunity it was held by a Dutch court that Dutch labor law applies to an allegedly wrongful dismissal of a Portuguese national as a teacher in a Portuguese school operated in Amsterdam by the Portuguese Ministry of Education (pp. 290–91). The usual amusing cases arising from invocation of the European Convention on Human Rights as Dutch law appear. One of these held that the requirement of seat belts for motorists did not violate the right of everyone (recognized in Article 8 of the Convention) "to respect for . . . private and family life, . . . home and . . . correspondence" (p. 307). That article did, however, forbid tapping defense counsel's telephone conversations by order of the *Untersuchungsrichter* in a criminal case (*ibid.*), but did not prevent deportation of a Yugoslavian woman whose 3-month relationship with a man was doubtfully to be regarded as "family life," and in any event could be continued in Yugoslavia (p. 308). Likewise, Article 10 protecting "freedom of expression" did not include the right to solicit money in the streets (pp. 309–10).

A number of environmental pollution cases are reported. One of particular interest held that Dutch nursery gardeners could obtain relief in a Dutch court against a French potash company for excessive and harmful saline discharge into an international river—the Rhine. The court concluded that Dutch law includes unwritten international law, and that the national judge must have recourse to the "general principles of law" prescribed for application by the International Court of Justice in Article 38(1)(c) of its Statute. Under this criterion the court followed as a precedent the *Trail Smelter* arbitration in 1941, which awarded damages to the United States for injuries caused by a Canadian smelter processing sulphur ores and discharging fumes harmful to crops across the border. The court retained jurisdiction for the development of an adequate factual record in order to determine the amount of damages (pp. 326–33). The U.S. Supreme Court reached the same result in *Georgia v. Tennessee Copper Co.* (206 U.S. 230, 237 (1907)) and *Georgia v. Pennsylvania Railroad Co.* (324 U.S. 439, 450 (1945)).

EDWARD DUMBAULD
U.S. Senior District Judge

The Canadian Yearbook of International Law. Volume XVII, 1979. Edited by C. B. Bourne. Vancouver: The University of British Columbia Press, 1980. Pp. 462. Index. $28.

The Canadian Yearbook of International Law. Volume XVIII, 1980. Edited by C. B. Bourne. Vancouver: The University of British Columbia Press, 1981. Pp. 425. Index. $32.

The 17th and 18th volumes of the *Yearbook* continue the tradition of quality scholarship its readers have come to expect. The 17th volume begins with an article by Shabtai Rosenne on the career of John Read, the first Commonwealth judge to sit on the International Court of Justice. The following three articles treat, respectively, the delimitation of the continental shelf between Canada and the United States in the Beaufort Sea (Frederick), the Northwest Passage in international law (Pharand), and water pollution in international law (Florio). Useful maps of the Beaufort Sea and the Northwest Passage are provided. Readers will find the discussion very interesting on the status of the Northwest Passage as a strait, its potential role as a transit route for oil tankers, and Canada's need to protect the Arctic environment.

L. C. Green offers an interesting discussion of war law and the medical profession, which examines the history of legal protection for medical personnel working in war situations. The final article (Blom), focusing on the choice-of-law methods in the private international law of contract, highlights a regular and awkward practice of the *Yearbook*, namely, breaking up long manuscripts into a serialized article continued through several volumes. Rather than ask readers to follow an article over a multi-year period, especially a good one, as this article is, it would seem wiser either to condense it for one volume or to publish it separately as a monograph.

The 18th volume includes two articles relating to hydrocarbon transport: recent developments in tanker control in international law (Popp) and international pipelines between Canada and the United States (Ballem; maps are included). Gregoire Lehoux offers a thorough study of the Third Law of the Sea Conference and the compulsory settlement of disputes. Two further articles examine Canada's role in the development of the law of armed conflict (L. C. Green) and the legal limits on the use of force by Canadian warships engaged in law enforcement (Fenrick). The remaining article is the concluding installment of Blom's study on choice-of-law methods.

The Notes and Comments section of the *Yearbook* is rather modestly labeled. Readers are always offered a broad selection of substantive and significant studies on international law topics. Each volume also regularly includes a valuable review of Canada's practice in international law, as well as a book review section and an index.

FOREST L. GRIEVES
University of Montana
Universität des Saarlandes

The Australian Year Book of International Law. Vol. 7. Edited by D. W. Greig. Canberra: Australian National University, 1981. Pp. xxix, 548. Index. $91.20.

Volume 7 of the *Year Book* is offered as "[a] survey of current problems of Public and Private International Law with a section of Australian Practice in International Law for the years 1976 and 1977." It contains no less than 13 essays of varying length, the longest being a learned discussion of the *Beagle Channel* arbitration by the editor.

As is usual in publications of this nature, private international law gets comparatively short shrift. It is represented by a brief note on recent developments by J. L. R. Davis of the Australian National University and an article on private remedies for transfrontier environmental damage by E. Willheim of the Attorney-General's Department.

The volume begins with an informative and moving obituary for Professor D. P. O'Connell that traces his distinguished career, outlines his contribution to international law, and provides us with some insight into Daniel O'Connell, the person. O'Connell spent most of his working life in Australia. But he was a New Zealander. He received his law degree from the University of Auckland.

The essays are all interesting, but not all of them can be mentioned. Some, like Professor R. D. Lumb's article on *The Timor Sea* and K. W. Ryan's on *The Torres Strait Treaty* between Australia and Papua New Guinea, are of special interest to Australians. But they should also interest anyone concerned with the law of the sea.

Other articles are of more general interest. Professor D. H. N. Johnson of the University of Sydney criticizes the ICJ Judgment of December 19, 1978 in the *Aegean Sea Continental Shelf* case,[1] which dismissed Greece's case against Turkey for want of jurisdiction. His most important criticism is that

[1] [1978] ICJ REP. 3.

the Court "failed in this case to grasp the nettle of how to deal with States who fail to appear." But he is also unconvinced by the Court's holding that a dispute about the boundary of the continental shelf related to the territorial status of Greece.

M. R. Burrowes, an honors student at the Victoria University of Wellington, New Zealand, contributed an article on the procedural aspects of implementing the UN Racial Convention. More articles of this nature on the practical aspects of human rights enforcement are needed.

In two contributions, R. P. Schaffer of the University of New South Wales criticizes the South African approach to treaty interpretation and discusses the Australian experience with Southeast Asian refugees.

In *Recent Developments in the Law of Foreign Sovereign Immunity*, Barrister P. Southerland argues for adoption by Australia of foreign sovereign immunity legislation that would incorporate features of the U.S. Foreign Sovereign Immunities Act of 1976 and the UK State Immunity Act, 1978.

J. D. Kindt of the University of Illinois at Urbana/Champaign writes about investment interdependence as a potential response to future Arab oil embargoes.

The always valuable section on Australian practice is enhanced in this volume by the contribution of Elihu Lauterpacht in his capacity as Legal Adviser to the Australian Department of Foreign Affairs.

J. B. ELKIND
The University of Auckland

BRIEFER NOTICES

International Law for Seagoing Officers (4th ed.). By Burdick H. Brittin. (Annapolis: Naval Institute Press, 1981. Pp. xvi, 483. Index. $21.95.) In contrast to its predecessors,[1] the fourth edition of this volume presents a more comprehensive treatment of international law, aimed at a more universal audience. That is, it is neither expressly designed nor exclusively intended for legal practitioners and governmental policy makers; rather, laymen, nonlaw professionals, and academicians will find in this work useful information about international law in general and law of the sea implications in particular.

On balance, Brittin has provided the reader with a traditional international law text, albeit not from a case-oriented approach. Instead, he specifically addresses concepts and principles underpinning international law, and in the process, relates them to various issues of salient interest to the international community. Accordingly, among the topics examined are the sources of international law; the rights and duties of states; diplomatic representation and responsibilities; territorial jurisdiction over land, water bodies, air, space, and the high seas; the law of war and armed conflict; and the notion of collective security.

Somewhat disturbing to this reviewer was the conspicuous absence of footnote

[1] Reviewed in 51 AJIL 656 (1957) and 67 AJIL 612 (1973).

citations; even so, this annoyance was assuaged by the inclusion of an impressive bibliographical supplement. Relatedly, as a research tool, readers will find this volume particularly helpful and convenient because of its 17 prominent appendixes. These encompass some 150 pages, and pertain to national security issues, as well as to the law of the sea. In the latter context, excerpts are drawn principally from the 1980 UNCLOS III Draft Convention. In sum, notwithstanding its title, persons broadly interested in international law should welcome Brittin's revised version as a timely, thoughtful, highly comprehensible contribution to the corpus of contemporary international legal literature.

CHRISTOPHER C. JOYNER
The George Washington University

The U.N. Convention on the Elimination of All Forms of Racial Discrimination (2d ed.). By Natan Lerner. (Alphen aan den Rijn: Sijthoff & Noordhoff, 1980. Pp. xvii, 259. Index. Dfl.75; $37.50.) While it may be difficult to find a single phrase in which to convey the essence of Lerner's theme, the book is diligent in its scholarship and persuasive in its judgment. If it is not overly provocative of argument, it is because the time when it was originally written followed the election of John F. Kennedy to the presidency of the United States and coincided with the great surge in the operational activities of the UN system. The accent was on production, including scholarship. The United Nations was striking out to combat all forms of racial discrimination; the effort was to make the law not merely negatively to compensate the victims, but to act positively to deter oppressors.

In the second edition we are dealing with a virtually new book. This reviewer does not propose to try to strike a balance between the extremes of uncritical adoration and unselective condemnation. I feel strongly, however, that had Lerner been able to free himself of the shackles of professional conformism and probe deeper into the records for the origins of the Convention, he might have revealed much of the evolution of the UN struggle against racial discrimination. The United Nations Convention on the Elimination of All Forms of Racial Discrimination neither was inevitable nor served a special purpose. It emerged out of the accidental coalescence of men and events with different destinies and purposes to create the pursuit of nondiscrimination. There is still room for a legislative history of the Convention to reveal its faults and virtues.

MOSES MOSKOWITZ
Secretary-General,
Consultative Council of Jewish Organizations

Utilization of Outer Space and International Law. By Gijsbertha C. M. Reijnen. (Amsterdam and New York: Elsevier Scientific Publishing Co., 1981. Pp. xvi, 179. Index. Dfl.150; $63.75.) This volume is a scholarly examination of selected legal problems in the developing regime of the law of outer space. It focuses on examining the basic need for a legal definition of rights, obligations, and responsibilities, with specific reference to current space documents. The documents utilized are the Outer Space Treaty, 1967; the Rescue Agreement, 1968; the Liability Convention, 1972; the Registration Convention, 1967; and the 1979 Moon Agreement. The problems identified are the issue of sovereignty in outer space; the role of international organizations, both governmental and nongovernmental; the issue of nuclear power and radiation; the problem of remote sensing satellites; direct television by satellite; and the commercialization of outer space.

Another problem implicit in the author's thought process, but not elaborated, concerns the very real dangers of private profit and the commercialization of outer space, along with the rapid development of technology, which renders the slowly developing legal regime for outer space obsolete and fundamentally alters life on the planet Earth.

The author presents solutions to identified problems ranging from the traditional devices of diplomacy to legal obligations in positive treaty law. One interesting suggestion stems from the view that the Liability Convention of 1972 fails to deal adequately with the compensation issue. Reijnen suggests establishing a UN *International Guarantee Fund* which would have responsibility for *no-fault* compensation. The monies would be supplied by all launchers. This suggestion is worthy of attention from space users.

It should be noted also that chapter V, a fascinating account of remote sensing, was coauthored with F. de Graaf and that chapter VIII on the Dutch system of municipal law and the incorporation of treaties, while well done and interesting, is out of place and unnecessary.

In conclusion, the volume is tremendously valuable for its technological expertise and document citation, and as a guide to the current morass of space law, agencies, and institutions. The author should be congratulated for the superb attention to detail and scientific clarity.

CAROLINE A. DINEGAR
University of New Haven

The Politics of Peace: An Evaluation of Arms Control. By John H. Barton. (Stanford: Stanford University Press, 1981. Pp. 257. Index. $18.50.) The author seeks to define a new agenda for arms control that will give it a greater impact than it now has on diminishing the likelihood of war. To achieve this laudable objective, he first defines what benefits arms control can bring, and second, examines "the theoretical arguments underlying arms control . . . to take the analysis back to a set of ideas that might be acceptable to at least some on both sides of the issue" (p. vi).

This approach differs from that of most current literature, which frequently concentrates on weaponry to the exclusion of political factors. Furthermore, the author's extensive research brings to the fore some excellent, but almost completely forgotten, past studies. All this is to thc good.

However, in constructing his framework—two-thirds of the book—he comes up with highly controversial fundamental assumptions. Some examples are:

> "The U.S. opposed arms control in the 1950's and supported it in the 1960's" (p. 66).
>
> "Both the supporters and critics of arms control generally agree that the intellectual framework developed in the 1950's that underlies the recent arms control effort is no longer adequate. The framework gave priority to U.S.-Soviet strategic nuclear issues" (p. vi).
>
> "It [history] also gives ground for special pessimism about the logic used to argue in favor of narrow arms control agreements—that one agreement can build on another step by step" (p. 206).

On the basis of his own philosophical framework, the author advocates "world centralization" as an alternative to the current order, and lists seven "immediately plausible institutional reforms," together with an immediate agenda of six more traditional measures. Many believe that such a universal approach rests on an exaggerated concept of the capability of a state with a few nuclear weapons to upset the world balance of power, and equally, on an erroneous view that the decline of U.S.-Soviet détente precludes their cooperation where their interests are virtually identical, such as avoidance of nuclear weapons proliferation.

Regardless of the validity of its fundamental thesis, the book does suggest techniques that might be useful in obtaining world support for measures already agreed upon by the United States and the Soviet Union, or alternatively in prodding great-power agreement.

BERNHARD G. BECHHOEFER

Volkenrechtelijke aspecten van Antilliaanse onafhankelijkheid. By H. Meijers. (Alphen aan den Rijn: Sijthoff & Noordhoff, 1980. Pp. 682. Index.) This volume contains the working papers, comments, and discussion generated by a conference on January 9–10, 1980, organized by the University of the Netherlands Antilles and the University of Amsterdam. In anticipation of the independence of the Netherlands Antilles, with the islands either continuing as a single state as under the internally autonomous status envisaged in the Kingdom Constitution of 1954, or possibly as two or more separate states (which would increase the difficulties experienced by "microstates" because of their small size), the material brought together here furnishes a useful "how to do it" manual for the officials involved in consummating independence. Eight topics are selected that are regarded as most important and indispensable for such officials to confront, either before or after independence. The topics are treated with respect to their international law aspects. Historical, political, and economic data are minimal (though the importance of oil, tourism, and "offshore" companies for the islands is made plain).

The topics include the mechanics of treaty formation and administration, state succession, self-determination, foreign business organizations, sea law, air law, rights of individuals (including human rights, nationality, and law of aliens), and international organizations. The chapters dealing with each of these rubrics furnish a clear, concise, and comprehensive review of the subject matter. The participants in the conference were drawn from academic, government, and professional circles, and maintain a high level of scholarly distinction in their exposition of the matters at hand.

EDWARD DUMBAULD
U.S. Senior District Judge

The Rule of Law in the Areas Administered by Israel. Israel National Section of the International Commission of Jurists. (Tel Aviv: TZATZ, 1981. Pp. 114.) This study was mostly the work of lawyers who, at the time, fulfilled their reserve duty in the Israel Defense Forces as legal advisers to the military commanders in the administered areas.

The slender volume purports, according to the foreword by Haim H. Cohn, to be a sober statement of law and fact, not a political pamphlet. Regrettably, in its attempt to cover most aspects of Israeli military occupation, much of the study must be held to be not only strongly biased in its approach (justifying in detail Israeli occupation policies in the West Bank, the Gaza Strip, and the

Golan Heights) but, at times, in error. To cite only two instances of the latter: the authors ignore the last part of Article 49 of the fourth Geneva Convention of 1949, prohibiting transfers of the occupant's population into occupied areas, even though the full text of that article is printed immediately above the assertion that an occupant's settlements in an occupied territory are not prohibited by the article (p. 54). Again, on pages 94 to 97, the authors deal with the asserted legality of imposing a *new* value-added tax in occupied areas—a subject of great interest in the territories in question in 1981 and 1982—and assert that Article 43 of the 1907 Hague Regulations outlines as the primary concern of an occupant the welfare of the indigenous population and that Article 48, which prohibits by its wording the imposition of new taxes, was derived from that primary concern and should yield to the latter in case of conflict. That interpretation must be deemed to be a clear negation of categorical treaty (and customary international law) provisions. And in several instances in the study, an admitted minority view by a single writer is cited as the basic support of an otherwise legally questionable practice by Israel.

Unfortunately for many assertions made by the authors in defense of Israeli policies covered in the study, governments, courts (including the Supreme Court of Israel in at least two well-known judgments), and writers have held that the Hague Regulations are declaratory of customary international law to which all states are subject, unless they objected to a rule from its beginning or, in the case of a new state, from the time it came into existence. This holding voids many of the defenses claimed by the authors of this study.

GERHARD VON GLAHN, *Emeritus*
University of Minnesota-Duluth

South African Yearbook of International Law, Volume 5, 1979. (Pretoria: The VerLoren van Themaat Centre for International Law, 1980. Pp. ix, 274. Index. R18,00.) This volume, the fifth in the series, follows the same format as earlier ones. One very welcome innovation is the inclusion of two articles on subjects not directly involving South Africa, both by university professors in the United States. One, by Matthew Lippman, *Human Rights Reviewed: The Protection of Human Rights under the International Covenant on Civil and Political Rights*, is a useful substantive piece on the history and content of this treaty; the other, by Paul Lansing and Robert Castle, *The Seizure of the American Embassy in Iran: How Should International Law be Applied?*, reviews the legal issues and outlines the legal dimensions of various possible U.S. responses. There are only three other papers, all of which deal with South African issues: (1) enforcement of foreign judgments in Transkei, Bophuthatswana, and Venda; (2) the independence of Venda; and (3) the administration of Walvis Bay.

Several of the regular sections will be of interest to students of international organization and South African politics: UN discussions and actions on South Africa, foreign policy and practice of South Africa as reflected in legislative and executive addresses, and a list of treaties ratified by South Africa in 1979. Scholars of international law may find some material of value in the sections on South African judicial decisions, foreign judicial decisions, and notes on the Third Law of the Sea Conference. By maintaining these sections, as well as broadening the content and analytic approach of the main articles, the *Yearbook* could continue to provide information on official South African policy while appealing to a wider audience, and thus could make a greater contribution to the dissemination of contemporary international legal research.

NATALIE K. HEVENER
University of South Carolina

China in the Global Community. Edited by James C. Hsiung and Samuel S. Kim. (New York: Praeger Publishers, 1980. Pp. xiii, 271. Index.) As stated in the preface, most studies of Chinese foreign policy have tended to be highly Sinocentric in orientation. This collection attempts to change that. Each essay is written from a global approach by taking advantage of the theories and methods of international relations research and, at the same time, interpreting the differences that often exist between a government's stated goals and its actual practices.

The authors, all men with strong backgrounds in both international relations and China, successfully discuss numerous topics such as China in the United Nations, Chinese foreign trade, and China's energy development, to mention a few.

A most worthwhile collection of essays, this volume also includes a thoughtful bibliography and would be of interest to the serious student of Chinese foreign policy as well as the more casual observer of world affairs.

MARY D. MCVEY
San Francisco

Annals of Air and Space Law. Vol. IV, 1979. By Nicolas Mateesco Matte. (Montreal: Institute and Centre of Air and Space Law, McGill University; Toronto: The Carswell Company Ltd., 1979. Pp. 711. In French and English.) This work, the fourth in a series, contains the distinguished contributions of scholars and practitioners with respect to air law and the law of outer space. It is particularly pertinent to the development of these two fields of law that they be considered together. Recent conferences, such as that of the Smithsonian Institution in Washington in 1981, reveal that the issues in air law, matured through the experience and accelerated use of airspace, are similar in many respects to those now arising in outer space—particularly problems of liability, fault, and insurance.

The volume commences with air law. The 50th anniversary of the Warsaw Convention is the occasion for bringing together several articles on that subject by Bin Cheng, René Mankiewicz, Peter Martin, and others. The next section—on space law—contains articles ranging from space policy in general to such space-associated activities as broadcasting and solar power generation. Dr. Matte's article *Space Policy Today and Tomorrow* can be singled out as a particularly valuable contribution.

The last two sections contain book reviews, comments on international organizations, and decisions in several of the leading cases on air law including *Haddad v. Air France* and *Miller v. American Airlines*.

While the volume is dated 1979, the materials presented are timely, set forth with adequate clarity, and useful for scholars and practitioners alike.

HARRY H. ALMOND, JR.
The National War College

BOOKS RECEIVED*

International Law—General

Akehurst, Michael. *A Modern Introduction to International Law* (4th ed.). Winchester: Allen & Unwin, Inc., 1982. Pp. 304. Index. $28.50, cloth; $12.95, paper.

Campbell, Dennis (ed.). *Transnational Legal Practice: A Survey of Selected Countries.* 2 vols. Deventer: Kluwer, 1982. Pp. xii, 387. Index. Dfl.180; $90.

Gnesa, Edi. *Die von Israel besetzten Gebiete im Völkerrecht.* Zürich: Schulthess Polygraphischer Verlag, 1981. Pp. xxvi, 223. Sw.F.42.

Langen, Eugen. *Transnationales Recht.* Heidelberg: Verlagsgesellschaft Recht und Wirtschaft mbH, 1981. Pp. 241. Indexes. DM 110.

Mukherjee, Sakti, and Indrani Mukherjee. *Major Issues in International Law.* Calcutta: The World Press Private Ltd., 1981. Pp. xiii, 302. Index. $8.50; £3.25; Rs.50.

Netherlands Yearbook of International Law. Vol. XII, 1981. T. M. C. Asser Institute, The Hague. Alphen aan den Rijn and Germantown: Sijthoff & Noordhoff, 1981. Pp. 438. Index. Dfl.80; $40.

Papakostas, Alkis. *International Law and the Case of Afghanistan.* Athens: Gutenberg Press, 1981. Pp. 44. In Greek.

Rey Caro, Ernesto J. *Estudios de Derecho Internacional.* Córdoba: Universidad Nacional de Córdoba, 1982. Pp. 250.

Thierry, Hubert, Jean Combacau, Serge Sur, and Charles Vallée. *Droit International Public* (3d ed.). Paris: Editions Mont-Chrestien, 1981. Pp. xvi, 780. Indexes.

International Economic Law & Relations

Buxbaum, David C., Cassondra E. Joseph, and Paul D. Reynolds (eds.). *China Trade: Prospects and Perspectives.* New York: Praeger Publishers, 1982. Pp. xx, 424. Index. $38.95.

Dam, Kenneth W. *The Rules of the Game: Reform and Evolution in the International Monetary System.* Chicago and London: The University of Chicago Press, 1982. Pp. xviii, 382. Index. $27.

Fordwor, Kwame Donkoh. *The African Development Bank: Problems of International Cooperation.* New York: Pergamon Press, 1981. Pp. xvi, 343. Index. $30.

Odle, Maurice A. *Multinational Banks and Underdevelopment.* New York: Pergamon Press, 1981. Pp. xi, 206. Index. $20.

Rosenn, Keith S. *Law and Inflation.* Philadelphia: University of Pennsylvania Press, 1982. Pp. xxxix, 451. Index. $40.

Vishny, Paul H. *Guide to International Commerce Law.* Vol. I. Colorado Springs: Shepard's/McGraw-Hill, 1981. Index.

Wood, Philip. *The Law and Practice of International Finance.* New York: Clark Boardman Co., Ltd., 1981. Index. $75.

Law of the Sea & Maritime Law

Johnston, Douglas M. (ed.). *The Environmental Law of the Sea.* Gland: International Union for Conservation of Nature and Natural Resources, 1981. Pp. 419.

Vitzthum, Wolfgang Graf (ed.). *Die Plünderung der Meere: Ein gemeinsames Erbe wird zerstückelt.* Frankfurt am Main: Fischer Taschenbuch Verlag, 1981. Pp. 327.

Use of Force & Law of War

Byrne, Edward M. *Military Law* (3d ed.). Annapolis: Naval Institute Press, 1981. Pp. xxiii, 790. Index.

Dispute Settlement

Van den Berg, Albert Jan. *The New York Arbitration Convention of 1958: Towards a Uniform Judicial Interpretation.* The Hague: T. M. C. Asser Institute; Deventer: Kluwer, 1981. Pp. xv, 466. Index.

* Mention here neither assures nor precludes later review.

Human Rights

Bonnicksen, Andrea L. *Civil Rights and Liberties: Principles of Interpretation*. Palo Alto: Mayfield Publishing Company, 1982. Pp. xi, 311. Indexes. $9.95.

Dinstein, Yoram (ed.). *Israel Yearbook on Human Rights. Vol. 11*. Tel Aviv: Faculty of Law, Tel Aviv University, 1981. Pp. 366.

Kavass, Igor I., Jacqueline Paquin Granier, and Mary Frances Dominick (eds.). *Human Rights, European Politics, and the Helsinki Accord: The Documentary Evolution of the Conference on Security and Co-Operation in Europe 1973–1975*. 6 vols. *Volume I: Stage I Helsinki 1973*. Buffalo: William S. Hein & Co., Inc., 1981. Pp. xix, 419. Bound: $285.

Liñán Nogueras, Diego. *El Detenido en el Convenio Europeo de los Derechos Humanos*. Granada: Universidad de Granada, 1980. Pp. 134. Indexes.

Sumner, Colin (ed.). *Crime, Justice and Underdevelopment*. London: Heinemann Educational Books Ltd., 1982. Pp. xvi, 345. Indexes. $55.

Tay, Alice Erh-Soon (ed.), in collaboration with Graeme Connelly and Roger Wilkins. *Teaching Human Rights*. Canberra: Australian National Commission for UNESCO, 1981. Pp. vi, 216. Index. $A8.80.

International Criminal Law

Contemporary Developments in the Definition and Punishment of Sex Offences. (Proceedings of the international colloquium organized and hosted by the Swedish National Section, International Association of Penal Law, held in Stockholm, May 31 to June 3, 1978.) Toulouse: Editions Erès, 1981. Pp. iv, 172.

Environment & Natural Resources

Auer, Peter (ed.). *Energy and the Developing Nations*. (Proceedings of an Electric Power Research Institute Workshop, Hoover Institution, Stanford University, March 18–20, 1980.) New York: Pergamon Press, 1981. Pp. xiii, 509. Indexes. $59.50.

Charney, Jonathan I. (ed.). *The New Nationalism and the Use of Common Spaces: Issues in Marine Pollution and the Exploitation of Antarctica*. Published under the auspices of The American Society of International Law. Totowa: Allanheld, Osmun & Co., 1982. Pp. ix, 343. Index. $39.50.

Chauhan, B. R. *Settlement of International Water Law Disputes in International Drainage Basins*. Berlin: Erich Schmidt Verlag, 1981. Pp. 480. DM 89.

Strategic Minerals: A Resource Crisis. Published by the Council on Economics and National Security. New York: National Strategy Information Center, Inc., 1981. Pp. 105. $5.95.

Air & Space Law

Gorove, Stephen (ed.). *United States Space Law: National and International Regulation*. Binder I. London, Rome, New York: Oceana Publications, Inc., 1982. 2 binders projected. $85/binder.

Air and Outer Space Law. Thesaurus Acroasium, Vol. X, 1981. Thessaloniki: Institute of Public International Law and International Relations of Thessaloniki, 1981. Pp. xvi, 842.

International Organizations

Dimitrov, Th. D. (comp./ed.). *World Bibliography of International Documentation. Vol. I: International Organizations. Vol. II: Politics and World Affairs*. Pleasantville: UNIFO Publishers, Ltd., 1981. Vol. I: pp. xii, 474; vol. II: pp. v, 352. Indexes.

Puchala, Donald J., and Frederic Eckhard (eds.). *Issues Before the 36th General Assembly of the United Nations 1981–1982*. New York: United Nations Association of the United States of America; New York: New York University Press, 1981. Pp. 150. Index. $17.50.

European Community Law

The Law of the European Communities and Greece. Thesaurus Acroasium, Vol. VIII. Thessaloniki: Institute of Public International Law and International Relations of Thessaloniki, 1981. Pp. xv, 668.

Private International Law

Casad, Robert C. *Civil Judgment Recognition and the Integration of Multiple-State Associations: Central America, the United States of America, and the European Economic Community.* Lawrence: The Regents Press of Kansas, 1982. Pp. xiii, 258. Index. $25.

Courbe, Patrick. *Les Objectifs Temporels des règles de Droit International Privé.* Paris: Presses Universitaires de France, 1981. Pp. 505. Index.

Giuliano, M., F. Pocar, and T. Treves. *Codice delle Convenzioni di Diritto Internazionale Privato e Processuale* (2d ed.). Milan: Dott. A. Giuffrè Editore, 1981. Pp. xiv, 1944. Index. L.60.000.

Arms Control & Disarmament

Dunn, Lewis A. *Controlling the Bomb: Nuclear Proliferation in the 1980s.* New Haven and London: Yale University Press, 1982. Pp. xii, 209. Index. $21, cloth; $6.95, paper.

Regional & Comparative Law & Politics

Auburn, F. M. *Antarctic Law & Politics.* Bloomington: Indiana University Press, 1982. Pp. xx, 361. Index. $32.50.

Bassiouni, M. Cherif (ed.). *The Islamic Criminal Justice System.* London, Rome, New York: Oceana Publications, Inc., 1982. Pp. xxii, 255. $30.

Dinstein, Yoram (ed.). *Models of Autonomy.* Tel Aviv: Faculty of Law, Tel Aviv University; New Brunswick and London: Transaction Books, 1981. Pp. x, 319. Index.

Gobbo, Mario. *The Political, Economic, and Labor Climate in Spain.* Philadelphia: Industrial Research Unit, The Wharton School, University of Pennsylvania, 1981. Pp. ix, 134. Index. $18.

Golbert, Albert S., and Yenny Nun. *Latin American Laws and Institutions.* New York: Praeger Publishers, 1982. Pp. xiv, 573. Index. $39.95.

The Criminal Justice System of the Federal Republic of Germany. (Proceedings of the Conference sponsored by the American National Section (U.S.A.) AIDP, the Goethe Institute of Chicago, De Paul University College of Law, and held in Chicago, April 12, 1980.) Published under the auspices of the International Association of Penal Law. Toulouse: Editions Erès, 1981. Pp. 134.

Streinz, Rudolf. *Meinungs- und Informationsfreiheit zwischen Ost und West: Möglichkeiten und Grenzen intersystemarer völkerrechtlicher Garantien in einem systemkonstituierenden Bereich.* Ebelsbach: Verlag Rolf Gremer, 1981. Pp. xxii, 290. Indexes. DM 89.

Strömholm, Stig (ed.). *An Introduction to Swedish Law.* Vols. I and II. Deventer: Kluwer, 1981. Pp. 436.

International Relations & Politics

Dolman, Antony J. *Resources, Regimes, World Order.* Published in cooperation with Foundation Reshaping the International Order (RIO). New York: Pergamon Press, 1981. Pp. xiv, 413. Indexes. $37.50, cloth; $10.95, paper.

Finger, Seymour Maxwell, and Joseph R. Harbert (eds.). *U.S. Policy in International Institutions: Defining Reasonable Options in an Unreasonable World.* Special student edition, updated and revised. Boulder: Westview Press, 1982. Pp. xv, 217. Index. $24, cloth; $12, paper.

Rona, Thomas P. *Our Changing Geopolitical Premises.* New York: National Strategy Information Center, Inc.; New Brunswick and London: Transaction Books, 1982. Pp. xi, 352.

Thorson, Thomas Landon. *Biopolitics.* Washington: University Press of America, 1982. Pp. vii, 216. Index. $21.50, cloth; $10.50, paper.

Treaty Law

List of Treaty Collections. United Nations, Office of Legal Affairs, Codification Division. A Symposia Press reprint, 1981. Pp. xv, 174. Index. $40. Distributed by Wm. W. Gaunt & Sons, Inc.

Miscellaneous

Biella, Friedrich, et al. *Die Wiedergutmachung nationalsozialistischen Unrechts durch die Bundesrepublik Deutschland. Vol. II: Das Bundesrückerstattungsgesetz.* Munich: Verlag C. H. Beck, 1981. Pp. xx, 819. DM 148.

Brunn, Walter, Hans Giessler, Heinz Klee, Willibald Maier, and Karl Weiss. *Die Wiedergutmachung nationalsozialistischen Unrechts durch die Bundesrepublik Deutschland. Vol. IV: Part I: Das Bundesentschädigungsgesetz*. Munich: Verlag C. H. Beck, 1981. Pp. xvi, 460. DM 98.

Cavelier, Germán. *Documentos para la Historia Diplomática de Colombia. Textos. Vol. II: 1830–1860*. Bogotá: Editorial Kelly, 1981. Pp. xxxii, 388. Index.

Dicey, Albert Venn. *Lectures on the Relation between Law and Public Opinion in England during the Nineteenth Century*. New Brunswick and London: Transaction Books, 1981. Pp. xciv, 506. Index. $29.95, cloth; $12.95, paper.

Leigh, L. H. *The Control of Commercial Fraud*. London: Heinemann Educational Books Ltd., 1982. Pp. xii, 339. Index. $50.

Levi, Michael. *The Phantom Capitalists: The Organisation and Control of Long-Firm Fraud*. London: Heinemann Educational Books Ltd., 1982. Pp. xv, 346. Index. $50.

The Immigrant's Handbook: A Critical Guide. By The Law Union of Ontario. Montreal: Black Rose Books, 1981. Pp. 263. $19.95, cloth; $9.95, paper.

Smith, Bradley F. *The American Road to Nuremberg: The Documentary Record, 1944–1945*. Stanford: Hoover Institution Press, 1982. Pp. x, 259. Index. $24.95.

OFFICIAL DOCUMENTS

United Nations Security Council Resolution 502 (1982)*

The Security Council,

Recalling the statement made by the President of the Security Council at the 2345th meeting of the Security Council on 1 April 1982 (S/14944) calling on the Governments of Argentina and the United Kingdom of Great Britain and Northern Ireland to refrain from the use or threat of force in the region of the Falkland Islands (Islas Malvinas),

Deeply disturbed at reports of an invasion on 2 April 1982 by armed forces of Argentina,

Determining that there exists a breach of the peace in the region of the Falkland Islands (Islas Malvinas),

1. *Demands* an immediate cessation of hostilities;

2. *Demands* an immediate withdrawal of all Argentine forces from the Falkland Islands (Islas Malvinas);

3. *Calls* on the Governments of Argentina and the United Kingdom to seek a diplomatic solution to their differences and to respect fully the purposes and principles of the Charter of the United Nations.

* UN Doc. S/RES/502 (April 3, 1982), adopted by the Security Council at its 2350th meeting.

INTERNATIONAL LEGAL MATERIALS*

CONTENTS

VOL. XXI, NO. 1 (January 1982)

PAGE

TREATIES AND AGREEMENTS

Belgium-Denmark-Finland-France-Federal Republic of Germany-Greece-Ireland-Italy-Netherlands-Norway-Portugal-Spain-Sweden-United Kingdom: Memorandum of Understanding on *Port State Control in Implementing Agreements on Maritime Safety and Protection of the Marine Environment* 1

Brazil-United Kingdom: Memorandum of Understanding on the *Development of Peaceful Uses of Nuclear Energy* 31

Canada-European Economic Community: Agreement on *Fisheries* 33

Gambia-Senegal: Agreement on a *Proposed Confederation* 44

Netherlands-United States: Treaty on *Mutual Legal Assistance* 48

Organization of African Unity: Banjul Charter on *Human and Peoples' Rights* 58

JUDICIAL AND SIMILAR PROCEEDINGS

International Court of Justice: Case concerning *Delimitation of the Maritime Boundary in the Gulf of Maine Area*

Order Constituting Special Chamber to Deal with the Case 69

Order on Written Pleadings Procedure 76

Iran-United States Claims Tribunal: Decision with regard to *Jurisdiction over Claims Filed by Iran against U.S. Nationals* 78

United Kingdom: House of Lords Decision in Buttes Gas and Oil Co. *v.* Hammer (*Act of State Doctrine*) 92

United States: Court of Appeals for the Fourth Circuit Decision in United States *v.* County of Arlington, Virginia (*Diplomatic Relations Act; Vienna Convention on Diplomatic Relations; Taxation; Foreign Sovereign Immunities Act*) 109

LEGISLATION AND REGULATIONS

China: Regulations on the *Exploitation of Offshore Petroleum Resources in Cooperation with Foreign Enterprises* 132

European Communities: Council Regulation on the *Common Organization of the Market in Fishery Products* 137

Israel: Law on *Golan Heights* 163

United States:

Export Administration Amendments Act of 1981 164

Foreign Assistance Appropriations Act, 1982 166

International Security and Development Cooperation Act of 1981 172

Multinational Force and Observers Participation Resolution 196

OTHER DOCUMENTS

Council of Europe: Recommendation concerning *International Cooperation in the Prosecution and Punishment of Acts of Terrorism* 199

Israel-United States: Statement on *Multinational Force and Observers* 202

* ILM subscription, $65; concessionary rate to ASIL members, $24. Address orders to ILM, 2223 Massachusetts Ave., NW, Wash., D.C. 20008. Outside U.S., please add $4.50.

PAGE

United Nations: General Assembly Resolutions
On *Arbitrary or Summary Executions* 203
On the Declaration on the *Elimination of All Forms of Intolerance and of Discrimination Based on Religion or Belief* 205
On the *Enlargement of the International Law Commission* 209
On a *Draft Code of Medical Ethics* 211
United Nations: Security Council Resolution on *Israeli Occupation of the Golan Heights* 214
United States: Department of the Treasury Office of Foreign Assets Control Notice for *Account Parties with Standby Letters of Credit in Favor of Iranian Entities* 216

RECENT ACTIONS REGARDING TREATIES TO WHICH THE UNITED STATES IS A PARTY .. 217
RECENT ACTIONS REGARDING TREATIES TO WHICH THE UNITED STATES IS NOT A PARTY 223
NOTICE OF OTHER RECENT DOCUMENTS (not reprinted) 224

VOL. XXI, No. 2 (March 1982)

JUDICIAL AND SIMILAR PROCEEDINGS
International Court of Justice: Case concerning the *Continental Shelf* (Tunisia/Libyan Arab Jamahiriya)
Judgment of February 24, 1982 225
Separate Opinions 264
Dissenting Opinions 288
United States:
District Court for the Southern District of Texas Memorandum and Order in the Matter of the Complaint of SEDCO, Inc. (*Foreign Sovereign Immunities Act; Jurisdiction in Offshore Drilling Disaster; Limitation of Liability Act*) 318
Court of Appeals for the Seventh Circuit Decision in Eain *v.* Wilkes (*Extradition; Political Offense Exception; Terrorist Acts*) 342
State of California Attorney General's Opinion on the *Hague Convention Abolishing the Requirement of Legalization for Foreign Public Documents* 357

TREATIES AND AGREEMENTS
Brazil-Iraq: Agreement on the *Peaceful Uses of Nuclear Energy* 367
Czechoslovakia-United States: Agreement on the *Settlement of Certain Outstanding Claims and Financial Issues* 371
Italy-Malta: Agreement on the *Neutrality of Malta* 396
Sri Lanka-Switzerland: Agreement for the *Reciprocal Promotion and Protection of Investments* 399

LEGISLATION AND REGULATIONS
Chile: Law on *Mining Concessions* 409
United States:
Czechoslovakian Claims Settlement Act of 1981 414
Department of the Treasury, Office of Foreign Assets Control Regulations *Unblocking Czechoslovak Assets* 419

OTHER DOCUMENTS
Council of Europe: Recommendation on *Payment by the State of Advances on Child Maintenance* 420
European Communities: Commission Proposal for *Informing and Consulting Employees of Multinational Corporations* (Vredeling Proposal) 422
France-United States: Notices concerning Reciprocity with regard to *Family Support, Child Custody and Visitation Rights* 430

PAGE

United Kingdom: Letters to U.S. concerning *Measures to Suppress the Unlawful Importation of Narcotic Drugs into the United States* 439
United Nations:
General Assembly Resolution and Notes Verbale on the *Extradition of Mr. Eain* 442
General Assembly Special Committee on the Charter of the U.N. and on the Strengthening of the Role of the Organization—Draft *Manila Declaration on the Peaceful Settlement of International Disputes* 449
United States: Letters concerning the *United States and the Multinational Force and Observers* 456

RECENT ACTIONS REGARDING TREATIES TO WHICH THE UNITED STATES IS A PARTY .. 472
RECENT ACTIONS REGARDING TREATIES TO WHICH THE UNITED STATES IS NOT A PARTY 475
NOTICE OF OTHER RECENT DOCUMENTS (not reprinted) 476

The views expressed in the articles, editorial comments, book reviews and notes, and other contributions which appear in AJIL are those of the individual authors and are not to be taken as representing the views of the Board of Editors or of the American Society of International Law.

Manuscripts in triplicate may be sent to the Editors-in-Chief of AJIL, Professors Oscar Schachter and Louis Henkin, Columbia University School of Law, New York, N.Y. 10027. Subscriptions, orders for back numbers, correspondence with reference to AJIL and books for review should be sent to the AMERICAN JOURNAL OF INTERNATIONAL LAW (ISSN 0002-9300), 2223 Massachusetts Avenue, N.W., Washington, D.C. 20008.

AJIL is published in January, April, July, and October and is supplied to all members of the American Society of International Law. The annual subscription to nonmembers of ASIL is $52.00, plus $2.50 for all foreign subscriptions (including ASIL Proceedings). Available back numbers of AJIL will be supplied at $11.00 each. ($21 of membership fee is allotted to AJIL subscription.)

EDITORIAL OFFICE:
BOX 44
COLUMBIA UNIVERSITY SCHOOL OF LAW
NEW YORK, N.Y. 10027

BUSINESS OFFICE:
2223 MASSACHUSETTS AVENUE, N.W.
WASHINGTON, D.C. 20008

LIST OF TREATY COLLECTIONS

UNITED NATIONS
OFFICE OF LEGAL AFFAIRS
CODIFICATION

PREFACE TO THE REPRINT EDITION

When this LIST OF TREATY COLLECTIONS was originially published in 1956, the United Nations Organization had some seventy-six members. The bibliography was a valuable new source of information on treaty collections concerning seventy states.

Twenty-five years later the membership of the United Nations has more than doubled with the last two decades having seen a dramatic increase in the number of new sovereign states. The number and role of intergovernmental organizations has expanded considerably. The process of internationalization, involving states and intergovernmental organizations in an ever-growing multitude of various treaty arrangements, continues with great intensity on a scale without precedent.

Research tools and bibliographies which contain up-to-date information about treaty sources have not kept pace with international developments. The U.N. LIST OF TREATY COLLECTIONS, which has proven its scholarly quality, reliability and usefulness, remains the most recent and useful general guide to treaty collections covering the majority of the world's largest treaty-making states. For many of the new states, this work had continued relevance due to historical and practical reasons of state succession, although it does not offer any data on current treaty collections for them. The LIST has been out of print for a long time.

This reprint edition of the U.N. LIST OF TREATY COLLECTIONS is now made available to researchers again in order to fill the existing gap in treaty bibliography and to stimulate efforts that might lead us to a comprehensive new bibliography of current treaty collections.

Adolf SPRUDZS
Foreign Law Librarian and Lecturer
in Legal Bibiography
The University of Chicago Law School

June 1981

$40.00 XV-174 pages ISBN: 0-918542-01-4 June 1981 Cloth

A Symposia Press Reprint 1981

EXCLUSIVE DISTRIBUTION BY

WM. W. GAUNT & SONS, INC.
Law Book Dealers & Subscription Agents
Gaunt Building - 3011 Gulf Drive
Holmes Beach, Florida 33510-2199

American Journal of International Law

October 1982

Vol. 76 No. 4

Published by

American Society of International Law

PATRONS OF THE SOCIETY

Honorable ARTHUR H. DEAN
Honorable HERMAN PHLEGER
GENEVIEVE E. TILLAR (deceased)
W. ROBERT MORGAN
BRUNSON MACCHESNEY (deceased)
ALONA E. EVANS (deceased)
JOHN N. HAZARD
Honorable JOHN R. STEVENSON
ARTHUR R. ALBRECHT

In Memoriam

DR. JAMES BROWN SCOTT
HENRY C. MORRIS
ARTHUR K. KUHN
ALEXANDER FREEMAN
STANLEY P. SMITH

PATRONAGE, GIFTS AND BEQUESTS

Upon donation to the Society of $5,000 or more by gift or bequest, any member of the Society or individual eligible for membership may be elected a Patron of the Society. Upon donation of at least $5,000 in the name of a deceased person, such person may be elected a Patron posthumously.

Gifts and bequests may be made in the name of the American Society of International Law, Washington, D.C. Such contributions are deductible from federal returns for income, estate and gift tax purposes. The Society is incorporated by Act of Congress approved September 20, 1950 (64 Stat. 869).

MANLEY O. HUDSON MEDAL

The American Society of International Law bestows from time to time without regard to nationality a gold medal to commemorate the life work of Manley O. Hudson. Such awards are made for preeminent scholarship and achievement in international law and in the promotion of the establishment and maintenance of international relations on the basis of law and justice. Medals have been awarded to Manley O. Hudson (1956), Lord McNair (1959), Philip C. Jessup (1964), Charles De Visscher (1966), Paul Guggenheim (1970), Myres S. McDougal (1976), Eduardo Jiménez de Aréchega (1978), Richard Reeve Baxter (1981), Oscar Schachter (1981), and Hardy Cross Dillard (1982).

Second-class postage paid at Washington, D.C. and additional mailing office

**Postmaster: If undeliverable, send notice on Form 3579 to: American Journal of International Law
2223 Massachusetts Ave., N.W. Washington, D.C. 20008**

Printed by Lancaster Press, Lancaster, Pa. 17604

AMERICAN JOURNAL OF INTERNATIONAL LAW

VOL. 76 October 1982 NO. 4

CONTENTS

PAGE

Discontinuance of International Proceedings: The Hostages Case *Gerhard Wegen* 717
The Plaintiff's Dilemma: Illegally Obtained Evidence and Admissibility in International Adjudication *W. Michael Reisman & Eric E. Freedman* 737
Norm Making and Supervision in International Human Rights: Reflections on Institutional Order *Theodor Meron* 754
The Law Governing Treaty Relations between Parties to the Vienna Convention on the Law of Treaties and States Not Party to the Convention *E. W. Vierdag* 779
Lawyers Who Established International Law in the United States, 1776–1914 *John M. Raymond & Barbara J. Frischholz* 802

Editorial Comment
The Inter-American System Snarls in Falklands War *John Norton Moore* 830
Correspondence 832
Contemporary Practice of the United States Relating to International Law *Marian Nash Leich* 836
Judicial Decisions *Monroe Leigh* 847
Current Developments
The Election of March 1982 to Fill One Vacancy on the International Court of Justice *Shabtai Rosenne* 863
The Australian-United States Agreement on Cooperation in Antitrust Matters *Marian Nash Leich* 866
Book Reviews and Notes *Edited by Leo Gross*
Young, Oran R. *Compliance and Public Authority* 868
Fisher, Roger. *Improving Compliance with International Law* 870
Perkins, John A. *The Prudent Peace: Law as Foreign Policy* 871
Mitchell, C. R. *The Structure of International Conflict* 872
O'Brien, William V. *The Conduct of Just and Limited War* 873
Stone, Julius. *Israel and Palestine: Assault on the Law of Nations* 875
Jennings, R. Y., and Ian Brownlie (eds.). *The British Year Book of International Law, 1979*. Vol. 50 876
Simon, Denys. *L'Interprétation judiciaire des traités d'organisations internationales* 880
Masquelin, Jean. *Le Droit des traités dans l'ordre juridique et dans la pratique diplomatique belges* 881
D'Herbes, Jean, and Jean Touscoz. *Les Contrats internationaux de coopération industrielle et le nouvel ordre économique international* 883
Njem, Jean-Claude. *Le Régime juridique et la nationalisation de concessions pétrolières et autres concessions d'immeubles. Une étude de droit international privé au regard des pays en voie de développement* 883
Rosenbaum, Alan S. (ed.). *The Philosophy of Human Rights: International Perspectives* 884

Nelson, Jack L., and Vera M. Green (eds.). *International Human Rights: Contemporary Issues* 886
Hoffmann, Stanley. *Duties Beyond Borders: On the Limits and Possibilities of Ethical International Politics* 888
Wilkins, William J. *The Sword and the Gavel* 895
Falk, Richard. *Human Rights and State Sovereignty* 897
Wirsing, Robert G. (ed.). *Protection of Ethnic Minorities* 899
Seara Vázquez, Modesto. *Derecho Internacional Público* (7th ed.) 900
Feuerstein, Peter, and Clive Parry (eds.). *Multum Non Multa. Festschrift für Kurt Lipstein* 901
Picone, Paolo, and Giorgio Sacerdoti. *Diritto Internazionale dell'Economia* 902
Barack, Boaz. *The Application of the competition rules (antitrust law) of the European Economic Community to enterprises and arrangements external to the Common Market* 903
Venturini, Gabriella. *La Responsabilità Extracontrattuale delle Comunità Europee* 904
Watson, Philippa. *Social Security Law of the European Communities* 904
Campbell, Alan. *EC Competition Law. A Practitioner's Textbook* 905
Rudden, Bernard, and Derrick Wyatt (eds.). *Basic Community Laws* 905
Gold, Edgar. *Maritime Transport: The Evolution of International Marine Policy and Shipping Law* 906
Nanda, Ved P. (ed.). *The Law of Transnational Business Transactions* 908
Barde, Jacques. *La Notion de droits acquis en droit international public* 909
Maki, John M. (trans./ed.). *Japan's Commission on the Constitution: The Final Report* 910
Fukuda, Moritoshi. *Legal Problems of Japanese-Americans: Their History and Development in the United States* 911
Cable, James. *Gunboat Diplomacy 1919–1979* (2d ed.) 913
Mickolus, Edward F. (comp.). *The Literature of Terrorism: A Selectively Annotated Bibliography* 914
Chiu, Hungdah. *Agreements of the People's Republic of China: A Calendar of Events 1966–1980* 915

Briefer Notices: Hevener (ed.), 917; Adachi, 918; Lodge (ed.), 918; International Chamber of Commerce, 919; Usher, 919; Wilson, 920; Dale, 920; *Netherlands Yearbook of International Law. Vol. XII, 1981,* 921.
Books Received 922
International Legal Materials. Contents, Vol. XXI, No. 3 (May 1982) and No. 4 (July 1982) 926
Table of Cases 929
Index 931

The views expressed in the articles, editorial comments, book reviews and notes, and other contributions which appear in AJIL are those of the individual authors and are not to be taken as representing the views of the Board of Editors or the American Society of International Law.

Manuscripts in triplicate may be sent to the Editors-in-Chief of AJIL, Professors Oscar Schachter and Louis Henkin, Columbia University School of Law, New York, N.Y. 10027. Subscriptions, orders for back numbers, correspondence with reference to AJIL and books for review should be sent to the AMERICAN JOURNAL OF INTERNATIONAL LAW (ISSN 0002-9300), 2223 Massachusetts Avenue, N.W., Washington, D.C. 20008.

AJIL is published in January, April, July, and October and is supplied to all members of the American Society of International Law. The annual subscription to nonmembers of ASIL is $52.00, plus $2.50 for all foreign subscriptions (including ASIL Proceedings). Available back numbers of AJIL will be supplied at $11.00 each. ($21 of membership fee is allotted to AJIL subscription.)

EDITORIAL OFFICE:
BOX 44
COLUMBIA UNIVERSITY SCHOOL OF LAW
NEW YORK, N.Y. 10027

BUSINESS OFFICE:
2223 MASSACHUSETTS AVENUE, N.W.
WASHINGTON, D.C. 20008

The American Society of International Law

The American Society of International Law was organized in 1906 "to foster the study of international law and to promote the establishment and maintenance of international relations on the basis of law and justice."

The Society serves as a meeting place and forum for scholars, teachers, officials, lawyers, and others, from some one hundred countries. In April, it holds a three-day Annual Meeting at which current problems of international law are discussed. The Society also sponsors regional meetings outside of Washington in cooperation with other institutions. Salient questions of international law and relations are considered in depth by panels and study groups organized by the Society's Board of Review and Development. Works of scholarship are often published under the Society's auspices in connection with studies sponsored by the Board, many in the Society's series of *Studies in Transnational Legal Policy*.

The Society periodically issues four publications:

The American Journal of International Law, the leading journal in the field of international law, has been published since 1907. The *Proceedings of the American Society of International Law* carries the papers and discussion of the annual meeting of the Society.

International Legal Materials, a bimonthly, is a unique international collection of texts of current official documents, including legislation, treaties, court decisions, and reports. Subscription rates are $24 a year for members of the Society, $65 for others.

The quarterly *Newsletter* provides members with news of the Society and other organizations in the field.

Society membership is open to all persons of whatever nationality and profession who are interested in its objectives. Dues are: regular, $55; special category, $30 for persons *not* resident in a member country of the Organisation for Economic Co-operation and Development; intermediate, $25; student, $15. Membership application form is printed at the back of each issue of AJIL.

DISCONTINUANCE OF INTERNATIONAL PROCEEDINGS: THE HOSTAGES CASE

*By Gerhard Wegen**

I. INTRODUCTION

On May 12, 1981, the President of the International Court of Justice ordered the discontinuance of the *Case concerning United States Diplomatic and Consular Staff in Tehran* (*United States of America v. Iran*) (*Hostages* case).[1] Following the indication of provisional measures in December 1979[2] and the Judgment in May 1980,[3] the present Order ended the proceedings in the case.[4] This is the first order to apply the (Revised) Rules of Court of 1978 concerning the discontinuance of proceedings.[5] It therefore appears to be an appropriate time to comment on this topic of international procedure.[6]

Within a highly political and emotional setting,[7] the United States instituted proceedings against the Islamic Republic of Iran by unilateral application. Iran did not appear before the Court. Among other requests, the ICJ was asked to adjudge and declare that the United States was

* Member of the German Bar; Research Associate and Instructor, University of Tübingen.

[1] United States Diplomatic and Consular Staff in Tehran, 1981 ICJ REP. 45 (Order of May 12), *reprinted in* 20 ILM 889 (1981) [hereinafter cited as Order].

[2] United States Diplomatic and Consular Staff in Tehran, 1979 ICJ REP. 7 (Order of Dec. 15), *reprinted in* 74 AJIL 266 (1980), 19 ILM 139 (1980). For comments, see, *e.g.*, Gross, *The Case Concerning United States Diplomatic and Consular Staff in Tehran: Phase of Provisional Measures,* 74 AJIL 395 (1980).

[3] United States Diplomatic and Consular Staff in Tehran, 1980 ICJ REP. 3 (Judgment of May 24), *reprinted in* 75 AJIL 746 (1980), 19 ILM 553 (1980) [hereinafter cited as Judgment]. For comments, see, *e.g.*, McLaughlin & Teclaff, *The Iranian Hostage Agreements: A Legal Analysis,* 4 FORDHAM INT'L L.J. 223 (1980–81); Redwine, *The Effect of Duress on the Iranian Hostage Settlement Agreement,* 14 VAND. J. TRANSNAT'L L. 847 (1981).

[4] For comments on the settlement, see, *e.g.*, Suy, *Settling U.S. Claims Against Iran Through Arbitration,* 29 AM. J. COMP. L. 523 (1981).

[5] Rules of Court, adopted on April 14, 1978, ICJ, ACTS AND DOCUMENTS CONCERNING THE ORGANIZATION OF THE COURT, No. 4, at 92 (1978), *reprinted in* 73 AJIL 748 (1979), 17 ILM 1286 (1978). *See also* DOCUMENTS ON THE INTERNATIONAL COURT OF JUSTICE 203 (S. Rosenne 2d ed. 1979) for both English and French versions, and *id.* at 278 for a table of concordance of the Rules of the Permanent Court of International Justice and the present Court.

[6] Only a few writers have dealt with discontinuance in any detail in recent years. *See* A. MARTIN, L'ESTOPPEL EN DROIT INTERNATIONAL PUBLIC 157 *et seq.* (1979); Giardina, *Arrangements amiables ed estinzione del processo di fronte alla Corte internazionale di Giustizia,* 14 COMUNICAZIONE E STUDI [COM. E STUD.] 337 (1975); A. DEL VECCHIO, LE PARTI NEL PROCESSO INTERNAZIONALE 229 *et seq.* (1975); Pecourt García, *El Desistimiento en el proceso internacional: A propósito de la doctrina establecida por el Tribunal internacional de Justicia en el caso de la "Barcelona Traction,"* 23 REV. ESPAÑOL DERECHO INT'L 231, 241 *et seq.* (1970); Suy, *Contribution de la jurisprudence internationale récente au développement du droit des gens,* 1966 REV. BELGE DROIT INT'L 68, 86 *et seq.*; S. ROSENNE, THE LAW AND PRACTICE OF THE INTERNATIONAL COURT OF JUSTICE 534 *et seq.* (1965) [hereinafter cited as ROSENNE, LAW AND PRACTICE].

[7] *See* Gross, *supra* note 2, at 395 *et seq.*

> entitled to the payment to it, in its own right and in the exercise of its right of diplomatic protection of its nationals held hostage, of reparation by the Islamic Republic of Iran for the violations of the above international legal obligations which it owes to the United States, in a sum to be determined by the Court at a *subsequent stage of the proceedings.*[8]

The Court found an obligation on Iran's part to make reparation and decided in May 1980 "that the form and amount of such reparation, failing agreement between the Parties, shall be settled by the Court, and reserve[d] for this purpose the subsequent procedure in the case."[9]

Under the settlement negotiated with the participation of Algeria (later known as the "Algiers settlement of the Iran hostage crisis") on January 19, 1981,[10] the United States agreed to the prompt withdrawal of "all claims now pending against Iran before the International Court of Justice."[11] In April 1981, the Deputy Agent of the United States, relying on Article 88(1) of the Rules of Court of 1978, asked the Court to discontinue all proceedings relating to U.S. claims against Iran for reparation, subject to a reserved right to reinstitute such proceedings if Iran failed to live up to its commitments under the Algiers settlement, and subject to a further reservation.[12] When the President of the Court objected to this conditional discontinuance, the Agent explained that the United States intended to withdraw all currently pending proceedings and that it accepted the normal procedural effects of discontinuance. The Order was thereupon issued.

Discontinuance is here conceived of as the voluntary cessation of proceedings before a court or tribunal by the parties jointly, separately, or unilaterally.[13] In municipal procedural law discontinuance comprises such different concepts as (amicable) settlement, withdrawal or abandonment of claims, dis-

[8] Judgment, *supra* note 3, at 7–8 (emphasis added).

[9] *Id.* at 45.

[10] DEP'T STATE BULL., No. 2047, Feb. 1981, at 1 *et seq.*, *reprinted in* 75 AJIL 418 (1981), 20 ILM 223 (1981).

[11] *Id.*, Declaration of Algeria relating to commitments, para. 11. Paragraph 11 reads:

> Upon the making by the Government of Algeria of the certification described in Paragraph 3 above, the United States will promptly withdraw all claims now pending against Iran before the International Court of Justice and will thereafter bar and preclude the prosecution against Iran of any pending or future claim of the United States or a United States national arising out of events occurring before the date of this declaration related to (A) the seizure of the 52 United States nationals on November 4, 1979, (B) their subsequent detention, (C) injury to United States property or property of the United States nationals within the United States Embassy compound in Tehran after November 3, 1979, and (D) injury to the United States nationals or their property as a result of popular movements in the course of the Islamic Revolution in Iran which were not an act of the Government of Iran. The United States will also bar and preclude the prosecution against Iran in the courts of the United States of any pending or future claim asserted by persons other than the United States nationals arising out of the events specified in the preceding sentence.

[12] Order, *supra* note 1, at 46. The further reservation stated: "Independently of the foregoing, the United States reserves the right to seek redress in the Court if Iran fails to return promptly the premises, property, archives and documents of the United States Embassy in Tehran and of its Consulates in Iran." *Ibid.*

[13] *See* BLACK'S LAW DICTIONARY 417–18 (5th ed. 1979).

continuance of proceedings, and renunciation of action (*arrangement amiable, désistement d'action*, and *désistement d'instance*).[14] Though introduced into international procedure on the basis of the respective national legal thinking of international lawyers,[15] discontinuance in international proceedings has developed its own idiosyncratic, genuinely international features, embodied most clearly in the 1978 Rules of Court of the ICJ.[16]

This is the first discontinuance of a case since 1973,[17] and the eighth in the history of the ICJ.[18] In only two previous cases was there discontinuance where the respondent failed to appear before the Court and was thus in default.[19] All discontinuance orders have been definite and final, except in the *Barcelona Traction* case, in which Belgium withdrew its unilateral Application in 1961[20] and reinstituted proceedings one year thereafter.[21] Instances of discontinu-

[14] For a survey of several major national legal systems and their municipal rules on discontinuance, see Commentary on the Draft Convention on Arbitral Procedure 80 *et seq.*, UN Doc. A/CN.4/92 (1955) [hereinafter cited as Commentary].

[15] *See* the elaboration and discussion of the discontinuance provisions in the Permanent Court of International Justice, especially at the early stages; 1922 PCIJ, ser. D, No. 2, at 83; 1926 PCIJ, ser. D, No. 2 (Add.), at 168; 1936 PCIJ, ser. D, No. 2 (Add. 3), at 314, 318 & n.2.

[16] Some judges in the Permanent Court emphasized very early that genuine structural principles of public international law required an independent conception of discontinuance in international procedural law; *see* 1922 PCIJ, ser. D, No. 2, at 84; 1926 PCIJ, ser. D, No. 2 (Add.), at 168–69; 1936 PCIJ, ser. D, No. 2 (Add. 3), at 319 n.2.

[17] The last order of discontinuance in the present Court was rendered in Trial of Pakistani Prisoners of War, 1973 ICJ REP. 347 (Order of Dec. 15).

[18] The remaining six cases of discontinuance in the ICJ are: Protection of French Nationals and Protected Persons in Egypt, 1950 ICJ REP. 59 (Order of March 29); Electricité de Beyrouth Co., 1954 ICJ REP. 107 (Order of July 29); Aerial Incident of 27 July 1955 (UK v. Bulgaria), 1959 ICJ REP. 265 (Order of Aug. 3); Aerial Incident of 27 July 1955 (U.S. v. Bulgaria), 1960 ICJ REP. 146 (Order of May 30); Compagnie du Port, et des Entrepôts de Beyrouth and Société Radio-Orient, 1960 ICJ REP. 186 (Order of Aug. 31); Barcelona Traction, Light & Power Co., Ltd., 1961 ICJ REP. 9 (Order of April 10) [hereinafter cited as Barcelona Traction, Order].

Cf. the discussion of the necessary formality of the request for the withdrawal of an application in Monetary Gold Removed from Rome in 1943, 1954 ICJ REP. 27 *et seq.*, esp. at 30 (Judgment). The discontinuance provisions have been applied, as well, in cases of *incidental proceedings* which are not included in the figures mentioned in the text. For example, preliminary objections in the ICJ were once withdrawn formally in accordance with discontinuance provisions: Rights of Nationals of the United States of America in Morocco, 1951 ICJ REP. 110 (Order of Oct. 31).

The present Order is the fifth to be issued by the President while the Court was not sitting. The others are Electricité de Beyrouth, Aerial Incident of 27 July 1955 (UK), Compagnie du Port, all *supra*, and Pakistani Prisoners of War, *supra* note 17. The President of the Permanent Court was not vested with this power, yet he assumed it in Electricity Co. of Sofia & Bulgaria, 1939 PCIJ, ser. A/B, No. 77, at 64, 67. He seemingly relied on his powers under the interim protection provisions: *cf.* Art. 63(3) of the Rules of Court of 1936.

The present Order is also the second to be based on an agreement and not on a unilateral withdrawal. The other was Compagnie du Port, *supra*.

[19] Denunciation of the Treaty of 2 November 1865 between China and Belgium, 1929 PCIJ, ser. A, No. 18; Pakistani Prisoners of War, 1973 ICJ REP. 347. These cases are good precedent that the Court in the present case should have followed in various respects.

[20] Barcelona Traction, Order, 1961 ICJ REP. at 10.

[21] Barcelona Traction, Light & Power Co., Ltd. (Preliminary Objections), 1964 ICJ REP. 6 (Judgment) [hereinafter cited as Barcelona Traction (New Application)].

ance must be distinguished from those cases which the ICJ removed from its General List *proprio motu*.[22]

In this article, the present Order will be analyzed in the light of the Court's previous practice on discontinuance.[23] Before turning to that analysis, the discussion will review the elaboration of discontinuance in the Rules of the World Court and the pertinent rules of procedure of other international courts and tribunals. Several key questions evolved in the course of the development of those rules. Is discontinuance a unilateral act independent of the wishes of the other party or the control of the court? Is a discontinuance subject to the principles of *res judicata* or estoppel? Does it have substantive consequences as renouncing the original claim?

[22] The PCIJ did not have that power; *cf.* G. GUYOMAR, COMMENTAIRE DU RÈGLEMENT DE LA COUR INTERNATIONALE DE JUSTICE. INTERPRÉTATION ET PRATIQUE 84 *et. seq.* (1973). *See,* however, the *Letitia* dispute between Colombia and Peru, which was not entered on the Court's General List; PCIJ, ser. E, No. 9, at 76 n.2.

Though the ICJ is not expressly empowered to do so, scholars agree that it has removed eight cases from its General List *proprio motu.* G. GUYOMAR, *supra,* at 84 *et seq.*; ROSENNE, LAW AND PRACTICE, *supra* note 6, at 472 and 540; *see also* S. Rosenne, *Some Reflections on the 1978 Revised Rules of the International Court of Justice,* 19 COLUM. J. TRANSNAT'L L. 235, 241 *et seq.* (1981) [hereinafter cited as Rosenne, *Reflections*]; M. DUBISSON, LA COUR INTERNATIONALE DE JUSTICE 239 (1964); I. SHIHATA, THE POWER OF THE INTERNATIONAL COURT OF JUSTICE TO DETERMINE ITS OWN JURISDICTION 58 n.3, and 86 n.2 (1965). In all eight cases the respondents had not accepted the jurisdiction of the Court, though they had been invited to do so in the applications. G. GUYOMAR, *supra,* at 85. Inclusion of this issue in the applications was done mostly for political reasons during the Cold War, to show the other parties' unwillingness to adhere to the principle of judicial settlement of disputes.

Although their removal from the General List had become accepted practice, a new Article 38(5) was inserted in the 1978 Rules providing that such cases would not be put on the list in the first place. *Cf.* the corresponding new requirement of Article 38(2) that the basis for jurisdiction be indicated precisely. For comment, see Rosenne, *Reflections, supra,* at 240 *et seq.* This change probably resulted from the recent tendency of respondents to deny the jurisdiction of the Court and not to appear before it, while still requesting the removal of the case from the list. *See* France's attitude in the Nuclear Tests cases, 1973 ICJ Pleadings (2 Nuclear Tests) 347 *et seq.*

[23] In the PCIJ 11 cases were discontinued. In all of them, discontinuance was based on an agreement by the parties to the dispute because unilateral discontinuance was provided for only in the Rules of 1936 (Art. 69). Yet, in fact, 7 out of the 11 cases were unilateral discontinuances. They were: Denunciation of the Sino-Belgian Treaty, 1929 PCIJ, ser. A, No. 18 (Order of May 25); Legal Status of the South-eastern Territory of Greenland, 1933 PCIJ, ser. A/B, No. 55, at 157 (Order of May 11) (two cases); Appeals from Certain Judgments of the Hungaro/Czechoslovak Mixed Arbitral Tribunal, 1933 PCIJ, ser. A/B, No. 56, at 162 (Order of May 12) (two cases); Prince von Pless Administration, 1933 PCIJ, ser. A/B, No. 59, at 194 (Order of Dec. 2); Polish Agrarian Reform and German Minority, 1933 PCIJ, ser. A/B, No. 60, at 201 (Order of Dec. 2).

The other four cases were (1) based on an agreement as to the solution of the dispute: Factory at Chorzów, 1929 PCIJ, ser. A, No. 19, at 11 (Order of May 25); and (2) based on an agreement as to discontinuance: Delimitation of the Territorial Waters between the Island of Castellorizo and the Coasts of Anatolia, 1933 PCIJ, ser. A/B, No. 51, at 4, 6 (Order of Jan. 26); Losinger, 1936 PCIJ, ser. A/B, No. 69, at 102 (Order of Dec. 14); Borchgrave, 1938 PCIJ, ser. A/B, No. 73, at 4, 5 (Order of April 30).

Owing to the outbreak of World War II, two cases were in fact, though not formally, discontinued. *See* Electricité de Sofia and Bulgaria, 1939 PCIJ, ser. A/B, No. 77, at 54 (Judgment), and PCIJ, ser. E, No. 16, at 171; Gerliczy, *id.* at 144. In one case a request for an advisory opinion was withdrawn but not officially discontinued by the PCIJ: Expulsion of the Oecumenical Patriarch, PCIJ, ser. C, No. 9-II, at 10, 110–12; *cf.* PCIJ, ser. D, No. 2 (Add. 3), at 809; PCIJ, ser. E, No. 3, at 185.

II. Discontinuance in the Rules of the World Court

The Permanent Court of International Justice

The bodies that laid the groundwork for the Permanent Court of International Justice did not consider the question of discontinuance,[24] nor was it treated in the Court's Statute (or in that of the ICJ).[25] Discontinuance was dealt with only in the Rules of Court.

When the original Rules were prepared in 1922, the temporary Secretariat drafted an article providing for consent judgment.[26] Judge Altamira raised the question, which he answered in the negative, whether the parties might have the right to withdraw a case after having brought it before the Court.[27] Thereafter, the Committee on Procedure prepared a further clause allowing for discontinuance agreed upon by the parties,[28] and referred the question to the full Court.[29] In the ensuing debate, the judges made a clear distinction between discontinuance by agreement and unilateral discontinuance.[30] Although Lord Finlay proposed requiring the Court's consent to a withdrawal, Judge Anzilotti's view prevailed, that the jurisdiction of the Court was based entirely on the will of the parties and that their wishes should in all circumstances be respected.[31] The Drafting Committee then shifted the focus from consent judgment and inserted a text providing that the Court should record agreements that either settled the dispute or discontinued proceedings.[32] The latter was ultimately adopted as Article 61, which remained in force through 1936.[33]

Nevertheless, Article 61 was discussed at length when the Rules were revised in 1926. The central problem was consent judgments and their *res judicata* effect. Lord Finlay stressed that in such a case the Court would have

[24] League of Nations, Minutes of the Proceedings of the Advisory Committee of Jurists, with Annexes (1920); Draft Scheme for the Institution of the Permanent Court of International Justice, League of Nations O.J., Supp. No. 2, at 4 *et seq.* (1920).

[25] (Revised) Statute of the Permanent Court of International Justice, PCIJ, ser. D, No. 1, at 12 (3d ed. 1936); Statute of the International Court of Justice, 15 UNCIO Docs. 355 (1945).

[26] Rules of Court, Draft Prepared by the temporary Secretariat, Art. 44: "If during the proceedings the parties come to an agreement concerning the subject matter of the dispute, and notify such agreement to the Court in writing before the oral proceedings are closed, the Court shall embody this agreement in a formal judgment." PCIJ, ser. D, No. 2, at 252, 265.

[27] Memorandum by Judge Altamira, *id.* at 272, 279.

[28] Rules of Court, Concluded by the Committee on Procedure, Art. 44, *id.* at 293, 304.

[29] *Id.* at 289, 291.

[30] *Id.* at 83 (Judge Huber).

[31] *Id.* at 83–84.

[32] *Compare* Art. 44 of the Revised Draft of the Secretariat of Feb. 25, 1922, *id.* at 399, 410, *with* Art. 64 (later Art. 63) of the Draft Rules of Court Prepared by the Drafting Committee, *id.* at 444, 469 (and later at 481, 495).

[33] Rules of Court, adopted on March 24, 1922, PCIJ, ser. D, No. 1, at 66. Art. 61 provides:

> If the parties conclude an agreement regarding the settlement of the dispute and give written notice of such agreement to the Court before the close of the proceedings, the Court shall officially record the conclusion of the agreement.
>
> Should the parties by mutual agreement notify the Court in writing that they intend to break off proceedings, the Court shall officially record the fact and proceedings shall be terminated.

the power to inquire into the circumstances that had led to the agreement.[34] He also argued against the Court's bare ministerial role, that it was bound simply to record the discontinuance. The prevailing view, however, was that Article 61 imposed "a mere formality" upon the Court;[35] accordingly, no changes were made.

The revision discussions of 1934 through 1936 resulted in a major change prompted by developing practice. The Third Commission, acting on a report by the Registrar of June 1933,[36] proposed a clarification[37] that led to Articles 61, 61 *bis*, and 61 *ter*,[38] which clearly distinguished an amicable settlement (agreement, *accord des parties sur la solution d'un litige*), an agreement to break off the proceedings (discontinuance, *accord des parties pour mettre fin à la procédure*), and unilateral withdrawal of an action (discontinuance, *désistement unilateral*).[39]

During the discussions, the question was raised whether the parties had merely to communicate the fact of an agreement or the terms of that agreement as well.[40] Unanimously, the Court voted to impose communication alone.[41] The majority also took the view that discontinuance by agreement could occur whether proceedings were instituted by *compromis* or by unilateral application,[42] and that unilateral discontinuance, for which it now expressly provided, should not be construed as an agreement but as an essentially unilateral act.[43]

The Court decided to extend the time period within which discontinuance might occur.[44] It also agreed to continue its previous practice of recording a discontinuance by an order of the Court.[45] These views of the Court were incorporated in Articles 68 and 69, adopted in 1936.[46]

The International Court of Justice

Articles 68 and 69 were included in the first Rules of Court of the ICJ in 1946 with a single change: the President was vested with the power to issue the order, the Court not sitting.[47]

[34] PCIJ, ser. D, No. 2 (Add. 1), at 168. *See* the persuasive argument of Judge de Bustamante against such consent judgment: the Court must give judgment from the standpoint of law, whereas the parties to the dispute may agree on the basis of political, diplomatic, and economic considerations. *Ibid.*

[35] *Id.* at 171 (President Loder).

[36] Report by the Registrar, PCIJ, ser. D, No. 2 (Add. 3), at 829.

[37] Report of the Third Commission, March 14, 1934, *id.* at 780.

[38] Report of the Coordination Commission, May 14, 1934, *id.* at 877, and its Project of Rules of Court, *id.* at 890–91.

[39] Rules of Procedure, Project by the Coordination Commission (French version), Arts. 75–77, *id.* at 895; and Memorandum by Sir Cecil Hurst, President (English), *id.* at 904.

[40] *Id.* at 314–15 (Judge Fromageot).

[41] *Id.* at 315.

[42] Thus, it was clear that the articles dealing with discontinuance were conceived of merely as a procedural device to terminate proceedings. *Id.* at 317.

[43] *Id.* at 317 & n.2.

[44] *Id.* at 653–54.

[45] Judge Anzilotti correctly pointed out that discontinuance by order was already well established in the practice of the Court and in conformity with Article 48 of the Statute. *Id.* at 316. On Art. 48, see text at note 110 *infra*.

[46] Rules of Court, adopted on March 11, 1936, PCIJ, ser. D, No. 1, at 31 (3d ed.).

[47] Rules of Court, adopted on May 6, 1946, ICJ, ACTS AND DOCUMENTS CONCERNING THE

Unfortunately, the Court has not published its internal discussions about revising the Rules of Court. With this reservation in mind, the 1978 Rules warrant two observations.[48] First, as in the past, the Court sought to the maximum extent possible to respond to the parties' will to facilitate an amicable settlement of their dispute, which limits its own role to a ministerial one. Moreover, the Court tried to simplify and reduce the procedural steps to be taken by the parties. Although it ultimately did not change the substance of the discontinuance provisions (renumbered Articles 88 and 89), the Court carefully revised and restructured them. It apparently intended to dismiss any scholarly conclusions drawn from previous Rules and practice that attributed an impact on substantive law to discontinuance. The Court in these Rules definitely established discontinuance as a mere procedural device to end proceedings.[49]

This clarification in the 1978 Rules is revealed by the heading of the section. From 1922 through 1936 it read "Agreement (*Accord*)," and from 1936 through 1978, "Settlement and Discontinuance (*Des arrangements amiables et des désistements*)." Now the section is plainly called "Discontinuance (*Désistement*)," which emphasizes the procedural character of the termination of proceedings, whether by agreement or otherwise.[50]

Article 89, which deals with discontinuance in cases of unilateral applications that the applicant wants to withdraw, remained unchanged. This article applies regardless of whether the respondent has already taken some step in the proceedings.[51]

ORGANIZATION OF THE COURT, No. 1, at 54 (2d ed. 1947). *See* G. GUYOMAR, *supra* note 22, at 400, as to the purely ministerial nature of the President's new power.

Articles 68 and 69 were renumbered 73 and 74 in 1972 but remained unchanged until 1978. Rules of Court, adopted on May 10, 1972, ICJ, ACTS AND DOCUMENTS CONCERNING THE ORGANIZATION OF THE COURT, No. 2, at 3 (1972).

[48] The comments already available on the 1978 revision do not deal extensively with the discontinuance provisions. *Cf.* Guyomar, *Le Nouveau Règlement de procédure de la Cour internationale de Justice*, 24 ANNUAIRE FRANÇAIS DROIT INT'L 321 (1978); Lachs, *The Revised Procedure of the International Court of Justice*, in ESSAYS ON THE DEVELOPMENT OF THE INTERNATIONAL LEGAL ORDER IN MEMORY OF H. F. VAN PANHUYS 21 (1980). *But see* Mosler, *Aktuelle Aspekte des Verfahrensrechts des Internationalen Gerichtshofes*, in VÖLKERRECHT UND RECHTSPHILOSOPHIE, INTERNATIONALE FESTSCHRIFT STEPHAN VEROSTA ZUM 70. GEBURTSTAG 249 (1980) [hereinafter cited as Mosler, *Aspekte*]; Mosler, *The International Court of Justice at its Present Stage of Development*, 5 DALHOUSIE L.J. 545 (1979); Oellers-Frahm, *Die Verfahrensordnung des Internationalen Gerichtshofs vom 14. April 1978*, 18 ARCHIV VÖLKERRECHT 309 (1979/1980); Rosenne, *Reflections*, *supra* note 22.

[49] *Accord*, (Judge) Mosler, *Aspekte*, *supra* note 49, at 252.

[50] Judge *ad hoc* Armand-Ugon attached much value to the heading in his dissent in Barcelona Traction (New Application), 1964 ICJ REP. at 117. Great importance was attached to it in the revision discussion in the PCIJ, PCIJ, ser. D, No. 2 (Add. 3), at 853, 877, 314, 652, and 734–35. Thus, Judge *ad hoc* Armand-Ugon's dissent would have had to reach the contrary conclusion about the new Rules of Court.

[51] 1978 Rules of Court, *supra* note 5. Article 89 reads:

> 1. If in the course of proceedings instituted by means of an application, the applicant informs the Court in writing that it is not going on with the proceedings, and if, at the date on which this communication is received by the Registry, the respondent has not yet taken any step in the proceedings, the Court shall make an order officially recording the discon-

The changes are found in new Article 88, dealing with discontinuance of proceedings following an agreement between the parties. It reads:

> 1. If at any time before the final judgment on the merits has been delivered the parties, either jointly or separately, notify the Court in writing that they have agreed to discontinue the proceedings, the Court shall make an order recording the discontinuance and directing that the case be removed from the list.
>
> 2. If the parties have agreed to discontinue the proceedings in consequence of having reached a settlement of the dispute and if they so desire, the Court may record this fact in the order for the removal of the case from the list, or indicate in, or annex to, the order, the terms of the settlement.
>
> 3. If the Court is not sitting, any order under this Article may be made by the President.[52]

This article abolishes the conceptual distinction between an *agreement as to the settlement of a dispute* and an *agreement as to the discontinuance of proceedings*,[53] which were treated separately in the former Rules. Now both are called simply discontinuance (*désistement d'instance*) and are treated alike in Article 88(1). Only Article 88(2) refers to amicable settlement, and it specifies that the Court may not disclose the nature of the agreement unless the parties so desire. Thus, paragraph 2 of new Article 88 renders obsolete attempts to attribute *res judicata* or quasi-*res judicata* effect to the order on the basis of communications by the parties to the Court.[54] Article 88 seems to require a formal understanding as to discontinuance, even if the parties reached a settlement of the dispute.[55] Moreover, Article 88(1) of the Rules now foresees joint notification or separate notification of discontinuance by both parties.

---

tinuance of the proceedings and directing the removal of the case from the list. A copy of this order shall be sent by the Registrar to the respondent.

2. If, at the time when the notice of discontinuance is received, the respondent has already taken some step in the proceedings, the Court shall fix a time-limit within which the respondent may state whether it opposes the discontinuance of the proceedings. If no objection is made to the discontinuance before the expiration of the time-limit, acquiescence will be presumed and the Court shall make an order officially recording the discontinuance of the proceedings and directing the removal of the case from the list. If objection is made, the proceedings shall continue.

3. If the Court is not sitting, its powers under this Article may be exercised by the President.

[52] *Ibid.*

[53] J. WITENBERG, L'ORGANISATION JUDICIARE, LA PROCÉDURE ET LA SENTENCE INTERNATIONALES 343–44 (1937); *cf.* STATUT ET RÈGLEMENT DE LA COUR PERMANENTE DE JUSTICE INTERNATIONALE. ELÉMENTS D'INTERPRÉTATION 406 *et seq.* (ed. Schenk von Stauffenberg 1934); Giardina, *supra* note 6, at 337; Pecourt García, *supra* note 6, at 241 *et seq.*

[54] *See*, however, Giardina, *supra* note 6, at 354 *et seq.* It was already understood in the Permanent Court that the parties were free to determine what to communicate to the Court. PCIJ, ser. D, No. 2 (Add. 3), at 318–19 n.2; *cf.* M. HUDSON, THE PERMANENT COURT OF INTERNATIONAL JUSTICE 1920–1942, at 295 (1943). For a more recent understanding that no *res judicata* effect can be accorded to an order of discontinuance, see J. SIMPSON & H. FOX, INTERNATIONAL ARBITRATION, LAW AND PRACTICE 216 (1959); A. DEL VECCHIO, *supra* note 6, at 235 *et seq.*

[55] In 1926 Judge Pessôa suggested dropping Article 61(1) of the Rules of Court of 1922 because "la procédure perd sa raison d'être" if the parties agree on a settlement of a dispute. PCIJ, ser.

The French version of Article 88(1) shows particularly well the clarification and the shift in emphasis of the new provision.[56] Whereas previously a distinction was made between *désistement d'instance* (withdrawal of action/discontinuance of proceedings) and *désistement d'action* (discontinuance of a claim/renunciation of a right),[57] now both are subsumed under *désistement d'instance.* Accordingly, the Court in its new Rules takes pains to stress the purely formal character as well as the mere procedural effect of discontinuance in all its forms. Moreover, in the French version the ICJ abandoned a distinction it had made regarding the English "to record": *donner acte* and *prendre acte.* Formerly, the Court *prenait acte* (understood as "took account") of an agreement to discontinue proceedings and of a unilateral discontinuance; it *donnait acte* (understood as "gave effect") to an amicable settlement of a dispute followed by discontinuance. This revision may have resulted from the elaborate scholarly conclusions about the use of the terms in the Court's practice, claiming *res judicata* effect for orders in which the Court *donne acte* to an agreement between the parties.[58]

The Rules of 1978 consolidate the marked tendency toward attributing a purely ministerial function to the Court and a merely formal role to its order of discontinuance. Yet the Order in the *Hostages* case shows some noteworthy aberrations from the wording and the purpose of the new Rules of Court.

III. Discontinuance in Other International Courts and Tribunals

Although this article is concerned primarily with the World Court, a brief review of the discontinuance provisions of other courts and tribunals may provide further insights.

D, No. 2 (Add.), at 271. Yet the Court continued to require definite procedural steps by the parties to put an end to a current set of proceedings. *Cf.* G. GUYOMAR, *supra* note 22, at 400.

[56] "Si, à un moment quelconque avant l'arrêt définitif sur le fond, les parties, conjointement ou séparément, notifient à la Cour par écrit qu'elles sont convenues de se désister de l'instance, la Cour rend une ordonnance prenant acte du désistement et prescrivant que l'affaire soit rayée du rôle." Art. 88(1), 1978 Rules of Court, *supra* note 5.

[57] The Barcelona Traction (New Application) decision centered on this distinction and ultimately refused to recognize it. 1964 ICJ REP. at 18 *et seq.* In their dissenting opinions Judge Morelli, *id.* at 101 *et seq.*, and Judge *ad hoc* Armand-Ugon, *id.* at 117 *et seq.*, discussed the point at length. (After that decision, it seemed that the notion of *désistement d'instance* was superfluous, yet in 1978 it was incorporated into the Rules.)

[58] Giardina, *supra* note 6, at 350 *et seq.*; *cf.* Suy, *supra* note 6, at 86 *et seq.*; Pecourt García, *supra* note 6, at 245. The Court used *donner acte* when it wanted to lend some "authority" to an otherwise slightly irregular discontinuance order, issued either at variance with its Rules or in the absence of an applicable rule. Examples are (1) cases of unilateral withdrawal before such action was provided for: Denunciation of the Sino-Belgian Treaty; South-eastern Territory of Greenland; Hungaro/Czechoslovak Mixed Arbitral Tribunal Appeals; Prince von Pless; Polish Agrarian Reform; (2) cases where discontinuance was sought in incidental proceedings, *e.g.*, interim protection: Prince von Pless; Electricity Co. of Sofia and Bulgaria; (3) cases where discontinuance was notified by the parties separately (before 1978): Compagnie du Port. The Court did not attach any difference in substance to such use of the French. *Contra* Giardina, *supra* note 6, at 343 *et seq.* For a detailed discussion, see A. DEL VECCHIO, *supra* note 6, at 229 *et seq.*

The regional Courts established pursuant to the Human Rights Conventions are a case in point. In keeping with the purposes of the Conventions and their importance to the regional community concerned, the rules of procedure allow the Court to refuse discontinuance, be it due to an amicable settlement or a unilateral withdrawal.[59] Here, an *ordre public conventionnel* has emerged that requires the previous consent by the Court to any discontinuance.[60]

In the European Court of Justice, two features of discontinuance are noteworthy. First, unilateral discontinuance of proceedings is allowed irrespective of consent by the other party or approval by the Court. More important, the Rules of Court provide that the case will be discontinued if "the parties reach a settlement of their dispute and intimate to the Court the *abandonment of their claims*."[61] Thus, the distinction between *désistement d'action* and *désistement d'instance* (waiver of claim and discontinuance) is fully maintained.[62]

The Mixed Arbitral Tribunals established after World War I provided in their rules of procedure for the discontinuance of proceedings. For the most part, consent judgments were allowed, or an amicable settlement could be embodied in an award.[63] The question frequently arose, however, to what extent private parties could dispose of the claims in dispute, and to what extent the agents of the governments involved, or the court, had to approve such a settlement. Unilateral discontinuance was generally allowed,[64] and sometimes a clearcut distinction between "*désistement par le demandeur de ses droits*" and a "*désistement d'instance*" was made.[65]

The United Nations Draft Convention on Arbitral Procedure of 1955 calls for a more restrictive approach; unilateral withdrawal is allowed only with the consent of the respondent,[66] and the arbitral tribunal is required to take note of an agreement to discontinue the proceedings. The tribunal is empowered to embody the settlement in an award, if it sees fit.[67]

[59] Art. 47, Rules of Court of the European Court of Human Rights, as amended, 1979 Bundesgesetzblatt, pt. 2, at 213; Art. 42(3), Rules of Procedure of the Inter-American Court of Human Rights, 20 ILM 1289 (1981), which follows the "European" example.

[60] The *ordre public* argument was advanced very early by J. WITENBERG, *supra* note 53, at 343–46.

[61] Arts. 77 and 78, Rules of Court of the European Court of Justice, 17 O.J. EUR. COMM. (No. L 350) 18 (1974).

[62] This distinction is well established in the French version. Article 77 speaks of "*renonciation à toute prétention*," whereas Article 78 mentions "*renonciation à l'instance*." 17 J.O. COMM. EUR. (No. L 350) 18 (1974). *Compare* the forerunner in the Rules of Court of the European Coal and Steel Community, which makes the same distinction. 1953 J.O. CECA 37, 53.

[63] On amicable settlement, see in particular the Rules of Procedure in 1 Trib. Arb. Mixtes 239–40, Art. 68 (1922); *id.* at 249, Art. 62; *id.* at 680, Art. 62; *id.* at 696–97, Art. 68; *id.* at 158, Art. 67; *id.* at 822, Art. 66; *id.* at 832, Art. 56; *id.* at 850, Art. 67. For a survey of Rules of Procedure of conciliation commissions in this respect, see A. DEL VECCHIO, *supra* note 6, at 232 n.7.

[64] 1 Trib. Arb. Mixtes 53, Art. 65 (1922); *id.* at 42, Art. 69; and *see* the Rules of Procedure cited *supra* note 63.

[65] Arts. 68 and 69, Rules of Procedure of the German-Belgian Mixed Arbitral Tribunal, 1 Trib. Arb. Mixtes 33, 41–42 (1922).

[66] *See* Art. 21 and the explanations in Commentary, *supra* note 14, at 80 *et seq.*

[67] Art. 22 and explanations, *id.* at 82. *See also* Model Rules on Arbitral Procedure, 2 Y.B. INT'L L. COMM'N 14 (1958).

The Centre for the Settlement of International Investment Disputes (ICSID) established under the World Bank Convention[68] makes broad provision for discontinuance under its Institution Rules and Arbitration Rules.[69] Rule 44, which provides for unilateral discontinuance, is noteworthy because it requires the other party's consent or acquiescence.[70] Rule 45 provides for *proprio motu* discontinuance by the tribunal, as the parties may be deemed to have discontinued the proceedings after the lapse of a certain time period.

The Arbitration Rules adopted by the United Nations Commission on International Trade Law (UNCITRAL Arbitration Rules) in 1976 provide in Article 34 for consent judgment if requested by both parties and accepted by the tribunal upon settlement of the dispute.[71] Article 34(2), however, in rather sweeping language, vests the power and the initiative for terminating the proceedings *proprio motu* in all other instances in the tribunal itself.[72]

IV. Practice of the World Court

Parties that resort to third-party settlement, whether by adjudication or another means, have generally assumed their right to agree to discontinue those proceedings.[73] The practice of the World Court on discontinuance re-

[68] Convention on the Settlement of Investment Disputes Between States and Nationals of Other States, 575 UNTS 159.

[69] ICSID Rules of Procedure for the Institution of Conciliation and Arbitration Proceedings and ICSID Rules of Procedure for Arbitration Proceedings, *reproduced in* 4 G. Wetter, The International Arbitral Process: Public and Private 486 and 496, respectively (1979).

[70] The notes to Rule 44 under "C" explain that an express or implied agreement is necessary for such discontinuance; ICSID Arbitration Rules, *supra* note 69.

[71] 15 ILM 701, 714 (1976), also *reproduced in* 4 G. Wetter, *supra* note 69, at 413, 427.

[72] This provision may prove to be of particular interest because the UNCITRAL Arbitration Rules are to be applied by the Iran-United States Claims Tribunal established by the Algiers settlement, except as modified by the parties or by the tribunal. Declaration of Algeria Concerning the Settlement of Claims, Art. III(2), *supra* note 10.

[73] In German Secular Property in Israel (Israel/Federal Republic of Germany), 16 R. Int'l Arb. Awards 1 (1962), the parties agreed upon an amicable settlement of their dispute over German property in Israel in accordance with the terms of settlement proposed by the mediator they had appointed (*see* 345 UNTS 92). Article 5 of the settlement agreement of 1962, 448 UNTS 228, provided that it should be communicated to the mediator with the request by both parties that the mediation proceedings be formally terminated. The mediator noted the communications from the parties and terminated proceedings under the special agreement. 16 R. Int'l Arb. Awards at 3. *See* Wühler, *German Secular Property in Israel Case*, in Encyclopedia of Public International Law 116 (Bernhardt ed., Installment 2, 1982).

In some cases the parties have specifically provided for termination. The United States and Canada provided in Article 1 of the Treaty to Submit to Binding Dispute Settlement the Delimitation of the Maritime Boundary in the Gulf of Maine Area of 1979, *reprinted in* 20 ILM 1377 (1981), for the submission of the dispute by Special Agreement to a Chamber of the ICJ; but under Articles 2 and 3, an agreement to submit the dispute to arbitration enters into force if the Special Agreement is terminated. This may be done by either party if the Chamber of the ICJ is not constituted in accordance with the Special Agreement within a specified time (Art. 2), or if a vacancy on the Chamber is not filled to the satisfaction of the parties (Art. 3). If the Special Agreement is terminated, "the Parties shall jointly notify the International Court of Justice that the proceedings under the Special Agreement are discontinued." Curiously, in the French, equally authoritative text, the term "*discontinuation*" is used, which is most unusual because the word is not found in international legal parlance.

veals that it has often tried to accede to the parties' will. In several cases, it recorded discontinuance at variance with the express language of its Rules.[74] Moreover, it seemed to encourage the parties' efforts to reach an agreement settling their dispute.[75]

The Parties' Influence on the Proceedings

The Court has always tried to comply with the parties' will and, at the same time, to word its orders carefully, following closely the language in the discontinuance provisions, *e.g.*, in the use of *prendre acte* and *donner acte* in the French text. No problem arose in cases where the parties conformed to the prescribed procedure:[76] *i.e.*, *donner acte* was used to record an amicable settlement, as was most common in international courts. Yet at times the Court phrased its orders differently. In particular, the term *prendre acte* was used in a purely formal sense, while *donner acte* was used to bolster the Court's "authority" for recording a discontinuance at variance with the Rules or in the absence of an applicable rule.[77] Still, the Court adopted the technique and the language that it thought most appropriate to the specific procedural situation.[78] The use of different formulations implied no substantive difference, as scholarly writing has recognized.[79]

In addition, the Court has regarded discontinuance under (new) Article 89 of the Rules as an essentially unilateral act, and not as a contract between the parties, either express or implied. It described aptly the difference between former Articles 68 (now 88) and 69 (now 89):

> One difference between the two provisions is, however, significant. Whereas Article 68 contemplates a discontinuance which not only is (in effect) an agreed one, but also takes the form of an agreed communication to the Court, Article 69 on the other hand contemplates a notification to the Court which, *whether it results from an agreed settlement of the dispute or from some other cause*, always takes the form of a unilateral communication from the applicant or claimant party, which is either immediately effective, if the case comes under paragraph 1 of Article 69 (the respondent party having taken no step in the proceedings), or which (if such a step has been taken) becomes effective in the absence of any

[74] *See* the cases cited *supra* note 58, under (1).

[75] The Court extended time limits fixed by it at the request of parties with a view to facilitating ongoing negotiations. Losinger, 1936 PCIJ, ser. A/B, No. 69, at 102 (Order of Dec. 14). *Compare* Free Zones of Upper Savoy and the District of Gex, 1929 PCIJ, ser. A, No. 22 (Order of Aug. 19); 1930 PCIJ, ser. A, No. 24 (Order of Dec. 6); 1932 PCIJ, ser. A/B, No. 46 (Judgment).

[76] Castellorizo and Borchgrave cases, *supra* note 23; French Nationals, Electricité de Beyrouth, Aerial Incident of 27 July 1955 (UK), all *supra* note 18; Pakistani Prisoners of War, 1973 ICJ REP. 347.

[77] *See* the cases cited, *supra* note 58.

[78] *E.g.*, interim measures of protection: Prince von Pless and Electricity Co. of Sofia, *supra* note 18.

[79] *See* Barcelona Traction (New Application), 1964 ICJ REP. at 21. *Compare* the very clear discussion by Scerni, *La Procédure de la Cour permanente de Justice internationale,* 65 RECUEIL DES COURS 565, 658 *et seq.* (1938 III). *See* further Mosler, *Aspekte*, *supra* note 48, at 252; Pecourt García, *supra* note 6, at 244–45; A. DEL VECCHIO, *supra* note 6, at 229. *Contra* Giardina, *supra* note 6, at 343 *et seq. Cf.* J. WITENBERG, *supra* note 53, at 343 *et seq.*

> objections from the respondent party within the time-limit fixed by the Court.[80]

Role of the Court

The Court has adopted a careful approach toward exercising its functions in the discontinuance of proceedings. It has confined itself strictly to the examination of formalities[81] and to the purely ministerial step of removing the case from the list.[82] In one case the Court seemed to examine the material content of an agreement, but the actual purpose was to establish its reality.[83] The Court clearly stated its view in the *Barcelona Traction* case:

> The role of the Court, there being no objection to the discontinuance, is simply to record it and to remove the case from its list. In connection with the discontinuance itself, the Court is not called upon to enquire into the motives either of the discontinuing or of the respondent party.[84]

The Procedural Effect of Discontinuance

In several orders the Court did indicate the content of the agreement reached by the parties or of their communications to the Court. Thus, the Court may have examined the validity, legality, and actual existence of the agreement reached. Giardina maintained that in eight cases the Court had examined the "*legitimitá del accordo*" (the legality of the settlement) and the "*effetto risolutivo della lite che all'accordo stesso si ricollega*" (the effect of such agreement on the proceedings).[85] Consequently, he concluded that the Court's orders pronounced with quasi-*res judicata* effect that proceedings had become without object, and that such orders were decisions on the merits.[86] In par-

[80] Barcelona Traction (New Application), 1964 ICJ REP. at 20 (emphasis added). *See* G. SALVIOLI, TUTELA DEI DIRITTI E INTERESSI INTERNAZIONALI 371 *et seq.* (1941).

[81] Castellorizo, *supra* note 23, at 6, where the PCIJ stated that after fulfillment of the formal requirements of Art. 61(2) of the 1922 Rules, "there is nothing to prevent the Court from recording this fact"; *cf.* Borchgrave, *supra* note 23, at 5; Hungaro/Czechoslovak Mixed Arbitral Tribunal Appeals, *supra* note 23, at 163; Factory at Chorzów, *supra* note 23, at 13: "constate que la procédure au sujet de ladite affaire *a pris fin*" (emphasis added). *See* the authors cited, *supra* note 79, except Giardina and Witenberg.

[82] Barcelona Traction (New Application), 1964 ICJ REP. at 20. *Cf.* ROSENNE, LAW AND PRACTICE, *supra* note 6, at 535.

[83] Compagnie du Port, *supra* note 18, at 187. The Court established only the reality of the agreement.

[84] Barcelona Traction (New Application), 1964 ICJ REP. at 20. *Compare* the discussion by Mosler in *Aspekte*, *supra* note 48, at 253, and especially Scerni, *supra* note 79, at 661 *et seq.*

[85] Giardina, *supra* note 6, at 359.

[86] *Id.* at 353 and 360. The eight crucial cases are: Chorzów Factory, Denunciation of the Sino-Belgian Treaty, Territory of South-eastern Greenland, Prince von Pless, all *supra* note 23; French Nationals, Electricité de Beyrouth, Compagnie du Port, all *supra* note 18; Pakistani Prisoners of War, 1973 ICJ REP. 347. Two basic considerations contradict Giardina's reasoning. Three of the cases were removed from the list by order of the President. It hardly seems possible to attribute quasi-*res judicata* effect to the President's orders. In two of the cases, a settlement of the dispute had not yet been reached when the order was rendered: *Sino-Belgian Treaty* and *Pakistani Prisoners of War*. An order of the Court could hardly pronounce with *res judicata* effect on a settlement of a dispute that had not yet been resolved.

ticular, Giardina relied heavily on the difference between *donner acte* and *prendre acte* as laid down in the Rules and the practice of the Court.[87] This argument has become obsolete since the eradication of this distinction by the 1978 Rules. Writing at an earlier date, however, Giardina maintained that only his reasoning could explain satisfactorily why the parties had communicated their reasons for discontinuance to the Court, and why the latter had indicated them in the order.[88] Yet these actions may be explained by procedural considerations, *e.g.*, a gap in the Rules,[89] or by political considerations,[90] *e.g.*, the applicant's interest in demonstrating his "success on the merits,"[91] his interest in openly facilitating a settlement by other means,[92] or the respondent's interest in showing his law-abiding behavior.[93] Thus, the Court held:

> Both the inherent character of these provisions [*i.e.*, old Articles 68–69, new Articles 88–89] and their drafting records show that the main object which they have in view is to provide a procedural facility, or rather—since it would in any event never be practicable to compel a claimant State to continue prosecuting its case—to reduce the process of discontinuance to order. But these provisions are concerned solely with the "how", not with the "why", of the matter.[94]

Substantive Effects of Discontinuance

In the *Barcelona Traction* case, the Court held that its discontinuance order did not dispose of the disputed subject matter of the proceedings.[95] In some cases the Court had been informed, and indicated, that the dispute at the time of the delivery of the order was not settled in all its aspects.[96]

Barcelona Traction (New Application) stands for the proposition that the order of the Court has no effect besides putting "an end to a current set of proceedings."[97] A distinct question is whether the discontinuance notification may have additional effects in substantive law, *e.g.*, as a waiver or renunciation of a claim, right, or action,[98] or as a basis for invoking estoppel principles with

[87] Giardina, *supra* note 6, at 340 *et seq.* and 354 *et seq.*

[88] *Id.* at 353.

[89] *See* the problems already mentioned and the cases cited, *supra* note 58.

[90] The factor of political or moral value in the incorporation of certain terms, communications, or undertakings was stressed very recently by Judge Mosler in *Aspekte*, *supra* note 48, at 252.

[91] *E.g.*, French Nationals, *supra* note 18; *cf.* absent step in proceedings by respondent, Denunciation of Sino-Belgian Treaty, *supra* note 19.

[92] *E.g.*, Pakistani Prisoners of War, 1973 ICJ REP. 347; Denunciation of Sino-Belgian Treaty, *supra* note 19; Barcelona Traction (New Application), 1964 ICJ REP. 6.

[93] *E.g.*, Compagnie du Port and Electricité de Beyrouth, *supra* note 18.

[94] Barcelona Traction (New Application), 1964 ICJ REP. at 19.

[95] *Id.* at 21. For scholarly support, see Pecourt García, *supra* note 6, at 245–46, and all other writers mentioned in notes 6 and 78 except Giardina.

[96] Denunciation of the Sino-Belgian Treaty, *supra* note 19; Pakistani Prisoners of War, 1973 ICJ REP. 347.

[97] 1964 ICJ REP. at 20–21 (denying quasi explicitly a possible *res judicata* effect with regard to Art. 69 of the 1946 Rules).

[98] *Cf.* G. SALVIOLI, *supra* note 80, at 371 *et seq.*; A. DEL VECCHIO, *supra* note 6, at 232 *et seq.*; ROSENNE, LAW AND PRACTICE, *supra* note 6, at 538 *et seq.*; *see* on the whole, A. TOMMASI DI VIGNANO, LA RINUNCIA IN DIRITTO INTERNAZIONALE (1960).

regard to the facts mentioned in the order.[99] In *Barcelona Traction* the Court refused to recognize as procedurally relevant the dichotomy of *désistement d'action* and *désistement d'instance* by characterizing discontinuance as a procedural, a neutral, act.[100] The Court observed:

> The real question is not what the discontinuance does—which is obvious—but what it implies, results from or is based on. This must be independently established, except in those cases where, because the notice itself gives reasons, or refers to acts or undertakings of the parties, or to other circumstances, its import is clear and apparent.[101]

The Court stressed that any substantive effect of discontinuance may not be established a priori but only in close relationship with each case.[102] As a guideline, the Court will look primarily to the wording and terms of reference of the notification of discontinuance.[103] If it does not express a clearcut renunciation of claim, then the respondent has the (very heavy) burden of proof as to such renunciation, because the presumption is rather against renunciation of claims.[104] Thus, the Court will examine all the historical and factual circumstances surrounding a discontinuance to assess whether a renunciation of rights exists or whether the claimant may be estopped from invoking his rights.[105]

V. The Order in the Hostages Case

Its Content

The President of the Court issued the Order on the basis of Article 48 of the Statute and Article 88 of the Rules. The Order makes reference to the Application by which proceedings were instituted and its subject matter. It briefly describes the course of the proceedings and their current status, *i.e.*, that determination of the form and amount of reparation was pending.

The Order sets forth the United States action requesting discontinuance by quoting extensively from the American notification.[106] In the next paragraph it acknowledges the transmittal of certified copies of the Algiers Declarations. The Order then reiterates the request of the Applicant based on Article 88(1) of the Rules of Court that "all proceedings pending before the Court relating to United States claims against Iran for reparation be discontinued."[107]

[99] *See* Mosler, *Aspekte*, *supra* note 48, at 253; A. Martin, *supra* note 6, at 157 *et seq.* S. Rosenne, The International Court of Justice 378 (1957), maintained that estoppel principles applied to the facts mentioned in an order pursuant to (former) Article 69, yet some years later he seemingly abandoned this idea; Law and Practice, *supra* note 6, at 535 *et seq.*

[100] Rosenne, Law and Practice, *supra* note 6, at 537.

[101] Barcelona Traction (New Application), 1964 ICJ Rep. at 21.

[102] *Id.* at 18.

[103] *Id.* at 21–22.

[104] *Id.* at 21.

[105] *See* the approach of the ICJ, *id.* at 22 *et seq.*

[106] The analysis that follows is preliminary inasmuch as the correspondence between the Court and the parties to the dispute has not yet been made available to the public by either the U.S. State Department or the ICJ.

[107] Order, *supra* note 1, at 45.

The Order next describes the attempt by the United States to reserve the right to reinstitute the proceedings;[108] the President's characterization of such a discontinuance as conditional and, hence, as not falling within the terms of Article 88; and the affirmation by the United States of its intention that "all currently pending proceedings . . . be discontinued."[109]

The Order then reports that all the communications were transmitted to Iran and that no observations on its part were received. Thereupon, the U.S. request is presented as falling within Article 88(1) by emphasizing that it was notified separately by one party "in the context of an agreed settlement arrived at between the two parties." The Order concludes:

> Having regard to the adherence by the Parties to the two Declarations of the Government of Algeria dated 19 January 1981;
>
> Being satisfied that it is the common intention of the Parties that the proceedings before the Court should now be brought to an end by their unconditional discontinuance, and being satisfied that the case should accordingly be removed from the list;
>
> [The President thus] *Places on record* the discontinuance of the proceedings in the case, following upon an agreement between the Parties; and
>
> *Directs* that the case be removed from the list.[110]

Critical Appraisal

The Court not sitting, the Order was duly rendered by the President, which he is empowered to do under paragraph 3 of Articles 88 and 89. It had regard to Article 48 of the Statute. Reliance upon Article 48 has been well-established practice ever since the first discontinuance, when the Rules did not yet provide for discontinuance by an order. While Article 48 does not authorize the Court to make general policy on discontinuance of cases, it does authorize the Court to "make orders for the conduct of the case."[111]

By repeating the statement in the Judgment that the form and amount of reparation are pending in the subsequent proceedings before the Court, the Order establishes that discontinuance was admissible because final judgment on the merits had not yet been rendered. Moreover, it is the Court's practice to relate briefly the stages in the proceedings leading up to discontinuance. Hence, one must not infer that undoubtedly important dicta in the Judgment about what the Court may assume without strict proof[112] are by such reference applicable to the present Order. An analogous application to discontinuance of Article 53 of the Statute is flatly contradicted by precedent.[113]

[108] *Id.* at 46–47.

[109] *Id.* at 45. "In seeking a discontinuance, we intend that all currently pending proceedings relating to the United States claims against Iran for reparation be discontinued, and that the Court issue an order recording the discontinuance and directing the removal of those proceedings from the list."

[110] *Id.* at 47.

[111] *See supra* note 45.

[112] Judgment, *supra* note 3, at 10–11.

[113] Denunciation of the Sino-Belgian Treaty, *supra* note 19; Pakistani Prisoners of War, 1973 ICJ REP. 347.

Peculiar to this Order is the attempt by the Applicant to *reserve the right to reinstitute proceedings* when requesting discontinuance. The President of the ICJ was very definite on this point: as a procedural act, discontinuance must be sought unconditionally. Reservations must be made between the parties "outside the act of discontinuance itself."[114] The practice of the ICJ shows that applicants reserved their substantive rights while discontinuance was sought.[115] Moreover, the Court had held unanimously that Iran was under an obligation promptly to return the premises, property, archives, and documents of the American Embassy and Consulates.[116] Thus, it seems that the United States could not attempt to reserve the right to reinstitute proceedings in order "to seek redress" if Iran did not return those premises promptly. Such a reservation raises either the question of reparation (already covered by the Judgment) or the separate problem of the execution of a judgment of the ICJ.

The President acted in accordance with well-established practice in transmitting the communications it received from the United States to Iran. The Court has always done so in order to enable the respondent—even a defaulting one—to participate in an agreed discontinuance.[117]

However, Iran did not react at all. Consequently, Article 88 of the Rules of Court is not applicable because there was no (1) joint or separate (2) notification (3) in writing, by (4) both parties, that they had agreed to discontinue the proceedings. Only since 1978 have the parties been allowed to notify their agreement to the Court separately. It is true that the Court was never too formalistic,[118] and that it allowed discontinuance formally *contra* its Rules.[119] But in view of the very cautious structure of Article 88(2), which spells out what can be mentioned in the order by consent, it is not formalistic to adhere to the wording of that article. In cases of default Article 89 is readily available. Moreover, Article 89 is not concerned with the reason for discontinuance, be it an amicable settlement, an agreement to discontinue, or simply the applicant's wish not to go on with the proceedings.

More specifically, Article 89(1) of the Rules was applicable, as Iran had not yet taken any step in the proceedings. The Court has consistently interpreted the appointment of an agent as a step in the proceedings. Here Iran had addressed only "irregular" communications to the Court,[120] which refused

[114] Barcelona Traction (New Application), 1964 ICJ REP. at 20.

[115] *Id.* at 20. *See* the letter of the Pakistani Agent to the Registrar of the ICJ, 1973 ICJ Pleadings (Trial of Pakistani Prisoners of War) 175–76. *Compare* Aerial Incident case (UK), 1957 ICJ Pleadings 698.

[116] Judgment, *supra* note 3, at 45.

[117] Denunciation of the Sino-Belgian Treaty, *supra* note 19, at 7; *see* PCIJ, ser. C, No. 16-I, at 355–56.

[118] Mavrommatis Palestine Concessions, 1924 PCIJ, ser. A, No. 2, at 34 (Judgment No. 2). *See* the critique by Judge Koretsky in Northern Cameroons, 1963 ICJ REP. 15, 39–40 (dec.).

[119] *See supra* note 58.

[120] *See* for similar instances of such behavior in the Court and its discussion, Lamberti Zanardi, *Forme nuove di contestazione della competenza della Corte internazionale di Giustizia e potere della Corte di aprire d'ufficio un procedimento sulla competenza*, 14 COM. E STUD. 439 (1975); Rosenne, *The Reconceptualization of Objections in the International Court of Justice*, *id.* at 735 [hereinafter cited as

to recognize such *communications à titre privé* as a step in the proceedings.[121] In applying Article 89 the Court prefers not to elaborate the parties' reasons for discontinuance, considering that they may wish the least publicity possible or the least "official" notice of their diplomatic actions.[122]

In applying the new Article 88, the Order did not maintain the restraint embodied in the spirit and the wording of the Rules, but gave at least the *impression* that the *Court had played an active role in the discontinuance*. This departure may not be explained by the default of Iran. In its previous practice the Court followed closely the "regular" procedure.[123]

Under Article 88(2) of the Rules the Court may not even *mention* that an amicable settlement was reached and is the basis for the discontinuance unless the parties so wish. The same applies, then, to mentioning receipt of copies of such a settlement.[124]

The Order, with some stretching, subsumes the discontinuance by the United States under Article 88. The President of the ICJ read "*separately*" as indicating that note could be taken of actions by parties out of Court who deliberately chose not to appear before it.[125] Thus, respect for the parties' wishes may have to lead to a more carefully balanced approach than that of the President here. Moreover, the Court may choose not "to penalize" the defaulting respondent[126] by treating procedural acts required of the respondent simply as not being mandatory in case of default.

Furthermore, the concluding considerations in the Order, quoted above,[127] are not warranted by the Statute or the Rules, and even contradict previous practice and the Rules. These statements are fashioned so as to suggest that the *Court had to examine the request* for discontinuance and *to approve* it. However, the Court is not allowed to concern itself in a discontinuance order with the adherence of the parties to an amicable settlement; the Court has no power to investigate the common intention of the parties (one not appearing). These two paragraphs should not have been inserted in the Order at all.

Similarly, the President deviated from a practice that has been uniform since 1929 by stating in the *dispositif* that the discontinuance was placed on record "following upon an agreement between the parties." This fact may be recorded in an order pursuant to Article 88(2), if the parties so wish.

Rosenne, *Reconceptualization*]; Sinclair, *Some Procedural Aspects of Recent International Litigation*, 30 INT'L & COMP. L.Q. 338 (1981).

[121] The ICJ was very firm in rejecting "irregular communications to the Court" as a step in the proceedings in Pakistani Prisoners of War, 1973 ICJ REP. at 348.

[122] Article 88 requires notification in writing; Article 89(2) speaks of a statement of opposition.

[123] *Compare* especially Pakistani Prisoners of War, 1973 ICJ REP. 347, which is proposed here as the precedent to be followed, and the pertinent correspondence with the Court, 1973 ICJ Pleadings at 175–76.

[124] The Order notes that certified copies of the Algiers settlement were furnished to the ICJ, and that the Declarations had been initialed by duly authorized Government representatives. This gives the impression that the Court examined the legality-validity of the Algiers settlement. Yet it is not empowered to do so at all, either under consistent previous practice or under the new Rules.

[125] *See* Rosenne, *Reconceptualization, supra* note 120.

[126] *Ibid.*

[127] *See* text at note 110.

Effects of the Discontinuance in Substantive Law

The effect of the discontinuance is to put an end to the current set of proceedings. The question remains what the discontinuance implies, resulted from, or was based on.[128]

It may well be argued that the renunciation of the claims pending in the ICJ was designed as part of a comprehensive scheme to settle the dispute as a whole with regard to all American claims mentioned in the Algiers settlement. Thus, the withdrawal would entail a waiver or a renunciation of the claim to reparation. This line of argument would first take into consideration the wording of the notification.[129] The circumstances of the case would then be considered, especially the wording of the settlement and the overall setting within which withdrawal was provided for, including the whole negotiation process. For example, the section of the Declaration relating to commitments that provides for the "withdrawal of all claims" is entitled "Nullification of Sanctions and Claims." Possibly, the parties to the dispute intended by the Algiers settlement that all claims to reparation should be settled, renounced, or arbitrated by the new Iran-United States Claims Tribunal. Here the Court's reasoning in the *Barcelona Traction* case may warrant the result that a waiver of the claims (renunciation) was intended.[130]

Iran may make a different argument about the principle of estoppel. Even if the undertakings between the United States and Iran are not watertight,[131] Iran may argue that the United States is estopped from reinstituting proceedings for the determination of reparations.[132] As there is no "*prima facie* and in principle renunciation"[133] of the claims in discontinuance, the burden of proof would fall on the Respondent. Though that burden is great,[134] Iran may be able to overcome it in the present case.

It may well be maintained that jurisdiction with regard to the interpretation and performance of any provision on the withdrawal of claims in the Algiers settlement is vested in the Iran-United States Claims Tribunal by paragraph 17 of the Declaration relating to commitments and Article II(3) of the parallel Declaration Concerning the Settlement of Claims.[135] If conceived as a *pactum separatum* or *pactum subsequens* among the multilateral and bilateral treaties

[128] *Cf.* Barcelona Traction (New Application), 1964 ICJ REP. at 21. A substantial interpretation and final assessment of these problems is not intended and not yet possible. The following is but a listing of critical issues to be considered.

[129] *Id.* at 21–22.

[130] *Id.* at 19 *et seq.*

[131] The validity of the Algiers settlement under the principles of the law of treaties has been questioned; *see, e.g.,* McLaughlin & Teclaff, *supra* note 3, at 226 *et seq.*; Redwine, *supra* note 3, at 847.

[132] Iran could take up the arguments advanced by the ICJ in the Barcelona Traction (New Application) case, 1964 ICJ REP. at 22 *et seq.*; *see* A. MARTIN, *supra* note 6, at 157 *et seq.* with abundant documentation.

[133] Barcelona Traction (New Application), 1964 ICJ REP. at 21; *cf.* ROSENNE, LAW AND PRACTICE, *supra* note 6, at 539. *Contra* Pecourt García, *supra* note 6, at 246.

[134] *See* ROSENNE, LAW AND PRACTICE, *supra* note 6, at 529; Barcelona Traction (New Application), 1964 ICJ REP. at 22 *et seq.*

[135] Algiers settlement, *supra* note 10. The Iran-United States Claims Tribunal in its recently published opinion on its own jurisdiction construed its jurisdiction precisely. 21 ILM 78 (1982).

possibly applicable in this instance, the Algiers settlement may deprive the ICJ of jurisdiction to entertain a new application by the United States with regard to all matters pertaining to the seizure of the American Embassy. By mutual agreement states may terminate a given jurisdiction unless jurisdictional instruments forbid such action.[136] The *perpetuatio jurisdictionis* principle is not applicable because the consent of the states parties to the dispute is the very basis of international jurisdiction.[137]

Even if concurrent jurisdiction is arguable in the present case, the conflict may be resolved in favor of the Iran-United States Claims Tribunal according to the principles of general treaty interpretation, *lex posterior* and *lex specialis*.[138]

VI. Conclusion

The history of the discontinuance provisions and the practice of the World Court show a constant and steady development, culminating in the Rules of Court of 1978. Discontinuance is now well established as a procedural device giving effect to the maximum extent possible to the will of the parties to end proceedings. Moreover, both the Rules and the previous practice evidence the Court's efforts to abstain from citing or communicating in its order any facts or statements by the parties (even remotely) prejudicial to their interest.

Unfortunately, the present Order did not refrain from commenting upon the settlement reached by the parties to the dispute. In addition, the President of the ICJ should have applied Article 89(1) of the Rules of Court of 1978 in this Order. He should have been more cautious in citing communications to the Court, and he should have avoided any impression that approval by the Court was either obligatory or in fact given. Some statements should not have been included in the Order. In general, however, it may be assumed that this case will not reenter the General List of the ICJ.

In the wider context of the Algiers settlement, it should be noted that shortly after, and almost simultaneously with, the issuance of the present Order discontinuing proceedings in the International Court of Justice, the process of forming the Iran-United States Claims Tribunal began in the very same building, the Peace Palace at The Hague. It is already on the way toward functioning as a very busy arbitral tribunal.[139] It will apply the UNCITRAL Arbitration Rules as modified by the parties and the arbitrators.[140] Thus, in elaborating its rules of procedure,[141] and in its subsequent practice, the tribunal may very well contribute substantially to the body of international procedure and to the further refinement of discontinuance in particular.

[136] *Cf.* M. Bos, Les Conditions du procès en droit international public 261 (1957), with a view to an all-encompassing derogation from a jurisdictional instrument.

[137] Judge Anzilotti in the Rules discussion of 1922, *supra* note 31.

[138] *See* von Mangoldt, *Methods of Dispute Settlement in Public International Law*, in Settlement of Space Law Disputes 15, 25–26 (ed. K.-H. Böckstiegel 1980). The Iran-United States Mixed Claims Tribunal did in fact have recourse to such principles in its recent opinion on its jurisdiction, 21 ILM 78 (1982).

[139] *See* Dep't of State Public Notices 764, 46 Fed. Reg. 37,418 (1981); 763, *id.* at 36,277; 753, *id.* at 25,026; 749, *id.* at 19,893.

[140] *See supra* note 72.

[141] *See* Dep't of State Public Notices 789, 47 Fed. Reg. 1,063 (1982); 783, 46 *id.* at 58,631 (1981); 779, *id.* at 55,468; 775, *id.* at 49,695; 772, *id.* at 45,051.

THE PLAINTIFF'S DILEMMA: ILLEGALLY OBTAINED EVIDENCE AND ADMISSIBILITY IN INTERNATIONAL ADJUDICATION

*By W. Michael Reisman and Eric E. Freedman**

A suit cannot be pressed, whether on the domestic or international level, without supporting evidence. The processes of gathering such evidence are carefully regulated in many developed legal systems, in part because experience has shown that too zealous a pursuit of evidence can easily transform institutions designed to resolve conflict into a rationalization and a setting for possibly even more rancorous conflict. When some part of the state apparatus is prosecuting a case, liberal democracies have often imposed more stringent regulations as part of what we may call, in a nondocumentary sense, the "constitutional" or "rule of law" tradition, that continuing compact between governors and governed about restraint in the use of official power.

In any system of "rule of law," norms permitting as well as norms restraining the overly zealous collection of evidence for judicial purposes are under continuing stress. Defendants plead that judicial inquiry is being exploited as an excuse to conduct wide-ranging interventions into protected private spheres. Potential plaintiffs claim that they cannot prove their cases unless evidence completely within the control of the defendant is discovered. If the gravamen of the dispute is not merely a personal injury, but an allegation that the defendant, in not "playing by the rules," is harming the entire community, the plaintiff may argue with some cogency that prosecution of the case to his advantage, as well as vindication of the relevant norms to the community's, will be rendered impossible. The government apparatus bringing criminal or civil suits on behalf of the community often lodges a similar argument. With the extraordinary growth in the technology of crime, government personnel frequently maintain that they are unable to gather evidence for prosecution and for the protection of public order unless restraints on the gathering of evidence are relaxed.[1] This claim eventually stirs and then is countered by the ancient fear that the apparatus of justice may degenerate into little more than another instrument of elite control over an intimidated rank and file.[2]

In international adjudication, the problem is, if anything, aggravated. Formally speaking, there is no public prosecutor *jure gentium*; virtually all adjudications are initiated and conducted by states and against states. Compulsory and effectively sanctioned methods for securing necessary evidence, devices such as the interrogatory, discovery, and the subpoena duces tecum found in

* Of the Board of Editors and of the California Bar, respectively.

[1] *See, e.g.*, Israel, *Legislative Regulation of Searches and Seizures: The Michigan Proposals*, 73 MICH. L. REV. 222 (1974).

[2] *See, e.g.*, Amsterdam, *Perspectives on the Fourth Amendment*, 58 MINN. L. REV. 349 (1974); Levin & Cohen, *The Exclusionary Rules in Nonjury Criminal Cases*, 119 U. PA. L. REV. 905 (1971); Weinreb, *Generalities of the Fourth Amendment*, 42 U. CHI. L. REV. 47 (1974).

many domestic legal systems, do not exist. The "rule in *Parker's* case,"[3] which admonishes states to yield all the information pertinent to the suit and under their control, is often an empty piety; even if the defendant-state were willing to inventory all the pertinent evidence it had, there is really no way a plaintiff-state can compel it to surrender evidence that may be indispensable to the prosecution of its case. Hence, in international law, even more than in domestic systems, pressure may mount for the unilateral (and in some instances unlawful) gathering of evidence. But unilateral methods can themselves become a new source of conflict. This is, in short, the plaintiff's dilemma.

The plaintiff's dilemma confronts international tribunals with difficult and important choices. A municipal court can have its cake and eat it, too: when confronted with evidence secured unlawfully by a government department, it has the option of accepting the evidence while at the same time penalizing the specific agent responsible for its acquisition. But since international tribunals cannot penalize particular officers within a state, they do not have this option. International decision makers, when presented with claims supported by illegally obtained evidence, must balance the needs of a good faith plaintiff to secure evidence for its case against the rights of the defendant to the integrity of its own processes of confidentiality and secrecy. Yet the decision maker must also consider the more general need of the international community to maintain respect for the "sovereignties" of states. Because world order may be seriously threatened by evidentiary incursions, the international tribunal must be very sensitive to the provocativeness of an unlawful gathering of evidence and the consequences it may precipitate, no matter how damning the evidence retrieved may be.

I.

It is commonly acknowledged that "the practice of international tribunals in the admission of evidence has developed a pattern comparable to that of the liberal system of procedure in the civil law countries."[4] But scholars differ as to the reasons. "Anglo-American law," writes Sandifer, a commentator quite representative of the general view, "has exerted only a minor influence

[3] *See* W. M. REISMAN, NULLITY AND REVISION 593–94 (1971):

> The most extreme statement of the international burden of disclosure is found in the *Parker Claim* before the United States-Mexican General Claims Commission in 1927. In this case, the commission held that the respondent government was under an "obligation to lay before the Commission all evidence within its possession to establish the truth whatever it may be" and proceeded to declare that:
>
> > the parties before this Commission are sovereign nations who are in honor bound to make full disclosures of the facts in each case so far as such facts are within their knowledge or can reasonably be ascertained by them. The Commission, therefore, will confidently rely upon each Agent to lay before it all of the facts that can reasonably be ascertained by him concerning each case no matter what their effects may be.
>
> The rule in Parker's case has been cited with approval by other tribunals, and similar high burdens of disclosure appear in many compromis [footnotes omitted].

[4] D. SANDIFER, EVIDENCE BEFORE INTERNATIONAL TRIBUNALS 176 (1975).

on the matter of the admission of evidence."[5] Sandifer suggests that this differential influence of civil and common law states derived from the relatively greater participation of civil-law-trained lawyers in the conduct of international tribunals.[6] Lauterpacht, in contrast, attributed the lesser influence of Anglo-American evidentiary rules to their inherent inappropriateness for international tribunals:

> The question of rules of evidence applied by international tribunals shows . . . that international judicial settlement may be relied upon to produce, independently of any particular system of law, rules appropriate to its own requirements and circumstances. Thus, the history of international arbitration shows that whatever may be the merits of the strict Common Law rules regulating the admissibility of evidence and of burden of proof, it is not practicable to follow them in international litigation. They are not followed there; in fact, they have been expressly repudiated. There are therefore in this matter no longer two schools of thought in international law; there is one rule of international law on the subject, which as it happens, does not coincide with that which Common Law courts apply in actions brought before them.[7]

In Anglo-American law, the party adducing challenged evidence bears the burden of establishing that the evidence satisfies all applicable rules regarding admissibility. In international practice, as in the civil law,[8] the burden is shifted; evidence offered within time limits established by the tribunal will normally be admitted unless the individual challenging its acceptance can show specific grounds for nonadmissibility.[9] Sandifer summarizes this underlying approach:

> In the absence of the provision of a specific ground of exclusion in the arbitral agreement, there is no rule of law that can be invoked as

[5] *Ibid.*

[6] *Ibid.*

[7] H. Lauterpacht, *The So-called Anglo-American and Continental Schools of Thought in International Law*, 12 BRIT. Y.B. INT'L L. 31, 41 (1931).

[8] *See* Damaska, *Evidentiary Barriers to Conviction and Two Models of Criminal Procedure: A Comparative Study*, 121 U. PA. L. REV. 506 (1973) ("It is said that while common law systems are mainly concerned with the issue of admissibility, civil law systems admit all evidence that is logically relevant." *Id.* at 513).

[9] Sandifer writes:

> The International Court of Justice has construed the absence of restrictive rules in its Statute to mean that a party may generally produce any evidence as a matter of right, so long as it is produced within the time limits fixed by the Court. Evidence submitted after those time limits may only be admitted with the consent of the other party and subject to the sanction of the Court. In practice, while the Court has placed few restrictions upon the rights of the parties to produce whatever evidence they see fit, it has upon occasion exercised its discretionary authority to refuse to accept evidence offered.

D. SANDIFER, *supra* note 4, at 184–85 (footnotes omitted).

Rosenne writes:

> The practical inability to deduce from the preceding survey of the practice of the Court—whether its administrative decisions or its judicial work—clear guidance on the material admissibility of evidence (beyond the general test of relevance) is to no small extent due to the nature of international litigation and the manner in which it is conducted. The truth is that material admissibility is rarely disputed, least of all on formal grounds, and the parties concentrate on attacking the weight of evidence brought by the other side.

2 S. ROSENNE, THE LAW AND PRACTICE OF THE INTERNATIONAL COURT 584 (1965).

> binding a tribunal to exclude particular evidence. In practice . . . tribunals have been unwilling to exclude evidence in reliance upon general rules or principles, drawn from the practice of other tribunals or from municipal law. Admission is a matter of right, and the burden is upon the party challenging any piece of evidence to show that the particular procedural law of the tribunal will be violated by a refusal to exclude it.[10]

Commentators agree that, in the words of one observer, "[e]vidence is seldom excluded by the [International] Court [of Justice]."[11] The Swiss Memorial in the *Interhandel* case[12] averred that the liberal standard of admissibility established by the Court meant that "[l]es parties sont . . . dans une large mesure libres de présenter les preuves qu'elles estiment nécessaires et opportunes."[13] That is the traditional practice in international arbitration.[14] Umpire Gutiérrez-Otero, in his opinion in the *Franqui* case[15] before the Spanish-Venezuelan Mixed Claims Commission of 1903, quoted Mérignhac[16] to the effect that "le tribunal arbitral demeurera libre d'employer, pour s'éclairer, tous les genres de preuves qu'il croira nécessaires; et il ne sera lié, à cet égard, par aucune des restrictions qu'on rencontre dans les lois positives, spécialement quant à l'administration de la preuve testimoniale."[17]

One explanation of the practice of liberal admission before international tribunals is that the nature of the cases presented and of the tribunals themselves demands an especially broad tolerance. After all, tribunals in international law have traditionally been viewed as creatures of the consent of the litigants with only those powers the litigants have accorded them. Perhaps judges have been hesitant to exclude evidence in view of the very difficulty often attending its acquisition. Others have theorized that the rules of admissibility are an integral part of the trial-by-jury system in Anglo-American procedure.[18] According to this rationale, it is appropriate for "the [interna-

[10] D. SANDIFER, *supra* note 4, at 189–90.

[11] Alford, *Fact Finding by the World Court*, 4 VILL. L. REV. 37, 81 (1958). *Cf.* M. HUDSON, THE PERMANENT COURT OF INTERNATIONAL JUSTICE §520, at 571 (1943) ("The occasions have been rare in which the [Permanent] Court [of International Justice] has excluded evidence proffered, and no general rules for exclusion have been formulated").

[12] Interhandel Case (Switz. v. U.S.), 1959 ICJ REP. 6 (Judgment of March 21).

[13] Mémoire du Gouvernement de la Confèderation Suisse, 1959 ICJ Pleadings (Interhandel) 79, 128 (Memorial dated March 3, 1958).

[14] J. RALSTON, THE LAW AND PROCEDURE OF INTERNATIONAL TRIBUNALS §§379–83 (1926); J. SIMPSON & H. FOX, INTERNATIONAL ARBITRATION 192–93 (1959).

> International tribunals usually allow the parties the greatest freedom in presenting evidence. In international law there are no general rules requiring the exclusion of categories of evidence. While it is open to the parties to agree upon rules of exclusion, the tendency has always been to give tribunals the widest discretion in the admission and assessment of evidence.

Id. at 192.

[15] Franqui Case (Spain v. Venez.), 10 R. Int'l Arb. Awards 751 (1903).

[16] A. MÉRIGNHAC, TRAITÉ THÉORIQUE ET PRATIQUE DE L'ARBITRAGE INTERNATIONAL §272, at 269–70 (1895).

[17] 10 R. Int'l Arb. Awards at 751.

[18] The assumption that restrictive rules of admissibility are an exclusively Anglo-American phenomenon, evolving in the law of evidence of common law countries only because of the

tional] tribunal to admit evidence that might normally be rejected in municipal litigation" because "the members of the tribunal, being jurists trained in the sifting of evidence, are [unlike jurors] competent to appreciate the evidence according to its intrinsic and relative value."[19]

But it would be wrong to say that there are no restrictions on admissibility of evidence. Although barriers to the admission of evidence have been relatively insignificant, they have not been entirely lacking. Commentators have pointed to considerations of internal procedural fairness and the orderly administration of judicial machinery ("good judicial order") as the most important policy limitation on the liberal evidentiary standard. Thus, evidence purposely withheld for late submission, with the intent of gaining an unfair advantage, has on occasion been rejected by international jurists. Different conceptions of what constitutes bad faith, however, have protected some such tardy submissions from rejection. In the *Island of Palmas* arbitration,[20] for example, Judge Huber found that the Netherlands had committed no impropriety in withholding documents mentioned in its memorandum until they were called for by the arbitrator in his discretion.[21]

Where arbitral agreements have limited the nature of the evidence to be considered, some tribunals have refused admission of other evidence, on the rationale that were exceptions made, opposing parties might ignore the decision of the tribunal on grounds of *excès de pouvoir*.[22] Article V of the arbitral agreement concerning the *Masica Incident*,[23] for example, specified that "neither government shall be entitled to put in any further evidence as to the events which occurred on the 16th June, 1910, beyond that which was given before, or taken into consideration by, the above-mentioned court of enquiry at La Ceiba."[24] On other occasions, tribunals have shown some reluctance to admit evidence not submitted within time limits fixed by them. At least twice,

---

institution of the jury, is widely shared among scholars. McCormick has written: "It is safe to say that without the jury there would be no law of evidence remotely resembling the rules of admissibility which make up its contents in English-speaking countries today." *Evidence*, in 5 ENCYCLOPEDIA OF THE SOCIAL SCIENCES 639 (1931). Wigmore is to the same effect:

> But chiefly it owes its origin, maintenance, and system to the separation of function between judge and jury. If this separation of judge and jury had not existed as it has, with all its history, nothing marked would probably have developed. Under the Continental systems, in which the jury is but a modern borrowing, little of the sort appears.

1 J. WIGMORE, EVIDENCE §28, at 409 (1940). Sandifer writes: "The radical difference in Anglo-American and in civil law rules relating to admissibility of evidence is generally attributed to the presence of the jury in the judicial system of the former and its absence in the latter." D. SANDIFER, *supra* note 4, at 177.

[19] D. SANDIFER, *supra* note 4, at 182.

[20] Island of Palmas Case (Neth. v. U.S.), 2 R. Int'l Arb. Awards 831 (Perm. Ct. Arb. 1928).

[21] *Id.* at 840–42. *See* D. SANDIFER, *supra* note 4, at 60–69.

[22] On nullity in general, see A. BALASKO, CAUSES DE NULLITÉ DE LA SENTENCE ARBITRALE EN DROIT INTERNATIONAL PUBLIC (1938); W. M. REISMAN, *supra* note 3; J. WITENBERG, L'ORGANISATION JUDICIARE, LA PROCÉDURE ET LA SENTENCE INTERNATIONALES (1937).

[23] Arrangement between the United Kingdom and Honduras Referring to Arbitration Matters relating to the Masica Incident, 10 AJIL, Supp. 98 (1916).

[24] *Id.* at 100.

for example, the Central American Court of Justice proved sympathetic to challenges to the admissibility of documents not submitted with the complaint, although in neither case did the Court find that it was necessary specifically to exclude the tardily proffered evidence.[25] Similarly, in the *Saint-Naoum* case,[26] the Permanent Court of International Justice refused to hear testimony offered by the Serb-Croat-Slovene representative after the close of proceedings, despite the earlier unavailability of the witness concerned.[27]

On at least one occasion, the Permanent Court of International Justice rejected documentary evidence because it was not filed in proper form. In the *Free Zones* case,[28] Switzerland offered documents that, although bearing indirectly on the case, were not annexed to any written proceedings and were therefore not formally presented either to the judges or to the opposing party, France. When the Swiss agent referred to the documents during oral argument, France objected and the Court, invoking Article 52 of its Statute,[29] refused to admit the evidence.[30] Under similar circumstances, in the *Mavrommatis Jerusalem Concessions* case,[31] the Court hesitated to receive into evidence specific documents that had not been annexed, and admitted the evidence only "by a special decision . . . under Article 33 of the Rules."[32]

Other policies have also animated decisions by international tribunals to exclude apparently relevant evidence. Several decisions of the Permanent Court of International Justice manifest a concern for maintaining the viability of efforts at extrajudicial settlement by insisting on the preservation of the

[25] Honduras and Nicaragua v. Guatemala and El Salvador, THE CLAIM INSTITUTED BEFORE THE COURT OF JUSTICE OF CENTRAL AMERICA BY THE GOVERNMENT OF HONDURAS AGAINST THE GOVERNMENT OF GUATEMALA 90–143 (1908); Felipe Molina Larios v. Honduras, 3 ANALES DE LA CORTE DE JUSTICIA CENTROAMERICANA 58, 60–61 (1913). *See* D. SANDIFER, *supra* note 4, at 185–86.

[26] Question of the Monastery of Saint-Naoum (Albanian Frontier), 1924 PCIJ, ser. B, No. 9.

[27] 1924 PCIJ, ser. C, No. 5-II, at 381–82; 1926–27 PCIJ, ser. E, No. 3, at 214.

[28] Case of Free Zones of Upper Savoy and the District of Gex, 1932 PCIJ, ser. A/B, No. 46.

[29] Article 52 of the Statute of the Permanent Court of International Justice read: "After the Court has received the proofs and evidence within the time specified for the purpose, it may refuse to accept any further oral or written evidence that one party may desire to present unless the other side consents." Article 52 of the Statute of the International Court of Justice is identical to that of the Permanent Court.

[30] 1929 PCIJ, ser. A, No. 22, at 14, 21.

[31] The Mavrommatis Jerusalem Concessions, 1925 PCIJ, ser. A, No. 5.

[32] 1929–30 PCIJ, ser. E, No. 6, at 290.

Article 33 of the 1926 Rules of the Permanent Court of International Justice read:

> The Court shall fix time limits in each case by assigning a definite date for the completion of the various acts of procedure, having regard as far as possible to any agreement between the parties.
>
> The Court may extend time limits which it has fixed. It may likewise decide in certain circumstances that any proceeding taken after the expiration of a time limit shall be considered as valid.
>
> If the Court is not sitting, the powers conferred upon it by this article shall be exercised by the President, subject to any subsequent decision of the Court.

Rules of Court, adopted on July 31, 1926, PCIJ, ser. D, No. 1, at 33, 46–47.

confidentiality of earlier efforts at settlement.[33] In the *Chorzów* case,[34] the Court refused to consider declarations, admissions, or proposals made by the parties in the course of prior, abortive direct negotiations.[35] During proceedings in the *Danube Commission* case,[36] the Court declined admission of the history of certain articles of the Versailles Treaty, since these were "confidential" and had not "been placed before the Court by, or with the consent of, the competent authority."[37] By special order in the *Oder Commission* case,[38] the Court ruled inadmissible, as *travaux préparatoires*, the minutes of the Commission on Ports, Waterways and Railways of the Paris Peace Conference.[39] And when, in the *Meuse* case,[40] the Netherlands objected to Belgium's offer into evidence of a treaty draft that the two parties had considered during abortive negotiations, the Court declined to make the document a part of the record.[41]

Beyond these scattered examples, international tribunals have displayed little interest in excluding evidence. Documentary, testimonial, and real evidence has frequently been accepted for consideration even when irregularly presented. Despite the intermittent storms over this matter in domestic law, strong opposition to the near lack of international evidentiary barriers has never really developed. The general consensus of practitioners and commentators alike is that stricter rules of admissibility are wholly inappropriate for international arbitration or adjudication.[42] In his opinion in the *Máximo Mora*

[33] This consideration is an important one on the domestic level as well. Rule 408 of the Federal Rules of Evidence provides:

> Evidence of (1) furnishing or offering or promising to furnish, or (2) accepting or offering or promising to accept, a valuable consideration in compromising or attempting to compromise a claim which was disputed as to either validity or amount, is not admissible to prove liability for or invalidity of the claim or its amount. Evidence of conduct or statements made in compromise negotiations is likewise not admissible. This rule does not require the exclusion of any evidence otherwise discoverable merely because it is presented in the course of compromise negotiations. This rule also does not require exclusion when the evidence is offered for another purpose, such as proving bias or prejudice of a witness, negativing a contention of undue delay, or proving an effort to obstruct a criminal investigation or prosecution.

According to the Advisory Committee's Note to Rule 408, "exclusion may be based on two grounds. (1) The evidence is irrelevant. . . . (2) A more consistently impressive ground is promotion of the public policy favoring the compromise and settlement of disputes."

See McCormick's Handbook of the Law of Evidence §274 (2d ed. E. Cleary 1972).

[34] Case Concerning the Factory at Chorzów (Claim for Indemnity) (Jurisdiction), 1927 PCIJ, ser. A, No. 9.

[35] *Id.* at 19.

[36] Jurisdiction of the European Comm'n of the Danube between Galatz and Braila, 1927 PCIJ, ser. B, No. 14.

[37] *Id.* at 32.

[38] Case Relating to the Territorial Jurisdiction of the Int'l Comm'n of the River Oder, 1929 PCIJ, ser. A, No. 23.

[39] *Id.* at 42.

[40] The Diversion of Water from the River Meuse, 1937 PCIJ, ser. A/B, No. 70.

[41] 1937 PCIJ, ser. C, No. 81, at 220, 224.

[42] *See, e.g.*, Alford, *supra* note 11, at 81:

> An exclusion of evidence by the [International] Court [of Justice] based upon the way in which it was secured would be unrealistic in view of the known barriers established by States

case[43] before the United States-Spanish Mixed Claims Commission of 1871, the Spanish arbitrator expressed a common attitude:

> It may be that under the strict English-American rules of evidence which prevail in trials where a court decides questions of law and a jury decides questions of fact, and the judge prescribes what witnesses can testify, and what description of evidence can be permitted to go to the jury, these newspaper clippings might not be admitted. But this commission is not bound by such English-American rules of evidence in jury trials. The arbitrators hear and decide questions of law and fact alike. The arbitrators are competent to decide for themselves as to the amount of credibility to be given to any evidence, and are not in danger of being misled, as juries may be. This objection to the reception of newspapers to prove facts of general and public notoriety seems, so far as I can see, to grow out of a very technical, artificial, and varying rule in English and American tribunals, which excludes all evidence which can be labeled as hearsay.[44]

More recently, Rosenne has asserted, with regard to documentary evidence submitted to the International Court, that "the restrictions upon admissibility of evidence sometimes encountered in municipal procedure (and connected with the system of jury trial) have no place in international adjudication, where the relevance of facts and the value of evidence tending to establish facts are left to the entire appreciation of the Court."[45]

The scholarly discussion is plainly not satisfactory. The resistance of international commentators and decision makers to more formidable evidentiary barriers stems from a constricted conception of the purpose of rules limiting the admissibility of evidence. As our review has shown, most arbitral and doctrinal discussions have characterized the problem of admissibility solely in terms of the differential skills of legal specialists and laymen in a courtroom. Strict rules of admissibility are typically viewed as having no rationale whatsoever in the absence of the jury trial. Since the institution of the jury is not part of international judicial practice, doctrinalists found no reason for strong restrictions upon the acceptance of evidence in that context. Whatever limitations were accepted were attributed to an overriding concern with internal procedural fairness and the orderly administration of judicial machinery. The concern for "good judicial order" obviously must figure prominently among the policies stimulating the exclusion of evidence. But it is neither the only nor the most important evidentiary policy.

International tribunals and judicial scholars err seriously when, relying purely on historical argument and rigidly textual interpretation, they ignore

---

to the flow of information. The Court is not faced with the problem of intermittent police abuses of individuals which national constitutional guarantees are designed to minimize. The Court must get its evidence when and by whatever means it can obtain it.

[43] Case concerning Antonio Máximo Mora (Spain v. United States), 16 RECORD, OPINIONS AND DECISIONS, UNITED STATES-SPANISH MIXED CLAIMS COMMISSION, Decision No. 48 (1871).

[44] Count Lewenhaupt, Umpire, Case of Antonio Máximo Mora, *quoted in* D. SANDIFER, *supra* note 4, at 182–83.

[45] 2 S. ROSENNE, *supra* note 9, at 557.

other significant policy implications involved in rules limiting admissibility. One such implication is the constitutional or rule of law dimension in which courts are supposed to function, *inter alia*, as a buffer between the other institutions of government and the other participants in the social process. While the structural features of the domestic decision process itself and, in particular, the presence or absence of the jury will unquestionably have some effect on rules of evidence, many of the restrictive principles of admissibility now derive from complex relationships between different branches of government. Restrictive admissibility is often an attempt to limit the power of the prosecutor and to protect the community from overly zealous invasions of privacy in the interests of gaining evidence for judicial purposes.[46] *Mutatis mutandis*, the same problems may apply on the international level. Indeed, international tribunals have not been entirely oblivious to this dimension. On two occasions, at least, the admissibility of relevant evidence has been questioned because it was secured in a manner that the court deemed harmful to public order and that it did not wish to encourage.[47]

II.

The question of the admissibility of evidence obtained by unlawful intervention was raised, in rather sharp fashion, in the merits phase of the *Corfu Channel* case[48] in 1949. British ships transiting the Straits of Corfu in a claimed right of innocent passage struck mines whose presence had not been made known by the Albanian Government. Thereafter, British minesweepers swept the Channel without securing Albanian permission. Later, in the International Court, the United Kingdom sought to use the mines that had been collected in the sweeping operation as evidence of Albanian responsibility.

The Court paid close attention to the question of the lawfulness of the November 1946 sweeping operation. "Operation Retail," as it was called by both the parties and the Court, had been preceded by a request from the United Kingdom to the Albanian Government for permission to sweep Corfu Channel. The Albanian Government had replied on October 31, 1946 that it did not consent to any sweeping within Albanian territorial waters, *i.e.*, in the Straits of Corfu. In the meanwhile, the United Kingdom had requested the permission of the International Central Mines Clearance Board for a sweeping of the Channel; the board indicated its judgment of its own lack of competence by approving the British request subject to Albanian consent.

[46] Such was the basic rationale for the United States Supreme Court's decision in Mapp v. Ohio, 367 U.S. 643 (1961), which held that the Fourteenth Amendment fully incorporated the Fourth Amendment's guarantee against unreasonable searches and seizures, on the ground that "the only effectively available way" that one could compel respect for the "constitutional guaranty" of the Fourth Amendment was to exclude from both state and federal criminal prosecutions all evidence obtained in violation of the Constitution. 367 U.S. at 656 (quoting Elkins v. United States, 364 U.S. 206, 217 (1960)). Stressing the importance of "the imperative of judicial integrity," the Supreme Court noted that "[n]othing can destroy a government more quickly than its failure to observe its own laws." 367 U.S. at 659.

[47] *See* notes 49–69 and accompanying text, *infra*.

[48] Corfu Channel Case (UK v. Alb.), 1949 ICJ REP. 4 (Judgment of April 9).

When Britain then informed Albania of its intention to conduct the sweep, Albania replied that a sweep within its territorial waters, where it claimed "foreign warships [had] no reason to sail,"[49] would be considered a deliberate violation of Albanian territory and sovereignty.

Despite the protest, Operation Retail was carried out on November 12 and 13. The British invited an officer of the French Navy to attend as observer. There seems to be no evidence that the sweep was conducted with any purpose other than its manifest objective, nor any dispute about the absence of formal authority for it. As the Court observed:

> The United Kingdom Government does not dispute that "Operation Retail" was carried out against the clearly expressed wish of the Albanian Government. It recognizes that the operation had not the consent of the international mine clearance organizations, that it could not be justified as the exercise of a right of innocent passage, and lastly that, in principle, international law does not allow a State to assemble a large number of warships in the territorial waters of another State and to carry out minesweeping in those waters. The United Kingdom Government states that the operation was one of extreme urgency, and that it considered itself entitled to carry it out without anybody's consent.[50]

The United Kingdom justified its action on two grounds. One related to an agreement among the United Kingdom, France, the Soviet Union, and the United States, allocating competence for mine clearance. The Court dismissed it summarily. The second justification related to the gathering of evidence. As the Court phrased it, the main defense of the United Kingdom was that "the *corpora delicti* must be secured as quickly as possible, for fear they should be taken away, without leaving traces, by the authors of the minelaying or by the Albanian authorities."[51] The justification for this defense rested on "a new and special application of the theory of intervention, by means of which the State intervening would secure possession of evidence in the territory of another State, in order to submit it to an international tribunal and thus facilitate its task."[52] The United Kingdom also justified Operation Retail as a method of self-protection and self-help.[53]

[49] *Id.* at 33.

[50] *Id.* at 33–34.

[51] *Id.* at 34.

[52] *Ibid.*

[53] In oral argument, Sir Eric Beckett, representing the United Kingdom, characterized his nation's intervention theory as follows:

> [W]e say that the United Kingdom had the right to sweep for the purposes of investigating the cause of the explosions under *Saumarez* and *Volage* in October, because (i) the United Kingdom did suspect, and had good reason to suspect, that a most serious international offence had been committed against ships of the Royal navy; (ii) the United Kingdom wished to bring a claim before the Security Council, if evidence was found to justify its suspicions; (iii) the United Kingdom feared, and had good reason to fear, that if very speedy action was not taken that evidence would be made to disappear by the party guilty of this offence.

Reply by Sir Eric Beckett, ICJ Pleadings (4 Corfu Channel) 542, 572 (Reply dated Jan. 18–19, 1949).

The legality of such intervention as its minesweeping operation represented, asserted the United Kingdom, was well recognized in international law:

> (*a*) There is recognized in international law the right of a state, when a state of affairs involving a serious and flagrant breach of the law has been brought about by another State

The International Court rejected both of these claims. It felt that the assertion of a right of intervention for these purposes would be abused by relatively stronger states and ruled that the principle of self-help would not apply even after "the Albanian Government's complete failure to carry out its duties after the explosions, and the dilatory nature of its diplomatic notes."[54] Nonetheless, the Court viewed those circumstances as extenuating to the point of virtually obliterating Britain's adjudged counter-delict. It declared "that the action of the British Navy constituted a violation of Albanian sovereignty,"[55] but the Court refused to apply any serious sanction against the United Kingdom. It decided unanimously that its declaration of the unlawfulness of the United Kingdom's act "is in itself appropriate satisfaction."[56] More important, it admitted evidence concerning the mines that had been unlawfully swept by the United Kingdom.

The phenomenon of a judgment that affirms a norm, while allowing the illegal fruits of its violation to be enjoyed by the violator, is not unusual. Courts doing this seem to wish to vindicate the norm, while establishing, by special jurisprudence, that some violations will be tolerated. In terms of strictest

---

or has been permitted to come about, to intervene by direct action. The purpose of such intervention may be to prevent the continuance of the situation which is in breach of the law, or, where the intervening State has suffered an injury of a nature capable of being redressed, to further the administration of international justice by preventing the removal of the evidence.

(*b*) In this case it was plain from the nature of the incident of 22nd October that a serious breach of international law had been committed by some State whether Albania or another. Not only had a dangerous obstruction been placed right across an international highway of navigation, thus constituting a threat to the shipping of all nations, but this obstruction took the form of a minefield the laying of which was a manifest breach of the Hague Convention VIII of 1907. Either of these grounds was in itself sufficient to justify intervention by the United Kingdom, the State which had suffered from it.

Reply of the United Kingdom, *id.* (2 Corfu Channel) 241, 282, para. 82 (Reply dated July 30, 1948).

The United Kingdom acknowledged that any right of intervention must be "exercised in a reasonable manner so as to cause the minimum interference with the sovereignty of the State concerned." *Id.* at 284, para. 82(*f*). It argued that this requirement had been fulfilled in Operation Retail because "the Government of the United Kingdom in fact took the utmost precautions to ensure that all aggressive and provocative acts were avoided and that Albanian sovereign rights were not infringed." *Id.* at 286, para. 84.

In response to the claims of the United Kingdom, Albania asserted that a right of intervention, if it existed any longer in international law, was a collective right of international organizations and not individual states. Reply of Albania, *id.* at 313, 372, para. 151 (Reply dated Sept. 20, 1948). According to Albania, the fact that British ships were victims of mine explosions did not excuse the sweeping operation. And even if Great Britain had possessed a right of intervention, the Albanians declared, the abusive manner in which the minesweeping operation was exercised would itself constitute an infringement upon the sovereignty of Albania. *Id.* at 372, para. 150. The Albanian representative warned that support by the International Court for the act of the United Kingdom would create a serious threat to world order: "Le Gouvernement albanais . . . ajoute qu'il serait fort dangereux pour la Cour de sanctionner par son autorité des pratiques qui ne correspondent pas à l'état actuel des relations internationales et sont la négation même de la justice internationale." *Id.* at 371, para. 147.

[54] 1949 ICJ REP. at 35. [55] *Ibid.*

[56] *Ibid.*

construction, mines illegally swept in another's territorial waters are admissible to prove sole responsibility for their explosion and injury to others. For precedential purposes one may say that unlawfully gathered evidence may at least on the facts of the *Corfu Channel* case be deemed admissible.[57] More broadly construed, the only practical interpretation of this aspect of the *Corfu Channel* judgment would seem to be that certain unlawful collections of evidence will be declared violations of international law, yet no sanction will be imposed on the gatherer, nor will the illegally gained evidence be deemed inadmissible.

It is noteworthy that the result achieved did not require these fine distinctions. The Court might have admitted the mines but substantially penalized the United Kingdom. Alternatively, it might have denied admissibility but imposed an onerous *praesumptio juris*, effectively requiring Albania to demonstrate either that it could not have known of the mines or that it had used all due diligence in seeking to clear the Corfu Channel. Either technique would have affirmed the normative principle prohibiting the unlawful gathering of evidence, while still confirming Albanian liability. We will speculate below on the reasons why the Court rejected these alternatives and the longer range political consequences of the way it formulated its decision.

III.

The issue of admissibility presents itself as a subtle factor in a different context in the *Iranian Hostages* case[58] of 1980. The Iranian Government, despite the compelling jurisdictional case submitted by the United States, chose not to appear in court, and availing itself instead of an interesting practice long countenanced by the Permanent Court and the International Court,[59] presented its arguments by letter delivered through diplomatic channels. A basic Iranian point, not always stated with optimum coherence, was that the invasion of the Embassy, the sequestration of the documentary material there, and the incarceration of the U.S. diplomats had to be put in context. As the Iranian letter explained:

> [I]t cannot be studied separately . . . [for it] involves, *inter alia*, more than 25 years of continual interference by the United States in the in-

[57] *But see* Shah, *Discovery by Intervention: The Right of a State to Seize Evidence Located Within the Territory of the Respondent State*, 53 AJIL 595, 612 (1959):

> Certain eminent writers are of the view that, despite what they term the somewhat general language used by the [*Corfu Channel*] Court, the observations of the Court could be confined merely to rejecting the right of self-help for the purpose of discovery of evidence, and self-help might still be regarded as legal in some circumstances. It is submitted that the learned authors, in their anxiety to retain the right of self-help for states till such time as the systems of pacific settlement of international disputes and of collective security established by the Charter can be rendered effective, read into the declaration of the Court an interpretation that it cannot bear. . . . [D]iscovery of evidence by intervention is not a method that is admissible in international law [footnote omitted].

[58] Case concerning United States Diplomatic and Consular Staff in Tehran (U.S. v. Iran), 1980 ICJ REP. 1 (Judgment of May 24).

[59] *See, e.g.*, Status of Eastern Carelia (Advisory Opinion), 1923 PCIJ, ser. B, No. 5; Nuclear Tests Cases (Austl. v. Fr.), 1973 ICJ REP. 99 (Order of June 22), 1974 ICJ REP. 253 (Judgment of Dec. 20); Fisheries Jurisdiction Case (UK v. Ice.), 1974 ICJ REP. 3 (Judgment of July 25).

> ternal affairs of Iran, the shameless exploitation of our country, and numerous crimes perpetrated against the Iranian people, contrary to and in conflict with all international and humanitarian norms.[60]

The Iranian claim might be reformulated as follows: The United States is alleged to have intervened in Iranian affairs for a quarter of a century and to have unlawfully influenced Iranian politics during that period. Evidence that would permit the Iranian Government to prove its allegation—excluding that which is in the United States and, of course, is classified and securely kept and is for all intents and purposes nonexistent for influencing international judicial proceedings—is available in the United States Embassy in Tehran and in other consular facilities throughout Iran.[61] If the principle of inviolability of diplomatic premises is taken as an absolute, the United States would be permitted to remove this information or to destroy it in place. Then the Iranian Government would never be able to prove its case, for it is most improbable, if not inconceivable, that the United States would voluntarily release such information or otherwise make it available to an international judicial process. The only way that the Iranian Government could establish its claim would be by a type of international discovery through self-help: precipitous entry into the U.S. facilities, sequestration of the documents there, their examination and filtering, and then their submission in an international process.

In these terms, the constructive Iranian argument can be seen as akin to the British argument in the *Corfu Channel* case and as one more manifestation of what we have characterized as the plaintiff's dilemma. If evidence cannot be gathered immediately, though unlawfully, the entire suit will be frustrated.

In contrast to its treatment in the *Corfu Channel* case, the Court did not explicitly consider the evidentiary dimension of the constructive Iranian claim.[62] In part, this may be because the Iranian Government did not make

[60] 1980 ICJ REP. at 8.

[61] No convincing evidence of illegal United States intervention in Iranian affairs seems to have been discovered in the American Embassy in Tehran. Barry Rubin explains the disparity between the expectations of the student militants who seized the Embassy and the reality of their findings in the following terms:

> None of [the leaders of the students who occupied the Embassy] had much experience with international politics or with the workings of embassies. This, coupled with their ideology, made their analyses of the United States Embassy's operations inaccurate in the extreme. For them, a State Department report on the Kurdish insurrection or on the anti-Khomeini Islamic terrorist group Forqan was proof that the United States was in contact with these movements, if not directing them. Any meeting between an Iranian official and embassy employees was proof of the former's treason and the latter's espionage. What was the most remarkable was their failure, after months in the embassy files, to produce any hard evidence of their accusations; some of the material circulated as evidence within Iran consisted of the most transparent forgeries.

B. RUBIN, PAVED WITH GOOD INTENTIONS 326 (1980).

[62] The *Times* of London found an inability independently to scrutinize the evidence to be one of the failings of the five-man United Nations Commission sent to Tehran in February of 1980. In an editorial entitled *A Meaningless Tribunal*, the *Times* criticized the Commission in part as follows:

> The United Nations has a fundamental responsibility to uphold and preserve international law. It also has the task of resolving international disputes by whatever peaceful means are

the claim clearly; in part, it may have been the Court's exercise of its own discretion in determining the pertinent and determinative issues to which it should address its attention. Certainly, the continuing detention of the diplomats was then perceived as a grave and combustible threat to world public order that urgently required defusing. Whatever the particular reasons, the Court responded in general terms that the gravity of a seizure of an embassy and its personnel could not be considered "secondary" or "marginal," considering the importance of the legal principles involved.[63]

> In any case, even if the alleged criminal activities of the United States in Iran could be considered as having been established, the question would remain whether they could be regarded by the Court as constituting a justification of Iran's conduct and thus a defence to the United States' claims in the present case. The Court, however, is unable to accept that they can be so regarded. This is because diplomatic law itself provides the necessary means of defence against, and sanction for, illicit activities by members of diplomatic or consular missions.[64]

The remedies supplied by diplomatic law to which the Court referred were (1) the declaration by the receiving state of a member of a mission as *persona non grata* under Article 9 of the 1961 Convention[65] and under Article 23 of

---

> appropriate. The continued captivity of the hostages in Iran has now compelled the United Nations to jettison one of those principles in pursuance of the other. In giving its imprimatur to the five-man Commission investigating the alleged crimes of the former Shah of Iran, the United Nations is playing a dangerous game. It is saying, in effect, that it is prepared to accept, and submit to, one of the most serious and blatant acts of international illegality of the century in the hope of gaining the release of the American hostages, and, as a secondary objective, promoting the normalization of relations between Iran and the United States, especially desirable in the context of the Soviet invasion of Afghanistan.
>
> . . . .
>
> The investigation will meet not even the most basic principles of natural justice. There will be no independent scrutiny of the evidence, no cross-examination of witnesses, no attempt to ensure that any denial or explanation or defence on the part of the former Shah is heard and taken into account. It will be an entirely one-sided affair, staged-managed by the Iranians to achieve a particular result.

The Times (London), Feb. 21, 1980, at 15.

[63] 1980 ICJ REP. at 38–43.

[64] *Id.* at 38. *See* CASE CONCERNING UNITED STATES DIPLOMATIC AND CONSULAR STAFF IN TEHRAN (UNITED STATES V. IRAN), MEMORIAL OF THE GOVERNMENT OF THE UNITED STATES OF AMERICA, pt. V, at 73 (1980):

> Various Iranian spokesmen have stated or implied that some of the members of the United States Embassy in Tehran may have been engaged in functions (specifically, information-gathering or intelligence work) that are not contemplated by Article 3 of the Vienna Convention on Diplomatic Relations and that such actions, and the use of Embassy premises for such purposes, justify Iran's failure to accord inviolability to United States diplomatic agents and premises under Articles 22 and 29–35 of the Vienna Convention on Diplomatic Relations. But even if—contrary to fact—the Government of Iran had proved to the Court that in one or more respects the United States or the members of its Embassy had violated one or more obligations under the Vienna Convention, there would be no ground for finding that such violations excuse Iran from the legal obligations . . . described in this Memorial.

[65] 1980 ICJ REP. at 38–40; Vienna Convention on Diplomatic Relations of 1961, 500 UNTS 95, 23 UST 3227, TIAS No. 7502.

the 1963 Convention,[66] with the coordinate obligation of the declaring state to provide for the safe exit of the departing diplomat and, (2) *in extremis*, "the power which every receiving State has, at its own discretion, to break off diplomatic relations with a sending State and to call for the immediate closure of the offending mission."[67] Even in this latter case, under Article 45 of the 1961 Convention,[68] the diplomatic premises of the erstwhile sending state would still remain inviolable.

In terms of the *Corfu Channel* outcome, all of these remedies fail to assure access to the evidence that the plaintiff has reason to suspect will be grounds for and will promise success in the judicial process. To be sure, the Court's holding cannot be considered dispositive of the plaintiff's dilemma. Only if Iran had released the hostages but retained the information seized when the militants penetrated the diplomatic premises, would the Court have been obliged to determine whether state responsibility was engaged, specifically for retaining the evidence, whether damages might be owing to the United States, and, most important, whether the evidence gained by this unlawful entry could be admitted in a possible suit before the International Court of Justice. Nevertheless, the Court's dispositive lends credence to the inference that the illegally gained evidence would have had to be returned unused, the plaintiff's dilemma notwithstanding. The Court decided unanimously that Iran "must immediately place in the hands of the protecting Power the premises, property, archives and documents of the United States Embassy in Tehran and of its Consulates in Iran."[69] In these terms, the implication would appear to be that that evidence would not be admissible.

IV.

National decisions seem to have yielded, in certain cases, to the admissibility of evidence gained illegally from diplomatic premises. In the well-known Canadian case of *Rose v. The King*,[70] the Canadian court permitted the admission of documents obviously taken from Soviet diplomatic premises in Ottawa against the wishes of the Soviet Government. That case, however, was complicated by the fact that the Canadian Government, though using the documents as evidence, had not itself taken them. Moreover, it was the defendant, a Canadian national, who raised the issue of admissibility; the Soviet Union made no effort to claim the documents or to protest their use in the trial. Given the extraordinary circumstances in which the documents reached the court, *Rose* and a number of similar incidents would not appear to be the sorts of incremental erosions of the physical immunity of diplomatic premises that signaled the alarm of the International Court of Justice in the *Iranian Hostages* case. As regards electronic monitoring, however, state practice now appears to tolerate—perforce—much, if not widespread, listening to communications

[66] 1980 ICJ REP. at 38–40; Vienna Convention on Consular Relations of 1963, 596 UNTS 261, 21 UST 77, TIAS No. 6820.

[67] 1980 ICJ REP. at 40.

[68] Vienna Convention on Diplomatic Relations, *supra* note 65.

[69] 1980 ICJ REP. at 44.

[70] [1947] 3 D.L.R. 618.

to, from, and within premises, inconsistent with the letter of the 1961 Vienna Convention.[71]

V.

The plaintiff's dilemma brings two inclusive interests into conflict. On the one hand, there is a desire to encourage the use of international adjudication for alleged violations of international law and, incident to this, a desire to permit a state to pursue its interests in the courtroom by gathering evidence that will lay the groundwork for a case. A contrary concern is that a state may be overzealous in gathering evidence. Retroactive validation of illegal seizures of evidence could encourage many more interventions into the territory and social processes of other states, many initially justified as good faith efforts to gather evidence. The result could then be more conflict and frustration of the fundamental purposes of international adjudication. Plainly, judges and scholars must begin to clarify policies regarding admissibility of evidence in international adjudications and arbitrations.

In the *Corfu Channel* case, the International Court seems to have yielded to the former interest. That decision may, in retrospect, have been less than optimum. The Court need not have relied on the mines gained in Operation Retail to permit the United Kingdom to pursue its case for injury and demand for damages. As we observed, other devices, such as an absolute presumption of the responsibility of a state for unpublicized mines in its territorial waters or in straits through which international traffic transits, could have achieved the same objective. If the absolute presumption seems too rigid and strains other policies that are appropriate, the Court might have also established an onerous rebuttable *praesumptio juris*. A shifting of the burden of proof would then have required Albania to come forward with evidence indicating that it was not responsible for the location of the mines; inability to shift this burden of proof would have rendered Albania responsible for the injury. In this fashion, the Court could have reached the same conclusion without having

[71] The practice of electronic and even more intrusive surveillance, *inter alia*, of diplomatic premises was defended by John Ehrlichman as authorized by 18 U.S.C. §2511. *Presidential Campaign Activities of 1972, Senate Resolution 60: Hearings before the Senate Select Comm. on Presidential Campaign Activities*, 93d Cong., 1st Sess. 2543 (1973–74). In part because of this, 18 U.S.C. §2511(3) was subsequently repealed. For a review of the alleged practice of government surveillance, see V. MARCHETTI & J. MARKS, THE CIA AND THE CULT OF INTELLIGENCE 204–05 (1974). The Foreign Intelligence Surveillance Act, 50 U.S.C. §1801 (1978), would appear to contravene the letter of the Vienna Convention on Diplomatic Relations, but may well represent a distressingly wide spectrum of national practice. The United States, as a "rule of law" system in which legislative-bureaucratic controls have been extended increasingly to the foreign affairs sector, may be singular among electronically eavesdropping nations only in that it must establish explicit and publicly acknowledged legislative authority to do things many other states are able to do secretly or discreetly. Hence the United States is singled out for blame for engaging in what may well be operationally accepted conduct. *See* W. M. REISMAN, FOLDED LIES, ch. 1 (1979). Be that as it may, the United States and other states that engage in such conduct must conclude, and presumably have concluded, that the need for and value of intelligence gained by electronic surveillance outweighs the incremental erosion of the norm upholding the inviolability of diplomatic premises and their communications.

had to approve, in effect, a United Kingdom intervention into Albanian territory.

In the *Iranian Hostages* case, one would have expected the Court not to follow the *Corfu* precedent. The importance the Court ascribed to the international diplomatic function, and to the immunity without which it cannot be effectively performed, required a blanket prohibition of the admissibility of any evidence gained unlawfully by a violation of diplomatic premises. This would certainly seem to be the better position. Indeed, if the diplomatic function is as important as the Court and many other authoritative statements have held, then any encouragement of a violation of its immunity would appear certain to jeopardize what international order exists. At least for embassies, if not for many other areas, any illegally gained evidence should be deemed inadmissible. The plaintiff's dilemma should be resolved against the plaintiff.

NORM MAKING AND SUPERVISION IN INTERNATIONAL HUMAN RIGHTS: REFLECTIONS ON INSTITUTIONAL ORDER

*By Theodor Meron**

I. Introduction

One of the characteristic phenomena of contemporary international life is the proliferation of human rights instruments and systems of supervision. In addition to the Charter of the United Nations and comprehensive global conventions such as the International Covenant on Economic, Social and Cultural Rights[1] (Economic Covenant) and the International Covenant on Civil and Political Rights[2] (Political Covenant), instruments have been adopted within the United Nations or the specialized agencies to govern particular aspects of human rights (*e.g.*, racial discrimination, rights of women) and within regional organizations (*e.g.*, the Council of Europe, the Organization of American States) to govern both general and particular aspects of human rights.[3] In the United Nations, the general practice has been for each normative instrument to create its own system of supervision whenever such systems have been established.[4] Typically, each organ of supervision applies

* Professor of Law, New York University School of Law. The author wishes to record his gratitude to Professor Louis B. Sohn for helpful suggestions.

[1] GA Res. 2200, 21 UN GAOR Supp. (No. 16) at 49, UN Doc. A/6316 (1966).

[2] *Id.* at 52.

[3] *See* Human Rights: A Compilation of International Instruments, UN Doc. ST/HR/1/Rev.1 (1978) (which lists 50 human rights instruments); Basic Documents on Human Rights (2d ed. I. Brownlie 1981) [hereinafter cited as Brownlie]. These compilations are necessarily selective. By the end of 1981, the International Labour Organisation (ILO) alone had adopted 156 international labor conventions.

[4] *E.g.*, the International Convention on the Elimination of All Forms of Racial Discrimination, 660 UNTS 195 (Racial Discrimination Convention) (which established the Committee on the Elimination of Racial Discrimination), *discussed in* Buergenthal, *Implementing the UN Racial Convention*, 12 Tex. Int'l L.J. 187 (1977); the Political Covenant, *supra* note 2 (which established the Human Rights Committee), *discussed in* Robertson, *The Implementation System: International Measures*, in The International Bill of Rights: The Covenant on Civil and Political Rights 332 (L. Henkin ed. 1981). *See generally* van Boven, *Human Rights Fora at the United Nations. How to Select and to Approach the Most Appropriate Forum. What Procedural Rules Govern?*, in International Human Rights: Law and Practice 83 (J. Tuttle ed. 1978). *See also* Franck & Fairley, *Procedural Due Process in Human Rights Fact-Finding by International Agencies*, 74 AJIL 308 (1980), for a critique of fact-finding by international agencies in the human rights area.

The trend to establish separate implementation organs for each UN human rights instrument is continuing. The Convention on the Elimination of All Forms of Discrimination against Women (Discrimination against Women Convention) provides for the establishment of a Committee on the Elimination of Discrimination against Women. GA Res. 34/180, 34 UN GAOR Supp. (No. 46) at 193, Art. 17, UN Doc. A/34/46 (1979). A proposal has been made to establish a new committee to implement the proposed convention against torture. *See* UN Doc. E/CN.4/1493 (1981). For a discussion of the pros and cons involved in the establishment of such a new supervisory body and for alternative proposals, see Report of the Working Group on a Draft Convention only the norms adopted in the specific "founding" instrument, rather than the entire corpus juris of international human rights or even all of the instruments comprising the International Bill of Human Rights,[5] *i.e.*, the Universal Declaration of Human Rights (Universal Declaration),[6] the Economic Covenant, the Political Covenant, and the Optional Protocol to the International Covenant on Civil and Political Rights.[7] This proliferation of normative instruments and systems of supervision, which is similar to the prolif-

---

against Torture and Other Cruel, Inhuman or Degrading Treatment or Punishment, UN Doc. E/CN.4/1982/L.40, at 12–15 (1982). *See also* text accompanying notes 47–49 *infra* and note 106 *infra*.

It may be recalled that Article 9 of the International Convention on the Suppression and Punishment of the Crime of *Apartheid*, GA Res. 3068, 28 UN GAOR Supp. (No. 30) at 75, UN Doc. A/9030 (1973), *reprinted in* Brownlie, *supra* note 3, at 164, provides that reports by states parties be considered by a group appointed by the Chairman of the Commission on Human Rights consisting of three members of the Commission who are also representatives of states parties to this Convention, which avoids establishing a new organ. It is more difficult to follow such a solution where members of a body (*e.g.*, the Human Rights Committee under the Political Covenant) are elected in their personal capacity and not as representatives of states.

[5] It is not clear whether this practice is always compelled by the language of the governing instrument or by considerations such as whether the other relevant instruments have been ratified by the state concerned. *Compare* this trend *with* the unified system of implementation and supervision followed by the ILO, Wolf, *Human Rights and the International Labour Organisation*, in 2 HUMAN RIGHTS IN INTERNATIONAL LAW: LEGAL AND POLICY ISSUES (T. Meron ed. forthcoming) [hereinafter cited as HUMAN RIGHTS IN INTERNATIONAL LAW]; Wolf, *Aspects judiciaires de la protection internationale des droits de l'homme par l'O.I.T.*, 4 REV. DROITS DE L'HOMME 773 (1971); the incorporation by reference in Art. 15 of the Convention on Human Rights and Fundamental Freedoms (European Convention on Human Rights), 213 UNTS 221, *reprinted in* Brownlie, *supra* note 3, at 242, of norms originating in human rights instruments established outside the framework of the Council of Europe, Buergenthal, *International and Regional Human Rights Law and Institutions: Some Examples of Their Interaction*, 12 TEX. INT'L L.J. 321, 324–25 (1977); and the broad principles that may be taken into consideration by the future African Commission on Human and Peoples' Rights under Arts. 60 and 61, African Charter on Human and Peoples' Rights, *approved* July 1981, *reprinted in* REV. INT'L COMM'N JURISTS, No. 27, Dec. 1981, at 76, 21 ILM 58 (1982). On the case law of the Court of Justice of the European Communities, see note 46 *infra*. *See* further discussion in text accompanying and following notes 46–50 and 102 *infra*.

It should be observed, however, that fact-finding bodies established by resolutions of international organs invoke "broadly recognized normative standards." Franck & Fairley, *supra* note 4, at 308. Thus, the Ad Hoc Working Group of Experts on Human Rights in Southern Africa of the Commission on Human Rights, when investigating allegations of infringements of trade union rights in South Africa, studied the applicable South African legislation in light of the UN Charter, the documents constituting the International Bill of Human Rights (*see* text following note 5), a number of relevant ILO conventions and declarations, the Racial Discrimination Convention, the International Convention on the Suppression and Punishment of the Crime of Apartheid, and the Standard Minimum Rules for the Treatment of Prisoners (GA Res. 415, 5 UN GAOR Supp. (No. 20) at 37, UN Doc. A/1775 (1950), ESC Res. 663 CI, 24 UN ESCOR Supp. (No. 1) at 11, UN Doc. E/3048 (1957)), UN Doc. E/CN.4/1486, at 3–5 (1982). These instruments were considered notwithstanding the fact that South Africa is not a party to the relevant conventions. The practice of fact-finding bodies of invoking instruments to which the "defendant" state is not a party has not been based on an articulated distinction between norms that have attained the status of customary international law and other norms. Have such instruments been invoked primarily as the applicable political rules or as the common law of mankind? These questions merit further study.

[6] GA Res. 217A, UN Doc. A/810, at 71 (1948).

[7] GA Res. 2200, 21 UN GAOR Supp. (No. 16) at 59, UN Doc. A/6316 (1966).

eration that has given rise to difficult questions of coordination within and between international organizations in the fields of budget, programming, and administration,[8] has led to overlapping jurisdiction and even to conflicts between the legislative and supervisory competence, or claims of competence, of various international bodies.[9] The object of this article is not to compile or map out all the possible conflict areas[10] or to undertake a detailed analysis of the conflicts, whether real or imaginary. Its more modest purpose is to present a broad panorama of the problems, directions, and policy. These matters merit attention, even though political and institutional reasons may make major reforms impossible for the time being. The questions to be discussed are relevant to three major fields of international law: treaties, human rights, and international organizations. While substantive problems of "legislation" or norm making are closely related to problems of supervision or implementation, normative problems will be focused upon first, and problems of supervision second.

II. Normative Conflicts

The development of an integrated system of international treaty law governing human rights has a number of goals. Such a system would prevent unnecessary duplication, conflicts between instruments, and variations in the interpretation and implementation of instruments adopted by different organizations; and it would ensure that statutory provisions on complex technical subjects are established and supervised by the most competent organizations.[11]

Attention must first be drawn to the fact that conflicts may arise between rights recognized in the same instrument, or between instruments of the same universal and hierarchical order, *e.g.*, the two Covenants,[12] particularly with

[8] *See, e.g.*, Sharp, *Program Coordination and the Economic and Social Council*, in UN Administration of Economic and Social Programs 102 (G. Mangone ed. 1966); Meron, *Administrative and Budgetary Coordination by the General Assembly*, in *id.* at 37; Meron, *Budget Approval by the General Assembly of the United Nations: Duty or Discretion?*, 42 Brit. Y.B. Int'l L. 91 (1967).

[9] For materials on this subject, see notes 43–45 and 72 *infra*.

[10] International Complaint System, Council of Europe Doc. CAHMP (80) 2 (1980), a Secretariat Information Memorandum prepared by the Directorate of Human Rights for the Ad Hoc Committee on the Multiplication of Complaint Procedures at the International Level of the Council of Europe, is a useful compilation.

[11] *See* Annual Report of the Administrative Committee on Co-ordination for 1973–1974, UN Doc. E/5488, at 51–52 (1974).

The 1973 report of the Ad Hoc Inter-Agency Meeting of Legal Experts on Co-ordination of Legislative Work of Organizations within the UN system suggested that the concept of "legislative work" should be interpreted

> in the widest sense as including all international and regional norms and standards designed to be applied by the member States of the various organizations, whether they were in the form of Conventions, Declarations, Recommendations, Resolutions and Regulations such as the International Health Regulations or Codex Alimentarius Standards, or model codes and other guides to national legislative activity.

Report of the *Ad Hoc* Inter-Agency Meeting of Legal Experts on Co-ordination of Legislative Work of Organizations, UN Doc. Co-ordination/R.1003, at 1 (1973) [hereinafter cited as Co-ordination Report].

[12] *See, e.g.*, Gastil, *quoted in* Meron, *A Report on the N.Y.U. Conference on Teaching International*

regard to the priority of classic human rights or social human rights.[13] While classic rights lend themselves, in principle, to immediate implementation, social rights can only be progressively implemented. This does not imply, of course, that classic rights are more important than social rights. It has been argued, not always bona fide, that developing states cannot be expected to implement the classic freedoms fully as long as they have not reached a level of economic development that enables them to implement social rights, and that those states must therefore give priority to social rights and to economic and social development in order to facilitate the realization of civil and political rights. However, the international instruments themselves attach equal weight to classic rights and social rights.[14] Furthermore, the UN General Assembly and the UN Commission on Human Rights have confirmed that human rights are indivisible and interdependent and that the same amount of attention should be given to civil and political as to economic, social, and cultural rights.[15] Nevertheless, on the political level this problem will continue to be troublesome.[16]

Another problem is posed by the overlap between comprehensive UN conventions and instruments of more limited scope adopted within the specialized agencies. Comprehensive UN conventions are often expressed in terms of general principles and the means of their implementation left to national discretion[17] or to the specialized agencies, particularly the International Labour Organisation (ILO). The ILO has argued that they might well result in eroding the more precise international obligations created by the more limited or specialized instruments, without formally contradicting them.[18] Jenks, who was in part responsible for the general language of the Economic Covenant, has observed that the two Covenants afford substantially less protection as regards certain stipulated rights than the relevant international labor con-

---

Protection of Human Rights, 13 N.Y.U. J. INT'L L. & POL. 881, 905 (1981) [hereinafter cited as Meron Report].

[13] For the distinction between classic human rights (civil and political) and social human rights (including economic and cultural), see MINISTRY OF FOREIGN AFFAIRS OF THE NETHERLANDS, HUMAN RIGHTS AND FOREIGN POLICY 93–94 (1979); Trubek, *Economic, Social and Cultural Rights in the Third World: Human Rights Law and Human Needs Programs,* in 1 HUMAN RIGHTS IN INTERNATIONAL LAW, *supra* note 5. The distinction between classic and social human rights should not be equated with that between individual and collective rights. *See* Humphrey, *Political and Related Rights,* in *id.*

[14] *See, e.g.,* the Preamble to the Economic Covenant; the Preamble to the Political Covenant.

[15] *See* GA Res. 32/130, 32 UN GAOR Supp. (No. 45) at 150, UN Doc. A/32/45 (1977), *discussed in* Donnelly, *Recent Trends in UN Human Rights Activity: Description and Polemic,* 35 INT'L ORG. 633 (1981); Comm'n on Human Rights Res. 36 (XXXVII), operative para. 2, UN Doc. E/CN.4/L.1561/Add.4, at 22, 24 (1981). *See also* Dinstein, *quoted in* Meron Report, *supra* note 12, at 891.

[16] *See generally* Alston, *Development and the Rule of Law: Prevention Versus Cure as a Human Rights Strategy,* in DEVELOPMENT, HUMAN RIGHTS AND THE RULE OF LAW 31, 47–54 (1981). *See also* Trubek, *supra* note 13, at nn.79–80.

[17] *See* Co-ordination Report, *supra* note 11, Ann. II, at 3.

[18] *Ibid. See* Jenks, *Human Rights, Social Justice and Peace: The Broader Significance of the I.L.O. Experience,* in INTERNATIONAL PROTECTION OF HUMAN RIGHTS 227, 246, 251–52 (A. Eide & A. Schou eds. 1968).

ventions.[19] Moreover, since each organization has its own machinery of supervision and many areas of human rights fall within the shared or concurrent competence of several organizations, governments may receive varying or conflicting guidance.[20]

Problems regarding the relationship between a convention adopted in one organization and a subsequent convention adopted in another cannot be resolved by the simplistic application of such provisions as Articles 30, 41, 58, and 59 of the Vienna Convention on the Law of Treaties;[21] more specific solutions are needed. The ILO has observed that many of the instruments adopted within the framework of the UN family create legal ties not only between ratifying states but also between such states and the organization concerned, which makes these provisions of the Vienna Convention largely inapplicable. The ILO has stated that "one cannot conceive of an international labour convention relating to one of the fundamental human rights . . . being modified in respect of the mutual relations of some of the parties thereto by an *inter se* agreement among them."[22]

Problems of overlap or conflict of norms can be avoided, or at least reduced, through appropriate drafting techniques. Whenever legislative abstention is not possible, legislative cross-references or saving clauses (such as Article 24 of the Economic Covenant[23] and its counterpart, Article 46 of the Political Covenant[24]) should be resorted to.[25] An early example of a legislative cross-reference, admirable in its simplicity, is Article 21 of the Regulations annexed to the fourth Hague Convention with respect to the Laws and Customs of War on Land of 1907.[26] It provides that "[t]he obligations of belligerents with regard to the sick and wounded are governed by the Geneva Convention."

Recent clauses designed to avoid conflicts have not been uniform. Some aim at saving only the more advantageous provisions of other instruments. Thus, the saving clause of the Convention on the Elimination of All Forms of Discrimination against Women (Discrimination against Women Convention) provides that nothing in it shall affect any provisions in any other inter-

[19] Jenks, *supra* note 18, at 252.

[20] Co-ordination Report, *supra* note 11, Ann. II, at 3.

[21] UN Doc. A/CONF.39/27 (1969), UN Doc. A/CONF.39/27/Corr.1 (1969), *reprinted in* 63 AJIL 875 (1969), 8 ILM 679 (1969) (Art. 30 concerns application of successive treaties relating to the same subject matter; Art. 41 concerns agreements to modify multilateral treaties between certain of the parties only; Art. 58 concerns suspension of the operation of a multilateral treaty by agreement between certain of the parties only; Art. 59 concerns termination or suspension of the operation of a treaty implied by conclusion of a later treaty).

[22] Co-ordination Report, *supra* note 11, Ann. II, at 10.

[23] Article 24 reads as follows:

> Nothing in the present Covenant shall be interpreted as impairing the provisions of the Charter of the United Nations and of the constitutions of the specialized agencies which define the respective responsibilities of the various organs of the United Nations and of the specialized agencies in regard to the matters dealt with in the present Covenant.

[24] The text is identical to Art. 24, *ibid.*

[25] *See* Co-ordination Report, *supra* note 11, Ann. II, at 7–8.

[26] 36 Stat. 2277, TS No. 539.

national agreement "that are more conducive to the achievement of equality between men and women."[27] Certain other saving clauses refer only to specific instruments. The Declaration on the Elimination of All Forms of Intolerance and of Discrimination Based on Religion or Belief provides that nothing in it "shall be construed as restricting or derogating from any right defined in the Universal Declaration of Human Rights and the International Covenants on Human Rights."[28] Should a similar provision be included in a future convention on religious discrimination, normative conflicts might arise between rights arising under that future convention and those conferred by other conventions. Suppose, for example, that the future convention on religious discrimination permits a certain type of discrimination against women to continue because of religious beliefs. Suppose, further, that the Discrimination against Women Convention prohibits this type of discrimination, but that such a prohibition is not adequately spelled out in either of the two Covenants. Which of the two conventions will prevail if such a question arises before a suitable control organ?

The drafting of pro forma avoidance-of-conflict clauses is therefore not satisfactory. The clauses must be phrased so as to avoid or resolve conflicts. If the difficulty is not resolved by drafting, it must be explained by substantive or political, rather than technical, considerations. These include lack of coordination within national governments, special interests of international organizations, and the "empire building" tendencies of international secretariats. (Drafting techniques will be further considered in section V below.)

Conflicts between the legislative activities of the United Nations and those of the specialized agencies reflect the overlap between certain provisions of the Charter and some of the broad constitutional provisions of the specialized agencies particularly concerned with human rights, *e.g.*, the ILO,[29] the United Nations Educational, Scientific and Cultural Organization (UNESCO),[30] and the World Health Organization (WHO).[31] This overlapping character becomes especially noticeable if one considers the goals of the organizations, the vagueness of the relationship agreements concluded between the United Nations and the specialized agencies,[32] and the autonomy and independent legal

[27] Art. 23, Discrimination against Women Convention, *supra* note 4. This may not always be easy to determine, as is shown by discussion of an earlier version of Article 23. *See* UN Doc. E/5938, at 2 (1977).

[28] GA Res. 36/55, UN Doc. A/RES/36/55, Art. 8 (1981).

[29] 62 Stat. 3485, TIAS No. 1868, 15 UNTS 35; *amended by* 7 UST 245, TIAS No. 3500, 191 UNTS 143 (1953); 14 UST 1039, TIAS No. 5401, 466 UNTS 323 (1962); 25 UST 3253, TIAS No. 7987 (1972) (ILO Constitution). The constitutions of the specialized agencies are collected in A. PEASLEE, INTERNATIONAL GOVERNMENTAL ORGANIZATIONS: CONSTITUTIONAL DOCUMENTS (3d rev. ed. 1974).

[30] 61 Stat. 2495, TIAS No. 1580, 4 UNTS 275; *amended by* 6 UST 6157, TIAS No. 3469, 575 UNTS 270 (1954); 10 UST 959, TIAS No. 4230, 575 UNTS 252; 22 UST 1699, TIAS No. 7197 (1968); 29 UST 3379, TIAS No. 9016 (1972); 29 UST 3384, TIAS No. 9017 (1976) (UNESCO Constitution).

[31] 62 Stat. 2679, TIAS No. 1808, 14 UNTS 185; *amended by* 26 UST 990, TIAS No. 8086 (1967); 28 UST 2088, TIAS No. 8534 (1973) (WHO Constitution).

[32] *See* Agreements Between the United Nations and the Specialized Agencies and the International Atomic Energy Agency, UN Doc. ST/SG/14 (1961). On the activities of the specialized

personality of each of the specialized agencies.[33] During the last few years the specialized agencies have increasingly complained that the General Assembly "is legislating more and more, and in ever greater detail" in fields that "are clearly the responsibility" of one of the specialized agencies,[34] which may lead to "confusion, overlapping of activities and even conflicting decisions."[35] With regard to UNESCO, for example, such conflicts have resulted from UN activities involving the right to education,[36] the right to information,[37] and the rights to science and technology.[38] UNESCO has asserted that these activities encroach on its Constitution and tend to modify the functionally decentralized system established by the UN Charter, the constitutive instruments of the specialized agencies, and the relationship agreements. Similar conflicts have also arisen between the United Nations and the ILO, for example, concerning the rights of migrant workers.[39]

---

agencies in the field of human rights, see UN Doc. E/CN.4/1193 (1976); UN Doc. E/CN.4/1433 (1980).

[33] For a proposal to review the various relationship agreements, see UN Doc. E/1981/3, para. 73 (1980).

[34] UNESCO Doc. 110/EX/19, para. 67 (1980).

[35] Director-General of UNESCO, *quoted in* UN Doc. A/AC.198/13, para. 20 (1980).

[36] *See* UN Doc. A/35/148 (1980); UNESCO Doc. 110/EX/19, para. 68 (1980).

[37] *See* UN Doc. A/35/362 (1980); UN Doc. A/AC.198/13, paras. 21–22 (1980).

[38] *See* UNESCO Doc. 109/EX/22 (1980); UNESCO Doc. 109/EX/Dec.5.3.2 (1980).

[39] Following the adoption of GA Res. 32/197, on Restructuring of the Economic and Social Sectors of the United Nations System, 32 UN GAOR Supp. (No. 45) at 121, UN Doc. A/32/45 (1977), the International Organisations Committee of the Governing Body of the ILO found it necessary to emphasize that the relationship agreement between the ILO and the United Nations recognizes the competence of the ILO, as defined in its Constitution, as an autonomous organization, with its own international personality. ILO Doc. GB.212/IO/1/9, para. 2(a) (1980).

Measures taken by the General Assembly towards formulating a new UN convention on the protection of rights of all migrant workers exemplify the conflicts in the legislative standard-setting context. GA Res. 34/172, 34 UN GAOR Supp. (No. 46) at 188, UN Doc. A/34/46 (1979). In response to that resolution, the ILO emphasized that its constitutional mandate had always included the protection of migrant workers and that "it would be preferable for standard-setting for the protection of migrant workers to continue to be entrusted to the ILO, as the agency with specific constitutional responsibility for this question." ILO Doc. GB.212/IO/1/8, para. 17 (1980). Many delegations at the General Assembly, however, were of the view that existing instruments had a "sectoral" approach, such as those of the ILO in labor and those of UNESCO in education. These delegations aimed at establishing a new instrument covering the whole range of political, civil, cultural, economic, and social aspects of the rights of migrant workers. *See id.*, para. 19.

On the work of the ILO for the protection of migrant workers, see UN Doc. A/C.3/35/1 (1980); INTERNATIONAL LABOUR CONFERENCE, SURVEY OF THE REPORTS RELATING TO CONVENTIONS NOS. 97 AND 143 AND RECOMMENDATIONS NOS. 86 AND 151 CONCERNING MIGRANT WORKERS (Report III, Part 4B, 66th Sess., 1980); INTERNATIONAL LABOUR OFFICE, INTERNATIONAL LABOUR STANDARDS 36 (1978). *See generally* Valticos, *The Role of the ILO: Present Action and Future Perspectives*, in HUMAN RIGHTS THIRTY YEARS AFTER THE UNIVERSAL DECLARATION 212 (B. Ramcharan ed. 1979).

Jenks was of the view that "[m]ost of the substantive rights provided for in the Covenant on Economic, Social and Cultural Rights fall, as the procedural provisions of the Covenant recognise, within the competence and specialised experience of one of the specialised agencies." Jenks, *supra* note 18, at 247. It was his expectation that fuller implementation of such rights would require the conclusion of further special conventions under the auspices of the appropriate specialized agencies, *e.g.*, the Convention against Discrimination in Education adopted by UNESCO in 1960, 429 UNTS 93, *reprinted in* Brownlie, *supra* note 3, at 234. Jenks, *supra* note 18, at 247. On the

In aiming at legislative coordination and the integration of systems of supervision of human rights, one must be careful not to prevent or impede the raising of standards. Regional organizations sometimes improve upon global conventions. For instance, the regulations of the European Communities regarding the social security of migrant workers go beyond the more general standards established in the relevant international labor conventions.[40]

One should not assume, however, that the rights recognized under regional instruments are necessarily more comprehensive than the rights recognized by the UN Covenants. Thus, the European Convention on Human Rights and its Protocols[41] safeguard 19 different rights, while the Political Covenant safeguards 23.[42] The two instruments protect a number of the same rights and their definitions are broadly similar. Yet, there is a risk of conflict between the regimes, resulting either from the lack of conformity between the definitions themselves or from differences in international procedures to protect the rights, particularly as interpreted by the control bodies.[43] The risk of substantive conflict may also be increased by divergencies in the interpretation and application of limitations that may be imposed on various rights, *e.g.*, in the name of public order or national security. It is in the development of control institutions and procedures, which involve adjudication and legally binding decisions, that the European system of protection of human rights is far in advance of the global system[44] (though the institutional inferiority of the Covenants has been partly compensated for by their normative superiority

---

basis of Articles 18, 20–22, and 24 of the Economic Covenant, Jenks concluded, with regard to implementation, that the specialized agencies "potentially" are "the executing agencies of the Covenant . . . with a major share of the responsibility for its effective implementation." *Id.* at 250. *See also Comparative Analysis of the International Covenants on Human Rights and International Labour Conventions and Recommendations*, 52 ILO O. BULL. 181 (1969).

[40] *See* Co-ordination Report, *supra* note 11, Ann. II, at 3. *See also* Jenks, *supra* note 18, at 248.

[41] The five Protocols to the European Convention on Human Rights are *reprinted in* Brownlie, *supra* note 3, at 257–65.

[42] *See* Council of Europe Doc. CAHMP (80) 1, at 5 (1980).

[43] *Contra*, Eissen, *The European Convention on Human Rights and the United Nations Covenant on Civil and Political Rights: Problems of Coexistence*, 22 BUFFALO L. REV. 181, 209 (1972).

[44] It should be noted that the Council of Europe is now exploring the possibility of extending the list of rights of the individual, notably rights in the social, economic, and cultural fields, which should be protected by the European Convention on Human Rights or any other appropriate means. *See* UN Doc. E/CN.4/1450, at 19–20 (1981). The present stage of the work being done on "extension" of human rights is described in Council of Europe Doc. H/ONG (82) 3. It may be observed, in this context, that the European Convention on Human Rights, which essentially covers rights that can be described as civil or political, is endowed with a machinery for judicial control, whereas the European Social Charter, Europ. TS No. 35, *reprinted in* Brownlie, *supra* note 3, at 301, which covers essentially economic and social rights, provides only for a supervisory machinery that may lead to adoption of recommendations. *See* Reply from the Committee of Ministers to Recommendation 838 (1978), Council of Europe Doc. H/Inf. (79) 4, App. III, at 21 (1979). *See generally* Report of the Committee of Experts on Human Rights to the Committee of Ministers on Problems Arising from the Co-existence of the United Nations Covenants on Human Rights and the European Convention on Human Rights, Council of Europe Doc. H (70) 7 (1970); COUNCIL OF EUROPE, DIRECTORATE OF HUMAN RIGHTS, PROCEEDINGS OF THE COLLOQUY ABOUT THE EUROPEAN CONVENTION ON HUMAN RIGHTS IN RELATION TO OTHER INTERNATIONAL INSTRUMENTS FOR THE PROTECTION OF HUMAN RIGHTS, ATHENS, 21–22 SEPTEMBER 1978 (1979) [hereinafter cited as PROC. OF THE COLLOQUY].

in some respects[45]). There is no policy reason why a regional organization should not be able to confer broader rights than universal organizations. The goal of uniformity should not lead to the acceptance of the lowest common denominator.

The multiplicity of norms may be advantageous, at times, because it allows the individual to seek out the most favorable provision. In certain cases it may be possible to apply the most favorable norm in procedure *A* even if it originates in system *B*. Through a gradual and rather indirect process, the Court of Justice of the European Communities has applied some of the substantive provisions of the European Convention on Human Rights when those provisions were more favorable to the individual concerned.[46] Unfortunately, as

[45] Eissen, *supra* note 43, at 184. Buergenthal points out that the American Convention on Human Rights contains a longer catalog of human rights than the European Convention. *The Inter-American System for the Protection of Human Rights*, in 2 HUMAN RIGHTS IN INTERNATIONAL LAW, *supra* note 5. *See generally* Buergenthal, *supra* note 5; Tardu, *The Protocol to the United Nations Covenant on Civil and Political Rights and the Inter-American System: A Study of Co-existing Petition Procedures*, 70 AJIL 778 (1976).

[46] The Luxembourg Court has applied not only the norms described in the Treaty of Rome, but also fundamental human rights contained in the general principles of Community law. *See* Stauder v. Ulm, 1969 ECR 419, 1970 Comm. Mkt. L.R. 112. The Court has also recognized that basic constitutional rights common to the member states of the Communities are part of the general principles of law that it protects. *See* Nold v. Commission, 1974 ECR 491, [1974] 2 Comm. Mkt. L.R. 338. In Rutili v. Minister of the Interior, 1975 ECR 1219, [1976] 1 Comm. Mkt. L.R. 140, the Court of Justice reached the question of the application of the provisions of the European Convention on Human Rights. The Court stated:

> [T]hese limitations placed on the powers of Member States in respect of control of aliens are a specific manifestation of the more general principle, enshrined in Articles 8, 9, 10 and 11 of the [European Convention on Human Rights], . . . which provide[s] . . . that no restrictions in the interests of national security or public safety shall be placed on the rights secured by the above-quoted articles other than such as are necessary for the protection of those interests "in a democratic society."

1975 ECR at 1232, [1976] 1 Comm. Mkt. L.R. at 155.

In Hauer v. Land Rheinland-Pfalz, 1979 ECR 3727, [1980] 3 Comm. Mkt. L.R. 42, which concerned a complaint that regulations promulgated by the Council of the European Communities prohibiting new plantings of vines violated Hauer's property rights, the Court of Justice referred to human rights treaties on which the member states of the European Communities had collaborated or to which they were parties, and discussed and interpreted Article 1 of Protocol No. 1 to the European Convention on Human Rights. In this further and more specific application to the law of the European Communities of human rights norms established outside of the framework of the European Communities, the Court of Justice stated that it had

> also emphasized in [Internationale Handelsgesellschaft, 1970 ECR 1125], and later in . . . *Nold* . . . , that fundamental rights form an integral part of the general principles of the law, the observance of which it ensures; that in safeguarding those rights, the Court is bound to draw inspiration from constitutional traditions common to the Member States, so that measures which are incompatible with the fundamental rights recognized by the constitutions of those States are unacceptable in the Community; and that, similarly, international treaties for the protection of human rights on which the Member States have collaborated or of which they are signatories, can supply guidelines which should be followed within the framework of Community law.

1979 ECR at 3744–45, [1980] 3 Comm. Mkt. L.R. at 64. The Court of Justice considered the right to property to be already indicated in the introduction and discussed further in the concluding observations, most supervisory organs apply only the body of norms stated in the instruments under which they were established. Where the scope of the applicable norms cannot be extended by the case law or rules of procedure of a particular organ, the possibility of doing so by a special protocol should be considered. Such extension requires, of course, that the state concerned accept the relevant norms through the special protocol.

A special protocol must be drafted with a view to avoiding conflicts with the founding or the constituent instrument. In some cases it may be difficult to reconcile the terms of these two instruments. This question has recently arisen over proposals to make the Human Rights Committee established under the Political Covenant an implementation organ of the proposed convention against torture and other cruel, inhuman or degrading treatment or punishment,[47] which would require it to apply norms created under this convention.

The Legal Counsel of the United Nations advised that the "legal validity [of such a solution] could be challenged on the ground that it constitutes a modification of the terms of the Covenant which has established the Human Rights Committee and defined its terms of reference. Such modification can only be effected by the procedure specified in article 51 of the Covenant."[48] He appeared to be suggesting that, as a treaty organ, the Human Rights Committee may function according to the terms of the Political Covenant only, and that it is "not sufficient . . . that there is a general concordance in

---

> guaranteed in the Community legal order in accordance with the ideas common to the constitutions of the Member States, which are also reflected in the first Protocol to the European Convention for the Protection of Human Rights.
>
> . . . .
>
> . . . [T]he second paragraph of Article 1 of the Protocol provides an important indication in so far as it recognizes the right of a State "to enforce such laws as it deems necessary to control the use of property in accordance with the general interest." Thus the Protocol accepts in principle the legality of restrictions upon the use of property, whilst at the same time limiting those restrictions to the extent to which they are deemed "necessary" by a State for the protection of the "general interest."

1979 ECR at 3745–46, [1980] 3 Comm. Mkt. L.R. at 64–65.

The Court of Justice then considered the constitutional rules and practices of the (then) nine member states, and particularly the legislative measures that have given concrete expression to the social function of the right to property, such as restrictions on the use of agricultural or forest land. It concluded that the relevant regulation could not be challenged in principle since it "is a type of restriction which is known and accepted as lawful, in identical or similar forms, in the constitutional structure of all the Member States." 1979 ECR at 3747, [1980] 3 Comm. Mkt. L.R. at 66.

See generally Lecourt, *Interferences Between the European Convention on Human Rights and the Community Law Concerning the Community and National Judicial Control*, in PROC. OF THE COLLOQUY, *supra* note 44 at 81, 92–94; E. STEIN, P. HAY, & M. WAELBROECK, EUROPEAN COMMUNITY LAW AND INSTITUTIONS IN PERSPECTIVE 136–40, 274–302 (1976); Dowrick, *Overlapping International and European Laws*, 31 INT'L & COMP. L.Q. 59, 81–82 (1982). Regarding the possible accession by the European Community to the European Convention on Human Rights, see Brown & McBride, *Observations on the Proposed Accession by the European Community to the European Convention on Human Rights*, 29 AM. J. COMP. L. 691 (1981).

[47] *See* UN Doc. E/CN.4/1982/L.40, para. 54 (1982). *See also* note 4 *supra* and note 106 *infra*.

[48] UN Doc. E/CN.4/WG.2/WP/6 (1981).

purpose between the proposed convention and article 7 of the [Political] Covenant."[49]

The question arises, however, whether a distinction should not be made between modifying the powers of the Human Rights Committee as a Covenant organ and conferring authority on it by means of another instrument concluded by members of the United Nations, apart from the Covenant, to apply other norms. It may be argued that the Human Rights Committee should be allowed to exercise such authority with regard to states that have so agreed through a special protocol or another instrument, especially since the Human Rights Committee is financed under the UN budget and is serviced by officials of the UN Secretariat.

Some might argue that the United States would be faced with a constitutional issue if such a special protocol incorporated other human rights instruments by specific reference and the United States became a party to it but not to the other instruments. Would the United States have to ratify the several incorporated instruments separately before becoming legally bound by them?[50] If the special protocol set out *de novo* the relevant norms, the constitutional issue might be avoided, but the special protocol would then be even more difficult to draft.

III. Supervision and Control

The purposes of rationalizing and coordinating the systems of supervision of human rights are similar to the goals of integrating the treaty law on human rights, as described in section II. Duplication and conflicts of interpretation should be avoided. Supervision of compliance should be entrusted to those organizations with the greatest technical competence in the field. Finally, conflicts should be resolved, both those regarding complaints submitted by one state against another and those regarding applications by individual complainants, which are of growing practical importance because of the multiplicity of existing procedures.

The UN General Assembly, the UN Commission on Human Rights, the UN Secretariat, and other international organs are committed to improving the coordination of their activities, but so far no significant reforms appear to have been made.[51]

It should not be assumed that jurisdictional conflicts arise only between the United Nations and the specialized agencies or between the organizations

[49] *Ibid.* Article 7 of the Political Covenant spells out the prohibition of torture.

[50] *See generally* U.S. Const. art. II, §2, cl. 2.

[51] *See* GA Res. 33/54, 33 UN GAOR Supp. (No. 45) at 144, UN Doc. A/33/45 (1978); GA Res. 34/25, 34 UN GAOR Supp. (No. 46) at 164, UN Doc. A/34/46 (1979); Comm'n on Human Rights Res. 22 (XXXV), 35 UN ESCOR Supp. (No. 6) at 128, UN Doc. E/1979/36 (1979). For an analysis of existing UN procedures for dealing with communications concerning violations of human rights, see UN Doc. E/CN.4/1317 (1979). Regarding coordination of systems of compliance, see UN Doc. E/CN.4/1193 (1976); UN Doc. E/CN.4/1433 (1980). A useful description of the practical measures of coordination and collaboration between international organizations in the area of human rights is contained in F. Wolf, Building the Law of the World: A Look at the Process (World Association of Lawyers of the World Peace Through Law Center, Washington, D.C., 1976).

belonging to the UN system and regional organizations. They also arise within the United Nations itself. Thus, in 1979 the Government of Chile asserted that the procedures of the Ad Hoc Working Group on the Situation of Human Rights in Chile, established pursuant to resolutions of the General Assembly and the Commission on Human Rights, conflicted with the procedure on Chile undertaken under Economic and Social Council (ECOSOC) Resolution 1503,[52] and that the situation in the country should be considered exclusively under the Political Covenant, to which Chile was a party.[53]

In replying to these claims, the special rapporteur on human rights in Chile, Abdoulaye Diéye, took the position that a government cannot stipulate under what procedure the domestic human rights situation should be examined. He stated that the procedure established under ECOSOC Resolution 1503 was complementary to other preexisting and subsequent procedures established by the United Nations, just as the procedure established under ECOSOC Resolution 1235[54] complemented that established under ECOSOC Resolution 1503.[55] He further pointed out that Chile had neither made a declaration under Article 41 of the Political Covenant nor ratified the Optional Protocol. Since the Human Rights Committee could only examine reports submitted by the Chilean Government, rather than communications from another party under Article 41 of the Political Covenant or from individuals alleging violations by Chile of Covenant obligations under the Optional Protocol, "[t]he Government cannot therefore plead that the procedures established under the International Covenant on Civil and Political Rights should be applied to the situation in Chile in exclusion of other procedures which the United Nations may consider appropriate to deal with that situation."[56] The special rapporteur thus strongly defended the multiplicity of investigatory procedures.[57]

Golsong has illustrated the complexity of these issues:

> If you take the possible overlapping of procedures . . . [of] supervision over states vis-à-vis freedom of association, the following provisions may be applicable: article 8 of the Covenant on Economic, Social and Cultural Rights, article 22 of the Civil and Political Rights Covenant, a variety

[52] 48 UN ESCOR Supp. (No. 1A) at 8, UN Doc. E/4832/Add.1 (1970). Under this resolution, the Sub-Commission on Prevention of Discrimination and Protection of Minorities of the Commission on Human Rights was empowered to appoint a working group that would consider communications "which appear to reveal a consistent pattern of gross and reliably attested violations of human rights and fundamental freedoms." *Ibid.* Consideration of such communications does not depend on whether the concerned state is a party to any of the instruments on human rights. *See* RESTATEMENT OF THE FOREIGN RELATIONS LAW OF THE UNITED STATES (REVISED) §702, Reporters' Note 8 (Tent. Draft No. 3, 1982). *See also* discussion at note 5 *supra*.

[53] *See* UN Doc. A/34/503, paras. 1–3 (1979).

[54] 42 UN ESCOR Supp. (No. 1) at 17, UN Doc. E/4393 (1967).

[55] *See* UN Doc. A/34/503, paras. 9–11 (1979). *See generally* Comm'n on Human Rights Res. 11 (XXXV), 35 UN ESCOR Supp. (No. 6) at 115, UN Doc. E/1979/36 (1979).

[56] *See* UN Doc. A/34/503, para. 12 (1979). For the consideration by the Human Rights Committee of the reports submitted by Chile under Article 40 of the Political Covenant and the question of admissible sources of information, see Robertson, *supra* note 4, at 347–48.

[57] For a similar view, see UN Doc. CCPR/C/SR.78, at 7 (1978) (statement by Uribe Vargas in the Human Rights Committee).

> of ILO standards and, if it is a question of freedom of association of teachers, various UNESCO documents. All of these are procedurally and substantively different. And on top of that you have the situation occurring in Europe—you can operate under article 11 of the European Convention on Human Rights, or under article 6 of the European Social Charter.[58]

Regarding implementation and supervision, attention must be called to Article 44 of the Political Covenant[59] (interstate complaints), and to Article 5(2)(a) of the Optional Protocol[60] (individual applications) and Articles 18 through 22 of the Economic Covenant as well. The Political Covenant probably does not prohibit states that are parties to it and that have recognized the competence of the Human Rights Committee with regard to interstate complaints under Article 41 from referring disputes over the interpretation or application of the Covenant to other means of settlement, including the International Court of Justice.[61]

Sohn has observed that the Political Covenant shows "preference for applying United Nations procedures only in cases where other procedures are not available. In particular, the procedures developed by the specialized agencies . . . are given triple protection."[62] In Sohn's view it would not be desirable to provide for an appeal to the United Nations from a final and binding decision rendered under the auspices of a specialized agency, but resort to appropriate UN procedures should be possible if no settlement is reached under a specialized agency's procedure or if that procedure does not result in a final and binding decision.[63]

In addition to the customary stipulation that individual cases will not be considered unless all available domestic remedies have been exhausted, some instruments provide that matters that are already being examined under another international procedure will not be considered. Although Article 44 of the Political Covenant does not specifically include the procedures of regional organizations among those that are not preempted by the Covenant, which deprives those organizations of the "preferred status" enjoyed by the specialized agencies under that article, Buergenthal has correctly suggested that this omission has little practical significance.[64] Article 5(2)(a) of the Optional

[58] Meron Report, *supra* note 12, at 930 (footnotes omitted).

[59] Article 44 reads as follows:

> The provisions for the implementation of the present Covenant shall apply without prejudice to the procedures prescribed in the field of human rights by or under the constituent instruments and the conventions of the United Nations and of the specialized agencies and shall not prevent the States Parties to the present Covenant from having recourse to other procedures for settling a dispute in accordance with general or special international agreements in force between them.

[60] *See* note 65 *infra*.

[61] *See* Robertson, *supra* note 4, at 355–56. It has been suggested that unless an international human rights agreement provides or clearly implies the contrary, special remedies under it generally supplement rather than replace the traditional remedies available between states. RESTATEMENT, *supra* note 52, §703, Comment *a*.

[62] Sohn, *Human Rights: Their Implementation and Supervision by the United Nations*, in 2 HUMAN RIGHTS IN INTERNATIONAL LAW, *supra* note 5.

[63] *See id.*

[64] *See* Buergenthal, *supra* note 5, at 327–28.

Protocol,[65] however, may be interpreted as embracing regional procedures.[66] The preference it assigns to other procedures should be interpreted as a temporary restriction, applicable while the case is pending before another international body, rather than as an absolute prohibition on examination of a particular matter.

These propositions are supported by the practice of the Human Rights Committee.[67] A case in point involved the argument by Uruguay that a matter communicated to the Committee was already being examined by the Inter-American Commission on Human Rights. The Committee regarded the communication as admissible because cases concerning the alleged victims had been withdrawn and were no longer under active consideration by the regional body.[68] The Committee therefore determined that it is not precluded from considering a communication if the same matter has been withdrawn from or is no longer being examined under another procedure of international investigation or settlement by the time that the Committee reaches a decision on the admissibility of that communication.[69] More important, in so doing, the Human Rights Committee recognized that cases considered by the Inter-American Commission on Human Rights under the appropriate governing instruments are examined in accordance with "another procedure of international investigation or settlement" within the meaning of Article 5(2)(a) of the Optional Protocol.[70]

The question of what constitutes "another procedure of international investigation or settlement" within the meaning of Article 5(2)(a) of the Optional Protocol has also arisen in other contexts. The Human Rights Committee has determined that the procedure set up under ECOSOC Resolution 1503 does not constitute such a procedure,"since it is concerned with the examination of situations which appear to reveal a consistent pattern of gross violations of human rights and a situation is not 'the same matter' as an individual complaint."[71] While agreeing with its conclusions, this author feels that the Committee has interpreted Resolution 1503 rather too narrowly as regards consideration of individual communications.[72] The Committee has also deter-

[65] Article 5(2)(a) provides that "[t]he [Human Rights] Committee shall not consider any communication from an individual unless it has ascertained that . . . [t]he same matter is not being examined under another procedure of international investigation or settlement."

[66] *See* Buergenthal, *supra* note 5, at 328; Sohn, *supra* note 62.

[67] *See* Rule 90(1)(e) and Rule 90(2) of the Rules of Procedure of the Human Rights Committee, UN Doc. CCPR/C/3/Rev.1 (1979). For a discussion of the interpretation of draft Rule 92(2) concerning later review of a determination of inadmissibility, see Report of the Human Rights Committee, 32 UN GAOR Supp. (No. 44) at 12–13, UN Doc. A/32/44 (1977). *See generally* Robertson, *supra* note 4, at 364–69.

[68] *See* Report of the Human Rights Committee, 34 UN GAOR Supp. (No. 40) at 124, 126, UN Doc. A/34/40 (1979). For similar rulings, see, *e.g.*, Report of the Human Rights Committee, 35 UN GAOR Supp. (No. 40) at 111, 112–13, 123, UN Doc. A/35/40 (1980).

[69] *See* Report of the Human Rights Committee, 33 UN GAOR Supp. (No. 40) at 100, UN Doc. A/33/40 (1978).

[70] *See id.* at 99–100.

[71] *Id.* at 100.

[72] For materials that support this criticism, see L. SOHN & T. BUERGENTHAL, INTERNATIONAL PROTECTION OF HUMAN RIGHTS 845–56 (1973); UN Doc. E/CN.4/1317 (1979). Tardu correctly suggests that the aim of the other procedure of international investigation must be to reach

mined that Article 5(2)(a) relates only to procedures implemented by interstate or intergovernmental agreements or arrangements; procedures established by nongovernmental organizations cannot bar consideration by the Committee of communications submitted to it under the Optional Protocol.[73]

A new problem is whether the procedure for the consideration of violations of human rights established in 1978 under Decision 104/EX/3.3 of the Executive Board of UNESCO constitutes a procedure of international investigation or settlement for the purposes of Article 5(2)(a) of the Optional Protocol. The UNESCO procedure allows examination both of massive and systematic violations and of individual and specific violations.[74] In presenting the new procedure to the UN Human Rights Committee, the representative of UNESCO argued that since the procedure had no "legal character," and since UNESCO's role was not that of an international judicial body, UNESCO did not consider it necessary to specify the conditions of admissibility of communications, as is done in Article 5(2)(a) of the Optional Protocol.[75] UNESCO's view seems to be that it will not be precluded from examining a communication submitted to its Committee on Conventions and Recommendations under Decision 104/EX/3.3 on the ground that the same matter is being examined by the Human Rights Committee.

Not surprisingly, UNESCO's position was questioned by several members of the Human Rights Committee.[76] The Committee has not yet reached a decision as to whether the UNESCO procedure constitutes "another procedure of international investigation or settlement," but it did state that the ultimate interpretation of Article 5(2)(a) fell within its jurisdiction.[77]

---

conclusions on specific cases. *See* 2 M. TARDU, HUMAN RIGHTS: THE INTERNATIONAL PETITION SYSTEM, pt. 1, §I, at 60 (1980). Regarding the examination by the Commission on Human Rights of the case of *Jehovah's Witnesses in Malawi* under ECOSOC Res. 1503, see Report of the Commission on Human Rights, 36 UN ESCOR Supp. (No. 3) at 91, UN Doc. E/1980/13 (1980). *See also* Robertson, *supra* note 4, at 358.

[73] *See* 1978 Report of the Human Rights Committee, *supra* note 69, at 100.

[74] *See* UNESCO Doc. 104/EX/Dec.3.3, para. 10 (1978).

[75] *See* UN Doc. CCPR/C/SR.78, at 6 (1978). The Director of the UNESCO Division of Human Rights and Peace stated:

> The problem of litispendence raised by Article 5, paragraph 2(a), of the Optional Protocol . . . concerned the procedure provided for in 104 EX/Decision 3.3 only in so far as the latter was regarded as constituting a "procedure of international investigation or settlement" within the meaning of that provision of the Optional Protocol. It was for the Human Rights Committee to decide on that point. In any event, UNESCO was not legally bound to suspend the examination of a communication in accordance with 104 EX/Decision 3.3 on the ground that it was already being examined by the Human Rights Committee.

UNESCO Doc. 107/EX/34, para. 45 (1979).

[76] *See* UN Doc. CCPR/C/SR.78, at 6–8 (1978). Paragraph 14(a)(x) of the UNESCO Decision 104/EX/3.3 procedure provides that communications relating to matters that have been settled by the states concerned in accordance with principles set forth in the Universal Declaration of Human Rights and the Covenants shall not be considered, but does not exclude examination of matters under consideration by another international body. *But see* the statement by the representative of UNESCO that paragraph 14(a)(x) was designed to avoid conflict with other bodies. UN Doc. CCPR/C/SR.78, at 9 (1978).

[77] *See* 1978 Report of the Human Rights Committee, *supra* note 69, at 105.

The UNESCO procedure has also aroused some concern about a possible overlap with the European system for the protection of human rights. The Council of Europe's Committee of Ministers has expressed the hope that, when implementing the new system, the competent authorities of UNESCO will not lose sight of the fact that some cases may have been or are being examined by another international organ, such as the European Commission of Human Rights.[78]

Problems of overlap and interaction arise not only between the various supervisory procedures of the United Nations and the specialized agencies, but also between global and regional instruments for the protection of human rights. The global instruments include not only the two UN Covenants, but also the more specialized UN conventions and instruments adopted under the auspices of the specialized agencies. The various investigatory procedures that originate in the resolutions of various organs,[79] rather than in treaties, should also be taken into account. Any one of them may conflict with parallel regional systems. In the inter-American system, the question of conflicts with procedures of other international organizations for the examination of petitions or communications is governed by Articles 46(1)(c) and 47(d) of the American Convention on Human Rights[80] and Article 36 of the Regulations of the Inter-American Commission on Human Rights,[81] which are discussed below in the concluding observations.

IV. The Interrelationship between the European and the Global Supervisory Systems

Sohn has rightly observed that the liberal attitude reflected in Article 44 of the Political Covenant and Article 5(2)(a) of the Optional Protocol can be

[78] *See* Council of Europe Doc. H/Inf. (79) 4, App. IV, at 27 (1979).

[79] *See* note 5 *supra*.

[80] OAS TS No. 36, *reprinted in* Brownlie, *supra* note 3, at 391, 9 ILM 673 (1970).

[81] *See* Buergenthal, *The Inter-American System for the Protection of Human Rights*, in 2 Human Rights in International Law, *supra* note 5. For the Regulations of the Inter-American Commission on Human Rights, see Organization of American States, Handbook of Existing Rules pertaining to Human Rights, OEA/Ser.L/V/II.50, doc.6, at 117 (1980).

For an interesting case of a waiver by the applicant government (Costa Rica) not only of the requirement of the prior exhaustion of domestic legal remedies but also of the application of Articles 48–50 of the American Convention on Human Rights, which require the prior exhaustion of procedures before the Inter-American Commission on Human Rights before a case may be referred to the Inter-American Court of Human Rights, see *In re* Viviana Gallardo, No. G 101/81 (Inter-American Ct. of Human Rights Nov. 13, 1981), *reprinted in* 20 ILM 1424 (1981), *discussed in* Buergenthal, *The Inter-American Court of Human Rights*, 76 AJIL 231, 239 (1982).

See also African Charter on Human and Peoples' Rights, *supra* note 5. The African Charter provides that the African Commission on Human and Peoples' Rights may only deal with communications from states concerning a violation of the African Charter if all local remedies are exhausted (Art. 50), but does not provide for matters being dealt with by another international procedure of investigation. However, the African Commission shall not consider communications from states parties that "deal with cases which have been settled by these [*sic*] States involved in accordance with the principles of the Charter of the United Nations, or the Charter of the Organization of African Unity or the provisions of the present Charter." Art. 56(7). These provisions increase the risk of overlap of procedures.

contrasted with the more restrictive approach reflected in Article 62 of the European Convention on Human Rights.[82]

Interstate Disputes

Under Article 62, the states parties to the European Convention on Human Rights may submit disputes arising out of the interpretation or application of the Convention only to a means of settlement provided for in the Convention (*i.e.*, the European Commission of Human Rights and possibly, after the Commission's decision, the European Court of Human Rights). They may not bring such disputes before other bodies such as the UN Human Rights Committee, the UN Committee on the Elimination of Racial Discrimination, the Conciliation and Good Offices Commission on Discrimination in Education of UNESCO, any of the various ILO organs, or even the International Court of Justice, except by special agreement.[83] The position of the Council of Europe and its organs has been that it is undesirable for states that have brought a case unsuccessfully under the European Convention on Human Rights later to refer the same matter to the Human Rights Committee. Even though the issue raised before the Committee would technically be a different one, because the complaint would allege a violation of a different treaty, the impression might be created that it is possible to appeal from the organs of the European Convention, which would weaken their authority.[84] In 1970, the Committee of Ministers of the Council of Europe adopted Resolution (70) 17 dealing with states parties to the European Convention that are also parties to the Political Covenant and have made a declaration under its Article 41. The resolution stated that such states should normally utilize only the procedure established by the European Convention for complaints against another party to the Convention that relate to an alleged violation of a right covered in substance by both the Convention (or its Protocols) and the Covenant. At the same time, the Committee of Ministers expressed its understanding that the procedure under the Covenant may be invoked for rights not guaranteed by the Convention or in relation to states that are not parties to it.[85]

Individual Applications

The effect of an acceptance of the Optional Protocol by states that have accepted the right of individual petition under Article 25 of the European Convention is that an individual alleging a violation of a right guaranteed by both the Political Covenant and the Convention would have the right to initiate proceedings under either instrument.[86] It has been suggested that such freedom of choice "can only strengthen the protection of human rights and fun-

[82] *See* Sohn, *supra* note 62.

[83] *See* De Meyer, *The International Control Machinery*, in PROC. OF THE COLLOQUY, *supra* note 44, at 241, 287. De Meyer suggests that reports that do not constitute a "settlement" of the dispute do not exclude any subsequent recourse to another form of settlement. *Id.* at 292.

[84] *See* Council of Europe Doc. CAHMP (80) 1, at 6 (1980).

[85] *See* Committee of Ministers Res. (70) 17, *reprinted in* Eissen, *supra* note 43, at 204–05; Council of Europe Doc. CAHMP (80) 1, at 6 (1980).

[86] *See* Council of Europe Doc. CAHMP (80) 1, at 6 (1980); De Meyer, *supra* note 83, at 292.

damental freedoms."[87] On the other hand, the principle of freedom of choice might lead to difficulties as a result, *inter alia*, of divergencies in the case law of the two systems.[88] In addition, does freedom of choice include the successive use by individuals of remedies open to them?[89] Under Article 5(2)(a) of the Optional Protocol, the Human Rights Committee appears not to be precluded from examining a complaint previously considered by the organs of the European Convention on Human Rights; but under Article 27(1)(b) of the Convention, the European Commission of Human Rights may not examine a complaint previously considered by the Committee unless there is relevant new information. In order to forestall the possibility of successive applications to the Commission and the Committee, the Committee of Ministers of the Council of Europe in its Resolution (70) 17, while recognizing the reasonableness of allowing an individual a choice of procedures under either the Convention or the Political Covenant, stated that no one should be able to bring the same case under both procedures, either at the same time or successively. To this end, the resolution suggested that the member states of the Council of Europe make a declaration of interpretation or a reservation when signing or ratifying the Optional Protocol to the effect that the competence of the Human Rights Committee would not extend to receiving and considering individual complaints relating to cases that are being or have been examined under the European Convention on Human Rights. Such a declaration would apply to complaints of violations of rights protected in substance by the two instruments.[90]

V. Concluding Observations

Coordination in international human rights is particularly needed in the United Nations family of organizations because of its decentralized structure. With regard to regional organizations, which have different memberships, it is possible to envisage a continued divergence in the character and scope of human rights undertakings.

In considering normative conflicts, it is best to recognize that the international community may have passed the zenith of its legislative activity in the area of human rights, at least insofar as broadly oriented global instruments are concerned. However, further "legislation" may be expected in certain fields, *e.g.*, rights of the child[91] and prohibition of torture,[92] and new subjects

[87] De Meyer, *supra* note 83, at 293.

[88] *See* Council of Europe Doc. CAHMP (80) 1, at 7 (1980).

[89] *See* De Meyer, *supra* note 83, at 293–95 (who asserts this is possible).

[90] *See* note 85 *supra* (as of February 1982, of the six Council of Europe states parties to the Optional Protocol, five had made such a reservation). *See* Multilateral Treaties Deposited with the Secretary-General, Status as of 31 December 1981, UN Doc. ST/LEG/SER.E/1, at 131 (1982).

[91] Regarding the proposed convention on the rights of the child, see GA Res. 36/57, UN Doc. A/RES/36/57 (1981); Report of the Working Group on a Draft Convention on the Rights of the Child, UN Doc. E/CN.4/1982/L.41 (1982).

[92] Regarding the proposed convention against torture and other cruel, inhuman, or degrading treatment or punishment, see GA Res. 36/60, UN Doc. A/RES/36/60 (1981); Report of the Working Group on a Draft Convention Against Torture and other Cruel, Inhuman or Degrading Treatment or Punishment, UN Doc. E/CN.4/1982/L.40 (1982).

suitable for legislation will no doubt come up. Work in more specialized fields such as labor rights will also continue, as well as some expansion of human rights norms within the European regional context that is now under way.[93] The problem of overlapping or conflicting norms is unlikely, therefore, to diminish.

Without exaggerating the severity or the dimensions of the problem, we should still consider ways of handling it. In this context, the suggestions made in 1973 by the ILO deserve attention.[94] To avoid duplication and conflict, the ILO proposed that, whenever possible, those organizations which had previously left a matter to other organizations should desist from any new legislative action. If the existing standards are unsatisfactory, or contain lacunae, the organization that adopted the original "legislation" should undertake to revise it. When a subject already covered requires legislative action, the new text should contain cross-references to the existing provisions, instead of establishing new texts as if dealing with a *tabula rasa*. One possibility would be to refer in a preambular clause of the new instrument to the existing provision and to refrain from "legislating" anew on the subject. Thus, no question would arise about the relationship between the obligations created by the two instruments. Another variant of a legislative cross-reference dealing with the subject matter of existing provisions is to state explicitly in the operative part of the new instrument that the existing provisions will continue to apply. Yet another technique is that of a saving clause, along the lines of Article 46 of the Political Covenant and Article 24 of the Economic Covenant, or—concerning freedom of association—Article 8(3) of the Economic Covenant.[95] Such saving provisions establish that the obligations arising from an earlier instrument or instruments are not affected by the adoption of the new instrument.

All of these various techniques have their pros and cons and may or may not be helpful in specific situations. A legislative cross-reference in the operative part of a new instrument may not be suitable where the existing provisions have not been widely accepted, because the indirect acceptance of the earlier instrument may make the acceptance of the new instrument more difficult. Going beyond these technical solutions,[96] we must ask what the desired goal of the international community is. Since the acceptance of various human rights instruments is as yet far from complete and some states have subscribed to certain instruments but not to others, maximizing accession by states is a desirable goal of the international community,[97] even at the cost of risking an overlap or conflict between instruments. In principle, this should

[93] *See* note 44 *supra*.

[94] *See* Co-ordination Report, *supra* note 11, Ann. II, at 5–9.

[95] Article 8(3) reads as follows:

> Nothing in this article shall authorize States Parties to the International Labour Organisation Convention of 1948 concerning Freedom of Association and Protection of the Right to Organize to take legislative measures which would prejudice, or apply the law in such a manner as would prejudice, the guarantees provided for in that Convention.

[96] *See* Co-ordination Report, *supra* note 11, Ann. II, at 5–9.

[97] *See, e.g.*, Weissbrodt, *A New United Nations Mechanism for Encouraging the Ratification of Human Rights Treaties*, 76 AJIL 418 (1982).

be done by raising the substantive international standard of the new norm and improving the efficiency of the control procedures, or at least making sure that the existing control procedures are not adversely affected by any new instruments.

However, the purpose of new treaties is not always to develop higher standards. If an organization has overreached and states are not willing to ratify a treaty that establishes high standards, it may be necessary for the organization to be less ambitious and prepare a treaty with lower substantive standards or less ambitious implementation provisions.[98] This problem has been presented by, *inter alia*, international labor conventions, which may not be ratified subject to reservations.[99] The ILO has therefore attempted to enable developing states to become parties to these conventions by adopting more flexible revised conventions and by embodying in new conventions so-called flexibility clauses.[100] An organization has to determine in each case what is more important: higher standards or more ratifications.

[98] An example of the lowering of standards with regard to implementation is found in the Protocol relating to the Status of Refugees (1967), Articles IV and VII, which allows reservations to the settlement of disputes clause. 19 UST 6223, TIAS No. 6577, 606 UNTS 267. The Convention relating to the Status of Refugees (1951), Articles 38 and 42, did not allow such reservations. 189 UNTS 137, *reprinted in* Brownlie, *supra* note 3, at 50.

[99] *See* Valticos & Wolf, *L'Organisation internationale du Travail et les pays en voie de dévéloppement: Techniques d'élaboration et mise en oeuvre de normes universelles*, in PAYS EN VOIE DE DÉVELOPPEMENT ET TRANSFORMATION DU DROIT INTERNATIONAL 127, 131 (Société Française pour le Droit International 1974).

[100] To date, approximately 40 international labor conventions have been revised. The purpose of the great majority of the revisions was either to raise the level of protection or to adapt the convention to changed conditions and new developments since its adoption or, frequently, a combination of these two objectives.

In a few cases, the most recent in 1949, the purpose of the revision was to eliminate rigidities or technical difficulties in the detailed provisions of the convention that were preventing its ratification. The conventions in question were mainly maritime conventions: *e.g.*, Nos. 72, 75, and 76 were revised by Nos. 91, 92, and 93, respectively, and the provisions causing difficulty did not involve the substantive level of protection. The only two major nonmaritime examples of revisions of this type are the revision in 1934, by Convention No. 41, and in 1948, by Convention No. 89, of the Night Work (Women) Convention (No. 4) of 1919, and the revision in 1949, by Convention No. 96, of the Fee-Charging Employment Agencies Convention (No. 34) of 1933. In both cases, the revision introduced greater flexibility into provisions that states had found to be unduly strict.

It was largely after this period that the flexibility devices currently used to permit ratification of ILO conventions by countries of differing levels of development were employed and refined, particularly following the entry of newly independent states into the ILO. The revised conventions that have since been adopted have made substantial use of the various flexibility devices, *e.g.*, the social security conventions adopted since 1952, which revised those adopted in the 1920's and 1930's, and the comprehensive Minimum Age Convention (No. 138) of 1973, but so also do the new conventions adopted during this period.

In one case, the revision of a convention that has hardly been ratified has been sought for the sole purpose of allowing a larger number of developing countries to ratify it through the introduction of greater flexibility. It is contained in the agenda item of the 1982 session of the International Labour Conference entitled "Revision of the Plantations Convention, 1958," which would enable ratifying states to limit the scope of the Convention by excluding small-scale agricultural undertakings from its application.

For a description of the flexibility devices, see generally N. VALTICOS, INTERNATIONAL LABOUR LAW 51–54 (1979); Valticos & Wolf, *supra* note 99. *See also* Wolf, *Une Nouvelle Dimension*

A modest proposal for rationalization would be to create an inter-organizational committee for coordination of human rights "legislation," composed of the legal advisers of the various international organizations and other experts. The committee would be charged with establishing an "early warning system" to identify possible "legislative" conflicts and formulating proposals to avoid or reconcile such conflicts. One problem would be how to give such a group adequate influence, especially when one of the organizations wishes to expand its "legislative" reach. A possible solution would be for the UN Secretary-General and the executive heads of the specialized agencies[101] to circulate the committee's reports to the legislative or governing bodies of all the organizations as official documents. Those bodies would thus at least be made aware of the problem.

In addition, ways should be found to permit judicial or other supervisory organs to apply a spectrum of human rights norms broader than those stated in the constitutive instruments of those organs.[102] When future instruments are drafted, this objective should be taken into consideration. As regards existing instruments, where their language compels the conclusion that the scope of the applicable norms cannot be extended by the case law or rules of procedure of a particular organ, the possibility of doing so by a special protocol should be considered.

A desirable long-range solution would be to establish through a special protocol a United Nations human rights tribunal, which would be empowered *ratione materiae* to apply not only the International Bill of Human Rights but the entire corpus juris of international human rights adopted under the aegis of the United Nations, or only such enumerated instruments as each state would accept. The (optional) *ratione personae* jurisdiction of the tribunal would extend to states that become parties to the special protocol. By consistently and rationally applying and interpreting human rights instruments, such a tribunal would greatly reduce the risk of normative conflicts.

It would also be desirable to avoid duplication and conflict regarding organs and procedures of supervision and control, and to entrust supervision to or-

---

du contrôle des autorités portuaires sur les navires au port: La Convention concernant les normes minima à observer sur les navires marchands, in LIBER AMICORUM ADOLF F. SCHNITZER 513 (Mémoires Publiés par la Faculté de Droit de Genève No. 61, 1979).

ILO conventions and recommendations through 1981 are collected in INTERNATIONAL LABOUR ORGANISATION, INTERNATIONAL LABOUR CONVENTIONS AND RECOMMENDATIONS, 1919–1981 (1982).

The author is grateful to the Office of the Legal Adviser of the ILO for the information contained in this footnote. The responsibility for its accuracy, of course, is the author's alone.

[101] On the machinery for inter-organizational coordination, see Meron, *Status and Independence of the International Civil Servant,* 167 RECUEIL DES COURS 289, 295 (1980 II). Should, as a recent UNITAR study suggests, an international legal research center be established, it could perform important coordinating functions in human rights "legislation." *See* M. ELBARADEI, T. FRANCK, & R. TRACHTENBERG, THE INTERNATIONAL LAW COMMISSION: THE NEED FOR A NEW DIRECTION 30–32 (UNITAR Policy and Efficacy Studies No. 1, 1981), *summarized in* 76 AJIL 630 (1982).

[102] *See, e.g.,* Arts. 60 and 61, African Charter on Human and Peoples' Rights, *supra* note 5. *See also* text accompanying and note 5 *supra,* and text accompanying notes 46–50 *supra.*

gans with the greatest technical competence in the subject. The drafters of international instruments concerning supervision of compliance must therefore try to prevent future overlapping or conflict, as much as possible. Coordination between organizations and bodies charged with supervision of compliance should be further developed, especially in the examination of reports submitted by states. While this article has not focused on the examination of such reports, attention should be drawn to the important suggestion by Sohn that the time is ripe for rationalizing reporting procedures by states in the UN context. He has proposed simplifying the many reporting systems and consolidating them into just one or two overall systems.[103] Work on this type of initiative could be started immediately. Eventually, the international community will have to try this approach in other areas of supervision by "legislating" the consolidation of supervisory systems into one or two organs, instead of maintaining the present multitude of organs. Such a consolidation would solve or reduce conflicts in supervision. It would also reduce normative conflicts through a more consistent and rational application and interpretation of human rights instruments.

Supervisory organs should also show due deference to other control organs and exercise a measure of "judicial restraint." A proper mapping out of possible conflicts and overlaps of jurisdiction in a scholarly study would make a contribution to the attainment of these aims. Gray zones should be clarified as soon as possible by rules of procedure or by case law. For example, Article 46(1)(c) of the American Convention on Human Rights provides that a petition or a communication shall not be admissible if its subject is pending in another international proceeding for settlement. Article 47(d) provides further that the petition or communication may not be substantially the same as one previously studied by another international organization. Article 36 of the Regulations, *i.e.*, the rules of procedure, of the Inter-American Commission on Human Rights has clarified these provisions by specifying that a petition concerning a case being considered by another international organization will not be admissible only if the respondent state is a member of the other organization and if those proceedings were instituted by the victim, a member of the victim's family, or someone with a mandate to act on the victim's behalf. Where these conditions are absent, for instance if the petitioner before the other organization is a nongovernmental organization acting on its own behalf, the Inter-American Commission may deem a petition admissible.

On the other hand, the UN Human Rights Committee has not yet fully spelled out in its Rules of Procedure the correct interpretation of Article 5(2)(a) of the Optional Protocol, which states that the Committee shall not consider any individual communication if "the same matter" is being examined by another procedure of international investigation or settlement. Do the words "the same matter" require the identity of the parties or not? For instance, suppose that one complex of facts involves several individuals alleging that they were victims of human rights violations by State *X*. Some of them initiate proceedings before the European Commission of Human Rights under

[103] Sohn, *supra* note 62.

the European Convention, and others submit communications to the UN Human Rights Committee alleging violations of the Political Covenant. Are the latter communications inadmissible as covering the same matter that is being examined by the European Commission? This point and other gray areas need to be clarified by the Human Rights Committee.

It will be interesting to see whether the Committee, following the example set by the Inter-American Commission on Human Rights, interprets the words "the same matter" as requiring both the same subject (*ratione materiae*) and the complete identity of the parties (*ratione personae*) (the same victim or someone authorized to act on the victim's behalf, as well as the same respondent state). In practice, it may not always be easy to determine whether initiators of individual communications before organ *A* have authorized actions on their behalf before organ *B*.

The Committee recently faced this very question. In 1982 it made a decision on admissibility that follows the trend established by the above-mentioned Article 36 of the Regulations of the Inter-American Commission. In that case, the author of the application submitted to the Human Rights Committee was also the subject of a complaint still under consideration by the Inter-American Commission on Human Rights. He claimed that he had no prior knowledge of the latter complaint. The Secretariat of the Inter-American Commission stated that the complaint had been submitted to the Commission by an unrelated third party. The Human Rights Committee decided that in view of these considerations, the other complaint did not constitute "the same matter" within the meaning of Article 5(2)(a) of the Optional Protocol and therefore could not block the applicant's access to the Committee.[104] The Committee has thus opened its doors wider, but in so doing it has increased the risk of conflict between itself and the Inter-American Commission. Both organs are now seized of the same case under different governing instruments. While in the circumstances one can sympathize with the decision, the question arises whether it would not have been preferable for the Human Rights Committee to await the disposition of the case by the Inter-American Commission.

In some situations simultaneous consideration of similar matters by different organizations may prove beneficial to the individuals concerned. But this cannot be taken for granted. States guilty of human rights violations could take advantage of conflicting opinions of control organs by hiding behind the milder opinion. On balance, it may therefore be preferable to encourage only sequential consideration, *i.e.*, organization *B* will act only if organization *A* does not succeed in settling the matter.[105] However, the difficulty is that the principle of sequential consideration—where it is not enunciated in the governing instrument—requires a measure of inter-institutional coordination, which is still grossly lacking. The fact that in a number of instances the same person serves on several implementation organs may somewhat remedy this institutional deficiency and encourage cross-fertilization; and increasing

[104] UN Doc. CCPR/C/WG(XV)/DR/R.18/74, at 5 (1982). For an earlier similar decision (1980) concerning a complaint submitted to the Inter-American Commission by "an unrelated third party," see UN Doc. CCPR/C/DR(XV)/R.2/10, para. 7.2 (1982).

[105] *See also* Tardu, *supra* note 45, at 793–98.

awareness of coordination needs may lead to efforts to institutionalize the "same person" phenomenon.[106] Another problem raised by sequential consideration is whether organization *B* should continue to desist from considering a human rights violation if the deliberations of organization *A* are unreasonably prolonged. Such a result would be clearly undesirable. This issue has been inconclusively discussed by the Human Rights Committee.[107]

What should the future policy be on possible overlap or conflict in supervision of implementation? The availability of international forums and international remedies for individual complainants is still limited. The law of human rights is as yet a weak instrument in the confrontation between individuals and sovereign states. In these circumstances, there may be advantages to double or even triple examinations of individual complaints, but such consideration should preferably be sequential rather than simultaneous. Subject to the language of the governing instruments, there is room for another body to examine a complaint in cases where the first examination has not produced an effective remedy for a serious violation, or where the first examination has been unreasonably prolonged. While sequential consideration is preferable, where the governing instrument leaves open the possibility of simultaneous consideration, it should not necessarily be excluded if it is required for the more effective protection of human rights. Until the procedures for the protection of human rights become comprehensive, effective, and generally accepted, there is room for such resort to complementary control mechanisms, even at the risk of overlap or conflict. Once international control procedures have gained further strength and there is no more danger that rationalization of the multiplicity of procedures will lead to the selection of a less effective implementation procedure, action aimed at the establishment of uniformity would be justified. However, the time for such an effort has not yet come.

The prevailing wisdom has been that it is important to improve coordination, to avoid conflict, and to avoid different interpretations. In addition, compelling a state to defend essentially the same case before several organs may increase cynicism about the system as a whole and give the impression of institutional chaos. Nevertheless, overzealous efforts to rationalize the existing multiplicity of procedures might cause the most favorable procedures to be brought into line with the least far-reaching ones. For instance, the Soviet Union has been pressing for the abolition of the ECOSOC Resolution 1503 procedure on the ground that the two UN Covenants have entered into

[106] It has thus been proposed that the future Committee against Torture should be composed, so far as possible, of persons who are also members of the UN Human Rights Committee. Report of the Working Group on a Draft Convention against Torture and Other Cruel, Inhuman or Degrading Treatment or Punishment, UN Doc. E/CN.4/1982/L.40, Ann. II, Art. 17(2) (1982). *See also* discussion of Art. 9 of the Apartheid Convention, *supra* note 4.

[107] *See, e.g.*, 1977 Report of the Human Rights Committee, *supra* note 67, at 14–15.

For a view based on the *travaux préparatoires* of Article 5(2) of the Optional Protocol that the provision allowing the Human Rights Committee to consider a petition if other proceedings have been "unreasonably prolonged" applies not only to Article 5(2)(b) (exhaustion of domestic remedies), but also to Article 5(2)(a) (competition with other international procedures), see *id.* at 13; M. TARDU, *supra* note 72, pt. 1, §1, at 67–69.

force and duplication of supervision should be avoided.[108] Given the Soviet refusal to become a party to the Optional Protocol, it is clear that this suggestion is aimed at weakening the existing implementation system rather than at improving coordination. As a study by the Government of the Netherlands has suggested, there may indeed be good reason "to allow the new procedures a certain amount of time to develop and consolidate themselves in practice. In the long run it may then prove possible to rationalize the numerous procedures, adapting the *less* effective to bring them into line with the better ones."[109]

A similar policy should apply to complaints submitted by one state against another and to investigations of human rights violations by states undertaken by international organizations. In the present formative stage of human rights supervision, multiplicity of recourse procedures, which leads to a greater observance of human rights, is more important than institutional order.

[108] HUMAN RIGHTS AND FOREIGN POLICY, *supra* note 13, at 80.

[109] *Ibid.* (emphasis in original). For a discussion of advantages inherent in double or triple examination and in seeking out the provision most favorable to the individual concerned, see Council of Europe Doc. CAHMP (80) 1, at 3–4 (1980). *See generally* Golsong, *To which Extent and for which Subject Matters Is it Advisable to Create and Develop Special Judicial Bodies with a Jurisdiction Limited to Certain Regions or to Certain Subject Matters?*, 62 BEITRÄGE ZUM AUSLÄNDISCHEN ÖFFENTLICHEN RECHT UND VÖLKERRECHT 99, 112 (1974).

THE LAW GOVERNING TREATY RELATIONS BETWEEN PARTIES TO THE VIENNA CONVENTION ON THE LAW OF TREATIES AND STATES NOT PARTY TO THE CONVENTION

*By E. W. Vierdag**

I. Introduction

The Vienna Convention on the Law of Treaties (the Convention), concluded on May 23, 1969,[1] entered into force on January 27, 1980.[2] It thus took more than 10 years for 35 states to ratify the instrument or to accede to it. Although its entry into force may hasten ratification and accession somewhat in other states, it will probably be a very long time before a large majority of states are parties to the Convention. Therefore, international treaty practice will long be faced with the conclusion of treaties between or among states that are parties to the Convention and other states.

The extent to which the Convention will actually govern treaty relations between states after its entry into force depends on a number of factors. Among these, Article 4 of the Convention is of prime importance. Article 4 reads as follows:

> *Non-retroactivity of the present Convention*
>
> Without prejudice to the application of any rules set forth in the present Convention to which treaties would be subject under international law independently of the Convention, the Convention applies only to treaties which are concluded by States after the entry into force of the present Convention with regard to such States.

This provision consists of two parts. It is intended to guarantee that the Convention shall not have retroactive effect. At the same time—*ex abundanti cautela*, as it were—it says that the Convention does not detract from the validity of the customary law governing treaties concluded before its entry into force.

However, still more can be read into Article 4, namely, that it also functions as a so-called general participation clause. As will be discussed more fully below, a general participation clause is a provision in an international legal instrument limiting its applicability to cases involving states that are parties to the instrument. If a state that is not a party becomes involved, then the instrument ceases to be applicable altogether, even among the states that are

* University of Amsterdam. The author is indebted to Professor H. Meijers and to Dr. H. H. G. Post of the University of Amsterdam for their critical comments on earlier versions of this paper.

[1] UN Doc. A/CONF.39/27 (1969), *reprinted in* 63 AJIL 875 (1969), 8 ILM 679 (1969).

[2] Multilateral Treaties in Respect of Which the Secretary-General Performs Depositary Functions, UN Doc. ST/LEG/SER.D/13, at 597 (1980). Article 84(1) requires 35 ratifications or accessions for the entry into force of the Convention.

parties to it. If Article 4 is read as a general participation clause, the words "with regard to such States" must then be read as "with regard to *all* such States." If this reading of "such States" is the correct one, then the "law" mentioned in the title of this paper would be customary international law, and not the law as laid down in the Convention (where this is not customary law).

The likelihood that numerous treaties will be concluded between states that are and states that are not parties to the Convention poses the following question: if Article 4 is not a general participation clause, then what law does govern such treaties? We will attempt to answer this question by examining the meaning of Article 4, and to that end, by first tracing its origins. We will then consider the provision, hypothetically, as a general participation clause and point out some of the consequences of this interpretation. Next we will inquire whether Article 4 should rather be understood as allowing the application of the Convention to a treaty as regards some parties *inter se*, even though other parties to the treaty would not be bound by the Convention, and their participation would thus be governed by customary law. It must then be asked whether the provisions of the Convention and rules of customary treaty law are compatible. Some provisions seem to be of doubtful compatibility, while others are probably incompatible and require general participation to function properly. Finally, we will attempt to indicate a possible solution to these problems.

One further introductory remark should be made. At the 34th plenary meeting of the UN Conference on the Law of Treaties, it was decided that the Convention should not contain special provisions on reservations to the Convention itself; the general articles on reservations (Articles 19 through 23) were thought to cover the matter adequately.[3] Thus, the makers of the Convention did envisage the possibility that differing Convention regimes would govern treaties, insofar as a particular reservation would modify the law of treaties laid down in the Convention for the reserving state.[4] The problems that may arise when two or more Convention regimes govern treaties as a result of reservations to the Convention will not be discussed as such in the present paper,[5] but rather the effect of Article 4: treaties governed simultaneously by the Convention and by the customary law of treaties—as is also the case under Article 3(c) of the Convention.[6]

II. Article 4 of the Convention

Origins of Article 4

Article 4 was not among the draft articles on the law of treaties submitted by the International Law Commission as the basic proposal for consideration by the Vienna Conference. As with other provisions not drafted by the ILC

[3] United Nations Conference on the Law of Treaties, Official Records of the Second Session [hereinafter cited as 2 Off. Rec.], UN Doc A/CONF.39/11/Add.1, at 296 (1969). Consequently, a Spanish proposal to insert into the Convention an article reading, "No reservation is permitted to Part V of the present Convention," was rejected.

[4] *See* 1 C. Rousseau, Principes généraux du droit international public 292, 298–99 (1944).

[5] *See* "Incompatible Provisions," *infra* p. 794. [6] *See* text at note 32 *infra*.

but proposed and adopted at the conference, the "legislative history" of Article 4 is very short.

At the 66th meeting of the Committee of the Whole, the Chairman of the United States delegation, discussing amendments to what is now Article 45, closed his statement with a remark that is recorded as follows:

> The United States was convinced that the only realistic way of achieving a codification of the law applicable to treaties concluded by existing and future States was to deal with the future, not with the past. . . . [I]t fully understood the desire of States facing current problems not to have their legal positions undermined by any of the provisions of the convention, and would have no objection to a proposal that the convention should apply only to future treaties.[7]

The term "future treaties," which is still occasionally used in the literature, is extremely ambiguous and unclear. What is simply a "treaty" to its parties is, or may be, a "future treaty" to a state contemplating ratification or accession, while a "future treaty" may also be one yet to be drafted, negotiated, concluded, or ratified.

Nevertheless, the notion turned up again, in slightly different form, in a Venezuelan proposal to insert the following new article (then numbered 77) into the Convention: "The provisions of the present Convention shall apply only to treaties concluded in the future."[8] This text was generally considered to be unsatisfactory, so a more elaborate and precise version was submitted to the committee by the Chairman of the Swedish delegation at the 101st meeting:[9] "Without prejudice to the application of the rules of customary international law codified in the present Convention, the Convention will apply only to treaties which are concluded by States after the entry into force of the present Convention with regard to such States."[10] Some further amendments were proposed. Then, following discussions among the several delegations concerned, seven delegations submitted a new version,[11] which was

[7] UNITED NATIONS CONFERENCE ON THE LAW OF TREATIES, OFFICIAL RECORDS OF THE FIRST SESSION [hereinafter cited as 1 OFF. REC.], UN Doc. A/CONF.39/11, at 392. R. D. Kearney and Robert E. Dalton state: "There had been a good deal of off-the-record concern expressed during the 1968 session regarding amendments whose major purpose seemed to be improvement of the position of one or another party to a treaty dispute." *The Treaty on Treaties*, 64 AJIL 495, 550 (1970).

[8] UNITED NATIONS CONFERENCE ON THE LAW OF TREATIES, OFFICIAL RECORDS, DOCUMENTS OF THE CONFERENCE [hereinafter cited as 3 OFF. REC.], UN Doc. A/CONF.39/11/Add.2, at 252, UN Doc. A/CONF.39/C.1/L.399 (1969). The representative of Venezuela declared that his proposal "had its origin in a remark made at the 66th meeting by the United States representative." 2 OFF. REC. at 333. One week earlier, however, the Swedish representative had also discussed the nonretroactivity of the Convention. *Id.* at 273 (para. 51).

[9] *Id.* at 321.

[10] 3 OFF. REC. at 252, UN Doc. A/CONF.39/C.1/L.400 (Brazil, Chile, Kenya, Sweden, and Tunisia).

[11] *Id.* at 252–53, UN Doc. A/CONF.39/C.1/L.403 (Brazil, Chile, Iran, Kenya, Sweden, Tunisia, and Venezuela):

> Without prejudice to the application of any rules set forth in the present Convention to which treaties would be subject, in accordance with international law, independently of the Convention, the Convention will apply only to treaties which are concluded by States after the entry into force of the present Convention with regard to such States.

adopted at the 104th meeting and was referred to the Drafting Committee.[12] The Drafting Committee placed the article in part I of the Convention, made a few minuscule changes in the text, and submitted it to the conference at the 30th plenary meeting. It was adopted by 81 votes to 5, with 17 abstentions.[13]

This summary reveals that none of the earlier versions of Article 4, and none of the changes made in the latest version, were concerned with the problems raised by the last two words of Article 4 as it now stands; nor were any remarks directed specifically to those two words during the discussions.[14] Moreover, the corresponding Article 4 of the draft articles on treaties concluded between states and international organizations or between international organizations, subsequently prepared by the ILC, does not shed any new light on the matter. It reads as follows:

> Without prejudice to the application of any rules set forth in the present articles to which treaties between one or more States and one or more international organizations or between international organizations would be subject under international law independently of the articles, the articles apply only to such treaties after the [entry into force] of the said articles as regards those States and those international organizations.[15]

The slight difference between this draft Article 4 and Article 4 of the Convention results from the attempt to adapt the text to the special designation of the treaties in question. Because "such treaties" is used, "those" replaces "such" at the end. No relevant conclusions can be drawn from these changes. Thus, the question raised here about the Convention on the Law of Treaties applies in exactly the same way to a future instrument on treaties concluded between states and international organizations or between international organizations.

Two Interpretations of Article 4

As far as could be discovered, no thorough analysis has yet been made of Article 4. Even comments that go somewhat further than merely stating that Article 4 limits the scope of the Convention to "future treaties," or similar

[12] *Id.* at 253; 2 OFF. REC. at 341.

[13] 2 OFF. REC. at 176. *Cf.* do Nascimento e Silva, *Le Facteur Temps dans les traités*, 154 RECUEIL DES COURS 215, 286–91 (1977 I).

[14] The main debates on what was then draft Article 77 (now Article 4) are in 2 OFF. REC. at 316, 320, 321, 323, 325, 327, 330, 332–35, 337, 338 (Committee of the Whole); and at 165–67 (plenary meetings). Article 77 was discussed together with draft Article 76, which is now Article 81. The controversies over which states should be entitled to sign the Convention or accede to it entirely dominated these meetings. The debates on Article 77 (Article 4) are summarized and commented upon in Rosenne, *The Temporal Application of the Vienna Convention on the Law of Treaties*, 4 CORNELL INT'L L.J. 1, 5–13 (1971).

[15] Report of the International Law Commission on the work of its 26th session, UN Doc. A/9610/Rev.1, at 137, *reprinted in* [1974] 2 Y.B. INT'L L. COMM'N 157, 298, UN Doc. A/CN.4/SER.A/1974/Add.1, pt.1. In the commentary, the ILC states that the text of Article 4 is repeated "subject only to the adjustments necessitated by draft article 1" (on the scope of the draft articles). The ILC's discussion of draft Article 4 did not touch upon the matter dealt with in this essay. [1974] 1 Y.B. INT'L L. COMM'N 234.

observations, are scarce. For each of the two interpretations of Article 4 mentioned in the introduction, only a few authorities can be cited.

Article 4 Is a General Participation Clause. H. W. A. Thirlway observes that "the whole field of the law of treaties . . . will continue to remain largely an area where customary law is supreme, notwithstanding the preparation of the 1969 Vienna Convention on the Law of Treaties." Mentioning both the time needed for the Convention to acquire "universal or quasi-universal acceptance by States" and Article 4, he concludes that it "is clear that it will be a long time before anything like the majority of existing treaties in effective operation will be treaties concluded between States both or all of which are parties to the Vienna Convention of 1969."[16] Clearly, Thirlway is suggesting that in the case of a bilateral treaty, both parties must be bound by the Convention, and that in the case of a multilateral treaty, all the parties must be bound by the Convention, if this instrument is to govern the treaties in question. This viewpoint is also apparent from his reference to the "[possibly very lengthy] period of time before [the] Convention acquires universal or quasi-universal acceptance."

At first glance, Thirlway's interpretation of Article 4 as a general participation clause is unexceptionable. If the canons of interpretation found in Articles 31 to 33 of the Convention itself are applied—especially that laid down in Article 31(1)—his position would seem to be quite correct: how could the "ordinary meaning" of "with regard to such States" in Article 4 ever be "with regard to some of those States, but not to some others"? (Or, in the case of a bilateral treaty, "with regard to one of those States"?) Not only is the text so unequivocal as to make further questioning of its true meaning almost inappropriate, but also the Convention seems to be based, as appears from a number of its provisions, on the hypothesis that the parties to a treaty will all be parties to the Convention.[17] Part V of the Convention also points to a general participation interpretation.[18] Additional support for this position may be found in Article 28, which contains the principle that treaties are generally supposed to apply to acts or facts occurring in the future, after their conclusion, and have no retroactive effect, unless the parties intended otherwise. However, this article does take into account that different situations may apply to the states involved: treaty provisions "do not bind a party in relation to any act or fact which took place or any situation which ceased to exist before the date of the entry into force of the treaty *with respect to that party*" (emphasis added).

As mentioned, general participation clauses limit the applicability of an instrument only to cases involving states that are parties to that instrument. They are sometimes referred to as *clausula si omnes.* This type of provision was regularly embodied in treaties codifying the laws of war, especially those

[16] H. THIRLWAY, INTERNATIONAL CUSTOMARY LAW AND CODIFICATION 108 (1972). D. P. O'Connell took the same stand. "Except in respect of those matters which can be regarded as codifications of the customary international law rules respecting treaties, the Convention [on the Law of Treaties] will only affect those treaties which are subsequently entered into by parties, all of whom have ratified the Convention." 1 INTERNATIONAL LAW 205 (2d ed. 1970).

[17] *See* "Provisions of Doubtful Compatibility," *infra* p. 789.

[18] *See* "Incompatible Provisions," *infra* p. 794.

adopted at the Hague Peace Conferences of 1899 and 1907.[19] For example, Article 2 of the fourth Hague Convention on the Laws and Customs of War on Land (1907) states: "The provisions contained in the Regulations referred to in Article 1, as well as in the present Convention, do not apply except between contracting Powers, and then only if all the belligerents are parties to the Convention."[20]

The Oppenheim/Lauterpacht treatise on international law makes the following observation about such clauses:

> The effect . . . was, in strict law, to deprive some of the Conventions of their binding force either from the beginning of the War or in the course of it as soon as a non-signatory State,[21] however insignificant, joined the ranks of the belligerents. . . . The effect might be that in a war in which a considerable number of belligerents are involved, the action of one State, however small, in a distant region of war, might become the starting point for a general abandonment of the restraints of the Convention.[22]

Little wonder that the clause stood in bad repute; its effect was even characterized as "fatal."[23] The Second World War gave this description still more substance; and the four Red Cross Conventions on the laws of war concluded in 1949 therefore abolished *expressis verbis* any notion of general participation as a condition of applicability.[24]

What would be the effect of Article 4 of the Convention on the Law of Treaties if conceived of as a general participation clause? First, the meaning of the term "concluded," which is not defined in the Convention, must be determined. It appears from certain of its provisions, *e.g.*, Articles 2(1)(a), 6, and 7(2)(a), that the term covers the whole procedure—simple or complex—that makes a treaty binding upon a state. Therefore, the states that have "concluded" in Article 4 are states that are bound by a treaty, *i.e.*, are "parties" to it in the sense of Article 2(1)(g), or are "contracting States" in the sense of Article 2(1)(f).

[19] *See* 2 L. OPPENHEIM, INTERNATIONAL LAW 234 *ff.* (7th ed. Lauterpacht 1952); *see also* Geck, *Allbeteiligungsklausel*, in 1 K. STRUPP, WÖRTERBUCH DES VÖLKERRECHTS 28 (ed. Schlochauer 1960–62).

[20] 36 Stat. 2277, TS No. 539. The 1899 version of this article is as follows:

> The provisions contained in the Regulations mentioned in Article 1 are only binding on the Contracting Powers, in case of war between two or more of them. These provisions shall cease to be binding from the time when, in a war between Contracting Powers, a non-Contracting Power joins one of the belligerents.

32 Stat. 1803, TS No. 403.

[21] *I.e.*, a state that is not a *party* to it, in the modern terminology of treaty law.

[22] L. OPPENHEIM, *supra* note 19, at 234–35 (footnotes omitted).

[23] F. VON LISZT, DAS VÖLKERRECHT 258 (12th ed. Fleischmann 1925).

[24] The common Article 2(3) of these Conventions states:

> Although one of the Powers in conflict may not be a party to the present Convention, the Powers who are parties thereto shall remain bound by it in their mutual relations. They shall furthermore be bound by the Convention in relation to the said Power, if the latter accepts and applies the provisions thereof.

See, e.g., the Convention for the Amelioration of the Condition of the Wounded and Sick in Armed Forces in the Field, 75 UNTS 31, 6 UST 3114, TIAS No. 3362.

The reading of Article 4 as a general participation clause would seriously reduce the *effet utile* of the Convention; its significance would be considerably limited. Its operation vis-à-vis a multilateral treaty would always be subject to the condition that no state that is not, or not yet, a party to the Convention could ratify that treaty or accede to it. For as soon as a state that is not a party to the Convention acceded to a treaty governed by the Convention, the applicability of the Convention to that treaty would end. The same would happen if a party to a treaty governed by the Convention denounced the Convention: the treaty in question would henceforth be governed by the rules of customary law. It goes without saying that these results would be highly detrimental to legal certainty in treaty relations. Problems such as those posed by this interpretation could only be avoided by barring states that are not parties to the Convention from treaties governed by it; but the universality and effectiveness of multilateral treaties would be jeopardized. Then the Convention could not very well serve the purposes intended by its makers. (They declared in the seventh preambular paragraph their belief that "the codification and progressive development of the law of treaties achieved in the present Convention will promote the purposes of the United Nations set forth in the Charter, namely, the maintenance of international peace and security, the development of friendly relations and the achievement of co-operation among nations.")

Of course, this interpretation of Article 4 only affects multilateral, and not bilateral, treaties: just as the Convention is always applicable to bilateral treaties concluded between parties to it, it is never applicable to other bilateral treaties unless the parties so specify.[25] In addition, as the Convention increases in authority in the course of time, it will generate rules that, though only conventional or contractual in origin, will pass into the general corpus of international law,[26] especially through the practice of the United Nations. Thus, the limitations imposed if Article 4 is understood as a general participation clause will gradually lose their severity, and with it their possibly paralyzing effect on the operation of the Convention in international treaty practice.

Though not insignificant, these considerations do not lead to the conclusion that Article 4 *must* be interpreted as a general participation clause. Above all, if the states that participated in the creation of the Convention had intended Article 4 to be such a clause, they would undoubtedly have spelled out this intention in so many words. It is most unlikely that such a far-reaching restriction on the operation of the Convention would be hidden away in the two closing words of Article 4.

No matter what the actual results of interpreting Article 4 as a general participation clause may be, they could be qualified as "unreasonable" under Article 32 of the Convention, as they would be most prejudicial to the object and purpose of the Convention. Some might even call the results "manifestly absurd." In such a case, Article 32 provides for recourse to "supplementary means of interpretation, including the preparatory work of the treaty and the circumstances of its conclusion."

[25] *See* text at note 30 *infra*.

[26] Phrasing borrowed from the Judgment of the International Court of Justice in the North Sea Continental Shelf Cases, 1969 ICJ REP. 4, para. 71.

Article 4 Is Not a General Participation Clause. Although the *travaux préparatoires* do not directly illuminate the matter discussed here, the *Official Records* of the conference contain a single statement that appears to be particularly relevant. It was made at the 30th plenary meeting (May 19, 1969) by the Chairman of the Swedish delegation, after the conference had voted on what was then Article 77. The Swedes had taken the initiative in drafting and sponsoring this article, which is now Article 4, in response to the general dissatisfaction with the Venezuelan proposal.[27] The statement is recorded as follows:

> Mr. BLIX (Sweden) said that his delegation, which had been a sponsor of the proposal just adopted as article 77, wished to explain its positive vote with a clarification on one minor point. It was his delegation's understanding that, when applied to a multilateral treaty, the article meant that the convention would be applicable between States which participated in the conclusion of a multilateral treaty after the convention had come into force for them, although there might be other parties to the same multilateral treaty for which the convention had not come into force.[28]

The legal weight of this declaration is not easy to assess. It was made in explanation of the delegation's vote, after the vote had been taken. The delegates to the conference did not react, either favorably or unfavorably, and the statement was announced as a clarification of a "minor point." Still, it would be erroneous to ignore its importance. It was made by the Chairman of the delegation that had played a crucial role in the drafting and adoption of the article in question. The clarification is in plain terms, and directly concerns the interpretation of the specific aspect of Article 4 that is under discussion here. As for the silence of the conference, the only conclusion that can be drawn from it is that it implied assent.

Thus, once again we are led to infer that the contracting parties did not intend, by adding Article 4, to include a general participation clause in the Convention. Consequently, the Convention does not itself preclude its applicability to treaties, only some of whose parties are parties to the Convention.[29] This conclusion, in turn, raises a number of questions, some of which will be discussed below.

III. A "Double Regime" Governing Treaties

The term "double regime" means that a treaty is governed by the Convention for one party or parties, and by the rules of customary law for the other party or parties. (The term "governed by" relates to the law governing the conduct of the parties in relation to a specific treaty.)

We must see whether the Convention is capable of governing a treaty simultaneously with the customary law of treaties. Obviously, it must allow

[27] 2 Off. Rec. at 321.

[28] *Id.* at 166–67 (para. 23).

[29] We suggest that I. M. Sinclair takes the same position—albeit implicitly—by observing: "How [Article 4] will apply in relation to future multilateral treaties remains to be seen, since it is difficult to see how the Convention can be fully operative in relation to some parties only to such a treaty." The Vienna Convention on the Law of Treaties 137 n.83 (1972).

for the preservation of a sufficient measure of reciprocity in the relations among the parties to a treaty. After all, the Convention has brought certain elements of precision, strictness, and even restriction into the law of treaties that are absent from customary law; most important, it prescribes rules of procedure for the settlement of disputes.

Article 34 on Third States

The point of departure in considering a double regime must be the general rule of the law of treaties that treaties do not bind third states. The rule is laid down in Article 34 of the Convention, as follows: "A treaty does not create either obligations or rights for a third State without its consent."

Obviously, this rule also applies to the Convention itself. When and how, then, can the Convention operate vis-à-vis treaties concluded by parties and nonparties to it, while preserving this rule? And when can it not do so? In the case of a *bilateral* treaty, the Convention cannot apply if only one of the parties is bound by it (unless the party that is not bound agrees that the Convention shall be chosen to govern the treaty[30]). The party that is bound by the Convention cannot invoke it against the other party both under Article 34 and under the general rule of international law; and the latter state cannot invoke it against the former under the general rule of international law. It may be recalled that Dr. Blix limited his statement on Article 4, quoted above,[31] to multilateral treaties. So a bilateral treaty, only one party to which is a party to the Convention, is governed by the customary law of treaties, and a "double regime" governing treaties will have legal relevance only with respect to treaties concluded by more than two states.

As the effect of the Convention is merely *inter se*, among the parties to it, it goes without saying that this conclusion only holds if at least *two* of the states concerned are parties to the Convention. A treaty concluded by three states, two of which are parties to the Convention, will be governed by the Convention as between these two states, and by the customary law of treaties as between these two states and the state that is not a party to the Convention. One is reminded of the complex situation in Article 3 of the Convention (on international agreements that are not within its scope). Subparagraph (c) of this article stipulates that, although the Convention does not apply to agreements to which subjects of international law other than states are also parties, this shall not affect "the application of the Convention to the relations of States as between themselves under [such] international agreements." This is not the place for an analysis of Article 3(c);[32] suffice it to say that the application of the Convention to a limited number of parties to an agreement was actually contemplated by the conference.[33]

[30] *See* further text at notes 67–71 *infra*.

[31] *See* text at note 28 *supra*.

[32] This remarkable provision originated with the Drafting Committee. 1 OFF. REC. at 146.

[33] Although not a word was said about Article 3(c) at the conference—*see* 2 OFF. REC. at 4—except for a short explanation by the Chairman of the Drafting Committee:

> The aim [of Article 3(c)] was to show more clearly the scope of the convention, particularly with regard to trilateral or mixed international agreements, the parties to which included

Compatibility of Convention Provisions with the Customary Regime

Not all the provisions of the Convention will cause awkward, impracticable, or untenable legal situations in cases where only some of the parties to a treaty are bound by the Convention. Several provisions would probably cause no embarrassment at all. Thus, in examining a possible double regime, we must distinguish among types of provisions.

"*Codificatory Provisions.*" This term designates provisions for which the double regime is a matter of form rather than substance, because they can be regarded as constituting codification in the strict sense of the term. These are the "rules set forth in the . . . Convention to which treaties would be subject under international law independently of the Convention," in the wording of Article 4. An example would be Article 26 (*pacta sunt servanda*), as would be, *inter alia*, Article 6 (capacity of states to conclude treaties), Article 27 (internal law and the observance of treaties), Article 34 (general rule regarding third states), Article 38 (rules in a treaty becoming binding on third states through international custom), Article 55 (reduction of the parties to a multilateral treaty below the number necessary for its entry into force), and Article 74 (diplomatic and consular relations and the conclusion of treaties).[34]

"*Compatible Provisions.*" These provisions are of a residuary nature, and they therefore contain such phrases as "unless the treaty otherwise provides," or "unless the parties otherwise agree." For example, when negotiating states agree that the treaty they are going to sign shall be subject to ratification (Article 14(c)), the position of the states parties to the Convention is the same as that of the other states involved: the means of expressing consent to be bound can be chosen freely under the Convention (Article 11), and under general international law as well. It may safely be assumed, therefore, that the double regime would not cause any difficulties. Similarly, a number of other provisions of the Convention appear more or less explicitly from their wording to cover matters that are wholly controlled by the will of the parties to the treaty.[35] Such matters are regulated first and foremost by agreement,

---

> not only States, but also other subjects of international law. It had been thought advisable not to exclude all such agreements from the scope of the convention. Where such agreements were concerned, the convention should govern relations between States, but not relations between other subjects of international law or between them and States. The object of subparagraph (*c*) was to state in explicit and non-controversial terms a conclusion which might have been reached by a reasonable interpretation of the text of the original article.

1 OFF. REC. at 147.

[34] If an interpretation of the rules in this category different from that adhered to by states that rely on customary international treaty law could be given by Convention parties, on the basis of the *travaux préparatoires* of the Convention, this category of "codificatory provisions" would not, of course, be a valid one. However, we believe that the *travaux préparatoires* do not contain indications to that effect.

[35] *See, inter alia,* Articles 10 (authentication of the text), 12 (consent to be bound expressed by signature), 13 (*idem* by ratification, acceptance, or approval), 15 (*idem* by accession), 16 (exchange or deposit of instruments of ratification, acceptance, approval, or accession), 17 (consent to be bound by part of a treaty, and choice of different provisions), 18 (obligation not to defeat the object of a treaty prior to its entry into force), 19 (formulation of reservations), 24 (entry into force), 25 (provisional application), 28 (nonretroactivity of treaties), 29 (territorial scope of

to which the Convention regulation yields. If the negotiating states that are not parties to the Convention do not object to a Convention regulation on a certain point, or if they actually prefer it to other possible regulations, it might suffice, in law, for them to remain silent on the matter. That would be completely in accordance with the intention of the parties to the Convention, as is evident from its wording, although it would be preferable if the Convention's regulations were chosen *expressis verbis*.[36]

"*Provisions of Doubtful Compatibility.*" Provisions of this type bring into the law of treaties certain formalities or specific requirements that are absent from customary law. How can the conduct of some parties, acting under these provisions, be reconciled with the position of other parties acting under the applicable customary law? And how does noncompliance with these Convention provisions by the latter parties affect the position of the former? Before turning to these questions, we should devote a few words to Articles 5 and 9.

Article 5 (on treaties constituting international organizations and treaties adopted within international organizations) does not take account of the possibility that not all of the prospective members (first part) or members (second part) of a given international organization may be parties to the Convention. The application of the Convention is "without prejudice to any relevant rules of the organization," but that proviso seems to be more relevant to the second than to the first part of Article 5. Still, the article does raise questions as to when and how it is to take effect. An international organization cannot, as such, be a party to the Convention. Its members can be parties, but how many must be bound by the Convention for Article 5 to become operative, either vis-à-vis the organization's constituent instrument, or vis-à-vis the treaties adopted within the organization? A two-thirds majority, as laid down in a different context in Article 9(2)? A simple majority? What if—on one of these bases—a treaty comes within the scope of the Convention? Will the international organization be notified that Article 5 and hence the Convention have become operative? But how? This task is not provided for by Article 77 (functions of depositaries), Article 78 (notifications and communications), or Article 85, which designates the Secretary-General of the United Nations as the depositary of the Convention.

The problem would not occur (or would be easily solved) if all the members of the international organization were parties to the Convention; but such a requirement could hardly be contemplated, as it would turn Article 5 into a general participation clause. One is left with the assumption that Article 5 will govern the constituent instrument of an international organization and the treaties adopted within it as regards the members that are parties to the Convention, but not the other members. But that assumption, however reasonable, is evidently impracticable.

The questions raised by Article 5 are by no means confined to the treaties

---

treaties), and 39 (general rule regarding the amendment of treaties). This list is not intended to be exhaustive.

[36] *Cf.* text at notes 67–71 *infra*, on choice-of-law clauses.

referred to in that provision. Such questions can come up in respect of all multilateral treaties governed by the Convention as far as some parties are concerned, and by customary law as far as other parties are concerned. The conclusion that this is a highly impracticable situation also appears to be valid for all multilateral treaties.

Similar questions are raised by Article 9(2) (on the adoption of the text of a treaty at an international conference). Like international organizations, international conferences are not, as such, subjects of the law of the Convention. Article 9(2) applies to conferences in which states that are not parties to the Convention may participate. Consequently, the validity of the adoption of the text of a treaty may be subject to differing legal appreciations. When invited to an "international conference," do the states that are not parties to the Convention automatically abandon the unanimity rule for the adoption of a text outside an "international conference," laid down in paragraph (1) of Article 9, by accepting the invitation?[37] How are they to accept the line—left undefined in Article 9—that will have to be drawn by the participating states between gatherings in the sense of Article 9(1) and gatherings in the sense of Article 9(2)? It may be true that Article 9(2) reflects an existing UN practice,[38] but that fact alone will not solve the problem if a controversy should arise. (However, as it will be in the interest of parties to the Convention as well as of states that are not parties that a decision be made at the beginning of a conference on the voting rule or rules that are to apply, it is hard to see why the rules set forth in Article 9 would not be appropriate in the making of that decision.)

Some examples will now be given of rules of treaty law from the Convention whose compatibility with customary law is doubtful. Among them is Article 20(3), which prescribes that a reservation to a treaty that is the constituent instrument of an international organization requires the acceptance of "the competent organ of the organization" unless the instrument provides otherwise. Suppose that the constituent instrument does not provide otherwise, that a reservation is made by a state not party to the Convention, and that the competent organ—equally not bound by the Convention—does not act. Is this reservation valid? There is no reason for the reserving state to query its validity, and this is in fact true for all the member states of the organization that are not parties to the Convention, if the reservation is not invalid for some other reason. Will it also be considered valid by the member states that *are* parties to the Convention? The principle of Article 34 (on third states), quoted above, clearly seems to compel them to accept its validity.

These circumstances, however, give rise to a further question: are the member states that are parties to the Convention bound to seek acceptance of reservations made by themselves to the instrument? If they are not, the Convention cannot work, as its functioning will be subject to a condition of general participation. If they are so bound, the rule of Article 20(3) will operate among parties to the Convention, but the reciprocity among the member states of

[37] *Cf.* the remarks by the Austrian delegate in 1 OFF. REC. at 81 (para. 12).

[38] [1966] 2 Y.B. INT'L L. COMM'N 195, UN Doc. A/CN.4/SER.A/1966/Add.1; *see also* 2 OFF. REC. at 17–23.

the organization will be impaired. Moreover, can the rule have its intended effect if only some member states are bound to observe it and others are not? Some members would be free to make reservations, while others would be obliged to submit their reservations to the competent organ for approval, which they might fail to obtain, even if the reservations happened to be the same as those made by the other states.

After the International Court of Justice issued its Advisory Opinion on *Reservations to the Genocide Convention* in 1951,[39] the so-called flexible system of rules concerning reservations to multilateral treaties soon became the *lex lata*.[40] Part of this system, according to the ILC's commentary on the 1966 final draft, was the "well-established" rule that "a State which within a reasonable time signifies its objection to a reservation is entitled to regard the treaty as not in force between itself and the reserving State."[41] This rule was formulated in the final draft as Article 17(4)(b): "An objection by another contracting State to a reservation precludes the entry into force of the treaty as between the objecting and reserving States unless a contrary intention is expressed by the objecting State."[42]

In the conference, the Soviet delegation proposed an amendment reversing this rule,[43] which was adopted at the 10th plenary meeting and embodied in Article 20(4)(b).[44] As the rule stands, the objecting state has to act twice: besides objecting to a reservation, it must state explicitly that it does not want any treaty relations with the reserving state. In diplomatic intercourse it would be much more convenient to obtain that result by remaining silent after the objection. (By the same token, it would probably not be unpleasant to inform the reserving state that treaty relations would be appreciated, despite the objection to the reservation; this position would have been brought about by the ILC's proposal.[45])

If at the conclusion of a multilateral treaty a state that is not a party to the Convention objects to a reservation made by another contracting state, but fails "definitely" to express its intention that the objection precludes the entry into force of the treaty between it and the reserving state, the objecting state can maintain that the treaty has not entered into force between it and the reserving state. If the objecting state is a party to the Convention, it would have "definitely" to express its intention in order to obtain that result. If the reserving state is a party to the Convention, it would seem to be obliged to infer from a rejection by a state that is not a party that since customary law applies, the treaty will not enter into force between it and the rejecting state unless that state notifies it to the contrary.

[39] 1951 ICJ REP. 15.

[40] *Cf.* P. IMBERT, LES RÉSERVES AUX TRAITÉS INTERNATIONAUX 72 *ff.* (1979). For a short survey, see, *e.g.*, I. BROWNLIE, PRINCIPLES OF PUBLIC INTERNATIONAL LAW 605–08 (3d ed. 1979).

[41] [1966] 2 Y.B. INT'L L. COMM'N, *supra* note 38, at 206.

[42] *Id.* at 202.

[43] 3 OFF. REC. at 265–66, UN Doc. A/CONF.39/L.3 (1969).

[44] 2 OFF. REC. at 35.

[45] *Cf.* P. IMBERT, *supra* note 40, at 152 *ff.*, especially 158–59, discussing the reversal of the presumption.

In this connection, what is the position of the other contracting parties to the treaty, both parties and nonparties to the Convention? These states, too, will have to assess the legal position as regards the above-mentioned reservation in the light of the specific legal regime that governs it. In particular, states that are parties to the Convention, and that may desire to further its applicability, must be mindful of the rule laid down in Article 34 (on third states). For the depositary of the treaty, all this adds up to a delicate and difficult task, whether or not he is himself a party to the Convention.

Similar situations will occur whenever states that are not parties to the Convention fail to conform to other requirements found in it. For example, Articles 22 and 23 prescribe certain formalities, such as notices and communications, that must be in writing. May a state that is a party to the Convention dispense with these requirements when none of the other parties to the treaty in question is a party to the Convention?

Article 35, on treaties providing for obligations for third states, requires the latter to accept the obligations in writing. What if a third state is not a party to the Convention and its acceptance consists of an oral statement by a competent representative in an international conference? May those parties to the treaty giving rise to the obligation which are parties to the Convention trust that the obligation has been validly accepted? Conversely, can a party to the Convention that is a third state with regard to a particular treaty make a valid oral acceptance of an obligation under the treaty if none of the parties to it is party to the Convention? May these states insist on an acceptance in writing? Must they insist on it?

In searching for answers to these and like questions, account should be taken of the award of the Franco-Mexican Claims Commission in the *Pablo Nájera* case of October 19, 1928. France, a member of the League of Nations, had failed to register the Franco-Mexican Claims Convention of September 25, 1924 with the Secretariat of the League in accordance with Article 18 of the Covenant. It was held that failure to register a treaty did not affect the position of a party to it that was not a member of the League:

> [L]'Etat non-membre est tout à fait étranger à l'engagement contracté par les membres; pour lui n'est obligatoire que la règle du droit international commun, d'après laquelle la force obligatoire d'un traité résulte généralement de l'échange des ratifications. . . .
>
> Le Mexique n'étant pas lié, en tant que ce soit, par la disposition de l'article 18, et cette disposition ne pouvant, par suite, lui nuire à aucun égard, il ne saurait, à l'inverse, non plus en tirer des arguments en sa faveur, pour se soustraire à des engagements internationaux qu'il a pris par une convention qui, pour ce qui le concerne, est pleinement valable.[46]

Questions of the same kind arise in connection with Article 40(5). According to this provision, a state that becomes a party to a treaty that has been amended shall be considered a party to the treaty as well as to the amending treaty if

[46] 5 R. Int'l Arb. Awards 466, 471–72; *cf.* C. ROUSSEAU, *supra* note 4, at 320–21, 457; and A. MCNAIR, THE LAW OF TREATIES 313 (1961). On Article 18 and states not members of the League, see especially the analysis in D. ANZILOTTI, COURS DE DROIT INTERNATIONAL 378–83 (trans. Gidel 1929).

the latter has entered into force, unless the state expresses a different intention. The state in question is bound in this way only vis-à-vis states parties to the treaty that are also parties to the amending treaty. The commentary to Article 40(5) reveals that the ILC was informed by the Secretariat of the United Nations

> that it is by no means uncommon for a State to ratify or otherwise establish its consent to the treaty without giving any indication as to its intentions regarding the amending agreement; and that in these cases the instrument of ratification, acceptance, etc. is presumed by the Secretary-General in his capacity as a depositary to cover the treaty with its amendments.

The ILC declared further that in the absence of any indication by the state, "it is desirable to adopt a solution which will bring the maximum number of States into mutual relations under the treaty."[47]

If some parties to a treaty that has been amended are parties to the Convention and some are not, accession by states to that treaty will lead to different legal results in the absence of expressions of intent. A Convention party will be a party to the treaty as well as to the amending treaty only vis-à-vis parties to these instruments that are also Convention parties. States that are not parties to the Convention cannot consider states that are parties as being bound by the amending treaty. Likewise, a state that is not a party to the Convention will not be considered a party to the amending treaty if it becomes a party to the treaty itself, either by parties or nonparties to the Convention.[48] Only among Convention parties, therefore, is the presumption by the Secretary-General—otherwise rebuttable—turned into a rule of law (failing an expression to the contrary); this rule does not apply in any situation involving a state that is not a party to the Convention. Thus, it is highly dubious whether the solution adopted in the Convention will indeed maximize the relations of states parties under an amended treaty, as was intended.

Article 41, on agreements to modify multilateral treaties between certain of the parties only, prescribes in its second paragraph that "the parties in question shall notify the other parties of their intention to conclude the agreement and of the modification to the treaty for which it provides" (unless the treaty provides otherwise). This is a procedural safeguard, intended "to add a further protection to the parties against illegitimate modifications of the treaty by some of the parties."[49] There does not seem to be any comparable customary rule on the procedure for the modification of treaties; customary law is concerned rather with questions of substance, that is, the compatibility of modifying instruments with the treaties they modify.[50]

When a number of parties to a multilateral treaty—some of them parties to the Convention, some of them not—negotiate a modifying treaty, the rule

[47] [1966] 2 Y.B. INT'L L. COMM'N, *supra* note 38, at 234.

[48] At the conference, Sir Humphrey Waldock, acting as expert consultant, explicitly referred to the *de lege ferenda* character of the presumption. 1 OFF. REC. at 204.

[49] [1966] 2 Y.B. INT'L L. COMM'N, *supra* note 38, at 235.

[50] *Cf.* C. ROUSSEAU, *supra* note 4, at 509 *ff.*, 764–814; E. HOYT, THE UNANIMITY RULE IN THE REVISION OF TREATIES. A REEXAMINATION (1959).

of Article 41(2) applies, but its scope is limited: states that are not parties to the Convention have no right to be notified, and such states have no obligation to notify if they participated in the negotiation. Article 41(2) will therefore be operative only among the parties to the Convention.[51] The very object and purpose of this provision is to afford protection to *all* the states parties to the treaty in question. However, the rule of general international law (also enunciated in Article 34 of the Convention) that treaties do not create rights or obligations for third states prevents Article 41(2) from fulfilling this function vis-à-vis states parties to the treaty that are not Convention parties. It cannot afford protection to *all* states parties to the treaty except in a situation of general participation.

"Incompatible Provisions." Part V of the Convention contains an elaborate system of rules concerning the invalidity, termination, and suspension of the operation of treaties. It opens with the following provision, set forth in Article 42:

> *Validity and continuance in force of treaties*
>
> 1. The validity of a treaty or of the consent of a State to be bound by a treaty may be impeached only through the application of the present Convention.
>
> 2. The termination of a treaty, its denunciation or the withdrawal of a party, may take place only as a result of the application of the provisions of the treaty or of the present Convention. The same rule applies to suspension of the operation of a treaty.

This is the first of the "General Provisions" that constitute section I of part V. In Article 30 of the 1963 draft, the idea was expressed that "the nullity, termination or suspension of the operation" of a treaty, or withdrawal of a particular party from a treaty, should result "from the application of the present articles."[52] The commentary to the corresponding article (Article 39) of the final draft (1966) explains that the words "only through the application of the present articles" and "only as a result of the application of the present articles" in draft Article 39 were intended "to indicate that the grounds for invalidity, termination, denunciation, withdrawal and suspension provided for in the draft articles are *exhaustive* of all such grounds, apart from any special cases expressly provided for in the treaty itself."[53]

In consequence, Article 69 opens as follows: "A treaty the invalidity of which is established under the present Convention is void." Does this not imply that the treaty is not void if the invalidity has been established otherwise? Part V of the Convention contains a number of substantive rules concerning the various modes of invalidity, withdrawal, and termination or suspension of

[51] Article 41(2) fails to indicate who is to perform the notification to the other parties. This may cause difficulties, especially in cases where the depositary of the treaty is not a party to the Convention. The same holds for Article 40(2), on notification of proposals to amend a multilateral treaty.

[52] Report of the International Law Commission covering the work of its 15th session, UN Doc. A/5509, at 3, *reprinted in* [1963] 2 Y.B. INT'L L. COMM'N 187, 189, UN Doc. A/CN.4/SER.A/1963/Add.1.

[53] [1966] 2 Y.B. INT'L L. COMM'N, *supra* note 38, at 237 (emphasis added).

a treaty, plus provisions on the procedures to be followed with respect to these matters. These procedures are found in section 4 of part V, Articles 65 through 68. Article 65, which many members of the ILC regarded as a "key article" for the application of the provisions of part V,[54] prescribes notification in writing to other parties when a party wishes to invoke a defect in its consent, or a ground for impeaching the validity of a treaty or for terminating it, withdrawing from it, or suspending its operation "under the provisions of the present Convention." The notification must indicate what the party proposes to do, and the reasons for its action. If other parties object (in writing) to the proposed action, a solution is to be sought through the means laid down in Article 33 of the Charter of the United Nations, unless other provisions on the settlement of disputes are applicable. If no solution is reached within a year, Article 66 provides that the dispute may be submitted to the International Court of Justice if it concerns a peremptory rule of international law (*jus cogens*: Articles 53 and 64 of the Convention), unless the parties agree to resort to arbitration. If the dispute concerns some other article of part V, any of the parties to it may request that the Secretary-General of the United Nations set in motion the procedure specified in the Annex to the Convention, which provides for settlement through a conciliation commission.

It is not necessary to recapitulate here the rules of the Convention on the various modes of and grounds for invalidity, termination, and suspension of the operation of treaties. These rules are not, as such, the subject of the present inquiry. Part V is considered here from the point of view of treaty relations between states parties to the Convention and nonparties.

The incompatibility envisaged does not occur as long as a dispute concerning a particular treaty originates among parties to it that are bound by the Convention and remains limited to them: in other words, as long as general participation obtains. But as soon as the dispute involves a state that is not a Convention party, the question of a double regime comes up. If that state is a member of the United Nations, Article 33 of the Charter seems to apply to the dispute with regard to that state also—though it should be recalled that Article 33 speaks only of "disputes, the continuance of which is likely to endanger the maintenance of international peace and security." Thus, the reference to Article 33 of the Charter in Article 65 of the Convention will affect a nonparty to the Convention only if it can be established that the dispute in question is a dispute in the sense of Article 33. Obviously, in principle, a treaty dispute can endanger international peace and security; but by no means all treaty disputes will have this effect.

Subject to this condition, and aside from the question of the precise meaning of the reference to Article 33 of the Charter for states that are parties to the Convention, the scope of the double regime is limited to two areas: the substantive rules and the procedural prescriptions.

As to the substantive rules containing the grounds, it is doubtful whether the ILC was correct in claiming[55] that its codification was exhaustive;[56] and

[54] *Id.* at 262.

[55] *See* text at note 53 *supra*.

[56] *See* Capotorti, *L'Extinction et la suspension des traités*, 134 RECUEIL DES COURS 417, 514, 536 (1971 III). The author draws the conclusion that the procedure of part V is not applicable when grounds are invoked that are not included in the Convention. *Id.* at 578.

it also introduced restrictive formulations that are probably absent from customary law. One is strongly reminded of the proposal by the Luxembourg Government in connection with Article 51 of the 1963 draft articles (Article 62 in the final draft of 1966, and Article 65 of the Convention) and the observations of the special rapporteur on that proposal.

Various governments had suggested that the provisions of part V should be applied only subject to independent determination, and that they were not to be invoked by states that refused to accept some form of compulsory means for the settlement of disputes. Luxembourg proposed the following provision as an intermediate arrangement:

> Upon acceding to these articles, States parties may, without prejudice to the general rules of international law, exclude from the application of the provisions relating to the defect in validity and the termination of treaties any State that has not accepted in their regard an undertaking concerning compulsory jurisdiction or compulsory arbitration, with respect to a treaty of which a defect in validity or the termination is alleged.[57]

The effect of this provision would have been that the articles regarding nullity and termination would have had full force as between states accepting compulsory adjudication, while in other cases "the general rules of international law would be applicable, so that the provisions contained in the articles would serve only for guidance and have no binding force."

The special rapporteur, in his response to this proposal, observed in part that he doubted the efficacy of this "intermediate solution." The general rules of international law regarding noncompliance with international law, lack of authority, fraud, error, etc., would have remained applicable. In consequence,

> the possibility of arbitrary recourse to grounds of invalidity or termination would still exist, and perhaps in aggravated form; for the strict definitions of the conditions for alleging grounds of invalidity or termination contained in the Commission's draft articles and the procedural safeguards at present contained in article 51 might be claimed not to apply.

The special rapporteur concluded with a remark that is particularly interesting in this connection:

> Indeed a serious objection to the proposal is the very fact that it involves drawing a distinction between "the general rules of international law" on the subject and the rules laid down in the draft articles. Although some elements of "progressive development" may normally be expected to be present in any codifying convention, the Special Rapporteur feels that it would, in some measure, defeat the object of codification if the resulting convention drew a distinction between the provisions of the code and the "general rules of international law."[58]

The implication is clear. There are several references to "general international law" in the Convention: in the eighth preambular paragraph and in Articles 3(b), 4, 38, 43, 53, and 64. In none of these provisions, however, do

[57] [1966] 2 Y.B. INT'L L. COMM'N, *supra* note 38, at 47.

[58] *Id.* at 49.

the Convention and general international law govern the same subject matter simultaneously, unless the relationship between the two systems is carefully specified. The adoption of the proposal by Luxembourg would have introduced into the Convention a "double regime" for the settlement of treaty disputes: parties to the same dispute would have been subject to different regimes. The special rapporteur was right in perceiving the problems a "double regime" could have generated: the object of the codification might indeed have been defeated "in some measure." The special rapporteur's response indicates that similar problems will almost certainly arise in the circumstances discussed in this paper.

Incidentally, although the Luxembourg proposal was not inserted into the Convention, at least one state declared its intention of acting in the spirit of the proposal. After the vote on what was to become Article 66 and the Annex, the Swiss delegation declared:

> [The delegation] wished to place on record that, should Switzerland sign the convention on the law of treaties, it would do so subject to the reservation that all the articles in Part V would only apply in the relations between Switzerland and those States parties which, like Switzerland, accepted the compulsory jurisdiction of the International Court of Justice, or compulsory arbitration, for the settlement of any dispute arising from the application or the interpretation of any of those articles.[59]

As judicial and arbitral settlement of disputes obviously requires procedural equality among the parties to the particular dispute,[60] it seems that the entire machinery for the settlement of disputes specified in part V of the Convention and the Annex cannot function properly unless all the parties to the treaty dispute are subject to it. States involved in the dispute that are not parties to the Convention might prefer, *e.g.*, to seek a settlement by political means, in an organ such as the UN General Assembly or in a regional political forum. (Of course, they may subject themselves voluntarily to the rules of part V, but willingness to do so must be expressed unequivocally.[61])

[59] 2 OFF. REC. at 194. On problems relative to part V of the Convention, see, in particular, Rosenne, *The Settlement of Treaty Disputes under the Vienna Convention on the Law of Treaties of 1969*, 31 ZEITSCHRIFT FÜR AUSLÄNDISCHES ÖFFENTLICHES RECHT UND VÖLKERRECHT [ZAÖRV] 1-62 (1971). The author does not directly discuss the matter dealt with here; in fact, it is only with respect to paragraph 1 of the Annex that he observes, at p. 49:

> The assumption of this paragraph is that the only disputes likely to involve Conciliation Commissions will be disputes between States which are either Members of the United Nations, or parties to the Vienna Convention. The possibility that only one of the parties to such a treaty-dispute will come within one or other of the categories is not contemplated. This may not be a theoretical matter.

Rosenne mentions a number of states that participated in the Vienna Conference but are not members of the United Nations.

[60] Witness the rule of reciprocity in, *e.g.*, Article 36(2) of the Statute of the International Court of Justice, and the strictness with which that rule is applied by the Court: Anglo-Iranian Oil Co. (Jurisdiction), 1952 ICJ REP. 93, 103; Norwegian Loans, 1957 ICJ REP. 9, 23-24.

[61] In the *Eastern Carelia* case the Permanent Court of International Justice declared: "It is well established in international law that no State can, without its consent, be compelled to submit its disputes with other States either to mediation or arbitration, or to any other kind of pacific

On the other hand, it would seriously disturb the procedural equality among the states parties to a treaty if some of the parties involved in the dispute were considered to be bound, *inter se*, by the rules of part V and the Annex, and others were not. By the same token, the latter could regard settlement in accordance with part V among the states that are bound by the Convention as *res inter alios acta*. What authority would the outcome of the procedure of part V have for them? Conversely, what authority would the settlement of the dispute outside part V have for states involved in the dispute that are parties to the Convention?

As a matter of fact, several states seem to have taken the position that part V requires at least reciprocity, if not general participation, by making reservations or objections to reservations to that effect upon ratification or accession. Two examples will be cited here. Finland declared:

> [A]s to its relation with any State which has made or makes a reservation to the effect that this State will not be bound by some or all of the provisions of Article 66, Finland will consider itself bound neither by those procedural provisions nor by the substantive provisions of Part V of the Convention to which the procedures provided for in Article 66 do not apply as a result of the said reservation.[62]

The Swedish Government objected to the reservation of the Syrian Arab Republic, which stated that its accession to the Convention did not include the Annex, and to that of Tunisia, which indicated that a dispute falling under Article 66(a) required the consent of all the parties involved in order to be submitted to the International Court of Justice for a decision.

> In view of these reservations, the Swedish Government considers, *firstly*, that the treaty relations between Sweden and the Syrian Arab Republic will not include those provisions of Part V of the Convention to which the conciliation procedure in the Annex applies and, *secondly*, that the treaty relations between Sweden and Tunisia will not include articles 53 and 64 of the Convention.[63]

The effect of such reservations may be more sweeping than the restrictive formulations seem to indicate, but their precise effect on the functioning of part V of the Convention as a whole remains to be seen. They do suggest the existence of yet another category of states in relation to the Convention. Apart from parties and nonparties to the Convention, there are states that are parties to a treaty dispute and to the Convention, and states that are parties to the same treaty dispute that are not bound by the Convention. Among the states

---

settlement." The dispute involved Article 17 of the Covenant of the League of Nations, concerning disputes between a member of the League (*in casu* Finland) and a state that was not a member (*in casu* the Soviet Union). "The submission, therefore, of a dispute between [states that are not members of the League] and a Member of the League for solution according to the methods provided for in the Covenant could take place only by virtue of their consent." 1923 PCIJ, ser. B, No. 5, at 27 *ff*.

[62] MULTILATERAL TREATIES, *supra* note 2, at 599.

[63] *Id*. at 601. (One wonders what the effect of the statement concerning Articles 53 and 64 can possibly be, considering the nature of rules of *jus cogens*!)

that are parties to the Convention as well as to the dispute, there are, however, some that are bound by part V of the Convention and some that are not. Moreover, some are only partially bound by part V as regards certain states as a result of objections to reservations with respect to part V, provided that the objecting states have not also expressed their definite intention that the Convention as a whole shall not enter into force between them and the reserving states (Article 20(4)(b)).

If the operation of part V is indeed subject to a condition of general participation, then a broader question arises: how can the operation of part V be reconciled with the *inter se* operation of a number of other provisions of the Convention? This question cannot be dealt with in abstracto; much less can it be answered here. But sometime in the future the Secretary-General, in his capacity as depositary of the Convention, may have to find answers to it.

Other Provisions. The list of articles discussed or referred to in the previous paragraphs may not be, and is not claimed to be, exhaustive.[64] Thus, an analysis of the articles on the interpretation of treaties (Articles 31 through 33) in the light of the problem discussed here might require a separate study, which would exceed the scope of this paper. The unsettled nature of the rules of interpretation in customary international law makes it probable that such a study would turn out to be rather unproductive.

IV. Conclusion

Although codifying conventions can settle the law not only for the parties to them, but also for states that—for whatever reason—have not become parties to them, it is nevertheless clear that, in a conflict between a state that is party to such an instrument and a nonparty, the latter will firmly deny that it is bound by the codified rules if the denial will make a difference in the conflict (as it did in the *North Sea Continental Shelf* cases[65]). This attitude was the point of departure of this paper. It was not meant, of course, to imply that codifying instruments cannot have the more positive effect: in paragraph 71 of the Judgment in the *Continental Shelf* cases, the International Court of

[64] At the end of his study, *La Conférence de Vienne sur le droit des traités. Une vue d'ensemble,* 15 Annuaire Français Droit Int'l 24–53 (1969), S. E. Nahlik asks what the meaning of the Convention can be for states that do not become parties to it, and for treaties concluded by states that do become parties, but were concluded before the entry into force of the Convention (Article 4). The answers to these two questions, Professor Nahlik says, will be more or less identical. He lists the provisions of the Convention that in his opinion are *not* applicable in either case, as they neither codify customary law nor are to be considered as "general principles of law recognized by civilized nations." They are: provisions that fix a term (Article 65) or a majority required for taking a decision (Article 9); that stipulate a particular form (Articles 23 and 67) or modalities of technique rather than substance (Article 79); that set forth the obligatory procedure for the settlement of disputes (Article 65 and the Annex); that choose one particular solution to a problem of the two or more that exist in practice, or at least in the relevant theory (Articles 31–32, Article 62); and finally, that "introduisent des droits ou obligations trop disparates pour qu'elles puissent être considérées comme engendrant des règles obligatoires." These latter are, in Nahlik's opinion, "especially" (*surtout*) Articles 37, 41(2), 44, and 60. *Id.* at 51–52.

[65] 1969 ICJ Rep. 4.

Justice observed that they can, and the Convention acknowledges this legal phenomenon in Article 38.[66]

The Convention does not contain any rules to avoid or solve problems arising from the adherence to a treaty of both parties and nonparties to the Convention. As far as can be ascertained, the matter was not discussed at the conference in Vienna. The Convention is framed as a self-contained instrument, as if it had only to function in situations of general participation. Several practical questions have been posed in the previous pages, though only a few could be answered. There may not be a clear-cut solution to the problem examined here, that of a double regime governing treaties—or indeed to that of a plurality of regimes governing treaties in general, *e.g.*, under Article 3(c) of the Convention or as a result of reservations to the Convention.

When parties to a contract are not certain what law will govern it, or fear disagreement on that question, they may insert a clause designating a particular legal system as the law of the contract. In international law this situation occurs notably when entities that are subject to municipal law contract with states, and it is preferred that the contract not be governed by a particular system of municipal law.[67] In some of these cases, the law chosen is international law, although the choice is hardly ever formulated in simple and clear terms.[68]

A similar technique is available to states negotiating a treaty, when some are parties to the Convention and others are not, which might give rise to doubts about the applicable international legal rules.[69] Two regimes qualify: the general international law of treaties and the law of the Vienna Convention (with its reference to "the rules of customary international law," which, according to the eighth preambular paragraph, "will continue to govern questions not regulated by the provisions of the present Convention"). Selection of the first regime will not be considered here. The choice of the second could be worded as follows: "The present treaty as well as the rights and obligations

[66] Article 38 reads as follows: "Nothing in Articles 34 to 37 precludes a rule set forth in a treaty from becoming binding upon a third State as a customary rule of international law, recognized as such." (Articles 34 to 37 concern "treaties and third States.")

[67] *See, e.g.*, F. MANN, *The Law Governing State Contracts*, and *The Proper Law of Contracts Concluded by International Persons*, in STUDIES IN INTERNATIONAL LAW 179 and 211 (1973).

[68] *See, e.g.*, clause 28(7) of the deeds of concession between Libya and two American oil companies:

> This Concession shall be governed by and interpreted in accordance with the principles of law of Libya common to the principles of international law and in the absence of such common principles then by and in accordance with the general principles of law, including such of those principles as may have been applied by international tribunals.

Quoted in 53 ILR 389, 402–04 (1979), 17 ILM 1, 11 (1978).

[69] H. Strebel observed as long ago as 1967:

> [The Convention] should expressly provide that both those who are parties to the Convention and those who are not, have the possibility to subject either all or certain treaty relations already in existence retroactively, either from the time they were entered into or beginning at a later date, to the new rules of the law of treaties, and also to do so under certain reservations.

Preliminary Remarks, 27 ZAÖRV 408, 409–10 (1967).

arising from it shall be governed by the Vienna Convention on the Law of Treaties, 1969."[70] In the case of an open treaty, to which states can accede, an article on reservations should prohibit reservations to the choice-of-law clause.

On the basis of such a policy, organs of international organizations, as well as international conferences, could adopt resolutions choosing the Convention as the governing law whenever they decide to draft a treaty. The choice-of-law clause mentioned above should then be embodied in the treaty. As a result of such policies, both the certainty of the law and the *effet utile* of the Convention would be greatly enhanced. So far, adherence to codifying instruments has been less than might have been expected, and only a limited number of states have become parties to them. The principal reason is not that states object to the law laid down in these instruments, but that they simply do not manage to complete the procedures required to become bound by them.[71] The device of subjecting a treaty to the law of the Convention by a simple clause embodied in that treaty would secure the operation of the Convention in a number of cases where the question of its operation could otherwise cause serious problems.

Finally, it was observed above[72] that the subject of this essay would apply to the future instrument on treaties concluded between states and international organizations or between international organizations in the same way that it applies to the Vienna Convention on the Law of Treaties. The preparatory work of the drafters of the articles for the future instrument suggests that they may not have paid attention to this point. However, even if they did, a convention on the law of treaties probably could not, of itself, solve the problems that could be generated by the fact that not all states (or international organizations) that conclude treaties do become parties to such a convention, and that those states or organizations which do become parties may make reservations. Nevertheless, it may be well to take this fact into account in drafting the articles on the settlement of treaty disputes under the instrument.[73] For example, the draft articles could make the right of a state or an international organization to invoke a ground for the invalidity or termination of a treaty conditional upon acceptance of the provisions in the convention on some form of compulsory settlement of disputes.

[70] If states want the Convention to apply retroactively to an existing treaty, the words "Article 4 of that Convention notwithstanding" might be added to the clause, because Article 4 does not contain the phrase "unless the parties otherwise agree."

[71] *See* M. NAWAZ, J. FRIED, & O. SCHACHTER, TOWARD WIDER ACCEPTANCE OF U.N. TREATIES (1971).

[72] *See* text following note 15 *supra*.

[73] The latest version of the draft articles, completed up to Article 80 plus Annex, and adopted by the ILC at its 32d session in 1980, is to be found in the ILC's report on that session, 35 GAOR Supp. (No. 10) at 139–81, UN Doc. A/35/10 (1980). The commentary to Articles 60–80 and the Annex is reproduced at pp. 181–236.

LAWYERS WHO ESTABLISHED INTERNATIONAL LAW IN THE UNITED STATES, 1776–1914

*By John M. Raymond and Barbara J. Frischholz**

In the late 18th and 19th, and the early 20th centuries invaluable contributions were made by lawyers to the establishment of international law in the United States. Their contributions took various forms, but all helped establish, clarify, or disseminate understanding of this branch of the law. Because of the ways international law develops, these people ranged from statesmen who established practices and doctrines in the international field that ultimately became the law, to those who participated in the development of important treaties and international agreements; and from judges who rendered significant decisions on points of international law, to scholars and others who were responsible for the gradual evolution of education and literature in the field.

THE 18TH AND EARLY 19TH CENTURIES

In the early days of the new nation there were no law schools as we know them today. Individuals trained for the law under the tutelage of an attorney, or by devoting long hours to the study, on their own, of the works of such authorities as Blackstone and Kent, or—if they wished to delve deeply into international law—Vattel, or even Grotius, the so-called father of international law. Through such training many young lawyers who were future leaders of our country learned, probably better than a great many of the present generation, the philosophical bases, the practical necessities, and the wisely oriented flexibility needed for the continuous adaptation of the law to new situations. It is these qualities that characterize Anglo-American jurisprudence at its best. Lawyers with the understanding and skills fostered by such a system had an enormous impact on the development of our law and set its course in the international field for the future.

The Judiciary

International law had been in the law of England, and hence in our colonial law, certainly since the Lord Chancellor Talbot said in 1735 that the "law of nations formed part of the law of England."[1] In 1784, between the Declaration of Independence and the adoption of the Constitution, Chief Justice McKean of Pennsylvania invoked the law of nations in holding an individual guilty of assault upon the secretary of the French Minister in the Minister's house.[2]

* Professorial Lecturer Emeritus, University of Santa Clara, and of the California Bar, respectively. Formerly, Mr. Raymond served as Deputy Legal Adviser, U.S. Department of State, and Ms. Frischholz as Research Attorney, California Court of Appeal, First Appellate District.

[1] Barbuit's Case, 25 Eng. Rep. 777 (Ch.).

[2] Respublica v. De Longchamps, 1 Dall. 111 (Pa. 1784); *see also* discussion of prize cases that arose during the period of the Continental Congress in Bourguinon, *Incorporation of the Law of Nations during the American Revolution—The Case of the San Antonio*, 71 AJIL 270 (1977).

At the national level after the adoption of the Constitution, the first official pronouncement on international law was made by Edmund Randolph, who was to become Secretary of State in 1794. In 1792 Randolph, then Attorney General, rendered an opinion which stated: "The law of nations, although not specifically adopted by the Constitution or any municipal act, is essentially a part of the law of the land."[3] Then in 1793 Chief Justice Jay, formerly Secretary of Foreign Affairs under the Continental Congress, speaking for the Supreme Court, announced that the United States "had, by taking its place among the nations of the earth, become amenable to the law of nations."[4]

These fundamental declarations were foreshadowed when the drafters of the Constitution incorporated in it the provisions on defense, diplomatic representatives, foreign commerce, punishment of "offences against the law of nations," and treaties, which were to be "the supreme law of the land."[5] International law had unobtrusively been woven into the fabric of our national existence.

The concept of "natural law"—what might be described as the conceptually reasonable and morally right law—had enormous influence on the 17th- and 18th-century theorists such as Grotius and Vattel. Although international law has retained its natural law roots, there was bound to be conflict as the practice of states, which creates customary law,[6] diverged from natural law principles. John Marshall settled the point for American jurisprudence. Sitting as Chief Justice in *The Antelope*, he stated that while the slave trade unquestionably was "contrary to the law of nature," nevertheless a "trade could not be considered as contrary to the law of nations which was authorized and protected by the laws of all commercial nations; the right to carry on which was claimed by each"; and he added that "the law of nations . . . is certainly to be tried by the test of general usage. That which has received the assent of all, must be the law of all."[7]

This is not the place to trace the history of the abolition of the slave trade, but it should be noted that the subject has long since been dealt with by multilateral treaties.[8]

[3] 1 Op. Att'y Gen. 26, 27 (1792).

[4] Chisholm v. Georgia, 2 U.S. (2 Dall.) 419, 473 (1793); *see also* Justice Wilson in Ware v. Hylton, 3 U.S. (3 Dall.) 199, 281 (1796); discussion in Dumbauld, *Independence under International Law*, 70 AJIL 425 (1976).

[5] U.S. CONST. art. I, cl. 8; art. II, cl. 2; art. VI.

[6] For a case illustrating the development of practice into comity, then into international law, see The Paquete *Habana*, 175 U.S. 677 (1900), discussed in text at note 105. For situations where unilateral claims, long asserted, developed into international law, see text at notes 25–28 and 35–41.

[7] 23 U.S. (10 Wheat.) 66, 115, 120–21 (1825). Three years earlier Justice Story on Circuit had followed natural law concepts and stated that the slave trade was "repugnant to the general principles of justice and humanity"; and he had held that therefore an American officer could properly capture a French slave-trading vessel on the high seas and proceed against her in an American court. United States v. *La Jeune Eugenie*, 2 Mas. 409, 26 Fed. Cas. 832 (No. 15,551) (C.C.D. Mass. 1822).

[8] General Act of July 2, 1890, for Suppression of the African Slave Trade, 27 Stat. 886, TS No. 383; Convention of Sept. 25, 1926, to Suppress the Slave Trade and Slavery, 46 Stat. 2183, TS No. 778, 60 LNTS 253. On natural law, see J. BRIERLY, THE LAW OF NATIONS 16–25 (5th ed. 1954).

Another basic contribution was made by Marshall in the internationally renowned case of *Schooner Exchange v. McFadden*,[9] which held that the French man-of-war *Exchange*, docked in the port of Philadelphia, was exempt from United States jurisdiction. The opinion opens with the frequently quoted postulate: "The jurisdiction of the nation, within its own territory, is necessarily exclusive and absolute. . . . All exceptions, therefore, to the full and complete power of a nation, within its own territories, must be traced up to the consent of the nation itself. They can flow from no other legitimate source."[10]

This clearly sets forth the most fundamental of all international legal doctrines, the territorial supremacy of the sovereign, sometimes characterized as "the touchstone of private and public international law."[11] Although hardly a novel proposition, nevertheless Marshall so clearly articulated the principle that it continues to be quoted as the law on the subject.[12]

Turning then to the exceptions to the doctrine, Marshall notes that the "mutual benefit [of sovereignties] is promoted by intercourse with each other," and that this necessitates relaxations of the exercise of absolute territorial jurisdiction in certain cases, which, having been consented to by sovereigns and tested by common usage, had become the law of nations.[13] He cites the exemption of the visiting sovereign from arrest or detention within a foreign country, and the like exemption of his ministers. Then follows the oft-quoted, but long misunderstood, language: a "sovereign is understood to cede a portion of his territorial jurisdiction . . . where he allows the troops of a foreign prince to pass through his domains," even "without any express declaration waiving jurisdiction," provided this right of passage has been granted to the foreign army.[14] Finally, Marshall said that while such exemption did not extend to merchant ships entering foreign ports, a public armed ship is part of the military force of the nation, and when it enters foreign waters under an implied license the license "ought to be construed as containing an

[9] 11 U.S. (7 Cranch) 116 (1812).

[10] *Id.* at 136.

[11] Mr. Justice White in his dissent in Banco Nacional de Cuba v. Sabbatino, 376 U.S. 398, 445–46 (1964).

[12] B. Ziegler, The International Law of John Marshall 64 (1939). *See also* Wilson v. Girard, 354 U.S. 524 (1957), discussed in note 14 *infra*.

[13] 11 U.S. (7 Cranch) at 136.

[14] *Id.* at 139. This was erroneously thought by some to mean that whenever our forces were stationed in friendly foreign territory they were exempt from foreign jurisdiction of every kind, a misconception left uncorrected for almost 150 years. But in Wilson v. Girard, 354 U.S. 524, 529 (1957), the Supreme Court straightened this out. It first reverted to Marshall's major premise and pointed out that "a sovereign nation has exclusive jurisdiction to punish offences against the laws committed within its borders, unless it expressly or impliedly consents to surrender its jurisdiction." It then proceeded to hold that while waiver might be implied from permitting a brief passage of foreign troops over a portion of a state's territory, or a temporary visit of a foreign public ship, the granting of permission to station friendly foreign troops in a state's territory for an indefinite period is different, and does not necessarily involve waiver of jurisdiction. The host state certainly can impose conditions on the entry of such troops, and may insist upon the exercise of its own territorial jurisdiction over the force. For an agreed waiver of jurisdiction by NATO countries, see note 32 *infra*, second paragraph.

exemption from the [jurisdiction of the] sovereign."[15] This was the case of the schooner *Exchange*.

Marshall thus both formulated and qualified the doctrine of absolute territorial jurisdiction of the sovereign. His clear statement of the law has been quoted and followed abroad as well as in this country.

Certain decisions on the effect of treaties deserve attention. In 1796 Justice Chase in *Ware v. Hylton*[16] established definitely that a treaty superseded a conflicting statute of one of the several U.S. states. In 1829 Marshall in *Foster v. Neilson*[17] dealt with the question whether a treaty with Spain operated as the law of the United States. Marshall stated that a treaty is "to be regarded in courts of justice as equivalent to an act of the legislature, whenever it operates of itself, without the aid of any legislative provision." Only the English text of the Treaty was before the Court, and as it did not show conclusively that it was intended to operate without the need of implementing legislation, the Treaty was held not to be self-executing. Four years later in *United States v. Percheman*,[18] the same Treaty was again before the Court. This time the Spanish text also was before the Court and it showed unmistakably that the Treaty was intended to operate without the need of legislation. As the English text could be interpreted either way, Marshall here held that the Treaty was self-executing and operated as law.

These decisions settled in our domestic law important effects of national conventional law established by our treaties.

The Executive

From the beginning, the Department of State has been responsible both for the negotiation of treaties and for the development of policies and practices in the field of customary international law. But in the beginning the Secretary of State was himself virtually the entire Department, and even when he later acquired additional staff, he was still for many decades his own legal adviser. Thus, the personal stamp of each Secretary can be seen in the shaping of legal policies and practices in the international field.

Many of the early Secretaries of State moved on to other influential positions where their statesmanship continued to guide the country. A footnote[19]

[15] 11 U.S. (7 Cranch) at 144.

[16] 3 U.S. (3 Dall.) 199, 234–37 (1796). John Marshall and Patrick Henry were counsel for the losing side. The decision did not deal with the effect of a treaty on an inconsistent *federal* statute. It was in 1870 in The Cherokee Tobacco, 78 U.S. (11 Wall.) 616, 621 (1870), that the rule was explicitly stated: "A treaty may supersede a prior act of Congress, and an act of Congress may supersede a prior treaty."

[17] 27 U.S. (2 Pet.) 253, 314 (1829).

[18] 32 U.S. (7 Pet.) 51 (1833).

[19] Robert R. Livingston was the first Secretary of Foreign Affairs under the Continental Congress, 1781–1783. Later he was Minister to France, 1801–1804. He was succeeded as Secretary of Foreign Affairs by John Jay, who held this post until after the adoption of the Constitution, when he was elevated to the position of Chief Justice of the United States, 1789–1795. Livingston and Jay had at one time practiced law together.

One of the first acts of Congress following the adoption of the Constitution was to establish the lists the roster of the Secretaries of State from the days of the Continental Congress to the middle of the 19th century. *All were lawyers*. They laid a solid foundation of doctrines of international law that has stood the test of time. The more notable instances will be mentioned.

On April 22, 1793, President Washington announced that we would be neutral in the hostilities then existing between Britain and France. He further stated that violations of "the law of nations with respect to the powers at war or any of them" would be prosecuted.[20] This position was based on the opinion of his Secretary of State, Thomas Jefferson, who described the rights and duties of a neutral power thus: "It is the right of every nation to prohibit acts of sovereignty from being exercised by any other within its limits and the duty of a neutral nation to prohibit such as would injure one of the warring Powers."[21] The enactment of the Neutrality Act of June 5, 1794 implemented our duty as a neutral nation by prohibiting the enlistment of American citizens or residents in foreign military service and the outfitting or arming of vessels in the United States for a foreign belligerent.[22] The Neutrality Act also established U.S. policy with regard to the sale of munitions by Americans to foreign belligerents, based on Jefferson's concept of the international law on the subject. He rejected the suggestion of Great Britain that all such export

---

position of Secretary of State. Up to the middle of the 19th century, the following, all lawyers, held that position (other positions of influence held by them are also indicated):

1790–1794. Thomas Jefferson. Vice President, 1797–1801; President, 1801–1809
1794–1795. Edmund Randolph. Attorney General, 1789–1794
1795–1800. Timothy Pickering. Secretary of War, 1795
1800–1801. John Marshall. Chief Justice of the United States, 1801–1835
1801–1809. James Madison. President, 1809–1817*
1809–1811. Robert Smith. Secretary of the Navy, 1801–1805
1811–1817. James Monroe. President, 1817–1825*
1817–1825. John Quincy Adams. President, 1825–1829
1825–1829. Henry Clay. Speaker of the House, 1811–1814, 1815–1820; Senator, 1806–1807, 1810–1811, 1831–1842, 1849–1852
1829–1831. Martin Van Buren. Vice President, 1833–1837; President, 1837–1841
1831–1833. Edward Livingston. Senator, 1829–1831; Minister to France, 1833–1835
1833–1834. Louis McLane. Senator; Secretary of the Treasury, 1831–1833; Minister to England
1834–1841. John Forsyth. Senator
1841–1843. Daniel Webster. Senator, 1827–1841, 1845–1850
1843–1844. Abel P. Upshur. Secretary of the Navy, 1841–1843
1844–1845. John C. Calhoun. Secretary of War, 1817–1825; Vice-President, 1825–1832
1845–1849. James Buchanan. President, 1857–1861

* Studied law, but no evidence of admission to the bar or practice as a lawyer.

NOTE: In these footnotes and in the text, biographic material is from *Scribner's Dictionary of American Biography*, unless otherwise noted.

[20] 1 MESSAGES AND PAPERS OF THE PRESIDENTS, 1789–1905, at 156–57 (J. Richardson ed. 1907); T. BROCKWAY, BASIC DOCUMENTS IN UNITED STATES FOREIGN POLICY 13 (rev. ed. 1968).

[21] AMERICAN STATE PAPERS, 1 FOREIGN RELATIONS 150; W. MOREY, DIPLOMATIC EPISODES 165 (1926).

[22] 1 Stat. 381. The Neutrality Act was particularly aimed at the French Minister to the United States, who had been trying to make the United States a base of operations against the British. T. BROCKWAY, *supra* note 20, at 14.

should be prohibited. The law of nations, said Jefferson, does not require the deprivation of a citizen's livelihood; however, such trade would be engaged in without protection from the United States Government and was subject to whatever punishment might be inflicted by the offended belligerent.[23]

These principles of neutrality, originally expounded by Jefferson, continued to be followed by the United States and were adopted by the 5th and 13th Hague Conventions.[24]

Jefferson was also responsible for laying the foundation for our jurisdiction over a territorial sea of 3 geographical miles in breadth. There had been some claims of territorial seas by other countries prior to our birth as a nation, but there was no consensus on the concept of a territorial sea, much less on its breadth. Claims varied from the distance a cannon ball would carry (said to be one sea league) to the distance a man could see (about 20 miles). Some European states claimed 4 nautical miles (about 9 geographical miles). On November 8, 1793, Jefferson, as Secretary of State, wrote to the British Minister on the subject. While reserving the possibility of extending our claim, he stated that the President had instructed his officers to limit the exercise of their authority "to the distance of one sea league or three geographical miles from the seashores."[25]

Largely because of this claim and the ensuing practice of the United States and Great Britain based on it, the idea of a definite 3-mile belt in which the coastal nation could exercise its jurisdiction became established and was followed by most maritime nations.[26] At least as early as 1862, the United States was denying others the right to claim more than 3 miles. In a note of December 16, 1862, addressed to the Spanish Minister, Secretary of State Seward stated that "the United States are not prepared to admit that Spain . . . can exercise exclusive sovereignty upon the sea beyond a line of three miles from the coast"; and this position was still being asserted in 1956 by Secretary of State John Foster Dulles.[27] It had become the U.S. view of the international law on the subject.[28]

The "*Caroline*" incident prompted two letters by Daniel Webster as Secretary of State that had a profound influence on public international law. During the 1837 revolt against the British Government in Canada, a Canadian military force crossed from Canada to New York State and set fire to the American steamboat *Caroline*, which had been running arms to the revolu-

[23] AMERICAN STATE PAPERS, *supra* note 21, at 147–48; W. MOREY, *supra* note 21, at 166–67.

[24] 36 Stat. 2310 and 2415; *see also* W. MOREY, *supra* note 21, at 168–75, 180–87.

[25] *Reprinted in* H. EXEC. DOC. NO. 324, 42d Cong., 2d Sess. 553-54 (1872), 1 J. MOORE, DIGEST OF INTERNATIONAL LAW 699–703 (1906). Jefferson also wrote a similar note to the French Minister. AMERICAN STATE PAPERS, *supra* note 21, at 183, 184.

[26] T. FULTON, THE SOVEREIGNTY OF THE SEA 21 (1911), *quoted in* 4 M. WHITEMAN, DIGEST OF INTERNATIONAL LAW 35 (1965).

[27] 1 J. MOORE, *supra* note 25, at 706, 707–08. Both Seward and Dulles are quoted in 4 M. WHITEMAN, *supra* note 26, at 61–62.

[28] United States v. California, 332 U.S. 19, 32–34 (1947); statement by Chairman of U.S. delegation to the Conference on the Law of the Sea at Geneva, March 11, 1958. *See* 4 M. WHITEMAN, *supra* note 26, at 35–37 and 91.

tionary elements in Canada. During the Canadian operation an American citizen on board the ship was killed. A Canadian was subsequently arrested in New York and charged with murder. This promptly brought an outraged demand by the British Government for his release.[29]

The British Government protested that what had been done was "a public act of [a person] in Her Majesty's service, obeying the order of [his] superior authorities" and could not be the subject of determination by an American court, but only a matter for diplomatic protest.[30] Webster conceded the following:

> That an individual, forming part of a public force, and acting under the authority of his Government, is not to be held answerable as a private trespasser or malefactor, is a principle of public law sanctioned by the usages of all civilized nations, and which the Government of the United States has no inclination to dispute.[31]

The underlying legal philosophy was that complaints of official governmental acts of representatives of a foreign government are not appropriate for judicial decision by our courts but should be relegated to diplomacy. This same philosophy underlies our act of state doctrine, formulated by the United States Supreme Court some 50 years later.[32]

But Webster took issue with the further British claim that the raid on the *Caroline* was justifiable as an act of self-defense. He pointed out that while self-defense may be an exception to the rule of inviolability of territory by agents of another power, the exception was limited to cases in which the "necessity of that self-defence is instant, overwhelming, and leaving no choice of means, and no moment for deliberation."[33] As this was not the situation in the case under discussion, Webster asserted that the attack on the *Caroline* was unjustifiable and that "the law which had been violated is the law of nations."[34] His formulation of the law of self-defense is still quoted.

The Monroe Doctrine, which bears the name of a very distinguished legally

[29] 2 J. MOORE, *supra* note 25, at 24–30, 409–14; W. MOREY, *supra* note 21, ch. II.

[30] Letter, Fox to Webster, March 12, 1841, THE DIPLOMATIC AND OFFICIAL PAPERS OF DANIEL WEBSTER WHILE SECRETARY OF STATE 120 (1845).

[31] Letter, Webster to Crittenden, U.S. Attorney General, March 15, 1841, *id.* at 133.

[32] "The courts of one country will not sit in judgment on the acts of the government of another done within its own territory. Redress of grievances by reason of such acts must be obtained through the means open to be availed of by sovereign powers as between themselves." Chief Justice Fuller in Underhill v. Hernandez, 165 U.S. 250, 252 (1897). For an earlier state court decision to the same effect, see Hatch v. Baez, 7 Hun 596, 599 (1876).

Webster's philosophy is also related to the modern practice which permits, by agreement, a friendly visiting force stationed abroad to try a member of that force for an act committed in line of duty, and subordinates the criminal jurisdiction of the host state over the offense. *See* NATO Status of Forces Agreement, 4 UST 1792, TIAS No. 2846, 199 UNTS 67, Art. VII, para. 3(a)(ii).

[33] Letter, Webster to Ashburton, Aug. 6, 1842, DIPLOMATIC AND OFFICIAL PAPERS, *supra* note 30, at 118, *quoted* in part *in* 2 J. MOORE, *supra* note 25, at 412. Webster had previously used the quoted language in a letter to Minister Fox, April 24, 1841.

[34] 2 J. MOORE, *supra* note 25, at 26; DIPLOMATIC AND OFFICIAL PAPERS, *supra* note 30, at 133–36. Fortunately for Canadian-American relations, the court that tried the Canadian found him not guilty, and the British apologized for invading American territory. W. MOREY, *supra* note 21, at 44.

trained statesman, is well known. It originated with another lawyer, Monroe's Secretary of State, John Quincy Adams, who incorporated its principle in a warning to Russia 5 months before Monroe made his pronouncement in his message to the Congress in 1823. These two lawyers and statesmen established "that the American continents . . . are henceforth not to be considered as subjects for future colonization by any European powers" and that "we should consider an attempt on their part to extend their system to any portion of this hemisphere as dangerous to our peace and safety."[35]

The doctrine has been invoked by the United States on numerous occasions.[36] It was thought by the Congress to be a binding commitment of the United States as late as 1967, when it included the doctrine among our commitments to foreign powers.[37]

As the Department of State said in 1960: "Although this concept was expressed by Monroe for the United States at the time as a unilateral declaration, the principle involved became, by a logical historical evolution, multi-lateral and mutual in acceptance throughout the American Republics."[38] In the Rio Treaty of 1947[39] and in the Charter of the Organization of American States of 1948,[40] the American states condemned intervention in the internal affairs of any state by any other power and agreed on mutual assistance should this occur. The Tenth Inter-American Conference of 1954 declared that extension by an extracontinental power of its political system to this hemisphere would "constitute a threat to the sovereignty and political independence of the American States."[41] The Monroe Doctrine, in substance, became a doctrine and commitment of the American states.

Finally, let us consider how certain problems of disarmament and peaceful settlement of boundary and other disputes were dealt with by our legal founders. The piecemeal technique developed by them is one perhaps far more likely to succeed in international disputes than the advancement of an overall solution for an entire problem, with the accompanying sense of bewildered frustration upon its rejection. As we shall see, such a solution has, over a span of several generations, achieved a truly outstanding result.

The Treaty of Peace of 1783 had left certain boundaries of the United States uncertain, and a number of other matters vague and controversial. The British refused to withdraw certain garrisons to the agreed boundaries. Damage claims by citizens of both countries arising out of the capture and confiscation of ships remained unsettled.[42]

John Jay, working with his British counterpart, Lord Granville, arrived at

[35] 2 MESSAGES AND PAPERS OF THE PRESIDENTS, *supra* note 20, at 207–20.

[36] 5 M. WHITEMAN, *supra* note 26, at 410.

[37] *U.S. Commitments to Foreign Powers: Hearings before the Senate Comm. on Foreign Relations on S. Res. 151*, 90th Cong., 1st Sess. 49–71 (1967), *reproduced in* 6 ILM 1123, 1134–36; HOUSE COMM. ON FOREIGN AFFAIRS, COLLECTIVE DEFENSE TREATIES 202 (Comm. Print 1967).

[38] 5 M. WHITEMAN, *supra* note 26, at 409.

[39] 62 Stat. 1681, TIAS No. 1838, 21 UNTS 77, Arts. 3 and 6.

[40] 2 UST 2394, TIAS No. 2361, 119 UNTS 3, Art. 15.

[41] Res. XCIII, Tenth Inter-American Conference (Caracas, Venezuela, March 1–28, 1954), *quoted in* 5 M. WHITEMAN, *supra* note 26, at 425.

[42] *See* W. MOREY, *supra* note 21, ch. I.

an agreement in 1794. Although subsequent developments were to prove its wisdom, the agreement was highly unpopular in this country at the time, as it left unresolved many points of irritation.[43] By far the most important long-range provisions were those for arbitration of certain remaining disputed issues by the use of a continuing forum for claims.[44] For the next hundred years or so, the use of arbitration commissions, a number of which were based on the Jay Treaty, resulted in the settlement of disputed matters by legal rather than by forcible means. One commission authorized by the two Governments, acting between 1799 and 1804, rendered 536 awards.[45] Later agreements, especially the Webster-Ashburton Treaty of 1842,[46] gradually settled the remaining disputed borders.

A notable development in remaining boundary disputes with Canada was the establishment of the International Joint Commission by the Treaty of January 11, 1909.[47] Elihu Root, to be mentioned again later, was the Secretary of State who brought this about. But much credit should also be given to Chandler P. Anderson, a lawyer of New York and Washington who served in diplomatic positions and on international bodies for many years. He was counsel to the Department of State when the 1909 Treaty with Great Britain on the Canadian boundaries was being developed, and he had much to do with its negotiation and ultimate content.[48] He will also be mentioned later.

A major part of our Canadian boundary runs through the St. Lawrence River, the Great Lakes, and the connecting waterways. The Commission established by the 1909 Treaty, consisting of three Commissioners from each country, was given certain authority over these waters. No new uses, diversions, or obstructions of the waters could be made without its approval (Article III). If the Commissioners failed to agree, separate reports would be made to their respective Governments for resolution (Article VIII). Here we have a standing body to deal with certain border disputes and to control action that might potentially cause difficulty. It has worked in a very satisfactory way for

[43] T. Bailey, A Diplomatic History of the American People 77–80 (8th ed. 1969); J. Dickey, The United States and Canada 38–39 (1964).

[44] 8 Stat. 116, TS No. 105, Arts. V–VII; *see also* A. Nussbaum, A Concise History of the Law of Nations 129 (rev. ed. 1954).

[45] A. Nussbaum, *supra* note 44, at 129.

[46] 8 Stat. 572, TS No. 119.

[47] 36 Stat. 2448, TS No. 548. A precedent for a boundary commission existed in the International Boundary Commission established by our Convention with Mexico of March 1, 1889, 26 Stat. 1512, TS No. 232. However, the type of problems that that commission was faced with was different. The bed of the Rio Grande (the boundary from El Paso to the Gulf of Mexico) changed from time to time, by erosion or by avulsion. The commission was to examine and decide all boundary questions that arose out of this situation, and questions concerning the construction of works affecting the boundary contrary to the treaty provisions. The decision was subject to veto by either Government within 1 month. As was the case with Canada, later treaties settled certain major boundary questions, notably the Treaty relating to the Utilization of Waters of the Colorado and Tijuana Rivers and of the Rio Grande, and supplementary protocol, 59 Stat. 1219, TS No. 994; and the Convention for the Solution of the Problem of the Chamizal, 15 UST 21, TIAS No. 5515, 505 UNTS 185. For the history of the *Chamizal* dispute, see Jessup, *El Chamizal*, 67 AJIL 423 (1973).

[48] Who's Who in America, 1926–27.

over 70 years. Some 80 major matters were dealt with between 1912 and 1964.[49] More recently, other agreements with Canada have dealt with such matters as the development of the Great Lakes–St. Lawrence Seaway, the division of the use of the waters of the Niagara River, and the cooperative use of the Columbia River.[50]

Together the foregoing developments, stemming directly or indirectly from the Jay Treaty of 1794, settled the Canadian-American boundary, provided standing means for considering new problems concerning boundary waters, and determined the division and cooperative use of the waters of certain rivers that flowed along the boundary or crossed it.

But Jay had also tried unsuccessfully to provide for demilitarization of the Canadian-American border. Following the War of 1812, a new attempt was initiated by Monroe, then Secretary of State. The negotiations culminated in 1817 in an exchange of notes between Richard Rush, then Attorney General but also Acting Secretary of State, and the British Minister, Charles Bagot.[51] The Rush-Bagot Agreement was the first disarmament agreement in the history of this country, possibly in the history of the world. Though falling short of achieving a completely disarmed border, it made a start. There were to be no naval fleets on the Great Lakes or Lake Champlain. With no warships there was no need for shore defenses. As time went on and boundaries were settled, the demilitarization of the Great Lakes was tacitly extended to the entire boundary; thus was created the longest unfortified border in the world.

The legal giants of the 18th and 19th centuries had vision. They and their successors employed both statesmanship and legal principles and techniques, which, given time, could turn their dream into reality. The result was that international boundary problems on this continent were solved in a way lawyers might wish to be a pattern for the rest of the world.

The Second Half of the 19th Century

The Executive

Between the middle and the end of the 19th century, there was not any shortage of legal talent in the office of the Secretary of State. John M. Clayton, a lawyer whose name survives as the negotiator of the Clayton-Bulwer Treaty with Great Britain,[52] held the office from 1849 to 1850. Later other lawyers of stature held the post:[53] William H. Seward (previously noted in connection with the establishment in our international law of a maximum breadth of 3

[49] 3 M. Whiteman, *supra* note 26, at 826–71.

[50] 54 Stat. 2426, EAS No. 187, 203 LNTS 267, in 1940, and 5 UST 1784, TIAS No. 3053, 234 UNTS 199, in 1952; 1 UST 694, TIAS No. 2130, 132 UNTS 223, in 1950; and 15 UST 1555, TIAS No. 5638, 542 UNTS 244, *signed* in 1961, *entered into force* 1964.

[51] 8 Stat. 231, TS No. 110½; 2 M. Miller, Treaties and Other International Acts of the United States of America (1776–1818), at 645–54 (1931–38).

[52] This Treaty concerned contemplated joint action of the United States and Britain in the construction of an inter-oceanic canal through Nicaragua or Panama. However, nothing was accomplished under it. In 1901 it was superseded by the Hay-Pauncefote Treaty. *See* text at note 109 *infra*.

[53] 21 Collier's Encyclopedia 501–02 (1968 ed.); *see* note 63 *infra*.

miles for the territorial sea); Hamilton Fish, William M. Evarts, James G. Blaine, and Frederick T. Frelinghuysen, who held office when our use of treaties expanded greatly; John W. Foster, Richard Olney, and William R. Day (later an Associate Justice of the United States Supreme Court) who, after they left office, were involved in the organization of the American Society of International Law; and finally John Hay who, as Secretary of State, secured the treaties giving us the Panama Canal Zone and Guantánamo, our first overseas military bases. These activities will be discussed below.

In 1886 John Bassett Moore, a lawyer expert in international law who was then with the Department of State, prepared a *Report on Extraterritorial Crime and the Cutting Case*. It was published by the Department[54] and became a landmark in our international law. Cutting, an American citizen, had published in Texas a statement alleged to be a libel on a Mexican national, which was a criminal act under Mexican law. Later, while temporarily in Mexico, Cutting was arraigned and prosecuted. Mexican law provided for prosecution if the victim of the crime was a Mexican national, regardless of where the act occurred. After an exhaustive review of the conflicting cases and authorities, Moore took the position that Mexico was without criminal jurisdiction in the case, that under international law a state cannot apply its law so as to render criminal an act of an alien committed abroad merely because the victim is one of its nationals. President Cleveland adopted this position in his annual message to Congress in 1886,[55] and it has been the United States position on the point ever since, although some states of the world continue to take a contrary view.[56]

A number of bilateral treaties concluded during this period opened the way and set the rules for such matters as trade and commerce, travel, and the opening of consulates. Numerous extradition treaties established the right and procedure for the retrieval of criminals who had sought refuge elsewhere.

There was one notable bilateral treaty of a different character. Although Great Britain was a declared neutral in our Civil War, British ships attempted to run the blockade of Southern ports, and British shipyards outfitted ships of war for use by the Confederacy in raiding Northern commerce. A number of diplomatic claims grew out of these practices. After the war, attempts to provide for arbitration of the claims finally reached successful culmination in the 1871 Treaty of Washington,[57] another example of the American tradition

[54] 1887 FOREIGN RELATIONS OF THE UNITED STATES [hereinafter cited as FOR. REL. U.S.] 757 (1887); *see also* 2 J. MOORE, *supra* note 25, at 228–42. In 1927 Moore, by then a judge of the Permanent Court of International Justice, had occasion to reiterate his position in his separate opinion in the S.S. *Lotus*, 1927 PCIJ, ser. A, No. 10.

[55] 1886 FOR. REL. U.S. at viii.

[56] The United States has never officially accepted the passive personality doctrine. *See* RESTATEMENT (SECOND) OF THE FOREIGN RELATIONS LAW OF THE UNITED STATES §30(a)(5); letter, Counselor of Dep't of State, Feb. 9, 1940, *quoted in* 6 M. WHITEMAN, *supra* note 26, at 104. However, it has come perilously close to following it, especially in the antitrust field, to the dismay of many friendly countries. *See* Raymond, *A New Look at the Jurisdiction in ALCOA*, 61 AJIL 558, especially 568 n.21 and 569 n.23 (1967); and Raymond, *The Exercise of Concurrent Jurisdiction: "Move with Circumspection Appropriate,"* 8 B.C. INDUS. & COM. L. REV. 673, especially 685–89 (1967).

[57] 17 Stat. 863, TS No. 133.

of settlement of disputed claims through arbitration. Hamilton Fish, an able lawyer and then Secretary of State, was the negotiator of the Treaty. It laid down certain basic rules to govern the arbitrators regarding the duties of neutrals, including a duty "to use due diligence" to prevent the arming of vessels within their jurisdiction.[58] The 1907 Hague Conference adopted the doctrine of the Treaty, but substituted "to employ the means at its disposal" for the more ambiguous "use due diligence."[59]

One bilateral agreement of this period led to something of a milestone in our international law of ecology and conservation. Fur seals had their rookeries on the U.S.-owned Pribilof Islands in the Bering Sea. Sealskin coats, hats, and muffs were much in demand toward the end of the 19th century, so the Canadian seal hunters would wait just outside the 3-mile limit of our territorial sea and kill the seals as they crossed into the high seas. The female seal could not be distinguished from the male while in the sea, and the death of a female usually meant the death also of an unborn pup or one on land. Furthermore, only about half the seals killed at sea were ever recovered, so for every female killed and recovered at sea, up to four seals may have died. This practice was decimating the seal population.

The Secretary of State, James G. Blaine, protested this practice, claiming that pelagic sealing (killing seals in the high seas) was "*contra bonos mores*" (against good public morals).[60] After a protracted controversy, Blaine secured an agreement to arbitrate the matter, which was signed February 29, 1892. In 1893 the arbitration tribunal rendered a decision rejecting some claims of the United States, such as that it had a protective role over the seals in the high seas and that the Bering Sea had become a *mare clausum* by prescription; however, the tribunal issued regulations prohibiting pelagic sealing by nationals of either party within 60 miles of the Pribilofs and forbidding *any* pelagic sealing during certain months. Here we see what is believed to be the beginning of our international law to conserve a species of wild animals.[61]

Multilateral treaties were few and far between. There were none before 1826, and the one then entered into dealt with the proper care of a cemetery in Algiers. The first significant multilateral convention to which the United States became a party was the Red Cross Convention of 1864. Several conventions set up international organizations and gave them legal power to set

[58] A. NUSSBAUM, *supra* note 44, at 217–18; 1 W. MALLOY, TREATIES, CONVENTIONS, INTERNATIONAL ACTS, PROTOCOLS AND AGREEMENTS BETWEEN THE UNITED STATES OF AMERICA AND OTHER POWERS (1776–1909), at 700–22 (1910); J. SCOTT, CASEBOOK ON INTERNATIONAL LAW 713 (1902).

[59] 36 Stat. 2415, TS No. 545, Art. 8; *see also* C. FENWICK, INTERNATIONAL LAW 745 (4th ed. 1965).

[60] Letter, Blaine to Pauncefote, Jan. 22, 1890, 1890 FOR. REL. U.S. 368. For the full story of this incident, see 1 J. MOORE, HISTORY AND DIGEST OF THE INTERNATIONAL ARBITRATIONS TO WHICH THE UNITED STATES HAS BEEN A PARTY 755 (1898); for a briefer account, see T. BAILEY, *supra* note 43, at 446–48.

[61] Although these regulations had only limited effect, they were the forerunner of what is now a multilateral agreement (the United States, the USSR, Canada, and Japan) to conserve the seal population of the North Pacific. 8 UST 2283, TIAS No. 3948, 314 UNTS 105; *amended* 15 UST 316, TIAS No. 5558, 494 UNTS 303; *extended* 20 UST 2992, TIAS No. 6774, 719 UNTS 313; *extended* TIAS No. 8368.

standards and require reports of practices in order to control certain matters of international concern: the General Postal Union and the International Office of Weights and Measures were established by the Conventions of 1874 and 1875; a Convention to Protect Industrial Property (*i.e.*, patents and commercial trademarks and trade names) was entered into in 1883, and one to protect submarine cables in 1884; and in 1890 the Pan American Union and the International Union for Publication of Customs Tariffs were established. This was the extent of the significant multilateral treaties entered into by the United States prior to 1900.[62] In their respective fields these treaties performed useful and necessary functions by establishing practical ways of handling certain matters of common international interest.

Treaties were now assuming a larger role in this country by establishing significant rights and duties under international law and by providing international mechanisms to handle matters of international concern. The Secretaries of State mentioned above should be given credit for their part in bringing about this enhanced role of treaty law during their respective terms of office.[63]

As the second half of the century began, there were other indications of the increasing importance of international law in the operation of the Department of State. Our claims against other countries and foreign claims against the United States were increasing in volume. To handle these the Department, in 1848, was authorized to appoint a Claims Clerk, the first semblance of legal assistance given the Secretary of State. More claims clerks were later authorized until, in 1866, a special position with the title Examiner of Claims was established. In 1891 the title was changed to the Solicitor of the Department of State, more properly to reflect his functions.[64]

Francis Wharton, as Examiner of Claims, pioneered one of the great advances in the literature of international law. Lawyers are quite familiar with the common law digests developed in the latter part of the 19th century; but for international law there was nothing really useful. The existing law digests more often than not buried points of international law under some totally different heading and, more seriously, were limited to judicial decisions—and then only those of American courts. Wharton perceived the need and proceeded to fill it. In 1886 he published his three-volume *International Law Digest*. Pertinent extracts from decisions of international as well as national tribunals, extracts from writings of leading authorities in the field, diplomatic notes, records of actions taken by states, significant provisions of treaties, policy

[62] 1 Bevans at v–vi. The Hague Conventions of 1899 did not enter into force for the United States until after 1899. *Id.* at 230, 247, 263, and 270.

[63] *See* text at note 53 *supra*. The terms of office of the Secretaries of State mentioned were: Seward (1861–1869), Fish (1869–1877), Evarts (1877–1881), Blaine (1881, 1889–1892), Frelinghuysen (1881–1885), Foster (1892–1893), Olney (1895–1897), Day (1898), and Hay (1898–1905). 21 COLLIER'S, *supra* note 53, at 501–02.

[64] In 1931 the title was once more changed to Legal Adviser of the Department of State. Woolsey, *The Legal Adviser of the Department of State*, 26 AJIL 124 (1932); Bilder, *The Office of the Legal Adviser: The State Department Lawyer and Foreign Affairs*, 56 AJIL 634–36 (1962); J. MATHEWS, THE CONDUCT OF AMERICAN FOREIGN RELATIONS 46–47 (1922).

pronouncements, all were set forth in an arrangement under headings that were serviceable for the international lawyer.[65]

The Wharton *Digest* became the pattern for three subsequent digests of international law: an 8-volume work by Judge John Bassett Moore in 1906, which included and updated the Wharton material; another of 8 volumes by (later Judge) Green H. Hackworth in 1940–1944, which supplemented the Moore *Digest* with material that had accumulated since the former publication; and finally a 15-volume *Digest* by Dr. Marjorie M. Whiteman, published in 1963–1973, bringing the Hackworth *Digest* up to date. The State Department has continued to supplement the *Digest* annually.

The authors were lawyers of great ability with lengthy practical experience in public international law. Moore was the first professor of law and diplomacy at Columbia University in 1891. After holding various arbitration and diplomatic posts he became Counselor of the Department of State, a position then carrying both legal and political responsibilities,[66] and from there he moved on through other important positions to become a judge of the Permanent Court of International Justice at The Hague under the auspices of the League of Nations.[67]

Hackworth was Solicitor of the Department of State from 1925 to 1931, when the title was changed to Legal Adviser; he continued to serve with that title until 1946. For over 20 years he was privy to every significant legal decision taken by the Department. In 1946 he was elected a judge of the International Court of Justice, the Court of the United Nations, where he served for 15 years.[68]

Dr. Marjorie Whiteman served for many years as Assistant Legal Adviser with dedication and distinction. She had been Hackworth's chief assistant in the preparation of his *Digest*. She not only contributed her own excellent *Digest* to the source materials of international law but in 1937 published a three-volume work on *Damages in International Law*, a subject comprehensively covered nowhere else.[69]

Education and Publications in International Law

Law schools as such did not begin to appear until nearly the end of the 18th century. The Litchfield (Connecticut) Law School founded in 1782 is traditionally accepted as the first.[70] The first law school connected with a

[65] In 1877 John L. Cadwalader, Assistant Secretary of State, published a book entitled *Digest of the Published Opinions of the Attorney General, and of the Leading Decisions of the Federal Courts, with Reference to International Law, Treaties, and Kindred Subjects*; but it was arranged alphabetically like a dictionary and was limited to only two sources of material. 1 M. WHITEMAN, *supra* note 26, at iii. Wharton changed the scope and arrangement of the material, which made it a useful reference work.

[66] Bilder, *supra* note 64, at 634.

[67] WHO WAS WHO IN AMERICA, 1943–1950, at 380.

[68] WHO'S WHO IN AMERICA, 1960–1961, at 1183; 1959–1960 ICJ Y.B. 20; 1960–1961 *id.* at 1, 13.

[69] WHO'S WHO OF AMERICAN WOMEN, 1968–1969, at 1308–09.

[70] YALE LAW SCHOOL CATALOGUE, 1969–1970. Law has been an undergraduate course from time to time in the political science department of various colleges and universities. This practice

university was the Harvard Law School, established in 1817.[71] Yale had an affiliated law school in 1824, although the first degree was not awarded until 1843.[72] The late Dean Harno found that "by 1850 there were fifteen [law schools]; by 1860 the number was twenty-one; and by 1870 it was thirty-one."[73] Information culled from law school catalogues indicates that by 1880 seven more had been added, and by 1890 another nine. During the decade ending in 1900 the number of law schools increased by 26—exactly the number added during the previous three decades—making a total of 73. The 1890's clearly saw a spurt in legal education.

During the last half of the 19th century, a practice began of teaching international law not only in a handful of law schools but also in some institutions as an undergraduate course in political science. At times it was presented by visiting distinguished professors giving a series of lectures, usually for a term or two; but the subject was not retained in the curriculum.[74]

Though by no means a complete list of those who gave courses in international law before 1900, the following individuals contributed greatly to the establishment of formal education in the discipline. Theodore D. Woolsey, the President of Yale University, taught international law there shortly after assuming the presidency in 1846, and continued to do so, possibly with gaps, until he retired in 1871, at which time he became lecturer in international law at Yale. The course became established in the law school, and in 1878 Woolsey was succeeded in teaching it by his son, Theodore S. Woolsey, who remained at Yale in that capacity over 30 years.[75] At Harvard Law School international law was offered from 1863 to 1865. Richard Henry Dana was lecturer there on the law of nations during the years 1866 to 1868. The course was also given in 1886–1887 by Henry Warren Torrey, followed by Dr. Freeman Snow in 1888. By this time, international law seems to have been firmly incorporated into the curriculum.[76] At the University of Michigan a course (probably undergraduate) in international law was given by James B. Angell, the President of the University, from 1871 until 1880, when he left the university on a diplomatic assignment. The course was again given in 1887, possibly earlier, but not until 1891 was it definitely incorporated in the curriculum.[77] Dr. Snow taught international law—emphasizing the law of war and neutrality—at the United States Naval Academy at least as early as 1884, and Col. William Winthrop did likewise at the United States Military Academy

---

was in effect as early as 1762, when George Wythe taught law to Thomas Jefferson at the College of William and Mary. 13 COLLIER'S, *supra* note 53, at 526.

[71] HARVARD LAW SCHOOL CATALOGUE, 1969–1970.

[72] YALE LAW SCHOOL CATALOGUE, 1969–1970.

[73] A. HARNO, LEGAL EDUCATION IN THE UNITED STATES 51 (1953).

[74] *See, e.g.*, note 85 *infra*.

[75] F. HICKS, YALE LAW SCHOOL, 1869–1894, at 7, 9 (1937); WHO WAS WHO IN AMERICA, 1897–1942, at 1381.

[76] HARVARD LAW SCHOOL ASSOCIATION, CENTENNIAL HISTORY OF THE HARVARD LAW SCHOOL 20, 41, 75, 76 (1918).

[77] SCRIBNER'S, *supra* note 19; E. BROWN, LEGAL EDUCATION AT MICHIGAN, 1859–1959, at 490–503 (1959).

probably as early as 1885, when he published his famous two-volume work on *Military Law*, still a standard reference work.[78]

Francis Lieber, a German who came to this country in 1827, taught for many years at the University of South Carolina and later at Columbia University. He became a well-known philosopher and political scientist. In 1865 he began teaching in the law school of Columbia, and his field became international and military law. It might be noted that he started a movement that ultimately led to the establishment of the Institut de Droit International.[79] In 1891 John Bassett Moore gave his first course in international law at Columbia University.[80] Also in 1891, George Grafton Wilson began teaching the subject as an undergraduate course at Brown University.[81] James Brown Scott, who was deeply interested in international law, probably started teaching it at the University of Illinois, where he was dean of the law school, just about 1899–1900.[82]

No list of law schools giving a course in public international law at any time in the last century was discovered. The earliest such list found was one by Professor Charles Nobel Gregory, one of the original editors of the *American Journal of International Law*. Professor Gregory wrote an article in 1907 in which he pointed out that for a number of years Professor Holland had been teaching the subject at Oxford and Professor Westlake at Cambridge. He then listed the following American law schools offering a course in it: Harvard, Yale, Columbia, Cornell, Chicago, Indiana, Washington University of St. Louis, the John Marshall School of Law in Chicago, George Washington University in Washington, D.C., and his own State University of Iowa.[83] As 8 law schools had come into the picture between 1900 and 1907, there were now 81 law schools in America, but as late as 1907 only 10 of them were scheduling international law. The subject was considered a "luxury." The spurt in legal education of the 1890's had not brought about a concomitant increase in the number of international law courses in law schools.

As for international law publications prior to 1900, the Wharton *Digest* and Winthrop's *Military Law* have already been mentioned. An extremely valuable work at the end of the century was John Bassett Moore's *History and Digest of the International Arbitrations to Which the United States Has Been a Party*, published in 1898.[84]

While there were foreign texts on international law, for example, those by the British writers Hall, Holland, Maine, Phillimore, Westlake, and others, there was a scarcity of American writers contributing to the literature. Of course, Chancellor Kent's *Commentaries* in 1830 contained some 200 pages of

[78] F. SNOW, CASES ON INTERNATIONAL LAW, preface (1893); W. WINTHROP, ABRIDGMENT OF MILITARY LAW, title page and preface (3d ed. rev. 1897).

[79] 14 ENCYCLOPAEDIA BRITANNICA 37 (1960); A. ROLIN, LES ORIGINES DE L'INSTITUT DE DROIT INTERNATIONAL, 1873–1923, at 9–10 (1923).

[80] THE BICENTENNIAL HISTORY OF COLUMBIA UNIVERSITY: A HISTORY OF THE SCHOOL OF LAW 169 (J. Goebel, Jr., 1955).

[81] WHO'S WHO IN AMERICA, 1926–1927.

[82] G. Finch, *The American Society of International Law, 1906–1956*, 50 AJIL 293, 295 (1956).

[83] Gregory, *The Study of International Law in Law Schools*, 2 AM. L. SCH. REV. 41, 45 (1907).

[84] In 1929 Moore also published a six-volume work on international adjudications.

material useful in the study of international law, but his work covered a much broader field. The earliest American text strictly on public international law is believed to have been the *Elements of International Law* by an eminent American diplomat and lawyer, Henry Wheaton, perhaps better known to American lawyers today as an early Reporter for the United States Supreme Court. The text first appeared in 1836 and was published and republished both here and in England. The eighth edition of 1866 edited by Richard Henry Dana is generally thought the best. It was reprinted in 1936 with an introduction by George Grafton Wilson.

The earliest text written and used by an academician was Theodore D. Woolsey's *Introduction to the Study of International Law*, published in 1860. Other American books on international law followed: by Professor J. W. Pomeroy,[85] Dr. Freeman Snow,[86] and Brigadier General H. W. Halleck.[87]

Dean Langdell had introduced at Harvard Law School what came to be the accepted method of teaching the law: the case method. The only American book in the international law field prior to the 20th century adaptable to a course taught in this manner was that of Dr. Snow. While his book consisted entirely of cases, he realized the value of recognized authorities, of pronouncements of policy having legal implications, and of historical precedents, and he attempted to cover those by a 27-page "syllabus," which cited material pertinent to the particular topics covered.

A noteworthy publication resulted from the Civil War. *The Instructions for the Government of the Armies of the United States in the Field*, issued as General Orders No. 100 of April 24, 1863,[88] was the first attempt in any country to humanize warfare, and to codify the customary law of war. It was based on a draft by Dr. Francis Lieber, mentioned above, and has frequently been referred to as Lieber's Code. The code greatly influenced the rules of warfare in other countries, and formed the basis of the later Hague Conventions on the Rules of War on Land. Lieber was a trusted adviser of two notable lawyers, General Halleck who approved General Orders No. 100 as Commander of the Union Forces, and President Lincoln who ordered it published.[89]

The Judiciary

The Civil War produced a flood of cases, the outcome of which depended on the validity of official acts of the Confederate States taken within the

[85] Pomeroy's book consisted of lectures he had given at the University of New York Law School and at Hastings College of the Law in San Francisco. J. POMEROY, LECTURES ON INTERNATIONAL LAW IN TIME OF PEACE, dedicatory page (T. S. Woolsey ed. 1886). There is no evidence that the subject continued in the curriculum of either school.

[86] F. SNOW, *supra* note 78.

[87] H. HALLECK, INTERNATIONAL LAW (1861). *See* bibliography in J. SCOTT, *supra* note 58, at lxv–lxvii; "standard modern authors" mentioned in F. SNOW, *supra* note 78, at xiii; and 10 SCRIBNER'S, *supra* note 19, pt. 2, at 40.

[88] The text of General Orders No. 100 appears as Appendix 2 in G. WILSON & G. TUCKER, INTERNATIONAL LAW (9th ed. 1935), and in earlier editions, and in G. WILSON, HANDBOOK OF INTERNATIONAL LAW, App. 2 (1910).

[89] Davis, *Doctor Francis Lieber's Instructions for the Government of Armies in the Field*, 1 AJIL 13 (1907). For Halleck's work on international law, see note 87 *supra*.

Confederacy during the rebellion. In the context of international law, the issue was the effect, if any, to be given to official acts of an unrecognized government taken within its own borders. There was, of course, no other government that could then have affected or determined the rights and duties of people living within the Confederate States, and a number of these acts were in no way hostile to the Union but were designed to settle private rights and duties of individuals. When the issue was presented to the courts after the war, the results seemed in many cases to be at odds with one another.

These cases were cited, discussed, and reconciliation attempted in a lengthy opinion by Mr. Justice Harlan in 1897.[90] Mr. Justice Cardozo, however, concisely explained the apparent conflict in 1926:

> Juridically, a government that is unrecognized may be viewed as no government at all, if the power withholding recognition chooses thus to view it. In practice, however, since juridical conceptions are seldom, if ever, carried to the limit of their logic, the equivalence is not absolute, but is subject to self-imposed limitations of common sense and fairness, as we learned in litigations following our Civil War. In those litigations acts or decrees of the rebellious governments, which, of course, had not been recognized as governments *de facto*, were held to be nullities when they worked injustice to citizens of the Union, or were in conflict with its public policy. . . . On the other hand, acts or decrees that were just in operation and consistent with public policy, were sustained not infrequently to the same extent as if the governments were lawful. . . .[91]

This explanation of our Civil War cases typifies the application of "the philosophical bases, the practical necessities, and the wisely oriented flexibility"[92] in which Anglo-American jurisprudence is rooted. Lawyers and judges who are able to understand the political practicalities while applying legal principles are needed in every branch of the law, but this is especially true in public international law where flexibility is critical.

The *Prize Cases*,[93] also arising out of the Civil War, offer another illustration of this flexibility. In 1861 President Lincoln announced that "an insurrection" had broken out, and proclaimed a blockade of Southern ports. The validity of the blockade was attacked. The contention was that the blockade was unsustainable since the "insurrection" was not a "declared war." The Supreme Court, in an opinion by Mr. Justice Grier, rejected this contention, taking judicial notice that there existed a "civil war," which "is never publicly proclaimed" but which warranted the proclamation of a blockade.[94]

Chief Justice Chase, speaking for the Supreme Court in two subsequent cases, established the doctrine that contraband cargo documented for a neutral port but destined ultimately for the Confederacy was subject to condemnation as prize; furthermore, that the ship itself could be condemned if it had acted in bad faith.[95] In the early days of World War I, the doctrine of "continuous

[90] Baldy v. Hunter, 171 U.S. 388 (1897).

[91] Sokoloff v. National City Bank, 239 N.Y. 158, 165 (1924).

[92] *See* p. 802 *supra*.

[93] 67 U.S. (2 Black) 635, 666–67 (1862).

[94] *Id.* at 667.

[95] The *Bermuda*, 70 U.S. (3 Wall.) 514 (1865); The *Peterhoff*, 72 U.S. (5 Wall.) 28 (1866). A similar case, The *Springbok*, 72 U.S. (5 Wall.) 1 (1866), was modified as to the detention of the

voyage," which had thus been established, was vigorously invoked by the British against U.S. shipping alleged by them to be destined for Germany.[96]

Three other decisions of the Supreme Court deserve comment. Chief Justice Waite in *Wildenhus's Case*[97] dealt with jurisdiction over crimes committed on foreign ships in our territorial waters. A writ of habeas corpus was sought by the Belgian consul on behalf of Wildenhus, a Belgian national, who had been charged with murdering another Belgian on board a Belgian ship docked in the port of Jersey City. It had long been a matter of tradition that events transpiring on board a foreign ship were matters for resolution by officials of the flag state as long as they did not directly affect those on the shore. Furthermore, a treaty between Belgium and the United States provided that consuls "shall have exclusive charge of the internal order of the merchant vessels of their nation, and shall alone take cognizance of all differences which may arise" between officers and crews, and "local authorities shall not interfere except when the disorder . . . is of such a nature as to disturb tranquillity and public order on shore, or in the port."[98] The question was thus posed: Under what circumstances is tranquillity in the port disturbed to the extent that the territorial sovereign is free to exercise his omnipresent authority?

The Court in *Wildenhus* proceeded to define the "peace of the port" doctrine. It held that the territorial state may assume jurisdiction if the "tranquillity of the port" is affected by "crimes which from their gravity awaken a public interest as soon as they become known"; and it further held that "the fact that only those on the ship saw [the crime] when it was done is a matter of no moment."[99] This decision keynoted the provisions dealing with the subject in the international Convention on the Territorial Sea of 1958.[100] Yet by its carefully expressed limitations, the decision left open the alternative for the flag state to take jurisdiction in such a case if the local sovereign chose not to do so.[101]

Another able jurist, Mr. Justice Gray, writing for the Supreme Court in *Hilton v. Guyot*,[102] addressed himself to the concept of "comity." Although the Court refused to give full faith and credit to a judgment of a French court since American judgments were reversible on their merits in French courts, its discussion of comity was a notable contribution. It stated:

> "Comity," in the legal sense, is neither a matter of absolute obligation, on the one hand, nor of mere courtesy and good will, upon the other.

---

ship itself by a claims commission established under the Treaty of Washington. For that Treaty, see text at note 57 *supra*. For the commission's decision, see 4 J. MOORE, *supra* note 60, at 3928–35; for a summary of the entire case, see 7 J. MOORE, *supra* note 25, §1261.

[96] *E.g.*, The *Kim*, The *Alfred Nobel*, The *Bjornsterjne Bjornson*, The *Fridland*, 1916 P. 38. And *see* T. BAILEY, *supra* note 43, at 325.

[97] 120 U.S. 1 (1886).

[98] 21 Stat. 776, TS No. 29, Art. XI.

[99] 120 U.S. at 12 and 17.

[100] 15 UST 1606, TIAS No. 5639, 516 UNTS 205, Arts. 1 and 19.

[101] The exact converse of *Wildenhus's Case* was presented when an American murdered another American on a U.S. ship in Belgian waters. In the absence of any demand for trial by the Belgians, the accused was tried in the United States. United States v. Flores, 289 U.S. 137 (1933).

[102] 159 U.S. 113 (1895).

> But it is the recognition which one nation allows within its territory to the legislative, executive or judicial acts of another nation, having due regard both to international duty and convenience, and to the rights of its own citizens or of other persons who are under the protection of its laws.[103]

The Court further stated that comity "contributes so largely to promote justice between individuals, and to produce a friendly intercourse between the sovereignties to which they belong, that courts of justice have continually acted upon it, as a part of the voluntary law of nations."[104] These extracts from the opinion of Mr. Justice Gray have become standard material to be quoted on the subject of comity. The opinion made a distinct contribution to friendly international relations, as well as to international law, by elaborating the meaning of and reason for the doctrine, while at the same time noting the circumstances that limit its application.

Five years later Mr. Justice Gray in *The Paquete Habana*[105] again considered comity; but his real contribution here was in showing how customary international law sometimes develops. The question before him was whether Spanish fishing vessels out of Cuba were liable to capture for running the blockade during the Spanish-American War. Gray began by pointing out that in 1403 and again in 1406, Henry IV had ordered his officers to treat French fishermen as exempt from capture. Gray then traced the history of this practice up to 1798, when Lord Stowell held that the exemption of small fishing vessels from seizure "was a rule of comity only, and not of legal decision."[106] "But," said Gray in 1900, "the period of one hundred years which has since elapsed is amply sufficient to have enabled what originally rested in custom or comity . . . to grow, by general assent of civilized nations, into a settled rule of international law."[107] After reviewing the practice of such nations and the writings of leading authorities during that hundred-year period, he held that "small fishing vessels . . . are exempt from capture as prize of war" by international law.

Overall, the last half of the 19th century witnessed a beginning of the American literature of international law, the introduction of formal study of the subject (though it had barely taken root), a few notable court and executive decisions that set some lasting precedents, and the expansion of American conventional international law. In all of these areas lawyers of the day played a leading role.

THE EARLY 20TH CENTURY

U.S. Global Interests and a Corresponding Interest in International Law

The turn of the century saw the sudden emergence of the United States as a power to be reckoned with in international affairs. We had defeated a

[103] *Id.* at 163–64.

[104] *Id.* at 165 (quoting Chief Justice Taney, Bank of Augusta v. Earle, 38 U.S. (13 Pet.) 519, 589 (1839)).

[105] 175 U.S. 677 (1900).

[106] The *Young Jacob* and *Johanna*, 165 Eng. Rep. 81.

[107] 175 U.S. at 694.

major European power in the Spanish-American War, and had acquired overseas interests and responsibilities stretching from Puerto Rico and Cuba in the Caribbean to Guam and the Philippines in the Far East.[108]

Soon after the war, the Secretary of State, John Hay, was able to secure important concessions in the Carribbean area owing largely to the rise in our global political stature. Hay was a lawyer who had served with Lincoln in the White House, and thereafter as Ambassador to Great Britain. He was now able to negotiate an agreement with the British, the Hay-Pauncefote Treaty of 1901,[109] forgoing their interest in any canal construction on the Isthmus of Panama, which had previously been obtained by the Clayton-Bulwer Treaty of 1850. This cleared the way for the United States unilaterally to construct and manage an inter-oceanic canal. Hay then procured from Panama an agreement granting the United States "in perpetuity" a zone across the Isthmus for the "construction, maintenance, operation, sanitation and protection" of a ship canal. We were also granted "all the rights, power and authority within the zone . . . which the United States would possess if it were [the zone's] sovereign," which laid the international legal foundation for the construction, operation, and defense of the Panama Canal.[110]

A few weeks later, Hay also secured an Agreement with Cuba to lease Guantánamo "for the purposes of coaling and naval stations." While recognizing Cuba's "ultimate sovereignty" over Guantánamo, the Agreement incorporated Cuba's consent that during the occupancy "the United States shall exercise complete jurisdiction and control over and within" the area.[111] We thus acquired our first two overseas military bases. From a legal standpoint the United States secured a unique degree of sovereignty over them, later approached only in the case of Okinawa.[112]

The United States was now becoming involved not only with the far-flung possessions recently acquired from Spain but in controversies between other nations in other parts of the world. In 1905 we became the peace broker in the Russo-Japanese War; and the following year our intervention at the Algeciras Conference prevented—for the time being—a serious outbreak between Germany and the British-French alliance.[113]

It is not surprising that, with these expanding interests and concerns of the United States fresh in their minds, a number of leading lawyers of the country

[108] T. BAILEY, *supra* note 43, at 483.

[109] 32 Stat. 1903, TS No. 401; T. BROCKWAY, *supra* note 20, at 68; T. BAILEY, *supra* note 43, ch. 33. *See* note 52 *supra* for the Clayton-Bulwer Treaty.

[110] Isthmian Canal Convention, 1903, 33 Stat. 2234, TS No. 431.

[111] TS No. 418, 6 Bevans 1113, Arts. I and III; *see also* TS No. 426, 6 Bevans 1120.

[112] Taft, as Secretary of War, thought Panama had reserved "titular sovereignty" in the Canal Zone by the 1903 treaty. The Agreement with Cuba, drafted by Hay, said Cuba had "ultimate sovereignty" over Guantánamo. Article 3 of the Treaty of Peace with Japan (3 UST 3169, TIAS No. 2490) stated that "the United States will have the right to exercise all and any powers of administration, legislation and jurisdiction over the territory and inhabitants" of Okinawa; and John Foster Dulles, the able lawyer and later Secretary of State who drafted the provisions of the Treaty dealing with Okinawa, thought Japan had "residual sovereignty." *See* 1 M. WHITEMAN, *supra* note 26, at 267–68. In each case the United States had secured for itself the present right to exercise sovereign power.

[113] T. BAILEY, *supra* note 43, at 517–19, 512.

began to think of developing our knowledge and study of international law, and of devising means of peaceful settlement of international disputes. To these ends, they undertook to form a society of people interested in the discipline and to stimulate such interest among representatives of law schools. They also initiated the drafting of treaties designed to provide for arbitration and other peaceful means to avoid war.

The International Law Society. In 1895 Albert K. Smiley, who operated the Lake Mohonk Mountain House in the Catskills, organized a conference at Lake Mohonk on international arbitration that was attended by a large number of prominent people, including many from the legal profession, and thereafter the Mohonk Conference was held annually until the outbreak of World War I. One of those invited to the Mohonk Conference was Professor James Brown Scott, who was deeply interested in the possibilities of arbitration. Scott had long been convinced of the urgent need for two things in the field of international law: first, an organization of those in the field, which would attest to its importance, provide a forum for an exchange of ideas, and foster new developments; and second, a journal of international law, which would contain information about current developments and publish the results of research, study, and reflective opinion on the subject.[114]

The Mohonk Conference provided Scott with a base from which to launch these projects. In 1905 he was at Columbia Law School, and that year at Mohonk he discussed his ideas with Columbia's dean, George W. Kirchwey, and with Robert Lansing, a distinguished lawyer who had represented the United States in arbitration proceedings and who was to become Secretary of State during World War I. They found themselves in agreement on the need for an international law society and a jounal of international law, and they gained the approval of the conference for the projects. Oscar S. Straus, a lawyer who had been Minister to Turkey and was soon to become Secretary of Commerce and Labor, was made Chairman of the organization committee, with Scott as Secretary. These two, with Dean Kirchwey, Lansing, Professor John Bassett Moore, Charles Henry Butler (Reporter for the Supreme Court of the United States), and Professor George Grafton Wilson of Brown University, made up the working team that planned and launched the organization. Other distinguished members of the bar associated with the project included Mr. Justice Brewer of the United States Supreme Court, Jacob M. Dickinson who was about to become President of the American Bar Association and also Secretary of War, former Secretary of State John W. Foster, Judge George Gray of the United States Circuit Court of Appeals, Professor Charles Nobel Gregory, and Professor Theodore S. Woolsey.[115]

At the organization meeting of the Society, which was held in New York City on January 12, 1906, Elihu Root, an outstanding lawyer who was by then Secretary of State, was elected President. Also elected were the following Vice-Presidents: Chief Justice Fuller and Associate Justices Brewer and Day of the United States Supreme Court; Secretary of War William Howard Taft, later to become President and finally Chief Justice of the United States; Oscar

[114] Finch, *supra* note 82, at 295.

[115] *Id.* at 296; 1 ASIL PROC. 23–27 (1907); 25 *id.* at 242–43 (1931).

S. Straus; former Secretaries of State John W. Foster and Richard Olney, both lawyers; former Attorney General John W. Griggs; United States Circuit Judges George Gray and William W. Morrow; and Andrew Carnegie and Joseph H. Choate, who will receive further mention below. Chandler P. Anderson[116] became Treasurer of the Society, and for many years was on the Board of Editors of its *Journal*. The American Society of International Law had been brought into existence.[117] No other single factor has contributed more to the study, the open discussion, the understanding, and the development of international law in the United States than this organization.

In 1906 James Brown Scott became Solicitor of the Department of State, serving in that capacity until 1910. Also in 1906 he obtained final approval of the Society for publication of a journal of international law and was forthwith appointed Managing Editor. The first issue of the *American Journal of International Law* appeared in January 1907.[118] It provided a means of communicating to members of the Society and others in the legal, diplomatic, and academic worlds current developments and thinking regarding problems of international law. From its inception the *Journal* established a notably high standard, carefully maintained over the years. It has made an outstanding contribution to American literature in the international law field.

For 18 years Elihu Root was re-elected President of the Society. The continuity of his capable and devoted leadership carried the organization through its early years. He was succeeded by another eminent lawyer and statesman, Charles Evans Hughes, soon to become the Chief Justice of the United States. He, in turn, was succeeded by James Brown Scott who, more than any other individual, was responsible for the existence of the Society and its *Journal*, and who had been active as an officer of the Society since its foundation and as Editor-in-Chief of its *Journal* until 1924. Scott was President of the Society for 10 years, to be succeeded by then Secretary of State Cordell Hull.[119]

The stature and loyal interest of these people, and of those who followed them, were in no small measure responsible for the fact that, despite the shattering of any hope of a legal resolution of every international dispute by the outbreak of World War I, the isolation that followed that war, the gathering clouds that culminated in World War II, and the later confrontations of the Cold War, Korea, and Vietnam, the American Society of International Law and its *Journal* kept the faith and have contributed so much to a better understanding of international law—of the problems with which it seeks to deal, of its substantive content and its procedural methods, and of its developing growth, its possibilities, and its limitations.

Conferences of Teachers. Though not himself a lawyer, one of the founders and a Vice-President of the American Society of International Law was Andrew Carnegie. He was sufficiently interested in international law and, in particular, in international arbitration to establish the Carnegie Endowment

[116] *See* text at note 48 *supra*.

[117] 1 ASIL PROC. at 28–33. The list of members of the Society in 1907 appears in *id*. at 11–12. There were 2 honorary members (from Europe), 17 life members, and 735 annual members.

[118] *Id*. at 35–38; Finch, *supra* note 82, at 296–98.

[119] Finch, *supra* note 82, at 299.

for International Peace. James Brown Scott became the director of its International Law Division. In 1911 the Endowment decided to take action to develop "sound, progressive and fruitful ideas" regarding arbitration and international law, "especially through lectures delivered before the leading universities." The task was delegated to Scott's division, which sought the assistance of the American Society of International Law. As a result, in 1914 the Society, with the support of the Endowment, assembled a Conference of Teachers of International Law and Related Subjects with a view to encouraging the introduction of international law courses in institutions of higher learning. Forty-four representatives from 41 American universities and colleges attended. Similar conferences were held in 1925 and in some later years.[120] Unquestionably, they stimulated academic interest in the subject, although the number of law schools offering a course in public international law did not substantially increase until after World War II.[121]

Efforts to Avoid War by Arbitration. Mention has already been made of the Mohonk Conferences and the interest of American lawyers in avoiding war by arbitration. During the last decade of the 19th and the first decade of the 20th centuries, this same interest grew rapidly throughout the world.[122] Our Government joined in the efforts to assure arbitration or conciliation of international disputes.

Early attempts by Secretary of State John Hay to accomplish this by bilateral treaties were nullified when the Senate inserted crippling amendments. Consequently, the President refused to ratify the treaties. Secretary Root tried to meet the basic objections of the Senate by adding an exemption from the obligation to arbitrate of any dispute that affected the "vital interests, the independence, or the honor of the two contracting States," and by further providing that a special treaty, approved by the Senate, would be required for every contemplated arbitration. Twenty-five such treaties were entered into in 1908 and 1909, but they could hardly bring about arbitration of international disputes when, by their very terms, a new treaty was required for every arbitration. Furthermore, in any serious dispute it would no doubt be claimed that the issue fell within the specific exceptions created for "vital interests" and matters of "independence" or "honor." In fact, the authors have not been able to discover a single invocation of any of the 25 treaties.[123]

[120] *Id.* at 300–02.

[121] As late as 1946, Professor Josef Kunz said his "search through catalogues of a considerable portion of about 100 law schools, members of the Association of American Law Schools, reveals that international law is given at only sixteen schools." Kunz, *A Plea for More Study of International Law in American Law Schools*, 40 AJIL 624, 625 (1946). Sixteen is only six more than Professor Gregory had found almost 40 years earlier. *See* text at note 83.

[122] For a fascinating account of this movement, including the 1899 and 1907 Hague Conferences, see B. TUCHMAN, THE PROUD TOWER, ch. 5 (1966).

[123] Letter, Department of State to author, May 18, 1970. The Arbitration Convention with Austria-Hungary, 36 Stat. 2156, TS No. 524 (1909), *extended* 38 Stat. 1783, TS No. 592 (1914), was not invoked in World War I, nor that with Italy, 35 Stat. 2091, TS No. 516 (1908), *replaced* 46 Stat. 2890, TS No. 831 (1928), in World War II. There was no such treaty with Germany or Japan. Arbitration treaties sponsored by President Taft in 1911 met the same fate as the Hay treaties. R. BARTLETT, THE RECORD OF AMERICAN DIPLOMACY 337–39 (1948); T. BAILEY, *supra* note 43, at 540–41.

William Jennings Bryan, though he achieved fame for his oratorical and political achievements, was a practicing lawyer in his early career. After becoming Secretary of State, in 1913 and 1914 he obtained 22 bilateral treaties of conciliation. These provided that there would be no resort to force until there had been an investigation by a conciliation commission, ordinarily within 1 year. The theory was that this would provide a "cooling-off" period. The compacts were rendered meaningless by the outbreak of World War I, and apparently have never been invoked.[124]

Europe as well as America had become interested in the possibility of avoiding war by means of arbitration. In 1899 the Tsar of Russia called a Peace Conference at The Hague, but the conventions drafted at that time were superseded as to many states (including the United States) by those adopted at a similar conference in 1907, also called by Russia at The Hague.

The United States delegation in 1907 was headed by Joseph H. Choate, one of the ablest lawyers of his time and a founder and Vice-President of the American Society of International Law. He had the assistance on the delegation of James Brown Scott and Charles Henry Butler.[125] The 1907 Hague Conference developed 14 multilateral conventions,[126] which may be briefly described as follows:

> (1) A Convention for the Pacific Settlement of International Disputes. The Convention urged the parties and all states to make use of mediation, commissions of inquiry, or arbitration to settle controversies, and it set forth a detailed procedure for arbitration. It retained the Permanent Court of Arbitration (set up by the 1899 Convention), something of a misnomer for what was, in fact, a panel from which arbitrators might be selected for a particular arbitration.[127]
>
> (2) A Convention renouncing the use of force to recover contract debts.
>
> (3) A set of 12 Conventions that codified the rules of land and naval warfare.

The outbreak of the Balkan Wars in 1912 and of World War I in 1914 were disillusioning to many who had so earnestly striven to prevent war by treaties calling for the peaceful settlement of disputes. Every nation involved in those conflicts was a party to such a treaty. Nevertheless, the rules of land and naval warfare drafted at The Hague remained the law in this area through two world wars. In its Judgment of September 30, 1946, the International Military Tribunal at Nuremberg declared that the provisions of its Charter under which German defendants were convicted of committing war crimes were "[i]n the main . . . merely declaratory of the existing laws of war as expressed by the [Regulations annexed to the fourth] Hague Convention" of 1907.[128] After 75 years the 1907 rules of land and naval warfare still basically

[124] R. Bartlett, *supra* note 123, at 339–40; T. Bailey, *supra* note 43, at 545–46. The conciliation Treaty with Italy, 39 Stat. 1618, TS No. 615 (1914), *modified* 47 Stat. 2102, TS No. 848 (1931), was not invoked in World War II. There was no other such treaty that might have been invoked in either World War I or World War II.

[125] 2 W. Malloy, *supra* note 58, at 2369–70.

[126] 1 Bevans 577–741.

[127] A. Nussbaum, *supra* note 44, at 221.

[128] 10 M. Whiteman, *supra* note 26, at 283.

represent the accepted law of war, even though they were slightly modified and considerably elaborated by the Prisoners of War Conventions of 1929 and 1949, the 1949 Convention relative to the Protection of Civilians in Time of War, and the 1977 Protocols thereto. They have proven their worth as ground-breakers in the codification of the international law governing the conduct of armed forces in time of war.

Publications in International Law

American literature in international law was growing. John Bassett Moore's *Digest of International Law*, published in 1906, has already been mentioned. In 1901 George Grafton Wilson and George Fox Tucker (former Reporter for the Supreme Judicial Court of Massachusetts) produced their treatise on *International Law*, published in nine editions over more than three decades. In 1902 James Brown Scott published his *Casebook on International Law*, patterned on Snow's work but considerably expanded.[129] For many years Scott's casebook was widely used in courses in international law. Also in 1902 Charles Henry Butler published a two-volume work on *The Treaty-Making Power of the United States*.

In 1906 Scott arranged for the Carnegie Institute of Washington to publish an English text of the Classics of International Law, previously published by Professor Holland in England. Scott was General Editor of the series in this country until his retirement in 1940.[130] In 1910 George Grafton Wilson, by then Professor of International Law at Harvard, published his *Handbook of International Law* in the Hornbook Series. It should also be noted that he succeeded Scott as Editor-in-Chief of the *American Journal of International Law*, and served as such until 1943.

Two other books just outside the time scope of this article should be mentioned. In 1915 Edwin M. Borchard, then Associate Solicitor of the Department of State, published *The Diplomatic Protection of Citizens Abroad, or The Law of International Claims*, which became a standard work; and in 1916 the first book appeared that might properly have used the modern terminology "Cases and Materials": the two-volume *International Cases, Arbitrations, and Incidents Illustrative of International Law as Practiced by Independent States*, by Professors Ellery C. Stowell and Henry F. Munro, both then of Columbia University. Stowell and Munro departed from the technique of Snow and Scott by including not only cases on international law but diplomatic notes, extracts from authoritative works, notes of the authors regarding the way certain matters had been handled in practice, and other materials that pertained to the law of nations and the way it had been applied.

Conventional International Law

Just a few examples of the multilateral treaties entered into in this era will serve to illustrate the expansion of this country's interests and activities internationally. In 1906 we joined the International Institute of Agriculture;

[129] Finch, *supra* note 82, at 295; Gregory, *supra* note 83, at 45.

[130] 1 H. GROTIUS, DE JURE PRAEDAE, preface by George A. Finch, at ix (Carnegie trans. 1949, reprinted 1964).

in 1907 we accepted the International Sanitary Convention; in 1911 we ratified the Convention on Repression of Circulation of Obscene Publications; in 1913 we joined in the Telecommunications Convention. The United States was also a party to two conventions sometimes referred to as human rights conventions: that on Suppression of White Slave Traffic in 1908 and that on Suppression of Abuse of Opium and Other Drugs in 1915.[131] The Solicitors of the Department of State who had the legal responsibility for these multilateral treaties were James Brown Scott (1906–1910) and J. Reuben Clark (1910–1913).

By 1914 the United States had come of age as a power in international affairs the world over, although in certain respects the development of the related field of international law in this country lagged somewhat behind. Nevertheless, important steps were taken during the early part of the century to foster international law, including the founding of a society and a journal devoted exclusively to the discipline. Scholarly conferences were held from time to time to stimulate interest in international law, but the number of law schools giving courses in it improved only slightly. Several notable publications in the discipline appeared.

The outstanding achievement in treaty law was the drafting, and acceptance by most nations, of the rules of land and naval warfare, which helped to ameliorate cruelties during two world wars and certain lesser conflicts. However, the principal effort of the combined legal, diplomatic, and academic communities had been aimed at developing treaties seeking to promote arbitration as a means of *avoiding* war. In the end, these valiant efforts failed to prevent World War I in 1914. We had not yet learned the hard reality that in international politics neither legal principles nor legal agreements by themselves can control courses of action that are motivated by overpowering national interests.

Summary

In the first century and a quarter of our existence as a nation, lawyers of this country built into U.S. jurisprudence a firm and sound foundation of international law. An early fundamental decision of the United States Supreme Court declared international law to be part of our law, and there followed other decisions on important points of international law. Certain actions and pronouncements of the executive branch established other points. After several decades, formal education in international law emerged, first as lectures by a mere handful of capable people, and at length as the offering of a small group of law schools (only ten by 1907). Books and articles dealing with various aspects of international law began to appear, as well as textbooks and casebooks for use in the study of the subject, and digests of international law for research.

A great boost to the discipline came with the founding in 1906 of the American Society of International Law and the publication of its *Journal*. The meetings of the Society and the contents of the *Journal* not only excited interest in the subject among lawyers and others but contributed greatly to the careful

[131] 1 Bevans 436, 359, 748, 883, 424, and 855, respectively.

refinement and definition of international law principles applicable in situation after situation.

The United States began to negotiate treaties expanding the scope of its rights and duties under conventional international law. We joined with other nations in treaties covering a multitude of matters of international concern, ranging from the International Red Cross to telecommunications, from the acquisition of military bases to the establishment of rules and procedures for the extradition of criminals; and we joined in producing the notable Hague Conventions designed to govern conduct during a war, which at least had an ameliorating effect in the major armed conflicts that followed, if for no other reason than the reciprocal self-interest of the warring parties.[132] But we were also faced with the fact that international law is inextricably interwoven with international politics, and that treaties can and will be disregarded when there are overriding national interests at stake.

By 1914 international law had established itself as a necessary and important component of our legal system. The contributions of the able, statesmanlike lawyers of the 18th, 19th, and early 20th centuries noted above laid a foundation that prepared the United States to deal with the novel challenges brought on by two world wars and the lesser conflicts and confrontations that followed; with the problems posed by the League of Nations, which affected this country although it was not a member of the League; and with the multitude of ramifications that ensued from the establishment of the United Nations and U.S. participation in the Organization.

[132] Philip Marshall Brown said the sanctions of international law are the "compulsive force of reciprocal advantage and fear of retaliation." P. BROWN, INTERNATIONAL REALITIES 21 (1917).

EDITORIAL COMMENT

The Inter-American System Snarls in Falklands War

With the end of the fighting in the Falklands war, scholars are beginning to assess the performance of the international community during the conflict. In this assessment, it is important that the actions of the Organization of American States (OAS) not be neglected. The OAS is the oldest and most successful regional organization under the United Nations system. Time and again, as in the Cuban missile crisis, it has acted to strengthen peace and freedom in this hemisphere. The core of its success is a shared belief that force shall not be used to settle disputes in international relations, that nations attacked in violation of this principle should act together in collective defense, and that peoples are entitled to self-determination. Sadly, in its actions in the Falklands-Malvinas war, and particularly in its resolution of May 29, the OAS lost sight of these great principles.[1]

The Falklands-Malvinas dispute is representative of many international conflicts concerning disputed sovereignty. In the world today there are at least 15 active island disputes and hundreds of land and sea boundary disputes. Nothing could be more fundamental under the Charter of the United Nations and the hemispheric Inter-American Treaty of Reciprocal Assistance (the Rio Treaty) than the principle that force may not be used to resolve these disputes. In the first article of the Rio Treaty the parties pledge "not to resort to the threat or use of force in any manner inconsistent with the provisions of the Charter of the United Nations or of this Treaty."

The Argentine invasion of the Falklands-Malvinas is in violation of this principle, regardless of the merits of the underlying Argentine claim. Moreover, the invasion is a use of force in disregard of the expressed preference of the peoples of the islands. International lawyers may be hard pressed to know whether Britain or Argentina would win sovereignty over the islands or how associated self-determination claims would be resolved if the dispute were submitted to an impartial arbiter. But there is no uncertainty on the more important issue of Argentine use of force in violation of the UN Charter and the Rio Treaty. If such use of force is not unequivocally condemned it could become a model for island and border wars all over the world, including many in Latin America. Indeed, in the background of the South Atlantic war are the more serious disputed claims to the Antarctic continent and offshore island groups south of 60° latitude, including a major dispute among Argentina, Britain, and Chile currently frozen by the Antarctic Treaty of 1959.

Against this background the OAS might have sought to reinforce the peace initiatives of the United States or to recommend that both parties accept

[1] Res. II, Serious Situation in the South Atlantic (resolution adopted at the 4th Plenary Session held on May 29, 1982), OEA/Ser.F/II.20, doc.80/82/Rev.2 (1982). All states voted in favor of the resolution with the exception of Chile, Colombia, the United States, and Trinidad/Tobago.

international arbitration or jurisdiction of a Special Chamber of the International Court of Justice as Canada and the United States have done in the *Gulf of Maine* dispute. At minimum, the Organization could have endorsed Security Council Resolution 502 calling for an immediate Argentine withdrawal, a cease-fire, and negotiations by all parties. Instead, it yielded to regional pressures, one-sidedly condemned "the unjustified and disproportionate armed attack perpetrated by the United Kingdom," and called on states parties to the Rio Treaty to give support to Argentina. It also urged the United States "to refrain" from materially aiding Britain in deference to the principle of "hemispheric solidarity." No mention was made that Argentine withdrawal was required by binding Security Council Resolution 502 or that Britain was acting under Article 51 of the Charter in defense against a prior Argentinian armed attack.

This OAS resolution of May 29 is not important for its legal effect. It is clear under Article 103 of the United Nations Charter and Article 10 of the Rio Treaty that regional actions that are inconsistent either with the obligations of the Charter or with binding action taken by the Security Council in dealing with a dispute are *ultra vires* and without legal effect. In this case the resolution of May 29 is inconsistent both with the Charter prohibition of the use of force in international relations (and the complementary right of defense against such an illegal attack inserted in Article 51 of the Charter) and with Resolution 502, particularly in its failure to call for an immediate withdrawal of Argentine forces.

But the May 29 resolution is profoundly important for the political implications of its tilt from fundamental Charter principles to a supposed overriding regionalism. Some—indeed the conventional wisdom—may say that actions such as that of May 29 are to be expected when regional solidarity is at stake or even that under the circumstances the OAS was moderate in not putting the United States more on the spot. I believe such arguments do a disservice to the greatness of the inter-American system. It is a tragic failure to place enduring Charter and regional principles—which are the real hemispheric protection—over vague calls for "hemispheric solidarity." The solidarity that counts is the willingness of North and South Americans to stand together for enduring principles of self-determination and avoidance of the use of force as a means of settling international disputes.

JOHN NORTON MOORE

CORRESPONDENCE

The *American Journal of International Law* welcomes short communications from its readers. It reserves the right to determine which letters shall be published and to edit any letters printed.

TO THE EDITORS-IN-CHIEF:

June 30, 1982

Professor Weissbrodt's discussion of *A New United Nations Mechanism for Encouraging the Ratification of Human Rights Treaties* (76 AJIL 418 (1982)) correctly draws attention to a critical weakness in postwar international efforts to protect human rights: the failure of a considerable number of states to ratify human rights treaties. Among the procedures he recommends for the rectification of this weakness is one drawn from the ILO. Technical difficulties impeding the ratification of ILO conventions by states are ironed out in informal discussions between government representatives and ILO staff, which apparently clears the way for a wider ratification of these conventions. This model, according to Professor Weissbrodt, has been "successful" because "the 152 member states of the ILO had reported over 4,856 ratifications of the then existing 153 ILO conventions" (p. 425 n.36). Without taking anything away from the work of the ILO and its contribution to the lives of working people everywhere, I think it is only fair to point out that the "success" that Professor Weissbrodt reports may only lie in the eye of the beholder.

The Chart of Ratifications of International Labour Conventions of January 1, 1980, updated by the ILO to June 1, 1980, shows 145 members (not all of them sovereign states) and a grand total of 4,808 ratifications for 153 conventions. Thus, on the average each state has ratified about 33 conventions, that is, one of every five. As may be expected, however, the "ratifying propensity" of states is not equal and the actual number of ratifications of the member states varies from a high of 104 (Spain) and 102 (France) to a low of 0 (Bahrain, Botswana, Namibia, and United Arab Emirates). The 15 states with the highest number of ratifications (11 European and 4 Latin American) contribute 1,177 ratifications, which is more than that (1,171) of the lower 71 states. Stated differently, 10 percent of the members at the high-ratifying end of the scale have more ratifications among them than 50 percent of the members at the low-ratifying end. Furthermore, no ILO convention adopted in the past 15 years has received more than 35 ratifications as of June 1, 1980.

It is submitted that far from suggesting "success," these statistics only reveal that the ILO membership comprises a small group of states that has ratified a large number of ILO conventions and a large group of states that has ratified few conventions. Indeed, the statistics *per se* would neither prove nor disprove "success." To make any claims of "success" for ILO procedures, one would have to demonstrate that these procedures changed the attitudes of states and resulted in larger numbers of ratifications than would otherwise have been the case. And, such a measure itself would hardly evaluate the extent to which ratified conventions were being implemented—the only true measure of success, it is suggested.

The above pattern of state ratifications may also be seen in ratifications of human rights treaties. A relatively small group of states has ratified most of these treaties, while a considerable number of states has more or less remained entirely outside the network formed by the major human rights treaties. The problem manifested by this common experience of human rights and ILO conventions is far more fundamental, it is submitted, than Professor Weissbrodt has recognized, and it is highly unlikely that it will be overcome through the mere resolution of technical difficulties. The basic problem is that despite the rhetoric and passage of numerous resolutions, most states have yet to accept the premise that the domestic treatment of individuals is a legitimate area for international action and one in which states may be under international legal obligations as distinct from political ones. The relatively low numbers of ratifications received thus far by the two Covenants and the generally hostile attitude of states towards even feeble implementation procedures cannot be explained otherwise. Professor Weissbrodt's recommendations are directed towards states that have already set themselves on the path to ratification of human rights treaties. They do not deal with the far larger group of states that thus far have refused to undertake and carry out international obligations on human rights.

FARROKH JHABVALA
Florida International University

David Weissbrodt replies:

Professor Jhabvala suggests that the success in obtaining ratification of ILO conventions is more apparent than real, and that, in fact, ILO membership includes a small group of states that have ratified a large number of ILO conventions and a large group of states that have ratified few conventions. It may be useful to analyze the ratification figures as set out in the most recently published ILO chart of January 1, 1982. (The following figures exclude the ratifications still registered for two states that withdrew from the ILO in the mid-sixties, Albania and South Africa. They include a number of states that joined the ILO in the last 5 years but have not yet ratified conventions or have ratified only very few—Bahrain (1977), Belize (1981), Botswana (1978), Cape Verde (1979), Equatorial Guinea (1980), Namibia (1978), and Zimbabwe (1980)—seven states with a total of 18 ratifications among them.)

At the beginning of 1982, the ILO had 146 member states. The total number of ratifications of ILO conventions by these states was 4,926, an average of 34 ratifications per state. Sixty-three states had ratified a number of conventions equal to or above the average: 27 were in Europe, 15 in the Americas, 13 in Africa, and 8 in Asia and the Pacific. These figures, both in absolute numbers and geographic spread, refute Professor Jhabvala's contention.

It is instructive to look at the distribution by region of ratifications of ILO conventions. The regional averages per member state are as follows: Europe, 57 (Western Europe, 61; Eastern Europe, 50); the Americas, 37; Africa, 26; Asia and the Pacific, 21.

These figures roughly reflect differences in levels of development. A conspicuous exception is the United States, with only seven ratifications—the last of which occurred almost 30 years ago. Only 11 member states—mostly poor developing countries—have fewer ratifications than the United States. If one looks at the position of certain other federal states, one finds Australia with 43 ratifications, Canada with 26, and India with 34.

While there are considerable variations in the number of ratifications received by the different conventions, a number of key instruments have been very widely ratified, as may be seen from the following figures:

Forced Labour Convention, 1930 (No. 29)	124 ratifications
Abolition of Forced Labour Convention, 1957 (No. 105)	107 ratifications
Right of Association (Agriculture) Convention, 1921 (No. 11)	102 ratifications
Freedom of Association and Protection of the Right to Organise Convention, 1948 (No. 87)	93 ratifications
Right to Organise and Collective Bargaining Convention, 1949 (No. 98)	110 ratifications
Equal Remuneration Convention, 1951 (No. 100)	100 ratifications
Discrimination (Employment and Occupation) Convention, 1958 (No. 111)	101 ratifications
Employment Policy Convention, 1964 (No. 122)	68 ratifications
Labour Inspection Convention, 1947 (No. 81)	100 ratifications
Protection of Wages Convention, 1949 (No. 95)	82 ratifications

In considering the ratification figures, one must bear in mind that a considerable number of conventions (over 40) have been revised by later ones. Some of those conventions are closed to further ratifications; others—even if theoretically still open to ratification—are superseded by the revising conventions and are therefore no longer relevant targets for ratification. A number of other conventions addressed themselves only to a limited number of states, *e.g.*, conventions concerning conditions in nonmetropolitan territories (ratified by only a handful of colonial powers for extension to their territories), conventions on indigenous workers (mostly relating to practices that have now disappeared), conventions concerning merchant seamen and fishermen, and a convention on plantation work.

Professor Jhabvala points out that conventions adopted since 1965 had, by 1980, in no case received more than 35 ratifications. It may be of interest to examine the ratification record of conventions adopted over the 30 years from 1951 to 1980. The average ratification per convention is as follows:

Conventions adopted from 1951 to 1960	42 ratifications
Conventions adopted from 1961 to 1970	26 ratifications
Conventions adopted from 1971 to 1980	17 ratifications

In considering these figures, one must bear in mind the subjects dealt with in the conventions concerned. The instruments adopted in the sixties included a number in the fields of social security and occupational safety that would not immediately be capable of implementation by large numbers of states. The same is true of certain instruments on occupational safety and conditions of seafarers adopted in the seventies. These ILO conventions set standards that are not just the common denominator of existing national practice, but for most countries require the raising or further development of national standards, a process that takes time. Thus, it is not true, as has occasionally been suggested in the United States, that many governments undertake ratification without a sufficient sense of the responsibilities resulting from their act.

There remains the question to what extent ILO measures aimed at promoting ratifications in fact influence government attitudes. This question would merit a separate article. It may be noted, however, that many statements are on record, by delegates to ILO meetings and by ILO deliberative bodies, emphasizing the usefulness of various means employed to promote the implementation and ratification of conventions (ranging from procedures involving reports on unratified conventions and their review by the Committee of Experts and the Conference Committee on the Application of Conventions and Recommendations to informal advice or advisory missions) and calling for increased resources to be devoted to such activities. ILO staff, who have been involved in providing such facilities, are also of the opinion that they have a significant impact. One illustration that may be mentioned concerns the request made in 1975 by six countries belonging to the Andean Group for direct contacts missions by ILO officials (which were carried out in 1976) to assess and advise on the possibilities of applying and ratifying 25 major ILO conventions as a means of harmonizing their labor policies and legislation; a number of ratifications have followed.

Finally, the question of effective implementation of ratified conventions is one on which a considerable literature exists. Reference may be made, for example, to E. A. Landy's exhaustive study, including statistical data, *The Effectiveness of International Supervision—Thirty Years of ILO Experience* (1966); to the ILO study, *The Impact of International Labour Conventions and Recommendations* (1976); and to the fact that the Committee of Experts on the Application of Conventions and Recommendations has since 1964 recorded more than 1,400 cases in which governments have taken action in response to the committee's comments to ensure the better application of ratified conventions.

Those concerned with human rights obviously would like to see an ever greater measure of acceptance and implementation of international human rights instruments. That aim is more likely to be attained by keeping these questions in the forefront of public discussion and by pressing for continuing review of government policies and attitudes than by assuming, pessimistically, that those who govern are impervious to any outside influence.

CONTEMPORARY PRACTICE OF THE UNITED STATES RELATING TO INTERNATIONAL LAW

MARIAN NASH LEICH*

The material in this section is arranged according to the system employed in the annual *Digest of United States Practice in International Law*, published by the Department of State.

STATE RESPONSIBILITY

(U.S. *Digest*, Ch. 9, §1)

Espousal of Claims—Continuous Nationality

In a letter from the Assistant Secretary of State for Congressional Relations, Powell A. Moore, to Congressman Clement J. Zablocki, Chairman of the House Committee on Foreign Affairs, dated August 5, 1982, the Department of State explained that the rule of continuous nationality in the international law of claims prevented it from recommending enactment of H.R. 2619.

The proposed amendment to Title VI of the International Claims Settlement Act of 1949, relating to claims of U.S. nationals against the German Democratic Republic, would have authorized the Foreign Claims Settlement Commission to receive and determine the validity of claims of certain "late" nationals, *i.e.*, persons who had been aliens lawfully admitted for permanent residence in the United States as of the date of the loss and who had acquired U.S. citizenship by September 4, 1974. The Department's letter pointed out that this provision would not "accord with long-established international law on state responsibility regarding claims against foreign governments, customary Department of State policy and practice, as well as consistent Congressional policy."

The letter continued:

> Under the long-established rule of international law of continuous nationality, no claimant is entitled to diplomatic protection of the state whose assistance is invoked unless such claimant was a national of that state at the time when the claim arose and continuously thereafter until the claim is presented. In effect, a claim must be a national claim not only at the time of its presentation, but also at the time when the injury or loss was sustained. (See Borchard, *Diplomatic Protection of Citizens Abroad*, 660 ff. (1928); 2 Hyde, *International Law Chiefly As Interpreted and Applied by the United States*, 893 ff. (2d ed., 1945); 5 Hackworth, *Digest of International Law*, 802 ff. (1943); 1 Whiteman, *Damages in International Law*, 94 ff. (1937); 8 Whiteman, *Digest of International Law*, 1243–1245, 1246–1247 (1967); Panevezys-Saldutiskis Railway, Judgment, 1939, P.C.I.J., Series A/B, No. 76; Nottebohm, Second Phase, Judgment, I.C.J. Reports 1955.)

* Office of the Legal Adviser, Department of State.

In 1939, the Permanent Court of International Justice stated:

"[T]he rule of international law . . . is that in taking up the case of one of its nationals by resorting to diplomatic action or international judicial proceedings on his behalf, a State is in reality asserting its own right, the right to ensure in the person of its nationals respect for the rules of international law. This right is necessarily limited to intervention on behalf of its own nationals because, in the absence of a special agreement, it is the bond of nationality between the State and the individual which alone confers upon the State the right of diplomatic protection, and it is as a part of the function of diplomatic protection that the right to take up a claim and to ensure respect for the rules of international law must be envisaged. Where the injury was done to the national of some other State, no claim to which such injury may give rise falls within the scope of the diplomatic protection which a State is entitled to afford nor can it give rise to a claim which that State is entitled to espouse." (Panevezys-Saldutiskis Railway, Judgment, 1939, P.C.I.J., Series A/B, No. 76, 4, 16–17.)

Innumerable international, domestic and mixed claims arbitral tribunals have followed and applied the international law rule of continuous nationality. It has been the constant policy and practice of the Department of State to decline to espouse claims which have not been continuously owned by United States nationals. Subsequent acquisition of United States citizenship by naturalization does not retroactively change the original legal defect. [See 6 Moore, *Digest of International Law*, 636–637.]

. . . .

It has always been the policy of the United States Government not to permit persons who were not citizens of the United States at the time of loss or damage to share in lump sums paid by foreign governments in settlement of nationalization claims or war claims. This policy rests upon the well-established principle of international law as stated above. This policy seems not to have been questioned before the enactment of the International Claims Settlement Act of 1949. Since the passage of that Act, however, bills have been introduced in the Congress to permit persons who were not citizens at the time of loss or damage to receive compensation out of vested Bulgarian, Hungarian and Romanian assets for nationalization and war damage in those countries. Bills have also been introduced to permit such persons with nationalization claims against Czechoslovakia to share in the proceeds of the sale of a steel mill of the Czechoslovak Government. Neither the executive branch nor the Congress favored any of such bills and none was enacted with the exception of a bill which permitted a small number of persons who were not citizens at the time of damage to share in the lump sum paid by Italy for war losses and damages outside of Italy. That bill was not opposed because the lump sum paid by Italy exceeded the amount needed to satisfy claims of persons who were citizens at the time of loss or damage.

An agreement settling claims of U.S. nationals against Czechoslovakia was initialed on November 6, 1981, and approved by Public Law 97-127, approved on December 29, 1981. Section 6 of that law directs the Foreign Claims Settlement Commission of the United States to reopen certain claims that had been denied by the Commission, on the ground that the claimants in question were not nationals of the United States on the date of taking, during an earlier adjudication of claims against Czechoslovakia carried out between 1958 and 1962 under the authority of Title IV of the International Claims Settlement Act of 1949, as amended. The particular claims arose from expropriations carried out between January 1, 1945, and February 26, 1948, by the Benes government, against promises of compensation that were later repudiated by the Communist government. The precise question before the Commission in those cases was whether the date of taking was the date of expropriation (when the claimants were not United States nationals) or the date on which it became clear that no compensation would be forthcoming (by which time the claimants had become United States nationals). The effect of Section 6 is to reconsider and resolve that question in favor of those claimants who had become nationals of the United States on or before February 26, 1948, the date of the Communist takeover. Given the particular facts involved, and the precise legal questions actually at issue, Section 6 cannot properly be regarded as an exception to the "continuous nationality" principle, which is expressly reaffirmed by subsection (a)(2)(B) of that section. That subsection provides:

> "The Congress reaffirms the principle and practice of the United States to seek compensation from foreign governments on behalf only of persons who were nationals of the United States at the time they sustained losses by the nationalization or other taking of their property by those foreign governments. In making payments under this section, the Congress does not establish any precedent for future claims payments." [95 Stat. 1677; 22 U.S.C. note prec. 1642.]

Bills have also been introduced in prior sessions of the Congress to amend the War Claims Act of 1948 to permit payment of compensation for imprisonment during the war out of vested German and Japanese assets to certain persons who resided in the United States and persons who acquired citizenship after their imprisonment. The Department of State opposed all of such bills on which its comments were requested and none was enacted.

The Department is not aware of any instance in which persons who were not citizens of the United States at the time of loss, with the exception of the small number who shared in the above-mentioned Italian fund and certain religious organizations in the United States, have been permitted to share in funds paid by foreign governments or funds derived from vested amounts either for the taking of property or for losses and damages as a result of the war.

This Congressional policy was most recently reiterated and followed in Public Law 96-606, approved on December 28, 1980, which amended the International Claims Settlement Act of 1949 to allow recovery by United States nationals for losses incurred in Vietnam. Section 704 provides:

> "A claim may be favorably considered under section 703 of this Act only if the property right on which it is based was owned, wholly or partially, directly or indirectly, by a national of the United States on the date of loss and only to the extent that the claim has been held by one or more nationals of the United States continuously from the date that the loss occurred until the date of filing with the Commis-

sion." [94 Stat. 3535; 22 U.S.C. 1645c. See also S. Rep. No. 94-1188, 94th Cong., 2d Sess. (1976), p. 3; 1976 U.S.C. C.A.N., Vol. 5 (1977), p. 5584.]

. . . .

Espousal of any kind of claims of persons who were not citizens of the United States at the time of loss or damage would establish a major departure in U.S. claims practice that would be inconsistent with international law.

. . . .

In 1974, upon the establishment of diplomatic relations, the United States and the German Democratic Republic agreed that private organizations designated in both countries shall directly conduct talks on so-called "humanitarian claims" of victims of Nazi persecution. (See statement of Congressman Bingham in the *Congressional Record* of September 30, 1976, 34109–34112.) At least some of the claims of "late" nationals proposed in the draft bill appear to be included in those "humanitarian claims." . . .

Even though the United States Government might not have the standing under international law to espouse a claim of a United States national and interpose it through diplomatic channels against a foreign government, in practice the Department and its missions abroad informally have exercised their good offices in behalf of such persons. Without adopting the claim as its own, or passing on the merits of the claim, the Department or the missions abroad would raise the matter informally with the appropriate authorities of the foreign government concerned to encourage an ex gratia settlement, not on the basis of legal right, but on humanitarian and equitable grounds. For example, in the case of the "humanitarian claims" of the Conference on Jewish Material Claims Against Germany, since 1974, both the Department and the American Embassy in East Berlin have acted on numerous occasions to encourage and facilitate direct talks between the Conference on Jewish Material Claims and the Anti-Fascist Resistance Fighters League to arrive at an amicable settlement of those claims without officially involving the United States Government and the German Democratic Republic Government.[1]

. . . .

Transnational Corporations

(U.S. *Digest*, Ch. 10, §4)

Conflicts of Jurisdiction—U.S. Economic Regulation

In an address at Columbia University's Parker School of Foreign and Comparative Law on June 30, 1982, the Legal Adviser of the Department of State, Davis R. Robinson, discussed a range of areas where conflicting claims of jurisdiction had arisen from U.S. economic regulatory actions, some taken for foreign policy or national security ends, others for essentially domestic purposes.

The Legal Adviser noted that such a jurisdictional conflict had recently

[1] Dept. of State File No. P82 0112-2405.

been occasioned by President Reagan's decision of June 18 to adopt further U.S. export sanctions against the Soviet Union because of its continuing deep involvement in Polish affairs, including Soviet responsibility for the prolongation of martial law and for suppression of human rights by the governing Polish military authorities.

Pointing out that there was no single "conflicts of jurisdiction" problem, Mr. Robinson then discussed several contexts, involving different facts and differing U.S. interests, in which U.S. controls having transnational effects had been formulated or enforced. He also described Department of State activity at the diplomatic level and within the U.S. Government, to minimize, reconcile, or obtain accommodation to the ensuing conflicts of jurisdiction.

Portions of the Legal Adviser's address follow:

> Consider, first, the area of antiboycott regulation. Conflicts between the U.S. and foreign governments often involve agencies' discretionary application of U.S. requirements to conduct abroad. The reach of antiboycott regulation, however, is not a matter of substantial agency discretion. Section 8 of the Export Administration Act of 1979 [50 U.S.C. App. 2407] specifically requires application to conduct abroad. That section bars United States persons engaged in interstate or foreign commerce from taking or knowingly agreeing to take any of a long list of specified actions "with intent to comply with, further or support any boycott fostered or imposed" by a foreign government against a country friendly to the United States. The Act then defines "United States person" to embrace foreign subsidiaries or affiliates which are found to be controlled in fact by domestic concerns.
>
> Congress judged that section 8 had to be extended to U.S. subsidiaries abroad in order to avoid evasion and frustration of the section's purposes. However, the application of section 8 to foreign subsidiaries has been objectionable to some other governments, particularly the United Kingdom. The U.K. argues that subsidiaries incorporated in the U.K. are U.K. persons, bound to follow only the laws and policies of the U.K. In the antiboycott area, the conscious and deliberate policy of the British Government is to leave decisions on compliance with foreign boycotts to the firms concerned. Hence, the U.K. argues, U.S. regulation of the boycott behavior of U.K. subsidiaries constitutes an unacceptable substitution by the United States of its own policy for British policy.
>
> This dispute is not academic. Commerce Department enforcement actions involving sanctions against a number of foreign subsidiaries have prompted vigorous protests from some of our allies.
>
> The Export Administration Act also provides broad authority to impose controls on exports for U.S. national security or foreign policy purposes or to meet problems of domestic short supplies. Such controls have produced recurring conflicts with foreign jurisdictions. The potential for conflict has increased since 1977, when Congress amended the Act to give the President the authority to control the export of goods or technical data subject to the jurisdiction of the United States or exported by any person subject to the jurisdiction of the United States.
>
> Controls imposed under the Export Administration Act can have far-reaching effects on foreign economic activity involving transactions in

U.S.-origin goods or technology. The Export Administration Regulations regulate re-exports (or sometimes even in-country transfers) of exported commodities and technical data. Foreign consignees may be required to obtain authorization before re-exporting or transferring U.S.-origin commodities or data (or in some cases, products manufactured using them). Under the Act and regulations, failure to comply with such requirements may expose foreign persons to U.S. criminal penalties.

In practice, the U.S. usually enforces its controls on foreign firms through Commerce Department action denying violators the right to receive future exports from the United States. Such "denial orders" promote compliance with U.S. requirements abroad for established firms which are dependent upon continued access to U.S. goods and technology.

A denial order normally operates to deprive the foreign person subject to the order of access to U.S. goods from either the U.S. or foreign suppliers. For example, a September 1981 Commerce Department denial order barring further U.S. exports to UAA [United African Airlines], a Libyan airline, also prohibited foreign persons from transferring any U.S.-origin goods or technology to UAA [see 46 Fed. Reg. 44,803]. These prohibitions covered U.S. goods, even if they had been exported from the United States before the denial order.

Certain Treasury Department regulations raise many of these same issues. Treasury maintains a variety of blocking controls, prohibitions on trade and restrictions on financial transactions with several countries and their nationals, including Cuba, North Korea and Viet Nam. These are "grand-fathered" vestiges of the President's authority under section 5(b) of the Trading with the Enemy Act. (The International Emergency Economic Powers Act of 1977 and the National Emergencies Act have continued the substance of the President's broad emergency economic powers under the Trading with the Enemy Act but place significant procedural and substantive restrictions on new future uses of these powers.)

These controls all involve extensive U.S. regulation of conduct in foreign territory by persons the U.S. regards as subject to its jurisdiction. U.S. nationals in the United States and abroad are barred from trading with proscribed countries or with their nationals. The controls also extend to subsidiaries of U.S. firms abroad. The most noted recent use of the President's broad emergency powers was the November 1979 blocking of Iranian assets in U.S. banks and their overseas branches and subsidiaries under the International Emergency Economic Powers Act.

. . . U.S. regulatory actions taken for essentially domestic purposes may also produce conflicts of jurisdiction.

The most familiar and widely noted illustration of this is U.S. antitrust law. Most of the professional writing and public and intergovernmental discussion of international conflicts of jurisdiction has dealt with antitrust. . . .

The international conflicts regarding U.S. antitrust jurisdiction follow from the long course of U.S. judicial decisions holding that U.S. antitrust jurisdiction extends to conduct abroad having direct and substantial effects upon United States commerce. The Federal Republic of Germany, the European Economic Community and other jurisdictions also make use of effects principles in defining their own antitrust jurisdiction. Indeed, some commentators have suggested that conflicts over "effects" jurisdiction may eventually disappear. For the foreseeable future, however, major U.S. trading partners, including the U.K., Canada and Australia, can be expected to have reservations with respect to the exercise of U.S. antitrust regulation on the basis of effects in the United States. Moreover, the possibility of private treble damage actions in the United States, which foreign officials often like to describe as "that rogue elephant," probably ensures the continuation of jurisdictional conflicts in the antitrust area.

Another prominent example of essentially domestic regulation raising conflicts with foreign jurisdictions is in the securities field. For example, with respect to the enforcement activities of the Securities and Exchange Commission, foreign bank secrecy legislation has impeded the Commission's ability to detect and correct insider trading or other abuses in U.S. markets. The problems involved are illustrated in two widely noted recent insider trading cases, *SEC* v. *Banca della Svizzera Italiana* [92 F.R.D. 111 (S.D.N.Y. 1981)], referred to as the "*St. Joe*" case because it involves options in St. Joe Minerals Corporation, and *SEC* v. *Certain Unknown Purchasers* [81 Civ. 6553, S.D.N.Y., filed Oct. 26, 1981], referred to as the *Santa Fe* case because it involves stock and options of the Santa Fe International Corporation. Both cases involve allegations that insiders used Swiss banks to effect purchases of stock and options in U.S. markets prior to the public announcement of takeover bids for these companies.

Heretofore, the identities of principals in insider trading transactions often have been shielded by Swiss penal laws barring disclosure of confidential banking information. However, in *St. Joe*, Judge [Milton] Pollack indicated his intention to order the Swiss bank to disclose its principals notwithstanding the possibility of sanctions under Swiss law. A client waiver was subsequently obtained and the information sought was produced. In *Santa Fe*, the SEC believes that extensive insider trading was carried on through several Swiss banks and has sought disclosure of the bank's principals.

Measures to protect the integrity of U.S. commodity markets have also posed jurisdictional conflicts. The Commodity Futures Trading Commission must seek information from foreign commodities traders about their principals in transactions on U.S. markets or other information necessary for the Commission to meet its regulatory responsibilities. Such measures have resulted in conflict with other countries, including particularly the U.K., both because of the importance of British commodities markets and because of the continuing U.K. objections to U.S. activities affecting persons or transactions in the U.K. Thus, a call by the Commission for information from a party in the U.K. triggered the first invocation of the 1980 British Protection of Trading Interests Act [see *In the Matter of Alan J. Ridge & Co., Ltd.*, C.F.T.C. Docket No. 80-16]. . . .

. . . .

Claims to regulatory jurisdiction by one country may, of course, give rise to objections from other countries. In this connection it is important to recognize that exercises of jurisdiction do not always present legal issues in the abstract. Rather, foreign governments' views of such actions will be affected by the factual and political context. Governments tend to be more receptive toward controls in situations in which common political objectives suggest that restraint and tolerance would be appropriate. For example, in the November 1979 blocking of Iranian assets conflicts were minimized because of a shared concern for the plight of the American hostages in Tehran.

In other contexts the reactions of foreign governments may be different. Some countries, such as the U.K., France, Canada and Australia, which have objected at one time or another to broad assertions of U.S. jurisdiction, have enacted or are considering "blocking statutes." These vary in form, but all permit foreign governments to block their nationals' or companies' compliance with foreign demands for document production or other regulatory measures.

To date, the blocking statutes have perhaps involved more symbol than substance. The British Protection of Trading Interests Act, enthusiastically enacted by Parliament in 1980 as a response to perceived American excesses, has until today only been invoked in the Commodity Futures Trading Commission investigation previously mentioned. However, the potential for enactment or implementation of blocking statutes stands as a warning to U.S. regulators. Indeed, some U.S. agencies have modified their investigatory actions to avoid triggering foreign blocking action. Such self-imposed limitations naturally help to avoid international controversy, but they may also be a complicating factor and, in some cases, impair valid U.S. law enforcement interests.

What is the State Department's view of these matters of jurisdictional conflict?

Our starting point is an analysis quite similar to that being followed by many U.S. courts. U.S. courts have recognized the need to take into account, in the exercise of jurisdiction, both the interests of the United States and the interests of other states concerned with a given transaction. We have supported the development of a "rule of reasonableness" in various fact situations involving threatening conflicts of jurisdiction.

This approach was articulated in 1976 in the Ninth Circuit's decision in the now famous *Timberlane* case [549 F.2d 597 (9th Cir. 1976)]. The Court there set out a range of factors to be weighed in situations involving competing state interests. The substance of the *Timberlane* balancing approach was subsequently taken up by the Third Circuit in the *Mannington Mills* case [595 F.2d 1287 (3d. Cir. 1979)]. Again the Court set out a variety of illustrative factors to be considered in determining whether jurisdiction is proper. The balancing approach has also been adopted by the Tenth Circuit in the *Amax* case [661 F.2d 864 (10th Cir. 1981)], a case dismissing an antitrust claim on the basis of a balancing analysis. Most recently, the Fifth Circuit, in the *Mitsui* case [594 F.2d 48 (5th Cir. 1979), *reh'g denied*, 599 F.2d 449, *cert. denied*, 445 U.S. 903 (1980)], noted and commended the *Timberlane* analysis. This balancing approach is likewise reflected in section 403 of the draft *Restatement of*

Foreign Relations Law of the United States, as revised under the auspices of the American Law Institute.[1]

This developing approach in given fact situations of weighing and balancing competing national interests in assessing a proposed exercise of jurisdiction is based on the recognition that a given transaction may be of legitimate interest to more than one state. The factors to be considered include, for example:

—the links, such as nationality, residence or economic activity, between the regulating state and the persons principally responsible for the activity to be regulated;
—the importance of regulation to the regulating state;
—the extent of other states' interest in regulating the activity; and
—the existence of potential or actual conflict with regulation by other states.

[1] Section 403 of the *Restatement of the Foreign Relations Law of the United States (Revised)*, together with Comment and Reporters' Notes, follows:

§403. Limitations on Jurisdiction to Prescribe

(1) Although one of the bases for jurisdiction under §402 is present, a state may not apply law to the conduct, relations, status, or interests of persons or things having connections with another state or states when the exercise of such jurisdiction is unreasonable.

(2) Whether the exercise of jurisdiction is unreasonable is judged by evaluating all the relevant factors, including:

(a) the extent to which the activity (i) takes place within the regulating state, or (ii) has substantial, direct, and foreseeable effect upon or in the regulating state;
(b) the links, such as nationality, residence, or economic activity, between the regulating state and the persons principally responsible for the activity to be regulated, or between that state and those whom the law or regulation is designed to protect;
(c) the character of the activity to be regulated, the importance of regulation to the regulating state, the extent to which other states regulate such activities, and the degree to which the desirability of such regulation is generally accepted;
(d) the existence of justified expectations that might be protected or hurt by the regulation in question;
(e) the importance of regulation to the international political, legal or economic system;
(f) the extent to which such regulation is consistent with the traditions of the international system;
(g) the extent to which another state may have an interest in regulating the activity;
(h) the likelihood of conflict with regulation by other states.

(3) An exercise of jurisdiction which is not unreasonable according to the criteria indicated in Subsection (2) may nevertheless be unreasonable if it requires a person to take action that would violate a regulation of another state which is not unreasonable under those criteria. Preference between conflicting exercises of jurisdiction is determined by evaluating the respective interests of the regulating states in light of the factors listed in Subsection (2).

(4) Under the law of the United States:

(a) a statute, regulation or rule is to be construed as exercising jurisdiction and applying law only to the extent permissible under §402 and this section, unless such construction is not fairly possible; but
(b) where Congress has made clear its purpose to exercise jurisdiction which may be beyond the limits permitted by international law, such exercise of jurisdiction, if within the constitutional authority of Congress, is effective as law in the United States.

RESTATEMENT OF THE FOREIGN RELATIONS LAW OF THE UNITED STATES (REVISED) 103–05 (Tent. Draft No. 2, 1981).

The State Department has sought to use this kind of approach in its own legal analyses and in our work with other agencies on their activities. In testimony and in comments on pending legislation, we have commended the principles reflected in the *Timberlane* decision to Congress. We have also supported the proper application of such principles in litigation. In the *Uranium* [*Antitrust*] *Litigation* [617 F.2d 1248 (1980)] my predecessor at the State Department [Roberts B. Owen] wrote to the Seventh Circuit in the spring of 1980 that "in future proceedings in this and other cases, the courts should give due consideration to the views of interested foreign governments and take into account appropriate considerations of comity where there is possible conflict between the laws or policies of nation states."[2]

The balancing approach is clearly not a failsafe procedure for resolving or preventing jurisdictional controversies. There will inevitably be instances in which the U.S. Government's national security needs and other predominant policy interests demand action even though it may create a conflict with foreign interests and claims to jurisdiction. The balancing approach to the resolution of jurisdictional conflict cannot prevent such outcomes. What it *can* do is help to ensure that decisions which implicate significant foreign concerns follow an informed and careful evaluation and weighing of the relevant U.S. and foreign interests.

There is also a wide range of practical steps that we are taking in order to prevent or resolve jurisdictional conflicts.

In some instances there are established procedures of intergovernmental cooperation which help significantly to prevent or mitigate conflicts. Both the Justice Department and the Federal Trade Commission regularly give, through our Embassies, prior notice to other governments potentially concerned before taking antitrust enforcement actions implicating their interests. The antitrust agencies likewise regularly consult with foreign governments concerning particular enforcement activities.

These practices derive from a set of agreed O.E.C.D. Guidelines on notice and consultation in the antitrust area.[3] They are sometimes supplemented by bilateral agreements with foreign governments. Notifications under these institutional arrangements have helped to prevent unpleasant surprises, while consultations have sometimes brought about moderation of either U.S. actions or foreign objections.

There has been an important recent development in this area. Yesterday [June 29, 1982], the Governments of the United States and Australia took a long step forward by concluding an agreement for antitrust cooperation containing significant provisions on notice and consultation, private treble damage actions, and blocking statutes.[4]

. . . .

Outside the antitrust area, other agencies engage in notification and

[2] *See* 74 AJIL 665, 667 (1980).

[3] Recommendation of the Council Concerning Cooperation between Member Countries on Restrictive Business Practices Affecting International Trade, OECD Doc. C (79) 154 (Final) (1979), on file in Dept. of State File No. P82 0105-2154.

[4] For a summary of the Agreement, see p. 866 *infra*.

consultation with affected foreign governments on an informal basis. For example, in the SEC's *Santa Fe* case . . . the SEC and the Justice and State Departments have carried on discussions with Swiss Government officials to attempt to devise a mutually acceptable procedure to identify suspected insider traders. Significant progress has been made on this issue. The Office of Antiboycott Compliance at the Commerce Department, too, has recognized the utility of the notice and consultation process as a means to deal with foreign interests and concerns involved in particular cases.[5]

[5] DEPT. STATE BULL., No. 2067, Oct. 1982, at 35.

JUDICIAL DECISIONS

MONROE LEIGH

Act of state doctrine—valuation standard in cases of expropriation—reduction of compensation to reflect lack of "going concern value"

BANCO NACIONAL DE CUBA v. CHASE MANHATTAN BANK. 658 F.2d 875. U.S. Court of Appeals, 2d Cir., August 4, 1981.

Defendant, Chase Manhattan Bank (Chase), was one of a number of American financial institutions whose properties were nationalized by Cuba following the revolution in the late 1950's. Plaintiff, Banco Nacional de Cuba (Banco Nacional), was the state-owned instrumentality designated to take over the assets and businesses of Chase and other American banks. Banco Nacional commenced the present action in 1960, asserting several claims against Chase totaling $9.8 million both in its own right and as successor in interest to other Cuban state-owned banks. While Chase did not contest the validity of these claims, it asserted counterclaims for $8.6 million for, *inter alia*, the expropriation of its Cuban branch offices.

The U.S. District Court for the Southern District of New York ruled that Chase had a justiciable counterclaim based on the expropriation of its branch offices and valued the property at $6.9 million.[1] The valuation standard applied by the district court was the "going concern value" of the branch offices, that is, compensation for the book value of the assets plus a premium for business good will. Accordingly, the court entered judgment for Banco Nacional in the net amount of $2.9 million and directed that the money be placed in a special account pursuant to the Cuban Assets Control Regulations.[2]

The U.S. Court of Appeals for the Second Circuit (per Hearse, J.) affirmed the district court's opinion except as to the valuation of Chase's Cuban branches. The appeals court held that Chase was not entitled to going concern value and therefore reduced the value of its counterclaim by the $1.4 million premium that the district court had allowed for business good will.[3]

The court began by confirming the district court's holding that Chase's branch-related counterclaim was not barred by the act of state doctrine and was therefore justiciable. The court explained that the decision of the Supreme Court in *Banco Nacional de Cuba v. Sabbatino* (376 U.S. 398 (1964)), which would appear to require that Chase's counterclaim be held nonjusticiable under the act of state doctrine, had been significantly modified by the High Court's decision in *First National City Bank v. Banco Nacional de Cuba* (406 U.S.

[1] 505 F.Supp. 412 (S.D.N.Y. 1980).

[2] 31 C.F.R. pt. 515 (1980).

[3] On the same day that it rendered this opinion, the Second Circuit (per Kearse, J.) decided three other cases relating to the property of American banks expropriated by the Cuban Government: Banco Para el Comercio Exterior de Cuba v. First Nat'l City Bank, 658 F.2d 913; First Nat'l Bank of Boston (Int'l) v. Banco Nacional de Cuba, 658 F.2d 895; Banco Nacional de Cuba v. Chemical Bank New York Trust Co., 658 F.2d 903.

759 (1972)) (*Citibank I*). Although in *Citibank I* the Justices did not agree on a single rationale, the Second Circuit cumulated the views of the majority in that case to arrive at the following "phenomenological rule":

> [W]here (1) the Executive Branch has provided a *Bernstein* letter advising the courts that it believes [the] act of state doctrine need not be applied,[4] (2) there is no showing that an adjudication of the claim will interfere with delicate foreign relations, and (3) the claim against the foreign sovereign is asserted by way of counterclaim and does not exceed the value of the sovereign's claim, adjudication of the counterclaim for expropriation of the defendant's property is not barred by the act of state doctrine.[5]

The court found all three of these conditions to be satisfied by Chase's branch-related counterclaim and held that it was therefore justiciable.

Banco Nacional next argued that even if the counterclaim was justiciable, the damage issue was nonjusticiable because of insufficient international consensus as to standards of required compensation. The court admitted that an international law standard regarding damages for expropriation could not be stated precisely. It concluded, however, that "when the Supreme Court in *Citibank I* held that Citibank's counterclaim was justiciable, it clearly indicated that a judgment should be reached as to the worth of that counterclaim for setoff purposes."[6]

As to the amount of compensation, the court modified Chase's counterclaim award to eliminate the premium granted by the district court for going concern value or good will. The court stated that in determining the standard of compensation for expropriated assets, principles of international law, not merely local law, must be applied. After reviewing the long and controversial debate that has taken place on this subject, beginning with the "Hull Doctrine" in 1938[7] and embodied in the actions taken by the General Assembly of the United Nations since 1962,[8] the court determined that international law requires the payment of either "appropriate" or "full" compensation. The court further determined that in the instant case application of either standard entitled Chase only to the net asset value of its branches, and not to a premium for their value as a going concern. The court observed that "going concern value" generally refers to the premium that a prospective buyer is willing to pay over book value in the expectation that the business will continue and that the new owner will receive the stream of earnings. The court reasoned that to award such value in this case would ignore the acknowledged state of the Cuban economy following the Castro revolution. In effect, the court concluded, the revolution had rendered the future prospects for Chase's banking

[4] The *Bernstein* exception to the act of state doctrine provides, in effect, that the doctrine does not apply when the executive branch expressly supports adjudication. *See* Bernstein v. N.V. Nederlandsche-Amerikaansche Stoomvaart-Maatschappij, 210 F.2d 375 (2d Cir. 1954); Bernstein v. Van Heyghen Freres Societe Anonyme, 163 F.2d 246 (2d Cir.), *cert. denied*, 332 U.S. 772 (1947).

[5] 658 F.2d 875, 884.

[6] *Id.* at 885.

[7] *See* Note of Secretary of State Hull, Aug. 22, 1938, 19 DEPT. OF STATE PRESS RELEASES, No. 465, Aug. 27, 1938, at 140.

[8] *See, e.g.*, UNGA Res. 1803 (XVII) on Permanent Sovereignty over Natural Resources, para. 4.

business so highly speculative that "we see no warrant for believing that, at a time when aliens were fleeing Cuba and many foreign businesses were being abandoned or nationalized, a potential buyer with his eyes open would have paid Chase a premium in anticipation of its future Cuban earnings."[9]

The court's rejection of a standard of valuation reflecting the going concern value of Chase's Cuban branches is highly questionable. It ignores the fact that the loss of good will was a direct result of the expropriatory action and permits the Cuban Government to create a loss of value by its own actions and then to profit from those actions at the expense of American investors. It also ignores the ongoing value of the expropriated banking business to the Cuban Government and the likelihood that Chase's operation, as conducted by Cuba, without competition and with liabilities canceled, was even more valuable than it would have been if Chase had remained in control. The court discounted these considerations, as it did the additional fact that the Foreign Claims Settlement Commission had previously ruled that Chase should be allowed compensation for the going concern value of its Cuban branches.[10]

Instructive in this regard is the model Bilateral Investment Treaty that has recently been developed by the Office of the U.S. Trade Representative and the U.S. Department of State as a basis for future negotiations with a diversity of foreign states. The treaty provides that the calculation of compensation for expropriation "shall not reflect any reduction in such fair market value due to either prior public notice or announcement of the expropriatory action, or the occurrence of the events that constituted or resulted in the expropriatory action."[11] As this model treaty reflects, fairness dictates that "full" or "appropriate" compensation be measured at a point prior to a foreign government's unilateral expropriatory action.

Boycott—invasion of Afghanistan by the Soviet Union—prohibition under National Labor Relations Act of secondary political boycott

INTERNATIONAL LONGSHOREMEN'S ASSOCIATION v. ALLIED INTERNATIONAL, INC. 102 S.Ct. 1656.
U.S. Supreme Court, April 20, 1982.

An American importer, Allied International, Inc. (Allied), had contracted with an American shipper for the transport of Russian wood products from the Soviet Union to the United States. The shipper employed an American stevedoring company to unload its ships. In protest against the Russian invasion of Afghanistan, the International Longshoremen's Association (ILA) ordered its members, including the stevedore's employees, to refuse to handle cargo arriving from or destined for the Soviet Union. As a result of this

[9] 658 F.2d at 894. Chase has not filed a petition of certiorari appealing this decision.

[10] The Commission held that "the evaluation of the loss should not be limited to the assets of the bank branches, but should also include compensation for the *ever increasing business activities of the branches and the substantial earning potential in connection with such activities.*" Claim of the Chase Manhattan Bank, N.A., F.C.S.C. Dec. No. CU-6295, at 2 (Oct. 20, 1971) (emphasis added).

[11] Treaty Between the United States of America and ______ Concerning the Reciprocal Encouragement and Protection of Investments, draft of Jan. 11, 1982.

boycott, Allied's shipments were disrupted, and it was forced to renegotiate its Russian contracts. Allied brought suit against the ILA in federal district court for damages under section 303 of the Labor Management Relations Act,[1] alleging that the ILA's action constituted an unlawful secondary boycott under section 8(b)(4)(B) of the National Labor Relations Act (NLRA).[2] The district court dismissed the complaint, holding that the union's activity constituted a purely political primary boycott and thus fell outside the scope of section 8(b)(4)(B).[3] The U.S. Court of Appeals for the First Circuit reversed on the ground that the activity, despite its political purpose, was within section 8(b)(4)(B)'s secondary boycott prohibition, and that resort to such behavior was not protected by the First Amendment to the U.S. Constitution.[4] In a unanimous decision (per Powell, J.), the Supreme Court affirmed the ruling of the court of appeals.

As a preliminary matter, the Court determined that the activity in question was "in commerce" and therefore within the scope of the NLRA. Because the union's refusal to handle the Russian cargo in no way affected the operations of foreign ships and did not seek to extend American constitutional protections to foreign workers, the Court held that the "longstanding tradition of restraint in applying the laws of this country to ships of a foreign country" was irrelevant to this case.[5]

The Court concluded next that the provisions of section 8(b)(4)(B) applied squarely to the undisputed facts of this case. The ILA's sole complaint was with the Soviet Union's foreign and military policy. The specific purpose of the union's action was not to disrupt business in order to achieve labor objectives, but rather to keep union members from handling goods from an objectionable source. Thus, however commendable the ILA's objectives might have been, its action had the effect of imposing a heavy burden on neutral employers—precisely the burden that the secondary boycott prohibitions were intended to prevent.

The Court also ruled that it was not a valid defense to the application of section 8(b)(4)(B) that the boycott was motivated by a political dispute with a foreign nation rather than a labor dispute with a primary employer. Section 8(b)(4)(B) on its face provides no such exception, and its legislative history does not suggest any.

As a final matter, the Court had no difficulty in disposing of the ILA's claim that the application of section 8(b)(4)(B) in this case infringed upon the First Amendment rights of the ILA and its members. The Court observed that it has consistently rejected the claim that secondary picketing by labor unions

[1] 29 U.S.C. §187 (1976).

[2] 29 U.S.C. §158(b)(4)(B) (1976), *amended by* 29 U.S.C.A. §158(b)(4)(B) (1980). Section 8(b)(4)(B) prohibits a labor union from engaging in activities designed to influence individuals employed by "any person engaged in commerce or in any industry affecting commerce" by inducing such employees to refuse to handle goods where the object thereof is "forcing or requiring any person to cease using, selling, handling, transporting, or otherwise dealing" in the products of, or "to cease doing business with any other person."

[3] 492 F.Supp. 334 (D. Mass. 1980).

[4] 640 F.2d 1368 (1st Cir. 1981).

[5] 102 S.Ct. 1656, 1662. *See, e.g.*, Windward Shipping (London) Ltd. v. American Radio Ass'n, 415 U.S. 104 (1974); Benz v. Compania Naviera Hidalgo, 353 U.S. 138 (1957).

in violation of section 8(b)(4)(B) is a protected First Amendment activity and concluded that "[i]t would seem even clearer that conduct designed not to communicate but to coerce merits still less consideration under the First Amendment."[6]

The ILA historically has used its boycott power as a weapon against foreign governments of which the union's leadership disapproved. Occasionally, its boycotts have conflicted with the prevailing attitude of the United States toward such governments.[7] In the wake of this decision, however, the ILA will be limited in the expression of its policies to the "many ways in which a union and its individual members may express their opposition to [a foreign government's] foreign policy without infringing upon the rights of others."[8]

Foreign Sovereign Immunities Act—immunity of a foreign state from prejudgment attachment—explicit waiver of immunity

LIBRA BANK LIMITED, ET AL. v. BANCO NACIONAL DE COSTA RICA, S.A. 676 F.2d 47.

U.S. Court of Appeals, 2d Cir., April 12, 1982.

This action arose out of a default on a $40 million loan provided by 16 banks, including the plaintiffs in this case, to the defendant Banco Nacional de Costa Rica (Banco Nacional). Prior to judgment in state court, plaintiffs caused the attachment of Banco Nacional's assets held by several New York City banks. Banco Nacional then removed the action to the U.S. District Court for the Southern District of New York and moved to vacate the attachment. The essential issue was whether Banco Nacional, by virtue of a general waiver clause in the loan agreement and similar provisions on various promissory notes, had "explicitly" waived its immunity from prejudgment attachment within the meaning of section 1610(d)(1) of the Foreign Sovereign Immunities Act of 1976 (28 U.S.C. §§1602–1611 (1976)) (the Act). The district court held that Banco Nacional's waiver of prejudgment attachment was not "explicit" within the meaning of section 1610(d)(1) and vacated the attachment. The U.S. Court of Appeals for the Second Circuit (per Timbers, J.) reversed, holding that section 1610(d)(1) does not require verbatim recitation of the words "prejudgment attachment" in order to constitute an "explicit" waiver. Rather, the court held, the focus should be on the intent of the foreign state, judged by the language of the waiver provision.

It was undisputed that Banco Nacional is an instrumentality of the Government of Costa Rica and therefore a "foreign state" within the meaning of the Act.[1] Accordingly, in the view of the court, under section 1609 of the Act, Banco Nacional's assets in the United States "in general are immune from attachment." However, section 1610(d)(1) provides by way of exception that the property of a foreign state used for a commercial activity in the United States shall not be immune from attachment prior to the entry of

[6] 102 S.Ct. at 1664–65.

[7] *See* N.Y. Times, April 21, 1982, at A1, col. 1.

[8] 102 S.Ct. at 1665.

[1] *See* 28 U.S.C. §1603.

judgment if the foreign state has "explicitly waived its immunity from attachment prior to judgment."

In obtaining the loan in this case, Banco Nacional entered into an agreement with the plaintiff banks that provided: "The Borrower can sue and be sued in its own name and does not have any right of immunity from suit with respect to the Borrower's obligations under this Letter or the Notes."[2] In compliance with the terms of this agreement, Banco Nacional made promissory notes in favor of each plaintiff. Each note provided: "The Borrower hereby irrevocably and unconditionally waives any right or immunity from legal proceedings including suit judgment and execution on grounds of sovereignty which it or its property may now or hereafter enjoy."[3] The issue before the court was whether the foregoing provisions constituted an "explicit" waiver of immunity from prejudgment attachment within the meaning of section 1610(d)(1).

The court began its analysis by observing that section 1610(d)(1) does not require the verbatim recitation of the words "prejudgment attachment." Rather, the underlying purpose of that section is "to preclude inadvertent, implied, or constructive waiver in cases where the intent of the foreign state is equivocal or ambiguous." Using this test, the court concluded that the immunity provision in the promissory notes "evinces a clear and unambiguous intent to waive all claims of immunity in all legal proceedings," including prejudgment attachment.[4]

Banco Nacional argued that such a ruling would eviscerate the distinction between explicit and implied waivers contemplated by the Act. Section 1610(a)(1) provides that the property in the United States of a foreign state used for a commercial activity in the United States shall not be immune from attachment in aid of execution or from execution if the foreign state has waived its immunity "either explicitly *or* by implication" (emphasis added). Section 1610(d)(1), by contrast, requires that waivers be "explicit." The court held, however, that "explicit" means "clear," and that section 1610(a)(1) makes the waiver provision of the promissory notes appear no less clear. "If anything, the contrast helps the plaintiffs, for the waiver here certainly is not 'implied'."[5] What Congress meant to preclude by section 1610(d)(1) was "*unintended*" waivers; and on the basis of the language of the promissory notes, it would be "absurd" for Banco Nacional to argue that it did not intend to waive its immunity from prejudgment attachment. "As in all contract cases," the court concluded, "we must ascertain the intent of the parties. Section 1610(d)(1) affects our interpretation of the operative language here only to the extent that that language might not be clear. . . ."[6]

[2] 676 F.2d 47, 49.

[3] *Ibid.*

[4] *Ibid.*

[5] *Id.* at 50.

[6] *Ibid. But see* New England Merchants Nat'l Bank v. Iran Power Generation Transmission Co., 502 F.Supp. 120, 127 (S.D.N.Y. 1980) (" '[t]he consent necessary to waive [a] traditional immunity must be express, and it must be strictly construed.' . . . Thus, application of merely the 'ordinary principles of construction' is inappropriate when the construction of a waiver of sovereign immunity is at stake") (quoting United States v. New York Rayon Importing Co., 329 U.S. 654, 659 (1947)).

This decision provides an authoritative and much needed interpretation of the Foreign Sovereign Immunities Act. Prior to *Libra Bank*, no federal court of appeals had squarely faced the issue as to what constitutes an explicit waiver under section 1610(d)(1), and the few decisions at the district court level have differed in their applications of the statutory requirement.[7] Whether other appellate courts will choose to follow the sensible lead of the Second Circuit remains to be seen.

Treaties—application of local law to wholly owned U.S. subsidiary of foreign corporation—Friendship, Commerce and Navigation Treaty with Japan—freedom of choice employment provision—employment discrimination

SUMITOMO SHOJI AMERICA, INC. v. AVAGLIANO. 102 S.Ct. 2374. U.S. Supreme Court, June 15, 1982.

Petitioner, Sumitomo Shoji America, Inc. (Sumitomo), is a wholly owned subsidiary of a Japanese general trading company, incorporated under the laws of the State of New York and operating in the United States. Respondents are past and present female secretaries employed by Sumitomo and, with one exception, are U.S. citizens. Respondents brought a class action suit in federal district court claiming that Sumitomo, by hiring only male Japanese citizens for the company's executive, managerial, and sales positions, had discriminated on the basis of sex and national origin in violation of 42 U.S.C., section 1981 and Title VII of the Civil Rights Act of 1964, as amended (42 U.S.C. §2000e *et seq.*). In response, Sumitomo asserted that its employment practices were protected by Article VIII of the Treaty of Friendship, Commerce and Navigation of 1953 between the United States and Japan (4 UST 2063, TIAS No. 2863) (the Treaty). Article VIII(1) of the Treaty states, in relevant part: "*companies of either Party* shall be permitted to engage, within the territories of the other Party, accountants and other technical experts, executive personnel, attorneys, agents and other specialists *of their choice*" (emphasis added).

The district court dismissed the section 1981 claim. However, it refused to dismiss the Title VII claim, finding that since Sumitomo was incorporated under the laws of New York, it was a company of the United States and therefore not covered by Article VIII(1).[1] The U.S. Court of Appeals for the Second Circuit reversed in part,[2] holding that Article VIII(1) was intended to cover both foreign parent companies and their locally incorporated subsidiaries operating within the territory of the host government. However, the court also held that the language of Article VIII(1) did not insulate Sumitomo's employment practices from Title VII scrutiny; consequently, Sumitomo would have to demonstrate that its practices fell within the "bona fide occupational

[7] *Compare* New England Merchants Nat'l Bank v. Iran Power Generation Transmission Co., 502 F.Supp. 120 (S.D.N.Y. 1980), *summarized in* 75 AJIL 375 (1981) (Treaty of Amity between the United States and Iran held not to constitute an explicit waiver of prejudgment attachment) *with* Behring Int'l, Inc. v. Imperial Iranian Air Force, 475 F.Supp. 383 (D.N.J. 1979) (Treaty of Amity between the United States and Iran held to waive immunity from prejudgment attachment).

[1] Avigliano [*sic*] v. Sumitomo Shoji America, Inc., 473 F.Supp. 506 (S.D.N.Y. 1979).

[2] 638 F.2d 552 (2d Cir. 1981), *summarized in* 75 AJIL 671 (1981).

qualification" exception to Title VII.[3] The Supreme Court, in a unanimous decision (per Burger, C.J.), reversed the Second Circuit Court of Appeals and held that Sumitomo was not a company of Japan and therefore was not covered by Article VIII(1) of the Treaty.

The Court first examined the language of the Treaty and observed that the phrase "companies of either Party" was defined by Article XXII(3), which states: "As used in the present Treaty, the term 'companies' means corporations, partnerships, companies and other associations. . . . Companies constituted under the applicable laws and regulations within the territories of either Party *shall be deemed companies thereof* and shall have their juridical status recognized within the territories of the other Party" (emphasis added). Since Sumitomo was constituted under the laws of New York, it was a company of the United States and not of Japan. Accordingly, the Court concluded:

> As a company of the United States operating in the United States, under the literal language of Article XXII(3) of the Treaty, Sumitomo cannot invoke the rights provided in Article VIII(1), which are available only to companies of Japan operating in the United States and to companies of the United States operating in Japan.[4]

Both the Japanese and United States Governments supported this interpretation of the Treaty.[5] Limiting its role to effectuating the intent of the Treaty parties, the Court stated: "When the parties to a treaty both agree as to the meaning of a treaty provision, and that interpretation follows from the clear treaty language, we must, absent extraordinarily strong contrary evidence, defer to that interpretation."[6]

Sumitomo, however, claimed that strict adherence to the language of the Treaty would overlook the Treaty's purpose. The Court disagreed. After tracing the historical evolution of U.S. commercial treaties, the Court observed that the purpose of such treaties was not to give foreign companies greater rights than domestic companies, but instead to assure them the right to conduct business on an equal basis without suffering discrimination based on their alienage.

The impact of the Court's decision on U.S. subsidiaries worldwide will be substantial. The language of Article VIII(1) is almost identical to the language in numerous other FCN treaties.[7] Although the Court purported to express

[3] *Id.* at 559. In a nearly identical case, the United States Court of Appeals for the Fifth Circuit agreed with the Second Circuit that a locally incorporated subsidiary of a foreign parent company was covered by Article VIII(1); however, contrary to the Second Circuit, the Fifth Circuit held that Article VIII(1) protects the local subsidiary's practices from Title VII liability. *See* Speiss v. C. Itoh & Co., 643 F.2d 353 (5th Cir. 1981), *summarized in* 75 AJIL 972 (1981), *cert. denied,* 102 S.Ct. 984 (1982). The district court decision in *Speiss* is summarized in 74 AJIL 195 (1980).

[4] 102 S.Ct. 2374, 2378–79.

[5] The Japanese Ministry of Foreign Affairs indicated its position to the American Embassy in Tokyo, which, in turn, relayed the information to the U.S. Department of State. The State Department articulated its view before the Court in a Brief for the United States as Amicus Curiae. *Id.* at 2379.

[6] *Id.* at 2380.

[7] *See, e.g.,* Convention of Establishment between the United States and France of 1959, 11 UST 2398, TIAS No. 4625, Arts. VI, XIV(5); Treaty of Friendship, Commerce and Navigation between the United States of America and Greece of 1951, 5 UST 1829, TIAS No. 3057, Arts. XII(4), XXIV(3).

no view as to the interpretation of these treaties,[8] the coincidence of treaty language may allow foreign governments, in reciprocal fashion, to subject U.S. subsidiaries abroad to onerous national employment laws and to deny them the right to employ necessary managers of their choice. While in former years, foreign companies generally operated abroad through branches that were not locally incorporated, local incorporation is now the predominant form for conducting foreign business activities. It therefore appears that international enterprises that wish to take advantage of Article VIII(1) of the Treaty will need to convert their foreign-incorporated subsidiaries into branch operations. Tax considerations, however, may make such action unattractive.

Treaty—definition—Base Labor Agreement of 1968 with the Philippines

WEINBERGER v. ROSSI. 102 S.Ct. 1510.
U.S. Supreme Court, March 31, 1982.

In 1968 the United States and the Philippines negotiated a Base Labor Agreement (19 UST 5892, TIAS No. 6542) (BLA), providing, *inter alia*, for the preferential employment of Filipino citizens at U.S. military facilities in the Philippines. In 1978 respondents, all U.S. citizens, were notified that their jobs at a U.S. naval facility in the Philippines were being converted into local national positions in accordance with the BLA, and that they would be discharged from their employment with the Navy. After exhausting their administrative remedies, respondents filed suit in the U.S. District Court for the District of Columbia alleging that the preferential employment provisions of the BLA violated section 106 of Public Law 92-129 (5 U.S.C. §7201 note (1976 ed., Supp. III)). Section 106, which was enacted in 1971, provides in relevant part that "[*u*]*nless prohibited by treaty*, no person shall be discriminated against . . . in the employment of civilian personnel at any facility or installation operated by the Department of Defense in any foreign country because such person is a citizen of the United States" (emphasis added). Respondents argued that the BLA was not a "treaty" within the meaning of section 106 because it had not been entered into by the President with the advice and consent of the Senate pursuant to Article II, section 2, clause 2 of the U.S. Constitution. The district court granted summary judgment for petitioner, the Secretary of Defense, but the U.S. Court of Appeals for the District of Columbia reversed.[1] In a unanimous decision, the Supreme Court (per Rehnquist, J.) reversed the court of appeals.

The single issue in this case was whether Congress intended the word "treaty" as used in section 106 to refer solely to agreements concluded pursuant to Article II, section 2, clause 2 of the Constitution, or whether the term included executive agreements such as the BLA.[2]

The Court began by observing that the word "treaty" has more than one

[8] 102 S.Ct. at 2380 n.12.

[1] Rossi v. Brown, 467 F.Supp. 960 (D.D.C. 1979), *summarized in* 74 AJIL 200 (1980), *rev'd*, 642 F.2d 553 (D.C. Cir. 1980).

[2] The Court expressly declined to consider whether the BLA violated Title VII of the Civil Rights Act of 1964 (42 U.S.C. §2000e) because the issue was neither raised in the petition for certiorari nor reached by the court of appeals. 102 S.Ct. 1510, 1518 n.18. However, in a somewhat

meaning. Thus, under international law, "the word ordinarily refers to an international agreement concluded between sovereigns, regardless of the manner in which the agreement is brought into force,"[3] while under the U.S. Constitution the word has a far more restrictive meaning. Turning to U.S. practice, the Court noted that Congress has not been consistent in distinguishing between Article II treaties and other forms of international agreements,[4] and has, in at least one case, used "treaty" to refer only to international agreements *other* than Article II treaties.[5]

The Court also observed that in the case of a statute such as section 106, which touches upon U.S. foreign policy, there is "even more reason" than in other cases to construe Congress's use of "treaty" to include executive agreements.[6] In this connection the Court observed that at the time section 106 was enacted, 13 executive agreements provided for the preferential hiring of local nationals on U.S. military bases overseas. The Court reasoned that if Congress had meant to limit the treaty exception in section 106 to Article II treaties, it must have intended to repudiate these executive agreements. In order to determine whether such an intent could fairly be attributed to Congress, the Court analyzed the legislative history of section 106. Based on this analysis, the Court determined that in enacting section 106, Congress was not concerned with limiting the authority of the President to enter into executive agreements with host countries, but rather with preventing certain ad hoc decision making by military commanders that had, in the past, resulted in financial hardship to dependents of American servicemen stationed overseas.[7] Thus, although admitting that the question was "not free from doubt," the Court concluded that the term "treaty" in section 106 extended to executive agreements such as the BLA.

While purportedly deciding an issue that was "solely one of statutory interpretation,"[8] the Supreme Court in this case evinced a clear recognition of the foreign policy implications of the issue before it. Thus, for example, the Court cited its previous recognition in *Dames & Moore v. Regan* (453 U.S. 654

---

related case decided this term, the Supreme Court analyzed a potential conflict between Title VII and the preferential employment provisions of an Article II treaty. *See* Sumitomo Shoji America, Inc. v. Avagliano, 102 S.Ct. 2374, *summarized at* p. 853 *supra*.

[3] 102 S.Ct. at 1514. *See, e.g.*, Vienna Convention on the Law of Treaties of 1969, Art. 2(1)(a), *reprinted in* 63 AJIL 875, 876 (1969); RESTATEMENT OF THE FOREIGN RELATIONS LAW OF THE UNITED STATES (REVISED), Introductory Note 3, at 74 (Tent. Draft No. 1, 1980).

[4] At times in this opinion, the Court uses the term "Article II treaties" to refer exclusively to treaties entered into by the President pursuant to Article II, section 2, clause 2 of the Constitution.

[5] 39 U.S.C. §407(a), authorizing the Postal Service, with the consent of the President, to "negotiate and conclude postal treaties or conventions."

[6] 102 S.Ct. at 1514, 1515. In this connection, the Court observed that "[i]t has been a maxim of statutory construction since the decision in *Murray* v. *The Charming Besty*, 2 Cranch 64, 117–118 (1804), that 'an act of congress ought never to be construed to violate the law of nations, if any other possible construction remains. . . .' " *Id.* at 1515.

[7] The Court failed to state whether respondents were dependents of U.S. servicemen stationed in the Philippines, although at least one reference in the opinion (*id.* at 1513) suggested that they were.

[8] *Id.* at 1513.

(1981)) that the President, in the interests of foreign policy, may enter into certain binding agreements with foreign nations without complying with the formalities of Article II, even when the agreement compromises commercial claims between U.S. citizens and a foreign power.[9] This and other references in the opinion strongly suggest that the Court recognized that Congress was aware in enacting section 106 that the Executive must, when appropriate, be permitted to exercise its discretionary powers in the interests of achieving long-term foreign policy goals.

European Economic Community Case Note

Transposing the interpretation of EEC Treaty concepts to agreements between the EEC and third countries—exhaustion of industrial and intellectual property rights

Polydor Ltd. and RSO Records Inc. v. Harlequin Records Shops Ltd. and Simons Records Ltd. Case 270/80, [1982] 1 Comm. Mkt. L.R. 677.

European Court of Justice, February 9, 1982.*

In a major judgment on the legal framework of the European Community's external relations, the European Court of Justice has further underscored the idiosyncrasies of the Common Market within the international legal order.[1] Even if agreements between the EEC and third countries contain the same concepts as the Rome Treaty, their respective interpretations may well diverge, according to the Court in its *Polydor* judgment.

The issue arose in the context of a copyright dispute. RSO Records Inc. (RSO) owns a number of copyrights in sound recordings by the well-known pop artists the Bee Gees. Polydor Ltd. (Polydor) is the exclusive licensee of RSO under the copyrights in the United Kingdom, and pursuant to its exclusive license manufactures and markets records and cassettes reproducing those recordings in the United Kingdom. Phonogram and Polygram Discos, which are members of the same group of companies as RSO and Polydor, are incorporated in Portugal and licensed by RSO to make and sell the recordings there. The defendants in the main action were Harlequin Records Shops Ltd. (Harlequin), a UK-based records retailer, and Simons Records Ltd. (Simons), a UK-based records importer and wholesaler. Since May 1979, Simons had imported from Portugal and Harlequin had retailed in the United Kingdom a large number of the copyrighted recordings below the current prices, without the consent of Polydor or RSO.

Alleging an infringement of the UK Copyright Act of 1956, Polydor sought

[9] *Id.* at 1514 n.6. *See* 75 AJIL 954 (1981).

* This analysis was prepared by Marco C. E. J. Bronckers, Member of The Hague Bar, the Netherlands.

[1] Already in an early judgment the Court pronounced that the "EEC Treaty is more than an agreement which merely creates mutual obligations between the contracting states" and that it "constitutes a new legal order of international law." Van Gend en Loos v. Nederlandse Administratie van Belastingen, Case 26/62, 1963 ECR 1, 12 (in which the Court introduced in Community law the notion of rights directly enforceable by individuals before national courts, which is more dynamic than the classic "self-executing treaty" doctrine).

an injunction restraining Harlequin from selling the records of Portuguese origin in the United Kingdom. By interlocutory judgment of December 21, 1979, the Chancery Division of the High Court of Justice issued the injunction requested by Polydor. On appeal, Harlequin argued that under Community law Polydor was not entitled to enforce the rights conferred upon it by the UK Copyright Act. Thereupon, the Court of Appeal requested a preliminary ruling under Article 177 of the EEC Treaty from the European Court of Justice.[2]

Harlequin based its defense on the free trade agreement between the EEC and Portugal of July 22, 1972 (the Agreement).[3] Similar agreements were concluded by the EEC with the other members of the European Free Trade Association (EFTA),[4] in part to ensure that they would continue to benefit in the United Kingdom and in Denmark from the reciprocal trade advantages enjoyed under the EFTA Convention after the latter two acceded to the EEC. The Agreement with Portugal provides, *inter alia*, for the abolition of quantitative import restrictions and measures having equivalent effect as of January 1, 1975. This prohibition and the relevant safeguard clause are virtually identical in wording to their counterparts in the EEC Treaty, *i.e.*, Articles 30 and 36 of the chapter on the freedom of movement of goods within the Community. The relevant safeguard clause (Article 23) of the Agreement reads in part:

> The Agreement shall not preclude prohibitions or restrictions on imports . . . justified on grounds of . . . the protection of industrial and commercial property. . . . Such prohibitions or restrictions must not, however, constitute a means of arbitrary discrimination or a disguised restriction on trade between the Contracting Parties.

Harlequin proposed that the Court's interpretation of the EEC Treaty govern the interpretation of comparable provisions in the Agreement. There is little doubt that if Harlequin's view had prevailed, Polydor would not have been able legally to block the "parallel import" of the litigious records from Portugal.

In a string of cases the European Court of Justice has struck a delicate balance between the freedom of movement of goods within the Common Market and the different national laws protecting intellectual and industrial property.[5] In essence, the Court has taken the position that Community law prevents the owner of an intellectual or industrial property right from relying on that right to restrain the import into one EEC member state of a product

[2] For the order of the Court of Appeal of May 15, 1980, requesting a preliminary ruling from the European Court of Justice, see [1980] 2 Comm. Mkt. L.R. 413. For the interlocutory judgment of the Chancery Division of Dec. 21, 1979, which, incidentally, declined to refer the matter to the European Court of Justice, see 1 *id.* at 669. For an instructive analysis of the procedural law of the European Communities, see H. G. SCHERMERS, JUDICIAL PROTECTION IN THE EUROPEAN COMMUNITIES (2d ed. 1979).

[3] 1972 O.J. EUR. COMM. (No. L 301) 166.

[4] The remaining EFTA members and the bilateral free trade agreements with the EEC are: Austria, 1972 J.O. COMM. EUR. (No. L 300) 2; Finland, 1973 O.J. EUR. COMM. (No. L 328) 2; Iceland, 1972 J.O. COMM. EUR. (No. L 301) 2; Norway, 1973 O.J. EUR. COMM. (No. L 171) 2; Sweden, 1972 J.O. COMM. EUR. (No. L 300) 97; and Switzerland, *id.* at 189.

[5] The Court's balancing act under Articles 30 and 36 of the EEC Treaty was clearly reflected for the first time in the Deutsche Grammophon v. Metro judgment, Case 78/70, 1971 ECR 487.

marketed by him or with his consent in another Community member state. To express it differently, once the marketing of a product within the Common Market can be attributed to the holder of an industrial or intellectual property right, he has *exhausted* his right to prevent the parallel importation of that product into another EEC member state. Recently, the Court forcefully reiterated the rationale of its case law on copyrights:

> The argument put to the Court by the Belgian and Italian Governments that in the absence of harmonization in this sector the principle of the territoriality of copyright laws always prevails over the principle of freedom of movement of goods within the Common Market cannot be accepted. Indeed, the essential purpose of the Treaty, which is to unite national markets into a single market, could not be attained if, under the various legal systems of the Member States, nationals of those Member States were able to partition the market and bring about arbitrary discrimination or disguised restrictions on trade between Member States.
>
> It follows from the foregoing considerations that neither the copyright owner [n]or his licensee . . . may rely on the exclusive exploitation right conferred by copyright to prevent or restrict the importation of sound recordings which have been lawfully marketed in another Member State by the owner himself or with his consent.[6]

In light of these judgments, Polydor could not have enjoined Harlequin from importing records manufactured and distributed by an affiliate of RSO into another EEC member state.[7] Harlequin sought to link the Court's case law under Articles 30 and 36 of the Rome Treaty with the interpretation of the Agreement's corresponding provisions, for the Court had already decided that these EEC Treaty provisions by themselves only affect intra-Community trade.[8] Consequently, Harlequin's sole defense to securing its supplies from Portugal rested in the Agreement.

In this case the Court was faced with two basic issues. First, did the provisions of the Agreement invoked by Harlequin indeed create directly en-

---

A recent study on the subject is D. GUY & G. LEIGH, THE EEC AND INTELLECTUAL PROPERTY (1981).

[6] Considerations 14 and 15 of the Membran v. GEMA judgment, Joined Cases 55 and 57/80, 1981 ECR 147.

[7] This would hold true even if Polydor itself had not "consented" to the manufacture and distribution of the records by another affiliate of RSO; the European Court of Justice imputes consent to all members of a corporate group. *See* the Court's judgment in Centrafarm v. Winthrop, Case 16/74, 1974 ECR 1183 (decision on trademarks).

[8] In 1976 the Court had allowed EMI (Europe) to resist the importation from the United States into various EEC member states of "Columbia" records, a trademark originally registered worldwide by CBS, but after a series of intricate agreements held by EMI within the EEC and by CBS in the United States. EMI v. CBS, Cases 51, 86, and 96/75, 1976 ECR 811, 871, and 913. CBS submitted that the import of its records into the Community could benefit from the "exhaustion" doctrine, apparently banking on an earlier judgment in a peculiar situation caused by nationalizations following World War II, where the Court had decided that independent holders of a trademark with a common origin could not prevent the parallel import of each other's products marketed under the common trademark. Van Zuylen Frères v. Hag, Case 192/73, 1974 ECR 731. The Court, however, rejected out of hand the extension of its case law to imports from outside the Community as proposed by CBS. It should be noted that at that time there existed no bilateral free trade agreement, such as the Agreement in issue in the *Polydor* case, between the Community

forceable rights? Second, how were these provisions to be interpreted? Logically, a positive answer to the first question would have had to precede a decision on the second question. The Court, however, rejected Harlequin's plea exclusively on the ground that Polydor's request for an injunction against imports of copyrighted sound recordings from Portugal was justified under the Agreement's safeguard clause (Article 23).

The Court did not consider a similarity of terms a sufficient reason to transpose the above-mentioned case law to the provisions of the Agreement. Harlequin had relied heavily on a judgment[9] in which the Court interpreted the prohibition on customs duties and charges having equivalent effect in the Yaoundé I Convention[10] between the EEC and various developing countries the same way it interpreted the corresponding prohibition in the Rome Treaty. The provision in the Yaoundé Convention, however, referred *expressis verbis* to the EEC Treaty principle; such a reference was lacking in the Agreement with Portugal.

The Court then advanced two arguments in support of its decision favoring Polydor's contentions. First,

> [i]t is apparent from an examination of *the Agreement* that although it makes provision for the unconditional abolition of certain restrictions on trade between the Community and Portugal, such as quantitative restrictions and measures having equivalent effect, [it *does*] *not have the same purpose as the EEC Treaty*, inasmuch as the latter . . . seeks to create a single market reproducing as closely as possible the conditions of a domestic market [excerpt from consideration 18; emphasis supplied].

Counsel to Polydor had been quick to point out that the type of relationships established between the Community and Portugal under the Agreement resembled more closely those established between the EFTA member states under the EFTA Convention than those established between the member states of the Community under the Treaty of Rome. The EFTA Convention purports to establish a "free trade area" between the contracting parties and not a "common market." Indeed, the "exhaustion" doctrine has no equivalent under the EFTA Convention, though it too incorporates a prohibition on "quantitative restrictions" and "measures having equivalent effect" in Article 10 and permits exceptions to this prohibition "necessary to protect industrial property or copyrights or to prevent deceptive practices" only if "such measures are not used as a means of arbitrary or unjustifiable discrimination between Member States or as a disguised restriction on trade between Member States" (Article 12).[11] Moreover, prior to the *Polydor* judgment, the supreme

---

and the United States, nor does one exist today. *See also* the 2d Bouhelier judgment, Case 225/78, 1979 ECR 3151 (the interpretation of Treaty provisions bringing about the complete liberalization of intra-Community trade cannot *as such* be transposed to relations with nonmember countries).

[9] Bresciani v. Amministrazione Italiana delle Finanze, Case 87/75, 1976 ECR 129.

[10] The two Yaoundé Conventions were the forerunners of the Lomé Conventions between the European Community and some 60 A(frican)-C(aribbean)-P(acific) countries, the second of which entered into force on Jan. 1, 1981. 1980 O.J. EUR. COMM. (No. L 347) 1. For the Yaoundé I Convention, see 1964 J.O. COMM. EUR. 1430.

[11] *See* Dittrich, *Die Verträge österreichs mit den Europäischen Gemeinschaften und das österreichisches Urheberrecht*, 26 ÖSTERREICHISCHE BLÄTTER FÜR GEWERBLICHEN RECHTSSCHUTZ UND UR-

courts of two EFTA countries, Austria and Switzerland, had refused to read the "exhaustion" doctrine into the free trade agreements between their countries and the Community.[12]

In its second argument, the Court said:

> It follows that in the context of the Agreement restrictions on trade in goods may be considered to be justified on the ground of the protection of industrial and commercial property in a situation in which their justification would not be possible within the Community.
>
> In the present case such a distinction is all the more necessary inasmuch as *the instruments which the Community has at its disposal* in order to achieve the uniform application of Community law and the progressive abolition of legislative disparities within the Common Market *have no equivalent in the context of the relations between the Community and Portugal* [considerations 19 and 20; emphasis supplied].

This institutional argument, which also distinguishes the Agreement from the Rome Treaty, embraces two aspects. The Agreement does not provide for a mechanism to ensure its uniform interpretation and application in the territories of the contracting parties. The only institution established under the Agreement (Article 33) is a quasi-political Joint Committee consisting of representatives of both contracting parties, whose recommendations and decisions have no direct effect on the municipal plane. In contrast, the uniform interpretation of the EEC Treaty throughout the Community is guaranteed by various judicial remedies leading to the European Court of Justice. In addition, Article 100 of the Treaty creates a legal basis for the harmonization of differing national laws, while the Agreement lacks such a provision.

Significantly, the Court was silent as to whether the litigated provisions of the Agreement could have been invoked by Harlequin in the first place, *i.e.*, whether they are enforceable by private parties in national court proceedings. The legal policy underlying the decision on the merits, however, may also have prompted the Court's restraint in dealing with the procedural question. It seems fair to say that the Court's judgment was inspired to some extent by the increasingly controversial notion of reciprocity. The Court was advised by several intervening member states and the EEC Commission that a unilateral grant of direct effect to the Agreement (and international agreements generally) would impair the Community's maneuverability in defending its interests and those of its member states through international negotiation. It was understood that the automatic extension of the Court's case law on intra-

---

HEBERRECHT 81, 86 (1977). Dittrich also observes that the "exhaustion" doctrine is not recognized under Article XX of the General Agreement on Tariffs and Trade (GATT), which he considers to have been a model for Article 12 of the EFTA Convention, implicitly for the Agreement's safeguards clause, and even for Article 36 of the EEC Treaty. *Id.* at 86–87. Both Portugal and the European Community are contracting parties to the GATT.

[12] Austro-Mechana v. Gramola Winter & Co., judgment of the Austrian Supreme Court of July 10, 1979, *reprinted in* 29 GEWERBLICHER RECHTSSCHUTZ UND URHEBERRECHT (Internationaler Teil) 185 (1980), with annotation by Eugen Ulmer (injunction against imports of copyrighted sound recordings lawfully marketed in West Germany granted to the copyright holder in Austria); Sunlight A.G. v. Bosshard Partners Intertrading, judgment of the Swiss Supreme Court of Jan. 25, 1979, *reprinted in* 28 *id.* at 569 (1979) (Swiss trademark owner may resist imports from the Netherlands and West Germany of products manufactured there under his license).

Community trade to imports of third countries, which would not necessarily reciprocate, could be expected to have an inhibitory effect upon the further development of intra-Community trade law itself. Such development would be likely to slow down if the member states realized that further trade liberalization within the Community would unilaterally improve the competitiveness of imports into the EEC, without compensatory export opportunities for Community products.

The *Polydor* judgment must have appeased those who worried that the speed of Community integration might slacken to the pace of extra-Community developments. Here the Court has brought out the distinctive features of the Common Market within the international economic order, though in so doing it has reduced the Community's exemplary role as a promoter of international integration. Yet the full impact of this decision remains to be gauged. Less than 3 months after rendering the *Polydor* judgment, the Court decided[13] that the prohibition on discriminatory taxation embodied in the Association Agreement concluded between the EEC and Greece in 1961[14] was directly enforceable in the Community because of its similarity to Article 95 of the EEC Treaty. One has to acknowledge that accession euphoria may have carried the day here. Still, this decision warns that the Court is prepared to judge each international agreement of the Community on its own merits.

[13] Pabst & Richarz v. Hauptzollamt d'Oldenbourg, Case 17/81 (Judgment of April 29, 1982, not yet published).

[14] 1963 J.O. COMM. EUR. 293. The Community has entered into Association Agreements with Cyprus, 1973 O.J. EUR. COMM. (No. L 133) 1; Malta, 1971 J.O. COMM. EUR. (No. L 61) 1; and Turkey, 1964 *id.* at 3687, as well. For a survey of all Community agreements in force or valid on Jan. 1, 1981, see App. 3 to A. PARRY & S. HARDY, EEC LAW 494–519 (2d ed. A. Parry & J. Dinnage 1981).

CURRENT DEVELOPMENTS

The Election of March 1982 to Fill One Vacancy in the International Court of Justice

The sudden death on December 12, 1981 of Judge Abdullah El-Erian (Egypt), who had been elected to the International Court in 1978 for a term of office to expire on February 5, 1988, created another vacancy in the Court, just after the election held in the 36th session of the General Assembly in 1981.[1] Under the requirements of Article 5 of the Statute, the election to fill this vacancy could not be held before the second half of March 1982. On December 21, 1981, the Security Council at its 2321st meeting adopted its Resolution 499 (1981), in which it decided that the election to fill the vacancy should take place at a meeting of the Security Council and at a meeting of the resumed 36th session of the General Assembly.[2] At the 12th meeting of the ninth emergency special session of the General Assembly on February 5, 1982, the President announced that the election would take place on March 19, 1982.[3]

On March 4, the Secretary-General issued his usual memorandum on the procedure for the election.[4] Here it was stated, *inter alia*, that pursuant to Article 5, paragraph 1 of the Statute the national groups had, on December 18, 1981, been invited to submit candidatures to be received by the Secretary-General by February 18, 1982, and that the absolute majority of votes required in the General Assembly "as at the date of the present memorandum" was 81, that is, 50 percent plus one of the 157 members of the United Nations at that date together with the three nonmember states parties to the Statute of the Court (in the regular election of November 1981 the absolute majority was 80).

Six candidates were nominated for this election, of whom four withdrew before March 19. As a consequence, the contest was between Ambassador Mohammed Bedjaoui (Algeria) and Ambassador Ahmed Esmat Meguid (Egypt).[5] The legal interest of this election lies in the reaffirmation by the General Assembly of the San Francisco compromise regarding the interpretation of the phrase "absolute majority" as applied in the General Assembly

[1] On that election, see my Note, *The Election of Five Members of the International Court of Justice in 1981*, 76 AJIL 364 (1982). The present Note may be regarded as a continuation of that Note.

[2] UN Docs. S/14799 (Dec. 17, 1981); S/PV.2321 (prov.) (Dec. 21, 1981). The suspension of the 36th session of the General Assembly was on the understanding that the occasional election would be one of the items to be taken up, as announced at the 105th meeting; UN Doc. A/36/PV.105, at 73 (prov.) (Dec. 18, 1981). The item of the elections was already on the agenda of the 36th session as agenda item 15(*c*).

[3] That emergency special session had been convened to deal with the situation in the Arab occupied territories by Security Council Resolution 500 (1982), Jan. 28, 1982. By Article 17 of the Rules of Procedure of the General Assembly (UN Doc. A/520/Rev.13 (1979)), the agenda of such a session shall consist "only" of those items proposed in the request for the holding of the session. The dealing by the emergency special session of any other matter on the agenda of the 36th session may not have been strictly in order.

[4] UN Doc. A/36/861-S/14885 (1982).

[5] UN Docs. A/36/862-S/14886 plus Corr.1 and Adds.1–4, replaced by A/36/862/Rev.1-S/14886/Rev.1 (1982).

(something never challenged since 1946) and in the new procedure of the Security Council to reduce the likelihood of a miscount such as occurred in 1981.

The General Assembly

Although the language of Article 10 of the Statute, with its use of the expression "absolute majority," is in this respect identical with that of the Statute of the Permanent Court, in fact the expression had been reinterpreted at San Francisco as part of the compromise then reached to retain unchanged the nomination and election systems. In the League of Nations it had been interpreted as requiring an absolute majority of the votes cast; blank ballot papers were not included in the count.[6] In the final stage of the San Francisco Conference (1945), the Co-ordination Committee agreed that the language should be retained "since the required majority was one half of the whole membership plus 1."[7] There are two ways in which the question could have been raised in the General Assembly. One would have been by a challenge to the number 81 based on the loss of the right to vote in the General Assembly through the application of Article 19 of the Charter (applicable to at least one member of the United Nations, both at the commencement of the 36th session of the General Assembly in September 1981, and on its resumption in March 1982). Another could have been based on the actual calculation of the majority required after the ballots had been counted and the number of abstentions or absentees ascertained, which would have led to a challenge of the President's announcement of the result of the ballot. Neither of these eventualities materialized.

The election was held simultaneously in the 107th meeting of the General Assembly at its 36th session and the 2333d meeting of the Security Council on March 19, 1982. At the commencement of the proceedings in the General Assembly the President (Ambassador Ismet Kittani, Iraq) announced that for the present election, 81 votes constituted an absolute majority in the General Assembly. No comment was made on this.[8]

Four ballots were required. On the first, 154 votes were cast, with the following result: Meguid, 79; Bedjaoui, 74; and one abstention. On the second ballot, 156 votes were cast: Bedjaoui received 79, and Meguid, 77. On the third and fourth, in which 156 ballots were again cast, the results were Bedjaoui, 80 and 87; Meguid, 76 and 69. Again, no attempt was made to challenge the result of the first ballot, in which Meguid received an absolute

[6] *See, e.g.*, para. 3 of the Note of the League Secretariat of 1930, quoted in INSTITUT FÜR AUSLÄNDISCHES ÖFFENTLICHES RECHT UND VÖLKERRECHT, STATUT ET RÈGLEMENT DE LA COUR PERMANENTE DE JUSTICE INTERNATIONALE: ELÉMENTS D'INTERPRÉTATION 37 (ed. Schenk von Stauffenberg 1934); M. HUDSON, THE PERMANENT COURT OF INTERNATIONAL JUSTICE, 1920–1942, at 245 (1943).

[7] Doc. WD 438, CO/202, 17 UNCIO Docs. 327, 330 (1945). Earlier, the Advisory Committee of Jurists, at its sixth meeting on June 12, 1945, had deferred decision on this matter. *Id.* at 411, 412. The categorical application of this interpretation compels me to retract any element of doubt that may be found in my 1 THE LAW AND PRACTICE OF THE INTERNATIONAL COURT 179 (1965). *See* further my Note, *The 1981 Occasional Elections to Fill Two Vacancies on the International Court of Justice*, 75 AJIL 349, 359 n.33 (1981).

[8] UN Doc. A/36/PV.107, at 6–10 (prov.) (1982).

majority of the votes cast by those present and voting. This was the second implicit reaffirmation of the continuing validity of the San Francisco compromise.

The Security Council

Only one ballot was required in the Security Council (absolute majority, 8), where Bedjaoui received 10 votes, Meguid, 4, with one abstention.

The procedure of the Security Council was altered in two respects in comparison with its earlier procedure. Firstly, to prevent a recurrence of the miscount, the system of independent countings by tellers drawn by lot from delegations represented on the Security Council was introduced. Secondly, the counting was not begun until the General Assembly had completed balloting in the sense of having cast the votes without yet counting them. The result of the balloting in the Security Council was announced as it became available.

This system was adequate for the present election because there were only two candidates for one vacancy, although four ballots were needed before the General Assembly elected a candidate who was the same as the one elected by the Security Council on its first ballot. It remains to be seen how this system would work in other circumstances, and particularly in a regular election for five members, the next of which is due to take place in 1984.

The Council of the League of Nations, following its usual practice, met in private for these elections and published the record of the meeting later. The Security Council of the United Nations has never followed that practice. In 1945 the Executive Committee of the Preparatory Commission of the United Nations proposed in draft Rule 27 of the provisional rules of procedure of the Security Council that the Security Council should meet in public unless it decided otherwise and that only when discussing any recommendation regarding the appointment of the Secretary-General should it meet in private (Rule 16).[9] Although this was queried as far as concerns the election of the members of the Court, the Preparatory Commission itself, in draft Rules 16 and 20, retained both those ideas, which are now incorporated in Rule 49 of the Provisional Rules of Procedure of the Security Council.[10] As far as is known, the Security Council has not discussed officially whether these elections should be held in public or private meetings—the latter being clearly exceptional in the general practice of the Security Council.

It is believed that it would be useful for the Security Council to reexamine this question, since the fact that the results of the voting in the Security Council are known in the General Assembly before it has finished its election seems to affect the eventual outcome of the election in the General Assembly if more than one ballot is required there. This may not be compatible with the original concepts.

Bedjaoui's election is another indication that there is no absolute rule or

[9] UN Doc. PC/EX/113/Rev.1, at 42, 43 (1945).

[10] UN Doc. PC/20, at 26, 27 (1946). The matter was discussed at the third and tenth meetings of Committee 2 of the Preparatory Commission (Security Council), Nov. 30 and Dec. 14, 1945. For the current version of the Provisional Rules of Procedure of the Security Council, see UN Doc. S/96/Rev.6 (1974).

practice calling for continuity in the nationality of a person elected to fill an occasional vacancy. Since 1946 the seat in question was first held by a national of Egypt, followed after an occasional election by a national of Lebanon. At the appropriate regular triennial election the seat was occupied by another national of Egypt, followed on this occasion by a national of Algeria.

SHABTAI ROSENNE*

THE AUSTRALIAN-UNITED STATES AGREEMENT ON COOPERATION IN ANTITRUST MATTERS

On June 29, 1982, the United States and Australia concluded an agreement to promote cooperation between the two countries on antitrust matters. The Agreement is designed to minimize jurisdictional conflicts in U.S. Government antitrust actions, as well as in private antitrust actions brought under U.S. law, that involve Australian Government policies and Australian companies.

Recognizing that conflicts have arisen, and may arise in the future, between interests reflected in U.S. antitrust laws and policies and those reflected in Australian laws and policies, the Agreement establishes a framework to facilitate resolution of such conflicts, giving mutual respect to each Government's sovereignty and due regard to considerations of comity.

The Agreement provides for each party to notify the other of antitrust-related actions or policies having implications for the other party's interests (Article 1, "Notification"). The two Governments agree to consult with respect to potential conflicts, to take each other's interests into account during such consultations, and to give the fullest consideration to modifying their respective policies or enforcement actions in order to avoid jurisdictional conflict (Article 2, "Consultation"). If, however, consultations under the Agreement have not developed means to avoid conflict between the two parties' laws, policies, or national interests, then each party is free to protect its interests as it deems necessary (Article 4, "Procedure after Consultations," paragraph 2).

Articles 5, "Cooperation in Antitrust Enforcement," and 6, "Private Antitrust Suits in United States Courts," contain provisions of particular importance or interest to the United States and to Australia, respectively. Australia agrees, in effect, under Article 5 that the mere seeking by legal process of information or documents located in Australian territory shall not be regarded *per se* as constituting a basis for invoking the Australian blocking statute, provided that Australia has been given prior notice of the issuance of such U.S. legal process. Under Article 6, the United States agrees upon request of the Australian Government to appear in private antitrust actions brought against Australian companies in U.S. courts, relating to conduct, or conduct pursuant to an Australian Government policy, that has been the subject of notification and consultations under the Agreement. In the event of such a

* Fellow of the Jewish Academy of Arts and Sciences (New York); Ambassador-at-Large and member of the Israel delegation to the 36th session of the General Assembly; honorary member of the American Society of International Law; member of the Institute of International Law. The views expressed here are the personal views of the author.

request, the U.S. Government is required to report to the court upon the substance and outcome of the consultations. The texts of Articles 5 and 6 follow:

ARTICLE 5

Cooperation In Antitrust Enforcement

1. When a proposed investigation or enforcement action under the antitrust laws of one nation does not adversely affect the laws, policies or national interests of the other, each Party shall cooperate with the other in regard to that investigation or action, including through the provision of information and administrative and judicial assistance to the extent permitted by applicable national law.

2. The mere seeking by legal process of information or documents located in its territory shall not in itself be regarded by either Party as affecting adversely its significant national interests, or as constituting a basis for applying measures to prohibit the transmission of such information or documents to the authorities of the other Party, provided that in the case of United States legal process prior notice has been given of its issuance. Each Party shall, to the fullest extent possible under the circumstances of the particular case, provide notice to the other before taking action to prevent compliance with such legal process.

ARTICLE 6

Private Antitrust Suits In United States Courts

When it appears to the Government of Australia that private antitrust proceedings are pending in a United States court relating to conduct, or conduct pursuant to a policy of the Government of Australia, that has been the subject of notification and consultations under this Agreement, the Government of Australia may request the Government of the United States to participate in the litigation. The Government of the United States shall in the event of such request report to the court on the substance and outcome of the consultations.[1]

MARIAN NASH LEICH*

[1] Dept. of Justice news release, June 29, 1982.

Article 3 of the Agreement, "Confidentiality," reads:

> Documents and information provided by either Party in the course of notification or consultations under this Agreement shall be treated confidentially by the receiving Party unless the providing Party consents to disclosure or disclosure is compelled by law. The Government of the United States shall not, without the consent of the Government of Australia, use information or documents provided by the Government of Australia in the course of notification or consultations under this Agreement as evidence in any judicial or administrative proceeding under United States antitrust laws. The Government of the United States shall not, however, be foreclosed from pursuing an investigation of any conduct which is the subject of notification or consultations, or from initiating a proceeding based on evidence obtained from sources other than the Government of Australia.

For other U.S. antitrust cooperative arrangements currently in effect, see, as to Canada, 6 M. WHITEMAN, DIGEST OF INTERNATIONAL LAW 159–60 (1968) and Dept. of Justice news release, Nov. 3, 1969 (to be found also at Dept. of State File No. INCO 15-1 CAN); as to the Federal Republic of Germany, Agreement between the Government of the United States of America and the Government of the Federal Republic of Germany Relating to Mutual Cooperation Regarding Restrictive Business Practices, *signed* at Bonn June 23, 1976, TIAS No. 8291, 27 UST 1956.

* Office of the Legal Adviser, Department of State.

BOOK REVIEWS AND NOTES

EDITED BY LEO GROSS

Compliance and Public Authority. By Oran R. Young. Published for Resources for the Future. Baltimore and London: The Johns Hopkins University Press, 1979. Pp. x, 172. Indexes. $12.95.

Any teacher of international law who uses simulation as one teaching method can attest to the surprise and shock of law students when they realize that one option available and likely to be proposed to government decision makers in particular cases is that they ignore or violate the law. In fact, in any legal system, both compliance in a variety of forms *and* noncompliance are options; each has its own constellation of short-, mid-, and long-term benefits for the system concerned, as well as for the self-perceived interests of the actor contemplating the choice. Because much of behavior is animated by self-interest (which need not and for many does not include concern for systemic effectiveness), the domestic model of a sheriff, suspended like a sword of Damocles over would-be violators, deterring potential and sanctioning accomplished violations of norms, is reassuring. But it does not obtain in the international system. Hence the inclination of many scholars over the years to reject international law as law and to view it, at best, as Austin's "positive morality."

In a provocative and cogently reasoned essay, Young observes that noncompliance may be no greater a problem in the international system than it is in domestic systems. He would largely transform the scholarly focus from a fixation on problems of enforcement to an examination of the scope, personal considerations, and social forces that lead to compliance. In the tradition of Malinowski, Young contends that decentralized systems may have effective legal arrangements, but rather than attributing them, as did Malinowski, to unorganized sanctioning by means of implications of reciprocity and retaliation, Young focuses on the calculus of conscious and, to a lesser extent, unconscious considerations of the complying actor. In two brief case studies, the Nuclear Test Ban Treaty and the International North Pacific Fisheries Convention (INPFC), he believes he finds high levels of compliance despite the highly decentralized character of the systems examined. On the basis of the insights gleaned from a very thorough survey of the literature and the case studies, he reconsiders some of the problems of compliance, observing that a binary choice is rarely involved, that normative generality and situational variety often permit multiple ways of complying, and that compliance *vel non* is not always easy to assess scientifically. Analyzing public authorities in the microeconomics terms of profit-maximizing firms, he explores how these authorities will compute the costs and benefits of investing in compliance, both theoretically and with brief reference to practice, and suggests normative guidelines for optimizing compliance (pp. 128–34) that appear sensible and unexceptionable. Young concludes with a consideration of the externalities of compliance mechanisms. The book includes a bibliographical note and a rather comprehensive reference list.

Young's essay is the more absorbing in that key parts of it are work-in-progress. The reader is invited into a seminar where the instructor is always refreshingly candid about problems, ambiguous cases, and matters yet to be considered. It is no criticism of the author's essay to draw attention to some of them. The effectiveness of the Nuclear Test Ban Treaty is gauged in the narrowest sense. As a means of retarding proliferation, a major goal, it could be a failure, indeed, may have been destined to be such. The INPFC case is cited for the proposition that "there is nothing in the record of the INPFC to lead to the conclusion that a centralized public authority with substantial enforcement capabilities is necessary to achieve high levels of compliance with prescriptions of this sort" (p. 93). But others might give INPFC much lower marks in both norm formulation and application precisely because of what was designed to be of limited effectiveness.

A more serious theoretical problem is the relative absence of consideration of the authority variable, a feature that unfortunately characterizes much of contemporary political science analysis. Young does incorporate H. L. A. Hart's rendition of Austin's "habit of obedience," but this barely touches the vigor and importance of authority. Nor is there much consideration of mythic as opposed to effective norms, what I have called the "myth system" and the "operational code"[1] and the fact that prospective ineffectiveness often shifts norms that were created to be effective from operationality to mythic status. Young states that a "behavioral prescription is a normatively compelling guide to action" (p. 104). That could characterize much of what is routinely ground out by formal international institutions and which, international lawyers know, is not operational.

Young also may attribute excessive *systemic* importance to norm compliance. Many will argue with his proposition that "it is a demonstrable fact that most acknowledged international prescriptions are complied with by the relevant actors most of the time" (p. 47), even without knowing what the referent of the word "acknowledged" is. More important is the fact, not treated by the author, that noncompliance is not necessarily system-destructive or even disruptive. If there is widespread and authoritative condemnation, the violation may reinforce the norm and the system within which it operates.

Nor is it always possible to separate compliance from enforcement. When Young writes that "[t]he principal burden of obtaining compliance with the prescriptions of the INPFC . . . falls on the governments of the Contracting Parties" (p. 88), he seems to be coming perilously close to the enforcement focus that he wishes to escape. When he defines a public authority "as an institutional arrangement that is vested with the task of eliciting compliance with some set of behavioral prescriptions in an identifiable social system" (p. 111), his readers will wonder how that differs from an enforcer.

Petrazhitski and his students Timashef and Sorokin were more concerned

[1] W. M. Reisman, Folded Lies: Bribery, Crusades, and Reforms (1979). Reviewed by J. Stone in 74 AJIL 483–85 (1980).

with uniformities in group behavior—sometimes referred to as compliance—than with deviance and enforcement. Timashef, the most systematic of the school, distinguished natural uniformities, mimetic uniformities, and imposed uniformities. It was only part of the last category that encompassed what he meant by law. For him and many others, law imported community deliberation about the desired behavior; the fact that the desirability was not self-evident and hence had to be prescribed; the fact that there were substantial rewards for some people in deviating from the prescription; and hence that the effectiveness and continuing "suetude" of the norm required some communication of an intention and capacity to make the norm controlling. Young's approach in including much of what is not Timashef's "imposed uniformity" may make the international legal system look better than it is and by terminological change obscure the inescapable enforcement problem even while emphasizing that it is only a part of systemic viability. Criticisms notwithstanding, this is a challenging and useful book.

W. MICHAEL REISMAN
Board of Editors

Improving Compliance with International Law. By Roger Fisher. (Vol. 14 in the Procedural Aspects of International Law series.) Charlottesville: University Press of Virginia, 1981. Pp. 370. Index. $20.

This book is a mélange. It deals with a variety of situations in which U.S. legal procedures can be used to impose compliance with international law. On the one hand, it contains a pragmatic suggestion of a "Dunn and Bradstreet" rating of nations as to their compliance with their international obligations based on findings by an international body comparable to the International Commission of Jurists. The author does not consider the international political problems of having such a body established, and appointed, on the high and nonpolitical level that he considers necessary. On the other hand, it has suggestions as to standing to sue in domestic courts for alleged violations of international law that are quite unrealistic.

The book is filled with interesting ideas that have very little relationship to political realities. If that were the only objection to the book, this review would end on a positive note, because many thinkers have advanced ideas that seemed "politically unrealistic" at the time but that later became an important part of our political institutions.

Two suggestions in the final chapter make it impossible to end the review on this pleasant a note. The first is that there might be a federal statute providing that a federal official, in continued noncompliance with an order of a federal court dealing with an international obligation, be put in a mental hospital for 60 days for a determination as to his sanity. The second suggestion is that such an official be suspended subject to a hearing on his loyalty to the United States.

This reviewer believes that many steps should be taken to improve U.S. compliance with international law. I do not believe, however, that these steps can be taken by imitating the Gulag Archipelago or the tactics of the late Senator McCarthy. Unless the author can suggest some better means of improving compliance with international law, I recommend that his views be given very little (if any) credence.

ADRIAN S. FISHER

The Prudent Peace: Law as Foreign Policy. By John A. Perkins. Chicago and London: The University of Chicago Press, 1981. Pp. xvi, 246. Index.

Perkins has written a praiseworthy brief for the rule of law as prudent foreign policy. He shares as a starting point the view so succinctly expressed by Montesquieu: "Le *droit des gens* est naturellement fondé sur ce principe, que les diverses nations doivent se faire, dans la paix, le plus de bien, et, dans la guerre, le moins de mal qu'il est possible, sans nuire à leurs véritables intérêts" (*De l'esprit des lois,* bk. I, ch. 3).

It is an unhappy commentary on our times, our leaders, and perhaps most of all our bar that Perkins is correct in perceiving the need to explain again what Montesquieu might be thought to have made clear 200 years ago. In between eruptions over a few treaties, there is not much evidence that the bar generally is much concerned with the role of law or lawyers in the elaboration and conduct of U.S. foreign policy.

Perkins's argument does not, however, stop at a minimalist notion of the role of law; rather, he perceives it as a means of change and as an ordered means of giving expression to the natural impulse to do what is right.

The positivist attacks on international law are correctly and briefly dismissed and implicitly denied by the persuasive case made in the remainder of the book for law as, *inter alia,* providing "the strategy by which a just and stable peace must be sought." Perkins does not attempt to argue the case in the abstract or solely from the standpoint of the moral philosophy that must motivate the policy of a free people if it is to remain free. Instead, his essay makes the case in specific contexts, such as the Bay of Pigs, the Cuban missile crisis, Vietnam, and U.S.-Soviet relations, and by taking into account the political realities. The author's brief analysis of the symbiotic relationship in today's world between law and the balance of power, including his illumination of the lacunae of such "realists" as George Kennan and the latter-day Acheson, is particularly well done.

It is not difficult to cavil with some of the points along the route sketched out in the book. The asserted "dichotomy between binding law and operational law" seems unpersuasive and subversive of the meaning of the term "law." It seems a distorted reflection of Austinian jurisprudence and even less enlightening. There are differences between political pressures and trends and legal obligation and it is a disservice to both to confuse them. After all, it is one thing to recognize that law must evolve to meet changing needs and quite another to grant lawmaking authority where it does not exist and then wonder why respect for law diminishes. Reference to "widely accepted principles not yet established as binding law that have character of law" is disturbing and unclear and thus a potential source of serious future problems.

To expect states to agree to having decisions made on such a basis seems unrealistic.

These criticisms and the reviewer's failure to be convinced of the contribution that would be made by the "Voluntary Adjudication Tribunal"—a new third-party dispute mechanism which would give a special place to justice or equity—may, in part, be due to the brevity of the book and the vastness of the subject it seeks to cover. Heaven knows, Perkins's concern with the failure of binding third-party dispute settlement processes to play a greater role is soundly based. At least initial focus on those gestures the United States could make to exercise greater leadership—repeal of the Connally reservations greatly enhanced efforts to insist on meaningful dispute settlement provisions in important bilateral treaties (their absence from the Panama Canal Treaty is noteworthy)—might be more practical. Nevertheless, it is also necessary for new ideas to be put forward.

Even if some of these flaws are as real as they seem to the reviewer, they by no means negate the utility of the book. *The Prudent Peace* is a brief, eminently readable, and thoughtful piece of first-rate advocacy in behalf of the rule of law. It has something to say to all members of the bar and all who are concerned with or otherwise interested in American foreign policy. There are few who would not be well advised to peruse its 164 pages and reflect on the issues raised.

ROBERT ROSENSTOCK
U.S. Mission to the United Nations

The Structure of International Conflict. By C. R. Mitchell. New York: St. Martin's Press, 1981. Pp. 355. Index. $35.

This book presents a good introductory survey of the major theories prevalent in the field of conflict studies. Like much of the social science literature in this area, however, the book operates under the fundamentally mistaken impression that international law and organizations are not relevant to the subject of international conflict. The system of international relations is characterized primarily as a Machiavellian struggle for power in which violence and coercion are the normal *ratio decidendi* for the settlement of international conflicts. The international legal order is perceived to be a relatively primitive and unsophisticated system for the performance of the crucial tasks of international conflict avoidance, management, termination, and resolution. Nations apparently still inhabit that Hobbesian state of nature where the threat and use of force are deemed legitimate means for governments to use as they see fit in pursuit of vital national interests.

No point would be served in attempting to refute this interconnected set of myths upholding the essential irrelevance of international law and organizations to international conflict. Suffice it to say that Louis Sohn's classic *Cases on United Nations Law* (2d ed. 1967) and the International Crises and the Role of Law series published under the auspices of the American Society of International Law should be required reading for any scholar pursuing serious research into the structure of international conflict. It is virtually impossible to analyze this subject meaningfully without a sound comprehension of the profound impact international law and organizations exert upon the structure and processes of international conflict.

The most dramatic confirmation of this proposition's veracity was the Iranian hostage crisis. I fail to understand how any scholarly analyst or governmental functionary could have prescribed a viable course of conduct for the United States during that conflict without possessing a thorough training in the rules of international law and the procedures of international organizations for the peaceful settlement of disputes. This is the reason why those American academics who publicly offered creative suggestions for the resolution of the crisis were international lawyers such as Richard Falk, Roger Fisher, and Alfred Rubin. The vast majority of commentaries generated by political scientists offered no solution other than the application of brute military force in order to redeem America's illusive national honor. Within the Carter administration this dichotomy between international law and Machiavellianism was typified by the diametrically opposed attitudes of Secretary of State Cyrus Vance, a lawyer, and National Security Adviser Zbigniew Brzezinski, a political scientist. The latter's Machiavellian approach only produced the disastrous hostage rescue mission aborted in the Iranian desert. By contrast, the patient continuation of Vance's international law approach by his successor ultimately resulted in the safe release of all the hostages. The Iranian hostage crisis demonstrates the glaring need for social scientists to overcome their inbred prejudices against international law and organizations in order to draw upon the rich body of literature on international conflict already written by international lawyers.

FRANCIS A. BOYLE
University of Illinois College of Law

The Conduct of Just and Limited War. By William V. O'Brien. New York: Praeger Publishers, 1981. Pp. xii, 495. Index and bibliography.

In the work under review, O'Brien sets out to describe two distinct but complementary concepts or doctrines, each related to the control of armed conflict: just-war doctrine and limited-war doctrine. He explains that whereas the just-war concept is of an "eclectic character," it is rooted in the contributions of Christian theology to the discussion of problems of world order (p. 15). Limited-war concepts, on the other hand, are said to have emerged mainly from post-World War II efforts at strategic studies, defined broadly (p. 208), and to be founded in "utilitarian rather than normative considerations" (p. 221). Each of the two major parts of the book is an analysis of the applicability of the respective doctrines to the appreciation of the controls upon the use of force, mainly in the practice of the United States, in the past 30 years.

A shorter third part of the book considers "how to" questions, questions of the relationship of either strategy for the limitation of the use of force to the tactical control of armed forces in situations of conflict. By way of conclusion, O'Brien asserts that the just-war doctrine, operating as it does "from perspectives of Christian realism," is the more effectual doctrine for limiting the incidence and scope of armed conflict (p. 329). He goes on, however, to call for steps to assure that the just-war doctrine "be more than a curiosity salvaged from the history of ideas," and to suggest that this be accomplished by merging the just-war doctrine, in some fashion, with modern and positivistic American limited-war policies (*ibid.*).

To the extent that the book demonstrates that ground may exist for discourse between theologians and moral philosophers on the one hand, and international relations theorists and strategists on the other, O'Brien has made a commendable contribution to the literature. His analyses of specific contemporary conflicts suggest that similar concerns and focuses of interest often are shared by both camps. This ought to rank the work as one of note.

But the book is troubling in certain respects. If it is O'Brien's aim to bring about the use of a revitalized just-war doctrine as a touchstone for the ordering of international affairs, then one would expect him to show the doctrine to be founded in notions of morality common throughout a pluralistic world, and not merely to be acceptable to those who are willing to look to Roman Catholic social thought for guidance in their geopolitical decision making. Regrettably, the same criticism seems apposite to many current analyses of world-order issues by those writing in this Catholic tradition.[1]

Even if one acknowledges that O'Brien's assessments of recent conflicts are presented for the limited purpose of showing the aptness of resort to just-war or limited-war analyses for the description of world affairs, certain of his comments still appear far too glib, standing as they often do without qualification. For example, one criterion for judging the justice of a war, we are told, is that the means selected for its pursuit not cause "superfluous suffering." Apparently intent upon finding America's recent wars to have been just wars, O'Brien dismisses out of hand arguments that resort to the use of nuclear weaponry above Japan and resort to the use of napalm in Vietnam might have been disproportionate measures. In the former instance, he says—without reference to medical literature—that "the subjective comparison of atomic radioactive fallout with the suffering caused by regular explosives and fire bombs is inconclusive" (pp. 85–86). More telling arguments for proportionality are lacking. Use of napalm by American forces in Vietnam, in the way that it was there employed, is justified as not resulting in superfluous suffering because the weapon is "part of the capabilities of most modern defense forces," and because "international practice has still not produced a positive-law *jus in bello* prohibition against the use of napalm" (p. 105). Such arguments do not convince one of the moral imperative underlying the just-war doctrine.

Similarly, in arguing that the Vietnam War was an instance of just war on the part of the United States, O'Brief sets himself the task of establishing that American forces were used by decision of "competent authority." To do so, he relies on the argument that assistance was rendered to a legitimate gov-

[1] *E.g.*, D. HOLLENBACH, RETRIEVING AND RENEWING THE CATHOLIC HUMAN RIGHTS TRADITION (1979). While this task is beyond the scope of such works, their influence is markedly limited by its absence.

ernment. The legitimacy of the Government of the former Republic of Vietnam is argued in this passage:

> [T]he fact remains that the South Vietnamese people supported their governments—*minimally*, to be sure—until the final collapse in 1975. As long as there was a South Vietnamese government in power, *substantially* supported by the people and willing to continue the war, it could not be said that the United States was imposing a disproportionately destructive war on Vietnam [p. 96, emphasis added].

Passages such as this do little to support the author's proposition that a just-war doctrine can be revitalized and used for moral and practical guidance by the world's decision makers.

The almost parochial attachment of the author to a theologically based moral philosophy has to be noted. At times, his review of American conduct in the post-World War II world seems to this reviewer to be decidedly partisan. Nonetheless, O'Brien is to be applauded for inviting a dialogue between the moral philosopher and the military strategist and for demonstrating areas where common discourse might prove productive. Thus, a reading of *The Conduct of Just and Limited War* leaves one with new hope for the future development of the laws of war.

J. DAVID FINE
Loyola University Law School, New Orleans

Israel and Palestine: Assault on the Law of Nations. By Julius Stone. Baltimore and London: The Johns Hopkins University Press, 1981. Pp. xiii, 223. Index. $17.50.

Readers in search of a balanced treatment of the legal issues in the Middle East will not find it in this book. In Stone's view, Israel's legal position is impregnable on virtually all issues separating it from its Arab neighbors. Arguments to the contrary are recognized only for their defects.

In large part, the book is an attempt to refute the positions taken by or under the auspices of the United Nations Committee on the Exercise of the Inalienable Rights of the Palestinian People. In particular, aim is taken at W. Thomas and Sally V. Mallison, coauthors of a study commissioned by the committee analyzing the legal significance of the UN resolutions on Palestine.[1] Stone's tactic essentially is to belittle or ridicule the Mallisons' analysis, occasionally by distorting what they say. For example, he attributes to them the position that assertions repeatedly found in General Assembly resolutions become international law by consensus (pp. 27–32, 38). They do not take that position, at least not at the point in their work to which Stone refers.[2] Although the Mallisons' analysis is not beyond criticism, they deserve better treatment than they get from Stone.

Shorn of its rhetoric, Stone's argument through the first four chapters is

[1] W. T. Mallison & S. Mallison, An International Law Analysis of the Major United Nations Resolutions Concerning the Palestine Question, UN Doc. ST/SG/SER.F/4 (1979).

[2] His reference is to UN Doc. ST/SG/SER.F/4, at 8.

that the Palestinian Arabs have no right of self-determination, or other valid territorial claim, anywhere in the area of Palestine formerly administered by the United Kingdom under the League of Nations Mandate after Transjordan was severed from it in 1922. This is because the post-World War I arrangements recognized a Jewish national home in all of Palestine, a large part of which was taken to form what is now Jordan. According to Stone, General Assembly Resolution 181 (II), which purported to partition Palestine west of the Jordan River, either had no legal effect in the first place, or, if it could have been legally significant, never took effect because it was "aborted" by Arab aggression. It is characteristic of the tone of the book that Stone refers no fewer than 22 times to the "abortion" of Resolution 181 by Arab aggression. It is characteristic of the style of the book that Stone relegates to an appendix the operative part of the 1948 Israeli Declaration of Independence relying on "our natural and historic right and on the strength of the resolution of the United Nations General Assembly."[3]

The book goes on to discuss the "right of return" (Stone's quotation marks) and the development of the self-determination principle since 1948, the meaning and effect of certain General Assembly resolutions—particularly insofar as they relate to the use of force in exercising a right of self-determination—and the status of Jerusalem. On the latter point, it is interesting to compare the dispassionate analysis of Elihu Lauterpacht with the approach taken by Stone. Lauterpacht holds that Israel has a right to remain in East Jerusalem.[4] Stone agrees, but he cannot resist accusing the authors of a UN study on Jerusalem (not the Mallisons) of "ghoulish dallying" when they espouse the *corpus separatum* principle for the city (pp. 107–08). On the merits, Stone concludes that Israel has strong legal grounds to claim vested territorial sovereignty not only over East Jerusalem, but over the entire West Bank and the Gaza Strip (p. 132).

Israel has some compelling legal arguments concerning its rights in Palestine. One must question, however, whether it is a service either to Israel or to scholarship to polemicize those arguments under the banner of legal analysis. Of course, Stone is not alone as a polemicist on Middle East issues, but that is hardly an excuse for fanning the flames. Scholarship in international law needs something better than that.

FREDERIC L. KIRGIS, JR.
Washington and Lee University

The British Year Book of International Law, 1979. Vol. 50. Edited by R. Y. Jennings and Ian Brownlie. New York: The Clarendon Press; Oxford University Press, 1981. Pp. ix, 419. Index. $98.

The British Year Book of International Law is always rewarding reading, but beyond that one can rarely generalize except to note the diversity of material.

[3] Declaration of Independence of the State of Israel, May 14, 1948, *reprinted in* the volume under review, at 152, 153.

[4] E. LAUTERPACHT, JERUSALEM AND THE HOLY PLACES (1968), *quoted* in part *in* the volume under review, at 107.

The present volume, however, permits a further generalization: it exhibits, rather strikingly, the extent to which British legal thinking in the international field (as in domestic law) focuses on the judicial process and the application of law *in concreto*. The first five articles are largely concerned with adjudication and nearly two hundred pages in the back summarize court decisions. The lawyer reading this material may find comfort in the practical uses and specificity of international law. In Brownlie's words, a harder edge is put on legal rights and duties when they are dealt with in litigated cases. It may also be true, as Brownlie suggests, that "the proliferation of unanchored and free-floating norms" (p. 41) dilutes standards of international law and that the softness of much international law is a threat to the status of its rules. On the other hand, an emphasis on adjudication is somewhat misleading since so little of international law is applied through litigation. We cannot, by wishing, anchor the free-floating norms by adjudication or eliminate the softness of many neutral principles. They, too, have a role in maintaining world order. "There is no need to throw to the dogs all that is not fit for the altar of the gods."[1]

Whether adjudication in international affairs should be likened to the "altar of the gods" may itself be debated. The question of the proper role of an international court is dealt with in the first article, a characteristically felicitous piece by Sir Gerald Fitzmaurice on Judge Sir Hersch Lauterpacht. Fitzmaurice reminds us of Lauterpacht's intellectual energy, his erudition and freshness of outlook; he considers him "without a peer" as an international jurist. On judicial philosophy, Fitzmaurice recalls Lauterpacht's rejection of *non-liquet* and his view that a tribunal should always come up with a decision that would deal with the substantive issues of law involved. Apparent gaps and uncertainties could always be filled by "recourse to principles and rules of private law in similar or analogous fields." To illustrate, Fitzmaurice refers to real property law, prescriptive rights, servitudes, and the like as having counterparts in international law, "which is really quite natural if States are visualized as akin to a congeries of landed proprietors whose estates are in greater or less proximity one with another, and who also have many similar business interests" (p. 9). His assumption that gaps in the law should be filled by visualizing states as large landowners is not wholly persuasive. The International Court of Justice did not think so in the *Rights of Passage* case (*Portugal v. India*). It would seem more reasonable to consider the ends to be served by the asserted rules than to be beguiled by a metaphor. Fitzmaurice also strongly favors Lauterpacht's view that judges should make "general pronouncements of law and principle that may enrich and develop the law." One of the reasons advanced by Fitzmaurice is that then the losing party "will have something to show for the risks they have taken by going to the law." There is a touching idealism about this remark, evidence of Fitzmaurice's devotion to the law. But can one imagine a government that has lost its case in the Court expressing appreciation for a new development of law it had vigorously opposed? Somehow the remark brings to mind the line of Charles Lamb (quoted by Fitzmaurice at the beginning of this essay) that "lawyers were children once."

[1] An aphorism of the Swiss jurist Tourtolon, *quoted in* M. R. COHEN, LAW AND THE SOCIAL ORDER 285 (1933).

Actually, it is not as clear to me, as it is to Fitzmaurice, that Lauterpacht was so fully committed to judicial development of the law through "generalization of principles." Lauterpacht had a keen sense of the limits of judicial power and I venture to suggest that in many cases he would have favored "individualization" (*i.e.*, narrowing) rather than generalization as the appropriate way for the Court to deal with unprecedented situations. Cardozo's comment that "the judicial web is woven in small knots"[2] is pertinent. In international law where the Court's authority is limited, "small knots" may strengthen the fabric of the law more than stretching it by judicial generalization.

The notion of small knots has relevance to Brownlie's lawyerly article, *Causes of Action in the Law of Nations*. The article looks closely at the submissions of parties in litigated cases before international tribunals and the ways the tribunals responded. Brownlie considers the "particularity" of the illegal acts and omissions complained of much more significant than the legal categories under which they are placed. Questions of causation, justification, and the relation between duties and forms of relief are more directly determined by the specific delict than by "general and autonomous principles" of state responsibility. This leads Brownlie to suggest (by way of a rhetorical question) that the "general apparatus" of state responsibility is a source of confusion and unhelpful. I did not quite see that this conclusion was supported by his analysis of the cases examined. His summaries are too brief to throw much light on the judicial reasoning, but they show that the causes of action pleaded involved such broad concepts as abuse of rights, discrimination, denial of justice, and violation of territorial sovereignty. It is doubtful that the International Court or an arbitral tribunal would pass on the application of these general concepts without recourse to principles of state responsibility taken from its "general apparatus." Surely the pleadings in the many International Court cases referred to (for example, *Barcelona Traction, Nottebohm, Corfu Channel, Norwegian Loans*) must have developed their claims by reliance in part on the general law of state responsibility. I would have liked a more ample and explicit exposition by Brownlie of his thesis, but this does not detract from the value of the innovative approach suggested by this article.

The utility of general ideas linked with specific precepts is well brought out by F. A. Mann in his article on the UK State Immunity Act of 1978. Here the main emphasis is on prospective litigation, which is of course highly appropriate in this context. Mann warmly welcomes the new Immunity Act. He favors applying the exceptions to immunity on the same level as the principle of immunity, without any priority to the latter. On this basis the law requires, in his view, a wide interpretation of commercial transactions irrespective of whether the act from which the claim arises (*e.g.*, breach of contract) was done in the exercise of sovereign authority. Mann also maintains that the foreign state claiming immunity must bear the burden of proving the facts on which it relies. While approving the Act generally, Mann takes strong exception to the provisions exempting foreign central banks from enforcement of judg-

[2] B. CARDOZO, THE NATURE OF THE JUDICIAL PROCESS 69 (1921).

ments and execution (even though the bank's assets may be used or intended to be used for commercial purposes). He attributes this exemption to the wish to attract foreign funds to the city of London and asks whether so "cynical" an attitude commends itself. "Does principle and financial and commercial probity no longer count?" The point is strongly put, but one wonders whether the legislative attitude in the United Kingdom, or for that matter in the United States,[3] is likely to be swayed by principle rather than by the practical competition for overseas funds.

Two articles deal with the Optional Clause of the Court's Statute. James Crawford returns to the much discussed issue of the automatic reservation (as in the Connally Amendment) and examines closely the position of Judge Lauterpacht expounded in his separate opinion in the *Norwegian Loans* case and in his dissent in the *Interhandel* case. Crawford takes issue with Lauterpacht's view of the inconsistency of the automatic reservation with Article 36. The argument is detailed. In Crawford's opinion, even if Lauterpacht's view is correct as regards Article 36(2), an automatic reservation is not void but is capable of supporting *pro tanto* the jurisdiction of the Court under Article 36, paragraph 1. He reasons that the declaration with reservation is intended to have effect vis-à-vis parties to the Optional Clause, but it requires such a party's consent or acceptance to operate as such (p. 85). He observes that this is similar to, but not the same as, recourse to *forum prorogatum*. It is not the same because, if an automatic reservation is accepted by another party, the other reservations in the two declarations remain relevant. Also, interim measures would be proper on the basis of such declarations, whereas they would not be possible simply on the basis of an *anticipated* ad hoc acceptance of jurisdiction under *forum prorogatum*.

J. G. Merrill's article provides a valuable analytical survey of the present (1980) state of the Court's compulsory jurisdiction under Article 36(2). Merrill notes the increase since 1955 in the number of states with declarations under the Optional Clause: 45 instead of 33. He points out that the increase has come from Asia, Europe, and most importantly, from Africa. Eleven African states had declarations in force in 1980. However, in 1955 the declarations represented 40 percent of UN membership; in 1980 that figure fell to 30 percent of the larger membership. As to the terms of the declarations, it is perhaps surprising that those with automatic Connally-type reservations have remained at six, thus proportionately representing a decline. However, an increase in other major reservations is less encouraging. There are more comprehensive reservations on issues of territorial sovereignty and more stringent reservations *ratione temporis*. Recent declarations also include more reservations and greater variety than those of earlier years; one reason is that declarations with reservations are often copied in later declarations by other states, which increases the number and variety of the reservations. A more hopeful statistic is that one-third of the current declarations are full and unequivocal acceptances of compulsory jurisdiction within the terms of Article 36(2). Merrill hopes that the improved UK declaration will be infectious for

[3] The U.S. Foreign Sovereign Immunities Act has a similar provision in its section 1611.

new declarations and that the U.S. declaration will be revised to remove the Connally reservation. One wishes that hope could be shared.

The remaining two articles are by Widdows, *What is an Agreement in International Law?*, and by Weis, *The Draft United Nations Convention on Territorial Asylum*. The latter, a characteristically scholarly paper by a leading expert in the field, deals with the disappointing results of the UN conference in 1977. Drafts of experts prepared over some years of effort were significantly weakened by the governments. For example, a stricter concept of "definite possibility of persecution" was made the criterion for the grant of asylum. Weis finds it unlikely that in the near future a Convention on Territorial Asylum that would constitute progress from a humanitarian standpoint could be concluded and widely ratified on a universal level. He believes regional conventions would be easier to achieve and cites favorable tendencies in Africa as well as in Latin America to sustain that hope.

The book reviews in this volume merit mention because they reveal a welcome tendency toward more critical and more searching reviews than have been common in the past in the *Year Book*. Reviews of Abi-Saab by Bowett, of Bokor-Szego by Crawford, of Gold by Mann, and of Cassese by Akehurst are good examples. Especially noteworthy is a detailed analytical review by the late Sir Otto Kahn-Freund of *Torts in Private International Law* by Morse. The review shows how a master in the field can illuminate a technical subject in a presentation that is both critical and appreciative of the author's effort.

OSCAR SCHACHTER

L'Interprétation judiciaire des traités d'organisations internationales. By Denys Simon. Paris: Editions A. Pedone, 1981. Pp. xv, 936.

When this reviewer finished reading Professor Simon's work, it became clear that it merited more than a brief book review, and could be the subject of a leading article in the *Journal*. Simon's book is almost one thousand pages long, contains 2,657 footnotes, an extensive bibliography drawn from multinational sources, and an exhaustive list of arbitral and judicial decisions spanning a period of 120 years (from 1858 through 1978). In a work of this magnitude, covering judicial interpretations of treaties of public international organizations, footnotes and tables sometimes serve as important a function as the text itself. Simon's work is no exception in this regard.

While the arrangement of the chapters, sections, titles, and conclusions (and there are over two hundred such headings) is cumbersome and difficult to follow, this should not detract from the demonstration of the skill and thoroughness of Simon's painstaking scholarship. The book, assuredly, is a worthy addition to such great works as McNair's *The Law of Treaties* (1961) and the major contributions of Hudson, Lauterpacht, Hyde, the Harvard Research, Oppenheim, and the many other authorities cited by Simon.

Simon performs a masterful task in tracing the development of the judicial art of treaty interpretation, drawing on the vast sources of the Permanent Court of International Justice (PCIJ) and its successor, the International Court of Justice (ICJ). The ICJ is not a mere continuation of the old one, but "it will not lightly disregard the wisdom and common sense embodied in the long practice" of its predecessor. Simon compares the World Courts with the Court of Justice of the European Communities and finds no radical difference in the respective modes of reasoning of their judges, with the important exception that the Treaty Establishing the European Economic Community (the Treaty of Rome, March 25, 1957) has become constitutionalized, and the supremacy of European Community law is recognized as an inherent quality of Community law.[1] While there may be some merit in Casper's statement that "as in the United States, the supremacy of law seems to mean the supremacy of judges," Simon points out that judges cannot freely interpret and that they are bound by certain basic guidelines, which they have followed scrupulously, of which the most important is "to give effect to the continuing consensus of the parties" (citing McDougal and Lasswell) and to adjudicate consistently with the promotion of the best interests of the public international organization involved. Simon cites with apparent approval the guiding words of Mr. Justice Holmes in the landmark case of *Missouri v. Holland* (252 U.S. 416 (1920)): "A constituent instrument will call into life a being the development of which could not have been foreseen completely by the most gifted of its begetters," with which the author could have coupled Holmes's earlier observation: "A word is not a crystal, transparent and unchanged, it is the skin of a living thought and may vary greatly in color and content according to the circumstances and the time in which it is used" (*Towne v. Eisner*, 245 U.S. 418, 425 (1918)).

As far back as 1946, "Pollux," in an article entitled *The Interpretation of the [UN] Charter*, observed that "[t]he accumulated literature on treaty interpretation is already so voluminous and some of it, at least, so adequate that it might seem presumptuous to add to it."[2] Much has happened, however, since then, and Simon has traced the growth of treaty interpretation through the labyrinth of commissions, international courts, the United Nations and the specialized agencies, and other public international bodies—not presumptuously, but laboriously, thoroughly, and admirably. Professor Simon's *magnum opus* brings to international legal scholars, jurists, and Foreign Office practitioners a complete analysis and reference work that is a major contribution to the fast-growing field of international law as developed by international tribunals.

SHELDON Z. KAPLAN
Of the District of Columbia Bar and formerly Staff Consultant, Committee on Foreign Affairs, U.S. House of Representatives

Le Droit des traités dans l'ordre juridique et dans la pratique diplomatique belges. By Jean Masquelin. Brussels: Etablissements Emile Bruylant, 1980. Pp. 674. F.3,396.

Masquelin's book (The Law of Treaties in the Belgian Legal Order and Diplomatic Practice) is a comprehensive work explaining the place of treaties

[1] *See* Ami Barav, 72 ASIL PROC. 193–97 (1978), and the cogent remarks of Gerhard Casper at page 175.

[2] 23 BRIT. Y.B. INT'L L. 54, 54–55, and 54 n.3 (1946).

in Belgian law. The work spans international law and the municipal law of Belgium, since as the author states, the law of Belgium has since 1831 foreseen the fact that treaties could bind Belgian citizens as individuals (p. 8). The starting point for an examination of the Belgian practice concerning treaties and their authoritative effect is Article 68 of the Belgian Constitution. This article provides that "[c]ommercial treaties and those which could burden the state or bind Belgians individually have effect only after having received the approval of the chambers [of the legislature]." While the language is quite different from Article VI of the American Constitution, one is nevertheless struck by the fact that this provision bears a definite similarity to the U.S. supremacy clause in that both provisions acknowledge that as to some treaties in some circumstances the treaty itself is acknowledged as the municipal law of the land.

The author raises the question of the "self-executing" effects of a treaty early in his book, and then returns to the question for specific treatment at approximately its midpoint. He states that a number of treaties have as their object not so much the creation of general obligations between states, but "the creation of rules which possess the character of normative legislative acts" (p. 390).

The general doctrine of self-executing treaties in Belgium is the same as is often set forth in American decisions.[1] The basic test is whether the treaty contains normative expressions that can be directly applied or will have direct effect. Nevertheless, the author concludes that it is indeed difficult to establish a single criterion that is sufficiently precise to distinguish between the self-executing and non-self-executing terms of a treaty.

Europe offers extremely interesting questions of the internal effect of treaties. For example, Belgian courts apparently went back and forth on the question of whether an international convention covering traffic signals was self-executing before finally coming to the determination that it was not, but imposed obligations only on the contracting states (p. 405). Masquelin sets forth what appears to be the complete decision in another case dealing with the imposition of commercial duties on cheese, which comes to a startlingly different conclusion (pp. 436–41). In this case, *Fromagerie Franco-Suisse*, decided May 1971, the Cour de Cassation held that a law imposing a duty on the importation of cheese that conflicted with an article of the Treaty establishing the European Economic Community was unenforceable, even though the legislature passed the law after the enactment of the Treaty. Thus, the Court held that the Treaty not only had domestic effect, but could not be contravened by a subsequent act of the legislature. This is strikingly different from the resolution that would obtain in the United States, where an act of Congress enacted subsequently to a treaty will prevail over conflicting treaty provisions.[2]

The book is a comprehensive treatise on the many aspects of the Belgian practice with respect to treaties. Its scope is revealed by a glance at some of the major topics listed in the table of contents: origin and nature of international legal norms, sources of the rights and obligations of states, ratification

[1] *See*, for example, Sei Fujii v. California, 217 Pa.2d 481 (1950).

[2] *See* 5 G. HACKWORTH, DIGEST OF INTERNATIONAL LAW 185 (1943).

of the law of treaties, characteristics of treaties, formation of treaties, legal effects, modification and termination of treaties. The book is well organized and a very useful reference for its subject matter.

HOWARD C. ANAWALT
The University of Santa Clara School of Law

Les Contrats internationaux de coopération industrielle et le nouvel ordre économique international. By Jean d'Herbes and Jean Touscoz. Paris: Presses Universitaires de France, 1980. Pp. 350.

Le Régime juridique et la nationalisation de concessions pétrolières et autres concessions d'immeubles. Une étude de droit international privé au regard des pays en voie de développement. By Jean-Claude Njem. Stockholm: Almqvist & Wiksell International, 1980. Pp. 295.

Few concepts arising in the United Nations are so laden with emotion as the "New International Economic Order." Adopted by the UN General Assembly in 1974 as a shopping list of measures that developing nations felt should be taken to redress a serious economic imbalance, it has begun to be thought of, at least in the United States, as an enemy war cry in the North-South struggle. So it is refreshing to see that a large group of French businessmen and academics can meet without emotional overtones to discuss how the business community can best work with developing nations to address some of these inequities in a practical way.

The d'Herbes-Touscoz volume is the record of a colloquium held at the University of Nice in 1979 to explore the techniques of industrial cooperation. While most of the 150 participants came from the business community, there was a healthy leavening of academics and government officials from the francophone states of Africa. Like the meeting itself, the book concentrates on three problems: equalizing the value of contributions to a cooperative venture, dealing with the guaranties of performance that may be demanded by one side or the other, and managing the cooperative venture itself. Quite wisely, many other issues of a philosophical, political, or legal nature are strictly excluded; one senses a welcome authoritarianism on the part of the chairmen.

A hypothetical contract of industrial cooperation between a multinational oil company and a developing state serves as the focus of discussion. There is heated debate on whether industrial cooperation is in fact something different from joint ventures, service agreements, concessions, or transfers of technology. As always, the multinational corporation seeks a return on its investment in technical expertise and trained personnel, while the developing country desires to acquire what the discussants neatly refer to as "la maîtrise industrielle." An ambitious goal, but the participants have many wise and diverse suggestions based on actual experience.

Much of this volume consists of summaries of remarks made by participants, which does not make for easy reading. But it does constitute a stimulating and largely pragmatic collection of ideas from a community that views North-South relations in a way different from that currently fashionable in the United States.

The Njem book is the fourth in a useful series of studies on international law published by the University of Uppsala. Njem is concerned with the principles of international law applicable to the nationalization of petroleum concessions from the standpoint of a developing country. Not surprisingly, he advances the thesis that, except in rare cases of denial of justice and a few other circumstances, no state liability for nationalization arises under public international law.

This conclusion is not, of course, a novel one, and but for the care and detail with which Njem builds his case, it would not be worth special attention. Like many dissertations, his work falls somewhere between a treatise and a brief, and one does encounter the occasional statement that is more partisan than scholarly. Still, there is much of interest in his analysis, especially as to the relationship between domestic law governing real and personal property and applicable doctrines of public international law; and of the difficult problems that arise when decrees of nationalization attempt to reach property in foreign jurisdictions. In considering resolutions of the UN General Assembly as giving birth to substantive rules of international law, Njem goes further than most scholars today, but the debate at the Third United Nations Conference on the Law of the Sea concerning the effect of the 1970 resolution characterizing deep seabed nodules as the common heritage of mankind shows that his views are widely shared in the developing world.

A perusal of these two volumes within a short time period leaves the reader with a bewildering range of notions as to how, if at all, the New International Economic Order is to be implemented. Shall it be by practical measures that aim to bring developing countries slowly into the developed world, or by legal measures which inevitably contain an element of confrontation? Experience suggests that we will deal with both, and so both of these volumes make a contribution to the process of orderly change.

William C. Brewer, Jr.
U.S. Department of Commerce

The Philosophy of Human Rights: International Perspectives. Edited by Alan S. Rosenbaum. Westport: Greenwood Press, 1980. Pp. xv, 272. Indexes. $27.50.

Rosenbaum's solid 38-page introduction to part I of this volume indicates the scope to which the editor aspired, by stating his own "perspectives on the philosophy of human rights" (pp. 3–41). That aspiration would certainly explain the reference both to "philosophy" in the main title and to "international" in the subtitle.

A number of the contributions do indeed offer coherent and even cogent starting points of thought. In part II Chaim Perelman offers "the idea of the reasonable" as the matrix of philosophical inquiry, and the dialectic of "the reasonable" in a community of rational human beings as the dynamic source of insights concerning both the factual and the normative ingredients of human rights (pp. 45–51, esp. 49–50). I. C. Sharma seeks to clarify the relations of human rights to "humanism" by seeing humanism as "comprehensive" rather than "scientific," grounded on each integrated human self as the pivot of "intellectual, emotional and volitional functions" (pp. 103–12). The part ends with "a metaphysical approach to human rights from a Chinese point of view" by Peter K. Y. Woo (National Taiwan University) (pp. 114–24), one of the few chapters presenting an international—or at least a cross-national—dimension. As Woo sees the Chinese version of human rights, it consists of mere relations of compassion and interdependence among members of the community, a view that he sees as balancing, if not neutralizing, the dominantly liberal concept in the West of human rights *as rights* (pp. 129 *ff*.). The offering on Judaism and human rights by Abraham Kaplan is homiletically rich and learned, but seems rather unfocused on this volume's themes.[1] R. J. Henle, S.J., in *Thomistic Reflection*, makes the powerful philosophical and also cross-national point that human rights formulations are finally no more than statements—for the time being consensually validated—of human relations that are just or "right," with reference to goods and actions (pp. 88–93, esp. 91–92). And S. H. Nasr, in *Concept and Reality of Freedom in Islam*, is at pains to explain (on the assumption that human rights have some relation to liberty) why it is "meaningless to try to study the notion of freedom in Islam, from the point of view of the meaning that has been attached to this term in the West since the rise of humanism" (see pp. 95–101, esp. 95, 101).

In part III, on "the meaning of human rights" (pp. 125–66), R. S. Downie asks whether "social equality" is acceptable as a human right (pp. 127–35, esp. 128). His answers are marred (for this reviewer) by rather unquestioning reassertions of much questioned criteria, such as distinctions between various modalities of equality, between "self-satisfactions" and "impersonal cultural values" (pp. 132–33), between "equal treatment" and "equal consideration," between "the good" of the community and "its goodness" (pp. 130–31), and between "welfare" and "culture," not to speak of a thesis that all "rights" are either "consumer rights" or "producer rights" (pp. 129–30). In the end, after a jousting tournament with Enoch Powell,[2] he ends by stressing people's "basic needs," from which spring "minimal social rights" and which alone deserve to prevail over "the claims of culture"; and the no less commonplace truth that "when we take social equality beyond minimum standards, it not only enters into competition with other goods, but may actually engulf them" (p. 138). Some years ago, indeed, the present writer gave reasons for doubting the usefulness of the equality notion in this area.[3] Downie's thesis is followed here by E. Shmueli's study of predicaments arising (for example) when an underlying right of "self-realization" is postulated for individuals, on the one hand, and a collectivity (when it is usually called self-determination), on the other.

Two of its more solid chapters, by D. P. Chattopadhyaya on *Human Rights, Justice and Social Context* (pp. 170–93) and by T. R. Machan on *Human Rights,*

[1] It originated as a lecture at Lewis and Clark University rather *alio intuitu*. One wonders why Professor Milton Konvitz's more juristic talents were not called on. *See* his JUDAISM AND HUMAN RIGHTS (M. Konvitz ed. 1972).

[2] Concerning Powell's article, *Human Rights*, in 3 J. MED. ETHICS 160–62 (1973).

[3] *See* Stone, *Justice in the Slough of Equality*, 29 HASTINGS L. J. 995–1024 (1978).

Feudalism and Political Change, conclude this volume. They contain virtually all that this book has concerning the relation of its theorizings to practice.[4] The former chapter concludes from its survey of contemporary performance that "the structural conditions necessary for the realisation of human rights are in most nations of the world, minimal, and in some cases almost absent" (p. 191). To prescribe the extension of human rights in a particular society can be rational only if we attend to "the states of affairs" and "the abilities and desires" of the persons concerned in the time and place. "Social context" in this sense is crucial both for understanding and for enhancing any given human rights performance, or any emulation of it in other times and places. Tibor Machan concludes the volume worthily by considering frontally some problems of practice affecting human rights. These are centered on identifying which "ethical imperatives" are "applicable to those living in societies, for example feudal or semi-feudal, that should be transformed into communities with a constitution of human rights" (see esp. pp. 236 *ff.*, 243); and the implications of such imperatives for foreign policy (pp. 239–43).[5]

While international lawyers should not, therefore, expect too much from the reference to "International Perspectives" in the subtitle of this work, they may find important underlying insights in this effort to "philosophize" about "human rights."[6]

JULIUS STONE
University of New South Wales

International Human Rights: Contemporary Issues. Coedited by Jack L. Nelson and Vera M. Green. Stanfordville: Human Rights Publishing Group, Earl M. Coleman Enterprises, Inc., 1980. Pp. xiii, 350. $25.

This volume of original essays, by a diverse group of scholars, emanated from an international human rights conference held at Rutgers University in late 1978. Some of the case material, perforce, is now dated. But the attempt to place the subject of human rights in a philosophical and legal framework

[4] R. S. Downie, at 133, does mention and summarily dismiss Maurice Cranston's theorem (in his *Human Rights, Real and Supposed,* in POLITICAL THEORY AND THE RIGHTS OF MAN (D. D. Raphael ed. 1967)) that a human right, to be such, must be practicable, of paramount importance, and universal in character. Elsewhere Andrew Levine, in a generally cogent, elegant, sometimes brilliant discussion (*see, e.g.*, pp. 143–47, on the tensions between human rights doctrine and the dominant [freedom] assumptions of "liberal" society) also seems to ask whether "right" in the human rights sense is a concept that has "viability" (p. 138). Alas, it soon appears that by "viability" he means only intellectual tenability, and not any empirically testable capacity to realize itself in the world.

[5] And *see* C. FRANKEL, HUMAN RIGHTS AND FOREIGN POLICY (1978); T. BUERGENTHAL, HUMAN RIGHTS, INTERNATIONAL LAW AND THE HELSINKI AGREEMENT (1978); and HUMAN RIGHTS AND WORLD ORDER (A. A. Said ed. 1978).

[6] The book contains a reading list (pp. 253–56). More directly in the international law concern, see M. GANJI, INTERNATIONAL PROTECTION OF HUMAN RIGHTS (1962); V. VAN DYKE, HUMAN RIGHTS, THE UNITED STATES AND WORLD COMMUNITY (1970); E. B. HAAS, HUMAN RIGHTS AND INTERNATIONAL ACTION (1970); INTERNATIONAL PROTECTION OF HUMAN RIGHTS (L. Sohn & T. Buergenthal eds. 1973); and Meron, *Report on the N.Y.U. Conference on Teaching International Protection of Human Rights,* 13 N.Y.U. J. INT'L L. & POL. 881–957 (1981).

remains valid, although, clearly, not all would agree with the perspective of several of the key contributors.

Christian Bay of the University of Toronto attempts to bridge the controversy of the primacy of political over economic rights by adoption of the concept of human need, defined as anything necessary for the preservation of human life, health, and basic freedom to enjoy well-being and self-expression. Human need should be provided by any type of political society to all of its members, since underlying the concept of human need is the fundamental proposition that all persons are held to be equal in human worth, and therefore all are entitled to the minimum human essentials. Even if one assumes that this is a universal precept, it nevertheless leaves open the fact that available resources are not equally abundant among nations or to the nationals within any given nation.

Bay easily dismisses this problem by his assertion that marketplace determination of access to resources is unjust if it thwarts the availability of basic resources to all on an equal footing. Accordingly, in rich societies he would allocate "only a fraction" of immense private corporate assets for the public benefit and thus resolve the dilemma; by what means and by what criteria remain undefined. He offers nothing but an inchoate hope as to reallocation of resources between the rich and the poor nations. Indeed, the latter part of Bay's essay degenerates into an amateur attack on colonialism, militarism, and other such evils which, if removed, would, according to Bay, allow for attainment of universal basic human needs.

James Nickel attempts to reconcile the philosophical approaches of H. L. A. Hart and John Rawls. Hart seeks the common "core of good sense" inherent in traditional natural law doctrines, which allow individuals to compete for limited resources on some basis of fairness by granting equal political opportunity while restricting the use of violence or bodily harm in the pursuit of these resources. Institutions and rules emerge to assure these ends and, presumably, to guarantee basic human rights in the process. Rawls accepts these premises, but goes beyond them by adopting an approach that characterizes economic and social rights as basic to any just society. He requires equality of "primary goods" for all persons in the society at the same time that equality of basic political rights is preserved. Any or all of the primary goods may be traded off for assurance of basic rights only in exceptional circumstances. Nickel himself concludes that the right to life, liberty, and freedom from torture are matched by the necessity to assure food, shelter, and health needs to all, and that both sets of rights and needs are fundamental; neither can have primacy over the other, for the absence of the one set will, in the end, negate the existence of the other.

The remaining essays attempt to place these basic rights and needs within a specific cultural context. *The Use and Abuse of Democracy in Islam* by Abdul Said and "Jamil Nasser" (a pen name) is the most interesting, as it contrasts the Western view of individual rights and self-fulfillment with that of collective well-being and submission to a higher will in all matters of life. The authors state that hardly any modern Islamic nation-state is politically viable, that the universalism of Islam has not been well adapted to contemporary political systems, and that governance in most Islamic states is an undigested combination of values inherited from Shariahic law, Western liberalism, and Marxist sources. As a consequence, both human rights and social justice are sadly neglected in most Islamic states, whose inhabitants enjoy neither high economic standards (other than in the oil-rich countries) nor basic political entitlements.

The Appropriateness of Political Democracy in Latin America by Robert J. Alexander is worthwhile reading, especially in light of current developments in much of the continent. It is followed by a now dated, but interesting, view by Lars Schoultz of U.S. economic aid as an instrument of foreign policy in the case of human rights violations in Latin America.

RITA E. HAUSER
Of the New York Bar

Duties Beyond Borders: On the Limits and Possibilities of Ethical International Politics. By Stanley Hoffmann. Syracuse: Syracuse University Press, 1981. Pp. xiv, 252. Index. $9.95, paper.

Stanley Hoffmann has written a brief for marrying American national interest and a liberal's moral impulse to produce an ethical statecraft. His opponents belong to the power-politics or "realist" faction in the school of international relations whose lugubrious viewpoint is captured in that marvelous and sinister line from Thucydides' Melian dialogue: "They that have odds of of power exact as much as they can, and the weak yield to such conditions as they can get."

Realpoliticians argue that a sense of ethical obligation is appropriate only within the framework of a national community. The relations of states exist in "the domain of necessity where the only rules are expedients dictated by prudence, where the only standard is efficacy and, again echoing Thucydides, where 'Justice and honor cannot be followed without danger.' "

Hoffmann apparently believes that at least in this epoch, a statesman who assesses every decision from the short and straight perspective of wartime leadership, who subordinates every value to the accumulation of coercive power, and who ignores the ethical and humanitarian consequences of policy must blunder as well as sin. He blunders because a monomaniacal emphasis on power threatens other interests: at least in a democracy, leaders are charged to preserve not only the nation but also its prosperity and freedom. He blunders because treating the world at all times as if it were in a state of war both aggravates the risk of conflict and eliminates any prospect of evolution towards a less dangerous international system. And he blunders, finally, because the state-of-war mentality hinders where it does not prevent political leaders from addressing problems like migration, pollution, and stagflation, which will not yield to the threat of force.

In the course of his effort to spell out the foreign policy consequences of a liberal philosophy, Hoffmann demonstrates many things but none more clearly than the difficulty of deriving from liberal principles a clear, consistent, and readily defensible set of policy prescriptions. Derivation for domestic purposes is difficult enough, given liberalism's internal strains. Being meliorist it accepts the essential institutional features of the status quo. But being reformist, committed to social adjustments that will expand the realm of real individual freedom, it must gnaw away at the status quo and limit the freedom to exploit. The consequent balance between coexistence and reform is always tense.

In the international realm the existence of states adds a deeply complicating factor. It haunts Hoffmann's prescriptions in at least two areas of policy: the use of force and human rights.

Like another recent liberal explorer of the morality-and-force terrain, Michael Walzer, Hoffmann argues that

> all states rights are based on . . . two kinds of [individual] rights: the right to a state of [one's] own . . . and the right to political and civil liberty. . . . The first right gives the people of the state a right against foreigners. . . . The second right is "meaningless" unless the state exists first: "as individuals need a home, so rights need a location" [p. 67].

Walzer concluded that since "the recognition of sovereignty is the only way we have of establishing an arena within which freedom can be fought for and (sometimes) won,"[1] it is necessary to deny a right of foreign intervention to assist a democratic revolution. Walzer no doubt thought he was saying something profound and conclusive, a judgment I have been unable to share. To support his deductive argument, Walzer added the empirical judgment that "foreign intervention, if it is a brief affair, cannot shift the domestic balance of power in any decisive way toward the forces of freedom, while if it is prolonged or intermittently resumed, it will itself pose the greatest possible threat to the success of those forces." While the latter may be self-evident, the former certainly is not. Brief foreign interventions have been decisive in civil conflicts. Certainly our 1965 Dominican intervention determined the outcome of that country's conflict, though not on behalf of what anyone other than Senator Helms and Jeane Kirkpatrick would call the "forces of freedom."

Hoffmann evinces greater sensitivity to the full range of conflicting liberal values. A moderate world order—one that is relatively stable and where states are not constantly teetering on the brink of war—expands the opportunities for the practice of ethical statecraft. Particularly in an ideologically divided world, authorization of intervention to assist the "forces of freedom" or what the Soviets would call "wars of national liberation" is a recipe for rampant instability and conflict, as well as one with extremely problematic consequences for authentic liberation. Thus, to make the world safer for liberal values it is necessary, in Hoffmann's judgment, to resist the temptation to promote a liberal outcome through direct military intervention, as distinguished from lower order forms of assistance. The same priority militates against the exception sponsored by Walzer for intervention to assist wars of secession, or cases where "a particular set of boundaries clearly contains two or more po-

[1] M. Walzer, Just and Unjust Wars (1977).

litical communities one of which is already engaged in a large-scale military struggle for independence."

The conceptual basis for this distinction is that such interventions do not challenge the idea that sovereignty implies the inviolability of nation-state boundaries. They respond, rather, to the conviction that one particular political shell houses two nations.

The practical moral basis for Walzer's distinction is an unarticulated assumption that a governing elite that sees itself and is seen by its subjects as alien cannot tolerate evolution towards democracy because it cannot hope to command a majority in free elections. Moreover, Walzer may believe, intervention to facilitate self-determination rather than self-government is a less threatening precedent, first, because in any given case it is a one-time thing, and second, because success is not a question of degree. Once a new state is recognized as such by a significant number of countries or is admitted to the United Nations, the justification for intervention expires. Self-government or "liberation" from oppressive class relations or a neocolonialist regime is necessarily a matter of degree. Ideology and interest cloud the eye of the beholder.

In his excessively acclaimed work, Walzer failed to develop these more functional supports for his rather airy distinction. But even if he had, Hoffmann would be right to disparage it. Most states, and particularly those states most vulnerable to intervention, house poorly assimilated and disgruntled tribal, racial, ethnic, linguistic, or religious communities. A large-scale revolt, Walzer's condition precedent to legitimate intervention, is generally a function of opportunity, not will. In other words, the fact of a revolt does not correlate closely with the community's oppression or alienation, with its passion for self-determination.

Secessionist movements rarely can and rarely want to restrict their claims to precisely that territory occupied by their group. Hence, if they succeed, they will generally contain within themselves the seed of yet another nation waiting to be born. So Walzer's distinction does not obviate the danger of continuing intervention in the same geographic area despite its changing political contours. (Moreover, history will not support the view that alien elites or alienated minorities are unassimilable.) The world-order threat springing from prosecessionist interventions may not be very much less, therefore, than the threat from interventions against tyrants.

Hoffmann says that both pose unacceptable threats to order in a world without any effective centralized institution to evaluate the intervenor's claims. So in this respect Walzer appears readier to bear risks to the system of order for the benefit of a liberal outcome in particular cases. On the other hand, Walzer's obsession with the theoretical nicety of his distinction leads him to authorize counter-intervention on behalf of tyrants when third parties have previously intervened to assist democratic rebels. This is more than Hoffmann can swallow. A refusal to license counter-intervention on behalf of tyrants is one technique for moderating the conservative rigor of his nonintervention rule. In addition, Hoffmann would legitimate military assistance other than the provision of troops "to resisters fighting for national liberation or for liberation from tyranny"; and under the rubric of "humanitarian intervention," he would even allow armies to cross borders "when the battle for self-determination or self-government entails large scale atrocities committed by a regime against the people."

While acknowledging the danger that these exceptions, particularly humanitarian intervention (which Walzer also would allow when atrocities reach genocidal proportions), could end up as fig leaves for garden-variety aggression,[2] Hoffmann implies that it will become transparent soon enough if foreign troops remain after midwifing the birth of a new state or government. And I suppose he therefore concludes that although they can be faked, his exceptions are unlikely to increase the incidence of aggression, rather as advocates of the insanity defense hope that its potential for abuse will not contribute to the dimensions of violent crime.

Hoffmann might have added a rather more telling argument. In a decentralized political system characterized by auto-interpretation of the law and self-help to enforce it, rules which invite evasion by cutting harshly against the grain of powerful interests often aggravate the risk of armed conflict. While in some cases a norm without exceptions may inhibit the compulsion to intervene, in the main I think it simply provokes confrontations between states moved to aid the rebels and states determined to treat that aid as a provocative challenge to "the law." Hoffmann's greater tolerance of military assistance to rebels is less likely to produce the explosions of self-righteousness and the tests of will that constitute the gravest threat to a moderate world order. So on balance I endorse them, although Hoffmann's own examples illustrate the risk.

Good francophile that he is, he cites "the case of France in the Central African ex-Empire—removing Bokassa, previously supported by Paris, and assuring thereby the continuation of French influence, but also the end of genocide" as an arguably acceptable case of legitimate humanitarian intervention. He contrasts it with Tanzania's liberation of Uganda from the thralldom of the unspeakable Idi Amin. To be sure, Nyerere became heavily entangled in postliberation Ugandan politics. At the same time, the extent and discrimination of Amin's killing did justify talk of genocide and the Tanzanian invasion had the additional justification of being a punitive response to Amin's armed attack, not all that easily distinguishable from Israel's occupation of the West Bank after Jordan entered the 1967 war. Bokassa was of course a disgusting politician who should have ended on the gibbet rather than as a permanent guest of the sanctimonious Houphet Boigny. Bokassa bled his country, made it a cornucopia for the man who was until recently President of France, and beat children to death for acts of lèse-majesté like not wanting to buy school uniforms from his relatives. For all that, he simply did not kill on a mass scale. I hope Hoffmann will find a happier illustration in the next edition of his book.

The issue of human rights refocuses the tensions coiled inside a liberal statecraft. On the one hand is the liberal's abiding concern for the dignity, welfare, and freedom of individual human beings. On the other, the liberal's

[2] It was one of the justifications invoked by Lyndon Johnson for the Dominican intervention.

concern for a moderate world order where the tempering of interstate competition expands the statesman's opportunity for cooperation and humanitarian choices. Arraigning a regime for human rights violations stabs at the heart of its legitimacy. All contemporary governments justify themselves as representatives of popular will. Grave violations imply a repressive rather than representative relation between governors and governed. As they multiply, the regime looks more and more like an occupying force, an image that acquired broad diplomatic currency in Somoza's final days and helped to seal his fate.

Against both Machiavellian and liberal objections Hoffmann marshals five arguments in defense of his conclusion that concern for human rights violations should exercise a continuing claim on the resources of American foreign policy. First, because "widespread domestic conditions of misery and tyranny . . . incite external intervention" and thereby aggravate international tensions; second, because those conditions tempt leaders "to find external diversions"; third, because regimes that violate international law in their domestic behavior are more likely to behave as outlaws in the international arena; fourth, because gross violations of human rights have costly spillover effects, particularly in their tendency to generate refugees who, more often than not, come knocking on America's door; and fifth, because such violations create or at least aggravate domestic turmoil, which in turn tends to endanger U.S. economic and security interests in the stricken country.

Opponents will contend that his list has three generic flaws: it assumes that grave violations are a cause of instability and revolt when they may in fact be a response. This is plainly the position of the Argentines, Chileans, and Uruguayans and their American partisans like Mrs. Kirkpatrick. It assumes that grave violations will not restore order; but at least in the short term they sometimes are awfully effective. And finally, it assumes that pressure to reduce violations will at least in the preponderance of cases have that effect without consequently unleashing still greater chaos or even more serious violations. Opponents can then press their attack by shillelaghing Hoffmann with some of his own acute analysis, including the frank concession that

> [v]iolations of human rights are the expression of deep structural problems . . . inherent in certain kinds of political regimes and in certain kinds of economic systems in many parts of the world. . . . [and] there is at present no way in which one can deal with those structural problems head on from the outside. We do not have the means for it, we do not have the knowledge, or we do not have the will [pp. 138, 139].

If violations are structural, it could be argued, then when we ask regimes to stop butchering, we are necessarily asking them either to stop doing what they deem necessary for survival, *i.e.*, to self-destruct, or to reform themselves radically, which may mean yielding a very large measure of status and wealth. If we are not doing that, if we ask only for the elimination of marginal, shall we say gratuitous, brutality, the deeper structures will continue to produce the destabilizing dissidence which a human rights policy is supposed to avert.

Hoffmann, who yields to no one in rhetorical ingenuity, would, I presume, respond along the following lines. Since he does not urge the subordination of all other objectives to the promotion of human rights, since he merely prescribes that day-to-day policy making should incorporate human rights concerns, giving them greater or less emphasis depending upon such factors as gravity of violation, capacity to influence (either with carrots or sticks), and the weight of competing interests, he is not logically obligated to demonstrate that in a clear preponderance of cases violations produce serious adverse consequences and that a U.S. response will reduce the violations and mitigate those consequences. As long as this is true in a significant number of cases, statesmen will ignore the issue at the peril of both national and humanitarian interests. Moreover, by raising the issue, U.S. policy makers moderate the electorate's dangerous tendency to romanticize marriages of convenience with ugly regimes, thereby complicating ultimate divorce.

Hoffmann concludes his book by returning to the world-order problem, above all to the competitive, enmity-filled relationship between the United States and the Soviet Union. If the writing is a little weary here, the prescriptions almost commonplace, and the supporting argument thinly clothed, no doubt it is the result of Hoffmann's having elaborated his views on a number of other occasions with rather less influence than that achieved respectively by the sycophants and mediocrities who in recent years have pressed their mouths against successive princes' ears.

He restates the incontrovertible proposition that unrestrained confrontation between the Soviets and ourselves will create precisely that Hobbesian environment of siege and survival which tends to lock ethical perceptions out of the domain of statecraft, as well as to encourage the erection of garrison states.

Despite his thinly veiled disdain for his former Harvard colleague, Hoffmann's prescriptions have a good deal in common with the Soviet strategy Henry Kissinger defended until discovering it did not correspond conveniently with the fantasies of Ronald Reagan. Both pre-Reagan Kissinger and contemporary Hoffmann see the Soviet Union as a dangerous but neither imminently omnipotent nor inexpiable power whose potential for creating disorder can be moderated through the maintenance of a well-proportioned military establishment and the construction of mutually beneficial economic links.

Détente was a process: of establishing links, of promoting communication so both sides could probe for common interests while recognizing each other's deep priorities, and of preventing dangerous instabilities from bubbling out of unrestrained arms programs. Hoffmann neither foresees nor urges evolution towards a de facto U.S.-Soviet global condominium. But I think he would go farther than Kissinger ever intended to test the possibility of Soviet participation in managing problems such as the Middle East or South Africa. And he fiercely opposes Kissinger's policy of treating left-wing movements in Third World countries as crazed enemies of American interests and therefore proper targets for liquidation.

Hoffmann would have strengthened his case for détente without tears if he had systematically reviewed the three assumptions that nominally inspire Western confrontationists: (1) that in the past decade the Soviets have made huge strategic gains; (2) that their military capacity now exceeds ours to an extent that imperils our most vital interests; and (3) that the decade-long enhancement of Soviet capabilities is explicable only in terms of a Soviet drive for global hegemony.

The first is transparently false. Surely the most significant geopolitical events of the past decade are Egypt's shift from a Soviet protectorate to a complaisant arm of the Western alliance and China's transformation from a supposedly mad-dog enemy of Western interests to a de facto ally. The Western Hemisphere remains safely capitalist in most of its parts, an important contributor of dynamism to the international capitalist system and a source of oil removed from the dangers and vicissitudes of the Persian Gulf. In Africa we and the Soviets have traded a few inconsequential clients, though most or all of theirs seemingly hunger for Western ties. And in Asia the passage of 10 years has transformed Vietnam from a vast sinkhole for our own resources to one down which the Soviets must pour theirs.

As for the military balance, the closest thing to an impartial expert body, the London-based International Institute of Strategic Studies, finds it still very close, far too close to allow the Soviets rationally to contemplate a challenge to vital Western interests.

The third assumption is as false as the first. A moderately intelligent Soviet planning establishment will always seek forces larger than those deployed by the West, in part because it has a two-front problem (those one billion irridentist Chinese who only a few years ago made the Pentagon plan for the contingency of fighting two major wars simultaneously) and permanently unstable regimes in Eastern Europe and, somewhere down the road, if some experts are right, fissiparous tendencies within its own, multiethnic body. When you add to its more varied security threats a second-rate technology, particularly in computers and electronics, and pervasive inefficiency and a marked breakdown in social élan (alcoholism, crimes against state property, increasing infant mortality rates, etc.), the felt need for large forces in being and large stockpiles of equipment might plausibly become yet more acute from the Soviet perspective. Moreover, in trying to understand Soviet motives one cannot overlook the persistent strength within the Western alliance of a faction anxious for confrontation and hopeful for the eventual reduction of the Soviet Union to a beleaguered, second-class state and even to its ultimate crack-up.

I, personally, have no objection to that denouement. Indeed, there is reason to believe that if all states were the size of Sweden and Austria, the world would be a considerably safer place. I simply do not think that that outcome is worth the risks that would attend efforts to promote it through a policy of unappeasable hostility. In any event, the issue is not what an American might like to see but rather what the Soviet elite may genuinely fear. Fear is as likely as ambition to inspire aggressive behavior. Hence the advantages of a policy that neither terrifies the Soviets nor induces hallucinatory ambitions.

When communication breaks down between two paranoid superpowers arming to the teeth and convinced that the balance of power is delicate, my anecdotal reading of history suggests that war usually results. For once I would like to be wrong.

The world, regrettably, is the only laboratory available to test hypotheses about foreign policy, and the guinea pigs are we. A nuclear holocaust will be the only conclusive proof of my thesis that the present dangerniks are dead wrong. In the absence of experience testing, we can only hope that books like Hoffmann's will manage to convince the understandably edgy electorate that a hysterical view of the present danger is the one best calculated to extinguish both our freedoms and ourselves.

TOM J. FARER
Board of Editors

The Sword and the Gavel. By the Last of the Nuremberg Judges, William J. Wilkins. Seattle: The Writing Works, 1981. Pp. vii, 328. Index. Ill. $14.95.

The special value of this book by the lone survivor of the 32 State judges who composed the 12 exclusively *American* tribunals at Nuremberg (1947–1949) lies in the fact that it does not deal exclusively with "Nuremberg" or the *Krupp* case on which the author sat. Its bulk is a frank and intensely personal self-portrait, *mutatis mutandis* not atypical of his fellow Nuremberg judges. It thus offers some answers to the essential but rarely asked question: who were the judges (sometimes themselves accused as the victors seeking revenge against the defeated) who came from far away to Hitler's favored city, with its ruins, black market, and cigarette currency (here vividly described) to decide exceedingly complex cases, staggering in their dimensions? (In the *Krupp* case 252 witnesses were heard, 4,935 exhibits were admitted, the transcripts not counting trial briefs covered 15,000 pages, and the judgment and separate opinions run to 157 printed pages.)

William Wilkins, one of nine children of a Cornish immigrant, grew up in northern Michigan; in 1918 saw battle in France; obtained a Doctor of Law degree from George Washington University; eventually became chief trial lawyer for the prosecution office, and since 1940 (with a hiatus as Judge Advocate, 2d Air Force, Colorado Springs with final rank as full colonel) judge for 32 years on the Superior Court Bench of Kings County in Seattle.

A man of conservative leanings, who has little patience with "bleeding heart" judges, he handed down four death sentences, but as chairman of Washington State's Prison Terms and Paroles Board he set up a pioneering program of "honor camps" for deserving convicts. At a mature age, he adopted the five young children of a deceased friend. His comments on the shortcomings of civil and criminal justice are as instructive as his intense loyalty to family and family homesteads, and his civic, patriotic, and Masonic activities. At Nuremberg, he felt uncomfortable with, and dismissed, the male servant ("butler") assigned to him and Mrs. Wilkins by the Army. What comes through is a warm-hearted, strict, gregarious, sometimes opinionated personality with an uncompromising demand for *rectitude.*

In its Judgment of July 31, 1948, the *Krupp* tribunal unanimously agreed with the International Nuremberg Tribunal in the *Goering* case that already under pre-1939 international law, participation in the preparation, initiation, and waging of aggressive war was the supreme international crime. Hence, arms production, in itself legitimate, becomes criminal if intentionally done for that purpose. The tribunal found that the prosecution had not proven such intent beyond a reasonable doubt, and it dismissed the crime-against-peace count.

Judge Wilkins felt this to be "a matter of such gravity" that he was "in conscience bound" to file a Special Concurring Opinion. A model of lucidity, it builds on the simple reminder that "the same elementary and basic principles applicable generally with respect to other crimes" apply to the crime against peace, namely, participation in the crime, and criminal intent. For arms producers like "the giant Krupp concern" this means "substantial participation in and responsibility for . . . building up the power of a country to wage war," and "intent" and "knowledge that the military power would be used in a manner which, in the words of the Kellogg Pact, includes war as an 'instrument of policy.' " To him, the evidence in these respects as to "several" of the indicted Krupp leaders was "well nigh compelling."[1]

On the two other charges, the defendants were found guilty. The first concerned unlawful spoliation and plunder of occupied territories: "The Krupp firm"—Wilkins summarizes (p. 211)—"took over various plants and their contents in Holland, France, Yugoslavia and Russia, the [movable] loot consisting of raw materials, tools and machines which were taken to Essen" where Krupp had almost a hundred factories.

On the second charge, unlawful exploitation and mistreatment of slave labor, the tribunal, again unanimously, found that over 100,000 men and women, including 25,000 prisoners of war and 5,000 concentration camp prisoners (partly employed by Krupp at Auschwitz) had to manufacture weapons to be used against their own and their allies' countries. "These pathetic people" were forced to work under "almost unbelievable" conditions of "hunger, overwork, diseases, beatings and frequent death" (p. 220). Wilkins adds that his summary of these Krupp policies "but scratched the surface" (p. 215) and refers for more material to the U.S. Government publication mentioned here in footnote 1.

These misdeeds, committed "not for Germany but for *Krupp private profit*" (emphasis in original, p. 220), prompted Wilkins and the third judge, W. J. Daly of the Connecticut Supreme Court, to sentence Alfried Krupp (with presiding Judge H. C. Anderson of the Tennessee Court of Appeals consenting) to 12 years' imprisonment and (with Anderson dissenting) to confiscation of the entire Krupp concern, of which he was the sole owner.

Now comes the book's climax: the Military Governor of the U.S. Zone of Germany, General Lucius D. Clay, confirmed this sentence on April 1, 1949. But in May 1951, Clay's successor, U.S. High Commissioner for Germany John J. McCloy, released Alfried Krupp from prison and restored to him all his properties, so that, Wilkins adds bitterly, he died in 1968 reputedly "the

[1] 9 Trials of War Criminals Before the Nuernberg Military Tribunals 455, 455–56, 466 (1950). Regrettably, the book only cites (p. 209) some passages of this 12-page concurring opinion, and omits mentioning Wilkins's Dissenting Opinion on the Dismissal of Certain of the Charges of Spoliation (*id.* at 1455–84), which also contains highly significant doctrinal statements on the law of armed conflict.

richest man in Europe" (p. 221). Now retired, Wilkins must "speak up" in fairness to the late General Clay, his fellow judges also deceased, and to himself. McCloy "might have" had authority to shorten Krupp's prison term, but to return to Krupp the forfeited property, much of which had been "stolen and pillaged . . . did not come within the category of clemency."[2] This action exceeded McCloy's authority, was reached without proper examination of the trial records, constituted inadmissible "political expediency," and was fostered by the very American whom the *Krupp* tribunal had excluded from the proceedings as an "alleged attorney" and whom Clay had expelled from the American Zone (pp. 217–22). At the least, McCloy should have demanded "restitution and damages to the unfortunate kidnapped slave laborers"[3] and to the owners of the properties "stolen by and on behalf of the Krupp firm" (pp. 217–22). Wilkins's sense of rectitude remains offended.

JOHN H. E. FRIED

Human Rights and State Sovereignty. By Richard Falk. New York and London: Holmes & Meier Publishers, Inc., 1981. Pp. x, 251. Index. $28.50, cloth; $15.75, paper.

Reading writings by Richard Falk is invariably a stimulating, if frustrating, experience. The reviewer finds himself dazzled by the brilliance of Falk's analysis and the incisiveness of his insights, while startled by his gaps in logic, imprecise statements, and highly questionable propositions.

Perhaps one should expect this to be particularly the case when Falk writes on the inherently controversial subject of human rights. For example, while reading the introduction to the book, one can applaud his observation on

> the danger that human rights would become the preserve of sentimentalist legalists and dogged propagandists, that is, of those who thought the world automatically became a better place every time platitudes were inscribed in a legal form and of Cold Warriors who used some of these platitudes to increase international tensions and military spending through their strident denunciations of "the enemy" state and its ideology [p. 1].

One may also appreciate his provocative question whether the state system is "compatible with the substantial realization of human rights" (p. 6). But then one comes upon his apparently inconsistent contention that "in a world of mass poverty and rising resource costs, it seems preferable, by and large, to move in a socialist direction to satisfy those human rights concerned with

[2] Art. III(6) of Allied Control Council Law No. 10 of December 20, 1945 under which the American Nuremberg trials were held, only authorized each Zone Commander to *distribute* property forfeited by the war crimes courts "as he may deem proper in the interest of justice" but not to set aside any court's forfeiting order.

[3] By 1973 (!), under a settlement reached by a Jewish organization after years of negotiations, eventually 3,090 still surviving former Krupp slave laborers received DM 10,050,900, equivalent to a maximum of $825 per person. Heirs of Jewish nonsurvivors, and non-Jewish survivors and their heirs, received nothing. *See* B. FERENCZ, LESS THAN SLAVES 100, 210 (1979). For a review of Ferencz's book, see this *Journal*, 75 AJIL 702–04 (1981).

the basic needs of people" (p. 7). A major problem with this statement, and one present throughout the book, is that Falk nowhere makes clear what he means by "socialism." There is a world of difference between the socialism represented by the Soviet Union and that characteristic of, say, the Scandinavian countries. Even if Falk is speaking in terms of the Scandinavian model, of course, his proposition is debatable.

The substantive chapters of Falk's book have all appeared previously in article or similar form in other publications, although he notes that "in each instance revisions have been made" (p. x). The subjects covered include "The Evolution of American Foreign Policy on Human Rights: 1945–1978" (ch. II), "Theoretical Foundations of Human Rights" (ch. III), "A World Order Perspective on Authoritarian Tendencies" (ch. IV), "Comparative Protection of Human Rights in Capitalist and Socialist Third World Countries" (ch. V), "Responding to Severe Violations" (ch. VI), "The Algiers Declaration of the Rights of Peoples and the Struggle for Human Rights" (ch. VII), "Keeping Nuremberg Alive" (ch. VIII), and "Human Rights after the Iranian Revolution" (ch. IX). The points made and the contentions advanced in this somewhat disparate collection are too numerous to cover in this brief review. Suffice it for present purposes to highlight a few salient themes.

Pertinent to the current administration's policies, Falk suggests that the policy objective of reducing suffering and producing a more humane world "is not effectively advanced by exposing Soviet failures, about which the United States can do little, and may even be counterproductive by creating more tension and less cooperation" (p. 26). In Falk's view the emphasis should be rather on encouraging liberal democratic values in non-Communist societies.

A major theme that Falk emphasizes throughout this book is one readers familiar with the World Order Models Project (WOMP) will recognize: the state system as it emerged from European regional politics in the middle of the 17th century is disintegrating and "a new world order system is emergent that will combine an organizational framework suitable for a planetary polity with appropriate new beliefs, values, and myths" (p. 61). According to Falk, this evolution may or may not result in an improved atmosphere for human rights, because under the "negative variant of the poststatal system, human rights will be denied in more systematic and flagrant ways than is currently the case" (*id.*). The hope of Falk and WOMP is that a worldwide populist movement will result in a positive variant of the poststatal system that promotes human rights. Falk does recognize that even a populist movement can be responsible for repressive intolerance.

Little enlightenment is to be found in Falk's discussion of his thesis that socialism is more attractive than capitalism from a human rights viewpoint for a Third World country. In addition to his failure to define his terms, Falk is not an economist, and he approaches the subject at a high level of abstraction with little reference to empirical data. Indeed, he acknowledges that "socialism *as applied* to date in the Third World deprives it of the moral advantage associated with socialism *as theory* or as an ideological perspective" (p. 127). Falk fails to recognize that consistent failure in application may indicate major problems with the theory.

Falk's comments regarding the Iranian revolution have been noted and challenged in other forums. His apologia for the Ayatollah Khomeini appears less and less impressive with the passage of time and the emergence of more evidence, including a report by Amnesty International, regarding the barbaric nature of the Khomeini regime.

In sum, this book is vintage Falk. Brilliant, idiosyncratic, provocative, and occasionally aggravating, his writings continue to challenge conventional wisdom and policy. In this they serve us well.

JOHN F. MURPHY
The University of Kansas

Protection of Ethnic Minorities. Edited by Robert G. Wirsing. New York: Pergamon Press, 1981. Pp. xii, 375. Indexes. $39.50.

This symposium provides a useful ethnic survey of today's world. Essays by well-qualified specialists cover every major region except Western Europe (a curious omission), either by offering an overview of the relations between ethnic majorities and minorities or by presenting case studies of the situation of particular ethnic minorities. For the student of comparative politics, this is a treasury of information and insight about such diverse matters as the contrast between the American melting pot and the Canadian mosaic, the theory and practice of Communism as it relates to ethnic policy in Eastern Europe, the Soviet Union, and China, and the rationale for African states' abandonment of support for the doctrine of the rights of ethnic collectivities in the aftermath of their successful campaigns for independence under the banner of national self-determination. The book makes a valuable contribution to general understanding of the status of ethnic minorities in the so-called national states of our time, of their grievances and demands, of the problems that they pose for ethnic majorities, and of the policies and programs instituted by majorities for dealing with both the problems that minorities endure and the problems that they present.

The title of the volume is somewhat misleading, for it does not focus on the protection of ethnic groups. There are only scattered and fleeting references to the scheme for international protection that was instituted after World War I, and in no sense does this work represent a systematic examination of the problems and possibilities of an international legal regime for protecting ethnic minorities. Indeed, the editor casually dismisses the system operated by the League of Nations as an abject failure (p. 10), and the writer of the concluding chapter, Pierre L. van den Berghe, considers it implausible that the United Nations, an organization of states, should display genuine interest in restricting states' freedom to deal with ethnic minorities as they wish (p. 346).

Even though the book is not really about the protection of ethnic minorities, it has value for those who are concerned with that issue. Most of the contributors resist the urge to idealize minorities as victims whose complaints and demands are always justified, and promote a balanced view of the often troubled relationships among ethnic groups within states. The reader repeatedly encounters the shrewd recognition that liberal concessions to the demands of minorities sometimes stimulate rather than satisfy their political appetites, that external efforts at protection are not always humanely motivated, and that the assimilative tendencies that trouble minorities may derive less from the malign intentions of their rulers than from the acceptance of their demands for freedom from discrimination and for full participation in the national economy. Moreover, these essays promote an awareness of the complexity and diversity of the global ethnic situation that ought to inspire a cautious approach to the notion of constructing an international regime that would prescribe a uniform set of rights for ethnic minorities and establish a standard form of relationship among the ethnic groups constituting states. This volume offers not a treatment of, but a solid body of material for thought about, the problem of the protection of ethnic minorities.

INIS L. CLAUDE, JR.
University of Virginia

Derecho Internacional Público (7th ed.). By Modesto Seara Vázquez. Mexico: Editorial Porrúa, S.A., 1981. Pp. 661. Indexes.

This is basically a text for undergraduate students. This assessment is corroborated, among other things, by questions printed at the end of individual sections, and a glossary of Latin terms used in international law, on pages 603–05 (but does it not go too far in offering explanations of ad hoc and de facto?). There are also a number of illustrative graphs, some of them quite useful, *e.g.*, those explaining the problems of delineations in the realm of the law of the sea.

Some 380 pages are taken up by the author's exposé, and some 280 by annexes and indexes. The first part, after an introduction, deals with the law of peace. It covers the sources of international law and its subjects: peaceful international relations, including a discussion of the "juridical instruments" and the "organs"; the *dominio espacial* of the activities of states (territory, sea, air, and outer space); pacific solutions of international conflicts; international responsibility; and the "state of pre-war" (*el estado de preguerra*). The second part deals with the law of war.

The annexes include the UN Charter, the Statute of the International Court of Justice, the Charter of the OAS, and the Inter-American Treaty for Mutual Defense of 1947, with the amendments of the San José Protocol of 1975. Finally, some 115 pages are taken up by the reproduction of passages from the Constitutions of 21 countries (Latin American, plus Spain and Portugal) that deal with international law and relations. The inclusion of these latter annexes, of course, is open to question; if only a few relevant samples were given, there would be space for reproducing such first-rank universal international treaties as, *e.g.*, the Vienna Convention on the Law of Treaties and the International Covenants on Human Rights—or for more of the author's own text.

The ever-growing body of international law, especially if one hopes to cover regional phenomena without limiting oneself to one's geographic area, poses increasingly difficult problems: squeezing everything into one volume, while keeping the material in just proportions; avoiding being too general or even superficial; sometimes not being fully up to date; and occasionally offering oversimplifications.

In the case of Seara's book some of these shortcomings may be mentioned. For instance, while approximately 20 pages are devoted to the law of the sea, why are only 3 given to international human rights law? Why, in giving information in the bibliography on "collections of treaties and documents," are those by Leibnitz, Martens, and some national collections mentioned, while the *Treaty Series* of the League of Nations and the United Nations are not included?

When one is offered, on page 126, a list of the universal documents in the field of the international protection of human rights, one misses the 1975 Declaration on the Protection of All Persons from Being Subjected to Torture and Other Cruel, Inhuman or Degrading Treatment or Punishment. When the Warsaw Treaty Organization and COMECON are briefly covered and their organs mentioned (pp. 169–71), such more recent and important bodies of the former as the Committee of the Defense Ministers and the Military Council (created in 1969), as well as the Committee of Foreign Ministers (created in 1976), are overlooked. As for the latter, there is no word on three committees: on Planning, on Scientific and Technical Co-operation, and on Material and Technical Supply (organs not to be confused with the Organization's 23 standing commissions). Also, the fact that Vietnam joined COMECON in 1978 seems to be unknown to the author.

Finally, one is a bit shocked by the notion of the "Johnson-Brezhnev Doctrine," used in the "State of Pre-War" chapter (pp. 335–36). Deeper study and reflection on the nature of the pertinent Soviet doctrine, better referred to by its official name—proletarian (socialist) internationalism—would probably lead to the avoidance of suggesting an American-Soviet tandem almost along a Kellogg-Briand line!

RICHARD SZAWLOWSKI
Vancouver, B.C.

Multum Non Multa. Festschrift für Kurt Lipstein. Edited by Peter Feuerstein and Clive Parry. Heidelberg: C. F. Müller Juristischer Verlag, 1980. Pp. xv, 383. DM 178.

This collection of essays, entitled *Quality not Quantity*, honors an exile from Nazi Germany who came to Cambridge University where he studied, taught, and wrote, eventually to assume the comparative law chair. The author of the highly regarded *The Law of the European Community* (1974), counsel in the *Nottebohm* case, and lecturer in private international law at the Hague Academy is celebrated by a number of former students and colleagues, mostly European. A short prefatory note indicates each editor's personal appreciation, by Feuerstein in German and by Parry in English. The book consists of 21 chapters and a four-page bibliography of Lipstein's major publications; 11 essays are in English, 7 in German, and 3 in French. Most of the chapters deal with comparative law or private international law, only a few with public international law. (The reviewers will focus on the last category.)

The essays to be noted briefly are the following: *Systemwandel und Theoriendynamik im Völkerrecht*, by Professor Konrad Ginther; *An International Lawyer Looks at the E.E.C.*, by Joyce A. C. Gutteridge; *Sur la notion de contrat international*, by Professor Pierre Lalive; and *Of Treaties*, by Professor Clive Parry. Ginther's rigorous essay will be of particular interest to political scientists, for he examines the concepts of order and world order, traces contextual changes since World War I, and develops a paradigm for analyzing the process of system change. He relies heavily on Thomas S. Kuhn's influential model of growth in science. Gutteridge convincingly demonstrates how Article 189 is central to the Treaty of Rome as a "peculiar phenomenon . . . which does not fit into any regular pattern of international law or federal law" (p. 57, quoting Lipstein), and determines that the delegation of sovereignty under this article makes the EEC's Council and Commission "autonomous legislative organs" (p. 60). Perhaps taking the same cue from Lipstein, Lalive argues that contracts between states and transnational enterprises are a matter of international law in degree determined by context. This refreshing departure from a particularly sterile debate over a priori notions unmasks subtly observed political considerations. Parry also makes a bow to legal indeterminancy. The centerpiece of his essay is an absorbing "historiography of treaties," in the course of which he notes that "though States have regarded treaties as important, and at least initially in some degree binding, they have not regarded them as constituting any particularly distinct category of acts in interstate relations"(p. 232).

N. G. ONUF AND L. C. WILSON
School of International Service, The American University

Diritto Internazionale dell'Economia. By Paolo Picone and Giorgio Sacerdoti. Milan: Franco Angeli Editore, 1982. Pp. 1156. Index.

This book is important both because of its excellent quality and because it is the first book published in Italian on international economic law. Professors Picone and Sacerdoti, two of the most brilliant of Italy's new generation of international lawyers, have produced a volume that will be invaluable to Italian diplomats, practicing lawyers, scholars, and students who need ready reference to international economic agreements and authoritative interpretations of them. This is a worthy Italian counterpart to the outstanding works in English by Andreas Lowenfeld (*International Economic Law*) and John Jackson (*Legal Problems of International Economic Relations*).

The book skillfully combines editorial essays by the coauthors and their collaborators (Dr. Manlio Frigo and Dr. Emanuela Agnoletto) with basic texts of international economic organizations (the GATT, IMF, IBRD, EC), UN resolutions, bilateral agreements, and national legislation affecting foreign economic relations. The book is divided into 12 parts, beginning with "Introductory Essays on International Economic Law," and moving on to "Permanent Sovereignty Over Natural Resources" (part II), "Regional Integration Agreements and Economic Cooperation" (part III), "International Trade" (part IV), "The International Monetary System" (part V), "Natural Resources, Raw Materials and Energy" (part VI), "States and Multinational Corporations" (part VII), "Capital Movements and Foreign Investments" (part VIII), "Protection of Competition" (part IX), "Problems of Development" (part X), "International Development Aid" (part XI), and "Italian Laws Concerning Foreign Economic Relations" (part XII).

Particularly to be commended is the high quality of the essays on these diverse subjects, which demonstrate an impressive understanding of international economics, international law, and international politics. The value of the essays is enhanced by meticulously edited footnotes, which cite basic authorities in English, French, German, and Spanish, as well as Italian. The authors have made a special effort to include the most up-to-date materials: part IV on international trade includes some of the major "codes" concluded during the Tokyo Round (one curious omission is the Code on Subsidies, probably the most controversial and economically significant).

The only major fault that I can find with this otherwise splendid volume is that the authors do not always distinguish sufficiently between different kinds of international economic law. UN resolutions such as the Charter of Economic Rights and Duties of States are set out at length, and the unsuspecting reader might be led to believe that this resolution of the UN General Assembly is equivalent to a multilateral agreement such as the Articles of Agreement of the International Monetary Fund. The authors might also have done more to emphasize the paradox that currently afflicts the world economy—namely, that the enormous number of international economic principles that have been negotiated during the last four decades have not produced a real consensus on many fundamental issues. They would have done well to emphasize that agreements like the GATT are not being observed by many of the world's countries and are also incomplete in their coverage (failing to deal with trade-distorting performance requirements imposed on foreign investment and on the increasingly significant volume of international trade in services). But it should be emphasized that these deficiencies in the book, if they may fairly be so described, are minor when weighed against the achievement of the authors in producing the first comprehensive work on international economic law in the Italian language at such a high level of professional quality.

RICHARD N. GARDNER
Columbia University School of Law

The Application of the competition rules (antitrust law) of the European Economic Community to enterprises and arrangements external to the Common Market. By Boaz Barack. Deventer: Kluwer, 1981. Pp. xxix, 433. Dfl.90; $45.

This is a very timely discussion of what is finally being recognized as an extremely sophisticated—and formidable—legal and regulatory system. The book is the published version of a doctoral dissertation submitted to Cambridge University and, as such, it suffers from some of the artificial adherence to form common to strictly academic studies. On the other hand, the academic nature of the work serves both to focus and to strengthen it. The table of cases is extensive and contains few notable omissions; the bibliography indicates extensive research in both European and U.S. sources and provides an excellent foundation for further study; and, though often ponderous, the footnotes add substantially to the textual material.

While the book does contain some unfortunate shortcomings in form, they are clearly outweighed by the substance of the study, for example, the excellent comparative analyses of EEC and U.S. antitrust policy in both law and practice. The major thrust of the work, however, is to examine the operation of Community competition policy, particularly from the viewpoint of its application to non-Community enterprises. Perhaps inevitably, the focus narrows to the very controversial and troublesome question of the extraterritorial application of the Community's laws and regulations.

The author approaches the subject of extraterritorial jurisdiction first by comparing the EEC and U.S. doctrines and then by measuring each against established international law principles. In brief, the Community has adopted an "effects" doctrine similar in most respects to that found in the U.S. *Alcoa* case and the *Restatement*. Needless to say, it follows that the Community antitrust authorities face most of the same problems of measuring whether effects are direct, substantial, foreseeable, and the like, as well as the same problems of enforcement jurisdiction, so familiar in the United States.

Interestingly, and quite unlike many other students of the subject, Barack observes that, despite the serious problems associated with extraterritorial jurisdiction, it is a practical necessity. Accordingly, the existence of conflicts, coupled with a greater recognition of the need to regulate, rationalize, and promote today's highly interdependent international trade system, should result in a greater recognition of the need for multilateral agreement and international lawmaking. Also noteworthy is the author's frank appraisal that, for all the raging furor over U.S. extraterritorial enforcement of its antitrust laws, the EEC laws are generally stricter. Moreover, the Community's attitudes toward cartels, industrial rationalization programs, and specialization agreements, and the negative clearance regulations, all operate with a bias favoring Community residents and raise serious issues in the context of U.S. antitrust practice.

Barack would not, however, seek to loosen the Community competition laws. He is quite skeptical, for example, of any jurisdictional balancing such as Brewster's jurisdictional rule of reason applied in recent U.S. cases such as *Timberlane* and *Mannington Mills*. Balancing, he asserts, looks too much to the jurisdictional base and not enough to the competition policy itself while losing sight of traditional—and reliable—conflict-of-laws rules. Though far from the last word, these observations alone make this book a useful addition to both the literature and the scholarly debate.

JOHN R. LACEY
Hartford, Connecticut

La Responsabilità Extracontrattuale delle Comunità Europee. By Gabriella Venturini. Milan: Dott. A. Giuffrè Editore, 1980. Pp. xii, 177. Indexes.

Social Security Law of the European Communities. (Vol. 5 of *Studies in Labour and Social Law.*) By Philippa Watson. London: Mansell Publishing, 1980. Pp. xi, 277. Index. $38.50.

EC Competition Law. A Practitioner's Textbook. By Alan Campbell. Amsterdam, New York, Oxford: North-Holland Publishing Company, 1980. Pp. xii, 345. Index. Dfl.110; $53.75.

Basic Community Laws. Edited by Bernard Rudden and Derrick Wyatt. Oxford: Clarendon Press; New York: Oxford University Press, 1980. Pp. xv, 301. $37.50.

The four books reviewed in this note have one thing in common: they all deal with the law of the European Communities. Otherwise, they differ widely in scope, purpose, and character.

Venturini's study of the noncontractual liability of the European Communities deals with an extremely complex and analytically fascinating subject. In contrast to the rather broad and general provisions for Community responsibility (inspired by French law) found in Article 40 of the Treaty establishing the European Coal and Steel Community, Article 215, paragraph 2 of the Treaty establishing the European Economic Community and Article 188, paragraph 2 of the Treaty establishing the European Atomic Energy Community impose noncontractual Community liability for damage caused by institutions and functionaries only "in accordance with the general principles common to the laws of the Member States." Obviously, as the author demonstrates, the import of that qualification becomes more difficult to determine with each enlargement of the Community.

The Court of Justice of the European Communities has developed the applicable principles and policies in a series of interesting judgments. Of particular significance is the case law recognizing liability for acts of a legislative nature. Since private parties can obtain annulment of illegal acts of general applicability only in the limited circumstances set forth in Article 173, paragraph 2 of the EEC Treaty and Article 146, paragraph 2 of the EAEC Treaty, or have their invalidity declared by way of the cumbersome preliminary question procedure under Article 177 of the EEC Treaty or Article 150 of the EAEC Treaty, the Court has admitted a supplementary and more direct remedy under Article 215, paragraph 2. It consists of an action for damages based on "legislative illegality," committed by the exercise of regulatory power under manifest and grave disregard of the limitations on the exercise of that power flowing from a superior rule of law protecting the individual. The fountainhead of this jurisprudence consists in the judgments in *A. Lütticke GmbH c. Commission*[1] and in *Zuckerfabrik Schöppenstedt c. Conseil.*[2] Venturini treats her subject in a comprehensive and systematic fashion with due regard for the stream of pertinent case law and the copious literature on the subject.

Watson's book is a scholarly and comprehensive study of the legal provisions on social security contained in, or enacted pursuant to, the Treaty of Rome. The creation of a Common Market guaranteeing freedom of movement within the Community to workers necessitated the insertion into the EEC Treaty of Article 51, giving the Community the power to adopt the necessary measures in the field of social security to protect migrant workers against loss or reduction of their protection. The cornerstone of the execution of that mandate

[1] Case 4/69, 1971 ECR 325.

[2] Case 5/71, 1971 ECR 984.

is Council Regulation (EEC) No. 1408/71, as amended. The bulk of Watson's study is a careful and critical exposition of the operation of this intricate and detailed piece of secondary Community law. Her work will be a welcome and helpful source of information for organizations dealing with that subject on a practical basis.

Even more practitioner-oriented is Campbell's textbook on EEC competition law. As is well known, the subject of the manual comprises a vast field of the law, whose complexity is due not only to the intrinsic difficulty in defining anticompetitive practices that threaten or impair the operation of the Common Market but even more to the fact that its administration lies in the hands of three sets of authorities: the Court of Justice of the European Communities, the Commission, and the municipal courts of the member states. Additionally, the Council is charged by Articles 87 and 94 of the EEC Treaty with the enactment of regulations and directives necessary for the implementation of the provisions of the Treaty. Campbell succeeds in presenting the involved and problem-rich matter in a comprehensive, succinct, and lucid manner. He arranges his text in five readable chapters, dealing with (1) the general scope and reach of Articles 85 and 86, (2) the interrelation between these articles and the articles of the Treaty according recognition to industrial property rights, (3) the role and practice of the Commission, (4) dumping and state aids, and (5) the jurisdiction of the municipal courts.

Special highlights of Campbell's exposition are his article-by-article commentaries on the basic Regulation No. 17 and his detailed attention to the functions and practice of the Commission. The text bristles with valuable hints and advice to the novice practitioner. Regrettable, though perhaps unavoidable, is the absence of any attention or reference to the pertinent literature.

The book by Rudden and Wyatt, in contrast to the three other works, aims primarily at classroom use. It is an effort to assemble under one cover the most important instruments constituting the primary and secondary Community law. Of course, an enterprise of that kind must be highly selective. Even the included treaty material had to be subjected to studious pruning. In general, the choices made are reasonable and properly explained in the preface. However, the international actions of the Communities should have deserved some documentary attention. The same is true with respect to the structural aspects of the common agricultural policy.

STEFAN A. RIESENFELD
Board of Editors

Maritime Transport: The Evolution of International Marine Policy and Shipping Law. By Edgar Gold. Lexington and Toronto: D.C. Heath and Co., 1981. Pp. xxi, 425. Index. $34.95.

It is paradoxical that at a time when the regime of the oceans is a most topical issue of international law, shipping, one of the most ancient uses of the sea, has somehow been relegated to the background both at UNCLOS III and in the literature of maritime law and policy. This neglect, now so thoroughly remedied by the author of *Maritime Transport*, can be attributed to the fact that upon the rise of sovereign nation-states much of what used to be general maritime law became "nationalized" and absorbed into the individual systems of municipal law with the resulting separation of private and public maritime law. The former regulated international seaborne trade, carriage of goods at sea, marine insurance, and the like, whereas the latter governed the public, "political" aspects of jurisdiction and the rights and duties with regard to the sea of the sovereign nations in time of peace and war. This split, otherwise only one aspect of the more general historical process of the separation of public international law from municipal law, is the central theme of this book by Professor Gold of the Dalhousie Faculty of Law and executive director of the Ocean Studies Programme of that major center for the study of ocean law and policy.

In his admirably conceived and executed work, the author, who is not only a marine lawyer and scholar but also a master mariner with 16 years of service in the merchant marine, brings his scholarship and experience to bear in tracing, in historical perspective but within the context of other oceanic considerations, the saga of maritime transport from its early beginnings of frail reed boats of ancient mariners to the present-day fleets of supertankers and other giant craft operating as part of a complex network of transnational shipping business. Organized in seven chapters, the narrative starts with the origins of shipping in the eastern Mediterranean where Phoenicians and Greeks laid the foundations for basic customary legal concepts and rules of maritime law, later developed by the Romans into a comprehensive legal system of ocean transportation. Public law was only peripheral to the regulation of maritime commerce. In the Middle Ages the Mediterranean, especially its western part, was the major focus of international shipping activities, producing the well-known international shipping law codifications of Amalfi, Oleron, and others. However, by the time of the great discoveries the European sea trade also had been well developed in the northwestern and northern seas of the European continent, as witnessed by the famous Hansa shipping ordinance.

In the early modern era the great overseas discoveries enlarged the shipping horizons and gave birth to the modern law of the sea associated with maritime rivalries and the gradual assertion of the principle of the freedom of the seas. Strategic and political considerations of the maritime powers were growing ever stronger. In the 19th century the emergence of Great Britain as the major maritime and naval power coincided with a revolution in shipping technology and the worldwide expansion of commerce and seaborne trade. The European system of maritime law was globalized and the split between private and public maritime law became an accomplished fact. By 1914 new maritime nations had joined Great Britain in the "rivalry for world power," which eventually led to the outbreak of the First World War.

The legal dimension of the maritime expansion was characterized by further isolation of private maritime law from the "public" law of the sea. At the same time, new aspects of international maritime transport and policy came into being: the institutionalization of shipping, a concern with safety at sea, and the search for uniformity in maritime law highlighted by the foundation of the Comité Maritime International in 1887. The maritime developments of the two world wars, when international law receded to a secondary level, and the interwar period, when private maritime law became even more isolated from the broader maritime policies, are comprehensively dealt with in one chapter of the volume. Of particular interest is the chapter that takes as its theme the internationalization of marine transport in recent decades and elaborates the role of international organizations in the development of the law of the sea and the emergence of the Third World as a new factor in international shipping. The final chapter brings together various aspects of the new challenges for maritime transport today: UNCLOS III, IMCO, UNCTAD, and environmental problems, among other issues.

The author's general conclusion is that in order to cope with all these political, organizational, and environmental challenges of the 1980's the law of maritime transport must overcome the division between private and public law so as to encompass all aspects of marine policy in an era of complex transnational operations of the most international of industries. A rich, but primarily English-language, bibliography, broken down into perhaps too many categories, complements the text. There are also a list of statutes and a list of cases, as well as an index and 16 tables in the text itself.

It is Gold's unique contribution to the study of marine law and policy to have provided a comprehensive historical background to one major, but neglected, aspect of this subject. His book combines high scholarship with superb style, which recommends it to marine lawyers, historical scholars, and policy makers, as well as to the general reader interested in one of the most fascinating stories in the development of human civilization.

BOLESLAW A. BOCZEK
Kent State University

The Law of Transnational Business Transactions. Edited by Ved P. Nanda. New York: Clark Boardman Company, Ltd., 1981. Index. $75.

This book is a useful contribution to the growing, but still too sparse, literature on the legal aspects of international business. Like many similar works, it consists of a collection of essays, 13 in number, each addressing a discrete topic, and each the product of a different pen. Also, like most of its relatives, its title is somewhat misleading, for, as Nanda says in his preface, the book addresses only "selected aspects of the subject"; but one volume could hardly be expected to do more in so vast and diverse a field.

The approach of the apparently able and highly experienced authors is largely a practical one; the book is principally addressed to the practitioner and the business executive. While the knowledgeable reader is likely to find little that is new, the book affords an excellent introduction to the topics covered for the general practitioner or the specialist roaming outside his area of expertise. While the authors make no pretensions to having produced scholarly articles, they have generally included enough citations to give the reader an entrée into the literature. One of the most useful features for the practitioner will be the sample forms and documents provided in several of the chapters.

The topics covered by the book will be familiar to those who have browsed in the literature on international transactions, as will the sometimes disconcerting gaps in the not entirely seamless web of the law that affects them. The opening chapters are the seemingly obligatory ones on the role of U.S. lawyers and the legal forms an enterprise might choose for doing business overseas—the latter an especially good treatment of the subject. There is a chapter on "United States Taxation of Foreign Investors," but not on taxation of foreign-source income. The chapter on "Selected Clauses in Transnational Contracts" contains no discussion of a choice-of-law clause, but that is remedied four chapters later by a treatment of "Forum-Selection and Choice-of-Law Agreements." There is a chapter on "International Technology Transfers" and a separate one on "International Technology Transfer Agreements." There is also a chapter on natural resource investments, three on aspects of antitrust law, one on U.S. trade law, and one on boycotts. The volume is looseleaf-bound, and the publisher promises periodic updating.

On optimistic (perhaps naive is a better word) days, one can still wish for the work that would bring a little more order into the crazy quilt that confronts the lawyer trying to practice in this field. This is not that work; but it is nonetheless a useful one.

RUSSELL B. STEVENSON, JR.
Securities and Exchange Commission

La Notion de droits acquis en droit international public. By Jacques Barde. Paris: Les Publications Universitaires de Paris, 1981. Pp. 349.

Jacques Barde is a young French professor who received his doctorate in public law from the University of Nancy. He finished this book in 1977 and it probably served as his thesis for his doctorate degree. It is a largely theoretical study of the subject of acquired rights in international public law.

"Acquired rights" is a term that international lawyers employ to escape from the difficulties created by the use of the municipal law concept of property. Acquired rights in international law is a concept somewhat similar to the concept of "property" as used in the Constitution of the United States; it is broader than the term "property" employed in some civil law systems where "property" is confined to ownership.

Professor Barde's work considers acquired rights in relationship to both private persons and states. He reviews both international law and domestic law with respect to each aspect of his subject; he sets forth in some detail the relevant international and national case law (including court decisions and arbitral awards) and the scholarly writings. This approach has the merit of collecting a substantial amount of information and citations (the book also contains a detailed bibliography). However, this approach also renders the work theoretical and, as such, it may be of primary interest to international law scholars rather than international practitioners.

After an introduction and a preliminary chapter on the acquired right of states, Barde turns to a consideration of the elements that constitute acquired right. He concludes that an acquired right must have these characteristics: it must be a part of the estate of a specific person acquired in a regular and proper manner, and it must be concrete and of a private nature. If a right has both private and public aspects, it can only be an acquired right where the private aspects predominate.

From this definition of an acquired right and his review of the body of international and national law bearing on this subject, Barde concludes that, for example, a person cannot obtain an acquired right with respect to a specific value of currency or a specific exchange rate; he also concludes that individual rights such as the right to trade and manufacture and business good will are not acquired rights. Thus, for example, a state may establish monopolies and thereby interfere with an alien's right to trade or manufacture, without interfering with acquired rights. A state can also abrogate gold clauses in contracts entered into with aliens without incurring an obligation to pay compensation.

Barde's work does not make an innovative or imaginative contribution to international law studies of acquired rights. Forced by the procrustean bed of his largely formalistic approach to deal with abstractions more than with concrete situations, he has produced a book that will not have a significant impact upon the subject he has chosen to consider. The international community today does not approach the issues posed by acquired rights and interference by states with such rights in a theoretical and abstract manner. Instead, issues of international, political, economic, and legal importance, such as sovereignty over natural resources, encouragement of investment in developing countries, and the protection afforded by international law to the individual, form the context within which the debate now takes place. In its largest framework, the issue of acquired rights in international law is part of the question of what limitations international law can and should impose upon national sovereignty and how the state should be held responsible when it breaches its obligations to others and interferes unlawfully with the rights of others. Professor Barde's treatise supplies a helpful collection of material with which to address these questions; it does not supply any significant insights, much less answers, to this important problem.

ROBERT B. VON MEHREN
Board of Editors

Japan's Commission on the Constitution: The Final Report. Translated and edited by John M. Maki. Seattle and London: University of Washington Press, 1981. Pp. x, 413. Biographical data, selected bibliography, and index. $25.

Professor Maki has achieved the monumental task of presenting, in clear and concise English, a necessarily much abridged translation of the Final Report of the Japanese Cabinet Commission, which, between 1957 and 1964, conducted a massive study of the workings of the Constitution of 1946 with a view to recommending its wholesale revision. The Japanese Cabinet Commission has been, undoubtedly, the intellectually most impressive and rigorous and exhaustive of all the select committees or constituent assemblies that have considered the introduction of new constitutional charters or the rewriting of old ones, in the case of Western or "received" Western constitutional systems, in the postwar era. This fact owes very much to the character and personality of the commission's Chairman, Dr. Kenzo Takayanagi, a distinguished law professor and specialist in Anglo-American law who had been Wigmore's student at Northwestern years before.

While the commission had originally been conceived with the intention of giving a more truly local and popular, Japanese root or *Grundnorm* to a charter whose historical origins were to be found in the era of Allied Military Government and occupation of Japan, its mandate soon became blurred by the bitter political debate, within Japan, over U.S.-Japan security arrangements and the proposed integration of Japan into the Cold War era Western military alliance system. So much of the commission's work, then, of necessity had to be focused upon what had been intended as only one point among many in its constitutional agenda: Article 9, and the renunciation-of-war provisions of the 1946 charter. In oral and written submissions made to the commission 20 years ago, the present reviewer and others had suggested that there was nothing in Article 9 preventing the Japanese Government from maintaining military forces for purposes of self-defense or in fulfillment of obligations under the UN Charter; and so it has proved to be.

The Japanese Constitution remains essentially the same today as it was in 1946, in spite of the excellent report of Takayanagi's commission, confirming several key propositions that other countries (including Canada, Switzerland, and West Germany) have come to recognize with their own attempts at constitutional revision in recent years: *first*, unless there is a substantial and continuing popular consensus as to objectives, direction, and pace of proposed constitutional novation, even the best prepared efforts are likely to be stillborn; and, *second*, provided a people is endowed, sufficiently, with pragmatism and common sense and what Learned Hand called the "spirit of moderation," even a not completely satisfying or up-to-date charter can indeed be successfully adjusted, on an incremental, case-by-case basis, to rapidly changing societal conditions and demands.

EDWARD MCWHINNEY, Q.C.
Simon Fraser University

Legal Problems of Japanese-Americans: Their History and Development in the United States. By Moritoshi Fukuda. Tokyo: Keio Tsushin Co., Ltd., 1980. Pp. xix, 220. Index.

Rarely have books written by Japanese scholars been reviewed in this *Journal.* With the single exception of Judge Shigeru Oda of the ICJ, much of the Japanese international legal thought has remained inaccessible to the outside world. As the hope of the Japanese elite for a more active role in world affairs commensurate to its economic power increases, the paucity of contemporary Japanese scholars' contribution to accessible international law literature presents a glaring contradiction. Dr. Fukuda happily breaks that silence.

The book is a product of Fukuda's JSD thesis presented to the University of Michigan Law School in 1978 under the supervision of Professor William W. Bishop, Jr. The book is divided into three chapters: "Naturalization and Immigration"; "Common Occupations and Alien Rights Not relating to Land Law"; and "Alien Land Laws: Constitutional and Treaty Issues." In each chapter the author examines trends in decisions and analyzes conditions that accounted for these decisions "from the standpoint of international law and civil rights awareness" (p. iv). The author carefully covers most of the legal problems encountered by Japanese immigrants in the United States, examining not only particular cases relating to Japanese but also cases of other immigrants similarly situated. But there is a conspicuous omission of one tragic event in the history of the treatment of Japanese-Americans and aliens: the relocation of Japanese during World War II. Discussing the McCarran-Walter Act of 1952 that finally allowed the Japanese the right to naturalization, the author makes a passing reference to "a certain amount of guilt feeling from the imprisonment of Japanese-American citizens and aliens in relocation centers" (p. 69). Why the question was omitted is nowhere explained. Professor Bishop simply notes in his preface that it is not treated in the book (p. vi). It is puzzling why such an important question was omitted from the history of the legal problems of Japanese-Americans. The relocation of Japanese-Americans during the war was a culmination of nonrecognition of minority cultures in the United States. Fukuda misses the overall context of U.S.-Japanese relations in which legal problems developed.

After the establishment of the modern state in 1868, Japan emerged as a power in the Pacific through the Sino-Japanese War of 1895 and the Russo-Japanese War of 1905. As the United States entered the Pacific arena by the annexation of Hawaii in 1898 and the subsequent acquisition of the Philippines in the wake of the Spanish-American War of 1898, Japan and the United States faced each other across the ocean as potential rivals. The history of U.S.-Japanese relations is a continuing conflict between the aspiration to power of Japan as an emerging state and the American desire to contain that aspiration. The Japanese efforts in 1919 to include, and President Woodrow Wilson's rejection of, the principle of racial equality in the preamble of the Covenant of the League of Nations epitomized that conflict.

Although immigration policy tends to vary in restrictiveness in accordance with changes in circumstances, Japanese immigrants in the United States for many years had to contend with a policy that negated and refused to recognize their culture. It was not until 1952 that this policy was altered in favor of human rights and freedom of movement for manpower, goods, services, and ideas. Such a shift will occur when elite groups feel secure economically and not threatened by violence. Thus, only after the surrender of Japan in 1945 and the conclusion of the U.S.-Japan Security Treaty of 1951 were Japanese granted the right to naturalization. In such a historical context, it is difficult to accept the author's attribution of "the origin of these discriminatory legal problems" to "times of inexperienced and unsophisticated diplomatic negotiations and weak treaty settlements" (p. x).

Notwithstanding these shortcomings, the book offers many useful points of reflection for both Americans and Japanese. As Japan's increasing economic power competes against American interests in many areas, it is for Americans to ask whether the present trade friction between the two countries allegedly caused by Japan's "unfair trade practices" is historically rooted in their own prejudices against the "nonwhites" or "cheap labor," often used to discriminate against Japanese immigrants in the past. As the early Japanese immigrants suffered in the United States, because of different cultural backgrounds on the basis of the principle that "the real assimilation of aliens depended on their cultural associations before entering the United States" (p. 60), so it is for Japanese to ask whether their own treatment of Indochinese refugees in the past few years was in fact a repetition of what Japanese immigrants in the United States suffered. Furthermore, it is for Japanese to ask themselves whether their treatment of Koreans in Japan[1] meets the criteria they demanded of the United States for the protection of Japanese aliens in the United States.

EISUKE SUZUKI
Asian Development Bank

Gunboat Diplomacy 1919–1979 (2d ed.). By James Cable. New York: St. Martin's Press, 1981. Pp. 288. Index. $25.

Anyone who believes that gunboat diplomacy is a thing of the past will do well to read this excellent book. In the first edition, which appeared in 1971, the author broke new ground by analyzing the political applications of limited naval force since the close of World War I. He carefully examined the 50-year period in order to support his thesis that the use or threat of limited naval force is still one of the important techniques used by governments to secure advantages or to avoid losses in their international relationships. His findings supported his thesis and his book rapidly became a classic in the field of naval history.

Now, 10 years later, he returns to his subject matter in order to determine whether his original findings have stood the test of time. Did the events of the 1970's destroy the validity of the conclusions he drew from his earlier research? He leaves no doubt on that score, for he points out that governments have either threatened or used naval force on more than 60 occasions between 1970 and 1979. During the last decade, in other words, limited naval force was employed with "undiminished frequence" and often achieved the purpose for which it was initiated. The revised edition contains a meaty chapter analyzing what has happened since the first edition appeared.

In approaching his subject matter, the writer attaches considerable importance to definitions. "Gunboat diplomacy," he points out, "is the use or threat of limited naval force, otherwise than as an act of war, in order to secure advantage, or to avert loss, either in the furtherance of an international dispute or else against foreign nationals within the territory or the jurisdiction of their own state."

[1] *See* C. LEE, G. DE VOS ET AL., KOREANS IN JAPAN: ETHNIC CONFLICT AND ACCOMMODATION (1981).

Throughout his book the author remains carefully within the confines of his own definition. He is not concerned with revolutionary acts, or acts of war, or the use of naval force by governments in the repression of their own subjects. Nor is he concerned with the moral issues involved in the use of naval force. The principal question he raises is how the major naval powers, in the years ahead, might wish, or be able, to use their naval resources in order to further their foreign policy objectives.

As we look into a very uncertain future, the importance of this book becomes apparent. There are a good many constraints on the use of American military power to exert our influence in the world—including the sensitivity in the post-Vietnam era to using our troops abroad, and all the implications involved in a rapidly changing nuclear balance. On the other hand, with Soviet expansionism in high gear, and with trouble arising all over the world, the United States will undoubtedly be confronted with a good many situations in which the use of limited naval force might appear to be the most effective method of protecting American interests.

Here we run head-on into the points raised by Cable in a new chapter (Appendix II) in which he outlines the sea changes that have taken place in the 1970's. The most striking feature of the decade, he writes, has been the decline in numerical superiority of the U.S. Navy. Of course numerical comparisons alone do not give us a very solid base for judging the relative naval strength of the United States and the Soviet Union. But the decline in numerical superiority—and the persistent growth in Soviet naval power—does impose certain limitations on any possible expansion of the use of limited naval force by the United States in the future. Even though the United States is "still the *prima donna* of limited naval warfare, it is no longer the *prima donna assoluta*."

I repeat what I said at the outset: this is an excellent book. Its value is greatly enhanced by a fine bibliography and by an updated table of some two hundred incidents illustrative of the use by governments of limited naval warfare in various parts of the world during the past 60 years. The author has every right to be proud of his product, for it is thoroughly researched, its content is interesting and important, and it is quite well written. I recommend it highly for students and practitioners of international relations, for diplomats and naval officers, and for others interested in the U.S. Navy and its relation to American foreign policy.

FRANCIS O. WILCOX
The Atlantic Council of the United States

The Literature of Terrorism: A Selectively Annotated Bibliography. Compiled by Edward F. Mickolus. Westport: Greenwood Press, 1980. Pp. xi, 553. Indexes. $55.

During the last dozen years there has been a numerical explosion of popular and academic terrorism studies, which in turn has brought forth the publication of several significant terrorism bibliographies. One of the largest and most extensive bibliographic surveys is that of CIA analyst Dr. Edward Mickolus, who has achieved a substantial reputation in terrorism scholarship. This compilation is based upon Mickolus's earlier CIA annotated bibliography published in December 1976, although considerably enlarged since then.

The book contains 14 major topical divisions, including special sections on terrorist tactics, state terrorism, responses to terrorism, the media and terrorism, guerrilla warfare, and even a brief survey of terrorism in fiction. All of the legal entries are included as subdivisions of the major category labeled "Responses," and contain sections on the law of war, extradition, domestic legislation, state responsibility, self-help, hijacking, and international legal conventions. Approximately half the references are annotated, though many of the annotations are quite brief, and there is a fair amount of cross-referencing. The great majority of entries are in English, but a number of foreign studies are cited as well.

The focus of the compilation is contemporary, emphasizing the literature of the past two decades. Several 19th-century Russian sources, such as the *Revolutionary Catechism* of Sergei Nechayev, are also scattered throughout the book. The sections on potential nuclear threats and on psychological and medical approaches are particularly noteworthy. However, the entries in the subsection entitled "Disaster Response" do not seem to be very relevant or useful.

Aside from a number of odd choices and several erroneous citations, the difficulty with this massive listing is that it often repeats the same entry in different sections, gives both the conference paper and the subsequent article, and sometimes lists items as being "in press" or "forthcoming," when in fact they were actually published several years earlier. Newspaper articles and "op-ed" columns are given from such papers as the *Christian Science Monitor* and the *Washington Post* without explanation for their inclusion, and there are similar references to *Time* and *Newsweek* articles. Inevitably, the author's selections do not always coincide with a reader's preferences.

In sum, this compilation is extensive, detailed, and useful. However, both students and scholars should apply some caution in relying upon it without also referring to the original sources.

ROBERT A. FRIEDLANDER
Ohio Northern University

Agreements of the People's Republic of China: A Calendar of Events 1966–1980. By Hungdah Chiu. New York: Praeger Publishers, 1981. Pp. xvii, 329. Index.

In 1968, Douglas M. Johnston and Hungdah Chiu co-compiled some two thousand titles of agreements concluded by the People's Republic of China (PRC) in *Agreements of the People's Republic of China, 1949–1967: A Calendar.*[1]

[1] Published by Harvard University Press and reviewed in this *Journal*, 64 AJIL 199–201 (1970), by this reviewer.

In the volume under review, one of the co-compilers has updated the compilation to 1980.

The present volume follows in general the methodology adopted for its predecessor: chronological arrangement of bilateral and multilateral agreements according to the dates of signature, grouping of bilateral and trilateral agreements under the alphabetical headings of non-Chinese parties, and listing of agreements by subject matter. Like the first *Calendar*, the present one contains some two thousand agreements, ranging from matters of local and semi-governmental nature, such as water supply from Dongjiang to Hong Kong, a tourism "contract" between Pan American Airways and China Travel Service, and the pairing of sister cities (*e.g.*, Tianjin-Melbourne, Beijing-New York, Venice-Xuzhou) and provinces (Hubei-Ohio, Guangdong-New South Wales), to the more politically significant events, such as military aid agreements with North Vietnam and North Korea and the PRC-U.S. Joint Communiqué establishing diplomatic relations effective January 1, 1979. Because of interruptions of many publications, including the *Treaty Series of the People's Republic of China*, during the Cultural Revolution, the present volume fills an important void, and is to be welcomed by all those interested in Chinese treaty law.

A methodological problem concerns the appropriateness of classifying periodic reports of an organization established by an agreement as "agreements" themselves. A case in point is the establishment of a Chinese-Tanzanian Joint Shipping Line in 1966 (items 66–31 and 66–82), whose Board of Directors meets once a year alternately in Beijing and Dar es Salaam and issues an annual report ("Protocol"). Such reports should either be classified as "agreements," and thus be included in the volume, or not so classified, and thus excluded. In actual fact, the volume includes only the reports of 1969 (3d meeting, 69–29), 1973 (7th meeting, 73–96), and 1979 (13th meeting, 79–91), leaving open the question of what happened to the 11 other reports (through 1980).

Similarly, under the U.S.-China Agreement on Scientific and Technical Cooperation signed in January 1979 (79–17), a number of protocols were adopted covering such subjects as atmospheric science and technology, fishery and marine science and technology, medicine and public health, and earthquake studies and environmental protection (totaling now 17 protocols, including three new ones in 1981). To implement these protocols, a number of joint working groups were established, meeting alternately in Beijing and Washington, whose reports are listed as "accords" or "documents" (80–13 and 80–14). But should these reports be properly classified as "agreements"? To do so would either clutter future calendars or detract from their completeness.

On the other hand, there is no question that these reports yield a wealth of valuable information on China's implementation of agreements. For example, access to the Chinese-Tanzanian reports would have revealed that the Joint Shipping Line has expanded from a fleet of two 10,000-ton ships, acquired with an initial Chinese capital of £1,500,000, to the present five-vessel fleet plying between Dar es Salaam and Chinese as well as European ports on a commercially competitive basis. In contrast to the recent bankruptcy of the East African Shipping Line and the near-bankruptcy of Ghana's Black Star Line, the prospering of the Chinese-Tanzanian Line must be deemed a remarkable feat and should provide useful lessons to development planners.

It is to be hoped that the compilation of the titles of agreements can be followed by that of the texts of the agreements themselves. In this regard, mention should be made of recent exchanges of legal materials between the Asia Foundation and Beijing and Jilin Universities, portending perhaps a beginning of a comprehensive compilation of agreements, for which the two *Calendars* published to date constitute an essential first step. Chiu is to be congratulated for his contributions to the development of these very useful research tools on Chinese treaty law.

LUKE T. LEE
U.S. Department of State

BRIEFER NOTICES

The Dynamics of Human Rights in U.S. Foreign Policy. Edited by Natalie Kaufman Hevener. (New Brunswick and London: Transaction Books, 1981. Pp. ix, 374. Index. $19.95.) This collection of essays includes contributions on diverse topics relating to the theme of the human rights concerns manifested in the foreign policy of the United States. Each essay was drafted as a contribution to a series of colloquiums held at the University of South Carolina during the 1978–1979 academic year. The authors are, in the main, academic lawyers and political scientists. A series of appendixes include the texts of the Universal Declaration of Human Rights, the two International Covenants of 1966, relevant portions of the U.S. Foreign Assistance Act of 1961, and a table of signatures to and ratifications of the Covenants.

The volume might be of use to the political science or law teacher seeking a one-volume book of supplemental readings for student use in a course on international protection of human rights. The first four essays, by Paul M. Kattenburg, Richard A. Falk, Robert L. Borosage, and Louis B. Sohn place the discussion in a general foreign policy context. Essays grouped in part IV of the collection explore the role of interest groups and Congress in creating U.S. human rights policy, and assess the net contribution of the United States in the field. The greatest portion of the book, seven essays, addresses American contributions to the advancement of specific rights in international law and diplomacy. Specific topics discussed in these essays include self-determination of peoples, economic and social rights, arms control, minority rights, apartheid, and political repression in the Americas.

The scope and quality of the essays collected vary significantly. Particularly thorough are the treatment of the role of interest groups (especially NGO's) in the formulation of U.S. policy, by David Weissbrodt, and Robert G. Wirsing's study of the evolution of the legal status of minorities from the

League of Nations era to the present day. The concluding essay, written by Richard B. Lillich in the closing months of the Carter administration, is a particularly effective summary of U.S. practices and laws that stand to advance the cause of international protection of human rights.

J. DAVID FINE
Loyola University Law School, New Orleans

Gendai Senso Hohki Ron (The Modern Laws of War). By Sumio Adachi. (Tokyo: Keiseisha Co., Ltd., 1979. Pp. vii, 380. Index. ¥2300.) This comprehensive introduction describes numerous aspects of the contemporary rules of conventional warfare. Sumio Adachi, lecturer at the National Defense Academy of Japan, provides not only an exacting descriptive analysis but also more than adequate bibliographical references throughout.

The underlying assumption of Adachi's study is that to understand the adequacy (and the recognized inadequacy) of law as a restraint on international violence it is necessary to understand the diversity of conflict. Part of the problem of understanding war in the contemporary world is the difficulty of classifying war and armed conflict according to legal and illegal uses. Consequently, Adachi not only defines acts of war and armed conflict but also applicable laws, rules, and regulations.

Beginning with an introductory consideration of war and armed conflict, Adachi proceeds to discuss fundamental principles and laws of warfare, modernization and development of the laws of war, hostilities, belligerency, methods of warfare, weapons and weapon systems, maritime and air warfare, treatment of the wounded and sick, medical care and installations, prisoners of war, protection of civilian populations, protection of cultural property, occupation, violations of the laws of war, war crimes, neutrality, terrorism, and civil war.

Each chapter explicates possible dimensions of each topic. For example, the chapter on weapons includes consideration of weapons inflicting unnecessary pain, incendiary weapons, biochemical weapons, mines, rockets, and missiles, nuclear weapons, and weapons directed at the destruction of humanity.

Adachi continually expresses his concern for the human costs of warfare, arguing that law should have as its primary purpose the protection of individual life. The result of this effort is the "handbook" nature of the presentation and the excellent opportunity for non-Japanese scholars to become familiar with Japanese terminology and vocabulary. If there is any flaw, it comes from the overwhelming dependence on established source material. But even in the presentation of these materials, there is an effort to include representation from all dominant schools of thought. Somewhat neglected is reference to Asian theories, rules, and principles of warfare. Inclusion of more Asian material would have made this study more useful.

L. JEROLD ADAMS
Central Missouri State University

Terrorism: A Challenge to the State. Edited by Juliet Lodge. (New York: St. Martin's Press, 1981. Pp. 230. Index. $25.) This book ought to be titled "A Challenge to the West European State," as it deals exclusively with Western

European nations and Western European collective political institutions. Chapters address terrorism problems in the Federal Republic of Germany, Italy, France, the Netherlands, and Ireland. The last two chapters describe the European Community's approach to terrorism with particular emphasis on domestic and international legal solutions.

The chapter on terrorism in France, written by Philip G. Cerny, is very useful. It provides both an analytical and historical viewpoint of a phenomenon that is not well understood in the United States. With the recent increase in international terrorism in France it is a particularly welcome addition to the literature in English on terrorism in France.

The stress in the last two chapters on legal aspects of the response by the EEC and the Council of Europe to the problem of terrorism will be welcomed by readers of this *Journal*. However, no mention is made of important activities in the field of intelligence cooperation, as well as senior-level, ministerial groupings such as the Trevi Group and the Club of Five.

This is a useful book for the student of European terrorism.

RICHARD J. HIGGINS
U.S. Department of State

Arbitration Law in Europe. By the International Chamber of Commerce. (Paris: ICC Services, 1981. Pp. 368. $65.) This book provides useful introductory information concerning the arbitration laws of 17 European countries outside the Soviet orbit, plus appendixes containing leading arbitration conventions. The format applied to the arbitration law of each country sets forth general characteristics of the national law, definitions of principal terms, and a brief description of practice, sources, and law on choice of law, place of arbitration, procedure, and enforcement.

Practitioners in arbitration are not likely to find the foregoing information a sufficient basis upon which to form substantial decisions. In the opinion of this reviewer, it is advisable, if not necessary, to consult with counsel experienced in the pertinent law before making any important decision with regard to it. However, as a short introduction to the law involved, and as a beginning point from which to explore it, the book is a good start.

ARTHUR R. ALBRECHT
Of the California Bar

European Community Law and National Law. The Irreversible Transfer? By John Usher. (Winchester: Allen & Unwin, Inc., 1981, for the University Association for Contemporary European Studies. Pp. 96. Index. $15.95, cloth; $6.95, paper.) This is a concise survey prepared for students following introductory courses on the European Communities. While there is a great deal of literature discussing the constitutional and theoretical relationship between Community law and the laws of the member states, Usher takes a more practical approach. He is concerned with the degree to which Community law produces effects in the member states' legal systems through the legal mechanisms making Community rules enforceable by or against individuals and enterprises. Usher states very clearly and concisely the distinction between the "direct applicability" of regulations, as provided for in the Rome Treaty, and the "direct effect" of directives, as developed in the case law. The importance of this distinction was again seen recently in the Court of Justice Judgment of January 19, 1982 in *Ursula Becker v. Finanzamt Münster-Innenstadt*.[1]

The survey also examines the actual practice of the transfer of power from the national to the Community level by discussing three selected areas: common organization of agricultural markets, common policies, and harmonization of laws. In this part we see how far Community legislation has gone, especially in the agricultural area, so that states now have only limited rights to act in many areas. Of great importance for the future is the manner in which the Community's powers have been expanding. What once was considered to be an organization of limited, defined powers has been able to extend its activities into other related areas. For example, much of the Community's work in the environmental area could be considered by a strict constructionist as falling outside the Community's competence. The Commission's activities in external representation of the Community are also often cited as another example of the Community's expanding powers.

THAD W. SIMONS, JR.
Brussels

International Business Transactions in a Nutshell. By Donald T. Wilson. (St. Paul: West Publishing Co., 1981. Pp. lvii, 393. Index. $7.95.) This volume is a welcome addition to the West Nutshell series. It reflects the increased recognition in this country of the growing interdependence of nations and their attendant interlocking trade and investment ties.

This ambitious work provides an overview of a number of subject areas of import to those interested in international commercial affairs. Of particular use to the practitioner are chapters describing the role of corporate counsel to a transnational corporation, the selection of local counsel in foreign lands, and the negotiation of written agreements. Of interest also to students of international relations are chapters delineating the framework of various regional institutions, such as the European Economic Community, the Andean Common Market, and the Association of South East Asian Nations. After discussing the competition law of the European Economic Community and the extraterritorial reach of U.S. antitrust laws, the author reviews the problems of moving goods, people, money, and information across national borders. Finally, there are discussions of the programs of the Overseas Private Investment Corporation, the act of state doctrine, the doctrine of sovereign immunity, and the increasingly important area of dispute resolution.

The author has accomplished the difficult task of distilling the important facets of a diverse and sometimes complex subject in an interesting and easily readable manner. This work should serve as a valuable resource tool for student and practitioner alike.

LEO H. PHILLIPS, JR.
Overseas Private Investment Corporation

Anti-Dumping Law in a Liberal Trade Order. By Richard Dale. (New York: St. Martin's Press, 1980. Pp. xv, 237. Index. $22.50.) This book will be valuable to both economists and lawyers. While the legal aspects of international trade, and especially of dumping, may be complex, the economics of

[1] Case 8/81, [1982] 1 Comm. Mkt. L.R. 499.

the subject are truly arcane. Fortunately, Dale succeeds in combining the two highly interrelated aspects of the subject into a marvelously readable and understandable text.

Dumping is generally defined as engaging in sales abroad at prices below domestic cost. Virtually all of the essential economic and legal doctrine on the subject relies on Jacob Viner's seminal work, *Dumping: A Problem in International Trade*, published in 1923. As Dale points out, and as is painfully obvious from the text, little has really been added in the 60 ensuing years, despite the radical changes in the international economy and the abundant literature on international trade.

The essential thrust of Dale's study is to question whether Viner's basic assumptions regarding the nature of dumping can apply in today's world. For example, he notes that Viner relies too heavily on notions of cost rather than those of duration and/or predatory conduct. While Viner claims that "dumping prices are presumptive evidence of abnormal and temporary cheapness," he finds this assertion unsupported by sufficient empirical study (p. 33). In questioning the economic foundations of dumping legislation, Dale raises serious questions regarding the usefulness of the laws themselves. His conclusions are bold and unambiguous: "anti-dumping provisions have, in their implementation, become an impediment to international trade and a threat to the liberal trade order" (p. 192).

Dale reviews the antidumping legislation of the major trading nations with a critical eye, and his proposals regarding cost definition and material injury deserve some serious consideration, particularly in light of his general indictment of antidumping regulation as it exists today. The author, however, does not ask that his analysis be accepted on mere faith. Each chapter has extensive footnotes and Dale includes a comprehensive bibliography and a series of appendixes to complement what is one of the better treatments of the dumping question in many years.

JOHN R. LACEY
Hartford, Connecticut

Netherlands Yearbook of International Law. Vol. XII, 1981. T. M. C. Asser Institute, The Hague. (Alphen aan den Rijn and Germantown: Sijthoff & Noordhoff, 1981. Pp. 438. Index. Dfl.80; $40.) In accordance with the arrangement followed in previous years, this useful volume includes, in addition to signed leading articles, a current account of Dutch state practice, treaties to which the Netherlands is a party, Dutch municipal legislation with international impact, judicial decisions involving international law, and scholarly literature. The articles deal with the law of the sea, the right to leave and return to the country, international maritime cartels, and the international energy agency.

Several interesting judicial decisions may be noted. In an action by the "Democratic Republic of East Timor" to prevent the Dutch Government from permitting delivery of war vessels to Indonesia, the court held, with respect to the standing of the "Republic" to sue, that this question must be decided by a Dutch court of law "on the basis of the factual criteria for statehood as laid down in international law." In that connection, "the fact that the Netherlands and practically the whole of the international community do not recognize the Republic is not of decisive importance" (p. 303). This stout assertion of judicial independence contrasts with the policy of American courts, which, since the days of John Marshall, have deferred to the executive branch on issues involving recognition of foreign states.

In determining that conscripts could be sent without their consent to Lebanon to take part in UN peacekeeping forces, the Supreme Court held that this was permitted by Article 33(1)(c) of a 1922 statute authorizing service outside Europe "in . . . exceptional circumstances, subject to authorization by the Crown," although not permitted by Article 33(1)(d), which authorizes such service "in normal times, provided it is to be anticipated that their period of service will not be exceeded." The Court reasoned that the mere fact that "normal times" prevailed in the Netherlands did not justify reliance on this provision, since the dangerous, abnormal circumstances in Lebanon must also be taken into account (pp. 355–56).

An interesting labor dispute involved a decision by the British-American Tobacco Company to transfer its Amsterdam branch to Brussels, with a loss of 250 jobs. The Amsterdam court of appeal annulled this decision since the company had acted "in breach of the basic principles of proper management." The chairman of the company at a stockholders' meeting had indicated its acceptance of "OECD guidelines as a basis for its policy." The guidelines are based on the principle that in cases of this sort the enterprise should consult with employee representatives. Hence the decision to transfer was premature and contrary to the applicable rules of collective bargaining (pp. 357–58).

EDWARD DUMBAULD
U.S. Senior District Judge

BOOKS RECEIVED*

International Law—General

Bothe, Michael, and Raul E. Vinuesa (eds.). *International Law and Municipal Law.* German-Argentinian Constitutional Law Colloquium. Berlin: Duncker & Humblot, 1982. Pp. 322. DM 116.

Jennings, R. Y., and Ian Brownlie (eds.). *The British Year Book of International Law, 1980.* Vol. 51. New York: The Clarendon Press; Oxford University Press, 1982. Pp. ix, 511. Index. $96.

Polish Yearbook of International Law, Vol. X, 1979–1980. Warsaw: Polish Academy of Sciences, Institute of State and Law, 1981. Pp. 345. Bibliography. Zl.130.

South African Yearbook of International Law, Volume 6, 1980. Pretoria: The VerLoren van Themaat Centre for International Law, 1981. Pp. xiii, 257. Index. R18,00.

Von Münch, Ingo, in collaboration with Philip Kunig. *Völkerrecht in programmierter Form* (2d ed.). Berlin and New York: Walter de Gruyter & Co., 1982. Pp. xv, 484. Index. DM 58; $29.

International Economic Law & Relations

Mann, F. A. *The Legal Aspect of Money. With special reference to Comparative Private and Public International Law* (4th ed.). New York: The Clarendon Press; Oxford University Press, 1982. Pp. lvi, 602. Index. $69.

* Mention here neither assures nor precludes later review.

Postlewaite, Philip F., and Michael P. Collins. *International Individual Taxation.* Colorado Springs: Shepard's/McGraw-Hill, 1982. Pp. xxv, 507. Index.

Reynolds, Paul D. *China's International Banking and Financial System.* New York: Praeger Publishers, 1982. Pp. xvii, 221. Index. $23.95.

Rubin, Seymour J., and Thomas R. Graham (eds.). *Environment and Trade: The Relation of International Trade and Environmental Policy.* Published under the auspices of The American Society of International Law. Totowa: Allenheld, Osmun & Co. Publishers; London: Frances Pinter (Publishers) Ltd, 1982. Pp. xi, 209. Index. $29.50.

Stoll, Jutta. *Vereinbarungen zwischen Staat und ausländischem Investor.* Berlin, Heidelberg, New York: Springer-Verlag, 1982. Pp. xi, 166. DM 49; $21.80.

VerLoren van Themaat, Pieter. *The Changing Structure of International Economic Law.* The Hague, Boston, London: Martinus Nijhoff Publishers; The Hague: T.M.C. Asser Institute, 1981. Pp. xxv, 395. Dfl.165; $72.

Law of the Sea & Maritime Law

Koh, Kheng-Lian. *Straits in International Navigation: Contemporary Issues.* London, Rome, New York: Oceana Publications, Inc., 1982. Pp. xi, 225. Index. $35.

Use of Force & Law of War

Levie, Howard S. *Protection of War Victims: Protocol I to the 1949 Geneva Conventions.* Vol. IV. Dobbs Ferry: Oceana Publications, Inc., 1981. Pp. xiii, 535. Index. $37.50.

Roberts, Adam, and Richard Guelff (eds.). *Documents on the Laws of War.* New York: The Clarendon Press; Oxford University Press, 1982. Pp. xi, 498. Index. $34.50, cloth; $17.95, paper.

Yin, John. *The Soviet Views on the Use of Force in International Law.* Hong Kong: Asian Research Service, 1980. Pp. 189. Index.

Dispute Settlement

Elkind, Jerome B. *Interim Protection: A Functional Approach.* The Hague, Boston, London: Martinus Nijhoff Publishers, 1981. Pp. xxiv, 287. Index. Dfl.140; $59.

Human Rights

Henkin, Louis (ed.). *The International Bill of Rights: The Covenant on Civil and Political Rights.* New York: Columbia University Press, 1981. Pp. x, 523. Index. $35.

Maneli, Mieczyslaw. *Juridical Positivism and Human Rights.* New York: Hippocrene Books, 1981. Pp. 406. Index.

Transnational Legal Problems of Refugees. 1982 Michigan Yearbook of International Legal Studies. New York: Clark Boardman Company, Ltd., 1982. Pp. xii, 646. Index. $55.

Morrisson, Clovis C., Jr. *The Dynamics of Development in the European Human Rights Convention System.* The Hague, Boston, London: Martinus Nijhoff Publishers, 1981. Pp. xii, 176. Dfl.100; $39.50.

Novak, Michael (ed.). *Liberation South, Liberation North.* Washington and London: American Enterprise Institute for Public Policy Research, 1981. Pp. 99.

Van Boven, Theo. *People Matter. Views on International Human Rights Policy.* Amsterdam: Meulenhoff Nederland bv, 1982. Pp. 186. Dfl.34.50; Sw.F.25; $13.

Environment & Natural Resources

Hakapää, Kari. *Marine Pollution in International Law. Material Obligations and Jurisdiction, with Special Reference to the Third United Nations Conference on the Law of the Sea.* Helsinki: Suomalainen Tiedeakatemia, 1981. Pp. 341. Indexes.

World Petroleum Arrangements, 1980. Vols. I and II. New York: The Barrows Company Inc., 1981. Vol. I: pp. 84; vol. II: pp. 492. $285 for 2 vols.

Air & Space Law

Gorove, Stephen (ed.). *United States Space Law: National and International Regulation.* Binder II. London, Rome, New York: Oceana Publications, Inc., 1982. $85.

Heere, Wybo P. (comp.). *International Bibliography of Air Law. Supplement 1977–1980.* The Hague, Boston, London: Martinus Nijhoff Publishers, 1981. Pp. xxxviii, 356. Indexes. Dfl.160; $69.50.

International Organizations

Galenson, Walter. *The International Labor Organization: An American View.* Madison: The University of Wisconsin Press, 1981. Pp. xi, 351. Index. $21.50, cloth; $7.75, paper.

Özgür, Özdemir A. *Apartheid: The United Nations and Peaceful Change in South Africa.* Dobbs Ferry: Transnational Publishers, Inc., 1982. Pp. xx, 220. Index. $25.

Rajan, M. S. *The Expanding Jurisdiction of the United Nations.* Bombay: N. M. Tripathi Private Ltd.; Dobbs Ferry: Oceana Publications, Inc., 1982. Pp. xii, 252. Index. $30.

Spencer, Robert, John Kirton, and Kim Richard Nossal (eds.). *The International Joint Commission Seventy Years On.* Toronto: The Centre for International Studies, University of Toronto, 1981. Pp. xiv, 158. Index. $10.

European Community Law

Bebr, Gerhard. *Development of Judicial Control of the European Communities.* The Hague, Boston, London: Martinus Nijhoff Publishers, 1981. Pp. xviii, 822. Index. Dfl.360; $150.

Touscoz, Jean, et al. *La Communauté Economique Européenne Elargie et la Méditerranée: Quelle Coopération?* Paris: Presses Universitaires de France, 1982. Pp. 471.

U.S. Law of Foreign Relations

Foreign Relations of the United States, 1950, Volume IV: Central and Eastern Europe; The Soviet Union. (Dept. of State Pub. 8987.) Washington: U.S. Govt. Printing Office, 1980. Pp. xi, 1548. Index.

Foreign Relations of the United States, 1951, Volume III: European Security and the German Question. Part 1, Dept. of State Pub. 8982. Part 2, Dept. of State Pub. 9113. Washington: U.S. Govt. Printing Office, 1981. Pp. xxxiv, 2065. Index in part 2.

National Security

Albinski, Henry. *The Australian-American Security Relationship. A Regional and International Perspective.* New York: St. Martin's Press, 1982. Pp. 257. Index.

Strengthening Deterrence: NATO and the Credibility of Western Defense in the 1980s. The Atlantic Council Working Group on the Credibility of the NATO Deterrent. Cambridge: Ballinger Publishing Co., 1982. Pp. xvii, 270. Index. $24.50.

Ebinger, Charles K., Project Director, The Center for Strategic and International Studies. *The Critical Link: Energy and National Security in the 1980s.* Cambridge: Ballinger Publishing Co., 1982. Pp. xxx, 260. Index. $29.75.

Gutteridge, William, assisted by Marion Dobrosielski and Jorma Miettinen. *European Security, Nuclear Weapons and Public Confidence.* New York: St. Martin's Press, 1982. Pp. 236. Index. $27.50.

Robertson, K. G. *Public Secrets: A Study in the Development of Government Security.* New York: St. Martin's Press, 1982. Pp. 216. Index. $25.

Regional & Foreign Law & Politics

England, Joe, and John Rear. *Industrial Relations and Law in Hong Kong.* New York: Oxford University Press, 1981. Pp. xviii, 421. Index. $45.

Horn, Norbert, Hein Kötz, and Hans G. Leser. *German Private and Commercial Law: An Introduction.* Translated by Tony Weir. New York: The Clarendon Press; Oxford University Press, 1982. Pp. xvi, 355. Index. $39, cloth; $24.95, paper.

Schulz, Eberhard. *Die Deutsche Nation in Europa.* Bonn: Europa Union Verlag GmbH, 1982. Pp. 272. Index.

Venkatachalam, Viswanathan, and Rajiva K. Singh. *The Political, Economic, and Labor Climate in India.* Philadelphia: Industrial Research Unit, The Wharton School, University of Pennsylvania, 1982. Pp. xi, 147. Index. $18.

International Relations & Politics

Atallah, Daad Bou Malhab. *Le Liban—Guerre Civile ou Conflit International?* Printed in Beirut. Pp. 284. Distributed by Librairie Générale de Droit et de Jurisprudence, Paris. F.102,70.

Hare, J. E., and Cary B. Joynt. *Ethics and International Affairs*. New York: St. Martin's Press, 1982. Pp. 208. $25.

Horowitz, Irving Louis. *Beyond Empire and Revolution: Militarization and Consolidation in the Third World*. New York: Oxford University Press, 1982. Pp. xxvii, 321. Index. $19.95, cloth; $7.95, paper.

Martin, Pierre-Marie. *Introduction aux relations internationales*. Toulouse: Editions Privat, 1982. Pp. 221. Indexes. F.60,00.

Plano, Jack C., Robert E. Riggs, and Helenan S. Robin (eds.). *The Dictionary of Political Analysis* (2d ed.). Santa Barbara: ABC-Clio, Inc.; Oxford: Clio Press Ltd., 1982. Pp. xvi, 197. Index. $19.75, cloth; $9.75, paper.

Plano, Jack C., and Roy Olton. *The International Relations Dictionary* (3d ed.). Santa Barbara: ABC-Clio, Inc.; Oxford: Clio Press Ltd., 1982. Pp. xxvi, 488. Index. $19.75, cloth; $9.75, paper.

Till, Geoffrey. *Maritime Strategy and the Nuclear Age*. New York: St. Martin's Press, 1982. Pp. 274. Index. $35.

Treaty Law

Ginsburgs, George, and Robert M. Slusser. *A Calendar of Soviet Treaties 1958–1973*. Alphen aan den Rijn and Rockville: Sijthoff & Noordhoff, 1981. Pp. xx, 908. Index. Dfl.300; $150.

Kavass, Igor I., and Adolf Sprudzs (comps.). *Current Treaty Index 1982: A Cumulative Index to the United States Slip Treaties and Agreements*. Buffalo: William S. Hein & Co., Inc., 1982. Pp. x, 253.

Miscellaneous

Antieau, Chester James. *Constitutional Construction*. London, Rome, New York: Oceana Publications, Inc., 1982. Pp. xxiv, 255. Index. $30.

The 1980s: Meeting a New Challenge. Selected Speeches of President Chun Doo Hwan. Seoul: Korea Textbook Co., Ltd., 1981. Pp. ix, 298. Index.

Makela, Klaus, Robin Room, Eric Single, Pekka Sulkunen, and Brendan Walsh. *Alcohol, Society, and the State. Vol. 1: A Comparative Study of Alcohol Control*. Toronto: Addiction Research Foundation, 1981. Pp. 143. Index.

Pooley, James. *Trade Secrets: How to Protect your Ideas and Assets*. Berkeley: Osborne/McGraw-Hill, 1982. Pp. 145. Index. $19.95.

Reukema, Barbara. *Discriminatory Refusal of Carriage in North America*. Deventer: Kluwer, 1982. Pp. 296. Dfl.160; $80.

Single, Eric, Patricia Morgan, and Jan de Lint (eds.). *Alcohol, Society, and the State. Vol. 2: The Social History of Control Policy in Seven Countries*. Toronto: Addiction Research Foundation, 1981. Pp. 200.

INTERNATIONAL LEGAL MATERIALS*

CONTENTS

VOL. XXI, NO. 3 (May 1982)

PAGE

TREATIES AND AGREEMENTS

People's Republic of China-Sweden: Agreement on the *Mutual Protection of Investments* 477

Eastern and Southern African States: Treaty for the *Establishment of a Preferential Trade Area* 479

LEGISLATION AND REGULATIONS

Andean Group: Commission Decision on *Andean Multinational Enterprises* 542

European Communities: Council Regulations and Decisions on *Suspending Imports from Argentina* 547

Union of Soviet Socialist Republics: Edict on Provisional Measures to Regulate *Soviet Enterprises for the Exploration and Exploitation of Mineral Resources* 551

JUDICIAL AND SIMILAR PROCEEDINGS

European Court of Human Rights:

Judgment in Dudgeon Case (*Criminal Laws in Northern Ireland; Interference with Private Life; Homosexual Restrictions*) 554

Judgment in Young, James and Webster Case (*British Rail Closed-Shop Agreement; Refusal to Join Trade Union; Freedom of Association*) 577

International Court of Justice: Corrected Order on the Written Pleadings Procedure in the Case concerning *Delimitation of the Maritime Boundary in the Gulf of Maine Area* 601

United States:

Court of Appeals for the Eleventh Circuit Decision in Haitian Refugee Center *v.* Smith (*Application for Political Asylum; Practices of the U.S. Immigration and Naturalization Service*) 603

Court of Appeals for the Second Circuit Decision in Libra Bank Limited *v.* Banco Nacional de Costa Rica (*Prejudgment Attachment; Foreign Sovereign Immunities Act; Waiver of Immunity*) 618

Court of Appeals for the Third Circuit Decision in Velidor *v.* L/P/G Benghazi (*Yugoslav Seamen's Claims; Foreign Sovereign Immunities Act; Service of Process*) ... 621

Supreme Court Case Sumitomo *v.* Avigliano—Brief for the United States as Amicus Curiae (*Employment Practices; Treaty of Friendship, Commerce and Navigation*) ... 629

Supreme Court Opinion in International Longshoremen's Association *v.* Allied International (*Russian Invasion of Afghanistan; Refusal to Unload Soviet Cargoes; Violation of U.S. Labor Law*) 652

Supreme Court Opinion in Weinberger *v.* Rossi (*Treaty Interpretation*) 660

OTHER DOCUMENTS

Council of Europe: Declaration on the *Freedom of Expression and Information* 667

Organization of American States: Twentieth Meeting of Consultation of Ministers of Foreign Affairs Resolutions on the *Serious Situation in the South Atlantic* 669

United Nations Environment Programme: Nairobi Declaration on the *State of Worldwide Environment* 676

* ILM subscription, $65; concessionary rate to ASIL members, $24. Address orders to ILM, 2223 Massachusetts Ave., NW, Wash., D.C. 20008. Outside U.S., please add $4.50.

PAGE

United Nations Security Council: Resolutions concerning the *Falklands Islands (Islas Malvinas)* 679
United States: Statements concerning *Assistance and Sales to Argentina* 682

RECENT ACTIONS REGARDING TREATIES TO WHICH THE UNITED STATES IS A PARTY 685
RECENT ACTIONS REGARDING TREATIES TO WHICH THE UNITED STATES IS NOT A PARTY 694
NOTICE OF RECENT DOCUMENTS (not reprinted) 696

VOL. XXI, NO. 4 (July 1982)

TREATIES AND AGREEMENTS
Asian Development Bank-Philippines: Agreement concerning *Asian Development Bank Staff Housing Requirements* 697
Australia-United States: Agreement relating to *Cooperation on Antitrust Matters* 702
Canada-Egypt: Agreement for *Cooperation in the Peaceful Uses of Nuclear Energy* 710
New York-Quebec: Agreement on *Acid Precipitation* 721

JUDICIAL AND SIMILAR PROCEEDINGS
International Centre for Settlement of Investment Disputes Arbitration Tribunal: *Award in the Case of AGIP Company v. Popular Republic of the Congo* 726
International Centre for Settlement of Investment Disputes Arbitration Tribunal: *Award in the Case of Benvenuti et Bonfant v. People's Republic of the Congo* 740
United States:
District Court for the Northern District of Illinois Decision in Jafari *v.* Iran (*Jurisdiction in Case Involving Former Iranian Nationals; Algerian Accords; U.S.-Iran Claims Tribunal; U.S. Foreign Sovereign Immunities Act*) 767
Court of Appeals for the Second Circuit Decision in Kunstsammlungen Zu Weimar and Grand Duchess of Saxony-Weimar *v.* Elicofon (*Act of State Doctrine; State Succession; Restitution of Art Treasures*) 773
Supreme Court Decision in Sumitomo Shoji America, Inc. *v.* Avagliano (*Friendship, Commerce and Navigation Treaties; Employment Practices of Japanese Subsidiary Incorporated in U.S.*) 790

LEGISLATION AND REGULATIONS
Canada: Act to Provide for *State Immunity in Canadian Courts* 798
China:
Foreign Enterprise Income Tax Law 802
Rules and Regulations to Implement the *Income Tax Law concerning Foreign Enterprises* 804
France:
Law on the *Exploration and Exploitation of Mineral Resources of the Deep Seabed* ... 808
Law of *Nationalization* 815
Federal Republic of Germany: Act to Amend the *Interim Regulation of Deep Seabed Mining* 832
United Kingdom:
Protection of Trading Interests Act 1980 and Exchange of Diplomatic Notes concerning the Act 834
Statement and Order concerning the *American Export Embargo with regard to the Soviet Gas Pipeline* 851
United States:
Department of Commerce International Trade Administration, Office of Export Administration—Foreign Policy Export Controls with Specific *Regulations concerning Trade with the U.S.S.R.* 853
Department of Commerce National Oceanic and Atmospheric Administration—Further Regulations on *Deep Seabed Mining* 867

PAGE

Federal Reserve System Rules concerning *International Banking Facilities*
Introductory Note 872
Final Rules 878

OTHER DOCUMENTS
Canada-European Communities-France-Federal Republic of Germany-Italy-Japan-United Kingdom-United States:
Final Communique of Eighth *Economic Summit* 882
Statement of *International Monetary Undertakings* 883
Council of Europe:
Recommendation on *Economic Crime* 884
Recommendation on the *Rights of Spouses relating to the Occupation of the Family Home and the Use of Household Contents* 887
Recommendation on the *Harmonisation of National Procedures relating to Asylum* . . 889
European Communities: Comments on the *U.S. Regulations concerning Trade with the U.S.S.R.* 891
North Atlantic Treaty Organization: Documents from the Bonn Summit
Declaration 905
Document on *Arms Control and Disarmament* 906
Document on *Integrated NATO Defense* 907
United Nations Security Council: Documents concerning the *U.N. Interim Force in Lebanon and the Israeli Incursion of Lebanon* 908

RECENT ACTIONS REGARDING TREATIES TO WHICH THE UNITED STATES IS A PARTY 921
RECENT ACTIONS REGARDING TREATIES TO WHICH THE UNITED STATES IS NOT A PARTY 925
NOTICE OF RECENT DOCUMENTS (not reprinted) 926

STATEMENT OF OWNERSHIP, MANAGEMENT AND CIRCULATION

(Act of August 12, 1970; Sec. 3685, Title 39, U.S. Code)

Filed October 1982, *American Journal of International Law* (issued quarterly, January, April, July, October), Prince & Lemon Streets, Lancaster, Pennsylvania 17603. Published by American Society of International Law, 2223 Massachusetts Avenue, N.W., Washington, D.C. 20008. Editors-in-Chief, Louis Henkin and Oscar Schachter, Columbia University School of Law, New York, N.Y. 10027. Owner, American Society of International Law. *Average* number of copies per issue, last 12 months: total printed, 8,044; paid circulation, 6,584; mail subscriptions, 6,584; total paid circulation, 6,584; free distribution, 128; total distribution, 6,712; office use, left over, unaccounted, spoiled after printing, 1,332. For *single* issue nearest to filing date: total printed, 7,884; paid circulation, 6,486; mail subscriptions, 6,486; total paid circulation, 6,486; free distribution, 128; total distribution, 6,614; office use, left over, unaccounted, spoiled after printing, 1,270.

Table of Cases

(*Italicized* page numbers indicate where decisions are excerpted or cases discussed at length. Abbreviations: arb., arbitration; Eur. Ct., Court of Justice of the European Communities; IACHR, Inter-American Court of Human Rights; ICJ, International Court of Justice; PCIJ, Permanent Court of International Justice.)

Alberta Gas Chemicals, Inc. v. United States, 175
Alfred Dunhill of London, Inc. v. Republic of Cuba, 162, *311–2*
Anglo-French Continental Shelf arbitration. *See* United Kingdom-France Continental Shelf
[The] *Antelope*, 803
Attorney General v. Burgoa (Eur. Ct.), *396–8*
Attorney General v. Irish Northern Aid Committee, *621–3*
Baker v. Carr, 392
Barcelona Traction (ICJ), 506, 719, *728–9*, *730–1*, 735
Banco Nacional de Cuba v. Chase Manhattan Bank, 163, *847–9*
Banco Nacional de Cuba v. Sabbatino, 162, 164, *310–1*, 312, 401, 847–8
Bay of Fundy (arb.), *537*
Benz v. Compania Naviera Hidalgo, 308
Blad's case, 401
[The] *Bremen* v. Zapata Off-Shore Co., *312–3*, 314
Broadbent v. Organization of American States, 623
Buttes Gas and Oil Co. v. Hammer and Others, *399–402*
Cabell v. Chavez-Salido, *616–7*
Carbon Black Export, Inc. v. The *Monrosa*, 313
Certain Expenses of the United Nations (ICJ), 424
Chorzów Factory (PCIJ), 743
Committee to Preserve American Color Television (a.k.a. Compact), et al. v. United States, *389–91*
I Congreso del Partido. See Marble Islands v. *I Congreso del Partido*
Corfu Channel case (ICJ), 506–7, 525, 543, 546, 644, 645, *745–8*, 749, 751, *752–3*
Cutting case, *812*
Dames & Moore v. Regan, 856–7
Danube Commission (PCIJ), 743
De Sanchez v. Banco Central de Nicaragua, *171–3*
Diversion of Water from the River Meuse (PCIJ), 743
Empresa Cubana Exportadora, Inc. v. Lamborn & Co., *162–5*
Fertilizer Corp. of India v. IDI Management, Inc., *166–9*
Filartiga v. Peña-Irala, 170–1, 175, 656
First National City Bank v. Banco Nacional de Cuba, 847–8
Foley v. Connelie, 617
Foster v. Neilson, 170, *805*
Franqui case (arb.), *740*
Free Zones (PCIJ), *742*
Frisbie v. Collins, 619
Government of Costa Rica (*In re* Viviana Gallardo) (IACHR), *239*
Grisbadarna case (arb.), *566–71*, 575, 577, 579, 586, 587
Gulf of Fonseca case, 537–8
Gulf of Maine (ICJ), 831
Gulf Oil Corp. v. Gilbert, *395–6*
Hanoch Tel-Oren v. Libyan Arab Republic, *169–71*
Hilton v. Guyot, *820–1*
Hostages case. *See* US Diplomatic and Consular Staff in Tehran
Illinois Brick Co. v. Illinois, 160
Industrial Investment Development Corp. v. Mitsui & Co., Ltd., 843
In re Alan J. Ridge & Co., Ltd., 842
In re Metzger, 391
In re Uranium Antitrust Litigation, 296, 845
Interhandel case (ICJ), 740
International Association of Machinists and Aerospace Workers v. Organization of Petroleum Exporting Countries, *160–2*
International Business Machines Corp. v. Commission (Eur. Ct.), 593
International Longshoremen's Association v. Allied International, Inc., *849–51*
Island of Palmas (arb.), 741
Ker v. Illinois, 619
Koster v. Lumbermen's Mutual Casualty Co., 395
Lauritzen v. Larsen, *304–5*, 306, 307, 309
Letelier v. Republic of Chile, 175
Libra Bank Ltd. et al. v. Banco Nacional de Costa Rica, S.A., *851–3*
Louisiana v. Mississippi, *562, 564*
Mannington Mills v. Congoleum Corp., 296, 843

Marble Islands v. *I Congreso del Partido, 402–4*
Markham v. Pitchess, 175
Masica Incident (arb.), 741
Mavrommatis Jerusalem Concessions (PCIJ), 742
Máximo Mora (arb.), *743–4*
McCulloch v. Sociedad Nacional de Marineros de Honduras, *308*
McMullen v. Immigration and Naturalization Service, *386–8*
Mitsui case. *See* Industrial Development Corp.
Monetary Gold Removed from Rome (arb.), 644
Monetary Gold Removed from Rome (ICJ), 645, 646
Montreal Trading Ltd. v. Amax Inc., 843
Nemetz v. Immigration and Naturalization Service, *165–6*
New England Merchants National Bank v. Iran Power Generation and Transmission Co., 175
North Sea Continental Shelf cases (ICJ), 321, 799–80
Nottebohm case (ICJ), 836
Nuclear Tests cases (ICJ), 371, *505–6*
Oder Commission (PCIJ), 743
Pablo Nájera (arb.), *792*
Pabst and Richarz v. Hauptzollamt d'Oldenbourg (Eur. Ct.), 862
Panevezys-Saldutiskis Railway (PCIJ), 836, 837
[The] Paquete *Habana, 821*
Parker's case (arb.), 738
Perez v. The Bahamas, *173–4*
Pfeifer v. United States Bureau of Prisons, 175
[The] *Philippine Admiral*, 403
Piper Aircraft Co. v. Reyno; Hartzell Propeller, Inc. v. Reyno, *394–6*
Polydor Ltd. and RSO Records Inc. v. Harlequin Records Shops Ltd. and Simons Records Ltd. (Eur. Ct.), *857–62*
Portland Channel (arb.), *561–2*, 573
Prize cases, *819–20*
Reid v. Covert, *626*
Reservations to the Genocide Convention (ICJ), 791
Rex v. Cia. Pervana de Vapores, S.A., *393–4*
Romero v. International Terminal Operating Co., *305–6*
Rosado v. Civiletti, 175
Rose v. The King, *751*
Saint-Naoum (PCIJ), 742
Scherk v. Alberto-Culver, *313–4*
Schooner *Exchange* v. McFadden, *804–5*
SEC v. Banca della Svizzera Italiana (St. Joe case), 842
SEC v. Certain Unknown Purchasers (Santa Fe case), 842, 846
South West Africa case (ICJ), 636
Strait of Juan de Fuca (arb.), 561
Sugarman v. Dougall, *616–7*
Sumitomo Shoji America, Inc. v. Avagliano, 175, *853–5*
Texas Trading & Milling Corp. v. Federal Republic of Nigeria, 173
Timberlane Lumber Co. v. Bank of America, 296, 843, 845
Tuck v. Pan American Health Organization, *623–4*
Tunisia/Libyan Arab Jamahiriya Case concerning the Continental Shelf (ICJ), 365: Application of Malta for Permission to Intervene, *371–2*
United City Merchants (Investments) Ltd. v. Royal Bank of Canada, *627–9*
United Kingdom-France Continental Shelf (arb.), 321, 336, 343
United States v. Aluminum Co. of America, *307*
United States v. Cordero, *618–9*
United States v. Mackin, *388, 391–2*
United States v. Mann, 175
United States v. McRary, *619–21*
United States v. Mitchell, *297–8*
United States v. Monroy, 175
United States v. Percheman, *805*
United States v. Perez-Herrera, 175
United States v. Rubies, 175
United States v. Toscanino, 619
United States v. Vetco, Inc., 297
United States v. Whiting, *624–6*
US Diplomatic and Consular Staff in Tehran (ICJ), *499–531, 717–36, 748–51, 753*
US-France Air Services case (arb.), *516*
Verlinden B.V. v. Central Bank of Nigeria, 173
Vishipco Line v. Chase Manhattan Bank, N.A., *385–6*
Ware v. Hylton, 805
Weinberger v. Rossi, *855–7*
Westinghouse Electric Corp. v. Rio Algom, 296
Wildenhus case, *820*
Wilko v. Swan, 314
Windward Shipping v. American Radio Association, *308–9*
Wisconsin v. Michigan, 583
Zenith Radio Corp. v. Matsushita Electric Industrial Co., Ltd., 175, 296
Zenith Radio Corp. v. United States, 390

INDEX

(The following abbreviations refer to sections of the *Journal*: *BN*, Briefer Notices; *BR*, Book Reviews and Notes; *CD*, Current Developments; *Corr.*, Correspondence; *CP*, Contemporary Practice of the US Relating to International Law; *Ed.*, Editorial Comments; *JD*, Judicial Decisions; *LA*, Leading Article; *NC*, Notes and Comments; *OD*, Official Documents. Other abbreviations include: EEC, European Economic Community; FCMA, US Fishery Conservation and Management Act; FCN Treaty, Treaty of Friendship, Commerce and Navigation; FRG, Federal Republic of Germany; ICJ, International Court of Justice; ILC, International Law Commission; IMF, International Monetary Fund; OAS, Organization of American States; PCIJ, Permanent Court of International Justice; UK, United Kingdom; UNCLOS III, Third United Nations Conference on the Law of the Sea; US, United States.)

Aaland Islands Convention (1921), sea boundary delimitation, 578
Abu Musa, offshore oil concession dispute, *JD*, 399–402
Act of state doctrine: and assets confiscated by foreign states, *JD*, 385–6; and international commercial system, 309, 310–2; and property nationalized by foreign states, *JD*, 162–5; *JD*, 847–9; UK judicial restraint regarding "sovereign transactions," *JD*, 399–402; US judicial restraint in foreign relations, *JD*, 160–2; 401–2
Adachi, Sumio. Gendai Senso Hohki Ron, *BN*, 918
Adami, Vittorio, 557–8, 565, 570
Adams, John Quincy, enunciation of Monroe Doctrine, 809
Adams, L. Jerold. *BN* of Adachi, 918
Aegean Sea, continental shelf dispute, 321, 343
Aerospace Industries Association, 416
Afghanistan, 266, 384, 408, 409, 411, 590, 849
Agreement on Reparation (Paris Agreement, 1946), 644, 645–6
Agreement Relating to the International Telecommunications Satellite Organization (INTELSAT Agreement, 1973), 62, 63, 64, 70, 76
Akinsanya, Adeoye A. The Expropriation of Multinational Property in the Third World, *BR*, 683
Albania, 153, 579: claims to monetary gold removed from Rome, 644, 646; UK minesweeping of territorial waters, 506, 745–8, 752–3
Albrecht, Arthur R. *BN* of International Chamber of Commerce, 919
Algeciras Conference (1906), 822
Algeria, 813, 863, 866: settlement of Iran hostage crisis, 718, 731–2, 735–6
Aliens, 657: state citizenship requirement for public employment, *JD*, 616–7; US-Haiti agreement on illegal migrants, *CP*, 374–7; US standards for deportation, *JD*, 386–8; US standards for naturalization, *JD*, 165–6
Allen, J. de V., A. J. Stockwell, & L. R. Wright (eds.). A Collection of Treaties and other Documents affecting the States of Malaysia, 1761–1963. Vols. I & II, *BR*, 218
Allied Control Council, 123, 127–8
Almond, Harry H., Jr. *BN* of Matte, Annals of Air and Space Law, 707
Altamira y Crevea, Judge Rafael, 721
American Bar Association, 414, 823
American Convention on Human Rights, 133, 231–2, 234–5, 246, 769, 775: jurisdiction of Inter-American Court under, 235–45
American Declaration on the Rights and Duties of Man (1948), 243
American Institute of International Law, on delimitation of territorial sea, 580
American Law Institute. *See* Restatement of Foreign Relations Law of the United States (Revised); Restatement (Second) of Conflict of Laws; Restatement (Second) of Foreign Relations Law of the United States
American Society of International Law: contribution of Hardy Cross Dillard, 595, 597; establishment and early history of and of *Journal*, 812, 817, 823–5, 826, 827, 828–9
American Trial Lawyers Association, 416

Amnesty International, 135–6, 147
Amram, Philip W. *Corr.* on Joe C. Barrett, 372
Anand, R. P. *BR* of Larson, 216
Anawalt, Howard C. *BR* of Masquelin, 881
Anderson, Chandler P., 810, 824
Angell, James B., 816
Anglo-American Claims Convention (1853), and sovereignty over Bay of Fundy, 537
Angola, 408
Antarctic Treaty (1959), 830: consultation on technology under, 94–5, 97, 113, 115, 116–7
Anti-Fascist Resistance Fighters League, 839
Antitrust: Extraterritorial Jurisdiction at a Crossroads, *LA*, 280; A Turnabout in Extraterritoriality, *Ed.*, 591; US-Australian agreement on cooperation, 845; *CD*, 866; US jurisdictional conflicts resulting from regulation, *CP*, 839–46; US law and foreign states' control over natural resources, *JD*, 160–2. *See also* Claims
Anzilotti, Judge Dionisio, on discontinuance in PCIJ, 721
Apollis, Gilbert. L'Emprise Maritime de l'Etat Côtier, *BR*, 690
Arab countries, 14, 533, 544–5
Arbitration: confirmation of foreign award by US court, *JD*, 166–9; evidentiary rules in international, 739–40, 741, 743–4; of sea boundary disputes, 561–2, 563, 566–73; under LOS treaty involving international organizations, 16; US treaties in early 20th century, 825, 828. *See also* Iran-United States Claims Tribunal; Mixed Arbitral Tribunals
Arbitration Law in Europe, *BN*, 919
Archer group, at UNCLOS seabed negotiations, 101–2, 104
Argentina, 346, 408: Beagle Channel dispute with Chile, 571–3; US security assistance to, 254–6, 259, 269–70, 271, 272, 274–5, 276. *See also* Falkland Islands
Aristotle, on man's political nature, 494, 497
Armed conflicts, effects on treaties, 176
Armenia, 130
Arsanjani, Mahnoush H. International Regulation of Internal Resources, *BR*, 675
Artificial islands, 176
Asian-African Legal Consultative Committee. Report of the Seventeenth, Eighteenth and Nineteenth Sessions, Held in Kuala Lumpur (1976), Baghdad (1977) and Doha (1978), *BR*, 461
Asylum, large-scale migrations of those seeking, *NC*, 598: definition of refugee, 606, 607–9; "temporary refuge," 603–6
Atkeson, Timothy. *BR* of van Lier, 689
Australia, 269, 420, 422, 426–7, 842: agreement with US on antitrust cooperation, 845; *CD*, 866; maritime boundary Treaty with Papua New Guinea, *LA*, 321; statement during pending ICJ case, 505–6; UN initiative on refugees, 603–6
(The) Australian-United States Agreement on Cooperation in Antitrust Matters, *CD*, 866
(The) Australian Year Book of International Law. Vol. 7, *BR*, 701
Austria, 861: Lake Garda boundary dispute with Venice, 557; 19th-century law on island delimitation, 557
Aviation: The Montreal Protocols to the Warsaw Convention on International Carriage by Air, *CD*, 412; US-France arbitration on reprisals, 516; US suspension of Polish and Soviet privileges, 380–3
Ayala, 482

Baccelli, Guido Rinaldi. La Collaboration Internationale en Matière Aéroportuaire, *BR*, 215
Bahamas, 173–4, 297–8
Bangladesh, 598
Barack, Boaz. The Application of the competition rules (antitrust law) of the European Economic Community to enterprises and arrangements external to the Common Market, *BR*, 903
Barde, Jacques. La Notion de droits acquis en droit international public, *BR*, 909
Barrett, Joe C. *Corr.* on, 372
Bartolus of Sassoferrato, 495
Barton, John H. The Politics of Peace: An Evaluation of Arms Control, *BN*, 704
Baruch Plan, 84, 88

Bassiouni, M. Cherif. International Criminal Law: A Draft International Criminal Code, *BR*, 661
Bath, C. Richard. *BR* of Ferrero Costa, 691
Bay of Fundy, arbitrator's ruling on sovereignty over, 537
Beale, Joseph Henry, on comity, 284–5
Bechhoefer, Bernhard G. *BN* of Barton, 704
Bedjaoui, Mohammed, 863, 864–5
Belgium, 124, 427–8, 743, 820, 859: discontinuance of proceedings before ICJ, 719; sea boundary delimitation practice, 564, 579, 586
Belize, 563: OAS Juridical Committee and claims to, 594–5
"Beneš" claimants, under US-Czechoslovak settlement, 649–51, 653, 837–8
Berlin Declaration (1945), by Allied powers, 121–2, 125
Best, Geoffrey. Humanity in Warfare, *BR*, 208
Bevan, Don, 27
Bibliography of International Humanitarian Law, *BN*, 223
Bilder, Richard B. Managing the Risks of International Agreement, *BR*, 658
Bishop, Wm. W., Jr. *BN* of Italian Yearbook of International Law. Vol. III, 1977, 222
Bizec, René-François, & Yves Daudet (eds.). UN Code de Conduite pour le Transfert de Technologie, *BR*, 678
Björksten, S. R., on sea boundary delimitation, 574
Black Sea, right of passage through, 536, 538
Blaine, James G., 812, 813
Blanco Gaspar, Vicente. El Voto Ponderado, *BR*, 695
Blocking statutes, 843, 845, 866. *See also* Documents
Bluntschli, Johann Caspar, on sea boundary delimitation, 560, 572
Boczek, Boleslaw A. *BR* of Gold, 906
Bodin, Jean, 478
Boggs, S. Whittemore, on methods of delimiting the median line, 581, 583–5, 587, 588
Boigu, 322, 327, 329, 333, 337
Bolivia, 408: US security assistance to, 269–70, 273
Book Reviews and Notes, 184, 430, 658, 868
Borchard, Edwin M., 827
Bosporus, passage through, 536
Botelho, Bruce M. *BN* of Riklin, 221
Bothe, Michael (ed.). Trends in Environmental Policy and Law, *BR*, 456
Botswana, 269
Boundary Treaty of 1661 (Norway-Sweden), arbitrators' interpretation in *Grisbadarna* award, 566–71
Bourne, C. B. *BR* of Teclaff & Utton, 692
Boyle, Francis A. *BR* of Mitchell, 872
Brazil, 254–5, 406, 408, 421, 422–3
Breuer, Georg. Weather Modification: Prospects and Problems, *BR*, 688
Brewer, David J., 823
Brewer, William C., Jr. *BR* of d'Herbes & Touscoz and of Njem, 883
Brisk, William J. *BN* of Caribbean Yearbook of International Relations: 1977, 222
(The) British Year Book of International Law, 1979. Vol. 50, *BR*, 876
Brittin, Burdick H. International Law for Seagoing Officers (4th ed.), *BR*, 702
Brownlie, Ian (ed.). Basic Documents on Human Rights (2d ed.), *BN*, 221
Bryan, Greyson. Taxing Unfair International Trade Practices, *BR*, 435
Bryan, William Jennings, 826
"Bryan Treaties" (1913–1914), 518, 826
Buergenthal, Thomas, 766: The Inter-American Court of Human Rights, *LA*, 231
Bulgaria, 107, 837
Burke, W. T. U.S. Fishery Management and the New Law of the Sea, *LA*, 24
Burmester, H. The Torres Strait Treaty: Ocean Boundary Delimitation by Agreement, *LA*, 321
Butler, Charles Henry, 823, 826, 827
Butler, William E. (ed.). International Law in Comparative Perspective, *BR*, 430
Buzan, Barry. Recipient of Deák Prize, 610
Bynkershoek, C. van, on breadth of territorial sea, 558

Cable, James. Gunboat Diplomacy 1919–1979 (2d ed.), *BR*, 913
Calogeropoulos-Stratis, Aristidis S. Droit humanitaire et Droits de l'Homme—La protection de la personne en période de conflit armé, *BR*, 669
Cambodia, 266
Cameroon, United Republic of, 427
Campbell, Alan. EC Competition Law. A Practitioner's Textbook, *BR*, 905
Canada, 131, 143, 332, 426–7, 627, 842, 843: admission of illegally obtained evidence, 751; *Caroline* incident, 807–8; domestic law and Civil and Political Rights Covenant, 151–2; salmon and fisheries agreements with US, 45, 346–7; and seabed mining negotiations, 100–1, 104, 115; territorial sea boundaries with US, 321, 325, 349, 586, 831; UN initiative on refugees, 599–603; US boundaries generally, 809–11
(The) Canadian Yearbook of International Law. Vol. XVII, 1979; Vol. XVIII, 1980, *BR*, 700
Cardozo, Benjamin, 819
Carey, John. *BN* of Dowrick, 223
Caribbean countries, 38–9, 54
Caribbean Dependency States, UK, 379
(The) Caribbean Yearbook of International Relations: 1977, *BN*, 222
Carlsten, Hans M. *BR* of Lindencrona & Mattsson, 440
Carnegie, Andrew, activities furthering international law, 824–5
Carnegie Endowment for International Peace, 824–5, 827
Carter, Jimmy, 414, 613: administration implementation of human rights legislation, 248–9, 253–4, 256–76; "doctrine" on external aggression, 590–1
Cassese, Antonio, & Edmond Jouve (eds.). Pour un droit des peuples. Essais sur la Déclaration d'Alger, *BR*, 451
Cattan, Henry. Jerusalem, *BR*, 696
Central American Court of Justice: admission of evidence by, 742; on passage through Gulf of Fonseca, 537–8
Centre for the Settlement of International Investment Disputes, rules on discontinuance, 727
Charney, Jonathan I. Technology and International Negotiations, *LA*, 78
Chase, Salmon P., 819
Chen, Lung-chu, Myres S. McDougal, & Harold D. Lasswell. Human Rights and World Public Order. The Basic Principles of an International Law of Human Dignity, *BR*, 184
Chetumal Bay, 532, 563
Chile, 402, 404, 408, 830: Beagle Channel dispute with Argentina, 571–3; UN human rights actions, 140, 144; UN supervision of human rights compliance, 765; US security assistance to, 254–5, 266
China, People's Republic of, 266, 408: boundary with Hong Kong, 560
Chiu, Hungdah. Agreements of the People's Republic of China: A Calendar of Events 1966–1980, *BR*, 915
Choate, Joseph H., 824, 826
Choice of forum, in transnational cases, 312–5: foreign plaintiffs in US courts, *JD*, 394–6
Choice of law: clause proposed for treaties, 800–1; early US development, 282–5; regarding deposits in foreign branches of US banks, *JD*, 385–6; regarding transnational events generally, 286–9, 292, 294, 300, 302–3, 304–9, 317; regarding transnational regulatory cases, 285, 287, 289–91, 292, 295–6, 297–9, 300–1, 317–9
Claims: antidumping, US Government authority to settle, *JD*, 389–91; "continuous voyage" doctrine, 819–20; settlement of US-Czechoslovak, *CD*, 639; US against Iran, 503, 718, 731, 735: reparation for, 717–8, 731, 732, 733, 735. *See also* State responsibility; United States, Civil War; Warsaw Convention of 1929
Clark, J. Reuben, 828
Clark, Roger S. *BR* of McDougal, Lasswell, & Chen, 184
Claude, Inis L., Jr. *BR* of Wirsing, 899
Codding, George A., Jr. *BR* of Matte, Traité de Droit Aérien-aéronautique, 214
(The) Codification and Progressive Development of International Law: A UNITAR Study of the Role and Use of the International Law Commission, *CD*, 630
Cohen, Stephen B. Conditioning U.S. Security Assistance on Human Rights Practices, *LA*, 246

Colombia, 147, 269, 379
Comity: applied to choice of law and extraterritorial jurisdiction, 281–5, 295, 308–9, 319, 845; Justice Gray on, 820–1; UK judicial enforcement of IMF Agreement based on, *JD*, 627–9
Commission for International Economic Cooperation, 80
Common heritage of mankind, 6, 9, 18
Communist countries, 632. *See also* Eastern Europe
Compensation, 240: amount due for nationalized property, 648, 656; ICJ on Iran's duty to compensate US, 502–3; under Czechoslovak nationalization laws, 641–2; valuation standard for nationalized property, *JD*, 847–9
Conciliation, 16–7: "Bryan Treaties," 518, 826; and good offices of UN Secretary-General, 132, 134
Conditioning U.S. Security Assistance on Human Rights Practices, *LA*, 246
Conference on Jewish Material Claims Against Germany, 839
Conflict of laws, 281, 314: early US development, 282–5; in private international law treaties, 176, 178–81. *See also* Restatement (Second) of Conflict of Laws
Constantinople Convention (1888), on Suez Canal, 547
Contemporary Practice of the United States Relating to International Law, 154, 374, 611, 836
Contempt, whether similar concept exists in international law, 504–9
Contempt, Crisis, and the Court: The World Court and the Hostage Rescue Attempt, *LA*, 499
Continental shelf. *See* Law of the sea
Contracts: explicit waiver of immunity under US sovereign immunity law, *JD*, 851–3; *Restatement* of US foreign relations law on "internationalization clauses," 656–7. *See also* Hague Convention respecting the Limitation of Force for the Recovery of Contract Debts
Convention on the International Maritime Satellite Organization. *See* INMARSAT Convention
Cook, Walter Wheeler, 285
Copyright Protection in the Americas. Binder I, *BR*, 458
Costa Rica, 232, 233, 234, 236, 237, 239, 240, 269: whether waiver of immunity by national bank "explicit," *JD*, 851–3
Council of Europe, 754: on overlapping human rights supervision, 769, 770, 771
Crawford, James. Execution of Judgments and Foreign Sovereign Immunity, *LA* Oct. 1981, correction to, 153
Crimea Conference (1945), 124, 127
Critical Defense Zones and International Law: The Reagan Codicil, *Ed.*, 589
Crosswell, Carol McCormick. Legal and Financial Aspects of International Business, *BR*, 682
Cuba, 266, 607, 619, 821, 830, 841: Guantánamo Agreement with US, 822; litigation over nationalized US property, *JD*, 162–5; 310–2; *JD*, 847–9; sovereign immunity defense in UK, *JD*, 402–4
Cultural Property, Convention on the Means of Prohibiting and Preventing the Illicit Import, Export and Transfer of Ownership (1970), State Department support of US bill to implement, *CP*, 611–3
Current Developments, 176, 405, 630, 863
Cyprus, 153
Czechoslovakia, 124, 131, 137, 408, 589: claims settlement Agreement with US, *CD*, 639; 837–8

Dale, Richard. Anti-Dumping Law in a Liberal Trade Order, *BN*, 920
Damages. *See* Compensation
D'Amato, Anthony. *BR* of Kalshoven, Kuyper, & Lammers, 188
Dana, Richard Henry, 816, 818
Dante, on world order, 477–9, 483, 493–5
Dárday, Deszö, on sea boundary delimitation, 565
Dauan, 322, 327, 329, 333
Daudet, Yves, & René-François Bizec (eds.). UN Code de Conduite pour le Transfert de Technologie, *BR*, 678
Day, William R., 812, 823
Decaux, Emmanuel. La Réciprocité en droit international, *BR*, 198

Deep seabed. *See* Law of the sea; United Nations Committee on the Peaceful Uses of the Sea-bed
Deep water ports, 176
de Lacharrière, Guy Ladreit, 368–9
de Magalhaes, Barbosa, on territorial sea delimitation, 575–6
Denmark, 304–5, 543, 858: sea boundary delimitation practice, 566, 576–7, 578, 580
DeSaussure, Hamilton. *BN* of Matte, Space Policy and Programmes, 471
Detention, 409: under US human rights legislation, 250–2, 267–8, 269, 276, 277
Developing countries, 38–9, 79, 86: implementation of human rights Covenants, 757; and reporting under Civil and Political Rights Covenant, 143, 148; and seabed mining, 87, 98, 102; and service on ILC, 634, 635, 636. *See also* Group of 77; New International Economic Order; Third World
de Waart, P. J. I. M. *BR* of Ress, 686
d'Herbes, Jean, & Jean Touscoz. Les Contrats internationaux de coopération industrielle et le nouvel ordre économique international, *BR*, 883
Dickinson, Jacob M., 823
Diéye, Abdoulaye, on UN human rights investigatory procedures, 765
Digest of United States Practice in International Law, 1978, *BR*, 437
Dillard, Hardy Cross. *Ed.* on, 595
Dinegar, Caroline A. *BN* of Reijnen, 703
Dinstein, Yoram (ed.). Israel Yearbook on Human Rights. Vol. 10, *BR*, 698
Diplomatic privileges and immunities: and collection of evidence in *Hostages* case, 512, 749–51, 753; Pufendorf on, 488–9; state practice on illegally obtained evidence, 751–2
Discontinuance of International Proceedings: The Hostages Case, *LA*, 717
Discrimination against Women, Convention on the Elimination of All Forms of (1979), 758–9
Dispute settlement, 182, 238, 801: good offices in, 131, 132, 140; under LOS treaty, 18–9, 22, 29; under Vienna Convention on treaty law, 787, 795–9; US boundary practice, 809–11. *See also* Arbitration; Conciliation; Contempt, Crisis, and the Court; Hague Conventions on Pacific Settlement of Disputes.
Documents, Convention abolishing legalization for foreign public, *CD*, 182; production of, 296–7, 298, 317, 524, 654, 843, 866–7. *See also* Blocking statutes; Evidence; Hague Convention on the Service Abroad of Judicial and Extrajudicial Documents
Dominican Republic, 410, 427–8
Dowrick, F. E. (ed.). Human Rights: Problems, Perspectives, and Texts, *BN*, 223
Du Bois, Pierre, on power of papacy, 495
Dulles, John Foster, 807
Dumbauld, Edward. *BN* of Fikentscher, 219; *BN* of Meijers, 705; *BR* of Netherlands Yearbook of International Law. Vol. XI, 1980, 699; *BN* of Vol. XII, 1981, 921; *BR* of van Dijk, 204; *BR* of van Panhuys, Heere, Josephus Jitta, Ko, & Stuyt, 463; on hindering execution of judgments, 511; on use of force and arbitral agreements, 518–9
Dungan, Malcolm T. *BR* of Fernández-Shaw, 457

Eastern European countries, 6, 14, 119, 266, 589: and reporting under Civil and Political Rights Covenant, 143, 148–9; settlements regarding nationalized foreign property, 639, 642–3
East Timor, 259, 268
Education, early US international law, 815–8, 825, 828
Egypt, 863, 866: access to Gulf of Aqaba under Peace Treaty with Israel, *LA*, 532; 614; Sinai Multinational Force and Observers, *CD*, 181; *CP*, 613–5
(The) Egyptian-Israeli Peace Treaty and Access to the Gulf of Aqaba: A New Legal Regime, *LA*, 532
ElBaradei, Mohamed. The Egyptian-Israeli Peace Treaty and Access to the Gulf of Aqaba: A New Legal Regime, *LA*, 532
———, & Thomas M. Franck. The Codification and Progressive Development of International Law: A UNITAR Study of the Role and Use of the International Law Commission, *CD*, 630
(The) Election of Five Members of the International Court of Justice in 1981, *NC*, 364
(The) Election of March 1982 to Fill One Vacancy in the International Court of Justice, *CD*, 863
El-Erian, Abdullah, 365, 366, 863
Elias, Taslim, 366

Elkind, Jerome B. *BR* of Greig, 701; *BR* of Mani, 660
El Salvador, 408–9, 537: US security assistance to, 254–5, 268–70, 272, 274–5
Energy, conservation and orbit/spectrum regulation, 77
Environment. *See* Law of the sea: Fisheries, Marine environment and resources; Rosencranz, Armin
Equatorial Guinea, 408
Equitable access, to orbit/spectrum, 59, 62–5, 76
Equitable considerations, in sea boundary delimitation, 560, 569, 570–1, 578, 581, 585–7
Equitable principles, in delimiting continental shelf, 14–5
Erasmus, 480
Ethiopia, 266, 272, 410, 427–8
European Commission of Human Rights, 135, 769, 770, 771, 775–6
European Convention on Human Rights, 133, 246: normative conflicts with other instruments, 761–2; supervisory system, 761, 766, 770–1, 776
European Court of Human Rights, 234, 770
European Court of Justice, 593, 762: on Community law vs. treaty obligations of member states, *JD*, 396–8; on EEC Treaty and agreements with third countries, *JD*, 857–62; rules on discontinuance, 726
European Economic Community (EEC), 21, 153, 842: Commission assertions of extraterritoriality, *Ed.*, 591; Commission on direct effect of agreements with third countries, 861; participation in LOS Convention, 15–6, 22. *See also* European Court of Justice
European Free Trade Association (EFTA), 858, 860–1
Eustis, Frederic A., III. *BR* of Wassenbergh & van Fenema, 693
Evarts, William M., 812
Evensen, Jens, on LOS negotiations, 4–5
Evidence: admissibility in international adjudication, *LA*, 737: barriers to, 741–5; when illegally obtained, 745–53. *See also* Documents; Hague Convention on the Taking of Evidence Abroad
Exclusive economic zone. *See* Law of the sea
Expropriation, judicial abstention and, 310–2. *See also* Compensation; Nationalization
Extradition, 177, 812, 829: political offense exception, 388; *JD*, 391–2; treaties and voluntary return of accused by states, *JD*, 618–9; US State Department guidelines, *CP*, 154–9
Extraterritorial Jurisdiction at a Crossroads: An Intersection between Public and Private International Law, *LA*, 280

Falk, Richard. Human Rights and State Sovereignty, *BR*, 897
———, & Samuel S. Kim (eds.). The War System: An Interdisciplinary Approach, *BR*, 186
Falkland Islands, war between Argentina and UK: *Ed.* on OAS Juridical Committee and, 594; *Ed.* on OAS resolution, 830; UN Security Council Res. 502 on, *OD*, 712; 831
(The) Falklands (Malvinas), International Law, and the OAS, *Ed.*, 594
Farer, Tom J. *BR* of Hoffmann, 888
Fawcett, J. E. S., & Audrey Parry. Law and International Resource Conflicts, *BR*, 675
Feinrider, Martin. *BR* of Bothe, 456
Ferencz, Benjamin B. *BR* of Majer and of Krausnick & Wilhelm, 448; *BR* of Rifaat, 446; An International Criminal Court. A Step Toward World Peace: A Documentary History and Analysis. Vol. I: Half a Century of Hope. Vol. II: The Beginning of Wisdom, *BR*, 211
Fernández-Shaw, Felix. La Difusión Internacional de los Programas Audiovisuales, *BR*, 457
Ferrero Costa, Eduardo. El Nuevo Derecho del Mar: El Perú y las 200 Millas, *BR*, 691
Feuerstein, Peter, & Clive Parry (eds.). Multum Non Multa. Festschrift für Kurt Lipstein, *BR*, 901
Field, David Dudley, on sea boundary delimitation, 560, 563
Fiji, 13, 14
Fikentscher, Wolfgang. De fide et perfidia—Der Treuegedanke in den "Staatsparellelen" des Hugo Grotius aus heutiger Sicht, *BN*, 219
Fine, J. David. *BN* of Hevener, 917; *BR* of O'Brien, 873
Finger, Seymour Maxwell. Your Man at the U.N. People, Politics, and Bureaucracy in Making Foreign Policy, *BR*, 443

Finland, 123, 125: reservation to Vienna Convention on treaty law, 798; reservations to Civil and Political Rights Covenant, 152; sea boundary delimitation with Sweden, 559, 578, 579
Finlay, Judge Lord, on discontinuance in PCIJ, 721–2
Fiore, Pasquale, on sea boundary delimitation, 577–8
Fischer, Dana D. Reporting Under the Covenant on Civil and Political Rights: The First Five Years of the Human Rights Committee, *NC*, 142
Fish, Hamilton, 812, 813
Fisher, Adrian S. *BR* of Roger Fisher, 870
Fisher, Roger. *BR* of McWhinney, 658; Improving Compliance with International Law, *BR*, 870
Fisheries. *See* Law of the sea
Fishing and Conservation of the Living Resources in the Baltic Sea, Convention on (1973), 332
FitzGerald, Gerald F. *BR* of Blanco Gaspar, 695
Food and Agriculture Organization, report on fishery management, 24–6
Force, use of, 410: and Falklands-Malvinas dispute, *Ed.*, 830; ICJ on US hostage rescue attempt, *LA*, 499; by UK in Corfu Channel, 506–7; UN Charter rules and treaties, 176
Ford, Gerald R., 414: administration implementation of human rights legislation, 248, 249, 256, 272; attitude toward such legislation, 253, 263
Foreign access to surplus fisheries, under FCMA and LOS treaty, 28–9, 33, 37–40, 51–2, 54
Foreign Relations of the United States, 1952–1954, Vol. XVI: The Geneva Conference, *BR*, 467
Forster, Isaac, 364
Foster, John W., 812, 823, 824
France, 21, 124, 128, 313–4, 420, 495, 516, 742, 746, 820, 822, 843: law on respect for judicial decisions, 508; and return of Czechoslovak gold, 640, 643–7; sea boundary delimitation practice, 562, 563, 565, 577, 578, 579. *See also* Franco-Mexican Claims Convention
Franck, Thomas M., & Mohamed ElBaradei. The Codification and Progressive Development of International Law: A UNITAR Study of the Role and Use of the International Law Commission, *CD*, 630
Franco-Mexican Claims Convention (1924), validity for Mexico as nonmember of League of Nations, 792
Frankowska, Maria. Umowy Międzynarodowe w Formie Uproszczonej, *BR*, 673
Fraser, Donald, and US human rights legislation, 250–2, 261, 267, 268, 272
Freedman, Eric E., & W. Michael Reisman. The Plaintiff's Dilemma: Illegally Obtained Evidence and Admissibility in International Adjudication, *LA*, 737
Frelinghuysen, Frederick T., 812
Frenzke, Dietrich. Die Rechtsnatur des Sowjetblocks: Eine juristische Entschleierung, *BR*, 674
Fried, John H. E. *BR* of Wilkins, 895
Friedlander, Robert A. *BR* of Mickolus, 914
Frischholz, Barbara J., & John M. Raymond. Lawyers Who Established International Law in the United States, 1776–1914, *LA*, 802
Fukuda, Moritoshi. Legal Problems of Japanese-Americans: Their History and Development in the United States, *BR*, 911
Fuller, Melville W., 823

Galiani, F., on breadth of territorial sea, 558
Gardeniers, Ton, Hurst Hannum, & Janice Kruger. The 1981 Session of the UN Sub-Commission on Prevention of Discrimination and Protection of Minorities, *CD*, 405
Gardner, James A. Legal Imperialism: American Lawyers and Foreign Aid in Latin America, *BR*, 196
Gardner, Richard N. *BR* of Picone & Sacerdoti, 902
Geertz, Clifford. The Theater State in Nineteenth-Century Bali, *BR*, 663
Gelberg, Ludwik. The Warsaw Treaty of 1970 and the Western Boundary of Poland, *NC*, 119
General Agreement on Tariffs and Trade (GATT), 647: Tokyo Round, 593
General Postal Union, 814
Geneva Convention on the High Seas (1958), 376
Geneva Convention on the Territorial Sea and the Contiguous Zone (1958), 820: straits passage provision and Gulf of Aqaba, 542–3, 544–5, 546, 550–1

Geneva Conventions for the protection of war victims (1929 and 1949), 758, 784, 827
Gentili, 482
Georges Bank, and US-Canada maritime boundary, 347
Germany, Democratic Republic of (GDR), 120, 125, 128–9, 408: claims of "late" US nationals, *CP*, 836–9; 1950 boundary (Zgorzelec) agreement with Poland, 123–4, 128
Germany, Federal Republic of (FRG), 13–4, 143, 313, 586, 841–2; Poland's western boundary under Warsaw Treaty, *NC*, 119; rights of US military personnel, *JD*, 624–6; UN initiative on refugees, 601–3
Germany, pre-1945, 641, 652, 820, 822, 838: existence and legal competence of, 120; current claims to maintaining boundaries of, 124, 127; sea boundary delimitation practice, 578; seizure of Czechoslovak and Albanian gold, 643–4
Giardina, A., on discontinuance practice of World Court, 729–30
Gidel, Gilbert, on sea boundary delimitation, 570, 573, 580, 583, 586
Gilas, Janusz. Systemy Normatywne w Stosunkach Międzynarodowych, *BR*, 674
Ginsburgs, George. *BR* of Frenzke, 674
Gold, Edgar. Maritime Transport: The Evolution of International Marine Policy and Shipping Law, *BR*, 906
Golsong, Heribert, on UN human rights investigatory procedures, 765–6
(The) Good Offices of the United Nations Secretary-General in the Field of Human Rights, *NC*, 130
Goodwin-Gill, Guy S. International Law and the Movement of Persons Between States, *BR*, 670
Gray, George, 823, 824
Gray, Horace, 820–1
Greece, 131, 137, 410: Association Agreement with EEC and Rome Treaty, 862
Green, L. C. *BR* of Bassiouni, 661; *BR* of Dinstein, 698
Gregory, Charles Nobel, 817, 823
Greig, D. W. (ed.). The Australian Year Book of International Law. Vol. 7, *BR*, 701
Grewlich, Klaus W. Transnational Enterprises in a New International System, *BR*, 679
Grier, Robert C., 819
Grieves, Forest L. *BR* of Canadian Yearbook of International Law. Vol. XVII, 1979; Vol. XVIII, 1980, 700; *BR* of Schaefer, 447
Griggs, John W., 824
Gros, André, 364
Gross, Franz B. *BR* of Ronen and of Cassese & Jouve, 451
Gross, Leo. *BN* of Brownlie, 221; *BR* of New Directions in the Law of the Sea. Vols. VII-X, 212; Book Reviews and Notes, 184, 430, 658, 868
Gross amendment, to US human rights legislation, 267
Grotian Society Papers. *See* Indian Year Book of International Affairs
(The) Grotian Vision of World Order, *LA*, 477
Grotius, 802, 803: on delimiting territorial sea, 555–6; on world order, *LA*, 477
Group of 77, 79, 114: on US LOS policy, 3, 5–6, 11, 12
Guatemala, 408, 410: claims to Belize, 594–5; sea boundary delimitation practice, 564–5; US security assistance to, 254–6, 269–70, 272, 273, 274–5
Guelff, Richard Kennedy. *BR* of Calogeropoulos-Stratis, 669
Guerra, Guillermo, on sea boundary delimitation, 572–3, 587
Gulf of Aqaba, regime under Egyptian-Israeli Peace Treaty, *LA*, 532
Gulf of Fonseca, 532: right of innocent passage through, 537–8

Hackworth, Green H., 815
Hague Codification Conference (1930), 82: on delimitation of territorial sea, 574, 576–7, 579, 580; on passage through inland seas, 538–40, 542
Hague Conference on Private International Law, 183
(The) Hague Convention Abolishing the Requirement of Legalization for Foreign Public Documents, *CD*, 182
Hague Convention on the Service Abroad of Judicial and Extrajudicial Documents in Civil or Commercial Matters, 183

Hague Convention on the Taking of Evidence Abroad in Civil or Commercial Matters, 183
Hague Convention respecting the Limitation of Force for the Recovery of Contract Debts, 518
Hague Conventions on law of war (1907), 813, 818, 826–7, 829: 4th Convention, 121: Regulations under, 758, 784, 826; general participation under, 784; 5th and 13th Conventions, 807
Hague Conventions on Pacific Settlement of Disputes (1899 and 1907), 132, 826
Hague Peace Conferences, 518, 784, 826
Haiti, 408, 607: agreement with US on illegal migrants, *CP*, 374–7; US security assistance to, 269–70, 273
Hall, W. E., 817
Halleck, H. W., 818
Halperin, Morton, 263
Hammarskjöld, Dag, 136, 137, 140
Hand, Learned, on extraterritorial jurisdiction, 306–7
Hannum, Hurst, Ton Gardeniers, & Janice Kruger. The 1981 Session of the UN Sub-Commission on Prevention of Discrimination and Protection of Minorities, *CD*, 405
Hardy, Michael. *BR* of Timmermans & Völker, 684
Harlan, John M., 819
Harno, A., 816
Harvard Research in International Law, on sea boundary delimitation, 574–5
Hauser, Rita E. *BR* of Lillich, 666; *BR* of Nelson & Green, 886; *BR* of Newberg, 667
Hay, John, 812, 822, 825
Hazard, John N. *BR* of Levin, 672; *BR* of Soviet Yearbook of International Law, 1979, 217
Helsinki accords, 246, 380
Helsinki Final Act, 380, 382
Henkin, Louis. Restatement of the Foreign Relations Law of the United States (Revised): Tentative Draft No. 3, *CD*, 653
Hevener, Natalie K. *BN* of South African Yearbook of International Law. Vol. 5, 1979, 706; *BR* of Nanda, Scarritt, & Shepherd, 668
——— (ed.). The Dynamics of Human Rights in U.S. Foreign Policy, *BN*, 917
Hickenlooper Amendment, 164
Higgins, Richard J. *BN* of Lodge, 918
Hobbes, Thomas, on law of nations and of nature, 483–4, 485, 486, 487, 488, 489, 490
Hoffmann, Stanley. Duties Beyond Borders: On the Limits and Possibilities of Ethical International Politics, *BR*, 888
Holland, Sir Thomas E., 817, 827
Holy Roman Empire: emperor and world order, 477–9, 483, 494, 495–6, 497; Supreme Court delimitation of Lake Sant' Andrea, 557
Honduras, 234, 236, 308, 537
Horn, Norbert (ed.). Legal Problems of Codes of Conduct for Multinational Enterprises. Vol. 1, *BR*, 191
House of Lords: on act of state doctrine, *JD*, 399–402; on contempt of court, 505; on restrictive theory of sovereign immunity, *JD*, 402–4
Hsiung, James C., & Samuel S. Kim (eds.). China in the Global Community, *BN*, 707
Huber, Ulrich, on comity in choice of law, 282, 284, 310, 319
Hudson, Manley O., award to Hardy Cross Dillard, 595
Hughes, Charles Evans, 824
Hull, Cordell, 824
Hull rule on compensation, 848
Humanitarian intercession, and good offices, 130–1
Human rights, 91, 647, 650–1, 828, 840: good offices of UN Secretary-General concerning, *NC*, 130; international norm making and supervision, *LA*, 754; private claims and access to US courts, *JD*, 169–71; *Restatement* of US foreign relations law on, 655–6; rules of regional courts on discontinuance, 726; and US military assistance and sales, *LA*, 246. *See also* (The) Inter-American Court of Human Rights; Large-Scale Migrations of Asylum Seekers; (The) 1981 Session of the UN Sub-Commission on Prevention of Discrimination and Protection of Minorities

Hungary, 123, 125, 589, 598, 641, 837
Huynh, Thi Huong (comp.). Bibliography of International Humanitarian Law, *BN*, 223

Imbart de Latour, Joseph, 563
Immunity. *See* Diplomatic privileges and immunities; sovereign immunity
Import prohibitions, by US for foreign fishery-related actions, 43–4, 54
India, 410, 598: broadcasting-satellite development, 67; judicial review of arbitral awards in, *JD*, 166–9
(The) Indian Year Book of International Affairs, 1980. Vol. XVIII, Part I; Part II: Studies in the History of the Law of Nations (Grotian Society Papers), *BR*, 464
Individual petition, under human rights treaties, 236–7, 239
Indonesia, 333, 340: broadcasting-satellite development, 67, 74; US security assistance to, 259, 268, 270
Industrial Property, Convention to Protect (1883), 814
INMARSAT Convention, 65
Institut de Droit International, 563, 817: the 1981 session, *CD*, 176
Inter-American Commission on Human Rights, 135, 234, 240–1, 243: submission of cases to Inter-American Court, 236–9, 242, 244, 245; supervisory conflicts with other organizations, 767, 769, 775, 776
Inter-American Convention on Private International Law (the Bustamante Code), 153
(The) Inter-American Court of Human Rights, *LA*, 231
(The) Inter-American System Snarls in Falklands War, *Ed.*, 830
Inter-American Treaty of Reciprocal Assistance. *See* Rio Treaty
International Atomic Energy Agency, 97, 360
International Bank for Reconstruction and Development (World Bank), 359
International Bill of Human Rights, 141, 755, 774
International Business Machines (IBM), proceedings against in US and Europe, 593
International Chamber of Commerce, 313: Arbitration Law in Europe, *BN*, 919
International Civil Aviation Organization (ICAO), 414, 418
International Committee of the Red Cross, 429: Convention of 1864, 813, 829; exercise of good offices, 133–4
International conferences, and Vienna Convention on treaty law, 790, 792, 801
International Convention on the Elimination of All Forms of Racial Discrimination, 423, 427
International Convention on the Suppression and Punishment of the Crime of Apartheid, 420, 426, 427
International Council of Scientific Unions, 115
International Court of Justice, 73, 177, 321–2, 328, 424, 427, 631, 636, 644, 646, 651, 766, 770, 795, 797, 798, 799–800, 815, 831: admission of evidence by, 740, 745–53; discontinuance of *Hostages* case, *LA*, 717: role of President in, 717, 718, 731–4, 736; election of March 1982 to, *CD*, 863; 1981 regular election to, *NC*, 364; on reservations to multilateral treaties, 791; service of Hardy Dillard on, 595–6; on US hostage rescue attempt, *LA*, 499
International Court of Justice, Rules of, 526: on discontinuance, 717, 718, 719, 720, 722–5, 728–30, 731–4, 736; elections to Court under, 365, 366
International Court of Justice, Statute of, 14–5, 73, 507, 520, 555: on discontinuance, 721, 731, 732, 734; elections to Court under, 364–5, 367–8, 863; sanctions under: to enforce interim measures orders, 526–30; for noncompliance with judgments, 525–6, 529, 530; for nondisclosure of documents 524–5
International Covenant on Civil and Political Rights, 133, 242, 246, 426–7, 428: normative conflicts, 756–9, 761–4; reporting practice during the first 5 years of the Human Rights Committee, *NC*, 142; 423; supervision under, 754–5, 761, 765–6, 769–72, 776
International Covenant on Civil and Political Rights, Optional Protocol, 427: examination of communications under, 143–4; supervision under, 755, 765–8, 769–71, 775–6, 778
International Covenant on Economic, Social and Cultural Rights, 242, 246, 426–7, 428: normative conflicts, 756–9, 761–2, 772; supervision under, 754–5, 761, 765–6, 769, 777–8
International Development Association, 359

International Institute of Agriculture, 827
International Institute of Humanitarian Law, on definition of refugee, 608–9
International Joint Commission, 810–1
International Labour Organisation, 146: Director-General and good offices, 133–4; encouragement of acceptance of conventions, 418, 424–5, 426, 428, 429: *Corr.* on, 832; 833; normative conflicts of conventions and other instruments, 757–61, 772–3; supervising convention implementation, 758, 766
International Law Association, proposals on sea boundary delimitation, 560, 563, 565, 572–3
International Law Commission, 18, 367, 369: draft articles on treaties between states and international organizations, etc., 782; draft articles on treaty law, 780–1, 791, 793, 794, 795, 796–7; on passage through inland seas, 540–2, 543, 544; on sea boundary delimitation, 555; UNITAR study of role and use of, *CD*, 630
International Legal Materials, 360: Contents, 230, 475, 713, 926
International Longshoremen's Association, US Supreme Court on secondary political boycott of USSR, *JD*, 849–51
International Military Tribunal (Nuremberg), 826
International Monetary Fund (IMF), UK court on unenforceable exchange contracts, *JD*, 627–9
International Oceanographic Commission, 107
International Office of Weights and Measures, 814
International organizations, 131: draft articles on treaties between states and, etc., 782, 801; and human rights norms and supervision, *LA*, 754; and negotiations involving technology, 80, 90, 109, 113–5; participation in LOS Convention, 15–7; and UN treaty registration and publication, 353, 355, 358–60; and Vienna Convention on treaty law, 789–90, 801
International Sanitary Convention, 828
International Sea-Bed Authority. *See* Law of the sea
International Telecommunication Convention (1973), and allocation of broadcasting-satellite frequencies, 59–62, 64, 67, 74
International Telecommunication Union (ITU), 59, 60, 63, 64, 66, 67, 68, 69, 73, 75–6, 80, 97: 1983 plan for Region 2, 73–4. *See also* World Administrative Radio Conference; World Administrative Radio Conference on the Uses of the Geostationary Orbit
International trade: liability of US banks for deposits in foreign branches, *JD*, 385–6; UK judicial enforcement of IMF Agreement, *JD*, 627–9; US Government authority to settle customs claims, *JD*, 389–91; US sanctions against Poland and USSR, *CP*, 379–84. *See also* Antitrust: Extraterritorial Jurisdiction at a Crossroads: Restrictive business practices
International Union for Publication of Customs Tariffs, 814
International Waterways Commission, on median line delimitation, 581
INTERPOL, 155, 410
Intertemporal law, choice of time in private international law, 176, 177–8, 179
Iran, 14, 408, 422, 427–8, 590, 841, 843: conduct re *Hostages* case, 717, 732, 733–4, 748–51; ICJ on US hostage rescue attempt, *LA*, 499; offshore oil concession dispute, *JD*, 399–402; UN Secretary-General and US hostages, 140; US security assistance to, 257, 259–60, 269, 270, 271
(The) Iran Crisis and International Law, *BR*, 460
Iran-United States Claims Tribunal, 735–6
Iraq, 266
Ireland, 14–5, 386–8, 621: relation of domestic law to treaty obligations under EEC law, *JD*, 396–8
Irish Northern Aid Committee, scope of registration requirement under US law, *JD*, 621–3
Irish Republican Army, 622: Provisional wing of, 386–8, 391
Irwin, Paul. General Chronological List 1648–1809. Vol. I of Index-Guide to Treaties (ed. Parry), *BR*, 466
Israel, 14, 408: access to Gulf of Aqaba under Peace Treaty with Egypt, *LA*, 532; 614; Sinai Multinational Force and Observers, *CD*, 181; *CP*, 613–5
Israel National Section of the International Commission of Jurists. The Rule of Law in the Areas Administered by Israel, *BN*, 705
Israel Yearbook on Human Rights. Vol. 10, *BR*, 698
(The) Italian Yearbook of International Law. Vol. III, 1977, *BN*, 222

Italy, 123, 125, 410, 427–8, 622, 859: claims of "late" US nationals, 837; claims to Albanian monetary gold, 644, 646; 19th-century law on river delimitation, 557; sea boundary delimitation practice, 565, 577, 580

Jackson, John H. *BR* of Bryan, 435
Jacobson, Harold K. *BR* of Pambou Tchivounda, 695
Jamaica, 13–4, 237
Japan, 21, 125, 269, 389, 560, 576, 822, 838: employment of nationals by US subsidiaries under 1953 FCN Treaty, *JD*, 853–5; proposed rules on sea boundary delimitation, 574
Jay, John, 803: boundary settlement with Britain, 809–11
Jefferson, Thomas, establishment of international law principles in US practice, 806–7
Jenks, C. W., 757–8
Jennings, R. Y., 368–9
———, & Ian Brownlie (eds.). The British Year Book of International Law, 1979, *BR*, 876
Jessup, Philip. *Corr.* on 1981 *Ed.* by, 371
Jhabvala, Farrokh. *BR* of The Indian Year Book of International Affairs, 1980. Vol. XVIII, Parts I & II, 464; *Corr.* on 1982 *CD* by Weissbrodt, 832
Jiménez de Aréchaga, Eduardo. El Derecho Internacional Contemporáneo, *BR*, 431
John of Paris, on world order, 495
Johore, 579
Jordan, position on Gulf of Aqaba, 532–3, 544–5, 552–3
Joyce, James Avery. World Labour Rights and Their Protection, *BR*, 205
Joyner, Christopher C. *BN* of Brittin, 702; *BR* of Ferencz, 211
Judicial assistance: Hague Convention on foreign public documents, *CD*, 182
Judicial Decisions, 160, 385, 616, 847
Jurisdiction: adjudicatory, of Inter-American Human Rights Court, 235–41, 244–5; advisory, of Inter-American Human Rights Court, 235, 242–5; extraterritorial, in public and private international law, *LA*, 280; federal, defenses to under Constitution and extradition law, *JD*, 618–9; high seas v. foreign commerce, under US kidnapping law, *JD*, 619–21; and ICJ enforcement of interim measures orders, 528; of territorial state and foreign ships, 820; private cause of action in US federal courts, *JD*, 169–71; tripartite division of in revised *Restatement* of US foreign relations law, 653–4; vessels on high seas, US-UK Agreement, *CP*, 377–9. *See also* Antitrust; Discontinuance of International Proceedings; Sovereign immunity
Jus gentium. See Law of nations

Kalshoven, Frits, Pieter Jan Kuyper, & Johan G. Lammers (eds.). Essays on the Development of the International Legal Order, *BR*, 188
Kampuchea, 408, 409
Kaplan, Sheldon Z. *BR* of Simon, 880
Kawa, 325, 328, 342
Kearney, Richard D. *Corr.* on Joe C. Barrett, 372
Kellogg-Briand Treaty, 519
Kent, James, 817–8
Kenya, 62, 144, 145, 269
Khan, Prince Sadruddin Aga, report on massive exoduses, 600–1
Kim, Samuel S., & James C. Hsiung (eds.). China in the Global Community, *BN*, 707
———, & Richard A. Falk (eds.). The War System: An Interdisciplinary Approach, *BR*, 186
Kirchwey, George W., 823
Kirgis, Frederic L., Jr. *BR* of Stone, 875
Kissinger, Henry S., 249–50, 263
Klein, Eckart. Statusverträge im Völkerrecht. Rechtsfragen territorialer Sonderregime, *BN*, 470
Knight, H. Gary, 47, 48, 51
Koh group, at UNCLOS seabed negotiations, 104–5
Korea, Democratic People's Republic of (North), 841
Korea, Republic of (South), 408: US security assistance to, 254–5, 269–70, 276

Krausnick, Helmut, & Hans-Heinrich Wilhelm. Die Truppe des Weltanschauungskrieges, *BR*, 448
Kruger, Janice, Ton Gardeniers, & Hurst Hannum. The 1981 Session of the UN Sub-Commission on Prevention of Discrimination and Protection of Minorities, *CD*, 405
Kulikov, R. O Mezhdunarodno-pravovoi otvetstvennosti za narushenie prav cheloveka, *BR*, 455
Kulski, W. W. *BR* of Sonnenfeld and of Frankowska, 673, of Gilas, 674
Kussa, 325, 328, 342
Kuyper, Pieter Jan, Frits Kalshoven, & Johan G. Lammers (eds.). Essays on the Development of the International Legal Order, *BR*, 188

Labouz, Marie-Francoise. L'Organisation des Nations Unies et la Corée. Recherches sur la fiction en droit international public, *BN*, 468
Lacey, John R. *BN* of Dale, 920; *BN* of Waldmann, 472; *BR* of Barack, 903
Lachs, Manfred, on hostage rescue attempt and US case before ICJ, 513, 515–6
Lake Geneva, Treaty of Lausanne (1564) delimitation, 557
Lakes, international, delimitation principles, 556–9, 570
Lammers, Johan G., Frits Kalshoven, & Pieter Jan Kuyper (eds.). Essays on the Development of the International Legal Order, *BR*, 188
Landlocked states and states with special geographical characteristics, and surplus fisheries of neighbors, 38–9, 54
Langdell, C. C., 818
Lansing, Robert, 823
Large-Scale Migrations of Asylum Seekers, *NC*, 598
Larson, Joyce E. (ed.). New Foundations for Asian and Pacific Security, *BR*, 216
Lasswell, Harold D., Myres S. McDougal, & Lung-chu Chen. Human Rights and World Public Order. The Basic Policies of an International Law of Human Dignity, *BR*, 184
Lauterpacht, Sir Hersch: on evidentiary rules of international tribunals, 739; on nationality principle of claims, 651. *See also* Oppenheim/Lauterpacht
(The) Law Governing Treaty Relations between Parties to the Vienna Convention on the Law of Treaties and States Not Party to the Convention, *LA*, 779
Law of nations (*jus gentium*): Grotius on, 481, 482, 488, 497–8; Pufendorf on, 486, 488–91, 492; Suárez on, 479, 488, 496
Law of the sea
  Archipelagic states: jurisdictional limits, 108–9, 110, 113
  Continental shelf, 18: Australia-Papua New Guinea maritime boundaries, *LA*, 321; defining outer limits of, 106–8, 110, 112, 116; hydrocarbon exploitation beyond 200 miles, 10, 12, 21; UNCLOS III on delimitation between states with opposite or adjacent coasts, 14–5, 321, 555
  Deep seabed, 4, 6: definition of the Area, 18; jurisdiction under Torres Strait Treaty, 322, 333–41; technology and UNCLOS negotiations, 83, 86–9, 90, 92, 96, 97–105, 109, 110–1, 112, 113, 115–6; US on UNCLOS mining regime, 9–12; Western countries on UNCLOS mining regime, 21
  Exclusive economic zone, 18, 21, 89: scientific research in, 49, 54–5; UNCLOS III on delimitation between states with opposite or adjacent coasts, 14–5, 321, 555; under Draft LOS Convention, 338–9; under Torres Strait Treaty, 338–40
  Fisheries, 4, 21: coastal state exception in dispute settlement, 19, 29; exemption of small vessels from capture, 821; jurisdiction under Torres Strait Treaty, 322, 328, 333–40, 342–7; relation of Irish law to treaty obligations under EEC law, *JD*, 396–8; US management and LOS treaty, *LA*, 24
  High seas: fishing under FCMA and LOS treaty, 41–3, 45–9, 54; freedoms and Egypt-Israel Peace Treaty, 550–1, 554; US interdiction of illegal migrants on, *CP*, 374–7; US-UK Agreement on vessels trafficking in drugs, *CP*, 377–9
  International Sea-Bed Authority, 100, 102, 105, 637: site selection, 13–4 (*see also* Deep seabed)
  Marine environment and resources: extraterritorial reach of US law on, 297–8; FCMA conservation and allocation measures, 35–40; FCMA conservation and allocation objectives, 25–

9, 31, 32–5; FCMA species coverage, 41, 43–8; fur seal arbitration of 1893, 813; UNCLOS negotiations and technology, 109, 110, 112; under Torres Strait Treaty, 331, 338–40
Territorial sea: claims in Gulf of Aqaba, 532–3; of islands in Torres Strait, 325–6, 327, 333–8, 342–4, 345, 347–9; passage through straits, 4, 21, 83, 348, 534–5: and inland seas generally, 533–45, 547–9, 553–4; and Gulf of Aqaba, 533–4, 541–2, 543, 544–54; sovereign immunity in, *JD*, 173–4; UK minesweeping of Albanian, 506, 745–8, 752–3
Territorial sea, delimitation: breadth of, 4, 18, 50, 55, 534, 558–9, 619–20, 807, 811–2; equidistance method, 580–5, 586, 587, 588; median line principle, 555–6, 558–64, 565, 566–88; perpendicular line, 565, 569–71, 574–7, 579–80, 582–3, 584, 586, 587, 588; proportionality rule, 556–8; the thalweg, 560–4, 569, 571–4, 576, 578–9, 580, 581, 586, 588
Tribunal: site selection, 13–4
See also United Nations Conference on the Law of the Sea
Law of the Sea Tribunal. *See* Law of the sea
(The) Laws of Armed Conflicts. A Collection of Conventions, Resolutions and Other Documents (2d rev. & completed ed.), *BR*, 209
Lawyers Who Established International Law in the United States, 1776–1914, *LA*, 802
Lay, S. Houston, Myron Nordquist, & Kenneth R. Simmonds (eds.). New Directions in the Law of the Sea. Vols. VII & VIII, *BR*, 212
League of Nations, 133, 369, 425, 526–7, 792, 829, 864, 865: Codification Committee on delimitation of territorial sea, 574, 575–6, 577; Covenant, on use of force and arbitral agreements, 518–20, 521; Secretary-General's role re minorities, 132; treaty registration and publication, 350, 353, 355, 356, 358, 362. *See also* Hague Codification Conference; Permanent Court of International Justice
Lebanon, 866
Lee, Luke T. *BR* of Chiu, 915
Legal effect, domestic, of judgments of Inter-American Human Rights Court, 240
Leich, Marian Nash. The Australian-United States Agreement on Cooperation in Antitrust Matters, *CD*, 866; Contemporary Practice of the United States Relating to International Law, 154, 374, 611, 836; Digest of United States Practice in International Law, 1978, *BR*, 437; The Hague Convention Abolishing the Requirement of Legalization for Foreign Public Documents, *CD*, 182; The Montreal Protocols to the Warsaw Convention on International Carriage by Air, *CD*, 412; The Sinai Multinational Force and Observers, *CD*, 181
Leicher, Bruce A., & Stephan M. Minikes. *BR* of Crosswell, 682
Leigh, Monroe. Judicial Decisions, 160, 385, 616, 847
Lerner, Natan. The U.N. Convention on the Elimination of All Forms of Racial Discrimination (2d ed.), *BN*, 703
Levin, D. B. Mezhdunarodnoe Pravo, Vneshniaia Politika i Diplomatiia, *BR*, 672
Liberia, 308
Libya, 145, 169, 266, 321–2, 841
Licari, Tania. *Corr.* on *Ed.* by Jessup, 371
Lie, Trygve, 137
Lieber, Francis, 817: code on law of war, 818
Liebesny, Herbert J. *BR* of Cattan, 696
Liechtenstein, 153, 313, 402
Lillich, Richard B. *BR* of Goodwin-Gill, 670
——— (ed.). U.S. Ratification of the Human Rights Treaties. With or Without Reservations?, *BR*, 666
Lindencrona, Gustaf, & Nils Mattsson. Arbitration in Taxation, *BR*, 440
Lipson, Leon, 84–5
Lipstein, Kurt. Festschrift for, *BR*, 901
Lodge, Juliet (ed.). Terrorism: A Challenge to the State, *BN*, 918
London Fisheries Convention (1964), 397–8
Lowenfeld, Andreas F. *BR* of Zagaris, 441
Luxembourg, 124, 427–8: proposal on invalidity and termination under Vienna Convention on treaty law, 796–7

Machiavelli, 478
Maier, Harold G. Extraterritorial Jurisdiction at a Crossroads: An Intersection between Public and Private International Law, *LA*, 280
Majer, Diemut. "Fremdvölkische" im Dritten Reich, *BR*, 448
Maki, John M. (trans./ed.). Japan's Commission on the Constitution: The Final Report, *BR*, 910
Malaysia, 598
Mali, 144
Malta, 13, 153
Malvinas, Islas. *See* Falkland Islands
Mani, V. S. International Adjudication: Procedural Aspects, *BR*, 660
Marshall, John, decisions incorporating international law principles, 803–5
Martens, Georg F. von, on sea, lake, and river delimitation, 558–9
Martin, David A. Large-Scale Migrations of Asylum Seekers, *NC*, 598
Masquelin, Jean. Le Droit des traités dans l'ordre juridique et dans la pratique diplomatique belges, *BR*, 881
Massachusetts Institute of Technology, study on seabed mining, 103–4, 115, 116
Mata Kawa, 325, 328, 342
Matte, Nicolas Mateesco. Annals of Air and Space Law. Vol. IV, 1979, *BN*, 707; Space Policy and Programmes Today and Tomorrow. The Vanishing Duopole, *BN*, 471; Traité de Droit Aérien-aéronautique (3d ed.), *BR*, 214
Mattsson, Nils, & Gustaf Lindencrona. Arbitration in Taxation, *BR*, 440
Mauritania, 410
Mbaye, Kéba, 368–9
McDougal, Myres S., 84–5, 89, 301
———, Harold D. Lasswell, & Lung-chu Chen. Human Rights and World Public Order. The Basic Policies of an International Law of Human Dignity, *BR*, 184
McKean, Thomas, Chief Justice of Pennsylvania, 802
McVey, Mary D. *BN* of Hsiung & Kim, 707
McWhinney, Edward. *BR* of Maki, 910; Conflict and Compromise, *BR*, 658
Mediterranean Sea, and LOS treaty, 548, 549
Meguid, Ahmed Esmat, 863, 864–5
Meijers, H. Volkenrechtelijke aspecten van Antilliaanse onafhankelijkheid, *BN*, 705
Melander, Göran, & Peter Nobel (eds.). International Legal Instruments on Refugees in Africa, *BR*, 453
Mérignhac, A., on evidentiary rules in international arbitration, 740
Meron, Theodor. Norm Making and Supervision in International Human Rights: Reflections on Institutional Order, *LA*, 754
Mexico, 38–9, 369, 427–8, 812: claims to Belize, 595; sea boundary delimitation practice, 563, 564–5. *See also* Franco-Mexican Claims Convention
Mickolus, Edward F. (comp.). The Literature of Terrorism: A Selectively Annotated Bibliography, *BR*, 914
Military assistance and sales, US, and human rights, *LA*, 246
Military Surrender, Act of (1945), 121
Minikes, Stephan M., & Bruce A. Leicher. *BR* of Crosswell, 682
Mitchell, C. R. The Structure of International Conflict, *BR*, 872
Mixed Arbitral Tribunals established after World War I: rules on discontinuance, 726; sanctions for nonperformance of litigant's duties, 524, 526
Mixed Claims Commission, US-Spanish (1871), on evidentiary rules in international arbitration, 744
Mohonk Conferences, 823, 825
Monroe, James, 809, 811
Monroe Doctrine, 589, 808–9
Montreal Agreement (1966), 413
(The) Montreal Protocols to the Warsaw Convention on International Carriage by Air, *CD*, 412
Moore, John Bassett, 563, 812, 815, 817, 823, 827
Moore, John Norton. The Inter-American System Snarls in Falklands War, *Ed.*, 830
Morocco, 269, 408, 427–8

Morozov, G., on hostage rescue attempt and US case before ICJ, 502–3, 504, 513, 515–6
Morrow, William W., 824
Moskowitz, Moses. *BN* of Lerner, 703
Münch, Fritz, on plotting a median line, 581–3, 587
Munro, Henry F., 827
Murphy, Cornelius F., Jr. The Grotian Vision of World Order, *LA*, 477
Murphy, John F. *BR* of Falk, 897

Nadelmann, Kurt. *Corr.* on Joe C. Barrett, 372
Nagendra Singh, 364, 368–9
Namibia, 408
Nanda, Ved. P. (ed.). The Law of Transnational Business Transactions, *BR*, 908
———, James R. Scarritt, & George W. Shepherd, Jr. Global Human Rights: Public Policies, Comparative Measures, and NGO Strategies, *BR*, 668
Nationalism, rise of, 478–80, 495–6
Nationality: dual, under US-Czechoslovak claims settlement, 651–2; exception in US-Czechoslovak claims settlement, 649–51
Nationalization: and act of state doctrine, *JD*, 162–5; US-Czechoslovak claims settlement, *CD*, 639; 837–8. *See also* Compensation; Expropriation
National liberation movements, 10, 13, 21
National Maritime Union, 308
Natural law, 480–1, 484, 485, 492, 496–8, 803: Pufendorf on, 486–93
Natural resources, conservation by foreign states and US antitrust law, *JD*, 160–2. *See also* Law of the sea: Fisheries, Marine environment and resources
Negotiation, of sea boundaries between states, 563
Negotiations, international, and new technology, *LA*, 78
Nelson, Jack L., & Vera M. Green (eds.). International Human Rights: Contemporary Issues, *BR*, 886
Netherlands, 420, 542, 544, 591–2, 741, 743: on overlapping human rights procedures, 778; sea boundary delimitation practice, 564, 586
Netherlands Yearbook of International Law. Vol. XI, 1980, *BR*, 699; Vol. XII, 1981, *BN*, 921
Newberg, Paula R. (ed.). The Politics of Human Rights, *BR*, 667
Newcity, Michael A. *BR* of Copyright Protection in the Americas. Binder I, 458
New Directions in the Law of the Sea. Vols. VII–X, *BR*, 212
New International Economic Order, 411, 648: and international negotiations, 78–81, 84, 89, 91, 117–8
(A) New United Nations Mechanism for Encouraging the Ratification of Human Rights Treaties, *CD*, 418; *Corr.* on, 832; *Corr.* in response, 833
New Zealand, 269
Nguyen, Quoc Dinh. Droit International Public (2d ed.), *BN*, 220
Nicaragua, 171–2, 537: US security assistance to, 255, 257, 269–70, 272
Njem, Jean-Claude. Le Régime juridique et la nationalisation de concessions pétrolières et autres concessions d'immeubles. Une étude de droit international privé au regard des pays en voie de développement, *BR*, 883
(The) 1981 Session of the Institut de Droit International, *CD*, 176
(The) 1981 Session of the UN Sub-Commission on Prevention of Discrimination and Protection of Minorities, *CD*, 405
(The) 1981 US-Czechoslovak Claims Settlement Agreement: An Epilogue to Postwar Nationalization and Expropriation Disputes, *CD*, 639
Nixon, Richard M., administration implementation of human rights legislation, 248, 249, 250, 256, 263, 272
Nobel, Peter, & Göran Melander (eds.). International Legal Instruments on Refugees in Africa, *BR*, 453
Nongovernmental organizations, 407, 408, 410: and fact-finding by Human Rights Committee, 146–7
Nordquist, Myron, & Kenneth R. Simmonds (eds.). New Directions in the Law of the Sea. Vols. IX & X, *BR*, 212

———, S. Houston Lay, & Kenneth R. Simmonds (eds.). New Directions in the Law of the Sea. Vols. VII & VIII, *BR*, 212
Norm Making and Supervision in International Human Rights: Reflections on Institutional Order, *LA*, 754
North Atlantic Treaty Organization (NATO), individual rights under Status of Forces Agreement, *JD*, 624–6
Northern Ireland, 408
Norway, 576: reservation to Civil and Political Rights Covenant, 152; sea boundary delimitation practice, 580: with Finland, 579; with Sweden, 558, 563, 566–71

O'Brien, William V. The Conduct of Just and Limited War, *BR*, 873
Obscene Publications, Convention on Repression of Circulation of, 828
Oder-Neisse line, and 1970 Warsaw Treaty, *NC*, 119
Official Documents, 712
Olney, Richard, 812, 824
Onuf, N. G. *BR* of Geertz, 663
———, & L. C. Wilson. *BR* of Feuerstein & Parry, 902
Opium and Other Drugs, Convention on Suppression of Abuse of, 828
Oppenheim/Lauterpacht, on general participation clauses, 784
Orbit/spectrum: basic legal regulatory principle, 57–65; planning allocation of, 67–9; planning considered jurimetrically, 70–3, 76
Order, international: and Catholic Church, 477–8, 494, 495; Dante on, 477–9, 483, 493–5; Grotius's vision, *LA*, 477; and Holy Roman emperor, 477–9, 483, 491, 495; John of Paris on, 495; Pufendorf on, 485–93; Spinoza on, 484–5, 487, 489, 490; Suárez on, 479, 482, 488, 493, 495–7
Organization for Economic Co-operation and Development (OECD), 845
Organization of African Unity, treaty definition of refugee, 606, 608–9
Organization of American States (OAS), 133–4, 231–6, 241, 242, 243, 244, 245, 656, 754, 809: Copyright Protection in the Americas. Binder I, *BR*, 458; Juridical Committee and Falklands-Malvinas sovereignty, *Ed.*, 594; resolution on Falklands-Malvinas war, *Ed.*, 830; treaty registration and publication, 360
Organization of Petroleum Exporting Countries (OPEC), 160–1
Otunnu, Olara, 369–70
Outer Space Treaty (1967), and allocation of broadcasting-satellite frequencies, 59–62, 68, 74
Oxman, Bernard H. The Third United Nations Conference on the Law of the Sea: The Tenth Session (1981), *LA*, 1

Pakistan, 139, 598
Palestine Liberation Organization (PLO), 10, 11, 169
Pambou Tchivounda, Guillaume. La Conférence au Sommet: Contribution à l'Etude des Institutions des Relations Internationales, *BR*, 695
Panama, 594: deportations by and extradition law, *JD*, 618–9; sea boundary delimitation practice, 565, 577. *See also* Panama Canal
Panama Canal, 402, 594; delimitation of Zone, 565, 577; treaties establishing Zone, 812, 822
Pan American Health Organization. *See* World Health Organization
Pan American Union, 814
Papacy. *See* Roman Catholic Church
Papua New Guinea, 428: maritime boundary Treaty with Australia, *LA*, 321
Paraguay, 171, 408, 656: US security assistance to, 254–5, 260, 269–70, 272, 274–5
Parry, Audrey, & J. E. S. Fawcett. Law and International Resource Conflicts, *BR*, 675
Parry, Clive (ed.). Index-Guide to Treaties. Based on the Consolidated Treaty Series and all other series therein utilised. Vol. I: General Chronological List 1648–1809, *BR*, 466
———, & Peter Feuerstein (eds.). Multum Non Multa. Festschrift für Kurt Lipstein, *BR*, 901
Pechota, Vratislav. The 1981 U.S.-Czechoslovak Claims Settlement Agreement: An Epilogue to Postwar Nationalization and Expropriation Disputes, *CD*, 639
Perkins, John A. The Prudent Peace: Law as Foreign Policy, *BR*, 871

Permanent Court of Arbitration, 826: delimitation of sea boundary between Norway and Sweden, 566–71
Permanent Court of International Justice (PCIJ), 368, 518, 815, 864: admission of evidence by, 742–3, 748; enforcement of interim measures, 526–7; on nationality and international claims, 837; on obligations of parties to a case, 510; Rules on discontinuance, 721–2, 723
Peru, 234, 236, 237, 393, 402: exchange control regulations and IMF Agreement, *JD*, 627–9
Pettman, Ralph. State and Class: A Sociology of International Affairs, *BR*, 190
Philippines, 370, 408, 422: US security assistance to, 254–5, 260, 269–70, 271, 276; whether executive agreement with preferential employment provision constitutes treaty, *JD*, 855–7
Phillimore, Sir Robert, 817
Phillips, Leo H., Jr. *BN* of Wilson, 920; *BR* of Akinsanya, 683
Picone, Paolo, & Giorgio Sacerdoti. Diritto Internazionale dell'Economia, *BR*, 902
(The) Plaintiff's Dilemma: Illegally Obtained Evidence and Admissibility in International Adjudication, *LA*, 737
Plischke, Elmer. *BR* of Foreign Relations of the United States, 1952–1954, Vol. XVI: The Geneva Conference, 467; *BR* of Irwin, 466
Poland, 131, 590, 840: US sanctions against, *CP*, 379–81; western boundary under Warsaw Treaty with FRG, *NC*, 119
Pomeroy, J. W., 818
Portugal, 13: free trade agreement with EEC and EEC law, *JD*, 857–62
Potsdam Agreement, 120–8
Preparatory Commission of the United Nations, 369, 865
Private international law: extraterritorial jurisdiction in public and, *LA*, 280; Hague Convention on foreign public documents, *CD*, 182; 1981 resolutions of Institut de Droit International, *CD*, 176. *See also* Hague Convention on Service Abroad; Hague Convention on Taking Evidence Abroad
Property rights, copyright restrictions vis-à-vis third countries and EEC law, *JD*, 857–62
Protected Zone, under Torres Strait Treaty, 322, 327, 330–2, 337, 343, 344–7, 348
Pufendorf, Samuel: on sea boundary delimitation, 556–7, 560, 570, 586, 587; on world order, 485–93
Puig, Juan Carlos. Doctrinas Internacionales y Autonomía Latinoamericana, *BR*, 431

Queensland, 1879 boundary, 324–6, 330

Raestad, Arnold, on *Grisbadarna* delimitation, 569–70
Ramcharan, B. G. The Good Offices of the United Nations Secretary-General in the Field of Human Rights, *NC*, 130
Randolph, Edmund, 803
Raymond, John M., & Barbara J. Frischholz. Lawyers Who Established International Law in the United States, 1776–1914, *LA*, 802
Reagan, Ronald, extension of "Carter doctrine" on external aggression, *Ed.*, 589. *See also* United States President
Recent Developments in United Nations Treaty Registration and Publication Practices, *LA*, 350
Recognition, validity of acts of US Confederacy, 818–9
Recognition and Enforcement of Foreign Arbitral Awards, Convention on, defenses to enforcement under, *JD*, 166–9
Recueil des Cours de l'Académie de droit international de La Haye, 1978. Vols. 1–3, *BR*, 199
Red Cross Conventions (1949), 784
Reese, Willis L. M., 302–3: *Corr.* on Joe C. Barrett, 372
Reformation, 478, 482, 492, 493, 495
Refugees, 132, 134, 374, 377. *See also* Asylum
Refugees, Convention relating to the Status of (1951), 598, 603–4, 606, 607–9
Refugees, Protocol relating to the Status of (1967), 374, 603–4, 607
Reijnen, Gijsbertha C. M. Utilization of Outer Space and International Law, *BN*, 703
Reisman, W. Michael. Critical Defense Zones and International Law: The Reagan Codicil, *Ed.*, 589; *BR* of Young, 868; on nondisclosure of documents, 525

———, & Eric E. Freedman. The Plaintiff's Dilemma: Illegally Obtained Evidence and Admissibility in International Adjudication, *LA*, 737
Renaissance, 482, 493
Reporting Under the Covenant on Civil and Political Rights: The First Five Years of the Human Rights Committee, *NC*, 142
Reprisals, US against Iran, permissibility *pendente lite*, 503, 515–7
Reservations, 179, 181, 243, 801: to Civil and Political Rights Covenant, 152; to LOS Convention, 14; to the Vienna Convention on treaty law, 798–9, 800; under the Vienna Convention, 780, 790–2
Respect for judicial process, as used by ICJ in *Hostages* case, 501, 504–15, 521–3
Ress, Georg (ed.). Souveränitätsverständnis in den Europäischen Gemeinschaften, *BR*, 686
Restatement of Foreign Relations Law of the United States (Revised), 280: Tentative Draft No. 2, 654: law applicable in domestic courts to transnational events, 300–3, 316, 317–20, 843–4; Tentative Draft No. 3, *CD*, 653: extraterritorial jurisdiction, 654–5
Restatement (Second) of Conflict of Laws, 280: law applicable in domestic courts to transnational events, 285–7, 290–1, 295, 302–3, 317, 319
Restatement (Second) of Foreign Relations Law of the United States, 280, 656: law applicable in domestic courts to transnational events, 285–6, 290–300, 302
Restrictive business practices, copyright restrictions vis-à-vis third countries and EEC law, *JD*, 857–62
Retroactivity, barring of under Vienna Convention on treaty law, 779–82, 783
Reunification of Germany, 127, 128–9
Reuter, Paul, on role of ILC, 633
Rhee, Sang-Myon. Sea Boundary Delimitation between States Before World War II, *LA*, 555
Riesenfeld, Stefan A. *BR* of Leich, 437; *BR* of Venturini, of Watson, 904, of Campbell, of Rudden & Wyatt, 905
Rifaat, Ahmed M. International Aggression. A Study of the Legal Concept: Its Development and Definition in International Law, *BR*, 446
Riklin, Alois (ed.). Internationale Konventionen gegen die Folter. St. Galler Expertengespräch 1978, *BN*, 221
Rio Treaty (1947), 809, 830–1
Riphagen, W., on LOS negotiations, 8–9
Rivers: international, delimitation principles, 555–6, 558–9, 570, 581; municipal law delimitation principles, 557
Roach, J. Ashley. *BN* of Huynh, 223; *BR* of Schindler & Toman, 209
Röhm, Eberhard H. *BR* of Bizec & Daudet, 678
Roman Catholic Church, papal power and world order, 477–8, 494, 495–6
Romania, 837
Ronen, Dov. The Quest for Self-Determination, *BR*, 451
Roosevelt, Franklin D., 263
Root, Elihu, 510, 810, 823, 824, 825
Rosenbaum, Alan S. (ed.). The Philosophy of Human Rights: International Perspectives, *BR*, 884
Rosencranz, Armin. The ECE Convention of 1979 on Long-Range Transboundary Air Pollution, *CD* Oct. 1981, correction to, 153
Rosenne, Shabtai, 520, 630: The Election of Five Members of the International Court of Justice in 1981, *NC*, 364; the Election of March 1982 to Fill One Vacancy in the International Court of Justice, *CD*, 863; on evidentiary rules in international adjudication, 744
Rosenstock, Robert. *BR* of Perkins, 871
Rothblatt, Martin A. Satellite Communication and Spectrum Allocation, *LA*, 56
Rubin, Alfred P. *BR* of Allen, Stockwell, & Wright, 218; *BR* of Recueil des Cours de l'Académie de droit international de La Haye, 1978. Vols. 1–3, 199
Rubin, Seymour J. *BR* of Gardner, 196; *BR* of Horn, 191; The Falklands (Malvinas), International Law, and the OAS, *Ed.*, 594
Ruda, José María, 364, 368
Rudden, Bernard, & Derrick Wyatt (eds.). Basic Community Laws, *BR*, 905
Ruddy, F. S. *BN* of Nguyen, 220

Rusk, Dean. *BR* of Finger, 443
Russell, Ruth B. *BN* of Labouz, 468
Russo-Japanese War, 822
Rwanda, 422, 427–8

Sacerdoti, Giorgio, & Paolo Picone. Diritto Internazionale dell'Economia, *BR*, 902
Saibai, 322, 324, 327, 329, 333, 337
Sanctions, availability of against ICJ litigant, 504, 523–30; economic, US against Poland and USSR, *CP*, 379–84; 840. *See also* Reprisals
Sandifer, D.: on evidentiary rules of international tribunals, 738–40; on nondisclosure of documents, 524, 525
San Francisco Conference (establishing the UN, 1945): compromise on meaning of "absolute majority," 863–5; on elections to ICJ, 865. *See also* Preparatory Commission of the United Nations
San Marino, 153
Satellite Communication and Spectrum Allocation, *LA*, 56
Saudi Arabia, 590–1: position on Gulf of Aqaba, 532–3, 543, 544–5, 552–3
Scarritt, James R., Ved P. Nanda, & George W. Shepherd, Jr. (eds.). Global Human Rights: Public Policies, Comparative Measures, and NGO Strategies, *BR*, 668
Schachter, Oscar. *BR* of Jennings & Brownlie, 876; Hardy Cross Dillard (1902–1982), *Ed.*, 595; The 1981 Session of the Institut de Droit International, *CD*, 176
Schaefer, Michael. Die Funktionsfähigkeit des Sicherheitsmechanismus der Vereinten Nationen, *BR*, 447
Schechter, Michael G. *BR* of Falk & Kim, 186
Schindler, Dietrich, & Jiří Toman (eds.). The Laws of Armed Conflicts. A Collection of Conventions, Resolutions and other Documents (2d rev. & completed ed.), *BR*, 209
Schücking, Walther, on territorial sea delimitation, 575
Schwarzenberger, G. *BR* of Bilder, 658
Scotland Yard, 387, 388
Scott, James Brown, 817, 823, 824, 825, 826, 827, 828
Sea Boundary Delimitation between States Before World War II, *LA*, 555
Seara Vázquez, Modesto. Derecho Internacional Público, *BR*, 900
Security assistance, US, and human rights, *LA*, 246
Self-defense: anticipatory, in 17th-century theory, 481, 490–1; in Falklands-Malvinas war, 831; Webster on law of, 808; whether barred *pendente lite*, 504, 519–23
Self-determination, Falklands-Malvinas dispute, *Ed.*, 594; *Ed.*, 830
Self-help measures: as defense to illegal gathering of evidence, 746–7, 749; during judicial proceedings, 511–2, 516
Senegal, domestic law and Civil and Political Rights Covenant, 152
Settlement of Investment Disputes Between States and Nationals of Other States, Convention on (World Bank Convention, 1966), 727
Seward, William H., 807, 811–2
Sharjah, offshore oil concession dispute, *JD*, 399–402
Shelton, Dinah. *BR* of Willamette Law Review. Vol. 17, no. 1, 697
Shepherd, George W., Ved P. Nanda, & James R. Scarritt (eds.). Global Human Rights: Public Policies, Comparative Measures, and NGO Strategies, *BR*, 668
Simma, Bruno. *BR* of Decaux, 198
Simmonds, Kenneth R., Myron Nordquist, & S. Houston Lay (eds.). New Directions in the Law of the Sea. Vols. VII & VIII, *BR*, 212
———, & Myron Nordquist (eds.). New Directions in the Law of the Sea. Vols. IX & X, *BR*, 212
Simon, Denys. L'Interprétation judiciaire des Traités d'organisations internationales, *BR*, 880
Simons, Thad W., Jr. *BN* of Usher, 919
(The) Sinai Multinational Force and Observers, *CD*, 181; presidential report to Congress on deployment, *CP*, 613–5
Singapore, 269, 579

Slim, Taïeb, 368
Smiley, Albert K., 823
Snow, Freeman, 816, 818, 827
Sohn, Louis, on international human rights procedures, 766, 769–70, 775
Solomon Islands, 333, 422
Somalia, 402, 598
Sommereyns, Raymond. *BR* of Tabory, 433
Sonnenfeld, Renata (ed.). Odpowiedzialność Państwa w Prawie Międznarodowym, *BR*, 673
South Africa, 137, 266, 408, 412
South African Yearbook of International Law, Volume 5, 1979, *BN*, 706
Southeast Asia, refugee migrations in, 604, 606
Sovereign immunity: and act of state, *JD*, 160–2; *JD*, 162–5; of foreign sovereigns under US law, *JD*, 171–3; *JD*, 173–4; and international commercial system, 309–10, 312; UK demarcation between sovereign and commercial acts, *JD*, 402–4. *See also* United States: Foreign Sovereign Immunities Act
Soviet Purchasing Commission (in US), 382, 383
Soviet Yearbook of International Law, 1979, *BR*, 217
Space law, 91, 97: early negotiations on, 84–5, 89; and new technology, 113–4, 115; Satellite Communication and Spectrum Allocation, *LA*, 56
Spain, 14–5, 305–6, 397, 410, 427–8, 740, 807, 821: sea boundary delimitation practice, 562, 563, 565
Spencer, John H. *BR* of Asian-African Legal Consultative Committee, 461; *BR* of Melander & Nobel, 453
Spinoza, on world order, 484–5, 487, 489, 490
Sri Lanka, 408
State responsibility, 751, 752: continuous nationality rule of claims, 649–51; *CP*, 836–9; ILC progress on codification, 634, 638; *Restatement* of US foreign relations law on, 656–7
Steele, Robert D. (ed.). The Iran Crisis and International Law. Proceedings of the John Bassett Moore Society of International Law, *BR*, 460
Stegenga, James A. *BR* of Best, 208
Stein, Ted L. Contempt, Crisis, and the Court: The World Court and the Hostage Rescue Attempt, *LA*, 499
Stevenson, Russell B., Jr. *BR* of Nanda, 908
Stockholm Conference on the World Environment, 92
Stockwell, A. J., J. de V. Allen, & L. R. Wright (eds.). A Collection of Treaties and other Documents affecting the States of Malaysia, 1761–1963. Vols. I & II, *BR*, 218
Stone, Julius. *BR* of Rosenbaum, 884; Israel and Palestine: Assault on the Law of Nations, *BR*, 875
Storni, Segundo R., draft articles on territorial waters, 572
Story, Joseph, on comity, 283–4, 295, 296, 319
Stowell, Ellery C., 827
Straus, Oscar S., 823–4
Strupp, Karl, on *Grisbadarna* delimitation, 570
St. Ville, Mary, & Josephine Cockrell Thornton. *BR* of Joyce and of Valticos, 205
Suárez, Francisco, on world order, 479, 482, 488, 493, 495–7
Suez Canal, under Egyptian-Israeli Peace Treaty, 547
Suriname, 422, 427–8: Constitution and Civil and Political Rights Covenant, 152
Suzuki, Eisuke. *BR* of Fukuda, 911
Sweden, 412, 421, 576–7: domestic law and Civil and Political Rights Covenant, 152; objections to reservations under Vienna Convention on treaty law, 798; on retroactivity and general participation under Vienna Convention, 781, 786, 787; sea boundary delimitation practice, 580: with Finland, 559, 578; with Norway, 558, 563, 566–71
Switzerland, 297, 740, 742, 842, 846, 861: on dispute settlement under Vienna Convention on treaty law, 797
Syria, 412, 421: reservation to Vienna Convention on treaty law, 798
Szawlowski, Richard. *BR* of Kulikov, 455; *BR* of Seara Vázquez, 900

Tabory, Mala. Multilingualism in International Law and Institutions, *BR*, 433; Recent Developments in United Nations Treaty Registration and Publication Practices, *LA*, 350
Taft, William Howard, 823
Taiwan, 269
Talbot, Lord Chancellor, 802
Tana Lagoon, 532
Tanzania, 144
Tarazi, Salah El Dine, on hostage rescue attempt and US case before ICJ, 502, 503–4, 512–3, 515–6
Tate letter (1952), 309
Technology and International Negotiations, *LA*, 78
Technology transfer, marine, and LOS convention, 9–10, 12, 21, 87
Teclaff, Ludwik, & Albert E. Utton. International Groundwater Law, *BR*, 692
Telecommunications, 828, 829: allocation of orbit/spectrum for satellites, *LA*, 56. *See also* International Telecommunication Convention; International Telecommunication Union
Territorial sea. *See* Law of the sea
Territorial sovereignty, John Marshall on, 804–5. *See also* Falkland Islands
Thailand, 269, 410, 598
Thant, U, 130, 137–8
(The) Third United Nations Conference on the Law of the Sea: The Tenth Session (1981), *LA*, 1
Third World, 599: on role and performance of ILC, 631–2, 635–6
Thirlway, H. W. A., on general participation under Vienna Convention on treaty law, 783
Thornton, Josephine Cockrell, & Mary St. Ville. *BR* of Joyce and of Valticos, 205
Timmermans, C. W. A., & E. L. M. Völker (eds.). Division of powers between the European Communities and their Member States in the field of external relations, *BR*, 684
Toman, Jiří, & Dietrich Schindler (eds.). The Laws of Armed Conflicts. A Collection of Conventions, Resolutions and other Documents (2d rev. & completed ed.), *BR*, 209
Torres Strait Treaty. *See* Treaty concerning Sovereignty and Maritime Boundaries between Australia and Papua New Guinea
(The) Torres Strait Treaty: Ocean Boundary Delimitation by Agreement, *LA*, 321
Torrey, Henry Warren, 816
Tortora, Manuela. Institution Specialisée et Organisation Mondiale: Etude des Relations de l'OIT avec la SDN et l'ONU, *BR*, 445
Torture, under US human rights legislation, 251–2, 267–8, 269, 275, 276, 277
Touscoz, Jean, & Jean d'Herbes. Les Contrats internationaux de coopération industrielle et le nouvel ordre économique international, *BR*, 883
Transnational corporations, proposed EEC rules having extraterritorial effect, 591–2. *See also* Antitrust; Restrictive business practices
(Les) Travailleurs Etrangers et le Droit International, *BR*, 687
Treaties: application of US local law under FCN, *JD*, 853–5; between states and international organizations, etc., governing law under, 782, 801; conflict of laws in private international law, 176, 178–81; definition under US Constitution, *JD*, 855–7; early US practice, 809–14, 822, 827–8, 829; effects of armed conflicts on, 176; extradition, US procedures under, *CP*, 154–9; human rights, and the Inter-American Human Rights Court, 242–3; human rights, normative conflicts and supervision, *LA*, 754; individual rights under, *JD*, 624–6; legal effect in early US practice, 805; negotiations and technology, *LA*, 78; private cause of action under, *JD*, 169–71; reporting US executive agreements to Congress, *CP*, 377; theories of Grotius and Pufendorf, 491; UN registration and publication, *LA*, 350. *See also* Extradition; (A) New United Nations Mechanism for Encouraging the Ratification of Human Rights Treaties; (The) Torres Strait Treaty: Ocean Boundary Delimitation by Agreement; Treaty of Peace between Egypt and Israel; (The) Warsaw Treaty of 1970 and the Western Boundary of Poland; Vienna Convention on the Law of Treaties
Treaty concerning La Plata River (1973), 346
Treaty concerning Sovereignty and Maritime Boundaries between Australia and Papua New

Guinea (Torres Strait Treaty, 1978), *LA*, 321: special needs of islanders, 322–4, 327, 329–32, 337, 347
Treaty of Corinto (1902), 518
Treaty of Peace between Egypt and Israel: deployment of Multinational Force and Observers, *CP*, 613–5; establishment of MFO, *CD*, 181; regime for Gulf of Aqaba, *LA*, 532
Treaty of Rome (1957): and agreements between EEC and third countries, *JD*, 857–62; standing of individual from nonmember state to invoke Art. 234, *JD*, 396–8
Treaty of Versailles, 491, 743
Tripartite Commission for the Restitution of Monetary Gold (France, UK, US), and Czechoslovak monetary gold, 640, 643–6
Truman Proclamation (1945), 555
Tucker, George Fox, 827
Tunisia, 268, 269, 321–2, 408, 577: reservation to Vienna Convention on treaty law, 798
Tunteng, P-Kiven. *BR* of Baccelli, 215
Turkey, sea boundary delimitation practice, 562–3, 580
(A) Turnabout in Extraterritoriality, *Ed.*, 591
Twiss, Travers, on sea boundary delimitation, 560, 563

Uganda, 138
Umm al Qaiwain, offshore oil concession dispute, *JD*, 399–402
UN Code de Conduite pour le Transfert de Technologie, *BR*, 678
Unification of Certain Rules Relating to International Transportation by Air, Convention for. *See* Warsaw Convention of 1929
Union of Soviet Socialist Republics (USSR), 107–8, 119, 122, 126, 137, 143, 266, 270, 271, 325, 370, 408, 421–2, 560, 579, 589, 590, 652, 751: on overlapping human rights procedures, 777–8; on US LOS policy review, 5, 6; proposal on objections to reservations under Vienna Convention on treaty law, 791; US sanctions against, *CP*, 379–80, 382–4; 840; US Supreme Court on US labor boycott of, *JD*, 849–51
United Kingdom, 143, 177, 312–3, 370, 391, 537, 542, 592, 652, 806–7, 820, 822: Agreement with US on vessels trafficking in drugs, *CP*, 377–9; *Caroline* incident, 807–8; choice of US forum by Scottish plaintiffs, *JD*, 394–6; copyright law vis-à-vis third countries and EEC law, *JD*, 857–62; early US treaty practice, 809–13, 822; enforcement of IMF Agreement, *JD*, 627–9; production and admissibility of evidence in *Corfu Channel* dispute, 506, 525, 745–8, 749, 752–3; restrictive theory of sovereign immunity, *JD*, 402–4; and return of Czechoslovak gold, 640, 643–7; "sovereign transactions" corollary to act of state doctrine, *JD*, 399–402; territorial sea delimitation practice, 560, 563: with US, 560, 561–2, 563, 572–3, 578; and US assertion of extraterritorial jurisdiction, 840, 842, 843. *See also* Falkland Islands
United Nations: encouragement of human rights treaty ratification, *CD*, 418; treaty registration and publication, *LA*, 350
United Nations Ad Hoc Committee on the Drafting of an International Convention against the Taking of Hostages, 632
United Nations Charter, 128, 176, 380, 424, 425, 500, 545–6, 552, 630–1, 712, 754, 759–60, 785, 795, 830–1, 861: good offices of Secretary-General under, 130, 134, 135–6, 137, 138, 141; on self-defense, 520; treaty registration and publication under, 350–1, 352, 355, 356, 358, 360, 361
United Nations Charter of Economic Rights and Duties of States, 648
United Nations Commission on Human Rights, 757: and good offices of Secretary-General, 134, 136; and large-scale refugee migrations, 599–602; supervision of compliance, 764–5; 34th session of Sub-Commission on Discrimination and Protection of Minorities, *CD*, 405; working group on encouraging acceptance of treaties, *CD*, 418
United Nations Commission on International Trade Law (UNCITRAL), Arbitration Rules, 736: on discontinuance, 727
United Nations Committee on the Elimination of Racial Discrimination (CERD), 145, 151, 770
United Nations Committee on the Peaceful Uses of Outer Space, 632
United Nations Committee on the Peaceful Uses of the Sea-bed, 2, 4, 632

United Nations Conference on the Law of the Sea (1958), 82, 106: on passage through inland seas, 542–5. *See also* Geneva Convention on the Territorial Sea

(Second) United Nations Conference on the Law of the Sea (1960), 82

(Third) United Nations Conference on the Law of the Sea, 321, 323, 348, 349, 360, 637, 655: passage through straits and inland seas, 546, 547–9, 550–1, 554; *Restatement* of US foreign relations law on progress and US sea law, 655; and technological change, *LA*, 78; The Tenth Session (1981), *LA*, 1; US fishery management and LOS treaty, *LA*, 24. *See also* Law of the sea

United Nations Conference on the Law of Treaties, 800: on general participation under Vienna Convention, 786; on nonretroactivity under Vienna Convention, 780–2; on objections to reservations, 791

United Nations Conference on Trade and Development (UNCTAD), 80, 114: reports on seabed mining, 97–9

United Nations Draft Convention on Arbitral Procedure (1955), on discontinuance, 726

United Nations Economic and Social Council, 134, 136, 146, 406, 407, 408, 412, 421, 423, 425, 429, 765, 767, 778

United Nations Economic Commission for Europe, 153

United Nations Educational, Scientific and Cultural Organization (UNESCO), 80, 410, 611: Director-General and good offices, 133–4; normative and supervisory conflicts with other human rights agencies, 759–60, 766, 768–9, 770

United Nations Emergency Force, and Gulf of Aqaba, 533

United Nations General Assembly, 4, 79, 80, 83, 84, 94, 130, 408, 411, 412, 418–9, 425, 428, 429, 632, 635, 648, 757, 760, 764–5, 797, 848: Declaration of Principles on Sea-bed, 18, 95; declaration on religious discrimination, 759; on good offices of Secretary-General, 131, 134, 136, 140; and large-scale refugee migrations, 601–2, 607–8; March 1982 ICJ election, *CD*, 863; 1981 ICJ regular election, *NC*, 364; resolutions and law development, 91–2; resolution on permanent sovereignty over natural resources, 642; 6th Committee's relationship with ILC, 630, 633, 635, 636, 638; and treaty registration and publication, 351, 353, 355, 356–8, 359, 361–2

United Nations High Commissioner for Human Rights, proposal to create, 405, 412

United Nations High Commissioner for Refugees, 139, 141, 429: exercise of good offices, 133–4; and large-scale influxes, 598–9, 603–8

United Nations Human Rights Committee, *NC*, 142: fact-finding capability, 146–7; independence of members, 142–4; influence on state law and practice, 151–3; power to make recommendations, 147–51, 153; proposal to broaden competence, 763–4; supervision of compliance, 765–8, 770, 771, 775–7

United Nations Institute for Training and Research (UNITAR), 426, 427–8: study on role and use of ILC, *CD*, 630

United Nations Juridical Yearbook, 362

United Nations Secretariat, 107, 369, 406, 764: reports on seabed mining, 97–9, 113, 115; staffing of ILC, 635, 637; treaty registration and publication by, 351–60, 362–3; on validity of amendments to treaties, 793

United Nations Secretary-General, 146, 152, 408, 410, 419–20, 421, 422, 423, 427, 428, 632, 774, 789, 793, 795, 799, 865: and elections to ICJ, 364–6, 367, 369, 863; good offices in human rights field, *NC*, 130; and large-scale refugee migrations, 600, 602; and treaty registration and publication, 352, 355, 357–8, 359, 361

United Nations Security Council, 128, 134, 135, 137, 181, 182, 362, 499, 531, 613: March 1982 ICJ election, *CD*, 863; 1981 ICJ regular election, *NC*, 364; Res. 502 on Falklands-Malvinas war, *OD*, 712; 831; resolutions and passage through Gulf of Aqaba, 545–7, 550

United Nations Treaty Information System (SIONUT), 354–5, 359, 360

United Nations Treaty Series and [Monthly] Statements, recent practices, *LA*, 350

United States

- Agreement on cooperation in antitrust matters with Australia (1982), 845; *CD*, 866
- agreement with Haiti on illegal migrants, *CP*, 374–7
- Agreement with UK on vessels trafficking in drugs, *CP*, 377–9
- Air Transport Agreement with Poland (1972), 380–1
- Alien Tort Claims Act, subject matter jurisdiction under, *JD*, 169–71

alleged human rights violations, 408
Arms Export Control Act, 273–4
Base Labor Agreement with Philippines (1968), 855–6
Boat Safety Act (1971), 376
Case-Zablocki Act, 377
Civil Rights Act (1964), 853
Civil War, cases and claims, 812–3, 818–21
Clayton Act, 160
Clayton-Bulwer Treaty (1850), 811, 822
Comprehensive Drug Abuse Prevention and Control Act (1970), 379
Czechoslovak claims settlement, *CD*, 639: Agreement on the Settlement of Certain Outstanding Claims and Financial Issues (1981), 639–42, 647, 648, 649, 653, 837; Czechoslovakian Claims Settlement Act (1981), 639, 648–51, 837–8
Export Administration Act (1979), 840–1
Extradition Treaty with Israel, 392
Extradition Treaty with UK, political offense exception, *JD*, 391–2
Federal Aviation Act (1958), 381, 382–3
Federal Kidnapping Act, high seas and foreign commerce jurisdiction, *JD*, 619–21
Fishermen's Protective Act, 44–5
Fishery Conservation and Management Act (1976), 174: and LOS treaty, *LA*, 24: amendments to regulations under, 52–3; distribution of state-federal authority, 49–51, 55
Foreign Agents Registration Act, scope of registration requirement, *JD*, 621–3
Foreign Assistance Act (1973), human rights provision, 250, 251–2, 258
Foreign Assistance Act (1974), human rights provisions: evolution of, 249, 250–4; Executive implementation, 247–9, 256–78
Foreign Sovereign Immunities Act (1976), 160–1: exceptions to jurisdiction, *JD*, 171–3; *JD*, 173–4; explicit waiver of immunity, *JD*, 851–3; immunity standards, *JD*, 623–4; jury trials and actions against foreign states, *JD*, 393–4
Hay-Pauncefote Treaty (1901), 822
Immigration and Nationality Act, 165–6, 376
International Claims Settlement Act (1949), 649: proposed amendment on "late" nationals, *CP*, 836–9
International Emergency Economic Powers Act (1977), 841
International Organizations Immunities Act (1945), immunity standards, *JD*, 623–4
Iranian *Hostages* case: barriers to collection of evidence by Iran and the ICJ, 748–51, 753; discontinuance of, *LA*, 717; rescue attempt and the ICJ, *LA*, 499
Jay Treaty (1794), 810, 811
Jones Act, 304–5
Labor Management Relations Act, 850
Lawyers Who Established International Law in, 1776–1914, *LA*, 802
Limitation of Liability Act, 313
Longshoremen's and Harbor Workers' Compensation Act, 393
Marine Mammal Protection Act (1972), 28, 32: extraterritorial reach, 297–8
National Emergencies Act, 841
National Labor Relations Act, 307–9: Supreme Court on secondary political boycott under, *JD*, 849–51
Neutrality Act (1794), 806
position on draft LOS treaty, 2–12, 14–5, 22
position on nonretroactivity of Vienna Convention on treaty law, 781
and ratification of human rights treaties, 422, 426–8, 764, 833–4
Reciprocal Fisheries Agreement with Canada (1977), 346–7
Refugee Act (1980), deportation standards, *JD*, 386–8
responses to European assertions of extraterritoriality, *Ed.*, 591
Rush-Bagot Agreement (1817), 811
sea boundary delimitation practice, 321, 325, 349, 559, 564–5, 577, 586, 831: with UK, 560, 561–2, 563, 572–3, 578

Securities Exchange Act (1934), 313–4
Sherman Act, 160
Sinai Multinational Force and Observers: deployment of, *CP*, 613–5; establishment of, *CD*, 181
Submerged Lands Act (1953), 49–50
Tariff Act (1930), 379: Government's authority to settle claims, *JD*, 389–91
Trade Act (1974), 647–8
Trade Agreement Act (1979), 390
Trading with the Enemy Act, 841
Treaty of Amity, Economic Relations and Consular Rights with Iran (1955), 502
Treaty of Friendship, Commerce and Navigation with Japan (1953), 853–5
Treaty of Washington (1871), 812–3
War Claims Act (1948), 838
Webster-Ashburton Treaty (1842), 810
United States Air Force, 624
United States Attorney General, 387–8
United States Civil Aeronautics Board, 380–3, 413, 415, 416–7
United States Coast Guard, 384: authority to board and search UK vessels on high seas, 377–8; high seas interdiction of illegal aliens, 375, 376–7
United States Commodity Futures Trading Commission, 842, 843
United States Congress, 43, 48, 49, 50, 52, 161, 166, 388, 390, 392, 394, 592, 620, 622, 639, 809, 845, 852: extraterritorial effects of legislation, 291, 293, 297, 299–300, 301, 304, 305, 307, 309, 314, 318, 840; human rights legislation, 247–8, 249–56, 261, 265, 273, 274, 275, 276, 277–8; implementation of Cultural Property Convention, *CP*, 611–3; law on Sinai Multinational Force, *CP*, 613–5; policy and role in Czechoslovak claims settlement, 646, 647–8, 650, 653; policy on claims settlement generally, *CP*, 836–9; reporting executive agreements to, *CP*, 377; whether statutory use of "treaty" includes executive agreements, *JD*, 855–7
United States Constitution, 376, 379, 802, 850–1: on choice of law, 287–8, 300; definition of treaty, *JD*, 855–7; forcible abduction and federal jurisdiction, *JD*, 618–9; incorporation of international law principles, 803; jury trials and actions against foreign states, *JD*, 393–4; *Restatement* of US foreign relations law principles from, 657; rights of military personnel abroad, *JD*, 624–6; state citizenship requirement for public employment, *JD*, 616–7; uniform rule of naturalization, *JD*, 165–6
United States Court of Claims, 183
United States Court of Customs and Patent Appeals, 183
United States Court of International Trade, 183: on Government's authority to settle customs claims, *JD*, 389–91
United States Court of Military Appeals, constitutional rights of US military personnel abroad, *JD*, 624–6
United States Department of Agriculture, 380
United States Department of Commerce, 384, 389, 840–1, 846: role of Secretary in fishery management, 28, 40, 47, 51, 52–3
United States Department of Defense, 855
United States Department of Justice, 156, 158, 392, 427, 593, 845, 846
United States Department of State, 2, 12, 40, 47, 52, 54, 164, 182, 183, 377, 379, 381, 383, 384, 392, 427, 646: on continuous nationality rule of claims, *CP*, 836–9; guidelines on extradition, *CP*, 154–9; implementation of human rights legislation, *LA*, 246: attitude of Foreign Service, 249, 257–61, 277–8; Human Rights Bureau, 249, 261–2, 266, 271, 275, 276, 278; on jurisdictional conflicts resulting from US economic regulation, *CP*, 839–46; model Bilateral Investment Treaty on compensation for expropriation, 849; on nationality principle of claims, 649–50; and negotiations involving technology, 90–1, 93; on Protocols 3 and 4 to Warsaw Convention, 416–8; role in establishing international law in US, 805–15, 824, 828; support of bill implementing Cultural Property Convention, *CP*, 611–3
United States Department of the Treasury, 263, 389–90, 646, 648–9, 841
United States Department of Transportation, 416
United States Drug Enforcement Agency, 155
United States Export-Import Bank, 380

United States Federal Trade Commission, 845
United States Foreign Claims Settlement Commission, 645, 647, 648–9, 836, 837–8, 849
United States House of Representatives, 250, 251, 252, 254, 273, 276, 379, 645, 650, 836: on registration by agents of foreign principals, 622–3. *See also* United States Congress
United States Immigration and Naturalization Service, 165–6: standards for deportation appeals, *JD*, 386–8
United States Internal Revenue Service, 297
United States International Communication Agency, 612–3
United States National Labor Relations Board, 308
United States President, 48, 415, 416, 612, 639, 806, 807, 812, 825, 840, 841: high seas interdiction of illegal aliens, 376–7; implementation of human rights legislation, *LA*, 246; power to enter into binding foreign agreements, *JD*, 855–9; report to Congress on Sinai Multinational Force, *CP*, 613–5; sanctions against Poland and USSR, *CP*, 379–84
United States Securities and Exchange Commission, 592, 842, 846
United States Senate, 48, 50, 53, 253, 273, 379, 426, 648, 825: action on Montreal Protocols to Warsaw Convention, *CD*, 412; and draft LOS treaty, 2, 7; safeguards for US servicemen in foreign courts, 626. *See also* United States Congress
United States Supreme Court, 48–9, 162, 165, 183, 391, 394, 626, 818, 823, 828, 848: on application of local law under FCN Treaty, *JD*, 853–5; on choice of US forum by foreign plaintiffs, *JD*, 394–6; Civil War cases, 818–21; on definition of "treaty" under Constitution, *JD*, 855–7; on extraterritorial jurisdiction of US courts, 280, 303–16, 318, 319; international law principles in early practice, 803–5, 808; on sea boundary delimitation, 562, 564, 583; on secondary political boycott of USSR by labor union, *JD*, 849–51; on state citizenship requirement for public employment, *JD*, 616–7
United States Trade Representative, Office of, model Bilateral Investment Treaty on compensation for expropriation, 849
Universal Declaration of Human Rights, 246, 600, 606, 651, 755
Uruguay, 346, 408, 767: US security assistance to, 254–5, 269–70, 272, 274–5
U.S. Fishery Management and the New Law of the Sea, *LA*, 24
Usher, John. European Community Law and National Law, *BN*, 919
Utton, Albert E. *BR* of Arsanjani and of Fawcett & Parry, 675
———, & Ludwik Teclaff. International Groundwater Law, *BR*, 692

Vagts, Detlev F. A Turnabout in Extraterritoriality, *Ed.*, 591
Valticos, Nicolas. International Labour Law, *BR*, 205
van Aggelen, J. *BR* of Travailleurs Etrangers et le Droit International, 687
van Dijk, P. Judicial Review of Governmental Action and the Requirement of an Interest to Sue, *BR*, 204
van Fenema, H. P., & H. A. Wassenbergh (eds.). International Air Transport in the Eighties, *BR*, 693
van Lier, Irene. Acid Rain and International Law, *BR*, 689
van Panhuys, H. F., W. P. Heere, J. W. Josephus Jitta, Ko Swan Sik, & A. M. Stuyt (eds.). International Law in the Netherlands. Vols. II & III, *BR*, 463
Vatican, 153
Vattel, Emmerich de, 802, 803: on breadth of territorial sea, 558
Venezuela, 14, 20, 234, 236, 237, 269, 408, 427–8, 740: deportations by and extradition law, *JD*, 618–9; proposal on nonretroactivity of Vienna Convention on treaty law, 781, 786
Venice, Republic of, Lake Garda boundary dispute with Austria, 557
Venturini, Gabriella. La Responsabilità Extracontrattuale delle Comunità Europee, *BR*, 904
Vienna Convention on Consular Relations (1963), 750–1
Vienna Convention on Diplomatic Relations (1961), 750–2
Vienna Convention on the Law of Treaties (1969), 5, 176, 361, 362, 656, 758: law governing treaty relations between parties and nonparties, *LA*, 779: amendments and modifications to treaties under, 792–4; compatibility with customary law, 788–99; effect on third states, 787, 788, 790, 792, 794; general participation interpretation of, 779–80, 783–6, 789, 790, 794, 795, 798, 799, 800; invalidity, termination, and suspension under, 794–9

Vierdag, E. W. The Law Governing Treaty Relations between Parties to the Vienna Convention on the Law of Treaties and States Not Party to the Convention, *LA*, 779
Vietnam, Democratic People's Republic of (North), 266, 270, 402, 403, 408, 607, 841: US claims, 838–9; whether liable for confiscated assets in local branch of US banks, *JD*, 385–6
Vitoria, 482
Völker, E. L. M., & C. W. A. Timmermans (eds.). Division of powers between the European Communities and their Member States in the field of external relations, *BR*, 684
von Glahn, Gerhard. *BN* of Israel National Section of the International Commission of Jurists, 705; *BN* of Klein, 470
von Mehren, Arthur, 315–6
von Mehren, Robert B. *BR* of Barde, 909
Vosburgh, J. A. *BR* of Apollis, 690

Waite, Morrison R., 820
Waldheim, Kurt, 130, 138–41
Waldmann, Raymond J. Regulating International Business through Codes of Conduct, *BN*, 472
Waldock, Sir Humphrey, 364–6
Walker, George K. *BR* of Steele, 460
Wallace, Cynthia Day. *BR* of Grewlich, 679
War, law of, 816, 828: early US assumption of neutrality, 806–7; Grotian theory, 480–3; Lieber's Code, 818; Pufendorf's theory, 489–91; Spinozan theory, 485. *See also* Armed conflicts; Geneva Conventions on protection of war victims; Hague Conventions on law of war
Warsaw Convention (1929): Guatemala City Protocol, 413; The Hague Protocol, 413; Montreal Protocols 3 and 4: US Senate action on, *CD*, 412
(The) Warsaw Treaty of 1970 and the Western Boundary of Poland, *NC*, 119
Wassenbergh, H. A., & H. P. van Fenema (eds.). International Air Transport in the Eighties, *BR*, 693
Watson, Philippa. Social Security Law of the European Communities, *BR*, 904
Weber, Max, 246
Webster, Daniel, enunciation of international law principles, 807–8
Wegen, Gerhard. Discontinuance of International Proceedings: The Hostages Case, *LA*, 717
Weiss, Edith Brown. *BR* of Breuer, 688
Weissbrodt, David. A New United Nations Mechanism for Encouraging the Ratification of Human Rights Treaties, *CD*, 418; *Corr.* on, 832; *Corr.*, response to Jhabvala, 833
Western countries, 632, 640: and reporting under Civil and Political Rights Covenant, 143, 148
Western Europe, 143, 269
Westlake, John, 817
Weston, Burns H. *BR* of Butler, 430; *BR* of Pettman, 190
Westphalia, Peace of (Treaty of, 1648), 478, 485, 493, 497, 555
Wharton, Francis, 814–5, 817
Wheaton, Henry, 818
Whiteman, Marjorie M., 815
White Slave Traffic, Convention on Suppression of, 828
Wickersham, George, on territorial sea delimitation, 575–6
Wilcox, Francis O. *BR* of Cable, 913
Wilhelm, Hans-Heinrich, & Helmut Krausnick. Die Truppe des Weltanschauungskrieges, *BR*, 448
Wilkins, William J. The Sword and the Gavel, *BR*, 895
Willamette Law Review. Vol. 17, no. 1. Symposium issue on International Law and Foreign Policy in the 1980s, *BR*, 697
Wilson, Donald T. International Business Transactions in a Nutshell, *BN*, 920
Wilson, George Grafton, 817, 818, 823, 827
Wilson, L. C., & N. G. Onuf. *BR* of Feuerstein & Parry, 902
Wilson, Woodrow, Fourteen Points, 350
Winthrop, William, 816–7
Wirsing, Robert G. Protection of Ethnic Minorities, *BR*, 899
Woolsey, Theodore D., 816, 818

Woolsey, Theodore S., 816, 823
World Administrative Radio Conference (1979) (WARC-79), on orbit/spectrum allocation, 62, 66–7, 69
World Administrative Radio Conference on the Uses of the Geostationary Orbit (GEO-WARC), 73, 75–6: tasks of, 69–70, 71, 74
World Food Conference (Rome), 92
World Health Organization, 759: immunity in US of Pan American regional office and director, *JD*, 623–4
Wright, L. R., J. de V. Allen, & A. J. Stockwell (eds.). A Collection of Treaties and other Documents affecting the State of Malaysia, 1761–1963. Vols. I & II, *BR*, 218
Wyatt, Derrick, & Bernard Rudden (eds.). Basic Community Laws, *BR*, 905

Yalta Conference (1945), 122
Yaoundé I Convention (1964), 860
Yemen, South, 266
Young, Oran R. Compliance and Public Authority, *BR*, 868
Yugoslavia, 13, 137, 576: sea boundary delimitation practice, 579

Zacklin, Ralph. *BN* of Zarb, 469; *BR* of Jiménez de Aréchaga and of Puig, 431; *BR* of Tortora, 445
Zagaris, Bruce. Foreign Inve$tment in the United States, *BR*, 441
Zaire, 408: US security assistance to, 254, 256, 260, 269–70, 276
Zarb, Antoine H. Les Institutions Spécialisées du Système des Nations Unies et leurs Membres, *BN*, 469
Zeballos, E. S., 572

American Journal of International Law

VOLUME 76
1982

Published by

American Society of International Law

AMERICAN JOURNAL OF INTERNATIONAL LAW

VOLUME 76 **CONTENTS** **1982**

[No. 1, January 1982, pp. 1–230; No. 2, April 1982, pp. 231–475; No. 3, July 1982, pp. 477–715; No. 4, October 1982, pp. 717–960.]

PAGE

The Third United Nations Conference on the Law of the Sea: The Tenth Session (1981) *Bernard H. Oxman* 1
U.S. Fishery Management and the New Law of the Sea *W. T. Burke* 24
Satellite Communication and Spectrum Allocation *Martin A. Rothblatt* 56
Technology and International Negotiations *Jonathan I. Charney* 78
The Inter-American Court of Human Rights *Thomas Buergenthal* 231
Conditioning U.S. Security Assistance on Human Rights Practices *Stephen B. Cohen* 246
Extraterritorial Jurisdiction at a Crossroads: An Intersection Between Public and Private International Law *Harold G. Maier* 280
The Torres Strait Treaty: Ocean Boundary Delimitation by Agreement *H. Burmester* 321
Recent Developments in United Nations Treaty Registration and Publication Practices *Mala Tabory* 350
The Grotian Vision of World Order *Cornelius F. Murphy, Jr.* 477
Contempt, Crisis, and the Court: The World Court and the Hostage Rescue Attempt *Ted L. Stein* 499
The Egyptian-Israeli Peace Treaty and Access to the Gulf of Aqaba: A New Legal Regime *Mohamed ElBaradei* 532
Sea Boundary Delimitation Between States Before World War II *Sang-Myon Rhee* 555
Discontinuance of International Proceedings: The Hostages Case *Gerhard Wegen* 717
The Plaintiff's Dilemma: Illegally Obtained Evidence and Admissibility in International Adjudication *W. Michael Reisman & Eric E. Freedman* 737
Norm Making and Supervision in International Human Rights: Reflections on Institutional Order *Theodor Meron* 754
The Law Governing Treaty Relations between Parties to the Vienna Convention on the Law of Treaties and States Not Party to the Convention *E. W. Vierdag* 779
Lawyers Who Established International Law in the United States, 1776–1914 *John M. Raymond & Barbara J. Frischholz* 802

Editorial Comments

Critical Defense Zones and International Law: The Reagan Codicil *W. Michael Reisman* 589
A Turnabout in Extraterritoriality *Detlev F. Vagts* 591

The Falklands (Malvinas), International Law, and the OAS *Seymour J. Rubin* 594
Hardy Cross Dillard (1902–1982) *Oscar Schachter* 595
The Inter-American System Snarls in Falklands War *John Norton Moore* 830

Notes and Comments

The Warsaw Treaty of 1970 and the Western Boundary of Poland *Ludwik Gelberg* 119
The Good Offices of the United Nations Secretary-General in the Field of Human Rights *B. G. Ramcharan* 130
Reporting Under the Covenant on Political and Civil Rights: The First Five Years of the Human Rights Committee *Dana D. Fischer* 142
The Election of Five Members of the International Court of Justice in 1981 *Shabtai Rosenne* 364
Large-Scale Migrations of Asylum Seekers *David A. Martin* 598
The Francis Deák Prize 610

Correspondence 371, 832

Contemporary Practice of the United States Relating to International Law *Marian Nash Leich* 154, 374, 611, 836

Judicial Decisions *Monroe Leigh* 160, 385, 616, 847

Current Developments

The 1981 Session of the Institut de Droit International *Oscar Schachter* 176
The Sinai Multinational Force and Observers *Marian Nash Leich* 181
The Hague Convention Abolishing the Requirement of Legalization for Foreign Public Documents *Marian Nash Leich* 182
The 1981 Session of the UN Sub-Commission on Prevention of Discrimination and Protection of Minorities *Ton Gardeniers, Hurst Hannum, & Janice Kruger* 405
The Montreal Protocols to the Warsaw Convention on International Carriage by Air *Marian Nash Leich* 412
A New United Nations Mechanism for Encouraging the Ratification of Human Rights Treaties *David Weissbrodt* 418
The Codification and Progressive Development of International Law: A UNITAR Study of the Role and Use of the International Law Commission *Thomas M. Franck & Mohamed ElBaradei* 630
The 1981 U.S.-Czechoslovak Claims Settlement Agreement: An Epilogue to Postwar Nationalization and Expropriation Disputes *Vratislav Pechota* 639
Restatement of the Foreign Relations Law of the United States (Revised): Tentative Draft No. 3 *Louis Henkin* 653
The Election of March 1982 to Fill One Vacancy on the International Court of Justice *Shabtai Rosenne* 863
The Australian-United States Agreement on Cooperation in Antitrust Matters *Marian Nash Leich* 866

Book Reviews and Notes *Edited by Leo Gross* 184, 430, 658, 868

Books Received 224, 472, 708, 922

Official Documents
Argentina-United Kingdom: UN Security Council Resolution 502 (1982) 712

International Legal Materials. Contents, Vol XX, Nos. 5–6 (1981); Vol. XXI, Nos. 1–4 (1982) 230, 475, 713, 926

Table of Cases 929

Index 931

The views expressed in the articles, editorial comments, book reviews and notes, and other contributions which appear in AJIL are those of the individual authors and are not to be taken as representing the views of the Board of Editors or the American Society of International Law.

Manuscripts in triplicate may be sent to the Editors-in-Chief of AJIL, Professors Oscar Schachter and Louis Henkin, Columbia University School of Law, New York, N.Y. 10027. Subscriptions, orders for back numbers, correspondence with reference to AJIL and books for review should be sent to the AMERICAN JOURNAL OF INTERNATIONAL LAW (ISSN 0002-9300), 2223 Massachusetts Avenue, N.W., Washington, D.C. 20008.

AJIL is published in January, April, July, and October and is supplied to all members of the American Society of International Law. The annual subscription to nonmembers of ASIL is $52.00, plus $2.50 for all foreign subscriptions (including ASIL Proceedings). Available back numbers of AJIL will be supplied at $11.00 each. ($21 of membership fee is allotted to AJIL subscription.)

EDITORIAL OFFICE:
BOX 44
COLUMBIA UNIVERSITY SCHOOL OF LAW
NEW YORK, N.Y. 10027

BUSINESS OFFICE:
2223 MASSACHUSETTS AVENUE, N.W.
WASHINGTON, D.C. 20008

The American Society of International Law

2223 Massachusetts Ave., N.W., Washington, D.C. 20008 (202) 265-4313 CABLES "AMINTLAW"

1982 APPLICATION

[ ] REGULAR MEMBERS .... $ 55

[ ] INTERMEDIATE MEMBERS (first 3 years of membership for *those under 30 years of age* at time of application) .... $ 25
Date of Birth ____________

[ ] STUDENT MEMBERS . . . Verification to be completed by a professor or administrative officer of your school: I hereby certify that the applicant is regularly registered in
(school) ____________
for academic year ________ Title ____________
Signature ____________ $ 15

[ ] SPECIAL CATEGORY (persons *not* resident in a member country of the OECD) .... $ 30

[ ] CONTRIBUTING MEMBERS .... $ 75

[ ] SUPPORTING MEMBERS .... $ 150

[ ] ANNUAL PATRON .... $ 500

[ ] LIFE $1,000

($21 of membership fee is allotted to AJIL subscription.)

Please enroll me as a member of the American Society of International Law for the calendar year starting January 1, 19____. My check, money order, UNESCO coupon, or payment in a convertible currency is enclosed $__________. I have checked membership category for which I am eligible.

(Please Print)

Name: ....

Address: ....

City: ....

State (or Country): .... Zip: ....

Member, U.S. Bar? .... State: .... Year: ....

Other Professional Affiliation: ....

Signature: ....

[ ] Please send me ILM at member rate of $24, plus $4.50 if outside U.S.

[ ] Check here if you would like to receive a list of Society publications.

PLEASE MAKE CHECKS PAYABLE TO *The American Society of International Law.* Contributions above obligatory dues, and all dues if membership is related to your work or profession, are tax deductible in the United States.

[ ] *Nonmember* subscription to AJIL (incl. ASIL Proceedings) ... $ 52

Please add $2.50 if you reside outside the U.S.

Oxford

The International Law of the Sea

Volume I

D. P. O'CONNELL; *edited by* I. A. SHEARER, *University of New South Wales*. This comprehensive exposition of the principles and doctrines developed by jurists, law-making institutions and diplomats during the past 400 years surveys the evolution of the freedom of the seas, and the growth of claims to national jurisdiction over territorial waters, the sea bed, and ocean resources. Critically analyzing the results of the United Nations third Conference on the Law of the Sea, convened in 1973, this study assesses the prospects for orderly change in light of the questions raised by the conference.
December 1982 520 pp.; maps; index; bibliog. $74.00

The International Law of Human Rights

PAUL SIEGHART. This is the first self-contained textbook of the substantive international law of human rights. It explains the subject; sets out, right by right and with full cross-references, the relevant texts of the eight major international instruments; presents their interpretation by competent independent international institutions and by the superior courts of thirty countries in nearly 1,000 decided cases; summarizes twenty-four subsidiary conventions; and presents the twenty-three established international procedures for the supervision, interpretation, and application of the substantive law.
December 1982 600 pp. $77.00

How Wars End

The United Nations and the Termination of Armed Conflict, 1946–1964

SYDNEY D. BAILEY, *formerly Quaker Representative at the United Nations*. There have been 150 "small" wars since 1945, mostly in the Third World. The international community, usually through an organ of the United Nations, seeks to bring the fighting to a halt. This book, based on studies of a number of such cases, examines the problems that are likely to arise and suggests how new or existing institutions can be used to end the fighting.
Volume I 1982 400 pp. $89.00 **Volume II** 1982 720 pp. $98.00

Documents on the Laws of War

Edited by ADAM ROBERTS, *University of Oxford, and* RICHARD GUELFF, *Coudert Brothers (an International Law firm)*. Armed conflicts and military occupations are the subject of a large body of international law, covering a wide variety of issues. This volume focuses on the major currently applicable agreements; it contains the texts of twenty-five formal international agreements, from the 1856 Paris Declaration to the 1981 U. N. Weapons Convention. Prefatory notes explaining the legal and historical contexts, complete listings of countries bound by the agreements, and any reservations or declarations which they have made are given for each document.
1982 432 pp. cloth $34.50 paper $17.95

Prices and publication dates are subject to change.

OXFORD UNIVERSITY PRESS
200 Madison Avenue, New York, New York 10016